PUBLIC PAPERS OF THE PRESIDENTS
OF THE
UNITED STATES

PUBLIC PAPERS OF THE PRESIDENTS
OF THE
UNITED STATES

George Bush

1990

(IN TWO BOOKS)

BOOK I—JANUARY 1 TO JUNE 30, 1990

UNITED STATES GOVERNMENT PRINTING OFFICE
WASHINGTON : 1991

Published by the
Office of the Federal Register
National Archives and Records Administration

For sale by the
Superintendent of Documents
U.S. Government Printing Office
Washington, DC 20402

Foreword

Enclosed in these pages you will find documents reflecting our advances in foreign and domestic policy. My State of the Union address to the Congress on January 29 emphasized four themes: investments for a competitive America, opportunity, stewardship, and democracy. Our challenge at home was to improve and reinvigorate our democratic system by investing in our people and our future—in short, to build a better America. Abroad, the new democracies that emerged in Europe and Latin America reflected, in many ways, the same cornerstones that anchor our own freedoms—freedoms which have been an inspiration to millions of people around the globe. We sought to continue to offer our helping hand to the world's emerging democracies so they too could enjoy a free and prosperous future.

Domestically, in these six months, we took major steps in our crusade to bring excellence to American education. Most important, in my State of the Union address I announced six national education goals, developed in close partnership with the Nation's Governors. These six ambitious goals for the year 2000 set as national objectives that all children will start school healthy and ready to learn; that our high school graduation rate will increase to over 90 percent; that American students will leave grades four, eight, and twelve having demonstrated competency in challenging subject matters; that American students will be first in the world in science and mathematics achievement; that all Americans will be literate and prepared for lifelong learning; and that every American school will be safe and drug-free.

During this period, we also made important progress on a broad range of other domestic issues. We extended our environmental stewardship by holding a White House Conference on Science and Economic Research Related to Global Change, proposing a public-private partnership to plant a billion trees a year through the year 2000, helping expand and protect Florida's wetlands, signing the Basel Convention on the dangerous international dumping of hazardous waste, and working vigorously to achieve a significant revision of the Clean Air Act to improve our air quality while keeping our economy competitive. My budget included $2 billion in new investments in environmental protection.

We continued to work to increase parents' choices in caring for their children and a market-oriented farm bill to continue the progress in agriculture begun with the 1985 farm bill. We presented the National Transportation Strategy, worked to pass the Americans with Disabilities Act and the Hate Crime Statistics Act, and continued to develop meaningful Federal budget reform.

Through our foreign policy, we furthered support for democratic governments in our own hemisphere. We welcomed the democratically elected governments of Panama and Nicaragua and developed economic assistance programs for both nations. In February I travelled to Cartagena, Colombia, where along with my counterparts from the Andean nations, we discussed a comprehensive and intensified strategy to stop the production and flow of illicit drugs and agreed on the importance of

v

increased economic cooperation as this strategy is implemented. In June I announced the Enterprise for the Americas Initiative, a historic new effort to bring economic growth to Latin America through trade, investment, and debt restructuring. Its eventual goal is a free trade zone throughout the hemisphere. As one part of that effort, President Salinas and I announced plans to work towards a free trade agreement between the United States and Mexico.

During the first half of 1990, we extended further assistance to Central and Eastern European nations to aid their transition to democratic governments and market economies. We initiated the Two Plus Four talks to lead to a unified Germany, signed an agreement to send Peace Corps volunteers to Poland, and announced the Citizens Democracy Corps to serve as a clearinghouse for Americans who wish to volunteer their expertise and assistance to aid Central and Eastern Europe.

Throughout these challenging times, we maintained close ties with our friends and allies in Western Europe and Asia. I met with Prime Minister Kaifu of Japan in Palm Springs, California, and in a commencement address at Oklahoma State University, I announced a balanced structure for Europe in a new world order. This address outlined my vision for the future of the North Atlantic Treaty Organization (NATO) and the Conference on Security and Cooperation in Europe (CSCE). We also proposed that the heads of government of the NATO member nations meet to discuss this vision, a proposal that our allies promptly accepted.

I also hosted a successful summit in Washington with President Mikhail Gorbachev of the Soviet Union. We had several days of intensive and rewarding talks. President and Mrs. Gorbachev also joined Barbara and me at Camp David. At this summit, we signed several significant bilateral agreements, made important progress on arms control and regional issues, and furthered the United States' goal of a Europe whole and free.

George Bush

Preface

This book contains the papers and speeches of the 41st President of the United States that were issued by the Office of the Press Secretary during the period January 1–June 30, 1990. The material has been compiled and published by the Office of the Federal Register, National Archives and Records Administration.

The material is presented in chronological order, and the dates shown in the headings are the dates of the documents or events. In instances when the release date differs from the date of the document itself, that fact is shown in the textnote. Every effort has been made to ensure accuracy: Remarks are checked against a tape recording, and signed documents are checked against the original. Textnotes and cross references have been provided by the editors for purposes of identification or clarity. Speeches were delivered in Washington, DC, unless indicated. The times noted are local times. All materials that are printed full-text in the book have been indexed in the subject and name indexes, and listed in the document categories list.

The Public Papers of the Presidents series was begun in 1957 in response to a recommendation of the National Historical Publications Commission. An extensive compilation of messages and papers of the Presidents covering the period 1789 to 1897 was assembled by James D. Richardson and published under congressional authority between 1896 and 1899. Since then, various private compilations have been issued, but there was no uniform publication comparable to the Congressional Record or the United States Supreme Court Reports. Many Presidential papers could be found only in the form of mimeographed White House releases or as reported in the press. The Commission therefore recommended the establishment of an official series in which Presidential writings, addresses, and remarks of a public nature could be made available.

The Commission's recommendation was incorporated in regulations of the Administrative Committee of the Federal Register, issued under section 6 of the Federal Register Act (44 U.S.C. 1506), which may be found in title 1, part 10, of the Code of Federal Regulations.

A companion publication to the Public Papers series, the Weekly Compilation of Presidential Documents, was begun in 1965 to provide a broader range of Presidential materials on a more timely basis to meet the needs of the contemporary reader. Beginning with the administration of Jimmy Carter, the Public Papers series expanded its coverage to include all material as printed in the Weekly Compilation. That coverage provides a listing of the President's daily schedule and meetings, when announced, and other items of general interest issued by the Office of the Press Secretary. Also included are lists of the President's nominations submitted to the Senate, materials released by the Office of the Press Secretary that are not printed full-text in the book, acts approved by the President, and proclamations and Executive orders. This information appears in the appendixes at the end of the book.

Volumes covering the administrations of Presidents Hoover, Truman, Eisenhower, Kennedy, Johnson, Nixon, Ford, Carter, and Reagan are also available.

The Public Papers of the Presidents publication program is under the direction of Gwen H. Estep. The Chief Editor of this book was Karen Howard Ashlin, assisted by Sheli Fleming.

White House liaison was provided by Marlin Fitzwater, Assistant to the President and Press Secretary. The frontispiece and photographs used in the portfolio were supplied by the White House Photo Office. The typography and design of the book were developed by the Government Printing Office under the direction of Robert W. Houk, Public Printer.

Martha L. Girard
Director of the Federal Register

Don W. Wilson
Archivist of the United States

Contents

Cabinet

Secretary of State.. James Addison Baker III

Secretary of the Treasury.............................. Nicholas F. Brady

Secretary of Defense...................................... Richard B. Cheney

Attorney General... Richard L. Thornburgh

Secretary of the Interior................................ Manuel Lujan, Jr.

Secretary of Agriculture .... Clayton Yeutter

Secretary of Commerce.................................. Robert Adam Mosbacher

Secretary of Labor .... Elizabeth Hanford Dole

Secretary of Health and Human Services ... Louis W. Sullivan

Secretary of Housing and Urban
Development.. Jack Kemp

Secretary of Transportation .... Samuel Knox Skinner

Secretary of Energy.. James D. Watkins

Secretary of Education .... Lauro F. Cavazos

Secretary of Veterans Affairs........................ Edward J. Derwinski

Director of the Office of Management and
Budget... Richard G. Darman

United States Trade Representative.............. Carla Anderson Hills

Administration of George Bush

1990

New Year's Message to the People of the Soviet Union
January 1, 1990

On behalf of the American people; my wife, Barbara; and my family, I bring you our warmest greetings.

A new year is dawning around the world, the first year of the last decade of the 20th century. And as the world looks back to nine decades of war, of strife, of suspicion, let us also look forward to a new century and a new millennium of peace, freedom, and prosperity.

Of course, there are no maps to lead us where we are going, to this new world of our own making. We can find our way only through cooperation beginning with a candid dialog. It is in pursuit of such a dialog that I met your President, Mikhail Gorbachev, near the island nation of Malta. Let me share with you some of the matters we discussed.

First, we agreed to redouble our efforts to diminish the horrible threat from weapons of mass destruction and to pursue with other nations an agreement to reduce conventional forces in Europe.

Second, we talked about ways we can end regional conflicts and alleviate the terrible toll in human suffering they bring.

Third, I want to assure you, as I did your President, that the West seeks no advantage from the extraordinary changes underway in the East. We talked about the magnificent efforts of the people of Eastern Europe to find a free and democratic future. And I told your President that I support the dynamic process of reform in the Soviet Union. We will work together to reduce barriers to trade, investment, and the free movement of goods and ideas.

In these ways, and as your economic reforms take place, the entry of the Soviet Union into the global market can be advanced—an historic goal that, once achieved, can improve the life of every Soviet citizen. But it is our belief that lasting peace and prosperity comes from a respect for human rights and the sharing of democratic values that are deeply rooted in the human spirit. Your own Leo Tolstoy said that if our hearts are empty, no law or political reform can fill them. The real law lives within our hearts. These values are not exclusively American or Western. They are not the possession of any people or any domain. They belong to all men and women, through all time, and in all places. They are the inalienable rights of man.

Of course, much remains to be done, but the progress of the past year gives me confidence that we are heading in the right direction. In this, President Gorbachev has been a good partner in peace. Given the war-torn history of this century, we should redouble our efforts to forge a new century of peace and freedom. Our nations have produced Abraham Lincoln, Leo Tolstoy, Martin Luther King, and Andrei Sakharov. We have persevered as allies in a terrible war. The challenges we face today are no less daunting, but with good will and determination on both sides, I am confident our two peoples will be equal to the task.

Thank you, God bless you, and have a happy New Year!

Note: The message was recorded on December 19, 1989, in the Map Room at the White House. It was televised in the Soviet Union on January 1.

Statement on the Tentative Settlement of the Labor Dispute Between the United Mine Workers and the Pittston Corporation
January 1, 1990

I am delighted with the news that the collective-bargaining process has produced a tentative agreement that will bring an end to the 9-month-old dispute between members of the United Mine Workers and the Pittston Corporation. Secretary Dole, [Federal mediator] Bill Usery, Rich Trumka of the United Mine Workers, and Paul Douglas of the Pittston Corporation deserve congratulations for their work in achieving this agreement. And I want to wish the families and communities of the mineworkers a very happy New Year, as they look forward to the benefits of a new contract.

Appointment of Deane Roesch Hinton as United States Ambassador to Panama
January 2, 1990

The President today announced the recess appointment of Deane Roesch Hinton, of Illinois, a career member of the Senior Foreign Service, with the personal rank of Career Ambassador, as Ambassador to the Republic of Panama. He would succeed Arthur H. Davis.

Since 1987 Ambassador Hinton has served as the U.S. Ambassador to the Republic of Costa Rica. Prior to this he served as Ambassador to the Islamic Republic of Pakistan, 1983–1987, and as Ambassador to the Republic of El Salvador, 1981–1983. From 1979 to 1981, he was Assistant Secretary of State for Economic and Business Affairs. Ambassador Hinton served as the Representative of the United States of America to the European Communities, with the rank and status of Ambassador Extraordinary and Plenipotentiary, 1976–1979. In 1975 he was senior adviser to the Under Secretary of State for Economic Affairs. Ambassador Hinton also served as Ambassador to the Republic of Zaire in 1974. From 1971 to 1974, he was Assistant Director, then Deputy Director on the Council on International Economic Policy at the White House. Ambassador Hinton served as Director and Economic Counselor at the Agency for International Development in Santiago, Chile, 1969–1971, and in Guatemala, 1967–1969.

Ambassador Hinton graduated from the University of Chicago (A.B., 1943). He served in the U.S. Army, 1943–1945. He was born March 12, 1923, in Fort Missoula, MT. He is married and has 12 children.

Letter to Congressional Leaders Reporting on the Cyprus Conflict
January 2, 1990

Dear Mr. Speaker: (Dear Mr. Chairman:)

In accordance with Public Law 95–384, I am submitting to you this bimonthly report, covering the period September 1 through October 31, 1989, on progress toward a negotiated settlement of the Cyprus question.

Since my last report to you, no formal intercommunal negotiations have been held. By the end of October, leaders in both communities were expressing a willingness to return to the negotiating table and to work in good faith toward completion of a draft outline for a Cyprus settlement.

To bridge the gap that existed between the two sides, the U.N. Secretary General met first with Cyprus President Vassiliou in New York on October 3 and separately a week later with Turkish Cypriot leader Rauf Denktash. A week after this second meeting, the Secretary General issued a statement indicating that he had ordered a review of the entire negotiating situation since August 1988, and that once this was completed, he would consult again with each of the parties with a view to inviting them to begin a further round of talks.

Both Mr. Vassiliou and Mr. Denktash used the occasion of their visits to the United States to spend two additional days in Washington. I met with President Vassiliou when he was here. Secretary of State Baker and National Security Advisor Scowcroft joined me in that meeting. Mr. Vassiliou also saw separately Members of Congress, Deputy Secretary of State Lawrence Eagleburger, and the U.S. Special Coordinator for Cyprus.

Mr. Denktash came to Washington on October 12 and 13. He met with Members of Congress and the U.S. Special Coordinator for Cyprus. Deputy Secretary of State Eagleburger hosted a luncheon in honor of Mr. Denktash.

In these Washington meetings, officials in my Administration stressed to both Cypriot leaders our unqualified support for continuation of the intercommunal negotiating process under the aegis of the Secretary General. Only this process, we emphasized, offered the possibility of success. We therefore urged both parties to return to the negotiating table as soon as possible to complete work on the draft outline for a settlement. Both parties also were told that the United States did not see continuation of the *status quo* as a solution to the Cyprus problem.

We also encouraged the Greek and Turkish Cypriot leadership to take advantage of other opportunities to pursue bicommunal cooperation. One such fruitful area is demanning of posts along the buffer zone, conducted under the auspices of the U.N. Peacekeeping Force in Cyprus, to follow on the successful demanning of posts in Nicosia agreed to last May.

In sum, both Cypriot leaders left Washington fully aware that U.S. interest in a negotiated settlement remained strong and that we would continue to give the most active support to U.N. efforts to resume the intercommunal negotiating process and keep it going in a meaningful manner.

Sincerely,

GEORGE BUSH

Note: Identical letters were sent to Thomas S. Foley, Speaker of the House of Representatives, and Claiborne Pell, chairman of the Senate Foreign Relations Committee.

Letter to Benjamin Hooks, Executive Director of the National Association for the Advancement of Colored People
January 2, 1990

On this the first day of a whole new decade, Barbara and I send to you our personal best wishes for a very happy new year and to the NAACP, I send my sincere hope that 1990 will be a great year for your most prestigious organization.

The recent bombings make it clear we have not totally beaten back the evils of bigotry and racial prejudice. We cannot let up in the fight against racism. Please assure your members I will see that the Federal Government does not let up as it works to bring the perpetrators of these hideous crimes to justice.

GEORGE BUSH

Note: An original was not available for verification of the content of the letter.

Remarks to the Republican National Committee
January 2, 1990

Mr. Atwater. See, Mr. President, they understand you're the best chairman this party ever had. [*Laughter*] Ladies and gentlemen, the leader of our party and the best chairman this party has ever had, President George Bush.

The President. Thank you all. And this has been a nostalgic return for me because, as Lee generously pointed out, I was chairman of the Republican National Committee years ago. And so, when I went back up to the fourth floor, it was like Yogi Berra said: deja vu all over again—[*laughter*]—and it was a nostalgic return—everything familiar. Some things never do change, except, of course, the Muzak. [*Laughter*]

I just wanted to come up here and really just, at the beginning of this year—we planned to do it at Christmastime—and I wanted to come up here and say thank you for all you've done to build and strengthen this party. And I appreciate it very, very much. We are, and proudly remain, the party of Lincoln, the Republican Party. And I am very grateful for the terrific support that you have given our administration—all of us, all Departments.

Needless to say that 1989 was the first year of new leadership—I'm talking about our very able chairman, Lee Atwater, and Jeanie Austin, too—both of them doing an outstanding job all around this country. And I am totally confident that when we look back after the upcoming elections, the work that they are engaged in and that you all are engaged in will clearly pay off.

This has been a year of tremendous excitement and achievement around the world, too, a remarkable time of change. And when we started the year and our work together by my declaring "the day of the dictator is over"—words, I believe, from the Inaugural Address—who imagined that the peoples of Eastern Europe would so swiftly vindicate that call? Who imagined that Václav Havel would start the new year by addressing the Czechoslovakian people not as a playwright but as the President of his country?

And in our own Western Hemisphere, democracy has spread from one country to another. But at the beginning of my term—not counting Chile, which has now had democratic elections—but at the beginning of the term, there were still three holdout dictatorships in Latin America. And thanks to the sacrifice and the courage of our American fighting men, today there are only two. And we're starting the new year with a free Panama—one more step towards a hemisphere that hopefully will be one day totally free, totally democratic.

I wish all of you could have been with me—or maybe I don't. [*Laughter*] Some of you might be like me. Seeing these kids in the hospital down in San Antonio the other day, it was just inspiring—19-year-old, 20-year-old, with this marvelous, marvelous attitude and approach towards their mission—the desire to go back—lying there in these hospital beds, wounded, some of them very, very seriously. But it was an amazing New Year's present for both Barbara and me. And I can't tell you how grateful I am to them and to our military for this superbly executed, highly complex operation down there.

The year offers us tremendous challenge and opportunity on the domestic front, as well as in the foreign policy field. But to make the most of it, we must get action from the United States Congress. And so, I would take this opportunity to call on Congress to pass our clean air legislation—our proposal, if you will, to harness the power of the market to fight acid rain and air pollution. And I call on the Congress to pass our anticrime package to make the streets safer, a step that Congress should have taken long ago and that they can now take when they return that will really bolster the fight against narcotics.

And finally—there are many other initiatives—but here today I'd like to call on Congress to act responsibly in favor of growth and opportunity and to lay aside all the political rhetoric and to go ahead and do that which the majority of the Congress said they want; and that is to cut the capital gains tax, to reestablish a capital gains differential, because that will mean jobs and opportunity for more Americans.

So, those are three areas domestically that we will be pushing for. There will be others, but those are three that I think the Congress should adopt as priority. We've got a great big job ahead of us this year, a full agenda, and each of you is critical to our efforts. In fact, the work of the national committee will be in much clearer focus nationally because of the congressional elections that are coming up.

I understand that Lee, generous fellow that he is, gave you a couple of days off at Christmas and New Year's. [*Laughter*] Hopefully, time to spend with your families, time to recharge the batteries. But now we're back and you're back, and we need you. We need you to face up to the challenge of 1990. The work that you're doing here is reflected in the field, and I've heard so many good reports from Republicans around the States about how the national committee is really backing them. People who see get this sense that the party is on the move. And with such a team, I am confident that this will be a great year—a Republican year.

Barbara joins me in wishing you the very best. Like Margaret Alexander, we know the new year will be prosperous—[*laughter*]—and a great success. I wish she'd lighten up just a little, though. I'll tell you, I'm getting tired—and so is everybody else—helping on this money-raising. But we want to continue—[*laughter*]—we want to continue—finance section quieted over here. [*Laughter*]

No, but we're very grateful to you. And I think I find in my job—sometimes—we don't adequately say thanks to those that are doing a lot of the heavy lifting. So, that's really what this little sojourn is all about: to express my confidence in Lee Atwater, my confidence in Jeanie Austin, my confidence in each one of you who is working to strengthen the Republican Party. It's going to pay off, you watch, in the elections of 1990. Thank you very, very much.

Note: The President spoke at 2:50 p.m. in the State Dining Room at the Capitol Hill Club. In his remarks, he referred to Jeanie Austin and Margaret Alexander, cochairman and finance director of the committee.

Nomination of Tommy G. Thompson To Be a Member of the Board of Directors of the National Railroad Passenger Corporation
January 3, 1990

The President today announced his intention to nominate Gov. Tommy G. Thompson to be a member of the Board of Directors of the National Railroad Passenger Corporation for a term of 4 years. He would succeed Robert D. Orr.

Since 1986 Governor Thompson has served as Governor of the State of Wisconsin. Prior to this he served as an assembly-man for the Wisconsin State Legislature since 1966.

Governor Thompson graduated from the University of Wisconsin at Madison (B.A., 1963; LL.D., 1966). He was born November 19, 1941, in Elroy, WI. Governor Thompson served as a captain in the U.S. Army. He is married, has three children, and resides in Madison, WI.

Nomination of Colin Riley McMillan To Be an Assistant Secretary of Defense
January 3, 1990

The President today announced his intention to nominate Colin Riley McMillan to be an Assistant Secretary of Defense for Production and Logistics. He would succeed Jack Katzen.

Currently, Mr. McMillan serves as chairman of the board and chief executive officer of the Permian Exploration Corp. In addition, he serves as managing partner of the Three Rivers Ranch and chairman of the board of the First Federal Savings Bank in Roswell, NM.

Mr. McMillan graduated from the University of North Carolina (B.A., 1957). He was born July 27, 1935, in Houston, TX. Mr. McMillan served in the U.S. Marine Corps, 1957–1960, and the U.S. Marine Corps Reserve, 1960–1972. He is married, has four children, and resides in Roswell, NM.

Statement by Press Secretary Fitzwater on the Attack on Religious Workers in Nicaragua
January 3, 1990

We deplore in the strongest terms this outrageous attack on religious workers and extend our deepest sympathy to the families of the victims. This is a tragic incident, one that further underscores the need to bring peace, stability, and democracy to Nicaragua.

The U.S. Embassy in Nicaragua has been in contact with local church officials to obtain information, including the Sisters of St. Agnes and the Capuchin Fathers. We are providing counselor services for the victims of the attack. We have no information on who is responsible for this attack, and we note that the church officials themselves have no indication, either. Our Embassies in Honduras and Nicaragua are attempting to find out further details. The Nicaraguan Government has provided no information to substantiate its charge that the *contras* launched the attack, and we hope the Sandinistas do not seek to obscure this tragedy by engaging in a propaganda battle.

The Nicaraguan resistance has condemned the attack. Its military commander has stated that the mining region where the attack occurred is outside of his force's usual operating area. But he also emphasizes that he has no information on the attack.

Note: Press Secretary Fitzwater read the statement to reporters at 11:11 a.m. in the Briefing Room at the White House.

Remarks on Signing the Earth Day Proclamation
January 3, 1990

It's good to see you all. Well, excuse the brief delay. Let me salute these distinguished gentlemen here: Admiral Truly, Mike Deland, Bill Reilly. Of course, it's a great, special pleasure to have Senator Chafee and Congressman Mo Udall here. And welcome to the White House on this special occasion. On April 22, 1990, America will celebrate Earth Day. I'm the guy that got mixed up on Pearl Harbor Day—

[*laughter*]—so I've got to be very careful that these people—Dr. Bromley, hi—understand. [*Laughter*]

No, but it is on April 22d that we celebrate Earth Day. And across the country, citizens will be asked to make a personal and collective commitment to the protection of the environment, to think globally and act locally. And April 22d also marks the 20th anniversary of the first Earth Day, giving each and every one of us a chance to reflect on the progress made over the past 20 years and set the environmental agenda for the next decade.

We've just started a new year. And 20 years ago this week, on another new year, President Nixon signed landmark environmental legislation—the National Environmental Policy Act—into law. The historic environmental laws of the seventies followed this step—the Clean Air Act, the Clean Water Act, the laws regulating pesticides and toxic substances and hazardous waste. And that act created the CEQ [Council on Environmental Quality], a voice for the environment that's been revitalized now, thanks to Mike Deland. And the EPA, established some 20 years ago under the leadership of Bill Ruckelshaus, is thriving under our able Administrator, Bill Reilly.

We've made much progress in the last 20 years, spending hundreds of billions of dollars to make pollution control work. In 1987 alone, we spent a total of $81 billion—over 62 of it in the private sector. I'm particularly proud that in 1989 we were able to take a number of new initiatives. We've signed legislation to protect wetlands and valuable waterfowl habitat. We've added funds to expand our parks, forests, and wildlife refuges; and we've banned the import of ivory. And we plan to host an international conference on climate change this spring. We've proposed to phase out CFC's worldwide, and a ban on unsafe hazardous waste exports. We've proposed a phaseout of asbestos by 1997. And we've introduced the first major overhaul of the Clean Air Act in over a decade—the most ambitious Clean Air Act proposed by any administration.

We need action on the revisions to the Clean Air Act we sent to Congress. The package was, in my view, carefully balanced to restore clean air for all Americans while sustaining job creation and competitiveness and economic growth. And I call on the Congress now to pass a Clean Air Act quickly, carefully, and responsibly—a Clean Air Act that harnesses the power of the marketplace to provide future generations with a cleaner, safer environment without jeopardizing the economy or the jobs on which all Americans depend.

I believe with all my heart that we can serve both of these important goals. And if the Congress cannot pass a bill that preserves both, then I would not be able to sign it; I'd have to veto it. But the Federal Government is only part of the story. It is in the city halls and State capitals, in schools and in the workplace, in this country and around the world, that real progress on the environment will be made. Environmental awareness—it's really got to be a second nature.

Earth Day can be part of the American tradition of private and public leadership that will help us reach that goal. In deciding to make this Earth Day proclamation the first proclamation of the new year—and the new decade, I might add—I want to make this point: Earth Day—and every day—should inspire us to save the land we love, to realize that global problems do have local solutions, and to make the preservation of the planet a personal commitment.

I now take great pleasure in signing this proclamation, recognizing April 22d, 1990, as Earth Day. So, come on over.

Note: The President spoke at 2:11 p.m. in the Roosevelt Room at the White House. In his remarks, he referred to Richard H. Truly, Administrator of the National Aeronautics and Space Administration; and D. Allan Bromley, Science Advisor to the President and Director of the Office of Science and Technology Policy. The proclamation is listed in Appendix E at the end of this volume.

Statement by Press Secretary Fitzwater Announcing the Surrender of General Manuel Noriega in Panama
January 3, 1990

General Scowcroft [Assistant to the President for National Security Affairs] notified the President at approximately 6 o'clock this evening that preliminary word had reached SOUTHCOM that General Noriega was willing to give himself up sometime tonight. We, of course, could not be sure that it would actually occur.

President Bush remained in the Residence until Secretary Cheney called him at approximately 9 o'clock this evening to say that General Noriega was in our custody. The President immediately came to the Oval Office to work on remarks, which he will be presenting to you in just a few minutes. I'll give you a 2-minute warning in just a second.

The President will not take questions following his statement, but General Maxwell Thurman, commander of SOUTHCOM, will hold a briefing in Panama on the details of the situation. General Thurman's briefing will follow the President's statement very soon. We'll be right back.

Note: Press Secretary Fitzwater spoke to reporters at 9:35 p.m. in the Briefing Room at the White House.

Remarks Announcing the Surrender of General Manuel Noriega in Panama
January 3, 1990

Well, on Wednesday, December 20th, I ordered U.S. troops to Panama with four objectives: to safeguard the lives of American citizens, to help restore democracy, to protect the integrity of the Panama Canal treaties, and to bring General Manuel Noriega to justice. All of these objectives have now been achieved.

At about 8:50 p.m. this evening, General Noriega turned himself in to U.S. authorities in Panama with the full knowledge of the Panamanian Government. He was taken to Howard Air Force Base in Panama, where he was arrested by DEA. A U.S. Air Force C-130 is now transporting General Noriega to Homestead Air Force Base, Florida. He will be arraigned in the U.S. District Court in Miami on charges stemming from his previous indictment for drug trafficking.

I want to thank the Vatican and the Papal Nuncio in Panama for their evenhanded, statesmanlike assistance in recent days. The United States is committed to providing General Noriega a fair trial. Nevertheless, his apprehension and return to the United States should send a clear signal that the United States is serious in its determination that those charged with promoting the distribution of drugs cannot escape the scrutiny of justice.

The return of General Noriega marks a significant milestone in Operation Just Cause. The U.S. used its resources in a manner consistent with political, diplomatic, and moral principles.

The first U.S. combat troops have already been withdrawn from Panama; others will follow as quickly as the local situation will permit. We are now engaged in the final stages of a process that includes the economic and political revitalization of this important friend and neighbor, Panama.

An economic team under the direction of Deputy Secretary of State Eagleburger and Deputy Secretary of Treasury Robson is just returning from Panama. A team of experts has remained on hand there to assess the full range of needs. We will continue to extend to the Panamanian people our support and assistance in the days ahead.

Panamanians, Americans—both have sacrificed much to restore democracy to Panama. The Armed Forces of the United States have performed their mission courageously and effectively, and I again want to express my gratitude and appreciation to all of them. And I want to express the special thanks of our nation to those servicemen who were wounded and to the families of those who gave their lives. Their sacrifice has been a noble cause and will never be forgotten. A free and prosperous Panama will be an enduring tribute.

Thank you all very, very much.

Note: The President spoke at 9:40 p.m. in the Briefing Room at the White House.

Presidential Determination No. 90–6—Memorandum on Multilateral Loans to China
January 3, 1990

Memorandum for the Secretary of the Treasury

Subject: Determination Pursuant to Title I of the Foreign Operations, Export Financing, and Related Programs Appropriations Act, 1990

Pursuant to provisions appropriating sums for the International Development Association in Title I of the Foreign Operations, Export Financing, and Related Programs Appropriations Act, 1990, I hereby certify that the International Development Association has not provided any new loans to China since June 27, 1989.

This determination shall be published in the *Federal Register.*

GEORGE BUSH

[*Filed with the Office of the Federal Register, 4:36 p.m., January 4, 1990*]

Note: The memorandum was released by the Office of the Press Secretary on January 4.

Letter to Congressional Leaders on Multilateral Loans to China
January 3, 1990

Dear _____:

As required by Title I of the Foreign Operations, Export Financing, and Related Programs Appropriations Act, 1990, I have determined that the International Development Association has not provided any new loans to China since June 27, 1989.

This determination, a copy of which is enclosed, shall be published in the *Federal Register.*

Sincerely,

GEORGE BUSH

Note: The letter was released by the Office of the Press Secretary on January 4.

Nomination of Malcolm S. Forbes, Jr., To Be a Member of the Board for International Broadcasting, and Designation as Chairman
January 4, 1990

The President today announced his intention to nominate Malcolm S. Forbes, Jr., to be a member of the Board for International Broadcasting for a term expiring April 28,

1992. This is a reappointment. Upon confirmation he will be designated Chairman.

Currently, Mr. Forbes serves as president and chief operating officer of Forbes, Inc., and deputy editor in chief of Forbes magazine. Prior to this he served as vice president and secretary of Forbes, Inc. Mr.

Forbes graduated from Princeton University (B.A., 1970). He was born July 18, 1947, in Morristown, NJ. Mr. Forbes served in the New Jersey National Guard, 1970. He is married, has five children, and resides in Bedminster, NJ.

Notice of the Continuation of the National Emergency With Respect to Libya
January 4, 1990

On January 7, 1986, by Executive Order No. 12543, President Reagan declared a national emergency to deal with the unusual and extraordinary threat to the national security and foreign policy of the United States constituted by the actions and policies of the Government of Libya. On January 8, 1986, by Executive Order No. 12544, the President took additional measures to block Libyan assets in the United States. The President transmitted a notice continuing this emergency to the Congress and the *Federal Register* in 1986, 1987, and 1988. Because the Government of Libya has continued its actions and policies in support of international terrorism, the national emergency declared on January 7, 1986, and the

measures adopted on January 7 and January 8, 1986, to deal with that emergency, must continue in effect beyond January 7, 1990. Therefore, in accordance with Section 202(d) of the National Emergencies Act (50 U.S.C. 1622(d)), I am continuing the national emergency with respect to Libya. This notice shall be published in the *Federal Register* and transmitted to the Congress.

GEORGE BUSH

The White House,
January 4, 1990.

[*Filed with the Office of the Federal Register, 12:53 p.m., January 4, 1990*]

Letter to Congressional Leaders on the Continuation of the National Emergency With Respect to Libya
January 4, 1990

Dear Mr. Speaker: (Dear Mr. President:)

Section 202(d) of the National Emergencies Act (50 U.S.C. 1622(d)) provides for the automatic termination of a national emergency unless, prior to the anniversary date of its declaration, the President publishes in the *Federal Register* and transmits to the Congress a notice stating that the emergency is to continue in effect beyond the anniversary date. In accordance with this provision, I have sent the enclosed notice, stating that the Libyan emergency is to continue in effect beyond January 7, 1990, to the *Feder-*

al Register for publication. A similar notice was last sent to the Congress and the *Federal Register* on December 28, 1988.

The crisis between the United States and Libya that led to former President Reagan's declaration of a national emergency on January 7, 1986, has not been resolved. The Government of Libya continues to use and support international terrorism, in violation of international law and minimum standards of human behavior. Such Libyan actions and policies pose a continuing unusual and extraordinary threat to the national security and vital foreign policy interests of the United States. For these reasons, I have determined that it is necessary to maintain in force the broad authorities necessary to apply economic pressure to the Government of Libya to reduce its ability to support international terrorism.

Sincerely,

GEORGE BUSH

Note: Identical letters were sent to Thomas S. Foley, Speaker of the House of Representatives, and Dan Quayle, President of the Senate.

Nomination of Three Members of the National Council on Disability, and Designation of Chairman
January 4, 1990

The President today announced his intention to nominate the following individuals:

Sandra Swift Parrino, of New York, to be a member of the National Council on Disability for a term expiring September 17, 1992. This is a reappointment. Upon confirmation she will be designated Chairman. Currently, Mrs. Parrino serves as Chairman of the National Council on Disability in Washington, DC. Mrs. Parrino received a bachelor of arts degree from Briarcliff College. She was born June 22, 1934, in New Haven, CT. Mrs. Parrino is married, has three children, and resides in Briarcliff Manor, NY.

Mary Matthews Raether, of Virginia, to be a member of the National Council on Disability for the remainder of the term expiring September 17, 1991. She would succeed Phyllis D. Zlotnick. Mrs. Raether attended the University of Texas. She was born June 17, 1940, in New Orleans, LA. Mrs. Raether is married, has two children, and resides in McLean, VA.

Alvis Kent Waldrep, Jr., to be a member of the National Council on Disability for a term expiring September 17, 1992. This is a reappointment. Currently, Mr. Waldrep serves as founder, president, and chief executive officer of Kent Waldrep National Paralysis Foundation in Dallas, TX. Mr. Waldrep attended Texas Christian University. He was born March 2, 1954, in Austin, TX. Mr. Waldrep is married, has one child, and resides in Plano, TX.

Statement on Receiving the Report of the President's Advisory Committee on the Points of Light Initiative Foundation
January 4, 1990

It is with a great deal of pleasure that I have today received the report of the President's Advisory Committee on the Points of Light Initiative Foundation.

Last summer I announced a three-part strategy to make community service central to the life and work of every individual, group, and organization in America. To help to implement this strategy, I announced that the Points of Light Initiative Foundation would be formed. I asked Gov. Tom Kean of New Jersey to head a committee to advise me on the structure of the Foundation and on the legislation needed to accomplish its goals. At the same time, the White House Office of National Service has developed recommended goals for the Foundation.

In addition to Governor Kean, this distinguished Presidential Advisory Committee is composed of Edward A. Brennan, chairman and chief executive officer of Sears, Roebuck & Co. and chairman of the board of governors of the United Way; Norman A.

11

Brown, president and chief programming officer of the W.K. Kellogg Foundation; Frances Hesselbein, national executive director of the Girl Scouts of the United States of America; and Vernon E. Jordan, Jr., senior partner of the law firm of Akin, Gump, Strauss, Hauer & Feld and former president of the National Urban League.

I am committed to making community service national policy of the highest priority. Drug abuse, illiteracy, homelessness, AIDS, environmental decay, and hunger must no longer be seen as someone else's problems for someone else to solve. To be a Point of Light is to measure your own success by what you do for someone else. Community service must become part of our daily pattern of living.

I am confident that the report I have received today from this distinguished group of Americans will assist us greatly in achieving these worthy goals.

Note: The Office of the Press Secretary issued a fact sheet on the same day which provided the following additional information on recommended goals for the Points of Light Initiative Foundation:

Points of Light Action Groups

Mission: To engage individuals from all walks of life and diverse groups and organizations who may never have worked together before in collaborating with one another to solve community problems.

a. To develop Points of Light Action Groups in all 50 States to determine pressing community problems, identify and mobilize community resources, and deploy them against these problems. Such groups would consist of new or strengthened partnerships among businesses, professionals, unions, schools, religious organizations, nonprofits, clubs, associations, and concerned individuals.

b. These groups will serve as catalysts for community action and as new engines for social change.

Youth Engaged in Service to America (YES)

Mission: To engage every young person, aged 5 to 25, in community service.

a. The Foundation will identify model community service projects in organizations of which young people are a part (schools, churches and synagogues, neighborhood organizations, clubs, etc.) and encourage similar organizations to replicate them.

b. The Foundation will help create youth service projects in a limited number of pilot areas (to be determined by the Board) that engage a wide variety of local groups and organizations and provide models which communities can replicate throughout the nation.

c. Every significant sector of American society (corporate, professional, labor, religion, nonprofits, clubs, and associations, etc.) not yet involved in youth development will work with young people to devise community service initiatives or participate in existing projects which are led by young people.

One-to-One Relationships

Mission: To form one-to-one mentoring relationships with people in need.

The Foundation will target a limited number of communities (to be determined by the Board) in which intensive efforts will be undertaken through the collaboration of a wide variety of community-based groups and organizations to develop one-to-one relationships with virtually every single individual in need.

Media Leadership/Support

Mission: To devote the distinctive capabilities of the local and national news and entertainment media to persuading people to engage in community problem solving.

a. Every segment of the news and entertainment media (e.g., television, newspapers, magazines, radio, cable, motion pictures) will provide examples of media groups and/or organizations that highlight community service continuously, spotlight successful service initiatives, profile outstanding community leaders, and inform the public of how to engage in community service.

b. In addition, in partnership with the Advertising Council, the Foundation will develop a nationwide advertising campaign to develop a new perspective on our social problems, to increase public awareness of the importance of community service, and to catalyze community action.

c. The Foundation will also create a mechanism to provide regular satellite feeds to local television stations containing stories about highly successful and newsworthy community service leaders and developments, and a wire print service to disseminate such information to local print media.

Finance/Resource Acquisition

Mission: To obtain the necessary resources from the private and public sectors to support the activities of the Foundation.

The Foundation will raise at least $25 million from the private sector in financial contributions and additional in-kind contributions. Also, the Foundation will seek $25 million in congressional funding.

The President's News Conference
January 5, 1990

The President. This morning I met with the Attorney General, Dick Thornburgh, to discuss the legal process related to the prosecution of General Noriega. We are committed to a fair trial and to providing all the protections guaranteed by the United States Constitution and laws. The Attorney General assures me that our case is strong, our resolve is firm, and our legal representations are sound.

Our government is not seeking a deal with Noriega. Our policy remains that we brought him to this country for prosecution. I will be ever mindful of this legal process in the days ahead and will not comment on any aspect of this prosecution or any matters that could even inadvertently affect the outcome of this case. And I'm going to ask others from this administration to do the same.

Deputy Secretary of State Eagleburger and Deputy Secretary of Treasury Robson have just given me a report on the economic reconstruction efforts in Panama. The first action that the United States took after General Noriega was removed from power was to release some $400 million in money that was withheld by virtue of our economic sanctions, sanctions which are now being lifted—$140 million, I believe, is already in Panama. The revitalization of the Panamanian economy is a major priority in the months ahead, as are our efforts for humanitarian assistance. And I would say here: I've been very grateful for the medical supplies that have gone to Panama.

I can report today that considerable progress has been made so far in returning Panama to a normal state of affairs. The new government has taken charge, and President Endara is working tirelessly to meet the needs of his people. Both Under Secretary Robson and Eagleburger were very high in their praise of Mr. Calderon, Mr. Ford, and of course, President Endara. They're discussing housing programs, business development, bank loans that will help spur economic growth. We are committed to be a part of that process.

I want to assure all of the countries of Latin America that United States policy remains one of a friendly, supportive, and respectful neighbor. We have worked hard and intensively to consult bilaterally and multilaterally with Latin America, and we will continue to do that. I personally will be involved in that. At the Latin American summit in Costa Rica, I pledged that we would work with the countries of this hemisphere to build a better life for their citizens. Our policy of cooperation is firm. Yesterday I had a lengthy discussion with Prime Minister Felipe González of Spain, who is so well respected in this hemisphere as well. And I share his deep, personal interest in seeing that the countries of this hemisphere pull together on behalf of democracy and economic freedom.

I know the yearnings of my fellow leaders in this hemisphere, leaders in Latin America, and I believe they will support the new government of Panama and they will support the United States as we work together in this hemisphere. I've asked the Vice

President, Dan Quayle, to visit a number of these Latin American countries within the next several weeks to personally deliver this message. I view this as very, very important diplomacy. And I am determined not to neglect the democracies in this hemisphere. Some have felt that we were so infatuated with the change in Eastern Europe that we were in the process of neglecting this hemisphere, and that is not the case. And the Quayle trip, in my view, will help. I have been undertaking consultations directly with leaders since I've been President. I will resume that, as I said, and the Vice President will be in a position to explain very clearly not only U.S. policy but our aspirations for Panama and, indeed, for this entire hemisphere.

So, that's where we are, and I'd be glad to take a few questions.

Q. Mr. President, you said that the Government is not seeking any kind of a deal concerning Noriega.

The President. Yes.

Q. Does that mean that you are irrevocably ruling out any reducing of charges, increasing of charges? And also, since the indictment runs from '81 to '86 and you had many contacts, apparently, with Panama during that period, were you ever aware of any drug activities on the part of Noriega?

The President. On the first part of the question, there's no such plan. The man's entitled to whatever is granted him under our law. So, there isn't any such plan.

Secondly, I have made some statements in reply to your second question, so punch it in the computer. And I'll have nothing more to say about it because I do not want, even inadvertently, to prejudice this case. But my actions are, in my view, totally unrelated.

Q. Mr. President, with General Noriega out of Panama and safely in custody in this country, it seems like you may have a difficult choice in deciding how to maintain order in Panama. Do you envision keeping a U.S. military peacekeeping force there beyond the usual contingent of 12,000 troops, or would you like to see the Panamanian Defense Forces reconstituted?

The President. One, I'd like to see their police forces, whatever emerges, reconstituted. Two, we will get our forces that went

in out as soon as possible. Three—I will just say this because your question obviously understands this—but to those listeners out there, SOUTHCOM has had a force there. And that force, under the treaty, will remain there. But the answer is: We want to get those additional augmented forces out as soon as possible, and we will.

Covert Diplomacy

Q. Mr. President, I'd like to try to follow up a question you were asked when you were here last about secrecy and the two missions by General Scowcroft to China. As I'm sure you may be aware, Secretary of State Baker was asked about what we then thought was the first China mission on one of the weekend talk shows, and he indicated that it was, indeed. It turned out to be the second. He has since acknowledged quite openly that his answer was false and that he felt constrained to give that answer to protect the secrecy of the mission. And I wondered first, sir, whether you felt it was worth it for him to have to do that? And second, whether that sort of thing is acceptable in your administration?

The President. Well, let me simply say that some things will be conducted in secrecy. And I know you don't like it. Your business is to get everything out in the open. And my business is to conduct the foreign affairs of this country in the way I think I was elected to, and for the most part, that will be in the open. But this move into Panama was held in secrecy, and I think the American people understand that.

My move to send people to China was controversial. Some think that the best way to make change for human rights in China is isolation—don't talk to them, try to punish them by excommunication. I don't feel that way, and so, I asked these people to go forward. And I don't think Jim Baker would ever deliberately mislead somebody, and so, I will stand with him.

Q. Sir, I believe he indicated that he felt he had to do that and that he knew what he was doing—that he had to do it. And I wondered how you felt about it.

The President. Ask him about it. I support my Secretary of State.

General Noriega of Panama

Q. You talk about your concern about prejudicing the case; but as you well know, you have called Noriega a thug, and other people in the administration have gone further. You've said he's poisoning our children. Haven't you already done that and——

The President. I think I've heard all kinds of characterizations of him in the press—columnists, even commentators, Presidents, Members of the United States Congress. He is now in custody. Time for rhetoric is over; time for answering hypothetical questions that might prejudice the trial is over. I would go back, Lesley [Lesley Stahl, CBS News], to help you on that, to Watergate, where there were hearings held, charges made over and over again, editorials written and voiced; and yet the people received a fair trial. So, I am convinced that our system of justice is so fair that the person will get a fair trial. But I can tell you, from my standpoint, I am going to bend over backwards and not answer hypothetical questions or not do anything that might prejudice that.

Q. Can I have a followup, please? I want to actually follow up on Helen [Helen Thomas, United Press International].

The President. Now, that's a separate question. [*Laughter*]

Q. But it's a followup. Reducing of charges—are you saying that if he wants to go for that, if he wants to try to go for reducing of charges, that we will entertain it? You said——

The President. No, I'm not saying that. I'm saying he has a right to do what he wants, and let the legal process determine how that should work out.

Q. You're not ruling it out.

The President. Well, I'm not ruling it in. I'm just saying he's got his rights, and we ought not to stand up here and try to define narrowly what they are.

U.S. Military Action in Panama

Q. Mr. President, based on your opening remarks and your comments about the Vice President's trip, it would indicate that you're concerned about relations with Latin America. Has the actions you've taken set it back?

The President. To some degree I am concerned because I am well aware of how our friends south of our border, including my friend President Salinas, look at the use of American force anywhere. So, I am concerned about it. I think it's something that's correctable, because I think they know that I have tried a lot of consultation, that we have exhausted the remedies in this particular case of multilateral diplomacy. But given the history of the use of U.S. force, I would be remiss if I didn't face up to the problem that we must go forward diplomatically now to explain how this President looks at the protection of American life; that we acted—in our view—well within our rights, but that we will continue consultation. But look, I felt strongly about the protection of American life. So, we've got to get them to understand that this isn't a shift away from what some had termed excessively timid diplomacy.

Q. Well, Mr. President, wouldn't that indicate that actually you were continuing old American policies that have upset the people in Latin America?

The President. Well, if there is that perception, then it's up to me and the Secretary—and in this instance, the Vice President's trip takes on enormous importance—to convince the people of the truth. And that is that we are not reverting to just a willful—what's the word I'm groping for here—use of force that has no rationale. But when it comes to the protection of American life, please—our friends south of the border—understand this President is going to protect it.

I'll tell you one thing that's helped on this, to the degree there is a problem at all, and that is the way the Panamanian democracy is now starting to move forward, the certification of the three people who had been deprived of their right to hold office by the previous regime. That's been of enormous help. And then I think the other thing is the public reception in Panama for our action. It has been overwhelming—overwhelming.

Q. On that, sir, Lee Atwater, the chairman of the RNC [Republican National Committee], says Panama is a political jackpot for you and it could well wipe out the disenchantment, for example, for the way you handled China. Without saying that's why you went into Panama, sending troops in, is one effect of it that it is a political jackpot?

The President. Well, Jesse Jackson doesn't think so. He talked to my wife. And so, there's differences of opinion on that. But I didn't do something for political reasons. That's not the reason I do that. I did it to protect American life. A President's called on to take certain actions. We're not going in to try to furbish a political image; that's ridiculous.

Q. Having said that, though, have you now neutralized the Democrats on foreign policy? Is this the last time [Senate Majority Leader] George Mitchell can ever accuse you of having a timid foreign policy?

The President. Knowing George, he'll find a reason, he'll find a way. And that's his job. Look, we're going into an election year. But I want to try, if I can, to separate the response. And he's been supportive of this— let's give the man credit. But I don't think it's laid to rest or put off-bounds any criticism of the President by Democratic opposition, if that's the question—no, absolutely not.

Q. Mr. President, do you anticipate that the bulk of the additional combat troops sent into Panama will indeed be out by the end of this month, as some administration officials have said? And secondly, and more broadly, do you now see an expanded role for the American military in small, regional issues like this one, or more particularly in the war against drugs, since there was a strong connection to this operation?

The President. I see no parallel between the situation here, where American lives are at stake and you had an indicted person who usurped power and declared war against the United States—I don't think you can draw a parallel between that unique situation and then other countries.

What was the other part of it?

Q. The bit about whether you see these additional combat troops able to come home, all of them.

The President. As soon as possible, and I have made clear to the Secretary of Defense, to the Chairman of the Joint Chiefs, who is down in Panama right now, I believe that this is what we should do. This is what

they themselves want to do. Some U.S. forces that went in are already out. So, I would look for an early return.

Q. General timeframe?

The President. Can't help you. But as soon as General Powell gets back, we'll have a more——

Q. What about the international law implications? Isn't this something that you are also going to talk to the Latin American countries?

The President. Absolutely.

Q. Isn't this setting a precedent? What is the explanation behind it?

The President. The right to protect American lives granted under the U.N. Charter. And we will protect lives of citizens, and we will go forward with that. The State Department, as I understand it, has already spelled that out. But I think you raise a good point. Yes, we should make very clear why we acted and under what authority we acted as we did.

Future American Military Action

Q. Mr. President, you just described Panama as a unique case. And I'd just like to ask you sort of a philosophical question. If the criteria you listed here—protecting American lives, having exhausted all the other diplomatic options—presented themselves again, should we look in a Bush Presidency for more such deployments in military force if your criteria were met?

The President. Yes, if you can spell out what the criteria is, and then if you can look to the future to see the situation surrounding it. I can't visualize another situation quite this unique. But let me just say when American life is threatened—we were concerned in El Salvador, for example. A civilian hotel could well have been occupied by a guerrilla force that would have threatened American life. That concerned me. And indeed, we moved forces not in some macho way but to try to protect the lives of American citizens. But I think most people understood that. But, David [David Hoffman, Washington Post], I don't see another real parallel here looming on the horizon at all.

China-U.S. Relations

Q. Mr. President, back to the issue of China. Your decision to send emissaries to China carried some cause for you. Have you seen any payoff yet? Have you had any response from the regime there that is productive or encouraging for you?

The President. Well, it does carry some, and I think some who are familiar with the situation have been quite supportive—and some quite critical; I will admit that. As I indicated, some favor isolation: Don't talk, and let them come to us. I think one of the great things that happened to us under the Shanghai communique and prior to that is the fact that we had a kind of contact, and they began to help facilitate the changes and the reforms that have taken place. So, I want to see those go forward again.

Is that responsive? I can't remember——

Q. Let me ask you specifically: Are we close to a resolution on the issue of the dissidents who are——

The President. I don't know the answer to that. They know my position, and it is one of adherence to human rights, I might add. The thing I object to about this whole one is the assigning of motives to the other person. You can question the tactics, but I refuse to let my political critics get me down in terms of they understand human rights and I don't.

I want to see, through the contacts that we've made, change that can be manifested in several ways. Now, there has been some. The Voice of America, for example, now has—they have a person permitted to go there. There's been a reiteration of the sale of missiles which we are very much in our—I think in the interest of peace in the world. So, there's been progress. I would like to hope that there would be more.

Soviet Reforms

Q. Mr. President, as you know, Mikhail Gorbachev has been visiting the Baltics in his country to deal with the growing independence or autonomy movement there. Have you encouraged him to allow those movements to continue, or do you consider that essentially an internal affair of the Soviet Union?

The President. Well, he's got his own internal affairs, but he knows of our advocacy of peaceful change. And to the man's credit, he has been the big advocate of peaceful change. He has been the advocate of reform. I mean, you've got to link it, Jerry [Gerald Seib, Wall Street Journal], to Eastern Europe to some degree. And I realize—and we can discuss this—that the problems are different. But give the credit that I don't think any of us a year ago from this day would have given in terms of Soviet adherence to change, given the dynamic upheaval in Eastern Europe.

Now, he's facing problems inside the borders of the Soviet Union—the Baltics, recently this other one—and he keeps reiterating his conviction about peaceful change. So, I support that. But we did have an opportunity to discuss in broad philosophical terms this question at Malta.

Q. Are you confident as a result that there's not going to be a crackdown?

The President. I'm certainly not buying into the hypothesis that there will, and I hope that this approach that he has taken—for which we give credit—will prevail.

Attack on Religious Workers in Nicaragua

Q. Yes, Mr. President, several times today you've made reference to the U.S. right to—indeed, your obligation to protect American lives. Today an American nun is being buried here in the United States. Even the Catholic order she represented there in Nicaragua claims that she was killed by *contra* forces.

The President. ——did claim that? I heard——

Q. Representatives of that group say the *contra* forces have been known to operate in that area using those tactics, and perhaps they didn't recognize the pickup truck that they were driving in. What do we know about who may have killed those nuns, and what are you doing to communicate to the *contra*—are you trying to call them off?

The President. Well, we're not calling them off because we don't know they were called on. And I'm interested in your hypothesis because you're telling me that some have concluded that it was the *contras.* The *contras* have denied that. Some have suggested it might be the other side. And the answer is: I deplore the loss of that nun's life. And similarly, there was another that I believe was killed that was a Nicaraguan there. And I deplore that loss of life. But it is murky. It is extraordinarily murky, similar to the situation in El Salvador.

But I want to take this opportunity to speak out against it. But we don't know the answer to it. And in El Salvador, we've said: Find out. We'll give you whatever technical assistance we can. And we want to find the answer to this question.

Q. But you're not confident then that the *contras* didn't——

The President. I don't know the answer to your question. They've said they didn't—others are accusing them. And I don't know, and I don't think our government knows. I'd share it with you if they did.

Women in Combat

Q. Mr. President, in Panama we saw women leading troops in combat for the first time. Are you comfortable with women in that role, and would you support changes in restrictions on women in combat?

The President. No, I'd willingly listen to recommendations from the Defense Department, but these were not combat assignments. But anytime you have a highly trained, gung-ho, volunteer force and they're caught up in some of the firefights that went on, a person—man or woman—can be put into a combat situation.

But it's my understanding, and I think Cheney took a question on that today, that these were not combat roles. And so, I would let the heroic performance of these people be weighed and measured and then see if the Defense Department wanted to recommend to the President any additional changes.

Soviet-U.S. Relations

Q. Do you have assurances from Moscow that the operation in Panama won't hurt U.S.-Soviet relations?

The President. Well, they didn't seem overly enthused about it, by Mr. Gerasimov's [Soviet Information Minister] statement. But on the other hand, I don't agree with him at all. But I don't think it's going to fundamentally flaw the relationships between ourselves and the United States [Soviet Union].

Military Action in Panama

Q. Do you think that the Latin leaders have been hypersensitive to the—given the fact that in back channels, apparently, they've been supportive of the invasion? Can you say if that is correct? And then also because of that, do you think they're hypersensitive in their public statements about U.S. force in the region?

The President. I like to feel that, given the way the situation is resolved, there is more support than has manifested itself in votes at the United Nations or in public statements. The Vice President's trip will help on this. My own consultations will help give me a clearer answer to your question. But I am absolutely convinced, given what happened and the reason why it happened, that if there's damage I can repair it, we can repair it, the State Department and whoever else is involved can repair it.

Q. But is it hypersensitive, their reaction so far?

The President. I think predictably so.

Q. Mr. President, some countries think the precedent now of Panama—feel that their sovereignty might be violated if the United States pursues drug dealers in their countries. And there has been some change in laws that they are worried about this—in the sense of the CIA, the FBI going out, being able to apprehend people outside the United States territory.

The President. And so, the question is what?

Q. Do these countries have reason to be worried that the precedent of Panama might serve as——

The President. Oh. Panama was more than that. Panama had, clearly, other ingredients that caused American action. It wasn't a simple case of going after a person who had been indicted for narcotics. And we know you had the abortion of democracy, but you also had this threat to the lives of Americans.

Let me do something in conclusion that may be a little risky. And it's a housekeeping detail, and it relates mainly to television.

I got a lot of mail after the last press conference; I had some calls. Because when I was speaking here in this room, juxtaposed against my frivolous comments at the time were some split-screen technique. It showed American lives—the bodies of dead soldiers, the caskets of dead soldiers coming home. And I would respectfully request that if the urgency of the moment is such that that technique is going to be used, if I could be told about and we'll stop the proceedings—or if it's something less traumatic. But that one—I could understand why the viewers were concerned about this. They thought their President—at a solemn moment like that—didn't give a damn. And I do, I do! I feel it so strongly. So, please help me with that if you would. Thank you all very much.

Note: The President's 32d news conference began at 1:08 p.m. in the Briefing Room at the White House.

Nomination of Anthony Hurlbutt Flack To Be a Member of the National Council on Disability
January 5, 1990

The President today announced his intention to nominate Anthony Hurlbutt Flack to be a member of the National Council on Disability for a term expiring September 17, 1991. He would succeed John F. Mills.

Currently Mr. Flack serves as president of his own firm, Anthony H. Flack & Associates in Connecticut. He was awarded the Bell Award for Outstanding Service in the field of mental health at the Bridgeport Chapter of the Connecticut Association of Mental Health. Mr. Flack attended Brown University. He was born September 7, 1923, in Greenwich, CT. Mr. Flack has two daughters and resides in Norwalk, CT.

Remarks on Signing the Proclamation Granting Special Trade Status to Poland
January 5, 1990

Let me just welcome the Secretary of State and, of course, Secretary Mosbacher and Derwinski. It's a great pleasure to have Carla Hills here—Ambassador Hills, our USTR—Chairman Boskin, the head of our economic advisers. Who am I missing? We'll get to the Ambassador in just a minute. Ed Derwinski, I mentioned. Let me just give a special welcome today, Mr. Ambassador, to you, Ambassador Kinast, and just say how pleased we are you're here.

The past year has been one of outstanding change in Eastern Europe. One country after another has embarked upon it, each in its own way, down the path of peaceful, democratic reform. But it was the brave people of Poland, under the banner of Solidarity, that led the way, beginning with the roundtable agreement of last spring and continuing with the formation of the first non-Communist government in Eastern Europe in more than 40 years. Poland has blazed the trail, the freedom trail.

And so, I'm here today to fulfill one of the pledges that I made during my visit to Poland in July, granting the nation access to our Generalized System of Preferences, the GSP. This special GSP treatment means that Polish exports will enjoy the most liberal access possible to the American market, and it will pave the way for increases in Polish exports to the United States—a vital contribution to Poland's economic recovery. It's going to open the door for investment, trade, and the interaction of two free peoples. And it's among the most important steps we could possibly take to help the people of Poland. And yet this measure is just one of many steps that the United States and our economic partners are taking to help Poland at this historic moment.

Let me outline just one other of these steps, if I might. As you know, in response to a request made last September by the new Polish government, I pledged that the United States would extend a $200 million grant as our contribution to a $1 billion stabilization fund to support Poland's economic reform program. Well, I said that I would encourage our economic partners to contribute the remaining $800 million so that Poland's needs would be fully met. And now I'm pleased to announce that on January 2d our goal was met in full. We joined our economic partners in the Group of 24, pledging to the Polish Government a fund of more than $1 billion, all to back its ambitious economic stabilization and reform program.

The United States now has developed a 3-year economic assistance program for Poland totaling more than $1 billion. And of this, nearly half will be provided this year alone in the form of grants. And take note:

The total financial commitments that we and our economic partners have made to Poland now add up to more than $8 billion. And that's $8 billion in Western economic assistance to Poland. Poland is not at the end but the beginning of a process of economic recovery and democratic change. The road they face is not an easy one. But the Polish people have already shown the courage and determination that they need to meet the challenges ahead. We will not let them face these challenges alone.

So, let me say it again, as I said out in Hamtramck last April: Poland is not alone, America stands with you. And now let me make all of this official, Mr. Ambassador.

Well, let me just at least say happy New Year to everybody. I know our other guests would like to do that.

Note: The President spoke at 2:04 p.m. in the Roosevelt Room at the White House. In his remarks, he referred to Secretary of Veterans Affairs Edward J. Derwinski; Michael J. Boskin, Chairman of the Council of Economic Advisers; and Polish Ambassador Jan Kinast. The proclamation is listed in Appendix E at the end of this volume.

Letter to Congressional Leaders on Amending the Generalized System of Preferences
January 5, 1990

Dear Mr. Speaker: *(Dear Mr. President:)*

I am writing to inform you of my intent to add Poland to the list of beneficiary developing countries under the Generalized System of Preferences (GSP).

The "Support for East European Democracy Act of 1989," P.L. 101–179, which I signed into law on November 28, 1989, amended Title V of the Trade Act of 1974 to allow Poland to be considered for GSP designation. I have carefully examined Poland under the criteria identified in sections 501 and 502 (b) and (c) of the Trade Act of 1974, as amended. In light of these

criteria, and particularly Poland's ongoing political and economic reforms, I have determined that it is appropriate to extend GSP benefits to Poland.

This notice is submitted in accordance with section 502(a)(1) of the Trade Act of 1974, as amended.

Sincerely,

GEORGE BUSH

Note: Identical letters were sent to Thomas S. Foley, Speaker of the House of Representatives, and Dan Quayle, President of the Senate.

Nomination of Richard F. Hohlt To Be a Member of the Board of Directors of the Student Loan Marketing Association
January 5, 1990

The President today announced his intention to nominate Richard F. Hohlt to be a member of the Board of Directors of the Student Loan Marketing Association. He would succeed Donald E. Roch.

Currently Mr. Hohlt serves as senior vice president of government affairs at the United States League of Savings Institutions in Washington, DC. Prior to this he served as executive assistant to United States Senator Richard G. Lugar.

Mr. Hohlt graduated from Milliken University (B.S., 1970). He was born December 4, 1947, in Indianapolis, IN. Mr. Hohlt served in the Air Force Reserves, 1970–1976. Currently he resides in Alexandria, VA.

Statement by Press Secretary Fitzwater on Disaster Relief for Areas Affected by the San Francisco Earthquake and Hurricane Hugo
January 5, 1990

At the direction of the President, the Office of Management and Budget is today distributing $184.6 million from the President's Unanticipated Needs for Natural Disasters Account. On October 26, 1989, the President signed the second continuing resolution for fiscal year 1990, which provided $2.85 billion in disaster relief funds for areas affected by the San Francisco earthquake and Hurricane Hugo. Of the $2.85 billion, $250 million was made available to the President to meet, at his discretion, unanticipated needs arising from both disasters.

The funds released today will be distributed primarily in California and South Carolina and be used for a variety of purposes, including school reconstruction; debris removal; transfer of patients to VA hospitals from damaged facilities; repair of damage to Federal parks, forests, wildlife refuges, and medical facilities; forest fire prevention; and stabilization of historic properties.

Agencies receiving funds today include the Departments of Agriculture, Veterans Affairs, Education, Interior, and Defense and the General Services Administration. The President has previously authorized distribution of $20 million from the account for earthquake preparedness planning and research activities at the Federal Emergency Management Administration, the U.S. Geological Survey, the National Science Foundation, and the National Institute of Standards and Technology.

After distribution of the funds today, $45.4 million will remain in the President's Unanticipated Needs for Natural Disasters Account. This contingency reserve will enable the President to respond to unanticipated disaster relief needs which continue to be identified as recovery from the disasters proceeds.

Remarks to the American Farm Bureau Federation in Orlando, Florida
January 8, 1990

Well, my thanks to my friend Dean Kleckner, Farm Bureau president, for that warm introduction. We're grateful for his leadership on that National Economic Commission and the tremendous support of you, the members of the Farm Bureau. My thanks, too, to Bob Delano out here, former Farm Bureau president, whose leadership and counsel have been so helpful to me.

I'm happy to have our distinguished Secretary of Agriculture, Clayton Yeutter, here at my side, doing a superb job for us. And I know you'll hear tomorrow from Ambassador Carla Hills [United States Trade Representative]. You talk about two people who understand the need to open up foreign markets to U.S. agricultural products—these two are tough, and they are the tops, and we're grateful to both of them.

My friend, Bob Martinez, Governor Martinez, it's always a pleasure to see you and visit your beautiful State. And of course, I'm very proud of the next two. Great to see Senator Connie Mack here—a new Senator making a national impression, I'll tell you—and next to him, or right near him, second from the end, my close friend and a long-time supporter [Representative] Bill McCollum—two outstanding voices for Florida in our Nation's Capital. I wish we had a lot more like them, I'll tell you.

I just returned from a little fishing and hunting over the holidays in Texas and Alabama, and I heard a story about the time that Mark Twain spent 3 weeks fishing in Maine after the fishing season had closed. On the way home, aboard the train, he told the man seated next to him about all the fish he'd caught. Finally, Mark Twain asked, "By the way, who are you, sir?" "I'm the State game warden," replied the man. "Who are you?" And after a long pause, Twain said, "Well, to be perfectly truthful, I'm the biggest damn liar in the whole United States." [*Laughter*]

I won't bore you with my fishing stories because I could reminisce with you all day long on this subject. It's a pleasure to be here because for 71 years now the American Farm Bureau has helped American farmers—over 3 million member families—to become the best in the world. And farming is a proud and noble part of our history. In fact, Thomas Jefferson himself wrote that "Agriculture is the most useful of the occupations of man." Today, nearly two centuries later, I'm here to give my first major address of the new decade, and I'm proud to begin this decade by talking to you about the future of farming in this country. But as we look forward, it's also important to reflect upon the past and what farmers have gone through, both good and bad.

You, America's farmers, deserve the credit for the rebound in U.S. farming, and I salute you again. I salute the board of directors up here, all farmers, who are leading this outstanding organization. You've been through the worst droughts and national disasters of the 1980's, and you've survived tough economic times. But you've worked with your minds and your hands to beat adversity with a kind of can-do commitment that's been the hallmark of American farming for generations.

Right here in Florida, we're seeing some of that can-do attitude as you face—Florida farmers—as you face the terrible loss of the citrus and winter vegetable crop. On the way down on Air Force One, Bob Martinez gave me the details of Florida's losses. But let me tell you—I'm sure you've heard this from Clayton—you will not be facing this alone. Clayton and I have talked, and I've asked the Secretary to personally oversee our efforts to provide assistance. And I know you can count on the USDA to be in there fighting with you.

It was a little over 4 years ago—seems like just yesterday—but a little over 4 years ago that the 1985 farm bill became law. Admittedly, the cost has been high, but it has worked. Since then, the news has been good. Surpluses have declined dramatically, and most of our good land has been brought back into production. Net farm income reached a record level last year, and the share of income that came from market sales continued to grow. The farm credit situation has greatly improved, bringing more financial stability to rural America.

As we face the future, the outlook is even better. Through sound fiscal policies and wise management of our resources, commonsense attitudes and, God willing, good weather, we can succeed. Together, we will keep rural America strong and American agriculture thriving in the 1990's.

But to do that—and Dean Kleckner alluded to this in his introductory remarks—to do that, our first priority must be to keep the American economy growing. That means fiscal and monetary policies that make sense. Today one of the best things we can do for farmers is to keep the interest rates low, and that is exactly what we intend to do.

This year, we will work with Congress on the 1990 farm bill. Getting a good farm bill through Congress is like milking a bull. [*Laughter*] But I can tell you that to be competitive we must have market-oriented farm policies that allow producers more flexibility to decide what crops to grow—and that because American farmers then can do what Americans do best, compete. At the same time, we've got to maintain a safety net to protect farmers from conditions beyond their control. But market-oriented farm policies are only a part of the agricultural picture; it is absolutely essential that we expand markets and enhance productivity.

We've got to assure the public that America's food is safest in the world, and we've got to protect our precious environment. America's farmers—I know this—America's farmers understand the importance of a clean environment. Many of you here today come from farms that have been handed down from parents and grandparents. You know that to protect the land is to protect not just your livelihood but your heritage.

We must recognize that productive agriculture and a sound environment can be compatible, especially in terms of water quality. The administration has initiated a concentrated 5-year effort to work with the Nation's farmers to protect our ground

water from contamination by fertilizers and pesticides. We'll spend close to a third of a billion dollars on research and support for farmers to stop contamination of our land and water. We must keep your good land in business without unreasonable burdens, but we must also keep it good land. I am counting on your leadership as we work to expand farm productivity while safeguarding our precious environment.

We must also make sure that all Americans are confident in the safety of our food supply. My administration is working hard to develop legislation to protect the food supply without overwhelming the agricultural industry.

But in the coming decade, the American farmer must have a level playing field in the international trade arena, too. And the way to fight trade barriers is through negotiation, not reciprocal protectionism. I know that many Farm Bureau leaders serve on the Agricultural Trade Policy Advisory Committee—and how important this issue is to you. Our administration has just made a bold proposal in the Uruguay round that would phase out export subsidies in 5 years and other trade-distorting practices in 10 years. But any agreement we sign—and I can guarantee you this—any agreement that we sign will be an agreement that is also good for American agriculture. You see, our goal is simple: open markets and free trade.

And it's beginning to work—international markets are improving. The value of U.S. agricultural exports has increased for the third year in a row; and sales to developing nations, the dynamic markets of the future, were up 13 percent last year.

We also support expanding our ties with Eastern Europe and the Soviet Union to open even more markets. Earlier this winter, Secretary Clayton Yeutter led a Presidential delegation to Poland to determine how American know-how can help Poland shift from that controlled economy to a market economy. It was a wonderful mission, and we're forging new partnerships between our agricultural industries and Eastern Europe's emerging economies.

But in today's global economy, America must also become more competitive through increased production, new uses for our products, and expanded markets at home. And so, this administration supports greater research into biotechnology for improved productivity, and we're encouraging alternative uses of farm products like ethanol and other new fuels and fuel additives. Just a few months ago, we proposed the expansion of the producer tax credit for alternative fuels to include ETBE. This will mean more markets for growers and cleaner air for all Americans.

But for us to reap the full benefits of a competitive economy we must cut the capital gains tax rate. With our capital gains tax proposal, we can help keep American agriculture dynamic and prosperous. And with continued economic growth, we can keep rural America going strong. Passage of our capital gains proposal, which would apply to the sale of farmland, will be one of my top priorities in this legislative year. Your support has been instrumental in the fight for the capital gains cut. And the fight isn't over yet. And I am sick and tired of the demagogs who call this a tax cut for the rich. It means jobs, it means savings, and it is good for all Americans.

And so, the farm bill, our international trade negotiations, and a capital gains tax cut will be high on my agenda for this great nation, because what's good for agriculture is good for America.

Let me talk just a little about some of the challenges facing all America. Like people everywhere in this great country, you work hard. You sacrifice to make good lives for yourselves and your children. Every one of us dreams of excellence in education; economic opportunity for all citizens; and a clean and healthy environment; and safe, drug-free streets, schools, and workplaces.

Together we are working to build a better America; but much remains to be done, and you're in the forefront. Rural America cares about education. You know, some say improving our schools is something for Federal money and Washington bureaucrats to handle, and I know you don't believe that. Whether it's a classroom on a rolling prairie in Nebraska or a busy New York street, improving education is a national challenge.

Last September, I met with the Nation's Governors at the education summit in Virginia to begin promoting educational restructuring in every State and determining national goals to attain excellence. The administration has sent the Educational Excellence Act to the Congress, and we want—and America needs—action on it soon.

Rural America is also battling the ravages of violence and drugs. Every citizen has the right to a safe home, the right to freedom from fear. Early in my administration, we sent the Comprehensive Violent Crime Control Act to the Congress. We proposed measures to improve enforcement and prosecution and strengthen current laws to put the drug dealers behind bars and keep them there. This critical crime legislation has been sitting on Capitol Hill for months. Brave citizens everywhere are standing up to crime, and it's a time for Congress to act quickly and responsibly because the war on drugs and crime will not wait. And I might say parenthetically, thank God we've got Bill McCollum in a key role in the House and Connie Mack, Senator. I again want to mention the support that we are getting from them and others like them for this approach I've outlined.

Let me just add a little more on our relationship with Capitol Hill. When I took office—Inaugural Address—I put out my hand to the Congress, to the Democratic majority, and reminded us all that the American people did not send us to Washington to bicker. As I've said, we sent proposals to Congress on clean air, combating crime, capital gains—responsible proposals, carefully thought out, based on principles. Now a year has passed. A new year has become. And it's time—it is past time—for Congress to tend to some of the unfinished business. Let me say to Congress as it comes back in a couple of weeks now: The hand of cooperation is once again extended. And I would only add: America wants it done right. America wants it done responsibly. And America wants it done now. We are always willing to listen to ideas and alternatives, but we are not willing to compromise on fundamental principles.

Finally, rural America does believe in liberty and democracy. Freedom-loving people everywhere are following the news reports from behind what used to be called the Iron Curtain. In fact, I read that the first thing to sell out in West Berlin on the day the Wall came down wasn't TV's or denim jeans. It was fresh fruit. In Romania, citizens knew freedom had arrived because for the first time in many years they saw food on the grocery store shelves. We reap what we sow, says the Bible, and what a bountiful harvest we are witnessing. It is a harvest of joy and opportunity that we will continue to support and encourage every step of the way. And let me add: This harvest is not just happening in Eastern Europe. Let's help the countries to our south, so that this hemisphere will be the first totally democratic hemisphere in the entire world.

I know I don't have to tell you this, but let me just tell you from the bottom of a grateful heart that I am mighty proud of our courageous fighting men who have helped Panama. And the joy shown by the people of Panama says it all, right there in the streets of Panama City.

And so, as I conclude my comments to the Farm Bureau, I can tell you I am optimistic about the coming decade, for I believe in the wisdom of our policies; I believe in the providence of the Almighty; and most importantly, I believe in the tough resiliency and the moral strength of the American people. Throughout our history, farmers—many in this room—have weathered disaster; and each time, like steel forged in a white-hot furnace, you are stronger with each testing by fire.

In the "Dirty Thirties" swirling clouds of dust ruined hundreds of farmsteads on the Great Plains. Many of the Dust Bowl farmers stayed on the land, and today their descendants have invented conservation techniques to catch and preserve the winter snows and the spring rains to carry their crops through the hot plains summer—a triumph of human courage and ingenuity. In the 1970's, an unheard-of disease, the southern corn leaf blight, swept through the fields of the Midwest. In a few days, the tall, green, tasseled corn was devastated, as if someone had taken a blowtorch to it. Over that winter, scientists and farmers developed resistant corn varieties in time for the next spring planting. A national food disaster was stopped dead in its tracks—a triumph of faith, science, and inventiveness.

And today, at the daybreak of the new decade, I want rural America to share in the promise and prosperity of our great nation. And in the months and years to come, as we approach the horizon of the new century, may we all share in the opportunity and optimism of a world at peace.

Thank you, and God bless the United States of America. Thank you very, very much.

Note: The President spoke at 10:47 a.m. in Hall D of the Orange County Convention/ Civic Center. Following his remarks, he visited the Land and the Living Seas Pavilions at EPCOT Center and then returned to Washington, DC.

Remarks Introducing the Presidential Lecture Series
January 7, 1990

Professor Donald and Mrs. Donald; Mr. Chief Justice and Mrs. Rehnquist; Chief Justice Burger, I understand, is here; Secretary Cheney and the Honorable Lynne Cheney; distinguished Members of the Congress; General Powell: Let me welcome you to the White House. And Barbara and I are very pleased to have you here. It's a privilege.

We're proud to host this lecture on the Presidency of the United States. And this is the first in a series of lectures on the men who have held this office. And it seeks to make them come alive: What were they like? How did they live? How was history, the history of America's house, molded by their dreams? To occupy this office is to ask those questions, and certainly to feel a kinship with those who have gone before—for each in his own way sought to do right and thus achieve good. And each felt a sacred trust with every American and often wondered, I suspect, how they could be worthy of that trust.

Perhaps no President had greater doubts or more brilliantly resolved them than the subject of this inaugural lecture: Abraham Lincoln, of Illinois. As President, Lincoln abolished slavery, and he saved the Union. Perhaps no leader has been so severely tested before or since. And yet we remember Abe Lincoln not merely for what he did; we revere him for what he was. Lincoln was a strong man—an arm wrestler, a rail splitter—and yet also a mix of kindness and humility. He was at once a hard and gentle person, a man of grief and yet of humor; for he knew, as he told Secretary of State Seward, that if he did not tell stories, he felt his heart would break.

Tonight we have with us a distinguished man who undoubtedly will tell stories. His name is David Donald, the Charles Warren professor of American history at Harvard University. A native of Mississippi, Mr. Donald graduated from the University of Illinois, where he was a student of the great Lincoln scholar J.D. Randall. He has taught at some of America's greatest universities and has written eight books about Lincoln and the Civil War, twice receiving the Pulitzer Prize in biography. Moreover, our guest is now working on a new biography of America's 16th President.

Earlier, I spoke of kinship. Well, I'm sure David Donald would agree any President's kinship with Lincoln is perhaps the most personal of all. So often Barbara and I go down to the Lincoln bedroom, which then served as Lincoln's cabinet room and office. And on his desk, to the left of the fireplace, is an original copy of the Gettysburg Address, written in his hand, which you will see in the East Room. And on the mantel is a plaque marking an equally noble legacy—

here the Great Unifier signed the Emancipation Proclamation.

Yet perhaps nowhere do we learn more about Lincoln even now than in a portrait that I talked about last month off the coast of Malta before meeting Chairman Gorbachev. It is, as this one is, by George Healy, and hangs on the wall of my office upstairs. And in it you see the agony and the greatness of a man who nightly fell on his knees to ask the help of God. The painting shows two of his generals and an admiral meeting near the end of a war that pitted brother against brother. And outside at the moment a battle rages. And yet what we see in the distance is a rainbow—a symbol of hope, of the passing of the storm. The painting's name: "The Peacemakers." And for me, this is a constant reassurance that the cause of peace will triumph and that ours can be the future that Lincoln gave his life for: a future free of both tyranny and fear.

One hundred twenty-nine years ago, leaving Springfield to assume the Presidency, Lincoln addressed his home people at Great Western railroad station. And he told them, "All the strange checkered past seems to crowd now upon my mind." Even now, the memory of Abraham Lincoln crowds upon our minds. It's a great privilege, then, to introduce a man who has devoted his lifetime to the study of its tragedy and its glory, one of the great scholars of perhaps our greatest President, Professor David Donald. And thank you, sir, for being with us.

Note: The President spoke at 5:30 p.m. in the State Dining Room at the White House. In his opening remarks, he referred to Secretary of Defense Richard B. Cheney; Lynne V. Cheney, Chairman of the National Endowment for the Humanities; and Gen. Colin L. Powell, Chairman of the Joint Chiefs of Staff. The remarks were released by the Office of the Press Secretary on January 9.

Remarks on Signing the Martin Luther King, Jr., Federal Holiday Proclamation
January 9, 1990

Well, let me salute Dr. Hooks, the able head of the NAACP. And I see our Director, Bill Bennett, here, and many others. Connie Newman is here somewhere. I see Dorothy Height, Art Fletcher, and Josh Smith, and others. But I want to welcome you to the White House—pardon the slight delay there—and bemoan the fact that some of the young people that were to be here couldn't make it because of the bus schedules and the weather.

This is an event that celebrates the greatness of a man whose life and legacy helped set America free. I refer, of course, to Dr. Martin Luther King. He would have been 61 years old next Monday. Since 1986 this day has been a Federal holiday, and I will shortly sign this proclamation. But first, just a few words from the heart.

Most of you weren't born yet—I was addressing myself to young people. I am going to have to modify that slightly, looking around. [*Laughter*] Certainly, the front row over here—[*laughter*]—but now, there's some that qualify. Let me rephrase it: Many of you weren't born yet when Dr. King was killed, and yet you know that his life was central to the story of America. Each day we write new chapters; and as we do, let us recall who Dr. King was, what he did, and what his lessons were. For you remain the trustees of all that he believed.

First, he was a crusader and an evangelist, bore the weight of a pioneer. He was a force against evil. His life was a metaphor for courage. His goal was an America where equality and opportunity could coexist and where goodness could prevail.

Next, what did he do? Well, he went to cities and towns, large and small, places like Selma and Birmingham and Montgomery—wherever he was needed. And wherever he found hatred, he condemned it. Wherever there was bigotry, he assailed it. And wherever there was segregation, he defied it. He endured death threats and these obscene phone calls in the dead of the night, but he refused to be intimidated. And through his courage, Dr. King changed forever America for the better.

Finally, what did this man teach? Well, he preached "love thy neighbor." He taught that before government there was man, and government arose to meet man's needs. He demanded rights central to all that's good about our country: the right of free expression; equal protection under the law; the right to vote as we choose; the right to think, dream, and worship as we please.

Those lessons did not die with Martin Luther King. But we must recall them daily, for while he did so much, there is much that remains to be done, in particular—and I know how strongly Reverend Hooks feels about this—particularly when we hear of bombings, obscene phone calls, hate mail. Each one of us must speak out. And there is no place for the baggage of bigotry in the United States of America.

Teddy Roosevelt called the Presidency the bully pulpit. Well, I will continue to use that pulpit, hopefully with sensitivity, always to denounce and work to bring to justice the bigots who stain this good and decent land. I am confident that Martin Luther King would support that goal, just as I know he would rejoice today that the civil rights anthem of "We Shall Overcome" has captured the hearts of millions as democracy begins to bloom in Eastern Europe.

And here at home, where Dr. King's call for nonviolent change is making America a better place—here, too, his lessons live. We see them in our neighborhoods, in our churches and, yes, in students—in you as students. But you are the dream that Dr. King spoke so movingly about. And you must fight for what he died for: a nation in which no one is left out. And I know you've made that fight your own.

For evidence, Darrell Webster, a graduate student at Catholic University, overcame a troubled childhood to mentor kids in his old neighborhood. Shavonna Brown, of Woodson Junior High, conquered a simi-

27

lar background to become a leader in her school. And then, Linda Lawson—in an age where too many are choosing drugs, Linda's choice was different: she chose education, becoming valedictorian of her high school and, today, a junior at prestigious American University. And next semester she's going off to England to study. Darrell, Shavonna, Linda—in a sense, I wish that Martin Luther King could see you now. For he often spoke of how education can spur excellence, and excellence, equality. He knew how higher learning could be the great uplifter, and he believed that education could help each American climb the ladder of self-respect and dignity.

And that's the lesson that I'd like to emphasize today: Take pride in what you've done, as I know Dr. King would. But remember, too, that we have not finished the work of making Martin Luther King's dream a reality for each child in America: that one day they would live in a nation where they were judged not by the color of their skin but by the content of their character.

So, let me address these closing remarks to you particularly, the students. Dr. King loved the young people of America, and so I wanted not only you to be here but others—some of whom could not make it— be here today. For while he's gone now, the children remain. And that, in essence, has become his legacy. For the youth have inherited his mantle and must help realize the dream. So, do right, as he would. Love justice, as he did every day of his life. And next Monday, of course, will be our special holiday. So, it is now my privilege to sign a proclamation naming January 15th of this year the Martin Luther King, Jr., Federal holiday.

Thank you all very much for being with us. And could you join me when we do the signing?

Note: The President spoke at 10:03 a.m. in Room 450 of the Old Executive Office Building. In his opening remarks, he referred to Benjamin Hooks, executive director of the National Association for the Advancement of Colored People; William J. Bennett, Director of National Drug Control Policy; Constance B. Newman, Director of the Office of Personnel Management; Dorothy Height, president of the National Council of Negro Women; Arthur A. Fletcher, Vice Chairman of the Pennsylvania Avenue Development Corporation and former Assistant Secretary of Labor; and Joshua Smith, chairman of the NAACP Task Force on Quality Education. The proclamation is listed in Appendix E at the end of this volume.

Statement on the Meeting With Benjamin Hooks, Executive Director of the National Association for the Advancement of Colored People
January 9, 1990

I met with the Reverend Benjamin Hooks today to personally express to him my outrage at the recent bombings, obscene phone calls, and hate mail that have threatened the NAACP headquarters and branch chapters around the country over the past weeks. I have also reassured him that my administration will not tolerate bigotry and racial prejudice. We must finally leave the tired old baggage of bigotry and racial hatred behind us. I have asked Reverend Hooks to let his membership know that this administration will not let up in the fight against racism and that we will work to bring the perpetrators of these hideous crimes to justice.

It is particularly appropriate at this time, as we celebrate Dr. King's birthday in this first month of the new decade, that we restate our dedication to fulfill the dream of opportunity for all of the American people.

Nomination of D'Wayne Gray To Be Chief Benefits Director of the Department of Veterans Affairs
January 9, 1990

The President today announced his intention to nominate D'Wayne Gray to be Chief Benefits Director for the Department of Veterans Affairs. This is a new position.

Currently Lieutenant General Gray serves as executive director of the Montgomery County Revenue Authority in Rockville, MD. Prior to this he served as a consultant for the Center for Naval Analysis in Falls Church, VA. In addition, he has served in the U.S. Marine Corps from 1952 to 1987 and was awarded a Distinguished Service Medal, Legion of Merit, a Bronze Star, Meritorious Service Medals, and Air Medals.

General Gray graduated from the University of Texas (B.A., 1952) and George Washington University (M.S., 1971). He was born April 9, 1931, in Corsicana, TX. General Gray is married, has three children, and resides in Falls Church, VA.

Nomination of Philip R. Lochner, Jr., To Be a Member of the Securities and Exchange Commission
January 10, 1990

The President today announced his intention to nominate Philip R. Lochner, Jr., to be a member of the Securities and Exchange Commission for the remainder of the term expiring June 5, 1991. He would succeed David S. Ruder.

Dr. Lochner has served in various positions at Time Warner, Inc., in New York, NY, including general counsel and secretary, 1988 to present; vice president, 1986 to present; and associate general counsel, 1978 to present. Prior to this, he served as an attorney with the law firm of Cravath, Swaine and Moore in New York City, 1973–1978, and associate dean and assistant professor of law at the State University of New York Law School in Amherst, NY, 1971–1973.

Dr. Lochner graduated from Yale University (B.A., 1964; LL.B., 1967) and Stanford University (Ph.D., 1971). He was also a Fulbright fellow at the University of London in 1968. Dr. Lochner was born March 3, 1943, in New Rochelle, NY. He is married, has two children, and resides in Greenwich, CT.

Statement by Deputy Press Secretary Popadiuk on President Bush's Telephone Conversation With President Virgilio Barco Vargas of Colombia
January 10, 1990

President Bush called President Barco today to express regret over the recent misunderstanding resulting from erroneous press stories about a proposed U.S. counternarcotics operation. President Bush explained that the U.S. had intended a cooperative effort with Colombia that could complement President Barco's courageous and determined effort to break up the narcotics cartels and bring traffickers to justice. President Bush assured President Barco that the United States never intended to conduct any activities within Colombian territorial waters, that no U.S. actions would be taken without the full cooperation and consent of the Colombian Government, that no blockade was ever contemplated, and that he had not authorized naval maneuvers, as incorrectly described in the press.

The two Presidents agreed that it was most unfortunate that inaccurate and confusing reports of tentative U.S. proposals for cooperation with the Colombian Government had created such a false impression. President Barco said that he regretted the erroneous press stories which had emanated from both Colombia and the United States and that he always knew that President Bush would never approve actions which impinged on Colombian sovereignty.

President Bush assured President Barco that the United States would take no actions without prior consultations with and the cooperation of the Government of Colombia. The two Presidents agreed to remain in close contact on this and other issues of mutual concern.

Statement by Press Secretary Fitzwater on the President's Meeting on Emergency Aid to Poland
January 11, 1990

Earlier this morning the President met with members of the Emergency Committee for Aid to Poland (ECAP). This committee was recently formed by a distinguished group of business, labor, civic, and academic leaders to provide humanitarian relief to the people of Poland to help them through the winter. In the meeting, members of ECAP briefed the President on the status of the organization's efforts. Over 50 tons of much-needed medical supplies and infant formula have already been donated by generous U.S. companies, and shipments of these goods have begun.

The President applauds the efforts of the committee, which is capably led by its co-chairmen, Senator Robert Dole and Dr. Zbigniew Brzezinski. The committee has also been assisted by Labor Secretary Elizabeth Dole, who met with Polish leaders to identify needs as part of the Presidential mission last year.

The work of ECAP exemplifies both a spirit of voluntarism and our nation's commitment to aid the people of Eastern Europe as they embark on their new journey into freedom. The President wishes ECAP every continued success in its important work.

Informal Exchange With Reporters
January 11, 1990

China-U.S. Relations

Q. Mr. President, has China done enough to restore good relations with the U.S.?

The President. We have a distinguished guest here, an old friend of mine who I am delighted to see, the Prime Minister of Portugal. And I'll tell you, we've got a lot of business to talk about, but just receiving him here is a great treat and honor for me. And Barbara's looking forward to lunch with Mrs. Cavaco Silva.

And I will say one thing on this subject you asked about. And we can't really do any more questions here. We have a new policy: We don't take questions at what we call photo opportunities. But we'll have a chance later on.

But inasmuch as there is interest in this, let me just say I view the lifting of martial law as a very sound step. For those that are interested in human rights and the reform that was on the move and that we'd all like to see go forward, there's no way you can look at that but not say it is very positive. And we will continue to watch this situation very closely. But I've taken a position that I do not want to isolate China by no contacts and set the clock back. And of course, we welcome the lifting of martial law; it's a good sign. That's all I've got to say about it. And I hope you'll excuse me, because we have no more time here.

Q. Does this mean you're preparing——

Television Interview of Helen Thomas

The President. I said that's the last question. You didn't hear what I said, Rita [Rita Beamish, Associated Press]? They've got their job to do, and I've got mine. [*Laughter*]

Helen [Helen Thomas, United Press International], you're a star. I would like to talk to you off the record.

Ms. Thomas. On what?

The President. Phil Donahue.

Ms. Thomas. Did you watch it?

The President. You've got a lot of stars here. I saw it. Did you see that show, Marlin [Marlin Fitzwater, Press Secretary to the President]? It was very interesting, actually.

Ms. Thomas. I was up against the TV pros.

The President. It was interesting. I did it at the house——

Ms. Thomas. You think so?

The President. I've got to argue with you about one point, but on some of it I was in agreement.

Ms. Thomas. When would you like to do that? [*Laughter*]

Meeting With Prime Minister Cavaco

The President. There's another star right there. Well, I don't know. You guys don't like off the record, so we can't talk about it.

Let me just say to our friends from Portugal that I'm very pleased to have an old friend of mine, the Prime Minister, right here in the White House. He graced my own house in Maine when I was the Vice President, long before I was President of the United States. I consider him a friend; I value his counsel. I respect his commitment to democracy in Eastern Europe and elsewhere. And so, I'm looking forward not only to a sound exchange of views but to renewing a friendship that Barbara and I treasure—and a friendship, frankly, that doesn't need day-to-day contact because it's good and solid. And so, I view our relationship important, and I want to hear from the Prime Minister his views.

The Prime Minister. You want to see me in Portugal? [*Laughter*]

The President. Well, I'd like to come. We want to see you back in Maine, too—[*laughter*]—where we get out of this formal setting here. Welcome, welcome to all of you who are not based here.

Note: The exchange began at 11:05 a.m. in the Oval Office at the White House prior to a meeting with Prime Minister Anibal Cavaco Silva of Portugal.

Remarks Following Discussions With Prime Minister Anibal Cavaco Silva of Portugal
January 11, 1990

The President. I was pleased to meet once again with a leader of a close and enduring ally—and a good friend, as well—Prime Minister Cavaco Silva of Portugal. This was at least our third meeting—a very productive, substantive meeting. In exchanging views on the full range of important bilateral and international issues, we found that

our relations are stronger than ever.

Today we're all witness to dramatic, momentous change around the world, especially in Eastern Europe. Future generations may call the present period a crucial turning point, but they will surely judge us on our ability to meet the challenge of change. Over the past two decades, Portugal has been an example of tremendous progress— in overthrowing a dictatorship, consolidating democracy, granting independence to former colonies, and undertaking economic reform. We see Portugal standing as an inspiration and an example to Eastern European countries as they emerge from the darkness of political and economic authoritarianism. The Portuguese experience has demonstrated that peaceful, democratic change and economic progress are possible.

Mr. Prime Minister, today your country is a stable democracy, with a strong economy and a dynamic society. As a valued NATO ally, Portugal's important contributions to the alliance have helped keep the peace for over 40 years. Today relations between your country and the United States are better than ever—based on equality, shared interests, and mutual respect.

As Prime Minister Cavaco Silva knows very well, security in today's world transcends armaments. It involves many factors: commerce, the environment, the fight against terrorism and narcotics, as well as military preparedness. The Prime Minister and I discussed these issues, and I'm glad to say we share a common perspective on strengthening our cooperation. We agreed on the need for close and constant consultations among our NATO allies and between the United States and the EC on the fast-paced changes that are sweeping Europe.

We also discussed the process of national reconciliation in Angola. Portugal has historic ties to the southern African region. We value the perspective and support they've given to President Mobutu's [of Zaire] efforts to mediate the Angolan conflict. When peace and stability come to that region, as certainly we hope they will, Portugal will have an important role in the reconstruction process.

You know, hundreds of years ago, Portugal's influence was felt in the furthest corners of the globe. From Macao and India to Brazil and southern Africa, Portuguese explorers showed the world what was possible. Today Portugal is again showing what is possible and serving as an example well beyond its borders.

Portugal's economy remains robust even as it undergoes reform. Foreign investment is growing. Nationalized firms are giving way to privatization. Through the Prime Minister's expertise, his own expertise, Portugal has opened up capital markets and cut taxes and brought to life a more flexible, dynamic marketplace. Portugal is clearly well on its way in developing its economy and deserves the support of all of its allies in its efforts.

Our two countries share much in common. Both traditional maritime powers, we value the marketplace of economic competition, and we treasure democracy. These common perspectives will serve us well as we approach EC economic union in 1992 and give us confidence that we can meet the challenge of change in the new decade, working together as allies.

It's been a great pleasure, sir, having you here at the White House. Good luck, and thank you for coming our way.

The Prime Minister. Mr. President, I would like to express to you my satisfaction for the meeting we had this morning which afforded the opportunity for yet another useful, open, and friendly exchange of views on our two countries' participation in the Atlantic alliance, the strengthening of our bilateral relations, and the new developments in the international situation.

Portugal's and the United States' positions are convergent as regards the new prospects, brought about by the recent developments in Eastern Europe, for the Atlantic alliance. As we have already seen at last December's NATO summit, the allies' cohesion and the reinforcement of its two pillars—the European and the American—are essential for the preservation of our security. I had the opportunity to stress to President Bush that the Portuguese Government is in favor of a continued commitment and presence of the United States in Europe, which is a key factor for Europe's own security.

We also concurred in our expression of solidarity with the peoples of Eastern Europe by furthering the ongoing democratization process and promoting adequate economic aid. I informed President Bush about the outcome of the recent meeting of the European Council in Strasbourg, where significant steps were made toward a European union and the building of a new

Europe, and where a plan of action to assist the Eastern European countries was devised. The Portuguese Government strongly hopes that relations between the European Community and the United States will reach a high level of cooperation and mutual understanding in a way that reflects the existing political and security relations between Europe and the United States.

As regards our bilateral relations, I reaffirmed Portugal's commitment to pursuing its privileged relationship with the United States. Portugal's location, reaching deep into the Atlantic Ocean, the preferential relationship we have in the framework of the Atlantic alliance, and the staunch defense of our common values naturally lead us to the establishment of a special relationship as allies, which should be reinforced and diversified. Thus, I had the opportunity to state the Portuguese Government's intention to expand the framework of our bilateral relations so as to establish a broader and deeper relationship while preserving the existing cooperation in the areas of defense and security, and to suggest formulas allowing the extension of the economic, cultural, and technological fields within the present political mutual understanding.

In the prospect of a single European market, we want to develop new forms of increased cooperation and to promote joint investment by the economic sectors of our two countries. I note with pleasure that President Bush has a similar purpose, and therefore, we must now set the direction

for more far-reaching and dynamic relations.

When we discussed the international situation, we addressed in particular detail the events in southern Africa, and especially the development of the peace process in Angola and Mozambique. I apprised President Bush of the conversations I had recently with the Presidents of those two countries and of the outcome of the ongoing consultations we maintain with the Angolan and Mozambican Governments, and expressed the hope that if all interested parties show a positive attitude it will be possible to put an end to the conflict that exacts such a heavy toll on the peoples of those two African countries.

Finally, Mr. President, I would like to thank you most especially for this opportunity to visit Washington and to meet with you, which I am sure has significantly contributed to our pursuing a very useful dialog on the ways in which we can strengthen the friendly relations that exist between our two countries.

Note: The President spoke at 1:21 p.m. at the South Portico of the White House. Prime Minister Cavaco spoke in Portuguese, and his remarks were translated by an interpreter. Prior to their remarks, the President and the Prime Minister met privately in the Oval Office and with U.S. and Portuguese officials in the Cabinet Room, and then attended a luncheon in the Family Dining Room.

Appointment of Richard G. Trefry as Military Assistant to the President and Director of the White House Military Office
January 11, 1990

The President today announced the appointment of Lt. Gen. Richard G. Trefry, USA, Ret., as Military Assistant to the President and Director of the White House Military Office.

General Trefry served in the U.S. Army from 1950 until 1983. A field artillery officer, General Trefry finished his military

career as the Inspector General of the Army. Following his retirement, General Trefry was a founder of Military Professional Resources, Inc. He has served as a senior fellow of the Institute of Land Warfare and as a lecturer and instructor to military service schools and colleges.

General Trefry graduated from the U.S.

Military Academy in 1950. He was born August 6, 1924, in Newburyport, MA. General Trefry is married to the former Jacquelyn Dahlkoetter and resides in Clifton, VA.

Question-and-Answer Session With the Youth Collaborative Mentor Group in Cincinnati, Ohio
January 12, 1990

Sister Jean Harrington. I have told the President that he has a very unique group of people sitting in front of him. He has 10 Taft High School students with their mentors or their tutors, 2 college students who are in college as a result of our Last Resort Scholarships, and a student from Porter Middle School and one from Bloom Middle School, and a teacher from Bloom Middle School who has coordinated the Earn and Learn Program. And I know the President's eager to hear about your experiences, and I imagine you're eager to hear about some of the things he does, too. So, it's open.

The President. When you either ask a question or tell me what you're doing, which I hope you'll do, just say where you are in life and what school you're in—college or mentoring or whatever. It would be helpful, and I think everybody here would be interested.

We've had a good briefing on this unique program. I keep talking about something called a Thousand Points of Light. At first, we had one guy who said, "Did he say 'a thousand pints of Lite'?" [*Laughter*] And I said, "No, it's a Thousand Points of Light." And that really means involvement of one person in the lives of others—helping. Then I come out here today and have had this wonderful briefing on how this program, in many ways, is just the epitome of a Thousand Points of Light—a lot of people helping kids get going or stay involved or pull themselves up.

And so, I don't know who wants to be first, but I'd be glad to answer any questions. I see somebody nicely put a picture of Barbara up there. She is very active in education, because, I'll tell you what, for you kids, you old kids, even—[*laughter*]—Ed, sorry about that—no, but her thing is literacy. And she's been involved in it for a long time. And I understand, of course, that—

obviously, much of this program, as it starts with these young kids—let's have everybody be literate. But I wish she were here, because the Sister had asked about her very generously.

Yes, sir?

Social Attitudes and Values

Q. Mr. President, I'm a mentor here at Taft High School. The question I have is a very difficult one. And it has been my perception in working with the young people that there is a sense of hopelessness, to the degree that it almost stunts the importance of the programs that we have. If they perceive that, in the community at large, no one really cares, and if I do my best, if there's a legitimate opportunity—my question is: What do you feel a U.S. President and administration can do to help create a more hopeful attitude or atmosphere or environment for our young people and those that are——

The President. It is a tough question. But you know, the more I think of it—and you're the experts, you're the guys with your sleeves rolled up, and you're the ones that are trying to learn—being right there in the front line, I would have to concede, gives you perhaps a better insight of this than I have being back there in the White House.

But as I look at it, a lot of it is family. A lot of it has got to be our—in some way, encouraging the strength of a family. And this is an awfully philosophical answer to a rather specific question. But I happen to think that some of the despair and some of the discouragement comes from the dissolution or the strains on the American family. Now, there are some answers to that, obviously. If we are successful in working with the local communities in the antinarcotics battle, I think that'll help enormously. If

34

programs like this are successful—and this is why this whole subject of education is priority—if programs like this are successful, I think through education itself kids will begin to get hope and see that, comparatively, as you look around the world, we're pretty well off—even those who are not doing very well. So, I guess what I can do about it is to encourage what I think of as fundamental values. I happen to be one who has learned in one short year that faith is important. And I have a philosophy, Ed, of what happened, a theory.

We came out of the Vietnam war; it was very divisive. We had that post-Watergate period that increased a certain national cynicism, it seemed to me. And that spills off on young people—maybe on their teachers. So, we're now coming into a new period. We look around the world, and we see the darnedest, most dramatic changes moving towards the values that have made this country the greatest: freedom, democracy, choice to do things.

So, I think we can now, with programs like you're engaged in, point to people coming our way around the world because they see we do have something very special. I'm not sure that's a totally satisfactory answer, but I get back to fundamentals—to values. We're trying in the education field to stress certain fundamentals. I had a marvelous meeting yesterday with a bunch of educators and businesspeople, because we've challenged the Nation's Governors to come up with educational goals. But they're going to get back to fundamentals of reading and writing and math, science, and now geography.

But on balance, I am optimistic. And yet I know there's an awful lot of reasons to be discouraged in part of some individuals. But I think I've got to keep an optimistic stance as President. I've got to keep talking about fundamental values. I've got to keep trying to do what we can in terms of not only funding educational initiatives but restructuring. So, we get back to ways that we can compete. And in the process, these kids will have a better opportunity.

Federal Role in Education

Q. First of all, sir, I'd just like to commend you on your efforts for the war on drugs.

The President. Tell me who you are and what grade, or what staff——

Q. What grade? I could kiss you, sir. [*Laughter*]

The President. Go ahead.

Q. Sir, I'm an adult volunteer mentor——

The President. Volunteer. Isn't that great?

Q. ——here at Taft High School. Yes, sir.

The President. Well, you do look like you're young. Come on, you are.

Q. Well, thank you, sir.

The President. I won't put you on the record here. [*Laughter*]

Q. What I'd like to say is: I'd like to commend your efforts on the war on drugs and say that we here as a people are behind you 100 percent. But what I would like to concentrate on is education. It seems to me that the drug problem that we're having is a result of the feeling of hopelessness in the educational programs. And my question is twofold. First is, a lot of the inner-city kids—even kids that aren't inner-city—can't afford higher education, and if there is some kind of Federal program that would lend itself to possibly giving every American a chance to attend higher education at no cost? Because we're pricing ourselves out of jobs and out of the world market.

The President. Let me put this in perspective—the answer. I'll bet you can't guess within 10 percent what percentage of the funding—the State, local, Federal—comes from the Federal Government. I'm not going to put anybody on the spot, but it is 7 percent. That means that 93 percent comes local and State. And then that doesn't even count the volunteers. It doesn't count what Ed's doing to help somebody—what you're doing to help somebody—which is impossible to price, because not only do you bring a certain number of hours a day but you bring a dimension for your own dedication that you can't purchase. You're doing it because you believe in something and you want to help somebody.

So, the Federal role is properly proscribed. It's not going to be much bigger. I think what the Federal Government can do is the things I was talking to him about. I think you're going to see a step-up on Head

Start, which doesn't get to your question, but I think helps where a Federal Government has a very specific and, I think, extraordinarily legitimate role in helping these early kids at the most formative ages. There are Federal programs that help on the Pell grants and things of that nature, for the Federal Government assists at the college level. There are certain tax things we can do to encourage savings—college saving bond program which we've now got into effect that helps people, even those that don't have a lot of money saved—interest-free—to educate the kids.

But I don't believe it is the Federal role to say the Federal Government will pay for every kid to be educated in college. I don't want to usurp the legitimate role of the States, the private institutions of the volunteer sector. And also we have very serious constraints on Federal funding. We're operating at a deficit of—this year, the target is to get it down to $63 billion or $64 billion. Who's next? Which one?

Award Presentation

Q. I would like to present a plaque to you.

The President. Sure. Come on. [*Laughter*] Somebody's got to hold my—this is getting overweight here.

Q. Mr. President, on behalf of Robert A. Taft High School, the Excel Mentors Program, and the Cincinnati Youth Collaborative, I would like to present this plaque to you, which says: "Presented to President George Bush from the Excel Mentors Program, the Cincinnati Youth Collaborative, and Robert A. Taft High School, Cincinnati, Ohio, on January 12th."

Mentor Program

The President. Now, Vickey, what about you, though? Now, because you—or, do you—having fouled this one up, I mean, do you go here?

Q. Yes, I do. I'm a 10th grade student.

The President. Let me ask you something. And I don't want to put you on the spot. But I mean, generally, when you and others that are your friends in school—do you share my optimism about the future, or are you a little discouraged because of the hurdles ahead?

Q. I'm not discouraged at all. I think the person has to, for one, have self-confidence, which is something that my mentor, Andrea Hughes—she's given me a lot.

The President. Is she helping you? Well, now, how does that work? I mean, does she come over in school and get you aside and say, "Here are the things I think you ought to concentrate on," or do you do it at your house? Maybe Andrea can tell us.

Q. We do a variety of different things together. Sometimes, we come over to the high school, and they have programs such as the Excel Day, where the mentors and the students get together and talk about different issues.

The President. In groups or just one-on-one—you and Vickey?

Q. The celebration is in a group. The one-on-one occurs throughout the month at any given time. Sometimes, we go to things such as plays together, or if there are particular functions going on in the city that I think will help broaden her growth and experience, we may attend those functions. We sometimes go out to dinner and talk about various different issues—current events and things of that nature. Sometimes we talk about what's going on in school. If she's getting prepared for a particular examination and she may need a direction on where to go, I work with her on that aspect. There's a variety of things that the mentor does with the student, and it's an individualized program—that portion of it. But also, we get together as a group, as a family, because we, too, believe that building a family atmosphere and environment encourages the children to go forward and to try to succeed in school.

The President. Does the mentor program concentrate on areas where a kid doesn't have the benefit of a two-parent family and all, or not necessarily?

Q. We involve everyone, those of single-parent families and also those of two-parent families, to get the parents involved in the program, too. So, we don't limit it or exclude anyone. Again, they all are welcome. What we do is, if we have children who may be in single-parent homes and need to have special tutoring, we have tutors in this particular program that we lend to the students.

The President. That's on a subject, like the kid's doing lousy in math and—yes. Who else has something to tell me about?

Q. On a subject-type of basis, yes.

The President. Who else has something to tell me about? Christie, you're looking nervous back there.

Federal Role in Education

Q. Mr. President, do you plan to continue or increase funding for educational programs?

The President. I think it'll be up. But as I say, there are constraints on it. There are constraints on what the Federal Government can do in almost every area of social need. Parts of the Federal budget will clearly be up in education. And I've expressed at the Governor's—and I've heard this from all of the Governors, incidentally—the need to do more in Head Start. That doesn't take care of Stacy's problem. But you have limited resources—do the best you can with them. So, you'll see it up in total, and you'll see it up in some categories, but not as much as if the Federal Government weren't operating at this big deficit. But it'll increase.

Shoot.

Q. I have another question.

The President. But to the degree it can't—Christie, here's the key point—to the degree it can't, programs like we're talking about here, programs like this, programs where individuals involve themselves in the lives of others, become even more important. I happen to think that the more involvement we have at the local level, the better. I don't think it is the role of the Federal Government to tell Ms. Powell—it is Ms. Powell, isn't it? The school—what's the school's——

Q. Dr. Powell.

The President. ——Dr. Powell exactly how the curriculum ought to work in the schools in Cincinnati—some guy sitting in a great, big bureaucratic building in Washington. I don't think so. I think that you ought to have controls of those things. I think we can have national goals that says, look, we're moving into a different era. Math is going to be more important. Obviously, reading has got to be fundamental, if you

will. So, I think we can help work with the Governors to set goals, but the control has got to remain, in my view, my concept of education, at the local and school board and parent and mentor and tutor level—and, obviously, teacher level.

You had what they call a follow-on. What is it? Are you finished? [*Laughter*] Who's next? Any of you guys?

Q. Mr. President, the two main goals of our mentor program is to help the students raise their self-esteem and also to help them to do better in the required testing in order to go into college. Now, we have right now on the burners—we're trying to have implemented into our program here at the school the ACT–SAT [American College Test and Scholastic Aptitude Test] preparation in the curriculum. And this is one of the things we're working on. The other, in raising self-esteem—we're trying to build into our young people the concept that they are of worth, they are somebody, and that there is hope. What I'd like to ask you is: Is there anything that you can do to lend support to a concept like this on a national level?

The President. Well, kind of like what I was talking to Ed about. I don't think it's a specific program, but I think it is encouragement. I think it is having confidence in people and not picking up this mantle that the young people are all off on some drug horizon and can't have—given up. It's the emphasis on—risk of repetition—on fundamental values. And I think it's in that kind of exhortation, rather than program, that a President can be helpful. I don't think you can design a curriculum to lift the self-esteem of a kid. It's got to come from peers. It's got to come from family. It's got to come from dedicated volunteers or workers who are saying, Hey, you are somebody. You can amount to something. So, it's in that broad, philosophical range.

Mentor Program

The President. Tell me, though, how are you involved in this? I think people would be interested—I know I would—in just the background. Just use you as a case example. I was going to give Andrea a chance. But I mean, are you just suddenly a guy that's concerned and want to pitch in, or how does it work?

Q. That's exactly how it starts.

The President. Yes.

Q. It starts with a general concern for the well-being and productivity of our young people, and we come in as volunteers. This is my mentee.

The President. Is he?

Q. And we work with Anthony, encouraging him. He's already taken his ACT test, and he's improved his scores. And these are the types of things that we do.

The President. How do you find Anthony? I mean, somebody say, "Hey, we've got a guy over here that really would like to work with you and needs some help"?

Q. We have a coordinator here at the school, and that person links both the mentor and the student together. And that's how it's done. And we're in the process of doing recruiting. Anyone who wants to help us—they're welcome to come on down.

The President. Well, I'd like to use this opportunity and this marvelous exposure to encourage this voluntarism, encourage this participation.

Let me ask him. I don't want to put you—you don't have to. This is not a classroom, where you've got to say something. [*Laughter*] But I mean, from your standpoint, are you doing better because this gentleman is helping out and stuff?

Q. Yes.

The President. Do you feel like you've got somebody that cares?

Q. Yes.

The President. What was it like before? You were just drifting around and didn't——

Q. I was pretty much the same. I always had my act together, you know? [*Laughter*]

The President. You did have it together? [*Laughter*] Well, that's good. A lot of guys that didn't. But how about the chemistry? Does it ever work on the mentor program that you have to shift around because the——

Q. We've been pretty fortunate; that has not occurred. You asked the question, how do the students get into the Excel Mentor Program. There are several ways. They could be referred by a teacher, a counselor—parents even call. And also, students

are self-referred. They want to be a part of this because they see that it is a helpful program. And they're excited about being in the program.

The President. But do the ones that need it the most see that? I mean, the guys that are really having the most trouble out there—maybe the drug scene, maybe the tough home situation? Do they say, hey, I need help, or do you have to go seek them out and say, Wait a minute, you're screwing up here, and if you don't——

Q. A lot of times, those individuals are referred.

The President. Yes.

Q. Mr. President, my name is Jim Brock. My favorite statement is, I'm a Taft High School graduate, and I'm in the mentoring program. I am a homeroom mentor, and that is how we address the majority of the students: through the homeroom mentoring program. During that time, we tell the students that there is help available for you. If you need a tutor, there is help available for you. If you need a mentor to give you a one-on-one approach, that is also available for you. And that is largely how we address the students.

We go out into the community. We have an outreach program where we go to many of the social organizations, we go to churches, we go to any community organization that will let us speak with them. We do that, and that's how we are branching out into the community.

The President. Do parents welcome the mentor approach, or do they say, wait a minute, you're getting in our turf a little bit?

Q. I know my mother welcomed Andrea a lot. And part of my getting into the mentoring program was because I was having trouble in history. And we went to Ms. Harris concerning my history. And when I got Mr. Sales as my history tutor, then she also asked me did I want a mentor? And I agreed to it, so that's how I met Andrea, was through my mother, because I was having trouble in a certain subject and we had wanted to get me a tutor. But as I got my tutor, I also got a mentor.

Q. And a part of that mentoring program requires that the parents meet with the mentors to determine whether or not they will be comfortable with this relationship with their child or the children. So, at the onset, the parents get involved in that decisionmaking process. And it has worked well. And Vickey's mother and I get along very well, and we sometimes get together and talk about issues that may have affected Vickey throughout the school year and get together on how can we help her deal with some of the issues that she's facing.

One of the issues that we had to address early on was the fact that she was coming out of a junior high school into the high school, and it was a new experience for her. And she was sort of getting steered in the wrong direction by being less academically inclined and more interested in what was going on socially. So, her mother and I worked with Vickey to get her back on the right track. And since we've done that, she's been doing very well academically.

The President. Who else?

Federal Role in Education

Q. Mr. President, my name's Maryanne. I am a sophomore at Xavier University. Before my freshman year of college there— college tuition is outrageous, and without the Youth Collaborative I couldn't have afforded the—I guess it's around $9,000 a year now. And I think that I've benefited greatly because Xavier is a private institution, and I get a more personal education that way, instead of having to go to—not that U.C. [University of Cincinnati] isn't a good school, but——

The President. No.

Q. ——it's more of a—not as one-on-one.

The President. That's right. You choose as best you can what you think is best for you.

Q. Please?

The President. No, I say—I can understand that.

Q. Yes. I mean, for me, I like to ask questions when I'm in a classroom, and the Youth Collaborative let me do that, let me follow the education that I wanted. And they help a lot. And I know that they're helping a lot of other college-bound students because we just opened a college information center, the Youth Collaborative did, down at the Lazarus in downtown Cincinnati. And it's kind of a guidance counsel-

ing center for students who maybe don't feel comfortable with their guidance counselors or who have been disconnected from high school guidance counselors. And it's a great program. They have videos of colleges, and they have scholarship information, and they have counselors that can speak to you and ask you where you want to go with your life, and stuff like that— help you to make decisions.

The President. Well, that's very helpful and interesting. And it gets back to Stacy's—whose role is it to give you a shot, give you a chance, give the kid she's trying to help a chance? And the answer is: I think it's everybody's. I think the Federal Government has a role in these programs. I think there are these programs—there's a friend of mine in New Orleans, Jay Taylor, who guarantees a certain class in a certain school, you're going to be educated. You do your job, you lead a good life, stay out of the difficulties that some kids face on narcotics or whatever, and we guarantee you— private, nothing to do with State, nothing to do—just helps do what Stacy was asking— how do we do this? Or what you're saying, that tuition is high. And these programs are springing up all over the country.

And you take them and multiply them in terms of dollars, and it's amazing what it results in. So, back to what somebody asked me—who was it—about what can I do. Ed, I think I can do more to encourage individuals and volunteers all over the country to—and it's far more than a Federal Government can do, far more in terms of total dollars brought to bear on the program. When you price out what each person here is doing and then try to multiply that, if you could project this program around the country, it would mind-boggle you in terms of Federal budget.

So, maybe I'm getting a little inspiration here that I need to make this point louder and clearer to others around the country.

Sister Harrington. Unfortunately, Mr. President——

The President. I'm being thrown out. I know. [*Laughter*]

Sister Harrington. The clock moves too rapidly. And so, in the name of all of the people here, I'm going to say thank you for them. And we're sorry that we can't get questions from everyone.

The President. Well, maybe we'll get another shot here. But I will follow this with keen interest and express to those who are giving your time like this—I'll tell you, you're doing the Lord's work. Because I am not pessimistic about the young people in this country, and I'm convinced that we can compete. I'm convinced that we can win this damn battle against narcotics that is just decimating a lot of families. And I get inspired by this. So, I am very, very grateful to all of you for what you're doing. Thank you very much.

All right, off we go.

Note: The President spoke at 12:52 p.m. in the library of Robert A. Taft High School. In his remarks, he referred to Sister Jean P. Harrington, director of the Cincinnati Youth Collaborative; Ed Sales, volunteer and Excel homeroom mentor; Vickey Williams, Christie Thompson, and Anthony Crockett, students at Taft High School; Lee Etta Powell, superintendent of Cincinnati Public Schools; Stacy Reid, mentor volunteer; and Tara Harris, school community coordinator of the Excel Mentors Program.

Remarks to Students and Faculty at Robert A. Taft High School in Cincinnati, Ohio
January 12, 1990

Thank you, Mr. Henderson. You know, no matter where I go or how old I get, it still makes me a little nervous to be talked about by a principal. [*Laughter*] But thank you, sir. And thank you, Superintendent Powell, and all of the students here today for such a kind welcome. As a ball fan, I'm sorry I didn't hear Tommy speaking and all. But I understand he did a first-class job. May his won-and-loss record go just up— ERA and all of that. But good luck to you, and thanks very much for being here. I want to particularly salute your two Congressmen: Congressman Luken and Congressman Gradison. Where are they? Here they are modestly standing in the back. I mentioned Superintendent Powell. Most of all, I want to thank the band. You know, I hear—[*applause*]—they had only a few days to practice that "Hail to the Chief." With talent like that, I expect to see them on MTV any day now. [*Laughter*]

It is great to be here. It's not often, frankly, that a President gets to stand in a gymnasium literally full of success stories. And Taft High School and the city of Cincinnati are showing the rest of the country what's possible when students and people in a community strive for excellence, but doing it together. And I don't mean just the Sena-

tors—though your Senators are racking up a better record than ours back in Washington, I might add. [*Laughter*] You've got students, parents, schools, business and religious groups all united in one great enterprise: the Cincinnati Youth Collaborative. It's a partnership that builds brighter futures every day—one kid at a time.

I'd like to recognize a very special person who's brought this concept—this whole CYC [Cincinnati Youth Collaborative]— brought it to life, a local heroine, Sister Jean Harrington. And let me offer congratulations to her and best wishes to the man who's taking over, Mr. John Bryant.

You know, you may not know this as a part of it because you're so close to everything, but you've got something truly unique going on here. On January 29th, I understand that every television station in greater Cincinnati, all six broadcasting companies and two cable channels, will be launching a 2-hour program called a Future-Thon. It's like a telethon for the schools of Cincinnati. But Future-Thon is asking for something even more precious than money. It's asking people to volunteer their talents and their time to be role models, to help Cincinnati students get the future they deserve. And the kids of Cincinnati deserve the very best.

If you've ever thought that school was a waste of time, then you ought to think about talking to one of the students in the CYC. They'll tell you better than I can what this program means. It means scholarships that add up to more than a quarter of a million dollars. It means skills that you can count on—take a job the day after you graduate. It means classes for college entrance exams that have sent scores soaring up by 25 percent, a new child-care center opening next fall, and training in computers for every student who goes to Taft. Here is an example for the entire Nation.

But it offers something even more important, because with every friendship you build with a CYC mentor and with every hour you spend with a tutor you're getting something more than skills: You're gaining power, purpose, a friendship you can count on, somebody to lift you up when you're a little bit down. And once you have that, you can never be stopped, never denied the potential that's yours and the success that's waiting for you.

Let me offer special thanks to those adults who are giving of themselves, who are serving as CYC mentors. Every adult in America can gain so much by developing a special relationship with a young person. When you lift the spirits of the young, you raise their horizons to the stars, you give them the promise of a future bright with possibility. I hope the adults here today are just the first of what will soon be thousands like you, helping the young people of your community.

One young woman, Loretta Englemon, recently said, "I know what I want out of life, and I know where I'm going." Every student here at Taft is at a point in life when there are a lot of choices to be made, important choices. And if life is the sum of the choices you make, whatever challenges you're facing, you understand that drugs only make them harder to handle. You already know how drugs destroy lives, and a few of you have seen it happen. Maybe you lost a good friend. Or maybe you see or hear about drug dealers making that big dough. But in the drug trade there are no benefits, no security, no retirement plan.

And sure, people have different ideas about success. Some think it's measured by what's parked in your driveway or hanging in your closet. But real success is something else. An educated man or woman gains so much more. With just a pen or a pencil and a desire to learn, there are no limits to success. Maybe it has to do with the finding of one's own talents, using them to reach your fullest potential—whatever path you choose, working to make a difference for yourself and those around you. If you stay in school, you'll find that the key to success is right next to you. And if you keep struggling to live up to your own expectations, you'll find the strength to succeed right deep in your heart.

So, let me congratulate every one of you. I hope by coming here I highlight the magnificent spirit that I see here. Congratulations for what you're doing. You're proving to yourselves and those around you that you have potential, that you are someone, that you can succeed.

That's why I'm pleased to announce today that the Cincinnati Youth Collaborative is the 40th White House daily Point of Light. On behalf of the Nation, thank you for showing that from now on in America any definition of a successful life must include serving others.

You go to a great school in a wonderful town, in the greatest nation on the face of the Earth. Your dreams are within your reach. And so, may every single one of them come true.

It's been a wonderful experience here for me today. And I feel motivated. I feel I understand a little bit better what one person can do in helping another. It's been well worth it, I'll tell you. Thank you. God bless you, and God bless the United States of America. Thank you very, very much. Thank you all. Thank you all. Good luck to you.

Note: The President spoke at 1:25 p.m. in the school auditorium. He was introduced by Orlando Henderson, principal of the high school. In his opening remarks, the President referred to Lee Etta Powell, superintendent of Cincinnati public schools;

Thomas Browning, pitcher for the Cincinnati Reds baseball team; and Sister Jean P. Harrington, director of the Cincinnati Youth Collaborative.

Remarks to the Chamber of Commerce in Cincinnati, Ohio
January 12, 1990

Thank you all for that welcome back. And, Joe, thank you, sir, for those very kind words. I'm very pleased that both Tom Luken and Bill Gradison made their flight out with us on Air Force One today, and they're both with us. And if it's not inappropriate, I would ask Joe if I could ask them both to stand up and be saluted by this audience of friends. [*Applause*] Where did Tom go? Okay, we'll let his son represent him—the mayor of Cincinnati. [*Laughter*]

But I'm delighted to be back in here. And it is a nonpartisan, nonpolitical gathering—first one I've attended in Hamilton County like that in a long, long time. [*Laughter*] And it's good to see State Senator Stan Aronoff over here; my friend Bob Taft, the commissioner; the mayor, who is doing a superb job, Charles Luken.

Delighted to be back here in Cincinnati. I will say to you, Joe, that, yes, I learned a lot from that spectacular program there at Taft. And I expect we all ought to salute the leadership of Procter and Gamble—my friend John Smale, always out front on what I call a Thousand Points of Light, trying to help somebody else. But for those of you in this community who have not had a chance to see what it is I'm talking about here— this new program of voluntarism interacting with the best in professionalism at a school to help lift these kids up—you ought to go take a look and you ought to get involved. It is stimulating in every single way.

Actually, I was hoping to get out here for the Reds' opening day. But they tell me I'm 3 months too early. [*Laughter*] Same problem I ran into on Pearl Harbor Day. [*Laughter*] But here I am. And we're not here to talk baseball. But you can claim him in Cincinnati, and I'll claim him from Houston, but I'm mighty proud of Joe Morgan making it into the Hall of Fame. You got Johnny Bench, and now you've got Joe.

And let me, colonel, thank you and the Air Force for that magnificent music and being with us here today.

You know, it is fitting in the days leading up to the State of the Union Address we should meet again in Cincinnati. The last time I visited was in November of '88, in the final days of the Presidential campaign. And earlier, Cincinnati was one of my last stops before the convention in New Orleans.

On the trip before that we spent a morning out at Procter and Gamble's R&D facility. They taught me a trick that every President should know—how to put toothpaste back into the tube. [*Laughter*] A marvelously educational experience. [*Laughter*]

All in all, I did come here four times during the Presidential campaign. I talked of America's future and of future generations. I talked of certain principles. And I told you that I was ready to make the tough calls and to take the heat. And today I've come back to tell you that I'm ready to make good on that pledge, because up on Capitol Hill some important business remains unfinished, promises have gone unfulfilled. We sent responsible proposals to Congress in a lot of areas, but certainly in four of America's most critical areas: capital gains, America's children, clean air, and combating crime.

In some cases, our proposals have been under consideration with Congress for the better part of a year. And these four issues are bogged down in the jungles on Capitol Hill. The clock is running, and America's patience is running out. And I'm not here to assign blame; I'm here to suggest that we need to move forward. America wants it done right. America wants it done responsibly. And America wants it done now. And these four initiatives represent only part of the way in which the events of 1989 will affect the coming year.

We've seen a lot of exhilarating changes

in recent months that offer new hope for world peace. It's an exciting time we're living in, and we like what's happening in Central Europe. But just as it would have been impossible 6 months ago to predict those thunderous changes, it's impossible today to know what will unfold in the next 6 months, let alone the next 6 years. But in this world of change, one thing is certain: America must be ready. And as excited as I am about the changes moving toward a more peaceful Eastern Europe, America must be strong. And a strong America means not only a strong economy; it still must mean a strong defense, a ready and highly effective defense force. And if proof of that were ever needed, we saw it in that superb, beautifully coordinated operation last month—we saw it in the courage of our troops in Panama.

I welcome the dynamic changes in Eastern Europe. I strongly support, as I bet we all do, Mr. Gorbachev's *perestroika* and his commitment to peaceful change and openness, *glasnost*. But this is not the time that we should naively cut the muscle out of our defense posture. And yet some think that all the answers to this year's problems can be found by spending what is called in Washington a peace dividend. It's like the next-of-kin who spent the inheritance before the will is read. And unfortunately, what is being packaged as a dividend is not money in the bank. It is more like a possible future inheritance, a legacy that will enable us to pass on a better world to our children; and like an inheritance, it's a special gift, a legacy not only of prosperity but also security earned by the hard work and sacrifice of those who came before.

Of course, whenever a potential inheritance looms, there are those eager to rush out and squander it—to buy new things, to spend, to spend, to spend—and spending funds they don't yet have. Then the bills start coming, and the inheritance may not. And what was promised as a bonus becomes a burden. In Washington, that burden comes in the form of a new spending program. That's not going to happen, because most Americans know we not only must maintain a strong defense but still must reduce the deficit. And reducing the deficit isn't just a good idea, a sound idea, an idea

of sound fiscal policy; it's what the American people want. And as our two Congressmen here today know, it's the law—it's required under the Gramm-Rudman-Hollings law.

The way to reduce the deficit is to restrain the spending growth and continue the economic growth. And it's not the time, as some like to say, to go on out and raise the taxes on the working men and women in this country. The new budget must meet Gramm-Rudman requirements. It must reduce barriers to economic growth. It must keep interest rates low. And I'm not satisfied yet—I'm encouraged, but I'm not satisfied at all—want to see them lower. And I say all this because the best poverty program—the best antipoverty program, if you will—is a good job. And the best jobs program is a sound, strong central economy.

A sound economy is a competitive economy. And to keep America competitive, to fuel our continuing growth—in some areas, boom—we also need an infusion of new venture capital. That's why we need a majority in both Houses of Congress—what they've already voted for, and I'm talking about a tax cut on capital gains.

As the world turns to freer markets—and you're seeing this happen, some solidifying their commitment to freer markets, countries that never had the benefit of free markets beginning to move, taking early steps towards free markets—but as the world moves in this direction, this is no time to become wishy-washy about where America stands. The jury is no longer out. Markets work. Government controls do not work.

And since the debate has all but ended on this issue, perhaps our most diehard ideologs can now turn their attention to the real question that divides America: Is it Texas or Cincinnati that produces the world's best chili? [*Laughter*] Of course, this is a question to be decided by the market— [*laughter*]—and that's what I'm trying to tell you all here today.

The economic challenge of the nineties is to make markets work better. And one of the best ways a government can do that is to do what people around the world are asking their governments to do: get out of the way—less regulation, fewer mandated programs from Washington that tie the hands of our health care providers, our educators, and so many others as well. You see, our ideas work here at home. We're in the midst of the longest peacetime expansion in the history of the United States, an 86-month expansion that has created an astonishing 20 million new jobs since 1982. That's due to the genius of places like Cincinnati and the solid American values that have flourished here and inspired the world from Central Europe to Central America.

The whole world is watching, and the whole world is ready. The headlines tell of other nations buying American. That's good news, not bad news. We've been urging our own people to "Buy American" for years, to invest in the greatest job-creating machine of the 20th century. And it's no surprise, then, the world investors are following suit. The results are in: America is the choice.

We don't have to look elsewhere to know what works. If you want to follow the smart money advice of the 1990's, go to where the Japanese and the Europeans are going. Look at the United States of America. Look at what the rest of the world calls the American miracle. You've seen it happen. You've made it happen. You've been a part of it happening right here in Cincinnati, U.S.A., the Blue Chip City, where 150,000 more people are at work than were working 6 years ago—150,000 more.

Cincinnati produced its miracle the old-fashioned way, the American way. It's an old tradition here. When he first opened his slaughterhouse in 1810, Richard Fosdick was warned that meat couldn't be cured in Cincinnati's climate. But he didn't know that it couldn't be done. He continued his experiments until he discovered the rock-salt process for curing meat and made this city the principal hog market of the world.

Renewing our emphasis on innovation is one of the ways modern Cincinnati has prospered. You've also built a diverse economic base, stripped away corporate fat, renewed our emphasis on quality. Fortune says Cincinnati makes some of the best jet engines in the entire world.

Ultimately, these are the kind of efforts that will determine how America fares in the competitive, free-trade world of the nineties. The way of the future is free people. And the way of the future, in my view, is and must be free trade. And free people and free trade is what America is all about.

Of course, it's not enough that we say that trade simply be free. It has also got to be fair. And I am not complacent; I am not satisfied with where things stand. We must do better in removing barriers to Americans' goods and services, whether those barriers be in Japan, in Western Europe, or anywhere else in the world. A global game is afoot, a game in which a Cincinnati businessman can now fly nonstop to London and Frankfurt any day of the week. If the rules are fair and the same for everybody, we can play this game. It's called free enterprise. And America is the free enterprise capital of the world.

Winning in the competitive nineties will take more than investing in products. We must also invest in people. And that was what was so moving about my experience today here at lunch. We must invest in people. And that means offering every American child an education second to none. Our Education Excellence Act remains a priority of my administration, sent to Congress almost 9 months ago. It calls for choice, flexibility, and accountability. And the time for study is past, and the time for action is now.

You in Cincinnati have acted, working to educate and train our people for the 21st century. Three years ago business, educational, and community leaders here came together to take on a mighty task: reduce the numbers of students at risk, that staggering 40-percent dropout rate in Cincinnati's public schools. The result was what I saw today—that Cincinnati Youth Collaborative, an intensive people-to-people mentoring program that many of you support. And it's already seen some fantastic, early success.

It has America talking. Your Governor visited one of the participating classrooms at McKinley Preschool before coming out to the education summit that I hosted there in Charlottesville, Virginia, last fall. And earlier today, as I said, I had this opportunity to see the tremendous programs at Taft High

School firsthand. I guess the most moving part of it for me today was the mentoring part—involvement of one Cincinnatian in the life of another; an older man, an older woman taking under his or her arm a kid, lifting them up, helping them when they're hurt. A beautiful experience.

There are other matters that require urgent attention when Congress gets back later this month. Our Clean Air Act proposals recognize that in an emerging global economy, environmental destruction knows no borders, and that a healthy economy goes hand in hand with a healthy environment.

And a kinder, gentler environment also means a society where every man, woman, and child can live and prosper in an environment free from fear. And that, then, means freedom from crime, and especially the increasingly violent crime that has been spawned by this plague of drug abuse, drug trafficking. Our anticrime package, as well—it's time for the Congress to act on it.

There's much to be done in the months ahead. But as a new year begins, Americans should also pause to take some pride in what we've all accomplished together. Let me suggest two areas. At home, more than anything else—if you had to define it—a kinder and gentler nation is one in which everyone who wants a job has a job. And today America has the lowest unemployment rate since 1973, and Ohio has reached its highest employment level in history.

Abroad, for more than 40 years, 3 generations has stood steadfast in an often hostile and tumultuous world. Firm in our belief in America's destiny as leader of the free world, our spirit did not falter; our troops did not flinch. And today, after the watershed events of 1989, the free world that we're leading is growing bigger all the time.

And in the past months we saw democracy restored to the brave people of Panama. We want to help them enhance it and strengthen it. We saw the powerful brought before the bar of justice. And we took pride in the skill and the courage and, yes, the sacrifice of American soldiers. The Panamanian operation was conducted by highly trained troops—the best, the finest, the best trained troops in the world. But it is not simply training; it's patriotism, and it's dedication.

I went to a couple of hospitals in San Antonio—Barbara and I did—to talk to some of our wounded. And I'll never, ever forget their spirit. One kid lying there severely wounded said, "My only regret," he said, "is that I'm here, not down there with the others." Pride in America, in my view, has never been higher.

And somehow, it is more than coincidence. In the same month, we hear that the bald eagle—the American eagle—may soon come off the endangered species list. How about that? [*Applause*]

In case you don't understand it, I love my job. [*Laughter*] We've got a lot to do. But as you see the changes in Eastern Europe, see Mr. Gorbachev struggling against what some would say just terribly difficult odds—things are coming our way. They're moving toward freedom. They're moving toward democracy. And I am proud to be at the helm.

Thank you all. God bless you, and God bless Cincinnati, and God bless the United States of America. Thank you very, very much.

Note: The President spoke at 2:16 p.m. in the ballroom at the Hyatt Regency Hotel. In his remarks, he referred to Joseph Head, chairman of the board of the Greater Cincinnati Chamber of Commerce; Representatives Thomas A. Luken and Willis D. Gradison, Jr.; Robert A. Taft II, president of the Hamilton County Board of Commissioners; Joe Morgan, former member of the Houston Astros and Cincinnati Reds baseball teams, and Johnny Bench, former member of the Cincinnati Reds, both recently elected members of the Baseball Hall of Fame; and Air Force Band commander Lt. Col. Richard A. Shelton. Following his remarks, the President returned to Washington, DC.

Statement by Press Secretary Fitzwater on the President's Meeting With Mr. and Mrs. William Rouse
January 12, 1990

Following his speech to the Chamber of Commerce, President Bush met with Mr. and Mrs. William Rouse, the mother and stepfather of James Markwell of Cincinnati, who was killed in Panama. Markwell's brother, Brandon, 17, and his sister, Dawn, 15, also met with the President.

Pfc. James Markwell was a U.S. Army Ranger medic killed by gunfire after landing in his drop zone during the Panama invasion. President Bush sent a letter of condolence to Private Markwell's family on January 4, as well as to the families of all those killed in Panama.

The President met with Mr. and Mrs. Rouse in a private room following his speech. The President expressed his gratitude on behalf of all Americans for the sacrifice Private Markwell made in service to his country. The President expressed his personal sympathy to the Rouses.

Private Markwell was a native of Cincinnati and was buried there on December 30, 1989.

Nomination of Frederick M. Bernthal To Be Deputy Director of the National Science Foundation
January 12, 1990

The President today announced his intention to nominate Frederick M. Bernthal to be Deputy Director of the National Science Foundation. He would succeed John H. Moore.

Since 1988, Dr. Bernthal has served as Assistant Secretary of State for Oceans and International Environmental and Scientific Affairs in Washington, DC. Prior to this, he served as Commissioner of the Nuclear Regulatory Commission in Washington, 1983–1988; chief legislative assistant to Senator Howard Baker, 1980–1983; legislative assistant to Senator Howard Baker, 1978–1979; associate professor of chemistry and physics at Michigan State University, 1975–1978; and assistant professor at Michigan State University at East Lansing, 1970–1975. In addition, Dr. Bernthal served as a visiting scientist for the Niels Bohr Institute at the University of Copenhagen, 1966–1977; staff postdoctoral scientist at Yale University, 1969–1970; graduate research assistant at Lawrence Berkeley Laboratory, 1965–1969; and research aide for the Argonne National Laboratory, 1964.

Dr. Bernthal graduated from Valparaiso University (B.S., 1964) and the University of California at Berkeley (Ph.D., 1969). He was born January 10, 1943, in Sheraton, WY. Dr. Bernthal is married, has one child, and resides in Washington, DC.

Statement by Press Secretary Fitzwater on the Vietnam-United States Special Resettlement Program
January 13, 1990

Beginning this weekend, the first group of former Vietnamese "reeducation camp" detainees and their accompanying family members (61 persons) will arrive in the United States. They are the first to depart under a bilateral agreement concluded last

July in Hanoi between the United States and Vietnam. The group arrived in Bangkok on January 5 and 6, where they have spent the last week completing their final processing before departure for the United States. A second group (88 persons) is scheduled to arrived next week.

All Americans rejoice at this event, but we particularly share the joy of those in the Vietnamese-American community who will now, at long last, be reunited with their family and friends in the United States.

The U.S.-Vietnam Special Reeducation Center Detainee Resettlement Program represents the culmination of years of intensive U.S. diplomatic effort to obtain permission for those persons and their families who were closely associated with the United States during the Vietnam War period to emigrate to the United States. We expect a total of 700 former detainees and their family members to depart Vietnam this month and 7,000 to enter the United States by the end of the current fiscal year on September 30.

Statement by Press Secretary Fitzwater on the Death of Hyman Schachtel
January 14, 1990

The President today called Mrs. Hyman Schachtel, wife of Rabbi Hyman Schachtel of Houston, TX, to express his sadness and condolences over the death of her husband. The President and Hyman Schachtel go back a long, long time. The President termed Rabbi Schachtel one of the great religious and civic leaders that he has known. He told Mrs. Schachtel that her husband had been an inspiration to him and a very good friend. The President and Mrs. Bush will miss him sorely.

Statement by Press Secretary Fitzwater on the Vienna Meeting of the Conference on Security and Cooperation in Europe
January 16, 1990

Today the United States and the 34 other nations of the Conference on Security and Cooperation in Europe (CSCE) begin a dialog that is unique in history. The military leaders of our respective countries will meet together in Vienna to discuss national military policies, forces, and budgets.

It is difficult to imagine a better time or forum for such a dialog. Six months ago the peoples of Eastern Europe embarked on a course of changing the governments which had for so long denied their legitimate rights and contributed to perpetuating the division of Europe. Those who are leading the forces for change frequently cite the principles of democratic process, economic justice, and personal freedom that were ar-

ticulated by the 35 CSCE states at Helsinki 15 years ago. It is natural, then, to turn to the CSCE and to the forum in which we discuss confidence and security-building measures to initiate a dialog among military experts on issues that are key to building a stable European security architecture for the coming decades.

The President has asked the Chairman of the Joint Chiefs of Staff, Gen. Colin Powell, to make the first presentation in the Military Doctrine Seminar on behalf of the United States. His presence in Vienna is tangible evidence of our transatlantic commitment not just to security but to openness and dialog among nations as a means to bring about peaceful change and a secure future for all of our peoples. We look forward to a fruitful exchange among all participants in this historic meeting.

Remarks on the United States Military Action in Panama and an Exchange With Reporters
January 17, 1990

The President. Well, let me just say that this is my first chance to, in person, thank General Thurman and his troops for the outstanding job they did for our country in Panama. Secretary Cheney and I are extraordinarily grateful to this, our commander. He served with great distinction—and General Stiner and General Cisneros and many others as well. But before our meeting we're having in here, I want to bring him out and publicly tell him how strongly I feel about the wonderful mission, the way it was accomplished, and the professionalism and, I guess, particularly, Max, the dedication of those kids. I'll tell you, it is so moving, as a parent, to visit with some of the parents of those that have fallen and wounded. And it's something you see all the time, but I'll tell you, these were remarkable young people.

And well done, and thank you.

General Thurman. Thank you very much, sir. You ought to be proud of them—soldiers, sailors, airmen, marines, coastguardsmen—they did a dynamite job.

The President. Yes, they did. Well, we're proud of you.

General Thurman. We appreciate your support.

The President. Very proud of you.

Q. When do you think the troops will be coming home—all the troops will be out?

The President. We'll be talking about that right now. And they're down substantially, and democracy is on the move. General Thurman's just briefed the Secretary and me very quickly here on the moves that Panama is taking. We want to give them economic help. We want to offer hope to the individuals there who are out of work— some of it because of the sanctions that we had to place upon Panama. So, we're committed. I think I speak for him, but I know I speak for me: We want them out of there as soon as possible. I think a large number are out now.

General Thurman. Yes, sir. We're down to 18,900 this morning, which is about 8,000 below what we had in country at the maximum 27,000.

The President. Eight out, and we've got about four or five to go. SOUTHCOM obviously will remain. It has a mission. We have rights and obligations under the treaty. And I'm sure that's agreeable to the Panamanian leadership.

Q. How much aid do you think you're going to get?

The President. Well, I don't know. We're going to be talking about that right now, Helen [Helen Thomas, United Press International].

Q. Do you want to get them all out before the drug summit so that it's not an obstacle, particularly for Peru?

The President. Well, I want to do what's right for Panama. I want to do what Panama wants. And obviously, there's still some security considerations that General Thurman was telling Secretary Cheney and me about. But it's Panama's show now. Panama is strengthening their democracy. And we want to know what they want; we want to work closely with them. It is my objective to get the troops out, to get back to the levels before this military action. We will do that. But it has nothing to do with the summit in Cartagena [Colombia] at all. This is prudent. It is right. And I'm not driven by the summit.

Vice President Quayle's Trip to Latin America

Q. Are you having trouble finding countries that will accept Vice President Quayle as a visitor because of——

The President. No.

Q. Is he going to Panama?

The President. I expect he will. I hope so. His itinerary I don't think has been set yet, but I hope so.

Note: The President spoke at 11 a.m. in the Colonnade at the White House. In his open-ing remarks, he referred to Gen. Maxwell R. Thurman, commander in chief of the U.S. Southern Command; Lt. Gen. Carl Stiner, commanding general of the 18th Airborne Corps; and Brig. Gen. Marc Cisneros, commanding general of U.S. Army South.

Remarks and an Exchange With Reporters Prior to a Meeting With Federal Law Enforcement Officials
January 17, 1990

The President. Well, welcome. And I'm meeting today with the heads of the various Federal crime-fighting agencies to renew our determination to defeat drugs, to defeat crime, and to destroy the kingpins behind them.

Over the past year, these agency chiefs were asked to take on even greater responsibilities, and they've answered the call with great distinction. And I only wish that Congress would finish the job that I asked them to do last spring. True, in fairness, more money has been provided for new prison space and more Federal law enforcement officers, but too much work has been left undone. And Congress must act now on the rest of our package to fight violent crime, to toughen the Federal sentencing for those using a firearm in the commission of a felony, to reform the rules of evidence, and to enact the death penalty proposal that I sent them. These agency heads and their agents face enough constraints, and the last thing that they need is for the Congress to not move or to tie their hands.

Seven months ago we were also drafting our initial drug strategy, and I must say we've since enjoyed success in getting our first strategy approved by the Congress. The American people have rallied behind our plan. Law enforcers from the Feds to the cops out there on the beat have joined together to make it work. And in short, our first strategy laid a solid foundation for our future efforts.

And we have seen great progress where it counts—in the streets, where record amounts of cocaine have been seized. And yet, we have yet to turn the corner. In this very city, January has been the month of murder, the deadliest month in the history of the District of Columbia.

So, we're going to press on, press hard in our second strategy, which is going to be released in advance of our budget. And all of this I will be discussing in this second annual luncheon today here.

Before we go inside, I wanted to thank three people especially: Secretary Brady, Attorney General Thornburgh, and my very able Director, Bill Bennett. They place teamwork before turf, giving crimefighters everywhere an example of how to cooperate against crime. I'm proud of them. I'm proud of all the rest of our law enforcement people here and those with whom we're associated all across this country.

So, what we want to do is get moving now. And now, if we'll go inside, we can hear from each and every one of you, if you will, as to how your work is going.

Hello, Jack. How are you? Good to see you.

Thank you all very much.

Extradition of Colombian Drug Dealers

Q. Mr. President, what about what happened in Colombia today, sir?

The President. What?

Q. The communication by these so-called extraditables claiming they would stop the cocaine trade, making that claim again in return for——

The President. Well, they've a credibility problem with me. But that's one point, and the other is, I've learned not to comment on matters that I have not seen verified. So, you're asking about a statement that I just don't know anything about.

Thank you all very much.

Note: The President spoke at 12:16 p.m. in the Rose Garden at the White House. In his remarks, he referred to William J. Bennett, Director of National Drug Control Policy, and John C. Lawn, Administrator of the Drug Enforcement Administration.

Nomination of Susan J. Koch To Be an Assistant Director of the United States Arms Control and Disarmament Agency
January 17, 1990

The President today announced his intention to nominate Susan Jane Koch to be an Assistant Director of the United States Arms Control and Disarmament Agency for the Bureau of Strategic Programs. She would succeed William H. Fite.

Since 1988 Dr. Koch has served as Principal Director of Nuclear Forces and Arms Control Policy in the Office of the Assistant Secretary of Defense for International Security Policy. Prior to this, she served as a staff analyst for Strategic Defense and Space Arms Control Policy in the Office of the Assistant Secretary of Defense for International Security Policy, 1985–1988; as a Special Assistant to the Deputy Assistant Secretary of Defense for Nuclear Forces and Arms Control Policy in the Office of the Assistant Secretary of Defense for International Security Policy, 1982–1985; branch chief in the Office of European Analysis and Office of Policy Analysis at the Central Intelligence Agency, 1980–1982; intelligence analyst in the Office of Political Analysis and Office of Political Research at the Central Intelligence Agency, 1975–1980; and an assistant professor in the department of political science at the University of Connecticut, 1971–1975. In addition, Dr. Koch has served as an instructor in the department of political science at Mount Holyoke College, 1970–1971.

Dr. Koch graduated from Mount Holyoke College (A.B., 1964) and Harvard University (M.A., 1968; Ph.D., 1971). She was born January 24, 1943, in Bridgeport, CT. Currently, Dr. Koch resides in Washington, DC.

Telephone Conversation With the Astronauts Aboard the Space Shuttle *Columbia*
January 18, 1990

The President. Hello, Fred, can you hear me? Dan? Are we talking to space?

Commander Brandenstein. Yes, sir, Mr. President. Welcome aboard *Columbia.* We hear you very clearly.

The President. Well, Dan, is that you, the captain, the boss of that outfit?

Commander Brandenstein. Well, that's what they say, but everybody contributes a lot, and I just kind of stay out of the way so they can get their jobs done.

The President. Well, listen, I just was calling you to congratulate you. Dan Quayle is sitting here next to me in the Oval Office, and as you know, he's taken a very active role in this Space Council. But what I'm calling to do is to congratulate you and the crew, after all those somersaults—but doing a superb job up there on this mission. And we followed the LDEF [Long Duration Exposure Facility] and the very exciting grab, and I just wanted to hear firsthand how it was going.

Commander Brandenstein. Well, Mr. President, I think it's going well. We've pretty much concluded most of the major objectives of this mission, and obviously, the retrieval of the LDEF was one of the highlights, and we're very happy we have it back onboard. We believe it's a real treasure that's going to help very much in designing future space satellites and shuttles and space stations.

The President. Well, I think that's wonderful. And how do all the new guys behave—Jim, Marsha, and David? Can they talk, or are you doing the speaking for this crowd?

Commander Brandenstein. I want to give them all a chance. In fact, we'll let G. David tell you how it is to be a new guy.

The President. All right, fire away, Dave.

Mr. Low. Well, Mr. President, it's a pleasure to be up here. I've enjoyed this flight very much. We've enjoyed a lot of success with a lot of help from all the folks on the ground. It's a real pleasure to be up here to contribute to our space program.

The President. Well, I'm delighted. How's Marsha doing? Is she near a mike there?

Ms. Ivins. Yes, sir, I have a mike. I think we new guys are really excited. We've waited a long time for this, and it's sort of a dream come true. The world—looking at it from up here—is incredible.

The President. I don't want to date your commander, the captain there, Dan, but I had dinner over at the White House 2 nights ago with Dick Truly, who reminded me that they had flown together sometime back. Dan, sorry about that.

Commander Brandenstein. That's true. And in fact, I've been taking my share of hits this mission. I just had a birthday yesterday, and I've been taking a lot of grief.

The President. All right. Well, listen, is Bonnie there? Who else have we not—I'd like to say hello to everybody.

Commander Brandenstein. Certainly. We'll let Jim Wetherbee tell you. He's the other new guy. And we'll let him tell you what he thought of it, and then we'll turn you over to Bonnie.

Lieutenant Commander Wetherbee. I'm proud to be here. It's a pleasure being part of this program. I'm happy to be part of watching Dan recover that satellite. He's about the best in the world at grabbing satellites at Mach 25.

The President. Unbelievable. Well, I'm glad to see a Navy pilot—could you use a 65-year-old Navy pilot up there?

Commander Brandenstein. Navy pilots don't get that old.

The President. Oh, yeah? I'm one. [*Laughter*] Hey, listen, there seems to be a long pause.

Ms. Dunbar. Well, I'm delighted to be here, Mr. President, and feel fortunate to do it again. But I know that it takes a lot of work on the part of many, many people. And I want to thank all the people at Johnson Space Center, and NASA in general, for making this possible. It's been an incredible mission.

The President. Well, you know, that's one thing that does come through. There you all are working, and people following very keenly what you're doing. But I think one thing the American people do see as a result of a highly complex mission like this is this enormously effective teamwork. And I must say, I'd like to join you in saluting everybody involved. And I wish you well as you wrap it up now and come on back. But we're proud of you, and I look forward to seeing you at the White House, as does the Vice President, when you can get around to getting up here after you get back.

So, well done. We're proud of you, and we will follow the rest of the mission, as we have the beginning, with great interest. And, Dan, to you and your wonderful crew, congratulations.

Commander Brandenstein. Well, thank you very much for taking the time and speak with us this morning, Mr. President. And we're proud to have had the opportunity to represent our country and to conduct this mission, and along with all the other people that make up the NASA and the space team in this country.

The President. Okay. Well, we'll let you go to work, and well done. Thank you very much. Over and out.

Commander Brandenstein. Goodbye.

Note: The conversation began at 7:39 a.m. The President spoke from the Oval Office. In his remarks, he referred to Richard H. Truly, Administrator of the National Aeronautics and Space Administration. The space shuttle crew included Capt. Daniel C.

Brandenstein and Lt. Comdr. James D. Wetherbee, both of the Navy, and mission specialists Bonnie J. Dunbar, Marsha S. Ivins, and G. David Low.

Remarks at the Bush Administration Executive Forum
January 18, 1990

Mr. Vice President and members of the Cabinet, Governor Sununu, all of you members of our team, thank you. Thank you very much for that warm reception, the pleasure of being here.

What a privilege it is to celebrate the first anniversary of an administration that you all helped make possible and that you enrich every day through your own hard work and your dreams. I wanted to stop the applause so you could get back to work. [*Laughter*]

I understand that every Cabinet member is here and preceded me. And I'm very proud of our Vice President, very proud of this Cabinet, very grateful to our Chief of Staff. You've done America proud, and you've made each of us proud. So, I would say to our Cabinet: Please, why don't you make me a little less lonely up here? As the noted philosopher says, "Come on down!" So, please, I'd like to invite the Cabinet members to come up here.

Well, thank you all. Please be seated. And again, I'm glad to be with you. I won't keep you long. Another pledge: My remarks will be on the record. After all, I'm getting tired of reading in the press that I'm too secretive. [*Laughter*] Let me tell you my views on that—I'd like to, but they're classified. [*Laughter*]

You know, a week from Sunday, America is going to come to a stop—the Super Bowl. And the bad news is that only one team there will triumph. But the good news is that today we salute an event in which—with your help—all America has triumphed: the first 12 months of this administration. And looking back, it's been quite a year.

First, there was Barbara. Americans got to know her. And I don't have to tell you how lucky I am to have her by my side and working with many of these Cabinet officers, particularly Secretary Cavazos, trying to help him and all of you make America better in education.

As far as accomplishments, minding the admonitions of my mother, I'm not going to dwell on my biggest feat of 1989. Suffice it to say that during the second year I hope to catch yet another fish. [*Laughter*]

One year ago this week, you and I began the work which led to even larger feats, like the lowest unemployment rate in 15 years and the 20 millionth new job since 1982; like inflation at less than 5 percent, falling interest rates, real per capita income, and investment at record levels. You have helped achieve the longest peacetime boom in our nation's history.

This prosperity, I really believe, has helped make America a kinder and gentler place. And we've nurtured it through pioneering initiatives, whether by working to solve the savings and loan crisis or to make our education system number one again, whether enhancing the quality of our environment or waging a stepped-up, all-out battle against drugs—and I'm sorry that Bill Bennett is not here today. Our goal has been, and remains, you see, to build a better America. These great objectives have been set down in our initial quarter. And now let's use the next quarter to make still greater progress.

Woodrow Wilson could have been describing our administration when he said, "It's always a beginning, not a consummation." In that spirit, let me simply observe: Just wait until the second-guessers see our second year.

You know, remember the old New England story about a man who was stuck in the mud with his car. The man was asked by this passing motorist whether he was really stuck. Finally, he responded with a shake of his head. "You could say I was stuck," he said, "if I was really going anywhere."

Well, America is going somewhere—toward a better future. It is not stuck. And much of the credit belongs to you, the people in this room. You are changing the way Americans view their government. Franklin had a word for it—not Ben, Aretha. It is "respect"—she and Rodney Dangerfield. And in your own way, you've helped ensure that just as millions have become free from tyranny abroad, millions more will know freedom from want, crime, and drugs at home.

Toward that end, we've sent proposals to the United States Congress to confront our most crucial issues. And while I'll listen to reasonable alternatives, I will not compromise on the principles upon which our proposals are based. And so, I call upon the Congress to work with the White House and complete the job that we were all sent here to do.

For instance—let me just give you some examples; I can't possibly spell out every initiative—for instance, our commitment to the environment is crystal clear. We have sent Congress legislation to reduce acid rain, air toxics, and urban smog. It is the first rewrite of the Clean Air Act in over 10 years. And I asked both Houses to preserve the careful balance in that bill—help clean up our air and preserve jobs. We've laid down a fairminded compromise, and now let's break the stalemate. Let's protect our environment for decades to come. Let's get moving.

But that isn't all—far, far from it. We've also made proposals to stem drug use and crime: proposals to ensure stiffer penalties for violent criminals, greater certainty in sentencing, an end to early release and easy parole. Eight months ago, I sent legislation to the Congress, and since then, more money has been provided for additional prison space and more Federal law enforcement officers. And yet Congress has left too much work undone. I see our Attorney General nodding, and he's been out in the forefront, and he understands that. And so, I call upon Congress to act now, quickly and responsibly. We need mandatory time for these firearm offenses—no deals when criminals use a gun. And for anyone who kills a law enforcement officer, no legal penalty is too tough, and that does mean the death penalty—not at some point, not sometime, but now.

Next is—another example—education. And here also we need the Congress to act. I sent legislation up to give greater choice to parents and students, reward excellence, and demand greater accountability. And so, let's ensure that every child in America grows up with a decent education.

I look at these Cabinet officers up here with me, and I see so many—I'm thinking as my mind is running—so many other initiatives that, with your help, they have taken in taking our program to Capitol Hill. But what it all adds up to is the future. The future is what I'm talking about, the future of our kids. And so, we've proposed child-care legislation to put choice in the hands of low-income parents and allow a grandparent to help, or a neighbor, or a local church. And when it comes to child care, let parents, not the Big Brother, decide how that job gets done.

Yes, the future, a future in which Americans are free to work, invest, save, and plan—so, our administration does want to cut the capital gains tax to spur investment and create jobs. And Americans have shown the world that the path to a strong economy is through innovation, investment, and enterprise. Come to think of it, what they create isn't a bad definition of America—opportunity for all.

Opportunity can come from the bipartisanship which puts America first. Perhaps Will Rogers said it best when he observed: "I love a dog. He does nothing for political reasons." [*Laughter*] Ask Millie. I'm not sure she'd agree. [*Laughter*]

Nevertheless, our proposals reflect America's best interests, not the interest of one faction or another. And I ask the Congress to respond in kind, spurring opportunity, not dependency, for a future free from fear.

Keep in mind—and I know this as well as any of us—the agenda is unfinished. The public awaits, expecting us, as I said last January, to act, not to bicker. And as we act, let's recall what we believe and who it is that we serve: not ourselves, not a party, but this nation and her people—moreover, all those for whom America is the conscience of mankind. The working mother in

San Antonio and the farmer in Nebraska and the teacher in New Jersey and the uniformed sons and daughters who keep us free—we serve them, every single one.

Yet the essence of America, that belief in the individual, eclipses language and border. And so, we must also champion the heroes of Prague and Warsaw, Bucharest and Berlin, and the thousands of people who last July—I saw it—greeted me there in Budapest, tears running down their faces, waiting hours in a driving rain, cheering for the principles of liberty and democracy, cheering for the United States of America.

Dwight Eisenhower, beloved Ike, once observed that we must help the cause of democracy summon "lightness against the dark." He was right. And so, we have helped Poland and Hungary, and we will help others in Eastern Europe. But let me be clear: I will not neglect this hemisphere, the Western Hemisphere. Our operation in Panama, Operation Just Cause, was a tremendous success. And I am very proud of the young men and women who served this country with such pride and courage. And, yes, there's going to be some second-guessing, Monday morning quarterbacks at work. But let's not forget: 92 percent of the people in Panama supported Operation Just Cause. And these people are our brothers and our sisters, and they deserve our help. And so do all our friends in Latin America and the Caribbean. And they'll receive it. For even as we rejoice in the changes in Eastern Europe, we've got to remember our friends in America's hemisphere.

Americans supported Operation Just Cause because democracy is a noble cause. And today it's on the move wherever people dream. Around the world, that cause endures, and the darkness lifts, and the light grows brighter by the day.

No President could have a finer group of people as part of his administration. I thank you from the bottom of a very grateful heart. No nation could have better public servants. And I thank you on behalf of every American. God bless you. God bless our beloved land, this morning star of freedom, the United States of America. Thank you very, very much.

Note: The President spoke at 11:26 a.m. at DAR Constitution Hall at the 9th annual Executive Forum for political appointees of the administration. In his remarks, he referred to singer Aretha Franklin and comedian Rodney Dangerfield.

Exchange With Reporters
January 18, 1990

Reallocation of Foreign Aid

Q. Mr. President, will you be discussing Senator Dole's plan to cut aid to Turkey and other countries?

The President. I won't be talking about that. I'll be talking about my delight that somebody understands that it is the President that ought to set these priorities, and that's what I'm very pleased about.

Q. Are you angry at Senator Dole?

The President. I'm pleased with him. What are you talking about?

Q. Does that mean the priorities are going to change?

The President. I want to see them put the power where it should be in this matter, and not mastermind foreign policy through 138 subcommittees—allocating funds. I'd like to see it done the way I think the Founding Fathers intended for it to be done. And don't worry about our friends, Turkey—we'll take care of that.

Q. Are you going to get the same amount?

The President. I want to get back what I want first.

Social Security Tax Cut

Q. What do you think of Senator Moynihan's plan, Mr. President?

The President. Hey, listen, we've got to get going. We've got a distinguished visitor here—what do you think of the Moynihan plan, Mr. President? [*Laughter*] He and I have the same feeling about it. We both draw a blank when we hear about it. [*Laughter*] This is an effort to get me to try to raise taxes on the American people by the charade of cutting them, or cut bene-fits. And I am not going to do it to the older people in this country.

Note: The exchange began at noon in the Oval Office at the White House, prior to a meeting with President Turgut Özal of Turkey.

Statement by Press Secretary Fitzwater on President Bush's Meeting With President Turgut Özal of Turkey
January 18, 1990

The President met for approximately 30 minutes in the Oval Office with President Turgut Özal of Turkey. The meeting was followed by a working lunch in the Residence.

The two Presidents discussed a wide range of issues, including changes in the Soviet Union, the negotiations at Vienna on conventional force reductions, and NATO's vital role in a changing Europe. They engaged in detailed discussions of the situation in the Middle East and the sweeping changes in Eastern Europe, with special reference to the Balkans.

President Bush and President Özal agreed to continue their pattern of close consultations and stressed the importance of U.S.-Turkish security cooperation at this time of rapid change in Europe and in East-West relations. The two Presidents also discussed Cyprus at some length and reaffirmed their support for U.N.-sponsored negotiations between Greek and Turkish Cypriots.

Remarks at the Bush-Quayle Campaign Reunion
January 18, 1990

Well, I'm delighted to see you all. And first, let me pay my respects to our chairman of the Republican National Committee and to Jeanie Austin, the cochairman. What a job they are doing for the party, and what a job they're going to do for winning in 1990.

I want to salute the "G–7"—two members of our Cabinet, and the others lined up here—great friends. I value their counsel still, and I know very well that if I hadn't had their counsel back then I probably would not be standing here as the 41st President of the United States. So, my heartfelt thanks to all of you.

Let me just say a word of thanks to our outstanding Vice President, Dan Quayle. He is doing a great job for our country, and I am delighted to see him. And of course, the Silver Fox. [*Laughter*] I think she's doing pretty well for the country, too. Forty-five years—some things never change. [*Laughter*]

I'm sorry if I'm late. The 18-wheeler got a flat. Then I got tangled up in the flag. Then the metal detector got set off by the silver foot. [*Laughter*] Does it all come back to you now? [*Applause*]

It's too bad a lot of our campaign staff couldn't be with us tonight. I understand that some of them are still waiting in the elevator in the Woodward Building over there. [*Laughter*] You remember those ritzy, patrician, Ivy League, elitist campaign headquarters—[*laughter*]—famous for its plush carpets, quiet telephones, priceless antiques—[*laughter*]—and that fine food you all ate? [*Laughter*] This is the truth.

They did an informal survey over at Domino's. True story—they said we ordered twice as much pizza as the Democrats. [*Laughter*] And true to our reputation, we tipped better, too. [*Laughter*] And now that we're in office, you might sum it up this way: We deliver. [*Laughter*]

It was a long, hard campaign. We all have our memories, but I remember riding in planes and kissing babies and hugging pigs and marching in parades and driving stagecoaches and tractor trailers and playing shuffleboard in Florida and standing under confetti cannons in California and waiting for yet one more balloon drop. But tonight, I really came over to thank you for one thing you did not ask me to do: You never asked me to make a video riding in a tank. [*Laughter*]

Some of the members of the press corps who had the good fortune—or ill fortune, depending on how they looked at it—of being assigned to our campaign would know that this is a true one, but I'll never forget it. Barbara and I were traveling in the car when they told us to look out the window to wave because these photo dogs were coming alongside for a photo opportunity. And so, we're both sitting there, smiling and waving and looking enthusiastic—you know how you do in campaigns. [*Laughter*] And the truck full of photo dogs pulls up next to us, and they all look over and say in unison, "Pardon me, sir. Do you have any Grey Poupon?" [*Laughter*] Don't say these guys don't have a sense of humor.

The Secret Service really never got into the act too well. They had one comedian, though. I'd been singing to myself in the car—this is also a true story—and as Barbara and I were getting out, she heard a quiet voice from behind the wheel in the front say, "If I were you, sir, I wouldn't give up your daytime job." [*Laughter*]

Barbara tells a story about staying in a hotel and not having her bathrobe with her. In the morning, the room service knocked on the door with coffee, and she looked all over for a robe—no luck. So, when the room service guy opened the door, the future First Lady was standing there, looking quite elegant, wrapped in a bedsheet. [*Laughter*] First Ladies do have a fashion effect, if you will, so start planning the toga

parties; we're coming into an election year. [*Laughter*]

But we know—she knows and I know and Dan knows and Marilyn knows—we know well where the real heavy lifting happened out there in the campaign—out in the field. And I'm talking about what you all know so well: the phone work, the signmaking, the all-nighters, the creative chaos, and the just plain making do with what you've got. I heard about the Orlando office scrambling to rent a forklift to unload 60,000 posters, only to find out that the forklift wouldn't come through the door. And so, for 2 hours—truth—in spite of blisters, sunburns, sore biceps—the crew carried and stacked every one of those posters, all 60,000, by hand. And I can never forget my gratitude to those people.

The toughest part, for me, was the debates. Some time has passed, so I want to take a moment to recognize my opponent. He was strong, tough, tenacious, a real fighter. I gained a newfound respect for Dan Rather. What a team. [*Laughter*] What a team we had. [*Laughter*]

I referred to some of these guys standing back here—Lee Atwater, the Republican master of R&B. [*Laughter*] He couldn't teach me rhythm, but he did teach the Democrats to sing the blues. And I believe they're just starting. [*Laughter*]

You know Bob Teeter. He promised me he'd always give us an accurate view of things. So, he tried to balance the good news and the bad news—you know, 1 month of good news, 18 months of bad news. [*Laughter*] But he served us with wonderful loyalty and dedication, and I valued his advice.

In biblical times, Noah heard a voice that told him to go build an ark. The hero, you remember, in "Field of Dreams" heard a voice that told him to go out and build a baseball field. Poor Rich Bond. He heard a voice that told him to go build momentum in Iowa. [*Laughter*] But again, what a job he's done, what loyalty, what dedication that he's given me and Barbara and our family—and all of us working together in the party.

Then we heard we were down by over 20 points, and a man named John Sununu predicted that we'd win New Hampshire by 10 points. What a kidder, right? [*Laughter*] But he did, literally. And he's versatile. He can take on the Democratic Party, bring in New Hampshire and, yes—you're not going to believe this—but he can even fix Xerox machines in the White House. [*Laughter*]

And then, over the course of the campaign, some say that it was Roger Ailes who gave me a personality. [*Laughter*] He made me seem more decisive. Well, I'm not sure about that. Maybe I am, and maybe I'm not. [*Laughter*] But he worked hard and was very well compensated. We paid him in pints of Haagen-Dazs [ice cream]. [*Laughter*]

And as for Craig Fuller, there's no way I can ever really express my gratitude to him—my former Chief of Staff, with me every inch of the way. We'd call in; they'd say, get us the plane. That meant get ahold of Fuller on the telephone wherever he was. But he did a magnificent job.

I don't need to tell you my respect for Nick Brady and Bob Mosbacher, both of them now serving with great distinction as members of, I think, the finest Cabinet a President has ever been blessed with.

We'll let this party get back to being a party, but before I leave, I want to thank each one of you. I hope you'll pass along my thanks to those who couldn't be here.

We set out to win an election in 1988 for a reason. America's work is unfinished, but her promise—I still believe it—is unlimited. We live, as Rick Klun, a bass fisherman from Montgomery, Texas, said one day to 7,000 bass fishing fans in Arkansas—he said—young kid, learned to bass fish, and following—in his jockey shorts—following his Dad in the creeks of Oklahoma—and he said, "Isn't it wonderful to live in a country without limits?" And that's exactly the way I feel about the United States.

You've seen people flocking to our commitment to freedom and democracy all around the world—wondrous changes, especially in Eastern Europe. And God bless those young kids that gave Panama's democracy a chance to be fulfilled now.

Here at home, in the '88 election, we sought power for its potential to help people. We wanted progress for a clean environment and the fight against drugs that savage our streets, and for the sake of the family, free institutions, free speech, and free markets, to make an America second to none in education, to ensure economic opportunity for all Americans. We knew what remained to be done.

So, we've introduced the first amendments to the Clean Air Act and a tough crime package and an innovative education bill. Carefully crafted for the S&L industry—we've worked that out, policies there, and trade, and conducted a foreign policy that we think our forebears would be proud of.

You and the many who aren't with us tonight pulled off incredible feats of endurance and faith during the campaign, day after day, for the sake of the party and the American people. And Dan Quayle, who put up with a lot during this campaign—I might say, nobody took more heat and did a better job for our ticket and our election than he did.

So, Barbara and I came over here literally to try as best we can, from the bottom of our grateful hearts, to say thank you. Thank you for giving us this fantastic opportunity to serve the greatest country on the face of the Earth. God bless you all. Many, many thanks.

Note: The President spoke at 6:10 p.m. in the International Ballroom at the Washington Hilton Hotel. In his opening remarks, he referred to the "G–7," a group of his leading campaign advisers which included Secretary of the Treasury Nicholas F. Brady and Secretary of Commerce Robert A. Mosbacher. The President also referred to Robert Teeter, campaign adviser and pollster; Richard N. Bond, deputy campaign manager and national political director; John H. Sununu, Chief of Staff to the President; and Roger Ailes, senior campaign media adviser. The Woodward Building was the 1988 Republican campaign headquarters in Washington, DC.

Remarks at the Annual Convention of the National Association of Home Builders in Atlanta, Georgia
January 19, 1990

Well, thank you, Shirley, Florida's gift to the Home Builders and trusted adviser to this President. I'm delighted to be with you. I'm delighted to see a fellow Houstonian—your next president, your incoming president. Marty, good luck to you in the travails ahead. I wish you the very best. And to other VP's here—Mark Tipton and Jay Buchert and Kent Colton and Bob Bannister—delighted to be with all of you. And, Patsy, what a job you've done on this convention. Thank you for including me in it.

It's great to see you. It hasn't been so long, has it, since that last meeting that Shirley referred to, in November. And of course, we have with us several other distinguished guests. Congressman Newt Gingrich is here, and Chalmers Wiley, so active in the housing business. [Representative] Steve Bartlett is over here, a fellow Texan. Kit Bond, Senator Bond—great leaders in the Senate—Senator Wyche Fowler flew down with me on Air Force One. So, you have a very distinguished congressional delegation here, and I expect I'm missing somebody.

Also with me on the plane—and doesn't have that much to do with housing, but he's here and I'm very proud of him—is Secretary Manuel Lujan, the Secretary of the Interior, who came with me—over here someplace—whoops, where is—there he is on the end—and other members of what I think is an outstanding Cabinet. And of course, I'd be remiss if I didn't single out an old friend of mine—one fatal flaw, he's a Democrat—[*laughter*]—but one old friend of mine, and that is Atlanta's old and yet new mayor, my friend—and I mean that—Maynard Jackson and his family are here with us today, too. So, Maynard, we wish you all the best in the job ahead.

And what a treat it is to be back in Atlanta. In fact, I believe that it was in this very hall about a year and a half ago that the party opposite from mine held their 1988 convention. And of course, I have fond memories of that convention. It gave me a very good excuse to go fishing in Wyoming with [Secretary of State] Jim Baker. [*Laughter*] And the question was appropriately raised, "Where was George?" Albeit a year and half later, I'm proud to say, "Here I am," proud to be with the Home Builders. Isn't it great to live in a country with no limits? Who would have thought that I would put my silver foot in the same place where Ann Richards talked? [*Laughter*]

In any event, it is great to be back among the Home Builders of America. I really hope you all appreciate one thing—it's not every day that this association gets to hear from one who actually lives in public housing. [*Laughter*] And let me say parenthetically, I'm very sorry that my favorite Silver Fox is not with me. She's doing literacy work in Florida. But I might add, I am very proud of Barbara Bush, and I wish she were with me here today.

You see, before we moved to the White House, Barbara and I were a home builder's and, yes, a realtor's dream. We lived in 28 places in 45 years. And yet in a real sense, wherever we lived—whether it was in Houston, Washington, New York, or China—our family had one true home that we took with us wherever we went.

I remember the first place Barbara and I lived in, when our son George was just a baby—a tiny, ramshackle shotgun house in the oil town of Odessa, Texas. It had a makeshift partition down the middle that cut the house into two apartments, leaving us with a small kitchen and a shared bathroom, an old water-drip window unit—you remember those cooler units they used to use out there—cranked up like a west Texas dust storm still couldn't drown out the noise of the all-night parties next door.

But that first house that Barbara and I lived in couldn't compare to those new "smart houses" that you in the NAHB are building. We were fortunate that the wiring even worked, while today you're putting telephone, television, and power together on one master cable, linked to a computer.

It is remarkable what free enterprise and American ingenuity can do.

Yet despite it all, Lord Byron was right—a home is a place in the heart. I can't speak for our neighbors, but for us that little tiny shack was home. And I have to wonder and worry how many families break apart because they can't afford to buy or rent a home even half as decent as that first place that we lived in. We cannot allow the high costs of housing to suffocate the financial life of America's young people. When it comes to housing, this must not become a society of haves and have-nots. And I salute your association, who understands that principle and is doing something about it.

The fact is that for the last decade and a half the cost of new homes—the cost of the American dream, if you will—has been escalating. Young couples just starting out, low- and moderate-income Americans, unmarried people trying to invest in the future—and many are finding themselves priced out of the home market, especially new homes. To create decent housing that people can afford, the Government and the private sector must cut some redtape. So, I've asked my able, distinguished Secretary of HUD, Jack Kemp—and what a job he is doing for housing in this country—to convene a blue ribbon commission to identify these barriers to affordable housing construction and to make recommendations on how to eliminate them.

And while I'm at it, let me just get something off my chest. As you know, as I travel around this country, I've encouraged the planting of trees, and even planted a few myself—half of which lived. [*Laughter*] But in these same travels, I see so many new suburbs that are utterly denuded of trees. Ironic, since the new owner's first instinct will be to plant as many trees as possible. Ironic also because trees clean out air. And so, I respectfully suggest as a former businessman that leaving the original trees might be a shrewd sales strategy. It's good for business, and it is very good for the environment.

But the truth is, there's one housing policy and one sales strategy that's better than all the others combined, and of course, I'm talking about a healthy, growing economy with low, long-term interest rates. This first month of the 1990's marks the 86th month of economic growth in America. And as Shirley says, it was housing that paved the way to the longest peacetime recovery in modern history. You built nearly 10 million single-family homes in the eighties and nearly 5 million multifamily units. And by working together, the housing industry will keep this country going strong in the nineties.

Now, you understand that the engine of homeownership in America is the private enterprise system. And by helping those entrepreneurs and risktakers, more Americans will have access to the dream of homeownership and decent housing. But to keep America moving—keep it moving—we will need the cooperation of Congress. And I can think of one simple action that Congress can take to give this economic expansion a boost. It has already been debated; it has already won the support of the majority of the Members in the House, the majority of the Members in the Senate. And what we need now is a simple up-or-down vote to cut the tax on capital gains.

Some call such a cut a favor for the rich, and they should know better. They should know what you know—that a capital gains tax cut favors economic growth, jobs, and opportunity for working America. It favors every American who makes a living day after day, brick by brick, hammer on nail; and it helps those get jobs—those who do not have jobs now. A capital gains tax cut will help every American who holds a job or owns a home. And so, I call on the Democrat leaders of Congress to give the American people a break and to let the House and Senate work their will by having an up-or-down vote on the capital gains tax cut—and do it soon after the Congress comes back.

Also vital to the home buyer and the home builder alike are low and stable rates of interest. A 1-percent increase in the rate of interest knocks millions of families out of the market. In the last few years, millions of families could afford a new home because mortgage interest rates have dropped from 18 percent in the early eighties to less than 10 percent today. But I want to see them come down even more. I am not satisfied at

10 percent.

The 1990's must be another decade of lower taxes and lower interest rates; but to have a stable economy, it must also be a decade in which Washington at long last adopts fiscal policies as sound as those of the average American household. None of us is allowed to spend our bonus before we earn it, nor should Congress start planning where to spend a possible peace dividend. To the extent that the world events allows us to cut defense spending, then we should recognize that cutting the Federal budget deficit would be a true dividend for America's taxpayers and our children's future. We must get that deficit down.

And too often we forget, Congress forgets, that every house is the handiwork of an architect, a surveyor, a mason, a plumber, a carpenter, painter—dozens of other working men and women. And if Congress levies new burdens on our economy, it's these very people who will be put out of work. But of course, even if we do cut the capital gains tax, and even if we do keep interest rates low and get them lower, and even if we do protect the economy, this is cold comfort for those Americans who languish in the projects—or the thousands of others who know no shelter at all. These Americans need help. They need hope. And so, that's just what I call our program that Jack and I are working on together: HOPE. It stands for Homeownership and Opportunity for People Everywhere. Our program addresses the full range of housing concerns—from shelter, the homeless, to affordable housing for low-income families, to greater access to jobs.

Let's start with what HOPE can do for first-time home buyers. It's time Congress let Americans use their IRA savings to get into that first house.

And then—God bless them—there are those who must live in the poverty and fear of public housing. They're disproportionately minority Americans. And they suffer abuse from drug-dealing predators within, and the last thing they need is abuse from without. One of the first and, I think, very best things that Jack Kemp did when he came into office was to change HUD procedures so the drug dealers can be kicked out of public housing. We owe that to those people living in these public dwellings.

And concerning abuse from without, let me say just one thing: Atlanta is a great and cheerful city. It has proudly risen from the ashes of a distant past. And so, for those who plan to revel in a rally of hate here tomorrow, let them know this: Atlantans, like all Americans, turn their backs on bigots.

To escape violence and crime, to live in decent housing, our public housing tenants must first be empowered, empowered to choose where they want to live, empowered by housing vouchers. Low-income families don't need us to build new public-housing horrors, these edifices. They need decent low-income housing. And that's why I call on the Congress to extend the low-income housing tax credit.

Earlier I discussed my capital gains cut proposal, but even this cut would not be enough for America's impoverished inner cities, often as desolate and as shattered as a war zone. No, for these communities, we've got to go one step further and eliminate the capital gains tax all together within these enterprise zones, because this surely will attract more investment and jobs and encourage more development in these areas.

There is something perverse about discriminatory lending practices that have kept the FHA out of the very places that need the most help. And so, my administration will ensure that FHA is true to its first mission: to make housing affordable for low- and moderate-income families. It's wrong to draw a red line around the inner city—it's not right or fair. And we're going to replace the red line with a green line of opportunity and jobs for the future.

The centerpiece of HOPE is to let all Americans live in dignity and control their destiny. And dignity is exactly what resident management projects allow. Tenant management and tenant ownership is not just an experiment, it's the future. But even more is needed. We're all going to have to work in a partnership to solve the problems of the helpless and the homeless. My administration is going to do its part by expanding homeless assistance. Late last year I signed a bill that boosts funding under the McKinney Act to reduce homelessness. Our

HOPE proposals will tie shelter with basic services for those in need. And Secretary Kemp, I know, will tell you later of the other steps we're taking.

You're doing your part. You certainly are, building and renovating shelters for the homeless, for battered women, for these troubled children and retarded adults. And you're working with the Job Corps, taking the unskilled, the out of work, and training them for lifetime careers in construction and maintenance. And again, I congratulate you on this commitment. What better Point of Light—one American helping another have a better life.

But our partnership needs a third element: that constellation of volunteers I referred to that I call the Thousand Points of Light. I couldn't come to Atlanta without taking note of one such Point of Light: a part-time carpenter and his wife, who have provided shelter for so many in this very city. And of course, I'm talking about the former President, Jimmy, and Rosalynn Carter. They deserve our thanks, as do all the people behind Habitat for Humanity. [*Applause*]

And he was President, and he deserves the applause you've given him. And so does a woman named Ella McCall. Ella, once a homeless mother—now she has her master's degree and serves the homeless as a social worker in a shelter in Washington, DC. And when the family strives to move out of a shelter into a home, they need her, they need Ella. When a homeless mother wanders lost with her children in tow, she needs Ella. And when I look out of the south window of the White House at dusk and see the distant figures of ragged men bedding down for the night, I pray to God that this country find more people like Ella McCall.

Your work in job training, Jack Kemp's work in tenant management and ownership, Ella McCall's work with the homeless—all of this ultimately saves the taxpayers money. But this isn't about money, it's about caring. And if it takes love to make a house a home, then perhaps the same could be said of a country. For the poorest among us, America must not just be a place to live in but a home for all.

Thank you. God bless you, and God bless the United States of America. Thank you very, very much.

Note: The President spoke at 11:45 a.m. in the Omni Coliseum. In his opening remarks, he referred to the following association officers: Shirley McVay Wiseman, president; Martin Perlman, incoming president; Mark E. Tipton, first vice president; Robert J. Buchert, vice president and treasurer; Kent W. Colton, chief executive officer; and Robert D. Bannister, senior staff vice president for governmental affairs. The President also referred to Ann Richards, one of the keynote speakers at the 1989 Democratic National Convention.

Statement by Press Secretary Fitzwater on Development of Wetlands Conservation Policy
January 19, 1990

President Bush today visited the Everglades National Park to emphasize his commitment to achieving the goal of no net loss of wetlands. On December 13, he signed into law the Everglades National Park Protection and Expansion Act of 1989, which expands the park by over 100,000 acres. The President believes this type of environmental stewardship can coexist with economic growth and prosperity as we face the challenge of protecting the Nation's wetlands.

At the President's direction, the Domestic Policy Council, which has created a task force on wetlands, is in the process of examining how best to implement the President's goal of no net loss. The Domestic Policy Council review is expected to lead to recommendations for revising Executive Order 11990, which was signed in 1977 and directs Federal agencies to minimize the loss of wetlands resulting from Federal actions, but does not address the broader issue of achieving no net loss. In addition, the task force will examine other methods to achieve the goal of no net loss and make recommendations to the President in late 1990.

The task force has been undertaking background studies and briefings on wetlands preservation. During the coming months, the task force will hold a series of public meetings around the country to solicit public comment on appropriate strategies for achieving the no-net-loss goal, including consideration of the effectiveness of regulatory programs and the use of nonregulatory approaches. The meetings will also focus on specific issues, such as losses which are related to agricultural production, losses of wetlands in the Mississippi River Basin and along the Louisiana coast, and the unique challenges posed in Alaska. Information gained at these meetings will be used in the development of recommendations to the President.

The task force will accomplish its work through the use of small interagency groups, each of which will develop options on a particular issue for consideration by the full task force. These groups will address a number of issues, such as: the scope and meaning of the no-loss goal; specific Executive order language required to ensure that Federal policies assist in achieving the goal; the important roles of State and local communities and private conservation groups in preserving wetlands; the role of market-based incentives in wetland protection; mitigation of wetlands loss through replacement elsewhere; and additional steps that may be necessary to implement the no-net-loss goal, including whether legislative changes are required.

Nomination of William D. Phillips To Be an Associate Director of the Office of Science and Technology Policy
January 19, 1990

The President today announced his intention to nominate William D. Phillips to be an Associate Director of the Office of Science and Technology Policy. This is a new position.

Since 1989 Dr. Phillips has served as president of the Missouri Advanced Technology Institute in St. Louis, MO. In addition, he has served as science adviser to the Governor of Missouri, 1987 to present, and a professor of chemistry at Washington University, 1987 to present. Prior to this, Dr. Phillips was senior vice president of science and technology for Mallinckrodt, Inc., in St. Louis, MO.

Dr. Phillips graduated from the University of Kansas (B.A., 1948) and the Massachusetts Institute of Technology (Ph.D., 1951). He was born October 10, 1925, in Kansas City, MO. He served in the U.S. Navy, 1943–1946. Dr. Phillips currently resides in St. Louis, MO.

Nomination of Eugene Wong To Be an Associate Director of the Office of Science and Technology Policy
January 19, 1990

The President today announced his intention to nominate Eugene Wong to be an Associate Director of the Office of Science and Technology Policy. This is a new position.

Dr. Wong has served at the University of

California at Berkeley as a professor of electrical engineering and computer science, 1969–present; as an assistant professor, 1962–1965; and as an associate professor, 1965–1969. He has served as a fellow at Harvard University, Imperial College, and the University of Cambridge. Prior to this, he worked for IBM Research Center in Yorktown, NY, 1960–1962, and for the IBM Research Laboratory in Poughkeepsie, NY, 1955–1956.

Dr. Wong graduated from Princeton (B.A., 1955; Ph.D., 1959). He was born December 24, 1934, in Nanking, China. He is married, has three children, and resides in Berkeley, CA.

Nomination of Edward W. Kelley, Jr., To Be a Member of the Board of Governors of the Federal Reserve System
January 19, 1990

The President today announced his intention to nominate Edward W. Kelley, Jr., to be a member of the Board of Governors of the Federal Reserve System for a term of 14 years, from February 1, 1990. This is a reappointment.

Since 1987 Mr. Kelley has served as a member of the Board of Governors of the Federal Reserve System. Prior to this, he was chairman of the board of Investment Advisors, Inc., in Houston, TX, 1981–1987.

In addition, he has served as chairman of board of the Shoreline Companies, Inc., and director of Texas Industries, Inc.

Mr. Kelley graduated from Rice University (B.A., 1954) and Harvard University (M.B.A., 1959). He was born January 27, 1932, in Eugene, OR. He served in the U.S. Naval Reserve, 1954–1956. Mr. Kelley is married, has three children, and resides in Washington, DC.

Nomination of Jessica L. Parks To Be a Member of the Merit Systems Protection Board
January 19, 1990

The President today announced his intention to nominate Jessica L. Parks to be a member of the Merit Systems Protection Board for the remainder of the term expiring March 1, 1995. She would succeed Samuel W. Bogley.

Since 1988 Ms. Parks has been Associate Regional Counsel for Litigation and Program Enforcement at the Department of Housing and Urban Development in Atlanta, GA. Prior to this, she served in various capacities at the Department of Housing and Urban Development in Atlanta: Associate Regional Counsel, 1987–1988, and Assistant Regional Counsel, 1985–1987. She also served as Administrative Judge for the Merit Systems Protection Board in Atlanta, GA, 1982–1985.

Ms. Parks graduated from Tulane University (B.A., 1974) and the University of Tennessee College of Law (J.D., 1980). She was born February 4, 1953, in Chattanooga, TN. She is married, has two children, and resides in Decatur, GA.

Remarks at a Fundraising Dinner for Governor Bob Martinez in Miami, Florida
January 19, 1990

Thank you very much, Bob. Thank you, Governor. In case you missed it, Bar and I are pretty proud of our son Jeb—smiling away when I think Bob honored him by asking him to be his campaign chairman. To Mary Jane Martinez and our chairman, Van Poole; our able Secretary of the Interior way down there, Manuel Lujan—was with me all day long today—and of course, to my old friend, the doer, Alec Courtelis—I'll tell you, he does everything to help others—and to our outstanding United States Senator, Connie Mack, who is doing a superb job up there in Washington; and Members of the U.S. Congress Mike Bilirakis and Bill Grant, Craig James, Clay Shaw, Bill McCollum, Porter Goss, and of course, your own—and Bar and I feel like our own—Ileana Ros-Lehtinen, right from this district here—and I might say, parenthetically, I am very proud of the team that her husband is putting together here in Miami to see that justice prevails—I'm very proud of Dexter Lehtinen.

You know, when it comes to standing by Bob Martinez, Barbara and I are not going to let anything get in our way, as much as we hate having to leave Washington in January to come south to Florida. We'll do anything that's required of us. [*Laughter*]

As you know, I originally intended to come here in December. But as I told Bar, in order to meet with the most important man in the Soviet Union, I had to postpone a get-together with the most important man in Florida. Barbara said, "You know Dennis Erickson?" [*Laughter*] Of course, those of us who are fans of Hurricanes, we're not alone. Every time you changed the TV channel this year, there was another team from Florida out there. I might say to Dennis and to Sam, I look forward to seeing you at the White House to salute your fantastic record. But tonight we're talking about another champion: my early supporter, my friend, a great Republican, and—as Jeb pointed out, and Alec, too—a great chief executive. And I'm talking about Bob Martinez.

You know, in the next decade Florida will need his leadership as never before. Every year, the equivalent of the population of a new city even larger than Bob's Tampa moves to Florida. And some say this growth is a mixed blessing. Everyone loves the new businesses and the new jobs, but growth can also bring problems—how to preserve the environment, to fight crime. Florida's growth is the proof of Florida's prosperity. So, what you need is a Governor who has always sought the best for Florida, who will carefully weigh the needs of nature and man, who will make the most of economic opportunity while protecting your own very special way of life. And that's the kind of Governor you need, and that's the kind of Governor you've got, and that's the Governor that we must reelect.

Some leaders look only for immediate political gain. Bob Martinez—he looks beyond the horizon to the stars. And this has been an incredible year of change—promises to be a decade of change, beginning with the successful mission of the space shuttle *Columbia*. And now, thanks to Bob Martinez, American business is on the launch pad with Spaceport Florida.

And a President, too, must look to the far horizons, and the other great frontier of our time is the freedom frontier. The world in January 1990 is a very different place, very different than it was in January of 1989. Then the Berlin Wall seemed to be an impenetrable veil between East and West; now that Iron Curtain is open. And then a dictator reigned in Panama, and now the people rule in Panama. In fact, there are only two holdouts preventing a totally democratic hemisphere. So, let Daniel Ortega and Fidel take note: Like the dinosaur, the day of the dictator is over. They are swimming against the tide.

But this is an era of brisk change abroad. Let us also make it a time of great achievement at home. And Bob and I began this year by working together to help Florida farmers recover from the terrible freeze.

And I was pleased at his suggestion to sign a major disaster declaration for southern Florida earlier this week authorizing Federal relief and recovery assistance. And we will work on a wide range of domestic issues, from the environment to crime fighting, sound economic policies and education.

But to be effective, we will both need the cooperation, not the opposition, of partisan legislators. Take clean air. Last summer, I proposed the first major revision of the Clean Air Act since 1977, one that uses market solutions to cut acid rain, smog, and other poisons in our air. And it was a balanced proposal. But Congress still hasn't acted, and so I call on Congress as soon as it reconvenes to preserve the balance, to keep costs under control, but to act on clean air.

And, yes, we have other environmental concerns. I know that every time I fish along the flats off Islamorada, I'm reminded of just how special Florida truly is. You have the longest coast of any State in the continental United States, some of it beautiful beaches, some of it lined with leafy mangroves; your interior landscape, a tropical jewel glistening with rivers and marshes and freshwater swamps, and the famous river of grass. Just this afternoon, as Bob referred to this, we toured the Everglades and saw sanctuaries for crocodiles and turtles. And this is the home of the royal palm and the bald cypress, the Florida panther, and so many other rare and endangered plant and animal species. And all these creatures, great and small, need very special protection.

So, Bob has been working with my administration to extend the Everglades eastward across the very land that we saw today. And this successful partnership between Florida and the Federal Government has been furthered by the able leadership of Manuel Lujan. Working with Secretary Lujan, Governor Martinez took the initiative necessary to make this major Everglades expansion a reality. He created the East Everglades Land Acquisition Task Force. And because the State of Florida was willing to set aside part of this land, I was able to sign into law a bill increasing the size of Everglades National Park by more than 100,000 acres. And because of our efforts together, we have ensured that the Everglades will remain an everlasting treasure for the children of America. In fact, I hear that even the alligators are pleased— [*laughter*]—so pleased they're wearing polo shirts with a little picture of Bob Martinez on their chests. [*Laughter*]

And we will go further to protect natural Florida, but we also need common sense to protect another delicate ecology, if you will—the ecology of an expanding economy with good jobs and good government. And as I start my second year as President, one of my prime economic goals is to cut the tax on capital gains. You see, I believe I know that such a tax cut would create even greater opportunities for more Americans. Now, of course, there's those who claim otherwise. They attack me for claiming this is a tax cut for the rich, but we know that such a tax cut will help every American who holds a job or owns a home. A majority, a majority—Connie knows this well—the Members of the United States Congress, Senate and House, are on record as wanting to cut capital gains. And therefore, I call on the political leadership in Congress to get out of the way of that majority. Let the will of the majority work on this important job-oriented piece of legislation.

Bob and I agree on other basic economic principles, as true in Tallahassee as they are in Washington, DC: When legislators send a spendthrift legislation, we send it back. But if legislators will work with us, we can devise creative new ways to use frugal means to achieve generous ends. And for those who say that we need to spend more money to get people off welfare, I say look to Florida—look to Florida. Thanks to your Governor's Project Independence, 31,000 men and women, all welfare recipients, were able to use State training and education to replace welfare with work. And this is the best kind of antipoverty program, one that saves the taxpayers' money—tens of millions of dollars—one that really does work.

Bob and I share yet another goal, and that's to beat the scourge of drugs, a menace to the very future of America. Bob is the lead Governor on the substance abuse and drug trafficking for the national task force for the National Governors' Association. He set a national precedent by appointing a State drug czar. And he has worked to make parolees undergo drug testing with counseling—to get straight and then to stay straight.

And Bob and I also share a philosophy about prison sentences: Make them at least as tough as the criminals you convict. And Bob has already stiffened the Florida code, added the prison space to enforce it. In Washington, Congress, to its credit, acted on part of my anticrime package. More money has been provided for additional prison space, more Federal law enforcement officers. But Congress has left too much work undone. And so, help Senator Mack and our Republican Congressmen here tonight—all of them supporters—our Members of Congress and me, help us all to get action on the rest of my violent crime package: to toughen Federal sentences for those using a firearm in the commission of a felony, to reform the rules of evidence, to support the police, to enact the death penalty proposal that I sent them. Join me in calling on Congress to take the shackles off the policemen, the courts, and the law.

Bob and I support an oppressed minority, one that's too often been stripped of its rights, and I'm talking about the victims of crime. I hope that each of you, one way or another, will try to help out what I call a Thousand Points of Light, try to learn a little more about these organizations to help the victims of crime.

I say a killer deserves something else, and I'm talking about justice. And justice is exactly what Bob Martinez is dispensing in this State. So, let those who value life so little know one sure thing—that when they come to Florida, they've reached the end of the line. We need to back up our law enforcement people.

But the challenges of the future also require vision and compassion, especially the challenge of preparing our children for the future. And if I might—I am in great admiration of Barbara for what she's done over the years in working to help make our country a literate nation. We have an Educational Excellence Act, and that Educational Excellence Act has been one of my top priorities since I sent this legislation to Congress almost 9 months ago. To make our schools work, we must give parents, teachers, and children choice and flexibility—and then hold everyone accountable for the results. And accountability should begin with the United States Congress. It's high time that Congress finished its homework and passed needed education reforms. When it comes to caring for children, perhaps Washington could learn a thing or two from Bob Martinez, who has worked so hard on behalf of children at risk, whose One Church, One Child program has placed so many foster children in loving homes.

I've spoken here at length about some of my hopes for this year because they mesh so well, you see—they mesh so well with your Governor's outlook. But Bob's achievements stand alone, from the environment to crimefighting to preparing the children of Florida for the future. His would be a remarkable record of achievement for any Governor, but for this Governor, it's all just another day at the office.

The bottom line is this—and this is what I came down to tell you—I need Bob Martinez. Florida needs Bob Martinez. So, let's hit the campaign trail, the trail to victory in November.

Thank you. God bless you, and God bless America.

Note: The President spoke at 7:26 p.m. in the main ballroom of the Omni International Hotel. In his remarks, he referred to the Governor's wife, Mary Jane Martinez; Van Poole and Alec Courtelis, chairman and finance chairman of the State Republican Party; Dexter Lehtinen, acting U.S. Attorney; and Dennis Erickson and Sam Jankovich, football coach and director of intercollegiate athletics at the University of Miami. Following his remarks, the President and Mrs. Bush traveled to Camp David, MD, for the weekend.

Remarks to Participants in the March for Life Rally
January 22, 1990

Well, at first I want to welcome all of you gathered in Washington from around the country for this year's March for Life. Before you begin the march, I want to take a minute to share my deep, personal concern about abortion on demand, which I oppose.

For 17 years, the March for Life has served as a poignant reminder to all Americans that human life in all its forms must be respected. And I think all of you know my deep conviction on *Roe* versus *Wade*. The continuing strong presence of the March for Life reminds those of us in decisionmaking capacities—in the White House and in the Congress and in the Court—that millions of Americans care fundamentally about this issue and are committed to preserving the sanctity of life.

Your movement also reminds Americans, especially young Americans, of the self-evident moral superiority of adoption over abortion. We should all be grateful to the families that adopt babies, giving them care and love and a chance for a wonderful life.

Ladies and gentlemen, let me assure you that this President stands with you on this issue of life and that my prayers go out to all of you for your faith and courage. God bless you, and God bless life. Thank you very much.

Note: The President spoke at noon from the Oval Office at the White House, via an electronic hookup with the rally site. Participants had gathered on the Ellipse for a march to the Supreme Court on the occasion of the 17th anniversary of the Court's decision of Roe v. Wade, *which legalized abortion.*

Statement on the Appointment of Arnold Schwarzenegger as Chairman of the President's Council on Physical Fitness and Sports
January 22, 1990

I am pleased to announce the appointment of Arnold Schwarzenegger as Chairman of the President's Council on Physical Fitness and Sports, and I challenge him to raise the consciousness of all Americans on the importance of good health through physical fitness.

The physical health of all Americans must have a stronger commitment than an annual New Year's resolution. We now know that individuals can influence their health, fitness, and productive prime of life through the active pursuit of regular exercise programs. I have asked Arnold to chair the Council because I believe he is uniquely qualified to address and influence national health and fitness issues, especially among our youth. Arnold has devoted much of his career to the pursuit and advocacy of physical fitness. His abilities have produced a broad range of career successes involving athletic competition, acting, and business ventures.

The continued success of the President's Council on Physical Fitness and Sports is in large part due to the efforts of past Councils and Chairmen, especially immediate past Chairman Dick Kazmaier. I have asked Dick to remain on the Council so that his experience and knowledge can be of benefit to the new Chairman. I will be announcing other new members of the Council in the very near future, and I know that through the Council's work and Arnold's leadership physical fitness will become a priority for all Americans in the 1990's.

Statement by Press Secretary Fitzwater on Rural Development Programs
January 22, 1990

Today the President ordered the implementation of a report from the White House Economic Policy Council's Working Group on Rural Development, formed in April 1989 to analyze and evaluate existing Federal rural development programs and develop policy options for improving their coordination and execution.

The President has instructed Secretary of Agriculture Clayton Yeutter to implement six proposals designed to improve the coordination of rural development programs and serve as a catalyst for future initiatives. They are:

President's Council on Rural America. A Presidential Council will be formed with membership drawn from farmers, State and local governments, rural businesses, and high-technology industries to advise the Federal Government on improving Federal rural development policy.

State Rural Development Councils. Each State will establish a rural development council to coordinate Federal rural development programs in its region. Council members will include representation from the Office of the Governor and the State representatives of all Federal departments administering rural development programs locally. The council will identify and assess local rural development needs and coordinate the delivery of Federal and State rural development programs to meet those needs.

Rural Development Demonstration Programs. Under existing budgetary resources and programs, a series of rural development demonstration programs will be organized to identify regional rural development needs, develop plans of action to meet those needs, bring together the necessary resources, and evaluate the process and its results for possible application on a broader basis.

Rural Development Technical Assistance Center and Hotline. The Department of Agriculture will establish a center to provide technical assistance and detailed information on Federal programs that serve rural communities. The Center will also link callers with Federal, State, and regional program officials who can provide additional assistance.

Target Federal Rural Development Programs. Given limited Federal budget resources, the Federal Government will attempt to target rural development programs on those activities that generate the maximum net economic benefits. While most Federal rural development programs allocate funds by formula, programs with discretionary accounts will allocate funds to those activities where the payoff is greatest.

Economic Policy Council's Working Group on Rural Development. This working group will become a standing committee of the President's Economic Policy Council and will implement any rural development initiatives developed by the President's Council on Rural America and approved by the administration.

Secretary Yeutter will hold a press availability at the Department of Agriculture today at 10:30 a.m. to discuss these initiatives.

Nomination of James L. Kolstad To Be Chairman of the National Transportation Safety Board
January 22, 1990

The President today announced his intention to nominate James L. Kolstad to be Chairman of the National Transportation Safety Board for a term of 2 years. He would succeed James Eugene Burnett, Jr.

Since 1988 Mr. Kolstad has served as Acting Chairman of the National Transportation Safety Board in Washington, DC. Prior to this, he served as Vice Chairman of the National Transportation Safety Board, 1988; member of the National Transportation Safety Board, 1987–1988; vice president of the Pat Thompson Co. in Denver, CO, 1986–1987; aviation management consultant in Denver, CO, 1986; and senior director of communications and public affairs for Frontier Airlines in Denver, CO, 1978–

1985. In addition, he served as Director of the Office of Community and Congressional Relations for the Civil Aeronautics Board, 1973–1978; Presidential advanceman for the White House, 1972–1973; Executive Assistant for Intergovernmental Relations for the Office of the Vice President at the White House, 1971–1972; Director of Intergovernmental Relations at the Department of Transportation, 1969–1971; and legislative assistant to Congressman James F. Battin, 1968–1969.

Mr. Kolstad graduated from the University of Montana (B.A., 1960). He was born March 3, 1939, in Washington, DC. Mr. Kolstad served in the U.S. Navy. He resides in Alexandria, VA.

Statement by Press Secretary Fitzwater on the Overseas Private Investment Corporation Mission to Panama
January 22, 1990

The U.S. Overseas Private Investment Corporation (OPIC) plans to recruit U.S. businesses for an investment mission to Panama, February 23–28. The OPIC mission will familiarize investors with the economic and political climate in Panama by providing direct access to representatives of Panama's new government and business community. The purpose of this mission is to help rebuild the Panamanian economy.

Panama's business infrastructure retains attractive features, such as transportation, communications, and financial services. It has excellent potential in agriculture, aqua-

culture, light industry, and tourism.

Preparation for the mission will begin with a preliminary trip to Panama by OPIC CEO and President Fred M. Zeder on January 31.

OPIC is the U.S. Government agency responsible for encouraging investment in some 110 developing countries worldwide. An increasingly vital tool of American foreign policy, OPIC encourages investors to explore overseas business opportunities. In the past year, OPIC has led investment missions to Poland, Hungary, Bolivia, sub-Saharan Africa, and other developing nations.

Nomination of L. Joyce Hampers To Be an Assistant Secretary of Commerce
January 22, 1990

The President today announced his intention to nominate L. Joyce Hampers to be an Assistant Secretary of Commerce for Economic Development. She would succeed Orson G. Swindle III.

Since 1985 Mrs. Hampers has served as an attorney with the law firm of Tierney and Manoil in Boston, MA. Prior to this, she served as the Republican candidate for the Massachusetts State Treasurer, 1986; attorney with the law firm of Rosales and Rosales in Boston, MA, 1983–1985; commissioner at the department of revenue for the Commonwealth of Massachusetts, 1979–

1983; partner with the law firm of Blake and Hampers in Boston, MA, 1978–1979; and associate commissioner and member of the State tax commission at the department of revenue for the Commonwealth of Massachusetts, 1975–1978.

Mrs. Hampers graduated from Boston College School of Law (LL.B., 1967) and Boston University School of Law (L.L.M., 1969). She was born September 30, 1938, in Mount Vernon, IN.. Mrs. Hampers is married, has three children, and resides in Chestnut Hill, MA.

Remarks at the American Spectator Annual Dinner
January 22, 1990

Thank you, David. And let me say that I deem it a high honor to be introduced by David Morse, a man I've known for a long, long time, a Nobel winner and extraordinary human being. And congratulations, sir, on the wonderful work of Libertad, the work that it's doing to advance the cause of freedom in the world. Let me also pay my respects and recognize Lord Henry Plumb over here, who is with us tonight, also a distinguished international figure—very proud to be with him and many members of my administration and Senators and Members of the House of Representatives— our whole team on Capitol Hill. And of course, I'm very pleased to be on Bob Tyrrell's kinder and gentler side. [*Laughter*] That's his right side, if any question about that.

I understand that this is actually the American Spectator's 1989 annual dinner. [*Laughter*] Now, that's true conservatism, you see. Wait until the year's over—completely over—until you decide whether it's worth celebrating about. [*Laughter*] But who am I to criticize? Actually, I've learned to be more forgiving about confusions in-

volving the calendar—ever since I made September 7th a date that would live in infamy. [*Laughter*]

But I am delighted to be here, and so is Barbara. We are to help celebrate tonight with all of you. Our nation's intellectual life would be more than a little poorer without the American Spectator surveying the scene. Your critical eye helps us see beneath the surface, see beneath and beyond the intellectual fads and fashions of the day, to the ideas and the enduring values that really matter in our society. That's a valuable service, especially today, because there is a tendency these days to mistake surface appearances for the substance of things.

Take an issue like homelessness. There is no condition more repugnant to the democratic values and the dignity of the individual, and there's no problem more susceptible to misunderstanding. We've all heard the law of unintended consequences. Well, what's at work here is what we could call the law of well-intended consequences. And in some ways, our difficulty with dealing with homelessness begins with the label, a label that tells us what the homeless lack is homes.

But the problem is far more complex— more complex because the real problem of homelessness is not one-dimensional. There are homeless families, cases where the husband and the wife and the children are all together, out on the street. But most often, homelessness is a symptom of a more pervasive problem: drug or alcohol addiction or chronic joblessness or mental illness or family problems—conditions that prevent the unfortunate people that we see on the streets from caring for their children, from keeping a home.

If our policy towards the homeless doesn't treat these causes, if it doesn't combine the basic need for shelter with other support services that reach the real reasons for homelessness, all the best intentions and all the housing in the world won't get the homeless off the street once and for all and back into society. There is no other way to truly help the homeless break the grip of life on the streets. And so, last November I announced what we call the HOPE initiative—Homeownership and Opportunity for People Everywhere. Along with help for first-time homebuyers, this new proposal brings other creative solutions to the difficult housing problems facing low-income families—not new public construction programs that too often prove to be expensive failures but more tenant ownership and housing vouchers to provide more options to more people.

But affordability is only one part of the problem—availability is the other. We must renew the low-income housing tax credit to spur needed private construction. We've got to go even further. We need policies that encourage the growth and investment that provide jobs, the jobs that translate into homes. And we need enterprise zones to stimulate entrepreneurship. And we need to cut the capital gains tax. And in these pockets of poverty, these special enterprise zones, we need to eliminate that tax altogether.

But the real answer for homeless with mental problems or dependent on drugs or alcohol—the real answer is shelter plus care. And you're familiar with the McKinney Act. It's now been signed into law and substantially increases funding to reduce

homelessness. But the solution to the problems of the homeless require partnership— Federal, State, and local. Through HOPE, we will improve coordination of basic needs, like shelter, with other social services to help the homeless get the support they need to control their own lives and find the jobs that mean the difference between a life of despair and a life of dignity.

But homelessness isn't the only issue where we need to look beyond superficial, quick-fix solutions. Take our schools, education. There is no single function more vital to society than what goes on in that classroom: cultivating the skills and intellect we need to succeed in the future, transmitting our values—centuries of experience and hard-won wisdom—from one generation to the next.

Now the conventional wisdom—current wisdom, I guess you call it on the back page of the Spectator—is that there's nothing wrong with our schools that can't be corrected, if only the Federal Government would just get out that checkbook and write a check. Well, we all know the bigger the pricetag, the better the quality, right? Well, the fact is, we already spend as much or more than the other industrialized societies and democracies on education—an average of almost $4,000 per student each year. And we all know the results: Our schools simply are not making the grade.

So, what's wrong? It's not a question of cash. We've got to use our resources more wisely—look to the schools that do work, find out why, translate their success into the goals that all schools can aim for. And then we've got to take two more crucial steps. We've got to give parents a choice in their children's schools, and we've got to give our schools the freedom and flexibility they need to strive for higher standards—and then hold them accountable.

There is no shortcut to better schools. And there's also no shortcut to the victory line in the race against drugs and crime. There's no simple solution to a problem as complex as this. And here again, it'll take a partnership of people reaching into every neighborhood and every school.

You know, at the Federal level, we've developed a comprehensive national drug strategy to attack this insidious plague on four fronts: enforcement, interdiction, education, and treatment. And I salute our drug czar, Bill Bennett—why we call people czars in the United States, I don't know. But if there's ever a guy that deserved the title, it's Bill.

But over the past year, we've sent Congress our proposals—and frankly, we have made progress in some areas. I'm pleased that Capitol Hill provided us with the reinforcements that we asked for—new agents, new prosecutors, new prisons—to catch, convict, and hold those who value America so little. But these new troops can't do it alone. Simply put, we must have tougher laws on the books. And that means increased mandatory time for firearms offenses, the death penalty for anyone who kills a law enforcement officer, and no more loopholes that let criminals go free.

Working together, the administration and Congress can make even more progress. But our drug and crime problems go beyond government solutions alone. Getting addicts off drugs or making sure that hardened criminals do hard time will take the commitment of everyone who cares about this country. And it will take a return to the values that have taught generations of Americans the difference between right and wrong. It's not an easy road to travel, but it is the surest route to a drug-free America.

And that's why, with all the flash and the fluff in the world today, there's something we can't afford to lose sight of, something deceptively simple: It's who we are that makes this nation what it is. You know—we all know—democracy is more than the machinery of government, more than just a system of checks and balances, clashing interests. More than anything else, democracy depends on the decency of its people. And I am convinced that there is in this country a deep reservoir of democratic decency—a respect for others, a sense of responsibility, a solid recognition that values matter. This reservoir of decency is there for us to draw on to renew our dedication to the fundamental ideals of a free government.

And it's not a matter of each individual waging a lonely battle against the impersonal forces of society—we're not alone. The values I'm talking about have a home in the family, in our churches, and in our communities. And these institutions are strong, much stronger than the alarmists out there would have us believe. Each of them contributes to our public life, enriches it in ways beyond measure. Each of them makes this nation strong, gives it a sense of purpose and a role in the world.

And this is the culture that sustains us, the culture that we must ourselves sustain. And that's our challenge today. I must confess, I worry at times about the dissolution of the family, about the diminution of the family. But fundamentally, the institution is strong. And our challenge, then: to see the values and institutions that endure beneath the kaleidoscope of modern culture.

The American people understand there are no snap answers, that the only solutions that succeed are ones consistent with these core values. And for all the noise and the clatter of contemporary culture, that's cause for optimism. The calendar offers each of us convenient launch points for a fresh start. Sometimes it's a new day, a new year— now, a brand-new decade. And the beginning of the nineties invites America to clearly put its signature on the 20th century, to write the next chapter in a book of spectacular achievements in freedom, economics, human advancement, world leadership. I welcome the nineties with a genuine sense of optimism. It's an ideal time to renew our vows and our values, time to look beyond the next paycheck and the next personal problem, time instead to look to the next generation.

And so, I am optimistic about our future for one compelling reason: To succeed, we do not have to acquire any new qualities. The courage, ingenuity, and compassion that made us the leader of the free world is still in every one of us. And we simply have to remember that the American adventure isn't over—it's just begun.

Thank you all very much. God bless you and the Spectator, and God bless the United States of America. And thank you for letting Barbara and me come by.

Note: The President spoke at 7:25 p.m. in the ballroom at the Willard Hotel. In his remarks, he referred to Lord Henry Plumb, former President of the European Parliament, and R. Emmett Tyrrell, Jr., editor of the American Spectator, a monthly magazine.

Remarks to the Law Enforcement Community in Kansas City, Missouri
January 23, 1990

Thank you, Mayor Berkley. Thank you very, very much, all of you. Thank you very much. But how did you know that our dog, Millie, was the most popular person in the Bush family? [*Laughter*] I'm delighted to be introduced by my friend Dick Berkley, and thank you for that warm introduction. As he confessed, we go back a long, long time, and I'm grateful to him for his friendship and his leadership. I also want to thank and pay my respects to two that flew out here with me on Air Force One: our distinguished Attorney General, Dick Thornburgh; and our drug policy czar—why we use the word in the United States, I do not know—but our able Drug Policy Director, Bill Bennett. Both here with me today, and both doing a superb job for our country.

It's always good to see the Governors, and be with them, of these two great States, both friends—John Ashcroft, from Missouri, and of course my friend Mike Hayden, from just across the line—I think it's just across the line—but both of them, side by side with us, recognizing that the States must have considerable influence, must take a lot of action, if we're going to solve the problems that I wanted to talk to you about today.

And of course, we also had some other travelers with me, friends of good standing flying out, your two able Missouri Senators, Jack Danforth and Kit Bond. Both—whoops, they're here—here's one. Where's Kit? Over here. And of course, Congressman Ike Skelton, my friend, and also Tom Coleman. And let me just say about this group of Representatives, Senate and House: All of them, all four, are taking leadership roles in this fight against crime. And I know that your Congressman from the district I just visited, Alan Wheat, wanted to be here. He is attending to duties in Washington. I hope he's doing the right thing back there, as Congress just reconvened. And of course, so many law enforcement and community leaders—the police chief has been at my side, and the respect with which he's held by people in the communities is very clear and obvious—Commissioner Ray Price.

And of course, I had a wonderful meeting with the Ad Hoc Group. I've known the leader of the group because he is serving on one of our most prestigious antinarcotics task forces in Washington, Presidentially appointed, working closely with Bill Bennett and me. Al, we're just delighted that you are willing to not only do what you are doing here but take the time to be a part of that. Al Brooks—an outstanding leader for this community.

Then I had a list—not to read off, necessarily, but I would be remiss if I didn't say how pleased I was with the briefing I received out here—the Ad Hoc Group. Inspiring presentations—and I won't mention them all, but Dr. Stacey Daniels, Dr. Mark Mitchell, one a Ph.D. psychologist, the other an M.D.; Cliff Sargeon, who just hitchhiked a ride with us somewhere along the line—I don't know where he is out there—and of course, Ron Finley and Vic, Majeeda, Aasim—so many others that just made this whole program come alive.

And now, before I get to my words, let me also salute the Army and thank the band from Fort Riley for that wonderful music. Outstanding, as always.

And I can tell you—and mean it—that it is great to be in the heartland, great to be back in Kansas City. And you know, Kansas City has so much of which to be proud. You've heard the tally: grassier than Ireland; built on more hills than ancient Rome;

more water, more fountains than Paris. But you also know what really sets Kansas City apart. It is not your parks. It's your people. They call it the Kansas City spirit—restless, idealistic, determined. It's the kind of spirit that pushed back frontiers and brought the railroads west, rebuilt a burned-down convention hall in 90 days, and survived three floods this century. And, yes, it's a community spirit, a spirit that emphasizes the value of collective well-being. Norman Rockwell captured—in a painting called just that—the "Kansas City Spirit." It pictures a brawny, sunburned man, feet firmly planted on the ground, eyes on the distant horizon. And one hand clutches a blueprint, and the other's rolling up his sleeves.

And thank God, it's a spirit that is very much alive today, because in recent years, it's not the convention hall that's caught fire but the streets themselves, burning with a new form of pain called crack and crackling with a burst of gunfire not heard in Kansas City since the outlaw days of the Old West.

But people in this town refused to surrender to the drug plague. You took back what's yours—took back your kids and took back your streets. It began like the spirit of Kansas City, when one man rolled up his sleeves and stepped forward with a blueprint—a blueprint that's become a model for our cities, an inspiration to people everywhere. I had the pleasure of meeting with him, as I alluded to earlier, and with his group this morning; and I know that many more than I mentioned are here with us this afternoon. They're a group of homegrown Kansas City heroes called the Ad Hoc Group Against Crime, and the man's name—you know him, Alvin to some, Al to me—Al Brooks.

Ad Hoc recognized early on that the war on drugs meant unconventional warfare, a battle to be fought day by day, house by house, family by family, child by child, because each kid saved is a victory won. Working closely with police, Ad Hoc members gather in force—gather by the dozen, using bullhorns, wooden coffins, street rallies—to warn drug dealers to get off the street. They're not subtle. I just saw them in action out there. But they are determined, and they are united, and they are clearly making a difference.

I spent a part of the morning here in the downtown inner-city area. I can't remember a more inspiring experience since I've been President. Went to 33d and Park—saw what they used to call the drug tree, an ancient, curbside oak where the drug dealers put up a basketball board to lure young children and cover up their own deadly operations. And it's still a rough area, still not free of crime. But a lot of crack houses are gone, and a lot of pride's come back. And block after block, house after house carries the sign of victory, Ad Hoc's six-word warning to the cowards of the night: "This neighborhood fights back against drugs."

Part of the solution to the drug menace lies in effective, community-based initiatives like the Ad Hoc Group here. Also, cooperation between local and Federal law enforcement is essential, as we saw last Friday when Kansas City police combined with Federal agents to bust what may be the biggest crack ring in town. Another part, an essential part, lies in the demand side: stopping drug use before it starts, and helping those who want to stop. And our national drug strategy calls for record levels of new funding for both education and treatment.

But demand-side solutions alone, important as they are, will never be enough. There are people out there intent on doing evil—cowardly, amoral. And when they spot someone vulnerable—the school kid who has to cross a drug-infested corner to get home—they see their fellow man the way a pack of jackals sees a wounded fawn.

A 4-year-old boy shot dead in a suspected crack house; an 11-year-old kid gunned down outside another drug den, allegedly at the hands of a 14-year-old guard; in a downtown bar, a mother sells her baby for crack; and a firebombing leaves three generations dead, including a grandmother and three little kids—the headlines are horrifying, sickening, outrageous. And though they come from Kansas City, they are tragically familiar in cities across America.

Strong families are an important element in a healthy, respectful society. Many of life's most important lessons are learned within the walls of our own homes, and we must do everything we can do to strengthen our families and help them cultivate character in our children. But let us also be clear about the role of personal accountability, of the responsibility of the criminal for his actions. The fact of the matter is, the criminal chooses his way of life, his companions, the kind of crimes he commits. He's not the victim; he is the victimizer.

And you who have struggled, worked hard for safe streets know this. It's time we protect the rights of our elderly, our kids, and our crime victims everywhere. The law-abiding community that you represent has a duty to punish wrongdoers. Punishment is not, as some may see it, an unseemly indulgence in revenge. Just punishment is a moral, civilized response to wrong. Punishment is necessary not only as a deterrent to future crimes but for its own sake—which is to say, for the sake of justice.

This tradition of justice speaks not of a society that disparages human life but, rather, one that treasures innocent human life as precious, as unique. In Larry McMurtry's—you remember it—classic western novel "Lonesome Dove," two Rangers finally put an end to a brutal gang's deadly rampage, and one of the outlaws turns out to be Jake Spoon, the Rangers' old partner. "It's a bad situation," says Captain Call, moments before arresting his old friend. "But there he is. He put himself in it." McMurtry's saga, like the lives of the real-life pioneers who inspired it, reveals some simple truths. Most Americans believe each of us faces the innate temptation to succumb to evil and yet always has the freedom instead to choose to do good.

Today too many law-abiding Americans are prisoners in their own homes, and we really have to change that. We have got to change it. The wrong people are behind bars. Go to the community I came from. Talk to the lady and her husband in a Christian home, a cross and the Bible inside, locked in for fear of what's on the outside.

The first line of defense will always be our local law enforcement. But as in the days of legendary U.S. marshals like Bat Masterson and Wild Bill Hickok, places like Kansas City again need the support of top-notch Federal lawmen. Congress deserves our thanks for providing the new Federal troops that we asked for—new agents, new prosecutors, new prisons to catch, convict, and contain those who prey on our cities.

But it's time for Congress, reconvening this very day, to finish the job, because it does no good to send the troops into battle wearing handcuffs. Shortly after taking office, I sent a comprehensive package to Congress to combat violent crime, to back up our new lawmen with new laws—laws that are fair, fast and final. Fair—an exclusionary rule designed to protect the truth and punish the guilty, and not good cops who have acted in faith. Fast—habeas corpus reforms to stop the frivolous appeals that are choking our courts. And finally—fair, constitutionally sound death penalty provisions, because for any drug dealer who kills a cop, no penalty, in my view, is too tough.

Major portions of our crime bill still await congressional action. But today there's another bill—a Trojan horse standing at the gates of Congress. It's called S. 1970. It looks like a real crime bill. It sounds like a real crime bill. But look at it—take a look at it. Go to the library and get it. In actuality it will be tougher on law enforcement than on criminals. And its so-called reforms of the exclusionary rule, habeas corpus, the death penalty, and the Justice Department itself will only entrench and extend the legal loopholes and the redtape that disrupt honest law enforcement and have angered the American people for far too long. It must be defeated. America needs a crime bill with teeth, yes, but this is a sheep in wolf's clothing.

We don't question anyone's motives. One of the things I don't like about politics—maybe I should expect it, get into the arena, as Teddy Roosevelt called it—it seems to be a charge and countercharge. I propose one agenda and somebody else, another. We don't have to question the other person's motives or integrity in making the proposal, but it is time to debate these differences openly. We can't accept anything—and I will not—that rolls back the clock on our ability to fight crime and punish wrong-doers. And good legislation shouldn't have to wait until the final weeks of an election year—as happened in 1984, 1986, and 1988, just by coincidence. And America wants it done right. And America wants it done responsibly. And America wants it done now.

You in Kansas and Missouri, right here, have set a personal example of courage in grappling with tough choices. In this city, you fought back and you got involved and you refused to look the other way. And you have my thanks and the gratitude of an admiring nation.

In the Norman Rockwell painting that I mentioned earlier, the man with the blueprints is looking sharply to one side. They say a young boy saw the picture in a book and asked his father, "Dad, Kansas City is in the center of America. Which way is the man facing—west or east?" The father's answer was pure Midwest: "Well, son, it sort of depends on which way you hold the book." [*Laughter*]

Of course, the truth is, it doesn't matter how you hold that picture. Because no matter how you look at it, the Kansas City spirit, the real Kansas City spirit, always faces the same way—forward to a brighter tomorrow, forward to the future ahead.

Thank you for an inspiring day. Thank you for this warm greeting on this January day. God bless you all as we begin a new year. God bless Kansas City, and especially, God bless the United States of America. Thank you all very, very much.

Note: The President spoke at 1:40 p.m. in the Kansas City Municipal Auditorium Music Hall. In his remarks, he referred to Larry Joiner, Kansas City chief of police; Ray Price, president of the board of police commissioners; and Stacey Daniels, Mark Mitchell, Cliff Sargeon, Ronald Finley, Victor Syng, Majeeda Baheyadeen, and Aasim Baheyadeen, members of the Ad Hoc Group Against Crime Steering Committee.

Nomination of Bradley Gordon To Be an Assistant Director of the United States Arms Control and Disarmament Agency
January 23, 1990

The President today announced his intention to nominate Bradley Gordon to be an Assistant Director of the U.S. Arms Control and Disarmament Agency for the Bureau of Nuclear Weapons and Control. He would succeed Kathleen C. Bailey.

Since 1987 Dr. Gordon has served as a legislative assistant for foreign policy, defense, and intelligence for Senator Rudy Boschwitz. Prior to this, he served as a professional staff member on the Senate Foreign Relations Committee, 1985–1987; political analyst for the Central Intelligence Office of Near Eastern and South Asian Analysis, 1979–1985; research assistant for the Middle East Institute at Columbia University, 1975–1976; and research assistant for the Bureau of Applied Social Research at Columbia University, 1975.

Dr. Gordon graduated from Brandeis University (B.A., 1971), the University of Vermont (M.A., 1974), and Columbia University (Ph.D., 1979). He was born May 22, 1949, in Burlington, VT. Dr. Gordon is married, has three children, and resides in Reston, VA.

Nomination of John Wesley Bartlett To Be Director of the Office of Civilian Radioactive Waste Management
January 23, 1990

The President today announced his intention to nominate John Wesley Bartlett to be Director of the Office of Civilian Radioactive Waste Management at the Department of Energy in Washington, DC. He would succeed Ben C. Rusche.

Since 1978 Dr. Bartlett has served as manager of nuclear technology at the Analytic Sciences Corporation (TASC) in Reading, MA. Prior to this, he served as manager of systems studies in nuclear waste for Battelle Pacific Northwest Laboratories, 1968–1978, and he was a Presidential exchange executive, 1973–1974. In addition, Dr. Bartlett served as a Fulbright professor of nuclear engineering at Istanbul Technical University, 1968, and as a faculty member at the University of Rochester, 1962–1968.

Dr. Bartlett graduated from the University of Rochester (B.S., 1957) and Rensselaer Polytechnic Institute (M.C.H.E., 1959; Ph.D., 1961). He was born October 18, 1935, in Camden, NJ. Dr. Bartlett is married, has two children, and resides in Lynnfield, MA.

The President's News Conference
January 24, 1990

The President. Good morning, good morning. Well, as you know, I'll soon present my budget to the Congress. And as I prepare to do so, it strikes me that our nation faces challenges on many fronts, so let's give each the attention it deserves. Tomorrow I'm going to announce the second phase of our strategy to fight drugs in the schools and the streets of America. The future of this country depends on whether we can give our children a chance to grow up drug-free.

And secondly, I will soon present our plan to restructure America's defenses in the wake of the dramatic changes that are taking place abroad. And I'm proposing a defense budget that begins the transition to a restructured military—a new strategy that is more flexible, more geared to contingencies outside of Europe while continuing to meet our inescapable responsibility to NATO and to maintaining the global balance.

And finally, Secretary Brady and Director Darman and Chairman Boskin will put the details of our budget before the American people. And as that occurs, other members of the administration, the Cabinet, key agencies will provide an in-depth outline of their efforts to address the many challenges of caring for the afflicted and uplifting the poor, cleaning the environment, educating our kids, as well as other important issues. All of this is a preparatory to the State of the Union, 1 week from today, in which I will speak to the broader issues that we face as a nation.

There are two items that I want to mention here today, and then take some questions. First, I've decided that the environmental challenges that face America and the world are so important that they must be addressed from the highest level of our government. And at the beginning of this century, President Theodore Roosevelt helped pave the way for the establishment of the National Park System. Twenty years ago, President Nixon established the EPA, Environmental Protection Agency, by Executive order. That is now one of the largest and most important regulatory agencies in the Government. And today I'd like to announce another step forward in this important tradition of support for conservation and environmental protection.

Many countries have environmental ministers with Cabinet status. And I'm convinced that that Cabinet status will help influence the world's environmental policies. So, with so many difficult decisions ahead I'll need Bill Reilly's counsel; I'll need him sitting at my side in the Cabinet. And I'm pleased to endorse the elevation of the EPA to Cabinet status by creating a Department of the Environment.

Senators Glenn and Bill Roth, chairman and ranking members of the Senate Governmental Affairs Committee, have introduced legislation that would create this Department. Congressmen Conyers and Horton are working on similar legislation, and I look forward to working with them and other interested Members of the House and Senate to enact legislation that would bring EPA to the Cabinet table, where it now belongs.

And now I'd like to address one other issue that I know is foremost on your minds. Every American should know—I want to take this opportunity to state this as strongly as I can—that I will not break faith with the Chinese students here. I've made that very clear from the very beginning. And right after Tiananmen, I moved to protect the Chinese students in this country. Not one was sent back. They were safe then, and they are safe now, and they will be safe in the future.

And when Congress passed the Pelosi bill last fall, I was faced with a choice. If I signed the bill, the students would still be safe, but China would retaliate and cut off future student exchanges. You see, I think the exchanges have brought forward the reforms that have taken place in China, if you look back over your shoulders for a starting point and compare it to the Cultural Revolution days. Some of the reforms have taken place; steps have been taken forward. And regrettably Tiananmen was a gigantic step back. But I want to keep contact; I do not want isolation.

If I vetoed the bill, I could take action to provide the students with even greater protection while keeping the door open for more Chinese scholars to study here. And the price of the Pelosi bill is lost opportunity for the Chinese scholars of tomorrow, and people should understand that very, very clearly. The bill is totally unnecessary,

the long-term policy consequences are potentially great, and Congress, in my view, will have only itself to blame. I can understand their emotion, but we've got to look at policy, and we've got to be fair in what has already been accomplished by the Executive order. It's a strong message. I want it to be seen exactly that way.

And now I'd be delighted to take any questions.

Soviet Civil Unrest

Q. Mr. President, how serious a crisis is the nationalist rebellion in Azerbaijan for President Gorbachev, and what are the chances that he'll survive this test and the challenge from the Baltics?

The President. Well, I think the answer to your question unfolds every day. We don't really know. And it is serious. Gorbachev has always indicated a desire for peaceful change inside the Soviet Union, and I refer to what he said on the Baltics. He's faced with an ethnic problem here and an internal problem of enormous dimensions. But I don't know, Terry [Terence Hunt, Associated Press]. I can't make predictions about that, but I know that I hope that he not only survives but stays strong, because I think it is in our interest that *perestroika* succeed and go forward.

Q. Could I just follow up on that? Do you think that he's gone too far in the crackdown in Baku?

The President. Anytime you have a use of force and the loss of life, we are concerned. But I don't believe I can judge that question right now.

Gun Control

Q. Mr. President, you're very concerned with drugs, and drugs are intimately connected now to guns. What do you tell your grandchildren on why you would ban semiautomatic foreign-made guns and not domestically produced? There were two students who were killed in the last 10 days—high school students here. Aren't you deeply concerned? I mean, where's the lethal legal justification?

The President. Yes, I am concerned. And I just don't happen to believe that banning of weapons will take them out of the hands of the criminals. And we've seen State law after State law violated by the bad guys getting the weapons, so I don't want to go for more Federal gun control. I'm not going to do it. We've taken some steps that I think are helpful.

Q. Well, we are sending weapons, though, to Colombia and so forth, that are made in this country. How do you stop that?

The President. To Colombia?

Q. And to other places where they're getting into——

The President. Well, if they're going to the Colombian Government, I wouldn't stop it, and if they're going to the bad guys, we would follow every possible avenue to stop it.

Chinese Student Relief Legislation

Q. Mr. President, back on China for a moment. It appears your veto will be overridden in the House today. That would require Senate actions for the job to be complete. I know you met with Senate leaders this morning.

The President. I did.

Q. Are you confident that just these remarks you've made out here today and whatever else you may have said will be enough; or do you really feel that the Chinese leadership, with whom you've dealt with so long, kind of let you down here and didn't give you a strong enough hand?

The President. Well, what I did to try to— in talking with the Senate leaders this morning, the Republicans—is to cite certain steps that China has taken. They've accepted the Peace Corps volunteers. You see, I think that's good. People will say, well, in the face of Tiananmen that's not good. I think it is good because I think cultural contacts, educational contacts will benefit, in the long run, democracy and reform in China. They've accredited a VOA correspondent—as you know, who were kicked out. They've muted the hostile propaganda against Americans and stopped harassing the U.S. Embassy. That's good. That's important to me, as President, who feels a certain responsibility for the people there. They've given some assurances on missile sales—want to see them follow up, but I think that's positive. They've reopened the Fulbright [student] exchanges. I think that's

good, and I think that's positive.

And I think if we let Congress have its head and do what is emotionally popular, these things would be changed. They've lifted martial law. I don't know a single Member of Congress that if I'd have said to them, look, we think by sending General Scowcroft [Assistant to the President for National Security Affairs] and Larry Eagleburger [Deputy Secretary of State] over there we can get martial law lifted; do you think it's worth it—I think most would have said sure, that would be a good step. It happens, and we see a lot of criticism of it. They've released 573 people that were detained after last June's events.

You can argue about any one of these points, but I ask the Senate and the House—it may be a little late for that one— the Senate to take a look at these things and put it in the totality of a policy. And you see, I think there are some real reasons—Asian reasons, if you will, Cambodia and Japan—that we should retain relations with China. That doesn't mean we endorse the lack of human rights.

I tell you, one of the criticisms that gets to me a little, and I vowed—I didn't tell you my New Year's resolution was not to let it get to me—but is the idea I don't care about human rights. That is absolutely ridiculous. I want to see China move forward. And some think isolation, some think a railroad up there in the Congress is going to do it. And I don't think so. I think we're handling it pretty well, Brit [Brit Hume, ABC News].

Q. Just to follow up, Mr. President: Did you in any way convey to the Chinese leaders the idea that these steps taken so far would be enough to head off this action taken by Congress, which they must find as unfavorable as you?

The President. No, we didn't give a timetable, but we've encouraged in every way we can these and more. But I'm just asking that people look at them. I have not seen them—maybe it's my fault—one account, on whatever media, of these steps put together as a package. I haven't seen one. So, I'd like to suggest to the Congress that are debating this to take a hard look at this and see whether it's progress, whether it adds up to anything or, as some of our critics would say, is pure boilerplate.

Q. Mr. President, in voting, in the House particularly—you seem to be conceding that that's gone for you—do you think that there's a problem of trust here with you? Are they saying they don't trust you to go forward on this student thing? After all, you told them you weren't going to have high-level exchanges, and while you were telling them that, you were sending a high-level delegation. Do you have a credibility problem?

The President. Where was the exchange in that? What the exchange was, Lesley [Lesley Stahl, CBS News], was when the Secretary of Commerce was going to go to China in an exchange visit arranged by their Commerce Minister. That was canceled.

Q. Yes, but they obviously thought it included high-level contacts. The question is——

The President. Who were they?

Q. ——do you think you have a problem with them not trusting you because of that?

The President. No, I don't think it's a question of trust. I think the students have done a very good job presenting their case to the Congress. I think there are some politics involved—crass politics. When you hear name calling, when you hear people saying "kowtow", that is not the kindest word to say we have an honest policy difference with this President. And so, there's some politics involved in this as well.

But I think there's some genuine feeling that these students have a very good case. And what I want to do is make the case that the way to continue reforms and have reform go forward is not through isolation and unilateral congressional action but through the kinds of contacts that I foresee and encouraging the kinds of steps that have already been taken.

Q. You talk about the lifting of martial law. What about the situation as it exists without the gesture? Are you at all disturbed that the repression goes on? Could you be——

The President. Yes, I'm very much concerned about the status quo. And I was terribly concerned at the time of the Cultural Revolution, when we made the original contact with China. And it was a good thing we did because you began, through contacts with the West, to see China pull out of this Middle Kingdom syndrome and move forward.

And I think I know enough about it: that in China you get a couple of steps forward and then somebody steps back. And a look at Deng Xiaoping's own history—I think he was out three times and in four. And some will argue, well, he's part of the problem. He's now retired. But the reforms, particularly on the economic side, that brought a new level of prosperity to the Chinese people really was started by him.

So, I'm not giving up—I mean, I'm not accepting the status quo at all, and China knows my position on this. But I do think that there's some indignation about students. There is some feeling—I'm talking about the Congress now—there's a lot of empathy with the students right here. But I think there's also a dose of political rhetoric up there that certainly has diminished the other side. And I will readily concede: Maybe I could have done better and sooner in presenting the facts of this case. The Attorney General's doing a good job showing the differences between the Pelosi bill and what we've already accomplished. I don't know where we'll come out, but I'm going to keep on working the policy.

The Nation's Economy

Q. Mr. President, given the weakness of the dollar and the turmoil in the financial markets and the recent poor economic indicators, what are you going to do to calm the markets and keep the economy from sliding into a recession?

The President. Well, one thing I'm not going to do is comment on levels of the market, except to say that there's been a substantial increase over the last year. And some are reading the recent couple of days as corrections, although I gather it recovered a little bit yesterday. And the market has always been an indicator, and it's been one that's been read quite positively. But I don't want to get into market levels. What I do want to do is establish sound policies. And I'm convinced that if we can get the cooperation of Congress that we need on reducing the deficit, that that will go a long way not in market prices but in terms of the fundamentals on the economy.

It's slowed down a little. There's a lot of prediction that it'll be slow for awhile and then have a rather robust step up, come summer. But I don't know. All I know is that we've got to not bash anybody but get out there and try to enact policies that will help keep the longest recovery in modern history going.

Q. You've said that you felt that there was room for further reduction of interest rates. Given the need to attract foreign investment from overseas where rates are high, how do you square that with your call for lower interest rates?

The President. You mean, to attract——

Q. Attract foreign investment to cover the U.S. deficit—and yet we're competing against the foreign investment.

The President. I think people see the U.S. still, regardless of what's temporary out there, as the safest haven for investment anywhere in the world. And I want to conduct the fiscal policies of this government so they will continue to see it that way.

China-U.S. Relations

Q. Going back to the vote on the Chinese student visas, you and your people have been trying to get that vote delayed. Is that because you have some indication from the Chinese that they may soon release Fang Lizhi [Chinese dissident]——

The President. No.

Q. ——and if this vote goes against you, it could hurt his chances?

The President. No, it is not, but I don't think it will help his chances. But I would love to see that step taken by the Chinese. I think we're reconciled to the fact that the vote will go forward tomorrow in the Senate.

Q. When you try to defend your China policy, one thing you never do is talk about the "China card." You seem to hate that expression, even though when Kissinger and Nixon were doing it, it was considered a master stroke of foreign policy, playing the Chinese off against the Soviets. If Gorbachev does fall from power and is succeeded by men whose role model is Joe Stalin, aren't you going to have to play the China

card, too?

The President. I don't think you play a card. I think that's gratuitously offensive to the Soviets and to the Chinese. But one of the reasons I want to stay engaged is that there are geopolitical reasons to have good relations—or improved relations, even under these unsatisfactory conditions. And it's going to be hard to do because of the human rights setback, but I want to have some contact. I want to retain contact because, as you look around the world—take a look at Cambodia, take a look at Japan, take a look at a lot of countries in the Pacific—China is a key player. And I'd like to think that our representations will have them move forward on the human rights side so we can have a more normalized relationship with them.

Soviet Civil Unrest

Q. Mr. President, regarding the Soviet Union, have you in the course of these events going on in Baku, or any of your senior people—I see General Scowcroft is here—been in touch with Mr. Gorbachev or his people to discuss how severe it is?

The President. Well, we've had contact with him. I don't remember when my last contact was with Mr. Gorbachev, but it didn't relate specifically to the Baku——

Q. Could I then follow, sir, to ask you to reconcile, if you can, the position that you've taken: that you say you want Mr. Gorbachev to survive and succeed; and on the other hand, you have areas of the Soviet Union, such as the Baltics, that you do not recognize as being part of the Soviet Union and where you say you favor independent pursuit of their own destiny. Does he succeed if they secede?

The President. Again, at this juncture the U.S. position is well-known, and you've stated it correctly: that we have not recognized the status of the Baltics. However, what I say that we want to do is to encourage Mr. Gorbachev's stand that peaceful change is the order of the day. And he's sorting out some very difficult internal problems in these three Baltic countries. And I don't think it helps facilitate things for us to fine-tune all that. They know our position. I talked to him about this, incidentally, at Malta. And the thing, I think, is that—in looking at the Soviet scene there—that he is still adhering as best he can to the concept of peaceful change in the Baltics. And that's got to dominate.

European Borders

Q. Mr. President, President Jaruzelski of Poland recently suggested that the four big powers reaffirm the frontiers of Poland irrespective of whatever happens to Germany. Would the United States join such a reconfirmation of the frontier?

The President. Well, we have recognized under Helsinki [accords] existing borders, and I have no problem reiterating that. But whether that requires some kind of an international action on it—I just have no judgment on that.

Czechoslovak Summit Proposal

Q. Mr. President, Havel, of Czechoslovakia, proposed yesterday a summit [in] Prague between Mr. Gorbachev and you. Do you think it's a good idea?

The President. Listen, I respect him so much, and I don't just give him the back of my hand. But we've got a summit set, and we have a very critical agenda that I want to see met—goals that I want to see met. And so, I think at this time that suggestion is not going to work out the way he suggests. But I was rather moved by the suggestion and by the conditions that make the suggestion possible. Who would have dreamed this a year ago, that the conditions inside Czechoslovakia would give them the freedom to make this kind of suggestion? I was rather moved by it. But I don't believe it's going to work for this summit.

Social Security

Q. Mr. President, you've opposed the Moynihan Social Security bill strongly. Would you endorse or work for or support a Republican alternative proposed by Congressman Porter that would take the Social Security increases for this next year and allow people to keep those tax increases and put them in a separate account?

The President. The Porter proposal has some interesting ingredients to it. I am not prepared to endorse it. We don't have provision for that in our budget proposals. It's

worthy, though, of consideration, of some study. But I'm not prepared to endorse that; no, I'm not.

Q. Is that not the first step to privatizing Social Security?

The President. Well, I don't think he would say that that's the inevitable goal, but it has certain aspects there. But the people are concerned about Social Security. So, when you have innovative thinking of that nature, I don't want to just gun it down. I am not going to support it.

Q. Mr. President, over the last few years there have been large increases in the Social Security tax. And even though it's a regressive tax, people supported it, or swallowed it, because they were told that that was necessary to make the system solvent for the next generation. But now everyone is finding out that, in fact, that money isn't there any longer, that it's been used for debt reduction. Given the fact that people are now realizing that this is happening, do you think it's fair to ask them to continue to pay this increased tax for even 1 month later?

The President. The Commission that reformed Social Security was well-aware of what you've just talked about. They considered it. I think the Commission included Mr. Moynihan—I may be mistaken, but I think it did. And they considered this point. And we will have some innovative suggestions as we go along here as to how to compensate for this understandable concern on the part of some. But for now, for this year, we will not alter the recommendations of that bipartisan commission.

Q. Could I just briefly—do you feel that this increase was sold to people under false premises?

The President. No, because I think these were intelligent people wrestling with a very, very difficult problem, and I can't accuse them of selling the Commission conclusions as under false cover.

Q. Well, as you know, the budget deficit has been coming down over the past few years solely because the Social Security surplus has been rising. In fact, your own budget projections show $200 billion a year deficits in the indefinite future when you remove the Social Security surplus. Given the fact that you have such a large deficit in every other program, when will you and the Congress stop both bickering and accountant gimmicks and deal with this problem that the American public has said for a decade——

The President. Thank you for the endorsement of our approach, Owen [Owen Ullman, Knight-Ridder Newspapers]. We would urge that we stop bickering and go forward with the proposal that we come out with, that I think will begin to address itself to Maureen's [Maureen Dowd, New York Times] question, that is very sound. And nobody's trying to conceal the fact that the Social Security Trust Fund is operating at a surplus. There wasn't any concealment by the Speaker of the House Tip O'Neill and others that entered into this bipartisan agreement.

Q. Well, wait. If I could follow, sir: Your own budget proposal that you will unveil on Monday, which shows a $64 billion deficit, in fact, if you remove Social Security, would be closer to $150 billion. Is that not correct?

The President. But you're making the old argument of taking the Social Security Trust Fund off budget. And at this juncture we're not prepared to do that. But wait until you see the detail, and I hope the American people will see something here that begins to address itself to these fundamentals that I think are properly being asked about.

Abortion

Q. Mr. President, could you confirm this week's published report that there are divisions within your own immediate family on the issue of abortion? And in particular, could you confirm the widely held view that your own wife supports abortion rights?

The President. No, I couldn't confirm that. And the meeting that I read about in one of the most respected publications was pure, unadulterated—[*laughter*]—malarkey is the word I like to use. It just wasn't there.

Q. Mr. President, if I could follow up: As I understand your position, you now say that the question of abortion is one of personal choice, one on which Republicans can have diverse views and still be good Republicans?

The President. I've always said that. I've campaigned for people that disagree with me on abortion.

Q. But my question is: You say it's an issue of personal choice and a question of conscience, and yet you support a constitutional amendment which would remove that choice for all Americans. How do you reconcile those two?

The President. I reconcile that I was elected to try to fulfill the platform and the programs that I believe in. And so, that's my personal choice, but that doesn't mean I have lack of respect for others and that I'm going to go out and not campaign for people that disagree with me on this issue, on foreign policy, or whatever it is. And so, that's how I explain it.

U.S. Military Action in Panama

Q. Mr. President, last time you took questions here, you were claiming success for the capture of Noriega and also that you had protected American lives in Panama. But what do you have to say to the Panamanians about more than 200 civilian Panamanians that were killed as a result of this invasion? And also, in your aid package to Panama, which hasn't been announced yet, do you plan to offer any compensation to the families of these people?

The President. Well, I'm not sure of the details on the aid package because I haven't signed off on it yet. But what I say to them is: Look, you lost some Panamanian lives. Innocent life was lost. And yet, 92 percent of the people in Panama strongly supported the action of the United States. Isn't that significant? And I mourn the loss of innocent civilians in Panama or anywhere else, and certainly mourn the loss of Americans. But you have to feel concerned about that, but you have to look at the broad picture, and then you have to—and I'm very pleased with the strong support from the Panamanian people—and then you've got to do what's right. You have to try to help repair the wounds, repair the damage.

We've got to go to the—I know most of you are very anxious to be at the arrival ceremony out there. And I have to be there.

Taxes

Q. Mr. President, another question that's been raised about the Moynihan proposal is the fairness of the tax system. Over the past decade, even as income tax has come down for high-paid people, Social Security taxes have gone up, mostly for lower and middle-income people. Do you think that's fair?

The President. Well, look, if we were all starting over, I think we could fine-tune the entire tax system. We're not starting over. And I think that system has been, in and out over the years, basically a pretty fair system. And while I'm here, don't think I've lost because of some political arguments on the Hill that capital gains reduction is only for the rich. I support it. But the reason I do is that in my view it increases jobs for people. So, you have to look at what individual—somebody has an idea that some individual deduction that encourages, say, drilling, when we are in an increasingly negative oil supply situation. And some would say, hey, that favors those who go out and drill. And I say, wait a minute. That's true. And that may not be fair to some taxpayer here, but the national interest is best served by the encouragement and development of domestic resources. We're all fat, dumb, and happy about our energy situation today—and I'm not. So, there's all kinds of provisions that some will argue are fair or unfair.

Q. But, sir, some of your favorite economists in think tanks say that the Social Security tax acts as a great disincentive to work and to employing people.

The President. Yes.

Q. Doesn't that serve the same end?

The President. Well, I think that's a legitimate complaint about some of it, and that's one of the reasons I favor holding the line on taxes. And one of the reasons I oppose Moynihan is I think it's a disguise for increased taxes around the corner. And I don't want to see the benefits of Social Security cut. It is odd that a Republican President, often accused by political opponents in an election year, is the one that is protecting the sanctity of the Social Security benefits. And I would say to those out around the country: Take a hard look now—don't let that rabbit be pulled out of the hat by 1 hand and 25 other rabbits dumped on you in another. This is a very complicated situation, and this is a sleight-of-hand operation here. And the very day Moynihan proposed it—or the next day, what do we get? We get the call from another prominent, respected Democratic Senator saying raise the sales tax on everybody.

Before we go making a lot of changes, let's know exactly where everybody's coming from in this. And I think Mr. Moynihan of a few years back ought to go out and discuss it with Mr. Moynihan of today, because he was a part, I believe, of a Social Security compromise that didn't correct some of the injustices.

Hey, listen, I've got to be out there looking very strict here at 10 a.m., and you guys have to be there.

Note: The President's 33d news conference began at 9:16 a.m. in the Briefing Room at the White House. In his opening remarks, he referred to Michael J. Boskin, Chairman of the Council of Economic Advisers.

Remarks at the Welcoming Ceremony for President 'Ali 'Abdallah Salih of the Yemen Arab Republic
January 24, 1990

President Bush. Mr. President, it is my great honor to welcome you to the White House and to extend to you the greetings of all Americans on this historic visit to our country, the first ever by the President of the Yemen Arab Republic.

And I know this is a proud day, too, for the over 40,000 immigrants of Yemeni heritage who have settled here in the United States, and I know that you'll be meeting with members of this American-Yemeni community during your stay. And, Mr. President, I want you to know that I share with them the hope that relations between our two nations will continue to prosper and grow.

Barbara and I remember our own visit to your nation back in 1986—a fascinating trip—our stay in San'a, your capital, the rich history of the Old City. And as an old drilling contractor, I won't ever forget the trip out to the Yemeni desert, near the ancient city of Marib, to attend the opening of the Alef oilfield. And all along the way, wherever we went, Barbara and I still remember the warm welcome that we received from the people of Yemen. We are delighted today to have this opportunity to return the genuine hospitality that we enjoyed in your country.

President Salih, in an era marked by great change in the Middle East and around the world, you have been a pillar of stability for your nation. Under your leadership, the past 11 years have brought the people of the Yemen Arab Republic genuine economic progress, progress that has meant real improvement in the living standards of all Yemenis. And I am proud that my country has been able to help Yemen develop its resources and begin to realize its full economic potential. And I also am gratified that the democratic trend now unfolding in so many nations around the world has taken root in Yemen with the free election of your nation's Consultative Assembly in 1988.

Mr. President, in just a few minutes we'll move inside to begin our discussions, discussions on issues of mutual interest ranging from strategic trends in the region and the world to bilateral aid to your rapidly growing role as an oil exporter. And let me assure you that America remains committed in the Middle East to help maintain security and to promoting the pursuit of peace.

There are few regions where the conflicts and challenges are so complex and where the United States finds such critical interests at stake—in the Gulf region, where the U.S. and so many other nations have an interest in unimpeded access to vital energy resources; in Lebanon, where we hope the present political impasse will be resolved so that the Lebanese people can at long last live in unity and peace; in the Arab-Israeli conflict, where the United States is and will always be committed to a lasting solution, a truly comprehensive and lasting peace that ends that long and costly conflict. And of course, on an issue of intense importance to the Yemen Arab Republic, I look forward to receiving President Salih's views on the prospects for improving relations between the two Yemens and the importance of these developments for regional peace and stability.

And so, sir, I look forward to our talks and to the opportunity that we'll have to build on what already is a strong and stable relationship. Once again, welcome to Washington. God bless you, and may God bless the Yemen Arab Republic. Thank you very much, and welcome.

All yours.

President Salih. President George Bush, Mrs. Bush, it gives me great pleasure to express my appreciation for your gracious invitation to visit the United States of America for the first time. Your beautiful country is also the country of freedom and democracy. I also wish to thank you for your kind words and this excellent welcome, which reflects the spirit of mutual cooperation between our two countries.

I look forward to your meetings with you. We shall discuss matters of mutual interests at the bilateral, regional, and international levels. I am sure that this visit will strengthen our cooperation with the United States of America. That cooperation has improved significantly since your visit to Yemen in 1986. I am confident that we will be able to open new avenues for economic cooperation and American investment in the Yemen Arab Republic. As you know, our country started its efforts in development and modernization 20 years ago with the lowest standard of living known in any developing country. However, with the diligence of our people and the help of our friends, we have been able to achieve considerable progress and improvements for our people in the economic, educational, and cultural aspects of their life. At the same time, the people of Yemen have strived to force their democracy and freedom as a prerequisite for the true development and progress.

Dear friends, our visit comes at an historic moment in the life of Yemeni people because we and our brothers in the South Yemen are embarking on reunifying our country in a democratic and peaceful way. That unity will be achieved under a new constitution to be approved by both legislatures and by universal referendum. This new constitution is based on democracy and freedom and establishes a multiparty system and direct elections of the legislative council on the basis of one man, one vote. Mr. President, I'm certain that united Yemen will become a positive factor in the security and stability of the Arabian Peninsula.

Meanwhile, our efforts in reunifying our country has not detracted us from participating in inter-Arab cooperation. Just about a year ago, we established the Arab Cooperation Council, which includes the Hashemite Kingdom of Jordan, the Republic of Egypt, and the Republic of Iraq. The main objectives of the Arab Cooperation Council is to expand economic, technical, and scientific cooperation among its members, as well as cooperation with international organizations and other regional economic communities.

Dear friend, I would like at this occasion, and in this capital of a nation which advocates with conviction the respect of human rights throughout the world, to remind the American people about the fate of the rights of Palestinian Arabs and their occupied territory since 1967, because you are fully aware of the suffering of Palestinians who wish to see an end to occupation and to live free on their land. Mr. President, despite all the suffering, we trust that the United States of America, which was established on the basis of justice, equality, and freedom and sponsored the right of self-determination for all nations and considers adherence to human rights as a prerequisite

for international legitimacy, will be able to convince the Israelis to accept peace initiatives and to abide by international decisions which give the Palestinians the right to self-determination under the leadership of their sole and legitimate representative, the Palestine Liberation Organization.

Dear friends, the cessation of hostilities in the Gulf war was heartily welcomed. However, the people of that region remain anxious about the final settlement and the establishment of permanent peace by direct negotiation between Iran and Iraq. Therefore, we hope that the international community and the United Nations Security Council will be able to establish permanent peace in the region through the implementation of Resolution 598.

Mr. President, dear friends, our world is now entering the last decade of the 20th century, a century which has witnessed the most violent wars in human history as well as the greatest scientific achievements of mankind. It is therefore our hope that this last decade will bring more freedom and democracy for our nations. We also hope to see wider economic cooperation among all nations, as well as a final resolution of the debt burden of the Third World countries, in order to achieve greater development for the world at large.

Finally, Mr. President, I hope that the cooperation between our two countries will continue to expand. And I wish you, dear friends, more happiness and good health. Thank you.

Note: President Bush spoke at 10:12 a.m. at the South Portico of the White House, where President Salih was accorded a formal welcome with full military honors. President Salih spoke in Arabic, and his remarks were translated by an interpreter. Following the ceremony, the two Presidents met in the Oval Office.

Remarks at a White House Briefing on Nonprofit Organization Assistance to Poland
January 24, 1990

Welcome. Please be seated, all you Points of Light out there. [*Laughter*] Thank you all very much for coming, and I understand you've had some discussion with our—I guess all three. John, have they all three been on? John Robson—let me salute him for the job he's doing on this, and Larry Eagleburger, of course, and Mike Boskin. We've got three of our strongest players, reflecting the interest that we all feel in Eastern Europe and trying to help figure out where various people in the United States can fit into helping in this change. So, I just came over for what is known in the trade as a cameo appearance—[*laughter*]—to salute you and to welcome your interest in Eastern Europe.

As I look back over my shoulder into 1989, I expect I have the same feeling that everybody here does: admiration at the astonishing change that took place in Eastern Europe, wonder as to how things are going to turn out, but confident that freedom and democracy cannot be rolled back in these countries. And so, we're at the end of one era, at the beginning of another one. And everywhere, from Sofia to Warsaw to wherever—to Prague—the new Eastern European agenda is a democratic agenda. And everywhere, though, there are extraordinary, difficult changes out there ahead.

The United States has an enormous stake in the success of these democratic movements—some of them further along than others, as you know. America's role in Europe depends importantly on how well we meet the challenges of Eastern Europe. And our government has now committed more than $1 billion to assist Poland and Hungary, and we are now actively considering additional support for the other countries of the region as they move down the path of democratic reform.

But the Government alone simply cannot get the job done—don't have the resources, cannot do it. And we need the private sector, nonprofit and profit, to engage its vitality and resources in this exciting process that's underway in Eastern Europe. This was my message at an earlier symposium last July in the White House on the eve of the visit that I took to Poland and Hungary. The response—I should say your response—has really been encouraging. And the nonprofit sector is playing a particularly important role.

I'm not sure the people in Europe understand that yet. I noticed a comment by a citizen in Romania that says the United States has only done—and had a price tag—I can't remember what it was—next to what we'd done. And there was one volunteer organization alone, in this case, taking medical supplies—Americare is well-known to some of you here—that had already taken in, I think, $1.2 million or $1.3 million. So, I don't worry about credit, but if we can be of more assistance in getting the totality of the message out, we want to be. I recognize that we're just in the very early stages of this, but when you add the interest of everybody sitting in this room, it's an enormous potential for helping alleviate human suffering and helping solve the problems of how best to assist in this inexorable move towards democracy.

So many of you here, I'm told, are already involved in Eastern Europe, doing work that the Government could not possibly begin to do on its own. But there's more, much more, to be done at this decisive moment in history. So, what I'd hoped that this symposium—which I understand continues into the afternoon—will do is to give you a better sense of how and where you can help, how the Government can support your efforts in a partnership for Eastern Europe.

We will continue to work with these emerging governments, including Mr. Gorbachev and others in the Soviet Union. I learned at Malta that we have a long way to go before we're even on the same plane in terms of how private markets work or how the private sector can involve itself in the solution to the problems that face these countries. But I will do my best to be sure that on the Soviet side that we continue on whatever exchanges that we have going to help increase the understanding. In some of the countries of Eastern Europe, we're ahead of where we are in others. But isn't it exciting to be here even discussing how we facilitate democracy and freedom in Eastern Europe in January of 1990. I think it's an amazing time of challenge, and I'm just very grateful to each and every one of you for taking the time and giving it the attention that it needs to get the problem done.

I just do not want to see things slip back. I think some countries are going to move ahead a little faster than others, but I don't see a chance to put the genie back into the bottle—that kind of Socialist-Marxist bottle out of which the genie has sprung.

And that's the good news. So, let's work together to try to facilitate the change. And, Carol, thank you for your role in bringing this distinguished group together.

That is the end of the cameo appearance, except one more time: Thank you very, very much. I'm very grateful to you.

Note: The President spoke at 11:57 a.m. in Room 450 of the Old Executive Office Building. In his remarks he referred to Deputy Secretary of the Treasury John E. Robson; Deputy Secretary of State Lawrence S. Eagleburger; Michael J. Boskin, Chairman of the Council of Economic Advisers; and Carol C. Adelman, Assistant Administrator for Asia and the Near East at the U.S. International Development Cooperation Agency.

Message to the Senate Transmitting the Treaty on the International Registration of Audiovisual Works
January 24, 1990

To the Senate of the United States:

With a view to receiving the advice and consent of the Senate to ratification, I transmit herewith the Treaty on the International Registration of Audiovisual Works done at Geneva on April 20, 1989. I also transmit, for the information of the Senate, the report of the Department of State with respect to the Treaty.

The Treaty establishes a multilateral system to facilitate enforcement of rights and to increase legal security concerning audiovisual works in foreign countries and to contribute to the fight against piracy. Essentially, the Treaty is administrative and procedural in nature; it is not a copyright treaty and therefore would not affect sub-

stantive national copyright laws. The registration system is voluntary and may be used at the option of the producer of audiovisual works.

As noted in the report of the Department of State, United States ratification of the Treaty would not require any amendments to the copyright laws of the United States or any other implementing legislation.

I recommend that the Senate give early and favorable consideration to the Treaty and give its advice and consent to ratification.

GEORGE BUSH

The White House,
January 24, 1990.

Message to the Senate Transmitting a Protocol to the Tunisia-United States Convention on Taxation and Fiscal Evasion
January 24, 1990

To the Senate of the United States:

I transmit herewith for Senate advice and consent to ratification the Supplementary Protocol to the Convention between the Government of the United States of America and the Government of the Tunisian Republic for the Avoidance of Double Taxation and the Prevention of Fiscal Evasion with respect to Taxes on Income, signed at Tunis on October 4, 1989. I also transmit, for the information of the Senate, the report of the Secretary of State.

The supplementary protocol amends the income tax convention with Tunisia that was signed on June 17, 1985, and transmitted to the Senate on March 13, 1986. The subsequent enactment of the Tax Reform Act of 1986 occurred before the Senate could consider the convention. The supplementary protocol amends the convention by incorporating changes in U.S. law enacted in the Tax Reform Act of 1986. Of particular importance are the provisions authorizing imposition of the new U.S. branch tax and limiting the benefits of the convention to residents of the two Contracting States by preventing their diversion to residents of third countries.

I recommend the Senate give early and favorable consideration to the convention and supplementary protocol and give its advice and consent to ratification.

GEORGE BUSH

The White House,
January 24, 1990.

Letter to Republican and Democratic Party Leaders on Support for the Nicaraguan National Opposition Union
January 24, 1990

The President today signed letters to Mr. Lee Atwater, chairman, Republican National Committee, and Mr. Ronald H. Brown, chairman, Democratic National Committee, encouraging the committees to provide assistance to the campaign of Violeta Chamorro and the Nicaraguan National Opposition Union (UNO). The text of the letter follows:

I am writing to ask your help in the common cause of furthering democracy in Nicaragua. The February 25 elections will determine whether Nicaragua's people will realize the promise of democracy to which the Sandinista government solemnly committed itself in the Esquipulas Accord. This also is the aim of the Bipartisan Accord on Central America, which embodied the Executive-Legislative agreement on the goals of democracy, security, and peace in that region. As President Arias of Costa Rica said in signing the Esquipulas Accord, "without democracy, there can be no peace in Central America." And without a level electoral playing field, there can be no true expression of the Nicaraguan people's will.

Violeta Chamorro and the National Opposition Union (UNO) are valiantly waging an electoral campaign and need the help of all democratic parties. In the crucial last weeks of the campaign, UNO is desperately short of funds needed for campaign rallies, distributing campaign literature, and media time. While Congress has made money available for UNO through the National Endowment for Democracy (NED), that money is limited by NED's charter to institution-building expenses and cannot be used to defray campaign costs. Moreover, the Sandinistas have imposed serious obstacles to delivery of the NED funds, and, to date, UNO has been permitted to make use of only a tiny fraction of them. For these reasons, Mrs. Chamorro's campaign runs the real risk of being crippled for lack of money. This result would undermine our bipartisan commitment to democracy in Nicaragua and frustrate the aspirations of the Nicaraguan people.

I am asking your help to give UNO a chance to let the Nicaraguan people achieve government by consent. The Democratic and Republican Parties have joined in supporting democracy in Eastern Europe, and once again we need to make our support felt with deeds. A joint contribution by both Parties to the UNO campaign would make an immediate difference at this critical moment, as would individual contributions by your Party's members. Time is short. The Department of State informs me that Nicaraguan law permits political contributions from foreigners so long as the Supreme Electoral Council is informed by January 31 that they are to be received. UNO would be responsible for satisfying applicable requirements under Nicaraguan law to employ such funds in the election campaign. The Justice and State Departments assure me that there are no general prohibitions under U.S. law on contributions to foreign political parties such as UNO. Of course, individual donors should ensure that they are not precluded from contributing by their tax status or other restriction specifically related to their particular circumstances.

If democratic peoples and organizations do not stand together to make democracy work, they can only blame themselves if democracy does not flourish.

GEORGE BUSH

Note: Identical letters were sent to Lee Atwater, chairman of the Republican National Committee, and Ronald H. Brown, chairman of the Democratic National Committee. An original was not available for verification of the content of the letter.

Continuation of Jeffrey M. Samuels as Assistant Commissioner of Patents and Trademarks at the Department of Commerce
January 24, 1990

The President today announced his decision to retain Jeffrey M. Samuels to continue to serve as Assistant Commissioner of Patents and Trademarks.

Since 1987 Mr. Samuels has served as Acting Assistant Commissioner of Patents and Trademarks at the Department of Commerce in Washington, DC. Prior to this, he served as managing editor of the Bureau of National Affairs' Patent, Trademark and Copyright Journal, 1982–1987;

legal editor of the Bureau of National Affairs' Patent, Trademark and Copyright Journal, 1976–1982; hearing officer for the New York State Department of Social Services, 1976; and an associate with a general practice law firm, 1975–1976.

Mr. Samuels graduated from Colgate University (B.A., 1972) and Albany Law School (J.D., 1975). He was born May 8, 1950, in Brooklyn, NY. Mr. Samuels is married, has two children, and resides in Fairfax,VA.

Nomination of Robert H. Gentile To Be an Assistant Secretary of Energy
January 24, 1990

The President today announced his intention to nominate Robert H. Gentile to be an

Assistant Secretary of Energy for Fossil Energy at the Department of Energy. He would succeed James Allan Wampler.

Since 1988, Mr. Gentile has served as Acting Director and Director of the Office of Surface Mining at the Department of the Interior in Washington, DC. Prior to this, he served as the liaison for coal affairs and Special Assistant to the Assistant Secretary for Land and Minerals Management at the Department of the Interior in Washington, DC, 1986–1988; chief executive officer of the Ohio River Collieries in Bannock, OH, 1982–1986; president of N&G Construction in Bloomingdale, OH, 1975–1982; management consultant for Lafferty Trucking Co. in Bannock, OH, 1975; Deputy Director of Operations and Director of Training for the Peace Corps in Brazil, 1973–1975; training program officer for the Peace Corps in northeast Brazil, 1972–1973; supervisory management information specialist for the Peace Corps in Washington, DC, 1972; evaluation officer in the Office of Program Development, Evaluation and Research for the Peace Corps in Washington, DC, 1970–1972; Peace Corps fellow, 1970; and resident adviser and assistant dean at the University of Toledo in Toledo, OH, 1966–1969.

Mr. Gentile graduated from the Franciscan University of Steubenville (B.A., 1966) and the University of Toledo (B.B.A., 1967; M.B.A., 1969). He was born February 5, 1944, in Steubenville, OH. Mr. Gentile resides in Arlington, VA.

Statement by Press Secretary Fitzwater on President Bush's Meeting With President 'Ali 'Abdallah Salih of the Yemen Arab Republic
January 24, 1990

President Bush met with President Salih of the Yemen Arab Republic this morning in a 30-minute private meeting followed by a half-hour plenary session. This is the first state visit by a Yemeni President. The two Presidents held discussions on a wide range of bilateral, regional, and international issues.

President Bush stated that he is pleased that the United States has been able to help Yemen realize some of its economic and development goals and noted that the United States has increased the PL480 program with Yemen this year.

President Bush reaffirmed the U.S. desire for peace and stability in the Middle East and reviewed continuing efforts to find a solution to the Arab-Israeli conflict. President Bush reaffirmed our strong belief that our diplomatic efforts with Egyptian and Israeli officials to develop a dialog between Israelis and Palestinians offer the best hope for moving the peace process forward toward direct negotiations between the parties on a comprehensive peace settlement.

The two Presidents also discussed South Yemen and President Salih's ongoing efforts to reunify the two Yemens. They also reviewed the current situation in Afghanistan and our shared support for self-determination for the Afghan people. The two Presidents agreed to work together in the continued search for peace throughout the Middle East region. President Bush took the opportunity to recall the warm hospitality he and Mrs. Bush received during their visit to Yemen in 1986.

Nomination of Donald Jay Yockey To Be a Deputy Under Secretary of Defense
January 24, 1990

The President today announced his intention to nominate Donald Jay Yockey to be Deputy Under Secretary of Defense for Acquisition. He would succeed Milton L. Lohr.

Since 1988 Mr. Yockey has served as a consultant for DJY Associates in Mountain Center, CA. Prior to this, he served in several capacities at Rockwell International, Inc., including senior vice president and special assistant to the president of Rockwell and as a member of the Rockwell management committee, 1986–1988; president of electronics operations, 1978–1986; president of the electronics systems group, 1977–1978; and vice president and general manager of the special telecommunications systems division of Collins Radio Co. and president of Collins government telecommunications group, 1972–1977. In 1966 he joined the autonetics division of Rockwell International, Inc., and served in the following positions: director of astrionics, assistant general manager of the electronic systems and sensor division, and vice president of the F–111 Mark II avionics program.

Mr. Yockey graduated from the University of Oklahoma (B.A., 1960). He was born January 6, 1921, in Buffalo, NY. Mr. Yockey served in the U.S. Air Force, 1947–1966, retiring with the rank of colonel. He is married, has four children, and resides in La Habra Heights, CA.

Appointment of John M. Engler as a Member of the Commission on Presidential Scholars, and Designation as Chairman
January 24, 1990

The President today announced his intention to appoint John M. Engler to be a member of the Commission on Presidential Scholars. He would succeed Ronna Romney. He will also be designated Chairman.

Since 1978 Senator Engler has been a State senator for the 35th senatorial district in Michigan and serves as the senate majority leader. Prior to this he served four terms in the Michigan House of Representatives.

Senator Engler graduated from Michigan State University (B.S., 1971) and Thomas M. Cooley Law School (J.D., 1981). He was born October 12, 1948, in Mount Pleasant, MI. He currently resides in Mount Pleasant.

Nomination of Charles M. Herzfeld To Be Director of Defense Research and Engineering
January 24, 1990

The President today announced his intention to nominate Charles M. Herzfeld to be Director of Defense Research and Engineering at the Department of Defense. He would succeed Robert Clifton Duncan.

Since 1985 Dr. Herzfeld has served as vice chairman of Aetna, Jacobs, Ramo Technology Ventures in New York, NY, and chairman of the board of directors of Westronix, Inc. Prior to this, he served successively as technical director, director of research, and vice president and director of research and technology of the ITT Corp., 1967–1985; and successively as the director of ballistic missile defense, deputy director, and director of the Advanced Research Projects Agency, 1961–1967. In addition, Dr. Herzfeld worked for the National Bureau of Standards, rising to the position of Associate Director of the Bureau, 1956–1961, and he served at the Naval Research Laboratory in Washington, DC, 1953–1956.

Dr. Herzfeld graduated from Catholic University (B.A., 1945) and the University of Chicago (Ph.D., 1951). He was born June 29, 1925, in Vienna, Austria. Dr. Herzfeld has two children and resides in Secaucus, NJ.

Toasts at the State Dinner for President ʻAli ʻAbdallah Salih of the Yemen Arab Republic
January 24, 1990

President Bush. Mr. President, Barbara and I are delighted to welcome you to the White House. And as I told you earlier today, we have many fond memories of that fascinating visit to Yemen almost 4 years ago. All of us here tonight recognize President Salih as a man of extraordinary accomplishment—a man who served his nation as a soldier and as a statesman, a man who's led his country at a time of great economic progress and is responsible for Yemen's growing role in Middle Eastern affairs.

Mr. President, as I hope you know by now, I value your views. I believe our discussions and your talks, both today and tomorrow, with so many key members of our administration and the Congress, will encourage understanding between our nations and help us advance the many interests that our nations share. It's been an opportunity to assure you of America's commitment to security in the Middle East and to the pursuit of a just and lasting peace in the region.

In the next few days, you'll be traveling across America—New York, San Francisco, and on to Dallas, in my home State. And I hope that at every step along the way, you encounter the warm welcome that Barbara and I enjoyed wherever we walked in the streets, in the markets of Sanʻa.

It has been a great pleasure, sir, to welcome you, to be your host on this historic visit—a visit that signifies the growing ties between our nations and a growing friendship between the people of Yemen and America. And so, tonight I ask all our guests to join me in wishing President Salih health and happiness. In the words of the old Arabian saying, "He who has health has hope, and he who has hope has everything." Once again, you are most welcome here in the White House, sir.

President Salih. Dear friend President George Bush; the First Lady, Mrs. Bush; distinguished guests: Allow me first, Mr. President, to congratulate you on the first anniversary of your first term in office. I also wish to express my great pleasure to visit your country, hoping to establish closer linkage between the very ancient in our country and the most modern in yours.

Mr. and Mrs. Bush, dear friends, in October 1962, Time magazine wrote about a country almost unknown to the outside world called Yemen. It said that in this country, which is just rushing toward the 13th century, a revolution took place against a despotic ruler. Since then, human ingenuity and mankind's ability to learn and adapt have made the impossibility an actual reality, because less than 25 years later—that is, in 1986—the people of that unknown country received the Vice President of the most modern and perhaps most famous country in the world.

Mr. President, it was then a wonderful occasion when you and the First Lady joined us in inaugurating our first refinery using Yemeni crude oil at the ancient town of Marib, which once was the cradle of one of the most advanced civilizations of the world. That visit was, in my view, a good omen because it came at the threshold of your campaign for the President of the United States of America. Therefore, I am extremely happy to greet you again and, through you, extend my greetings to the friendly people of the United States.

Thank you, Mr. President.

Note: President Bush spoke at 8:15 p.m. in the State Dining Room at the White House. President Salih spoke in Arabic, and his remarks were translated by an interpreter.

Nomination of C. Anson Franklin To Be an Assistant Administrator of the Agency for International Development
January 25, 1990

The President today announced his intention to nominate C. Anson Franklin to be an Assistant Administrator of the Agency for International Development for External Affairs, U.S. International Development Cooperation Agency. He would succeed Thomas R. Blank.

Since 1987 Mr. Franklin has served as Assistant Secretary of Energy for Congressional, Intergovernmental, and Public Affairs at the Department of Energy. Prior to this, he served as Principal Deputy Assistant Secretary for Congressional, Intergovernmental, and Public Affairs, 1986–1987; Director of Communications at the Department of Energy, 1985–1986; Assistant Press Secretary at the White House, 1982–1985; campaign manager for the Marshall Coleman for Governor Committee in Richmond, VA, 1981; director of administration in the

office of the attorney general of Virginia, 1978–1981; campaign manager for the Coleman for Attorney General Committee, 1977; campaign manager for Steelman for United States Senator in Dallas, TX, 1976; district representative for Congressman Alan Steelman, 1974–1975; and consultant in the Office of the Special Assistant to the Secretary of Housing and Urban Development in Washington, DC, 1973. In addition, Mr. Franklin has served as director of the telephone canvass for the Texas Committee to Reelect the President in Austin, TX, 1972; and press secretary for Congressman Bill Archer, 1971–1972.

Mr. Franklin graduated from the University of Virginia (B.A., 1969). He was born April 17, 1947, in Richmond, VA. Mr. Franklin served in the Army National Guard, 1969–1975. He is married, has two children, and resides in Washington, DC.

Message to the Congress Transmitting the 1990 National Drug Control Strategy
January 25, 1990

To the Congress of the United States:

Consistent with section 1005 of the Anti-Drug Abuse Act of 1988 (Public Law 100–690), I am today pleased to transmit my administration's 1990 National Drug Control Strategy for congressional consideration and action.

This report should be viewed as a companion volume to the National Drug Control Strategy that I sent to the Congress last September. In it you will find a comprehen-

sive blueprint for Federal drug control activities for the next fiscal year. The principal goal of our strategy, however, remains the same: to reduce the level of illegal drug use in America. To help determine the most effective means of pursuing that objective, my administration has once again been aided by broad consultation with Members of Congress, Federal, State, and local officials, experts in the fields of drug prevention, treatment, and enforcement, and hundreds of interested and public-spirited citizens. The result, I believe, is a truly national plan to combat the illegal use of drugs, one that will bring us success in this new decade.

I am grateful for the enthusiastic and bipartisan support that the Congress gave to the National Drug Control Strategy last year, and I turn to you for that support again. I know that every Member of Congress shares my desire to overcome the terrible scourge of drugs. And so I ask you to join me in moving quickly to fund and implement the proposals and initiatives contained in this report. Full congressional support of this national strategy is essential if we are to give Americans the thorough and effective drug control policy they expect and deserve.

GEORGE BUSH

The White House,
January 25, 1990.

Message to the Congress Reporting on the Economic Sanctions Against Libya
January 25, 1990

To the Congress of the United States:

1. I hereby report to the Congress on developments since my last report of July 19, 1989, concerning the national emergency with respect to Libya that was declared in Executive Order No. 12543 of January 7, 1986. This report is submitted pursuant to section 401(c) of the National Emergencies Act, 50 U.S.C. 1641(c); section 204(c) of the International Emergency Economic Powers Act, 50 U.S.C. 1703(c) ("IEEPA"); and section 505(c) of the International Security and Development Cooperation Act of 1985, 22 U.S.C. 2349aa–9(c).

2. Since my last report on July 19, 1989, there have been no amendments to the Libyan Sanctions Regulations, 31 C.F.R. Part 550 (the "Regulations"), administered by the Office of Foreign Assets Control ("FAC") of the Department of the Treasury. Additionally, since July 19, 1989, there have been no amendments or changes to orders of the Department of Commerce or the Department of Transportation implementing aspects of Executive Order No. 12543 relating to exports from the United States and air transportation, respectively.

3. During the current 6-month period, FAC has issued a limited number of specific licenses to individuals and corporations to permit them to engage in activities that would otherwise be prohibited by the Regulations. Under FAC licensing procedures, 23 individuals registered to travel to or remain in Libya with Libyan immediate family members. Fewer than 15 licensing actions were taken with respect to Libya.

4. Various enforcement actions mentioned in prior reports continue to be pursued. As reported previously, seven former officers of a Libyan student group operating under FAC license were convicted in November 1988 for the unauthorized use of student funds in violation of the Regulations. In May 1989, in the U.S. District Court for the Eastern District of Virginia, seven individuals associated with the student group were convicted of related charges of conspiracy, wire fraud, aiding and abetting, and credit card fraud. Their sentences ranged from 60 days' to 7 years' imprisonment with fines of up to $8,000.

In July 1989 the U.S. Customs Service seized a shipment of U.S.-origin electrical distribution and control equipment in Buffalo, New York, valued at $7,679 for an attempted illegal transshipment from Canada to Libya through the United States. In October 1989 the U.S. Customs Service seized a shipment of computer equipment valued at $7,500 for an attempted illegal transshipment to Libya through the Netherlands. Redelivery of the goods from the Netherlands to New York was effected prior to the seizure of the goods in New York.

In August 1989, in the U.S. District Court

for the District of Minnesota, a Federal grand jury returned a four-count criminal indictment charging a U.S. firm and two of its corporate officers with unlicensed shipment of 43,400 pounds of chemicals to Libya in April 1986. Guilty pleas were entered by two corporate officers and on behalf of the corporation at a December 4, 1989, hearing. Sentencing is expected in January 1990.

During the current reporting period, FAC determined that the Government of Libya had illegally transferred certain of its physical assets in the United States to a Libyan student organization at the time the sanctions were imposed. In October 1989 FAC ordered the assets sold at auction with the proceeds deposited into a blocked account in the name of the Government of Libya.

5. The expenses incurred by the Federal Government in the 6-month period from July 19, 1989, through the present time that are directly attributable to the exercise of powers and authorities conferred by the declaration of the Libyan national emergency are estimated at $425,776. Personnel costs were largely centered in the Department of the Treasury (particularly in the Office of Foreign Assets Control, the Customs Service, the Office of the Assistant Secretary for Enforcement, the Office of the Assistant Secretary for International Affairs, and the Office of the General Counsel), the Department of State, the Department of Commerce, the Department of Justice, the Federal Reserve Board, and the National Security Council.

6. The policies and actions of the Government of Libya continue to pose an unusual and extraordinary threat to the national security and foreign policy of the United States. I shall continue to exercise the powers at my disposal to apply economic sanctions against Libya as long as these measures are appropriate, and will continue to report periodically to the Congress on significant developments as required by law.

GEORGE BUSH

The White House,
January 25, 1990.

Remarks and a Question-and-Answer Session at a Luncheon for Newspaper Publishers
January 25, 1990

The President. Well, please be seated, and please continue with your coffee. But it's an honor to have you all here. There may be no group in America more aware of the challenges this country is facing. So, my first thought was to give you a general outline of our agenda after our first year. But then I decided to focus on the first item on the domestic agenda: illegal drugs. And they remain this nation's number one concern, and so I chose this forum to announce the second phase of our fight against drugs. This booklet is on our national drug control strategy that I hope we can get distributed to all of you.

As you know, last September for the first time, we launched a comprehensive, coordinated and, I think, coherent national strategy to stop the distribution and use of illegal drugs. We've made some notable progress in the months since that plan was unveiled. Attitudes continue to change. Here in Washington, the number of those arrested who test positive for drugs has dropped dramatically over the past 3 months, especially among juveniles. And abroad, Colombia has extradited 14 of the world's major drug merchants to stand trial here in the United States.

Given the headlines we've seen recently, though, it's clear that we're only really getting started. And the plan we laid out last fall outlined what we intend to do. And today I want to announce the second phase, as I said, of our strategy which explains how we intend to do it, agency by agency, task by task, dollar by dollar. And today we're releasing what I think of as a blueprint for success.

Our outstanding Director, Bill Bennett, the Drug Control Policy Director, will discuss the program later in depth. Right now, I want to sketch out, if I might, a few highlights and then open the floor to questions.

Our approach remains consistent. We're committed to the same aggressive goals and principles that we outlined last September: to reduce use through an integrated mix of supply- and demand-side approaches. And that means doing everything that works.

Our strategy calls for about a third of its funding to go toward drug education, prevention, treatment, and research. We're calling for more prevention programs in schools and workplaces, as well as grants for communities to set up education programs. In our treatment strategies, we're also emphasizing what works with careful and constant evaluation of treatment regimes and a new Office for Treatment Improvements at HHS.

We're funding new research in areas like law enforcement technology, treatment, and drug use forecasting that will help us spot trends and then target our resources and measure the impact of our strategies. And this spring, we're going to be releasing the first of an annual State-by-State status report measuring progress.

Roughly another third of the budget is devoted to domestic enforcement, prosecution, incarceration. To help local law enforcement initiatives, the '91 fiscal budget calls for nearly $500 million for State and local law enforcement grants, an increase of 228 percent over the last 2 years. We want to get the right resources to the right people, on the right level: street level.

Today we'll be announcing five high-intensity drug trafficking areas—cities and areas that are already doing a great deal but need more support. We want to help them map out a more comprehensive, coordinated approach to fight drugs.

We're also increasing the number of DEA and FBI agents and personnel, as well as more funding for assistant U.S. attorneys. We support an increase in Federal judgeships. We're proposing the death penalty for drug kingpins and those responsible for

drug-related killings and even, in some cases, attempted killings. We want there to be absolutely no doubt about the certainty of punishment.

The final third of our budget is earmarked for border interdiction and the international operations side. We want the multinational criminal organizations that produce and distribute drugs to be more than disrupted—we intend to see them dismantled and destroyed because we don't make deals with these dealers.

We have multilateral programs underway in many parts of the world. Throughout Central and South America, particularly, we're engaged in expanded and unprecedented levels of cooperation and assistance. We applaud the efforts of President Virgilio Barco of Colombia and also of our neighbor, President Salinas of Mexico. And I will reinforce our support for the courageous leaders of the region at the upcoming drug summit in Cartagena.

Among the steps we're taking to intensify border control, up to an additional 1,000 customs agents, who are already on the job, will be given authority to conduct drug investigations to better assist the DEA, the Drug Enforcement Administration. With interdiction in particular, coordination is absolutely crucial. We're putting an end—I hope and I believe we are—putting an end to turf battles. I met with all our top law enforcement people the other day, and they said they had never seen better cooperation between these—powerful in some instances—but between all the agencies.

Our budget for all international activities has increased from $419 million to nearly $700 million. We're creating a new National Drug Intelligence Center to ensure all enforcement agencies get the strategic and organizational intelligence that they need. Treasury's newly created Financial Crimes Enforcement Network will improve financial intelligence. And the Department of Defense has been increasingly effective in its expanded detection and monitoring roles.

Now, I imagine the news in this chapter of the war on drugs may be its price tag. Spending, understandably, gets a lot of attention. In this case, outlays continue to increase. But I want to emphasize our determination to win this fight without adding to the budget deficit—and, yes, I repeat, without raising taxes.

In 1990 drug funding totaled almost $9.5 billion—that was in 1990, the largest increase in history. Funding for fiscal '91 will be expanded by more than $1 billion, to over $10.5 billion, and outlays will increase 41 percent this year. In fact, with this request, the Federal drug budget will be 69 percent higher than it was when I took office in 1989.

To those who say that our program looks topheavy on the interdiction side, remember that many of the efforts to limit supply are exclusively Federal and inherently more expensive than demand reduction. We're willing to spend more to limit the drug supply. Simply put, we're willing to do whatever it takes.

But the real issue, of course, is not how much—it has got to be how well. And here the distinction between Federal and national is crucial. A truly national drug control strategy demands that we tap resources of every description—public and private; civilian and military; local, State, and Federal; volunteer, professional, and personal.

Let me tell you about a man that I know many of you in this room know, but some may not—Jim Burke, a corporate leader, former CEO of Johnson & Johnson, who's been applying the power of the media to unsell drugs through the Media Partnership for a Drug-Free America, the largest volunteer, private-sector ad campaign since the war bond drives of World War II. He's energized, and he's doing a superb job.

You're all familiar with those hard-hitting ads to discourage drug use. Many of you already contribute space to run them. And that's supporting the Partnership's current goal to raise $1 million a day in advertising time and space every day for the next 3 years—a remarkable goal indeed.

And I know that some of you—Joe Williams, of the Memphis Commercial Appeal, to take a notable example—has made a promotion of voluntarism an important part of your newspaper's mission. And that's also very, very important. A free press has a right and a responsibility to comment and report on a nation's problems. But your newspapers may also contribute to the progress of the communities they serve by pointing to solutions. And there may be no better outlet for America's volunteer effort, volunteer spirit, than saving those being lost to drugs. It's too early to tell how our efforts will be judged, but if more concerned Americans become involved Americans, I believe we will succeed.

Today I'm particularly interested in your thoughts and your ideas, so I'd like to open up the floor to suggestions, but certainly we'll be glad to answer questions on this subject or any other subject that enters your mind. And if it's highly technical, I may, if you'll excuse me, rely on my strong right arm, Bill Bennett.

Federalism

Q. Mr. President, you mentioned increasing spending without increasing the deficit. Do you agree or disagree with the principle that if the Federal Government mandates a program, be it in drugs or in other areas, the Federal Government also ought to provide the resources for accomplishing the goal rather than shifting the burden down to other levels of government?

The President. I am concerned about mandated programs. I particularly got this driven home to me at the recent educational summit in Virginia. The subject wasn't simply drugs, although there was a lot of discussion about it there. And they were pleading for flexibility. And I think Bill Bennett has tried to build into our requests a certain flexibility for local areas. And that's a hallmark of our philosophy here: to reduce the number of mandated Federal programs because they do not take into consideration the diversity of this country and the diversity of the communities in the country.

War on Drugs

Q. Mr. President, George Shultz [former Secretary of State] has just linked his considerable prestige to the ranks of those advocating the legalization of drugs. What do you feel are the most cogent arguments against these growing numbers of people advocating decriminalization?

The President. I just think that it would

increase, regrettably, the habit; and I strongly oppose it. Bill has very forthrightly been speaking out against it. And I'm just going to hold the line against legalization.

Q. Mr. President, what criteria were used to determine which five cities are going to get special attention under your proposal?

The President. May I defer to Bill on that?

Director Bennett. A number of things, but principally we use the FBI and DEA—Drug Enforcement Administration's criteria for investigation—level 1, level 2, level 3—various levels of investigation and intensity, that is, how many cases in major drug trafficking they have in certain areas. The areas we've designated are all level 1 areas, that is, areas where we think we will find the greatest concentration of major drug trafficking organizations.

The President. You'd better—while you're standing—maybe—that was very good—[*laughter*]—I may need more support. But please, ask as technical as you want.

Arrest of Mayor Barry of Washington, DC

Q. Mr. President, did you know in advance, sir, about the sting operation that led to the arrest of the mayor of Washington the other night? And can we ask you, sir, what was your personal reaction when you heard that the mayor of the town you live in had been arrested for drug——

The President. The answer is: No, I didn't. And the second part of the question is: great sadness, great tragedy. I think it would be most inappropriate for a President to prejudge a matter that's obviously in the courts, and I'm going to refrain from doing that. But you know what, my thought went to the kids in the schools. And it's a matter of sadness. And Barbara shares my view on that.

State of the Union Address

Q. Mr. President, what other areas of interest can we watch for in your State of the Union Message?

The President. Now, Jerry—[*laughter*]—you know that it seems that we're getting close to the date of that, but it is not in final form. And I'll just give you a little insight into the thought process. How much do you dwell on a shopping list of things that I want to see accomplished, a legislative shopping list? And how much emphasis do you place on the state of the Union? It's almost state of the Government versus state of the Union. And I've never been accused of being an overly eloquent fellow, but I am optimistic about our country, the state of the Union. And that isn't to say that I'm not deeply concerned about some of the problems.

We had a fascinating discussion at our table on environmental concerns and how you balance them with a person's right to a job in an expanding economy. And I guess I'd have to say the final draft has not been worked, but I expect you will see a combination of—I wouldn't call it a shopping list, but certainly spelling out what I think should be priorities for the state of the Government and what I'd like to see the Federal Government do, and then on a broader sense, my perceptions and observations about the state of the Union.

And I'll tell you, having visited with some of the families of the fighting men that went down to Panama, I have a renewed feeling that the country is going to be in pretty good shape down the road if we can handle our part of the Government right. I mean, there's a wonderful feeling in some parts of this country. And that isn't to say there's not a lot of hopelessness and a lot of despair that goes with some of these enormous social problems. But the underpinnings of the United States, the state of the Union, is not bad.

When you look around the world and see these countries coming our way—democracy, freedom—and then see the younger generation willing to serve as they do in a voluntary way with the courage and the patriotism that some of these kids showed in Panama, I'll tell you, there's something happening that's good about our country.

Soviet Reforms

Q. Mr. President, on a little different subject, a couple of respected Sovietologists lately, notably George Kennan and Mr. Brzezinski—Mr. Kennan has said that Mr. Gorbachev's position is precarious. Mr. Brzezinski has said the Soviet system is doomed. How do you react to those statements?

The President. Which were the two? I heard somebody saying that the Soviet system is doomed.

Q. Brzezinski, I believe, lately. And Mr. Kennan, George Kennan, said that Mr. Gorbachev's position was precarious.

The President. Well, on the Soviet system doomed, I think Mr. Gorbachev has already—in strongly supporting *glasnost* and strongly supporting *perestroika*—has confirmed the fact that the Marxist-Leninist model simply does not work. And all you have to do is look at an economy that's in egregiously bad shape, and you'll understand why he's reached that conclusion. And then if you needed additional confirmation, all you have to do is take a cursory look at Eastern Europe, and you'll see that people are opting for pluralism and for openness, *glasnost*, and for reform. So, I think that's a given, that's obvious.

In terms of Mr. Gorbachev, I was asked yesterday about it, and I said I want very much to see him succeed. I think he has conducted himself in an extraordinarily difficult situation very well. He remains committed to peaceful change, and I don't think anyone is faulting him for the difficulties that he's encountered in Azerbaijan. You see blockades of your ports, and the man has to respond. I'm not encouraging that course because we would like to see peaceful change wherever possible. But in talking about the ferment for change in the Baltics, he still is talking peaceful change. And I think he's done a remarkable job. It's not for some President of the United States to start saying who he thinks ought to be in that job. But as I look around, I think Mr. Gorbachev is really the best hope for what our interests are. We want to see peaceful change continue. We want to see the democratization of Eastern Europe. We want to see openness bring about market-force economies inside the Soviet Union. And all of these things, I think, are in our interest.

Now, it is my hope that he will emerge, that they can get this recent disorder under control and restoration of peace there and tranquillity, and then that the process can go forward in a democratic mode, a more democratic mode. So, I wouldn't speculate on totality of survival, but I think we have a lot at stake in continuing to deal with this man.

Defense Budget Cuts

Q. Mr. President, on the subject of defense, you have suggested that we will probably have to cut back on the budget in that area. And in order to help the Soviet Union, this cutting of the defense will affect our industries, such as shipbuilding industries in Boston, where we build outstanding cruisers. What are your plans if you have to do that to help these industries and the labor people that are employed there?

The President. Where bases have been closed there has often resorted vigorous private enterprise activity. I was asking about this, because under the Base Closing Act, we've had to make certain suggestions, and the Defense Department is wrestling with this whole concept of what facilities will remain as fully funded in the future as they have been in the past.

So, I think a lot of what the best thing a Federal Government can do is keep a strong and vigorous economy so you can accommodate private sector productive growth where theretofore there has been a government activity of some sort. So, it's that. I think there are government programs to help transitions, to help the States in transition, and of course, I want to continue those.

But let me simply say this: We're all familiar with what happens. Everybody says cut, and then when somebody has to make the call, they say, please cut in this other guy's district; don't cut in mine—mine's absolutely essential. And I was guilty of the same thing when I was a Member of Congress, and so I understand it. [*Laughter*]

But I think we have an able team. I think we have a team that is committed to working with the key leaders in the Congress, in the opposition party, and I think we can come up with a formulation of where we have to cut, doing it in a way that we don't cut into the muscle of our defense, the muscle—we may need a different kind of force in the future. As the threat diminishes in Eastern Europe, we may need a more rapidly deployable force. But it's got to be robust, it's got to be well-trained, it's got to be highly professional. So, I just want to be sure that we do this not on just kind of a squeaking-wheel, political way but that whatever we do in the future is done in a very thoughtful and, I would add, compassionate way where we do help the communities as best we can to move into this era of change—but also remember, still an era of challenge.

War on Drugs

Q. Mr. President, on your drug program: I'm from Chambersburg, Pennsylvania, about 90 minutes up the road from you, and we have a pretty severe drug problem there. But what happens is, all of these programs that come in, by the time the money is spent in the metropolitan areas, very little of it reaches our borders. Is there anything in Phase II that would provide money to the small communities of the country like Chambersburg?

The President. Bill, can you respond to that?

Director Bennett. It's interesting, because we heard from the big-city mayors this morning that all the money is going to the rural areas and they're not getting their share. [*Laughter*] What we're doing is, of course, essentially through our block grants, giving the money to the States and the State legislatures. Those State legislatures and Governors have the responsibility to decide how that money should be apportioned in the State. And from the way we look at it, there's a drug problem in rural America, suburban America, as well as urban America. And the people who should make that judgment should be the Governor and State legislators.

The President. Bill, in response to the earlier question, we are doing that, as you say—blocking it so we do not mandate a specific answer so that Chambersburg has to adapt to a program designed for some big city.

Director Bennett. There are very few mandates, in fact, in our drug strategy, or drug policy. And one thing that doesn't happen is that when a lot of districts receive their money, they aren't told that this is money from the Federal Government. And when the money goes into the State capital, it's combined with State sources and sent out. And we don't require Governors

to say, this is from George Bush and not from the Governor, and so we think some Governors may let the constituents think they deserve all the credit for it. But there's Federal money going out.

Q. Mr. President, how soon do you expect to see meaningful results from the implementation of Phase II? And how do you propose to deal with the already overcrowded facilities in the event that the results are even more successful than you anticipate?

The President. Well, I will give Congress credit for moving on additional facilities, prison facilities. And I think in some of this, certainly I hope we'll get early enactment on this program. I'd like to see it implemented, crossing the t's and dotting the i's, the way Bill Bennett has proposed. I'm not naive enough to believe that will happen.

But I was talking to Bill coming in, and we do sense a desire on the part of Congress to cooperate. We may have a problem on the Senate side with spending levels, but in terms of the objectives of this strategy, we're in pretty close accord with both Democrats and Republicans on the Hill. So, I think we can get early action, and we're already getting it in some of these programs that are in effect right now. I'm thinking backing up law enforcement; I mentioned increasing prison capacity, et cetera.

Arrest of Mayor Barry of Washington, DC

Q. Mr. President, given the fact that you have talked a lot about discouraging drug usage and given the fact that you said just a minute ago that your thoughts ran to the children when you heard about the arrest in Washington, do you think Mayor Barry should resign?

The President. No, again, I don't want to get into the case because I think it would be inappropriate to intervene. And that isn't actually asking me to get into the legal process, but let's let the system work. And I think the city is capable of making that determination and trying to achieve their consensus goal.

Gun Control

Q. Mr. President, last night I came up

with my wife to Washington, and on TV we saw four individuals who were shot. Through the drug program you talked about, wouldn't it also be hand-in-glove to make some further pronouncements towards gun control, especially towards the semiautomatic pistols that seem to be coming out?

The President. Were they shot in States that had controls on these pistols, or—I can't remember.

Q. They were in Washington, DC.

The President. In Washington? I think we have some rather stringent controls here against this. So, my position really has not changed on gun control. I realize there's plenty of room for difference of opinion on it, but I think the thing is to enforce the laws that are on the books. And in this instance, we've pointed to one that might have been more effective. But I don't believe that the answer is going to be more Federal gun control.

Pardons for Iran-Contra Figures

Q. Mr. President, a different subject with two points. Is it a possibility that you will pardon Poindexter? And if legal procedure falls through, would you consider a pardon for Ollie North?

The President. I have said before and will repeat that, again, while these matters are in the courts, I will not make any statement one way or another on the question; I don't think I should do that. And so, we'll just have to—Ollie's under appeal, and the Poindexter matter is now before the jury.

Chinese Student Relief

Q. Mr. President, would you mind speaking, if you will, sir, about the vote on China this afternoon in the Senate?

The President. [*At this point, the President raised his hand and crossed his fingers.*] [*Laughter*] A week ago if you would have asked me that question, having faithfully read my regional newspapers and my big-city newspapers and my newspapers from the west coast to the east coast, I would have thought there was a very minimal chance of achieving this. But we made the case, and I have pointed to—albeit small steps—certain steps that I think are encouraging as a result of the contact that

we have had.

The acceptance of Peace Corps volunteers—you might say, well, that's not too big a deal. You see, I think the contacts between students and the people, or students studying here and the American people, is a good thing. They've now said they'd do that, very recently. The accrediting of a VOA correspondent—not a major step by itself, but it reverses a period where all they did was blast the VOA for having an unsavory role, in their view, in Tiananmen Square. They are muting the whole concept, in terms of world propaganda by them was that it was the fault of the United States. And everybody here knows it wasn't the fault of the United States. It was the quest for democracy and for freedom of expression. That criticism has been dramatically muted—ask your editors to collect it for you.

They've given us certain assurances on missiles sales overseas. And I happen to be one that's still concerned about the proliferation of missiles, and I hope they'll follow through on that now, but I think that was a direct response to the able work of General Scowcroft [Assistant to the President for National Security Affairs]. Fulbright [student] exchanges have been reopened, or the discussions are on to get them officially—put a mandate on that. And that's good, if you believe that the contacts of that nature facilitate understanding of democracy and freedom.

They've lifted martial law. And now some of my severest critics on the Hill—I'd say to them, let me ask you a question now. Suppose I sent an emissary, and the only, one thing that could result would be the lifting of martial law. Do you think it's a good idea or not? Some of these people that are pounding my brains out up there, on both sides of the aisle, would have been the first to say, I think it's worth it. But that's been done. I'm not saying there's perfection and we can all walk around over in Tiananmen Square or anyplace else the way we can in the United States, but it's an improvement.

They've released 573 people from jail— an amnesty, if you'd want to call it such. And as they did it, they kicked them as they went out of the jail and said you're a bunch of lawbreakers—but the people are out. They're not in jail. I want to keep this going. I care about human rights. I care about the students. I care about reform. I am committed to the concept that the world is moving—what I would say, hopefully not chauvinistically—our way in terms of freedom and democracy. And I believe that contact is the way to go about doing this.

We have taken care of the fact that no student, as long as I'm President, will be sent back against his or her will. There is a strong Executive order, a strong implementation letter from the Attorney General saying this. I don't know why I'm giving you all this detail; the vote is in only 5 minutes, I think, and—no, wait a minute—yes, 5 minutes.

The world looks like everything's tranquil in some ways, some broad ways. There is a reason. We are a Pacific power. China is a billion-some people. We've got enormous differences with their leadership on what happened over there and on a lot of things. But in regional areas there, we've got to work with them. Cambodia's a good example. Japan to some degree is a good example. Some are so relaxed about the changes in the Soviet Union that they think that you don't have to worry about the broad geopolitical or geostrategic relationships. But I haven't reached that view. I think there's reason to still—not play some card—I've always found that an offensive statement—play the China card or play the Russian card. That's stupid, and I think it's bad statesmanship as well as bad diplomacy. But the contact and being able to impress on the leaders the U.S. view, I think, is good, sound diplomacy.

I had a lot of reasons for doing what I've done. I will say what I told some of your reporters yesterday: I think, in retrospect, I could have done a better job of it. I think I could have made more clear my own heartbeat in terms of the change, my own concerns about the things that went wrong, and my own desire to see this relationship move forward. But back to your question—you asked the time, I've told you how to build a watch—*[laughter]*—we may pull it out. And if we do, though, it will be for the reasons that I have outlined here.

Assistance for the Homeless

Q. Mr. President, people in our community are struggling to develop a strategy to deal with the problems of the homeless. This is happening all over the country. What can you do to help us address this issue?

The President. Well, we've got a new approach to housing that touches on the homeless: home ownership opportunity. We've got a fully funding for the first time of the McKinney Act, which is specific—a specific approach to the homeless including shelter, including rehabilitation. I think we can do a little more in terms of the rehabilitation aspect because I think there are, regrettably, some people out there—given the change in the law that took place a few years ago—that need help and attention, and maybe we can do a better job of persuading them. But I think the full funding of the McKinney Act, which I pledged to do, incidentally, in the campaign, is the best role for the Federal Government because it was fully debated and passed by the Congress, both Democrats and Republicans, as the best way to go. And we have now funded it, and I hope that that will be enacted in our budget. And I hope it will make a difference, because you go upstairs and you look out that window and you see some pretty heartrending sights. And then you go have those people interviewed, as has taken place by enterprising reporters, and you find that there's some very great complications as to why those folks are there. So, we've got to get to the cause, whether it's economic deprivation or whether it's some other problem that the folks have that lead them to that state of hopelessness.

Thank you all very, very much for being with us. I'd better push on. But thank you.

Note: The President spoke at 1:21 p.m. in the East Room at the White House. In his remarks, he referred to John M. Poindexter and Lt. Col. Oliver North, USMC, Ret., national security advisers during the Reagan administration who were convicted in the Iran arms and contra aid controversy.

The President's News Conference
January 25, 1990

The President. Two subjects I'd like to address myself to: First, I want to acknowledge the vote in the Senate upholding my veto this afternoon and reaffirming our commitment to Chinese students in this country, as well as the goal of improving relations with China. No Chinese student in this country is going to be sent back against his or her will. And we will continue to urge the People's Republic of China to recognize the human rights of its citizens, to participate in the affairs of the world community. And I do want to express my personal thanks to the leadership of the Republican Party in the Senate—Senator Dole, Senator Simpson—who lead this effort with courage and determination. And a special thanks to all those Members who voted for the values of justice and human freedom that I believe were at stake in this question.

Secondly, this morning I called President Endara of Panama to assure him of our continuing support of his efforts to establish democracy in Panama. Part of this effort involves the establishment of a healthy economy, and I'm deeply impressed with his commitment to reform Panama's economy. And based on this commitment and the report I received from Larry Eagleburger [Deputy Secretary of State] and John Robson [Deputy Secretary of the Treasury], with us here, I informed President Endara that we'd arrived at an economic assistance package to help assist Panama in its economic recovery.

Our plan, valued at about $1 billion, includes $500 million in humanitarian assistance for housing, emergency public works, business assistance, loans, guarantees, and export opportunities, and then $500 million in an additional assistance package for balance of payment support, public investment, and economic restructuring.

The Vice President will review the details of this plan with President Endara on his visit to Panama. We're going to work closely with the Congress on this package to ensure its prompt implementation. The economic challenges that Panama faces are great, but we will work with the people to build a prosperous, democratic nation.

I've just met again with Secretaries Robson and Eagleburger, and they believe, given the history in Panama on the business side, that this economic assistance can, indeed, result in the short run in a vastly improved economic situation.

China-U.S. Relations

Q. Mr. President, isn't it about time that you told the American people what were the results of two secret missions to China, whether you got any kind of promise from Beijing for loosening up and becoming a more tolerant society, and will this victory lead you to trying to lift the sanctions against China?

The President. Well, I think I addressed myself to that yesterday, but let me repeat: I was very pleased at their lifting of martial law; I was very pleased at the release of 573 people from jail in a kind of an amnesty. I've said that these weren't all the steps that need to be taken. I'm very pleased that they've stopped harassing the United States Mission there, our Embassy in Beijing. I'm very pleased that they've lightened up on the areas where I think we can really move things forward, and that is the Peace Corps and the Fulbright [student] exchanges.

So, this was all part of the debate on the Hill. And I must say that I think that the fact that they had made those moves carried some weight with some of the Senators.

Q. Is that the promise that you were given? I mean, they say now that martial law is really——

The President. There were no promises. I'm looking for action, not words.

Q. Well, how about the sanctions?

The President. That's the third question, and—what sanctions? Which part of the sanctions?

Q. Military and technical assistance and so forth.

The President. Well, we're looking at the whole performance scale, and I expect they are, too. But I'm very, very pleased with the results on the Hill today.

Q. Mr. President, out of 535 Members of Congress, 62 supported you on this veto. Do you view that as a mandate for your policies?

The President. Yes, because you've got to give disproportionate weight to how the executive branch feels. We're an equal branch. So, you add to that the support on the Hill—we come out more than equal.

Q. And does it give you any support for new initiatives toward China?

The President. The thing I like about it, given the mournful predictions of some a couple of weeks ago, is that it gives me the confidence that I'm going to go forward the way I think is correct here. And I've had a lot of chance to talk to people that voted with us and some that didn't, and I understand their sensitivities. And I vow to do a better job of informing them as these things develop, as to what it is we're intending. But I'm very, very pleased with the result, for reasons that I'm sure everybody out here can understand.

Q. Mr. President, back to the Chinese students for a moment. Does your commitment that no Chinese student would be sent back against his or her will—does that run absolutely, or is that something that will run until such time as you feel that China has changed its ways in some way that meets your approval?

The President. Against his or her will——

Q. Ever?

The President. ——is the controlling statement, yes.

Assistance for Panama

Q. Mr. President, on the aid to Panama, some assessments say $1 billion is only a fraction of what it will need to restore the effects down there. What is your assessment, and what are people saying? Is this the first step toward what?

The President. Well, I'm basing my judgment on what President Endara said and on the recommendations of the economic mission that went there. And President Endara seemed very pleased at this. I said to him, "If there is additional categories in which we can be helpful, please let me know." But I think he was very pleased, and I think

both Larry and John feel that it is a very good step. Whether it's the last step or not, I don't know. We've got to see how that private sector responds and how the economic recovery goes forward. But I wouldn't say this is the end of the road in terms of what we can do to help them.

Q. But is there a full assessment of what the total cost will be?

The President. Well, I think they feel that this is—let's go here, see what happens, and then take another look. Some may come up with higher figures, but this is what we think is a good and full program to give them the help they need right now.

Q. Mr. President, have you been personally briefed on the exact number of people left homeless as a result of the U.S. invasion of Panama? And when specifically, sir, can they expect to get new homes to replace those destroyed?

The President. I think these programs will give instant—or as close to instant relief as we can hope for here. In fact, there's a provision—I'd like to ask Larry and John to take a couple of questions, after I bail out on this, that will address themselves in more specificity because I don't have the exact number there. But I would like to help as best I can with the reconstruction.

War on Drugs

Q. I know you're talking about foreign policy, but may I ask you a drug question since you were talking about that today, though?

The President. Yes, sir.

Q. Given the fact that in your Inaugural Address you promised to stop the scourge of drugs, and given the fact that today you told the newspaper publishers that drugs was at the top of your agenda, is this going to be the primary test for your administration—in its first 4 years at least—the primary domestic test, assuming the economy doesn't fall apart? Is this the big one?

The President. I think it's the big one, and I think it's the test not for the administration but for every community in the country, every State, every local government—for the people. And somebody asked me, if you had to set goals, changes in the education system or—but where could you most readily hope to see results? I would say in the antinarcotics fight. I think it's really that kind of priority.

China-U.S. Relations

Q. Mr. President, going back to China. You gave us an accounting of why General Scowcroft [Assistant to the President for National Security Affairs] went in December, but I wonder if I could ask you to go back to July? Could you give us an accounting of that trip? What happened? What did you learn? Why did you send him then?

The President. To make clear to the Chinese leadership that the relationship is important, but that it could not go forward until certain changes had taken place. And that, in sum, is what it was about.

Q. Was it your initiative, or theirs, sir?

The President. Mine. Mine, I should say.

Q. Back to the override vote. Does this suggest to you—your victory today—that if you can win here, you can win on anything with Congress?

The President. No, because I think we had a very good case here. If I took a case up there that wasn't any good, why, I'd probably get beat. But this one I think people were willing to listen—some that had been positioned opposed to it, opposed to my position. And I think when they heard the full argument, I think they decided, well, we should support the President on this one.

Q. Could you extrapolate a little bit on that, Mr. President? Given that you've pointed out repeatedly that you have done administratively what Congress ought to do legislatively, why was it so important to win this vote?

The President. Well, I said yesterday—I mean, for several reasons. One reason—I think there was a political ingredient in it, and nobody likes to get pounded on that. And also, I think—from a foreign policy standpoint—I think it's better to do it this way. I think there's a trust factor that hopefully will result in changes that are satisfactory to the American people and to me—a trust factor in the administration. And I hope that I can use that, having won this now, to further the kinds of things that I think will help move China forward.

You see, I think that the unilateral deci-

sion by President Nixon to send Kissinger on a secret mission to establish contact in days when there were far darker in China's U.S. relations was a good decision. And I think the decisions I've made are good decisions. I can understand the controversy, and I can understand why there wasn't a unanimous endorsement. But I view it as a very good step. I will pledge right here to work with the Congress. I love the way the debate ended with both Senator Mitchell and Dole saluting each other for the way in which the matter was discussed. And I think that's a good signal for the political fights that may lie ahead.

Q. If I could follow up on David's [David Hoffman, Washington Post] question: You said that Mr. Scowcroft's trip in July—the Chinese were told certain things had to happen for the relationship to go forward. Can you elaborate on those things and tell us if they've happened?

The President. No, because I think that we've seen China take certain steps. In diplomacy, I don't think you make progress by throwing down a list of things, telling somebody else how to behave. I do think you adhere to your own principles, and I think sometimes you have to undertake the kind of diplomacy that I engaged in here to reiterate principles and to explain the severity of problems to people. But if you do it publicly all the time and you do it so you're painting somebody into a corner, I don't think you get results. And that's why I did what I've done.

Q. Is the status of Mr. Fang [Chinese dissident] one of those things that needs to be resolved? And can you give us any information on that?

The President. It certainly is a matter that I would like to see resolved.

Q. Mr. President, on capital gains you've pointed out on several occasions that because of parliamentary rules you've been thwarted. You've asked that Congress give the majority the right to exercise their will by passing capital gains. Now, in this case, you technically won on this veto because of parliamentary rules, but the vast majority voted against you on this. Don't you believe that that is, in fact, a repudiation of your Chinese policy?

The President. No, I don't see a parallel. This is executive branch. You are equal with the legislative branch. The whole ball game is entitled to have the veto process. Part of the election is about the veto process. It's not a question of whether—but when you have a majority of Senators up there doing one thing, that's fine, provided the President agrees with it. But that's what I'm saying.

Q. But I'm talking specifically about what Congress did over the last couple of days.

The President. Surprised you, didn't it?

Q. The majority of Congressmen in both the House and the Senate voted against you on this issue. Do you believe that that's a repudiation by Congress of your Chinese policy?

The President. No. They're entitled to do their thing, and the executive's entitled to do its own thing. And it worked, and we're going to stay right on track. And I think the process worked very well. I don't view it as a repudiation at all.

Q. Mr. President, I understand that Transportation Secretary Skinner was among those making calls on this vote.

The President. I hope so.

Q. Well, that suggests a little pork-barrel persuasion as well. Was there something more than just the pure——

The President. Highways in China? What are you talking about?

Q. Well, I mean, was it just the pure merits of the case that won the day, or was it win one for the——

The President. I think there were some politics in it. I think there was politics in it.

Q. Both sides?

Q. On both sides?

The President. Yes, both sides.

Q. That you used?

The President. Yes, because some of them said, look, let's stand with the President. Some that may have had a slight difference of emphasis on our side—and clearly there was plenty on the other side when you don't see one single vote come across the aisle—not one, not one.

Q. Did you make specific promises to anyone on help on any other issue?

The President. No.

Q. Did you play hardball?

The President. Softball—great, big, fat one coming over the plate. Excuse me.

Q. You spoke of a trust factor. I wonder if I can apply that to the American people, sir. What can you say to convince the people that the missions to China weren't secret simply to avoid the overwhelming public opposition to them?

The President. I say I think what I'm doing is correct, and I say I think I was elected to do in foreign policy what I think was correct. And you have the checks and balances of the Congress. They had a shot to say that it wasn't correct in this instance. And so, I say that I feel encouraged that the process worked out this way, and I point back to the original relationship with China. And I don't believe you would have ever had it if there hadn't been some secret diplomacy.

Q. If I could ask the question again, sir——

The President. You might. You'll get the same answer if you ask the same question.

Q. Were the missions not kept secret to avoid the overwhelming public opposition to them?

The President. No. The missions were kept secret because I believe this is the best way in dealing with China to effect change—positive change.

Q. Mr. President, as you're aware, China issued an angry statement overnight over the House action yesterday, referring to their vote as interference in China's affairs. You warned yesterday about China's action if your veto was not sustained. What I don't understand is why China would—since you've promised to do the same things administratively that the Pelosi bill would have done—why China would regard that as interference, but you doing it they wouldn't?

The President. I think they would see it as a further public slap at a time when they feel some steps have been taken that are positive. And I think that is probably what—but let there be no mistake about it, I'm sure they're not very happy with my Executive order. I mean, they're entitled to their view, and we're entitled to ours. And I have a mandate to protect these students, and China, as you know, has a very different view on it. But I think that's the only thing I can think of.

Middle East Peace Process

Q. Let me ask on a different topic: on the Middle East. You've had 3 press conferences in 2 days now, and there's been no questions at all about the Middle East. Is this a signal that your administration and that the American public as a whole is disgusted with the slow pace of events toward the peace process?

The President. No, because I don't write the questions for the press conference. I mean, I can't help it if I had no questions. But I don't think anything in the status quo should be interpreted as a lack of interest in trying to be helpful on the talks going, if that's what you mean. In fact, there is discussion going on. We had discussions with our most recent visitor, President Salih. I've just concluded a meeting with Senator Specter, who is just back from Syria and from Iraq, and there's a lot going on. I wish I could tell you I felt that there was demonstrable progress. But no, please don't assume because I have addressed myself in the statements to the China question and the question of Panama or the question of our domestic agenda that we have lost interest in trying to be a catalyst in the Middle East.

Q. Do you think one side is being more recalcitrant than the other?

The President. I don't think it would be helpful to quantify recalcitrance. I think what we ought to do is what Jim Baker is trying to do right now, and that is to facilitate the talks, to get them started.

China-U.S. Relations and Chinese Student Relief Legislation

Q. Mr. President, with this victory in the Senate, do you anticipate sending General Scowcroft or perhaps some other envoy back to China to talk again, perhaps in open this time?

The President. I'm not sure Scowcroft and Eagleburger want any more grief like this. [*Laughter*] There are no plans to do—let me be very clear, again. And I'm not dodging your question. One, there are no plans for anything of that nature. Secondly, this was my idea, for good or for bad. And these are seasoned diplomats and seasoned people

in national security, and we talk about these matters. And when the President makes a decision, why, they do what I suggest here. And so, I don't want to be doing anything other than expressing total confidence in them and in their mission, and I know it's been controversial.

But I'm not somebody that's always looking for a way to do something in secret. When I see, though—back to the question I was asked—that in my judgment a quiet conversation might lead to progress, I hope I will continue to feel I have the flexibility to pursue such conversation.

Q. Mr. President, when you sent your memorandum of disapproval on the China students bill, you characterized it as a pocket veto and said that the constitutional provision precluded it becoming law. Yet we haven't heard you object to the fact that the Congress took the vote to override. Have you changed your mind on that?

The President. I need a lawyer on that one. I don't——

Q. I'd certainly like to follow it up somehow.

The President. I think you should get——

General Scowcroft. You need a lawyer.

The President. I really do. [*Laughter*] It's technical, and I can't——

Q. Some people said that by sending the message back, you undid your pocket veto and actually gave them a veto to override. But I don't think the White House accepts that, and I'd certainly like to get an answer to it.

The President. Yes, let me get you an answer, because we're not seeking to do some clever parliamentary maneuver to have people have to vote on this question when I would rather have seen the matter lie dormant.

Q. You indicated in the beginning of your statement that you feel you do have a mandate now on this China policy. A lot of people have criticized it as a secret policy. You also indicated that perhaps you might do more to keep Congress informed. Why not keep them informed of these secret missions, and what do you plan to do in terms of keeping them informed?

The President. Well, I think we do. We bend over backwards to keep people informed in the Congress. And I think once in a while there is something that is done quietly, and then when it is proper, why, we'll give a thorough and full briefing. And I think in this one, when this matter was disclosed by us, we immediately briefed Congress on what it was we had intended to do, why we did it. And so, I don't think there's any real lack of consultation. In fact, I pride myself on the fact that we have had outstanding consultation. And I've had these leaders down here over and over again—bipartisan—and I'm going to continue to do that.

Q. The July trip, Mr. President—it was 6 months before Congress found out about it.

The President. That's right.

Q. Why not inform the people?

The President. Because we were working on some initiatives, and in my judgment, it was better that it be quiet. And I've cited some examples in history, particularly the China trip, the opening to China, that I think was best served by the way it was done.

Q. Mr. President, as you analyze the outcome today and the vote itself, how much of it was a vote on the Chinese student issue, and how much of it do you perceive to be a vote on your overall approach to China?

The President. Or on the political side—I don't know. I don't know how you measure it. But I do think this: As I had an opportunity to discuss it with individuals, and as our team did, I think there was much more understanding of the merits than had been granted originally. And I think we'd all agree—everybody here—that a couple of weeks ago it just was kind of written off and getting pounded on the merits as well as on the politics. So, the consultations and the discussions to try to get support for this, I think, have increased understanding even by those that didn't vote for me.

At least I think they understand that there were some merits to what I was trying to do. They may have disagreed with it. Some may have agreed with what is the thrust of some of these questions, on the secrecy question. Some may have felt that legislation is better than the executive branch authority doing it. But I think I was given the benefit of the doubt by some in

terms of knowledge of the importance of a relationship with China. I think I've hopefully dissuaded some in terms of some of the propaganda on the other side—that I didn't care about human rights.

So, it was an interesting development here: taking a project that many had considered extraordinarily difficult and then seeing it resolve itself in this way. But there's no intention on my part to crow about it. I mean, it was a very close vote, and it worked out better than many had felt it would. And now we've got to go forward. Tomorrow it's something else. I'm not going to live there on this thing forever.

Q. If I may follow: Was there not a broader issue in regard to the China policy here than just the situation with the students?

The President. I'm not sure——

Q. Was this not a congressional mandate or a Senate mandate on the way you've handled the overall China policy more than just the student issue?

The President. Some of it was. Some of it was political. We'd already accomplished by Executive order what the Pelosi bill was going to do, so some of it was a feeling that maybe it would be better to lock it in on legislation. Some of it was they wanted to make a statement. There's a lot of reasons. You have to just ask those who voted as they did.

Q. Mr. President, a lot of the emotion over your China policy had to do with the famous Scowcroft toast on videotape. It angered a lot of people to see him toasting people responsible for the Tiananmen Square massacre. Will you say that at least that part of it was a mistake, that if——

The President. No, because when you go to China, that is—I don't know of anybody that's been there that doesn't engage in that activity. And if you read the full context of what was said, I think it was a very unfair shot. But I agree with you—some people used that as something that was outrageous. But they ought to go over to China and just understand how it works.

Q. If people had only known that he went over there and that he had talks, do you think the public reaction would have been different than it was when they saw him toasting on television?

The President. No, I think the people that are outraged by it and expressed themselves were concerned about my whole approach to it, I think. But I can say that I think that it may have affected one or two. I don't really know the answer to that one.

Panama

Q. Back to Panama, sir. The election last May was the one that never really resulted in a full count because of General Noriega, yet that's the same election on which the Endara government is basing its legitimacy. Is it time, sir, for another election in Panama?

The President. Well, I think, fortunately, the Endara government has been endorsed by the Electoral Commission. They were kind of diverted from their normal course of business by Mr. Noriega a while back. But I think that's a matter for the Panamanians to decide. I think it would be a little bit outrageous for us to come charging in and tell them when they ought to have an election.

Q. But what is your opinion on it?

The President. Well, I'm not going to have an opinion. I want this to be the Panamanian system. The emphasis from now on ought to be Panama's democracy, Panama determination, let Panama figure out—and then we'll try to help, or if they ask for criticism or suggestions, fine. But I don't want to be appearing that we are trying to run the new democracy in Panama from up here. That would be the worst thing we could do.

El Salvador

Q. On another topic, several key Democratic Senators say they don't believe President Cristiani has control of the military any longer. What is your response to that? They are also drafting legislation which would kill future military aid. Do you think you will be as successful in defeating that package as you were today?

The President. I hope so because Cristiani is trying hard. And I think there is some evidence that he doesn't control all his military. The very fact he's trying to bring some to justice who at least have been accused of wrongdoing demonstrates that. But the man was elected—certifiably free elec-

tions. He is trying very hard. He has taken some extraordinarily courageous and tough steps, and he has my full support.

U.S. Military Action in Panama

Q. My question is about Mexico and Venezuela and other countries in South America that have been offended by the invasion in Panama.

The President. Yes.

Q. I wonder if you have spoken with their leaders and used some of your personal diplomacy to convince them that you didn't intend any—and won't be invading any other countries anytime soon. [*Laughter*]

The President. Well, I haven't given them my invasion list, but I have—[*laughter*]—no, but seriously, it's a very important question diplomatically; it's a good question. First place, as of today, because of what's happened since the fighting began, things are better. Some of it may be just that time heals. Secondly, I think that they have been informed—some by me, mail, phone calls when these actions took place, and our State Department and our representatives—as to what our intention was, what the cause was, what we're doing. They've seen a lot of forces come out now, which I think is helpful. There's a history. And anytime you undertake an engagement like I authorized, you've got to assess what the down side is because of the history.

But, Jessica [Jessica Lee, USA Today], I am pleased with where we are now. And I have not engaged in the last week or so in a lot of diplomatic activity with my friends, but I've sent enough communications that I think they know what my heartbeat is on this. And I hope now, when they saw what happened with the Panamanian people, that that made a profound impression on them. And they've seen Endara go forward, and they've seen the stamp of approval given to his democracy. And they see that now, as of today, that we're determined to help not just with rhetoric but with a means of recovery. So, things are better—and I think, given the action that I authorized, in pretty good shape. I'm not suggesting I have no diplomacy ahead.

Chinese Student Relief Legislation

Q. Mr. President, it was a surprise victory to start the year. Will this transfer to other issues, and is this what someone once called big Mo, momentum, starting off 1990? [*Laughter*]

The President. Listen, I learned a lesson not to talk about that. And I learned it the hard way—took it right on the chin. And I'm coming in here in the spirit of cooperation, and excuse me if the adrenaline flew on one or two of the questions because things didn't look too bright a little while back. But, no, this is too serious a business, especially as it relates to this China policy. And so, I'm not in a mode of talking about momentum or something of that nature.

I do think because of the way it worked out it's going to be helpful in reaching accommodation in the Senate and in the House on certain of our objectives. By that I mean I offer out that hand of cooperation, but it is a two-way street. I simply cannot accept legislation that is opposed to principles I believe in.

So, I don't know where it will fall out, but there is—and I promise you, I don't come in here with some sense of gloating or anything of that nature at all. It was too tough a vote for a lot of my friends on both sides of the aisle.

Ellen [Ellen Warren, Knight-Ridder Newspapers], last one.

Assistance for Panama

Q. Mr. President, in announcing $1 billion for Panama—that's an awful lot of money. So, what countries are going to get less money as a result of our generosity to Panama?

The President. Well, there will be offsets; and we will at the appropriate time, which is fairly soon, tell the Congress where we think those offsets should come from. But let me reiterate my philosophical approval for the Bob Dole position, which is to give the President more flexibility on this concept of earmarking [foreign aid].

I've boycotted the back benches, so we're going to end with this one right here.

Racism

Q. Mr. President, do you agree with the NAACP and other organizations that there is a rising tide of racism in this country?

The President. I had a long talk with some of the executives of the NAACP the other day, and they expressed to me their concerns. And I share their concerns, but I like to think that there isn't a rising tide. I think that there are some very ugly incidents, and if I can use this platform, the White House, to speak out against that bigotry and against that ugliness, perhaps it will help. But I will tell you that several of those leaders felt that there was a growing pattern of racism, and as your question said, a rising tide. I don't know that I agree with it, but I do agree there is some very ugly incidents lately, and we all ought to do what we can to make clear that is not the American way.

Thank you, I really do have to go. Thank you. You guys have been stiffed, but I'll get you next time, I promise.

Note: The President's 34th news conference began at 3:24 p.m. in the Briefing Room at the White House.

Statement on Economic Assistance to Panama
January 25, 1990

In early January, I sent Deputy Secretary of State Lawrence Eagleburger and Deputy Secretary of the Treasury John Robson to Panama to discuss with President Endara, Vice Presidents Ford and Arias Calderon, and their advisers ways the United States could help in Panama's economic reconstruction. They returned enormously impressed with the commitment of President Endara and his economic team to reform Panama's economy and get it moving again. I share their enthusiasm. Yet the economic challenges Panama faces are great and will require the help of its many friends around the world.

To assist Panama, I have approved a far-reaching economic recovery plan, valued at about $1 billion. The plan has two main parts:

- loans, guarantees, and export opportunities valued at over $500 million to strengthen Panama's private sector and to help create jobs, including $42 million in humanitarian assistance for housing those displaced from the Chorillo area, for emergency public works, and to help businesses affected by the looting;
- a $500 million assistance package for balance of payments support, public investment and restructuring, and to assist Panama to normalize its relations

with the international financial institutions.

The Vice President will personally review the details of this plan with President Endara during his visit to Panama.

Through these and other programs I am announcing today, the United States has made good on its word to assist the Government of Panama and the Panamanian people in their efforts to restore the health of Panama's economy. Private sector initiatives, supported by the Government's economic reform policies, will be the key to Panama's recovery, enabling the entrepreneurial talents of the Panamanian people to flourish. We will continue to work with the people of Panama to build a prosperous, democratic nation.

White House Fact Sheet on the Partnership With Panama: Action Plan To Foster Economic Recovery
January 25, 1990

The President today announced the following action plan to foster economic recovery in Panama:

I. *Humanitarian Assistance*

The Agency for International Development (AID) will initiate a $42 million humanitarian assistance program for Panama, covering:

- replacement housing for the former residents of the Chorillo area;
- an emergency public works program, principally for Panama City and Colon, but also including rural areas;
- small business rehabilitation to assist those businesses affected by the looting; and
- technical assistance to Government of Panama (GOP) agencies.

The Departments of the Treasury and Defense will develop ways to assist U.S. firms wishing to donate products to Panamanian businesses.

II. *Loans, Guarantees, and Export Opportunities to Strengthen Panama's Private Sector and to Create Jobs*

The Export-Import Bank (Exim) will pro-

vide up to $400 million in short-term and medium-term guarantees, through Exim and its affiliate, the Foreign Credit Insurance Association, to finance sales of American products.

AID will use $15 million in Trade Credit Insurance Program funds authority to support additional Exim lending to private sector borrowers.

The Overseas Private Insurance Corporation (OPIC) will reopen its insurance and finance programs to support American private investment in Panama. This program is valued at $50 million.

The Department of Agriculture will initiate a $15 million P.L. 480 title 1 program and a $15 million Commodity Credit Corporation program for Panama.

The United States Trade Representative will:

- restore Panama's suspended 1990 sugar quota and, consistent with U.S. policy, compensate Panama for its foregone 1989 quota. This is estimated to be worth a total of $28 million;
- initiate an educational program to ensure Panama makes full use of trade

benefits under the CBI and GSP programs; and

• remove the quota on cotton pants.

The Department of Transportation will arrange for the Federal Aviation Administration to negotiate a Memorandum of Agreement with the GOP on the provision of technical assistance in order to ease air travel to and from Panama.

The Department of State will, if the GOP so wishes, arrange that the already-negotiated bilateral investment treaty be resubmitted to Congress.

The Department of the Treasury will:

• discuss with the GOP the conclusion of a Tax Information Exchange Agreement (TIEA), thus permitting U.S. firms, under established tax guidelines, to deduct expenses of conventions held in Panama. A TIEA would also make Panama eligible for section 936 funds;

• working with other interested agencies and organizations, offer technical assistance to the Panamanian banking sector; and

• initiate discussions with the GOP with the view toward concluding an agreement pursuant to section 4702 of the Anti-Drug Abuse Act of 1988 for the exchange of large currency transaction information.

The Department of Commerce will lead a business development mission to Panama and undertake other efforts to stimulate trade and investment with Panama.

The Department of Defense will:

• resume promptly preferential buying of Panamanian goods and services by U.S. military authorities in Panama, the Panama Canal Commission, and all other U.S. entities, in accordance with

the provisions of the Panama Canal Treaty of 1977; and

• authorize the return of U.S. military dependents to Panama when the military situation permits.

In addition, Panamanian flag vessels will continue to have full access to U.S. ports.

III. *Promoting Sustained Economic Recovery*

Significant but temporary external economic assistance will be required to assure that Panama's economy returns to a sustained growth pattern. This undertaking will be a partnership involving the United States, Panama, other donor countries, and international financial institutions (IFI's).

The administration will seek an additional $500 million in FY '90 for U.S. assistance to Panama. This amount shall be offset from other programs. The $500 million would be used to help Panama normalize relations with the IFI's, for balance of payments support and business credit, for a public investment program, for public-sector restructuring, and for development support.

The Administration will also:

• work to establish a support group of friendly donor countries to help clear Panama's arrears to the IFI's;

• seek an early and generous rescheduling of Panama's debt to foreign governments under the auspices of the Paris Club; and

• take steps to assist the conclusion of a satisfactory financing package for Panama's commercial bank debt that addresses the amount of debt and the level of debt service payments in the context of the strengthened debt strategy.

Nomination of John R. Dunne To Be an Assistant Attorney General
January 25, 1990

The President today announced his intention to nominate John R. Dunne to be an Assistant Attorney General for the Civil Rights Division at the Department of Justice. He would succeed William Bradford

Reynolds.

Currently State Senator Dunne serves as a partner with the law firm of Rivkin, Radler, Dunne and Bayh in Uniondale, NY. Prior to this he served as a New York State senator from District 6, 1966–1989. Senator Dunne served as chairman of the senate judiciary committee and was ranking majority member on the senate insurance committee, the rules committee, and the committees on environmental conservation, housing and community development, and social services. In addition he served as deputy majority leader, 1987–1988, and chairman of the senate environmental conservation committee, 1982–1984.

Senator Dunne graduated from Georgetown University (A.B., 1951) and Yale Law School (LL.B., 1954). He was born January 28, 1930, in Baldwin, NY. Senator Dunne is married, has four children, and resides in Garden City, NY.

Remarks to the United States Conference of Mayors
January 26, 1990

Thank you very much for that welcome. Mayor Whitmire, Secretary Skinner, Director Cochran, Mayor Isaac, Mayor Ray Flynn, and other distinguished mayors, and ladies and gentlemen, thanks for the reception and for the pleasure of being here. The mayors group is known as a pretty tough group. And maybe that's why in 10 years no President has been here. [*Laughter*] But all I ask is that the warmth be the same when I leave as when I arrived here. [*Laughter*]

Look, in particular, let me thank Kathy Whitmire—reelected over and over again in our hometown—thank her for that warm introduction. Kathy is my hometown mayor, and so I welcome the chance to ask her respectfully about one of the most pressing problems facing the city we love: room service in my hotel suite there in Houston—[*laughter*]—which is my legal residence, as you all know. Actually, in the South we do it differently: you don't run with a Republican or Democratic label. But I've suspected that possibly, even though we're in opposing political parties, Kathy and I have always gotten along. For instance, she's never held it against me that a member of my family owns the other baseball team in Texas. [*Laughter*] And for my part, I've tried to return her kindness. So, I picked up the phone when she called a couple weeks ago. She asked me to declare a disaster area, and I told her I did not think that the Houston Oilers were that bad. [*Laughter*]

But, Kathy, to you and all of your colleagues; your successor, Ray; others here; and all of you, it is an honor to address this 58th annual U.S. Conference of Mayors, your winter meeting, and to talk to you about the ways that you and I, the White House and the mayors, can do a better job of building a better America.

Nineteen months ago, I sent you a letter expressing my thoughts on urban policy, and wrote, "As we prepare to enter the 1990's, it is clear that America needs a new working relationship between the Federal Government and the cities." I meant it then and I mean it now. And we do need to forge a new relationship, a relationship—a partnership—which realizes that as mayors you are on the front line in the war against urban problems, a partnership which can achieve the promise of America.

That promise depends, first, on maintaining our economic resources, just as we have during the longest peacetime boom in American history. Next week I'll be doing what you've had to do: next week I'll release a budget for fiscal year 1991 that hopefully builds on this prosperity. Together we can create opportunity for all.

The promise of America also depends on safeguarding our natural resources, just as mayors are doing through programs like Chicago's "Plastics on Parks" or in Virginia Beach, generating electricity from that city's landfill—you're doing your part, and we intend to do ours by strengthening the Clean Air Act, preserving our wetlands, improving America's parks, and others—domestic and international initiatives. And Wednesday, I announced my support for the Glenn-Roth legislation to elevate the EPA to Cabinet status. Together, we must protect our environment for decades to come.

Then there are human resources. Today an estimated 15 million families are headed by working parents or single mothers. But when it comes to child care, Washington doesn't automatically know best. I am resisting mandated Federal programs. And so, I urge the Congress to pass my child-care legislation. Let's put the choice in the hands of the low-income parents.

Each of these initiatives will nurture the promise of America. Yet urban problems won't fade until we meet the challenges that I discussed in that letter in 1988, the challenges that you face every single day: drugs and crime, education, housing, and the plight of our homeless. Can we meet them? I believe that we can because I believe in America, nothing is impossible. Perhaps an ex-baseball player put it best. "When I was a little boy," Craig Nettles said, "I wanted to be a big-league player and join the circus. With the Yankees, I've accomplished both." [*Laughter*]

I do believe that as partners we, too, can accomplish what some might deem impossible. So, let us assault the drugs and crime that form the first of our challenges. Rescuing our kids from crack and cocaine will not be easy, but it can be done.

As proof, consider that in 1985, 23 million Americans used illegal drugs on a current basis—at least once in 30 days. But last year that number fell by more than a third. That means almost 9 million fewer Americans are casual drug users. Good news. It's up to us to make it better.

And that's why yesterday I released the 1990 Drug Control National Strategy, Phase II of the Comprehensive Drug Policy that we unveiled last September. We're asking Congress to spend over $10.5 billion in fiscal '91 for education, treatment, interdiction, and enforcement. That is a 41-percent increase in outlays over the current year, and it means a 69-percent increase in drug-related spending overall since our administration took office.

I ask you to support our strategy to take back the streets from crime and drugs. We need—we really do, I believe—need mandatory time for firearms offenses—no deals when criminals use a gun—and, as Phase II proposes, an expansion of the death penalty for drug-related crimes. In that context, I ask you to urge your State legislatures to approve the same penalty for the killing of local law enforcement officers. Let's work together to stop the hooligans and the thugs.

Phase II aims to help the teenager tormented by crack or the pregnant mother whose drug use imperils her child. Yet drugs are not only a Federal problem. So, you, too, have responded. Macon, Georgia, started the "Macon-Bibb war on drugs." In Houston, local officials and residents of an area in our city called Acres Homes Project have teamed to pursue "drug-free tomorrows." I visited out there last month with Kathy, and the courage of that community is absolutely inspiring. Same inspiration from what's happening in downtown Kansas City and so many other cities all across this country.

And so, now let's join hands to inspire the millions of Americans who want to help America get clean and stay clean. According to the Gordon Black poll—it was released just yesterday—10 percent of all families are already involved in volunteer anti-drug programs. But what's really startling is that an unbelievable 60 percent of Americans would volunteer 5 hours each week to stop the sale and use of drugs. And the same percentage would donate from $20 to $100 to their community to stem drug use. Now, why haven't they? Maybe it's my fault; maybe it's yours; maybe it's the private sectors. But they simply have not been asked.

One American who was asked and who got involved is a man that many of you know, his name is well-known: Jim Burke, former head of Johnson & Johnson. Let me tell you about him. Yes, he was the chief executive and the former chairman of Johnson & Johnson, but he decided on his own to do something about drug use. He decided to unsell drugs through the Media Partnership for a Drug-Free America. And his partnership already made dramatic strides, but it aims to raise $1 million a day in advertising time and space every day for the next 3 years to discourage drug use. That is an amazing goal—$1 billion. But I am absolutely convinced he's going to make it. And it's a great example of what can be accomplished when an individual is asked to help.

So, get out your pocket calculators. The Gordon Black poll figures mean that Americans are willing to donate more than 500 million hours per week and $5 billion, nationally. They want to serve, they want to give, but they have to be asked before they can do either. A promise: I will use the bully pulpit to ask them to do both, and I urge you to do the same thing. Together— and that isn't just Federal Government spending and municipal spending. I am talking proudly of the Thousand Points of Light. We need to get more involved. Together let's defeat public enemy number one.

Ending the scourge of drugs will not only save lives. It will also help meet that second challenge that I talked about: the education of our kids. You know how central education is to urban America. Bright minds can find solutions to your Rubik's cube of problems. Remember, nothing is impossible. Yet look at today's box score of so-called higher learning: a dropout rate that is totally unacceptable, erratic standards, unsafe schools wracked by drug use and trafficking, kids ill-equipped to read or write. And so, let's be honest: Our educational system is not making the grade.

To go from fail to pass will require school boards, teachers, and parents to work together with all levels of government. So, I applaud the mayors who have started programs like Step Up in Kenner, Louisiana, providing learning incentives for students, or the program in Colorado Springs which helps dropouts and at-risk kids finish high school; mayors who head the more than 350 cities which enriched America on your National Education Day.

So far, so good—and yet still so much to do. For while education is mostly a local and State responsibility, the Federal Government must help. That's why I call on the Congress to pass our Educational Excellence Act, legislation which seeks, first, to encourage excellence; second, to see that Federal dollars serve those most in need;

and third, to demand educational accountability; and fourth, to support flexibility and choice.

For instance, we want to create a $500 million program, when fully funded, to reward schools that improve the most. Then there's our new Magnet Schools of Excellence program; our plan to reward schools which create a drug-free environment and reduce the dropout rate; and a National Science Scholars initiative in science, math, and engineering. And recently, I was very pleased to sign into law legislation to help urban schools hit hardest by drug use.

These initiatives can and will make America competitive in the international marketplace of ideas. But the promise of America also depends on meeting the third and fourth challenges that I mentioned earlier: making housing affordable and accessible, and providing help for the homeless.

Basic shelter—affordable housing—should be every American's reality, not merely a dream. So, 2 months ago, I announced an initiative to make the Federal Government a more effective urban partner. Its name: HOPE, Home Ownership and Opportunity for People Everywhere, a new comprehensive housing and urban development agenda. HOPE will help first-time homebuyers by allowing them to draw without penalty on IRA savings as a downpayment for that first home. It will also help tenants become homeowners, as public housing sites have done in St. Louis, Washington, east Los Angeles, and other places as well— each with tenants in control. For other low-income families, we want housing vouchers that increase housing options. And toward that end, I have asked Secretary Kemp to convene a commission to identify barriers to affordable housing.

Yet for many, the problem of housing is availability, not just affordability, so we want Congress to renew the tax credit to aid the construction and rehabilitation of low-income housing. But we must also create incentives for growth in those areas of need, for growth means jobs, and jobs mean homes. So, we've urged Congress to help the dream along by passing our enterprise zone legislation, proposing at least 50 urban enterprise zones over the next 4 years to fuel the engine of job creation. There's more. We want to cut the capital gains tax for the Nation. And for enterprise zones, we've got to abolish the tax altogether to spur investment, jobs, and enterprise that can turn dark corners of despair into neighborhoods lit by opportunity and hope.

Finally, let us provide hope for those whose roof is the sky above, whose floor is the street below. We see them everywhere—next door on 15th Street, in our suburbs, and in our small towns. I'm talking, of course, about the homeless.

The homeless need emergency shelter, food, and medical care. And to reduce homelessness, 2 months ago I signed a bill that increases funding under the McKinney Act—Democrat, Republicans supporting it overwhelmingly in the Congress. And we want to find new ways to put part of our FHA foreclosures into the hands of nonprofit groups and to coordinate basic needs like shelter with other social services.

It won't be easy; we know that. But we also know the real answer to the homeless is shelter plus care. And we know that to help the homeless, like improving education or stopping drugs, will require a combined Federal, State, and local effort. Only then can we unleash the resources of the private and public sectors, showing, as a writer said, how "America is a willingness of the heart."

I believe there is a willingness of the heart in this room. I know there's a discussion, a lively discussion, over resources, over direct grants—subjects that the mayors and the Governors and the Presidents in days gone by have fought about for a long, long time. But the main thing is there is this willingness of the heart among Democrats and Republicans, the White House and the mayors, a willingness to put aside partisan concerns. And so, I came over here today to say let us sit down together and do what needs to be done to achieve the promise of America and, thereby, make the impossible possible.

Thank you for this occasion. Thank you all very much, and God bless you. God bless your important work in the community. Thank you.

Note: The President spoke at 10 a.m. in the Presidential Ballroom at the Capitol Hilton Hotel. In his opening remarks, he referred to Secretary of Transportation Samuel K. Skinner; Thomas Cochran, executive director of the U.S. Conference of Mayors; Mayor Robert Isaac of Colorado Springs, CO; and Mayor Raymond Flynn of Boston, MA.

Statement by Press Secretary Fitzwater on President Bush's Meeting With President-Elect Fernando Collor de Mello of Brazil
January 26, 1990

President Bush met with Brazilian President-elect Fernando Collor de Mello for approximately an hour this morning. The two leaders exchanged views on a wide range of bilateral and regional issues, including trade, investment, debt, and the environment. The President expressed strong support for President-elect Collor's plans to reform and revitalize Brazil's economy and stated that the United States would work closely with Brazil toward this goal.

President Bush told President-elect Collor that he recognized Brazil's important role in hemispheric affairs, and expressed the desire to maintain close contacts with him on regional matters in the future.

In the discussion of environmental issues in Brazil, President Bush reviewed our own efforts to address environmental problems in the United States and expressed a desire to work with Brazil and other countries so that a proper balance can be worked out between development and environmental concerns, with full respect for every nation's sovereignty and with the need to base deliberations on the best scientific data available.

Remarks to Special-Needs Adopted Children and Their Parents
January 26, 1990

Richard Middleton. Good evening, boys and girls, and mothers and fathers. My name is Richard Middleton. I'm 11 years old. I adopted my father—[*laughter*]—at least a year ago. I love my father. And I'm very glad that the President and Mrs. Bush are helping more children like me to find parents to love. That's why it's such a great honor for me to introduce to you, boys and girls, moms and dads, the President of the United States.

The President. Richard, good job. Well, good afternoon. And thank you, Richard, a wonderful introduction. You only had to use your cards for one sentence, and I have to use it for the whole speech here, see. [*Laughter*] But you did a great job.

And to Secretary Sullivan, thank you, sir. It's always a pleasure to be with you. And thank you, everyone, for traveling here today—especially the Orsi family, who drove all the way from Connecticut with their 21 children, 19 of whom are adopted. And I'm glad all of you could join me here in the White House. You know, in fact, this has got to be the most unique event ever held in the White House, I think. It's like a fishpond, moving around. It's very good, and I'm glad to have you all here.

You know, this time last year, when Barbara and I became the official caretakers of the White House for 4 years, the first thing we did was invite all of our children and our grandchildren to spend our first night here together upstairs as a family. And my family is very, very important to me, and I feel lucky to have been blessed with a wonderful wife and children and, of course, now 12 grandchildren. But all of you here today are just as lucky because you, too, are part of a family of your own—to grow with you, share with you, and most of all, to love you.

Each of your moms and dads know just how special you are when they picked you out to go home with them. And now you've got some of the greatest parents around. And they have so much love to give you, and they feel the warmth and joy of your

own love in return. The kids who are still waiting to be adopted don't have parents yet, but they're not alone. They have many friends, people who have spent their lives helping children just like you find families just like you all—helping them find families of their own.

Let me tell you about some of them here with us today. First, there are business leaders, corporate leaders who have committed to helping children like you find loving homes. For example, how many of you watch cartoons? Quite a few. Do you know the Jetsons? Or the Flintstones? Or Yogi Bear? Well, the people who work at Hanna-Barbera created those cartoons. And now they're creating a new character who will encourage families to adopt children.

And some of you may be aware of a TV program in which children who want to be adopted go on television in cities across America. It's called "Wednesday's Child," and it is very successful. Almost three-quarters of all the kids who appear on this show find families. And so, NBC network is going to work with us to get more kids on TV and more stations to show "Wednesday's Child" so more families will see these children.

There's a man here today who is very committed to helping other children just like you. He's a friend of mine for a long time, and his name is Dave Thomas, and he was an adopted child. And he grew up to be a successful businessman with a family of his own. Now he's the head of Wendy's Hamburgers—and by the way, he really does have his own daughter named Wendy. Now, where is Dave? He was—here he is, right over here. And he's going to make information available to help put loving parents together with special needs children in Wendy's all across the country.

And now I'd like to tell you about another man whom I've just met, and what an inspiring man he is. Taurean Blacque is a noted actor with an impressive list of credits. But he deserves even more credit for what he does in real life. He has adopted 10 special-needs children, 10 children. You know, single people and older Americans can be great adoptive parents. And Taurean's not married. He says that having 10 kids will probably keep him too busy to get married for a long time. [*Laughter*] I don't know if he qualifies as an older American yet—[*laughter*]—but I hear that his hair started going gray the minute he got all these kids. [*Laughter*] But he says he wouldn't change it for the world. He proves that love is something you do every day; love is something that takes hard work and commitment—because he had to fight to get every one of those children. Taurean asked me to do a head count and make sure nobody got left behind in the Green Room. Are all 10 of you here? [*Laughter*] Okay, I can't take a count here; I'm too busy here. [*Laughter*] No, all 10 are, I'm sure. And you've got a very special dad.

You know, people like Taurean, who open up not just their homes but their hearts, are amazing people. And I know that we have a number of adoptive parents among us today as well. And you're a breed apart because, while so many people shout about how to make the world a better place, you quietly lead by example, changing the world in a very special way—one child at a time. Truly, yours is a gift of limitless love.

This guy's got to go real bad here. [*Laughter*] That's okay, we're used to that around here. That's okay, big guy.

Okay, where were we? [*Laughter*] No, but seriously, not all children are as lucky as the ones here today. There are thousands of kids in America who still need a home and a family to care about them. This year, an estimated 30,000 children available for adoption spent their Christmas holidays waiting for a permanent home. And most of these kids, about 60 percent, are special-needs children. To find families for these kids, our administration has sent to Congress our Special Needs Adoptive Assistance Act to help individuals meet the financial commitment involved in adopting special-needs children. We've also taken steps to encourage Federal employees wanting to give loving homes to these children, who often wait for years to be adopted.

Every children in America deserves a loving home and a family, and they deserve

something else: the chance to succeed in school and in life. Government cannot substitute for a supportive home. But some children do need extra help to prepare them for the challenge of learning.

At the education summit, the Governors and I agreed that through the Head Start program we are making real progress towards preparing disadvantaged children for school. And I am pleased to announce that my 1991 budget will propose the largest increase ever: half a billion additional dollars for Head Start. This new funding will increase the Head Start enrollment to 667,000 children and bring us to the point where we can reach 70 percent of this nation's disadvantaged 4-year-olds through Head Start. I urge the Congress to fund our Head Start proposal in full because every American child with special needs, whether physical, emotional, or material, deserves the opportunity for a full and happy life.

Our children are precious. And you're the reason all of us came together here today: to tell you how special you are to us and how glad we are that you are in the family. You know, our son Marvin and his wife, Margaret, just adopted their second child, a little grandson, our grandson Walker. And if I do say so myself, this guy is really something. And so is his sister, Marshall, who's also adopted. And they're an important part of our family, and we love them.

Through my wonderful experiences with adoption in the Bush family, I've learned something. I've learned this: Adoption is good for our country; and for the children who need a loving home; and for the birth parents, who want the best for their children; and for the adoptive parents, by giving them the joy of raising and loving a child.

See the sign behind me: "Adoption Works—for Everyone." And that is true. Adoption works because each one of you is so special, and because you adopted very special parents. And it works because everyone in this room loves you very much.

From my family to yours, Barbara and I say thank you, and God bless you. And now, Barbara, I understand we're going to invite this whole gang into the State Dining Room for cookies and lemonade, so why don't we go on in there. And thank you all for coming to the White House. Glad to have you.

Note: The President spoke at 2:39 p.m. in the East Room at the White House.

Letter to Congressional Leaders Transmitting Certification of Panama's Cooperation in the Control of Illegal Narcotics
January 26, 1990

Dear Mr. Speaker: (Dear Mr. Chairman:)

I am transmitting to you my certification that Panama is fully cooperating with us on the war on drugs. In addressing the urgent issues connected with rebuilding virtually every aspect of Panamanian society since coming into office, the Government of President Guillermo Endara has made the war against drugs a centerpiece of its program. Panamanian leaders have demonstrated their commitment by cooperating in returning Manuel Noriega to face trial in the United States, by freezing hundreds of bank accounts at U.S. request, and by concluding a comprehensive narcotics control agreement with us.

I am convinced that the Panamanian people and their government recognize that it is in their direct national interest to end their association with the scourge of drugs. I have firmly concluded that the vital national interests of the United States require that assistance and benefits be provided to Panama, and that the United States support multilateral development bank assistance to that country.

I therefore urge you to enact a joint resolution approving my determination immediately.

Sincerely,

GEORGE BUSH

Note: Identical letters were sent to Thomas S. Foley, Speaker of the House of Representatives; Claiborne Pell, chairman of the Senate Foreign Relations Committee; and Dante B. Fascell, chairman of the House Foreign Affairs Committee.

Presidential Determination No. 90–9—Memorandum on Narcotics Control Certification for Panama
January 26, 1990

Memorandum for the Secretary of State

Subject: Narcotics Control Certification for Panama

By virtue of the authority vested in me by Section 481(h)(6) of the Foreign Assistance Act of 1961, as amended (the FAA) (22 U.S.C. 2291(h)(6)), and Sections 802(b)(4) and 803 of the Trade Act of 1974, as amended (the Trade Act) (19 U.S.C. 2492 (b)(4) and 2493), I hereby determine and certify that Panama has fully cooperated with the United States, or taken adequate steps on its own, to control narcotics pro- duction, trafficking, and money laundering, as defined in Section 481(h)(2) of the FAA and Section 802(b) of the Trade Act, and that Panama does not have a government involved in the trade of illicit narcotics.

In making this determination, I have considered the factors set forth in Section 481(h)(3) of the FAA and Section 802(b)(2) of the Trade Act.

You are hereby authorized and directed to publish this determination in the *Federal Register.*

GEORGE BUSH

Nomination of Richard J. Hankinson To Be Inspector General of the Department of Justice
January 26, 1990

The President today announced his intention to nominate Richard J. Hankinson to be Inspector General of the Department of Justice. This is a new position.

Since 1986 Mr. Hankinson has served as Assistant Commissioner in the Office of Physical Security and Law Enforcement at the General Services Administration in Washington, DC. Prior to this, he served in various positions for the U.S. Secret Service at the Department of the Treasury, including Deputy Assistant Director of Investigations, 1985–1986; Special Agent in Charge of the Vice President of the United States, 1983–1985; Deputy Special Agent in Charge of the Vice President of the United States, 1982–1983; Assistant Special Agent in Charge of the Vice President of the United States, 1981–1982; Special Agent in Charge in Richmond, VA, 1978–1981; Assistant Inspector in the Office of Inspection, 1976–1978; Special Agent for Vice President Nelson Rockefeller's Secret Service Detail, 1975–1976; Resident Agent in Canton, OH, 1971–1975; and Special Agent in Richmond, VA, 1966–1971.

Mr. Hankinson graduated from the University of Richmond (B.A., 1965). He was born September 11, 1942, in New Baltimore, PA. Mr. Hankinson is married, has three children, and resides in Vienna, VA.

Message to the Congress Transmitting the Fiscal Year 1991 Budget
January 29, 1990

To the Congress of the United States:

I have the honor to present the *Budget of the United States Government for Fiscal Year 1991.*

The American economy is now in its eighth consecutive year of expansion and growth. It is essential that the growth of the economy continue and increase in the future. The budget is designed to achieve that goal.

The budget has five broad themes:

• *Investing in Our Future*—With an eye toward future growth, and expansion of the human frontier, the budget's chief emphasis is on investment in the future. It proposes: a capital gains incentive for long-term private investment and new incentives for family savings; record-high amounts for research and development, space, education, and Head Start; a major investment in civil aviation; and a large increase in spending to attack the scourge of drugs. At the same time, the budget maintains a strong national defense while reflecting the dramatic changes in the world political situation that are taking place; and it fulfills responsibilities to protect the environment, and preserve America's cultural heritage.

• *Advancing States as Laboratories*—The budget recognizes the emergence of new ideas and initiatives originating at the State and local level. The Federal Government will foster such innovation and experimentation in numerous fields, from transportation to health, through waivers of certain rules and regulations, and through demonstration grants.

• *Reforming Mandatory Programs*—Entitlement and other mandatory spending now constitutes nearly half the budget, not counting an additional 14 percent for interest. The budget provides for full payment of social security benefits and funds growth in health, low income and other mandatory programs. However, it proposes reforms where warranted to slow the growth in some of these programs and thus leave more room in the budget for priority initiatives.

* *Acknowledging Inherited Claims*—The budget faces up to such inherited claims as the cleanup of decades old environmental damage at nuclear weapons facilities. It analyzes potential claims from unfunded annuities and Federal insurance programs. It assesses the growing volume of defaults in Federal credit programs and proposes essential credit reforms.

* *Managing for Integrity and Efficiency*—The budget contains suggestions for reforms in the way Congress deals with the budget. It provides more resources and suggests improved methods for managing the vast Federal enterprise better. It identifies low-return domestic discretionary programs where a smaller investment of budgetary resources is warranted.

The budget meets the deficit target of $64 billion for 1991 established by the Gramm-Rudman-Hollings law, without raising taxes. It would balance the budget by 1993 as required by that law, begin reducing debt, and protect the integrity of Social Security.

Each of the themes outlined above is discussed in more detail in Section One of the budget, the Overview. The customary tabular and appendix material is contained in Section Two.

I look forward to working with the Congress in the weeks and months ahead to produce a budget that meets the Gramm-Rudman-Hollings target, advances the Nation's essential interests, and keeps the economy on the path of continued growth.

January 29, 1990

GEORGE BUSH

Message to the Congress Reporting Budget Deferrals
January 29, 1990

To the Congress of the United States:

In accordance with the Impoundment Control Act of 1974, I herewith report two new deferrals and four revised deferrals of budget authority now totalling $8,251,604,695.

The deferrals affect International Security Assistance programs, as well as programs of the Departments of Agriculture, State, and Transportation.

The details of these deferrals are contained in the attached report.

GEORGE BUSH

The White House,
January 29, 1990.

Remarks at the Annual Convention of the National Religious Broadcasters
January 29, 1990

Thank you all very much. Thank you, President Rose. Thank you very much. Thank you for that warm welcome. And President Rose, Director Cook, new Director Gustavson, friend Pat Robertson, Dr. Robertson: my greetings to you all. And I certainly want to salute your leadership, all the leadership of the NRB. And ladies and gentlemen, it's often said of a group or individual that he hasn't got a prayer. Well, I'm pleased to be with an audience about whom that will never be said. [*Laughter*]

This marks the fourth time that I've had the honor of addressing the annual convention of the National Religious Broadcasters. And once again, it is a delight to be back, and I know I speak for Barbara in that regard as well. In the spirit of the occasion, I want to make two vows. First, I'll be brief. And I know there's a mention in the Bible about the burning bush. [*Laughter*] But I also know—and I say this not with humility but with objectivity—compared to most around me here, I'm not that hot a speaker. [*Laughter*] So, I won't burden you. But the second promise is for those of you way off in the back of the room: I'll try to speak up. Pat Robertson warned me that the agnostics in this room are very bad. [*Laughter*]

Let me begin with some good news for modern man. There is no denying that America is a religious nation. And sure, differences exist over sect and theology. I'm reminded of what that French statesman Talleyrand once said of America: "I found there a country with 32 religions and only 1 sauce." [*Laughter*] Well, you know these Frenchmen. [*Laughter*]

And yet you know that what unites us eclipses what divides us. For we believe that political values without moral values, a moral underpinning, cannot sustain a people. And this afternoon I'd like to talk to you about those moral values. I speak of the qualities of tolerance and decency, courage and responsibility, and of course, faith—values which remind us that while God can live without man, man cannot live without God. And today, amid political and economic upheaval, these values have not changed, nor will they be more crucial than in the 1990's.

I hope you know by now—you know me—I am an optimist; and after all, last year I had the experience that renewed my faith. I was running out of prayers. I had almost given up. Then a miracle occurred: I caught a fish! [*Laughter*] So, it won't surprise you that I'm convinced we can and will uphold the values that I'm referring to. For as Americans we always have. Consider that for more than two centuries America has endorsed, properly so, the separation of church and state, but it has also shown how religion and government can coexist; and that, to paraphrase our founding document, "All men are endowed not by government but by their Creator with certain unaliena-

ble rights." And these rights include the freedom of expression and to think, dream, and worship as we please; equal protection under the law and the right to choose our leaders and our destinies; the inherent dignity of the individual. And we must manifest that dignity by the policies that we pursue.

For example, I believe that we should help parents obtain the best child care for their kids, and so we have sent legislation to Congress to make good that goal. But I want to ensure that parents, not bureaucrats, are the ones who decide how to care for these children. I will not see the option of religious-based child care restricted or eliminated. I will fight that every inch of the way.

And next there is the concern of every child, the quality and the diversity of America's schools. Our pioneering legislation, the Education Excellence Act of 1989, will spur excellence and demand accountability. For our kids' sake, let's help American education make the grade.

We come next to an issue on which many Americans disagree, but for my part let me be very clear: I support the sanctity of life. We need policies that encourage adoption, not abortion. And that comes right from the heart.

Finally, I continue to support a belief held by the overwhelming majority of Americans: the right to voluntary school prayer. And so, I continue to support a constitutional amendment restoring voluntary prayer. You see we need the faith of our fathers back in our schools.

So, as we struggle to find answers to our pressing social problems, I will endorse policies that reflect the rights of the individual, a concept as old as the scriptures. Rights which form the essence of America and that to other nations have become the message of America, for our freedoms have been carried to every corner of the Earth. One year ago in my Inaugural Address I said, "The day of the dictator is over." And indeed, the last year has been a victory for the freedoms with which God has blessed the United States of America. We've seen the rights of men move mountains or, as in East Berlin, even move a wall. And think of

Central America, where men and women facing great personal risk work for human rights and against tyranny of any ideology. And let me add, I am especially proud of our troops in Panama. Americans supported Operation Just Cause for a lot of reasons, but because democracy is a noble cause. And to the young soldiers who serve this country, every American thanks you.

Think next of South Africa and the Philippines where the values of church leaders have been a force for democratic change. And, yes, in Eastern Europe too, where for centuries, faith has sustained those striving for freedom amid adversity. You know, 8 years ago, one of the Lord's great ambassadors, the Reverend Billy Graham, went to Eastern Europe and the Soviet Union, and upon returning, spoke of a movement there toward more religious freedom. And perhaps he saw it before many of us, because it takes a man of God to sense the early movement of the hand of God. And yet, who could predict that in 1989 freedom's tide would also be economic, political, and intellectual? Or that the walls of bayonets and barbed wire, the walls of tyranny, would come tumbling down?

Look, first, at East Germany, where in 1982, long before last November's mass demonstration, members of Leipzig St. Nicholas Church—1982—members of that church began a weekly prayer for peace. In the services, students were taught nonviolence, and started the candlelight vigils that one day would rouse a continent. And the police came and threatened them. But the students vowed to stay, and did, becoming a light unto the world. And ultimately, that light spread to Dresden and East Berlin. And as it shone, a Wittenberg pastor said: "I would rather see a thousand drops of candle wax on the marketplace than one drop of blood." And there was no blood—only the stirring sight last October of 70,000 workers in the streets and squares of Leipzig. And weapons? They carried candles. And their light was likened to a blizzard of fireflies in the night. Ask anyone that evening. They sought what we Americans enjoy: free markets, free elections, and the exercise of free will unhampered by the state. And they were propelled by many things, faith not the least of them. And as they and others

marched across Eastern Europe, the day of the dictator did end, and the day of democracy began.

Look at Bulgaria, where last month the state press agency conceded. People were wishing Merry Christmas to each other maybe for the first time without fear they would be accused of being religious. And Czechoslovakia—there too, a victory for the rights of man. For years police chased carolers from Prague's Kings Road. And this Christmas, carols warmed the heart of the city, and there was wonder in the air. In the Soviet Union last year, Moscow hosted the first nationwide gatherings of Jews since the fall of the czar. And in Romania, still further victories—Christmas songs on the radio for the first time since 1946. And heroes who showed that you can't lock people behind walls forever when moral conviction uplifts their hearts.

And let me close, then, with a story of two such heroes, both Romanian, and how their example illumined decency, courage, and love. The first was a Lutheran minister, Laszlo Tokes, who dared to speak of freedom. So last November in Timisoara, masked thugs broke into the small apartment of Tokes and his pregnant wife. And they beat him. And they stabbed him. And the Government allowed them no food, and even parishioners were not permitted to bring bread. And finally, the police arrived to deport the pastor, but the flock protected him, forming a human chain around his apartment. And in time, the chain grew across the land until, as we celebrated Christmas, Romania's quest for freedom summoned lightness against the dark. Today, Laszlo Tokes ministers to ever larger numbers preaching his faith, but now preaching it without any fear at all.

As does another, Gheorghe Calciu, a Romanian Orthodox minister. His story proves you can't kill an idea, or you can't destroy the human will. Father Calciu has spent 21 of his 64 years in jail—21 of his 64 years, a third of his entire life, in prison. And in fact, he found God there while in prison for opposing the Government. Released, he risked his freedom by preaching a series of Lenten sermons. And for that he was imprisoned again, tortured beyond belief. Yet

Father Calciu had faith. He refused to break and was sentenced to death. And as he stood in the corner of the prison yard praying for his wife and son, awaiting death, it was then something remarkable occurred. His two executioners called to him, and surely he thought, this was the end. But instead they said, "Father,"—that was the first time they had called him that—"we have decided not to kill you." And 3 weeks later he asked permission to celebrate the Divine Liturgy, and while making preparations heard these same two men approach. And he turned around and was astonished—his would-be executioners were on their knees on the cold concrete of the cell.

Father Calciu is with us today. Father, it is an honor to salute you, and I'm sure you're glad to be here, but I know, too, you hope to return to your native land. And in the season of miracles, who can doubt you will? For today, the times are on the side of peace because the world increasingly is on the side of God.

For my own part, I know this is true. For although I've been President for barely a year, I believe with all my heart that one cannot be America's President without a belief in God, without the strength that your faith gives to you. Another President, Dwight Eisenhower—beloved Ike—once said: "Free government is the political expression of a deeply felt religious faith." Let each of us use his faith to express the noblest values of America so that together we can then serve the inalienable rights of man.

Thank you for your work, for your kindness to Barbara and me, and God bless you. And God bless our beloved land, the United States of America. Thank you very, very much.

Note: The President spoke at 2:13 p.m. in the Sheraton Washington Ballroom at the Sheraton Washington Hotel. In his remarks, he referred to the following officials of the National Religious Broadcasters: Robert Cook, interim executive director; Brandt Gustavson, newly appointed director; and Pat Robertson, member of the board of directors.

Nomination of Gerald A. Cann To Be an Assistant Secretary of the Navy
January 29, 1990

The President today announced his intention to nominate Gerald A. Cann to be Assistant Secretary of the Navy for Research, Development, and Acquisition. He would succeed Thomas F. Faught, Jr.

Since 1988 Mr. Cann has served as vice president of the undersea warfare center of the General Dynamics Corp. in Arlington, VA. Prior to this, he served as president of Gerald A. Cann, Inc., 1985–1987; Principal Deputy Assistant Secretary of the Navy for Research, Engineering, and Systems, 1979–1985; Deputy Assistant Secretary of the Navy for Systems, 1977–1979; staff assistant

for ocean surveillance in the Office of the Director of Defense Research and Engineering, 1970–1977; assistant program manager for surface ship sonar systems and program manager for undersea surveillance for TRW, Inc., 1965–1970; and in various positions with the American Machine and Foundry Co.

Mr. Cann graduated from New York University (B.A., 1953). He was born April 29, 1931, in New York City. Mr. Cann served in the U.S. Army Signal Corps, 1953–1955. He resides in Rockville, MD.

Statement by Press Secretary Fitzwater on President Bush's Upcoming Meeting With President Alfredo Cristiani Buckard of El Salvador
January 29, 1990

President Bush will meet with President Alfredo Cristiani of El Salvador on Thursday, February 1 in the Oval Office. President Cristiani is on a private visit to the United States to meet with congressional leaders, and will also meet with U.N. Secretary-General Perez de Cuellar to discuss possible U.N. involvement in further talks with the FMLN guerrillas. President Bush and President Cristiani are expected to discuss prospects for peace in El Salvador in the context of the Central American peace process, and the progress of the investigation into the killing of the Jesuit priests.

Nomination of Jacqueline E. Schafer To Be an Assistant Secretary of the Navy
January 29, 1990

The President today announced his intention to nominate Jacqueline E. Schafer to be an Assistant Secretary of the Navy for Installations and Environment. She would succeed Everett Pyatt.

Since 1989 Ms. Schafer has served as a member of the President's Council on Environmental Quality. Prior to this, she served as Regional Administrator for Region II of the Environmental Protection Agency, 1982–1984; legislative assistant to United States Senator James L. Buckley and a professional staff member of the Senate Committee on Environment and Public Works, 1971–1982; assistant to the director of research of the Buckley for Senator committee, 1970; and banking studies analyst and research assistant with the Federal Reserve Bank of New York, 1967–1970.

Ms. Schafer graduated from Middlebury College (A.B., 1967). She was born October 12, 1945, in Greenport, NY. Ms. Schafer resides in Arlington, VA.

Nomination of Michael Lorne Moodie To Be an Assistant Director of the United States Arms Control and Disarmament Agency
January 30, 1990

The President today announced his intention to nominate Michael Lorne Moodie to be an Assistant Director of the United States Arms Control and Disarmament Agency for Multilateral Affairs. He would succeed Lynn Marvin Hansen.

Currently, Mr. Moodie serves as a senior fellow and special adviser to the President at the Center for Strategic and International Studies in Washington, DC. Prior to this, he served as Special Assistant to the Ambassador for the U.S. Mission to the North Atlantic Treaty Organization, 1985–1987; Assistant for Special Projects at United States NATO, 1983–1984; chief program officer for the Center for Strategic and International Studies at Georgetown University, 1980–1983; consultant on the President's Foreign Intelligence Advisory Board, 1982–1983; research fellow and assistant to the chairman at the Center for Strategic and International Studies at Georgetown University, 1978–1980; research associate at the Institute for Foreign Policy Analysis in Cambridge, MA, 1976–1978; research analyst and associate for the Foreign Policy Research Institute in Philadelphia, PA, 1973–1976; and visiting lecturer at Chestnut Hill College in Philadelphia, PA, 1976–1977.

Mr. Moodie graduated from Lawrence University (B.A., 1971) and the Fletcher School of Law and Diplomacy at Tufts University (M.A., 1973). He was born November 12, 1948, in Superior, WI. Mr. Moodie is married, has one child, and resides in Silver Spring, MD.

Nomination of Joyce T. Berry To Be Commissioner on Aging at the Department of Health and Human Services
January 30, 1990

The President today announced his intention to nominate Joyce T. Berry to be Commissioner on Aging at the Department of Health and Human Services. She would succeed Carol Fraser Fisk.

Since 1989 Dr. Berry has served as the Acting Commissioner on Aging at the Department of Health and Human Services in Washington, DC. Prior to this, she served in various positions for the Administration on Aging at the Department of Health and Human Services: Associate Commissioner for State and Tribal Programs, 1987–1989; Associate Commissioner for Program Development, 1984–1986; Deputy Associate Commissioner for Program Development, 1983–1984; and Associate Commissioner for Education and Training, 1980–1983. She was Special Assistant to the Assistant Secretary for Rural Development at the Department of Agriculture, 1978–1980. In addition, she has served as an adjunct professor at the Catholic University of America, 1987; an education and training officer for the Administration on Aging at the Department of Health and Human Services in New York, 1974–1977; adjunct professor at the New School for Social Research in New York, 1976; manpower development specialist at the Department of Labor, 1971–1974; and an education program officer at the Agency for International Development at the Department of State, 1970–1971.

Dr. Berry graduated from Howard University (B.A., 1969; M.A., 1970), Fordham University (Ph.D., 1976), and Georgetown University Law Center (J.D., 1983). She was born November 17, 1947, in Washington, DC. Dr. Berry resides in Washington, DC.

Message on the Observance of National Afro-American (Black) History Month, February 1990
January 30, 1990

Each February, we observe National Black History Month in recognition of the remarkable achievements of Black Americans and the many contributions they have made to our nation's heritage.

In 1926, the respected historian, Carter G. Woodson, initiated "Negro History Week" in order to increase public appreciation for the important role Black Americans have played in shaping American history.

This year, during Black History Month, we once again pay tribute to those courageous men and women who have triumphed over the bitter legacy of slavery and discrimination and become full partners in America's great experiment in self-government.

Throughout our nation's history, Black Americans have continued to demonstrate the strength of their beliefs and the wealth of their abilities. The career of Dr. Daniel

Hale Williams, the first physician to perform successful open-heart surgery, and the beloved poetry of Langston Hughes and Sterling Brown provide powerful examples of the honor Black Americans have earned in virtually every field of endeavor. This month, we also celebrate the lasting influence of courageous individuals like Rosa Parks and Dr. Martin Luther King, Jr., who led the way in the struggle against bigotry and segregation. Their efforts helped open the doors of opportunity for millions of their fellow Americans.

Standing on the threshold of a new decade, we look to the future with high hopes, confident that it will be marked by ever greater achievements among Black Americans and by continued progress in our efforts to promote equal opportunity and racial harmony in the United States.

Today, I encourage all Americans to join me in saluting the tremendous achievements of Black Americans. They strengthen and enrich our entire nation.

GEORGE BUSH

Note: An original was not available for verification of the content of the message.

Remarks at a White House Ceremony Commemorating the 25th Anniversary of VISTA
January 31, 1990

Let me welcome all of you and pay my respects to Bernie Aronson, our Assistant Secretary of State, who is with us today; ACTION Director Jane Kenny; Pat Rodgers, the VISTA Director. Sarge Shriver was supposed to be here. Now, whether the man is here or not, I don't know. I don't see him. But I do see Senator Chris Dodd and Senator Jay Rockefeller, and we are delighted that you came for this. And is Tribal Chairman Nicola Larsen here? I think. Right here. Welcome, Nicola. I know this must be a special day for everybody, particularly for the 25 VISTA volunteers who are our special guests of honor.

We're here today to celebrate the 25th anniversary of VISTA, though some will tell you that remembering dates isn't my strong suit. [*Laughter*] But I wouldn't miss this anniversary for the world.

It was a quarter of a century ago, shortly after President Johnson signed VISTA into law, that the first volunteers started their service. And today 100,000 Americans of all ages and backgrounds can proudly say: "I was a VISTA volunteer." And even at this very moment, there are more than 3,000 volunteers at work in more than 650 neighborhoods. From the hollows of Appalachia to the mountains of New Mexico to the city streets of New York and Los Angeles, these volunteers work long, long hours on very short pay; and they work one community, one block, one child at a time.

Twenty-five years ago, President Johnson charged the VISTA volunteers with a tough mission, committing you—and here's what he said—"to guide the young, to comfort the sick, to encourage the downtrodden, to teach the skills which may lead to a more rewarding life." That was your mission then and that certainly is your mission today. Every time a kid learns to read, you make a difference. Every time a homeless family finds shelter, you make a difference. And every time a troubled person stays off drugs, you make a difference for all Americans.

I know how much Barbara's work in literacy means to her and to others. And she often talks about what volunteers are doing around the country. So, I know you do give a lot. But you are not giving dignity, for that cannot be conferred, or education, because that must be acquired. You're not bestowing ambition, because ambition's got to come from within. What the men and women of VISTA do achieve is even more miraculous: You impart to so many disadvantaged Americans the means to build pride, to earn a degree or a skill, to believe in themselves.

For an individual, dignity comes when he realizes that he's the true author of his destiny; for a troubled community, it comes by finding leadership from within. So, your achievements come as much from the power of self-confidence as they do from the material side—from material assistance. Sounds like a miracle. Maybe it is. It is a miracle that comes from caring.

Now, a few who care enough to volunteer are with us today—many, as a matter of fact—but Andrew Jacob, who works with at-risk street youth in Brunswick, Maine; Damita Wells, who recruits tutors for prison inmates in Nashville; and finally, Nick Flores, who counsels poor rural residents out in New Mexico, who is deeply involved in drug and alcohol abuse prevention, and who helps direct a food service for the hungry. I regard Nick as a very special volunteer because he suffered a terrible injury in a car accident prior to his assignment with VISTA. And I suppose no one would have blamed him if he had focused only on himself, only on his own needs. But not Nick Flores. He would rather serve others. And so, now he's out on the front lines, helping, building, and caring for people from Las Cruces to Santa Fe.

Perhaps he believes, like so many VISTA volunteers, that recognizing something greater than ourselves is what really matters. Or to put it as I have before: "From now on in America, any definition of a successful life must include serving others." And that's what attracts men and women to

VISTA—true activists. You don't often see them because they're off helping others in the most unlikeliest places. You don't often hear from them because they're too modest to brag. And you don't often notice them at work because theirs is a quiet mission—but together, helping move this country forward. So, when I talk of the Thousand Points of Light, please know that no light is more dazzling, brighter, than the VISTA volunteers.

I dropped by with Barbara to say thank you for all you do, and God bless you. Of course, God bless the United States. Thank you very much.

I forgot to mention the person with whom I work most closely in the White House involving voluntarism, and that's Gregg Petersmeyer here, who I know takes the same great pride in your work that Barbara and I do. But lest you didn't know who he was—this big, tall guy in the front—that's who it is. [*Laughter*] And he spends all his time trying to help stimulate this service to others that you've all made the hallmark of your lives.

Thank you all very, very much.

Note: The President spoke at 1:05 p.m. in the Roosevelt Room at the White House. In his remarks, he referred to Sargent Shriver, former Director of the Peace Corps, who was involved in the formation of VISTA; Nicola Larsen, tribal chair of the Tule River Tribal Council in Porterville, CA; and Gregg Petersmeyer, Deputy Assistant to the President and Director of the Office of National Service.

Address Before a Joint Session of the Congress on the State of the Union
January 31, 1990

Mr. President, Mr. Speaker, Members of the United States Congress:

I return as a former President of the Senate and a former Member of this great House. And now, as President, it is my privilege to report to you on the state of the Union.

Tonight I come not to speak about the state of the Government, not to detail every new initiative we plan for the coming year nor to describe every line in the budget. I'm here to speak to you and to the American people about the state of the Union, about our world—the changes we've seen, the challenges we face—and what that means for America.

There are singular moments in history, dates that divide all that goes before from all that comes after. And many of us in this Chamber have lived much of our lives in a world whose fundamental features were defined in 1945; and the events of that year decreed the shape of nations, the pace of progress, freedom or oppression for millions of people around the world.

Nineteen forty-five provided the common frame of reference, the compass points of the postwar era we've relied upon to understand ourselves. And that was our world, until now. The events of the year just ended, the Revolution of '89, have been a chain reaction, changes so striking that it marks the beginning of a new era in the world's affairs.

Think back—think back just 12 short months ago to the world we knew as 1989 began.

One year—one year ago, the people of Panama lived in fear, under the thumb of a dictator. Today democracy is restored; Panama is free. Operation Just Cause has achieved its objective. The number of military personnel in Panama is now very close to what it was before the operation began. And tonight I am announcing that well before the end of February, the additional numbers of American troops, the brave men and women of our Armed Forces who made this mission a success, will be back home.

A year ago in Poland, Lech Walesa declared that he was ready to open a dialog with the Communist rulers of that country; and today, with the future of a free Poland in their own hands, members of Solidarity lead the Polish Government.

A year ago, freedom's playwright, Václav Havel, languished as a prisoner in Prague. And today it's Václav Havel, President of Czechoslovakia.

And 1 year ago, Erich Honecker of East Germany claimed history as his guide, and he predicted the Berlin Wall would last another hundred years. And today, less than 1 year later, it's the Wall that's history.

Remarkable events—events that fulfill the long-held hopes of the American people; events that validate the longstanding goals of American policy, a policy based on a single, shining principle: the cause of freedom.

America, not just the nation but an idea, alive in the minds of people everywhere. As this new world takes shape, America stands at the center of a widening circle of freedom—today, tomorrow, and into the next century. Our nation is the enduring dream of every immigrant who ever set foot on these shores, and the millions still struggling to be free. This nation, this idea called America, was and always will be a new world—our new world.

At a workers' rally, in a place called Branik on the outskirts of Prague, the idea called America is alive. A worker, dressed in grimy overalls, rises to speak at the factory gates. He begins his speech to his fellow citizens with these words, words of a distant revolution: "We hold these truths to be self-evident, that all men are created equal, that they are endowed by their Creator with certain unalienable Rights, and that among these are Life, Liberty and the pursuit of Happiness."

It's no secret that here at home freedom's door opened long ago. The cornerstones of this free society have already been set in place: democracy, competition, opportunity, private investment, stewardship, and of course leadership. And our challenge today is to take this democratic system of ours, a system second to none, and make it better: a better America, where there's a job for everyone who wants one; where women working outside the home can be confident their children are in safe and loving care and where government works to expand child-care alternatives for parents; where we reconcile the needs of a clean environment and a strong economy; where "Made in the USA" is recognized around the world as the symbol of quality and progress; where every one of us enjoys the same opportunities to live, to work, and to contribute to society and where, for the first time, the American mainstream includes all of our disabled citizens; where everyone has a roof over his head and where the homeless get the help they need to live in dignity; where our schools challenge and support our kids and our teachers and where all of them make the grade; where every street, every city, every school, and every child is drug-free; and finally, where no American is forgotten—our hearts go out to our hostages who are ceaselessly on our minds and in our efforts.

That's part of the future we want to see, the future we can make for ourselves, but dreams alone won't get us there. We need to extend our horizon, commit to the long view. And our mission for the future starts today.

In the tough competitive markets around the world, America faces the great challenges and great opportunities. And we know that we can succeed in the global economic arena of the nineties, but to meet that challenge, we must make some fundamental changes—some crucial investment in ourselves.

Yes, we are going to invest in America. This administration is determined to encourage the creation of capital, capital of all kinds: physical capital—everything from our farms and factories to our workshops and production lines, all that is needed to produce and deliver quality goods and quality services; intellectual capital—the source of ideas that spark tomorrow's products; and of course our human capital—the talented work force that we'll need to compete in the global market.

Let me tell you, if we ignore human capital, if we lose the spirit of American ingenuity, the spirit that is the hallmark of the American worker, that would be bad. The American worker is the most productive worker in the world.

We need to save more. We need to expand the pool of capital for new investments that need more jobs and more growth. And that's the idea behind a new initiative I call the Family Savings Plan, which I will send to Congress tomorrow.

We need to cut the tax on capital gains, encourage risktakers, especially those in our small businesses, to take those steps that translate into economic reward, jobs, and a better life for all of us.

We'll do what it takes to invest in America's future. The budget commitment is there. The money is there. It's there for research and development, R&D—a record high. It's there for our housing initiative—

HOPE—to help everyone from first-time homebuyers to the homeless. The money's there to keep our kids drug-free—70 percent more than when I took office in 1989. It's there for space exploration. And it's there for education—another record high.

And one more thing: Last fall at the education summit, the Governors and I agreed to look for ways to help make sure that our kids are ready to learn the very first day they walk into the classroom. And I've made good on that commitment by proposing a record increase in funds—an extra half-a-billion dollars—for something near and dear to all of us: Head Start.

Education is the one investment that means more for our future because it means the most for our children. Real improvement in our schools is not simply a matter of spending more: It's a matter of asking more—expecting more—of our schools, our teachers, of our kids, of our parents, and ourselves. And that's why tonight I am announcing America's education goals, goals developed with enormous cooperation from the Nation's Governors. And if I might, I'd like to say I'm very pleased that Governor Gardner [Washington] and Governor Clinton [Arkansas], Governor Branstad [Iowa], Governor Campbell [South Carolina], all of whom were very key in these discussions, these deliberations, are with us here tonight.

By the year 2000, every child must start school ready to learn.

The United States must increase the high school graduation rate to no less than 90 percent.

And we are going to make sure our schools' diplomas mean something. In critical subjects—at the 4th, 8th, and 12th grades—we must assess our students' performance.

By the year 2000, U.S. students must be first in the world in math and science achievement.

Every American adult must be a skilled, literate worker and citizen.

Every school must offer the kind of disciplined environment that makes it possible for our kids to learn. And every school in America must be drug-free.

Ambitious aims? Of course. Easy to do?

Far from it. But the future's at stake. The Nation will not accept anything less than excellence in education.

These investments will keep America competitive. And I know this about the American people: We welcome competition. We'll match our ingenuity, our energy, our experience and technology, our spirit and enterprise against anyone. But let the competition be free, but let it also be fair. America is ready.

Since we really mean it and since we're serious about being ready to meet that challenge, we're getting our own house in order. We have made real progress. Seven years ago, the Federal deficit was 6 percent of our gross national product—6 percent. In the new budget I sent up 2 days ago, the deficit is down to 1 percent of gross national product.

That budget brings Federal spending under control. It meets the Gramm-Rudman target. It brings that deficit down further and balances the budget by 1993 with no new taxes. And let me tell you, there's still more than enough Federal spending. For most of us, $1.2 trillion is still a lot of money.

And once the budget is balanced, we can operate the way every family must when it has bills to pay. We won't leave it to our children and our grandchildren. Once it's balanced, we will start paying off the national debt.

And there's something more we owe the generations of the future: stewardship, the safekeeping of America's precious environmental inheritance. It's just one sign of how serious we are. We will elevate the Environmental Protection Agency to Cabinet rank—not more bureaucracy, not more red-tape, but the certainty that here at home, and especially in our dealings with other nations, environmental issues have the status they deserve.

This year's budget provides over $2 billion in new spending to protect our environment, with over $1 billion for global change research, and a new initiative I call America the Beautiful to expand our national parks and wildlife preserves that improve recreational facilities on public lands, and something else, something that will help keep this country clean from our forestland

to the inner cities and keep America beautiful for generations to come: the money to plant a billion trees a year.

And tonight let me say again to all the Members of the Congress: The American people did not send us here to bicker. There is work to do, and they sent us here to get it done. And once again, in the spirit of cooperation, I offer my hand to all of you. Let's work together to do the will of the people: clean air, child care, the Educational Excellence Act, crime, and drugs. It's time to act. The farm bill, transportation policy, product-liability reform, enterprise zones—it's time to act together.

And there's one thing I hope we will be able to agree on. It's about our commitments. I'm talking about Social Security. To every American out there on Social Security, to every American supporting that system today, and to everyone counting on it when they retire, we made a promise to you, and we are going to keep it.

We rescued the system in 1983, and it's sound again—bipartisan arrangement. Our budget fully funds today's benefits, and it assures that future benefits will be funded as well. The last thing we need to do is mess around with Social Security.

There's one more problem we need to address. We must give careful consideration to the recommendations of the health-care studies underway now. That's why tonight I'm asking Dr. Sullivan, Lou Sullivan, Secretary of Health and Human Services, to lead a Domestic Policy Council review of recommendations on the quality, accessibility, and cost of our nation's health-care system. I am committed to bring the staggering costs of health care under control.

The state of the Government does indeed depend on many of us in this very chamber. But the state of the Union depends on all Americans. We must maintain the democratic decency that makes a nation out of millions of individuals. I've been appalled at the recent mail bombings across this country. Every one of us must confront and condemn racism, anti-Semitism, bigotry, and hate, not next week, not tomorrow, but right now—every single one of us.

The state of the Union depends on whether we help our neighbor—claim the problems of our community as our own. We've got to step forward when there's trouble, lend a hand, be what I call a point of light to a stranger in need. We've got to take the time after a busy day to sit down and read with our kids, help them with their homework, pass along the values we learned as children. That's how we sustain the state of the Union. Every effort is important. It all adds up. It's doing the things that give democracy meaning. It all adds up to who we are and who we will be.

Let me say that so long as we remember the American idea, so long as we live up to the American ideal, the state of the Union will remain sound and strong.

And to those who worry that we've lost our way—well, I want you to listen to parts of a letter written by Private First Class James Markwell, a 20-year-old Army medic of the 1st Battalion, 75th Rangers. It's dated December 18th, the night before our armed forces went into action in Panama. It's a letter servicemen write and hope will never be sent. And sadly, Private Markwell's mother did receive this letter. She passed it along to me out there in Cincinnati.

And here is some of what he wrote: "I've never been afraid of death, but I know he is waiting at the corner. I've been trained to kill and to save, and so has everyone else. I am frightened what lays beyond the fog, and yet do not mourn for me. Revel in the life that I have died to give you. But most of all, don't forget the Army was my choice. Something that I wanted to do. Remember I joined the Army to serve my country and ensure that you are free to do what you want and live your lives freely."

Let me add that Private Markwell was among the first to see battle in Panama, and one of the first to fall. But he knew what he believed in. He carried the idea we call America in his heart.

I began tonight speaking about the changes we've seen this past year. There is a new world of challenges and opportunities before us, and there's a need for leadership that only America can provide. Nearly 40 years ago, in his last address to the Congress, President Harry Truman predicted such a time would come. He said: "As our world grows stronger, more united, more attractive to men on both sides of the Iron Curtain, then inevitably there will come a time of change within the Communist world." Today, that change is taking place.

For more than 40 years, America and its allies held communism in check and ensured that democracy would continue to exist. And today, with communism crumbling, our aim must be to ensure democracy's advance, to take the lead in forging peace and freedom's best hope: a great and growing commonwealth of free nations. And to the Congress and to all Americans, I say it is time to acclaim a new consensus at home and abroad, a common vision of the peaceful world we want to see.

Here in our own hemisphere, it is time for all the peoples of the Americas, North and South, to live in freedom. In the Far East and Africa, it's time for the full flowering of free governments and free markets that have served as the engine of progress. It's time to offer our hand to the emerging democracies of Eastern Europe so that continent—for too long a continent divided—can see a future whole and free. It's time to build on our new relationship with the Soviet Union, to endorse and encourage a peaceful process of internal change toward democracy and economic opportunity.

We are in a period of great transition, great hope, and yet great uncertainty. We recognize that the Soviet military threat in Europe is diminishing, but we see little change in Soviet strategic modernization. Therefore, we must sustain our own strategic offense modernization and the Strategic Defense Initiative.

But the time is right to move forward on a conventional arms control agreement to move us to more appropriate levels of military forces in Europe, a coherent defense program that ensures the U.S. will continue to be a catalyst for peaceful change in Europe. And I've consulted with leaders of NATO. In fact, I spoke by phone with President Gorbachev just today.

I agree with our European allies that an American military presence in Europe is essential and that it should not be tied solely to the Soviet military presence in Eastern Europe. But our troop levels can still be lower. And so, tonight I am announcing a

133

major new step for a further reduction in U.S. and Soviet manpower in Central and Eastern Europe to 195,000 on each side. This level reflects the advice of our senior military advisers. It's designed to protect American and European interests and sustain NATO's defense strategy. A swift conclusion to our arms control talks—conventional, chemical, and strategic—must now be our goal. And that time has come.

Still, we must recognize an unfortunate fact: In many regions of the world tonight, the reality is conflict, not peace. Enduring animosities and opposing interests remain. And thus, the cause of peace must be served by an America strong enough and sure enough to defend our interests and our ideals. It's this American idea that for the past four decades helped inspire this Revolution of '89.

Here at home and in the world, there's history in the making, history to be made. Six months ago, early in this season of change, I stood at the gates of the Gdansk shipyard in Poland at the monument to the fallen workers of Solidarity. It's a monument of simple majesty. Three tall crosses rise up from the stones, and atop each cross, an anchor—an ancient symbol of hope.

The anchor in our world today is freedom, holding us steady in times of change, a symbol of hope to all the world. And freedom is at the very heart of the idea that is America. Giving life to that idea depends on every one of us. Our anchor has always been faith and family.

In the last few days of this past momentous year, our family was blessed once more, celebrating the joy of life when a little boy became our 12th grandchild. When I held the little guy for the first time, the troubles at home and abroad seemed manageable and totally in perspective.

Now, I know you're probably thinking, well, that's just a grandfather talking. Well, maybe you're right. But I've met a lot of children this past year across this country, as all of you have, everywhere from the Far East to Eastern Europe. And all kids are unique, and yet all kids are alike—the budding young environmentalists I met this month who joined me in exploring the Florida Everglades; the little leaguers I played catch with in Poland, ready to go from

Warsaw to the World Series; and even the kids who are ill or alone—and God bless those boarder babies, born addicted to drugs and AIDS and coping with problems no child should have to face. But you know, when it comes to hope and the future, every kid is the same—full of dreams, ready to take on the world—all special, because they are the very future of freedom. And to them belongs this new world I've been speaking about.

And so, tonight I'm going to ask something of every one of you. Now, let me start with my generation, with the grandparents out there. You are our living link to the past. Tell your grandchildren the story of struggles waged at home and abroad, of sacrifices freely made for freedom's sake. And tell them your own story as well, because every American has a story to tell.

And, parents, your children look to you for direction and guidance. Tell them of faith and family. Tell them we are one nation under God. Teach them that of all the many gifts they can receive liberty is their most precious legacy, and of all the gifts they can give the greatest is helping others.

And to the children and young people out there tonight: With you rests our hope, all that America will mean in the years and decades ahead. Fix your vision on a new century—your century, on dreams we cannot see, on the destiny that is yours and yours alone.

And finally, let all Americans—all of us together here in this Chamber, the symbolic center of democracy—affirm our allegiance to this idea we call America. And let us remember that the state of the Union depends on each and every one of us.

God bless all of you, and may God bless this great nation, the United States of America.

Note: The President spoke at 9:05 p.m. in the House Chamber of the Capitol. He was introduced by Thomas S. Foley, Speaker of the House of Representatives. The address was broadcast live on nationwide radio and television. Prior to his address, the President attended a reception in the Speaker's Conference Room hosted by the congressional leadership.

White House Fact Sheet on the President's Conventional Armed Forces in Europe Initiative
January 31, 1990

After initial discussions with NATO allies, the President concluded that changes which have taken place in Europe over the last 3 months have made it possible to propose lower levels in the area of greatest concentration of forces: Central and Eastern Europe. However, the United States will maintain significant military forces in Europe as long as our allies desire our presence as part of a common security effort.

Therefore, in his State of the Union Address to Congress on January 31, President Bush proposed to revise NATO's current position in the Conventional Armed Forces in Europe (CFE) negotiations to lower substantially the levels of U.S. and Soviet ground and air force manpower in Central and Eastern Europe to 195,000 on each side. Forces withdrawn will be demobilized. There would be approximately 225,000 U.S. ground and air force personnel in Europe

after CFE reductions are completed. The proposal responds to rapid changes in Eastern Europe and is designed to help propel the CFE negotiations to an early conclusion in 1990.

The President's initiative would supersede an earlier proposal establishing a level of 275,000 each of U.S. and Soviet ground and air force manpower stationed outside of their respective national territories in the Atlantic to the Urals region.

The President has concluded that this proposal reflects the minimum level of U.S. forces needed in Europe to protect American interests and to sustain NATO's strategy of forward defense and flexible response. Even if—as we expect—Soviet forces in this region are reduced even further, the United States does not envision the further reduction of its forces in Europe below this new level.

Remarks at the Annual National Prayer Breakfast
February 1, 1990

Thank you, ladies and gentlemen. Thank you all. Thank you very, very much. Vice President and Mrs. Quayle, and Chuck Grassley, Sam Nunn, and my dear friend Billy Graham, and Ruth. Jim Baker, that was a very inspiring testament of faith. I also want to salute our very special guests who have traveled far to join us in a prayer for peace and understanding: President Moi of Kenya; President Ershad of Bangladesh; Major Buyoya, the marvelous head of Burundi; President Cristiani, a longtime friend; the Prime Minister Kisekka. And I just express for all of us a very hearty welcome, and to President Ershad, a happy birthday greeting to go with Bev Shea's. We're delighted you're here.

And I want to thank Bev Shea and Billy. It'll probably read: prayer breakfast, Bev Shea; supporting cast: secretary of state

Billy Graham. [*Laughter*] A lot of Presidents out here, Senators and Congressmen. He was magnificent. [*Laughter*] Magnificent music.

It's often said in my line of work that a candidate or a proposal hasn't got a prayer. Well, I'm pleased to be with an audience about whom that will never be said. [*Laughter*] And this breakfast is the result of years of quiet diplomacy—I wouldn't say secret diplomacy—quiet diplomacy by an ambassador of faith, Doug Coe. And I salute him.

And I was moved once again by what Sam and Liz told us of Members and staffers on the Hill who like to regularly meet to share a few quiet moments of prayer and Bible reading. The values that spring from our faith certainly tell us a lot about our country. And consider that for more than two centuries Americans have endorsed, and properly so, the separation of church and state. But we've also shown how both religion and government can strengthen a society. After all, our Founding Fathers' documents begin with these words: All men are endowed by their Creator with certain unalienable rights. And Americans are religious people, but a truly religious nation is a tolerant nation. We cherish dissent, we cherish the fact that we have many, many faiths, and we protect even the right to disbelieve.

A truly religious nation is also a giving nation. A close friend of mine sent me a poem recently which eloquently embodies this spirit of giving. "I sought my soul, but my soul I could not see. I sought my God, but my God eluded me. I sought my brother and found all three."

Thousands of Americans are finding their soul, finding their God, by reaching out to their brothers and sisters in need. You've heard me talk about a Thousand Points of Light across the country. Americans are working through their places of worship, through community programs, or on their own to help the hungry or the homeless, to teach the unskilled, to bring the words of men and the Word of God to those who cannot even read.

And so, I believe that this democracy of ours is once again proving, as it has throughout our history, that when people are free they use that freedom to serve the greater good and, indeed, a higher truth. As freedom blossoms in Eastern Europe—and Jim was talking eloquently about that—I am convinced that the 1990's will be the decade of the rebirth that he so beautifully spoke about, a rebirth of faith and hope.

And one example: I met this week Father Calciu, a Romanian Orthodox minister. Father Calciu had spent 21 of his 64 years in jail—a third of his entire life in prison. And in fact, it was while in prison for opposing the Government that he found God. And once released, he risked his freedom by preaching a series of Lenten sermons. And for that, he was imprisoned again and tortured beyond belief. And yet Father Calciu had faith, and he refused to break. He was sentenced to death. And as he stood in the corner of the prison yard, praying for his wife and son, awaiting death, it was then that something remarkable occurred. His two executioners called to him. And surely, he thought, well, this was the end. But instead they said, "Father,"—and that was the first time they had called him that—"we have decided not to kill you." And 3 weeks later, he received permission to celebrate the Divine Liturgy. And when he did, he saw these same two guys—the same two guards—approach, and to his astonishment, his would-be executioners got on their knees and joined him in prayer. This is one man's story, a humble priest.

And today the times are on the side of peace because more and more brave men and women are on the side of God. And so, that is the end of these few words. That is my prayer: that we will continue to recognize the power of faith. Thank you all, and God bless you.

Note: The President spoke at 9:25 a.m. in the International Ballroom at the Washington Hilton Hotel. In his remarks, he referred to Senators Charles E. Grassley and Sam Nunn; Representative Elizabeth J. Patterson; Secretary of State James A. Baker III; evangelist Rev. Billy Graham and his wife, Ruth; President Alfredo Cristiani Buckard of El Salvador; Prime Minister Samson Kisekka of Uganda; religious singer George Beverly Shea; and Doug Coe, a participant in the prayer breakfast.

Remarks on Transmitting Proposed Savings and Economic Growth Legislation
February 1, 1990

Well, today I'm transmitting to Congress an important initiative that was outlined last night in the State of the Union Address: the Savings and Economic Growth Act of 1990. And this important legislation will increase national savings, lower the cost of capital, create jobs, increase our international competitiveness, and improve our standard of living.

There are three elements to the act: family savings account, capital gains tax rate reduction, and then the homeownership initiative.

First, the family savings account will give Americans an important incentive to save for their futures. I believe Americans will save more if given this opportunity, and by doing so, they will generate new funds for investment that strengthen our economy.

Second, the permanent tax-rate reduction for long-term capital gains will lower the cost of capital and provide an incentive for long-term investment. And this will create jobs and make American business more competitive in the international arena.

And third, the homeownership initiative will allow individuals to withdraw without penalty up to $10,000 from an IRA, from an individual retirement account, prior to retirement if the funds are used to purchase a first home.

And this legislative package will help millions of Americans invest in their children's education, buy a first home, and then set money aside for family emergencies. And this will also strengthen our economy, create jobs, and make America more competitive internationally.

I'm grateful to those of you here—and up here—who have worked so hard to craft this legislation, and I look forward to working closely with Congress towards its enactment.

And now I'll sign the transmittal that signs and sends the Savings and Economic Growth Act up to the Congress.

Note: The President spoke at 10:07 a.m. in the Roosevelt Room at the White House.

Message to the Congress Transmitting Proposed Savings and Economic Growth Legislation
February 1, 1990

To the Congress of the United States:

I am pleased to submit for your consideration and passage the "Savings and Economic Growth Act of 1990." This legislative proposal would enact a permanent reduction in the capital gains tax rate, establish a new family savings program, and permit penalty-free Individual Retirement Account (IRA) withdrawals for first-time home buyers.

This proposal would encourage savings, investment, and economic efficiency, thereby creating jobs and providing other economic benefits to all citizens.

A permanent tax rate reduction for capital gains will lower the cost of capital and provide an incentive for long-term investment in the American economy that will create jobs and make American business more competitive in the international economy.

A new Family Savings Account will give most American families an opportunity to save through a simple and understandable tax-exempt savings incentive program. The resulting savings boost will also strengthen our economy and create jobs and opportunity for all Americans.

Permitting Americans to withdraw funds

from their IRAs prior to retirement without penalty for the purchase of their first home will assist individuals in saving for that first home, while providing additional stimulus to the construction of affordable housing in our country.

I look forward to working with the Congress on these important matters.

GEORGE BUSH

The White House,
February 1, 1990.

White House Fact Sheet on the Proposed Savings and Economic Growth Act of 1990
February 1, 1990

Today President Bush transmitted to the Congress the Savings and Economic Growth Act of 1990. This act will increase family savings, stimulate job-creating long-term investment, and strengthen the competitive position of American business. It contains three parts:

- *Family Savings Account.* This new savings program will give Americans an opportunity to save for their long-term goals in a tax-free manner.
- *Capital Gains Tax Rate Reduction.* This act will provide for a permanent partial exclusion from tax of gains on long-term investments in productive assets.
- *Home Ownership Initiative.* This will allow millions of American families an opportunity to save for their first home through the existing IRA program.

The Savings and Economic Growth Act provides a comprehensive and balanced program to stimulate our domestic savings rate and lower the cost of capital to American business. This, coupled with President Bush's proposed dramatic reduction in the Federal budget deficit, will allow more funds to flow into productive investment in this country.

The President calls upon the Congress for speedy enactment of these provisions. The sooner we can provide incentives for American families to save and for American business to invest for the long term, the more certain we can be that the current record-setting peacetime recovery will continue.

Family Savings Account (FSA)

- Married couples with adjusted gross income (AGI) under $120,000, singles with AGI under $60,000, and taxpayers who are heads of household with AGI under $100,000 are eligible if they have earned income and are not dependents on another return.
- Each person may contribute, per year up to $2,500 (couples up to $5,000) or the amount of their compensation that year, whichever is less.
- Contributions are not tax deductible when made. The funds deposited in the account must be made in cash (existing securities may not be used) and may be invested in any investment vehicle except for insurance contracts or collectible items such as stamps or artwork.
- Contributions are never subject to tax when withdrawn.
- Earnings on deposits at least 7 years old may also be withdrawn tax free. Earnings are taxed only if they are attributable to money on deposit less than 7 years. Earnings on deposits at least 3 years old are taxed like regular interest income when withdrawn. Earnings on deposits made less than 3 years prior to withdrawal will be subject to income tax and also to a 10-percent penalty tax when withdrawn.
- The Family Savings Account program is particularly beneficial to those who make a habit of saving. A family that contributes $2,500 each year to a Family Savings Account paying 8 percent interest would have over $73,000 saved after 15 years.

Capital Gains Tax Rate Reduction

- The President proposes a phased-in exclusion of up to 30 percent of the capital gain on an asset. Eventually only assets held at least 3 years would receive the full exclusion.

	Years held		
	1	2	3
Year sold:			
1990..	30 percent	30 percent	30 percent
1991..	20 percent	30 percent	30 percent
1992..	10 percent	20 percent	30 percent

- A 30-percent exclusion would effectively lower the capital gains tax rate to 19.6 percent for a taxpayer in the 28-percent tax bracket. The effective tax rate would be reduced to 10.5 percent for a taxpayer in the 15-percent tax bracket and to 23.1 percent for a taxpayer in the 33-percent tax bracket.
- Corporations would not be eligible for a capital gains tax rate reduction.
- In general, all capital assets held by individuals, except for collectibles, will be eligible for the capital gains exclusion.
- This reduction benefits a wide cross section of Americans. In 1987, 72 percent of the tax returns with capital gains were filed by taxpayers with other income of less than $50,000.

These taxpayers reported fully 41 percent of the net gains reported that year.
- The Department of Treasury estimates that this change will permanently increase tax revenue without taking into account the positive effects this change will have on economic growth.

Home Ownership Initiative

- Americans will be able to withdraw up to $10,000 from an IRA for a first-time home purchase without penalty. The home must cost less than 110 percent of the median home price in the geographic area in which they are buying.
- This could save an American family seeking to buy their first home up to $1,000 compared to current law. Current law imposes a 10-percent excise tax, on top of any regular tax owed, for withdrawals from an IRA account.
- This proposal is targeted toward low- and moderate-income families who do not currently own their own home. Higher income families are not eligible for the up front deduction on an IRA under current law unless they are not covered by another pension plan.
- More families will make use of the IRA as an investment tool. Evidence indicates that younger families do not make as great a use of the IRA as do older couples. This provides an incentive for taxpayers of all age groups to participate in the IRA system.

Remarks Prior to a Meeting With President Alfredo Cristiani Buckard of El Salvador
February 1, 1990

Reporter. President Cristiani, are you worried that Congress is going to cut your aid because of the human rights situation?

President Bush. The President is going to take some questions outside—of course, we believe in free speech, so he can take them here, too—but he is going to be available and take some questions outside.

And what I'd like to do is establish that this is what we call a modified photo opportunity—modified only that I'd like to say that I know this man. I know of his commitment to democracy. I support him now. I will support him in the future. And the success of democracy in El Salvador is a very important thing to us, to this country. And

I've been very impressed with the courage he has shown in going after those who have broken the law in his country. And that's been a shining example to all of us.

So, let there be no mistake about where I stand or where our administration stands in terms of support for President Cristiani and for the democracy in El Salvador, a democracy certified by the people not so long ago, when they had certifiably free elections.

He'll take some questions later on when we're going to have a little press gathering out there.

Welcome again.

Note: President Bush spoke at 2:02 p.m. in the Colonnade at the White House.

Message to the Congress Transmitting a Report on Aeronautics and Space Activities During 1987
February 1, 1990

To the Congress of the United States:

I am pleased to transmit this report on the Nation's progress in aeronautics and space during calendar year 1987, as required by section 206 of the National Aeronautics and Space Act of 1958, as amended (42 U.S.C. 2476). Aeronautics and space activities cut across many sectors of our Federal Government, and this report highlights the major programs of the 14 contributing departments and agencies, with the National Aeronautics and Space Administration (NASA) and the Department of Defense (DOD) the major contributors.

In 1987, as furtherance of the recovery of our space launch capability, studies were completed concluding that a mixed fleet, consisting of the space shuttle and expendable launch vehicles, would be required for continued U.S. operations and access to space. Remote sensing capability continued to make impressive progress to further our understanding of the ozone depletion in the atmosphere, the impact of weather patterns on agriculture, and the damage to the forest ecosystem caused by acid deposition. A new initiative was launched to study the Earth system, including the oceans and the atmosphere, on a worldwide scale.

During the year, technology products continued to flow to the user industries. Results of aeronautics research reached a new level of application. The NASA-developed computational fluid dynamics techniques coupled with drag reducing concepts were applied to hull/keel design. Aircraft safety continued to receive priority, with requirements being levied for equipment to alert pilots of collision threat.

The defense of our country was enhanced by the successful demonstration of target interception in space. Great strides were made as the United States moved closer to agreement with its partners in the permanently occupied space station project. Bilateral and multilateral discussions on space arms control were held in Geneva. Because of advances made in worldwide communications, information on space technology and exploration is now reaching 134 countries and in 44 languages.

There is great promise in our Nation's vision to be at the forefront of advancement in aeronautics, space science, and exploration, for it is this advancement that ultimately makes a significant contribution to the quality of life on Earth. Our challenge is to continue on an aggressive course of exploration that will provide the international leadership and climate for cooperation for which this great Nation has become so well known.

GEORGE BUSH

The White House,
February 1, 1990.

Appointment of Joy A. Silverman as a Member of the Board of Trustees of the John F. Kennedy Center for the Performing Arts
February 1, 1990

The President today announced his intention to appoint Joy A. Silverman as a member of the Board of Trustees of the John F. Kennedy Center for the Performing Arts.

Last year, Mrs. Silverman was nominated by the President to be U.S. Ambassador to Barbados, accredited also to Dominica, Saint Lucia, and Saint Vincent and the Grenadines. She has asked, however, that, for family reasons, the President not return her name to the Senate for this post. The President remains fully confident in Mrs. Silverman and her capacity for public service and is pleased she has agreed to devote her considerable energy to the Kennedy Center.

Mrs. Silverman was a full-time participant in President Bush's 1988 campaign and assisted the New York State campaign director. From 1987 to 1988, she served as a member, and later as chairman, of the advisory council to the New York State Commission on the Bicentennial of the United States Constitution. Mrs. Silverman has served as a member of the New York City mayor's commission for protocol. In addition to extensive work for various educational institutions, she has served actively with various charitable organizations in the New York metropolitan area. Mrs. Silverman attended the University of Maryland. She is married, has two children, and currently resides in New York City.

Statement by Press Secretary Fitzwater on South Africa
February 1, 1990

President Bush has been closely following the situation in South Africa. He believes that President de Klerk has taken a number of courageous and important steps aimed at ending apartheid and moving toward a democratic and nonracial South Africa. Should Mandela be released, President Bush would plan to invite both Mandela and de Klerk separately to meet with him at the White House so President Bush can determine how the United States can best help South Africa move forward toward a nonracial government and society.

Nomination of Erich W. Bretthauer To Be an Assistant Administrator of the Environmental Protection Agency
February 1, 1990

The President today announced his intention to nominate Erich W. Bretthauer to be an Assistant Administrator of the Environmental Protection Agency for Research and Development. He would succeed Vaun A. Newill.

Since 1988 Mr. Bretthauer has served as Acting Assistant Administrator in the Office of Research and Development at the Environmental Protection Agency in Washington, DC. Prior to this, he served in various positions at the Environmental Protection Agency, including Deputy Assistant Administrator in the Office of Research and Development, 1987–1988; Director of the Environmental Monitoring Systems Laboratory in Las Vegas, NV, 1985–1987; and Director of the Office of Environmental Processes and Effects Research in Washington, DC, 1982–1985. In addition, he served as a professional staff assistant at the United States Senate Committee on Environment and Public Works in Washington, DC, 1981–1982; a Congressional fellow at the United States Senate on the Environment and Public Works Committee, 1981; and a member of the special detail to the United States Radiation Policy Council, 1980–1981. Mr. Bretthauer has served in various positions at the Environmental Protection Agency in Las Vegas, NV, including Director of the Nuclear Radiation Assessment Division, 1979–1980; Director of the Monitoring Operations Division, 1978–1979; chief of the methods development and analytical support branch, 1975–1978; and chief of the contact monitoring methods branch, 1968–1975.

Mr. Bretthauer graduated from the University of Nevada at Reno (B.S., 1960; M.S., 1962). He was born September 12, 1937, in Denver, CO. Mr. Bretthauer is married, has four children, and resides in Las Vegas, NV.

Nomination of Glen L. Bower To Be a Member of the Railroad Retirement Board, and Designation as Chairman
February 1, 1990

The President today announced his intention to nominate Glen L. Bower to be a member of the Railroad Retirement Board for the remainder of the term expiring August 28, 1992. He would succeed Thomas J. Simon. Mr. Bower will serve as Chairman of the Board.

Since 1983 Mr. Bower has served as assistant director and general counsel at the department of revenue for the State of Illinois. He also served on the review board of appeals as chairman, 1986–1987, and member, 1985–1986. Prior to this he was a member of the Illinois House of Representatives, 1979–1983.

Mr. Bower graduated from Southern Illinois University (B.A., 1971) and IIT/Chicago-Kent College of Law (J.D., 1974). He was born January 16, 1949, in Highland, IL. He currently resides in Effingham, IL.

Nomination of Charles J. Chamberlain To Be a Member of the Railroad Retirement Board
February 1, 1990

The President today announced his intention to nominate Charles J. Chamberlain to be a member of the Railroad Retirement Board for the term of 5 years from August 29, 1989. This is a reappointment.

Since 1977 Mr. Chamberlain has served as a labor member of the Railroad Retirement Board in Chicago, IL.

Mr. Chamberlain was born August 7, 1921, in Ashton, IL. He is married, has two children, and currently resides in Crystal Lake, IL.

Order on the China National Aero-Technology Import and Export Corporation Divestiture of MAMCO Manufacturing, Incorporated
February 1, 1990

ORDER PURSUANT TO SECTION 721 OF THE DEFENSE PRODUCTION ACT OF 1950

By the authority vested in me as President by the Constitution and statutes of the United States of America, including section 721 of the Defense Production Act of 1950 ("section 721"), 50 U.S.C. App. 2170,

Section 1. Findings. I hereby make the following findings:

(1) There is credible evidence that leads me to believe that, in exercising its control of MAMCO Manufacturing, Inc. ("MAMCO"), a corporation incorporated under the laws of the State of Washington, the China National Aero-Technology Import and Export Corporation ("CATIC") might take action that threatens to impair the national security of the United States of America; and

(2) Provisions of law, other than section 721 and the International Emergency Economic Powers Act (50 U.S.C. 1701–1706), do not in my judgment provide adequate and appropriate authority for me to protect the national security in this matter.

Section 2. Actions Ordered and Authorized. On the basis of the findings set forth in section 1 of this Order, I hereby order that:

(1) CATIC's acquisition of control of MAMCO and its assets, whether directly or through subsidiaries or affiliates, is prohibited.

(2) CATIC and its subsidiaries and affiliates shall divest all of their interest in MAMCO and its assets by May 1, 1990, 3 months from the date of this Order, unless such date is extended for a period not to exceed 3 months, on such written conditions as the Committee on Foreign Investment in the United States ("CFIUS") may require. Immediately upon divestment, CATIC shall certify in writing to CFIUS that such divestment has been effected in accordance with this Order.

(3) Without limitation on the exercise of authority by any agency under other provisions of law, and until such time as the di-

vestment is completed, CFIUS is authorized to implement measures it deems necessary and appropriate to verify that operations of MAMCO are carried out in such manner as to ensure protection of the national security interests of the United States. Such measures may include but are not limited to the following: On reasonable notice to MAMCO, CATIC, or CATIC's subsidiaries or affiliates (collectively "the Parties"), employees of the United States Government, as designated by CFIUS, shall be permitted access to all facilities of the Parties located in the United States—

(a) to inspect and copy any books, ledgers, accounts, correspondence, memoranda, and other records and documents in the possession or under the control of the Parties that concern any matter relating to this Order;

(b) to inspect any equipment, containers, packages, and technical data (including software) in the possession or under the control of the Parties; and

(c) to interview officers, employees, or agents of the Parties concerning any matter relating to this Order.

(4) The Attorney General is authorized to take any steps he deems necessary to enforce this Order.

Section 3. Reservation. I hereby reserve my authority, until such time as the divestment required by this Order has been completed, to issue further orders with respect to the Parties as shall in my judgment be necessary to protect the national security.

Section 4. Publication. This Order shall be published in the *Federal Register.*

GEORGE BUSH

The White House,
February 1, 1990.

[*Filed with the Office of the Federal Register, 4:52 p.m., February 2, 1990*]

Note: The order was released by the Office of the Press Secretary on February 2.

Message to the Congress on the China National Aero-Technology Import and Export Corporation Divestiture of MAMCO Manufacturing, Incorporated
February 1, 1990

To the Congress of the United States:

1. I hereby report to the Congress on my decision to order the China National Aero-Technology Import and Export Corporation (CATIC) to divest all its interest in MAMCO Manufacturing, Inc., a company located in Seattle, Washington, and incorporated under the laws of the State of Washington. I have taken this action under the authority vested in me as President by section 721 of the Defense Production Act of 1950 ("section 721" or "the Exon-Florio provision"), 50 U.S.C. App. 2170. This report is submitted pursuant to subsection (f) of section 721. A copy of my order is attached.

2. The United States welcomes foreign direct investment in this country; it provides foreign investors fair, equitable, and nondiscriminatory treatment. This Administration is committed to maintaining that policy. There are circumstances in which the United States maintains limited exceptions to such treatment. Generally these exceptions are necessary to protect national security. Of those foreign mergers, acquisitions, and takeovers which have been reviewed under the Exon-Florio provision to determine effects on national security, this is the first time I have invoked section 721 authority. My action in this case is in response to circumstances of this particular transaction. It does not change our open investment policy and is not a precedent for the future with regard to direct investment in the United States from the People's Republic of China or any other country.

3. Section 721 requires me to make certain findings before exercising the authority conferred by that provision. Specifically, I must find that:

(1) there is credible evidence that leads me to believe that the foreign interest exercising control might take action that threatens to impair the national security, and

(2) provisions of law, other than section 721 and the International Emergency Economic Powers Act (50 U.S.C. 1701–1706), do not in my judgment provide adequate and appropriate authority for me to protect the national security.

I have made the findings required by section 721. Specifically, confidential information available to me concerning some of CATIC's activities raises serious concerns regarding CATIC's future actions. It is my determination that this information constitutes the "credible evidence" required by the statute. Moreover, I have determined that no law, other than section 721 and the International Emergency Economic Powers Act, provides adequate and appropriate authority to protect against the threat to the national security posed by this case.

4. MAMCO voluntarily notified the Committee on Foreign Investment in the United States ("CFIUS") of CATIC's intention to acquire MAMCO. CFIUS has been designated by Executive Order No. 12661 to receive notifications and to review and investigate to determine the effects on national security of foreign mergers, acquisitions, and takeovers. On November 30, 1989, CATIC purchased all of the voting securities of MAMCO. The acquisition was consummated while CFIUS review of the transaction was in progress, an action not prohibited by the statute.

CATIC is an export-import company of the Ministry of Aerospace Industry of the People's Republic of China. CATIC has business dealings with various companies in this country, in several sectors including commercial aircraft. The Ministry engages in research and development, design, and manufacture of military and commercial aircraft, missiles, and aircraft engines.

MAMCO machines and fabricates metal parts for aircraft. Much of MAMCO's production is sold to a single manufacturer for production of civilian aircraft. Some of its machinery is subject to U.S. export controls.

It has no contracts with the United States Government involving classified information.

5. On December 4, 1989, CFIUS made a determination to undertake a formal investigation and so informed the parties to the transaction. CFIUS undertook the investigation in order to assess MAMCO's present and potential production and technological capabilities and the national security implications of CATIC's purchase of MAMCO.

6. During the investigation, CFIUS asked for and received information from MAMCO in addition to that provided in the initial filing. Officials of the Departments of Commerce and Defense, representing CFIUS, visited MAMCO to gather information to assist CFIUS in its assessment of MAMCO's current production and technological capabilities.

7. In its investigation, CFIUS also considered the adequacy of all laws, other than the Exon-Florio provision, to deal with the national security concerns posed by the transaction.

8. Because of the sensitive nature of the evidence in this investigation, CFIUS will be available, on request, to provide the appropriate committees, meeting in closed sessions, with a classified briefing.

GEORGE BUSH

The White House,
February 1, 1990.

Note: The message was released by the Office of the Press Secretary on February 2.

Statement by Press Secretary Fitzwater on the China National Aero-Technology Import and Export Corporation Divestiture of MAMCO Manufacturing, Incorporated
February 2, 1990

The President announced his decision today to order the China National Aero-Technology Import and Export Company (CATIC) to divest its interest in MAMCO, Inc., a company located in Seattle, WA, that machines and fabricates metal parts for aircraft.

The President took this action pursuant to a section of the 1988 Trade Act often referred to as the Exon-Florio provision. That provision amended the Defense Production Act of 1950 to give the President the power to suspend or prohibit an acquisition of a U.S. company by a foreign party if the President makes certain findings with respect to that acquisition. The President made the requisite findings in this case. Specifically, based on credible confidential information, the President determined that CATIC's continued control of MAMCO might threaten to impair the national security. Moreover, the President determined that no other provision of law provided him

with adequate and appropriate authority to protect the national security in this case.

The United States welcomes foreign direct investment in this country; it provides foreign investors fair, equitable, and nondiscriminatory treatment. This administration is committed to maintaining that policy. There are circumstances in which the United States maintains limited exceptions to such treatment. Generally these exceptions are necessary to protect national security. Of those foreign mergers, acquisitions, and takeovers which have been reviewed under the Exon-Florio provision to determine effects on national security, this is the first time the President invoked Exon-Florio authority. The President's action in this case is in response to circumstances of this particular transaction. It does not change our policy and is not a precedent for the future with regard to direct investment in the United States from the People's Republic of China or any other country.

Question-and-Answer Session With High School Students at a Biotechnology Demonstration at the University of Tennessee at Knoxville
February 2, 1990

The President. What year of high school are we talking about?

Q. Junior and senior.

The President. Juniors and seniors? Well, let me start before she reads me her Gettysburg Address here and before she unloads on me, too. [*Laughter*]

Are you all in high school? Are you beginning to get more emphasis on science courses? Everybody? I mean, that's a common thread here. You wouldn't be here if you weren't already taking—what?—chemistry, biology, physics. What else, what other subjects? Math—yes, math would be fundamental. Have most of you made up your mind, when you go to college—going into science or math? You've already determined?

Dr. Monty. That's why they are here. They are those who have been selected because they are interested in science or mathematics.

The President. Okay, you get equal time. Go ahead. [*Laughter*]

Education Reform

Q. I loved your State of the Union Address on improving education. I was wondering, do you have any plans to get ideas internationally to improve education?

The President. Well, I'm going to kick that one right into the end zone of the Secretary of Education. But, yes, we have all—he travels a good deal, goes abroad. We have a lot of people in the Department that does that. We're having an international—this is not as much education as dealing with the environment—a big international conference coming up. And we get it all the time—exchanges of ideas.

But I think we've got—we set out there—and I want to give credit to your Governor McWherter and to your former Governor Lamar Alexander—we've gotten great ideas for a national goals program from—in this country—from the Governors who were responding to, maybe, the principal of your

high school, for heaven's sake. But I think we now don't need as many of the ideas from abroad as we do to implement these broad goals that are now set in place. Not that we can't learn from others, because some other countries are doing a whale of a job in education. But I think we've got our priorities set.

I still believe that a lot of the emphasis has to be at the local and State level. The Federal Government cannot dictate to your high school the curriculum or exactly what your teachers have to teach. We've learned a lot from those who have been successful abroad, but now I think we've got the information; we've got to go forward—is about the way I answer that.

Q. I would like to know, what plans do you have to fund scholarships for students who excel in math and science?

The President. Well, I'll give that one to him. But we have stepped up that in our budget; we've stepped it up. But go ahead, Larry.

Secretary Cavazos. We certainly have—quite a bit. That's one of the key points in the President's Excellence Act in Education: to identify outstanding students in mathematics and science, and provide scholarships for them for 4 years of college. That's the first step. But actually, it's right down the line. On top of that, we have increased funds for Pell grants, as well as for guaranteed student loans. So, we're certainly looking to that aspect of it and putting major emphasis on math and science.

The President. The first part, Jeanine—we haven't got it through yet. We've made the proposals. I think we've got a good chance in the Congress, but we have not got it passed. I think the Federal Government has a legitimate role there, just as we do in—you guys are past this stage—but in Head Start. One of the things that—when I first got working on this was back when Lamar Alexander was Governor. He kept talking about "ready to learn." And as I say, you all are past that, but there's a lot of kids out there that need to be ready to learn when they go to the first grade. So, along with the things that Jeanine was asking about, we think we must do better. And this is one of our national goals in terms of Head Start—getting people ready at the very beginning.

Who else has something they want to say? Yes, Stephanie.

Q. I was wondering if you were planning on starting the younger students in school with math and science, getting them a stronger base before high school and further education.

The President. We're trying to do that. Again, the curriculum must be set by the schools; but the emphasis—the goals of fluency in math and science, if you would—at an early age is out there now. And what the President should do, our Secretary, and then a Secretary like Secretary Watkins—whose whole success of the Department of Energy relates to—an awful lot relates to science and, thus, math feeding into that—is to exhort. I don't think we can dictate to the school level, the early school levels. We can't do that. But when you set the goals—and the Governors, for the most part, are on board. I think Governor McWherter approves of our broad goals. And all of us have a job of encouraging what you're talking about. So, I think we'll see that result if our national goals—as they move towards implementation, I think we'll see those things come into play.

I have a technical question here. I wonder why it's only the women, only the girls, that ask questions. Now, Daniel, I don't know whether you've got one.

Q. Is the Federal Government increasing in spending for special interest education programs?

The President. Let me ask the Secretary.

Secretary Watkins. Well, the answer is yes. And the President will be presented from his Domestic Policy Council with an entirely new initiative: that we in the Federal Government open our hearts and minds a lot more than we have in the past. For example, we have 23,000 scientists in our national laboratories—two-thirds of the intellectual potential of the Nation in science. And therefore, the reason you see

them so involved with you, in Oak Ridge and here in Knoxville, is that we have this kind of capability to bring new motivation and excitement, particularly to minorities and young women who in many areas of the country have been really denied math and science. And in fact, many are afraid.

And so, this whole program is going to be set up to get us involved, open our facilities to the local school districts—not to set curriculum, as the President said, at all but to get us involved. His Thousand Points of Light program—that's what we're talking about: getting our scientists to teach in the classroom, to teach teachers, to provide you with opportunities to go to the laboratories and see the excitement of science and be involved in it.

This decade will be the decade of science and research. And the President has opened that door with the most incredible research program and enhancement of education—and leading the way in the Nation with your speech before the joint session of Congress the other night.

So, this is the excitement. We're very much involved. You'll see much more coming up as this begins to unfold.

The President. I'm sure I would have got a lot better audience for the State of the Union, but I made the mistake in scheduling when Vanderbilt was playing Tennessee in basketball. [*Laughter*] So, I'm sure all you students watched the State of the Union, but I don't know. [*Laughter*]

Stanley, what do you got?

Q. I would just basically like to know that, since the population of black male students enrolled in colleges has dropped over the past decade, would that mean greater or lesser chances of us receiving money from the Government?

The President. I think what Dr. Cavazos was talking about will impact heavily in some minority areas that had not had too good a shot. And also, some of that depends on how the output goes not just for black people but white as well—how they do in the elementary schools.

So, as we move toward programs in—I mentioned Head Start. A lot of kids coming out of the background where they haven't really had much dough in the family, or a broken family, or something—those kids really need Head Start more than others. And so, I think if we get the whole elementary thing moving so that the kids—a lot of the kids you're talking about are like you, who have demonstrated an ability and have demonstrated excellence. I think you'll find there will be just more acceptance under existing programs. But I think we have some emphasis here that will benefit minority students, whether it's blacks or Hispanics or whatever.

Secretary Cavazos. There's quite a bit of it. It's there. And of course, as you point out, Mr. President, we're looking at the whole stance, from early childhood right on through the other end of college and on into adult education. And we have to put a special emphasis—you are so correct. The numbers are going down in terms of black males in colleges. We have to turn that around. We're losing a lot of very, very fine potential students out of the system, so we have to stop and back up to the beginning. So, we will find—dedicating in that direction.

The President. One thing we've done that really isn't directly responsive, but I've long been interested in historically black colleges, and we've stepped up the help for them, their endowment funding, which a lot of the black presidents of these colleges feel is very, very important. I think it's gone way up this year, maybe by 66 percent or something.

So, anyway, that's another—but it's not directly responsive, but it's so—the idea that everybody should be able to get a good education.

Dr. Monty. Mr. President, we probably have time for one or two more questions. Two of those here are outstanding math and science teachers, and they're probably holding back, trying to give the students a chance.

The President. I'd love to hear how you think it's going. I'm on a listening mode here on this trip, so I'd like to know—or if you had any specific suggestions as to how you see our departments interacting.

Q. Mr. President, there's tremendous positive advances taking place. But in education, we sort of get a mixed message sometimes. There's much discussion in many circles about catching up with European countries as far as science and math education is concerned. As a rule, that's related to standardized test scores. So, we're getting, on the one hand, that we need to increase standardized test scores and, then on the other hand, we need to increase problemsolving and creative thinking skills at the same time.

Now, they are certainly compatible to teach at the same time. But as a rule, it takes experience and training to take the subject matter and teach creativity mutually, or at the same time. And I'm wondering if there are any plans for special training that would be related to special programs? But it's a mixed message. And for clarification, particularly for inexperienced teachers, I think it's going to take some kind of a training program.

The President. Special training for teachers? Larry, do you have anything on the Federal side on that?

Secretary Cavazos. Well, in terms of the current budget that we have in front of us, we have about a 62-percent increase in the math and science education area, and it approaches almost $300 million that we'll be putting in next year in this direction. We're also going to have another program that we've requested money for—to also prepare principals, give them a special education, because, obviously, they're the people involved in the curriculum and the kinds of things that go on on a day-to-day basis.

So, this is a partnership. And we really have a commitment to help out in the area of math and science and the preparation of those teachers—but we're also going to include the principals.

The President. Now some of the States are doing—go ahead. You were going to say something.

Q. Just in followup. If there was a direction, should it be toward the problemsolving and creativity—the kind of creativity and creative thinking that it takes to come up with solutions to problems—developing this kind of research? Or should it be in the direction toward the standardized test scores, where basically, it's just the foundational material that——

Secretary Cavazos. I think a lot of that

can be worked out as we develop these programs with the people. However, my own instincts toward problemsolving and comprehension—as you recognize, our students can read, but oftentimes when we look at our national tests, they don't comprehend at adequate levels. And I think until we can really comprehend and understand what we're dealing with, all the rest of this will give us no purpose.

The President. Mary, do you want to add something?

Q. Well, I would just follow up to Tom. I, too, am concerned about the quality of teachers that we're going to be getting into science and math. And that has such far-ranging implications for just the quality of the high school, but also for elementary education—getting kids interested in science and math. And I, too, am very concerned about just the quality of teacher that we're going to get into science and math, and encouraging young people to go into the science- and math-related fields, but also to go into teaching, too.

The President. Again, just so you know where I'm coming from philosophically, I think we can encourage; but I think it's the responsibility of the States and then of the local organizations to actually sign people up and—I just don't want to see our federalizing our elementary, secondary, and higher education. The Federal Government has a distinct role, but I don't want to misrepresent to these kids that I think the Federal Government should undertake all the training for teachers, for example, or set the levels of pay for teachers—I worry—or curriculum. And I think we've got a pretty good balance right now.

Let me say to you kids, because we've got—I know you know a lot about the Government, but you met with—this is Secretary Cavazos, who is the Secretary of Education; Secretary Watkins, who is the Secretary of Energy. But I don't know that you met—we have four Members of Congress here. You guys may be math and scientists, but I'm a political guy, see. So, I've got to—but I hope sometime you will save a little time for the public service kind of things that—but over here is Congressman Quillen, Congressman Duncan, and Congressman Sundquist, and over here, Congress-

man Lloyd. So, they, too, are along with us today and are very interested. They don't happen to be all from Tennessee, but I wanted to put in a plug for them down the line—and public service as well.

I don't want to undermine all these Oak Ridge scientists here and get away from the subject at hand, but I'm very pleased these Congressmen are with us.

Q. I would like to commend the State for having our school. School of the Sciences made science, many times, fun. It showed that science is not just a textbook study: it's something that can change the world, literally. And I think it influenced a lot of the kids here who were going to school. I think it made us more interested and got us enthused to go forward in science and not just hold back.

The President. See, here, that's a very important point he's just made, because now, with the encouragement of the State, encouragement of the university, then other States and other communities—we were talking about this coming in in the car with the two Governors—other States and other communities can see the example here.

This is, I think, a first, actually—at least the summer program that you're talking about. I'm glad that you feel that way because it gives me the thought that if we can just get the message out, others on their own will take up this kind of a program—kind of approach, you mean, to science and math.

Dr. Monty. Mr. President, I feel like a schoolbell, but I've been asked to tell you that it's time for you to move on. These are exceptional students and exceptional teachers, and we're privileged that you would take time, along with the Secretaries, to visit with us.

The President. I'm glad you all came. Thanks. Thanks for taking the time.

Do you all know exactly where you want to go to college and exactly what you want to do? [*Laughter*] No? I never did, either—really. But anyway, thank you all for your time. I bet we had some other questioners or speakers we did not hear from.

Computers

Q. I'd just like to ask, what role will computers play in the school system in the future?

The President. More and more. And I don't even know how to turn one on—hardly. [*Laughter*] But, no, I can do that. I can write a letter. But, no, I think you're going to see that everybody is going to have to be computer literate. I think that's a given in the nineties, absolute given, for whatever you want to be—liberal arts, science and tech. So, I think you're going to see that just all over.

All right. Thank you. Thanks a lot.

Note: The President spoke at 2:25 p.m. at Carolyn Brown University Center. In his remarks, he referred to Kenneth J. Monty, professor of biochemistry; high school students Jeanine Fulton, Stephanie A. Burriesei, Daniel H. Chang, and Stanley Dean; Mary Boldon, biology teacher at Maryville High School; and Tom Ferguson, biology teacher at Farragut High School. Prior to the demonstration, the President met with university professors and scientists at the center.

Remarks to Students and Faculty of the University of Tennessee at Knoxville
February 2, 1990

Thank you, Lamar Alexander. You all may remember this, but when Lamar Alexander was the Governor, out of all the 50 Governors he probably did more to take action in the field of education than any other Governor. And now he's bringing his talents to bear at this great university system. I'm very proud of him.

And I'm very proud to be with Governor McWherter. And I noticed the enthusiastic reception to your latest addition to the educational scene—latest support for it. I salute you. I'm very proud of my Secretary of Education, a former university president himself, Dr. Larry Cavazos, who's with us today—doing a superb job. And of course, Admiral Watkins, bringing to the Energy Department as Secretary not only expertise in the nuclear field and certainly, based on his background in the military, military expertise, but a strong commitment to education. And both of them are doing a great job for our country. I'm pleased that Alvin Trivelpiece, the Oak Ridge National Lab Director, is here with us today; also four Members of the United States Congress—Jimmy Quillen and John Duncan, Don Sundquist, Marilyn Lloyd. And I, of course, am very pleased to see another old friend, longstanding, your mayor, Victor Ashe; and, of course, Howard Baker. I don't believe we've had a public servant of his decency

and honor in the arena for a long time. He is outstanding—was, still is. And so, Howard, I'm delighted to see you again.

And I'm sorry we were a little late getting in here. But you know how it is on this campus. Even I couldn't find a parking place. [*Laughter*]

It's great to be back in Tennessee. I'm very proud of this State and this university. And I noticed that Lamar said some of you noticed the T-shirt that I had on while I was jogging down in Texas in December—the Big Orange colors of the Tennessee Volunteers. Well, back in Washington, they debated which move took more guts, invading Panama or going to Texas wearing a Big Orange T-shirt. [*Laughter*] I got the shirt in Washington when Pat Summitt came to the Rose Garden last April with Tennessee's Lady Volunteers, the 1989 NCAA national champions. And it was a great day.

And when they came to Washington the Lady Vols had only one request. Not to see the Oval Office. Not to see the Smithsonian, the Wright brothers' plane. Not even Georgetown at night. What they wanted to see was Millie's new puppies. [*Laughter*] And that's a fact, too.

Of course, we said yes, but now it's my turn. And as long as I'm at UT, it seems I ought to get to meet Smokey, from what they tell me. [*Laughter*]

I'm proud of Tennessee and your great sports traditions. But the truth is what makes this university so special says a lot about what makes America so special. It's not the winner's trophy at the end of the quest: It's the quest itself. And in Tennessee, as in America, that means the quest for excellence. At UT, the quest for excellence starts not on the basketball court or the football field but in the classroom. Maybe you heard that at the White House I bragged as much about the Lady Vols' 14 years with a 100-percent graduation rate as I did about that fantastic basketball championship.

Earlier this week, I issued my first formal budget as President, a blueprint for the year ahead. And 2 days ago, I stood in the U.S. Capitol, stood before the American people, and reported to you on the state of the Union. Don't worry. If you missed the speech, you're not going to hear the two words that strike terror in the hearts of every college student: pop quiz. [*Laughter*] You have an excuse, because our timing was not exactly fortuitous. I understand that while I was orating there before the Congress the Vols were playing—what was it?—Vanderbilt in basketball, and some of you had your priorities all screwed up. [*Laughter*] So, I understand that.

But at the heart of the address, though, was a sense of confidence that America today is second to none—and sense of commitment, a plan to keep America second to none in the years ahead. The foundation for our plan, the foundation for our future, is anchored by a cornerstone we call educational excellence. Education really is our most enduring legacy, vital to everything we are and can become. And my budget calls for record funding, reflecting this belief. But as I said Wednesday night, real improvement in our schools is not simply a matter of spending more: it's a matter of asking more—expecting more—of our schools, our teachers, our kids, and ourselves.

You in Tennessee know that goals and high expectations work. Five years ago, Governor Lamar Alexander told Tennessee's eighth-graders, "If you want to go to State universities, you're going to have to take more math and science." And there

was a good deal of grumbling—a little grumpiness about that at first, but today almost all freshmen are meeting those requirements. And as a result, admissions scores are up; retention rates are up; and best of all, 41 percent more students are taking science and math in the high school than were taking those subjects 5 years ago. You expected more, so you got more.

I believe what worked for Tennessee will work for America. And Wednesday night, I announced America's education goals, goals developed in close cooperation with the Governors of the 50 States. And I thank your Governor for participating so actively in these deliberations.

Part of the answer means getting back to basics. Recently one kid was asked if he knew what the three R's were. He said, "Sure. Reading, writing, and remote control." [*Laughter*]

Well, just as we're redoubling our efforts to boost education, so we've doubled the three R's, as well. We have six goals, "six R's," for education in the nineties.

And the first: readiness. By the year 2000, every child in America will start school ready to learn. And we've called for a record increase, a half-billion dollars, to ensure a fair start through Project Head Start.

And our next goal might be called "search and rescue." We will target America's most at-risk youth and get them the help that they need—they deserve. Our 10-year goal: to raise America's high school graduation rate to at least 90 percent.

And third, it's time to reestablish excellence. By the new century, American students will leave grades 4, 8, and 12 having demonstrated competency over the world in which they live—the world of math, science, history, and geography.

And we're calling for a new renaissance in science and math, to make America's students first in the world by the year 2000.

And next: reading. A competitive America must be a literate America, where every man and woman possesses the knowledge and skills necessary to succeed in a global economy.

And then last and most fundamental: In every school in America, we've got to create an environment conducive to learning; and that means disciplined schools, that means—and it must mean—drug-free schools. The solution to chaos in our classrooms is no mystery. Franklin had a word for it—not Ben, Aretha Franklin. She calls it R-E-S-P-E-C-T. Respect. And kids need respect for our wonderful teachers, respect for learning, respect for themselves. And all six goals are important.

And, Lamar, I was thrilled to learn that Tennessee—a major research university and a pillar of the science-rich Oak Ridge Corridor—has already taken the lead in responding to our challenge to use science and technology to boost America's competitiveness. And thanks to Governor McWherter, again, and Norm Augustine, Martin Marietta, and Jim Watkins, the Department of Energy, you will have a new Summer School for Math and Science and a new academy for America's top elementary and high school teachers. And it will be a model for the entire Nation. Unbelievably, it was all put together in a week. And the speed of Tennessee's response proves what we've been saying since I first sent my Educational Excellence package to Congress last spring. The time for study is past; the time for action is now.

You know, building our competitive strength today also means that we need quick congressional action on our other proposals for investing in new capital—intellectual capital. And that includes everything from reforming product liability laws to doubling the budget of the National Science Foundation. It means a record-high increase in funds for research and development, R&D; new help for R&E, research and experimentation, by making the R&E tax credit permanent; and funds to improve education—the Eisenhower Education Grants for math and science would grow by 70 percent to $230 million.

In science and technology, the United States is today—and we should take great pride in this, and there are many men in this room and women in this room today who have made a significant contribution to this—the United States today is the undisputed heavyweight champion of the world. We produce more scholarly works, more breakthroughs, more international prizes than any other country.

But like any champion, we cannot rest on our reputation. More than 30 years ago, "Ike," Dwight Eisenhower, used his State of the Union speech to address a similar challenge. "Our real program," said Ike, "is not our strength today: it is rather the vital necessity of action today to ensure our strength tomorrow."

And today I am taking action by appointing the members of the President's Council of Advisors on Science and Technology. Indeed, my Vice President, Dan Quayle, who's doing such an outstanding job as Chairman of both the National Space Council and the Competitiveness Council, is swearing in the members of this new Council this afternoon. And it's comprised of some of the best scientific minds in the country. We'll meet tomorrow at Camp David to discuss ways to maintain U.S. supremacy in these fields.

One way to do that is by challenging the impossible. And that brings to mind another challenge that will probably mean more to strengthening the educational system and competitive edge than any other single endeavor—and I am talking about space. For in the coming century, first in space will mean first on Earth. And America intends to stay number one.

We need to find ways to do things faster and more efficiently in space. And that's why NASA and our Space Council have called on America's great universities and research centers to put their brightest engineers and scientists to work on coming up with bold, innovative ideas—new technologies for a new tomorrow in space.

Tennessee has already made important contributions to the space program. Rhea Seddon, one of America's first women astronauts, is a graduate of UT's College of Medicine. And researchers at UT's Space Institute in Tullahoma are working with NASA to develop advanced space propulsion systems for the next generation of manned and unmanned missions.

In the new century—your century—those new systems may help take Americans back to the Moon and beyond. Our goal: to place Americans on Mars, and to do it within the working lifetimes of scientists and engineers who will be recruited for the effort today. And just as Jefferson sent Lewis and Clark to open the continent, our commitment to the Moon-Mars initiative will indeed open the universe. It's the opportunity of a lifetime and offers a lifetime of opportunity.

Yet some wonder if America has lost its competitive edge and ask if we must now look overseas for the answer. They point to last week's launch in Japan—a new satellite sent to orbit the Moon. They forget 26 years ago today, long before some of you were born, America's Ranger Six landed on the Moon—26 years ago.

The United States is the "defending world champion." But we have to defend our title day by day, week by week, year in and year out. The Tennessee of Bob Neyland and Johnny Majors, of Wade Houston and Pat Summitt, knows something about defending athletic dynasties. Here it's done the old-fashioned way, the Tennessee way, the American way. You can play smart, but there are no shortcuts. It takes hard work and grit. It demands the constant renewal of new talent and ideas, always tempered by veteran coaching. And it means sweating harder, reaching higher, and seeing farther than the other guy.

It's never easy keeping that number one ranking. Pat Summitt said it in 1984, just before bringing the U.S. Women's Basketball Team to an Olympic Gold Medal. She said, "We're expected to win. That's a greater challenge than when you're expected to finish second." But she's right. Pat's right. We're going to need as never before that "can do" attitude that brought our ancestors to America and that brought Amer-

ica to greatness. In World War I, when they asked your own Sergeant York how he captured 132 enemy prisoners and 32 machineguns all by himself, he answered, "I surrounded 'em." [*Laughter*] And that's what some might expect from a Tennessean. [*Laughter*] But really, it's that kind of spirit that is going to carry us into the 21st century and beyond.

And as we approach the challenges of tomorrow, in a world increasingly hungry for yesterday's values, I hope that you'll continue to give voice to this State's frontier virtues: hard work; loyalty; love of faith, family, and the Volunteer State.

And when we hear America singing, it is often the sound of Tennessee: bluegrass fiddling in the mountains; the gospel and country sound of Nashville; the jazz, the blues of Memphis. It's the stuff of legend, the spirit of faith and hope. And with spirit like that, America's going to do a Tennessee waltz all over our competition.

So, thank you for this warm welcome. Thank you for this welcome. And God bless you, and God bless the United States of America. Thank you all very, very much.

Note: The President spoke at 3:25 p.m. in Alumni Memorial Gymnasium. In his remarks, he referred to Norman R. Augustine, chairman and chief executive officer of Martin Marietta Corp.; and Robert R. Neyland, John T. Majors, and Wade Houston, former head football coach, current head football coach, and head coach for men's basketball at the university. Following his remarks, the President traveled to Camp David, MD, for the weekend.

Appointment of the Members of the President's Council of Advisors on Science and Technology, and Designation of the Chairman and Vice Chairman
February 2, 1990

The President today announced the appointment of the President's Council of Advisors on Science and Technology (PCAST), comprised of 12 distinguished scientists and engineers. This panel will provide high-level advice directly to the President on a wide range of important issues concerning science and technology.

PCAST will be the first Presidential scientific advisory group in many years to report directly to the President. Its establishment is a measure of the Bush administration's high esteem for science and a recognition that advances in science and technology contribute in a major way to increased economic competitiveness. It also reflects the President's desire to strengthen Federal science and technology policy, enhance Federal research and development activities, and encourage private sector involvement in research and development.

The United States scientific community leads the world in creating new knowledge. Through PCAST, the President is seeking to provide the best obtainable private sector advice to executive branch decisionmaking in science and technology.

PCAST will be chaired by Dr. D. Allan Bromley, Assistant to the President for Science and Technology. PCAST was established January 19, 1990, by Executive Order 12700. Its members will be sworn in later today by the Vice President at the White House. They include the following individuals:

Norman F. Borlaug, of Texas, is a Nobel laureate and currently leader of the Sasakawa-Global-2000 agricultural program in sub-Saharan Africa, distinguished professor of international agriculture at Texas A&M University, and a senior consultant to CIMMYT. He was director of the wheat research and production program of the International Maize and Wheat Improvement Center, Mexico, from 1964 until his retirement in 1979. Dr. Borlaug's career began in 1935 in the Forest Service, and he subsequently worked as an instructor in plant pathology at the University of Minnesota in 1941, where he received his Ph.D. From 1942 through 1944, he was a microbiologist with E.I. DuPont de Nemours & Co. He also served as research scientist in charge of wheat improvement with the cooperative Mexican agricultural program, Mexican Ministry of Agriculture and the Rockefeller Foundation, 1944–60, and later as associate director of the foundation assigned to the inter-American food crop program, 1960–63.

D. Allan Bromley, Chairman, of Connecticut, is Assistant to the President for Science and Technology and Director of the Office of Science and Technology Policy (OSTP). Dr. Bromley carried out pioneering studies on both the structure and dynamics of nuclei and is considered the father of modern heavy ion science. He has played major roles in the development of accelerators, of detection systems, and in computer-based data acquisition and analysis systems. He is currently on leave from his position as Henry Ford II professor of physics at Yale University, where he was founder and director of the A.W. Wright Nuclear Structure Laboratory. Dr. Bromley has been a leader in the national and international science and science policy communities for more than 20 years, serving as a member of the White House Science Council throughout the Reagan administration and as a member of the National Science Board in 1988–89. He received the President's National Medal of Science in 1988 and the Presidential Medal of the New York Academy of Sciences in 1989. He has served as president of the American Association for the Advancement of Science and of the International Union of Pure and Applied Physics. Dr. Bromley received the B.Sc. degree in 1948 at Queen's University, Canada, the M.Sc. degree from Queen's University in 1950, and the Ph.D. degree in nuclear physics from the University of Rochester in 1952. He has since been awarded 10 honorary doctorates.

Solomon J. Buchsbaum, of New Jersey, has been senior vice president, technology systems, at AT&T Bell Laboratories since 1979. His early career included work at the MIT Research Laboratory of Electronics. He received his Ph.D. in physics from MIT in 1957. He joined Bell Laboratories in 1958 as a member of the technical staff and later became department head and director of the Electronics Research Laboratory. In 1968 he was named vice president for research at the Sandia Laboratories and served in a number of different capacities. He returned to Bell Laboratories in 1971 as an executive director. In 1976 he became vice president, network planning and customer systems. Dr. Buchsbaum is a member of the National Academy of Sciences and of the National Academy of Engineering. He was the recipient of the President's National Medal of Science in 1986.

Charles L. Drake, of Vermont, has been the Albert Bradley professor of earth sciences at Dartmouth since 1984 and professor of geology since 1969. Dr. Drake's professional career began at Columbia University in 1953. He joined the staff at Dartmouth in 1958 after receiving his Ph.D. in geology from Columbia University, where he has continued his career, including service as professor and chairman of the department, 1967–69; as dean of graduate studies, and as associate dean of the science department, 1978–81. Dr. Drake is a recipient of the G.P. Woollard Award, Geophysical Division of the Geological Society of America.

Ralph E. Gomory, of New York, is president of the Sloan Foundation and, until his recent retirement, was senior vice president for science and technology, IBM Corp. He received his Ph.D. in mathematics from Princeton in 1954. Dr. Gomory's professional experience includes teaching and research at Princeton from 1957 to 1959. In 1959 he joined the research division of IBM and was named director of the mathematical sciences department in 1965. In 1970 he became IBM director of research and held that position until 1985, becoming IBM vice president in 1973, senior vice president in 1985, and IBM senior vice president for science and technology in 1986. He has been awarded a number of honorary degrees and prizes, including the John von Neumann Theory Prize in 1984 and the National Medal of Science in 1988.

Bernadine Healy, Vice Chairman, of Ohio, is chairman of the Research Institute of the Cleveland Clinic Foundation, a position she assumed in 1985, and is a staff member of the clinic's department of cardiology. Prior to that time, she was Deputy Director of the Office of Science and Technology Policy at the White House and, until that appointment, had been a professor at the Johns Hopkins University School of Medicine and Hospital. Dr. Healy received her medical degree from Harvard Medical School in 1970. Her medical career continued at Johns Hopkins from 1976 to 1984, where she was professor of cardiology and medicine, director of the coronary care unit, and assistant dean for postdoctoral programs and faculty development. Dr. Healy is a member of the Institute of Medicine of the National Academy of Sciences. She is the immediate past president of the American Heart Association and a former president of the American Federation for Clinical Research.

Peter W. Likins, of Pennsylvania, has been president of Lehigh University since 1982. His professional career began as a development engineer with the Jet Propulsion Laboratory, California Institute of Technology, in 1958. In 1964 he joined the faculty at the University of California at Los Angeles, where he became professor of engineering and, later, associate dean. Dr. Likins received his Ph.D. in engineering mechanics from Stanford in 1965. In 1976 he became professor and dean of Columbia University, serving until 1980, when he became provost of the university.

Thomas E. Lovejoy, of Virginia, is the Assistant Secretary for External Affairs, the Smithsonian Institution. His previous experience includes service as a research assistant at the University of Pennsylvania, 1971–74, after receiving his Ph.D. in biology from Yale University in 1971; as executive assistant to the science director and as assistant to the vice president for resources and planning of the Academy of Natural Sciences, 1972–73; as the vice president for science of the World Wildlife Fund-U.S., 1973–87; and as executive vice president, 1985–89. Dr. Lovejoy is president of the Society for Conservation Biology.

Walter E. Massey, of Illinois, has been the vice president of the University of Chicago for research and for Argonne National Laboratory since 1984. He has also been professor of physics at the university since 1979. Dr. Massey previously served as a physics instructor at Morehouse College, 1958–59; and after receiving his Ph.D. in physics from Washington University in 1966, as a staff physicist with the Argonne National Laboratory until 1968; as assistant professor of physics, University of Illinois at Urbana, 1968–70; and as associate professor of physics and dean of the college, Brown University, 1975–79. He is vice president and president-elect of the American Physical Society and is the past president and chairman of the American Association for the Advancement of Science.

John P. McTague, of Michigan, is vice president-research, Ford Motor Co., and has served in that position since 1986. In 1983 Dr. McTague was appointed Deputy Director of the Office of Science and Technology Policy, becoming Acting Science Advisor to the President and Acting Director of OSTP in 1986. Prior to that, he was chairman of the national synchrotron light source department, Brookhaven National Laboratory, 1982–83. He was professor of chemistry and a member of the Institute of Geophysics and Planetary Physics, University of California at Los Angeles, 1970–82. Dr. McTague began his professional career as a member of the technical staff, North American Aviation Science Center, on receiving his Ph.D. in physical chemistry from Boston University, and remained there until 1970. He is U.S. Chairman of the U.S.-Japan Joint High Level Advisory Panel on Cooperation in Research and Development in Science and Technology.

Daniel Nathans, of Maryland, is a Nobel laureate, and a professor of molecular biology and genetics at the Johns Hopkins University Medical School and senior investigator of the Howard Hughes Medical Institute. He has been on the faculty of the Johns Hopkins University Medical School since 1962. After receiving his medical degree from Washington University in 1954, he served as medical resident at the Columbia-Presbyterian Medical Center in New York, 1955, 1957–59; as clinical associate at the National Cancer Institute, 1955–57; and guest investigator in biochemistry at the Rockefeller University, 1959–62. Dr. Nathans received the Nobel Prize in physiology or medicine in 1978 for his research with enzymes that cut DNA into specific pieces, one of the basic tools of genetic engineering.

David Packard, of California, has been chairman of the board of the Hewlett-Packard Co. since 1972. Mr. Packard received his B.A. and B.S.E.E. degrees from Stanford University in 1934 and 1939, respectively. His professional experience includes service as an engineer with the vacuum tube engineering department, GE Co., 1936–38; cofounder and partner, the Hewlett-Packard Co., 1939–47; president, 1947–64; and chairman and chief execu-

tive officer, 1964–69. Prior to his present position, Mr. Packard served as U.S. Deputy Secretary of Defense from 1969 to 1971. Mr. Packard received the Vannevar Bush Award of the National Science Board in 1987, and the President's National Medal of Technology and the Presidential Medal of Freedom in 1988.

Harold T. Shapiro, of New Jersey, has been president of Princeton University since 1988. Dr. Shapiro's previous academic experience has been with the University of Michigan, after receiving his Ph.D. in economics from Princeton in 1964, first as an assistant professor of economics. His career progressed from associate professor, 1967–70; professor, 1970–76; chairman of the department of economics, 1974–77; professor of economics and public policy, 1977; vice president for academic affairs, 1977–79. Dr. Shapiro was president of the University of Michigan from 1980 to 1987. He has served as a member of many industrial, governmental, and academic boards and commissions.

Appointment of Katherine E. Boyd as a Member of the Advisory Council on Historic Preservation
February 2, 1990

The President today announced his intention to appoint Katherine E. Boyd to be a member of the Advisory Council on Historic Preservation for a term of 4 years expiring June 10, 1993. She would succeed Jennifer B. Dunn.

Since 1965 Mrs. Boyd has been president

of her own interior design business, Katherine E. Boyd Interior Decoration in California.

Mrs. Boyd was born February 1, 1921, in San Francisco, CA. She is married, has three children, and currently resides in Hillsborough, CA.

Message to the Senate Transmitting the Federal Republic of Germany-United States Convention on Taxation and Fiscal Evasion
February 5, 1990

To the Senate of the United States:

I transmit herewith for Senate advice and consent to ratification the Convention between the United States of America and the Federal Republic of Germany for the Avoidance of Double Taxation and the Prevention of Fiscal Evasion with respect to Taxes on Income and Capital and to Certain Other Taxes, together with a related Protocol, signed at Bonn on August 29,

1989. I also transmit the report of the Department of State on the convention.

The convention replaces the tax convention that was signed with the Federal Republic of Germany on July 22, 1954, and amended by the protocol of September 17, 1965. It is based on model income tax treaties developed by the Department of the Treasury and the Organization for Economic Cooperation and Development. However, it includes a number of new provisions to accommodate important aspects of the Tax Reform Act of 1986, such as the imposition of a branch tax and strong measures to prevent "treaty shopping."

I recommend the Senate give early and favorable consideration to the convention, together with a related protocol, and give its advice and consent to ratification.

GEORGE BUSH

The White House,
February 5, 1990.

Message to the Senate Transmitting the Finland-United States Convention on Taxation and Fiscal Evasion
February 5, 1990

To the Senate of the United States:

I transmit herewith for Senate advice and consent to ratification the Convention between the Government of the United States of America and the Government of the Republic of Finland for the Avoidance of Double Taxation and the Prevention of Fiscal Evasion with Respect to Taxes on Income and on Capital, signed at Helsinki on September 21, 1989. I also transmit the report of the Department of State on the convention.

The convention would replace the existing income tax treaty with Finland that was signed on March 6, 1970. It is based on the model income tax conventions of the Organization for Economic Cooperation and Development and the Department of the Treasury and takes into account the changes in United States income tax law resulting from the Tax Reform Act of 1986.

The convention contains provisions designed to prevent third-country residents from taking unwarranted advantage of the convention by routing income from one Contracting State through an entity created in the other. The convention also provides for the exchange of information by the competent authorities of the Contracting States.

I recommend the Senate give early and favorable consideration to the convention and give its advice and consent to ratification.

GEORGE BUSH

The White House,
February 5, 1990.

Remarks to the Intergovernmental Panel on Climate Change
February 5, 1990

Thank you, Dr. Bolin, and thank you for all you're doing in leading this very important effort here. To Professor Obasi and Dr. Tolba and all the delegates of the World Meteorological Organization and the UNEP, the United Nations Environment Programme, let me commend all of you for coming together to examine an issue of such great importance.

I also want to salute Bill Reilly, our able EPA Administrator. He will become the next Cabinet official in the U.S. Government. I want to thank Assistant Secretary [of State] Bernthal for his leadership from the U.S. side of things and also salute my able Science Advisor, who is with us today, Dr. Bromley, who many of you know.

The recommendations that this distinguished organization makes can have a profound effect on the world's environmental and economic policy. By being here today, I hope to underscore my country's and my own personal concern about your work, about environmental stewardship, and to reaffirm our commitment to finding responsible solutions. It's both an honor and a pleasure to be the first American President to speak to this organization, as its work takes shape.

You're called upon to deliver recommendations which strike a difficult and yet critical international bargain: a convergence between global environmental policy and global economic policy, a bargain where both perspectives benefit and neither is compromised. As experts, you understand that economic growth and environmental integrity need not be contradictory priorities. One reinforces and complements the other; each, a partner. Both are crucial. A sound environment is the basis for the continuity and quality of human life and enterprise. Clearly, strong economies allow nations to fulfill the obligations of environmental stewardship. Where there is economic strength, such protection is possible. But where there is poverty, the competition for resources gets much tougher; stewardship suffers.

For all of these reasons, I sincerely believe we must do everything in our power to promote global cooperation—for environmental protection and economic growth, for intelligent management of our natural resources and efficient use of our industrial capacity, and for sustainable and environmentally sensitive development around the world.

The United States is strongly committed to the IPCC process of international cooperation on global climate change. We consider it vital that the community of nations be drawn together in an orderly, disciplined, rational way to review the history of our global environment, to assess the potential for future climate change, and to develop effective programs. The state of the science, the social and economic impacts, and the appropriate strategies all are crucial components to a global resolution. The stakes here are very high; the consequences, very significant.

The United States remains committed to aggressive and thoughtful action on environmental issues. Last week, in my State of the Union Address, I spoke of stewardship because I believe it's something we owe ourselves, our children, and their children.

So, we are renewing the ethic of stewardship in our domestic programs; in our work to forge international agreements; in our assistance to developing and East-bloc nations; and here, by chairing the Response Strategies Working Group.

I have just submitted a budget to our Congress for fiscal 1991. It includes over $2 billion in new spending to protect the environment. And underscoring our commitment to your efforts, I am pleased to note that funding for the U.S. Global Change Research Program will increase by nearly 60 percent, to over $1 billion. That commitment, by far the largest ever made by any nation, reflects our determination to improve our understanding of the science of climate change. We are working with our neighbors around the world to enhance global monitoring and data management, improve analysis, reduce the uncertainty of predictive models, and conduct regular reassessments of the state of science.

Our program allows NASA and her sister agencies and all our international partners to move forward with the Mission to Planet Earth. That will initiate the U.S. Earth Observing System, in cooperation with Europe and Japan, to advance the state of knowledge about the planet we share. Furthermore, even as we wait for the benefits of this research, the United States has already taken many steps in our country that bring both economic and environmental benefits, steps that make sense on their own merits in terms of responsibility and efficiency, which help reduce emissions of CFC's and carbon dioxide and other pollutants now entering the atmosphere. Let me outline them very briefly:

We are pursuing new technology development that will increase the efficiency of our energy use and thus reduce total emissions.

We're crafting a revised Clean Air Act with incentives for our private sector to find creative, market-driven solutions to enhance air quality.

We've launched a major reforestation initiative to plant a billion trees a year on the private land across America.

And we're working out a comprehensive review and revision of our national energy strategy, with initiatives to increase energy efficiency and the use of renewable sources.

These efforts, already underway, are the heart of a $336 million Department of Energy program and are expected to produce energy savings through the year 2000 of over $30 billion while achieving significant pollution reduction. Quite a return on investment.

We're also working, through diplomatic channels with our colleagues in other countries and through innovative measures like debt-for-nature swaps, to do more than simply reduce global deforestation. We hope to reverse it, turn it around, not unilaterally but by working with our international neighbors.

The economics of our response strategies to climate change are getting intensive study here in our country, in the United States. We're developing real data on the costs of various strategies, assessing new measures, and encouraging other nations to follow suit. And we look forward to sharing this knowledge and technical support with our international colleagues. As we work to create policy and agreements on action, we want to encourage the most creative, effective approaches. Wherever possible, we believe that market mechanisms should be applied and that our policies must be consistent with economic growth and free-market principles in all countries. Our development efforts and our dialog can help us reach effective and acceptable solutions.

Last December at Malta, in my meeting with President Gorbachev, I proposed that the United States offer a venue for the first negotiating session for a framework convention, once the IPCC completes its work. I reiterate that invitation here and look forward to your cooperation in that agenda.

We all know that human activities are changing the atmosphere in unexpected and in unprecedented ways. Much remains to be done. Many questions remain to be answered. Together, we have a responsibility to ourselves and the generations to come to fulfill our stewardship obligations. But that responsibility demands that we do it right. We acknowledge a broad spectrum of views on these issues, but our respect for a diversity of perspective does not diminish our recognition of our obligation or soften

our will to produce policies that work. Some may be tempted to exploit legitimate concerns for political positioning. Our responsibility is to maintain the quality of our approach, our commitment to sound science, and an open mind to policy options.

So, the United States will continue its efforts to improve our understanding of climate change—to seek hard data, accurate models, and new ways to improve the science—and determine how best to meet these tremendous challenges. Where politics and opinion have outpaced the science, we are accelerating our support of the technology to bridge that gap. And we are committed to coming together periodically for international assessments of where we stand. Therefore, this spring the United States will host a White House conference on science and economic research on the environment, convening top officials from a representative group of nations to bring together the three essential disciplines—science, economics, and ecology. They will share their knowledge, assumptions, and state-of-the-art research models to outline our understanding and help focus our efforts. I look forward, personally, to participating in this seminar and to learning from its deliberations.

Our goal continues to be matching policy commitments to emerging scientific knowledge and a reconciling of environmental protection to the continued benefits of economic development. And as Secretary Baker observed a year ago, whatever global solutions to climate change are considered, they should be as specific and as cost-effective as they can possibly be. If we hope to promote environmental protection and economic growth around the world, it will be important not to work in conflict but with our industrial sectors. That will mean moving beyond the practice of command, control, and compliance toward a new kind of environmental cooperation and toward an emphasis on pollution prevention rather than mere mitigation and litigation. Many of our industries, in fact, are already providing crucial research and solutions.

One corporation, for example—and there are others, but I'll single out one of them—3M started an in-house program called Pollution Prevention Pays—one company. And that has saved the company well over a half a billion dollars since 1975, prevented 112,000 tons of air pollutants, 15,000 tons of water pollutants, and almost 400,000 tons of sludge and solid waste from being released into the environment. They've done it by rewarding employees for coming up with ideas, and they have clearly demonstrated the benefits of doing it right.

Where developing nations are concerned, I know some argue that we'll have to abandon the free-market principles of prosperous economies. In fact, we think it's all the more crucial in the developing countries to harness incentives of the free enterprise system in the service of the environment. I believe we should make use of what we know. We know that the future of the Earth must not be compromised. We bear a sacred trust in our tenancy here and a covenant with those most precious to us—our children and theirs. We also understand the efficiency of incentives and that well-in-formed free markets yield the most creative solutions. We must now apply the wisdom of that system, the power of those forces, in defense of the environment we cherish.

Working together, with good faith and earnest dialog, I believe we can reconcile vitality with environmental protection. And so, let me commend you on your outstanding work and wish you all deliberate speed in your efforts to address a very difficult but very important human concern.

Thank you all very much. It is a great pleasure to be the first President to address this distinguished group. Thank you very much.

Note: The President spoke at 10:20 a.m. at Georgetown University's Leavey Center. In his remarks, he referred to Bert Bolin, Chairman of the Intergovernmental Panel on Climate Change; G.O.P. Obasi, Secretary General of the World Meteorological Organization; and M.K. Tolba, Executive Director of the United Nations Environment Programme.

Statement by Press Secretary Fitzwater on President Bush's Meeting With President-Elect Luis Alberto Lacalle of Uruguay
February 5, 1990

President Bush met with Uruguayan President-elect Luis Alberto Lacalle for approximately 40 minutes this morning. The two leaders exchanged views on a wide range of bilateral and regional issues, including trade, investment, debt, and the fight against narcotics traffickers. President Bush expressed support for President-elect Lacalle's plans to reform and strengthen Uruguay's economy and stated that the United States would work closely with Uruguay toward this goal. The two Presidents took note of plans for the negotiation of a mutual legal assistance treaty and agreed that such a treaty would be mutually beneficial.

Nomination of Richard E. Bissell To Be an Assistant Administrator of the Agency for International Development
February 5, 1990

The President today announced his intention to nominate Richard E. Bissell to be Assistant Administrator for Science and Technology of the Agency for International Development, U.S. International Development Cooperation Agency. He would succeed Nyle C. Brady.

Since 1986 Dr. Bissell has served as Assistant Administrator for Program and Policy Coordination at the Agency for International Development in Washington, DC. Prior to this, he served as executive editor of the Washington Quarterly, Center for Strategic and International Studies, 1984–1986; Director of Research and Director of Program Development at the U.S. Information Agency in Washington, DC, 1982–1984; and managing editor of ORBIS and director of economic security studies at the Foreign Policy Research Institute in Philadelphia, PA, 1974–1982. In addition, Dr. Bissell served as an adjunct professor and lecturer at Georgetown University, 1984–1986; Johns Hopkins School of Advanced International Studies, 1982; University of Pennsylvania, 1978–1982; Temple University, 1975–1979; and Princeton University, 1974–1976.

Dr. Bissell graduated from Stanford University (B.A., 1968) and the Fletcher School of Law and Diplomacy (M.A., 1970; Ph.D., 1973). He was born January 25, 1946, in Palo Alto, CA. Dr. Bissell is married, has three children, and resides in McLean, VA.

Message to the Congress Transmitting the 1989 Science and Engineering Indicators Report
February 5, 1990

To the Congress of the United States:

Pursuant to 42 U.S.C. 1863(j)(1), I am pleased to submit to the Congress a report of the National Science Board entitled *Science & Engineering Indicators—1989*. This report is the ninth in a continuing series examining key aspects of the status of American science and engineering.

The importance of scientific and engineering research to the well-being of our Nation is widely recognized. Science and engineering play a vital role in maintaining our Nation's defense, improving its health, and increasing its economic productivity.

I commend *Science & Engineering Indicators—1989* to the attention of the Congress and those in the scientific endeavor.

GEORGE BUSH

The White House,
February 5, 1990.

Message to the Congress Transmitting the 1990 Economic Report
February 6, 1990

To the Congress of the United States:

The United States enters the 1990s as a prosperous nation with a healthy and dynamic economy. Our living standards remain well above those of other major industrialized nations, and our prosperity is spread widely. Since 1982, American firms and workers have produced the longest peacetime expansion on record and created more than 20 million jobs. The containment of inflation during this long economic expansion is a milestone in postwar U.S. history.

In 1989, we regained our position as the world's leading exporter and retained our position as the world's leading job creator, with the fraction of the population employed reaching its highest level ever. In all, 2½ million jobs were created in 1989. The unemployment rate fell to levels not seen since the early 1970s, as did jobless rates for blacks and teenagers. The unemployment rate for Hispanics was the lowest since 1980, when the United States began regularly reporting it.

We have proven to the world that economic and political freedom works. After years of economic decline, the people of Eastern Europe are turning toward free markets to revive economic growth and raise living standards. I remain strongly committed to aiding the efforts of these brave men and women to transform their societies—and thereby to change the world.

Despite our successes, we cannot be satisfied with simply sustaining the strong record of the 1980s. We must improve on that record, deal with inherited problems, and meet the new challenges and seize the new opportunities before us.

Goals and Principles

The primary economic goal of my Administration is to achieve the highest possible rate of sustainable economic growth. Achieving this goal will require action on many fronts—but it will permit progress on many more. Growth is the key to raising living standards, to leaving a legacy of prosperity for our children, to uplifting those most in need, and to maintaining America's leadership in the world.

To achieve this goal, we must both enhance our economy's ability to grow and ensure that its potential is more often fully utilized than in previous decades. To these ends, as explained in the *Report* that follows, my Administration will:

- Reduce government borrowing by slowing the growth of Federal spending while economic growth raises revenue until the budget is balanced, and reduce the national debt thereafter;
- Support a credible, systematic monetary policy program that sustains maximum economic growth while controlling and reducing inflation;
- Remove barriers to innovation, investment, work, and saving in the tax, legal, and regulatory systems;
- Avoid unnecessary regulation and design necessary regulatory programs to harness market forces effectively to serve the Nation's interest; and
- Continue to lead the world to freer trade and more open markets, and to support market-oriented reforms around the world.

In advancing these principles, we must be both ambitious and realistic. There is room to improve, and there is much to be done to prepare for the next century. We must not fear to dream great dreams. But we must not fail to do our homework; the American people are ill-served by promises that cannot be kept.

Macroeconomic Prospects and Policies

The economy's performance during 1989, the seventh year of economic expansion, has set the stage for healthy growth in the 1990s. Growth in national output was more moderate in 1989 than the very rapid pace in 1988 and 1987. But, in sharp contrast to most past periods of low unemployment and high capacity utilization, inflation was kept firmly in check. Measured broadly, the price level rose 4.1 percent during 1989, down from 4.5 percent during 1988.

If my budget proposals are adopted, and if the Federal Reserve maintains a credible policy program to support strong noninflationary growth, the economy is projected to expand in 1990 at a slightly faster pace than in 1989. Growth is projected to pick up in the second half of the year and to continue at a strong pace as the level of output rises to the economy's full potential.

Fiscal and monetary policies should establish credible commitments to policy plans aimed at maximizing sustainable growth over the long run. A steady hand at the helm is necessary to produce rapid and continuous increases in employment and living standards.

My budget proposals reflect a strong commitment to the principles of the Gramm-Rudman-Hollings law, which has helped reduce the Federal deficit from 5.3 percent of GNP in fiscal 1986 to 2.9 percent in fiscal 1989. That is why I insisted last fall that the Congress pass a clean reconciliation bill and stood by the sequestration order that resulted from my strict adherence to the Gramm-Rudman-Hollings law.

I have also proposed a fundamental new rule for fiscal policy that would ensure that projected future Social Security surpluses are not spent for other purposes but are used to build the reserves necessary to guarantee the soundness of Social Security. Moreover, it would transform the Federal Government from a chronic borrower, draining savings away from private investment, to a saver, providing funds for capital formation and economic growth by reducing the national debt.

I remain strongly committed to the principles of low marginal tax rates and a broad tax base developed in the Economic Recovery Tax Act of 1981 and the Tax Reform Act of 1986. Steady adherence to these principles reduces government's distorting effect on the market forces that drive economic growth.

I strongly support the Federal Reserve's goal of noninflationary growth and share with them the conviction that inflation must be controlled and reduced in a predictable fashion. Accelerating inflation not only erodes the value of families' savings, it produces economic imbalances and policy responses that often lead to recessions.

The United States is part of an increasingly integrated global economy, in which domestic fiscal and monetary policies affect the economies of other nations, though the main impacts are on the domestic economy. My Administration remains committed to participating actively in the valuable process of coordinating macroeconomic policies internationally.

Encouraging Economic Growth

As we begin the 1990s, a central focus of my economic policies will be to build on the successes of the 1980s by creating an environment in which the private sector can serve as the engine that powers strong, noninflationary economic growth.

America's continued economic progress depends on the innovation and entrepreneurship of our people. I will therefore continue to press for a permanent research and experimentation tax credit, for increased Federal support of research with widespread societal benefits and that private firms would not have adequate incentives to undertake, for removal of regulatory and legal barriers to innovation, and for a lower tax rate on capital gains.

We must remove impediments to saving and investment in order to enhance the economy's growth potential. The fiscal policy I described earlier will raise national saving. In addition, I have asked the Congress to enact the Savings and Economic Growth Act of 1990, which contains a comprehensive program to raise household saving across the entire income spectrum. This program would help American families plan for the future and, in the process, make more funds available to finance investment and spur productivity, thus raising living standards, enhancing competitiveness, and expanding employment opportunities.

One of my highest legislative priorities this year is to reduce the capital gains tax rate. This tax reform would promote risk-taking and entrepreneurship by lowering the cost of capital, thereby encouraging new business formation and creating new jobs. A capital gains tax cut would stimulate saving and investment throughout the economy.

Government can encourage economic growth but cannot manage it. I remain strongly opposed to any sort of industrial policy, in which the government, not the market, would pick winners and losers. Second-guessing the market is the way to raise government spending and taxes, not living standards.

The growth of our Nation's labor force is projected to slow in the 1990s, and demands for skilled workers are expected to continue to increase. These developments will shift attention away from worries about the supply of jobs that have haunted us since the 1930s and toward new concerns about the supply of workers and skills.

We cannot maintain our position of world leadership or sustain rapid economic growth if our workers lack the skills of their foreign competitors. As I demonstrated last fall at the Education Summit, the Federal Government can lead in improving the inadequate performance of our elementary and secondary schools. Because school systems must be held accountable for their students' performance, the Nation's Governors and I have developed ambitious national education goals. To meet these goals, we must give students and parents the freedom to choose their schools, and we must give schools the flexibility to meet their students' needs.

More disadvantaged Americans must be brought into the economic mainstream, not

163

just to enhance our Nation's economic growth, but as a matter of simple decency. To this end, I have supported legislation to open new opportunities for the disabled, increased assistance to the homeless, helped implement welfare reform, proposed more effective job training programs, and introduced initiatives that will bring jobs and better housing to depressed inner cities. I have proposed substantial increases in spending for Head Start to prepare children from disadvantaged families for effective learning.

Those who cannot read and write cannot participate fully in the economy. Mrs. Bush and I will continue to support the difficult but important struggle to eliminate adult functional illiteracy.

Regulatory Reform

The improved performance of U.S. markets that were deregulated during the 1980s showed clearly that government interference with competitive private markets inflates prices, retards innovation, slows growth, and eliminates jobs. But in some cases, well-designed regulation can serve the public interest.

My proposals for reform of food safety regulation and the Clean Air Act follow the two key principles that apply in these cases: the goals of regulation must balance costs and benefits; and the methods of regulation must be flexible and cost-effective. One of my top legislative priorities is to improve the Clean Air Act in a way that preserves both a healthy environment and a sound economy.

When confronted with a threat to the solvency of our thrift institutions, my Administration moved swiftly to resolve the crisis. We must continue to reform the regulation of financial institutions and markets to preserve the soundness of the U.S. financial sector while encouraging innovation and competition.

The Global Economy

The 1980s have underscored the increased importance of global economic events in shaping our lives. We have all been touched by the movements toward political and economic freedom in Eastern Europe. We have been impressed by the rapid growth of market-oriented Asian economies. And we have great expectations for the movement in the European Community toward a single, open market by 1992.

Reductions in trade barriers between nations have raised living standards around the world. Investment has become more globally integrated, as citizens of other countries recognize the great strength and potential of our economy, and as Americans continue to invest abroad.

My Administration is strongly committed to supporting the historic efforts of the governments and people of Eastern Europe to move toward market-based economies. Similarly, under the Brady Plan, we will continue to support heavily indebted nations that adopt sound economic policies to revive economic growth. In both cases, reform must be comprehensive to succeed, but the rewards of success will be great.

America will continue to lead the way to a world of free, competitive markets. Increased global competition is an opportunity for the United States and the world, not a threat. But we cannot remain competitive by avoiding competition. My Administration will therefore continue to resist calls for protection and managed trade. To serve the interests of all Americans, we must open markets here and abroad, not close them. I will strongly resist any attempts to hinder the free international flows of investment capital, which have benefited workers and consumers here and abroad. And my Administration will work to reduce existing barriers to international investment throughout the world.

My highest trade policy priority is the successful completion this year of the current Uruguay Round of negotiations, aimed at strengthening and broadening the General Agreement on Tariffs and Trade (GATT). Successful completion of these negotiations will expand the world's gains from free and fair trade and raise living standards in all nations.

Looking Ahead

When I look back on the 1980s, on what the American people have accomplished, it is with pride. And when I look forward to the 1990s, it is with hope and optimism. Our excellent economic health will allow us to build on the successes of the 1980s as we prepare for the next century. Clearly, there is much work to be done. But with the economic principles and policies that I have proposed, I am confident that the United States can enjoy strong, sustainable econom- ic growth and use the fruits of that growth to raise living standards, solve longstanding problems, deal with new challenges, and make the most of new opportunities.

GEORGE BUSH

The White House,
February 6, 1990

Message to the Congress Reporting Budget Deferrals
February 6, 1990

To the Congress of the United States:
In accordance with the Impoundment Control Act of 1974, I herewith report 19 deferrals of budget authority now totalling $2,193,850,000.
The deferrals affect programs of the Department of Defense. The details of these deferrals are contained in the attached report.

GEORGE BUSH

The White House,
February 6, 1990.

Note: The attachment detailing the proposed deferrals was printed in the "Federal Register" of February 14.

Remarks to United States Troops at the National Training Center at Fort Irwin in Barstow, California
February 6, 1990

Good afternoon, General Bergeron, and good afternoon to the men of the 3d Brigade, the 9th Infantry Division, Motorized, from Fort Lewis, Washington; the pilots and the airmen of the Tactical Air Command; and the opposing force and the observer controllers.

It's great to be here at this first stop on a trip that's going to take me to San Francisco tomorrow and then to the banks of the Missouri in Nebraska and finally to the heartland of Ohio on Thursday. I appreciate the opportunity to witness firsthand the rigorous training that has made the American Army the premier land force in the world today. And these realistic battles that you wage here in the Mojave Desert forge tactical expertise, leadership, and a fighting spirit—and that's what we need.

No less an authority than General MacAr-thur put it this way: "Wars may be fought with weapons, but they are won by men. It is the spirit of the men who follow and of the man who leads that gains the victory." And I might add that nowhere was this more true than in Panama.

I'm grateful to Secretary Cheney and to General Powell and the Joint Chiefs for their brilliant leadership of Operation Just Cause. All Americans are grateful and proud of those courageous and patriotic young Americans who fought with unwavering devotion to liberty. Thanks to them, yet another country is free.

Never before has the importance and power of training been on more prominent display than in Panama. When I ordered the U.S. forces into action there last December, I didn't have to call my friend, our able Chief of Staff, Carl Vuono, to find out whether the Army was ready. I knew that the Army was well-trained, prepared to carry out any mission, anytime, anywhere. And the stunning performance of the Army and our other outstanding services more than justified my confidence and that of the American people.

Your work here at the NTC reflects the state of training throughout the Army—demanding, tough. But whether you are defending along the Whale or attacking up the Valley of Death or polishing gunnery skills back at your home station, remember that you are—all of you—preparing yourselves for combat and, by doing so, making a direct and lasting contribution to the preservation of peace.

You know, lasting peace stems from strength that is moral and intellectual, economic and military. Lasting peace comes from partnership with allies who are resolute in the defense of liberty. And it comes from a determination that makes a fragile peace strong, a temporary peace permanent. And lasting peace is our goal.

Now I'm sure that, like many Americans, you've been following the fascinating meeting taking place in Moscow. I can speak for all Americans when I say we are pleased to see Chairman Gorbachev's proposals to expand steps toward political pluralism in the Soviet Union. As a free and democratic people, Americans will always welcome measures which promote the growth of democracy. And it's especially encouraging to see anything which might bring the day of true democracy a bit closer for the Soviet people.

As we enter the nineties, the United States is shaping its military to meet a changing international environment, one that may be potentially safer, but one that will almost surely have its share of uncertainties and dangers. We see our active forces smaller but more agile and flexible—well-suited and ready for the demands of likely contingencies. The events of Eastern Europe and in the Soviet Union have changed our strategic defense posture. I have proposed an additional reduction of U.S. and Soviet troops in Central and Eastern Europe to a level of 195,000. At the same time, Secretary Cheney has laid out a very reasoned and steadfast approach to reducing military expenditures in the U.S. But it is important not to let these encouraging changes, political or military, lull us into a sense of complacency, nor can we let down our guard against a worldwide threat. The Soviet Union still does maintain formidable forces. Military challenges to democracy persist in every hemisphere. America must always be prepared to fight for freedom and security. When I decide we must use military forces to protect American lives and interests, I need to know, as I did in Panama, that you are ready and you are ready now.

Thousands of dedicated Americans are working for peace around the world—at Livermore Labs, where I'm going to visit tomorrow, to the troops training here at NTC to the worldwide alert crews that I'll be talking to there at Offutt SAC [Strategic Air Command] Headquarters on Thursday.

I congratulate each of you on your professional achievements, your personal commitment to the defense of America. As I watch you train with a "We can, we will" attitude, I want to make sure the men and women of Old Reliable, Gold Devils, Mung-Ho, Scout Out, Always First, Task Force Sabre, Active Support, the OPFOR, and the OC's all realize how very proud and thankful the American people are. God bless our great country, and thank you, colonel. And now back to war.

Note: The President spoke by radio at noon from the Communications Room at the Training and Feedback Center at Fort Irwin. In his remarks, he referred to Col. A.J. Bergeron, commander of the 3d Brigade, 9th Infantry Division; Gen. Colin L. Powell, Chairman of the Joint Chiefs of Staff; and the following military units present at the Center: Old Reliable, the 9th Infantry Division; the Go Devils, the 3d Brigade, 9th Infantry Division; Mung-Ho, the 3d Battalion, 47th Infantry Regiment; Scout Out, the 2d Battalion, 60th Infantry Regiment; Always First, Company C, 2d Battalion, 1st Infantry Regiment; Task Force Sabre, 1st Battalion, 9th Cavalry Regiment; Active Support, the 99th Forward Support Battalion; OPFOR, Operations

Forces; and OC, observer controllers. Following his remarks, the President watched war games at the Center and spoke with *some of the participants in the battlefield exercise. He then traveled to Los Angeles.*

Letter to Congressional Leaders Reporting on the Cyprus Conflict
February 6, 1990

Dear Mr. Speaker: (Dear Mr. Chairman:)

In accordance with Public Law 85–384 (92 Stat. 739; 22 U.S.C. 2373), I am submitting to you this bimonthly report on progress toward a negotiated settlement of the Cyprus question.

This report covers the 2 months between November 1 and December 31, 1989. This was a period marked by intensified activity, centering on the Secretary General of the United Nations, aimed at reconvening the stalled Cyprus intercommunal negotiations. In mid-November the U.N. Secretary General invited Cyprus President Vassiliou and Turkish Cypriot leader Rauf Denktash to meet with him separately in New York. The Vassiliou meeting with the U.N. Secretary General took place on November 29; the meeting between Denktash and the U.N. Secretary General occurred on December 4. At both meetings the U.N. Secretary General stressed the importance of a commitment "to resume talks on a meaningful basis," and then sketched out procedures for doing so at a negotiating session in February 1990 at which work on an outline for a Cyprus settlement might continue. The U.N. Secretary General also suggested that ways be found to encourage mutual trust and goodwill between the two communities.

These themes were also reflected in the required report of U.N. operations in Cyprus for the period June 1 to December 4, 1989, which the U.N. Secretary General sent to the U.N. Secretary Council on December 7, 1989. In the concluding "observations" section of this report (copy attached), the U.N. Secretary General reaffirmed that "a basis for effective negotiations exists provided both leaders manifest the necessary goodwill and recognize that a viable solution must satisfy the legitimate interests of both communities." The U.N. Secretary General then went on to express the hope that "after further discussions with my Special Representative, a way will be found whereby both leaders will soon be able to inform me of their willingness to continue the work agreed to on 29 June and proceed as I suggested during my last meeting with them."

The U.N. Security Council considered the Secretary General's report on December 14, and the President of the Council, speaking for all 15 Security Council members, including the United States, expressed full support for the U.N. Secretary General, urged both community leaders to proceed as suggested by the U.N. Secretary General during their most recent meetings with him, and to cooperate in completing work on an outline for a settlement. The President of the Council also urged the two parties to make a further, determined effort to promote reconciliation, including the adoption of goodwill measures. Finally, he asked the U.N. Secretary General to report back to the Security Council by March 1, 1990, on what progress had been made in resuming intensive talks and drafting an outline of an overall agreement.

Activities at the United Nations in New York were matched by the efforts of the U.S. Special Cyprus Coordinator, Nelson Ledsky, to promote the resumption of meaningful negotiations. The Coordinator met separately with Mr. Vassiliou and Mr. Denktash in New York. In mid-December, he traveled to Cyprus for some 6 hours of separate meetings each with Mr. Vassiliou and Mr. Denktash. At each meeting, Mr. Ledsky urged the parties to follow the procedural suggestions of the U.N. Secretary General and return to the negotiating table under U.N. auspices without preconditions.

He also outlined to the two communities a series of possible confidence-building measures, aimed at fostering bicommunal cooperation in such fields as education, health, and economic and social development. He suggested that these projects be managed by U.N. agencies, with funding coming from U.S. assistance monies that had been set aside for bicommunal projects. At the top of this list was the proposal to examine the feasibility of a bicommunal, English-language university for Cyprus.

The U.S. Coordinator also welcomed actions taken both by Cypriot authorities on November 15 to prevent a breach of the demarcation line and recent relaxation of travel restrictions by the Turkish Cypriots. He suggested that both sides examine further measures that would promote contact and travel between the two parts of the island. Both Greek Cypriot and Turkish Cypriot authorities agreed to examine with-

out commitment the concept of confidence-building and goodwill measures of the kind the U.S. Coordinator had suggested and to see whether these were compatible with efforts to arrive at a negotiated settlement of the overall Cyprus problem. We would expect discussion of these questions to continue in the months ahead.

Finally, toward the end of December, the U.N. Secretary General sent letters to President Vassiliou and Mr. Denktash proposing a meeting in February 1990. It is our expectation that both sides will attend the meeting with the U.N. Secretary General in New York.

Sincerely,

GEORGE BUSH

Note: Identical letters were sent to Thomas S. Foley, Speaker of the House of Representatives, and Claiborne Pell, chairman of the Senate Foreign Relations Committee.

Remarks at a Republican Party Fundraising Dinner in Los Angeles, California
February 6, 1990

Thank you, Frank, and Governor Deukmejian. Duke, always a pleasure to see you. To the California State delegation, many of whom are here, thank you for coming. And it's great to see our party chairman, Lee Atwater, with us tonight. He's doing an outstanding job. He plays that rhythm and blues—I'd rather hear Vicky Carr sing, but nevertheless. [*Laughter*] And thank you for the beautiful rendition of "The Star-Spangled Banner." Johnny, the honorary mayor of Hollywood. And all of you who are supporting this marvelous effort for our party, headed by Frank Visco—and, Frank, thank you for the introduction. I see that we have a lot of celebrities here tonight. Bob Hope, thank you, sir, for your remarks. When I first saw this star-studded audience, I thought I'd wandered into a Lakers' game. [*Laughter*] I don't think there have been so many celebrities in one place since they used to be there at Dodgers Stadium—at Tommy Lasorda's office before they al-

lowed the visitors—kicked the visitors out of there.

And, of course, Arnold Schwarzenegger is here. He was up visiting Barbara and me the other day at Camp David. I call him "Conan the Republican." And he has taken on big job for us as Chairman of this Fitness Council, and it's very, very important—he's taking it seriously. We saw his beautiful new daughter up there at Camp David—I bent over to kiss her and she tried to bench-press me. [*Laughter*] Where is he? Oh, right. Sorry about that. [*Laughter*] That's when I realized that any kid who has her own set of free weights doesn't need a teddy bear. [*Laughter*]

Now, there's one more person I'd like to mention tonight, even though he's not here—a friend of everybody in this room—tonight he's celebrating his 79th birthday, and I would like to simply say, happy birthday, President Reagan, wherever you are, and best wishes from all of us. This is my first trip out here on behalf of the California State party. I want to thank all of you for the victory that you gave us here on election night. I'll never forget the close win here. You have my gratitude—Duke, certainly, Governor, you do—and my appreciation for your hard work and commitment for a job well-done.

But tonight, I want to talk to you about another job: the job of preparing our great country for the future. Last Wednesday, I made my first State of the Union Address to the Nation. I covered a lot of ground because our country faces diverse challenges that will test every American as we enter this new decade. Around the world, there is, as we've heard here tonight, rapid and welcome change, as people from Panama to Prague strive for democracy. Self-determination is contagious. They even want it in Malibu, I understand. [*Laughter*] But millions of people are leaping over their volleyball nets to free them. [*Laughter*]

No, but seriously—[*laughter*]—millions of people are looking to America for the hope and encouragement they need as they seek the same freedom we have here—freedom of expression, security, and opportunity we enjoy. And America will be there to help. But if America is to continue its traditional leadership role, we've got to be competitive enough to take on the job, and strong and smart enough to do it right. Today——[*at this point, the President was interrupted by a demonstrator.*] She's pretty tough. [*Laughter*] You know, economic times are reasonably good and we're enjoying the greatest economic expansion in peacetime history. But to maintain the growth that has provided better lives for millions of Americans, we've got to make sure that America becomes even stronger. We've got to invest in our future.

And first, a sound education for our kids must be the first and foremost, and it is. And we have proposed the largest education budget in history. But real improvement in our schools is not simply a matter of spending more. It's a matter of asking more of our students, our teachers, our parents, our schools. And while the Federal Government is going to help meet its national challenge, the States—the "laborato-ries" of democracy, as Justice Brandeis put it—will do a much better job than we ever can. And that's why we've announced new education goals for our country, developed working with Governor Deukmejian and the other 49 Governors. By the year 2000, every child must start school ready to learn, and we've got to increase our high school graduation rate to no less than 90 percent. And we're going to make sure that our schools' diplomas mean something. In critical subjects—at the 4th, 8th and 12th grades—we must assess our students' performance. By the year 2000, U.S. students must be first in the world in math and science skills. And every American adult must be a literate worker and citizen. Every school in America must offer the kind of disciplined environment needed for our kids to learn. And this other goal—every school in America must be drug-free.

Here in California, we've designated Los Angeles as a "high intensity drug trafficking area" to help this great city rid itself of the scourge of drugs. And we've got to get PCP and crack off the streets and out of the schools. And it's time we got more Federal resources into the hands of those on the front lines. If we are to compete internationally, America must be drug-free, well-educated, and ready to do the job right.

And there's another investment we must make for the future of this country to keep competitive, and I'm talking about R&D, research and development. California can be proud of its great research institutions. Schools like these will dream the dreams and create the ideas that form the cornerstone of our economic power in the years to come. And that's why our 1991 budget includes a record-high $71 billion proposal for research and development. And with the best young minds of the next generation on our side, America will win the research and development race.

Education, a drug-free workplace, and research and development are part of the mix for economic competitiveness. But there's one more important ingredient—and many here know this—savings and investment. And together, they create jobs and promote opportunity for all Americans. And so we've proposed the Savings and Economic

Growth Act, which includes our family savings account proposal and provisions to allow first-time home buyers to make an early withdrawal from those IRA's without penalty. And it does one more thing—it proposes a cut in the rate in the capital gains tax. Last year, a majority in both Houses of Congress showed their support for this capital gains tax cut. And this year, with your help, we'll pass that tax cut to give our competitors a run for the money and keep the American economy going strong.

But to remain competitive, government must also reflect the new world emerging around us—like the National Training Center base I've just visited in Barstow— that Barbara and I were at today, and later going to the Strategic Air Command base near Omaha. As the nature of the threats to the American security change—and they are changing—so, too, must our response change. Our forces will remain robust, well-trained, highly professional, but geared to the new challenges of the nineties. And I believe that we can do that. I'm in a big battle in Congress, and I'd like to have your support to keep reasonable levels of defense. I'm not going to miss an opportunity to cut, but I want to do it prudently, and I want to get something from the other side when we do it.

Finally, one more thought here—kind of competitiveness I'd like to talk to you about. Let me tell you a story about a summer night, 1981, when a group of California Democrats sat in a restaurant in Sacramento with a pencil and a paper, redesigning California's political landscape. They drew what one of them called at the time their "contribution to modern art"—it was their words. Well, we've got a name for it, and we call it gerrymandering. Lines were drawn across communities, towns, even streets, into twisted, contorted, crazy shapes—without the slightest regard for either the will of the people or the rules of elementary fairness. Since those lines went into effect, there have been 135 general elections for California's congressional seats, and only once has a seat changed party control.

In 1984, in fact, Republican congressional candidates together received more total votes than the Democratic candidates and yet won nine fewer seats. The 1990 census may, and probably will, give California up to seven new congressional seats—meaning that nearly one out of every eight Congressmen in Washington will represent California. And all existing California congressional district lines will have to be redrawn—this time not with pencils in a restaurant but by state-of-the-art advanced computers. The time has come for redistricting reform. And we've got to end the charade of that Phil Burton Democratic gerrymandering that has deprived this State of fair representation.

Look, unlike the Democrats, we don't need gerrymandering, because Republicans can win on the issues. You heard Duke say it. In fact, we can put the Democrats out of business—on the issues. Look at what this Governor's Republican administration has accomplished since 1983: the unemployment rate was 11, cut to 5.2 percent; 2.7 million new jobs created in this great State. The list keeps growing: 14 new and expanded prisons open in 1991, education funding more than doubled, drug education now included in every school from grades four to eight. California now has some of the toughest environmental laws in the Nation, with thousands of acres of sensitive lands acquired and preserved. And thanks to commonsense policies and strong leadership, California is better off than it ever has been. Let's keep it that way. Let's keep it Republican, and let's elect Pete Wilson next November to be Governor of this great State.

Unfortunately, Pete couldn't join us tonight. He's in Washington—a crucial vote in the Senate on education. I appreciate his work, for he's a proven winner—and the voters know it. And he's a strong environmentalist, a leader of the war on drugs, key member of our team in the United States Senate. And believe me, we'll miss Senator Wilson, but come to think of it, I really like the sound of Governor Pete Wilson. You know Pete will be leading a solid team of candidates for State office to victory, and with him they'll be the ones to keep the taxes low, the environment clean, and the economy strong. People say I'm a cautious guy, and I can understand that—well, I really can't understand it. I'm going to go out on a limb tonight and make a prediction: 1990 will be a great year for the Golden State because Pete Wilson will be your next Governor. So my plea, in the tradition of Ronald Reagan and George Deukmejian: Let's keep California great and keep it Republican.

Barbara and I are delighted to be with you. Thank you for what you're doing for this party, thank you for what you're doing for the campaign for Governor and the other statewide races. Thank you all, God bless you, and God bless the United States of America. Thank you very much.

Note: The President spoke at 8:26 p.m. in the L.A. Ballroom at the Century Plaza Hotel. In his opening remarks, he referred to Frank Visco, chairman of the California Republican Party, and Tommy Lasorda, manager of the Los Angeles Dodgers.

Nomination of Admiral Frank B. Kelso II To Be Chief of Naval Operations
February 7, 1990

The President today announced his intention to nominate Adm. Frank B. Kelso II, USN, to be Chief of Naval Operations. He would succeed Adm. Carlisle A.H. Trost, whose term expires June 30, 1990.

Admiral Kelso is presently serving as commander in chief, United States Atlantic Command, and supreme allied commander, Atlantic. Previously he was commander in chief, U.S. Atlantic Fleet, 1986–1988, and commander, 6th Fleet, 1985–1986. Admiral Kelso graduated from the U.S. Naval Academy in 1956. He was born July 11, 1933, in Fayetteville, TN.

Remarks to the Staff of the Lawrence Livermore National Laboratory in San Francisco, California
February 7, 1990

Thank you, Mr. Nuckolls and Dr. Wood, of course, Secretary Watkins, our Secretary of Energy, in whom I have great confidence and who is my trusted adviser on matters that affect your lives on a day-to-day basis. I'm delighted to be here. And I'm told that my visit represents a milestone, a rare phenomenon: one of the very few presentations without a viewgraph. [*Laughter*]

But before I speak about the programs I've just seen at Livermore Labs, I want to say something about the people here, about your response, actually, in the wake of the earthquake back in October. I am told that Livermore employees raised over $100,000 in contributions for disaster relief, and you did it in just 2 days. So, I thank all of you for your strong commitment to community. I think people are beginning to understand what I mean when I talk about a Thousand Points of Light. And that is a wonderful example of how this whole concept works: one American pitching in to help another. So, you've really set a wonderful example.

It's very exciting for me to have a chance to visit this institution and the people who bring it to life. I loved that spontaneous welcome when I drove in here—people lined up out there. I don't know how long they've been whipped into shape to be standing there, but—[*laughter*]—I can tell you, it made me feel good anyway. [*Laughter*] So, if you were in line out there somewhere, thank you for your heroic work.

171

Yours are the minds that are rarely at rest—sometimes blessed, sometimes burdened with a flow of ideas that simply won't quit. Maybe even when you're out fishing or at 3 in the morning when you just want to get some sleep—maybe that works differently. But like the Bells and the Edisons and the Tellers before you, your ideas, your ability to deliver on them, are America's best.

The Livermore's technical prowess is well-known, truly remarkable. And I now have a better feel for it just from kicking the tires and being here for just a few minutes. For nearly 40 years, you've been at the leading edge of scientific knowledge. And I'm delighted that one of the Lab's founders is here today, one of the great pioneers in the national security field, leading minds in science; and of course I'm talking about my friend of longstanding, Dr. Edward Teller. Glad to see you, sir. Let me thank all of you at the Lab for your role in preserving the peace and keeping the world stable and America secure.

You're aware of the tremendous changes—Mr. Nuckolls referred to them—that have swept the world over the past 2 years—past year, actually. In my address to the Nation 2 weeks ago, I referred to it as the "Revolution of '89," a remarkable and hopeful transition that continues even now. What I didn't mention, and what you also understand, is how the world's movement toward democracy and freedom is a direct result of our ability to stand firm in the face of threats to stability and peace.

Just over an hour from now, I'm going to be talking to the Commonwealth Club in San Francisco, making an address on our national security strategy at this time of change. But let me say right now that the strength of the U.S. nuclear deterrent, developed through the effort of our national labs and the Department of Energy and Department of Defense, has helped to guard the peace and freedom so precious to all of us.

Now the labs are also developing technologies to strengthen deterrence through strategic defenses. Together with strategic modernization and arms control, programs like SDI, the Strategic Defense Initiative, and one of its most promising concepts,

"Brilliant Pebbles," complement our ability to preserve the peace into the 1990's and beyond. If the technology I've seen today proves feasible, and I'm told it looks very promising, no war planner could be confident of the consequences of a ballistic missile attack. The technologies you are now researching, developing, and testing will strengthen deterrence.

Even as we work to reduce arsenals and reduce tensions, we understand the continuing, crucial role of strategic defenses. Beyond their contributions to deterrence, they underlie effective arms control by diminishing the advantages of cheating. They can also defend us against accidental launches or attacks from the many other countries that, regrettably, are acquiring ballistic missile capabilities. In the 1990's, strategic defense makes much more sense than ever before, in my view.

So, a vigorous research, development, and testing program at our national labs will be as crucial as ever, as we adapt both the size and shape of our nuclear deterrent. We're working on a significant reduction in arms. I think that's what the world wants. I believe in it strongly. But to protect the American people, we will settle for nothing less than the highest confidence in survivability, effectiveness, and safety of our remaining forces.

The scientific expertise of laboratories like Livermore will also serve the national interest in other areas—problems like economic competitiveness, education, energy, space exploration, waste cleanup, sound environmental practices. These will be enormously important challenges in the future, challenges that your skills, your talents—those flashes of insight matched with long hours of labor—will help us meet squarely and well. I'm confident that the Livermore Laboratories will be a crucial part of our ability to meet the challenges of the new decade and the new century.

So, I came out here to learn, and I also came out here to say thank you very much. I have a funny feeling that because of the nature of the work, it is somewhat underappreciated by the average man on the street in our country. But I want to assure you of my support. I want to assure you, as President, of my gratitude for the dedication that you bring and, really, the service to country that exemplifies the best in America.

Thank you all very much for what you're doing. Thank you.

Note: The President spoke at 10:35 a.m. in *the Laboratory's auditorium. In his opening remarks, he referred to John H. Nuckolls, Director of the Lawrence Livermore National Laboratory, and Lowell L. Woods, the facility's special studies programs leader. Prior to his remarks, the President was briefed on the "Brilliant Pebbles" project and toured the weapons vault.*

Remarks and a Question-and-Answer Session at a Luncheon Hosted by the Commonwealth Club in San Francisco, California
February 7, 1990

The President. Thank you, Dr. Fink. Modesty may not be his long suit, but I like the introduction. [*Laughter*] And very candidly, I like the pride he takes in his institution, and he gave me a good lecture up here as to how I should be supportive of these smaller and independent colleges. And it struck home to me, I'll tell you.

And Governor Deukmejian, I'm glad to be with you, sir. And our Commonwealth Club president, Joe Perrelli, thank you for your hospitality. And let me just single out our former Secretary of State, George Shultz. I'm honored to see him here and be with him.

I'm going to get in real trouble here, but another San Franciscan who served his country at a very high level is now giving of his time to work with me on the prestigious Science Advisory Committee, and I'm talking about your own and my friend, David Packard. I'm delighted he's here.

And just two more. I'm pleased to see the mayor of San Francisco here—Mayor Agnos—delighted to see him. And of course, another who I read in the paper had re-retired, or was about to re-retire, and I'm talking to the former head of the World Bank, Tom Clausen, an old friend who I'm delighted to see him here.

So, I feel encompassed by friends and delighted to be back for, I think it is, my seventh—Joe, seventh?—seventh appearance before this prestigious group. A few minutes ago, I asked a 49er fan what he thought was the turning point in the Super Bowl. [*Laughter*] He said, the national

anthem. [*Laughter*]

Of course not all the recent memories—as Art knows—in the Bay area have been pleasant ones. I'm sure you remember the last time I was here, after this city suffered tragedy. And I'm talking about a clutter of car wrecks and a flattened freeway and a terrible black cloud rising from the Marina district. And I know that some damage remains, and certainly some heartache and some hardship. But today I've sensed and felt something else: renewal. The people of the Bay area have stood up and dusted themselves off and are rebuilding because you came together. And San Francisco will be as beautiful and vital as ever. So, I think it's fair to say, from having been here for about 45 minutes, San Francisco is back, and we can understand that. [*Laughter*]

But I've come here today to California for another reason: to give you a no-nonsense—you hardnosed business men and women that you are—a straightforward and hopeful message about the national security of our country. Yesterday at Fort Irwin, I also thanked our men and women in uniform—not just because they keep America safe and free, but I came to thank them because they help to make possible the wonderful changes that are sweeping the world. I wish every man and woman here could have been with me as I talked to the young troops out there in the desert. It's very clear why every one of our Joint Chiefs keep telling me our services all have the finest, most dedicated young men and women to ever serve in the uniform of the

173

United States.

And as the threats to our security change, so, too, must our defense strategy. In 1986 defense expenditures consumed 6.3 percent of our gross national product. As you know, I just submitted my 1991 budget to Congress, which holds down defense spending for the fifth year in a row, down to just above 5 percent of gross national product. I'm submitting this budget at a time when the postwar world that we have known, the world that began in 1945, is changing before our very eyes. So, to understand then where we're going, let me first review where we've been and where I think we are today.

The free world's first generation of postwar leaders had the cautionary example of their predecessors. They remembered that the Great War, the war to end all wars, was followed by chaos and conflict. They remembered that visionary statesmen after the First World War had tried to limit large navies, even outlawed war itself. But soon these great hopes faded in the face of unchecked aggression, and no pact could prevent World War II.

So, by 1945 our leaders had acquired a realism, a realism born of bloody experience, a pragmatism born of a sober appraisal of the world as it was. And from Harry Truman to Ronald Reagan, our strength became the world's shield; our ideals of freedom and democracy, the world's hope. We paid dearly for the defense of liberty with our national wealth and with many of our youngest and bravest.

And so, over the past 40 years, our leaders continued to provide for war even as they sought peace. It was during the Truman administration, in this very city, that men and women of great vision and high ideals came from around the world to create an assembly of nations. And so it was, in San Francisco, 45 years ago, that the United Nations was born. Then, as now, the United States strove to balance its role as peacekeeper with that of peacemaker. We helped create the United Nations and NATO. And we encouraged Soviet change even as we thwarted Soviet expansion.

Those who crafted this new policy had a name for it. They called it containment and predicted that if we blocked the easy path of expansion, the Soviet Union would one day have to confront the contradictions of its inhumane, illogical system. The purpose of containment was not to defeat or humiliate the Soviets. The purpose was to preserve and extend liberty. The hope was someday to see, as George Kennan put it in 1947, "the gradual mellowing of Soviet power." It took nearly a half a century to vindicate this strategy, but we can now see the results: today the cold war is in retreat. That is good news, for no sane man or woman is nostalgic for the cold war.

We're inspired by this Revolution of 1989—heartened, for example, to see a man of letters and conscience in Prague move from prison to the Presidential palace. We are heartened to see the Berlin Wall fall, setting off a shockwave that upended a tyrant in Romania. And we're grateful for something more. Now, because of our strength and that of our allies—now, thanks to the march of freedom and democracy in Eastern Europe and even in the Soviet Union itself—now the prospects for an enduring peace are greater than ever before. We can now envision a new destiny for the nations of the Continent—that of a Europe truly whole and free.

We are taking the first steps across a bridge begun by others long ago. And it's a bridge that can lead us from seemingly endless conflict to the promise of a lasting peace. But no matter how great the promise, we must be certain that the bridge is secure. As President, every morning I receive an intelligence briefing, and I receive the best information available to any world leader today. Yet the morning news is often overtaken by the news that very same evening. And the world is moving too fast to forecast with absolute certainty what will happen next. Our challenge is to manage this period of transition from the world of today to the world of tomorrow and safeguard the security of America in the process. When it comes to the security of this country, I would rather be called cautious than I would be called reckless. Our pursuit of this promising future must start with an understanding of today's realities.

Take, for example, our most recent proposal, warmly received by our allies and

President Gorbachev. I proposed reducing the troop levels on both sides in Central and Eastern Europe to 195,000 troops. That balance, that balance encourages the less threatening future we envision, and it holds great promise. But right now, right now, the Soviets still have more than 560,000 men under arms in Central Europe.

On the issue of strategic weapons, we've made progress in the START negotiations. And again, I'd like to salute George Shultz for his very important part in this. And we now hope to slash dramatically the number of strategic weapons on both sides. It is these important reductions that Secretary Baker is seeking this very day in Moscow. That's the future we envision, and it, too, holds great promise. But let us not forget that right now the Soviets still have more than 10,000 strategic weapons. They are modernizing them, they have developed two new mobile ICBM's, and their spending on strategic defense is comparable to their spending on strategic offensive forces.

The President of the United States is the Commander in Chief, bound by the Constitution to defend and protect the United States of America. Now, some would have me predicate the defense of our people on promising but as yet unfulfilled hopes for the future. I will not do that. I am determined to seek with the Soviets the collateral to implement a new peace. In international terms, collateral means soldiers discharged, tanks dismantled, nuclear missiles demolished, and chemical weapons banned from the face of the Earth. Some see our measured approach as endangering the process of change. I see our approach as essential to change, essential to the security of this nation, and as the only way to a lasting peace. We have shown that American resolve can help further Soviet reform. And we've shown that American strength is the catalyst for arms control. And we've shown that the idea called America can inspire change. And now we must not let impatience, born of euphoria, jeopardize all that we hope to achieve in the future.

First, as Americans have always believed, our foremost goal is to prevent another world war. To do so, we will still need to remain fully engaged. European security, stability, and freedom, so tied to our own,

requires an American presence. Western Europeans all want us to stay there—every single country—want us to avoid pulling back into an uninvolved isolation. I have the feeling that when the dust settles, the new democracies of Eastern Europe will feel exactly the same way. We must remain in Europe as long as we are needed and wanted. And the prospect of global peace, therefore, depends on an American forward presence.

Second, we will, of course, continue to reduce the likelihood of nuclear war. And that's why I will vigorously pursue the START talks with the Soviet Union. But arms control and strategic modernization are not competing strategies. Rather, they can work together to make the world a safer place. Just this morning, I went out and visited Lawrence Livermore Labs and met those visionary men and women who strive to make a nuclear strike on our country, whether from a nuclear superpower or some renegade nation or terrorist group, even more unlikely than it is today. And if the technology I have seen today proves feasible—and it looks very promising—no aggressor could be confident of the success of a ballistic missile attack. And that's what deterrence is all about.

And let's be clear: This purely defensive concept doesn't threaten a single person anywhere in the world—the life of a single person anywhere in the world. God forbid, if it ever had to be used, it would be used against missiles, not against people. When some complain of the cost of developing such technologies, they should first consider the cost of not doing all we can to deter conflict and protect the cities and the citizens of America. And that's why I will seek to persuade the Soviets, through our defense-in-space talks, that, in fact, greater reliance on strategic defenses will contribute to a safer world.

Now let me now tell you something about the strategy behind our 1991 defense budget. First, new threats are emerging beyond the traditional East-West antagonism of the last 45 years. These contingencies must loom larger in our defense planning. Remember the threats of Libyan and Iranian terrorism. And remember the liberation of Grenada and Panama. And remember the dedication of our American servicemen on duty in the Persian Gulf 2 years ago, safeguarding not only the flow of oil—safeguarding the flow of oil to the industrial democracies—but an action also welcomed by many small nations over there who were afraid that the Iran-Iraq war would adversely affect their own freedom.

And remember, too, that there are more than 15 countries in the world that will have developed ballistic missiles by the end of the decade—15 countries, many with chemical and biological capabilities. Nuclear weapons capabilities are proliferating, much to my regret and the regret of everybody here. And inevitably, high-tech weapons will fall into the hands of those whose hatred of America and contempt for civilized norms is well-known. We will continue to work hard to prevent this dangerous proliferation. But one thing is certain: We must be ready for its consequences. And we will be ready.

Then there are the narco-gangsters that concern us all, already a threat to our national health and spirit. Now they are taking on the pretensions of a geopolitical force—whole new force to effect change—and they must be dealt with as such by our military: in the air, on the land, and on the seas.

Clearly, in the future, we will need to be able to thwart aggression—repel a missile or protect a sealane or stop a drug lord. We will need forces adaptable to conditions everywhere. And we will need agility, readiness, sustainability. We will need speed and stealth. And we will need leadership.

In short, we must continue to deter both a global war and limited conflicts in new conditions. And for this reason, we doubly need to continue the modernization of our forces. I pray that it will not be my sad duty to commit American fighting men again into combat. But if I do, on my watch, the lives of American fighting men will not be shortchanged.

As I mentioned, just yesterday I visited the National Training Center at Fort Irwin, near Barstow, where our fighting forces prepare for action. It was at this very base that we trained many of our troops who fought with such distinction in Panama.

And they were courageous. But being prepared is also the best way to ensure that wars are prevented. And after seeing our men and women again and talking with them, they are indeed up to the challenges of the future.

You know, I once read that Khrushchev once spoke to the Commonwealth Club for 3 hours. [*Laughter*] Perhaps he began this speech with these words: "Let me make just a few brief observations before taking your questions." [*Laughter*]

So, I will get to my final concern: how all this change in our defense budget affects us at home. Many speak of the peace dividend. Few discuss the short-term cost of peace. There will be costs as we cross the bridge to a better future—for dislocated industries and workers, for communities—painful personal adjustments to be made. But America has always been willing to pay the price of peace. I know that some of the bases that have been proposed for cutbacks are in this area, just as many of them are in my home State of Texas. But let me state right here and now: There have been no politics in these proposals. Some talk about bases in Democratic districts here. Well, they're also in the same State as a great Republican Governor over here. I ask Congress to join me in a spirit of fairness. Longstanding critics of defense spending should not turn around and block the closing of a base in their home district. There's something just a little bit ironic about certain Members of Congress whose philosophy seems to be, make deep cuts, but be sure to cut in somebody else's State or somebody else's district. And we can't have that anymore. This is too important. I can't accept that. The taxpayers deserve better, and so do those affected by our decisions.

So let me assure you: If a base closes, it doesn't close Federal concern and commitment. You know, civilians who are laid off will receive top priority for placement in other DOD positions. The Homeowners Assistance Program will protect military and civilian personnel from falling real estate prices. And the Office of Economic Adjustment will work with communities to develop powerful new economic assets, new ways to use old bases. The Bible speaks of beating swords into plowshares. We're transforming military runways into municipal airports, and military bases into industrial parks and community colleges, and missile hangars into factories. I don't know how the pruning hook business is going out there, but we may go back into that too, cast them into pruning hooks.

You know, I know the American people will support these measures for a continued strong defense. My travels around this country tell me that. But to have the means to negotiate reductions and ensure peace, I will need the support, the cooperation, and consultation of Congress. We can now envision a time when the world is more secure than ever, when all the competitive instincts of modern man will be diverted to commerce—even to football.

You know, I started joking about the 49ers winning the Super Bowl during the national anthem. But it's not how many passes Joe Montana completed, it's that he knew better than to rest on his laurels at the beginning of the fourth quarter. So, so should we. I will work with Congress to build a bridge to a more secure world. And if we work together, then peace itself will be the greatest dividend of all.

Thank you for inviting me to San Francisco. And God bless you all.

Strategic Defense Initiative

Q. Having reviewed SDI at Livermore Lab today, do you support moving ahead with the project?

The President. Yes, I do. And our budget calls for that. And again, I would remind the critics that it is defensive; that the science and technology from it will benefit not just this concept of a reasonably priced way of intercepting somebody else's missile, whether it's from a major power or from some renegade hand, but that the science will benefit, I believe, the environment. I believe it has enormous potential for other uses. I feel more strongly about that than when I went to Livermore.

Defense Spending

Q. Will the expected troop reductions bring about a savings that can be used to offset the increased cost in strategic arms?

The President. Yes, and I hope that there will not be a greatly increased cost in strategic arms. The Soviets have modernized. They've modernized their systems, and we have not yet. But I would hope that the resulting reductions in the strategic arms, which I am pledged to and which I will work for, will have beneficial effect on and will result in savings.

You see, I am convinced that if politics of international change are handled correctly and if things go more forward, we will eventually have far lower levels of spending. But I've spelled out for you here why I think that should be approached in a very prudent manner.

Trade and Competitiveness

Q. With the recent events in Eastern Europe, do you think we should now again prepare for a world economic struggle rather than be preparing unnecessarily for a military struggle?

The President. Well, I wouldn't necessarily shift priorities. I've told you the priority I place on defense. But when it comes to competitiveness of the United States, we should be struggling with that on the front burner right now—and I think we are. And that's one of the reasons I increased dramatically R&D spending in our budget. It's one of the inevitable byproducts of a better education system. It's why we're putting more emphasis on math and science. It's why I'm imposing on great scientists like David Packard and others to give us the advice on how we can become more competitive. It's why my trade negotiator, Carla Hills, and our Secretary of Commerce are doing their level best to convince people that if we are going to have free trade, that has to be fair trade.

And so, this competition on the economic front is big. It's going to get even bigger, in my view. And we've got an enormous job to do—not just the Federal Government. We can't do this. Many businesses have already moved into much more—in the sense of quality product—moved much more into the sense of automation and modernization. So, it is a national goal that we be more competitive, but it can't wait until we get our defense program in line. It's right now. It's urgent.

177

And let me just throw in one, Joe, on the success of the Uruguay trade round, for those who are a little more technically oriented than some. The success of this Uruguay trade round is very, very important to our ability to enhance the rest of the world and ourselves by free trade. But we've got some big barriers out there. We've got some problems we have to overcome.

Budget Deficit

Q. Can you pledge that a certain amount of dollars from armament reduction be transferred as a reduction in the debt?

The President. No, I can't pledge that, but I am pledged to get the deficit down in accordance with the Gramm-Rudman targets. We will have that if we get our way with Congress, which doesn't exactly do things the way I want, I've found out. [*Laughter*] But if we get that done, I stated in my State of the Union Message that that should be an objective and to move right into it, the minute we are in balance, which would be in 3 years. Now, I expect there will be a lot of pressure on. You hear pressure today on what is referred to alluringly as a peace dividend. And it appeals to me. There are things that I'd love to be able to say—we can put a little more in this research, or we can help this homeless person a little more, or whatever it is. The pressures will be on, but I think that it would be a very good thing to do because as a grandparent of 12 I must confess, like a lot of people here, you feel that we are burdening the generations to come with a debt that does nothing but click off at the beginning of each year an enormously high and even higher rate of interest that we're pledged—interest account that we're pledged to pay on the national debt. So, yes, as I said in the State of the Union, that's what I want to do.

Defense Policy

Q. If the Soviet Union and others in the Warsaw Pact substantially scale back their military commitment, doesn't the U.S. run the risk of moving in the opposite direction of the world? Are we prepared to stand alone?

The President. No, because I think as I mentioned to you earlier—and this is the truth—our allies want us involved. They don't want to see us decouple or delink from Europe. They see the changes and welcome them. All the allied leaders—and I talk to the leaders of NATO on a fairly regular basis—they see and welcome the change, but they do not want to see the United States pull back into what would be perceived worldwide as some kind of a neo-isolationist decoupling.

And I am not suggesting that we can't save money; indeed, we will. If our proposal—the proposal that I put forward—is accepted by the Soviets and we negotiate out all the details and get a CFE, conventional force agreement, as we are proposing, I think we will see substantial savings that are made by the—what do you call it?—suddenly gone blank—in terms of when you bring a guy back and he no longer is in the army. [*Laughter*] But it's not just transferring: it's a question of having fewer troops on both sides. And that will inevitably result in some savings.

So, we're aware that there's a chance to save, but it is not that we are going to be swimming against the tide with our European allies. And as I said in the speech—and I recognize his question didn't indicate the guy that asked the question was asleep. He probably wrote the question before the speech, I hope. [*Laughter*] But what I also said is that I hope and believe that many of the new fledgling democracies in Eastern Europe are going to welcome a stabilizing presence on the part of the United States. Now, some will say that's sacrificing. And I say, no, it is in our interest because we provide a certain stability that wouldn't be there if we, the United States, weren't there.

Environmental Protection

Q. Do you see the freedom of the Communist country as a threat to the globe? That is, if they all want the comforts we have, will we use up the resources of our Earth at an even greater rate?

The President. No. I think there's an environmental awareness in the world today that is encouraging. I will readily concede there are some in what is known as the Third World—I'm not thinking so much as the evolution of Eastern Europe into the arms of democracy—but I think there's a feeling in some Third World countries: Don't you big guys from the United States who have raped, pillaged, and plundered the environment now come and tell us what we can't do. We understand that, but we've got to work with them and share our tremendously advanced technology, existing technology, as we work to find even greater technological breakthroughs to protect the environment.

But I don't think you're going to necessarily see that is because of the evolution of Iron Curtain countries into, hopefully, growing democracies. I think there's an awareness now in Europe about the need to have sound international environmental practice based on science—not on myth but on science.

German Reunification

Q. As Eastern Europe and the U.S.S.R. progress toward democracy, do you foresee any potential military alliances being formed that could threaten the free world, such as a united Germany and Japan?

The President. No, I don't. And I think everybody that's interested in foreign affairs, I'm sure, has an opinion one way or another as to what happens on the reunification of Germany, but I think that can be—well, let me recite, just as background, the U.S. position, which is self-determination—and this is the NATO position—self-determination. And then when it comes to borders, I believe Helsinki says no alteration in borders without agreement of the parties. So, that gives you a rather stable framework.

Now, you can read every day about the rapidity of change and what might happen in terms of German reunification. But I think it can be managed in such a way that it will not be a threat to Western Europe or to what was termed in the question, I think, the free world. And when I hear both West German Foreign Minister Mr. Genscher and West German Chancellor Kohl talking about a Germany that remains tied into NATO in some way—maybe not a NATO in exactly the same form it is—but that's encouraging. That's encouraging.

Soviet Role in the Middle East

Q. In the past, smaller countries used to play the U.S. versus the U.S.S.R. to get military and economic aid. Now that relations have improved with the U.S.S.R., and if we can anticipate continued improvement, what are the chances of the U.S. and the U.S.S.R. working together to solve some of the world's problems, such as the Middle East?

The President. Better, far better. And I think there's certain things that the Soviet Union could do that would facilitate their role as a catalyst for peace in the Middle East. One of them would be to assist more, through transportation—direct flights—for Soviet Jews wishing to leave the Soviet Union to go to Israel. I think that would send a sign that their interest in the Middle East is not just on the side of—what heretofore has been the side of the more radical states in the area. So, they can do something like that. I'd like to see them normalize diplomatic relations with the State of Israel. I think that would be helpful. But I would think that as the Soviet Union evolves in a more democratic fashion that some of the concerns we've had in the past will be lessened.

So, I wouldn't say that at some point they wouldn't have a useful role. I've cited two areas where I think they can have a useful role in building credibility not just with the State of Israel but with other states as well. So, let's hope that they can do something.

Soviet Reforms

Q. How can we help Mr. Gorbachev in his quest for a unification of his country—in demonstration of his country?

The President. I think we can avoid doing dumb things. [*Laughter*] And that's my cautious approach. You know, he's facing some enormously difficult internal problems. And you may have noted that I have been—hopefully on behalf of most the people in our country—supporting *perestroika.* When for a few months into our Presidency—mine—why, people wondered: What does he really care? Does he understand these changes? Does he really mean it when he says, I support *perestroika*? I do—and *glasnost,* the openness concept, as well.

But in the last press conference or so—a couple of them, maybe—I referred to support for Gorbachev. And I have felt that he has handled some extraordinarily complicated internal problems, problems inside the Soviet Union, with a certain restraint and finesse that I think demonstrates a real commitment to peaceful change. The last thing I think any United States citizen needs to do when you have the Central Committee meeting is to try to fine-tune it from San Francisco or Washington as to how they ought to conduct themselves. [*Laughter*] So, I want to be very careful about picking winners and losers or saying how they ought to do things.

But I do think that, generally speaking, it is in our interest to support *perestroika*. And I will say again: I think Mr. Gorbachev has shown a considerable restraint. And frankly, the dealings that I've had with him here, and then on the sidelines when George [George Shultz, former Secretary of State] and President Reagan were dealing with him, is that he's a man who you can talk to; he's quite open in his negotiations. He damn sure will tell you if he doesn't agree with you. [*Laughter*] I mean, you're not under any doubt about that. [*Laughter*] But it's a new approach. I mean, it's very different than dealing with some of the previous Soviet leaders.

So, I'm not here to anoint or try to shape the deliberations of the Central Committee proceedings in the Soviet Union this very day—or that will commence again tomorrow, maybe. But I do think that there's an awful lot to be hopeful about there because I find we can talk quite openly. And I'm looking forward to a summit meeting. I don't know why all meetings have to be called summits. [*Laughter*] We tried to call the Malta meetings something else, and it lasted for about 2 days. [*Laughter*] And I mean it, because I think summit projects the idea that you have to have some massive breakthrough, or else you disappoint the rest of the world. And I've changed my thinking on this. I think maybe communications where you don't have to do that is better. And that's why I was on the phone with him the other day on a couple of matters. So, I'm optimistic about our dealings with him, but I cannot predict and nor can any of you, with any degree of accuracy, exactly what's going to happen inside the Soviet Union.

Soviet Chairman Gorbachev

Q. Please comment on Mikhail Gorbachev's nomination for the Nobel Peace Prize.

The President. I'd hate to say I wasn't aware of it, but I wasn't aware of it. [*Laughter*] And I don't follow those proceedings too closely. [*Laughter*] But I've told you I would salute the man for his adherence to peaceful change in Eastern Europe. I mean, that, I think, is dramatic and, I think, worthy of a positive note. But far be it for me to try to influence the gurus that decide who wins a Nobel Prize. [*Laughter*]

War on Drugs

Q. As far as the issue of drug trafficking goes and the world drug problem, could you please address the issue of whether or not military forces will be used in a more direct way in the enforcement of international drug traffic?

The President. No, not in a more direct way. Military forces have been used over the years. The arrest power rests with the Coast Guard. The coastguardsmen can be aboard naval vessels. But we have an interdiction network that is manned and operated by our military. But what the question implies to me at least, of a quantum leap forward in terms of this—I don't know.

One of the things I have felt is that sometimes the military says, well, we can't undertake this mission or that because of readiness. It is my view that sometimes an exercise that results in the interdiction of aircraft coming into this country on an illegal mission is a good mission and should not be detracted from the readiness. So, I think that we're always looking at the mission of the military in this regard, but I don't want to give the military more arrest powers. I think we've got a very proper justice system in this country. I do think that they can be extraordinarily useful, and have been, in interdiction and in working with countries that want their cooperation.

Q. Are you prepared to use troops in the

United States to enforce the laws against drug consumption, to cut down on the demand which entices the supply?

The President. Well, not to cut down on the demand. I don't think that's a function of the U.S. military. We have police powers in this country; they are properly defined; and that should not, in my view, be altered.

Q. There are many questions that ask why do you find it necessary——

The President. The demand—let me be sure—the demand side really relates also to education, to people—this is bad; you should not do this. We've condoned things in this country that we should have condemned long ago in terms of narcotics.

Drug Summit in Cartagena, Colombia

Q. There are several questions that have asked why do you find it necessary to physically go to Colombia?

The President. Well, let me explain that to you because I think it's on the minds of a lot of people. I went to a barbecue in Beeville, Texas—*[laughter]*—and there were 800 people there—not quite this big a mob. And I thought, well, these people are doing this to welcome me back to south Texas. And I decided I would shake hands with everybody there. We politicians are all alike, you know—go out there and shake hands. Art, you know how that is. *[Laughter]* So, out I went. And I think about 15 percent of them at that point said, hey, you know, we're hoping you don't do this.

Let me explain it to you. In the first place, I am not going to do something stupid or macho. *[Laughter]* I love—the guy they used to call timid is now "macho man" or something. *[Laughter]* It has nothing to do with that; it doesn't have anything to do with personal. It has a lot to do with the support for a courageous leader in Colombia.

And I believe, and I think this goes for those who have the responsibility of protecting any President of the United States, that the security of the President can be protected on this naval base, a place where the man has his own home that is cut off from the mainland except by one entrance.

And I don't want to send a signal on your behalf or my behalf that the United States says to this great President, look, our Presi-

dent can't come there, even though we think the security can be guaranteed; and thus push him, perhaps inadvertently, to make a kind of deal that he has resisted making with these narco-traffickers.

I talked to a foreign leader the other day from South America, and he agrees with this rationale. So, it isn't whimsical or a desire to be in harm's way. I think we've got good arrangements, and I think it is good, sound antinarcotic policy to support President Barco [of Colombia], who is doing an awful lot to protect our kids from the scourge of narcotics.

War on Drugs

Q. There are claims that the removal of General Ortega will improve our efforts at interdicting international drug trafficking. Do you agree with this?

The President. Yes, I do, because there's some symbolism there. And just as I think the extradition of Carlos Lehder and the Colombians' pursuit of the drug lord that was recently killed down there in battle in Colombia—those things help, because if they see major participants, traffickers going about their life without threat, why, I just think it sends the wrong signal.

Mexico-U.S. Relations

Q. Since the Panama invasion, have our relations with Mexico improved?

The President. Yes. And I'll tell you one thing that was good. Our Secretary of the Treasury went down there—I don't know whether you saw it on Sunday—and signed with President Salinas, the very fine young President of Mexico, an agreement on Third World debt. I think that was a good sign.

Look, I think I know enough about this hemisphere to know that anytime a United States force is used in Central America, or wherever else in this hemisphere, there are going to be concerns built on a foundation of history that concern our friends and those who are less friendly to us in this hemisphere. But I've explained as best I can, through letter and by phone, to these leaders why we acted the way we did.

I will tell you that I am convinced not only is the relationship with Mexico good and is it strong, I see nothing but making it even better. And I'm going to work at that because Mexico—we must not take for granted the fact that we have marvelously strong allies to our north and friends to our south. Sometimes, blessed as we are by our own geography, we forget that. And there could be an inclination to neglect our neighbors, and I don't want to do that. And I can't tell you that there has been no strains, but I think some of what you've been reading about South American reaction has been overstated. And I base that on some contact with the individual leaders in this hemisphere. But it's an exciting hemisphere. This hemisphere can be, in the next couple of years, totally democratic. We must not neglect it.

So, if somebody disagrees with me on Panama and South America or Central America, that just redoubles my desire to make it right, make them understand that the President of the United States is going to protect American life, make them understand that 92 percent of the people in Panama support what I did, make them understand that democracy now has a chance, and make them understand that we're going to assist that democracy. Once I do a better job of that, I think any last concerns about what happened there will be laid to rest.

General Noriega of Panama

Q. Why are we wasting time with Noriega when he cannot possibly receive a constitutionally fair trial without compromising national security? Why not send him to exile in a country willing to take him? [*Laughter*]

The President. Well, the line is not very long, for one thing. And secondly—[*laughter*]—secondly, look, I would just disagree with the person writing the question that the given is he can't get a fair trial. Of course he can get a fair trial—and we've seen that over and over again in highly controversial cases. And so, our justice system that bends over backwards to be fair will, indeed, acquit itself well in this case.

Q. Is your administration——

The President. And should. The man's entitled to a fair trial.

Foreign Policy

Q. Is your administration prepared to accept governments you dislike, even if they carry their public support, such as the Sandinistas in Nicaragua?

The President. Please define acceptance. [*Laughter*] I mean, my aspiration is to help and assist those countries in this hemisphere that want to walk down democracy's road— freedom, democracy, the very changes that we see coming forward in Eastern Europe. Who would have thought we'd be talking about trying to assist Czechoslovakia a year ago? Or Romania? Or some of these other countries? So, I don't think we can dictate exactly what kind of system somebody else has. It's not our business, particularly if they have free and certifiably fair elections. But I think one's inclination is to help those who have the same reverence for democracy and freedom that we have.

Education Reform

Q. You stated in your State of the Union Address that you wish to improve education and to implement the goal of best by the year 2000. How do you plan to implement your goal of having our graduates be the best by the year 2000?

The President. Well, we have a sound program, what I call the Education Excellence Act, before the Congress today. It's complex legislation, but I want to see it passed. Probably get amended, probably get changed, but it challenges people to think anew. We've gotten the Governors together in a Governors conference that was more than just frill. What it did was get—agree to set national goals. And in the speech the other night, I spelled out four of the national goals that the Governors have agreed should be national. And they themselves will get to work and redouble their efforts in their States and try to encourage the localities to implement the program that we've spelled out.

But let me be careful here, because it isn't the role of the Federal Government to do this alone. It can't do it. Seven percent of the educational spending in this country is Federal. And the rest, for very understandable and, I think, wonderful reasons, belong at the State and local level or private educational institution level.

And so, we can exhort; we can push for the kind of legislation; we can push for implementation of the national goals through the use of the bully pulpit in the White House. And then we've got to encourage the Governors and the local school boards and our teachers, when it comes to alternative certification and all of these things, to think anew. And we can do this. But we're trying to put some emphasis on things like math and science, so we can guarantee our ability to compete in the future. But the Federal Government isn't going to do it alone. It wouldn't be good, either, for the Federal Government to try to do it alone.

Mrs. Bush

Q. President Bush, this is your last question. And before I ask the question, I wish to remind our audience to please remain seated until President Bush and Governor Deukmejian have left the room. This is a summary of many different questions that I've received, President Bush, and that is:

Where is Mrs. Bush, and how is she? [*Laughter*]

The President. I know you'll never believe this, but I'm getting a terrible inferiority complex. [*Laughter*] She's fine. And we both have something in common now—the vision thing—because she has this eye problem. But she is doing very well. There is no hidden agenda to her health. And today she is down as one of the Thousand Points of Light, which she's been for a long time, helping on literacy in southern California. And I'll meet her tonight in Omaha. But she's doing just great, and thank you for asking about her.

Thank you very much.

Note: The President spoke at 12:35 p.m. in the Grand Ballroom at the San Francisco Hilton Hotel. He was introduced by Joseph Fink, president of Dominican College and quarterly chairman of the Commonwealth Club. Following his remarks, the President attended a reception at the hotel and then traveled to Omaha, NE.

Statement by Press Secretary Fitzwater on the President's Remarks to the Commonwealth Club in San Francisco, California
February 7, 1990

In the President's reference to Chancellor Kohl and Foreign Minister Genscher [of the Federal Republic of Germany] today, he meant that Germany would remain as a member of NATO, but NATO may have a changing mission. This changing mission, involving an increased political role for NATO, was discussed in Brussels following the Malta summit.

Statement by Press Secretary Fitzwater on the Presidential Election Monitoring Commission on Nicaragua
February 7, 1990

Senator Richard Lugar, cochairman of the Presidential Election Monitoring Commission on Nicaragua, has announced this afternoon that the refusal by the Government of Nicaragua to issue visas to the entire group has prevented the Commission from carrying out its functions. We are disappointed that Sandinista stonewalling has brought this about. The President's bipartisan Commission reflects the full spectrum of opinion in the Congress on Nicaraguan issues and is universally regarded to be fair and impartial. It is hard to understand why a government that claims to be committed to a free and fair election would fear permitting such a group to observe the electoral campaign and balloting.

Nicaragua's refusal to permit official U.S. observers chosen by the President, in consultation with the Congress, follows a series of other actions which bring into question the Sandinista commitment. These include continued violence and coercion against opposition activists, imbalance in access to the media, and the use of state resources to help the Sandinista candidates. Politically motivated delays by the Sandinistas to disbursement of nonpartisan campaign funds to the opposition for such activities as voter registration and election monitoring have forced cancellation or curtailment of critical election-support programs. These funds, which were approved by the U.S. Congress,

have the sole objective of facilitating the conduct of an open campaign in which the maximum number of Nicaraguans can participate, vote in a secret ballot, and have their vote honestly counted.

We believe that a free and fair election and Nicaraguan adherence to its other commitments under the Esquipulas process offer the possibility for a stable peace in Nicaragua and for improved relations with the United States. The United States Government has undertaken a policy for the last year, on a bipartisan basis, which has aimed at doing all that is possible to enhance that possibility. Sandinista actions thus far are troubling, but we continue to remain hopeful that the desire of the Nicaraguan people for full freedom will prevail.

Remarks at a Fundraising Breakfast for Governor Kay Orr in Omaha, Nebraska
February 8, 1990

The President. Thank you all. It's sure nice to be back. Thank you, thank you. Thank you very, very much. Kay, thank you so much. And to P.J., the mayor, delighted to be with you, sir. I remember sitting in that Oval Office just before you were elected. I liked his confidence; I liked his strength. And he's doing a great job. I want to salute our congressional delegation. I don't think Virginia or Doug are here today, but they're doing a superb job in Washington, steadfast in support of the principles Kay just was enunciating.

I'm delighted to see my friend and, in a sense, mentor, your former Governor, Charlie Thone, way down here—and a good friend he is, and great Governor he was for this State. And then I salute Norm Riffle and Duane Acklie, Sallie Folsom. I'm especially pleased to have our [Republican] national chairman out here, Lee Atwater, who is doing a superb job for the party all across this country. The national committee has never been stronger.

And, of course, my friend and the future Senator, Hal Daub. I've worked with him; I

know him well. His wife was extremely active in supporting me in the early days of the last campaign. And I'm grateful to both of them. And I know he'll make a fine Senator. Hal, good luck to you.

I'm delighted to be here at this relatively early morning breakfast. It reminds me of the time I told our oldest grandkid that the early bird gets the worm. He says, "I think I'll sleep in and have pancakes." [*Laughter*] You know how these 12-year-olds are.

Well, this morning, appropriately, we're going with Special K—and, yes, in honor of a very special woman who has come a long way since she first worked for the Republican Party in—I don't want to date you, Kay, but I'm told it was 1963. And she's gone from ringing doorbells to making history—the great Governor of the State of Nebraska, Kay Orr. And I am so proud to be with her today. And a confession: We've known each other since 1976. I wanted to come here, and so did Barbara, to personally and enthusiastically endorse her. I'm here because she's made the tough choices and, in my view, the right decisions—and because her first term has produced not rhetoric, not empty rhetoric, but solid results for Nebraska. Dwight Eisenhower once said, "Our best protection against bigger government in Washington is better government in the States." So, let's guarantee that that keeps going. Let's help Kay keep making government better, and let's be sure that she wins a second term.

I was going over some of the economic statistics, and I believe that this election will decide whether Nebraska enjoys continued prosperity and whether you continue to have the leadership it takes to win in the battles we're in: the war on crime and drugs. It will decide whether Nebraska has farm policies that work—we want a Governor we can work with and listen to as we try to adapt our farm policies to the needs of these States—an education system that makes the grade. Those are the questions. And I am absolutely convinced that the answer lies in "Four More for Orr."

Barbara and I love Bill, Kay's husband. And I'm told that he likes to tell—he went to the bank to cash a check and the teller looked up and said, "Are you the wife of the Governor?" [*Laughter*] Then she got a little flustered and tried to make amends. "What I mean," she said, "are you Mr. Kay Orr?" [*Laughter*] Look, Bill, I know what you mean here. Kay said, "It's fine you're here, Mr. President, but if you really want to get this crowd fired up, bring Barbara." So, here she is. [*Laughter*] We've got a lot in common, my man. [*Applause*] Not too much—look, I've got to live with her, please.

No, but as America's first Republican woman Governor, Kay has become a household name. And why not—with stats that rival the Big Red. Let me tell you, more than 23,000 new jobs and $2.4 billion in new investment since 1987—those are Kay Orr victories. And so is net farm income, nearly tripled, and an unemployment rate—what's the rate you told me?

Governor Orr. At 2.7.

The President. Two-point-seven. If there ever is full employment in the United States, it has to be an unemployment rate of 2.7 percent. And that's cut in half from what it was. Nebraska's first-ever child care credit, crusade to improve secondary and higher learning—still further victories—and so are our Drug Advisory Council. And then, we all know of her commitment to wetlands and to wildlife preservation.

These triumphs have helped the working people of Nebraska. And Kay needs a second term to finish the job that she's so effectively begun. And yet the need, as Ike said, is not a State's alone—in this instance, not Nebraska's alone. I need her, too, to support the work of our administration. And I mean it, we do want to make America a kinder and gentler place and get more results for more Americans than at any other time in our history. Last Wednesday night I talked of this in my State of the Union Address and of the triumphs of 1989, like the lowest unemployment rate nationally in 16 years, inflation at less than 5 percent, the longest peacetime economic growth in the history of the United States. And yet what I call the "idea called America" is like Nebraska: It's something to build upon, not to rest upon. I feel that our administration is really just beginning. And I think Kay would concede that although she's been Governor 4 years, she's got a feeling of commencement as well.

And so, we have sent legislation to the Congress now to confront at the national level our most crucial issues. For example, prosperity does mean little if our kids aren't free from drugs. So, last month I announced a 1990 National Drug Control Strategy: Phase II of the comprehensive drug policy we unveiled last year. And I'm very pleased with the support it is getting all across the country. We're asking Congress to spend over $10.5 billion in fiscal year 1991 for education, treatment, interdiction, and enforcement, about a 70-percent increase since I took office in 1989.

We also want mandatory time for firearms offenses—no deals when criminals use a gun—and as Phase II proposes, an expansion of the death penalty for these drug kingpins. I believe it's long overdue. And then we have requested significant increases in Federal assistance to States and localities in drug use prevention, treatment, and law enforcement. And we've already made considerable progress in adding more police, more prosecutors, more prisons. Kay

Orr supports these steps. Her initials aren't K.O. for nothing. [*Laughter*] And that's what she intends to help to do to crime and drug use. I need her. I need her as Governor to work with the local police and the mayors in this great State to take back the streets.

Then there's another priority, and one in which Barbara's been standing for for a long, long time. I'm talking about the education of our kids. Kay Orr knows, as I do, that the future of the country really fundamentally begins with education. So, she supports our Educational Excellence Act of 1989, which can help achieve, by the year 2000, the education goals that I announced in that State of the Union speech last Wednesday—goals, incidentally, that were developed with almost the unanimous support of the Governors—certainly, Kay in the forefront of helping us develop these national goals. And let me be clear: They're not trying to dictate to the local school systems or get into the curriculum or to the pay level for teachers; we're talking about broad national goals that respect the concept of federalism that properly has guided our education system for a long time.

We must ensure that every student in America starts school ready to learn. There is a Federal role here. And that's why I've proposed a record increase in funds, an extra half a billion dollars, for a program which has and continues to work: Head Start. And we must see that each school has an environment where kids can learn. That means making every school drug-free. Our graduation rate must be no—these are goals by 2000—no less than 90 percent, and we've got to make these diplomas mean something. So we want U.S. students to be first in the world in math and science achievement. And we've got to guarantee that each American is a skilled, literate worker and citizen. Together, I believe that we can make this idea called America mean a decent education for all.

The idea called America also means that working parents should have increased child care options. Our legislation will achieve that goal. I don't want to see the Federal Government dictate where a kid has to be looked after in a child care program. I want to give the parents the choice to be able to take care of those kids as best they can, give them the ability to provide the day care; and that's what our approach is all about.

It also means a cleaner America. Kay touched on this. And we have sent up the first rewrite of the Clean Air Act in over 10 years. We also want to make a more abundant rural America, where Americans work, invest, and save. In the late 1980's, farm income hit near-record levels. Now we want to build on that good news, make it even better, and keep Nebraska strong by keeping agriculture thriving in the 1990's. And Kay was in there now discussing with me some new ideas she has on crop insurance, expressing, incidentally, her—hope this won't betray the confidence of our talk—her confidence in our great Nebraskan who is the Secretary of Agriculture, Clayton Yeutter. I depend on him. He's good. He knows agriculture, and I'm proud he's at my side.

But speaking of agriculture, first, I hope to negotiate a new trade agreement with the Soviet Union by the time of our 1990 summit, not too many months away. This will relax trade barriers between East and West, expanding markets for American exports. I feel strongly that selling our grain to the Soviet Union is in America's interest as well as in the interest of the Soviet Union. And next, we are going to write a new farm bill this year. It must emphasize market-oriented farm policies giving producers more flexibility to decide what crops to grow. And we need the investment created by passing our capital gains tax cut proposal, which would apply to the sale of farmland and, in my view, will create jobs all across the economic spectrum in this country. Together, these decisions will show what's good for agriculture is good for America.

What's good for all of us, naturally, is that I not talk too long here, with you all having to get to work. [*Laughter*] So, let me tell you one of my favorite fishing stories. It concerns Mark Twain, who, like all fishermen, loved to brag about his exploits.

Twain once spent 3 weeks fishing in the Maine woods, ignoring the fact that the State's fishing season had closed. On the way home, aboard the train, he sat next to a stranger and immediately started telling about all the fish he'd caught. Finally, Mark Twain asked, "By the way, who are you, sir?" The stranger said, "Well, I'm the State game warden. Who are you?" With that, America's greatest writer nearly swallowed his cigar. And after a long pause he answered, "Well, to be perfectly truthful, warden, I'm the biggest damn liar in the whole United States of America." [*Laughter*]

Twain loved to brag. But then, he had much to brag about. And so does Nebraska when it comes to your first elected woman Governor. And let me conclude simply by saying she has my full confidence. She's made tough decisions, right decisions. And

their results have enriched Nebraskans from the banks of the Missouri to the Wyoming line.

So, let's ensure "Four More for Governor Orr" and pledge to support one of our truly great Governors. Thank you very much for this occasion. Thanks for your support for Kay. And God bless you all. Thank you very much.

Note: The President spoke at 8:35 a.m. in Peony Park Ballroom. In his remarks, he referred to P.J. Morgan, mayor of Omaha; Norm Riffle, Nebraska Republican Party chairman; Duane Acklie and Sallie Folsom, members of the Republican National Committee; and Cindy Daub, wife of senatorial candidate Hal Daub.

Nomination of Keith McNamara To Be a Member of the Board of Directors of the State Justice Institute
February 8, 1990

The President today announced his intention to nominate Keith McNamara to be a member of the Board of Directors of the State Justice Institute for the remainder of a term expiring September 17, 1992. He would succeed Joseph Wentling Brown.

Since 1952 Mr. McNamara has been an attorney with McNamara and McNamara in

Columbus, OH.

Mr. McNamara graduated from Amherst College (B.A., 1950) and Ohio State University (J.D., 1953). He was born October 12, 1928, in Upper Sandusky, OH. He is married, has four children, and resides in Columbus, OH.

Remarks to Strategic Air Command Personnel
February 8, 1990

Well, good morning. This is the President speaking to you from the new command post at SAC Headquarters at Offutt. I know it's not morning for all the SAC troops listening in on this call, and that it is very early in the morning for some of you. Now I'm in the middle of a visit at your headquarters to discuss with General Chain your mission, the critical need to continue our strategic modernization program, and strategic arms control.

Earlier this week I visited Fort Irwin, the

Army's National Training Center, and spoke to a group in California about strategic defense. All of these subjects are vital. And yet what I am always impressed with in my visits to our military bases around the world is the people who serve. No matter how capable our system, it is the professional men and women of our military who makes them work. The dedicated, skilled individual is the foundation of deterrence. You spend time away from your families and homes so that other Americans can sleep safely in theirs. Thank you for that—and for braving conditions that are not always the best, especially the weather at some of the bases.

I also want to salute your role in shaping history, for the historical changes we are seeing in the Soviet Union are in no small part due to the vigilance and sheer hard work of the men and women of the Strategic Air Command. Your practice of deterrence has kept the peace and defined the basis for positive change in the Soviet Union. You should be proud of your role in that. But we still live in a time of uncertainty. So, as we push for a major new arms agreement with the Soviets, to increase stability we will continue to modernize strategic forces. Any time day or night, in the missile field or the flight line, in a command post, or in an office, you are deter-

rence.

So, on behalf of all Americans, I thank you for your sacrifices. For you air crews, keep 'em flying. And for you missile crews, the pointy end is up, and keep 'em in the green. God bless you all, and thank you for your wonderful service to this, the greatest country on the face of the Earth. God bless you.

Note: The President spoke by telecommunications network at 10:41 a.m. from the Command Center Operations Room at Strategic Air Command Headquarters at Offutt Air Force Base, Omaha, NE. In his remarks, he referred to Gen. John T. Chain, commander of Strategic Air Command Headquarters. Following his remarks, the President traveled to Columbus, OH.

Remarks at a Briefing for Head Start Volunteers in Columbus, Ohio
February 8, 1990

Ms. Clark. What I would like to do, President and Mrs. Bush, is to officially welcome you to our Head Start program and to Columbus on behalf of our board of trustees, our executive director, our policy council chairperson, the children of Head Start and their families, the staff, all of our community who work so very closely with us. We'd just like to say welcome.

The President. Well, we're very pleased to be here. Barbara—the two of us in the family, see, this level of the family—she knows much more about this because she's visited many Head Start programs. But I do want to say that when the Governors had the education meeting, education summit, everybody agreed that being ready to learn, the concept of—what do you give, 18 years to it, or 20-some years? No, but some of us are just really getting out front now in something that many of you worked for a long time, and it is a national objective now. It's one of the key objectives. And so we have increased the funding and all of that for it.

But I really want to hear about parental involvement—I know some are parents here—and the whole volunteer aspect of it, as well as the way it just works in practice. Because we believe—the whole administration—and it's not Republican or Democrat—I think on this one it gets way across any partisan politics. And people are saying, Look, the time has come to put even more emphasis on that which a lot of you have given your lives to doing. So we're here to learn and listen and say thank you, too.

Ms. Clark. Okay. What I think—what I would like to do now is to go around and introduce all of us who are here. And I also think that our group is very representative of what you've just mentioned—that it's not about partisanism between the parties, but that we're all here and we're working for one common cause.

I would like to introduce our president of our board of trustees, Mr. Richard Trelease.

The President. I met Richard.

Ms. Clark. One of our Head Start directors, Mrs. Christine Franklin, of our John XXIII Head Start program. One of our very faithful parents of John XXIII, Ms. Tamara

Scruggs. My assistant director, Mrs. Mary Kay Dailey. The chairperson of our policy council, Mrs. Orlinda Jabbar. Our executive director, Mr. Curtis A. Brooks. And also a former Head Start student who has received an award from you for academic achievement in 1989—she received a Presidential award and letter—Ms. Senta Clark.

The President. How old are you, Senta?

Senta Clark. Seven.

The President. Seven—all right!

Mrs. Bush. Oh, it's beautiful.

Ms. Clark. And her father, Mr. Nordholm Clark.

The President. How are you, sir?

Ms. Clark. Our Head Start director at Southwestern Head Start, Mrs. Jo Bostic. Our deputy executive director, Mr. William Conley. Another very faithful parent at Southwestern, Mrs. Shelly Cantrell. And I would like to introduce Mayor Veronika Shepard, from the village of Urban Crest, who started out as a Head Start parent. And Veronika may have started out about 22 years ago, I think, with myself. And since that time, she has elevated herself through the years. She is now the mayor of Urban Crest. And she has also just recently returned from a tour in Africa.

The President. Fantastic. I just want to be sure that when we're doing the introducing—I know you all know, probably, Don Casey and Chalmers—just so you—we're so proud of them and glad they're with us. Chalmers Wiley.

Ms. Clark. Absolutely. And they are individuals who definitely give support to our program. Senator Casey and Congressman Wiley. Also at our State legislative level, we have Senator Eugene Watts, Representative Ray Miller, and also Representative Dave Gilmore. And I'd like to commend our State legislative branch because through the sponsorship of Representative Ray Miller, the State of Ohio now is providing funding to Head Start for Head Start expansion to the tune of $19 million. So this is something really great for Ohio, and I really just thank everyone.

The two in the back row——

The President. Smiling proudly.

Ms. Clark. ——smiling proudly—[laughter]—are my parents. Absolutely. Mrs. Alberta Clark and Mr. Spencer Clark.

Mrs. Bush. Your mother's the one who got you interested?

Ms. Clark. Absolutely. My mother's the one who got me interested. My mother is the one that, when Mr. Curtis Brooks came to our church, the Union Grove Baptist Church, and asked our minister, Reverend Phil Hill, if he could put a Head Start center in our church, and Phil Hill, Reverend Hill, said yes. And then my mother was called out and asked to serve on the committee that was reviewing. So I was very proud.

The President. And that was close to 18— how many years ago?

Mrs. Bush. Twenty-three, she said.

The President. Twenty-two. I missed it, yes.

Ms. Clark. I don't think I told you how old I was at the time. [*Laughter*]

The President. No, no you didn't.

Ms. Clark. Twenty-two years ago.

Mrs. Bush. Ten. [*Laughter*]

The President. Okay, well. But who's going to tell me how the—am I supposed to just kind of ask questions, because I'm dying to ask a few questions. And I'd love to hear from the parents exactly how it works, how many parents end up getting involved. The more the better, we think, because it emphasizes not only—helps when the kids go home and all, but it also is, I think, very good for strong family. But do you want to help me with that one?

Ms. Clark. Can I start you out just a little bit——

The President. Yes.

Ms. Clark. ——by saying that out of our entire staff—which we have a staff of 161 individuals—50 percent are former Head Start parents.

The President. That's marvelous.

Ms. Clark. So, that gives us the beginning as to what our parents' involvement level is. And now I'm going to turn it over to our parents. I do want to say that we also have a home-based program. We recently converted over the past 2 years to home-base services, so we have a home-based parent; we have a center-based parent. And we have a parent who has done national training at our national Head Start conference.

The President. Tamara, tell us how it

works.

Ms. Scruggs. Parent involvement is very important. It's important for the kids because the kids are always excited to have their parents come into the classroom and into the center to help.

The President. Just give me an honest percent. It is a hard—it is tough. But what kind of percentage? Would 50 percent of them—I mean, say, you have a room full of kids—would 50 percent of their parents in one way or another try to be involved, or is that too high, or is that too low? Too high. So some don't, in other words.

Ms. Franklin. Some don't because—that it's a low income program and the parents are just having so much trouble with things at home that sometimes it's kind of hard. We do have a very good parent involvement. The staff is very instrumental in bringing parents into the school——

The President. Maybe I could ask Mr. Clark—obviously, your daughter, Senta, is doing pretty darn well—don't be embarrassed—[*laughter*]—pretty darn well. What do you think she got in Head Start that maybe other kids that didn't get to go to Head Start program would?

Mr. Clark. Well, I think it prepared her for—it's almost like when a kid is in high school getting ready for college. Head Start prepared her for elementary school. And it taught her a lot of things that probably I couldn't have taught her at home at 3 years old. And, therefore, as she got further on in school she excelled and, one day, turned around and you sent her a letter. [*Laughter*]

The President. The expression, Mr. Clark, that we use on that—and I expect all the pros around here know this—but it's "ready to learn." I mean, it's not the final, obviously, learning experience, but the concept is, let's get these kids ready to learn. And perhaps that's exactly what happened.

Did you like it, Senta? Do you remember—you're too old now, but do you remember much about the program? Did you want to go when your dad said, hey, you're going to go to Head Start? Or were you saying, no, I'd rather hang out here at home? When you were little, I mean.

Senta. I wanted to go.

The President. Yes. And then liked it when you were there?

Senta. Yes.

The President. That's great. Now what do you do? What's your interest now that you're older? Any one subject, or anything?

Senta. Math.

Mrs. Bush. That will please the President. [*Laughter*]

The President. Math. That's great. Who else wants to chip in on this and how it works from teachers, or volunteers, or——

Mrs. Bush. I wanted to ask about the parents, if you—because I'm into literacy—if you have programs for furthering education.

The President. And the response down there?

Ms. Shepard. I would like to touch base on that. Even though I'm a past parent, if it hadn't been for the Head Start program encouraging and giving me the incentive to further my education, I really feel that I wouldn't be now in the position I'm in as mayor of Urban Village. And that's one thing Head Start does promote with parents, is to further your education, right along with your child. So it gives a holistic approach when you go into the Head Start program. It touches the whole family, everybody.

Mrs. Bush. The other thing—I've been briefed on Head Start—but I'm so thrilled that they get physicals and dentals and hot meals. I mean, it's a wonderful program.

Ms. Clark. Absolutely—the total comprehensive approach. But to get back to the question in regards to literacy: We do have GED classes that are operating in our program. And what we're finding, and most especially I've seen this in the last couple of weeks—we have parents that are attending the GED classes. And then some of them are coming to me, letting me know that individuals from their community, or neighbors, are wanting to know, can they attend the classes? So, they're coming back and saying, "Ms. Clark, can someone else come?" Or, "I have a friend, she would like to come into the GED class." And we're opening up the doors, of course, and saying yes. And when Senta talks about math being a likable subject to her—we also have a math and science program that we're initiating. And we're doing this through the National Urban Coalition, who is promoting math and science. And what we're hoping to do through the GED classes is to also extend that into our math and science——

Mrs. Bush. That's wonderful.

Mr. Conley. One of the things I would like to just add, too—when you talk about parents—is that we recognize that it's not sufficient to just work with the children. That's wonderful, but you've got to do something about the environment from which the families come. And as the overall agency preparing for Head Start, we've been instrumental in accessing other kinds of resources that can impact on the family. As an example, specifically with the parents, is a new program that we have called Project HOPE. That stands for Head Start Opportunities for Parents through Education by Employment.

What we have done was to write for competitive—which we would receive from the HHS. And with that we were working intensively with a group of parents. We work with 150 people—well, actually, 75 will be an experimental program because this is a demonstration effort. And we hope by that to be able to show through intensive case work, through education, that we can involve the parents in some kind of a training and job placement and so on. That's going to make them more successful——

The President. Good point.

Mr. Brooks. Our goal, of course, is self-sufficiency. Bill is right there. We look forward to a more advanced kind of family planning. I think the leader is doing something magnificent right now. And we just basically believe in the holistic approach. The Head Start child is there because the family is poor. And we're trying our best to come up with strategies to get them out of poverty. One of the problems we, of course, have is that our operating funds come out of community service—and, of course, that is not in the budget. I talked to the national office this morning and they said that Senator Mark Hatfield would be by to see you to discuss that with you, because he's sponsoring that——

The President. You know, it is tough when you have to make choices—this funding for Head Start dramatically up and then

some of these other things. So we'll have to see what we can be helpful in.

Mrs. Bush. How about volunteers in the private sector? Do they get involved?

Ms. Clark. Yes. Yes, they do.

The President. And you're talking about Head Start?

Mrs. Bush. In Head Start, yes. But what—I mean, do corporations get involved and help? Or—with equipment? Or volunteers as one on one?

Ms. Clark. Well, we have a lot of one-on-one volunteer efforts that take place. We see the involvement of other community agencies and organizations that work with us. And I think very recently we've had several different agencies that have been calling or sent letters, and maybe Mary Kay might want to speak to a couple of them—some of the sororities that have come in and one of the sororities.

Ms. Dailey. The Methodist children's home here called and they wanted to know if they can send some young ladies. And they were 14 to 17 years old.

Mrs. Bush. Perfect.

Ms. Dailey. I saw that as a beautiful age for the children. And seven of them came last Friday to one of the centers, and the ladies that came were fantastic. Now, what are they going to do? I think if they just go in and sit down with the children, they don't need to tell you what they'll do. And they just went in and they sat a minute, but the children came to them and they went to the children, and they went right off into the afternoon's activities.

The President. What will they do if they keep up their interest? They'll come back once a week or——

Ms. Dailey. Yes.

The President. Something like that?

Ms. Dailey. This group will come back once a week every Friday.

The President. Yes.

Ms. Dailey. They gave a commitment to them. So that was really, really a good thing.

Mr. Trelease. As president of the board I guess that makes me the chief volunteer. [*Laughter*] Your presence and what you just said should help strengthen further efforts getting our community involved. All local people in the room would honestly tell you Columbus is in an era of growth and development unparalleled in its history. That will only remain as strong as the youth in our communities and the involvement of more people in our community. And I think your visit here is—I can really salute both of you for being here because it underscores the relationship that's needed to move us even further.

Ms. Franklin. I would like to add to that. We have six of our high school children in West Side and in our centers working with our—what we call the bottom—who are in our program—and we're working on a way to eliminate that through the—[*inaudible*]. It's been very, very fine in the classrooms.

Mrs. Bush. I hope some corporations will get involved and help you, too.

Ms. Clark. Yes, we're hoping that also.

Mrs. Bush. Maybe with jobs for the parents—in some fringe way or——

The President. You were going to say something, and I think you got preempted, Ms. Jabbar? Or were you? Maybe I had it wrong, but I thought you were getting up there on the edge—[*laughter*]. What end of it are you in now?

Ms. Jabbar. I'm a parent in the program, and I'm the policy council chairperson. And the policy council——

The President. Here in this installation here?

Ms. Jabbar. Yes.

The President. So, it's a neighborhood—it's not citywide, in other words?

Ms. Jabbar. It's a countywide.

The President. Countywide. Yes, yes. You have a kid in Head Start now?

Ms. Jabbar. My child was in——

The President. Was in, yes.

Ms. Clark. Because she had a 2-year turn as a chairperson.

The President. I see, I see.

Ms. Jabbar. But I've had two kids go through the Head Start program. And when they finished, like Veronika said was that I've grown being involved in the Head Start program and volunteering and so forth. I have grown, and I think with the Head Start program they have given me marketable skills that I know that I can go out and use in the outside world.

The President. You know, a lot of pressure

in the communities, of course—financial, you mentioned a lot of the kids out of impoverished homes and all—but do you detect a—is there more interest in parents in trying now, given all the pressures from narcotics in communities all across the whole country? I mean, these pressures—it's not one neighborhood. I mean, do you find that the pressures of society are making parents more like you, more willing to volunteer and get involved, or not? Or is it—do we just have to do a lot better in that? Maybe Veronika could help? I mean, I don't know. I'm really asking; I don't have an opinion. I wish your answer was, look, people are waking up, realizing they got to hold these families together, and they're going to do what you did. I'm not sure that we're there yet. We want to try to help as best we can in encouraging this approach. But you get a feeling on it?

Mr. Brooks. Mr. President, I can simply say that when we recruit for this program every year, I have watched the parents grow. And they are growing to a point now where—we only used to talk to maybe 200 or 300—and I went in the room the other day when the recruiting session came, and there were about 700 parents in there.

The President. That is encouraging.

Mr. Brooks. So, I think that the emphasis that you're putting on education is reaching a lot of people. And I don't think you need to shortchange yourself on that. You are causing some things to happen.

The President. Do you all have a program called Cities in Schools in Columbus? New York has it—one of these where they get—it's not a Head Start necessarily, but it's to encourage—it's a mix where the city government and private sector gets involved in trying to get almost—it's not replacing parents but bolstering——

Mrs. Bush. At-risk children.

The President. ——at-risk children. Encouraging them to go, seeing that they're not just totally neglected when they leave school and go home. But you don't have that particular program here, I guess. It's a volunteer——

Ms. Clark. High school level.

The President. Yes, that's good.

Mr. Trelease. But I think one of the aspects you'd be interested in is the home-based part of the program. We have a parent who is——

The President. Shelly, you're on. [*Laughter*] Your big moment. Address yourself to Dan Rather, wherever he may be. [*Laughter*]

Ms. Cantrell. Well, I'd like to say about the home base is that it's important for us because we live in a rural area and the bus doesn't come to us. And without the home base, my child wouldn't be in Head Start. And I have a time now each week where we have a one-on-one together. And it helps every day, because we have an activity to work on. And I don't think without the Head Start I would be as conscious of what my children need for their education.

Mrs. Bush. Does someone come to your house one day a week?

Q. Every Monday she comes for an hour and a half and she tells us an activity to work on. And it could be colors or shapes. This week we're working on matching.

Mrs. Bush. But she sets you up for the week?

Q. Yes. And then she'll come back and she'll ask us how we did—if my child is ready to do that part. There was an activity that she just wasn't ready to do yet, and so we changed it to something that my child is ready to do. And it's like you say, ready to learn—she's getting ready.

The President. That's encouraging.

Mrs. Bush. You have more than one child?

Q. I have three.

Mrs. Bush. That keeps you pretty busy.

The President. Ms. Bostic, you've been strangely silent here. Now, you're entitled—equal time here.

Ms. Bostic. Okay. I was thinking in terms of Head Start really, unlike a lot of programs, reaches out to parents. And we do have families that have very serious problems, more serious than years ago when I first started. But we don't give up on them, and we do go out—and we have a lot of opportunities for them to get involved. Maybe not necessarily in the classroom, but doing things at home, coming to meetings, or even working with an individual. So, I think our approach to reaching out has made a difference. We don't wait for par-

ents to come to us.

Ms. Clark. Some of that we can see in our average daily attendance. You know, with the Head Start regulations, we have a triggering point, which is 85 percent average daily attendance, that we know we must maintain. And what we've been seeing over this past school year is that we had parents that are sending their children 100 percent of the time. And then we have—outside our council level, we let the different centers know, so parents are now beginning to compete with one another—their center against another center as to how many of us can get our kids here every day. So, when we talk about parent involvement, to me that's a part of the starting point. When I see that parents are bringing their children every day, that's a starter. Then there are some that do work in the classroom or some who come to the parent meetings, but we know that they are all involved to some degree.

We're going to have to begin to wrap up, right after my supervisor speaks. [*Laughter*]

Mr. Conley. I see that you're on a schedule and I saw the cue for us to begin to wrap up, but I think we would be remiss if we didn't point out to you the drawings that the children did.

The President. Let's see these.

Mr. Conley. Some of which are portraits of you and Mrs. Bush. [*Laughter*]

Mrs. Bush. I don't see me yet.

The President. Here you are. [*Laughter*]

Mrs. Bush. What's your waiting list?

Ms. Clark. Our waiting list? We've been maintaining something like about 800 children on a waiting list. So, we're really looking forward to the expansion, because we have a lot of individuals that call and we just aren't able to serve them all.

Mrs. Bush. I think yours is better than mine is. [*Laughter*]

The President. What are you talking about?

Ms. Clark. There's another one up there.

Mrs. Bush. Identical. [*Laughter*]

The President. So sweet.

Mr. Conley. And we'd also like you to know that we're extremely proud of our Head Start staff and——

Ms. Clark. Child Development Associate

Credential—that's a competency-based credential that HHS encourages our staff to receive. And at the present, 80 percent of our staff are to be degreed or credentialed with the competency-based credentials.

The President. That's great. Well, everybody I hope had a say, but I really appreciate this opportunity to learn. It's funny, you go—you wonder—all the lights and the kind of hustle and the holding rooms—but it all adds up. I mean, you do this and then, tomorrow, well, maybe have a chance. And Barbara will come home and say what she did at the hospital or the school, you know. And I think it's a wonderful thing that we feel kind of uplifted when we get—we love living in this beautiful house that this guy drew over here. [*Laughter*] It's got two windows and a door. But it is wonderful, and I appreciate you all taking the time to help explain it to us.

Q. Okay, and on behalf of all of us here in our total program, I would like to thank you and Mrs. Bush very, very much. And I hope that God will continue to bless you in your leadership, to protect us and to lead us.

The President. Well, thank you so much.

Note: The President spoke at 3:02 p.m. at St. Aloysius Family Service Center.

Remarks at a Fundraising Dinner for the Ohio Republican Party in Columbus
February 8, 1990

Thank you all very, very much. I'm delighted to be here, and so is Barbara. Thank you, Tim, for all you do for the party and for the outstanding leadership you've brought to this dinner and everything you touch out here. I'll tell you, I'm delighted to be with you once again. I want to salute our Congressmen that are here. We've got outstanding Republican Congressmen in the House, and up at the head table here is Chalmers Wylie. I don't want to date him, but he and I were elected to Congress on the same day a thousand years ago. And John Kasich, Bob McEwen—all doing a great job. And then, with uncharacteristic modesty, I spot Ralph Regula and Mike Oxley out here—not even at the head table, but here—strong, both of them, wonderful Representatives. So, I feel surrounded by friends and former colleagues.

I also want to pay my respects and just tell you from my heart what a good job Lee Atwater is doing as chairman of the Republican National Committee—sitting over here. I know that the Ohio party is on the move, but I can tell you that that National Committee has taken a real leadership in a lot of these races, in recruitment—finding good people—and doing the best job that I can remember the party ever doing there. I want to pay my respects to a lot of the powerhouses of Ohio that are with us—Stan Aronoff, the president of the Ohio State Senate, a friend of mine of long standing from Cincinnati, is with us here. I thought Corwin was going to be here, but he's not—Corwin Nixon—or is he? I don't think so. But Joanne Davidson, ably representing—where is she? Way down here. Joanne, please pay my respects to Corwin. And I'm just delighted that you're here and have great respect for the job you're doing.

I, too, want to salute the organizers of this dinner—John Wolfe and Les Wexner and John McConnell. The great Ohio team also that we have on the national committee: our chairman, Bob Bennett; Martha Moore; Mike Colley—they're all doing an outstanding job. Incidentally—is this your birthday? This might well be the chairman's birthday today. So we want to wish him a happy one. And, of course, I'd be remiss if I didn't single out my old friend—still get a little free advice from him, but there's no one quite like him—Jim Rhodes, over here. Where's Jim? There, he's standing there—former Governor of this State.

And who would have thought, football and baseball and sports nut that I am, that I'd get a chance to get in there and have my picture taken with Archie Griffin, the two-time Heisman Trophy winner. You talk about a record—the only one, right? The only two-time winner of the Heisman. And so here we are—and I also want to single out another friend of mine who headed my campaign some time ago. I want to just announce that my dear friend, Keith—Keith McNamara, who was with us here a minute ago, has just been appointed to a position on the Board of Directors of the State Justice Institute. It's a very important job, and I'm delighted that he's willing to undertake that. But I want to salute him and thank him for his past support. And finally, I do want to pay my respects to one who is not here tonight—the mayor of Columbus, Buck Rinehart. Right now he's Captain Buck Rinehart, U.S. Marine Reserves. He's out at Twenty-nine Palms Base, in California. So even his Commander in Chief couldn't talk him out of that one. Twenty-nine Palms in the middle of February—don't tell me that Buck isn't willing to undertake those hardship assignments. [*Laughter*] But there he is. And again, in all seriousness, I do salute him.

I'm delighted to make one of my first fundraising stops of this decade right here in Ohio. And I congratulate you on the record-breaking success of this event. I'll never forget the help that all of you and this State gave to me and Dan Quayle in 1988. Memories of the Ohio campaign are still very fresh in my mind. Pitching horseshoes out there at the Ohio State Fair was one of the highlights. Riding on a campaign stop with Anne Hayes, who's right here with us tonight. She and her son, Steve—Judge Hayes. We had a marvelous trip, and all that does—seeing Anne here—is make me very nostalgic and very sentimental about Woody Hayes. What a wonderful man he was and what a great friend of mine. I'll never forget it.

And, of course—I'll get over this reminiscing in just a minute—but one of my final campaign stops was right here just before the election in Columbus at the rally finale, with a fellow who believes as deeply as I do in keeping America strong—I'm talking about Arnold Schwarzenegger. He was with us that day. And Conan the Republican, we call him. [*Laughter*] But I thought they were there to see a guy that might be the next President of the United States. But never—it was the best thing that ever happened because I was getting a little egocentric then—and all they wanted to do was see Schwarzenegger out here. But I had a marvelous time campaigning here. I spent so much time here that I met people who said that I had their vote—for Governor. [*Laughter*] I rode in a firetruck, kissed the babies, even threw out the first ball at the All-Star game. Seems like the only thing I did not do was to dot the "i" on the "Script Ohio." [*Laughter*]

But this is a critical year, as Tim said—and said it very well, indeed—Ohio always, but this year a critical State. What happens here is key to the Republican majority that we want to build all across this country. And I'm delighted to see that the party is making great gains here. I brought along a news clipping tonight, a story reporting the results of a new statewide poll on party preference. Apologies to John Wolfe—it's from the Dayton Daily News. [*Laughter*] But it says here that of all Ohioans between the ages of 18 and 25, 59 percent identify themselves as Republicans. And here's another statistic that makes the 59 percent even more impressive: Just 6 years ago, that figure was only 30 percent. A dramatic and amazing turnaround. That's a tribute to every one of you in this room tonight—and every one of you who are working so hard to make the Republican Party the majority party here in Ohio.

You know, last weekend, the Democratic leadership in Washington went on a retreat—that was their word, not mine—and they spent a weekend trying to find themselves—find themselves—work through an identity crisis that they're having. I read that some of the leadership thinks the problem is that people just don't know what their party stands for. I disagree with that. I think the problem for the national Democrats is that people know exactly what they stand for, and they don't want any more of that—more government, more taxes, and more Washington-knows-best bureaucracy. And that's their problem. And I really believe that that's why we're seeing these amazing changes in terms of party identification.

People are looking for something new in the nineties—and that's why they're looking at a new GOP generation. More Americans are turning to the Republican Party because our party really does have more of the new thinking, more of the answers—the answers people are looking for to help maintain the competitive edge in this global economy, to clean up our environment, to keep crime and drugs off our street, and to lead a new crusade for excellence in our schools—to see that every American enjoys the opportunity to live and work, to prosper and advance as far as his or her own efforts will take them.

When we hear from the opposition that there's nothing wrong that can't be fixed with a little redtape and a tax hike—we know better than that. We know all the answers are not found in Washington, DC. And we know about the vital work that gets done at the State level—in Columbus and in every other city and town in Ohio. We know the power of the private sector—the source of growth and jobs. And we know the power of individual citizens—people in every community across this country who don't wait for the word from Washington before they dig in and make a difference. And we know something else: We know that there is more than enough Federal spending. Ask your neighbors. I mentioned this in the State of the Union Message— some people still believe that $1.2 trillion is a lot of money, and that's the amount of this year's budget. We Republicans know it's up to us to see that it's spent wisely— that we measure success not by what we spend, but what kind of results we get. The challenges we face here at home are only half the story. More and more people trust this party to cope with the challenges that we face in the world today.

We've seen a world of change this past year—unbelievable, unpredictable change— triumph of democracy from Prague to Panama, the Revolution of '89 now spreading in 1990, perhaps in the Soviet Union itself. I know you followed carefully the deliberations of the Central Committee. Now we've seen them take their first step toward pluralism—multipartyism, if you will—inside the Soviet Union.

And we see the need all the more for American leadership—the need for an America strong enough and sure enough to defend our interests and our ideals, and to make the most of the opportunities now emerging for a more peaceful world, a freer world. You know, in the last few days, I've had an opportunity to visit with some of the men and women who have made the defense of peace and freedom their mission. I'm talking about the young troops in our armed services out at Fort Irwin, California—the Army's National Training Center— where our troops hone their battle tactics under the most realistic simulated battle conditions anywhere in the world. And then yesterday, I was at the Lawrence Livermore Labs there in San Francisco, which has such a rich history in helping defend our country, and where today so many of the top minds in science are engaged in pathbreaking work on the Strategic Defense Initiative. The Strategic Defense Initiative doesn't put people at risk; it puts incoming missiles at risk. And the science is mind boggling, and the fallout from that science will benefit a lot of peaceful pursuits, such as the environment and other areas that need the most advanced science in the world.

And then, finally, just this morning before I came here to Columbus, I paid a visit to the SAC Headquarters there at Omaha, Nebraska—the Strategic Air Command. I spoke on the SAC network to men and women at SAC bases all around the world— people who serve as our first line of defense. At every one of those stops, I thought about how much we owe to those dedicated men and women, about their sense of duty—and about our duty to each of them. This voluntary military that we have today has never, never been better. They are the best—and every single member of the Joint Chiefs tells me that over and over again. And I just wish you could have been with me to see the spirit of these young people.

I remember the words of one of the great field marshals of the 20th century—yes, I'm talking again about Woody Hayes—the saying he loved to repeat: "You can never pay back. You can only pay forward." That's true for our parents and our teachers, and it's true for the men and women in our Armed Forces. We show our thanks for all they've done for us by the good we do for generations yet to come. And that means taking the necessary steps today to make sure that this nation remains strong in the nineties and into the next century. It means making sure our Armed Forces are capable enough to meet our longstanding commitments—to deter war—and flexible enough to cope with whatever new contingencies we might face in the future.

That does not mean dismantling the solid foundation of military strength, alliance solidarity, and international security that has really brought us to this new moment of promise. But it will mean changes to respond to new conditions. It will mean hard choices between defense programs. But we've got to be careful; we've got to do our cutting with a scalpel and not with a meat ax. We're going to have to close some bases, consolidate some others. And I know we're in for a war up on Capitol Hill on this one—just mention base closing and Congress mans the battle stations. Doves become instant hawks. But let me tell you something: We are going to reorder our defense budget on the basis of our strategic needs, in response to the challenges we will still face in a world of many uncertainties and dangers. There will be no politics in this. It will be done with the best military minds that we can muster to be sure that we do it in an orderly, prudent way. And let's put politics aside and get on with making these tough decisions. [*Applause*] And for me, I will do my level best to encourage Congress to change that old adage—cut defense spending, but make the cuts in somebody else's district or in somebody else's State. We can't do that anymore. It's getting too critical now. I want to see prudent cuts, but I want to see it done in an orderly way so what emerges is a strong, robust, vital force. And I believe we can do it.

We're also going to push forward with arms control. And I had a chance to visit with some of you all who are helping on this dinner earlier on, and I told you that I am somewhat optimistic now about our negotiations with Mr. Gorbachev. We're going to push forward with strategic, chemical, and conventional weapons. I'm convinced

we can ease tensions, especially in Europe, and remain every bit as effective in preserving the peace—at lower levels of troops. That's why I proposed in the State of the Union Message that we would reduce our forward forces to 195,000, provided the Soviet Union would come way on down as well.

I am convinced we can do this. The initial reaction from Mr. Gorbachev has been quite positive. I think that today Secretary Baker had a very positive meeting with Foreign Minister Shevardnadze, and we're hoping, in the course of his discussions over there, to make significant progress towards a START treaty. So, we've seen great change; we've seen great promise this past year—the promise of the great Revolution of 1989: a freer world, a more peaceful world for us and for our children.

So, tonight, I really want to ask for your support as we work toward that better world—and I promise you mine in all the many challenges that we face here at home. I know we can succeed, provided that we uphold that proud Republican heritage that has served this nation so well. I'm an optimist about our country. I believe we are living in some of the most fascinating times, certainly the most promising and fascinating times since World War II. And I want to do my level best to keep this country on a forward course, but do it in a prudent manner so that we don't undermine, inadvertently undermine, the change that's taking place around the world—not just in Europe but the exciting changes that are taking place in this hemisphere. Who would have dreamed that in 1990 we might be on the verge of seeing a totally democratic, free and democratic Western Hemisphere, our own hemisphere?

And so, now we've got to turn to the politics at hand. And I urge you to do your level best to capture the governorship in this State, to win these statewide offices. Because it all ties in—the more confidence the President has in the State's ability to solve these local problems, the better the relationship. And I see a great change now coming. And I might say, in conclusion, we've got a redistricting problem ahead. And I am sick and tired, when I look at some of the congressional maps and see these wiggles and these turns and these aggressive moves that make these congressional districts look like pretzels. And we want to change that. And the best way to change that and guarantee that the people are fairly represented in this State is to elect a Republican Governor and to elect Republican majorities in both the Houses of your State legislature. And I want to come back and help. I pledge you my support, Mr. Chairman and Tim and others in this room. And we need you. Thank you for this wonderful sendoff for the State party. God bless all of you. Thank you very, very much.

Note: The President spoke at 6:47 p.m. at Ohio Center. In his opening remarks, he referred to Representatives John Kasich, Bob McEwen, Ralph Regula, and Mike Oxley; Corwin Nixon and Joanne Davidson, minority leader and minority whip of the Ohio House of Representatives; John Wolfe, owner of the Columbus Dispatch; Les Wexner, president of Worthington Industries; Martha Moore and Mike Colley, vice chairman and former chairman of the Ohio Republican Party; Anne Hayes, widow of Woody Hayes, former Ohio State University football coach; and Arnold Schwarzenegger, Chairman of the President's Council on Physical Fitness.

Nomination of Robert H. Swan To Be a Member of the National Credit Union Administration Board
February 8, 1990

The President today announced his intention to nominate Robert H. Swan to be a member of the National Credit Union Administration Board for the term of 6 years expiring August 2, 1995. He would succeed David L. Chatfield.

Since 1983 Mr. Swan has been president and chief executive officer with Tooele Federal Credit Union in Tooele, UT. Prior to this, he was vice president for Western

United Mines, 1982–1983; deputy director of finance for the State of Utah, 1977–1982; and owner/operator for Swan's Market, 1962–1976.

Mr. Swan graduated from the University of Utah (B.S., 1957; M.B.A., 1961). He was born July 19, 1935, in Tooele, UT. He served in the U.S. Army, 1958–1960. He is married and resides in Tooele.

Remarks to Members of the National Conference of State Legislatures
February 9, 1990

Thank you very much. Welcome to what is known as the White House complex. Don't ask me why. And I'm sorry about the delays that I understood some of you had getting in here. You do not have to show a picture I.D. to get out of here, I guarantee you. But I'm very pleased you all are here.

Delighted, of course, that Nick Brady left the national security meeting over there to come here. It, I hope, demonstrates our sense of priority and feeling that it is impor-

tant that you're here. I salute my Secretary of Education who's with us here, Larry Cavazos, and I'll say a little bit about his line of work in a minute. And, of course, Bill Reilly, who's doing such an outstanding job at EPA and will, indeed, be the first Cabinet Secretary for EPA when we get that change taken care of. Clayton Yeutter was to be here. Deb, is he coming? And I guess he'll be on over. Many of you—I see some Midwesterners here—know him very well.

And again, as we go to redo the farm bill, I feel very comforted having a person who really understands agriculture as well as he does.

And, of course, I'm delighted to welcome all of you. I'm told it's almost 50 States represented here. Lee Daniels, of course, your president; your former president, Sammy Nunez; and then also, one of your own up here whom I see almost every day, it seems like—Deb Anderson, the former speaker from the South Dakota House. And proof if there ever was one of Finley Peter Dunne's rule: Every now and then an innocent person gets sent to their legislature. And there she is right there. [*Laughter*] But I am glad to have this chance to drop in.

State legislatures are America's most practical and resourceful leaders, close to the grassroots, close to the people, close to America's concerns. And each of you has earned a special position of leadership and trust, and not by mastering the tricks of the trade but by mastering the trade itself. And many of you have been leaders in one of the most important and effective revolutions of the past 10 years: the return of the American political power to the States. That's where it began; that's where it belongs. I'm not saying it's done yet, but I want to reassure you we are concerned about further implementation of this broad, philosophical commitment to federalism.

I want to take this opportunity to renew that commitment and to the rights of the States, but also to States as laboratories, forging ahead at the cutting edge of the world's greatest experiment in freedom and security. It's, of course, a continuing experiment. From criminal justice to education, from child care to the environment, State and local governments are looking for new approaches to solving old problems—and looking not just at our problems but also at the possibilities. And in many cases, my budget will support new demonstration projects, both fostering and financing experimentation in the States. In other cases, my administration is granting waivers from Federal redtape to encourage new experimentation. But at the bottom line, my formula for federalism comes down to four words: "more flexibility" and "fewer mandates."

Last week, I submitted my first complete budget as President and gave the first report on the state of the Union. And we do face some big problems, and we've responded with big increases. Record funding for education—it's up overall, but I'm talking about the discretionary funds up significantly. Drug enforcement, the environment—other top priorities. We don't need a quick fix, but we do need quick action. More Federal money should not, in my view, automatically mean more Federal management.

In education, the solution to the problem is not reinforcing the Federal bureaucracy but reinforcing the American tradition of State and local education. Because real improvement in the schools is not simply a question of spending more—and Larry, I believe, is going to talk about that in a bit, and some of you were there when I spoke at your Indianapolis meeting almost 3 years ago—where we need to provide more, but we also need to demand more, expect more of our schools, our teachers, our kids, and ourselves. Last week, I announced the education goals that was developed in very close consultation with the Nation's Governors. I'll tell you, it was a wonderful team effort, if you will. Not three R's, but six R's—six goals for the year 2000.

Readiness in America where every child starts school ready to learn, and of course, much more emphasis in spending for Head Start in that regard. Rescuing those most at risk by raising our high school graduation rate to at least 90 percent. Reestablishing excellence. A new renaissance in science and math—and that's critical if our country is going to be competitive. I don't know, Nick, whether you got into that in your remarks at all, but this whole concept of competitiveness ties in to education, particularly in science, in math—first in the world by the year 2000. Reading, literacy for every American—and here we addressed ourselves to the question not just to the kids in school being sure they could read but to adult literacy as well. And then respect—schools that are disciplined, schools that in that context are totally drug-free.

A drug-free America, a safe America is, of course, one of our top concerns. And we get it from you all. We get it from those that are elected at the local levels, and we get it from the police chiefs, and we get it from the mayors. And it is priority. And there is an increasing and important Federal role in the fighting of crime. I recognize that, and I think our budget gives realization to that. But it is—with educating our kids—protecting our streets is one of those fundamental rights, duties that the Founding Fathers reserved for the States you represent.

Last May, I asked Congress to join me in launching a new partnership with America's cities and States, a partnership to ensure that those who scorn justice are brought to justice. A partnership—we call it "Take Back the Streets." And I'm here today to ask your help, take a leading role in the States in helping put away the violent, repeat, and fugitive offenders who plague American streets. Your role is essential. State and local cops back home need the same tools that we've proposed or ordered for the Feds. And I, again, go into this—mandatory time for firearms offenses, no deals on gun charges. We can't plea-bargain away the lives of the cops and the kids. And those who commit the ultimate crime—and a strongly held view of mine—must expect to pay the ultimate price.

At the Federal level, I've asked Congress for more than $10 billion for Phase II of our drug strategy, a strategy worked out by Bill Bennett, working with our top Cabinet officials. A 70-percent increase this is, since I became President—70-percent increase. It includes an unprecedented $500 million request for assistance to State and local law enforcement. And I am counting on you to match us with the same kind of hard-hitting resources—police, prosecutors, and prisons—to ensure that on this crime side, these violent thugs will be put away for good. We've got other parts of this drug strategy, as I'm sure you know: rehab and obviously a major interdiction effort, but which is involving certain military assets. But it's got to be across the board.

In these new partnerships, education and law enforcement, and in all your efforts, you really do—I get back to where I started—have my respect and gratitude and support. You have a special sense of belonging and place and sense of duty, or you wouldn't be doing this, you wouldn't be serving in these legislatures. And as public servants, you, too, have learned the simple truth: What we do for ourselves dies with us; what we do for others remains. And so, we're in a very interesting period where a lot of our major problems in this country, domestic problems, can best be solved with a major input from those of you in this room. And, again, education, crime, drug fight, whatever it is—I'm grateful to you.

I'm delighted you came by. And thank you very much for your support. And God bless you all. Thank you very much.

Note: The President spoke at 11:13 a.m. in Room 450 at the Old Executive Office Building. In his remarks, he referred to Debra Anderson, Deputy Assistant to the President and Director of the Office of Intergovernmental Affairs, and William J. Bennett, Director of National Drug Control Policy.

Nomination of Jonathan Moore To Be the United States Representative at the Economic and Social Council of the United Nations
February 9, 1990

The President today announced his intention to nominate Jonathan Moore to be the Representative of the United States of America on the Economic and Social Council of the United Nations, with the rank of Ambassador. He would succeed Lester B. Korn.

Since 1989 Mr. Moore has been Alternate

Representative of the United States for Special Political Affairs in the United Nations, with the rank of Ambassador. Prior to this, he was the United States Coordinator for Refugee Affairs and Ambassador-at-Large and Director for Refugee Programs, 1986–1989. He has served as director of the Institute of Politics and lecturer in public policy at Harvard's John F. Kennedy School of Government, 1974–1986. In addition, he has served as Associate Attorney General at the Department of Justice, 1973; and counselor at the Department of Health, Education, and Welfare, 1970–1973. He was Deputy Assistant Secretary of State for East Asian and Pacific Affairs, 1969–1970; executive assistant to the Under Secretary of State, 1969; special assistant to the Assistant Secretary of State for Far Eastern Affairs, 1964–1966; and special assistant to the Deputy Assistant Secretary and to the Assistant Secretary of Defense for International Affairs, 1963–1964.

Mr. Moore graduated from Dartmouth College (A.B., 1954) and Harvard University (M.P.A., 1957). He was born September 10, 1932, in New York City. He is married, has four children, and resides in Washington, DC.

Nomination of Shirin Raziuddin Tahir-Kheli To Be Alternate United States Representative for Special Political Affairs at the United Nations
February 9, 1990

The President today announced his intention to nominate Shirin Raziuddin Tahir-Kheli to be the Alternate Representative of the United States of America for Special Political Affairs at the United Nations, with the rank of Ambassador.

Dr. Tahir-Kheli has served as Director for Near East and South Asia at the National Security Council Staff at the White House, 1986–1989. Prior to this, she was Director for Political-Military Affairs at the National Security Council at the White House, 1984–1986. Dr. Tahir-Kheli was an adjunct professor for the School for Advanced International Studies at the Johns Hopkins University, 1988–1989. In addition, she has served in several capacities at Temple University in Philadelphia, PA: associate professor for political science, 1980–1982; assistant professor for political science, 1973–1979; and academic adviser in the Office of the Dean, 1972–1973.

Dr. Tahir-Kheli graduated from Ohio-Wesleyan University (B.A., 1961) and the University of Pennsylvania (M.A., 1963; Ph.D., 1972). She was born August 24, 1944, in Hyderabad, India. She is married and has two children.

Remarks at the Presentation Ceremony for the Flo Hyman Award
February 9, 1990

The President. Well, this is very brief, but I just couldn't be more pleased to see everybody here, and I want to welcome you to the White House.

This morning I want to use this occasion to present the Flo Hyman Award to Chris Evert. Now, Chris, you have long represented not just the game of tennis but your country. And you've done it so very well and with grace, dignity, and good sportsmanship, so today it's only fitting that you receive this award.

I know that all of your friends and colleagues here will agree that you certainly are the role model for our nation's young women, and we all miss you on the professional tennis circuit. Maybe Pam and Martina won't miss you on the tennis circuit, but the rest of us certainly will. [*Laughter*] And as you head off into this new phase of your career, I know that you will continue to serve as a tremendous example to our young people and to all of us.

So, let me speak for all Americans when I say we're very proud of you, and I thank you for your leadership and inspiration. And I'm just tickled to death to be able to present this award to you.

Ms. Evert. Thank you, President Bush. I'm very honored to receive this award, first of all because Flo Hyman, I think, meant so much to all of us who knew her—and all of us who didn't know her, by her spirit. And also because you presented it to me, and I know that you had to juggle a few things around. Your schedule's really tight at this moment, but I just want you to know it means a lot to me for you to present this.

And you know, I think we had a great day yesterday. It was Women's Sports Day and Girls' Sports Day, and I think one of the things that we tried to get across was a big issue, which was the physical education. And since you, as President, have done so much for education and are doing so much for education, I think it was great that we tried to tie it in with physical education—trying to make it a little more mandatory in schools, and I personally think it'd really help the kids to be mentally a little more alert. And you know, it's just food for thought for you and for all the Senators and everyone to really think about.

But, I'd just like to say thank you to the Women's Sports Foundation, and I'm just really honored to receive this. So, thank you very much.

The President. Congratulations. Thank you all.

Ms. St. James. I'm Lyn St. James——

The President. You want the final word? Get over there, come on. Everybody's entitled. Equal play around here.

Ms. St. James. President Bush, thank you.

I'm Lyn St. James. I'm the new president of the foundation. And on behalf of the foundation, but also on behalf of every girl and woman that participates in sports, we want to thank you for taking the time and the opportunity to share this day with us, this moment with Chris.

And we are—besides Chris representing it—we have a number of athletes out here and all over the country that are participating in sports and realizing their potential and finding out what they're all about because they do participate—and hope that you'll continue to carry that message. And we certainly know that you are a living example of it, and your family as well. But sports affects every part of our lives, and education certainly is a part of that. Drugs, everything that we're worried about—sports is an alternative. So, we really appreciate your support.

The President. You know, there's something Chris said on that. Arnold Schwarzenegger's the new head of the Fitness Council. He was in here—you probably noticed the change—[*laughter*]—but he was making the point, seriously, he was making the point how little of physical education goes on in the schools today—much less, he feels, than it used to be. So, we're going to try to use that Council to put more emphasis on women's sports, men's sports, and sports for the kids or fitness. I mean, it is very, very important, and of course, I'm just delighted to hear your thoughts on that.

Ms. St. James. It's something I think our generation didn't know. I thought it was mandatory when I went to school. So, that's something that's gotten, I think, sloughed aside. So, we need to kind of bring it back to the forefront.

The President. Well, that's the end of the formalities. Now can I say hello? Come on up and say who everybody is.

Note: The President spoke at 11:46 a.m. in the Roosevelt Room at the White House.

Nomination of John J. Adair To Be Inspector General of the Resolution Trust Corporation
February 9, 1990

The President today announced his intention to nominate John J. Adair to be Inspector General of the Resolution Trust Corporation. This is a new position.

Since 1984 Mr. Adair has served as an Associate Director of the Audit Oversight and Policy Group at the General Accounting Office in Washington, DC. Prior to this he served as a legislative assistant to Senator Peter H. Dominick, 1974. In addition,

Mr. Adair worked in the Philadelphia and Washington regional offices of the General Accounting Office, 1964–1974.

Mr. Adair graduated from Duquesne University (1963) and George Washington University (M.B.A., 1969). He is also a graduate of the National Defense University, 1982. Mr. Adair was born July 25, 1941, in McKees Rocks, PA. He is married, has five children, and resides in Springfield, VA.

Statement on the Release of Nelson Mandela
February 10, 1990

President de Klerk has announced his intention to release Nelson Mandela [African National Congress leader] on Sunday. I welcome this move and view it as another significant step on the road to the nonracial, democratic South Africa which we all desire. President de Klerk has shown bold and imaginative leadership in recent days

which has earned the admiration of many of us who hope for swift and peaceful evolution in South Africa.

As I stated earlier, I look forward to meeting independently with State President de Klerk and Mr. Mandela in the coming months as part of my continuing dialog with South African leadership.

Statement by Press Secretary Fitzwater on President Bush's Telephone Conversation With State President Frederik Willem de Klerk of South Africa
February 10, 1990

President Bush called South Africa State President de Klerk today to congratulate him on the announcement of the release of Nelson Mandela tomorrow. In the course of the 5-minute conversation, President Bush extended a personal invitation to State President de Klerk to meet with him at the White House. He also expressed his admiration for the significant initiatives announced by the South African Government in recent days, and reiterated his hope there would be continued progress toward a negotiated

solution in an atmosphere of nonviolence. The two Presidents discussed the challenges that face all South Africans in this time of impending transition. President Bush stated U.S. willingness to help create a climate for negotiations and his plan to continue meeting with a broad spectrum of South African leaders. In this connection, he emphasized his intention to invite Mr. Mandela to meet with him to exchange views on how best to move rapidly toward a negotiated solution. Nelson Mandela has given more than 27 years of his life to the cause of human dignity and has inspired millions around the world who value freedom.

Statement by Press Secretary Fitzwater on the President's Meeting With Secretary General Manfred Woerner of the North Atlantic Treaty Organization
February 11, 1990

The President met this weekend with Manfred Woerner, the Secretary General of the North Atlantic Treaty Organization, at Camp David. The President's wide-ranging discussions with Secretary General Woerner began on Saturday, February 10, and concluded on Sunday morning, February 11.

They talked about the recent political developments in Europe, including [West German] Chancellor Kohl's extraordinarily successful weekend visit to Moscow. The President complimented the Secretary General on his recent speech in Hamburg on the Atlantic alliance and German unity, and the Secretary General provided a further elaboration of his views. They expressed their gratification that the Government of the Federal Republic of Germany had affirmed that a unified Germany would remain a member of the North Atlantic alliance. They agreed that NATO, in addition to maintaining the common defense, should adopt new political roles: in helping guide Western policy toward the emerging democracies of Eastern Europe, in coordinating the negotiation and monitoring of arms control agreements, and in developing Western policy for regional and transnational issues.

Both leaders continue to attach a high priority to rapid conclusion of an agreement in the negotiations on conventional forces in Europe (CFE), and the President praised the Secretary General's efforts in winning full allied support for the President's recent CFE initiatives on military troop strength and the treatment of combat aircraft. Looking ahead to the conference that begins on Monday, February 12, in Ottawa, on "Open Skies," the Secretary General noted the rapid progress that has been made in advancing the President's "Open Skies" proposal.

Remarks at the Welcoming Ceremony for President Denis Sassou-Nguesso of the Congo
February 12, 1990

President Bush. Well, Mr. President, it is a great pleasure to welcome you and Mrs. Sassou-Nguesso to the United States and to the White House. The last time you visited, 3 years ago, you and I met at the United States Capitol Building, and today we meet at the White House.

In the 3 years since your last visit, southern Africa has seen significant progress towards peace and stability. Namibia is on the verge of independence. And in Angola, Cuban troops have begun the process of leaving. And while our support for the UNITA [National Union For the Total Independence of Angola] freedom fighters continues undiminished, we continue to hope for a negotiated settlement to that tragic war. Nelson Mandela's release from prison yesterday, which we've waited for and worked toward for so long, is another important sign that South Africa may soon begin negotiating a democratic, nonracial society and at last be on the way to ending apartheid once and for all.

Mr. President, to a considerable degree, many of these happy developments resulted from your involvement. As Chairman of the OAU [Organization of African Unity] in 1986, you used your prestige and diplomatic skill to convince those involved to come to Brazzaville to resolve their differences through the Angola-Namibia accords. And just as our diplomats worked ceaselessly to assure the accords were signed, you worked ceaselessly to assure the accords would succeed. Africa, America, and the rest of the world congratulated you for your role in this extraordinary achievement, a major diplomatic milestone in southern Africa. And today it is my privilege, on behalf of the American people, to thank you again for your efforts and ongoing commitment to regional stability.

We also appreciate your support for the continuing African effort, under the mediation of Zaire's President Mobutu Sese Seko, to achieve peace and stability in Angola. Those negotiations have not always gone smoothly, and some continue to believe that war is preferable to peace. Nevertheless, we remain confident that African statesmen, such as yourself, Mr. President, will be able to bring about national reconciliation in Angola and greater peace and stability in your entire region.

Mr. President, as we talk about the world's problems and their peaceful resolution, I would like to use this occasion to send two messages to the people of Africa. Some have suggested that events in the rest of the world, including Central Europe, mean that the United States will no longer pay attention to Africa. I can assure you and everyone in Africa that this is not the case. I had the pleasure of visiting Africa three times while I was Vice President and hope to be able to do so again. And Africa is the ancestral home of many Americans. And Africa is a major contributor to the world's supply of raw materials and minerals and a repository of many of the world's environmental riches, such as the lush, natural beauty of the Congo's tropical forests. Africa's our friend, and friends don't forget one another. Rather, they provide help and work closely in common endeavors. And I hereby renew the commitment of the American people and Government to continue to do so in partnership with Africa.

Today America celebrates the birthday of one of our greatest Presidents, Abraham Lincoln. Shortly before he took office, Lincoln stopped in Philadelphia to speak at Independence Hall, and he spoke of war and revolution and of America's birth certificate, the Declaration of Independence, signed in that hall less than 100 years earlier. "The Declaration," he said, "gave liberty not alone to the people of this country, but hope to all the world for all future time." And today another century has passed, and today liberty and hope are alive in the world as never before.

We welcome the steps Africa has taken to recognize and nurture this trend in recent years. And we encourage more rapid movement in this direction, for as recent events have proven from Central Europe to Central America, free people and free markets are the way of the future and essential ingredients of a successful, thriving, and truly developed nation. These are among the ideas I plan to share in our dialog over at the White House today.

And I believe that the leaders of Africa are reaching out to the United States, reaching out for a new partnership based on mutual responsibility and mutual respect. And so, the message of freedom and cooperation in my meetings with you, Mr. President, is also a message to the leaders of Africa.

Thank you, sir, for coming to the White House. We look forward to our visit and to mutually beneficial talks. Thank you very much.

President Sassou-Nguesso. Mr. President, as I step on American soil for my first state visit, I wish first of all to salute a great nation which has inspired so many ideals and dreams for mankind now for over 200 years. I wish to pay a well-earned tribute to your great people, who achieved its own freedom in order to spread values which continue to remain today the ideological foundation of contemporary societies. You, Mr. President, are one of the great figures who have inherited this rich legacy which has enabled your country to build a civilization which looks towards progress, which means it looks to the future, and does so in liberty and democracy.

The many highly positive initiatives which your ongoing consultation with your Soviet counterpart, President Mikhail Gorbachev, continue to result in, fall within the very happy prospect of a future that is less uncertain and more serene. We the people of Africa are convinced that such a fruitful dialog can only benefit all of mankind for peace and security as well as for economic development.

Because my visit coincides with the celebration of African-American Month, it gives me, a son of Africa, a chance to extend a respectful and grateful salute to the memory of President Abraham Lincoln and of Dr. Martin Luther King. Their lives, their struggle, represent for us Africans a never-ending source of admiration, pride, and hope. And I should like to include a great symbol of dignity for African men, Nelson Mandela, whose very recent release ushers in great prospects for the negotiations on the future of South African society. From this day on, the Congo can look for-

ward with optimism to the future of its own relations with South Africa.

May this happy coincidence usher in a period of ever more encouraging prospects for the strengthening of friendship and cooperation between our two worlds, between America and the Congo. And as I thank you, Mr. President, for the very wonderful welcome you have extended to me and the message of friendship you have just addressed to me, may I tell you how very happy I am to be today in this great, beautiful capital, where there is so much history and where there is so much hope.

Long live the United States. Long live the Congo. I thank you.

Note: President Bush spoke at 10:12 a.m. at the South Portico of the White House, where President Sassou-Nguesso was accorded a formal welcome with full military honors. President Sassou-Nguesso spoke in French, and his remarks were translated by an interpreter. Following the ceremony, the two Presidents met in the Oval Office.

Remarks Upon Receiving the Boy Scouts of America Report to the Nation
February 12, 1990

Well, let me just say how pleased I am to be here. And thank you, Curtis, and thank you, Secretary Skinner—Sam proudly proclaiming what we all are reminded of around here all the time: that he is an old Eagle Scout, and he's working on a new merit badge for national transportation policy. We hope that it—*[laughter]*. But to Harold and Ben Love and Earl Graves and the members of my administration and, of course, especially to the Scouts who've come here today, it is my pleasure to welcome all of you and to participate once again in this tradition that dates all the way back to 1910, when President Taft received the first Boy Scout delegation right here in the White House.

Let me say to all how deeply honored I am to receive this highest award: the Silver Buffalo. I live with a Silver Fox—*[laugh-*

ter]—and now she lives with a Silver Buffalo. But I'm honored because down through the years I've seen what the Boy Scouts mean in the lives of young men. And scouting is more than learning how to build a campfire or to tie a knot. And scouting teaches a love of outdoors and appreciation of our environment. It teaches the spirit of serving others, and self-respect. And let me make it pure and simple: It teaches lessons that last a lifetime. And so, when I hear about Boy Scouts that are out there helping the homeless or feeding the hungry or cleaning up our cities and towns or helping other kids stay drug-free, when I hear about boys as young as 8 and 9, Cub Scouts, doing things like that, I see a glimpse of the future—what this nation can be like if we follow the lead of the Scouts.

And I know the Scout slogan is "Do a

good turn daily"—and every day you do. And that's why right now, with you here representing the national Boy Scouts organization, I want to recognize the work of the Montana Council of Boy Scouts for an environmental program they call Project Good Turn. In the past 5 years, Project Good Turn has collected over 5,000 tons of trash from all across Montana and involved more than 30,000 young people in the cleanup effort. And the Montana Scouts have made this a real community project, enlisting everyone from the Girl Scouts to the State Highway Patrol and the Montana National Guard. And so, today I take great pleasure in naming Project Good Turn the 65th daily Point of Light, a shining example of the kind of community engagement that makes a difference, the kind we've come to expect from the Boy Scouts of America.

I'm proud to accept this year's report to the Nation, the new edition of the handbook, and to have this opportunity to thank you all for the wonderful works done by the Scouts all across this country. Thank you all very much, and God bless you. Thank you for coming.

Note: The President spoke at 11:50 a.m. in the Roosevelt Room at the White House. In his remarks, he referred to Eagle Scout Curtis W. Hawkins; Secretary of Transportation Samuel K. Skinner; Harold Sokolsky, assistant to the chief scout executive; Ben Love, chief scout executive; and Earl Graves, national commissioner.

The President's News Conference
February 12, 1990

The President. Good afternoon. Well, this has been an extraordinary and positive week in East-West relations. In the Soviet Union, progress was made at the Central Committee plenum on moving the Soviet political system toward pluralism and genuine respect for the views of the Soviet electorate. I commend this development, which demonstrates once again why our administration has supported Chairman Gorbachev's efforts to extend *glasnost* and *perestroika* through the Soviet Union.

Secretary Baker's visit to Moscow made solid progress in pushing the U.S.-Soviet agenda forward in preparation for the June summit here. We made important headway on conventional arms control, START, nuclear testing, and chemical weapons and continue to explore ways to reduce our differences on regional issues, especially concerning Central America and Afghanistan. All in all, Secretary Baker's talks in Moscow accomplished much of what Chairman Gorbachev and I intended when we set the goals for this meeting during our discussions at Malta. I am confident that if we continue this kind of momentum in our bilateral relationship with the Soviet Union, the June summit will be a major success.

And finally, I want to congratulate [West German] Chancellor Kohl for his successful visit to Moscow. His visit reflects the accelerating pace of German self-determination; and the statements on German unity, on the Soviet side, by the Soviet side, were most welcome. And we support Chancellor Kohl's position that a unified Germany should remain a member of NATO. Let me also express my appreciation of Chairman Gorbachev's statesmanlike view that decisions regarding German unity should be left to the people of Germany. I made a statement this morning on the wonderful news of the release of Mr. Mandela [African National Congress leader], so I will leave that to the question period.

But, Terry [Terence Hunt, Associated Press], I understand you have the first question today.

Conventional Force Reductions in Europe and Arms Reduction Agreements

Q. Yes, Mr. President. What is your reaction to Mr. Gorbachev's counterproposal for troop cuts in Europe? And in the wake of Secretary Baker's visit to Moscow, what do you think the likelihood is that there will be three treaties to be signed this year—chemical, strategic, and conventional?

The President. Let me take the last one first. I'm not sure that there will be three treaties to be signed by the time we have this summit, but I think there's going to be progress towards all three, and it's still our goal to get that CFE [conventional force reductions in Europe] agreement signed. On the troop—where Gorbachev wanted to have either 195,000 or 225,000—we're going to stay with our proposal because we don't see this linkage to that degree.

We're talking about the forward deployment there in Europe, the 195,000, and that's what we're challenging him to reduce. And we've got a big ocean between us and Western Europe. And so, the argument that we should always have a linked reduction is one that I want to get away from now. I think we've made some real progress on this, and I was very pleased with his reaction to our proposal, but I don't think we need to have exact linkage from this point on.

Q. Well, if you're rejecting his counterproposal, is there an impasse now?

The President. I wouldn't call it an impasse. This is the way it works when you're discussing these arms control things. No, I don't think we've got an impasse.

U.S. Military Presence in Europe and Defense Spending

Q. With the breakup of the Soviet empire, and you want Germany to remain in NATO, who's the enemy? [*Laughter*]

The President. What was that?

Q. Who's the enemy? Who are they supposed to be fighting against?

The President. Who?

Q. The NATO troops? U.S. troops in Germany?

The President. The U.S. troops are there as a stabilizing factor. Nobody can predict, Helen [Helen Thomas, United Press International], with total certainty, what tomorrow's going to look like. I've been wrong. You've been wrong. He's been wrong. She's been wrong—on how it's going to go. And we don't know in our——

Q. Do you expect the Soviet——

The President. May I finish, please.

Q. Okay.

The President. Our European allies want us there. I have a feeling that some of the Eastern Europeans want us there because they know that the United States is there as a stabilizing factor. And we will be there for a long time to come—hopefully, at significantly reduced numbers.

Q. May I just add, Mr. President, that there's a wide perception that your whole military budget is out of sync, that you're tone-deaf into what's been happening, and that there is a possibility of this money going for distressing domestic needs.

The President. I don't think that perception is widespread with the American people. I think the American people want a cautious approach to this. I don't think any of us think we can see with clairvoyance what's going to happen the day after tomorrow. And we are reducing our defense expenditures. We sent a budget proposal up there that makes good sense. You're right: Some of the Democrats are jumping all over us. But that's all right; that just goes with the system. The main thing is the Europeans, our staunchest allies, want us there because they see the U.S. as a stabilizing presence. And so, we are going to remain there. Now, as I say, I hope our negotiations go so well that we can have substantially reduced numbers over the years.

South Africa

Q. Mr. President, does the release of Nelson Mandela and the other steps announced by President de Klerk in South Africa alter in any way your views towards the United States economic sanctions which, of course, the Reagan administration, and you as a part of it, were never very enthusiastic about?

The President. What do you mean? In the sense of—alter my views as to what we ought to do in the future?

Q. Well, as to whether they work or not?

The President. Well, I don't know that one can attribute all the change in South Africa to sanctions. Now, we've got some sanctions on there, and by law, they remain on until the South Africans have taken certain steps. Somebody asked me about this yesterday, and I said, well, I can't judge.

Frankly, I think some are counterproductive. I happen to think American jobs there make good sense. And I don't think they perpetuate the status quo. But I think what's really changed is the mindset of the South African leadership. And I think that we ought to give Mr. de Klerk certain credit for being able to look much more realistically about political change and, hopefully, more favorably about a society that eventually eliminates this racism that is equated with apartheid.

Q. Well, would you be willing to push for the lifting of any of the sanctions before all of the conditions set forth in the law have been met?

The President. We can't do that. I'm bound by the law. And what I do want to do is discuss these provisions with Mr. Mandela and with Mr. de Klerk, and I've invited both of them to come here. And I also want to see them continue to talk with each other. And then out of that I think we'll have a much more realistic picture of what the United States might do in the future.

Q. Nelson Mandela continues to call for armed struggle to overthrow apartheid. When he comes to the White House, would you urge him to adopt the nonviolent tactics of Martin Luther King?

The President. Yes, I would. But what I—and I hope I didn't misread it—I read his statement to be more on the defensive side when I looked at it this morning. Yes, we've always advocated nonviolence, and I think the United States ought not to move away from that.

Q. Could I just follow up on the question about the sanctions? Are there things that you can do for the South African Government apart from lifting sanctions? We realize that by law you can't lift the sanctions unilaterally. Are there other things you can do other than just asking de Klerk to come to Washington?

The President. Well, I would say out of the meeting with Mr. de Klerk I would have a clearer perception of what other things might be. I think having him here is a major step; I think it's a very important step. And so, I would simply have to defer on that question until I have a chance to talk to him.

Q. Mr. President, there are those who

say—keeping on with sanctions—that now is more of a time than ever to keep all the pressure on and, if not keeping the pressure on, even go one step further. I wonder if you intended your invitation to Mr. de Klerk as a reward for what he's done, given that no South African President has ever been here before? And secondly, do you think it time, regardless of what you think of sanctions, to reward them in some other way?

The President. Reward?

Q. Reward South Africa?

The President. Well, I don't know about rewards. I think his coming here evidences the fact that we see in him a new brand of leadership, a man who is making dramatic changes in South Africa. The freeing of Mandela clearly is a very positive sign. And so, I think there's more to be done, but there are things that he has done that I think deserve our support and, I'd say, appreciation because I think these steps he's taking move South Africa down the road towards racial equity.

German Membership in NATO

Q. Mr. President, on Germany, would you be willing to consider a situation where a united Germany was not necessarily a full member of NATO?

The President. No, I think that Chancellor Kohl is absolutely correct, and we ought to support him—NATO membership. And I think it's stabilizing. I think it's good.

Q. But full——

The President. There might be some flexibility, obviously, on the deployment of NATO forces; but in terms of membership, I think that is the most reassuring and stabilizing concept. I happen to believe that it is the most reassuring and stabilizing in terms of how the Eastern Europeans will eventually look at it. Maybe not today.

Q. But you mean the same kind of membership that West Germany now has?

The President. Sure. There's some flexibility on deployment of NATO forces into Eastern Europe. Nobody wants to threaten the Soviet Union. As I was trying to say to Helen, the U.S. presence is a stabilizing presence.

South Africa

Q. Mr. President, on the de Klerk visit that now seems to be almost a fait accompli, are there any conditions on that? Does he have to lift the state of emergency? And in your conversation with him, did he tell you when he would do that?

The President. There's no conditions on my invitation, if that's the question—absolutely not.

Q. Well, would he come if the state of emergency has not been lifted? He hasn't done that.

The President. I don't know. I don't know whether he would or not.

Q. You didn't discuss that element with him?

The President. I didn't discuss any conditions. I said I want him to come. You have freed Nelson Mandela, you have taken certain steps that are positive, and we want to see more. We want to see you go further, but you're welcome. And that's the way——

U.S. War Games and Soviet-U.S. Relations

Q. Mr. President, do you have any second thoughts about——

The President. I was trying to identify the lady next to you, but go ahead.

Q. It happens all the time.

Q. Do you have any second thoughts about the trip last week [National Training Center, Fort Irwin, on February 6]? I'm especially thinking of the war games with the Soviet tanks, particularly when your views on the defense budget are well-known and the Central Committee was meeting at the same time?

The President. No, I think it was a good trip. And I've read some ticktock inside here, but it doesn't bother me a bit. I think that those people that were there understood that that training has applications elsewhere—we've seen recent areas where military force was used because it was well-trained. And so, I stand by that as a very good trip. You see, I support our defense budget; I think it makes sense. And the fact that we've got some critics up there that don't like it—that's too bad. I think the American people want to see us stay strong.

Q. What signal does that send to Mr. Gorbachev, however, who you just praised a few minutes ago?

The President. Well, it sent a pretty good one, I guess, because we came out of that meeting with some forward motion. And I salute him. I can't say the trip to the State of California's desert had a heck of a lot to do with it, but if you'd listen to some of the critique from Capitol Hill, you'd have thought it had been a disaster. And yet I've told you we've just completed one of the most successful ministerial summits that we've had with the Soviets. So, the critics up there on the Hill can't have it both ways.

German Membership in NATO

Q. I just wanted to follow up on the Germany question. You said you thought that the Eastern Europeans would ultimately come to see this alliance with NATO as a positive thing, too. Are you suggesting, sir, that there's something less threatening about a Germany that is in alliance—any alliance—rather than a neutral Germany?

The President. I think so, because I think a Germany inside the NATO alliance—they're good NATO partners now, and they'll be good NATO partners then. And they are very closely linked to the United States, and I think that's a very good thing.

Q. If I could just turn that around: Do you think that a neutral Germany does pose a threat potentially to its neighbors?

The President. Well, I know that's the concern of many Europeans, but it's a concern that would be allayed by having a unified Germany inside of NATO.

Conventional Force Reductions in Europe

Q. Mr. President, you indicated you don't think the conventional talks are at impasse. Would you be willing to consider an agreement in which the U.S. was able to keep extra troops in Europe, but at a number somewhat less than the 30,000?

The President. Well, we've made our proposal. I don't make these proposals without consulting the allies, and there's agreement that these are the proper levels. It's a level that has been scrubbed by our military, and I think there's a happiness within our own military about this. For this time in history, I think it's the right level. And so, we're not out there trying to trade that away.

South Africa

Q. Mr. President, you talk often about the importance of free markets to democracy. But Nelson Mandela supports the ANC view about nationalizing South African industries, including banks and mines. How do you feel about that? And does that pose a problem for real democracy in South Africa?

The President. We are not for nationalizing. We're for privatization across the—for free markets. And so, if we have a difference there, that's fine; we'll discuss it with him. But I am not about to embrace the idea that what we want to do is go down to more socialism when socialism is folding its hand and going over to the other side all across the world. I mean, you see this. So, this is a difference that we—if that's his view, why, certainly we're not going to embrace that.

Q. Is that a severe obstacle, though, to having a successful democracy there?

The President. Nationalization of all the— I don't necessarily associate nationalization—socialization of industry, the goods and services produced belonging to the state—I don't see that as particularly helpful towards democracy, if that's what you mean. But what I do agree with Mandela is, is to try to get a society that is not a racist society, doesn't support a concept of apartheid.

Q. On South Africa, the question is: How willing are you to become personally involved—your administration become personally involved in facilitating negotiations between Mr. Mandela and President de Klerk? Are you ready to play a role like President Carter did in the Camp David accords in the Middle East?

The President. If such a role would be productive, I certainly would. But I have the feeling from the talks with both men— just the short phone conversations with both Mr. de Klerk and Mr. Mandela—that they feel they can talk to each other without the U.S. catalytic role. But, sure, if we could be helpful in a way of that nature, we certainly would.

Conventional Force Reductions in Europe

Q. Mr. President, there are some people who are questioning the need for a conventional forces treaty at all at this point. The argument being that we're at a situation in which the East European countries are going to invite all the Soviet troops to go home anyway, and all that we'd be doing is codifying a Soviet presence that isn't even wanted in Eastern Europe. What's your response to that argument?

The President. Say it's very interesting, and it may well be that the pressure on the Soviets will have them withdraw to lower levels. I don't think there's great sentiment in the Warsaw Pact countries for continued Soviet presence. I'm not sure that it would negate the need to have an agreement. I think the Soviets would like to get our commitment, too. But you see, those troops are not wanted in Eastern Europe anymore. Our troops are wanted by the free world. And I suspect—can't prove it—that some countries in the Warsaw Pact countries today would see us not as a threatening presence but as a stabilizing presence.

Q. But is it possible the Soviets might use a treaty as an excuse to keep troops where they're not even wanted?

The President. I don't think they can do that. I think they've got a problem of a CFE treaty with us and others, but they also have the problem of opinion inside these countries. And they have enormous budgetary problems that make things very difficult.

South Africa

Q. Mr. President, what was your reaction to the rather effusive embrace of the South African Communist Party and the presence of the Communist Party flag on the balcony when Mr. Mandela made his speech yesterday?

The President. I didn't notice that. But you see, I think these Communist parties, for the most part, are sliding downhill. And I think what's coming uphill, and triumphantly so, is democracy and freedom. And I would hope that the steps that Mr. de Klerk is taking and is suggesting be taken would enhance the view that democracy and freedom are on the move.

Q. A followup, sir: If Mr. Mandela persists in allying himself with the Communist Party, would that change your view of his——

The President. Too hypothetical. I mean, what's good is that he's out there. Been in jail a long time. And it's an interesting question back here, but I'm not embracing every position of the ANC or some of the positions that are represented here today as Mr. Mandela's positions. What I am doing is embracing the concept that it's good that he's out of jail and that it's good that the South Africans seem to be moving towards a more equitable society.

German Reunification

Q. Do you think it's time for a conference of the Four Powers on Germany?

The President. No, not at this juncture. I know that idea has some credibility right now, but I think it's moving along pretty well. And we have always favored self-determination and that the Germans have to sort this out. At some point, clearly, the Four Powers will have to have some say. There's no question about that. Whether it's two-plus-four or what the formulation is, we're not locked on that at all.

Q. If Gorbachev continues to insist on German neutrality, Mr. President, do you think that could create a dangerous impasse that would spawn a neutrality movement in West Germany?

The President. Not necessarily. But I think that we've seen the Soviet Union's position change on the whole concept—or the whole acceptability of German reunification. It wasn't so long ago that Mr. Gorbachev and the Soviet system were positioned very skeptically about any reunification. And that's what was so symbolic about the Kohl-Gorbachev meeting, so important about it. And I might say that it was a very emotional day for people in Germany— GDR [German Democratic Republic] and FRG [Federal Republic of Germany]— highly emotional. Brother separated from brother, cousin from cousin, and all of this—now with a chance to have peaceful reunification.

And so, I don't want to buy into any real hypothesis on what might happen, but I think we ought to applaud the fact that the Soviets demonstrated a real flexibility on this question that we didn't think they had a few months ago.

Q. Can I just follow: Do you now think, then, that German unification is unstoppable and that Gorbachev will back off his demands?

The President. Well, I think, again, I'd just refer it to the will of the people there. And it seems to be moving very fast in that direction.

Israeli Trade Minister Sharon's Resignation

Q. Sir, what is your visceral reaction to the resignation of Ariel Sharon and its effect on the peace process? And is this part of the pattern of the hard-liners losing out around the world?

The President. You know, I just heard about this, and I have to understand more about what went on there. But Mr. Shamir [Prime Minister] was the proponent of these talks, and if this clears the way for the talks to go forward, that would be in keeping with U.S. policy.

South Africa

Q. When you talked with Mr. de Klerk and Mr. Mandela, did you talk about—when you talked about democracy and freedom, did you make the point that in our understanding of democracy, the majority rules? I'm really wondering about de Klerk. Or will you talk with him about that when he comes?

The President. I'm sure we will—and with Mr. Mandela. But that did not come up in these conversations. None of the detail here on the various sanctions or anything of that nature came up.

Q. Is that what you would tell him? De Klerk, I'm speaking——

The President. Well, let's wait and see what happens when he gets here.

Yes, Sarah [Sarah McClendon, McClendon News]? You haven't had one for a long time.

Military Base Closings

Q. Thank you so much. Sir, we have a big problem in this country with the bases that we have to close and the tens of thousands of personnel we have to let go out of the military, and out of civilian roles, too. I wonder if you would be for taking these military bases and turning them into prisons rather than building new prisons, and if you'd be for using the extra housing for the homeless?

The President. Well, Sarah, let me say this: that when military bases close, various communities historically seem to prosper. And I think the one in Waco, Texas, where a base was closed—it was years ago—all kinds of speculation that this would be the end of the world, and then gradually found out that it doesn't work that way. And so, I think there will be socially redeeming uses for these benefits that municipalities and county governments and others—these bases—that these entities may want to use them for.

And so, I would say it's a good question, because we can say to others this is not the end of the world. But let me say, on base closings: These suggested closings were made without political favor; and I would hope that we could get the Congress convinced that the age-old adage "cut here, cut there, but don't cut in my district" could be laid aside now. And I hope that that's what will prevail.

I said out there in San Francisco that instant doves become feathery instant hawks on base closings—[*laughter*]—only if it's in their district. And I want to see that changed, and I've got to convince these folks that we're not doing this in some vindictive political way. We're doing it to try to accommodate to what will be a new kind of defense force in this country.

Arms Reduction Agreements

Q. Mr. President, I wonder if you could clarify your position on your hopes for the June summit. Is it your view that it may be possible there if not necessarily to sign formal treaties but to substantially complete the CFE and the START and even maybe the chemical?

The President. Chemical. I'd hope we'd be substantially completed—that's a good way to phrase it.

South Africa

Q. Your Assistant Secretary for Africa seemed to suggest that some sort of gestures were now needed towards South Africa. Has there been any discussion of that or have you pretty much ruled it out, any concrete move, until the state of emergency is lifted?

The President. Well, we have certain provisions in the law that have to be met. But I would hope people would see the invitation to Mr. de Klerk, certainly, as a gesture, but one that will have, after the discussions with him, I think, considerable more substance to it.

German Membership in NATO

Q. Can you support a situation—back to Germany—where there is membership, let's say political membership, in NATO, but not a military relationship that exists now, with the possibility of no foreign troops on German soil and a reunified Germany?

The President. I don't think we're contemplating a neutralized Germany, and I have stated my position in terms of the alliance. And that's the way we view it, and I'm sure that's the way our allies look at it.

Q. Can I ask—since you had mentioned that unification is a matter to be left to the German people—if there were some referendum where they wanted a configuration without foreign troops on German soil, how would you deal with it?

The President. I would cross that bridge when I came to it. But I would point out that Helmut Kohl, to his credit, is not considering that.

Drug Summit in Cartagena, Colombia

Q. Mr. President—in a different hemisphere. Over the past couple of months, when asked why you're going to Cartagena this week, you've said you want to show support for the Government down there. Now that you're just a couple days away, do you expect to do anything more than that—than show the flag? Do you expect anything concrete to come out of it, perhaps increased use of military down there?

The President. Well, I do think that we want to support Mr. Barco [President of Colombia], a courageous leader, and I think going there will certainly indicate how strongly I feel about that. But I think there'll be more than that come out of it. I hope we can get agreement in terms of support for the antinarcotics efforts in these three countries: Peru, Bolivia, and Colombia.

What was the last part?

Q. Anything in particular, like the increased use of the military—the plan that seemed to have been scuttled earlier—to use U.S. warships off the coast of Colombia?

The President. Well, what happened on that plan was some mischievous stories that suggested blockade. So, one of the things I'll try to do—because there's never any intention of a blockade—absolutely absurd. And yet that threw a panic amongst many of the Colombians, who said we don't want a blockade off our coast. And that wasn't whatever had been intended. But in terms of interdiction, what I'd like to convince them is we can be extraordinarily helpful, particularly to Colombia in their courageous fight against narco-traffickers, by a sophisticated interdiction effort.

Q. Mr. President, on the same subject. Some observers and some headlines recently have talked about we're winning the war on drugs. And I believe your last statement—you said we're just starting on the war on drugs.

The President. Starting to win.

Q. Starting to win.

The President. Combined the two statements. [*Laughter*] We'll meld them.

Q. As you head for the drug summit, what will you tell the other leaders about the status on the war on drugs in this country?

The President. One of the points I'll emphasize at the beginning is: Look, I know you three leaders think that this is all the fault—not entirely, but a lot of the fault because of the demand in the United States. And let me assure you, we're not just talking about interdiction, we're not just talking about anticrime aspects of this in the United States, we're talking about major efforts on the demand side, a major initiative—and most of it is out in the private sector or in the schools, to educate people against the use of narcotics—because they think that the United States is causing all this problem. It's changed a little bit, because some of them are beginning to see user problems inside their own countries or neighboring countries or countries that have—across the ocean even. So, I think we've got to convince them that we are going out on all fronts, and I think I can do that.

Q. As a followup, they're—from what we've heard—going to ask you for more money for crop substitution, to substitute other goods for the coca crop down there. Will the U.S. put its money where its mouth is on that?

The President. Well, we'll listen to what they have to say on it, but they ought not to be condoning the growth of crops that are illegal in some areas, and certainly crops that are clearly used in the cocaine trade. And so, that's a moral question. I'd try to put it on that kind of emphasis and then see what we can do over here in terms of trying to help financially.

Warsaw Pact's Future

Q. Yes. You've said that the Eastern European countries want the Soviet troops to leave, and you've also pointed to the progress in talks about conventional force reductions. But the fact of the matter is, virtually all those Soviet troops are still there now in Eastern Europe. Can you point to any real progress on the ground, in terms of any changes in Soviet troop deployments in Eastern Europe? And to what extent do you see the continued threat for reversals, politically, inside the East bloc, that could cause those troops to continue to be deployed?

The President. To be wanted? I can't see a political change inside the Eastern European countries that would have an invitation go out to please remain. I don't see any politics or any political changes that would make me think that that is a likely scenario right now. And I do think that you put your finger on something—they have not—I don't know; I was looking for Brent [Brent Scowcroft, Assistant to the President for National Security Affairs] to see if any have been pulled back at all.

General Scowcroft. Yes, they have.

The President. He says some have, so we'll have to get you the information on exactly what withdrawals have taken place.

Soviet-U.S. Summit

Q. Mr. President, do you have a date for the summit with Mr. Gorbachev yet?

The President. Do what?

Q. Do you have a date?

The President. I don't think we've set the exact date.

China

Q. Mr. President, when you won the China veto vote, you said there were signs things were easing up in Beijing. Now they say that before students can leave the country to study abroad they'll spend 5 years at work. Isn't this backsliding, or is there some evidence that you have that things are easing up in China?

The President. Well, I'm disturbed by that statement. I don't like that statement because I feel that student exchanges are very good things to have between our countries. I know that some visas have recently been given to students, so I'd want to check the statement against the reality. I know that some students over there have been issued visas to come to the United States. But I saw the statement, and if you just want me to comment on the statement, I thought that was counterproductive, very much so.

Offshore Oil Lease Sales

Q. Mr. President, has the current oilspill out in southern California in any way changed your thinking about the wisdom of further development of offshore oil lease sales? And what is your timetable for when you're going to make the decision on those lease sales?

The President. A freighter or tanker has a hole punched in it, and I see a whole bunch of guys jumping up and down saying this proves you can't have any offshore drilling. I'm saying to myself, I'm not sure I understand the connection between tankers. Do they want to cut off all tankers, or do we just want to do our level best to make tankering safer?

I have said that we're not going to have drilling in highly environmentally sensitive places. But I'll be darned if I think we ought to shut down all offshore drilling everywhere. And I don't see that a spill from a tanker really has much to do with whether you can drill an offshore well safely, because it's going on all the time. And this country depends on it. We depend on offshore oil domestically for our own energy requirements. But I tell you what it does

do: It reinforces my view that we've got to be very careful about leasing in sensitive areas, even though there's no connection between a tanker spill and a drilling of a well.

Q. But when do you plan to make your decision on those lease sales?

The President. Fairly soon. I read the recommendations and the report. It should be fairly soon.

Meetings With South African Leaders

Q. Mr. President, did Mr. Mandela and Mr. de Klerk accept your invitations? And if so, when are they coming?

The President. I have to go back and look at my notes, but I felt they accepted in principle, both of them. I think Mr. Mandela said he wanted to talk, I thought he said, to his executive council or something. But anyway, he wanted to talk to some others that came right out the first few hours. I must say he seemed very pleased at that, and I think Mr. de Klerk the same way. But there wasn't any time set on either of those invitations.

NATO Military Doctrines

Q. Mr. President, is this the time to reexamine the "flexible-response" doctrine of NATO and, particularly, the wisdom of continuing work on the Lance missile?

The President. Well, that decision will not be taken until 1992. That was an agreement between all the NATO partners. And I see nothing to change that at this point.

Q. But could I just follow up? How can you, under current circumstances, justify possible deployment of the Lance, which would hit with nuclear warheads East Germany, perhaps Poland and Czechoslovakia?

The President. If you have these dramatic changes get effected, then you take a new look at all these considerations. That's what I would say.

Troop Cuts

Q. Yes. You talked a lot about troop cuts, but nobody is explaining how tens of thousands of soldiers would physically be removed from the armed services. What are your suggestions?

The President. Well see, I was talking to Marlin [Marlin Fitzwater, Press Secretary to the President] when I should have been listening. Excuse me. What was your question? The first part of it?

Q. A lot of people are talking about troop cuts, but you have not proposed a way to get many thousands of soldiers out of the armed services. How do you propose getting people out of uniform? Should we turn them all into DEA [Drug Enforcement Administration] agents or force a lot of early retirement? Do you want a lot of the people to go into the Reserves?

The President. Well, I'll tell you, in our defense budget, we did propose reductions. They'll come up over the years, not necessarily all at once. Eighty-one thousand troops, 2 active Army divisions, and then 2 battleships, 14 B–52's, all of which have personnel with them, M–1 tanks, Maverick missiles, sea-launch system, Apache helicopter—several different systems that will eventually result in lower personnel. Maybe I'm missing the question.

Q. So, you're only talking about reducing forces by attrition?

The President. Oh. I would hope a lot of it could be done by attrition because of the highly trained, dedicated men and women in the Armed Forces. I would hope a lot could. You have relatively high attrition rates in spite of pretty good retention. But there's still attrition. And I would like to think that a kid that went in to make a career out of this would not be unceremoniously dumped from the armed services. No, that's a good point. And I would hope that attrition can take care of the cuts that inevitably would be coming.

I'm told by Marlin this has got to be the last one.

Antiapartheid Activism

Q. Mr. President, what role did antiapartheid demonstrations in this country play in the release of Nelson Mandela and other political prisoners?

The President. I don't know, because you had antiapartheid demonstrations in many countries. So, I think if people get the feeling in South Africa that apartheid itself is abhorrent to the United States—through whatever way they get that feeling, whether it's a statement by the President, whether it's some legislative action, or whether it's some demonstration—that's helpful. But I can't help you on how you would quantify that.

Thank you all. Really, I've got a 2:30 p.m. meeting. But thank you very, very much.

Note: The President's 35th news conference began at 2:01 p.m. in the Briefing Room at the White House.

Remarks on Signing the United Nations Convention Against Illegal Traffic in Narcotic Drugs and Psychotropic Substances
February 13, 1990

Well, I'm pleased today to sign the United States instrument of ratification for the U.N. Convention Against Illegal Drugs. In doing so is a key international goal of our initial drug strategy way back last September. And this important convention lays down clear norms for all nations to criminalize the production, cultivation, and trafficking in the drugs that are poisoning our kids: cocaine, heroin, marijuana, and other dangerous drugs. It calls for outlawing money-laundering and controlling essential and precursor chemicals, the chemical tools for producing the illicit drugs. And it provides for the seizure of drug-tainted assets, the extradition of drug traffickers, and other important measures of international cooperation.

This convention helps equip the international community with the coherent, tough legal authority to stop the flow of illicit drugs. And it says something very important—sends a message—and that is that this scourge will stop. And we will stop the criminals that deal drugs, and we'll take back the streets.

As we continue preparations for the Andean drug summit and on the eve of the U.N. General Assembly, I'd like to urge all nations to join the United States in ratifying this United Nations convention, to join us in working together to rid the world of this menace—the menace from drugs. And now I'll sign the documents.

Thank you all very much. Thank you.

Note: The President spoke at 11:50 a.m. in the Roosevelt Room at the White House.

Statement on Signing the United Nations Convention Against Illegal Traffic in Narcotic Drugs and Psychotropic Substances
February 13, 1990

I am most pleased today to sign the United States instrument of ratification for the United Nations Convention Against Illicit Traffic in Narcotic Drugs and Psychotropic Substances.

We have labored long and hard to create through this Convention stringent international norms for the criminalization of drug trafficking, the forfeiture of drug proceeds, the control of chemicals essential to the manufacture of dangerous drugs, and cooperation among nations in combating drug trafficking. United States legislation already in place in each of these areas is a model for the rest of the world and indeed formed the basis for many of the central provisions of the Convention.

By signing this instrument of ratification, we move one important step closer to placing in the hands of all signatory nations to this Convention a new and formidable weapon in our continued struggle against international drug traffickers.

The Convention will obligate all participating countries to criminalize each link in the chain of activities with which these dealers in death seek to enslave our citizens, from drug production to the final laundering of drug profits. It will remove the drug lords' shield of bank secrecy and establish effective measures to seize and forfeit the billions of dollars in proceeds realized by their commerce in misery. It will place controls on the international flow of essential chemicals necessary for the production of these poisons. It will mandate unprecedented cooperation in the investigation and prosecution of drug-trafficking offenses and facilitate the extradition of drug traffickers to stand trial for their crimes.

On the eve of our Andean Drug Summit and the United Nations General Assembly Special Session on drugs, we call upon all nations to join us in ratifying this Convention and undertaking its solemn obligations to work together as never before to rid our world of the threat to our freedoms that drug trafficking represents.

The fight against drug traffickers is one that we must win, and this Convention can give us new hope that we will.

GEORGE BUSH

Nomination of Herman J. Cohen To Be a Member of the Board of Directors of the African Development Foundation
February 13, 1990

The President today announced his intention to nominate Herman J. Cohen, of New York, to be a member of the Board of Directors of the African Development Foundation for the remainder of the term expiring September 22, 1991. He would succeed Chester A. Crocker.

Currently, Mr. Cohen serves as Assistant

Secretary of State for African Affairs in Washington, DC. Mr. Cohen graduated from City College of New York (B.A., 1953). He was born February 10, 1932, in New York, NY. Mr. Cohen served in the U.S. Army, 1953–1955. He is married, has two children, and resides in Washington, DC.

Remarks on Signing the Urgent Assistance for Democracy in Panama Act of 1990 and a Question-and-Answer Session With Reporters
February 14, 1990

The President. Well, let me first give this statement. And I want to congratulate Secretary Baker for his superb job at Ottawa and also for following through on his meetings in Moscow on the agenda that President Gorbachev and I set out at Malta. And I'm delighted that the 23 members of the Vienna negotiations on conventional forces in Europe accepted the NATO initiative, which I proposed in my State of the Union Address on January 31st, to resolve the issue of manpower.

The United States and the Soviet Union each will station no more than 195,000 troops in the central zone in Europe. And this will be the overall ceiling for Soviet troops stationed on foreign territory in Europe. The U.S. will be permitted to station the additional 30,000 troops in Europe, outside the central zone. Now, this is an important breakthrough which removes a major obstacle to the early conclusion of a CFE treaty. And it also establishes the principle that U.S. forces in Europe are not to be treated as equivalent to Soviet forces in Eastern Europe.

The other major breakthrough was on German unification. And I called [West German] Chancellor Kohl yesterday to discuss the final details of the agreement that Secretary Baker reached at Ottawa. We and our German allies are in full accord. Things moved quite fast there. And the agreement we've reached calls for the Foreign Ministers of the two German States to meet with the Foreign Ministers of the Four Powers— the United States, France, the United Kingdom, and the Soviet Union—to discuss the external aspects of the establishment of German unity. This brings us a step closer to realizing the longstanding goal of German unity. And as I said in Mainz last May, it's a goal we and our allies have shared with the German people for more than 40 years.

These steps, along with the inspiring march of democracy in Eastern Europe, bring within sight the objective that I have stressed throughout the first year of my Presidency: a Europe that is whole and free.

Another subject that's related to the march of democracy in our own hemisphere—I think it's appropriate that the Secretary of State is here with me today as I sign into law the Urgent Assistance for Democracy in Panama Act of 1990. And I want to thank Congress for acting rapidly on this legislation. And I'm pleased to see such strong bipartisan support for the task of helping Panama rebuild and strengthen its economy and its democracy. With the signing of this legislation, we'll move forward with the broad range of activities to assist Panama, including AID and OPIC, Ex-Im Bank and other assistance in restoring Caribbean Basin Initiative and GSP trade benefits.

I look forward to working with Congress on these particular initiatives and on implementing the second phase of our economic recovery program for Panama. This legislation is an important step in our continuing effort to cooperate with the Panamanian Government and the people there, as they work to build a new and better life for themselves in freedom and democracy.

And thank you, and now I'm pleased to sign this statement. Maybe you want to give a couple of these to the congressional leaders.

[*At this point, the President signed the bill.*]

All right. Thank you all.

Conventional Force Reductions in Europe

Q. Mr. President, why do you think Chairman Gorbachev acceded to your proposal on the troop levels?

The President. I think he saw that it made very good sense. I have Jim's [Secretary of State Baker] comment; he discussed it with [Soviet Foreign Minister] Mr. Shevardnadze. But we've stayed firm on this proposal. We think it's a very sound proposal; it has the strong support of our allies. Events are moving awfully fast there, and I think they see this as good for them, and I hope they see it as a stabilizing agreement for Europe.

Q. Mr. President, on Monday——

Germany

Q. Mr. President, Mr. Shevardnadze has said up in Ottawa that he could foresee a united Germany with a role for both NATO and the Warsaw Pact. You've always said that NATO has to have its role. I assume that's still your position, but could you see the Warsaw Pact having a role as well?

The President. Well, the way it looks to me is that the allies want the stability of U.S. forces and a united NATO—U.S. forces in Europe and a strong NATO. The Eastern European countries that make up the Warsaw Pact want the Soviet troops to leave. You have a different equation now. And we are talking about Germany remaining in NATO—flexibility on where the troops in Germany are, but a strong NATO. And as I said the other day, I think it stabilizing, certainly as far as Western Europe looks at it, and also I think you're going to find a lot of countries in Eastern Europe see us as a stabilizing factor there.

Q. So, no Warsaw Pact?

The President. Well, these things are being discussed. I think changes are going on so fast there that it's hard to keep up with them all. But, again, I salute Secretary Baker and our people who went with him on this trip because a lot of things happened that happened more quickly than

certainly I would have thought. This troop agreement is one of them.

Q. You said on Monday——

The President. ——think we set out some——

Q. On Monday you said that the time was not right for a Four Power conference on Germany. Did something change between Monday and the agreement on Tuesday?

The President. Well, I'd let Jim address himself to that, but, yes, I think there was a lot of change—not about change but certainly there was a feeling on the part of Chancellor Kohl, who told me this on the phone yesterday that the agreement that Secretary Baker had been discussing and details of which he worked out with Shevardnadze and the allied leaders was a very sound step. And we're not trying to dictate to anybody over there how it would work; I left that question open. But, yes, it moved very, very fast.

Do you want to add something to that?

Secretary Baker. No, sir, I think that's it.

Q. Were you not aware on Monday that things were moving in that direction that—on Tuesday?

The President. Not aware on Monday that we were going to have a deal on Tuesday, absolutely not.

Secretary Baker. Nor were we in Ottawa, I might add.

The President. And nor were we on the troop deal. I mean, you've got to realize, Norm [Norman Sandler, United Press International], we're dealing with historic change; and we need to be very elated about this. [*Laughter*] Seriously. And it's very, very fast. And the fact that the Secretary was able to close this deal in such a short period of time—I say short from the time we last talked about it—I think is evidence of this. But he can't do that alone; he has to have the change from the Germanys. But you've got to remember, [East German Prime Minister] Modrow has talking to Kohl, and Jim's been talking to Shevardnadze. The NATO people were meeting. We had this conversation over the weekend with Woerner [Secretary General of NATO]. And so, there's a lot of diplomacy going on.

But, no, this surprised me that they were

willing to make an agreement on that, as it did troops. But I thought it was right to stay firm on it.

Conventional Force Reductions in Europe

Q. In light of that, what about some of the—I guess it is criticism—that by agreeing to a CFE agreement with 195,000 that you're legitimizing their keeping that number of troops in Eastern Europe? And is it time to lower that——

The President. We're dealing with a period of dynamic change. We are trying to project, as I think I conveyed the other day, and Jim has been conveying, a sense of stability to the question. Our allies view this certainly as a good, sound number.

Now, what hasn't been taken into consideration—and it takes time to work its way through the system, and it will happen after elections are held in various countries—is how those countries feel about the presence of Soviet troops. So, what the Secretary was able to do here through the acceptance of our proposal is delink the weapons. And that's good because the Western Europeans—and again, I repeat, I think some of the Eastern Europeans—want us there, seeing us not as a threat but as a stabilizing influence. The Eastern Europeans appear not to want the Soviets there, and I have a feeling that Mr. Gorbachev will not want to stay against the general feeling there in Eastern Europe. And also, he has enormous problems on his own economic front.

So, the thing to do is, we got a good deal, a steady, stabilizing deal, and then see what events come along if we go. But now let's close the deal; that's what I want to do. Conclude this CFE agreement and get it done and signed. And there's still some technical problems in it.

Secretary Baker. ——a major disproportion in reductions, too.

The President. Yes. The original proposal had the Soviets taking down an awful lot more than we did. Now we've got what I think of as a delinked—again, I think that is stabilizing. Somebody at the press conference the other day—I had a question that at least implied to me they thought it may be destabilizing, that you want it linked to equal numbers. I don't agree with that. I think it's just the opposite.

Q. How soon does that get wrapped up now—CFE?

The President. Jim?

Secretary Baker. The President has stated he wants it this year, so that's what we're shooting for.

Q. How about START? Are you preparing to propose any new initiatives at the START talks? There's been talk about a ban on mobile MIRV's.

The President. Well, I haven't had a chance to talk to General Scowcroft [Assistant to the President for National Security Affairs] in detail since the Secretary has been back, and I haven't had a chance to talk to him about it. But now guess what we're going to do? We're going to go in and talk about this.

Q. He wants it——

Q. Will we have trouble finding countries accepting 195,000?

The President. Oh, no. No, no, that's—all right. Thank you.

Note: The President spoke at 1:45 p.m. in the Roosevelt Room at the White House. Parts of these remarks could not be verified because the tape was incomplete. H.R. 3952, approved February 14, was assigned Public Law No. 101–243.

Statement on Signing the Urgent Assistance for Democracy in Panama Act of 1990
February 14, 1990

I have signed today H.R. 3952, the "Urgent Assistance for Democracy in Panama Act of 1990."

I would like to express my appreciation to the Congress in passing this legislation, which will allow us to proceed expeditiously on Phase I of our plan to foster economic recovery in Panama. We plan now to proceed with the broad range of activities that officials of my Administration have been discussing with interested Members of Congress in consultations that have taken place over the last several weeks. This program contains a range of AID, OPIC, Eximbank, and other assistance, as well as restoration of Caribbean Basin Initiative and Generalized System of Preferences trade benefits for Panama.

I am further appreciative of the provisions that will permit us to provide certain assistance for Panamanian law enforcement agencies on an expedited basis. This will facilitate our efforts to have the Panamanians assume the law enforcement responsibilities now being shouldered by our military forces.

I look forward to working with the Congress on the necessary legislation to implement Phase II of our economic recovery program for Panama.

Finally, I note that Section 104(b)(3) of the Act requires me to report on agreements with Panama "in the process of negotiation." The Constitution, however, commits to the President the responsibility of negotiations with foreign governments and necessarily provides the President with discretion to determine whether and when to disclose information concerning agreements that are in the process of negotiation. Accordingly, I will construe this section consistent with my constitutional responsibilities.

GEORGE BUSH

The White House,
February 14, 1990.

Note: H.R. 3952, approved February 14, was assigned Public Law No. 101–243.

Nomination of Arthur E. Williams To Be a Member and President of the Mississippi River Commission
February 14, 1990

The President today announced his intention to nominate Brig. Gen. Arthur E. Williams, USA, to be a member and President of the Mississippi River Commission. He would succeed Thomas Allen Sands.

Currently, Brigadier General Williams is commander of the Lower Mississippi Valley Division in Vicksburg, MS. Prior to this he served as commander of the U.S. Army Engineer Division, Pacific Ocean Division, at Fort Schafter, HI, 1987–1989.

General Williams received his bachelor of science degree from Saint Lawrence University and from Rensselaer Polytechnic Institute. He received his master of science degree from Stanford University. He was born on March 28, 1938, in Watertown, NY. General Williams served in the U.S. Army, 1962–present. He is married, has three children, and resides in Vicksburg, MS.

Statement on the Drug Summit in Cartagena, Colombia
February 15, 1990

It is truly a great pleasure for me to be in Colombia today. As I have said so many times, my admiration for President Barco, his colleagues, and all the citizens of Colombia who have joined in this difficult struggle to fight international narcotics traffickers have earned my profound admiration and that of the American people. We are deeply grateful.

I am looking forward to a fruitful and productive exchange of views with President Barco, President Garcia [of Peru], and President Paz Zamora [of Bolivia] in Cartagena. The Document of Cartagena, which we will sign, will establish a broad, flexible framework which will help guide the actions of our four countries in the years to come as we fight this war together.

In addition to signing the document, it is just as important that the four of us have an opportunity to exchange views candidly among ourselves concerning this international scourge that affects all of our countries. Frankly, I look forward to learning from my three colleagues today and expect to take home new ideas.

I would like to report this morning some very good news: that we appear to be making headway in the United States in our effort to reduce the demand for cocaine. Some very encouraging statistics were released Tuesday indicating that, on a wide front, drug use is declining, particularly among our young people, which is so important. Drug use among U.S. high school seniors has declined from a high of 32.5 percent in 1982 to a 1989 figure of 19.7. As I know there is great concern with regard to the use of drugs in the United States, I simply wanted to pass that good news on to you this morning.

Note: In the morning, President Bush arrived at Ernesto Cortissoz Airport in Barranquilla. He then went to the Guest House near the Naval Academy in Cartagena. There, President Bush participated in the arrival ceremony, a bilateral meeting with President Barco, and working sessions with the other summit participants.

Declaration of Cartagena
February 15, 1990

The Parties consider that a strategy which commits the Parties to implement or strengthen a comprehensive, intensified anti-narcotics program must address the issues of demand reduction, consumption and supply. Such a strategy also must include understandings regarding economic cooperation, alternative development, encouragement of trade and investment, as well as understandings on attacking the traffic in illicit drugs, and on diplomatic and public diplomacy initiatives.

The Parties recognize that these areas are interconnected and self-reinforcing. Progress in one area will help achieve progress in others. Failure in any of them will jeopardize progress in the others. The order in which they are addressed in the document is not meant to assign to them any particular priority.

Economic cooperation and international initiatives cannot be effective unless there are concomitant, dynamic programs attacking the production of, trafficking in and demand for illicit drugs. It is clear that to be fully effective, supply reduction efforts must be accompanied by significant reduction in demand. The Parties recognize that the exchange of information on demand control programs will benefit their countries.

The Parties recognize that the nature and impact of the traffic in and interdiction of illicit drugs varies in each of the three

Andean countries and cannot be addressed fully in this document. The Parties will negotiate bilateral and multilateral agreements, consistent with their anti-narcotics efforts, specifying their responsibilities and commitments with regard to economic cooperation and intensified enforcement actions.

A. UNDERSTANDINGS REGARDING ECONOMIC ASPECTS AND ALTERNATIVE DEVELOPMENT

The Parties recognize that trafficking in illicit drugs has a negative long-term impact on their economies. In some of the Parties, profits from coca production and trade and from illicit drug trafficking contribute, in varying degrees, to the entry of foreign exchange and to the generation of employment and income. Suppression of coca production and trade will result in significant, immediate, and long-term economic costs that will affect, in various ways, each of the Andean countries.

The President of the United States will request Congress to authorize new funds for the program during fiscal years 1991 to 1994, in order to support the Andean Parties' efforts to counteract the short- and long-term socio-economic impact of an effective fight against illicit drugs. This contribution by the United States would be made within the framework of actions against drug trafficking carried out by the Andean Parties. The Andean Parties reiterate the importance of implementing or strengthening sound economic policies for the effective utilization of such a contribution. The United States is also prepared to cooperate with the Andean Parties in a wide range of initiatives for development, trade and investment in order to strengthen and sustain long-term economic growth.

Alternative development, designed to replace the coca economy in Peru and Bolivia and illicit drug trafficking in all the Andean Parties, includes the following areas of cooperation. In the short term, there is a need to create and/or to strengthen social emergency programs and balance of payments support to mitigate the social and economic costs stemming from substitution. In the medium and long term, investment programs and measures will be needed to

create the economic conditions for definitive substitution of the coca economy in those countries where it exists or of that sector of the economy affected by narcotics trafficking. It is necessary to implement programs to preserve the ecological balance.

1. Alternative Development and Crop Substitution

In order to foster increased employment and income opportunities throughout the entire productive system and implement or enhance a sound economic policy to sustain long-term growth, the United States will support measures aimed at stimulating broad-based rural development, promoting non-traditional exports, and building or reinforcing productive infrastructure. The Parties, in accordance with the respective policies of Bolivia, Colombia, Peru and the United States, shall determine the economic assistance required to ensure sound economic policies and sustain alternative development and crop substitution, which in the medium term will help replace the income, employment and foreign exchange in the countries in which these have been generated by the illegal coca economy. The United States is prepared to finance economic activities of this kind with new and concessional resources.

In order to achieve a complete program of alternative development and crop substitution, the Parties agree that in addition to the cooperation provided by the United States, economic cooperation, as well as greater incentives to investment and foreign trade from other sources, will be needed. The Parties will make concerted efforts to obtain the support of multilateral and other economic institutions for these programs, as the three Andean Parties implement or continue sound economic policies and effective programs against drugs.

The Parties are convinced that a comprehensive fight against illicit drug traffic will disrupt the market for coca and coca derivatives and will reduce their prices. As success is achieved in this fight, those employed in growing coca and in its primary processing will seek alternative sources of income either by crop substitution or by changing jobs. The Parties will work together to identify alternative-income activities for external financing. The United States is ready to consider financing of activities such as research, extension, credit and other agricultural support services and support of private-sector initiatives for the creation of micro-enterprises and agro-industries.

The United States will also cooperate with the Andean Parties to promote viable domestic and foreign markets to sell the products generated by alternative development and crop substitution programs.

2. Mitigation of the Social and Economic Impact of the Fight Against Illicit Drug Trafficking

As the Andean Parties implement or continue to develop effective programs of interdiction of the flow of illicit drugs and of crop eradication, they will need assistance of the fast disbursement type to mitigate both small- and large-scale social and economic costs. The Parties will cooperate to identify the type of assistance required. The United States is prepared to provide balance of payments support to help meet foreign exchange needs. The United States will also consider funding for emergency social programs, such as the successful one in Bolivia, to provide employment and other opportunities to the poor directly affected by the fight against illicit drugs.

3. Trade Initiatives, Incentives to Exports and Private Foreign Investment

An increase in trade and private investment is essential to facilitate sustained economic growth and to help offset the economic dislocations resulting from any effective program against illicit drugs. The Parties will work together to increase trade among the three Andean countries and the United States, effectively facilitating access to the United States market and strengthening export promotion, including identification, development and marketing of new export products. The United States will also consider providing appropriate technical and financial assistance to help Andean agricultural products comply with the admission requirements.

The Parties may consider the establishment of economic and investment policies,

as well as legislation and regulations to foster private investment. Where favorable conditions exist, the United States will facilitate private investment in the three Andean countries, taking into account the particular conditions and potential of each.

B. UNDERSTANDINGS REGARDING ATTACKING ILLICIT DRUGS

The Parties reaffirm their will to fight drug trafficking in a comprehensive manner attacking all facets of the trade: production, transportation and consumption. Such comprehensive action includes the following:

—Preventive actions to reduce consumption and therefore demand.

—Control and law enforcement activities against illegal cultivation, processing, and marketing of illicit drugs.

—Control of essential chemicals for the production of illegal drugs and the means used for their transport.

—Seizure, forfeiture, and sharing of illegal proceeds and property used in committing narcotics-related crimes.

—Coordination of law enforcement agencies, the military, prosecutors and courts, within the framework of national sovereignty of each of the Parties.

—Actions to bring about a net reduction in the illegal cultivation of coca.

The Parties undertake to engage in an ongoing evaluation of their cooperation, so that the President of the United States, as appropriate, may request Congress to provide additional assistance to the Andean Parties.

Given that the Parties act within a framework of respect for human rights, they reaffirm that nothing would do more to undermine the war on drugs than disregard for human rights by participants in the effort.

1. Prevention and Demand

The Parties undertake to support development and expansion of programs on comprehensive prevention, such as preventive public education in both rural and urban areas, treatment of drug addicts, and information to encourage the public opposition to illegal drug production, trade and consumption. These programs are fundamental if the drug problem is to be successfully confronted.

The Parties recognize that prevention efforts in the four countries will benefit from shared information about successful prevention programs and from bilateral and multilateral cooperation agreements to expand efforts in this field.

To this end, the Parties undertake to contribute economic, material and technical resources to support such comprehensive prevention programs.

2. Interdiction

A battle against an illicit product must focus on the demand for, production of and trade in that product. Interdiction of illegal drugs, as they move from producer to consumer, is essential. The Parties pledge to step up efforts within their own countries to interdict illegal drugs and to increase coordination and cooperation among them to facilitate this fight. The United States is ready to provide increased cooperation in equipment and training to the law enforcement bodies of the Andean Parties.

3. Involvement of the Armed Forces of the Respective Countries

The control of illegal trafficking in drugs is essentially a law enforcement matter. However, because of its magnitude and the different aspects involved, and in keeping with the sovereign interest of each State and its own judicial system, the armed forces in each of the countries, within their own territory and national jurisdictions, may also participate. The Parties may establish bilateral and multilateral understandings for cooperation in accordance with their interests, needs and priorities.

4. Information Sharing and Intelligence Cooperation

The Parties commit themselves to a greater exchange of information and intelligence in order to strengthen action by the competent agencies. The Parties will pursue bilateral and multilateral understandings on information and intelligence cooperation, consistent with their national interests and priorities.

5. Eradication and Discouragement of Illicit Crops

Eradication can play an essential part in the anti-drug fight of each country. In each case, eradication programs have to be carefully crafted, measuring their possible effect on total illicit drug production in each country; their cost-benefit ratio relative to other means of fighting illicit drugs; whether they can be most effective as voluntary or compulsory programs or a combination of the two; and their probable political and social consequences.

The Parties recognize that to eradicate illicit crops, the participation of the growers themselves is desirable, adopting measures that will help them obtain legal sources of income.

New economic opportunities, such as programs for alternative development and crop substitution, shall be fostered to help to dissuade growers from initiating or expanding illegal cultivation. Our goal is a sustained reduction in the total area under illegal cultivation.

Eradication programs must safeguard human health and preserve the ecosystem.

6. Control of Financial Assets

The Parties agree to identify, trace, freeze, seize, and apply other legal procedures for the disposition of drug crime proceeds in their respective countries, and to attack financial aspects of the illicit drug trade. In accordance with their respective laws, each of the Parties will seek to adopt measures to define, categorize, and criminalize money laundering, as well as to increase efforts to implement current legislation. The Parties agree to establish formulas providing exceptions to banking secrecy.

7. Forfeiture and Sharing of Illegal Drug Proceeds

The Parties pledge to implement a system for forfeiture and sharing of illegal drug profits and assets, and to establish effective programs in this area.

In United States cases related to forfeiture of property of illegal drug traffickers where Bolivia, Colombia, and Peru provide assistance to the United States Government, the Government of the United States pledges to transfer to the assisting government such forfeited property, to the extent consistent with United States' laws and regulations. The Parties will also seek asset sharing agreements for Bolivia, Colombia, and Peru, with other countries.

8. Control of Essential Chemicals Used in the Production of Illicit Drugs

The control in the United States of the export of chemical substances used in the processing of cocaine is vital. In addition, there is a need for greater control of the import and domestic production of such substances by the Andean Parties. Joint efforts must be coordinated to eliminate the illicit trade in such substances.

The Parties agree:

—to step up interdiction of the movements of essential chemicals that have already entered the country, legally or illegally, and are being diverted for illicit drug processing. This includes controlling choke points as well as establishing investigative and monitoring programs in close cooperation with all the Parties' law enforcement agencies.

—to further develop an internal system to track essential chemicals through sale, resale and distribution to the end user.

—to cooperate bilaterally and multilaterally to provide each other with information necessary to track domestic and international movements of essential chemicals for the purpose of controlling their sale and use.

—to support the efforts under the Organization of American States (OAS) auspices to develop and implement a regional inter-American agreement on essential chemicals.

9. Control of Weapons, Planes, Ships, Explosives and Communications Equipment Used in Illegal Drug Trafficking

Illicit drug trafficking is heavily dependent on weapons, explosives, communications equipment, and air, maritime and riverine transportation throughout the illicit cultivation and the production and distribution process.

The Parties agree:

—to strengthen controls over the movement of illegal weapons and explosives

and over the sale, resale and the registration of aircraft and maritime vessels in their respective countries, which should be carried out by their own authorities.

The Parties agree to establish within their own territory control programs that include:

—the registration of ships and aircraft;

—the adoption of legal standards that permit effective forfeiture of aircraft and vessels;

—controls on pilot licenses and training;

—registration of airfields in their respective countries;

—development of control measures over communications equipment used in illegal drug trafficking to the extent permitted by their respective laws and national interests.

The United States agrees to work with the Andean Parties to stem weapons exports from the United States to illegal drug traffickers in the three Andean nations.

10. Legal Cooperation

The Parties pledge to cooperate in the sharing of instrumental evidence in forms admissible by their judicial proceedings. The Parties also agree to seek mechanisms that permit the exchange of information on legislation and judicial decisions in order to optimize legal proceedings against the traffic in illicit drugs.

The Parties recognize the value of international cooperation in strengthening the administration of justice, including the protection of judges, judicial personnel, and other individuals who take part in these proceedings.

C. UNDERSTANDINGS REGARDING DIPLOMATIC INITIATIVES AND PUBLIC OPINION

The scourge of illicit drug trafficking and consumption respects no borders, threatens national security, and erodes the economic and social structures of our nations. It is essential to adopt and carry out a comprehensive strategy to promote full awareness of the destructive effects of illegal production, illicit trafficking and the improper consumption of drugs. Toward this end, the Parties commit themselves to use all political and economic means within their power to put into effect programs aimed at achieving this goal.

1. Strengthening Public Opinion in Favor of Intensifying the Fight Against Illegal Drug Trafficking

Public awareness should be enhanced also by means of active and determined diplomatic action. The Parties pledge to strengthen plans for joint programs leading to the exchange of ideas, experiences, and specialists in the field. The Parties call upon the international community to intensify a program of public information stressing the danger of drug trafficking in all of its phases. In this regard, the Parties undertake to give active support to Inter-American public awareness and demand reduction programs, and will support the development of a drug prevention education plan at the Inter-American meeting in Quito this year.

2. Economic Summit

The 1989 Economic Summit in Paris established a Financial Action Task Force to determine how governments could promote cooperation and effective action against the laundering of money gained through illegal drug trafficking.

The United States will host the next Economic Summit on July 9–11, 1990, in Houston. The United States will use this opportunity to seek full attention on a priority basis to the fight against illegal drug trafficking. The Parties call upon the Economic Summit member countries, and on the other participants in the Financial Action Task Force, to give greater emphasis to the study of economic measures which may help to reduce drug trafficking. In particular, the Parties call upon the Economic Summit countries to take the steps necessary to ensure that assets seized from illicit drug trafficking in Bolivia, Colombia and Peru are used to finance programs of interdiction, alternative development and prevention in our countries.

3. Multilateral Approaches and Coordination

The Parties intend to coordinate their actions in multilateral economic institutions in order to ensure for Bolivia, Colombia and Peru, broader economic cooperation within the framework of a sound economic policy.

4. Report to the UN Special Session on Illicit Trafficking in Drugs

The United Nations has recognized that the problem of drug trafficking presents a grave threat to the security of the states and economic stability. It has called for a Global Action Plan and it has convened a Special Session, February 20–23, 1990, to discuss the magnitude of this problem. This will be a proper occasion to reiterate the need to bring into force as quickly as possible the UN Convention Against Illicit Traffic in Narcotic Drugs and Psychotropic Substances, which provides for energetic measures against illegal drug trafficking, while recognizing the ancestral and traditional uses of coca leaf.

The Parties request that consideration be given during the Special Session to the inclusion of the cooperative efforts outlined in this document to develop concrete programs for strengthening multilateral responses to the drug problem, as recommended in Resolution No. 44/141 of the United Nations General Assembly.

5. Report to the OAS Meeting of Ministers and CICAD

The Organization of American States has called an Inter-American meeting of Ministers responsible for national narcotics programs, to be held on April 17–20, 1990 in Ixtapa, Mexico. The Parties urge that the meeting of Ministers and the Inter-American Drug Abuse Control Commission (CICAD) give priority to the understandings set forth in this document and lend support to their early implementation within the context of regional cooperation against drugs.

6. Madrid Trilateral Meeting

The Parties stress the importance of the document issued by the Trilateral Meeting in Madrid and the efforts undertaken in Europe, particularly the participation of the European Community, with a view to adopting specific policies and initiatives against illicit trafficking of drugs.

7. World Ministerial Summit to Reduce Demand for Drugs and to Combat the Cocaine Threat

The Parties note with satisfaction the convening of a World Ministerial Summit to Reduce Demand for Drugs and to Combat the Cocaine Threat, to be held on April 9–11, 1990 in London. This meeting will serve to highlight the role demand reduction must play in the international community's efforts to reduce the trade in illicit drugs and will underline the social, economic and human costs of the trade. The Parties agree to coordinate their actions and future strategies in this area with the objective of building upon this important initiative.

8. Demarches to Transit Countries

Through specialized agencies of the United Nations such as the Heads of National Law Enforcement Agencies, our countries participate in important coordination efforts. The Parties undertake to strengthen cooperation with transit countries on interdiction of traffic in illicit drugs.

9. World Conference Against Illicit Drug Trafficking

In order to progress towards the goals agreed upon at the Cartagena Summit, the Parties call for a world conference in 1991 to strengthen international cooperation in the elimination of improper consumption, illegal trafficking and production of drugs.

10. Follow-Up Meeting to the Cartagena Summit

In order to follow up on progress of agreements arising under the foregoing understandings, the Parties agree to hold a high level follow-up meeting within a period of not more than six months.

Note: President George Bush of the United States, President Virgilio Barco Vargas of Colombia, President Jaime Paz Zamora of Bolivia, and President Alan Garcia Pérez of Peru met on February 15 in Cartagena, Colombia. This declaration was issued jointly by all of the participants in the summit. The declaration was made available by the Office of the Press Secretary but was not issued as a White House press release.

White House Fact Sheet on the Bolivia-United States Essential Chemicals Agreement
February 15, 1990

The U.S. and Bolivia signed a bilateral agreement on essential chemicals today. William J. Bennett, Director of the Office of National Drug Control Policy, signed on behalf of the United States, and Minister of Foreign Affairs Carlos Iturralde signed on behalf of Bolivia.

The agreement:

- specifies certain information to be collected by the parties and provides for information sharing, mutual cooperation, and the coordination of investigative and enforcement efforts with respect to essential chemicals;
- requires parties to promptly investigate the intended consignee or destination to confirm that the essential chemicals will be used solely for legitimate purposes;
- requires the enactment of domestic legislation, where necessary, to implement the agreement, including the ability to seize illicit shipments of essential chemicals;
- obligates the parties to invite key nations and international organizations to join these efforts and to support them fully;
- is consistent with and complements the Organization of American States' proposed Inter-American Drug Abuse Control (CICAD) agreement on pre-

cursor and other chemicals.

The agreement complements existing U.S. legislation and should provide us with additional tools to control movement and usage of those chemicals key to the processing of illicit drugs.

The Declaration of Cartagena reaffirms the need to enhance cooperation in the areas of monitoring, investigation, and enforcement with respect to illicit shipments of essential chemicals. The United States hopes to conclude similar agreements with other countries.

White House Fact Sheet on the Peru-United States Extradition Agreement
February 15, 1990

The United States and Peru signed an exchange of notes on extradition today. Secretary of State James A. Baker III signed on behalf of the United States. Guillermo Larco Cox, Prime Minister and Foreign Minister, signed on behalf of Peru.

This exchange of notes will:
- confirm our bilateral commitment to extradition;
- confirm explicitly that narcotics trafficking and related drug offenses are incorporated by reference in the 1899 United States-Peru Extradition Treaty.

This agreement represents the mutual desire of our countries to try to enhance effective law enforcement cooperation and to recognize the importance of the return of fugitives to stand trial as part of this effort. The exchange of notes should lead to further discussions between the two Governments with respect to extradition and the return of fugitives generally.

White House Fact Sheet on the Bolivia- and Peru-United States Public Awareness Measures Memorandums of Understanding
February 15, 1990

The United States signed two bilateral public awareness measures memorandums of understanding today in Cartagena, one with Bolivia and one with Peru. Secretary of State James A. Baker III signed both agreements on behalf of the United States. Minister of Foreign Affairs Carlos Iturralde signed on behalf of Bolivia. Guillermo Larco Cox, Prime Minister and Foreign Minister, signed on behalf of Peru.

These understandings will promote concrete measures reflecting the Declaration of Cartagena's emphasis on the need to raise public awareness and support for the measures we need to take to combat drug trafficking and consumption by:
- encouraging collaboration on initiatives to build public support for countering narcotics production, distribution, and use;
- recognizing that cross-fertilization of ideas, experience, and activities are essential to the success of counternarcotics efforts;
- encouraging parties to establish and share the International Narcotics Information Network (ININ), a computerized data base, so that antidrug activities can be made easily obtainable to those needing this information;
- promoting joint cosponsorship of mass media projects that promote the sharing of information about drug problems and solutions in the four countries.

The United States is discussing the possibility of similar understandings with other countries.

White House Fact Sheet on the Peru-United States Tax Information Exchange Agreement
February 15, 1990

The United States and Peru signed a tax information exchange agreement (TIEA) today. Secretary of State James A. Baker III signed on behalf of the United States. Guillermo Larco Cox, Prime Minister and Foreign Minister, signed on behalf of Peru.

This agreement will:

- permit the exchange of tax records, bank statements, and other information in order to uncover illicit drug profits, trace drug money-laundering, and generally to further civil and criminal tax investigations;
- encourage prosecution for tax evasion as an effective way to put drug dealers behind bars;
- improve tax compliance, through exchanges of technical know-how, development of new audit techniques, identification of new areas of noncompliance, and joint studies of noncompliance areas.

The agreement is responsive on a bilateral basis to the pledge in the Declaration of Cartagena to tighten monitoring of financial transactions. We are discussing similar arrangements with other countries.

White House Fact Sheet on the Bolivia-United States Weapons Export Control Memorandum of Understanding
February 15, 1990

The United States and Bolivia signed a weapons export control memorandum of understanding today. Secretary of State James A. Baker III signed on behalf of the United States. Minister of Foreign Affairs Carlos Iturralde signed on behalf of Bolivia.

The memorandum of understanding will help diminish the flow of U.S. light arms and other items to drug traffickers in the Andean countries by providing a framework for:

- the Department of State's Office of Munitions Control to condition issuance of a U.S. firearms export license upon the presentation of an import certificate validated by the importing government;
- subsequent discussions that will specify the weapons and other items to be covered by the understanding.

The U.S. Government is also working domestically to suppress the flow of smuggled arms, which are an important part of the narcotics trafficking problem. We are pursuing discussions with other governments also concerned about limiting the flow of U.S. weapons to illegitimate end users in the Andean countries.

Joint News Conference Following the Drug Summit in Cartagena, Colombia
February 15, 1990

President Barco Vargas of Colombia. The multilateral agreement we have just signed opened a new era in this struggle against drugs. It is the first time that we developed a common scheme for common action. In— [*inaudible*]—we have agreed upon a very clearcut goal to be followed, and it has been agreed that it is necessary to adopt commercial measures to strengthen our economies, with the purpose of confronting the drug problem in all its scope and extension. I am also very pleased because the progress attained here today coincides with an integral policy that I have defended on behalf of the Colombian Government. This summit meeting undoubtedly has been a success. I would like to thank each and every one of my fellow Presidents for having expressed themselves so openly throughout our discussions.

Before beginning the dialog, I wish to say that it is not true, the rumors of certain negotiations with drug traffickers. That is completely untrue and false. The government policy has not changed. It is very clear that drug traffickers must put an end to their illegal activities and submit themselves to the Colombian legal and justice systems. You all know that the Colombian laws will not be negotiated. Thank you very much.

Q. Mr. President, the United States recently halted its plans to deploy naval forces in international waters off Colombia to help trap drug trafficking aircraft. Are you now willing for these operations to resume, and if not, can you tell us why?

President Barco Vargas. The answer is a very clear one. There is territorial maritime area in which—or which belongs to, and cannot be altered by, nor crossed without permission from Colombia. There are other areas which in order to board or to cross a vessel they must request permission from Colombian authority. That permit is authorized. They will grant that permit. But this has certain legal implications which implies that a vessel in these international waters

cannot be attacked.

Q. Sir, my question was U.S. naval forces in international waters off Colombia—are you now willing for those operations to take place?

President Barco Vargas. No, it's not necessary. We don't need them. Colombian territorial waters are being patrolled by us and controlled by us. *Muchas gracias* [Thank you very much].

Q. President Bush, with all this security system that has been established, you showed that there is sort of a lack of trust regarding the Colombian authorities; perhaps you thought that we were not able to preserve your life and the people that came with you. So, now we would like to know: Will we also have lack of trust regarding the cartel of drug users in the United States and people who are being bribed in the United States? Are you willing to fight against those cartels in the United States? It seems that your commitment is not as real as our President's commitment in this struggle against drug traffic.

President Bush. In the first place, I don't think I'd be here if I didn't have any lack of trust in President Barco. I wouldn't be here if I didn't strongly support his efforts to fight drugs. And I wouldn't be here if the best security experts in our country felt that there was undue risk. So, I'm here, and that should answer the first part of your question.

Secondly, fighting any cartel in the United States that has—you want me to start over? Starting from scratch. The question related to my lack of belief in security here. I wouldn't be here if I had any such lack of belief. I am here. I have great respect for what President Barco is doing in the war on drugs. And I hope that my coming here, as with President Garcia and President Paz, demonstrates a solidarity of support for him. And the security arrangements have been very good. And I will say that there's been a lot of speculation about that in our country that's probably compelled you to ask the question.

Secondly, I don't know what cartel you're talking about, but I owe it to the children of America, the United States—and I owe it after this cooperative meeting to these three Presidents—to guarantee them that we will do everything we can to cut out the demand for narcotics in the United States. And that means going after any cartel, any individual, any lawbreaker of any kind who is violating the laws of the United States or, indeed, international law, when it comes to narcotics.

Q. Mr. President Jaime Paz, one of the means of putting an end to the scourge of drug trafficking is through the substitution of coca leaf plantations in a country such as my own. Nonetheless, the coca growers have shown and expressed their concern because of the destiny of trading the products that could substitute the coca leaf plantation and crops. They would like to see a fixed market with fair prices for their new products. Have you reached some type of agreement with the President of the United States of America so that this country will invest in buying the products that will substitute the coca plantations?

President Paz Zamora of Bolivia. Mr. journalist, regarding the point you have just touched, allow me before answering your question in a very specific manner to share with you an impression I had after having finished discussions in the meeting. Regarding the conception of the fight against drug trafficking, in Cartagena, we have begun some type of *perestroika*, even though I wouldn't say that I am acting as Gorbachev here. But we have given way to a great *perestroika* because we have reassessed and readdressed many things at the level of what used to be the idea we had not very long ago regarding how we should confront and broach this problem.

And I feel that all of us have changed. This has been a process that has become a reality here in Cartagena because the Presidents of the countries attending this meeting have begun to understand the true scope of this problem and the way to confront it also. And it is within this context that I would like for you to know—and you will see this in the document that we have signed here in Cartagena—you are going to see that the third part of the document deals with the need to have some type of alternate development vis-a-vis the problems posed by the surplus cultivation of coca leaves.

Therefore, we have expressed a concept that is very clear. It is not a mechanical substitution of a hectare of coca leaf for a hectare of cacao but rather of a concept related to the economy of the coca. But we have to develop a alternate development scheme that will bring about some type of alternate economy. And supposedly, it will be an economy with the ability to insert itself efficiently and in a competitive manner in the international market.

Therefore, questions such as the one you have just addressed will probably be reduced to a couple of—[inaudible]—or three, as can be the case of coffee and sugar at this specific point in time, for they do have fixed quotas in the American market. But the objective, the purpose, is to have an alternate development that will produce in my country an alternate economy, an alternative to the coca economy. But it must be an efficient and competitive economy that must not be subsidized by the international market. That, therefore, means that it must be some type of collaboration, some type of investment, in order to be able to substitute this alternate economy and lead us to have a sound and competitive economy in the international markets. So, it's a different way of approaching the problem in the terms in which we used to do a few months ago.

Q. Mr. President Garcia, your responsibility as President of a large amount of producer of the coca leaf is a total responsibility, vis-a-vis a country that is—[inaudible]—have depended for a long time on this crop. And second, you have a responsibility vis-a-vis the welfare of human beings, because you have said that narco-traffic is a crime against humanity. So, within the context that you yourself find in this summit meeting, are you being loyal to these two—[inaudible]

President Garcia Pérez of Peru. I think that this meeting is of the utmost importance. And using the title of an old friend: We are searching for lost time. And after much time, we are reinserting and reformulating here in a very loyal manner the problem of drug traffic and the illegal production of coca. And I do believe—[*inaudible*]—that we are starting with a new chapter not only in terms of—[*inaudible*]—but also in terms of the relations between the United States of America and Latin America.

With the documents that are signed, there is a whole reformulation and reinterpretation as to how we struggle with the drug traffic, a comprehensive and economic—[*inaudible*]. And for the first time, it has been acknowledged that drug traffic is an economic aspect of our relations and that the struggle against drug traffic implies we compensate the overall disturbances and disorders that this struggle might produce in our economies. It also acknowledges that the substitution of crops has to be supported by a—[*inaudible*]—of countries. [*Inaudible*]—responsibility as producers, we commit ourselves to the struggle both at the productive level and in terms of humanization.

And we hope that where it is most important—[*inaudible*]—is that for the first time we have come together with the President of the United States, and at a multilateral level, to discuss and debate one of the many problems that we are confronting in Latin America and which unite our hemisphere. And just as we are—[*inaudible*]—Bolivia, Colombia, and Peru—[*inaudible*]—in order to deal with a problem that has been considered to be a security problem in the United States, I think that this is the first chapter of a multilateral approach to the problems of Latin America and its relations with the United States. And I do hope, Mr. President, that we will have the occasion to hold multilateral meetings to discuss problems such as foreign debt or in the commercial relations of our countries in the future. I think a new chapter of multilateral relations between Latin America and the United States—and we are overcoming past stages at a bilateral level which have made the solutions—[*inaudible*].

In answering your question, I feel very certain that we are recovering at a time—[*inaudible*]—because we have—[*inaudible*]—participation and because we are as-

suming our responsibilities, and as we discussed this morning, we are assuming a commitment of struggling, despite the fact that we are developing countries. And the United States of America—that its contribution and its aid is not an aid but rather an investment for its future—[*inaudible*]—economic disaster occurring in the United States in view of the problem of drug use and abuse. And I think that in Cartagena every possible step has been taken. [*Inaudible*]—we make slow, gradual—[*inaudible*]—in discussion of this issue, but what is important is that we have taken this to a multilateral level.

Q. Mr. President, in your welcoming remarks this morning, you mentioned that the problem of drugs is a problem of the world community. It mainly affects South and North America and Europe. From diplomatic sources in Europe, I've got the information that in an early stage European countries wanted to take part in this summit but have been blocked away. Why was it not possible that any European country could take part in this summit meeting?

President Barco Vargas. The answer to your question of why the European countries did not participate in this meeting is due, first, to the fact that that opportunity was never raised; and it was not logical for us to meet a series of concerns that are different. Whenever Europe wishes to talk with us, the Latin Americans, it will be indeed a great pleasure for us to agree to a meeting with the Europeans.

Q. President Paz Zamora, in Colombia, there are important leaders who consider that the repression against the drug cartels have failed and who encourage a dialog with drug traffickers. Which is your opinion regarding this position? Would you be willing to attempt a dialog in Bolivia?

President Paz Zamora. As a result of my political vocation and ideology, I personally am willing and happy to have a dialog with everyone. But specifically, in the case we are discussing at this point, undoubtedly, we have come together here to Cartagena on the basis that the four heads of state and four countries agree and accept what is necessary now is to confront drug traffic as a threat against humanity. So, within the context of this meeting, I would say that if you think about, possibly—the dialog is not something that is possible. We have come together in order to coordinate a joint comprehensive effort in order to struggle against drug traffic, which is considered to be a scourge against humanity.

Q. Mr. President Bush, we're seeing all kinds of military and material assistance to South American countries against drug cartels. Would you agree it's a kind of intervention of internal affairs to other countries? Why don't you invite more of these other countries to form any kind of independent, international organization to provide those kinds of assistance, rather than single, direct involvement?

President Bush. No, I don't agree with the gentleman at all. He asked whether I agree or not that this is some intervention in the affairs of these countries. And I think that's absurd on the face of it. And you've heard the welcome given this summit by President Garcia saluting the multilateralism. You heard President Barco call it this morning an unprecedented agreement—no, this is President Paz—an unprecedented agreement achieved in record time. And President Barco—this meeting is the dawn of a new era in the war against drugs.

So, how anybody could suggest it was an intervention in the internal affairs is ridiculous. What we're trying to do is cooperate starting through this multilateral forum, this important summit of four nations. And then, I am pledged to work bilaterally with each of the countries because the problems are different here. But now, in terms of other countries around the world, I hope the United States will always be concerned about the problems of others and try to assist. And we are assisting. But this meeting should not be characterized as some intervention in the affairs of this country when I, along with two other Presidents, accepted the very gracious invitation—I might thank you for the hospitality—from the President of Colombia.

Q. President of Peru, Alan Garcia, our President, has asserted that this is the beginning of a new era; President Paz Zamora, who said that this is sort of a *peres-*troika. You have said that this is a significant event because it is the first multilateral meeting on this level. When you go back to Peru, what will you be telling the people of your country in terms of a practical and real result in terms of the favored solution of their problem? And what could you say to the people of South America—that they will be witnessing this exchange and that it will not be relevant—*[inaudible]*?

President Garcia Pérez. Thank you very much for your question. Personally, I would like to—*[inaudible]*—the problems of—*[inaudible]*—at a multilateral level. And most probably, I and President Bush will continue doing this on topics such as foreign debt and in our—*[inaudible]*—but certainly in responding directly to this.

We are doing a reformulation, a reinterpretation, of the struggle against drug traffic which calls for restriction in supply and demand, and substitution crops, and police control—this is true. But it also predisposes the huge amounts of economic resources as an investment for the future. President Bush—*[inaudible]*—this problem of deciding on alternative crops—how much will it cost now and how will the—*[inaudible]*. As they say in the United States: "Where is the hamburger?" I think that—*[inaudible]*—before it was a military—*[inaudible]*—and where will these resources liberated by disarmaments, where are they going—*[inaudible]*?

And in defense, I have confidence—this is why I'm here. I think that this has been a desired effect in terms of confidence and—this one—in terms of we shall all make in terms of solving problems. And this is what I will be telling my country. We will start by solving the problems when you understand these problems, and the next step is to make investments to allocate resources for these problems. But what is seen here is the concept. Basically, what I started to say earlier, we have new relations between Latin America and the United States, and we hope that's forever.

Note: The joint news conference began at 4:31 p.m. at the Guest House near the Naval Academy in Cartagena.

The President's News Conference Following the Drug Summit in Cartagena, Colombia
February 15, 1990

The President. We depart Cartagena having forged an unprecedented alliance against the drug trade. This afternoon, my colleagues, President Barco [of Colombia] and President Garcia [of Peru], President Paz Zamora [of Bolivia], and I signed the Document of Cartagena which sets forth the principles of this alliance.

In signing the document we've committed ourselves to the first common, comprehensive international drug-control strategy. We, in fact, created the first antidrug cartel. The document, which creates a flexible framework under which the four of us will coordinate our activities, covers the major issues of economic assistance; demand reduction; expanded law enforcement and interdiction activities; the involvement of military resources, where possible, appropriate; and the control of precursor chemicals, automatic weapons, and other key components of the narcotics trade; the pursuit of profits and sharing of seized assets; and a commitment on the part of all of us to continue together regularly to coordinate our activities.

In addition to signing this Document of Cartagena, we begin the process of executing bilateral agreements in support of the document today. Secretary of State Baker executed the agreements with Peru on tax information exchange, public awareness, and extradition, and with Bolivia on public awareness and the export of defense articles. Director [of National Drug Control Policy] Bennett executed a bilateral agreement with Bolivia on the control of precursor chemicals. Equally important, the four of us today had an opportunity to discuss in total candor the problem that illegal drug trafficking and use presents to each of our societies.

I also had the opportunity to review with my colleagues the greatly expanded counternarcotics activities of the U.S. Government. The $2.2 billion, 5-year program to which the United States is committed to support our partners in this struggle was discussed in some detail. In addition, I had the opportunity to explain our plans to expand to $7.5 billion inside the United States on treatment, prevention, and criminal justice support.

I believe they were impressed with the major increase in resources, which we've committed to reducing demand in our country. I must say, I also listened very carefully to the challenges that each of the three countries face, and have come away with the new ideas worthy of consideration with a better personal understanding and appreciation of the problems that my allies face in this struggle.

And I cannot leave this beautiful country, Colombia, without once again emphasizing that President Barco and all of his citizens who joined him in this brave fight against drug trafficking are an inspiration to me and an inspiration to the American people. I came here today to make the point as clear as I could that they do not and will not stand alone; they will have the steady and sustained support of the United States. We want to try to help them in the multilateral institutions, help President Barco in asset sharing and opening up markets as best we can. I want to thank him and his many colleagues for the most hospitable arrangements that we encountered here in Barranquilla and over in Cartagena. It was a great pleasure to be here—albeit, very, very briefly.

So, thank you, again, President Barco. And I offer you my profound appreciation for your steadfast efforts in the fight against narcotics. I'll take just a few questions because we're scooting on.

Q. Mr. President, how long do you think it will take to replace the coca plant? And how much will it cost?

The President. Well, I know we did not go into the replacement costs. And I expect any program that tries to shake their economy, to move it out of planting, which is very difficult for those governments to control, is going to take some time. And I can't give you a time estimate on that.

Q. Mr. President, are you surprised that the narco-terrorists didn't strike today, that there was no attack on you or any bombing in this country just to register displeasure with your visit?

The President. Well, you know, I got a question at the press conference over there on security; and I want to thank not only the security people here but our own security people, Secret Service and others, who are concerned with the security of the President. And I am not surprised.

Q. Mr. President, I gather you chose not to raise today that rather ticklish question of a U.S. Navy radar net somewhere off the coast here. Why not, sir?

The President. Well, there was no discussion of a radar net. There is so much misunderstanding over what was intended in the first place that it's not timely to do that. However, there was discussion of interdiction and my reasserting to those countries, all three of them, my intention to interdict narcotics coming into this country [United States]. But the stories on the U.S. task force were so distorted that I felt it was better to keep talking in general terms about our military interdiction efforts rather than asking for support from any one of the three countries.

Q. Sir, do you feel that now, after this meeting, that your understanding with these leaders may have been enhanced to the point where you might soon be able to raise that topic again?

The President. Well, it depends in what way, yes, in the first place, I'd feel the understanding is enhanced. And it was a frank meeting—I mean, very frank with us on things that maybe they wanted me to do more of, or disagreed with. But I think that the idea of working cooperatively for interdiction is very important. You heard President Barco's answer there at Cartagena on that question. So, we're not going to push. We're not going to do something of that nature without a cooperative effort. But there are efforts in terms of interdiction on the high seas that the United States will continue to do.

Q. Mr. President, you acknowledged in the document today that the U.S. has a responsibility to help these economies wean themselves from the drug trade. Do you see that responsibility as job for job and dollar for dollar?

The President. No. But I see us making every effort we can to help them because they do have some severe problems. And I mention now trying to help Colombia, for example, in the multilateral agencies, for example. There's a lot of ways to try to help, but I don't think it is a job-for-job kind of approach. I don't think we can do that. I don't think there's a way the United States can do it or that any of the individual leaders can do it. We had a long discussion about the supply and demand of cocaine, how market prices affect what the farmers do in Peru or Bolivia. So, it isn't a job-for-job question.

Q. Mr. President, any successful interdiction strategy would require increased military-to-military cooperation. Is the U.S. already installing a ground radar system in Peru—I mean, in Bolivia or Colombia—I'm sorry—or in any way helping the Colombians now to install a ground radar system?

The President. No, but I'd have to defer that question to somebody here. I know nothing of it. But I know there was a report that was written up that proved to be totally inaccurate, because I was just told there was a report saying there was some 200 people building a ground radar station. But I simply don't know of it. If there is, I'd be surprised, frankly.

Q. Do you know to what extent the U.S. and Colombia are, in fact, cooperating militarily now, in terms of interdiction efforts?

The President. Yes, I know that.

Q. Can you share that with us?

The President. No.

Q. Why not, sir?

The President. Because I don't feel like it, and because some of the things we do with Colombia—if I shared it with you, maybe the drug narco-traffickers would find out about it, and I don't want to do that.

Q. Mr. President, the declaration calls for you to go to Congress for more money over the next several years. Does that go beyond the $2.2 billion, and if so, how much?

The President. Well, we're going to stay with this figure right now, but I expect the effort will continue to grow.

Q. Mr. President, perhaps—for the sake of our children—perhaps the United States wait too long to take this stand on the drug summit. And what is the timetable from now on?

The President. Well, you raised a very good point. And I think it has been too long before countries get together and try to work on this problem. But we're remedying that. The good news is—and I shared a dramatic graph with the Presidents—that we are making progress at home. One of the things that President Barco impressed on me some time ago was the need to do something about demand, and I believe we're making headway. I'm not happy with it, but we're making headway in the United States on that question.

Q. Mr. President, in addition to the good will, to paraphrase President Garcia, "Where's the beef?" What are these Presidents taking home to their own countries about the war on drugs?

The President. Read the communique, and I think you'll see.

Last one.

Q. Mr. President, how can we expect the Bolivians and Peruvians not to grow coca if we block their exports of flowers, citrus, sugar?

The President. I don't know if you heard the question. The question is: How can we expect them not to grow coca if we have other trade problems? And you mentioned sugar and flowers. I think the leaders here recognize that growing coca for the international drug market is immoral and wrong. And I think they believe that, and so they need assistance. If we have a flower problem, and we do—I think we take 80 percent to 90 percent of the cut flowers from Colombia—we've got to try to help on it. I don't know that we can solve it.

Coffee is a major problem for Brazil and the other countries—I mean, for Colombia and also Brazil and the other countries with whom met—please, just 1 minute; I'm not going to get to you, I don't think, because this may be the last one. And so, we have to work with them very cooperatively in trying to get a coffee agreement. But what I did get from these people—and I think I knew it ahead of time, but had it reinforced—was that these economies are hurting because of the kinds of export problems they are encountering. I have a problem and tried to explain it to them—that consumers in the United States, the largest market for coffee, don't necessarily want to pay higher prices for it. And the same for flowers.

So, what we did on the flowers is explain the procedures that the Commerce Department—and say that we would try to help in negotiating that. But the point is: It shouldn't be linked to whether people condone the growing of a crop that is illegal and that they're trying to stop, as a matter of fact.

Q. What about sugar, Mr. President? Will you address that?

Q. Europe and Japan in future negotiations.

The President. You're the guy. Yes. We're going to talk about that at the G–7 [economic summit] in Houston, just as we did in Paris last year. It's a very important agenda item for the G–7. And the more they get involved—because they're user countries—the better it'll be. So, I'll give a full report to the G–7 and other European countries on this ice-breaking meeting here. And you can be sure it'll be on the agenda at the G–7 summit in Houston.

Listen, thank you all very much. It's been a long day.

Note: The President's 37th news conference began at 6:10 p.m. at Ernesto Cortissoz Airport in Barranquilla, Colombia.

Letter to Congressional Leaders Transmitting a Report on the General Agreement on Tariffs and Trade Negotiations on Agricultural Trade
February 15, 1990

Dear Mr. Chairman:

As required under section 4301 of the Omnibus Trade and Competitiveness Act of 1988, I am enclosing a report on the status of the General Agreement on Tariffs and Trade (GATT) negotiations concerning agricultural trade. The report contains information on the progress that has been made to date in the negotiations, the general areas of disagreement, the anticipated date of completion of the negotiations, and the changes in domestic farm programs that are likely to be necessary on conclusion of the negotiations.

I certify that significant progress has been made in the negotiations, and that implementation of the marketing loan program described in subsection (b)(1) would harm further negotiations, and that implementation of the export enhancement program provided for in subsection (c)(1) would be a substantial impediment to achieving a successful agreement under the GATT.

I understand that Ambassador Hills (the Office of the U.S. Trade Representative) has consulted with your committee about this certification.

Sincerely,

GEORGE BUSH

Note: Identical letters were sent to Senators Lloyd Bentsen, chairman of the Committee on Finance, and Patrick J. Leahy, chairman of the Committee on Agriculture, Nutrition, and Forestry; and Representatives Dan Rostenkowski, chairman of the Committee on Ways and Means; Dante B. Fascell, chairman of the Committee on Foreign Affairs; and E de la Garza, chairman of the Committee on Agriculture.

Memorandum on Federalism
February 16, 1990

Memorandum for the Heads of Executive Departments and Agencies

Subject: Federalism Executive Order

I wish to take this opportunity to reaffirm an important Executive order, issued when I served as Vice President, and call for your personal commitment in ensuring your department's or agency's compliance with its provisions. This order, which is entitled "Federalism" (No. 12612, October 26, 1987), establishes fundamental principles and criteria to guide you in developing and implementing policies that have substantial direct effects on States and local governments. Let me note a few of the order's more important provisions:

• In most areas of governmental concern, the States uniquely possess the constitutional authority, the resources, and the competence to discern the sentiments of the people and to govern accordingly.

• The nature of our constitutional system encourages a healthy diversity in the public policies adopted by the people of the several States according to their own conditions, needs, and desires. In the search for enlightened public policy, individual States and communities are free to experiment with a variety of approaches to public issues.

• Federal action limiting the policymaking discretion of the States should be taken only where constitutional authority is clear and certain and the national activity is necessitated by a problem of national scope.

- With respect to national policies administered by the States, the national Government should grant the States the maximum administrative discretion possible.
- When undertaking to formulate and implement policies that have Federalism implications, Federal executive departments and agencies should (1) encourage States to develop their own policies to achieve program objectives and to work with appropriate officials in other States; (2) refrain, to the maximum extent possible, from establishing uniform national standards for programs and, when possible, defer to the States to establish standards; and (3) when national standards are required, consult with appropriate officials and organizations representing the States in developing those standards.

The Executive order has special requirements dealing with preemption and with legislative proposals. It also requires that, when a proposed policy has sufficient Federalism implications, the agency must prepare a Federalism Assessment. This assessment is intended to provide the agency and the Administration with an evaluation of the extent to which the policy imposes additional costs or burdens on States and local governments. You are to consider the Federalism Assessment before adopting and implementing the policy.

The order also requires that you designate an official to be responsible for ensuring your agency's implementation of the order. Please ensure that your agency has provided the name of the designated official to the Director of the Office of Management and Budget.

I want to stress that the principles of this order are central to my Administration. I ask that each of you personally review the provisions of Executive Order No. 12612 and assure that the mechanisms necessary to ensure their implementation are in place.

GEORGE BUSH

Statement on Signing the Foreign Relations Authorization Act, Fiscal Years 1990 and 1991
February 16, 1990

I have signed today H.R. 3792, the "Foreign Relations Authorization Act, Fiscal Years 1990 and 1991." This Act authorizes funding for the Department of State at a level sufficient to cover appropriations for this fiscal year. The levels authorized for Contributions to International Organizations and Contributions for International Peacekeeping Activities are those requested by the Administration. These authorizations provide for full funding of our assessed obligations in the international area.

This Act, which provides the Department's basic operational authorities, includes welcome new authorities for the Department, many of them included at the Administration's request. I am pleased that this Act does not contain a provision that compelled me to veto an earlier version of this legislation (Section 109 of H.R. 1487).

Additionally, H.R. 3792 also waives a number of restrictive earmarks that would otherwise apply. I regret, however, that the Congress has included several provisions in the Act that raise constitutional difficulties.

The Constitution vests in the President the executive power of the United States. The executive power includes, among other things, the authority to receive and appoint ambassadors and to conduct negotiations on behalf of the United States with foreign governments. Thus, pursuant to the Constitution, the President is entrusted with control over the conduct of diplomacy. The content, timing, and duration of negotiations with foreign governments are also within the President's control. Unfortunately, many provisions of this Act could be read to violate these fundamental constitutional principles by using legislation to direct, in various ways, the conduct of negotiations with foreign nations.

Section 102 of the Act would prohibit the use of certain appropriated funds for any U.S. delegation to any meeting within the framework of the Conference on Security and Cooperation in Europe unless individuals representing the Commission on Security and Cooperation in Europe, a body controlled by the legislative branch, are included in the U.S. delegation. By purporting to deny certain funds for the negotiation of certain arms control agreements unless representatives of the Commission are included in the U.S. delegation to such negotiations, this section impermissibly intrudes upon my constitutional authority to conduct our foreign relations and to appoint our Nation's envoys. I therefore shall construe it to express the sense of the Congress but not to impose any binding legal obligation, and as severable from the ability to continue the critically important negotiations at issue.

Section 108 would restrict the expenditure of appropriated funds for carrying on "the current dialogue on the Middle East peace process with any representative of the Palestine Liberation Organization if the President knows and advises the Congress that that representative directly participated in the planning or execution of a particular terrorist activity which resulted in the death or kidnapping of a United States citizen." I have frequently emphasized my determination to work to eliminate the scourge of terrorism, and I have no intention of negotiating with terrorists. This provision demonstrates that the Congress shares my concern. However, if this section were interpreted to prohibit negotiations with particular individuals under certain circumstances, it would impermissibly limit my constitutional authority to negotiate with foreign organizations. Accordingly, I shall construe this section to preserve my constitutional discretion for the conduct of foreign negotiations.

Section 407 of the Act is similarly subject to inappropriate interpretation. This section purports to require that no individual may be admitted to the United States as a representative to the United Nations if the individual "has been found to have been engaged in espionage activities directed against the United States or its allies and may pose a threat to United States national security interests." In effect, this provision could constrain the exercise of my exclusive constitutional authority to receive within the United States certain foreign ambassadors to the United Nations. While espionage directed against the United States and its allies is a problem of the utmost gravity, curtailing by statute my constitutional discretion to receive or reject ambassadors is neither a permissible nor a practical solution. I therefore shall construe section 407 to be advisory.

Section 134 is consistent with the Administration's planned course of action and improves on prior law. Nevertheless, it infringes upon my constitutional authority to conduct foreign relations and receive representatives of foreign governments by purporting to permit the Soviet Union to occupy a consulate facility in the United States only upon certification that the U.S. mission in Kiev is able to occupy an interim facility. I also shall treat this section as advisory.

A number of other provisions might be construed to require the executive branch to contact foreign governments and espouse certain substantive positions regarding specific issues. *See e.g.,* Sections 115, 210, 902(a)(7). My constitutional authority over foreign affairs necessarily entails discretion over the timing and subject matter of such contacts. Accordingly, I shall construe all these provisions to be merely precatory as well.

Similarly, several sections, in particular section 804, impose significant reporting requirements on the Secretary of State to inform the Congress of specified diplomatic contacts. Such blanket reporting requirements could be read to compel the disclosure of the contents of sensitive ongoing negotiations and may, therefore, compromise my constitutional authority over such negotiations. I am also concerned that such provisions tend to undermine the spirit of cooperation and trust between the executive and legislative branches that I have been laboring to foster. In reporting to the Congress, therefore, I shall construe these provisions in light of my constitutional duties.

Section 206 of the Act would establish a United States Advisory Commission on Public Diplomacy. Several of its provisions would impermissibly interfere with the President's control over the deliberative processes of the executive branch. Section 206 clearly contemplates that the Commission shall report to the Congress about deliberations within the executive branch and, indeed, shall monitor the executive branch in its execution of the laws. I shall interpret these provisions consistent with my authority as head of the unitary executive branch to "take care that the Laws be faithfully executed," U.S. Constitution, Article II, Section 3, to coordinate and supervise my subordinates, and to have the executive branch speak with one voice to the Congress.

Certain provisions of the Act could be construed to require impermissible racial preferences. In order to avoid legal challenge, these provisions will also be construed in accordance with the Constitution.

On a different matter, it is my understanding that section 128, removing the sunset provision on section 901 of the 1988-89 Authorization Act, which prohibits the exclusion of aliens on certain grounds, has no effect on the substance of section 901 or on the way the executive branch has applied it since its enactment.

Finally, with regard to Title IX, I want to reiterate that legislatively mandated sanctions represent an unwise constraint upon the President's ability to conduct foreign policy. I note, however, that the section provides flexibility, by permitting a Presidential waiver to lift suspensions, in whole or in part, when it is in the national interest of the United States.

GEORGE BUSH

The White House,
February 16, 1990.

Note: H.R. 3792, approved February 16, was assigned Public Law No. 101–246.

Remarks Following Discussions With President Václav Havel of Czechoslovakia
February 20, 1990

President Bush. Well, welcome to everybody. And it's been my great pleasure to welcome to the White House a man of tremendous moral courage, one of the heroes of the Revolution of '89, the President of Czechoslovakia, Václav Havel.

Mr. President, your life has been one of miraculous transformations from the world of drama to the world of dissent, from the life of the artist to the life of the activist, and of course in the space of just 1 short year, the most miraculous journey of all, from prison to the Presidency. And of course it's possible to measure profound change in more personal terms. For years, as a dissident subject to arrest and imprisonment at any time, you could never go out without your toothbrush in your pocket. But now, as President, you can never go out without one of these neckties. [*Laughter*]

And many years ago you made a choice. You chose to live your life in keeping with your conscience not for others but for yourself. But others drew strength from the life you led, and your life was a tribute to the difference one man can make, powerful proof of the democratic idea. On the one side stood the state with its prisons and secret police; and on the other, Vaclav Havel, one man alone but with the strength of his convictions, always free with the freedom that comes from living in truth. First one man, and now millions.

President Havel never stopped believing in what he called this unbelievable thought: that any one of us can shake the Earth. Shake the Earth, Mr. President, and part the Iron Curtain. Shake the Earth and knock down the Berlin Wall. Shake the Earth and set in motion a process of change

241

from Budapest to Bucharest, from Warsaw to Wenceslas Square.

And that was the Revolution of '89, and our task now in the 1990's is to move forward from revolution to renaissance, towards a new Europe in which each nation and every culture can flourish and breathe free—a Europe whole and free.

President Havel, Czechoslovakia has turned to you to lead the way, and is it not fitting for a nation that each day writes a new page in its history to have elected a playwright as its President?

And I am pleased that we've had this opportunity to meet, to speak together about the changes that are taking place from Prague to Moscow, and about Czechoslovakia's place in the heartland of the new Europe now emerging. We know there is no room for illusions. Difficult work lies ahead. The damage of four decades of fear and repression cannot be repaired in a day. But we know something more: We know that the people of Czechoslovakia have waited long enough, and they know it's time to move forward to freedom.

Czechoslovakia and Europe are at the threshold of a new era. And I know I can speak for all Western leaders when I say that the Atlantic alliance will continue to play a vital role in assuring stability and security in Europe at this great and historic moment. And America will continue to play its part, including a strong military presence for our security and for Europe's.

Mr. President, you've not asked for American economic aid, and you made it clear that democratic Czechoslovakia wants the opportunity to do business on an equal footing. And in that regard, I am pleased to announce that I signed today letters notifying our Congress that I am waiving the Jackson-Vanik amendment for Czechoslovakia. Today our trade representatives began negotiating a trade agreement. Pending passage by your Parliament of new liberal emigration legislation, these measures will permit us to extend the most-favored-nation status to Czechoslovakia without the requirement of an annual waiver, granting your country the most liberal access to the American market possible under United States law.

Mr. President, you've also explained the enormous tasks that you face in rebuilding a democracy on the ruins of the one-party state that you inherited. And you've identified several areas where help is needed, and we are ready to respond. Let me just mention two specifics. First, in response to your request, I am asking Peace Corps Director Paul Coverdell to take the initial steps to bring the Peace Corps to Czechoslovakia by this fall. And second, I am delighted that we will soon reopen our consulate in Bratislava, as well as new cultural centers there and in Prague.

Mr. President, I assure you the United States will be part of your nation's democratic rebirth. Everything I've seen this past year tells me that Czechoslovakia can meet the challenges ahead. And as you've said in your first address as President on New Year's Day, so many times we've heard politics defined as the art of the possible; and this year has taught us something new, something more: It taught us, as you put it, that politics can be the art of the impossible.

Mr. President, before you leave us today, I would like to present you with a lithograph of your illustrious predecessor, Czechoslovakia's first President and author of your nation's Declaration of Independence, Thomas Masaryk. This portrait was done in Prague Castle and kept by President Masaryk until his death, when he gave it to his successor at Charles University's department of philosophy, President Jan Kozak.

In 1939, at the time of the Nazi invasion, Professor Kozak had 2 hours to pack his belongings and to flee Czechoslovakia. Among the items he took with him, this portrait of his friend. Professor Kozak settled in Ohio at Oberlin College, and so did this portrait until today. And now, with freedom returning to Czechoslovakia, so, too, should this portrait of President Masaryk, Czechoslovakia's first President and champion of freedom.

Once again, Mr. President, it has been my privilege to welcome you to Washington and to the White House. And God bless you, and may God bless the people of Czechoslovakia. We are pleased to have you here.

President Havel. Mr. President, I am very moved by your speech. I thank you very much for this drawing. I promise you it will be very soon back in our castle.

We had with Mr. Bush very important negotiations. We had very warm, very open, very friendly discussions. I am very glad that I had the opportunity to be here to explain what happened in Czechoslovakia, to explain our viewpoint, our policy. And thank you very much that we could be here. Thank you for the invitation. And of course I invite you to us in Prague, in Czechoslovakia. And you will see this nice drawing in my office on Prague Castle.

President Bush. Thank you, sir. Godspeed.

Note: President Bush spoke at 1:35 p.m. at the South Portico of the White House. Prior to their remarks, the two Presidents met privately in the Oval Office and with U.S. and Czechoslovak officials in the Cabinet Room, and then attended a luncheon in the Old Family Dining Room.

Presidential Determination No. 90–10—Memorandum on Trade With Czechoslovakia
February 20, 1990

Memorandum for the Secretary of State

Subject: Determination under Section 402(c)(2)(A) of the Trade Act of 1974—Czechoslovakia

Pursuant to section 402(c)(2)(A) of the Trade Act of 1974 (the "Act") (19 U.S.C. 2432(c)(2)(A)) I determine that a waiver of the application of subsections (a) and (b) of section 402 of the Act with respect to Czechoslovakia will substantially promote the objectives of section 402.

You are authorized and directed to publish this determination in the *Federal Register.*

GEORGE BUSH

Message to the Congress on Trade With Czechoslovakia
February 20, 1990

To the Congress of the United States:

Pursuant to subsection 402(c)(2) of the Trade Act of 1974 (the Act) (19 U.S.C. 2432(c)(2)), I have determined that a waiver of the application of subsections (a) and (b) of Section 402 with respect to Czechoslovakia will substantially promote the objectives of section 402. A copy of that determination is enclosed. I have also received the assurances with respect to the emigration practices of Czechoslovakia required by section 402(c)(2)(B) of the Act.

Pursuant to section 402(c)(2), I shall issue an Executive Order waiving the application of subsections (a) and (b) of section 402 of the Act with respect to Czechoslovakia.

GEORGE BUSH

The White House,
February 20, 1990.

Note: The Executive order is listed in Appendix E at the end of this volume.

Letter to Congressional Leaders Transmitting a Report on the Canada-United States Free-Trade Agreement
February 20, 1990

Dear Mr. Chairman:

Pursuant to section 103 of the United States-Canada Free-Trade Agreement Implementation Act of 1988 (Public Law 100–499), I am pleased to submit the attached report and related documents pertaining to a proposed action to accelerate elimination of duties on designated products under the United States-Canada Free-Trade Agreement.

Sincerely,

GEORGE BUSH

Note: Identical letters were sent to Lloyd Bentsen, chairman of the Senate Finance Committee, and Dan Rostenkowski, chairman of the House Ways and Means Committee.

Nomination of E.U. Curtis Bohlen To Be an Assistant Secretary of State
February 20, 1990

The President today announced his intention to nominate E.U. Curtis Bohlen to be Assistant Secretary of State for Oceans and International Environmental and Scientific Affairs. He would succeed Frederick M. Bernthal.

Since 1981 Mr. Bohlen has served as senior vice president of World Wildlife Fund in Washington, DC. He served as a consultant to World Wildlife Fund and vice president of Eastern Environmental Controls, Inc., in Chestertown, MD, 1979–1981, and as a consultant on the Committee on Merchant Marine and Fisheries at the House of Representatives in Washington, DC, 1977–1978. In addition, he served in several positions at the Department of the Interior from 1969 to 1977 in Washington, DC, including Assistant to Secretary Cecil D. Andrus, Chairman of the Alaska Planning Group, Acting Assistant Secretary for Fish and Wildlife and Parks, Deputy Assistant Secretary for Fish and Wildlife and Parks, Assistant to Secretary Rogers C.B. Morton, Assistant to Secretary Walter J. Hickel, and Assistant to Under Secretary Russell E. Train. From 1955 to 1969, Mr. Bohlen served in several positions at the Department of State in Washington, DC, including political analyst for east African affairs; second secretary and political officer for the U.S. Embassy in Cairo, Egypt; desk officer for Afghanistan affairs; and economic officer at the U.S. Embassy in Kabul, Afghanistan.

Mr. Bohlen graduated from Harvard University (B.A., 1951). He was born September 29, 1927, in Boston, MA. Mr. Bohlen served in the U.S. Army, 1952–1954. He is married, has three children, and resides in Washington, DC.

Remarks at the Presentation Ceremony for the Charles Stark Draper Prize for Engineering
February 20, 1990

Thank you all. Thank you, Jack. I got worried there when Jack was saying, "When we want somebody that is well known to present the prize." I was thinking, Barbara's not here. [*Laughter*] But, Jack, thank you for those very kind remarks.

To our honorees, Kilby and Noyce; and to Ambassador Dubinin, our Soviet Ambassador here, who's doing such a good job for his country; and Dr. White; Dr. Charyk; and my old friend Dr. Seamans; also another old friend, Steve Bechtel; Mr. Morrow; and the Under Secretary, Ivan Selin; and Don Atwood here from the Defense Department; and members and guests of the National Academy of Engineering:

I'm reminded of the famous story of the guy that called the insurance company after it closed one evening. A voice answered, and he said: "Sir, I'd like to talk to you about converting my 20-pay-life into the cash value immediately. And further, I've heard more about your key man insurance that insures the very key people, and we'd like a little more information on that. And lastly, we have this family—I have six kids, and we want a family health plan." The voice on the other end said, "Look," he said, "I'm the janitor around here just cleaning up, and after I said hello, that's all I know at all about insurance."

I feel the same way about engineering here tonight—[*laughter*]—surrounded by all this brainpower. It's overwhelming. But I am pleased to be here. I deem it a very great pleasure to help honor and celebrate National Engineers Week. And of course it is an honor to salute the first two recipients of this, engineering's highest international award, the Charles Stark Draper Prize.

Let me begin with a story that will show you my understanding of engineering, that I see it. It concerns three men that were scheduled to be executed on the same day of the French Revolution. One was a lawyer, another a politician, the third an engineer. First, came the lawyer. He put his head in the guillotine, and the blade went two-thirds of the way down the track and then stopped. The man was set free. Next, the politician. When the guillotine stopped short of his head, he, too, was spared. Finally, came the third man, the engineer, and he focused on the matter at hand. "I think that guillotine has a problem," he told the executioner. "But don't worry; I think I have the solution." [*Laughter*]

I say that with respect. [*Laughter*] But as you see, engineers just can't help themselves. Whatever the cost—[*laughter*]—they keep aiming for perfection. And they've helped make our century a time of extraordinary exploration, opening doors into an age where mankind not only moved into the future but reinvented it.

Tonight we honor Jack Kilby and Bob Noyce and their landmark work—the microchip, an invention which has already taken its place among the greatest of all time. Not to date myself, but when I was growing up, PacMan was a hiker, not a video game. The microchip came along and changed all of that and helped America change the world.

Think, for example, of a computer the size of a room shrunk down to the size that fits on your lap—the microchip made all that possible—or a calculator slashed from the size of a refrigerator to the size of a wristwatch. Think, finally, of our planet, and how the microchip has stirred the new breeze of democracy.

Maybe it's a good day to salute that because today the President of Czechoslovakia, Vaclav Havel, came over to the Oval Office and then was our guest at the White House for lunch. And what a stirring moment—I'll just divert for one second—I took him up to the Lincoln Bedroom, which is not normally the thing when you have these official visits. But I wanted him to see the room in which Abraham Lincoln had signed the Emancipation Proclamation. And I think I detected tears in his eyes, this playwright who not so many months ago was in jail and here he is the President of a fine, new, burgeoning democratic country. It was a very moving experience.

As I talked with him, I thought of how images of the past year have linked the peoples of Prague and Warsaw and Budapest and Berlin, images of bravery and defiance, of humanity's quest for freedom. And it was the microchip which carried them from one nation to another, becoming an instrument of liberty, the symbol in this information age. Integrated circuits have enabled us to do the unimaginable. Now it is unimaginable to believe we could ever live without them.

Already, the microchip has helped America not to deindustrialize but reindustrialize. To paraphrase Churchill, never has something so small done so much for so many. Yet remember, too, that if we are to lead the world, we must provide that world with further breakthroughs; for engineering is always a beginning, never a consummation.

I know that the National Academy of Engineering shares this belief. So, it has studied how America's engineering talent enhances our competitiveness and is exploring new ways to protect the globe from environmental abuse. You realize that truly informed decisions on issues like climate change require us to better integrate science, technology, and engineering into the policy equation. Our administration agrees and, so, supports research and development in all areas of science, technology, and engineering. We've asked for a record-high $71 billion for R&D in our budget for fiscal 1991. And to short-circuit the prediction that America will run short of engineers, we've introduced a National Science Scholars Initiative to give kids a new incentive to excel in science, math, and engineering. And I have announced an ambitious goal, one of our national goals reached after great consultation with the Governors, but a goal that we can achieve: that U.S. students will be number one by the year 2000.

You can tell—I hope you can tell from looking around—that I have great respect for people who have an understanding of science. Jim Watkins is a member of our Cabinet, Secretary of Energy. I'm pleased to see Dr. Bromley here and Secretary Rice and of course my own Chief of Staff, John Sununu, such a man—engineer. Yet, ultimately, I am convinced—not that we duck our responsibility in the Federal Government—but ultimately, I am convinced that it is the private sector that not only has shaped American opportunity but will continue to bring opportunity to the new millennium.

Look at—Jack, I don't want to embarrass you—but look at GE, spending $1.2 million a year on minority science scholarships, and a $20 million commitment to involve more inner-city kids in engineering, or Mobil, launching grant programs to help students enhance America's technological ability. I know that I'm going to, just through omission, risk embarrassing others because so many in this room are responsible for programs of this nature.

These efforts, both private and public, will sustain the computer revolution, for they rely on the qualities of American drive and determination, qualities that will contribute, as your Academy says, "to the advancement of engineering and the well-being of all humanity" and that are central to the man for whom this evening's prize is named.

Charles Draper was, first, an idealist pushing back the boundaries of mankind's technological future, and yet at the same time a practical man. I'm reminded of a writer who was asked what he would take if his home were on fire and he could remove only one thing. "I would take the fire," he replied. [*Laughter*] Dr. Draper knew that Yankee ingenuity revolves around what works.

Finally, he was indomitable, a fighter who looked to himself for inspiration. Albert Einstein once spoke of this genius of engineering, which explains in turn the greatness of Dr. Draper. He said: "Only men who are free create the inventions and intellectual works which make life worthwhile." Working in freedom, Charles Draper well used that freedom: used it to create and to inspire, to make history move his way.

This evening, we honor two men who themselves have made history and made each American proud. So, let me now present to Jack Kilby and Bob Noyce engineering's highest award, the Charles Stark Draper Prize, and say thank them, thanks to both of you, for your inspirational leadership.

Thank you all, and God bless the United States of America. Thank you very much.

Note: The President spoke at 8:50 p.m. in the ballroom at the Department of State. In his remarks, he referred to Jack Welch, Jr., chairman of the National Academy of Engineering; Jack Kilby, a consultant; Robert Noyce, president and chief operating officer of Sematech; Robert M. White, president of the National Academy of Engineering;

Joseph V. Charyk, chairman of the Charles Stark Draper Laboratory, Inc.; Robert C. Seamans, Jr., chairman of the Charles Stark Draper Prize Committee; Stephen D. Bechtel, Jr., chairman of the Bechtel Group, Inc.; Richard M. Morrow, chairman and chief operating officer of Amoco Oil Corp.; Under Secretary of State for Management Ivan Selin; Deputy Secretary of Defense Donald J. Atwood; D. Allan Bromley, Science Advisor to the President and Director of the Office of Science and Technology Policy; and Secretary of the Air Force Donald B. Rice.

Statement by Press Secretary Fitzwater on President Bush's Meeting With President Václav Havel of Czechoslovakia
February 21, 1990

The President and President Vaclav Havel of Czechoslovakia met for approximately 45 minutes today in the Oval Office. This was a continuation of their discussions yesterday. They talked at some length about the future of Europe and agreed to stay in close touch at this time of rapid change. Both expressed their support for

President Gorbachev's reforms and his encouragement of peaceful change in Eastern Europe, and both agreed that the presence of American troops is a factor for stability and security in Europe. Although it was anticipated that economic issues would be discussed, most of the conversation focused on political and East-West issues.

Nomination of Nelson C. Ledsky for the Rank of Ambassador While Serving as Special Cyprus Coordinator
February 21, 1990

The President today announced his intention to nominate Nelson C. Ledsky, of Maryland, a career member of the Senior Foreign Service, Class of Minister-Counselor, for the rank of Ambassador during his tenure of service as Special Cyprus Coordinator.

Since 1989 Mr. Ledsky has served as Special Cyprus Coordinator at the Department of State. He served as Deputy Senior Director and then Senior Director for the National Security Council, 1987–1989. In addition, he served in various capacities at the Department of State, including Deputy Direc-

tor of the Policy Planning Staff, 1985–1987; U.S. Minister in Berlin, Germany, 1981–1985; Director of the State Department's Olympic Boycott Office, 1980–1981; Deputy Assistant Secretary of Congressional Relations, 1978–1980; Director of the Office of Southern Europe, 1976–1978; Deputy Director of the Office of Southern Europe, 1974–1976; Deputy Director of the Office of Central Europe, 1972–1974; Berlin desk officer, 1970–1972; senior watch officer, 1969–1970; second secretary at the U.S. Embassy in Bonn, 1964–1969; consul at the U.S. consulate in Enugu, Nigeria, 1962–

1964; African language training program, 1961–1962; vice consul at the U.S. consulate in Georgetown, Guyana, 1957–1961; and an analyst at the Bureau of Intelligence and Research, 1957–1959.

Mr. Ledsky graduated from Western Reserve University (B.A., 1951) and Columbia University (M.A., 1953). He was born September 30, 1929, in Cleveland, OH. Mr. Ledsky is married, has three children, and resides in Bethesda, MD.

Nomination of LeGree Sylvia Daniels To Be a Member of the Board of Governors of the United States Postal Service
February 21, 1990

The President today announced his intention to nominate LeGree Sylvia Daniels to be a Governor of the United States Postal Service for the term expiring December 8, 1998. She would succeed John Lathrop Ryan.

Since 1987 Mrs. Daniels has served as Assistant Secretary for Civil Rights at the Department of Education in Washington, DC. Prior to this, she served as a staff assistant to former Senate minority leader Hugh Scott; chairman of the Pennsylvania State Tax Equalization Board; commissioner of the Pennsylvania Bureau of Elections; and deputy secretary of the Commonwealth of Pennsylvania.

Mrs. Daniels attended Temple University and Central Pennsylvania Business School. She was born February 29, 1920, in Denmark, SC. Mrs. Daniels is married, has three children, and resides in Harrisburg, PA.

Remarks and a Question-and-Answer Session at the Annual Dinner of the Business Council
February 21, 1990

The President. What I want to do is just make a few remarks, and then respond to a few questions, and then get out of here so you all can eat. But first I want to salute the former Chief Justice—I still refer to him as Chief—Warren Burger, and the members of my Cabinet that are here—many of you met them—other top officials in the White House scattered through the audience here. All, I might add, doing a first-class job.

I want to pay my respects to the Speaker, who is here tonight, Tom Foley, an outstanding, decent human being. I don't know where he is, but I don't want to overdo it because tomorrow I've got to fight with him on one or two things, but he's here somewhere. And to the other Members of Congress—the House—I saw John Dingell, I saw my old friend Chairman Don Riegle here. I know I'm going to miss, so I better stop right here, but I'm delighted that the Members of the Congress are here.

I also know how I got into this line of work, and when I look around this room— and I seldom speak for Barbara, but I will this time—we are very, very grateful for the terrific support that I had from so many in this room that have given me this opportunity, now going into the second year being President of the United States. And I will never forget how the political process works, and I will never get over being grateful to many of you friends of long standing.

We're living, as Roger [Roger B. Smith, chairman of the Business Council] pointed out, in fascinating times. President Havel just left here, and I just wish that each and every one of you could have been a fly on the wall or standing at his side to see his feeling about our institutions or our country when he came to the White House yesterday, using the expression "pinching himself to believe that it was really happening." To see him when I took him up to Lincoln's Bedroom to show him the very room in which Abraham Lincoln had signed the Emancipation Proclamation—it was a tremendously moving experience, and a privileged one, for me to witness this son of freedom, this playwright, who not long over a year ago was languishing in a prison and who is now the President of a free and, hopefully, democratic country. And it is mind-boggling, and I wish I could tell you that any of us in this room were smart enough to foresee the rapidity of change.

So, what I am trying to do, as your President, is to manage it in a prudent fashion to avoid moves that will inadvertently encourage some kind of a bad action out of the Soviet Union. We have a lot at stake in the success of *perestroika.* In this room we have some that pioneered doing business with the Soviet Union and were ahead—a lot of us here—in terms of understanding this new generation of Soviet leaders. But my view is, and I've said this in my public statements, we have a major stake in seeing *perestroika* succeed. And of course it has a major effect on the playwright, now President, that was here today. And it has the same kind of effect on a lot of other countries not only in Eastern Europe but in Western Europe.

I've elevated—or moved a little bit in the comments I've made and mentioned Gorbachev by name a time or two. And we're doing that deliberately, not to try to intervene into the internal affairs of the political process of the Soviet Union but rather to express our belief in the way in which he himself has managed the rapidity of change. Who would have thought that they would have not only accepted but encouraged the peaceful evolution that we now see has taken place all through Eastern Europe?

Somebody says to me—you know, when we get up into a big fight on trying to keep what I think are reasonable levels of defense, the big new question, the hot one they think they're going to really burn you with it in these press conferences is: Okay,

who's the enemy? It's not a bad question. But the enemy is, in my view, complacency or arrogance or something of this nature. So, I will try to manage these fascinating times, changes, in a prudent fashion; but I will be encouraging the Congress to keep prudent levels of defense because it isn't all that clear as to what is exactly going to happen.

At the same time, we'll be working on an arms control agenda with the Soviet Union that I think will result in sound agreements on conventional forces. [Secretary of State] Jim Baker got a major breakthrough the other day on the chemical weapons, and I think we can do something there. And of course the START talks—I see Cap [former Secretary of Defense Caspar W. Weinberger] here—that he was instrumental in, now. I hope we can bring a deal to fruition on that before too long. And so, I'm looking forward to our visit with Gorbachev that will happen this spring or early summer. And I think we can have some real progress going with the Soviet Union.

On the domestic side, I would be remiss if I didn't start these few remarks by thanking so many of you in this room. I still talk about a Thousand Points of Light. And I think the American people are beginning to understand that this isn't an escape from the responsibility of the Federal Government; rather, that it is an attempt to enlist the noblest impulses of the American people in one helping another, the concept that you shouldn't measure a successful life without throwing in the equation of doing something for someone else.

And I look around this room, and I think of some of our priorities, one of them education, another the fight against drugs. And in this room, just sitting here, are people that, when they pool the resources—and I'm not just talking about money; I'm talking about talent and mobilizing people—can do more just in this room combined than the Federal Government can do, particularly in the field of education.

And I am grateful to those who are in the forefront of this educational reform. I have in my mind a set role for the Federal Government. I don't believe the Federal Government needs to take over the local school boards. I don't believe we should set curriculum. I don't believe that we need to intervene in a salary dispute for teachers—God bless them because they do do a good job. But I do think that we have a proper role in joining with the Governors, as we did, in defining national education goals.

And several people in this room—I won't embarrass them by singling them out—have been extraordinarily helpful to me and to my team in the White House by making recommendations on the goals, recommendations that, for the most part, have been accepted by the Governors as we have set out national goals as to where we want to do the achievement levels, testing levels, excellence in math and science—that certainly will render us more competitive in the years ahead.

And so, I will press forward on an educational agenda. We have got to keep pushing the Congress to think anew. Many want to stay with the old programs that have failed and plow more money into those, and I think we've come to a point where we really have to come up with, as I say, not only these goals but the implementation of them. And it will not be done by the Federal Government alone, although the total dollars on educational spending is up.

On the antinarcotics fight, it's a prime fight. And I am grateful for the fact that Bill Bennett [Director of National Drug Control Policy] is our drug czar. I've never understood why we refer to people here as czars, but nevertheless, he is doing a good job. And we went down to Cartagena the other day and met with the Andean Presidents and Barco of Colombia. And we could show them that we are beginning to make progress on the demand side of the narcotics problem. I think we disarmed Barco and Alan Garcia [President of Peru] and Paz Zamora [President of Bolivia] by saying right up front: "Look, we know we're a problem. We know we're the big market. But let me tell you what we're doing about it."

And I bragged on the work of Jim Burke [chairman of the Partnership for a Drug-Free America] and others in this room who are out front trying to—in a private way, no government involvement—making the American people and the kids, particularly,

aware that this use of narcotics cannot be condoned. And once we got by the demand side, then we spelled out a rather broad agenda of working with those countries not only to abort but to interdict what was left of the supply of coca coming into this country.

But as I see many business people here that do business in that area, I remain convinced that the best answer to helping in Colombia and Peru and Bolivia is your end of the line: the business. And we've got to remove some of the regulatory burdens that we have. And it isn't easy because there are strong political influences for very legitimate reasons that are protecting, but we have got to have viable economies there that depend less on growing these insidious coca leaves. But again, the reason I want to mention that subject is because I think the business community has an enormously constructive role to play. And I am, once again, very grateful to you.

I'll mention just one more topic. There are many, many subjects. I see Don Riegle here, and I am very grateful to him for his leadership in the Senate on the savings and loan business. And all these things we can talk about briefly in a question period, but there is another area I want to mention, and that has to do with the environment. I am very pleased that the business community—large business and small—are in general support of our efforts to do something about clean air in this country. Today there was an attack leveled mainly against John Sununu [Chief of Staff to the President]. That suits me just fine, but they'll get around to me tomorrow. [*Laughter*] But the point I want to make is this: that there are no divisions in all of this. And I, obviously, must accept responsibility. But I believe that we are in a proper position.

I want to see market incentives, as much as we possibly can, in terms of cleaning up the environment. I do not want to throw people out of work, and yet I proudly proclaim that I am an environmentalist. And we've got a clean air bill that we've sent up, which is a first, and—several of you had a very important input into this very important legislation. And now we find that it's being pulled one way or another by the congressional process. And some of it I might be able to accept. Nobody's going to cross the "t" exactly the way we want or dot the "i", but there's certain limits beyond which I should not go if I remain true to my belief that we have got to find a balance between economic growth and environmental protection. And yet I'm optimistic that we can do that. And we're in a big battle now, and I would ask either your indulgence or support, depending on how you come down on these questions.

But I think we have a pretty good package, and I am convinced that we can do a good job for the environment. But it cannot be driven by the extremes. And it will not be driven by the extremes as long as I have something to say about what legislation becomes law. So, we're working on these issues.

There's others that I will be glad to take questions on, but I'll make just a general comment. I'm glad that my wife, Barbara, is working for so many of you—or put it the other way around, that you are working for her—I'm not sure which. But you have been fantastic in terms of the support for literacy and for putting an emphasis where it belongs in terms of the children of the United States of America. And I know that Bar joins me in that sentiment, and I am very grateful for the support that she has received from so many in this room in her work on literacy, other facets of education, the homeless, and just plain caring about the American people.

So, there we are. Thank you very much for inviting me up here. And now, with no further ado, I will be glad to take a few questions until Roger gives me the hook and I will go peacefully. Who's got one?

German Reunification

Q. *[Inaudible]*

The President. Well, first place, there is concern about it, that you properly put your finger on. I think there is more concern in certain of the Western European countries and in Poland than perhaps in some other countries. The Soviets, obviously, have expressed their concern, mainly on the timing. They have now accepted the concept of reunification. What we are doing is to back [West German] Chancellor Kohl

in the concept and let the Germans sort out the time. The longstanding NATO position, just for history, has been self-determination. Let the people decide, and then the border should not be changed without agreement of all the parties. But Kohl is talking about, and I think properly so, a Germany reunited but that remains a part of NATO.

And NATO will take on a broader role. It will have more of a political role; and that is, I think, a very stabilizing thing. I had a long talk with [Czechoslovakian President] Havel, who came here with an approach: Well, let's get all of the Soviet troops out and all the U.S. troops out, and life will be beautiful. Everything will be pruning hooks and plowshares. But I think I convinced him that the United States—wanted by Western Europe and, indeed, by some of the countries in Eastern Europe—is there as a stabilizing force. And my approach will be—and Helmut Kohl is coming up this weekend to Camp David—to support the concept, let the Germans make the determination. You may remember the formula two-plus-four: Let the two Germanys discuss it, and then we go to the Four Powers that have responsibilities under the post-World War II peace agreement—their agreement there—sort out the details.

But the way we see it is a Germany that is unified, a U.S. presence in Western Europe, no advance of what are known as allied troops into the GDR [German Democratic Republic], and a withdrawal of Soviet troops from places where they are not wanted. And that, I think, will take place regardless of what happens to Germany, just given the momentum and the feeling of these newly found democracies. And I think that will provide a rather stable environment.

Now, some of you do an awful lot of business in the Federal Republic, and you know that the German political scene is sometimes highly volatile. And we can't foresee what's going to happen with the Socialists in Germany; and when they align with the Socialist Party, SPD, in East Germany, you're going to have an equation that nobody can analyze. Are the East Germans Socialists—are they going to join automatically with their brethren in the Federal Republic? Or are they going to say: Hey, wait a minute, we have no linkage there because we're the ones who now want to throw off the yoke of socialism in a classic sense.

So, I still think unification—we're not going to do anything about it; nothing can be done about it—a U.S. presence, forces in the Federal Republic but that do not move in any threatening way to the Soviet Union—and I believe the Soviets have accepted this pretty much.

And then the other question is the Polish border. All of us know that could be highly contentious and emotional and inflammatory. But there I think we're going to see an agreement out of the two-plus-four—the six—that there will be no changes in that border certainly without the consensus and agreement of all the countries involved. And that would include in that instance the Soviet Union.

So, that's the way we're going, and I think it will result in stability. I hope it will. But we are not pressing the timetable. We're not pushing it, nor do I think it's the role of the United States to try to impede it. Gorbachev did that for awhile, and he felt something was moving awful fast. And that's why he said what he did to Kohl about 10 days ago in Germany—which was, look, in principle, we understand reunification. I can tell you that a month and a half ago he didn't feel that way, because I talked to him directly about it, and they were urging a real cautionary approach to German reunification.

Education

Q. In the area of education, first, I think we all want to commend you for your leadership in this area. Do you have any suggestions which the private sector—particularly the major companies of our country—can do to give some help in this area?

The President. Yes, and there's a lot of great examples in this room. I will refer you to John Akers [chairman, International Business Machines Corp.] or David Kearns [chairman of the executive committee, Procter and Gamble Co.] or John Smale [chairman and chief executive officer of Xerox Corp.] or so many others because there are some marvelous examples of how a corporation can get involved in programs

like mentoring. I understand that many companies have agreed to actually take a significant role in working with the localities and freeing up corporate personnel to go in and help on some of these programs. And I think that's an important area. But I think right in this room there are some marvelous examples of corporate involvement. And we have a program at the White House, an office, Thousand Points of Light—a young man, a dedicated, idealistic guy named Gregg Petersmeyer [Deputy Assistant to the President and Director of the Office of National Service]. Some of you knew his dad when he was in the communications business. And Gregg, if you just get in touch with him, can send you the best of what small business and large are doing. And I think and hope it would be helpful. And maybe the council staff itself could be involved in disseminating some of that information.

Defense Spending

Q. [*Inaudible*]

The President. Well, I'm concerned about it. And they have some legitimate questions. We're up for two missiles, and that may be a difficult—the Soviets having modernized a couple of really advanced type of missiles. And we're up for that. We're going forward with requests on the B-2 and the SDI. And the question we get back is: Who's the enemy? And the answer I send back up there is: Well, let's be prudent and careful until we can see extraordinarily clearly where we're going. And I'm not suggesting that Ligachev [Soviet Politburo Member and Chairman of the Agrarian Policy Committee] will come in and you'll have a diametric, different approach or that Soviet military's going to take over.

But we just don't know, and therefore, we have to have prudent levels. And we may have to take some hits. We're way down from what the previously recommended levels were in defense spending. And I know very well that the constituency is being whittled away all the time. And we're rethinking the kind of force we need. But until, one, the international situation is clear, and until we have completed the review of the kind of force we need—and

General Powell [Chairman of the Joint Chiefs of Staff] is involved in that right now—I will simply be urging that we not make imprudent cuts in defense.

But in the areas that I've mentioned it's going to be a hard hold for me. It's going to be difficult because people are looking at it that we have to choose between one missile, not two. Or you have to—here's Don Atwood [Deputy Secretary of Defense]. The poor guy lives with this every single day. And I might say I'm glad one of your former members is willing to undertake, really, the sacrifice involved to come into a high level in this government. But we're under fire. He can talk to you later about the details of it. But I think there's a recognition that we don't want to do anything silly, and we don't want to make cuts that are too drastic.

Having said that, I think our troop level, CFE proposal has been well received. Our allies are saying: Please, until we get CFE done, let's have that as a floor, not some ceiling, and let's hold it. And I think we need to do that to keep our allies together on it. But that's a hard sell because people say: Hey, the Soviets are going to have to get out. Why don't we do more? So, there's another area that we're going to have some difficulty. But I want to see a CFE agreement brought to fruition and, hopefully, to be signed at a CSCE meeting this summer. I think we can do that, as a matter of fact.

But Soviets are making representations of declined spending on defense. And yet a big percentage of the GNP—Bill Webster [Director of Central Intelligence] can give you a close number—I think 17 percent, maybe more, going into defense. And you might say, Well, if everything [is] plowshares and pruning hooks, why are they doing this? So, my innate caution says, Let's have a sound defense program. But those areas I mentioned are the ones that are going to be the toughest to hold, I think.

And we got another question. And I see Don here. And I expect John Dingell would agree there is still a sentiment up there in the Congress that perhaps I would have indulged in if I were still a Member from the 7th District of Texas, and that is if you're going to close a base, that's great, but be sure to close it in somebody else's State or somebody else's congressional district. We've got in [Secretary of Defense] Dick Cheney and Don Atwood, people that have looked at this without any politics involved at all. Some say: Hey, that's a Democratic congressional district. And I say: Yes, and it's a Republican Governor in the State of California. So, come on with something else; don't give me that one. And so, what we're going to try to do is have a prudent approach to defense spending in this country as well. And it isn't easy, as Don knows, but we're going to keep with it and try to encourage the American people to support what we're doing there.

And then we need a lot of programs to help alleviate the suffering or the economic reversal that goes with the closing of a base. But if you look at some of the places, they have been closed, the record is pretty good on economic diversification. But that one is one where we'll be taking the offense. And I've been around here long enough to know that it's not going to be easy, but I'm determined to go forward with it.

China

Q. Just a minute on your thoughts about China, the direction they're going?

The President. Well, I'll have to confess to a certain discouragement. And I would point—a turning point, as what happened to the Ceausescus [former Romanian first family] in Romania and what happened to that Romanian revolution. But as you know, I was in a different posture—a fairly lonely one—with the Congress in terms of whether the way to handle the students in this country was through legislation or through Presidential Executive order. I maintain to this day that the Executive order that I signed and put into effect did more than the legislation, the Pelosi bill, would have done.

But the students sent everybody Christmas cards. Three of the student groups—the two biggest ones, ironically—were supporting the President's position, and so were some of the biggest benevolent associations in China-America—I'm thinking in the San Francisco, Steve—and some of these groups gave me strong support. But the Chinese students, those that were most

253

vociferous, were well-financed from someplace and did a very good job, saying the only way to guarantee their ability to stay in this country was through legislation.

And my view is, in dealing with China the way I did, I am not condoning tyranny. I am not doing as the Democratic leader said up there today: turning my back on human rights. What I am trying to do is preserve enough contact so the United States can have some influence. And it is my belief that the Fulbright program, the fledgling Peace Corps program is the way you approach bringing about change, and especially with China. And when Mr. Fairbank, a very distinguished Chinese scholar, said the worst way you deal with China—they are different, and if you think the way to do it is to slap them publicly in the face, that's not the way to do it.

But I cannot tell you that I'm happy about it, David [Kearns], because since the Romanian thing, there has been less forward motion. There's been some. They lifted martial law, and then the liberal press jumped all over me, saying it didn't amount to anything. It did, in my view. They've done a few other things, but they're small. But I can't tell you that the results of trying to keep contact have been totally satisfactory, but I'm going to do it because I believe that we will be in a position to effect change in China by this kind of at least having some contact with them.

And the idea that China is exactly the same as these other countries—I don't believe it. So, I'm on a little different wavelength with many, and yet I'm convinced that someday this policy will pay off. It hasn't. We want to see the release for Fang Lizhi, this dissident that's in the American Embassy. That has not taken place. They have lifted the ban on VOA [Voice of America] coming in there, but they're still jamming it.

So, there's a mixed review at this point. And yet I have a feeling that China works in more mysterious ways than other countries. And I don't know what internal struggles are going on right now, but I'll guarantee you there are some. And Deng Xiaoping [Chairman of the Central Military Commission] was out three times and bounced back four. And who knows what's going to happen to Zhao Ziyang [former General Secretary], who has not been stripped of all his party powers. He's still a member of the Communist Party there. And let's just see how it works. But I say, it's a little lonely.

Thank you all very much.

Note: The President spoke at 8:03 p.m. in the Great Hall at the Library of Congress.

Nomination of James Henry Michel To Be an Assistant Administrator of the Agency for International Development
February 22, 1990

The President today announced his intention to nominate James Henry Michel to be an Assistant Administrator of the Agency for International Development for Latin America and the Caribbean, U.S. International Development Cooperation Agency. He would succeed Dwight A. Ink.

Since 1987 Ambassador Michel has served as Ambassador to the Republic of Guatemala. He served in several positions at the Department of State in Washington, DC, including Principal Deputy Assistant Secretary for Inter-American Affairs, 1983–1987; deputy legal adviser, 1978–1982; assistant legal adviser for politico-military affairs, 1974–1977; deputy assistant legal adviser for politico-military affairs, 1971–1974; and attorney-adviser in the Office of the Assistant Legal Adviser for Administration, 1965–1971.

Ambassador Michel graduated from St. Louis University School of Law (J.D., 1965). He was born August 25, 1939, in St. Louis, MO. He is married and has four children.

Remarks at the Presentation Ceremony for the American Institute of Architects Gold Medal Award
February 22, 1990

The President. Now, officially, welcome to the White House. I'm delighted to see Bill Reilly here, our head of the environment; John Frohnmayer, the arts; and so many others. I might single out Rex Scouten, the curator of the White House, sitting behind you. Some know him, but Barbara and I have great respect for him.

As early as 1909, the Presidents, including Taft, Harding, and Franklin Roosevelt, have presented the Gold Medal of the American Institute of Architects to the best of the world's architects; and I am honored and very pleased to continue this tradition.

Architecture holds up a mirror to the soul of any nation; and American architecture, with its rich variety of styles and regional differences, is as diverse and as dynamic as the American people themselves. We recognize that the quality of our lives is shaped by the quality of the environment we create. We understand that the spirit of our country can be seen in our architecture. From the majestic monuments of this, our capital city, to the gentlest main street in smalltown America, our buildings speak to us of who we are, where we have been, and where we're going.

In the spirit of celebrating the best of our nation's architecture, we are here to honor a very special architect, Fay Jones, who has dedicated his life to shaping the American landscape, to making our country a better place to live through the power of the creative mind.

Through humble materials and simple forms, Mr. Jones has created architecture of great power and space. His reverence for the land and his respect for the inner needs of the people who visit or dwell in his buildings give his architecture rare beauty and dignity. In the Nation's heartland, in places like Eureka Springs, Arkansas, and Picayune, Mississippi, he has built masterworks of design that touch the heart as well as the mind. Grounded firmly in his Ozark roots, Fay Jones has created a truly American architecture that is respected the world over.

I would also like to recognize the other distinguished architects here with us today who are past recipients of the Gold Medal Award: Mr. I.M. Pei, Pietro Belluschi, Arthur Erickson, Joseph Esherick.

I am very pleased now to present the Gold Medal to Fay Jones. Mrs. Jones, would you please join me for the presentation. Do I do the honors here?

Mr. Damianos. Yes, indeed.

The President. All right, sir. I don't want to mess anything up, but here we go. Congratulations, sir.

Mr. Jones. Thank you, Mr. President. To be so honored by one's peers and to have this medal presented by you is really the honor of a lifetime. And I'm sure that architects everywhere are pleased that you have now reestablished a tradition, after over 50 years, of having this medal presented at the White House by the President. And certainly we applaud your recognition of the very important and vital role that architects must play in improving our living environment, an environment that should be more supportive and more healthful and more beautiful.

This medal, of course, I know signifies and represents a great deal; and I know I shall spend the rest of my life trying to live up to the challenges that go with something like this. [*Laughter*] So, to all who've had a part in my selection for this signal honor, for this medal and what it represents, my sincerest thanks and my deepest, deepest appreciation. Thank you very much.

Mr. Damianos. Mr. President, if I could steal a few minutes. Mr. President, I'd like to thank you on behalf of the American Institute of Architects because this is a very special occasion. I'm not going to steal anybody's thunder; I think all the good words have been said. However, you may know already that Teddy Roosevelt helped us establish this medal some years ago. Now, he wasn't able to award it, but I'm sure he'd be delighted that we're able to do it again. And it does represent the highest form of excellence that we have. We are trying to reach the public more than we ever have before, and you're certainly giving us that opportunity. And we thank you very, very much.

The President. Well, it's a pleasure. For those of you who may be here for the first time, this is the Nobel Prize won by Teddy Roosevelt, and this is the Roosevelt Room. And if you didn't know it, you could guess from looking at the pictures. [*Laughter*]

Thank you all very much.

Note: The President spoke at 1:12 p.m. In his remarks, he referred to William K. Reilly, Administrator of the Environmental Protection Agency; John E. Frohnmayer, Chairman of the National Endowment for the Arts; and Sylvester Damianos, president of the American Institute of Architects.

Remarks at the Centennial Celebration of the Johns Hopkins University Medical Institutions in Baltimore, Maryland
February 22, 1990

Thank you very much, Dr. Muller. Just before coming out, Steven asked me to get one thing right: the name of the university. [*Laughter*] It's Johns Hopkins. I don't know why he thought an elitist from Yale would miss that one, but nevertheless. [*Laughter*] Now, he was given his great-grandmother's last name as his first name. I told Dr. Muller: "You don't need to explain family names to somebody called George Herbert Walker Bush." [*Laughter*]

I am so glad that Dr. Louis Sullivan, our distinguished Secretary of HHS, could be here with me today. I am very proud of him. And it's always good to be with my admired friend—wrong political party, but admired friend—Governor Schaefer, who's doing an outstanding job for this State; and of course my dear personal friend, with whom I've served in the trenches, Maryland's great Congresswoman, Helen Bentley, with us here today; and of course my fellow honorees, so many distinguished scholars and guests, here to honor both the founding of this historic institution and the 100th anniversary of Johns Hopkins Medical Institutions.

I'm very pleased to be here, and I want to salute the society of scholars—the new ones, the old ones—and this distinguished group. And if I could be permitted one anecdote: When I heard the citations of my fellow honorees, this distinguished five, I was reminded of the story of the kid that threw a rope around his mongrel dog and started heading over to Madison Square Garden. And they said, "Well, where are you going?" He said, "Well, I'm going to enter him in the Madison Square Garden pet show." And they said, "Well, do you think he has a shot at winning?" He said, "No, but he's going to be in some damn fine company." [*Laughter*] When I listened intently to those citations, I'll admit I didn't know what half the words meant. [*Laughter*] But I know excellence when I see it, and I am very honored.

I was a bit nervous when I heard I'd be in a gown before a group of doctors. [*Laughter*] At least this one buttons up the front, though. [*Laughter*]

Gathered up here and out there are some of the best health-care professionals in America. And best in America means best in the world. You know, sometimes when we talk about the best of anything, we add the phrase "that money can buy." But in medicine, that doesn't quite fit. There's an unease in the health-care community that for all this nation's wealth, for all the money put into the system, American medicine still faces unprecedented problems.

Medical malpractice. Uninsured families. An aging population. Cancer, heart disease, AIDS, drug addiction, Alzheimer's, mental illness—the price tag is staggering. Today over 11 percent of our gross national product goes to health care, and we rank number one in the world in per capita health-care expenditures. Yet we do remain behind other industrialized countries in life expectancy. And in the developed world, we rank 22d in infant mortality rates—22d.

Clearly, we have our work cut out for us. And yet because of great institutions like Johns Hopkins, we can face these challenges with a sense of optimism and a sense of confidence. Those who think our medical problems today are unsolvable or solvable only by money ought to understand how far we've come.

For example, 19th-century hospitals were not so much centers of healing as of horror. And medical schools of the 1880's were deplorable and dangerous places—no labs, no patients, no questions permitted. Rookies became doctors after just 18 months, often without ever seeing the inside of a hospital.

Today's date marks Washington's birthday, but some scholars here today may recall his death. Diagnosed with a sore throat, the doctors bled him four times before he succumbed to its effects, thus depriving our young nation of perhaps years of service from its most revered statesman.

In the primitive days of early medicine, change did come slowly until Johns Hopkins revolutionized the way medicine was taught for all time and launched a movement that brought America from medical backwater to world leader. Hopkins' influence was completely out of proportion to its age or resources. It found its wealth at the source of America's wealth: in its ideas, in its people. New and powerful ideas, dedicated and farsighted people, linking a medical school with a hospital, teaching at the bedside, developing new methodologies to fight terrible disease, bringing scientific research to medicine, seeing what works— Johns Hopkins demonstrates what one biomedical research establishment can do to change and improve health care in thousands of hospitals for millions of people.

Yet in our country today, there is a growing awareness that to make this country as healthy as it can be, all of us—all of us— must accept a share of the responsibility: government, the health-care profession, and the American people themselves. First, the Federal Government. In my State of the Union Address, I asked Dr. Louis Sullivan to lead a Domestic Policy Council review of options on the accessibility, the costs, and

the quality of America's health-care system. This administration is committed to health-care policies that improve health-care quality while trying to restrain the costs. For example, last December we enacted significant new Medicare physician payment reform, and recently, we announced the first large-scale program to study medical treatment effectiveness. But better, more affordable health care must also be more accessible. Expanded efforts to reduce infant mortality and expanded Medicaid eligibility to cover more women and infants are just two of the steps that we are taking to help.

Yet if American medicine is to continue to do the job, we must maintain our world leadership in medical research and development. It was Hopkins that first isolated a substance that American Government and medicine can always use: adrenaline. The clock is ticking, and medical breakthroughs tomorrow depend on action today. This administration has committed itself and this nation to not only the largest overall R&D budget but the largest biomedical research budget in our history. We must encourage the development of new technologies to prevent disease and avoid the expense of long-term treatment. A good example of this occurred right here at Johns Hopkins, where the discovery of three types of polio virus made the polio vaccine possible. Ultimately, this high-tech solution, the vaccine, costs only a few cents per patient, versus the tens of thousands of dollars that might be required for a lifetime of care in an old iron lung.

Of course, here at Hopkins you are the leading recipient of Federal research dollars, more than $500 million in the last fiscal year. You won that support the Johns Hopkins way, the American way, the same way that your lacrosse team makes the rankings: by being the very best.

But to keep American medicine the best in the world, individual health-care professionals and institutions must make our medical system responsive and responsible. You are the guardians of your profession—its ethics and its quality. Your standards must be high, and they must be enforced. The same sense of fiscal discipline that we must apply to government you must apply also to the medical world in a time of rising costs.

And I ask you today to avoid the understandable urge to practice "defensive medicine," where doctors, fearing litigation, too often dictate treatment that is unnecessary, where the threat of lawsuits threatens the very research that is so desperately needed to save lives. In return, we've got to restore common sense and fairness to America's medical malpractice system. I have directed the Domestic Policy Council to determine steps that the Federal Government can take to help alleviate this serious situation. We've got to remember a simple truth: Not every unfortunate medical outcome is the result of poor medicine. You cannot make life risk-free. No risk means no progress, and that's not the American way.

One of Hopkins' founders, Dr. William Halsted, was the gifted surgeon who introduced rubber gloves. In an age of surgical slashing, he used his scalpel carefully, reducing shock and trauma—a kinder, gentler surgeon, if you will. [*Laughter*] But he was not without boldness. And Halsted conceived and perfected a daring feat of surgery, the radical mastectomy, that to this day saves the lives of thousands of women afflicted with breast cancer.

The procedure in that time was unprecedented—unprecedented in its time. And yet in today's atmosphere of fear of malpractice, it probably would never have been attempted. This fear has not only hurt medical innovation and treatment, it also hurts medical voluntarism. Many doctors used to give a day a week to the needy, and I'm convinced that if not for the liability issue many more would donate time today. And I also worry that the fear of malpractice limits the access of too many Americans in our rural areas to quality medical care, particularly those with high-risk cases. Clearly, we must find a fair and reasonable solution to the malpractice crisis.

But government and health-care professionals alone cannot make this the healthy and productive country we want it to be. America's health-care system will be best in the world only when every American cares about his own health. It is estimated that 40 to 70 percent of the causes of premature death in America are preventable deaths—unnecessary deaths. And common sense tells us what that means. It's not complicated. Eat sensibly. Exercise. Wear seatbelts. Don't smoke, and if you do smoke, stop. Don't abuse alcohol, and don't use illegal drugs.

We're not talking about lifestyle: We're talking about life. And the best prescription for better health in America is a strong, daily dose of individual responsibility. This sense of responsibility is nothing new. Not far from here, I'm told, is the famous John Singer Sargent painting of the founding fathers of Johns Hopkins medicine. Sargent began by painting the four doctors, but something, he said, was missing. It came as an inspiration. He knocked down a studio wall to get his new props in, and he added a huge Victorian globe and, above the globe, a painting within a painting: St. Martin giving his cloak to a beggar. The globe should remind us of the global responsibilities of American medicine, reaching out to relieve the terrible suffering of innocents like the AIDS babies in Romania or the children of famine in Africa. And St. Martin's gesture should remind us of the special responsibilities of the medical community to reach out to those most in need.

We live in an age of miracles. We really do—medical miracles as dramatic as the artificial heart, everyday miracles as commonplace as the healing power of love. I believe in miracles and that wondrous accomplishments, wondrous breakthroughs, wondrous days are ahead. And I am privileged to be honored at a place where those wonders will continue to unfold. God speed you in your work, and God bless medicine and those who practice. And God bless the United States of America. Thank you for this esteemed honor. Thank you from the bottom of my heart.

Note: The President spoke at 4:02 p.m. at Shriver Auditorium. In his opening remarks, he referred to Steven Muller, president of the university.

Statement by Press Secretary Fitzwater on the President's Telephone Conversation With Prime Minister Yitzhak Shamir of Israel
February 22, 1990

Prime Minister Shamir of Israel phoned the President this morning. The Prime Minister thanked the President for U.S. support of Jewish emigration from the Soviet Union, for opposing anti-Semitism, and for supporting the restoration of diplomatic relations as well as the establishment of direct flights between the U.S.S.R. and Israel. The President said that the United States would continue to support these policies.

The Prime Minister stated that Jewish immigration into Israel was a separate matter from the question of settlements and that the Israeli Government had no policy of directing where the new immigrants would live. The President thanked the Prime Minister for his statement and said that the United States would continue to support free emigration from the Soviet Union. At the same time, the President reiterated U.S. opposition to any settlement activity. The President also expressed his hope that the peace process could move forward so that the U.S., Israeli, and Egyptian foreign ministers could meet and that a meeting of Israeli and Palestinian delegations would take place in Cairo soon.

The President expressed his appreciation to the Prime Minister for his call, which both leaders described as helpful and constructive.

Remarks on Signing the American Red Cross Month Proclamation
February 23, 1990

Thank you very much, Chairman Moody, and all of you, ladies and gentlemen. It's a great pleasure for me—long drive over— [*laughter*]—but I'm willing to make the sacrifice. [*Laughter*] Literally, it took us about 30 seconds. But what a pleasure to address the Red Cross. One reason is that if my speech is a disaster, relief is close at hand. [*Laughter*] Moreover, you prove what Emerson said: "The greatest gift is a portion of thyself."

Seventy-seven years ago it was, William Howard Taft began a great and generous tradition. And since then, every President has been privileged, as I am, to serve as American Red Cross Honorary Chairman and, since 1943, to proclaim March as American Red Cross Month.

To Franklin Roosevelt, the Red Cross embraced in its membership all races and creeds. To Dwight Eisenhower, it mirrored the warm heart of a free people. And another great President, Ronald Reagan, rightly observed that the Red Cross volunteers have proved equal to the challenges of the times. This spirit is crystallized in the three windows beside me, windows commissioned by the Red Cross in 1917, which represent the theme of ministry through sacrifice. These windows tell the Red Cross story, from collecting blood to combating disaster, and what this has meant to Americans and people throughout the world for generations.

Let me tell a story which illustrates that meaning. It's about a violent winter snowstorm and a remote mountain cabin all but covered by snowdrifts. I'm afraid most Red Cross volunteers have heard it. A Red Cross rescue team was carried by helicopter to these snowdrifts, within a mile of the cabin, and then struggled to the cabin, shoveling a path through the snow. Finally arriving at the door, the lead rescuer knocked. It was opened by a crusty mountaineer. "We're from the Red Cross," the rescuer explained. To which the mountaineer responded by scratching his head. "Well, it's been a right tough winter," he said at last. "I don't see how we can give anything this year." [*Laughter*]

A few moments later, obviously, the mountaineer got the message that rescue team was there to help. Just as for millions of people in need, from that snowbound mountaineer to families made homeless by floods and hurricanes, the Red Cross is what I like to refer to as a brilliant point of light, part of that vast galaxy of individuals, businesses, schools, churches, synagogues, voluntary associations working together to solve problems.

A point of light, a star of hope across the globe—for 109 years that star has shone anytime there has been a need, anywhere there is a need. And today it dazzles still, in 2,800 chapters, in thousands of towns and cities and at our military bases around the world, providing light at the end of the tunnel, a rainbow through the clouds.

Look, first, here at home. When forest fires seared the State of Michigan in 1881, or the Dust Bowl ravaged lives, the Red Cross star of light, if you will, helped millions of people. And that legacy continues from Hurricane Hugo in South Carolina to the earthquake in north California. Through CPR, AIDS education, and programs for the elderly, the Red Cross star casts a glow of love and caring, showing that any definition of a successful life must include serving others.

And look around the world. In the late 1800's, the Red Cross sent food and medical supplies to a starving Russia, and since then, has served from San Juan Hill to Hamburger Hill. In 1987, 1,200 Red Cross volunteers assisted when the tiny country of Bangladesh suffered from floods. In 1988, you sent the first international disaster relief to the Soviet Union in 65 years. And today, just take a look at Eastern Europe, where you're providing emergency food, clothing, and medical aid to new refugees. These efforts prove anew that a world without the Red Cross would be a terrible cross to bear and show how the Red Cross star of hope can shine forever by helping the volunteers of today become the leaders of tomorrow.

For evidence then, look at these men and women, each a star player honored by the Red Cross, or as you say, each playing your part: Dorothy Campbell-Bell of Nashville, teaching law in the classroom and the disabled to swim; or Rochester, New York's Joe Delgado, next here, father of the Organization of Latin American Students. In Philadelphia, Bill Gallagher is a Red Cross leader and full-time medical student. And in Cape May, New Jersey, Karen Maiorana started Operation Mail Call. Then there's Ben Robinson, of Hartford, Connecticut, one of Ebony's 10 Young Leaders of America; and then Debra Johnson, of Ashtabula, Ohio, the 1988 Volunteer of the Year.

That's some battalion, some lineup, I'll tell you. And today they're leading a cavalry charge of hope and healing. They're among the more than 1 million volunteers who grace settings from day care centers to inner-city schools and who are buoyed by the donors who last year raised nearly $145 million for the Red Cross disaster relief fund.

I began with a story about such service to others, and so let me close with another. It's about a man, President Woodrow Wilson, who so admired the Red Cross that he once told Admiral Grayson to gather up sheep and put them grazing on the White House lawn. "He appointed me shepherd of the flock," Grayson recalled. "When shearing time came, I reported to him that we had a little over 100 pounds of wool." With that, Wilson ordered him to send 2 pounds of wool to every State, telling the Governors to have it auctioned for the benefit of the Red Cross. The auction raised $50,000, and in time, Admiral Grayson went on to become Chairman of the Red Cross. For like you, he believed that we succeed in life only when we make a difference in someone else's life.

You live that belief and have made the Red Cross a star of hope unto the world. This table was used by Red Cross Chairman William Howard Taft when he was President. So, it's my honor now to use it again as I sign this proclamation making March American Red Cross Month.

Thank you for all you do, and thank you for inviting me. God bless the Red Cross. Thank you all.

Note: The President spoke at 11:42 a.m. in the Board Room at American Red Cross headquarters. In his remarks, he referred to George Moody, Chairman of the Board of Governors of the American Red Cross. The proclamation is listed in Appendix E at the end of this volume.

Message to the Senate Transmitting the Tunisia-United States Consular Convention
February 23, 1990

To the Senate of the United States:

I am transmitting, for the Senate's advice and consent to ratification, the Consular Convention between the United States of America and the Republic of Tunisia signed at Tunis on May 12, 1988. I am also transmitting, for the information of the Senate, the report of the Department of State with respect to the convention.

The signing of this convention is a significant step in the process of enhancing and broadening the relationship between the United States and the Republic of Tunisia. Consular relations between the two countries currently are not addressed by a bilateral agreement. The convention establishes clear obligations with respect to matters such as notification of consular officers of the arrest and detention of the nationals of their countries and protection of the rights and interests of the nationals of their countries.

The people of the United States and Tunisia have a tradition of friendship and cooperation. I welcome the opportunity through this consular convention to promote further the good relations between the two countries. I recommend the Senate give early and favorable consideration to the convention and give its advice and consent to ratification.

GEORGE BUSH

The White House,
February 23, 1990.

Appointment of Arthur A. Fletcher as a Member of the Commission on Civil Rights, and Designation as Chairman
February 23, 1990

The President today announced his intention to appoint Arthur A. Fletcher to be a member of the Commission on Civil Rights for a term expiring November 29, 1995. He would succeed Sherwin Chan. Upon appointment he will be designated Chairman.

Currently, Mr. Fletcher serves as president of Arthur A. Fletcher and Associates in Washington, DC. Prior to this, he served as Deputy Assistant to the President for Urban Affairs at the White House, 1976–1977, and president of Arthur A. Fletcher and Associates, Inc., 1973–1976. Mr. Fletcher served as executive director of the United Negro College Fund, 1972–1973. He was Alternate Delegate of the United States of America to the 26th Session of the General Assembly of the United Nations, 1971; Assistant Secretary of Labor for Employment Standards in Washington, DC, 1969–1971; special assistant to the Governor of the State of Washington in Olympia, 1968–1969; member of the city council in Pasco, WA, 1967–1968; and an employee relations consultant at Hanford Atomic Energy Facility, 1967–1968. In addition, he has served as a teacher in public schools in Berkeley, CA, 1961–1965; reports control manager at Aerojet-General Corp. in Sacramento, CA, 1957–1961; and an assistant director in the public information office of the Kansas State Highway Department in Topeka, 1955–1957.

Mr. Fletcher graduated from Washburn University (B.A., 1950). He was born December 22, 1924, in Phoenix, AZ. Mr. Fletcher served in the U.S. Army, 1943–1945. He is married and resides in Washington, DC.

Statement by Press Secretary Fitzwater on Peace Corps Programs in Eastern Europe
February 23, 1990

The President is pleased to note that today in Warsaw the United States and Poland signed a formal agreement for a Peace Corps program in Poland. Under the program, which was arranged in response to a request from the Polish Government, 60 American volunteers will go to Poland in June to provide English language training.

Under a similar agreement with Hungary, signed on February 14, the Peace Corps will send another 60 volunteers to Hungary in June. Czechoslovakia has also requested a Peace Corps English language program, and the President has asked Director of the Peace Corps Paul Coverdell to go to Prague soon to lay the groundwork for such a program. As the Peace Corps expands its activities into Eastern Europe, it will also offer assistance in such areas as the environment, computer training, and small business development.

The President welcomes these programs, which will be of direct benefit to the emerging democracies as they rejoin Europe and the community of democratic states.

Statement on the Death of José Napoleón Duarte of El Salvador
February 23, 1990

The President and Mrs. Bush are deeply saddened to hear of the death of former President Duarte. President Duarte was the father of Salvadoran democracy, a dedicated servant to the people of El Salvador, and a firm friend of the United States. His wisdom and dedication to the growth of democracy in Central America will be long remembered. President Duarte was also a strong supporter and exponent on behalf of human rights and social justice and has left a strong legacy in this area.

President Bush enjoyed a warm, close working relationship with President Duarte. President Bush admires the courage he exhibited in building the foundation of democracy in El Salvador and the message of hope he brought to all of Central America. The American people join the people of El Salvador in mourning their loss.

Letter to Congressional Leaders Transmitting the Report on Soviet Noncompliance With Arms Control Agreements
February 23, 1990

Dear Mr. Speaker: (Dear Mr. President:) Pursuant to section 1002 of Public Law 99–145 (22 U.S.C. 2592a), I am forwarding herewith the classified version of the Administration's report to the Congress on Soviet Noncompliance with Arms Control Agreements. Also enclosed is the unclassified version of the report.

This is the fifth in a series of reports on Soviet compliance with their international obligations. On the whole, our compliance policy has made progress since last year's report. The report notes certain constructive steps the Soviets have taken, such as the destruction of the radars illegally deployed at Gomel and Soviet Foreign Minister Shevardnadze's commitment to correct the Krasnoyarsk radar violation of the ABM Treaty. At the same time, the report details several issues that continue to concern the United States.

I intend to continue to press for scrupulous Soviet compliance with their arms control treaty obligations. The principle of scrupulous compliance is particularly important as we near completion of new arms control treaties.

I value the strong congressional support for our compliance policy to date, and look forward to working closely with the Congress on these issues in the future.

Sincerely,

GEORGE BUSH

Note: Identical letters were sent to Thomas S. Foley, Speaker of the House of Representatives, and Dan Quayle, President of the Senate.

Continuation of Timothy L. Coyle as an Assistant Secretary of Housing and Urban Development
February 23, 1990

The President today announced his decision that Timothy L. Coyle will continue to serve as an Assistant Secretary of Housing and Urban Development for Legislation and Congressional Relations.

Since 1988 Mr. Coyle has served as Assistant Secretary for Legislation and Congressional Relations at the Department of Housing and Urban Development in Washington, DC. Prior to this, he served in several positions at the Department of Housing and Urban Development, including Deputy Under Secretary for Field Coordination, 1986–1988, and Deputy Assistant Secretary for Legislation, 1984–1986. In addition, he served as Assistant to the Chairman at the Federal Home Loan Bank Board in Washington, DC, 1983–1984; Executive Assistant for Field Operations in the Office of Housing for the Federal Housing Commissioner at the Department of Housing and Urban Development, 1981–1983; consultant for the Presidential Inaugural Committee in Washington, DC, 1980–1981; and general manager for Richert Steak Houses, Inc., 1977–1980.

Mr. Coyle graduated from San Diego State University (B.A., 1976). He was born August 29, 1953, in Los Angeles, CA. Mr. Coyle is married, has two children, and resides in Alexandria, VA.

Appointment of Jose E. Martinez as Special Assistant to the President and Associate Director of Presidential Personnel
February 23, 1990

The President today announced the appointment of Jose E. Martinez to be Special Assistant to the President and Associate Director of Presidential Personnel.

Since January 1990 Mr. Martinez has been Associate Director of Presidential Personnel for National Security Matters. Prior to this he was president of J.E. Martinez & Associates, Inc., a consulting firm located in Alexandria, VA. Mr. Martinez served in the U.S. Air Force from 1961 to 1981. His assignments included congressional liaison officer for the Secretary of the Air Force and country manager for foreign military sales. From August 1981 to March 1985, Mr. Martinez served as a professional staff member for the Senate Committee on Armed Services. His responsibilities included the au-

thorization of the Department of Defense requests for other procurement, military construction, and ammunition. He also served as special assistant to the committee chairman and as committee press secretary. In 1984 Mr. Martinez was Texas campaign director of Hispanics for Reagan/Bush. In 1988 and 1989, he served as national campaign director of Hispanics for Bush-Quayle and codirector for outreach programs in the office of the President-elect, respectively.

Mr. Martinez, of Brownsville, Texas, obtained his B.A. in 1976 from Our Lady of the Lake University in San Antonio, TX, and his M.A. in 1979 from the Catholic University of America in Washington, DC. He is married to the former Shirley Ann White and has five sons.

Joint News Conference Following Discussions With Chancellor Helmut Kohl of the Federal Republic of Germany
February 25, 1990

The President. Barbara and I met on February 24th and 25th here at Camp David with Helmut Kohl, the Chancellor of the Federal Republic of Germany, and his wife, Hannelore. And we were just delighted to have them here.

The Chancellor and I had an opportunity to talk at length about recent political developments in Europe and about East-West relations, and I am pleased to say that we share similar views on the most fundamental issues. We both welcome the prospect of further movement toward German unification, beginning with the steps toward economic and monetary union that are proposed for the period immediately following the elections in the GDR [German Democratic Republic] on March 18th. If events are moving faster than we expected, it just means that our common goal, for all these years, of German unity will be realized even sooner than had been hoped.

We share a common belief that a unified Germany should remain a full member of the North Atlantic Treaty Organization, including participation in its military structure. We agreed that U.S. military forces should remain stationed in the united Germany and elsewhere in Europe as a continuing guarantor of stability.

The Chancellor and I are also in agreement that in a unified state the former territory of the GDR should have a special military status, that it would take into account the legitimate security interests of all interested countries, including those of the Soviet Union. At the same time, the Chancellor and I agreed that we must continue to press hard for arms control efforts which would sharply reduce military forces in Europe from the Atlantic to the Urals.

We want to work together to have a CFE agreement ready for signature this year at a summit meeting of all 35 CSCE member states. The summit could also endorse our proposal for CSCE guidelines on free elections to help show the way and protect the emerging democratic institutions of Eastern Europe.

Chancellor Kohl and I had a good discussion on East-West relations. We both support Chairman Gorbachev's program of *perestroika*, his efforts to reform his country's political and economic system. Chairman Gorbachev has shown true statesmanship in respecting the will of the people in Eastern Europe, in trying to build new relationships based on cooperation instead of coercion.

Since those difficult days following World War II when America joined hands with the German people in their effort to build a new state and a new society, the United States has been their partner in a common dream; and that dream was to build a free, democratic, and prosperous German republic committed to peace and working in close harmony with its closest neighbors. That enduring German-American partnership has never been stronger as Chancellor Kohl, the leader of one of the world's greatest democracies, steps toward a golden moment in the history of his nation.

Mr. Chancellor, it was a pleasure to have you with us. And now for your statement, sir.

The Chancellor. Mr. President, ladies and gentlemen, my first word is thank you. I wish to thank you, Mr. President, and your wife, Barbara, in my own name as well as on behalf of my wife, for the very cordial and friendly reception here in Camp David.

The atmosphere, the climate of our meeting, is symbolic of the excellent German-American relations. In particular, now, when the day of unity is drawing near for us Germans, we are conscious with profound gratitude of the fact that all of this would not have been possible without the close friendship and the confident partnership with the United States of America.

In the spirit of this friendship, the two of us, Mr. President, in the course of these hours in Camp David—we have discussed a vast list of political issues; and the center of our conversations was the future of the transatlantic relations and, embedded therein, the hope of the Germans towards national unity.

Against the background of historic changes on the European continent, we have reconfirmed our common belief. First, the alliance of a free democracies in Europe and North America—and included therein the German-American partnership—are of fundamental importance for peace and security. This is true now. This will be true in future.

Second, the security link between North America and Europe is and continues to be today and in future for us Germans—that is to say also for a united Germany—of vital importance. That is why we need the presence of our American friends in Europe, in Germany—and that includes the presence of American forces.

Also for a united Germany and future, maintaining the friendship with the United States of America and the expansion of relations with them will be an important task. We are happy about the ever closer economic cooperation and economic exchange, exchange in the fields of science and culture, and about the ever more meaningful meetings between people—in particular, of the young generation.

We are convinced that transatlantic relations must systematically be expanded in all fields. It is common security in the alliance which is part of this—the ever closer contact between the European Community, including political cooperation, and the United States. And this includes, also, our joint efforts to make our way towards a European peace order within the framework of the CSCE.

Seeing the major changes in central Europe, east Europe, southeast Europe, the European Community continues to be an indispensable anchor of European stability. That is why we, the Federal Republic of Germany and, in particular, myself, do not only want to expand European integration but we want to accelerate this process wherever possible.

Beyond the big internal market, which is to be achieved after the 31st of December, 1992, beyond an economic and monetary union, primordial, the aim continues to be political union in Europe. That was the objective of the treaties of Rome, and nothing has changed in that area.

It is our joint interest that the reform policy in central, east, and southeast Europe and, in particular, the policy led by Secretary General Gorbachev in the Soviet Union will be successful. Europe and North America are and continue to be open for cooperation as partners, in particular with the reform states, and I welcome, particularly, what you have just said about the subject, Mr. President.

In the course of our conversations, we were also agreed that disarmament negotiations must energetically be pursued and be led to a success.

On the path towards German unity, ladies and gentlemen, what we need in particular now is reason and a good judgment. We Germans walk along this path with a particular responsibility in the center of Europe, and we're doing so, if you like, along two tracks which are of equal importance. On the one hand, we are leading intensive talks with the GDR, and at present we will, in particular, have to concentrate on the customs union and the economic community. On the other hand, we do have to consider that the link with our transatlantic partners, that European unity and comprehensive cooperation between East and West are being linked up with the development.

We do respect the legitimate security interests of all states, and we respect people's feelings, especially the feelings of our neighbors. And I am saying this particularly addressing our Polish neighbors. The border question will be settled definitely by a freely elected all-German government and a freely elected all-German Parliament. But let me repeat here what I have recently said in Paris already—it was in January of this year: Nobody has any intention of linking the question of national unity with changes of existing borders.

In the course of our talks, I have informed President Bush about the situation in the GDR and the talks I have had a couple of days only with Secretary General Gorbachev. And I wish to seize this opportunity, Mr. President, to thank you publicly today, and here before the press, that on the eve of my trip to Moscow you sent me a letter which did not only speak about supporting our policy and was not only marked by the habitual friendship but which will be going down in history as an important document of German-American friendship.

Let me conclude by thanking you very much again for your friendship and for the lovely hours we have been able to spend with you here. I think this will mark our future cooperation as well.

The President. Helmut, if agreeable to you, might I suggest to the press that we alternate the questions between us? Is that agreeable with you, sir?

German Reunification and Developments in Europe

Q. You have declared, Chancellor, that you do not want a change of borders. Does this mean that you consider the Polish border as final?

The Chancellor. My answer is very clear. It is contained in the text, and I am sure it has been translated correctly. According to the legal situation in our country, it is a freely elected Parliament—thus sovereign— of the people, which has to decide this question. And this is laid down also in the treaties of 1970 and has been mentioned in the conversations which took place in those years again and again.

Beyond this point, I have again and again declared during the past month that—and I do want to repeat—nobody wants to link the question of national unity with changes in existing borders. And nobody is permitted to doubt my attitude there.

Q. Then do you consider to exclude that before German unity a treaty be concluded with the Poles about the Polish border—do you consider this excluded?

The Chancellor. If I interpret the wish of the Polish Government correctly, and I think I do, then the Polish Government has a very national wish that the legally competent sovereign take that decision. In Poland, there are certain circles who wish that before such a decision to be adopted by an all-German Parliament, decisions be taken in the two German States. In the West German Parliament, we have already pronounced ourselves and confirmed our line about the nonchanging of borders.

The President. Might I just add the U.S.

position, with your permission, Mr. Chancellor? The U.S. respects the provisions of the Helsinki Final Act regarding the inviolability of current borders in Europe. And the U.S. formally recognizes the current German-Polish border. I just wanted to get that in.

Q. Do you think there is some difference between what you have just said and what the Chancellor said? There seems to be some bit of equivocation on his part. Do you think there is any difference in the U.S. view and what the Chancellor is saying today?

The President. I think we're in alignment. I would not interpret what he said as equivocating at all, and I have just given you the U.S. position.

Q. Can you explain for us at this stage precisely how the two-plus-four works and what the sequencing is? Whether they're consecutive, consultative? There has been so much confusion about that. Who has got what rights?

The President. No, those details have not been fully worked out in terms of timing of meetings and things of this nature; they have not been worked out. This formula was approved by the Foreign Ministers in Ottawa, and we simply have not tried to sit here in Camp David and fine-tune the procedures for the two-plus-four. Have you got a follow? I'm not sure I was responsive, Charles [Charles Bierbauer, CNN].

Q. Well, I'm not sure that I know any more than when you started. And that may be part of the problem here: that it is not clear whether the Germans hold their meetings simultaneous with you, whether you're in adjacent rooms, whether you run back and forth.

The President. No, those details have not been worked out. And it would be wrong for the United States to try to sit on its own and work out with the German Chancellor all these technical matters that involve others. So, we did not get into those details here today.

Q. Can I get the Chancellor to comment on how it should proceed?

The Chancellor. I would like to make a brief remark about the subject, all the more so since I don't believe that there is any reason for considering the situation with mistrust.

I'm very happy with the decision adopted in Ottawa: two-plus-four. It is only natural that the two states in Germany, in particular after the 18th of March elections in the GDR, will be discussing the subject in a particular way. This is a subject which concerns the Germans in particular. But I spoke about the two tracks a moment ago, along which things have to proceed. We will then, at the level of two-plus-four, have to discuss things very frankly. And we're not trying to exclude anybody—that was sort of the background of what you were saying—but we will have to discuss things in every necessary detail. And I think that is possible within a reasonable timeframe. If we talk to one another, we have a good chance of understanding one another.

Q. Mr. President, how do the Poles come into this process? Are they just one of the 35 at the end of it?

The President. Well, I know of Poland's feeling to want to make two-plus-four into two-plus-five. Is that what you're asking about? The two-plus-four has been agreed upon clearly. No agreement would ever be reached that affects the Polish borders without Polish involvement. But there is no change. We don't sit up here and try to change an agreement that was taken by several countries at Ottawa.

But I should add there will be a lot of consultative mechanisms to deal with the interests not just of Poland but of our allies and everyone else. And the Chancellor is very good about that, and I hope we've been good about it. And it is essential that we stay on the same wavelength with our allies and friends.

Excuse me, Helmut. I interrupted you, sir.

The Chancellor. Let me underpin what the President just said. I do realize that there is a particular interest on the part of the Poles. And I'm certain that in the course of this process we will find ways and means of adopting a solution satisfactory to everybody. I think every one of us has a feeling that there is a particular situation there, but I don't consider it useful that the two of us, when nobody else from amongst our party is here, try and decide on things and make a declaration today.

Q. ——seems to be growing across Europe, from Poland to Britain, and our own former Director of Intelligence, Mr. Helms, has called the German unification march a runaway freight train. Given the history, the role that Germany played in two wars in this century, shouldn't there be some assurances before this marriage takes place on borders and security?

The President. I think all those matters will be discussed in the various consultative mechanisms that we've brought up. But I prefer to look at Germany's 45 years of contribution to democracy and to the security of the West, and that's what we are focusing on. I've stated the U.S. position, which is not to be afraid of German reunification but to understand when peoples—brother on one side, brother on another—want to get together as one country, as they were before this artificial division that resulted out of World War II. So, we've already crossed that bridge. We welcome reunification. But it's not for the United States to set a timetable. It's not for us to say how fast. It is for us to guarantee as best we can, in consultation with our allies, that whatever evolves will be stable and that peace will be the result.

So, I've already given you the view in my statement about the U.S. toward unification, and we are not in a process of trying to speed it up or slow it down. It's a matter for the German people; it's a matter for the discussions that will be taking place in multilateral fora.

The Chancellor. Just a second. Let me say something about this, because this is a very central question. The question of German unity is a question of the right of self-determination. And all peoples of this Earth have the right of self-determination. It's a part of the Charter of the United Nations. It corresponds to the principles of CSCE. It corresponds to the major democratic traditions of our world. In all documents, all treaties which have been concluded with the Federal Republic, the will to reform the unity of the German nation had always been confirmed.

The second point is that the people in the two parts of Germany do want to unify, want to overcome the artificial division.

The people in the GDR, in a peaceful revolution—I think the most peaceful revolution of history—have made it clear that they want it by shouting, "We are the people. We are one people." Now, if I have a particular feeling seeing and hearing this, I believe that we do have a responsibility to be conscious of the fact that we are situated, geographically speaking, in the center of Europe. We have a certain history. We must understand that there are certain fears on the part of our neighbors, and I'm talking about serious fears and not only the pretended fears—because there are people who pretend they have fears but what they mean is that they fear the economic power of the Federal Republic plus GDR.

The President very rightly said last year the Federal Republic was 40 years of age. In the course of 40 years, it was a loyal and reliable partner in human rights and the defense of freedom. In 1983, I put my political existence at stake by agreeing that arms be deployed—NATO arms, American arms—and missiles be deployed on German soil. So, nobody has to tell me what a reliable partner is.

But I do take all the other data into consideration, and I've also made it clear—that's part of my answer to you—that I am amongst those who want to pursue the political union of Europe. The Federal Government is a government which is ready to delegate further competencies to the European Parliament. In other words, we want this united Germany to be ever more embedded in an integration process with its neighbors. So, nobody needs to be afraid.

And as regards economic strength, I can only say that the European Community has been able to draw great advantage of the economic strength of the Federal Republic and will be able to enjoy more advantage from the economic strength of a united Germany.

Q. Mr. President, I'd like to know perhaps the core question: Do you trust that Germany will never become an aggressive, resurgent military power? And if I might ask Mr. Kohl: Mr. Kohl, do you forsake such a power?

The President. I have stated that the U.S. position is that we welcome unification.

And clearly, that would not be the position if we held the fears that your question alluded to. I do think that one way to help with stability—not in relation to this question but European peace and stability—is to have a strong NATO and to have U.S. troops, if wanted, stationed in Europe. But if I shared the fears that you're talking about, clearly we might well have a different policy.

Let me take this one, Chancellor, because I recognized two at once.

Q. I would like to ask Chancellor Kohl how durable we can see the commitments to NATO and the continued presence of U.S. troops on German soil, given the broad support in the Federal Republic right now for a neutral unified Germany, given the probable outcome of the East German elections, and given some of the political pressures that you may come under later this year with elections in December?

The Chancellor. First of all, it's my affair, these elections in the Federal Republic of Germany in December, and I'm looking forward to them very calmly. A moment ago, I gave you the example. Had I been standing here in the fall of 1982 or in January '82, most of your colleagues would have doubted that the Germans would deploy. We did deploy American missiles, and that is why I really don't think we need to be told what reliability means. Neutralism would be a very false solution for us. I can't see that there would ever be any majority in the Federal Republic nor in the united Germany for a neutralized Germany. I think we have learned lessons, and we do not want to repeat the errors of history. But one mistake in the times of the Weimar Republic, of course, was that Germany was isolated in Europe. One must make Germany a part of the whole.

Q. How would you assess the results of your Camp David meeting? Has this accelerated the way towards German——

The Chancellor. I don't think that this was our subject, really. Actually, I must say, I don't quite understand this discussion on who accelerates and who does the contrary. At one point in time, I proposed these 10 points. At that time, the situation was quite different in November, and that is only a couple of weeks back. We had thought that

on the path towards German unity we would be able to take certain steps, that we would have an opportunity of concluding this contractual community first and then have further joint structures and then have a confederation.

It is the attitude of the people in the GDR and their exodus which has accelerated things. You must consider the fact that between the 1st of January and today some 110,000 people have left the GDR to come over to the Federal Republic—I think that equals the figure of inhabitants of Philadelphia—in the matter of 8 weeks. So, this movement must be stopped. That is why I made this offer of concluding a monetary union—in order to stop this movement, in order to hold people back, in order to make them stay at home.

If you ask me, we now need a possibility of proceeding along this path towards unity step by step with good judgment. We need this for ourselves. We also need this because of our neighbors. Because the dynamism which has been caused now has been caused by the people in the GDR, but not because anybody wanted to accelerate that movement. I do hope that in a few days, that is to say shortly after the 18th of March, the newly elected Parliament will soon form a government with whom we can agree on how we want to proceed. But I'm not interested in this being so very fast.

The President. The gentleman in the German press asked—I thought he said for both of us to comment on the nature of the talks. In diplomacy, they always say full and frank, and you can interpret that any way you want. But the benefit of this kind of meeting for me is you can talk in a very informal setting about any subject at all. And the relationship that I have personally with Chancellor Kohl and that the Federal Republic has with the United States enables us to talk very frankly.

But what I come out with, in addition to this statement that I made, is the importance to keep our allies involved. I believe the Chancellor shares with me the importance of the United States and the Soviet Union staying in very close touch. I know he shares with me the importance of our making progress with the Soviets on arms control and on other areas. So, as this meeting winds down, it was extraordinarily frank. We can talk as one does with friends. But we have so much common ground here, including how we're looking at unification and including the need to be sure that it doesn't look like either one of us is dictating to allies security arrangements or anything else for the future. So, it was a very good meeting.

Q. Mr. President, I wonder if each of you gentlemen could comment on whether you would anticipate that a reunited Germany will see fit to develop an independent nuclear weapons capability?

The Chancellor. No. This discussion is over in Germany. We are not at all longing to be an atomic power.

Q. Mr. President, if I could follow up on the question you were actually asked a week or two ago about who the enemy is these days. It seems that less and less it is the Soviets. So, would one purpose of keeping NATO intact and keeping U.S. troops within NATO in Germany be, as some analysts have said, to keep the Germans down?

The President. No. The enemy is unpredictability. The enemy is instability. And it is for that reason that there are agreed security provisions. And that's the answer to it.

Who out here was smart enough to predict for fact-certain the changes that have taken place any time in the last year? Certainly no one up here. Maybe Chancellor Kohl, but not the President of the United States. And so, what I think we want to do in a period of exciting change is to have a stable Western Europe.

The Eastern European countries are throwing off the yoke of communism. The policy of NATO has prevailed. The Soviet Union is engaged in dramatic change, but nobody can predict for fact-certain what will come. And so, what we want to do is use our good offices and our alignment with NATO to help with stability. And that is in the interest of the United States of America.

Some are saying in our country—and the Chancellor and I talked about this—well, we ought to take all the troops out. Or some are saying, take all Soviet troops out and all the U.S. forces out of Europe. In my judgment, that would not provide for a stable Europe. And so—back to your question—the enemy is instability and unpredictability as this rapid change continues to unfold inside the Soviet Union and inside Eastern Europe.

The Chancellor. I would like to join up with this term "instability." I think this is one of the major talks of all those responsible in East and West, and it's particular, too, for us in Germany. We must do everything possible in order to avoid destabilization in Europe, in particular in Eastern Europe. I will do whatever I can to respond to that aim. As a matter of fact, I do not only agree with the President on this but also with Secretary General Gorbachev.

Regarding the relationship between NATO and the Federal Republic, you seem to have made a mistake in your calendar. This is not 1945; this is 1990.

Q. Mr. President, going back to what you were saying before about keeping allies informed, would you like to see a NATO summit called together to discuss the unification?

The President. Well, I will let Chancellor Kohl also respond to that.

I don't think at this juncture we need a NATO summit. Jim Baker just had a very successful and forward-looking meeting up in Ottawa. And I wouldn't say that what's called for now is a NATO summit. We're talking about a CSCE summit, provided there's a CFE agreement.

I have—as the Chancellor knows, and we discussed this—a one-on-one meeting with Mr. Gorbachev in the late spring. We have a G–7 meeting [economic summit]. So, we've got all kinds of consultative mechanisms set up in addition to the two-plus-four, and there'll be a lot of bilateral talks. And maybe the Chancellor would like to respond about the need for NATO, in concert, to do more. But the big point is: Keep each other informed. And I don't think it has to be done at a NATO summit because I think most NATO allies share common ground. There's a concern here or a different suggestion there, but generally speaking, I think we're pretty much on the same wavelength with our allies.

Did you want to add to that here, Herr Chancellor?

The Chancellor. I fully agree with what the President has just said, but let me elaborate on that. What is happening now to many is a surprisingly new situation, including for those who have always talked about it but never thought the day would really come. Now the day is coming. That is why it is so important that we talk to one another as much as possible—so that there be no mistrust. And that is particularly important for us Germans. I agree that this is not the time to convene a NATO summit, but I do agree that we need many detailed conversations within the European Community.

On the 28th of April, we will have an informal summit, an extra summit, just as we have had it in Paris in the beginning of December. The forthcoming one is going to take place in Dublin, Ireland. Now, having the Presidency, I will inform people there. I will also be at the disposal of the representatives of the NATO member states. I have had, and I will be having, a number of contacts. Not long ago, I met with my Italian, Luxembourg, and Dutch colleagues in Italy. Before I came here, I called my friend [Canadian Prime Minister] Mulroney. I had a long telephone conversation with him.

What matters to me is that we make it clear that we play very frankly and fairly and want to cooperate with all our friends and partners, and the result will be good.

Q. For you and for me Germany must be a full member of NATO. And, Mr. President, do you think that at the end of the two-plus-four process there will be a peace treaty—that a peace treaty will then no longer be necessary?

The Chancellor. I can give a very simple answer to the first part of your question: Yes.

The President. And we agree with that. And eventually, the Four Powers that were set up right at the end of the war—that'll have to be resolved. But whether it requires a formal treaty or something of that nature, I'm not sure. But there will be a resolution, so there will not be a continued need for this Four Power arrangement, looking over the shoulders of a democratic, unified Germany.

Q. One question. In these conversations which were so frank and free, did you also discuss what needs to be done in the event that the Soviet Union would not agree to Germany being a member of NATO?

The Chancellor. We talked about many things, and also about what we need to discuss with the Soviet Union.

The President. We will do what Lyndon Johnson did—we will reason together. And it'll all work out.

Nicaragua

Q. Mr. President, with apologies to your guest, a question on another subject. If Daniel Ortega is elected in Nicaragua today, will the United States deal with him as the legitimate leader of Nicaragua? What will your policy be, sir?

The President. Policy will be, short-range, to wait and see how free, how fair the election is. I don't know whether this is going live into Managua, but the last thing I want to do is make any hypothesis about a victory of that sort, because our view is we'd be better off with those who have professed democracy as the route to go. And so, I will cross that bridge when we get there.

However, let me say this: If these elections are certifiably free and fair, whoever wins the election will find a better climate in which to improve relations with Nicaragua. We've had difficulty because Nicaragua has said that they're not giving arms to the FMLN. Now they say, well, if we're elected we won't give arms to the FMLN. There are certain things that are unacceptable not just to the United States but to other countries in this hemisphere. So, we've got to see where we go. But clearly, a free and fair election that is certified as such in spite of the shortcomings that have been reported to me by observers would be very, very helpful in this relationship.

Q. If I may follow: Would such an election call for a U.S. response, an American initiative?

The President. Well, again, it's too hypothetical, because we've got to know not only how an election works out but we also need to know what follows on. I thought the Secretary of State put it very well in testimony before Congress the other day when he said, look, there's got to be a period of establishing—he didn't put it this way, but I will—a bona fides. And I would cite the FMLN as one clear area where there should be change.

A democratic process is important; but what follows on in terms of freedom of the press, freedom of institutions there, freedom to protest, freedom to speak your mind, is also important. And so, all I'll say is that whoever wins that election, if it is certifiably free and fair, that's good. That's a positive thing, and we would certainly take that into strong consideration, the will of the people having been expressed, as we determine what steps next to take. But I would love to see Nicaragua living peacefully within its own borders, not trying to subvert its neighbors, and giving its people a shot at democracy. Once all that was sorted out, why, I can guarantee you there will be better relations with Nicaragua.

German Reunification and Developments in Europe

Q. Chancellor, you talked about elections in December. Seeing the developments in Europe, in Germany, can you foretell that there will be a Federal election, or whether it's an all-German election?

The Chancellor. I do assume that we will have a Federal election as it corresponds to a constitution.

Q. Have you talked about nuclear short-range missiles over the weekend?

The Chancellor. We have talked about how the process should be developed in the near future and what decisions we'll take with regard to the decisions taken in Brussels in spring, last year.

Q. Mr. President, you said you were surprised that perhaps unity was coming sooner than you yourself had expected. Do you believe that those of your other allies within Europe who are cautious about the pace of that unity are wrong, ill-informed, or do they not understand what you have been talking about?

The President. I think they will rejoice in the agreements in what we've said here today. I can understand individuals looking at a problem in a different way. But I can tell you that the alliance is pretty firmly together on the security matters. I think they're going to be very firmly together on what the Chancellor said here today about

NATO membership. And so, I can understand individual countries wanting clarification or raising questions; this doesn't trouble us at all. I have stated the United States position, and I will keep restating it, and I will be discussing this with our allies.

But look, none of our allied leaders have predicted the rapidity of this change or the dynamics of the change in Eastern Europe. And so, we're all trying to sort it out. But the main point is not that there's not nuances of difference but that there is so much common ground as to the way we look at the problems and as to the way we look at it with the Federal Chancellor.

Q. The question is for both leaders. I noticed in your opening remarks you were more specific than the Chancellor in referring to NATO. I wondered if that's an indication that there is some discussion or perhaps some sentiment among the Germans that NATO may somehow fade away or be transformed into a different kind of European security arrangement, and whether that was discussed this weekend?

The President. Well, we ourselves, Jerry [Gerald Seib, Wall Street Journal], have talked about a broader or slightly different roles. Clearly, the stability through the military aspects is part of it. But we've talked— and we've talked up here with Manfred Woerner [Secretary General of NATO] the other day—about a broader role for NATO. But I don't feel at the end of these talks that the Chancellor and I are looking at this differently. If there's some nuances there, I'll let him say so, but I don't think so.

The Chancellor. I can only say this is a very natural thing—that seeing the dramatic changes in the world with which we're confronted. Think only of the Warsaw Pact and its present situation—we are talking with the Warsaw Pact, NATO versus Warsaw Pact, United States versus Soviet Union—we are talking about our future. Manfred Woerner, when he was here, indicated, quite rightly so, that the political importance of the NATO alliance will increase. I think this is important.

And there are quite a few people, including in the reformed states of Central and East Europe, who do not feel threatened by NATO at all, but do consider NATO as a fortress of stability and security. And one has to take that into consideration when one talks about future development. I'm quite optimistic there.

Without developing these ideas further, we will not make any headway in disarmament. And this year we do have the good chance of being able to make headway in disarmament. I do not think that this is the time for pessimism.

Q. Chancellor, of the desire on both of your parts to have a unified Germany remain in NATO, you also said that there should be some kind of special arrangement to provide certain security guarantees for Eastern Europe and the Soviet Union. Does that preclude any participation at all with a unified Germany vis-a-vis the Warsaw Pact? And would it be conceivable that there could actually be Soviet troops in a unified Germany?

The Chancellor. One thing is clear: A united Germany cannot belong to two different pact systems. The other point is a question of sovereignty. We will have transition situations, and that is the subject about which one has to negotiate it. At present, there are 380,000 soldiers of the Soviet Army. Seeing the reductions, one has agreed upon half of that number will be remaining there for the time being. Many things will have to be looked into, and I cannot and will not give any final position here. A united Germany has its own sovereignty—that is quite clear. But then, in the transition period, one can still think about things which will be helpful.

Q. Can you give any more details of what you discussed in terms of providing these security assurances beyond what you've said so far?

The Chancellor. I don't think that is what a press conference is about, because we first must negotiate and then have a press conference about the results.

The President. Let me ask—I notice Mr. Fitzwater looking—that we may have overextended our time. Would it be agreeable, Chancellor Kohl, if we each took one more question?

Q. Mr. President, can you envision a situation where U.S. troops are still deployed in Germany while the Soviet Union has withdrawn all its troops from German soil?

The President. Yes, I can. And the reason I can envision such a situation is that if that's what the Germans want, that's what ought to happen. The U.S. troops are not in Europe against the will of any single country in which they're deployed—not one. And the Soviet troops have been for years inside the territory of countries that haven't wanted them. This is a fundamental difference. So, my answer is yes, I can so envision it.

Q. Mr. Chancellor, both of you have talked about U.S. troops and Soviet troops, but I'd like to ask a question about Germany's own troops. Both the Federal Republic and East Germany, the GDR, have substantial armies. I know a final decision about those armies won't be made until the united Germany is formed, but as you look ahead, what's your personal feeling? Do you think it will be necessary for Germany to retain an army of this size, or in the future will it be likely that those forces will be scaled down?

The Chancellor. Let me say, first of all, that's the question of the strength of forces which concerns us directly, but this question must be embedded in the overall situation, the overall security development. I do hope very much that in the area of disarmament we'll advance in leaps and bounds. And I do hope that we Germans will be able to profit from that.

That is why today I cannot answer that question, in particular since I am not the representative of an old German State. And I cannot tell you at all, in what I mentioned, a future German State would conceive of these things. In this question of will, one has to consider the effect that the answer will have on all our neighbors. I have spontaneously answered to the questions put to me by one of your colleagues. He asked, did we want to have nuclear arms? And I spontaneously said no. And that is of greatest importance. There shouldn't be any fears in that direction.

By the way, this and many other questions I consider to be able to be solved. We have had more difficult questions to solve—if I consider legal questions of private property in GDR, the social structure. So, the task ahead of us is enormous. And that is again why I'd plead it shouldn't be put under time pressure, but we should be advancing and solving these problems step by step.

The President. Thank you all very, very much.

Note: The President's 38th news conference began at 11 a.m. at Camp Greentop, MD. The Chancellor spoke in German, and his remarks were translated by an interpreter. Marlin Fitzwater was Press Secretary to the President.

Remarks to Members of the National Governors' Association
February 26, 1990

Before I talk about the issues that we've been discussing with the Governors, I'd like to make a brief comment on yesterday's election in Nicaragua. Any friend of democracy can take heart in the fact that Violeta Chamorro won the election. And the election process, by all accounts free and fair, is a credit to the people of Nicaragua, who chose to determine their nation's future at the ballot box—and that is a victory for democracy.

Yesterday's election moves us one step closer to the day when every nation in this hemisphere is a democracy. And I'll soon send messages—I think they may have already gone out—to Mrs. Chamorro, congratulating her on her victory; to President Ortega, congratulating him on the conduct of the election and on his pledge to stand by its results; to President Carter and his counterpart on that one, Dan Evans, to Mr. Soares of the OAS, to Perez de Cuellar and Elliot Richardson of the United Nations for their leading roles in observing the elections.

In the next few days I'll be speaking with Central and South American leaders. This morning I talked to President Carlos Andrés Pérez of Venezuela about appropriate trade and economic measures that we can take to support the new government of Nicaragua. We hope now for a peaceful transition, for the institutionalization of the democratic process in Nicaragua. And there is space in a democratic Nicaragua for all political points of view. Given the clear mandate for peace and democracy, there is no reason at all for further military activity from any quarter, and we hope the ceasefire will be reestablished without delay and

respected by all sides. For years the people of Nicaragua have suffered, and today the people of Nicaragua have spoken, and now is the time for Nicaragua to move forward to freedom.

And now back to our agenda at hand. I am very pleased to be with you on this occasion, an occasion which I believe will be viewed in years to come as a dramatic turning point for our country. You've come to Washington for this annual meeting with an uncommon agenda. Today we're launching a new era in education reform. Its focus—high expectations. Its hallmark—results. Its energy—derived from the people of our great nation, who will insist on a world-class education for our kids. For the first time in America's history, we now have national education goals and objectives, goals that pave the way to a decade-long commitment to excellence in education for all Americans, goals that will guide us on the journey toward an American renaissance in education.

We made the commitment to develop national goals last fall there in Charlottesville, Virginia. Five months later, I'm glad to see that the spirit of cooperation and bipartisanship, so much in evidence there at Charlottesville, is still very much alive. That spirit has got to endure. And over the coming months and years, the spirit must serve as a signal to America that our commitment to these common goals remains unshakable, very strong, not for just today, not just tomorrow, but for the rest of the decade, to the year 2000, until we get the job done and get it done right.

You know, only a year or so ago, the

notion of the President and the Governors agreeing on education goals was considered a bold step for America to take. Even now, there are some who say the goals we've established are too ambitious. I think they're mistaken. They've failed to appreciate the depth of our commitment to restructuring and change.

We've all been following the extraordinary events which have unfolded before our eyes in Eastern Europe over the last year, and there is a lesson in those events for all of us in this room and for all Americans. And that lesson is: When people unite behind common goals and demand the freedom to pursue their dreams, no system can stop them. And nothing will stop us.

There is nothing more important to the long-term stability and stature of America than establishing a first-class education system. Nothing is more important to a competitive America in the 21st century. Nothing is more important to improving the quality of life for our citizens. And nothing is more important than the promise inherent in these goals that all children in America can realize their fullest potential and reach out for their dreams.

I want to see these goals posted on the wall in every school so that all who walk in—the parents, students, teachers—know what we're aiming for, so that everyone knows the goal we have set for ourselves the goal that every child will be ready to learn from the first day they walk into the classroom; the goal of raising the graduation rate to 90 percent by making our schools meaningful, challenging, and relevant to the needs of our students; of setting high standards of achievement among our students, seeing that they leave the transition grades of 4, 8, and 12 having mastered the important subject matter; the goal of achieving first place in math and science among industrialized nations; of every American adult being skilled and literate, equipped to be a productive worker and a responsible citizen; and finally, the goal of every school in America being safe, disciplined, and drug-free.

These goals and objectives have been developed with a great deal of energy and effort over these past 5 months and with the input of hundreds of citizens from all sectors of society. And I want to thank everyone who has participated in this process. Governor Branstad and the members of your education task force, I thank you for your commitment, your dedication, and all the hundreds of hours of hard work—that as we acknowledge this first step, we've also got to recognize that hard work lies ahead.

Over the next few months, I know you'll be looking at strategies in your States which will move us forward to these goals, and strategies that will focus on measuring progress by results, by how well students are doing. One of the Governors encouraged me in the meeting in there to encourage the people of this country to support State and local initiatives that have to do with making the educational system better. And certainly I am prepared to do that, just as I am grateful to the Governors for their participation in setting these goals.

In the coming months, we'll work together with Congress on legislation to increase flexibility in Federal funding in return for enhanced accountability. And you, the Nation's Governors, have committed to break the bureaucratic shackles that smother innovation and stand guard over the status quo. Although the Federal Government traditionally has a limited role in education—and we all respect and acknowledge that it is the dynamism at the State and local level that achieves excellence—I promise you that this administration is determined to walk with you every step of the way.

When I next meet with my Cabinet, many of whom were with us there in Charlottesville, I'll ask each to work with our domestic policy adviser to devise strategies that can support your efforts and those of your communities in helping to achieve these goals. I will work with you to establish a bipartisan group to ensure that proper and constructive measurements of our educational performance are developed where they don't already exist. And this group is going to report to me each year on the progress we make.

And I'm calling on America's private sector to be a third party in this enterprise. We need to know from them what the workplace will need and expect of our citizens in the 21st century. And we need their talent and their commitment to help move this reform effort forward. And finally, I will do everything I can to provide the national leadership and energy to keep education in the forefront of America's domestic agenda.

The work ahead will not be easy. We're traveling uncharted waters. And never before have we as a nation set such goals for education. And never before have the Nation's leaders stepped forward to say we are willing to be held accountable for the results of this process. And never before have the President of the United States and the Governors joined together in a partnership and a long-term commitment on a single issue.

If we can accomplish just one thing today—and it may be the simplest and yet most valuable of all—it is to send a message to parents, teachers, community leaders, and every other American: These goals are not the Governors' goals. They're not the President's goals. They are the Nation's goals. And we are rejecting the status quo, raising our sights, investing our faith in the American people. And so, today I hope the Governors and the Cabinet will join me in extending a challenge to all Americans to adopt these goals as their own and to take aim now at the year 2000 and to enlist every ounce of American innovation, energy, resolve in the effort to achieve these education goals and prepare this nation for the challenges of a new century.

Thank you all very, very much for your superb cooperation.

Note: The President spoke at 11:59 a.m. in the East Room at the White House. Prior to his remarks, the President met with members of the association in the Blue Room.

Remarks Announcing the Publication of "Growing Up Drug Free: A Parent's Guide to Prevention"
February 26, 1990

The President. Thank you, all of you. And welcome, all of you, and welcome to the White House. We are here, as Secretary Cavazos, our outstanding Secretary of Education, said, to unveil this little book. And I must say I cheated—I saw it ahead of time. [*Laughter*] I saw it when we were walking over, and I think it's going to do a lot of good. It's titled "Growing Up Drug Free: A Parent's Guide to Prevention," published by the Secretary's Department. And it's written for parents who are concerned about their kids and illustrated by a number of promising young artists who are with us today. And this guidebook is being released because we all care about kids, about keeping their futures bright with promise and keeping them free of the enslavement of drugs.

And you, like all Americans, understand that our children are our best and brightest hope. But you don't get a prep course before becoming a parent, and kids don't come with owner's manuals. They have minds and problems of their own. So, the best thing parents can do is talk to them; just as important, listen to them; and know the facts about drugs and the warning signs that a kid's in trouble. And above all, we parents can make sure that our actions are as good as our words. Where illegal drugs and alcohol abuse are concerned, for too long we have condoned what we should have condemned. And that's what this book is about—knowing when and how to talk to your kids, when to listen, where to draw the line, and when to get help.

This guidebook sets forth simple steps that parents can take for their kids from preschool to high school. It talks about how to make your values and your high expectations known to your kids, how to remind the children that drugs kill dreams and destroy lives, how to make rules and then stick with them. And it emphasizes the importance of telling your kids when they're doing right, because every time you do, every time you help to cultivate character, you're providing another reason not to do drugs.

Schools, churches, synagogues, community groups, law enforcement—all can help us turn the tide on drug and alcohol abuse, but none can take a parent's place. Drug education must begin at home and in the neighborhood long before the classroom.

I want to thank the young people here today, those up here and some that I see scattered out there, and thank those who did the artwork that they've done for this book—and for the example that you all are setting for other kids all across the country. And I want to urge parents everywhere to read—hold this for me, would you?— [*laughter*]—to read "Growing Up Drug Free." With open minds and listening hearts, parents need to hear what their kids

have to say. So, show your kids how ready you are just to listen. And it's often surprising how much they want to do the right thing.

And now I'd like to take this one, and one of the first copies of this parent's handbook to Ann Lynch, the president of the National PTA. Ann, it's good to see you. And that one is for you, you lucky duck.

Ms. Lynch. Thank you. I am so pleased. Thank you. On behalf of the parents, I thank you. Now I have to figure out what to do with it.

The President. Thank you all very much.

Note: The President spoke at 3:05 p.m. in Room 450 of the Old Executive Office Building.

Statement on the Election of Violeta Chamorro as President of Nicaragua
February 26, 1990

In this remarkable year of political change, democracy won another victory yesterday. I am most pleased that there has been a free and fair election in Nicaragua and that the results are being accepted by both sides.

I am sending messages to Mrs. Chamorro congratulating her on her victory and to President Ortega congratulating him on the conduct of the election and his stated willingness to abide by the results. The United States looks forward to working with Mrs. Chamorro's new government in support of her stated goals of national reconciliation and economic reconstruction, and with President Ortega in helping ensure a peaceful transition of power. I have talked this morning with Venezuelan President Carlos Andrés Pérez, and we agree completely on the need to help all parties in Nicaragua to achieve a peaceful reconciliation and transfer of power.

We also congratulate the international observer delegations whose activities, which took place at the request of the Sandinista

government, helped ensure an open and safe electoral process. There were many, but I want to mention delegations led by former President Jimmy Carter and former Governor Dan Evans, the United Nations delegation led by former Secretary Elliot Richardson, and the OAS delegation led by Secretary General Baena Soares.

We hope that all sides in this hotly fought contest will extend the hand of reconciliation and cooperate together in rebuilding their country for the good of all Nicaraguans. There is space in a democratic Nicaragua for the expression of all political points of view. We also hope that the cease-fire will be reestablished immediately and respected by all sides. Given the election's clear mandate for peace and democracy, there is no reason at all for further military activity from any quarter.

We are confident the international community will strongly support the results of yesterday's elections and will join in the effort to help all Nicaraguans to rebuild their country.

Statement by Press Secretary Fitzwater on the Nicaraguan Presidential Elections
February 26, 1990

President Bush called President-elect Chamorro of Nicaragua to congratulate her on her election victory. President Bush noted that this is a great day for the people of Nicaragua. President Bush said the election reinforces the Nicaraguan people's commitment to the peace process and towards building a free and open society.

In addition, President Bush called Prime Minister Thatcher [of the United Kingdom], President Mitterrand [of France], and President Salinas [of Mexico] to thank them for the support they had exhibited over the past months for the return to a democratic process in Nicaragua. Prime Minister Mulroney [of Canada] called President Bush to discuss the Nicaraguan election and to express his support on behalf of the transfer to democratic rule.

Statement by Press Secretary Fitzwater on the White House Conference on Science and Economics Research Related to Global Change
February 26, 1990

President Bush today invited a number of countries, the European Community, and the Organization of Economic Cooperation and Development (OECD) to send official delegations to a White House Conference on Science and Economics Research Related to Global Change. The Conference will be held in Washington, DC, April 17–18, 1990.

The President announced his intention to host this Conference during his meeting with President Gorbachev and again recently in a speech to the United Nations Intergovernmental Panel on Climate Change.

The Conference will be devoted to science and economics issues relevant to policy on global environmental issues, including climate change. It is designed to substantially enhance and broaden international understanding of the important science and economics research issues related to global change.

The Conference will also assist in framing a strategy for implementing a joint international understanding of this science and economics research effort, and linking that knowledge to the policy process both nationally and internationally. The administration considers the Conference a vital next step in a joint international approach to address possible changes in the global environment.

Conference participants have been invited to send delegations consisting of their senior scientific, environmental, and economic officials. The President has designated the Director of the Office of Science and Technology Policy, Dr. D. Allan Bromley; the Chairman of the Council of Economic Advisers, Dr. Michael Boskin; and the Chairman of the Council on Environmental Quality, Mr. Michael R. Deland, to serve as Cochairmen of this Conference.

Message to the Senate Transmitting the Algeria-United States Consular Convention
February 27, 1990

To the Senate of the United States:

I am transmitting, for the Senate's advice and consent to ratification, the Consular Convention between the United States of America and the Democratic and Popular Republic of Algeria signed at Washington on January 12, 1989. I am also transmitting, for the information of the Senate, the report of the Department of State with respect to the convention.

The signing of this convention is a significant step in the process of enhancing and broadening the relationship between the United States and Algeria. There currently does not exist a bilateral agreement on consular relations between the two countries. The convention sets forth clear obligations with respect to matters such as notification of consular officers of the arrest and detention of nationals of their country and protection of the rights and interests of nationals of their country.

The people of the United States and Algeria have a tradition of friendship and cooperation. I welcome the opportunity through this consular convention to promote the good relations between the two countries. I recommend the Senate give early and favorable consideration to the convention and give its advice and consent to ratification.

GEORGE BUSH

The White House,
February 27, 1990.

Remarks Following Discussions With Charles Haughey, Prime Minister of Ireland and President of the European Council
February 27, 1990

The President. Well, it's been a great pleasure to meet today with Prime Minister Haughey. The last time we met was almost a year ago, as we celebrated St. Patrick's Day here at the White House and renewed the shared values and kinship that have bound our two nations together for over 200 years. Nine signers of the Declaration of Independence proudly claimed Ireland as their ancestral home. And so, it's an honor to welcome the Taoiseach to America's home—designed by an Irishman, I might add.

And today the Prime Minister is visiting Washington, though, in another capacity: as the President of the European Council. And with the rapid change we're witnessing across Eastern Europe and the Soviet Union, the relationship between the United States and the European Community has never been more important.

The Revolution of '89 brought with it new opportunities and challenges, and it is critical that we work to make the strong bonds between this nation and its European friends even stronger. The Prime Minister and I had a productive discussion of the many issues of great interest to the United States, to the EC, to Ireland, including the prospect of German unification, regional issues around the world; and we touched on Northern Ireland as well.

I was especially interested in the Prime Minister's views on the new architecture of Europe. He and I agree on the principles that should guide the design of the new Europe. First, we both welcome the prospect of overcoming the artificial division of the continent and building a Europe whole and free, united by universal values that are based on freedom and democracy. And second, there is no question that Western solidarity protects stability in this time of change and that transatlantic cooperation now is more important than ever. As I've said before, the United States will remain a European power. Third, we both look to the Conference on Security and Cooperation in Europe, the CSCE, to play a greater role in Europe's future, including guidance for the conduct of truly free elections and the transition from planned economies to pluralistic systems. Fourth, we believe the EC must play a vital role in the new Europe.

A more united Europe, able to take its rightful place in world affairs, is good for the United States of America. And we'll look for ways to improve our ties to the Community so a new Atlanticism will be teamed with a new Europe.

And today's meeting takes us forward in building new structures for the U.S. relationship with the Community. We committed ourselves to regular meetings between myself and the President of the EC to provide overall political guidance for the relationship. We agreed to twice yearly meetings between the EC Foreign Ministers and our Secretary of State. And we committed ourselves to joint efforts in the war against drugs and our hopes to preserve the global environment.

We do not expect perfect agreement between the United States and the EC on every issue, but we do agree that our inherent belief in the value of freedom, democracy, opportunity binds us together and that our mutual cooperation can benefit all. And we also agree that the historic ties of friendship between our two countries, the United States and Ireland, can serve the cause of peace in the international arena.

We're grateful for Ireland's efforts to encourage and enhance U.S.-EC cooperation. And we also appreciate Ireland's efforts to promote economic development, security, reconciliation, and peace in Northern Ireland. In a time when all things seem possible, all Americans hope for an end to the conflict that has brought such sadness to your beautiful land and your wonderful people.

Mr. Prime Minister, we wish you Godspeed on your journey home. The days ahead are exciting ones, full of expectations, and together, they can be days of great cooperation and great progress for all people. Thank you, sir, for your leadership. Thank you for your friendship. And God bless the United States and Ireland. Thank you, sir.

The Prime Minister. Mr. President, ladies and gentlemen, my visit to Washington takes place at a time of profound international change. The President and I, in my capacity as President of the European Council, discussed U.S.-European Community relations and their future evolution in the context of the Community's increasingly important role on the international, political, and economic scene.

The President and I agreed, at this time, to strengthen the links between the European Community and the United States. We agreed for that purpose, as the President has said, that a meeting between the U.S. President and each President in office of the European Council should become a regular feature of the U.S.-European Community relations, and that one such meeting should be held each Presidency of the European Council. And I'll be recommending that to my European colleagues, the heads of state or government of the European Community, immediately on my return. We also agreed that the Foreign Ministers of the Community will meet the U.S. Secretary of State on two occasions a year, at least. In addition, the European Commission is taking steps to increase the frequency of its formal meetings with the U.S. Cabinet. This arrangement will give us both a better overall structure and direction to the wide variety of existing contacts and discussions, and they will also provide a new framework for enhanced political and economic ties between the Community and the United States. We are, in fact, building a broader bridge across the Atlantic.

We also, the President and I, discussed areas for specific cooperation; and we agreed that the fight against international drug trafficking and the international movement of drug funds are areas very appropriate for specific cooperation. We shared common concerns on the need for continuing efforts to protect the environment in areas such as global climate change, the depletion of the ozone layer, and endangered species. And may I say that I think it's entirely appropriate that I, who have set myself the aim of being of a green Presidency of the European Community, should be having these discussions at this stage with President Bush, who has set for himself the role of environmental President in the United States.

During our meeting, we also reviewed developments in Central and Eastern Europe; in particular, implications of German unification. The President and I agreed that the United States and the Community have a pivotal role to play in overcoming the divisions between East and West and in laying the foundations for a Europe united in its commitment to peace, prosperity, democracy, and above all a respect for human rights and fundamental freedoms.

The President and I also discussed a number of bilateral issues, including immigration, super royalties, passive foreign investment companies, and of course the situation in Northern Ireland. And I greatly appreciate the President's deep personal concern for the situation in Northern Ire-

land and his constant wish to be of any possible assistance he can in bringing forward a solution to that intractable and difficult and tragic problem. I expressed my appreciation for constructive U.S. interest and support for Anglo-Irish relations.

Mr. President, it has been for me a great pleasure to have had the benefit of talking to you and receiving the benefit of your views and your insights into European and, indeed, international affairs at this very exciting time for all humanity. Thank you very much, indeed.

The President. Well, thank you, sir. Well spoken, and thank you very much. It's a great pleasure to have you here. Holler if we can do any more.

Note: The President spoke at 1:24 p.m. at the South Portico of the White House. Prior to their remarks, the President and the Prime Minister met privately in the Oval Office and with U.S. and Irish officials in the Cabinet Room, and then attended a luncheon in the Old Family Dining Room.

Joint Statement by President Bush and President Charles Haughey of the European Council
February 27, 1990

We meet at a time of historic international change. Our discussions focused on U.S./E.C. relations and their future evolution, in the context of close transatlantic cooperation and of the E.C.'s increasingly important role on the international political and economic scene.

Today's meeting took place against the background of U.S. interest in enhancing its relations with the European Community as outlined in President Bush's speech last May and Secretary of State Baker's speech in Berlin in December. The President of the European Council expressed the Community's appreciation of the positive attitude of the U.S. administration to the Community's role and development. He also emphasized that the Community and its Member States share the U.S. interest in developing our relations.

We agreed on the significance of our meeting for strengthening relations between the U.S. and the E.C. We also agreed that such meetings between the President of the United States and the President of the European Council should become a regular feature of U.S./E.C. relations and that at least one such meeting should be held during each Presidency of the European Council.

These meetings will serve to give overall political direction to the further development of consultation and cooperation.

The arrangements will also include twice-yearly meetings between EC Foreign Ministers and the U.S. Secretary of State. We agreed that such a meeting should take place in the first half of 1990.

We see the arrangements discussed today as important first steps in an evolving process towards a new framework for enhanced political and economic ties between the E.C. and the U.S.

We both agreed that areas of common interest meriting further examination as subjects for practical cooperation should be identified. At this stage, we agreed that the fight against international drug trafficking and the international movement of drug funds are areas appropriate for specific cooperation. The same is true of our continuing efforts to protect the environment in areas such as global climate change, the depletion of the ozone layer, and endangered species. We agreed that there will be further contact at the appropriate levels to follow up our discussions on these areas and to identify other areas of common interest.

At our meeting, we also reviewed devel-opments in Central and Eastern Europe, in particular the implications of German unification. We also discussed the CSCE, and the progress towards and prospects for European integration. We both agreed that, with their political ideals and common values, the U.S. and the E.C. have a pivotal role to play in overcoming the divisions between East and West and in laying the foundations for a Europe more united in its commitment to peace, prosperity, democracy, and respect for human rights and fundamental freedoms. Our meeting today makes a valuable contribution to enhancing that pivotal role.

Note: The joint statement referred to the Conference on Security and Cooperation in Europe (CSCE).

Remarks Congratulating the Super Bowl Champion San Francisco 49ers
February 27, 1990

The President. Who was it—Yogi [Berra] used to talk about deja vu all over again. Well, here we are, and Barbara and I are just delighted. It seems, really—and the talk in coming through the line—that only just yesterday it seemed that we celebrated the last Super Bowl victory, and now here we are. So, to Eddie DeBartolo and the staff, certainly Coach Seifert and all the players of the 49ers and families, congratulations and welcome to the White House. It's a joy to have you here.

You know, when I first heard that this occasion was in honor of one of the greatest victories in American championship history, I couldn't help but look around and wonder: So, where's Buster Douglas? [*Laughter*]

But we do have with us the man that I know all you guys recognize. And I hope all of you saw my friend and our new Chairman of the President's Council on Physical Fitness, larger than life himself, but confessed that he felt like Danny DeVito standing next to these guys. [*Laughter*] And I'm talking about our friend and a man who is undertaking a very important job for this country, heading the President's Fitness Council, Arnold Schwarzenegger. Arnold, thank you very much for being here. I think Arnold and my old colleague from the Congress, the guy sitting next to him—used to pitch in the major leagues, Senator Ben Mizell—And we're having a meeting on national fitness tomorrow, so you guys be careful. We may need you for a little leadership for the kids in this country.

But today we're here, though, to honor the 'Niners. Coach Seifert, I hesitate to call this your rookie year. Your team is carrying into the nineties the title the Steelers carried into the seventies: Team of the Decade. I won't mention America's team, the Cowboys—[*laughter*]—but we'll come back someday.

Of course, this last Super Bowl seemed to have been over sometime around the end of the national anthem. [*Laughter*] And in fact, I was asked to do—this is true—public service commercial aired twice during the game, once in the first quarter, once in the fourth. And the five people who saw it the second time—[*laughter*]—been invited as special guests to the White House. All of them work for me. [*Laughter*]

Joe Cool—where did Joe go? Where's Joe Montana? I don't spot him back there. There he is, hiding in the back row. But I was impressed by your performance once again—unsurprised, however. You see, back in '79, Joe played against the University of Houston in the Cotton Bowl. And down by 22 in the fourth quarter and sick with the flu, he still brought Notre Dame back for a win. As a Houstonian there are some things you never forget. [*Laughter*] Joe, go right back where you came from. [*Laughter*]

Now you're MVP for '82, '85, and '90. And in the Super Bowl XXIV, you threw for a record five touchdowns. Cooler than the other side of a pillow. [*Laughter*] Fair to say he's the most accurate passer in the NFL—70 percent. Never thrown a Super Bowl interception.

And Jerry Rice—three touchdown passes in one game. And of course, I couldn't fail to mention John Taylor, wide receiver, tight end Brent Jones—each with a touchdown to his credit.

And what I said last year applies today: While Joe and Jerry handled the aerial attack, Roger Craig ground out that tough yardage on the ground. And once again, he's shown what the words "Gold Rush" mean. And Tom Rathman, with whom I've just spoke in the line there, you've had an outstanding season, topped off by two bulldozing touchdowns. The only thing is, Tom, I wish you could get over this Mr. Nice image that you've recently developed on the playing field. [*Laughter*] Mike Cofer, seven for eight—that's about as close to perfection as a player can get.

The offensive line—superb, a five-man strategic defense initiative, really, protecting Joe. And here's to the powers of the 'Niners defense, led by Ronnie Lott. I understand that Ronnie gave the team a boost even before the national anthem, with his usual stirring pregame speech. Funny how guys named Ronnie—[*laughter*]—seem to have a knack for this "Win one for the Gipper," you know, kind of thing. [*Laughter*]

You have all impressed America with a truly awesome performance. In the mean-time, let me say—and I know you guys will understand it—express my appreciation for the Broncos. They are true sportsmen. You clobbered them. But they're a good team, and they came on to get into the Super Bowl. They're also—though you beat them—number two in the NFL, a considerable honor.

But the greatest honor should go to a 49er who's always at your side, someone who's shown great determination, someone with valor—your defensive back, Jeff Fuller.

It's a little wonder that many are calling the 49ers a dynasty. You've shown us that to excel in football, as in anything, a team must be passionately dedicated to excellence. When asked about this, Joe simply says: "I see myself as a man struggling in a business that's very competitive." Well put—a bit understated, but very well put. This fighting spirit is the hallmark of each and every member of this team and, I might add, the entire staff of the 49er organization. So, I want to congratulate you, and I'd be remiss if I didn't make one concluding pitch. You don't have too much time off now, with some of you going back to your communities—a lot of fellow Texans up here, several from Georgia, many, of course, from the coast. But I urge you to take some of this fame that you have earned and help the kids in this country stay off of drugs and learn to read and grow up to be the kind of sportsmen that each and every one of you are.

Thank you for coming to the White House. We're just delighted to have you all here, really. Now, where's Eddie? Oh, here he is. Good.

Mr. DeBartolo. Thank you very much, Mr. President. Thank you, Mr. President and Mrs. Bush. Thank you so much for having us back here and for your hospitality. And I know how very busy you are. We have a little present for the youngest member of your family to help her nights at Camp David to stay a little bit warmer. This [49er sweater] is for Millie.

Mrs. Bush. Oh, it's so cute. He wouldn't let me bring her down.

Mr. DeBartolo. I know. We saw her in the backyard.

The President. Well, thank you all.

Note: The President spoke at 2:50 p.m. in the East Room at the White House. Edward J. DeBartolo is owner of the San Francisco 49ers.

Exchange With Reporters on the President's Telephone Conversation With Chairman Mikhail Gorbachev of the Soviet Union
February 28, 1990

The President. Well, I just wanted to mention that this morning I had a very good talk with President Gorbachev. We touched on matters relating to Nicaragua and Central America and also matters relating to the changes in Europe. I'm not going to say any more on the details of the talk, but it was a very constructive conversation. I thanked him for his reception of Jim Baker and the time he gave him, and told him that Jim had filled me in on the details on the arms control agenda, and reassured him that I wanted to conclude the agenda as set out by the Secretary with Mr. Shevardnadze [Soviet Foreign Minister]. And as I say, we discussed the matters here in this hemisphere and in Eastern Europe.

So, it was a good talk, and I'm going to continue to try to have consultation. He agreed that these kinds of conversation are very useful. And so, I just wanted to get that on the record.

Q. Did you call him?

The President. Yes, I called him, yes.

Q. You talked about the Nicaraguan elections and then——

The President. Well, no, just to review these two areas. And I think we need to be doing a little more of that kind of thing, and I think he agrees. So it was—the mood of it, that's hard to define, but it was very good, very forthright. Where we differ, we can spell out the differences without rancor. And I think that's important in the Soviet-U.S. relationship.

And as Chancellor Kohl [of the Federal Republic of Germany] impressed on me up there at Camp David, the importance to the world of how the U.S. and the Soviet Union interact just cannot be overemphasized. So, it was good.

Q. Why did you want to call him? Generally, you have something specific that you want to request of him.

The President. Well, just to discuss these two areas. No, nothing specific, just these two areas. And I'm not going to go into the details of the talk. But I think it's important that there be some confidentiality if we're going to be able to speak as frankly as we did today. And so, I can't give you the full agenda, but I can tell you it was a very good one.

Q. How long did you talk?

The President. I'd say it was about 40 minutes, something like that.

Q. Did you have trouble getting through to him when you called?

The President. No, we set a time to take the call. He had matters on his mind yesterday that we've all read about, and so, we decided to do it today. But we touched on a lot of matters, and it was good.

Q. Did you talk about the Presidential powers bill?

The President. No, not in detail.

Q. Do you want Gorbachev to impress on Ortega [President of Nicaragua] the importance of turning over control——

The President. Well, I was very pleased with the Soviet statements about recognizing the winners of the election. And I think a lot of that stems from leaders in this hemisphere, to be sure that peaceful transition takes place.

Note: A tape was not available for verification of the content of the exchange, which occurred in the morning aboard Air Force One, en route to Staten Island, NY.

Remarks at a Fundraising Luncheon for Congressional Candidate Susan Molinari in Staten Island, New York
February 28, 1990

Thank you very, very much for that warm Staten Island welcome. Thank you all. Please, be seated. Susan, thank you for that warm welcome back. And let me say to those citizens of this marvelous part of New York, I was deeply touched, and I believe Susan was, when we rode in from the landing zone out here, to see the kids in the streets. And I want to thank everybody involved with this visit: first off, the firefighters that were there to greet us; the police officers, who do so much for every one of us, regardless of the politics, every single day; and then the kids that turned out. And I learned something long ago—it isn't George Bush; it's the Presidency. And I wish you all could be in that beautiful black limousine with Susan and me and just see the respect for the institution, the job, really, that I'm proud to hold. It was very, very moving for us, just as this welcome back is very moving for me.

I'm delighted that our able State chairman is with us, Pat Barrett, the guy that did it all in business and then rolled up his sleeves and put something back in the system by taking on this enormously important organizational job as chairman of the State party.

I had a chance a minute ago to visit with one of my dear friends and supporters, who was one of his predecessors, George Clark, who's here today someplace, too.

And I want to pay my respects to Olga Igneri, Richmond County Republican chairman, and Fred Pantaleone [Kings County Republican chairman], from over across the way—I've known for a long time, and another great party leader. Mike Long, the State Conservative Party chairman, is here, and we're grateful to him. And I'm so pleased to be with another young old friend of mine, Nelson Rockefeller; I want to see this guy involved in politics, too. I keep telling him that, but he's—[*applause*]. But of course we're here today to salute the 14th Congressional District's next Representative, and I'm talking about the one in

blue here, Susan Molinari. It's essential that she be elected.

And I also would be remiss if I didn't at least mention—[*laughter*]—another Molinari, one of the outstanding leaders on Capitol Hill, who is now back home to stay, tearing them up right here at home, Guy Molinari, my friend. And what a job he's doing, and I will always be grateful to him.

Deputy Borough President Jim Molinaro is also here today, and I salute him—a man I've known a long time.

But one more word about Guy. He was there very early on for me. And this room is full of a lot of politicians—a lot of statesmen out here, too, I see—but there's some politicians out here. And you never forget how you got where you're at. And Guy Molinari was at my side long ago when the going was tough and the pollsters had it figured out just about the way they had figured out Nicaragua. [*Laughter*] And so, I'm proud that he's here with us.

The Silver Fox sends her best. She didn't want to put her hairdo up against Guy Molinari's, so she stayed home. [*Laughter*] Sorry about that.

But look, the only reason we're kind of imposing on you before lunch is that this is the first stop on a cross-country trip—on our way to California as soon as I leave here, talking to Californians about some of the things Susan mentioned—fighting drugs, fighting crime—issues which certainly concern all New Yorkers, and I want to mention them to you today, too. I'll also be meeting with the Prime Minister of Japan on Friday and then again on Saturday morning to discuss another important issue. It's an issue of concern to everybody in this country and certainly in this dynamic area: the American competitiveness in the Pacific Rim.

It's been—well, I guess Susan touched on this—almost 25 years since a President came to Staten Island—President Johnson dedicating the bridge. And today I'm here to talk about another bridge, a bridge to the future, an election that will determine whether Staten Island gets the experience and leadership and independence that it deserves, the election of the next Congresswoman from New York: Susan Molinari.

So, here I am in the middle of the battle right here in New York, where one of the great contests of 1990 will take place. A lot at stake—there's been a lot of money spent on both sides, a lot of press attention. But I'm not here to talk about the Trumps. [*Laughter*]

You know, I'm here to talk about this congressional race. And look, you know it and I know it and the people know it here: Guy has left some big shoes to fill. But I can think of no one better to do the job than Susan. And this isn't kind of Johnny-come-lately because Barbara and I have known her for a long, long time. Like her dad, Susan is going to have that hands-on leadership the voters have come to expect from the name Molinari.

Speaking of names, I'll tell you a true story. Susan found a scrawny little mutt on election day 1988. We were all waiting for the returns to come in, but the dog wasn't doing well, and they didn't think it would make it. But it was a good dog—loyal, cautious, prudent, some would say timid—and it pulled through. I still can't figure out why Susan named the dog George. [*Laughter*] But she did. And being a female pup— [*laughter*]—she'll have it even tougher. Life ain't easy for a girl named George. [*Laughter*] Let me give you a little serious, political, inside advice, one single word: puppies—worth 10 points, believe me. [*Laughter*]

I understand that Susan's opponent is charging that she'll do nothing but follow in her father's footsteps. That's a marvelous endorsement as far as I'm concerned, a very good endorsement.

But look, she's established it here—an independent, tough leader—the determination, the understanding, and the experience to get the job done. And when she was 27, she was already making history: youngest member ever elected to the New York City Council, first Republican elected from her district, the only Republican elected to the council—and she beat her Democratic opponent for reelection 3 to 1. Susan is the

new generation of leadership. And she's been tested. She has been tested. During her tenure as minority leader on the council, she's held her own as the toughest "minority of one" that anybody's ever seen.

The effects of her leadership will be felt for many years. She opened the door for other Republicans to follow. She gave this party a voice where, literally, there was none. A great bipartisan leader, she proved that the only fair system is a two-party system.

Her opponent says that she can't possibly be effective in Congress because she's not in the majority party. Poor guy, he doesn't understand that there's a direct correlation between effectiveness and experience, between effectiveness and leadership, between effectiveness and independence. And Susan is the only candidate in the race with all three. Plus she has something else—a friend in the White House. And that's not going to hurt her a single bit.

The Republican leadership needs her in Congress because they need her drive, they need this initiative, and they need this experience I've been talking about. And I need her because we agree fundamentally on the issues: a strong economy; schools and streets free from drugs and violence; a clean, safe environment. We both agree that we need action on these issues and that we need it now.

Drug abuse—we had a little receiving line down there for some of the heavy hitters or heaviest lifters or whatever it was, I don't know. [*Laughter*] But more people came through the line: "Don't give up on the fight against drugs." I'm not about to. Drug abuse is a threat to all America, and it's an especially threat here, I'm told, right here in Staten Island. Only a few miles from here, remember the name Everett Hatcher, a veteran DEA agent brutally murdered by cocaine cowards. In the days after his death, his wife put the blame for his death squarely on the shoulders of the so-called casual drug users. We have to win the war on drugs for Everett Hatcher and all those who have given their lives to free America of drug abuse. And we will. And we are making progress, and I need Susan to help out on the legislative side of things.

One of the most vital issues—and she's been talking about that in the campaign—is the protection of our planet. Staten Islanders face some of the toughest environmental problems in this country, and Susan will fight, and fight hard, to reduce those air toxics and urban smog.

Right now, we have clean air legislation that I sent up to the Congress. It's strong. It's the toughest revision of the Clean Air Act that's been proposed in a long, long time. And the legislation is up there in both the House and the Senate. I think Susan will take the oath in time to make a difference. We've laid down what I would call a fairminded compromise to help clean up our air and yet not throw everybody in Staten Island out of work in the process. We've got to be able to grow, and we've got to be able to protect clean air and protect our environment. And that's what I'm fighting for, and that's what I want her help on in Washington, DC. What I want to see is break this stalemate. Let's protect our environment for decades to come. We've already shown we can get the lead out. And now, let's finish the job.

Susan gets action on the environment. You know, when that Exxon spill left sludge on the shores of Staten Island, she got the company officials into her office. By the time they left, the company had agreed to the Molinari nine-point plan for cleanup. And that is tough, effective leadership, and that's what I call results.

There's another result we ought to briefly talk about, and that's the result of 9 years of Republican leadership at the Federal level: lower taxes, the greatest economic expansion in history. And we've got to keep this economy strong so we can keep America strong. Susan and I believe that holding the line on taxes is the key to making America competitive in the global marketplace. She and I know we can outproduce and outmarket and outsell everybody else if we can keep the taxes low on the American working man and working woman and business people. I am going to keep my word and keep those taxes down.

Susan understands what the voters want, because like Staten Island, she does have a proud heritage and this brilliant future I've told you about. Let me tell you a story.

Eighty-six years ago, a battered steamer pulled into New York Harbor, and a 6-year-old boy—one of 14 kids—and his mother stepped off onto Ellis Island, ready to join his father and siblings after leaving their home on the coast of southern Italy. Looking across the harbor to the Statue of Liberty, little Bob Molinari took the oath of allegiance and became an American. Years later, that small boy became a successful businessman. He taught his five children the value of education and of hard work. He held down three jobs, put himself through night school, and then decided that it was time to give something back to this new land that had given him so much. He entered public service, serving Staten Island tirelessly in the State assembly.

Guy says that his dad was terribly proud of the United States; then he added, "and he never let us forget it." Guy felt the same way about education, about being an American, about his service to his country. When he was sworn into office not far from here, he, too, took his oath at the foot of the Statue of Liberty. The light that glows from the huge statue's torch shines over Staten Island—and beside this great community she stands, looking forward to the world and to the future. Now the time has come for Susan Molinari to lead Staten Island forward.

America has given her a lot. I bet she'd agree with that—a wonderful family, an education, and the opportunity to be the best that she can be. And so, now, like her granddad and her father before her, she wants to give something back, some of the blessings that America has given her. She cares about this country, and she has served you, the people of Staten Island, well. And it is a time now, in this very important seat, for a new generation of leadership.

Your future and that of your children are precious. They're very precious, indeed. We need experience, we need independence, we need honest leadership for a strong Staten Island, of course, and a strong United States. We need her kind of total commitment. And that's why I came up here to tell you we need Susan Molinari in the United States Congress.

Thank you all. And God bless you, and

thanks for the welcome back.

Note: The President spoke at 12:44 p.m. in *the Grand Ballroom at Shalimar Hall. Following his remarks, he traveled to San Francisco, CA.*

Message to the Senate Transmitting a Protocol to the International Civil Aviation Convention
February 28, 1990

To the Senate of the United States:

With a view to receiving the advice and consent of the Senate to ratification, I transmit herewith the Protocol Relating to an Amendment to Article 56 of the Convention on International Civil Aviation, done at Montreal on October 6, 1989. I also transmit, for the information of the Senate, the report received from the Department of State with respect to the protocol.

Article 56 of the convention concerns the composition of the Air Navigation Commission of the International Civil Aviation Or-

ganization and currently provides that it shall be composed of 15 members. The present protocol would increase the membership of the Commission to 19 members.

I recommend the Senate give early and favorable consideration to the protocol submitted herewith and give its advice and consent to ratification.

GEORGE BUSH

The White House,
February 28, 1990.

Remarks at a Fundraising Dinner for Gubernatorial Candidate Pete Wilson in San Francisco, California
February 28, 1990

Thank you so much for that welcome. And, Pete, oh, how strongly I feel about this gubernatorial race. And I came out here to wish you the very best and to state with confidence, especially after talking to some of your most enthusiastic supporters before dinner, that you will indeed be the next Governor of the State of California. And I am delighted to predict that right here. Just don't use the same pollster Ortega [President of Nicaragua] did. [*Laughter*]

To you and Gayle, Barbara and I send our very best. The Wilsons were just upstairs and talked to Barbara at home. And sorry she is not here tonight—she is going to meet me in a day or so as we receive the Prime Minister of Japan in California.

I want to salute Lee Atwater, who is doing an outstanding job as the chairman of the Republican National Committee. And, Frank, I'm not upstaging you, but I'm

saying nice things about you it seems just yesterday and the day before. But I'm glad you're here, sir, and I appreciate the work you're doing for the party. I'm delighted to once again be with Bill Walsh, who's been such an example not just in the field of athletics but in his commitment to helping others. And I also think we would be remiss if we didn't thank the Lowell High School Band for their participation here tonight.

And as some of you know, I was just in San Francisco 3 weeks ago. But as Kipling said, San Francisco, like all of California, has one drawback—it's hard to leave.

So much has happened, even since my last trip right here to San Francisco. And Bishop Swing, my old, dear friend, our pastor, now a bishop out here—it's not that we find that hard to believe, sir, but I'm so glad to see you again. But he was our pastor in Washington. Would it seem presumptuous of me to say that many of our prayers seem to be answered? From Moscow to Managua, change is in the air. And the Revolution of '89 has continued into a new decade, a decade of democracy.

Time and again in this century, the political map of the world was transformed. And in each instance, a new world order came about through the advent of a new tyrant or the outbreak of a bloody global war, or its end. Now the world has undergone another upheaval, but this time, there's no war. We've seen a bold Soviet leader initiate daring reforms. We've seen a playwright—humble man that I received in the White House the other day—Václav Havel, move from prison to the Presidential palace in Czechoslovakia. We've seen both the Berlin Wall and the Romanian dictatorship tumble into ruins. And I think it's fair to say that the day of the dictator is over.

Victor Hugo said that no army can match the might of an idea whose time has come. In the Revolution of '89, an idea overcame armies and tanks, and that idea is democracy. This has been true in the East. Now it is becoming true throughout the Western Hemisphere—first in Panama after Operation Just Cause, and now, at long last, for the brave people of Nicaragua. And how could we ask for more?

Another symbol of change: This morning I called President Gorbachev, and we had a long talk on matters affecting Nicaragua and Eastern Europe. And after the call and this highly rational and, I would say, cordial discussion with this dynamic new Soviet leader, my mind went back to those days not so many years ago when a talk of this nature would not have been possible. The mood of the day back then—confrontation, rhetorical overkill, tension bordering on hostility.

Yes, we've got some problems with the Soviet Union. But today's talk was so different—no polemics. Where we differed, we vowed to discuss the differences further. And the point is: Reason and calmness have replaced rhetoric. And as your President, I am determined to consult often with President Gorbachev to keep open the door to negotiation and peace. These indeed are exciting times, and I'm proud to be your President in these times of change.

But we're gathered here tonight to celebrate events closer to home. As I said, California is hard to leave, and for me, it's been hard to leave even when I'm back at the White House. You see, it was just yesterday, Bill, that for the second time in my Presidency, Barbara and I had the pleasure of entertaining the winners of the Super Bowl; and once again, our guests were the San Francisco 49ers. And just a few months earlier, Barbara and I hosted the Oakland A's after their great World Series victory. Something about monopoly—there's something in the books about cornering the market here—a little antitrust action. [*Laughter*] But when it comes to champions, I'm beginning to think you have cornered the market.

Yet I'm here on behalf of another champion, a champion for the victims of crime and drug-related violence, a champion for the environment, a champion for California, a champion for a sound and growing economy. And I'm talking about the next Governor of your State: Pete Wilson. And in this critical—critical for the Nation—election, with Pete at the top of the ticket, come November, California will go Republican in a big way.

California is prized for more than its political importance or the size of its GNP that Pete in a slightly braggart fashion there was talking about. We must win the State because California really does represent the future. California is at the forefront not just regionally and nationally but, as he rightfully pointed out, internationally, and needs a special kind of leadership—and Pete Wilson's kind of leadership it is. Twenty-three-year career in public life—it began under the dome in Sacramento, and today he is a lawmaker still, this time in Washington, DC. But it was as mayor of San Diego that Pete first showed a flair, a talent, for executive leadership. And it is exactly this kind of executive leadership that the whole State of California needs to take it to the threshold of a new millennium. You've got a good Governor. In my view, we have a great Governor, and I want to see that tradition continue with Pete Wilson.

And sadly, California needs something else. It needs to continue a crime-fighting tradition. It needs a Governor who will continue the war against violent crime. California needs a Governor who shares our philosophy about crime. And our philosophy—relatively simple—prison sentences should be at least as tough as the criminals we convict.

At the Federal level, I relied on Pete's help to pass a major part of our anticrime package. More money has been provided for prison space and more Federal law enforcement officers. But Congress has left too much work undone. We need action on the rest of our proposals to fight violent crime—by toughening Federal sentences for those who use a firearm in the commission of a felony. And if the kingpins who deal drugs are dealing death, then let's judge them for what they are—murderers. It's time we took the shackles off the policemen, the courts, and the law. I am convinced we must be tougher on these drug criminals.

And a Governor has to be as tough as the times. But the challenges of the future will also require vision and compassion if we're to protect a fragile coastal ecology or educate a new generation of children.

From the urban canyons of Los Angeles to the Yosemite beloved by Ansel Adams, Californians were among the first to stand up for the environment, and Pete Wilson was among the first environmentalists to hold office. He's added thousands of acres to the California wilderness system, saved canyons, protected urban recreation sites. And he supports our "America the Beautiful" initiative to plant a billion trees, to expand our national parks and wildlife preserves, and to make this more like the unspoiled green continent our forebears knew.

Right now Pete is working with me on our administration's proposal to enact our clean air bill, the first significant change since 1977, one that will clean up the smog and curb acid rain and cut back on the air toxics that plague California's air. Cleaner cars, cleaner fuels, cleaner factories—that's what we're striving for. And with Pete Wilson at the helm, you'll have a Governor who works for a cleaner California, just as he has in the United States Senate.

Education is also critical to the future, and it's a critical responsibility, I'd say, an increasingly critical responsibility of every Governor. Governors across the country are disturbed that there are still many American children—often in the inner city, often immigrants—who are denied the American dream because of a lack of literacy, a lack of job skills. This is unfair, this is unjust, and this is unacceptable. And that's why Pete Wilson backs our proposal for a half-billion-dollar increase for Head Start to give these children a hopeful start in life. I need that through the United States Congress.

Almost a year has passed since I sent the Educational Excellence Act to Congress. It's based on a few basic concepts: To make our schools work, we must give parents, teachers, and children the power to choose. To make our system work, States, schools, and individuals will need greater flexibility in the way in which they can pursue these goals. And then we must all be accountable for the results.

Last April I asked Congress to pass these measures to reform our educational system. And look, thanks to Pete's help and that of others, education reform has already passed the United States Senate. Now it's time for the House to finish its homework and pass our education reform now.

The political future of California and all of America rests on yet another issue—an issue that affects the voting rights of every Republican, every Independent, every Democratic voter—an issue of fundamental fairness, and I am talking about reapportionment. Some say reapportionment has been a political gold mine for both parties. They may be right. The Democrats get the gold and we get the shaft. [*Laughter*]

Remember, after the 1990 census almost one out of eight Members of Congress will represent the State of California. Remember that. This is bigger than party politics. Gerrymandering violates the spirit of one man, one vote. On a summer night in 1981, a group of California Democrats sat in a restaurant in Sacramento with pencil and paper and redesigned your political future. Lines were drawn—crazy, twisted lines—that cut across communities, towns, and even streets without the slightest regard for the will of the people. Since those district lines went into effect, there have been 135 general elections for California's congressional seats, and only once has a seat changed party control. And remember, this same brand of political manipulation that hurts Republicans also hurts every minority voter in the State of California.

So, isn't it ironic, if a little sad, that in the very decade democracy dawned around the world a small group sitting around a table in a restaurant who called themselves Democrats infringed on voting rights in America? Still, Republicans do not seek revenge, don't seek a gerrymander of our own. No, with fair lines, we can win on the issues, and we can also win on the strength of our candidates.

You know, in the early days of our great nation, some Americans stayed in the cities of the East and built great industries—and they have every right to be proud. And some Americans came halfway across the continent and farmed our rich and fertile plains—and they, too, have every right to be proud. But then there were those who pressed ever forward until they reached the sea. Gumption, gold, and glory took them all the way to the shore of the shining Pacific. We call these people Californians. Some

found gold; most didn't. But all Californians found something precious: the future. So, today's State of California is tomorrow's state of the Union. And there's no one better to lead California into that exciting future than Pete Wilson.

It's been said that "if you would test a man, first give him power." For 23 years, Pete Wilson has been tested. He's used power not to glorify self, to glorify one man, but to make a better life for millions. He's a great Senator today, a sterling example of California's passion for excellence. Tomorrow, the Golden State will be proud to call him Governor.

Thank you, and God bless you all. Thank you for having me here once again. Thank you very much.

Note: The President spoke at 7:48 p.m. in the Grand Ballroom at the St. Francis Hotel. In his remarks, he referred to Gayle A. Wilson, wife of Senator Wilson; Frank Fisco, California Republican Party chairman; and William Walsh, former coach of the San Francisco 49ers football team. A tape was not available for verification of the content of these remarks.

Presidential Determination No. 90–12—Memorandum on Narcotics Control Certification
February 28, 1990

Memorandum for the Secretary of State

Subject: Certifications for Major Narcotics Source and Transit Countries

By virtue of the authority vested in me by Section 481(h)(2)(A)(i) of the Foreign Assistance Act of 1961, as amended by the Anti-Drug Abuse Act of 1986 (P.L. 99–570), the Anti-Drug Abuse Act of 1988 (P.L. 100–690), and the International Narcotics Control Act of 1989 (P.L. 101–231), 22 U.S.C. 2291(h)(2)(A)(i), I hereby determine and certify that the following major narcotics producing and/or major narcotics transit countries/area have cooperated fully with the United States, or taken adequate steps on their own, to control narcotics production,

trafficking and money laundering:

The Bahamas, Belize, Bolivia, Brazil, Colombia, Ecuador, Hong Kong, India, Jamaica, Laos, Malaysia, Mexico, Morocco, Nigeria, Pakistan, Panama, Paraguay, Peru and Thailand.

By virtue of the authority vested in me by Section 481(h)(2)(A)(ii) of the Act, I hereby determine that it is in the vital national interests of the United States to certify the following country:

Lebanon.

Information for this country as required under Section 481(h)(2)(B) of the Act is enclosed.

I have determined that the following major producing and/or major transit countries do not meet the standards set forth in Section 481(h)(2)(A):

Afghanistan, Burma, Iran and Syria.

In making these determinations, I have considered the factors set forth in Section 481(h)(3) of the Act, based on the information contained in the International Narcotics Control Strategy Report of 1990.

You are hereby authorized and directed to report this determination to the Congress immediately, and simultaneously to transmit to the Speaker of the House of Representatives and to the Committee on Foreign Relations of the Senate the report required by section 481(e) of the Act for 1990. This memorandum shall be published in the *Federal Register.*

GEORGE BUSH

Note: The memorandum was released by the Office of the Press Secretary on March 1.

Statement by Press Secretary Fitzwater on Narcotics Control Certification
March 1, 1990

The President has decided today to certify by Presidential determination that the following major drug-producing and/or major transit countries have fully cooperated with the United States or taken adequate measures of their own to combat drug production, trafficking, and money laundering:

The Bahamas, Belize, Bolivia, Brazil, Colombia, Ecuador, Hong Kong, India, Jamaica, Laos, Malaysia, Mexico, Morocco, Nigeria, Pakistan, Panama, Paraguay, Peru, and Thailand.

The certification of Lebanon has been determined by the President to be of national interest to the United States. The President has decided not to certify Afghanistan, Burma, Iran, and Syria.

In addition to sending a clear message to countries which are not committed in any way to fighting drugs, decertification precludes the receipt of assistance, except for antidrug programs, from the United States.

The President's decision is based on the State Department's annual International Narcotics Control Strategy Report (INCSR), which is presented to the Congress on March 1 of each year.

Remarks on Legislation To Amend the Clean Air Act and an Exchange With Reporters in Los Angeles, California
March 1, 1990

The President. Let me just say I wanted to make one comment, and then we're going about our business here. A compromise has been worked out in a bipartisan fashion on a clean air bill, and I'm grateful to the Senators who participated in this compromise. It is the best in bipartisanship.

I'm also grateful to those in the administration—the EPA, our Chief of Staff, Roger Porter—who worked with the leadership and rank-and-file Senators to hammer out this compromise. And now I would encourage the Senate, this hard work having resulted in a good clean air bill, to move forward promptly; and then let's get it over to the House and do something to clean up the air in this country. It's a very big forward step; and I am very proud of the team, in the Congress and in the administration, that achieved these results. It took a lot of hard work, a lot of compromise.

Q. Mr. President, even as this compromise was reached today, as you're no doubt aware, many in the environmental community are questioning your commitment as an environmentalist because of the continuing reports of infighting between your Chief of Staff and your EPA Administrator over watering down such things as global warming and this compromised legislation. What do you say to that?

The President. I say they're crazy. I say they're wrong. You can't play to the extremes. I say take a look at this compromise in this landmark clean air legislation. It has been agreed to by the Democratic leaders, the Republican leaders, and a lot of the rank-and-file Senators in the Senate; and that lays to rest any such ridiculous allegations. Our EPA Chief is doing a great job. My Chief of Staff is doing a great job. This always trying to get on the inside baseball stuff—the American people are not interested in that. What they're interested in is cleaning up the air. And now we've made a good breakthrough on that. So, that's what I'd say to them.

And look, I've learned something. You're never going to keep the extremes happy. I'm not going to shut down this country. But I am going to help clean up the air, and that's exactly what this compromise results in.

Now, I've got to run because we're off for a very—one final question.

U.S. Hostages in Lebanon

Q. There are all kinds of reports that there's some kind of a breakthrough and that you have been involved in direct, indirect, secret talks over the hostages. Can you enlighten us?

The President. Well, I don't spend a day that I don't think about the hostages, but there are no secret talks going on. And I have read some of the most ridiculous stories, printed with anonymous sources, failing to do anything other than repeat rumors. I hope the hostages will be released. And if I see an opportunity to talk in private or in public about this to get them released, I'll do it. But I can tell you, Lesley [Lesley Stahl, CBS News], that it's not—I saw a report the other day printed—I hope it wasn't on the air—about talking to the French President about something of this nature. There never was such a conversation. I said so. I believe we shot it down, and then today I see it comes up again. There's something going on that's crazy. But there are no talks going on.

I saw ones in Geneva. I saw that there were talks in Geneva. And so, I immediately got a hold of our top people, Brent Scowcroft, and said: Look, work through the system. Are there any talks? Have there been any—direct, indirect—in Geneva? And he said no.

Now, let me tell you something. If I thought a talk in Geneva would result in letting people go free, I would undertake the talk. And if I thought the way to conduct that talk was to do it quietly, I would do it in that manner. If I thought the best way to get the hostages out were to publicly have talks in Geneva, I would do that. But there aren't any, and I'm glad to have this opportunity to be as definitive as possible.

Q. How come you wanted to ask Scowcroft?

The President. Because he's the one that works through the system. He's the one that calls the State Department. He's the one that does the President's bidding when it comes to national security matters.

Q. Are there talks underway now between the U.S. and the Syrians on the hostage issue?

The President. No talks. I've told you there are no talks underway that I know about.

Q. Is there any movement at all?

The President. I hope so. I sure hope so. I'd love to see them release these hostages. And I will do everything I can, privately, openly—whatever it takes—to get them out of there without trading for hostages. We're not in the negotiating process. But Iran knows from the very first day I've been President that good will will beget good will, and good will means releasing kidnaped prisoners. And so, that's where it stands.

Meeting With Japanese Prime Minister Kaifu

Q. Are you going to get something with Kaifu tomorrow, Mr. President?

The President. I'm looking forward to visiting with the Prime Minister in a very important relationship. I look forward to it.

Nicaragua

Q. Mr. President, are you worried that the *contras* are not going to lay down their arms?

The President. No, I'm not worried. They will.

Note: The President spoke at 9:40 a.m. at the Century Plaza Hotel, prior to his departure for the North Los Angeles County Correctional Facility. In his remarks, he referred to John H. Sununu, Chief of Staff to the President; Roger B. Porter, Assistant to the President for Economic and Domestic Policy; President François Mitterrand of France; and Brent Scowcroft, Assistant to the President for National Security Affairs. A tape was not available for verification of the content of these remarks.

Remarks at the Dedication Ceremony for the North Los Angeles County Correctional Facility in Santa Monica, California
March 1, 1990

Thank you all very much, ladies and gentlemen. Thank you, Sheriff Block. Thank you all for that warm welcome back. And, Sherm, let me just say once again the respect that I feel in my heart for you and others that are serving with you in this important work. I understand your daughter, Barbara, is here—Sergeant Persten, I believe, of the sheriff's department. If it's not inappropriate, I'd like to see her as long as I'm talking about her. There she is, right there—sorry to embarrass you. And, of course, to all the members of the sheriff's department, and to Mike Antonovich and old friend Pete Schabarum and all the supervisors, delighted to be here. Sybil Brand was introduced to me as our Points of Light lady. And I know that all interested in law enforcement are grateful for all she's done.

And now, I'm going to offend others by being exclusive, except I want to single out my friend, the Congressman Elton Gallegly from this area, doing a superb job in Washington. I wish we had more like him when it comes to support for law enforcement. And to all the other members of the Los Angeles law enforcement community that are here today, it is my view that all too often, you are the unsung heroes on the war on crime, of our assault on drugs. And, yes, it is my honor to visit you here today.

I've visited, as President, many education programs, rehabilitation programs, Head Start programs designed to, through education, help kids from the very beginning. And now, I've just completed the tour of Super Max, the 900-block maximum security prison. And I'll tell you, it does concentrate the mind.

It was a short tour, very short, but I won't ever forget it. It was long enough to bring anyone face to face with the reality of what institutions like this represent. Jails and prison do testify to something in the nature of man that most people put aside, prefer not to think about: the capacity for violence, the power of corruption, the ability to turn our back on what's right and do wrong. But they are also the ultimate proof of the community's determination to protect itself and serve justice. One of this nation's Founding Fathers said, "If men were angels, no government would be necessary." Well, I'm sure that no one here would suggest that men were angels. And that's why there's government to write the laws we live by and correctional facilities like this one for the people who break them.

When this ceremony is over, it will be time for many of you to go back to business. Go after the people who turn our cities into battlegrounds and our kids into drug users. Help our communities fight back.

This facility was built to meet the needs of L.A. County. Every penny—every penny—produced by State and local funding. And that's a sign that your vibrant community, the Los Angeles community, the Los Angeles taxpayer, knows that in the fight against crime and drugs, tough talk is simply not enough. And if you're going to be tough on crime you've got to be tough on the criminals. Talk to any law enforcement officer and they'll tell you what that means: No more revolving door. No more criminals out on the street because there isn't enough cell space to hold them.

And I'm here to tell you, citizens and law enforcement officials of Los Angeles County, that the Federal Government is doing its part to combat crime. Right now we're making a new effort in this area. That means more Federal prisons. And this year alone, over $1.5 billion will be devoted to prison construction to build over 24,000 new beds. And that's just this year. I've urged Congress to add another $374 million for more Federal cell space in 1991.

Fighting to win against crime and drugs means tougher laws. I've called on Congress to pass a tough, no-nonsense anticrime package. I'll tell you something. I feel deep in my heart that I owe that to each and every law enforcement officer that's here today and those that are serving all across this country. And so, today, though, let me call on you: Keep working with us and with all the elected officials at every level of government so that every American citizen can have faith that the law is on their side, not the criminal's. And that does mean tougher State and Federal laws, stiffer penalties for crime and violence—more for crimes of violence, and more certainty in sentencing; an end to easy parole; no deals for criminals carrying a gun; and for anyone who murders an officer of the law, justice means nothing less than the death penalty.

I know every law enforcement officer here today wants only one thing: the chance to do his duty, uphold the law. And for that, you deserve our thanks. Now, I know there have been difficulties. I've read the papers and I've seen the stories this past week about the indictments here.

Don't let it get you down. Yours is the largest sheriff's department in the world—11,000 people fighting the good fight. Keep your heads high. If some bad apple turns up, if an officer abuses your trust or ours by doing wrong, we must be that much more dedicated to supporting the countless officers, the millions across this country who honor the law by doing what is right.

You are, as I said a few minutes ago, society's unsung heroes. And I thank you for your service not just to your community but to our country. And I've got to tell you, as I walked through that facility with Sheriff Block just now and met some of the young officers in there who are doing this kind of work, I'm saying to myself: This isn't the easy way. There would be other ways that they could find to make a living that might be more easy. But it is the dedicated way. It is a way that really upholds the best in America's tradition of service.

Let me close by paraphrasing William Blake: "Prisons are the concrete of justice." Prisons are very much about the real world. There's a tendency, particularly among people of great sensitivity, to think about justice in airy and abstract terms: the idea, for example, that in spite of crime, all people are basically good. But it is unwise to think in the abstract when it comes to crime. Most people are good. But some, let's face it, are not. And today, I've visited perhaps the most modern facility in the country. And to think, I would say to my fellow Americans, to think concretely about crime, you should visit a facility, a prison facility.

I salute you for your work. I appreciate the opportunity to have made this visit. I am grateful to all of you for this warm welcome. And now, Sheriff Block, with your permission, sir, I'll cut the ribbon and officially open the North County Correctional Facility. God bless each and every one of you. Thank you very, very much.

Note: The President spoke at 11:09 a.m. at the facility. In his remarks, he referred to Los Angeles County Sheriff Sherman Block, county supervisors Michael D. Antonovich and Peter F. Schabarum, and institutional inspection commissioner Sybil Brand. Fol-

lowing his remarks, the President attended *luncheon in Los Angeles.*
the Republican Governors Association

Letter to Congressional Leaders Transmitting a Report on International Agreements
March 1, 1990

Dear Mr. Speaker: (Dear Mr. Chairman:)
Pursuant to subsection (b) of the Case-Zablocki Act (Public Law 95–426; 1 U.S.C. section 112b(b)), I transmit herewith a report prepared by the Department of State concerning international agreements.
Sincerely,

GEORGE BUSH

Note: Identical letters were sent to Thomas S. Foley, Speaker of the House of Representatives, and Claiborne Pell, chairman of the Senate Foreign Relations Committee.

Statement by Press Secretary Fitzwater on Legislation To Amend the Clean Air Act
March 1, 1990

The President is pleased that agreement has been reached between the administration, the Senate leadership, the Senate Environment and Public Works Committee, and a bipartisan group of other Senators on the major elements of legislation in the Senate on the Clean Air Act. The President is particularly gratified that this agreement is consistent with the legislation he submitted to Congress and is within the parameters and guidelines the administration felt were necessary for an environmentally sound, effective Clean Air Act. The agreement covers provisions relating to acid rain, air toxics, alternative fuels, and ozone attainment for stationary and mobile sources. All parties to the agreement are committed to its passage in the Senate.

The administration has participated for the past month in bipartisan discussions on the Clean Air Act at the request of the majority and minority leaders of the Senate. The administration team included representatives from the White House, the Environmental Protection Agency, the Office of Management and Budget, the Council of Economic Advisers, and the Departments of Energy and the Interior.

The provisions in this agreement are environmentally aggressive and will achieve significant and permanent reductions in pollutants that cause acid rain, will ensure annual improvements to bring our nation's cities into compliance with standards relating to urban smog and carbon monoxide, and will greatly reduce the risk to the public's health from toxic emissions.

This agreement is environmentally sound and strong. It is also designed to effectively achieve these reductions in an economically efficient and innovative way. It will for the first time establish a market-based system of incentives for reducing the pollutants that cause acid rain. It provides for the use of state-of-the-art technology to control toxic emissions. It includes strong incentives for the development and adoption of clean-coal technologies. It will establish a framework for encouraging the use of cleaner fuels to reduce pollution from automobiles.

By incorporating flexibility and innovation in its approach to achieving pollution reductions, it will allow environmental and health standards to be met in a way that creates maximum choice for both States and regulated industries and places fewer bur-dens on consumers. It will thus improve the Clean Air Act in a way that promotes both a healthy environment and a sound economy.

Exchange With Reporters at a Meeting With Ronald Reagan in Los Angeles, California
March 1, 1990

U.S. Hostages in Lebanon

Q. Mr. Reagan, there are reports out of Geneva that some secret talks are underway to help the release of the hostages in Lebanon. What kind of advice or words of caution do you have for President Bush?

President Reagan. Well, the way most leaks turn out, the caution, I think, would be: Wait until somebody could prove it.

Nicaragua

Q. President Reagan, since the *contras* were pretty much a creation of your administration, is it time now for them to lay down their arms?

President Reagan. Don't you think it might be time enough for us to wait and make sure that there is a civilian government in place in Nicaragua? Because the Sandinistas had their arms and their weapons long before any Nicaraguan citizens picked up guns and became the *contras*.

Q. Do you think they should wait, then, until Mrs. Chamorro is inaugurated April 25th?

President Reagan. Well, I don't know whether to wait that long or not, but things could take place foreshadowing what the situation is going to be earlier than that.

Q. Do you share that concern, Mr. President?

President Bush. I've expressed myself on this, and at this photo op I've elected not to take any questions. So, we have a slight differences in policy.

President Reagan. Oh, I was just sitting there. And, yes, he's doing exactly what is right for him. I just have a little more freedom.

President Bush. That's right. Exactly.

Meeting with Japanese Prime Minister Kaifu

Q. President Bush, can you comment on what you hope to accomplish with the Prime Minister tomorrow?

President Bush. It's going to be interesting to meet with Prime Minister Kaifu—coming because he's just solidified his position in the party and he's been reanointed. And we've got to convince him that we've got to move forward with some of the tough problems, as you know.

President Reagan. Have you met him before?

President Bush. Yes, sir. I've been there a couple of times.

President Reagan. I met him in Japan, too.

President Bush. Yes, impressive. I'm impressed with him. He's a very good man—good man.

Reel them in there, gang.

President Reagan's Health

Q. How are you feeling, Mr. President?

President Reagan. Just fine.

Q. You look very good, sir.

President Reagan. Well, thank you. I'm back riding horses now and then.

Q. Are you?

President Reagan. Yes.

Q. You've got to get back on them, right? Once they throw you, get back on them. Right?

President Reagan. Yes. And as I've told some of you—the old cavalry saying—there's nothing so good for the inside of a man as the outside of a horse. [*Laughter*]

Upland Earthquake

Q. Did you feel the earthquake?

President Reagan. No, I was traveling. Nancy did. She was on the phone. She hung up. [*Laughter*]

Note: A tape was not available for verification of the content of the exchange, which occurred in the afternoon at President Reagan's office in the Fox Plaza.

Remarks at the California Chamber of Commerce Centennial Dinner in Los Angeles
March 1, 1990

Thank you, Governor Deukmejian, for those kind words. It's great to be back in California and to be invited to such a wonderful party. I got to L.A. yesterday, and they told me I'd be appearing before the movers and shakers. [*Laughter*] I thought they were talking about people, not houses. But nevertheless—[*laughter*]—Steve, I want to congratulate you as the dinner chairman. And to Chairman Stanley Wainer, thank you, sir, for inviting me here tonight.

You know, when we landed at the airport, I was deeply touched to see a red carpet rolled out, 21-gun salute, balloons, confetti—truly moving. And then I looked around and realized it was the L.A. Coliseum Commission welcoming Al Davis back from Oakland. [*Laughter*]

Some of you all were up in San Francisco, some of the members of the Chamber, and last night we had some demonstrators there. And on the way over here, I did encounter a few demonstrators. One protester from UCLA was shouting, "U.S. out of Panama! U.S. out of El Salvador! USC out of Los Angeles!" [*Laughter*]

But something that really impresses me about California is the west coast's will to survive, even triumph, in adversity. New ways to cope spring up, no matter what kind of disaster strikes. Somebody told me there's even a new support group in Malibu called Parents Without Perrier. [*Laughter*]

What brings me here tonight, though, is the same appeal that brought so many to California a century ago: a sense that something powerful is happening here in this State. Your heritage was borne by those with the imagination and courage to press westward. After the century of shared progress that you celebrate tonight—from

sailing ships to silicon chips—you're still the State that sets the pace, breaks the barriers, and defines the future.

The gold rush never really ended in California; it just took on new and truer colors—from the green abundance of agriculture to the black gold in the earth, the silver screen, the wealth of the blue Pacific. The list of California's first-place rankings reads like the what's what of American business—number one in aerospace; construction; exports; in business owned by women, by black and Hispanic Americans; in numbers of college graduates, scientists, engineers, Nobel laureates, patents, and Ph.D.'s—California leads America. And America leads the world.

But California in business isn't just first-class; it's world-class—home to over 40 Fortune 500 firms, a dynamic job-creating small business sector, and a gross State product that the Duke referred to—my friend George Deukmejian—that outside of America ranks among the top 5 nations.

So, if California is the rock-solid edifice of America's economic strength, the California Chamber should be a room with a view, with a vision for the future, where decisions are made and actions taken that will lead the rest of the country in the coming century. You understand that California's economic prospects are strong, thanks to your natural resources and your geographic position on the Pacific rim. Let me add, it's fitting that I'll be meeting in California tomorrow and for the weekend with Prime Minister Kaifu of Japan. We have very important business to do with Japan, and these will be important meetings; I think they're fitting that they be held in California.

But what will truly lead California to success in the new century is her people and the way they do business. As our economy continues to grow and labor markets continue to tighten up, businesses like yours will need to turn to sources of talent once left untapped: youth at risk, who need to see the connection between school and work; the underskilled, who need training; older and more experienced workers, who need new skills; the disabled, who need only a chance to prove their abilities; and dual-career families, who need flexible, creative child-care solutions.

Flexible workplace policies will allow you to find and keep the best talent. And one of the most promising of these new business frontiers is telecommuting: taking advantage of new technology to enable your people to work at home 1 or 2 days a week. Clearly this exciting concept will not apply to every business or every kind of employee, but consider: A typical 20-minute roundtrip commute to work over the course of a year adds up to 2 very stressful 40-hour weeks lost on the road. But if only 5 percent of the commuters in L.A. County telecommuted 1 day each week, they'd save 205 million miles of travel each year and keep 47,000 tons of pollutants from entering the atmosphere. So, telecommuting means saving energy, improving air quality and quality of life—not a bad deal.

This administration is profoundly committed to protecting the environment that we all share. That's why I'm pleased to say that today we've reached an agreement with a bipartisan group of leaders in the United States Senate for environmentally aggressive and still economically sound revisions to the Clean Air Act. It's a new approach to clean air that will permanently reduce emissions that cause acid rain; greatly reduce the threat from air toxins; and bring clean, healthy air to every city in America, including this important city, Los Angeles.

I know that many of your companies, many represented right here tonight, are involved in forward-looking stewardship efforts for our precious environment. That's a measure of the enlightened management here in California. Along with looking inward for better ways to run your operations, you're also looking outward as active partners in your communities. And we all

know that some of your communities will demand—the problems—long-term, consistent, collective effort—work involving worthy sacrifice, but with profound, long-term results.

To make sure our educational system gives our kids the skills they need to thrive in the future, new partnerships between schools and, yes, businesses need to be expanded. Projects to improve schools, like the California Compact, show great promise and deserve all the help you possibly can give them. In fact, I understand there are already over 3,000 educational partnerships here in California, from multimillion-dollar projects for sweeping reform to adopt-a-school programs to low-cost volunteer efforts. Our schools need your time and talents, and if you're already involved, keep at it—and if you're not, this is your decade to do it.

And where the most troubling challenge to our communities is concerned, the enslavement of illegal drugs, your members can help us turn the tables against the dealers, turn them forever. So-called casual users and their money keep these merchants of death in business. So, anyone who still considers drugs a victimless diversion needs to hear this: You shame yourselves, and you shame your great country. And America now condemns what has too long been condoned. The country has had enough. And I believe we can and will win this battle against drugs. Many of you and your businesses already do preemployment drug screening. Let me encourage all of you: We need to make it very clear to every American that if you do drugs you don't get hired.

Those of you who are involved with the nationwide Partnership for a Drug-Free America are getting far-reaching results. But let me also encourage you to get involved with local efforts, at street level. On every block, in every town, in every city in America, there should be a home or a business willing to serve as a safe house for kids, where they can go for help; for information about drugs; for refuge from dealers; or just for the comfort of somebody who cares, of a caring, listening heart.

As I think of my job, I often think an

important priority—our kids need our help. And that will mean a lot to your communities. But there's one thing more that we should consider for the sake of the world community. We've all watched with wonder and delight the transformations that took place in Eastern Europe during the Revolution of 1989. We greet the triumph of democracy like a miraculous dawn that might somehow cast the whole world in its light at once. But it is not ordained and will not be the work of miracles. It must be the work of the newly liberated peoples themselves, and it must be America's work.

Forty years ago a world wounded, rent asunder by war, was built with America's leadership. In this decade, nations impoverished by ideology and ravaged by dictatorship—in Eastern Europe, in Latin America—are also ready to be reborn and rebuilt with the tools of free enterprise, the wisdom of free markets, and the skills of American business. As the political dust settles, the real struggle now begins. The cry for democracy, the redemption of the individual voice, is only the first step. As I said in my State of the Union Address, democracy is a cornerstone of free societies that must be joined with competition, opportunity, private investment, stewardship, and of course, leadership.

Now is the time for our country, for America, to provide that leadership, to do her quiet but crucial work to help lay the cornerstones of free societies and to widen the circle of freedom. We can rely on what we know. We know that prosperity preserves peace, that the troubled waters of political turmoil are calmed by economic growth, and that our economic influence can be a force for great good.

We are using that influence at the international level, marshaling assistance for nations making a courageous break from their totalitarian past. We're providing direct U.S. aid. And we're working with the Congress and with other nations to do more for these exciting fledgling democracies. But America's leadership in the world does not depend solely on government initiatives. Our influence is profound because our private sector has shown the leadership, and we need your engagement again today.

Every business and community organization, here in California and across the country—business leagues, Rotaries, clubs of every kind—all can find ways to help the people of Eastern Europe and Central America as they make this transition to market economies. In this, your national chamber is on the right track. Consider donating some time and expertise to the emerging businesses that are now struggling in Eastern Europe. Work with our important friends and neighbors to the south, in Panama and now in Nicaragua, as the transfer of power takes place. Whatever your specialty—strategic planning, marketing, inventory, line operations—it is needed now. Find a sister city or a business that would benefit from what you know of free enterprise and free markets and put your talents to work. Today there is an unprecedented opportunity, certainly an urgent need, for American business leaders to lead the world toward free enterprise.

You know, back in 1890, there were a lot of newspaper articles suggesting that California was in decline or, as one observer put it, "in a state of decadence." The critics claimed that industry and agriculture were struggling, and it looked like the gold had all been rushed. You know what happened. You know the history. California became a world-class economic superpower. Today you are called upon and privileged as few have been before to bring the world new and unprecedented prosperity. Show the world that commerce has conscience, that prosperity has a purpose, and that any definition of a successful life really must include serving others. In your own businesses, in your communities, and in the community of nations, gather strength and use it to help people.

I am privileged to be President of the United States at this terribly exciting time in not only our history but in the history of freedom and democracy around the world. Let me just say I feel that all of you in this room have an important part to play in this new decade in helping solidify the freedom that people have struggled for, the democracies that they revere, and the future they deserve.

Let me wish this chamber a very happy

100th birthday. Thank you for inviting me. God bless you, and God bless the United States of America. Thank you very, very much. Nice to be with you. Sorry to eat and run like this, but I'm still on Eastern Time.

Note: The President spoke at 7:50 p.m. in the Los Angeles Ballroom at the Century

Plaza Hotel. In his remarks, he referred to Steven Mersamer, dinner chairman; Stanley Wainer, chairman of the board of the chamber; and Al Davis, owner of the Los Angeles Raiders football team. A tape was not available for verification of the content of these remarks.

Remarks to the Academy of Television Arts and Sciences in Los Angeles, California
March 2, 1990

The President. Thank you all very much. Chuck, thank you, sir, for those kind words. And good morning to all of you. I want to thank you for being here at this very early hour. It's great to see such an all-star cast assembled. We Bushes are basically name-droppers. [*Laughter*] We like this kind of event. And wait until Barbara hears about it. [*Laughter*] I'm glad to see my good friend, Jerry Weintraub; and, Leo, to you, sir, the president of the academy, thank you very much. In fact, we've got a roomful of presidents: Bob Iger, ABC; Arthur Hiller, DGA; George Kirgo, WGA; Sidney Sheinberg, MCA; George Bush, USA. [*Laughter*]

And over my shoulder I feel the presence of Roger Ailes, my good friend and trusted adviser whose help was so important to me in my quest for the Presidency. I'm not sure I hit that line just the way Roger wanted me to do it, but the eye contact was superb. [*Laughter*]

Being President does have its advantages. And this is true: I have a TV set there in the White House with five screens, one big one in the middle, four small ones around it, all of them on at once. Now I don't have to miss the nightly news while I watch "Wheel of Fortune." [*Laughter*] It's a wonderful thing.

There's no escaping the fact that we live in the age of television. You know, in my State of the Union, I announced six national education targets to be met by the year 2000. And this morning I want to add a seventh goal: By the year 2000, all Americans must be able to set the clocks on their VCR's. [*Laughter*]

I know that your industry faces some real challenges right now—I had a chance to talk to some of the officials at the head table a little earlier—cable and satellite deals, the controversy surrounding the financial interest rules, the exploration of new revenue streams, regulatory hurdles. The list is a long one. But that's not what I came to talk to you about this morning, interested as I am in those problems facing the industry. I came here this morning to make a serious point about a different kind of opportunity—about the tremendous power of television and how it can help us meet some of the most pressing social challenges that we face. And I know this industry is more involved than ever in focusing on some of our nation's most serious problems, whether it's hunger or homelessness or drug abuse. And there's tremendous potential in that because every one of us in this room knows that television does more than entertain. It informs, and it educates.

This morning, I want to focus on public enemy number one: illegal drugs. Two weeks ago, I went down to Cartagena to the Andean drug summit—a country on the front line of the drug war. Their courageous President, Virgilio Barco, and the people of Colombia have made a courageous choice: Colombia versus the cartels. The battle is far from over. But for the first time, the drug runners are on the run. We're going to keep the pressure on, work with those Andean allies—Peru, Bolivia, Colombia—to cut the supply lines that run from the jungles of South America right into the heart of our cities. And we will. Two nights ago, we just learned that in Orange County, two cars were just pulled over carrying nearly 900 pounds of cocaine. Four million doses; street value—$30 million.

The supply side is a massive, serious problem. And I will continue to address myself to that side of the equation. But if we want to win this war, big busts won't be enough. We've got simply to drive down demand, dry up the market for illegal drugs right here in our own country. We do that by increasing awareness, education—providing people, especially young people, information that helps them separate fact from fiction when the subject is drugs. That really is why I was so pleased to accept your invitation, Leo and Chuck, to come over here this morning—to thank you, the leaders in the television industry, for enlisting the power of TV as a force for positive change. Each of you is a Point of Light, with a unique ability to inform and to change attitudes and to catalyze public action in our fight against drug abuse.

This morning, I want to thank so many of you for the work you're doing with my friend Jim Burke, the head of Media Advertising Partnership for a Drug-Free America. We see those hard-hitting antidrug commercials every day, and really, they are hitting home. We're starting to see a shift in attitudes in the regions where those spots are on the air. But it's not just the commercials that are getting the antidrug message across; increasingly, it's also your regular programming, the shows themselves. And that's important.

Most people have no idea how many kids watch those Saturday morning cartoons. This is one group that does. Well, I am astonished at the number: 20 million kids between the ages of 5 and 11, sitting on the living room floor every Saturday morning watching cartoons. Twenty million kids, impressionable, just asking to be entertained. And let me tell you something: Those 20 million kids in front of their TV's on any Saturday are the same target audience for every schoolyard drug pusher 5 days a week.

Today, drugs are an unfortunate fact of life in every city and town across America.

And our kids face pressure from their peers——

Audience member. Talk about AIDS. Why don't you lead the country on AIDS like you do on drugs? You never talk about it.

Audience members. Sit down! Sit down!

Audience member. Why don't you appreciate people who are fighting AIDS? Why aren't you going to address the AIDS conference?

The President. One of the reasons that we've increased Federal help to an all-time high on AIDS is to try to help people that are concerned. And we will continue to try to help people that are concerned about that subject.

You know, I think—I'll ad lib here for a minute—but I think of the dramatic changes in Eastern Europe and the dramatic changes towards democracy in this hemisphere, and I have come a long way in my own political maturity. This guy's interdiction doesn't bother me one little bit. And I'm glad we live in a country where we can all speak up, even if it takes advantage of the hospitality of you all.

But our kids do face peer pressure from their peers, pressure from the pushers out there to snort coke or smoke pot or even a killer called crack cocaine. "Just once can't hurt." "Everybody does it." "It's cool." And that's what our kids hear. That's what they're up against. For too many of our kids, regrettably, that is the real world. And we've got to help our children develop the power to say no, power that comes from self-confidence. We've got to arm our kids with the facts: Drugs aren't part of life in the fast lane; drugs are a dead-end. And that's why I am so delighted that the academy is taking the lead in producing a show called "Cartoon All-Stars to The Rescue"—a story about a boy who, with the help of more than a dozen of today's most popular cartoon characters, learns that he can draw the line against drugs, that every kid can be drug-free.

And that's a great message. And I hope that on Saturday, April 21st, the day that that show is first broadcast all across the United States and all over North America, every TV set is on and every kid is watching. And I want to thank all of you associated with the Academy of Television Arts and Sciences for taking part in this collaborative effort. Barbara and I are proud to participate with you. Never before in cartoon history have Bugs Bunny and Daffy Duck worked with the Teenage Mutant Ninja Turtles, the Muppets, and the Smurfs— [*laughter*]—and all the other stars of the cartoon world. And my hat's off to Roy Disney and Buzz Potamkin for keeping all those colorful egos in line. [*Laughter*]

One thing more while we're talking about cartoons: Every one of us knows those scenes where a character falls off a cliff or gets hit by a truck and then bounces right back up, dusts himself off, and moves right on to the next scene. Kids see that stuff, and they know it isn't real. But how many kids and young adults today have seen the programs or movies that show a character take drugs and, just like the cartoon characters, survive without a scratch? That isn't real, either. And in the real world, whether it's Hollywood or Harlem, or out in the heartland, smalltown America, we know what drugs do. And the simple truth is they destroy. And thank goodness the days when popular culture glorified and glamorized drug use are fading fast. Public opinion is turning around. We used to hear that drugs were fashionable and fun and risk-free. Not anymore. Now we're hearing something different. We're hearing that it's okay—no, that it's great, really, to be drug-free.

And I think that change is taking place because we all see the damage that drugs can do. We've seen too many sports stars, too many entertainers, too many of the men and women we look up to, too many of our heroes pulled down, destroyed by drugs. Drugs and success simply do not mix. And I really want to thank every one of you in this room for helping smash that stereotype. Because the truth is: Drugs don't care who you are, how famous you are, how much you earn. Drugs are deadly for everybody.

So, this morning, I want to make sure that I'm understood by all the writers and producers and actors in this room. I'm not asking you to compromise your art. I'm not asking TV producers or filmmakers to portray some kind of a fantasy world where drugs don't exist. Sugar-coating isn't going to solve anything. What I'm suggesting is that you have an opportunity to help your country. And I'm with those of you who believe the answer is to treat drugs with the same degree of realism TV brings to so many other subjects, to show what happens in the real world. When someone does drugs, show what happens: how what starts out as a high turns into the lowest form of self-abasement, where drugs mean more than family, friends, self-respect—to show in the real world how drugs destroy, how drugs kill every single day.

And that's the real message. It's a message that can save lives. And thanks to you, thanks to you, it's a message that's getting through to the children of the United States of America, to the children of many other countries as well.

Leo and Chuck, thank you for this opportunity to address this exceptionally prestigious and influential group. And I am grateful to all of you. And thank you for all you're doing, and God bless you. And now I'll go over and try to represent you properly as I meet the Prime Minister of Japan. Thank you very, very much.

Note: The President spoke at 8:28 a.m. in the Los Angeles Ballroom of the Century Plaza Hotel. In his remarks, he referred to Charles Fries, chairman of the Academy of Television Arts and Sciences; Leo Chaloukian, president of the academy; Jerry Weintraub, chief executive officer of Weintraub Entertainment Group; Robert Iger, president of ABC Entertainment; Arthur Hiller, president of the Directors Guild of America; George Kirgo, president of the Writers Guild of America; and Sidney Sheinberg, president and chief operating officer of MCA, Inc.

Remarks at an Antidrug Rally in Santa Ana, California
March 2, 1990

Thank you, Jim Everett. And let me say how much I respect you and appreciate the work you're doing to help the young people not just here but all across the country. You are an inspiration to all of us, and thank you very much for welcoming me. I'm also glad to be with Governor Deukmejian, who has done an outstanding job for the State of California—outstanding. And I want to thank Fred Travalena and my old friend and supporter, Chuck Norris, for being here with you all today—great examples for the young people. And there are some people up here with me that certainly deserve our thanks for making this fantastic day possible—another friend of mine, a man I respect, Sheriff Brad Gates, over here. And Mike Hayde, the president of "Drug Use Is Life Abuse"—what a job he's doing. And the board of directors of that great organization, including Dr. Robert Schuller, Georgia Frontiere. Also up here is some of Orange County's congressional delegation, and others as well—Bob Dornan, Dana Rohrabacher, Chris Cox, Dave Dreyer. And I also have to salute one of America's best teachers, my old hero—singled him out a couple of years ago—Jaime Escalante.

Thank you, and Jim Everett, again, thank you for that warm introduction. I heard that someone asked Jim if he was excited about being with the President here today, and he said, "No, not as excited as I'll be next year when we're invited to the White House after the Rams win the Super Bowl." No matter what team you like, you've got to admit that Georgia Frontiere has built one of the toughest teams in pro football. Who says there's no role for women in combat? I've got a confession. Although I love pro football, my first love is pro baseball. And if the Angels are looking for replacement players, I hope they'll remember that I played first base. But I have a confession to all the Angels fans. My son is the managing owner or partner of the Texas Rangers. And I asked him if I could come try out for the club, and he said, "Sure, Dad. You can come down and throw the ball around. But don't give up your daytime work." [*Laughter*]

It's great to be back in Orange County. Southern California is a place of both beauty and bounty, blessed with some of the greatest wonders of nature and some of the most wondrous works of man. And it's home to many of America's oldest traditions and newest ideas—the computerized pirate ships of Walt Disney, the real-life cowboys of the Irvine Ranch. And Orange County is a special place—a place that boasts productive lands, productive minds, and productive people and one of the youngest and hardest working populations in the entire country. And standing here today in Orange County, leading the way into a new decade and a new century, it's easy to see why many young people are looking to the future with a new sense of hope and seeing a world of limitless possibilities.

Something is happening in the world—something new, something powerful, something wonderful. Czechoslovakia's Václav Havel, who began the year as a prisoner and ended it as President of Czechoslovakia, summed it up in his visit to Washington last month. Things are happening so fast, he said, that "we have literally no time even to be astonished." And today the wind rushing down from the mountains is not the fierce menace called the Santa Ana wind, but the new breeze that I spoke about when taking office a year ago. It has swept around the world, bringing new hope in Europe, new hope in Africa, new hope in the Americas. Václav Havel, free at last. Nelson Mandela, free at last. And Nicaragua and Panama, free at last.

And just as people around the world are casting off the oppression of dictators, so people across America are casting off the oppression of drugs. Week by week, day by day, millions of Americans in thousands of towns are standing up to make the same courageous choice: drug-free neighborhoods, drug-free schools, and drug-free kids. And anyone who thinks that our great country lacks the will to win the drug war better take a look at the spirit that we have here today in this stadium right here in Orange County. It is fantastic. I know you'll win this war. You have what a longtime resident of Orange County, John Wayne, had—true grit. In one of his classic western movies, John Wayne spelled it out in his simple, all-American, pointblank style. He said: "There's right and there's wrong. You gotta do one or the other. You do the one, and you're living. You do the other, and you may be walking around, but you're as dead as a beaver hat."

As he did in the conduct of his own life, in that movie John Wayne stood for right; he stood for life. And today in Orange County, thousands of you have made that same choice. You've stood up for right. You've stood up for life. And you sum it up in a phrase: "Drug Use Is Life Abuse." That slogan—the power of that slogan—the slogan is powerful in its simplicity. And the logo itself is apt. In it, the word "life" is literally torn apart, just as the lives of our young are torn apart and destroyed by the nightmare called cocaine.

While visiting Orange County last spring, I commended the Los Angeles Rams for having every player wear a "Drug Use Is Life Abuse" patch on his uniform—a move that was copied by tens of thousands of local fans and student athletes here. The Rams wore the patches for a year. And a Rams spokesman said, "If it dissuaded one young man or young girl from doing drugs, it was worth the whole year." And I agree. In order to win, America's war on drugs must be total war—waged from the boardroom to the classroom, from the White House to your house. No element of our society is immune—certainly not the world of professional sports. And I think the patches were a mighty good idea. Fighting drug abuse isn't a personal message; it's a public service. "Drug Use Is Life Abuse" is the right message because its goal is not punishing those who are hooked on drugs, but deterring kids from ever getting started. That message is beginning to sink in. By now just about everybody knows this simple truth: Drugs aren't the answer. They never were. And they never will be.

And recently, we've seen some scattered but hopeful new signs of progress against the horror of drugs. It began last summer, when a major nationwide survey found that the number of current drug users in America had dropped by almost 40 percent in just 3 years. And then just 2 weeks ago, another new survey showed that the number of high school seniors using drugs declined again last year, a long-term trend that has brought seniors' drug use to its lowest level in 15 years. Let's keep it going.

There are so many other hopeful signs, visible in every city in America. In my old congressional district in Houston, Texas, the people got together and took back a park from the drug dealers. In Alexandria, Virginia, I visited a neighborhood where they hold all-night vigils every Friday to keep the pushers away from the kids. And then in the heartland, Kansas City, I saw these boarded-up crack houses bearing the six-word victory banner of the local activists— the words "This neighborhood fights back against drugs."

And right here in Orange County, thousands are doing their part. I think of heroic cops like Santa Ana police investigator Henry Cousin. Although severely wounded in a drug raid 3 years ago, Henry wouldn't quit. He joined a special Federal task force and recently helped take down the biggest drug seizure in Orange County history. And I think of heroic mothers like Santa Ana's own Rosa Perez, who fought in Santa Ana for 6 years to rid her neighborhood of pushers.

But the battle isn't only being fought in the streets. About a year and a half ago, I came to Los Angeles for one of the most critical moments in the campaign: the 1988 Presidential debate up there at UCLA. And they asked if there were any heroes left in America. I named an astronaut, an AIDS researcher, a freedom fighter. And I named a high school mathematics teacher from East L.A., a teacher who helped his Hispanic students see beyond poverty and neglect to the real potential of their own minds. Jaime Escalante, Investigator Henry Cousin, Mrs. Rosa Perez—three heroes, two cities, one dream. All three are here today, and all three deserve our heartfelt thanks. No, with your help, we've covered a lot of ground in the drug war. But tough challenges remain.

It's like when the Rams offense crosses the 50-yard line: with every yard you gain, your opponent digs in and progress gets that much harder, not easier.

Make no mistake. Drug abuse in this country is still far too widespread. There's far too much suffering, far too many wasted lives. But we're going to beat drugs the same way the Rams beat many of their opponents: relentless offense, a defense that refuses to give up a single yard to the opposition—or a single child to these merchants of death. And I might add that I was delighted to be greeted earlier on by so many law enforcement officers from this area. God bless them, and God bless those line officers out there in the streets, helping every one of you kids up here in the stands. Thank you all. Against drugs, a good defense means reducing demand—and through efforts like the record funding my administration has devoted for increased drug education, treatment, and criminal justice. And a tough offense means an attack on all fronts.

Last month's drug summit in Cartagena, Colombia, marked a good day for the rule of law and a very bad day for the cocaine cartels. I was glad I went to Colombia to support that courageous President of Colombia who was trying to keep the drug dealers where they belong—in jail. President Barco's courageous crackdown has seized or destroyed their cash, their homes, their labs, and their drugs. And 14 accused traffickers have been extradited to the United States and now face American justice in courtrooms in Miami, in Tulsa, Atlanta, and in San Francisco. The days of the drug lords may not be over yet, but their days are numbered. And we're going to keep up the fight on the supply side.

You heard the Governor mention it, but let me repeat it. Here at home, my administration recently named the Los Angeles Orange County as one of the Nation's five "high intensity drug traffic areas," a designation that means increased Federal enforcement manpower for the region. And nationwide, Congress—and bless these Congressmen here that are supporting our efforts—Congress has approved funding for the new agents, new prosecutors, and new prisons that we asked for to catch, convict, and contain America's most dangerous drug offenders. But Congress also needs to act, and act soon, on my new anticrime proposals. Congress needs to provide tough laws to deal with a tough problem. Working together, we can—we will—defeat this scourge.

America has earned her victories through determination and desire. And we will win the war on drugs because we must. Just 2 nights ago, right here in Orange County, two cars were pulled over carrying nearly 900 pounds of cocaine. And thanks to your courageous antinarcotics efforts, four million doses, with a street value of $30 million, will not poison our kids. And that is desire and that is determination. And let no one doubt the commitment we have in Washington as well. The White House has declared war on the crack house. And the only enemy response we'll accept is unconditional surrender.

Thank you for your warm greeting. God bless you all. Keep up the fight. And God bless the United States of America. Thank you all very much.

Note: The President spoke at 12:35 p.m. in the Santa Ana Bowl. In his opening remarks, he referred to Jim Everett, quarterback for the Los Angeles Rams; entertainer Fred Travalena; and actor Chuck Norris.

Nomination of John C. Foltz To Be Administrator of the Federal Grain Inspection Service
March 2, 1990

The President today announced his intention to nominate John C. Foltz to be Administrator of the Federal Grain Inspection Service, Department of Agriculture. He would succeed W. Kirk Miller.

Since 1979 Mr. Foltz has served as executive director of the Ohio Grain and Feed Association in Worthington, OH. Prior to this, he served as chief of the division of markets at the Ohio Department of Agriculture, 1977–1978; Assistant Administrator for Market Development at the Foreign Agricultural Service, 1976; Deputy Under Secretary for Legislative Affairs at the Department of Agriculture, 1973–1975; deputy director for agriculture for the Committee to

Re-elect the President, 1972; Director of Congressional Relations for the Cost of Living Council in the Executive Office of the President, 1971; legislative assistant in the Office of the Secretary at the Department of Agriculture, 1969–1971; and staff member and manager of public relations for the Future Farmers of America, 1958–1968.

Mr. Foltz graduated from Ohio State University (B.S., 1955; M.S., 1971). He was born February 23, 1933, in West Lafayette, OH. Mr. Foltz served in the U.S. Navy, 1955–1957. Mr. Foltz is married, has two children, and resides in Worthington, OH.

Statement by Press Secretary Fitzwater on the President's Meeting With Prime Minister Toshiki Kaifu of Japan in Palm Springs, California
March 2, 1990

The President and Prime Minister Kaifu met for approximately 1 hour this afternoon. Their meeting began with a brief one-on-one session, followed by a plenary. In their private session, the President and the Prime Minister took the opportunity to reaffirm the close and friendly bilateral relationship of the two countries and the growing significance of their global partnership. The President congratulated the Prime Minister on his recent electoral victory. The President noted that the pillars of the relationship are the U.S.-Japanese security relationship, the global partnership, and the bilateral economic relationship.

The plenary session was devoted to a discussion of security issues of common concern. The President and the Prime Minister noted the mutual benefits that the security relationship brings to both countries and noted that it continues to be the best guarantee for stability and prosperity in the Pa-

cific region. The President stated that the adjustments the United States is contemplating in its defense posture in the Pacific area will not affect either deterrence or stability, nor its commitment to its Asian allies. The two leaders discussed the issue of burden sharing, noting the need for suitable arrangements for balanced cost sharing. The President reaffirmed the United States support for the Northern Territories issue, and noted that Secretary Baker had raised the subject during his Moscow ministerial and that the U.S. would continue to raise the Territories with the Soviet Union.

The President emphasized that this summit should lay the conceptual framework through which the two countries could realize the full potential of the already close bilateral relationship. The Prime Minister stressed the importance to coordinate our policies and tackle the issues from the standpoint of mutual cooperation.

Remarks Following Discussions With Prime Minister Toshiki Kaifu of Japan in Palm Springs, California
March 3, 1990

The President. Well, I was very pleased to welcome my friend, the Prime Minister of Japan, here to Palm Springs for 2 days of very useful and far-reaching discussions about the critically important relationship between the United States and Japan. In the first instance, I wanted to see Prime Minister Kaifu again and extend personally my congratulations for his victory in the recent elections. I also want to express my very high regard and admiration for the outstanding leadership he has given his country and his party since he was propelled into office just 6 months ago. We first met last September, and in the intervening months we've seen some of the most momentous changes in recent world history. It is important that the leaders of the United States and Japan come together and review the entire scope of their relationship at this time of profound change in the world.

There are three things that are very clear to me: that our relationship with Japan will become even more important to us and to the world in the coming decades; that Japan is moving rapidly to assume a leading role in the world, as was evident in Prime Minister Kaifu's recent trip to Eastern Europe and the nearly $2 billion in assistance that he pledged to the nations of Poland and Hungary; and that no matter where we look around the world—from Eastern Europe to Panama to Cambodia—the United States and Japan are working together to promote political and economic transformations that will strengthen democracies and market economies.

Our meetings these 2 days were not formal negotiations. This has been an opportunity to come together and take stock of the entire range of our dealings—from security, to economics and trade, to foreign policy—and to talk about where we're going together as we move toward the 21st century. We talked about how we can expand even further our global partnership. I believe that in the coming years we have

a unique and challenging opportunity to expand even further our cooperation on international issues across the board; to strengthen the political "trialog" among the United States, Japan, and our European allies; to expand our aid cooperation to embrace a larger effort aimed at promoting economic and social development in the Third World; and to think about how Japan can more fully play a leading role in the world's political and economic institutions.

We talked about developments of recent months in Europe and in U.S.-Soviet relationships. And I believe that we're agreed that our two countries must work closely together to promote the same kind of positive changes in Asia. I reaffirmed to Prime Minister Kaifu, as did Secretary of Defense Cheney during that successful visit of his to Tokyo, that the United States is, and will remain, a Pacific power; that the United States attaches great importance, the greatest importance, to its security and political alliance with Japan; and that our two countries must continue to strengthen our defense cooperation. At a time of great change in the world, our treaty of mutual cooperation and security has become even more important to ensuring continued peace and prosperity as democracy and free markets spread across Asia and the Pacific.

We also discussed our economic relationship—one of the most broad-ranging and complex set of commercial and financial interactions in the entire world. And there are many economic areas in which we have close cooperation. I think of the Third World debt problems, economic policy coordination—collaborated there. And we reaffirm our commitment to that process, including cooperation in exchange markets.

We must also remember that Japan is the second largest market in the world for our manufacturers, and the largest market in the world for our farmers. Our exports to Japan already total $44 billion—only Canada buys more from us—and our exports to Japan are going up faster than our sales to the rest of the world. The Prime Minister and his government are very aware of the mood and concern in this country about the continuing impediments to further growth of our trade relationship. Even with that 18-percent growth in our exports to Japan last year, we still have a $49 billion bilateral trade deficit. Make no mistake about it: I want to see that deficit come down, not by restricting our markets or managing trade but by further increasing our exports to Japan. And so, in the coming months, our common task must be to further open markets and expand trade.

In addition to increasing our exports to Japan, our other key task is to ensure the success of the Structural Impediments Initiative that we launched last summer. We're facing some important deadlines, and the Prime Minister and I are calling on our officials to redouble their efforts to achieve meaningful interim and final results. We must make the SII, the Structural Impediments Initiative, and our other trade discussions a success. We must put our economic relationship on a solid foundation if we're to achieve the full promise of our relationship. We feel that we presented some valid ideas about removing structural impediments in Japan that will improve market access and reduce our trade imbalances, and we look forward to the Japanese response. But let's face it, these talks are a two-way street. We Americans must increase our savings, reduce our budget deficit, provide more incentive for our investors, strengthen our educational system, focus on producing goods of the highest quality. So, our task is to make the American economy even stronger and even more competitive, and that is a task for America, not for Japan.

So, Mr. Prime Minister, I am delighted that we had this opportunity to discuss all these matters. I am confident that during our time here together, we have launched a process that will continue throughout 1990 and the coming years—a process that will create a breakthrough relationship and lead to an era of even greater cooperation between our two countries. Together, we must master our problems and expand our opportunities. By working together, in partnership, the United States and Japan have the chance to lead not only our two peoples

but the whole world into a new era of peace, freedom, and prosperity. So, Mr. Prime Minister—Toshiki, my friend, thank you for coming. And I wish you a safe journey home. May you have great success in your efforts in the coming months. You have our full support.

The Prime Minister. George, thank you very much, first of all, for your warm remarks. I would also, first of all, like to express my appreciation for the heartwarming hospitality extended to me by you, George, and Mrs. Bush. I am particularly pleased to have had the opportunity to come together in scenic Palm Springs and to discuss issues at such length that our two countries face and that relate to peace and prosperity of the world.

My meeting with you was a meaningful opportunity to discuss coordination between Japan and the United States as we move into a new era of turbulent international situation in search of a new order based on freedom and democracy. I am fully satisfied that I was able to share fundamental thoughts with you through in-depth exchange of views. I value very highly the careful but bold initiatives taken by the President to foster desirable changes in the East-West relations and to promote arms control and disarmament negotiations. I am determined that Japan must share responsibility from the standpoint of its being one of the countries who are responsible for maintaining and strengthening international order.

During my recent visit to Europe, I have pledged in concrete terms support to the East European countries who are seeking to establish freedom and democracy and introduce market economies. On the German reunification issue, the President explained to me that he conveyed the U.S. position to the Federal Republic of Germany at the recent meeting between the President and Chancellor Kohl concerning the adherence of the unified Germany to NATO and the continued presence of U.S. forces on German soil. I expressed my appreciation for his explanation and expressed my admiration for the efforts by the President. The President and I exchanged views on the Asia-Pacific situation, and we shared the view that the diplomacy of new thinking of the Soviet Union needs to be actively applied in this region as well, and that it is important for both Japan and the U.S. to endeavor together to ensure the political stability and economic prosperity of this region.

This year marks the 30th anniversary of the conclusion of the Japan-U.S. security treaty. Recognizing the roles played by the Japan-U.S. security arrangement for peace and stability of Japan as well as the Asia-Pacific region, I, together with the President, confirmed the increasing importance of the treaty into the future. Furthermore, the President and I share the view that the Japan-U.S. security arrangements continue to be the important basis of Japan-U.S. cooperation in the search for peace through deterrence and dialog at the time of the evolution of the new international situation. I value the continued role of the United States in this vision as a Pacific power which is irreplaceable by any other country. I expressed to the President my determination to extend the cooperation required to secure the continued smooth operation of the Japan-U.S. security arrangements, including host nation support for U.S. forces in Japan.

With regard to Japan-U.S. economic relations, the President and I agreed to continuously enhance our relations with the understanding that the sound development of economic relations between our two countries is indispensable to the development of not only our economies but that of the world economy. Although negative aspects of the issues and problems in our bilateral economic relations tend to be emphasized, as the President said with profound insight, the two markets are extremely large for each of us and our economies are moving in the right directions, due to the adjustment efforts in the past several years. Both the U.S. budget deficit and Japan's current surplus are being reduced, and their ratios to GNP have been halved. However, the imbalances are still very large, and we should continue to work harder. The SII is extremely important to consolidate this positive trend. I am determined to firmly tackle structural reforms of Japan as one of the top priorities of my new

Cabinet, with a view to improving the quality of Japanese life with further stress on the consumer-oriented economy. I hope that the U.S., on its part, will promote structural adjustment as the President has just said. I told the President of my determination to maintain such policies as expansion of domestic demand, the improvement of market access, and deregulation.

The President and I agreed that both Japan and the U.S. will make the maximum efforts for the early solution of pending issues in the spirit of cooperation and joint efforts between our two countries. The President expressed that Japan and the U.S. have worked closely in dealing with debt problems and economic policy coordination and reaffirmed his commitment, including cooperation in exchange markets. The President's statement convinces me to make maximum efforts for Japan-U.S. cooperation in these areas, including in exchange markets. Having in mind that our solid bilateral relations are indispensable to the future stability and prosperity of the world, the President and I shared the recognition of the importance of consolidating our bilateral relations to be the constructive cooperation. In this context, we shared the recognition that it is important and necessary to further strengthen and expand the constructive relations in the 1990's, including educational and cultural exchanges, science and technology cooperation, and two-way technology transfers.

U.S.-Japan relations of today, transcending our bilateral framework, have acquired the significance of a global partnership with responsibilities for tasks facing the world. The President and I welcome that the Japan-U.S. global partnership is bearing specific fruit in such a broad range of fields as a response to regional problems, the management of world economy, economic cooperation for developing countries and debt problems, environment, drugs, and the fight against international terrorism. On the problem of drugs in particular, I highly appreciate the series of initiatives of the President and the courageous determination shown at the Cartagena drug summit. I expressed my determination to the President that Japan will actively participate in the international efforts to eradicate illicit drugs.

I conveyed my intention to the President to promptly implement concrete measures in support of the democratic government in Nicaragua and my belief that an early economic recovery is important for the stabilization of Panama. I expressed Japan's position that Japan would look into economic assistance for the reconstruction of the region as the peace process in Central America progresses. The development of the South Africa situation contains the possibility towards dismantling apartheid. The President and I agreed that Japan and the U.S. will continue to consult with each other on how to eliminate apartheid.

This year marks the final year of the Uruguay round. The President and I agreed that the successful conclusions of the negotiations is extremely important for the fight against protectionism and for the construction of the basis for the continued progress of the world economy as we move toward the 21st century. The President and I reaffirmed our convictions that we should closely cooperate for the success of the round.

Japan and the United States are faced with enormous challenges and opportunities in the strong current of history. Having in mind the significance of the Japan-U.S. partnership as a foundation for the stability of the world, I am fully determined to courageously pave the way, together with the President, toward the 21st century. Thank you.

Ladies and gentlemen, I understand that George will stay on here and have a most wonderful time answering your questions in a press conference. I, however, will have to leave this spot in order to return home in time to answer the questions that will be raised to me in the Diet, and also just in time to arrive in Tokyo before the night landing time limit arrives at 11 p.m. in Tokyo. Well, I hope that you will not call this night landing time limit another structural impediment.

The President. Thank you very much. That was a wonderful statement.

Note: The President spoke at 1:10 p.m. at the Morningside Country Club. Prime Minister Kaifu spoke in Japanese, and his remarks were translated by an interpreter.

The President's News Conference Following Discussions With Prime Minister Toshiki Kaifu of Japan in Palm Springs, California
March 3, 1990

Japan-U.S. Trade

Q. Mr. President, are you satisfied that the Prime Minister has given a sufficient political commitment to break the impasse in trade talks? And did he offer any trade concessions?

The President. You heard his statement, which I thought was very good. And all I can tell you is we had perhaps the best opportunity that I've seen to have genuinely frank discussions. I met with him in a one-on-one yesterday, and then last night sat next to him at dinner. So, I had an opportunity to continue the business part of the discussion.

Then I heard this statement—we had our other talks, too, but I heard this statement

today. And I'd say that the Japanese side knows how important it is to move forward, and clearly I have a renewed feeling of how important it is for us to do some of the things that they were talking about on this structural impediment side. So, I can't tell you in terms of a specific commodity or a specific date. But we were just talking here, and all of us are very pleased with the frankness as well as the spirit of cooperation that I think was reflected by the Prime Minister's statement.

Q. Do you think he went far enough, sir?

The President. Well, nobody ever goes far enough to do everything exactly the way we want it. But I think for those who understand the complexities of this relationship at this juncture, we got everything out of this meeting that we had hoped for. Obviously, we've got things to do, and clearly the Japanese side has things to do. I want to say something on that meeting, if I could. The fact that he came here now—finished a tough campaign, just given a big speech to the Diet; indeed, he gets home at 11 p.m. and has to go to answer questions in the Diet the very next morning—should be interpreted by Americans in this manner, that the Japanese feel this relationship is very important. And to the Japanese side, the fact that I invited him when I did should send a very important signal that we have this right up in the forefront of relationships that are critical. And I was very grateful that he accepted—in such short notice and in a complicated timeframe—this invitation.

Q. How confident are you that he can produce——

The President. Well, he's just won a good victory there. He's solidified his party's position. He, himself, emerges as a, I would say, dynamic new leader. And so we will simply wait and see. But I wish him well.

Israeli-Palestinian Peace Talks

Q. Mr. President, there are reports out of Israel that [Prime Minister] Yitzhak Shamir is prepared to accept the U.S. formula for Israeli-Palestinian peace talks. Do you know anything about that, and if so, what shape will it take?

The President. Well, as you know, we have been working on this for 8 months. And Jim Baker and I were just talking about it, and I might say I commend him for staying in there, trying to be a catalyst to get this process going. So, we don't know any of the details of that; we just talked to our top officials here. But I hope it's true and I hope we can move forward. And if we do, I'll be glad to salute our Secretary of State and others, including Mr. Shamir, Mr. Mubarak [Egyptian President], for hanging in there, trying to get something moving toward peace.

Q. Has there been any movement, sir? If you don't know about his final commitment, has there been any movement toward acceptance of the U.S. formula?

The President. Well, there has, over the

months. But just like the real world, you take two steps forward and take one step back. I hope we're going to go forward now.

Soviet Military Capability

Q. Mr. President, a question about some testimony last week on the Soviets. Secretary Cheney said he still believes they are continuing with modernization. Director [of Central Intelligence] Webster said in some testimony he thinks that the military threat seems to be receding in some significant respects. With your experience in intelligence, how do you explain these divergent views, and have you adopted either of them? What would you tell the American people about what to think about this?

The President. You know, I get asked—the question is, who is the enemy? And I answer: uncertainty, unpredictability. And I don't see a great disconnect between the way you phrased the question as to whether they are modernizing or as to whether the threat has receded. Clearly, as you see those troops starting to move out of various Eastern countries, and as you've seen the democracies coming in, that results in a diminished threat. But it doesn't say that everything is certain and that stability is guaranteed. I was asked that question in relation to why I felt we ought to continue to have troops in Europe and why I felt that it would be good to have a unified Germany in NATO. And the answer is: stability. Safeguard against unpredictability or instability.

So, I haven't gone into, David [David Hoffman, Washington Post], the testimony of each—haven't read it, but I really don't see a big conflict there.

Japan-U.S. Relations

Q. How long do you give Mr. Kaifu to produce? It seems we've heard these types of assurances he gave today before. What are you looking for specifically, and when are you looking for it?

The President. Well, we have some timeframes. We have some March talks that I'd like to see successful. But look, we weren't here to throw down definitive deadlines. That's not the way you deal with Japan, in my view. But the sooner the better, is the way I answer the question.

Q. But were there any new initiatives, Mr. President? For example, I mean, you emphasize that this wasn't a negotiating session. But were there any new initiatives on either side—any new proposals, for example, that you'd recommend some way that he could be of assistance in Nicaragua?

The President. Well, yes, there was a good discussion of that. And I was very pleased with his receptivity to helping the new democracies here. They pledged $1.95 billion to help in the reconstruction in Eastern Europe, help with the democracies there. And he was very openminded in response to my plea to be of similar—to be of assistance to Nicaragua and to Panama. So, yes, we had some detailed discussion about that, but it wasn't, like, by a certain date we expect a certain—like to see a certain amount of money, or anything.

Q. Could you tell us about any details— for example, a new way to be of assistance?

The President. Well, just that I felt a commitment on the part of the Prime Minister of Japan to assist democracy. And I think that is very important, and frankly, I think that will help the U.S.-Japan relationship. Because I think the people in our country, as I told him, want to see the Chamorro [Nicaraguan President-elect Violeta Chamorro] government succeed, want to see democracy in Panama succeed. So, in that particular subject matter, I was very pleased with the forthcoming comments from Prime Minister Kaifu.

U.S. Foreign Assistance

Q. Will you work to reduce some of the foreign aid to the largest recipients, like Egypt and Israel, so that the United States can give more to Eastern Europe, Nicaragua, and the countries——

The President. Well, I am against earmarking. I am for more flexibility. We have had discussions with our Congressmen, including the chairman of the House Foreign Affairs Committee. Some of those discussions encourage the concept of a fund that gives the President the flexibility to determine a certain amount of foreign aid money. So, I'm less interested in reducing somebody than I am getting the flexibility— so that when you see a country come for-

ward and try to solidify their democracy or work cooperatively with us in the Caribbean as, say, Mr. Manley in Jamaica is doing, we'd like to be able to help him more.

Israeli-Palestinian Peace Talks

Q. Would it be a bad signal right now with Israel trying to move toward talks with the Palestinians?

The President. Would what be a bad signal?

Q. Would the reduction of aid to Israel?

The President. I don't know that moving towards peace need be totally equated with aid. I mean, we're talking about a quest for peace that comes not just in Israel but in Egypt and everything else. So, I'm not tying those two subjects. But Israel has some big economic problems; they've got some big problems facing them that require a very generous apportionment of aid money, and they are getting that.

Resettlement of Soviet Jews

Q. To follow on the question of aid to Israel, Secretary Baker has suggested that we might tie aid to resettle the Soviet Jews to the Israelis' willingness to not settle the West Bank and to withdraw some of its settlements from the West Bank and Gaza. Then the State Department seemed to equivocate on that. What's your position?

The President. Well, I'm not sure there was equivocation. My position is that the foreign policy of the United States says we do not believe there should be new settlements in the West Bank or in East Jerusalem. And I will conduct that policy as if it's firm, which it is, and I will be shaped in whatever decisions we make to see whether people can comply with that policy. And that's our strongly held view. We think it's constructive to peace—the peace process— if Israel will follow that view. And so, there's divisions in Israel on this question, incidentally. Parties are divided on it. But this is the position of the United States, and I'm not going to change that position.

Q. So, will you link aid to resettle the Soviet Jews?

The President. I will just simply reiterate that the policy right here—that we are not going to look favorably upon new settlements.

313

Japan-U.S. Trade

Q. Mr. President, before coming to this meeting, the Prime Minister outlined in his speech to his own Parliament new measures to increase foreign exports to Japan. And he alluded to that in his departure statement just a few minutes ago. Did you discuss those with him, and how significant and serious do you see them to be?

The President. New measures to increase——

Q. Foreign exports—U.S. sales to Japan?

The President. Absolutely. It was discussed by me, and the Secretary of State had a good chance to discuss it with the Foreign Minister. At dinner, our various participants, including our trade people, had a chance to discuss that whole concept with the rest of the Japanese delegation, and I had every opportunity to discuss it. And so it's something they're quite clear on. We want to and we must increase exports. I covered that in my statement, and I listened carefully to what he said about the deficit we have and the surplus they have.

Q. Do you feel that he has begun to make some good moves in the direction of——

The President. Well, I'm very encouraged, as I told you—or, I'm encouraged by the talks we've had, and I am encouraged with the trend that seems to be taking place. We've got to do more.

U.S. Hostages in Lebanon

Q. Mr. President, regarding the hostages, is there any new movement to report? Is any third country, particularly the French—there are reports that perhaps French mediaries are working on behalf of the U.S. to negotiate with people in either Iran or Syria.

The President. Nice try. Let me tell you all something. You people reported that I called [French President] François Mitterrand to discuss the release of some guy that I had never heard of before, and we denied it, and you keep coming back at me. I'm not sure—I think it's good for you to do that, though, because I have said that if I find a way to get these hostages released, and the way to do it is through quiet diplomacy with the French, the British, the Ira-

nians, or anybody else, I will do it. I want those hostages out of there. So, keep asking. But on this case, the answer to your question is no.

Japan-U.S. Trade

Q. What new ideas came out of your talks to propel the trade dispute so that you get more progress down the road? Any new ideas you put on the table or that the Prime Minister——

The President. What's that?

Q. ——new ideas that you put on the table, or the Prime Minister did, to propel the trade talks?

The President. I don't know that we need new ideas. We just need new energy on both sides. And I did say this—I said, you've got a new Cabinet, and some of your top Cabinet officials that will be engaged in trade negotiation are not here. And I will tell you that our Cabinet officials—and I was thinking of Carla Hills, thinking of Mosbacher, as well as Secretary Brady and as well as Secretary Baker—would be on the next plane if it will help solve this problem. And he seemed to take on board that sense of urgency. We'll see where we go.

Q. Mr. President, I'm a little confused. In your statement, you said you did put forth new ideas and you were awaiting a response from the Japanese. I'm wondering if you could——

The President. That was one of them.

Q. Okay. Is that it?

The President. No, that's not entirely it. But there is some—I think we've covered the subject very well.

Q. May I ask you, sir, if you believe now, based on your discussions here, that these two countries will be able to avoid the punitive actions specified under congressionally mandated deadlines?

The President. We had a chance to review that and to review the question of Super 301. And we did discuss that. We discussed the timeframes involved. We discussed product specificity—and we all know what they are—satellites and forest products and supercomputers and semiconductors. And so, yes, we did get a chance to go into all that.

Q. Do you think he'll be able to avoid the

sanctions?

The President. Well, I'm hopeful we will, because it is going to require progress. But again, both sides understand the U.S. law on this, and I think their side understands it more clearly right now.

Q. Mr. President, 36 Senators wrote you a letter on forest products. What do you tell them and the thousands of timber workers who think they will lose their jobs if Japan takes our logs and not our finished lumber?

The President. I tell them the U.S.-Japanese relationship is important. I tell them I want to see open markets. I tell them I want to see progress made in that category, along with the other three, and many others that I have referenced here. That's what I would tell them.

Q. Mr. President, why did Mr. Kaifu not bring his Trade Minister?

The President. I'm not even sure—I don't know what their confirmation process—that they were all totally in place.

General Scowcroft. They are, but just barely.

The President. They are, but just barely. They were appointed, and they had 8 hours to pack up, and I guess that wasn't enough time. I think it was that when I sent them the invitation and when we started dealing with who was going to come, he wasn't quite sure that everything would be in place. I guess I'd prefer that the Japanese side answer that question.

Q. Mr. President, do you think that these talks are going to be able to diffuse protectionist moods in Congress?

The President. I hope so, but I don't know. I think that depends on the results. I oppose protectionism. I'm going to continue to fight against it. I want to open markets, I want to see a successful Uruguay round, and I will do from the executive branch side what I can. But, look, I'm not unsympathetic to those that say let's have markets open further. And that's what was good out of the meeting. We had a chance to say that. But I think the proof of the pudding is in the eating.

Q. It's up to the Japanese?

The President. Yes. And us on some areas. I mean, if you're talking about structural impediments, let's get on with some of the suggestions they make about us—on the

deficit and some other areas. I've told them that we're trying to be more competitive in going forward with an education program. They happen to support the idea of capital gains reductions, and I'd like to see that take place. So it's not just a one-way street.

Q. Mr. Bush, a great deal of American money flows out of the United States through American companies purchased by the Japanese. Did you discuss the question of restraint by Japanese investment in this country?

The President. No.

Q. Why? Why is that not——

The President. Because I welcome Japanese investment in this country. Do you know why? Jobs. American jobs—people working that wouldn't have a job necessarily if there wasn't that investment. And the Japanese are not number one in terms of foreign investment. And so the big thing is—and also, the other reason, Frank, is I don't want to see barriers thrown up to U.S. investment in other countries. So, that's why. It's a free trade concept, plus jobs for the American working man and woman in this country.

But it also has to do with financing a deficit that I'd like to see Congress help me get down.

Q. Did you talk about the corollary of lowering barriers to American investment in Japan?

The President. Yes, we did.

Q. And to what effect?

The President. Well, you've heard me discussing that.

Q. According to Mr. Fitzwater's statement, you emphasize that this summit should raise a conceptual framework. What is the meaning of a conceptual framework?

The President. Well, I think I touched on that in the calling for a trialog. We've asked the Secretary of State to meet with the Foreign Minister of Japan to discuss how we can—this is the global effort that we've been discussing—and so I think that language relates to that particular part of our discussions.

Q. Are you looking for some new structure for dialog?

The President. Well, yes, but it's going to require now more conversation between our foreign ministries. But I think as we see the world developing into the nineties, it is essential that Japan be included—U.S., Europe, and Japan—in a lot of these economic—discussion of these economic areas. And so, that's what we were talking about there. It's the global approach to some of these problems. But Japan is a key player there, and we've got to structure some of these organizations accordingly.

I think it's thoroughly understandable that Japan, with its contributions and the size of its economy, wants to have a stepped-up influence in some of the multilateral institutions. Well, that would be a discussion—that subject would be something that would come under these discussions that I've just outlined. You can't follow up on his question, you get a new one. No, you get a new one.

Q. Mr. President, when you used conceptual framework, you had in mind the SII talks and the Super 301?

The President. Excuse me?

Q. When you used the word "conceptual framework."

The President. Well, I thought I just explained that to this gentleman here—probably not as clear as I should have been—but we believe that Japan will have more of a voice in these international matters, and we're moving accordingly to expand what traditionally or heretofore has been dialog, and the three major factors having an input into it.

Mr. Fitzwater. We'll take a final question, please.

Q. Mr. President, you mentioned that the Japanese were aware of sentiment in the United States and in Congress. Did you specifically mention that to them? There have been some letters in the past week, as you probably know—Senator Bentsen and Congressman Gephardt have said—did you specifically tell them, "Congress is pushing very hard on this—we've got to do something"?

The President. I had—in that one-on-one had the opportunity to be just as clear as any Congressman would have liked me to be on what needs to happen to keep this terribly important relationship on track. And similarly, Prime Minister Kaifu was as frank with me as to how some of what we

do is viewed in Japan. So, it was very good in that regard. And I hadn't seen probably all the letters from Congress, but you're right, there's a tremendous amount of interest on that. And those letters were, in a sense, helpful to me because—the ones that I saw—because they depicted a sense of urgency that I hope I was able to convey and that others in our party were able to convey to our Japanese counterparts. So, I think in that role, in that context, those inputs were very helpful.

Thank you all very much.

Panama

Q. The bombing in Panama—are American servicemen at greater risk?

The President. We oppose terrorism, and that seems to be a terroristic action. And it happens, regrettably, all around the world, and that would be the only answer I could give you, Ann [Ann Compton, ABC News]. So, I would hope not. The process of democratization is still strongly popular in Panama, so I don't know what that was even about. But if it was some protest against democracy, why, so be it. But it must be condemned by all.

Thank you all very much, and I hope you have a pleasant day. I know I will.

United Negro College Fund

Q. What do you think of Mr. Annenberg's $50 million gift?

The President. Well, it's a little premature. We were planning to discuss that. But I think it's a wonderful thing. I've long been a supporter of the United Negro College Fund. Our administration has stepped up support for historically black colleges and universities and the endowment concept there, and I think that generosity, which is a challenge gift, as I understand it, will bring on well-deserved support from others. It's most generous, and one of the most brilliant Thousand Points of Light I can think of.

Note: The President's 39th news conference began at 1:46 p.m. at the Morningside Country Club. Brent Scowcroft is Assistant to the President for National Security Affairs, and Marlin Fitzwater is Press Secretary to the President.

Remarks at the Presentation Ceremony for a Donation to the United Negro College Fund in Palm Springs, California
March 4, 1990

The President. I'm delighted to be here today with Ambassador Annenberg; Adele Hall, a very active member of the UNCF family; Chris Edley, of course, the head of the United Negro College Fund; and our old friend Dr. Cook, the president of Dillard. And as many of you know, my own personal relationship with the UNCF dates back to my senior year at Yale University, 42 years ago. Bill Trent, who you all remember, was then the head of the United Negro College Fund—went on to become a senior vice president at Time, Inc.—but a dedicated individual. And he first got me interested way back then in working with the fund and the historically black colleges and universities. And I must say, on a personal basis, he and I remain very close friends to this day.

But this year I am pleased to serve as honorary chairman of the United Negro College Fund Capital Campaign. And I'm delighted to know that my good friend Walter Annenberg has set such a significant and marvelous example with his gift to this excellent cause. I also want to salute my friend Adele Hall, who has been so active in this important work. Although black colleges represent about 3 percent of American colleges, they enroll about 20 percent of all black students attending colleges and universities. And support for the UNCF provides precious opportunity for thousands of America's most promising students. It's an important effort. It's a noble effort. And our mission must be to strengthen our historically black colleges and universities to meet the challenges of the 21st century. This administration and the many supporters of UNCF around the country are committed to doing just that. And so, spectacular gifts like this one to the UNCF will enable these schools to continue to ensure the highest academic standards.

Walter, I just can't tell you how inspired I am by your generosity, exemplifying the very best of what I call the Thousand Points of Light. And, Chris, thank you for your inspired leadership of the United Negro College Fund. And, Dr. Dillard, thank you for your—I mean, Dr. Cook, thank you for your hospitality at Dillard. I'll never forget that. And now I'm pleased to turn the podium over to Walter Annenberg.

Mr. Annenberg. Well, I'm indeed delighted to have an opportunity to participate in this very significant role of support for underprivileged human beings.

I'm not going to say a great deal, but I do want to point out that it is the obligation, the responsibility of those who have been fortunate in life to support those who are less fortunate. And if you don't understand that, you're not very much of a citizen. The Navy has a great expression—I say the Navy because I want to comment on something that I was sure would appeal to the President. In life, you can reduce it to just a simple phrase: Shape up or ship out. That's it. [*Laughter*]

Mr. Edley. Ambassador Annenberg, Mrs. Annenberg, Mr. President, Adele Hall and Sam Cook, and ladies and gentlemen of the press: This is the most momentous occasion in the history of the college fund up to this point. And I know that this is a launching pad. Mr. Ambassador, we thank you from the bottom of our hearts for this tremendous gift. I am sure that it will capture the imagination of the Nation—the foundations, the corporations, other wealthy individuals who can make a difference.

As our country approaches the 21st century, we know that two-thirds of the entrants in the work force will be members of minority groups—including blacks—and that two-thirds of those minority groups will be blacks. And we know that as we approach the middle of this decade, a little over 4 years from now, that for the first time in decades, the number of black teachers in the public schools will drop below 5 percent. And even as we speak, there is a tragic decline in the number of blacks participating in all levels of education. We need a crusade not just to raise the money for the sake of raising money but to educate the people who will guarantee a prosperous America in the 21st century. We must not fall behind.

And that is the real significance of what we do today. And I sincerely hope that all Americans will watch to see what is the response to this magnificent challenge as we seek to raise $250 million to meet the challenge that Ambassador Annenberg has given us this day. I thank you all. And again, I thank Mr. and Mrs. Annenberg.

Note: The President spoke at 8:46 a.m. at the Annenberg residence. Following his remarks, he returned to Washington, DC.

Statement on the Economic Situation in Argentina
March 5, 1990

The actions announced yesterday by Argentina's President Carlos Menem indicate that he clearly is determined to bring about economic recovery in Argentina. President Menem called me last Thursday, March 1, to tell me that he would be announcing new economic measures designed to bring stability to his country's economy. The United States encourages him in this effort and in his support for democracy. We realize, however, that this process is not easy and respect the efforts that President Menem is making. We will be studying closely the reforms he has announced, and will look for ways to continue helping the Argentine people to achieve economic recovery and prosperity.

Statement on the 20th Anniversary of the Treaty on the Non-Proliferation of Nuclear Weapons
March 5, 1990

Twenty years ago today, the Treaty on the Non-Proliferation of Nuclear Weapons (NPT) entered into force. One hundred and forty states have joined the treaty, making it the most widely accepted arms control instrument in history. The NPT represents the primary legal barrier to nuclear proliferation and thus constitutes a principal foundation of international security. Later this year, the parties to the NPT will convene the Fourth Review Conference of the treaty. In the context of this review, I reaffirm the determination of the United States to carry out its treaty commitments and to work to assure its continuance in the interest of world peace and security.

The NPT has been not only a significant arms control instrument, it has also facilitated international cooperation in a wide variety of peaceful uses of atomic energy under international safeguards applied by the International Atomic Energy Agency. These applications have included using nuclear technology to improve health conditions as well as to increase agricultural output, electric power generation, and industrial capabilities. The United States will continue to play a leading role in nuclear cooperation pursuant to the treaty. Our longstanding commitment to serious arms control negotiations has helped to bring forth a number of important arms control agreements, including the Intermediate Nuclear Forces Treaty concluded in 1987. At this very moment we are making significant strides toward concluding far-reaching arms control agreements in the nuclear and conventional areas.

It is essential in these times of great change and great promise, and of major progress in arms control, that the community of nations works together even more diligently to prevent nuclear proliferation, which poses one of the greatest risks to the survival of mankind. I urge all states that are not party to the NPT to join and thereby demonstrate their support for the goal of preventing nuclear proliferation, and I call upon all states party to the treaty to join our efforts to secure the integrity of the NPT, which benefits all countries.

Nomination of Lynne Vincent Cheney To Be Chairperson of the National Endowment for the Humanities
March 5, 1990

The President today announced his intention to nominate Lynne Vincent Cheney to be Chairperson of the National Endowment for the Humanities, National Foundation on the Arts and the Humanities, for a term of 4 years. This is a reappointment.

Since 1986 Dr. Cheney has served as the Chairman of the National Endowment for the Humanities in Washington, DC. Prior to this she served as senior editor for Washingtonian magazine.

Dr. Cheney graduated from Colorado College (B.A., 1962; M.A., 1964) and the University of Wisconsin (Ph.D., 1970). She was born August 14, 1941 in Casper, WY. Dr. Cheney is married to Richard B. Cheney, has two children, and resides in McLean, VA.

Statement by Press Secretary Fitzwater on President Bush's Telephone Conversation With Seymour Reich of the Conference of Presidents of American Jewish Organizations
March 5, 1990

The President talked by telephone this afternoon with Seymour Reich, president of the Conference of Presidents of American Jewish Organizations. The President urged Mr. Reich and all those who shared his concern for the Middle East to continue to devote themselves to bringing about as soon as possible a pre-elections dialog between Israelis and Palestinians. This remains the surest path available to promoting a peace that would ensure Israeli security and the legitimate political rights of Palestinians.

The President also reiterated that U.S. policy toward Jerusalem is unchanged. The United States supports a united Jerusalem whose final status is determined by negotiations. The President also made clear U.S. support for Jews as well as others to live there in the context of a negotiated settlement. The President also reiterated longstanding U.S. policy that all parties avoid unilateral actions, including settlement activity.

The President also used the occasion of his conversation with Mr. Reich to state his strong support for the immigration of Soviet Jews to Israel, and made it clear that the United States will oppose any efforts designed to frustrate this human right. The President expressed his administration's support for proposed housing investment guarantees, provided the United States and Israel can work out assurances that satisfy the United States on settlement activity.

Remarks to Members of the National PTA Legislative Conference
March 5, 1990

The President. Under Secretary Sanders and Roger Porter, distinguished guests—and Ann, especially to you and the leaders of the PTA—welcome to the East Room of the White House. Barbara and I are delighted that you're here. It's been said that education is what remains when we've forgotten all we've been taught. By this reckoning, I guess I've become quite a scholar over the years. [*Laughter*]

But the truth is, we may have forgotten our algebra lessons, but we haven't forgotten logic. We may have forgotten a history lesson from high school, but we haven't forgotten the lessons of history. So, our first concern is for those Americans who never get the chance to learn. No one feels this concern more than you, you who serve on the school boards and work with the PTA all across this country. Since the founding of the PTA in this very city 92 years ago, later merged with the heroic National Congress of Colored Parents and Teachers, the men and women of the PTA have struggled to make this nation fully educated. And you've for years been a strong voice in support of standards of higher achievement.

Well, I'm here today to tell you that your Governors and your President have listened and that the vision of the PTA is now the vision of America. As you know, I met with the Governors last fall at an education summit, the first of its kind. And at Charlottesville, we forged a national compact on education reform. We resolved to put progress ahead of partisanship, the future before the moment, and our children before ourselves. And I am pleased to tell you that in our meeting last week, judging from the enthusiasm of the Governors and education leaders like Ann Lynch, the spirit of Charlottesville is growing ever stronger. Our resolve is strong because we are agreed: The time for rhetoric is past; the time to seek results, at hand.

We did not meet for yet another conference, more speeches, more white papers. No. We met to establish the first national education goals in American history. Our nation is committed, as we have never been before, to a radical restructuring of our schools. And we are committed to this national effort because nothing less than our national future is at stake. And as I speak just a week and a half after the Governors' meeting, I am pleased to announce that a United States delegation headed by former Governor Tom Kean is on its way to a World Conference on Education for All way over in Thailand. And I have charged them to share America's commitment to and enthusiasm for education reform. Both Barbara and I look forward to hearing from these delegates when they return. By the way, two of the delegates, Tom Kean and Jim Duffy from Project Literacy U.S., have something in common with Ann Lynch—they're all members of my Education Policy Advisory Committee. And Ann, I do want to thank you for your hard work with this group. We have a good one; this is a working group.

And so, as the nations of the world gather this week to discuss goals, we're getting to work right here at home to ensure a bright future for our children and our country. We've got to meet six new goals by the end of the century.

First: American children must be ready to learn from the first day of school. And of course, preparing children for school is a historic responsibility of parents. But where parents are absent or where they're unable to help, we need to provide the right kind of assistance to help children, especially in those early years. And that's why I proposed a record funding for Head Start.

Second: High school graduation rates have improved, but I think we'd all agree they're still unacceptably low. And so, we will raise the graduation rate to at least 90 percent by making our schools meaningful, challenging, and relevant to the needs of the students.

Third goal: We will expect that every child can learn and raise our expectations of what they can accomplish. When our children leave the transition grades of 4, 8, and

12, it is not too much to expect that they will read at the 4th-grade level, and the 8th-grade level, and then the 12th-grade level. And it's not too much to expect that they will have the appropriate mastery of English, math, science, geography, and history.

Fourth: When it comes to math and science, America will no longer settle for the bottom of the list, or even third or second place among the industrialized nations. When it comes to math and science achievement, we will accept only one prime number: number one in the world.

Fifth: Every American adult must be literate and have the skills needed to compete in a global economy. This country has such a marvelous system of junior and vocational colleges ready to teach new skills—from learning Spanish to car mechanics to computer literacy. And there's no reason that education should end with the conferral of a diploma. And of course, there are many adult Americans who have yet to master the very basics. Barbara has been a leader of the campaign for literacy for 8 years now. And through her, I have learned that a simple lack of letters is a silent sorrow, but it need not be a lifelong tragedy.

Our sixth and final goal is the most basic of all: to free every school in America from drugs and violence. It is no coincidence that the words civility and civilization come from the same Latin root. You're looking at one who studied Latin for 4 years—don't remember a thing—[*laughter*]—except that it is no coincidence that the words civil and civilization come from the same Latin root. For if rudimentary civility is lost in our schools, then our civilization itself really is in danger.

Every time I meet with teachers and administrators, I am told the same thing: Every State, every district, every school is unique. So, to make our goals work, we will need to relax the Federal regulations that try to force every State, district, and school into exactly the same mold. The Governors impressed on me the need for flexibility.

Last year I met with many teachers to prepare for the education summit. And I was told no two students are exactly alike, and no two schools face exactly the same challenge. And so, while we work to devel-

op appropriate measures and to monitor progress, you must work school by school, class by class, child by child. To raise scores is important, but no statistic can match the thrill of watching the brightening face of a learning child. And yet, when too many strings are attached to Federal funding and by the States, educators and students alike are treated like puppets. And so, I promise to continue to work with the Governors and Congress to cut you loose from excessive Federal regulation.

In return for greater flexibility, we will seek, of course, accountability. Accountability begins when we quit kidding ourselves. We must stop measuring our efforts by what goes into our schools and start measuring our efforts by what comes out of them. So, we will no longer grade ourselves by dollars spent, classrooms filled, chairs occupied: no more A's for effort. We must have the courage to be graded on our results, just like our children. In a very real sense, we will be graded along with our children.

Again, these are not just my goals or the Bush administration goals, nor are they the handiwork of the Governors alone. These are the national goals, and it will take an act of national will to make them stick. So, let's start inside every school by posting these goals so that all who walk in—parents, students, the teachers—know where we're going. And to make these goals work, I'm asking you to rethink school procedures and course requirements—even that challenge, the academic schedule itself. We've inherited hallowed academic traditions from the agrarian age, traditions of discipline that should be strengthened. But when hallowed tradition proves to be hollow convention, then we must not hesitate to shatter tradition.

Parents, perhaps, have the greatest task ahead of them. True, Head Start can work wonders. But too many parents have fallen into the habit of thinking of education as a service we can hand over to the school boards, to you leaders, much in the same way we expect our cities to provide electricity or water or some other service. Education is not a utility. Education is a national mission. It really must include the parents. And that's why we need the leadership of this marvelous organization, the PTA. After all, a school program can't kiss away the pain from an injured knee. And a school program won't calm the fears of a child about to get a first shot. And a school program alone can't instill a lifelong love of learning. But parents can spark the flame of curiosity by reading to their children every night. And you can best reach all the parents of America. You can recruit them as educators not just for their preschool children but to help their children do their homework all the way through school.

The PTA has more than 6.6 million members in 27,000 local units in every State, here in the District of Columbia, and in Defense Department schools abroad. And there is no organization in America that can reach as many schools and as many parents as you can—not State governments and really not even the Federal Government. Success in education starts with you, from every parent and every teacher who will settle for nothing less than a world-class education for our kids.

And so, what I wanted to do was to come over here today to this lovely East Room—Barbara at my side, because I think we would all agree she's doing a great job out there in this literacy—what we both wanted to do was to come over here and say that for all that you do, and for all that you will do, you have our most sincere thanks. God bless you and God bless the United States of America. Thank you very much.

Ms. Lynch. You only need to stand for one President, not for me. [*Laughter*] Mr. President, we wanted to take this occasion because it's not often that groups such as ours gets to come to this East Room, to correct a wrong that we think has caused some difficulty in your family.

Several years ago, Mrs. Bush received a national honorary membership from the National PTA. [*Laughter*] And since we believe strongly that it takes two to really provide good parenting when there are two in the family, we felt to put you on an even keel and to express our appreciation for being truly the education President and for sharing the time and energy and enthusiasm in a world that has so many other problems and excitement for you—that you have taken this time for education—we would like to make you a member, an honorary member of the National PTA.

The President. Thank you very much.

Note: The President spoke at 2:33 p.m. in the East Room at the White House. In his remarks, he referred to Under Secretary of Education Ted Sanders; Roger Porter, Assistant to the President for Economic and Domestic Policy; and Ann Lynch, president of the National Congress of Parents and Teachers (PTA).

Remarks at the Welcoming Ceremony for Prime Minister Giulio Andreotti of Italy
March 6, 1990

The President. Mr. Prime Minister and Mrs. Andreotti, and friends of Italy. Barbara and I are pleased to welcome the President of the Council of Ministers of the Republic of Italy, Giulio Andreotti, and his wife, Livia, to the United States and to the White House. Prime Minister Andreotti's public career is rich in achievement, unrivaled in modern Europe. He served his nation with distinction as statesman and diplomat and, of course, as Prime Minister. But Prime Minister Andreotti is also a man of letters, known for his humor and integrity. And here in America, he's known as a good and close friend—the leader of a strong nation and a strong people. And we are proud and honored to have him as our guest today.

Forty-five years ago the giants of modern history—Churchill, Truman, and de Gaulle—were embarking on the great task of rebuilding Europe, what would later be known as the Marshall plan. And another giant worked with them, a man who helped build the strong Atlantic community we have today—Prime Minister de Gaspari of Italy. I mentioned that Prime Minister Andreotti is a renowned author. Well, he wrote a biography of de Gaspari, and it is in the tradition of his subject that Prime Minister Andreotti leads Italy today.

Like his predecessor, Giulio Andreotti is a leader who fights for freedom, peace, and democracy in an evolving Europe. This week's visit by the Prime Minister bears witness to Italy's continued leadership in the swift-moving stream of events in Europe and to America's steadfast partnership with Italy and Europe through it all. I look forward to exchanging views with you, Mr. Prime Minister, this time on the dramatic developments in Europe—East and West. Over the past two decades, we've seen Italy's role in world affairs grow under your leadership, both as Foreign Minister and as Prime Minister. And during that time, the United States and Italy have been the firmest allies. Our dialog is constant; it is substantive; it is productive.

We agree on the foundations of a new Europe. We welcome the prospect of overcoming Europe's artificial division and building a Europe whole and free. We look to the Conference on Security and Cooperation in Europe, the CSCE, to play a greater role in Europe's future, particularly in guiding the economic and political transformation of the rising democracies in Eastern Europe. We agree that the EC must play a vital role in new Europe. A more united Europe, able to take its rightful place in world affairs, is good for the United States of America. As Italy assumes the Presidency of the European Community beginning in July, Prime Minister Andreotti and I will work to improve economic and political ties between the United States and the Community. In this role, Italy will have the opportunity to lead the EC in the battle against organized crime and narcotics trafficking—a fight in which our two nations remain strong, determined, and united.

Above all, we share a common commitment to NATO and the conviction that the United States must and will remain a European power. We are true partners in the Atlantic alliance which serves as the foundation for stability and our common security. So, Prime Minister Andreotti and I have

much to discuss about Germany, the alliance, East-West relations, U.S.-EC ties, and other topics. And I am confident that we share the commitment that Chancellor Kohl and I expressed at Camp David 9 days ago: that a united Germany should remain a full member of NATO, including participation in its military structure. In all these areas I look forward to serious and productive talks with Prime Minister Andreotti, a true and valued friend of the United States.

Americans have always held a special place in our hearts for Italy. It was the American novelist Henry James who once wrote: "We go to Italy to gaze upon certain of the highest achievements of human power, representing to the imagination the maximum of man's creative force." Well, together we can achieve even more, and today's visit will strengthen the deep bonds between us. And we share 12 million Americans who proudly call Italy their ancestral home, and because of them, America is a richer place—because of their commitment to family and faith and their zest for life. Let me, in closing, express to you, sir, my hope that you have a most successful visit, a safe journey, and a delightful time here. Mr. Prime Minister, welcome back to Washington, DC.

The Prime Minister. Thank you very much for your warm words of welcome. In return, I would like to express to you the great esteem in which you are held by the Italian government and people. My visit is but a continuation of a solid tradition of alliance and cooperation between our governments, a tradition which forms part of the much broader alliance and solidarity between Western countries to which we owe this extraordinarily long period of peace in Europe and prosperity in the world. Within this framework Italy is actively working, as it deems the alliance to be ever more valid and necessary.

The very close links between the United States and Europe is still, for Italy, an essential point of reference in a world in which ideological confrontation is waning and military tensions will everywhere have to yield to a new climate of dialog. We rejoice to see the dawn of democracy in Eastern Europe. We look forward with hope towards a new relationship with the Soviet Union under Gorbachev. These are fresh and exciting prospects that are awakening in Europe today. New balances lie on the horizon, full of promise, yet also fraught with problems. By updating and reviving the spirits and the models of NATO and Helsinki, we must all together seize the challenges that are facing us.

And what challenges: the backwardness in so many parts of the world, the dreadful degradation of the environment, organized crime and, above all, the scourge of drugs that so deeply jeopardizes our society. This is the message of our nation that is profoundly committed to building up a European Community soundly founded on the values of freedom and progress; a country that is open to the world, including those parts of it which are less fortunate, and sensitive to its needs and problems; a country, lastly, that has always been an integral part of the great mosaic of Europe, but also one which is vitally interested in the problems of the Mediterranean area towards which our attention shall not be lessened following to what is now occurring in Eastern Europe.

Mr. President, I am now thinking about what links America and Italy by history and culture. I'm not referring only to the role of that ingenious Italian Renaissance man, Christopher Columbus, in marking the birth of this country, an event which we shall be delighted to celebrate with the American people on its anniversary in 1992. I'm also thinking to the many millions of Americans of Italian descent whom you have recalled, Mr. President, who are such an important and active part of this country today. My message goes out to them also in the hope they may look more and more to Italy's tradition as well as its contemporary reality for a precious heritage and cherished sense of belonging.

Mr. President, in conclusion I wish to say that Italy desires to continue looking to the United States with sentiments of solidarity that long decades of shared political and military partnership have made so strong and rich, and with that friendship that is now an invaluable asset of both our peoples. It is with these same feelings, Mr. President, that I wish to thank you for your welcome and extend to you my best wishes for the prosperity and well-being of all the American people.

The President. Sir, thank you very much.

Note: The President spoke at 10:10 a.m. at the South Portico of the White House, where the Prime Minister was accorded a formal welcome with full military honors. The Prime Minister spoke in Italian, and his remarks were translated by an interpreter. Following the ceremony, the two leaders met in the Oval Office.

Exchange With Reporters Prior to a Meeting With Prime Minister Giulio Andreotti of Italy
March 6, 1990

German Reunification

Q. Mr. Prime Minister, do you believe the two-plus-four formula will give Italy a sufficient voice in the possible reunification of Germany?

The Prime Minister. No, it's not a problem which belongs to Italy. I think that all the member countries of the Atlantic alliance must handle together these problems, and provided that the specific problems related to Berlin must be handled by the four countries.

Q. Mr. President, are you concerned or hopeful about what's happening in Afghanistan?

Baseball Strike

Q. Mr. President, do you think anything should be done about the baseball strike?

The President. We have a strike, and our son owns one of the teams—or is the managing owner or managing partner of one of the baseball teams, and she's asking me about the strike, knowing that I don't take questions at a photo opportunity. However, she got close to something I might answer—very close there. I was tempted.

Meeting With Prime Minister Andreotti

Q. Mr. President, are you going to approve a NATO meeting here on Germany next month?

The President. I'm not going to take any questions at a photo opportunity, except to say this to the Italian journalists: Welcome back to the United States, and we are delighted you're here. And frankly, I view this as a very important meeting with a respected friend. But other than that, I won't take any questions in here. However, the Prime Minister is free to do anything he wants in here.

Note: A tape was not available for verification of the content of the exchange, which began at 10:35 a.m. in the Oval Office at the White House.

Remarks to the American Society of Association Executives
March 6, 1990

Neil, thank you, sir. Thank you all. Thank you, Neil Milner, chairman, for that warm welcome and challenge. And Bill [Taylor], the president, the other president here today, thank you, sir. [*Laughter*] Let me just say I really am pleased and privileged to be with this group of people that do so much. You know, I really feel comfortable talking to this group because most people think I've been free associating for years. [*Laughter*]

I heard that last year I accidentally caused panic among your executive directors. They thought I pledged no new faxes. [*Laughter*]

Believe it or not, there are still some Americans who don't know what the "association for associations" is. That's why next week they're doing a bit on you for TV's "Unsolved Mysteries." [*Laughter*]

Because really, only your organization is big enough and broad enough to include the Leafy Greens Council and the Association of Tongue Depressors. [*Laughter*] That happens to be a fact.

But I guess it's only natural for the heads of organizations like yours to get together themselves. Some people think of our great country as a nation of rugged individualists alone against the odds. And that is part of the American tradition, but only a part. There's another tradition, a tradition as old as America itself, as old as Pilgrims and the Mayflower Compact, as old as the pioneers who settled the West. It's the tradition that Tocqueville described more than 150 years ago when he came to America, observed the scenes, and wrote that "Americans of all ages, all conditions, and all dispositions constantly form associations."

That shouldn't surprise us, because the act of association is nothing less than democracy in action: individuals translating common interests into a common cause. And you know, today we see the power of democracy, and isn't it an exciting time to be alive, seeing this change in Eastern Europe and in Managua, Nicaragua? We see that power of democracy and we see fresh evidence every day that the democratic ideal we cherish, the idea we call America, is alive everywhere: in the Revolution of 1989 that brought down the Berlin Wall and brought freedom to Eastern Europe; here in our own hemisphere, in the great victories for democracy in Panama and then again in Nicaragua—and millions of people now enjoying the freedoms that America has known for two centuries.

Here at home, we've got to see what these transforming changes in the world mean for us. And those changes carry a challenge, a challenge to us to find in our freedoms new ways to solve the problems that threaten our society and our continued leadership in the whole world community. Look around at the problems we face: drug abuse, hunger, homelessness, illiteracy, despair in our inner cities, the breakdown of the family. There's a role, a critical role for government in finding solutions, but we know government doesn't always have the answers. If we could eliminate these problems, solve them once and for all with more programs, more bureaucracy, these problems would have disappeared a long time ago.

The fact is, government isn't the only organized entity out there with the powers to change things, the power to make a difference. Everyone in this room is well aware of the advantages of association. But I don't know whether you are really aware of the full extent of your own power, of the resources, the expertise, the potential energy your organizations can bring to bear on these problems—your ability to help solve community problems.

I know most associations are already active in community service, and I've heard about some of the wonderful work being done: the Medical Association of Atlanta, working after hours to provide free medical care to the homeless; by the Oregon Remodelers Association out there in Portland, Oregon, in Project Pride, a program to do home repairs for the low-income elderly; by the Hotel Association of New York, with its ongoing commitment to donate surplus food to feed the hungry. These are just three, just three of countless community service projects that your associations are engaged in, a commitment of time and talent mirrored in similar community efforts by millions of Americans across the country.

In fact, one study in 1988 found that Americans who volunteered in formal organizations gave almost 15 billion hours valued at an estimated $150 billion. Now that's tremendous, but it's just the tip of the iceberg, just a fraction of all the good works we are capable of. Because the fact is, coping with the problems we face is within our power. There is no problem in America that is not being solved somewhere. Think about it: the programs I've just mentioned—New York, Atlanta, Portland—thousands more. Think about ways that your organization, every one of your members, can make this mission of serving others your

very own.

The story I want to tell you today—a story that Martin Luther King, Jr., told in his speech he made the night before that terrible day in Memphis, 22 years ago—it's a story about serving others and the courage that takes. It's a familiar story about the Good Samaritan and the stranger he helped. But there's another part of the story we don't always remember. Before the Good Samaritan stopped that day, two other men saw the injured stranger and passed him by. And Dr. King thought long and hard about it, and he used to ask himself: Why didn't the others stop to help? And Dr. King came up with some good reasons: They didn't stop because they were too busy, had more important work waiting in Jerusalem of far more consequence than helping one unfortunate man; and so, on they went.

And then one day, Martin Luther King put himself in their shoes. At the age of 30, on his very first trip to the Holy Land, he and his wife, Coretta, traveled that road from Jerusalem to Jericho. And Dr. King saw the story of the Good Samaritan in a new light. That road starts off more than 1,000 feet above the sea level and ends in Jericho 2,000 feet below sea level—a twisting road, full of blind curves. He imagined the road 2,000 years ago, each curve a perfect ambush for robbers. And at the moment, Dr. King realized why the two men didn't stop. It had nothing to do with the reasons he had imagined. They didn't stop because they were afraid.

The way Dr. King imagined it, one asked himself: "If I stop to help this man, what will happen to me?" And he went on about his way. But then the Good Samaritan came along and he asked himself a different question: "If I don't stop to help this man, what will happen to him?" And he asked himself that question, and he found the courage to stop, the courage to help, the courage to serve.

So which question, then, do we ask ourselves about going down to the soup kitchen in that dangerous neighborhood; about stopping on a dark street to help a homeless man; about reaching out to those desperate kids out there, kids who have no home life, who are hooked on drugs, who live a nightmare we can't begin to imagine? Doing any of these things isn't easy. Every one takes an act of courage. But unlike the Good Samaritan, we don't have to act alone. Each one of you understands the power of collective action: how much we can get done when we work together, pool our resources, combine our talents.

And don't think it won't take courage. It's going to take courage to go back to your member organizations, back to their CEO's and boards of directors, and suggest that they place community service at the center of their agenda. It's going to take courage to insist that community service has a place at the very heart of every organization. It will take courage to make each one believe that from now on in America, any definition of a successful life must include serving others. But that's just exactly what I'm asking you to do.

Today, I want to lay down some challenges, challenges to associations all over America to take up community service. First, build on a firm foundation. Find out what's working in your industry, in your profession, in your community; let your members know which community service programs are most effective; and then, challenge them to make those programs the blueprint for their own efforts. Find new ways to use existing assets. I understand that one of the ASAE's great strengths is its allied societies structure—69 State and local organizations, thousands more association executives. And I'm asking each of these allied societies to take the lead in their

community for solving social problems, become what we call Points of Light action groups.

And second, set a target of 100-percent participation in community service. Challenge your constituents to call on every employee and member at every level of every organization, from the CEO on down to the newest hire, to make community service their personal mission.

And finally, a third challenge—recognize those members who are what I like to call Points of Light. I've belonged, as many of you have, to many associations in my life, and I know one of the things you do best is to recognize outstanding performance. And so, I ask you to turn the spotlight on community service in your newsletters, your magazines, at your annual meetings—on individuals who give 110 percent helping people in need and on those organizations who demonstrate 100-percent participation in community service.

I'm counting on you, each one of you, to take these challenges to heart. People in this room represent thousands of associations, organizations of all sorts and sizes, a combined membership of 100 million Americans. And so today, I'm asking you: Channel that energy into community service, tap that power, and transform a nation.

Once again, my thanks for all you are doing and all that you're going to do. God bless you, and God bless the United States of America. Thank you all very, very much.

Note: The President spoke at 2:12 p.m. in Hall A at the Washington Convention Center.

Nomination of Jo Anne B. Barnhart To Be an Assistant Secretary of Health and Human Services
March 6, 1990

The President today announced his intention to nominate Jo Anne B. Barnhart to be Assistant Secretary for Family Support at the Department of Health and Human Services in Washington, DC. This is a new position.

Since 1986 Mrs. Barnhart has served as Republican staff director for the Governmental Affairs Committee of the United States Senate. Prior to this, she served as campaign manager for Senator William V. Roth, Jr., in Wilmington, DE, 1987–1988;

consultant in the Office of Policy Development at the White House in Washington, DC, 1986; Associate Commissioner for Family Assistance at the Social Security Administration at the Department of Health and Human Services, 1983–1986; and Deputy Associate Commissioner for Family Assistance at the Social Security Administration, 1981–1983. In addition, Mrs. Barnhart served as legislative assistant for Senator William V. Roth, Jr., 1977–1981; project di-

rector for SERVE Nutrition Project at the Wilmington Senior Center, 1975–1977; legislative liaison for the Mental Health Association of Delaware, 1973–1975; and a space and time buyer for deMartin-Marona and Associates in Wilmington, DE, 1970–1973.

Mrs. Barnhart graduated from the University of Delaware (B.A., 1975). She was born August 26, 1950, in Memphis, TN. Mrs. Barnhart is married, has one child, and resides in Arlington, VA.

Statement on Signing a Bill Extending the Authorization for School Dropout Demonstration Programs
March 6, 1990

I am pleased to sign today H.R. 2281, a bill that will help to attack the unacceptable dropout rate in our Nation's schools. This bill extends an important Department of Education program, which provides funds to local school districts to devise and demonstrate innovative strategies to reduce dropout rates and to encourage those who have dropped out to return to school. Successful strategies can then be shared with other schools.

We all know that the dropout problem afflicting our educational system is both chronic and severe. Only about 70 percent of our young people graduate from high school on time, and the statistics are even worse for minority children and those in urban areas. The consequences of our high dropout rate are tragic for the individuals who drop out and harmful for our Nation's productive capacity and competitive position in the world.

But this alarming situation can be turned around. As I have previously announced, the Nation's Governors and I have agreed on a wide-ranging set of goals for the future of American education. Among those goals

is increasing our high school graduation rate to at least 90 percent by the year 2000. The Governors and I recognize that this is an ambitious target, but we are convinced that it can, and must, be met. The bill before me today acknowledges that meeting this goal is primarily a State and local responsibility, which will also require the commitment and dedication of our Nation's teachers, principals, and business and community leaders. It also recognizes that the Federal Government has an important role to play by funding experiments to develop innovative local projects that can serve as models for other school districts. I have already asked the Congress to more than double the funding for this program over its fiscal year 1989 level. H.R. 2281 will authorize the Congress to meet that request, and I am very pleased to sign it.

GEORGE BUSH

The White House,
March 6, 1990.

Note: H.R. 2281, approved March 6, was assigned Public Law No. 101–250.

Toasts at the State Dinner for Prime Minister Giulio Andreotti of Italy
March 6, 1990

The President. Ladies and gentlemen, we're going to get this part out of the way early. [*Laughter*]

Mr. Prime Minister and Mrs. Andreotti and distinguished guests, friends of Italy, all: Barbara and I are very pleased to welcome you to the White House tonight to honor the President of the Council of Ministers in the Republic of Italy, our friend Mr. Andreotti. And later on this evening, we will be celebrating Italy's national pastime with a performance by one of the world's greatest opera singers. We'll leave it as a little bit of a surprise. [*Laughter*]

But I am reminded of a story concerning America's national pastime. It seems that great Italian tenor, Enrico Caruso, was asked by a group of American reporters what he thought of Babe Ruth. Caruso, ever polite, replied that he didn't know, because unfortunately he had never heard her sing. [*Laughter*]

One American writer called Italy "The Land of the Immortal Gods"—not just the land of mythology but the home of eternal ideas symbolized by the immortal genius of Da Vinci and Michelangelo, Raphael; the timeless architecture—the Piazza San Marco in Venice; the classic strains heard in La Scala, in Milan. And Italy is the spiritual home of millions—St. Peter's in Rome—and the ancestral home of 12 million Americans. And many are here tonight, including our OAS Ambassador Luigi Einaudi, who is also the grandson of Italy's first President.

And Mr. Prime Minister, you are one of America's closest friends, and you know our country well. And we are proud and honored to be with you. We certainly agree on the key role that Italy plays in the new, emerging Europe. And in my discussions with Prime Minister Andreotti today and over the past months, we have shared the excitement on the remarkable changes that we are seeing. I can think of no time in modern history when our strong transatlantic partnership was more crucial.

They say that all the roads lead to Rome,

and so Italy was appropriately my first stop on my first visit to Europe as President of the United States. And together we set the tone for critical arms reduction proposals, now even closer to fulfillment. We totally agree that a strong NATO is vital to our collective security in the new Europe. German unification with a unified Germany remaining a full member of NATO, support for the rising democracies in Eastern Europe, and the continued role of the United States as a force for stability in Europe are all part of our agenda today. And as we've done so often in the past, we found much agreement. But we also have much to look forward to.

This summer, we will meet again at the Houston economic summit. And then, beginning in July, Italy becomes Chairman of the European Community, and our two governments will work to develop stronger economic and political ties between the United States and the EC. But most important of all, there is perhaps the toughest issue between our two nations, a meeting which will take place this summer in Italy. And our side has already made bold advances against other nations involved, but we must be allowed to compete on a level playing field. And that's right, I'm talking about the 1990 World Cup in soccer. [*Laughter*]

And so, Mr. Prime Minister, and our friend, our discussions today reinforced my deep admiration for you and your nation. To our noble and strong union, and to you and the citizens of the Republic of Italy, I ask our guests to join me in a toast. A salute to you and to your great country, sir.

The Prime Minister. Mr. President, the number of our Cabinets, which is a feature of Italy's political life but does not affect the stability of our democracy, has provided me with other opportunities to come to the White House in the last years, although in different ministerial capacities.

Being back in the United States today after more than a decade as President of

329

the Council of Ministers of the Italian Republic is indeed a source of great satisfaction to me. Many decisive events have taken place in the meantime which our continents have often lived through, side by side, in a relationship of alliance and cooperation which has been strong and vital. The world has become increasingly complex and interdependent and certainly not easier to manage today.

I am especially happy to be visiting Washington at this moment when the world, and Europe in particular, are living through such an exciting and crucial time. On the European continent, a decades-long ideological and military confrontation is giving way with astounding speed to new balances and to the promising establishment of democracy in the Eastern European nations. A new Europe is coming into being, in which we trust that a reduction in tensions will make the presence of armaments less disquieting.

We Italians have always believed that Atlantic solidarity would one day bear fruit. My seniority as a politician would enable me to reel off every single stage in this long process, both of resistance and of political cohesion. And we Italians have always held the view that the political and military commitment of the United States and Europe was an indispensable condition for the ultimate success of our common endeavor. Well, Mr. President, Italy is still convinced today—more than ever before, if it were possible—that this solidarity must continue to inspire our action. The continuing military and political presence of the United States in Europe is basic to ensuring stability and balance for the whole world.

As ideological and military confrontations wane, Europe needs a broader framework for cooperation, a form which by strengthening the Helsinki formula develops into a system for comprehensive dialog with the participation of the United States and Canada. And together with NATO, this is the institutional framework in which we can together tackle issues related to the growth of the budding democracies in the East, the reunification of the two Germanys, and the development of the new relationship with the Soviet Union—in short, and to borrow your own words, Mr. Presi-

dent, the construction of that whole and free Europe which is already taking shape and to which we all look forward with hope.

Italy feels it is part of this Europe—and indeed, an essential one. But I would like to recall that Italy, by its nature in history, is also part of the Mediterranean world. We shall continue to follow the problems of that area very closely, including longstanding ones such as the Arab-Israeli conflict, the Lebanese crisis, and the problems related to the future development of each people in this important area.

Naturally, Mr. President, what we need today is a new solidarity. By this, I mean a solidarity between the United States and Europe that is newer and subtler than the one tested so successfully at a time when we were threatened from the exterior. This kind of solidarity is today both indispensable and urgent to enable both Europe and the United States to jointly take up other challenges, whether regional or global in scope. I'm referring to the backwardness and indebtedness of developing countries, to environmental protection, and to the fight against drugs, which you, Mr. President, very clearly stated to be an absolute priority issue, showing your solidarity to the Latin American countries which are most suffering at the hands of drug traffickers.

Mr. President, all kinds of dictatorships have failed, even those which believe that by sacrificing freedom they would succeed in solving the economic and social problems of their peoples. To a nation such as the United States that has provided and is providing a generous and sustained contribution to freedom in all continents, we renew the expression of our convinced friendship, genuinely rooted in our hearts and minds and inspired by constructive spirit.

Mr. President, I ask you and all your guests here to make a toast to your health and that of Mrs. Bush. And also, I would like to invite you, if the American soccer team is going to win, to come to Rome and assist to the last game. [*Laughter*] Thank you, Mr. President.

The President. Well done, sir. Thank you. Very nice. Thank you so much.

Note: The President spoke at 8:12 p.m. in the State Dining Room at the White House. The Prime Minister spoke in Italian, and his remarks were translated by an interpreter. Following the dinner, soprano Roberta Peters performed in the East Room.

Remarks at the American Electronics Association Luncheon
March 7, 1990

Mitchell, thank you. After listening to him, I'm glad it was the other guy from Massachusetts that I ran against a couple of years ago. [*Laughter*] But really, thank you for that warm welcome, and I'm delighted to be here and, of course, delighted to see Dick Iverson and so many familiar faces out here. Many of you came a long way to be here, and so I won't ask you to sit through a long speech. The punishment should fit the crime. [*Laughter*] Jim Baker stole my favorite story—you remember about the kid who went to church with his grandfather, and he said, "Granddad, what are all the flags along the side of the church for?" And the grandfather said, "Well, that's for those who died in service." The kid said, "Oh, really? The 9 a.m. service, or the 11 a.m. service?" [*Laughter*] Wasn't this Duke Ellington Band great? Listen, thank you. The choir—just fantastic. Thank you.

And it is an honor—really, I mean it—and pleasure to be here back with this association. And you are the leaders of a vital range of our most innovative and interrelated industries, from semiconductors, microprocessors, and circuit boards to PC's and mainframes, supercomputers, telecommunications, and defense electronics. But at every stage of that impressive technological food chain, yours are the people and the products that really keep this country competitive. I'd add a special tip of the hat to President Gary Tooker of Motorola, winner of last year's Malcolm Baldrige Quality Award. It's a prestigious award and sets a great example for the rest of this country. So, congratulations. Where is he? I can't see with the light. Gary, congratulations to you.

But for almost 50 years now, your industries have been at the center of a remarkable revolution in the way work is done, the way ideas are managed, even the way time

and the vast reaches of space are understood. And along the way, you've also become the Nation's largest manufacturing employer, creating jobs for over two and a half million Americans, modernizing services and industries of every kind, assuring our national security, and providing a vital export market.

As technologies, economies, and geopolitics change almost weekly, your industries stand at a threshold of tremendous opportunity. Our first priority is to encourage productivity gains, savings, long-term investment in high-tech industries, by lowering the cost of capital. And we believe that one of the most crucial Federal priorities is to encourage planning for the long term because for too long, where investment is concerned, the Federal Government has been more of a hindrance than a help. And so, we intend to work with you closely, constantly, and consistently to see that American electronics and technologies regain and retain a permanent position in world markets.

Last month we sent to Congress our Savings and Economic Growth Act, which includes an innovative family savings plan to stimulate capital formation, new incentives for IRA's to help first-time home buyers, and a business-building, job-creating, revenue-enhancing cut in the capital gains tax. Without it, every business in America, of every size, is at a competitive disadvantage abroad. Now, let me read you, lest you have forgotten, a list of the maximum long-term capital gains tax rates for some of America's competitors: Japan, about 5 percent; South Korea, zero; Taiwan, zero; West Germany, zero; Singapore, zero; Hong Kong, zero. And the list goes on. And why some American politicians don't understand the importance of this capital gains differential, I do not know. It's pure politics. And so, we're going to fight hard, with your continued support, for that crucial tax cut.

Along with encouraging investment, we've proposed a budget that will bring the deficit down below those Gramm-Rudman-Hollings targets without raising taxes. And we're committed to unprecedented support for R&D, research and development efforts. We believe that the R&D tax credit should be made permanent. And our budget includes a record-breaking $70 billion in Federal direct investment for research and development.

Our budget also devotes unprecedented resources to space, education, the fight against drugs, environmental initiatives, and other crucial investments in our own future. Such investments over the years have ensured that this country has retained its leadership in terms of the basic research and fundamental discoveries underlying your industry. This administration is also committed to working with you in the critical pre-competitive development stage where the basic discoveries are converted into generic technologies that support both our economic competitiveness and our national security. Here again we can help to level the international playing field on which you compete.

But we understand, as you do, that no investment is more important than our human resources. So, together with the Nation's Governors, we have set ambitious national goals for America's students. As one incentive, we've proposed a new National Science Scholars program. We have also requested a 70-percent increase for the Eisenhower Math and Sciences Educational Program and a $100 million increase in the National Science Foundation education budget. By the year 2000, our kids can be first in the world in science and math achievement; and with enough involvement and leadership from groups like this, they will be first.

Your industries face some unique challenges. The marketplace is tough enough without undue constraints and unfair restrictions. So, we've pledged to make sure that trade is fair and free by judiciously but firmly implementing the 1988 Trade Act. We're moving forward with Japan through

the Structural Impediments Initiative and by working to develop a more productive relationship overall. Just last weekend, as Mitch referred to, I met with Prime Minister Kaifu and specifically discussed satellites, telecommunications, supercomputers, forest products, and yes, semiconductors. I hope, I fervently hope, that on the basis of our talks Japan will be moving toward early resolution of these problem areas. We agreed that we must both do our very best to make these SII talks a success. We've presented ideas for removing structural impediments in Japan, and they have presented ideas to us about our own structural impediments. We remember, therefore, that it is a two-way street.

Our task must be to make the American economy even stronger and even more competitive. But we're also committed to strengthening and expanding the multilateral trading system through the Uruguay round. I just can't tell you how important a successful conclusion of that round is for American business, for business all around the world. We've proposed far-reaching reforms of the global trading system, working to bring a wide range of new trade areas under the GATT. These crucial negotiations will help us create a more equitable, more efficient trade climate, worldwide.

I've made it a priority to review and modernize our export controls to provide vital help to the emerging democracies without compromising national security. Given the pace of political change, rapid advances in technology, and the competitive position of American industry, we must ensure that export controls are effective or eliminated. I am happy to report this week we have a team at COCOM in Paris negotiating the modernization of export controls on computers. These controls have been an important part of our security for decades, and I know our allies want to work with us to ensure their relevance in the 1990's.

To provide a further competitive edge for American firms, we will support legislation to reduce the antitrust uncertainty that may discourage joint production ventures. Under such a proposal, the courts would weigh, on a case-by-case basis, the competitive benefits as well as costs of joint production ven-

332

tures. In addition, joint production ventures announced to the Government would be liable only for actual damages in private antitrust suits. Such an initiative would build on the competitive strength of American business by allowing firms to pool their skills, build new production facilities, and share investment risks.

One risk you all face—and it's not just business—citizens working in associations and volunteer organizations, in schools, everyplace—one risk that you all face at an intolerable level is liability. In your case, I'm talking about product liability. And the Council on Competitiveness, ably chaired by Vice President Quayle, has already begun a concentrated effort to significantly reform our cumbersome and expensive product liability system. It's about time that we made ourselves more competitive by getting rid of those lawsuits and claims that are purely frivolous and patently unfair.

And so, today I'm going to give the Competitiveness Council another challenge: to find ways that American industry can better translate new ideas and technologies into marketable products. So many of the world's most advanced technologies, from

robotics to the VCR, were first developed here. And yet, so many of those concepts were ultimately brought to the marketplace by our competitors. We can do better. And I am determined that we will do better.

Today I've outlined some of what we're doing to level the playing field. But it will be leaders like you right here in this room that have to take the ball and run with it. You represent the vital core of America's competitive potential, with over 3,500 of the most dynamic, technologically advanced, forward-thinking companies in the country. Your ideas are important to us. And your success is absolutely crucial to America's future. So, let me encourage you to work together, and with us, on a long-term program to meet the competitive challenge of a new century.

It's a great pleasure to have been here with you. Thank you very much, and God bless you all. And thank you, again, to the Duke Ellington choir.

Note: The President spoke at 11:42 a.m. in the Grand Ballroom at the Washington Court Hotel. In his remarks, he referred to Mitchell Kertzman and J. Richard Iverson, chairman and president of the association.

Remarks at the National Drug Control Policy Luncheon
March 7, 1990

Bill, thank you. Thank you all. Well, I heard about this luncheon, and I have talked to Bill about your really heroic work. And I'd like to just say a word about his heroic work to start with, because I've never seen a fellow come in and take a tremendously difficult assignment like this, hit the ground running, and accomplish a great deal. And I think we all owe Bill Bennett a vote of thanks. He's out there in the trenches. He's in the boardrooms. He's everywhere. He's like Batman. [*Laughter*] So, thank you for all you're doing.

No, and I'm very sorry about the delays getting everybody in here. The good news, however: You don't have to show an ID to get out of this place. [*Laughter*] And I

apologize for being a couple of minutes later than I had intended in coming over here.

But I'm glad to see that so many of you could come to Washington. I see Al Brooks and, of course, Erma—having been and seen their projects I feel a kinship with them—and really, indeed, with all the rest of you from what Bill has told me. In the past year, I have spent a lot of time praising those involved in service to others. And I'm grateful for this opportunity to salute you not only as what we call Points of Light but as also points of courage.

When I was in Kansas City, in the Baptist church basement where Al has his headquarters, there was a banner on the wall that asked a four-word question. It went like this: "Is This Dream Possible?" And when I look around this room and when I talk to the Director, I know the answer to that one. In this room are 28 folks who refused to surrender, 28 reasons why I really now believe, as Bill does, that we are going to win.

A few months ago, Bill Bennett wrote a booklet called "Fighting Back." And many of you here were profiled in that piece. Almost every story was different. But almost every story began the same way. It began when one man or woman threw down the hat, took off the gloves, stepped forward, armed with the most powerful force known to man: the force of an idea. You fought back. You got involved. You made a difference, and you proved to America that this war can be won.

So, I think you are America's hometown heroes—unconventional warriors, but this is an unconventional war. You've shown how the communities under siege can be united in a battle for life and how they can be restored to health and safety, doing it your way, on your turf.

It's sometimes hard to see with all these lights, but the ceiling here is decorated, and you can see it, with a field of golden stars. Just like real stars, we often forget to notice them. You are the stars in America's war on drugs. You shine through the dark, you give

hope in the night. And we're here today really to say that someone noticed. Bill Bennett noticed. And I noticed. And I hope all of America will notice.

This used to be the Navy's library right here, and of course, stars have a special significance to those who navigate on the seas. And in this sense, stars like you do far more than fuel hopes and prayers. You are also beacons to thousands of other people, immovable lights by which they can chart their course to victory. So, I just wanted to stop by here to say thanks, to assure you that we're going to keep on fighting against drugs and fighting for you, for your neighborhoods, and most of all for the kids, the children out there. And we're going to remember the rallying cry of Chicago's Father George Clemens: "There are more of us than there are of them."

Congratulations and thank you all for what you're doing. Thank you very much.

Note: The President spoke at 1:39 p.m. in the Indian Treaty Room at the Old Executive Office Building. In his remarks, he referred to William J. Bennett, Director of National Drug Control Policy; Alvin L. Brooks, director of the Kansas City, MO, Human Relations Department and executive director and founder of the Ad Hoc Group Against Crime; and Erma Scales, chairwoman of the Acres Homes War on Drugs Committee in Houston, TX.

Statement by Press Secretary Fitzwater on the President's Space Exploration Initiative
March 8, 1990

On July 20, 1989, in a speech commemorating the 20th anniversary of the *Apollo* Moon landing, the President announced three major space policy objectives of the administration: the completion of Space Station *Freedom*, a return to the Moon to stay, and a manned expedition to Mars. In that speech, he asked the Vice President to lead the National Space Council in developing policies and plans to accomplish these objectives.

The President announced today he has approved the first of a series of policy decisions for the long-term space exploration initiative he announced on July 20. Acting upon the recommendation of the Vice President and the National Space Council, the President has approved a program that will give early focus to technology development and a search for new and innovative technical approaches to the Moon and Mars missions.

The policy consists of the following elements:

- The initiative will include both lunar and Mars program elements.
- The early program will focus on technology development with a search for new and innovative approaches and technologies.
- The program will include investment in high leverage innovative technologies with potential to make a major impact on cost, schedule, and/or performance.
- The program will take at least several years defining two or more significantly different human space exploration reference architectures, while developing and demonstrating technology broad enough to support all. Selection of a baseline program architecture will occur after that time.
- The program will perform mission, concept, and system analysis studies in parallel with technology development.
- The program will include robotic science missions.
- By spurring research and development in high technology fields, the space program will help promote American economic leadership.
- The program will require the efforts of several agencies. NASA [National Aeronautics and Space Administration] will be the principal implementing agency. The Department of Defense and the Department of Energy will also have major roles in the conduct of technology development and concept definition. The National Space Council will coordinate the development of an implementation strategy for the exploration initiative by the three agencies. To facilitate coordination, the Department of Energy will be added as a formal member of the National Space Council.

Remarks at a Presentation Ceremony for the Panama Campaign Streamer at Fort Myer, Virginia
March 8, 1990

Thank you all very much, Secretary Cheney and General Powell, and all the members of the Joint Chiefs, service secretaries, men and women of the Armed Forces. We are here today to add another campaign streamer to the rollcall of glory, the roster of great American campaigns: Yorktown, Gettysburg, Normandy, and now, Panama. Let us never forget that our Armed Forces have always fought for the children of America, for they are America's future. Panama was no different. The children of Panama deserve a future of freedom and democracy. And the people of that nation, Panama, needed us to stand with them to defend that struggle for democracy and for the opportunity that Americans have enjoyed for over 200 years.

The moment of decision came from me when the lives of America's servicemen stationed in Panama and the lives of American citizens there were threatened. That's when a silent phrase passed the lips, I think, of every American: Enough is enough. Our Armed Forces united in an operation appropriately labeled Just Cause, and 27,000 of America's finest sprang into action. They descended in C–130's, choppers, parachutes. They came in the cover of darkness, and they came in frontal assault with the sun at their backs. All braved death. All fought with distinction. So, it is especially fitting that the fabric of this streamer is woven with the colors of all the services.

Just last week, General Powell and General Thurman brought a few of these service men and women over to the White House. I heard tales of heroism, all of them told with reluctance, all of them told plainly and as matters of fact. And it was a matter of duty, they told me. I met an Army medic who, though wounded, pulled one serviceman after another from the line of fire before collapsing. This medic now wears

335

the Silver Star and the Purple Heart. I met a corporal whose proudest achievement is not that he stormed the PDF [Panamanian Defense Forces] barracks, but that his unit took the barracks while protecting the lives of a frightened family. Then I met a sergeant, a jump master, whose unit withstood withering fire and suffered severe casualties. But the sergeant told me that he and his men drew courage and conviction from the wild enthusiasm of the Panamanian people and from support that they were getting from back here, back here at home in the United States.

So, it's out of recognition of their bravery that we affix these streamers. But the greatest tribute goes to the soldiers, the sailors, the marines who fell. This streamer is, most of all, for them. It will adorn the service flags standing just a few feet from the Oval Office next to the American flag—a flag already lined with the crimson color of sacrifice. It is in honor of every American who died in the defense of liberty that we honor our flag. That is why I am determined that the American flag will be consecrated, not desecrated.

Panama was another chapter in a great epic, an act of free men and women in the Revolution of '89—a revolution that also swept the East and that is now sweeping

the globe. Because of Panamanians whose yearning for freedom is so strong that they will brave beatings to go to the polls, because of young Americans whose commitment to freedom is so strong that they will brave death to fight for it—it is because of them that the day of the dictator truly is over. And the revolution continues. The people have spoken in Nicaragua. When they speak in Cuba and Haiti, our Western Hemisphere will be entirely within the compass of freedom. And when that day comes, it will be the ultimate tribute to those who have protected our freedom so well for so long.

It is a great privilege, indeed an honor, for me to be here today to salute our Secretary, Dick Cheney; our Chairman, Colin Powell; the other members of the Chiefs; General Thurman; General Stiner; and the men and women who fought so bravely in Panama. Thank you, God bless you, and God bless the United States of America.

Note: The President spoke at 10:25 a.m. in the Ceremonial Hall. In his remarks, he referred to Gen. Colin L. Powell, Chairman of the Joint Chiefs of Staff; Gen. Maxwell R. Thurman, commander in chief of the U.S. Southern Command; and Lt. Gen. Carl Stiner, commanding general of the XVIII Airborne Corps.

Remarks at the National Transportation Policy Meeting
March 8, 1990

Well, Sam, thank you very, very much. And Deputy Secretary Elaine Chao and to our able Commandant of the Coast Guard and to Dr. Larson, who did such heroic work on all of this, thank you all for being here—Governor, so many Members of Congress here. And as some of you may know, after Sam Skinner, our able Secretary of Transportation, became Secretary, he took time to earn a license as a jet pilot. I've wondered: if I'd named him Secretary of Agriculture would he have been out milking the cows? [*Laughter*] But nevertheless, here he is.

But his leadership derives from experience. And it's experience and solid analysis that has shaped this transportation policy that we're unveiling today. No sector is more important to the American economy than transportation. It's an $800-billion-a-year business with $5 trillion worth of assets. To say that it's important to our quality of life, the flow of commerce, and really to our national security, is a gross understatement. As world trade grows even larger, as we continue our leadership in an increasingly global society, we will become even more dependent on transportation than we are today. And when transportation lags or is congested, when people and goods are stranded in traffic or in airports, we'll suffer. And when people and goods flow through a responsive, well-maintained, and efficient transportation system, our quality of life improves with it.

For over 200 years, since the days of barges and riverboats, America has grown and prospered with our transportation system. Our competitive stake will depend no less on American transportation leadership in the future. And still, too often we take for granted the highways that bind America together, and the airports and harbors that bind America to the world. The institutions our forebears created, the technologies they developed, and the transportation systems they built created a new and mobile society far different from the life they knew. For example, as a young man, Dwight David Eisenhower had a vision of a nation united, of an America in which goods and people would flow from city to city, from State to State with great ease. And the vision of his youth became the reality of his Presidency.

Today, Eisenhower's vision of an interstate highway system, the most ambitious public works project in the history of man, is virtually complete—a fitting tribute in this, his centennial year. Just as the Model T and the Kitty Hawk prepared the way for today's millions of cars and thousands of passenger jets, so it is now our turn to invest in America's future, to begin to create the transportation system of the 21st century. On the ground, over the waterways, and in the air and space, our mission for this decade and the next century is to build on our achievements, to link the nations of the world as we've linked the States of this great country.

The national transportation is our blueprint, if you will, for this new world. And as I said in the State of the Union last month, it's time to act and it's time to give our State and local governments the flexibility that they need to best use Federal funds. We also have a strategy for airports and for removing economic regulation of the trucking industry—you heard the Secretary talk about those—and most of all, we have a strategy to unleash the creative genius of American technology.

This technology took us to the Moon, and now it must make travel to space economical and commonplace. And this genius built a network of highways, and now we must support and encourage advanced technologies in the whole field of transportation, from magnetically levitated trains to intelligent vehicles and highways to advanced materials and engineering.

Finally, sometimes the best transportation policy means not moving people but moving their work. Last week in Los Angeles I spoke of the growing trend in this country toward working outside the office, a trend known as telecommuting. Millions have already found their productivity actually increases when they work nearer the people they're really working for: their families at home. The benefits in reducing congested highways and mass transit are obvious. Think of it as commuting to work at the speed of light.

As we look ahead, it's not enough to have a partnership between Federal, State, and local government. We must have the dynamic fourth partner—and that's where many of you fit in—the private sector. Such a partnership has already built a transportation system that is the envy of the world. And if we work together in this joint venture, America can continue to be the world leader in transportation.

I'm delighted to be with you. I want to congratulate the officials from the Department of Transportation. And now, let's go to work. Thank you all very, very much.

Note: The President spoke at 11:41 a.m. in Room 450 of the Old Executive Office Building. In his remarks, he referred to Deputy Secretary of Transportation Elaine L. Chao; Adm. Paul A. Yost, Jr., Commandant of the Coast Guard; Federal Highway Administrator Tom Larson; and Gov. Wallace G. Wilkinson of Kentucky.

White House Fact Sheet on the National Transportation Policy
March 8, 1990

President Bush today joined Secretary of Transportation Samuel K. Skinner in releasing "Moving America," the first statement of national transportation policy issued by the Federal Government in over a decade.

Last year, President Bush made development of a new national transportation policy statement one of the administration's major objectives. In developing the policy, the Department of Transportation (DOT) conducted an extensive outreach effort involving over 100 hearings, field visits, and meetings to hear the views of the transportation community and the general public. Reflecting the central role of transportation in Americans' lives, and the broad range of their transportation needs and concerns, the statement issued today is designed to improve America's competitiveness, advance American technology, unleash private sector resources and initiatives, rebuild and expand the transportation infrastructure, and improve the quality of life of all Americans.

The new statement of national transportation policy is a comprehensive framework of policies for all aspects of transportation and a strategy to carry the policies into action. The policies and action strategies reflect new initiatives, such as major increases in funding for Federal aviation and research and development programs, as well as the renewal and extension of sound policies and programs that have worked well in the past, such as increased efforts to reduce highway fatalities and to achieve economic deregulation of transportation industries.

The policy provides a framework for Federal decisions. Federal actions to carry out the new policy will be built on the foundation of a strengthened transportation partnership in which Federal, State, and local governments and the private sector all participate in financing, maintaining, and operating the transportation system.

The policy statement and the action strategies focus on six themes:
- Maintain and expand the Nation's transportation system.
- Foster a sound financial base for transportation.
- Keep the transportation industry strong and competitive.
- Ensure that the transportation system supports public safety and national security.
- Protect the environment and the quality of life.
- Advance U.S. transportation technology and expertise.

Maintain and Expand the Nation's Transportation System

The policy provides a framework for reauthorizing Federal transportation programs by focusing Federal resources on facilities and projects of national significance, reducing categorical grants, and providing greater flexibility to recipients. The policy gives priority to maintaining needed transportation infrastructure, encourages effective management and pricing techniques to improve use of assets and enhance capacity, promotes increased attention to intermodal and rural connections, and supports addition of new capacity where required. The Federal Government will work with its partners, State and local governments and the private sector, to address the projected transportation needs.

Strategies for action include:
- Increase Federal research and development funding and aviation capital improvements—air traffic control modernization and airport grants—by 70 percent over the amount funded during the previous 5 years.
- Focus Federal-aid highway programs on systems and projects of national significance, and provide greater flexibility to State and local governments.
- Restructure urban mass transportation programs to provide greater flexibility and increased State and local matching shares.

Foster a Sound Financial Base for Transportation

The policy supports increased reliance on user fees, reduced spending from the General Fund, and use of transportation trust funds in a fiscally responsible manner. It proposes to foster State and local financing by permitting greater use of tolls on highways and passenger facility charges at airports. It also promotes greater private investment in transportation by supporting the removal of legal and regulatory barriers to private participation in financing, building, owning, and operating facilities and services such as roads and transit systems. The policy encourages joint public-private projects at the State and local level.

Strategies for action include:
- Spend transportation trust funds for transportation purposes.
- Increase aviation user fees to finance an expanded program.
- Allow local passenger facility charges at airports, to finance increased airport capacity.
- Increase private sector participation in transportation, including local transit and airports.
- Increase State, local, and private funding of highways by, for example, opening up opportunities for toll roads.
- Establish new Federal user fees to recover a portion of Coast Guard and Federal railroad safety activities.

Keep the Transportation Industry Strong and Competitive

The policy encourages increased productivity and competitiveness in transportation. Federal budgets and programs will emphasize more cost-effectiveness and competitiveness for mass transit, the U.S. merchant marine, and commercial space services. The policy supports elimination of unnecessary and outmoded Federal regulations, including remaining ICC regulation of trucking, inconsistent State requirements and standards for truck regulation and tax reporting, and Federal requirements that impose unique cost burdens on railroads. DOT will reassess Federal user charges and subsidies affecting competition among modes and will review maritime, aviation, and other

programs to ensure free and equitable competition. DOT will also participate in negotiations to improve access of U.S. transportation companies to international markets and to encourage harmonization of equipment technologies and standards domestically and internationally. Finally, the Federal transportation work force will be enhanced by increasing the number of air traffic controllers and improving the recruitment and training of controllers.

Strategies for action include:
- Encourage uniform international standards for air traffic control, aircraft, and airports.
- Encourage more open skies in international agreements.
- Promote uniformity in State registration and reporting requirements for motor carriers.
- Eliminate remaining economic regulation of trucking.
- Support repeal of the Federal Employers' Liability Act for railroads.
- Achieve Amtrak self-sufficiency.
- Review and restructure maritime programs to improve competitiveness of U.S.-flag ships in world trade.

Ensure that the Transportation System Supports Public Safety and National Security

One of the chief objectives of the policy is to improve transportation safety. A major focus is reducing highway fatalities. The policy also focuses on effective handling of hazardous materials, aging aircraft and aviation security, and standards and procedures for safe construction and operation in all modes. To support national security, the policy commits DOT to work with the Department of Defense to identify defense transportation needs and carry out the new national sealift and airlift policy. Other policy commitments include working with other agencies in fighting terrorism and in battling domestic and international trafficking in illegal drugs.

Strategies for action include:
- Support reauthorization of highway safety programs to reduce highway fatalities.
- Increase the number of Federal avia-

tion, railroad, and motor carrier safety inspectors.
- Increase public awareness and promote enforcement of State seatbelt, child safety, and motorcycle helmet laws.
- Reduce drunk and drugged driving.
- Improve safety standards for passenger cars, light trucks, and vans.
- Enhance marine safety by reducing the incidence of boating while intoxicated and supporting other safety initiatives.
- Support legislation strengthening oversight of the transportation of hazardous materials.
- Expand safety inspection and enforcement for pipelines with greatest risk.
- Improve disaster preparedness.
- Increase the level of effort for DOT drug enforcement by 10 percent in FY 1991.

Protect the Environment and the Quality of Life

An essential consideration in transportation is its effect on the environment and on the quality of life, including access and mobility for all citizens. The statement recognizes the importance of minimizing adverse effects of transportation on the environment, and supports the administration's clean air initiatives as they relate to transportation. Under the policy, DOT will promote stronger measures for oilspill prevention, effective means of responding to spills that occur, and liability requirements for damages caused by oilspills.

Strategies for action include:
- Carry out transportation elements of the administration's clean air initiatives.

- Support and implement enhanced oil-spill protection and liability legislation.
- Support no net loss goal for wetlands affected by transportation projects consistent with administration policy.
- Enforce mobility rights of disabled citizens.

Advance U.S. Transportation Technology and Expertise

The policy emphasizes the importance of renewed attention to technology and innovation, and supports increased Federal spending for transportation research, including magnetic levitation and intelligent vehicle/highway systems. The policy commits DOT to working with the academic and business communities to build awareness of transportation as a career and increase cooperative programs to prepare professionals for technologically advanced careers in transportation. The policy calls for coordination among Federal agencies and State, local, and private interests to improve collection of transportation-related data, foster more effective dissemination of data, and share knowledge of techniques for applying data in transportation planning and decisionmaking.

Strategies for action include:
- Increase overall funding for DOT research and development activities by 17 percent in FY 1991.
- Increase funding for new aviation technology and human factors research.
- Increase highway research, including intelligent vehicle/highway systems.
- Conduct research on magnetic levitation and high-speed rail.
- Develop a comprehensive assessment of data needs and priorities of DOT and the transportation community.

Remarks at a Fundraising Dinner for Senator John Warner in Tysons Corner, Virginia
March 8, 1990

Thank you all very much. My introduction to rap. John Warner, thank you for that introduction. [*Laughter*] And you did say Washington Post. [*Laughter*] And to Senator Laxalt, my old friend—boy, do we miss him in the United States Senate, I'll tell you. But I'm delighted he's here with us tonight. And I want to pay my respects to—I see Congressman Bateman and Congressman Parris. Somebody told me Congressman Slaughter was here. We have a great Virginia delegation, incidentally, in the House. Secretaries Derwinski and Lujan were supposed to be here, and I hope they are someplace. And I'm delighted that they are. We've got a good Cabinet, too, and I'm proud of both of them, both former Members of the United States Congress.

Our vice chairman of our Republican National Committee, Jeanie Austin, is over here. And I'm delighted to see her, and I hope you'll tell Lee Atwater that I'm wishing him all the best when you see him on Monday. I think he'll be going back to work.

I want to pay my respects to Committeewoman Traywick, Marshall Coleman—an old friend. I felt somewhat overwhelmed by the members of the Redskins that were here earlier, but I was delighted to see all good candidates for the Secret Service these days, I think. [*Laughter*] Giants.

And Moe Bandy—that John introduced you to—he and Barbara and I, along with Loretta Lynn and Crystal Gayle, traveled all through Illinois and Iowa campaigning, and I am grateful to him, and he's a wonderful American. Besides that, he's a fellow Texan, so I've got to brag on him. But, Moe, thank you very, very much.

And it's great to be back in the heart of America—at least two blocks outside the beltway—[*laughter*]—and to return, though, to one of America's fastest growing areas, certainly Virginia's. I discount the rumors that Tysons Corner will soon be changed to Buster Douglas Corner. [*Laughter*]

But, nevertheless, we're here to salute Virginia's great Senators. You know, John is Virginia's senior elected statewide official. But more than that, he's in what I think of as the Virginia tradition, and he mirrors that superb mix of qualities that makes Virginians second to none. The first of these qualities, and Paul touched on it, is honor. As Casey Stengel would say, you can look it up. Virginia boasts a tradition of conscience and public honesty, public integrity. From Patrick Henry to our beloved friend Lewis Powell, the record is clear: Virginians ask and get integrity from their public officials.

Let me share a story—and again, Paul touched on it, and let me elaborate—that illustrates that tradition. Happened at the Republican convention in Richmond in 1978—four men vying for the GOP Senate nomination, and no one could get a majority. Many of you in the room were there, I know, as delegates, and I was following it very closely. And late Saturday night, one ballot following another, and finally about 11:30 p.m., before the deciding ballot, an aide suggested an idea to John. "Mr. Warner," he said, "these are principled delegates. A lot of them won't participate on a Sunday, and a good number of them aren't backing you. Just filibuster, just wait until midnight." And John's response, I think, in the great Virginia tradition I referred to, spoke rather eloquently about his character. He said, "I'd rather lose the nomination than win it that way."

And you know the rest. He did lose that nomination. He promptly endorsed the winner, Dick Obenshain, that we all remember later lost his life in a terrible accident. And the party then turned to John, and he achieved an upset victory in just 11 weeks of campaigning. First in defeat, and then in victory, he was a symbol of Virginia at its best. It is absolutely essential that he remain in the United States Senate.

Even Virginians who supported others on the other side in '78 are backing John. Honor is one reason. And another is a second quality which this State has cherished throughout its history—experience. Experience almost really unrivaled in the United States Senate. Ask anyone, John Warner is among the top in terms of being a respected Senator. Pick any issue. Invariably, he's there with calm talk and reasoned thought. And there's a word for that, and it's the third quality which makes John such a superb public servant: the wisdom that will be so crucial to the 1990's.

Nowhere is this sagacity more evident than in foreign policy. And nowhere could that wisdom be more important. Five weeks ago I talked in the State of the Union message about an idea called America. Well, that idea called America is the idea of democracy. And around the world, through what I've called the Revolution of '89, that idea has allowed brave men and women to counter bayonets and conquer barbed wire. The Hungarian playwright Imre Madach once wrote a work entitled, "The Tragedy of Man." And today, we celebrate the victory of man. Look at Berlin, where a wall is falling, and Panama and Romania, where tyrants fell. Look at Poland and Czechoslovakia and Nicaragua or, yes, at the events of just 2 days this week.

Who could have dreamt it? On Monday, Romanians toppling a statue of Lenin that had stood in a Bucharest square for 30 years. And in the Soviet Union last Sunday and over the past few months, another sight that even Ripley wouldn't believe: that nation's first multicandidate elections at the local or republic level. And think of it: Communist candidates accepting the will of the popular ballot, a ballot which included, incidentally, independent candidates. And even in Moscow, totalitarianism is on the wane because of a dynamic Soviet leader willing, as Lincoln said, "to think anew." And because we have been resolute, liberty is on the march, for a strong America is an America at peace.

And John Warner is encouraging peace as the ranking Republican on the Senate Armed Services Committee, where he's helping arms control get done, but done right. John is one of the few Members of the Senate who once negotiated an executive national security agreement with the Soviets. And I'm looking to him to help guide new treaties and new budgets

through this new decade of unprecedented change. But our administration has still other priorities because change here at home is just as important as change abroad.

And the first—John referred to it with his vote when he summarily dismissed his Senators. I've never seen so many Senators told to do something and then do it. [*Laughter*] I've got to find out the formula. But the first is the environment. And last week, we reached an agreement in principle with the Senate leaders on the first rewrite of the Clean Air Act in over a decade, to cut urban smog and acid rain and air toxics. And John helped negotiate that deal. And like any northern Virginian, he knows that less traffic congestion is needed for clean air.

And in that spirit, earlier today Sam Skinner, our Secretary of Transportation, presented me with our National Transportation Policy. And I'm proud to say that among its many parts will be a strategy to build roads and streamline traffic, and something we especially need in northern Virginia: more flexibility in how Federal transportation funds are spent. Only then can we win the daily battle against gridlock, crashes, and bumper-to-bumper conditions. And as a guy said to me, "It gets worse after you leave your driveway." Think about it. [*Laughter*] I'll repeat it. [*Laughter*] No, I won't. [*Laughter*]

Another administration priority is the elderly, and John, as you know—most of you, his close friends know—serves on the Special Committee on Aging. And I need him to help stop those who would mess around with Social Security.

And for the less elderly, I need him as Senator to support our bill to boost child-care choice through tax incentives, not Federal meddling in child care across this country. And though Barbara and I are veterans in the field—a personal note—last month John had the same child-care privilege I've enjoyed. He became a grandfather.

Finally, two priorities concern Americans of every age. One is education, and the other—you know what I'm going to say, because it's a national priority—the fight against crime and drugs. In January, I announced the 1990 National Drug Control

Strategy, Phase II of the drug policy that we unveiled last year. We're asking Congress to spend over $10.5 billion in fiscal '91 for education, treatment, interdiction, and enforcement, about a 69-percent increase just since I have taken office.

And John supports this strategy, just as he supports such Phase II steps as an expansion of the death penalty for those drug kingpins. And our budget request to increase Federal assistance to States and localities has his support. Let others soft-pedal the need to be hard on crime. I say, as Virginians do: If you do crime, you'll do time. And we intend to take back the streets. We must be successful in the name of our young people of this country.

And at the same time, I hope you know how interested we all are in education. We've got to take back our schools. And last fall, I convened an unprecedented event: this nation's first education summit, appropriately held at the University of Virginia. And UVA's founder, Thomas Jefferson, once said simply, "I cannot live without books." And so, we met, as Jefferson would have wanted, to find new ways to propel America's love of learning. And from that summit arose the education goals the Nation's Governors and I announced recently—unanimous approval by the Nation's Governors. And among them, we must see that every student in America starts ready to learn—and I'm talking about Head Start and great emphasis and great increase in Head Start—and that each school has an environment where kids can learn, and that means making every school drug-free. These are goals for the year 2000. Our graduation rate must be no less than 90 percent. And we want U.S. students to be first in the world in math and science by the year 2000.

Like Jefferson, John knows that education is America's most enduring legacy and,

moreover, that to preserve it we must give our all, as he did during three separate times of war and now does in time of peace.

Let me close then, as I began, with a story, this tale about giving your all. Eleven years ago last month, as Virginia's newly elected Senator, John was scheduled to give the annual reading of George Washington's farewell address. A snowstorm hit Washington, the worst since 1922. The city was paralyzed. Not our Senator—he put on his boots, began the long walk from his home to the Capitol, stopping to push stalled cars and finally hitching a ride to the Hill on a tractor still here as a part of a protest by farmers. [*Laughter*] And to John, such tenacity was all in the line of duty. He figured if George Washington could make it to Valley Forge, a freshman Senator could certainly appear. And after 3 hours in the cold, he did appear. And others might not have thought it was very important, but he did, motivated by patriotism and respect for the traditions in the United States Senate. And that day was just one of many that he has made his friends proud.

And so, let's roll up our sleeves, keep in the Senate a man whose honor, experience, and wisdom have so enriched this very special Commonwealth in which you all are privileged to live. God bless you, and thank you very much. I know I speak for Barbara, too, when we said, John, if you need a little extra campaign work, call the White House. We're ready. It is national priority that this man be returned to the Senate.

Thank you all very, very much.

Note: The President spoke at 7:13 p.m. in the ballroom at the Sheraton Premier Hotel. In his remarks, he referred to National Republican Committeewoman Flo Traywick and former Virginia gubernatorial candidate J. Marshall Coleman.

Remarks at the Swearing-In Ceremony for Antonia Novello as Surgeon General
March 9, 1990

The President. Justice O'Connor and Secretary Sullivan, Senator Hatch and Congressman Conte and Dr. Mason, and other distinguished guests, in a few minutes we're going to make history three times over. Surgeon General Novello will be the first woman, first Hispanic, and first Puerto Rican to become Surgeon General of the Public Health Service. Lou Sullivan, our outstanding Secretary, and I agree that women and minorities who serve in vital and visible posts in government also serve as role models for our young people. And Toni, your success as Surgeon General will be an inspiration to millions of people.

Dr. Novello's life is already an amazing success story, a vibrant example of the American dream. Twenty years ago, she graduated from the University of Puerto Rico School of Medicine, and 12 years ago she joined the Public Health Service and rose quickly through the ranks. Dr. Novello is a teacher, scholar, administrator, and a physician who has firsthand knowledge of the Public Health Service and the National Institutes of Health. This ceremony is more than a celebration; it is the beginning of a solemn commitment to the American people. Dr. Novello, you have the privilege, in my view, of working with the very best. And my respect and appreciation of my good friend Lou Sullivan grows every day as he fights for the good health of our people. In your hands, too, we now place the health of our people.

The paths ahead are difficult. And in a few minutes, just the few minutes we've been here, 11 people have died from smoking—390,000 people each year. And we must also do all we can to put an end to drug abuse, alcohol abuse, and AIDS. And because so many of these problems begin with our children it is only right that we ask a pediatrician to help. There is one thing each of us can do to live longer and live better, and that is to emphasize health promotion and disease prevention, and it's the best way to save lives and reduce the cost

of medical care. Ultimately, we are all responsible for our own health. And we look to you, Dr. Novello, to help guide us in that effort. Godspeed and good luck in this important new assignment. And now we'll ask Justice O'Connor to do the honors. I guess I'll wedge in on my little toe mark here. All right.

[*At this point, Surgeon General Novello was sworn in.*]

Dr. Novello. Mr. President; Justice O'Connor; Mr. Secretary; my husband, Dr. Joe Novello; my mother, Ana Delia Flores; Dr. Mason; distinguished guests; my dearest family and friends: The American dream is well and alive today, and I might say today the "West Side Story" comes to the West Wing. [*Laughter*] When I was a little girl attending public schools in Puerto Rico, I looked beyond the Caribbean and beyond El Yunque and beyond everywhere that I could. And all I wanted to do when I dreamed was to become a pediatrician, a doctor for the little kids in my hometown. I never told anyone that I wanted to be that. It seemed too grand of a notion. Well, dreams sometimes come true in unexpected ways, and today I stand before you with pride and humility as the first Puerto Rican, Hispanic, female Surgeon General of this country.

Mr. President, you have bestowed a great honor and a great responsibility on me. By doing so, you have also sent a message. You have sent a message that somewhere this very morning, anywhere in San Francisco, San Antonio, Boston, Biloxi, there's another minority girl or boy who can dream the dreams that I just dreamed yesterday of becoming the Surgeon General of this country. I do not aspire to be the Surgeon General of the Hispanics, or the Surgeon General of the women, or the Surgeon General of the children. I aspire to be the Surgeon General of every American of this great country. As a practicing physician, I learned what patients want from their doctor. They don't care if the doctor is male or female, if the doctor is black or white, if the doctor is Anglo or Hispanic, or even how they voted in the last election. What they do care is that the doctor has compassion, scientific excellence, availability at all times—the good ones and the bad ones. That's the definition of a good doctor.

Once a dream, it is now my pledge to be a good doctor for all who live in this great country. My motto as your Surgeon General will be "good science and good sense." And so, I ask for your help and the grace of God as I strive to give something back to the Nation that has been so good to me. Thank you very much. *Dios lo vendiga,* and God bless America.

Note: The President spoke at 11:28 a.m. in the Roosevelt Room at the White House. In his opening remarks, he referred to James O. Mason, Assistant Secretary for Health.

Remarks Upon Meeting the University of Miami Hurricanes
March 9, 1990

What a day in the Rose Garden. And welcome, all of you especially—and all of you to the White House. It's great to see Senator Gramm and Senator Mack, and distinguished Members of the United States Congress here, Dante Fascell and Congressman Bennett. Sam Jankovich, the director of athletics at Miami; and, of course, Dennis Erickson and his staff; and then the number one football team in America, the Miami Hurricanes. For all of us name-droppers, it's been 2 great weeks. Last week, the San Francisco 49ers—[*laughter*]—were in here, and the NFL's team of the eighties. And now, we've got the college football team of the decade. The 'Canes have lost five football games in the last 5 years; that's all. A 55-and-5 record. And your Sugar Bowl win this year marked the University of Miami's seventh straight trip—seventh—to a New Year's Day bowl game.

And when sports fans think of a college bowl over the last 10 years, they think of two of the biggest games in college football history. January 1, 1984, your team started making college football history when you went 10 and 1, and then upset Nebraska 31–30 in the Orange Bowl—one of the greatest wins ever. And then one that some of you young guys remember, November 25th, 1989. Your titanic struggle with the Fighting Irish at Notre Dame this year resulted in a 27-to-10 win over the then top-ranked defending national champion in what many consider the game of the year.

But with Miami, there's also great memories of great championships. Back in 1984, the Nebraska game at the Orange Bowl brought you your first national championship—national title. And then you beat O.U. in the Orange Bowl to win the 1987 national title. And just when the opposition thought the storm had passed, you beat the Crimson Tide soundly in this year's Sugar Bowl. Three national titles, three great championship games.

And not only have you played great games, but you've produced some of football's greatest players. Take a look at the Miami dynasty of quarterbacks. What is it about the water in Miami? Jim Kelly of Buffalo, Bernie Kosar of the Browns, Vinnie Testaverde—Tampa Bay, and Steve Walsh of the Cowboys. No wonder they call it Quarterback U. Well, the team of the eighties heads for the nineties with Craig Erickson as quarterback, and your passing game is taking full flight. In fact, some say that when Craig throws the ball, anything that flies that far should be showing an in-flight movie and serving a meal. [*Laughter*]

But behind this Erickson Express, if you will, this offense is the number-one-ranked defense in the country, led by All-American defensive linemen Greg Mark and Cortez Kennedy. And I hear it's easier to get a tax cut through Congress than a ball carrier through that defense. The man behind it all is right here, Coach Erickson. It was your rookie year as Miami's coach, and yet you made them national champs. And coaching is never easy, but that first year is always the toughest, and you did a great job. And congratulations to all of you. In the best American tradition, the Hurricanes have shown that they won't settle for second best. Thank you and God bless you all. Welcome to the White House.

Coach Erickson. President Bush, first of all, we'd like to thank you for the Miami weather that you brought with us today. It's very nice. And secondly, we've had a lot of honors and a lot of accolades since winning the national championship, but for us to have the honor to come to the White House and visit with you is truly the greatest honor that any football team could ever

have. And we've got a lot of great young guys here that worked very hard to win the national championship. Five of them were here in 1987 with President Reagan. We've got a lot of other young ones here that hopefully will be here in 1990, 1991, 1992. [*Laughter*] But on behalf of the University of Miami, the administration, my coaching staff, and the football team, we would like to present you with this jersey which signifies that we were number one in the country.

The President. Well, congratulations again, and thank you all. That's terrific.

Note: The President spoke at 11:40 a.m. in the Rose Garden at the White House.

Letter to Congressional Leaders on Nuclear Cooperation With EURATOM
March 9, 1990

Dear Mr. Speaker: (Dear Mr. President:)

The United States has been engaged in nuclear cooperation with the European Community for many years. This cooperation was initiated under agreements that were concluded over 3 decades ago between the United States and the European Atomic Energy Community (EURATOM) and that extend until December 31, 1995. Since the inception of this cooperation, the Community has adhered to all its obligations under those agreements.

The Nuclear Non-Proliferation Act of 1978 amended the Atomic Energy Act of 1954 to establish new nuclear export criteria, including a requirement that the United States would have a right to consent to the reprocessing of fuel exported from the United States. Our present agreements for cooperation with EURATOM do not contain such a right. To avoid disrupting cooperation with EURATOM, a proviso was included in the law to enable continued cooperation until March 10, 1980, if EURATOM agreed to negotiations concerning our cooperation agreements. EURATOM agreed in 1978 to such negotiations.

The law also provides that nuclear coop-

eration with EURATOM can be extended on an annual basis after March 10, 1980, upon determination by the President that failure to cooperate would be seriously prejudicial to the achievement of U.S. nonproliferation objectives or otherwise jeopardize the common defense and security and after notification to the Congress. President Carter made such a determination 10 years ago and signed Executive Order No. 12193, permitting nuclear cooperation with EURATOM to continue until March 10, 1981. President Reagan made such determinations in 1981, 1982, 1983, 1984, 1985, 1986, 1987, and 1988, and signed Executive Orders Nos. 12295, 12351, 12409, 12463, 12506, 12554, 12587, and 12629 permitting nuclear cooperation to continue through March 10, 1989. I made such a determination in 1989 and signed Executive Order No. 12670, permitting nuclear cooperation to continue through March 10, 1990.

In addition to numerous informal contacts, the United States has engaged in frequent talks with EURATOM regarding the renegotiation of the U.S.-EURATOM agreements for cooperation. Talks were conducted in November 1978, September 1979,

April 1980, January 1982, November 1983, March 1984, May, September, and November 1985, April and July 1986, September 1987, September and November 1988, July and December 1989, and February 1990. Further talks are anticipated this year.

I believe it is essential that cooperation between the United States and the Community continue and, likewise, that we work closely with our allies to counter the threat of proliferation of nuclear explosives. Not only would a disruption of nuclear cooperation with EURATOM eliminate any chance of progress in our talks with that organization related to our agreements, it would also cause serious problems in our overall relationships. Accordingly, I have determined that failure to continue peaceful nu-

clear cooperation with EURATOM would be seriously prejudicial to the achievement of U.S. nonproliferation objectives and would jeopardize the common defense and security of the United States. I therefore intend to sign an executive order to extend the waiver of the application of the relevant export criterion of the Nuclear Non-Proliferation Act for an additional 12 months from March 10, 1990.

Sincerely,

GEORGE BUSH

Note: Identical letters were sent to Thomas S. Foley, Speaker of the House of Representatives, and Dan Quayle, President of the Senate. The Executive order is listed in Appendix E at the end of this volume.

Letter to Congressional Leaders Transmitting a Report on Telecommunications Trade Negotiations With the European Community and Korea
March 9, 1990

Dear _____:

Pursuant to section 1376(c)(2)(B) of the Omnibus Trade and Competitiveness Act of 1988 ("the Act") (Public Law 100–418; 102 Stat. 1221), I am hereby transmitting my report that finds that substantial progress has been made in telecommunications trade talks conducted under section 1375 of the Act with the European Community (EC) and Korea and contains the reasons why an extension of the negotiating period with the EC and Korea is necessary.

Sincerely,

GEORGE BUSH

Note: Identical letters were sent to George J. Mitchell and Robert Dole, majority and minority leaders of the Senate; Lloyd Bentsen and Bob Packwood, chairman and ranking Republican member of the Senate Finance Committee; Thomas S. Foley and Robert H. Michel, Speaker and minority leader of the House of Representatives; John D. Dingell and Norman F. Lent, chairman and ranking Republican member of the House Energy and Commerce Committee; Dan Rostenkowski and Bill Archer, chairman and ranking Republican member of the House Ways and Means Committee.

Nomination of Karen L. Gillmor To Be Director of the Women's Bureau
March 9, 1990

The President today announced his intention to nominate Karen L. Gillmor to be

Director of the Women's Bureau at the Department of Labor. She would succeed Jill

347

Houghton Emery.

Since 1987 Dr. Gillmor has served as manager of physician relations at the Ohio State University Hospitals in Columbus, OH. Prior to this, she served as chief of management planning and research at the Industrial Commission of Ohio, 1983–1986; advancement officer for the Ohio Republican Finance Committee, 1982–1983; vice president for public affairs and governmental relations and assistant to the chairman at the Huntington National Bank in Columbus, OH, 1981–1982; special assistant to the dean of the Ohio State University College of Law, 1979–1981; research assistant at

Burke Marketing Research, Inc. in Indianapolis, IN, 1978–1979; and assistant to the president for Indiana Central University in Indianapolis, IN, 1977–1978. In addition, Dr. Gillmor has served as assistant to the vice president, and dean at the Ohio State University, 1972–1977, and director of guidance at the Fairfield Union Local Schools in Lancaster, OH, 1970–1972.

Dr. Gillmor graduated from Michigan State University (B.A., 1969) and the Ohio State University (M.A., 1970; Ph.D., 1981). She was born January 29, 1948, in Cleveland, OH. Dr. Gillmor is married and resides in Columbus, OH.

Statement by Press Secretary Fitzwater on the Restoration of Lithuanian Independence
March 11, 1990

The United States has never recognized the forcible incorporation of the independent states of Estonia, Latvia, or Lithuania into the U.S.S.R. We have consistently supported the Baltic peoples' inalienable right to peaceful self-determination.

The new Parliament has declared its intention to restore Lithuanian independence. The United States would urge the Soviet Government to respect the will of the citizens of Lithuania, as expressed through their freely elected representatives, and expects the Government of Lithuania

to consider the rights of its minority population.

The United States believes it is in the mutual interest of Lithuania, the Soviet Union, and all CSCE countries to resolve this issue peacefully. We call upon the Soviet Government to address its concerns and interests through immediate constructive negotiations with the Government of Lithuania. We hope that all parties will continue to avoid any initiation or encouragement of violence.

Statement by Press Secretary Fitzwater on the President's Meeting With Former Prime Minister Noboru Takeshita of Japan
March 12, 1990

The President met for approximately 1 hour with former Japanese Prime Minister and current LDP [Liberal Democratic Party] leader Noboru Takeshita. They discussed the whole range of issues underpinning the overall U.S.-Japan relationship. The discussion focused on bilateral economic issues, the U.S.-Japan security arrangement, and the global partnership between the

United States and Japan. Much of the discussion concerned economic issues currently existing between the two countries and the fact that their solution will require extraordinary efforts on both sides of the Pacific. Mr. Takeshita indicated that the government of Prime Minister Kaifu has become increasingly aware of the urgency of the problems facing the two countries and that Mr. Kaifu has created a new team within the Office of the Prime Minister for coordinating solutions for the Structural Impediments Initiative (SII) talks. The two leaders also discussed the public pressures on both sides of the Pacific concerning the U.S.-Japan relationship and the necessity for leaders in both countries to reinvigorate the relationship.

Nomination of Julian W. De La Rosa To Be Inspector General of the Department of Labor
March 12, 1990

The President today announced his intention to nominate Julian W. De La Rosa to be Inspector General of the Department of Labor in Washington, DC. He would succeed James Brian Hyland.

Currently Mr. De La Rosa serves as secretary to the board of police commissioners at the metropolitan police department in St. Louis, MO. Prior to this, he served in various capacities at the Federal Bureau of Investigation, including Special Agent in Charge in St. Louis, MO; executive at the headquarters in Washington, DC, 1987–1988; Special Agent in Charge of the San Antonio Division, 1979–1986; supervisory position at the headquarters, 1972–1979; Special Agent, 1963–1972; and support employee, 1959–1963.

Mr. De La Rosa graduated from St. Mary's University (B.A., 1963). He was born September 12, 1939, in San Antonio, TX. Mr. De La Rosa is married and resides in San Antonio, TX.

Appointment of Deborah Amend as Special Assistant to the President for Communications
March 13, 1990

The President today announced the appointment of Deborah Amend as Special Assistant to the President for Communications.

Since 1985 Ms. Amend has served in several capacities at the National Republican Congressional Committee in Washington, DC, including deputy campaign director, 1989 to present; Midwest regional campaign director, 1986–1989; and incumbent field representative, 1985–1986. In addition she has served as press secretary for Congressman E. Clay Shaw, 1982–1985; deputy press secretary for Senator Bob Packwood, 1980–1982; and on the national field staff for George Bush for President, 1979–1980.

Ms. Amend graduated from the University of Iowa (B.S., 1979). Currently she resides in Alexandria, VA.

The President's News Conference
March 13, 1990

The President. We began this administration by saying that the day of the dictator is over. And now restless millions have spoken and have elected, or prepare to elect, new governments—their governments. As long as we live, the images of this revolution, the

Revolution of '89, will always be with us: a playwright President in Prague, the tumbling of the Berlin Wall, crumbling of a Romanian dictatorship.

But this revolution leaves us with a new challenge: how to best support newborn democracies. This challenge is utterly unlike the task of rebuilding Europe after the Second World War, for no single great plan will do. We need a flexible approach, one that will meet the needs of each country we seek to help.

Today I want to speak about how we can best help two democracies in our hemisphere: Panama and Nicaragua. We should take great pride in the way in which our leadership—Congress and the administration—helped the democratic spirit take hold in these two countries, but this is no time to bask in self-praise. These nations need our help to heal deep wounds inflicted by years of strife and oppression, years of loss and deprivation. And we must act, and act soon, to help the peoples of these new democracies in two great and historic tasks: reconstruction and reconciliation.

I've taken an important step today. As a demonstration of our resolve to be part of the process of reconciliation, I just signed an Executive order to end the economic embargo against Nicaragua. Americans are determined to help the people of Nicaragua.

And next I'm asking the Congress and the American people to join me in crafting a bipartisan agreement to help both countries. After all, bipartisanship did work well last year to put the focus on free elections and end the fighting in Nicaragua. Bipartisanship also helped bring an end to the tyranny in Panama. And we need to work again in that same spirit to put together an assistance program for both countries.

I'm proposing the creation of a fund for democracy to assist in the reconstruction and development of these two countries. And I'm requesting the Congress to approve by April 5th a package of assistance of $800 million for these two countries, using funds from the defense budget. This package consists of $500 million for Panama, already requested in that January 25th proposal to Congress, along with $70 million for refugees, and an additional $300

million for Nicaragua. I'm asking the Secretary of State and the Secretary of the Treasury to work together on the economic assistance aspects of these packages and, of course, to consult with the United States Congress.

In addition, under existing authorities, I am initiating immediate action to provide $21 million of previously appropriated economic aid, principally for food and humanitarian assistance. I also will be sending to the Congress in the future a budget amendment for an additional $200 million in fiscal '91 for Nicaragua, consistent with the approach that we've taken this year.

Moreover, I've instructed the Secretary of Defense and Dick Darman at OMB to begin negotiations immediately with the Congress on mutually acceptable offsets from the defense budget that can be used for this democracy fund without having an unacceptable impact on national security. I further propose that in the event that an agreement on offsets cannot be reached by March 27th, the Congress authorize me to select offsets from the defense budget. And should neither of these alternatives prove to be workable, I am prepared, because of the dire need of these funds, to ask for a waiver of the budget act to allow this critical program to proceed on the required timetable.

I urge the Congress to move quickly and also urge in the strongest terms that it not add any extraneous items to this request. It is urgent to advance the prospect for democracy and reconciliation in Nicaragua and Panama. Damage to both economies has been great. We must help, and we want to help. Our help is needed swiftly to bring about demilitarization and advance the whole Central American peace process. If bipartisanship prevails, we will be able to meet this goal and respond to the expectations of our neighbors.

Let me save the details for congressional briefings and give you the three broad categories of assistance: aid for democracy, for development, and for demilitarization. We want to help democratic institutions take root in each country, but democracy begins with the rule of law and respect for human rights. It needs the support of courts that are fair and free of every influence but the law. It needs the support of police forces that are upright and honest. And it needs our support. Development and demilitarization—they go hand in hand. They start when we provide textbooks for children, when we create thousands of new jobs, when the hand that held a gun guides a plow. In short, as we demobilize the military, we must mobilize the market.

This is a great and historic task, but we are inspired by the courage of our neighbors. We're close—very, very close—to a hemisphere that is completely democratic, a compass of freedom that spans half the world, from Alaska to Argentina. And facing this enormous challenge, we are not alone. Other nations can and must help. But only America can take the lead on this one. I stand prepared to work with the Congress to do our part for reconstruction and reconciliation for democracy.

And now I'd be glad to respond to questions. And, Helen [Helen Thomas, United Press International], I believe you have the first one.

Deficit Reduction Plan

Q. Thank you, Mr. President. Your warm reception of the Rostenkowski plan—does that mean you're ready to negotiate tax increases and a freeze on Social Security benefits, things you have never gone for in the past? And I have a followup.

The President. No, it doesn't. The answer is no. Followup?

Q. A followup? You are not willing to negotiate, or what is your——

The President. Overall feeling? Look, I think he—without rancor, without a lot of rhetoric—made a very broad proposal. We've made a proposal—the administration. We now would like to hear from the budget process on the Hill what their proposal is, and then we'll talk. But perhaps, as I told some reporters yesterday, in being receptive through not knocking the things in it we don't like—and there are plenty—I was somewhat colored by the way in which Chairman Rostenkowski approached this and with, I think, the evident good will on his part and determination to try to break the ice and move the process forward.

Q. But you're not saying you would go for a tax increase?

The President. No, I'm not for a tax. Let me——

Q. How about a freeze on Social Security?

The President. Well, there are a lot of things I'm not for that are in his proposal—a lot, including taxes.

Lithuanian Independence

Q. Mr. President, the United States has never recognized the forced incorporation of Lithuania into the Soviet Union. Now that Lithuania has declared its independence, the United States seems to be moving tentatively toward full recognition. Is that because we're afraid of offending Mr. Gorbachev or don't want to alienate him?

The President. It's because we want to see the evolution of the control of the territory there, and also we want to see peaceful resolution to the question.

Q. Well, do we still regard Lithuania as a captive nation, along with the other Baltic States?

The President. We might not use that word, but we never have regarded Lithuania as incorporated into the Soviet Union. That's been our policy. And we rejoice as people are permitted the free expression that we take for granted in this country. And clearly, I think, there is a great deal of interest in this concept of Lithuanians working it out with the Soviets to achieve what they want. And so, we're not standing in that way. But in terms of recognition, there is a standard of control of one's territory that I've been advised should guide this.

Nicaragua

Q. Mr. President, are you concerned about the apparent reluctance of the *contras* to disband, and what can you do about it?

The President. Yes, I am concerned about it, and I'm also concerned about certain military action by the Sandinistas. But I'm also encouraged, Brit [Brit Hume, ABC News]. And I'm encouraged because yesterday I talked to Dan Quayle, and he told me of his visit with Ortega [President of Nicaragua], where Ortega seemed willing to transfer the Defense Ministry, seemed willing to transfer the Interior Ministry, and was open about the discussion of reducing—I want to be careful here I don't overstate it—but reducing a military action on both sides.

There is a United Nations vehicle that can be helpful, ONUCA [United Nations Observer Group in Central America], which could have a useful role to play in the separation of forces and in getting done what Violeta Chamorro [President-elect of Nicaragua] wants, which is both sides start laying down their weapons. That ONUCA has support from other leaders in this hemisphere—Carlos Andrés Pérez [President of Venezuela], I believe, supports it. I know Mrs. Chamorro wants us to give more support to this, so I've asked the State Department to look into that immediately.

So, I'm less concerned than I was about the peaceful transfer of power, including the military. But I think to the degree both sides can start laying down weapons and moving towards the kind of market economies we're talking about and with less reliance on military, it's better. So, I can't say I'm not concerned, but I am encouraged the way it's going so far.

Israeli Settlement in the Occupied Territories

Q. Mr. President, do you regret, the other day, raising the issue of settlements in East Jerusalem?

The President. No, I don't regret it. I think all the speculation and commentary of the last 10 days have blown things way out of proportion. What I was doing was reiterating United States policy. But let me say this: Right now in Israel, there's internal developments taking place in the political scene there, and I do not want to look in any way like we're trying to mingle into the internal affairs of Israel as they're going through this difficult political problem right now—right now. So, I will answer no more on it—well, try to clarify it because you have the followup. But it's so sensitive and it is so emotional that I just think any further speculation on this question would certainly not be useful, given what's happened just in the last few hours.

Q. Well, can I just ask then——

The President. Yes, you can ask.

Q. I'm not really clear why you raised the issue at all. Was there a particular reason?

It's long been part of U.S. policy, but it hasn't been talked about a lot.

The President. Well, I understand that. That's why I will speculate no further on it. I think it is highly emotional. But I think any speculation and any commentary at this juncture—a lot of developments since I made that comment—would be counterproductive.

Deficit Reduction Plan

Q. Mr. President, following up on Helen's question, could I ask, beyond your well-known friendship with Chairman Rostenkowski, what elements of the plan do you see as meritorious?

The President. The fact that it's aimed at getting the deficit down. Does that help you any?

Q. No, because it doesn't say what—do you have any ideas to throw in beyond his? Is a 1-year freeze——

The President. We've thrown our ideas out on the table, John [John Mashek, Boston Globe], and he's now thrown his out. And now we'd like to have the leaders of the budget process on the Hill throw theirs out, and then perhaps we can talk. Look, there's a lot of changes in the world, a lot of changes out there in terms of Eastern Europe and the requests that I'm making today—a lot of things going on. And so, I don't want to appear totally inflexible, but I'm not about to stand here and give Dan or the Congress the idea that I want to accept several of the things that are in his approach. But will I be willing to talk when they get all these proposals out there? Certainly. Are we prepared to negotiate? Absolutely.

China

Q. Mr. President, you've opened your comments today by saying that the day of the dictator was over and speaking of the moves for democracy in 1989, and yet the exception to that rule is the situation in China, where since the crackdown at Tiananmen Square we've seen little moves toward democracy and freedom there. Do you have any second thoughts about the approach that you took for the situation in China and your sending of your high-level envoys there, and any thoughts that this policy must now change because of the lack of response from the Chinese Government?

The President. No, but I'm not happy with the evolution of reform in China, but I'd have no regrets about that. And I'm reinforced by a lot of expert opinion that feels the approach I took—accomplishing something by Executive order that the Congress wanted to do dramatically later on through legislation—was the proper approach. And so, I hope our policy will bear more fruit. But, no, I am not happy with the status quo.

Q. Well, Mr. President, if you're not happy with the status quo, why not change your policy now to take a tougher line toward the Chinese regime?

The President. Because I'm familiar with China and I think we're on the right track and I hope that we'll see an evolution of more reform. And that's exactly why not change it now.

Deficit Reduction Plan

Q. Mr. President, back to the surprising administration reaction to the Rostenkowski proposal: Regardless of whatever negotiating positions are being drawn now or politics is being played, can you today assure the American people that there will be no tax increase, no new taxes this year?

The President. I'm only one player, but you know my position, and I have no intention of changing that position.

Q. Under what circumstances might you——

The President. Too hypothetical. Nice try. Too hypothetical.

Right here, lady in the front row.

Assistance for Nicaragua and Panama

Q. Thank you. I'd like to ask you something about your Nicaragua/Panama proposal.

The President. Yes?

Q. But in light of what the majority leader of the House says—that you have not shown strong leadership—you do not propose in your——

The President. Who said that?

Q. Mr. Gephardt, the majority leader of the House. [*Laughter*]

The President. Thank you for your clarifi-cation. I have a follow-on. [*Laughter*]

Q. I would like you also to comment on that. The Nicaragua question is: You are not proposing to Congress exactly where to cut in the defense budget; you're basically leaving that to them. Why don't you tell them where they should cut specifically?

The President. On offsets?

Q. Yes.

The President. From the defense budget?

Q. Why don't you say: Here's a B–2; take it?

The President. We are. We are doing that. And what I'm saying to them——

Q. But where?

The President. ——well, that's in negotiation up there. But what I've also said here is: If you're not willing to do it, give me the authority on March 27th, and it'll be done like that. I am willing to do it. We're going to take the hits. We're negotiating with Congress now.

Q. Why not tell the American people, then?

The President. We'll tell them on March 27th if they turn it to me. And right now I don't know how much of it's confidential, but I'll let the Secretary of Defense answer the question—but I don't see any great secrecy in this.

What we're trying to do is to give the Congress the ball and say: Here's what we recommend. Now you tell us what you want to do, but don't go making a lot of add-ons. Do it the way we feel is necessary to keep the focus on Nicaragua and Panama. I think Congress has a very legitimate role here; but if they're not willing to fulfill it, Lesley [Lesley Stahl, CBS News], we have no problem giving you a list that would take care of it just like that. But I think it's the Congress' role now to work with our people.

Representative Gephardt

Q. Why does Gephardt get under your skin so much? You've got—I don't know, an 80-percent approval rating. He makes a speech attacking you, and——

The President. Well, what have I said? What would make you think that he gets under my skin? [*Laughter*]

Q. He says you're not a strong leader.

The President. Oh, I know. I know. That's so discouraging. [*Laughter*]

Q. And all the people around the White House and——

The President. But why do you think it gets under my skin? The honest answer is—I know you won't believe this—it doesn't. It doesn't. I think we're going in the right direction. We're talking substance and policy. I think many in the Congress think that we are being responsive. But look, I expect that. I expect that kind of political criticism. But I think if you want to talk about the substance of his ideas: Do I think it's a good idea to loan money to the Soviet Union today? No. We have no request for food aid to the Soviet Union; you just want to put it on a ship and send it over there? No, I don't think that's a particularly brilliant idea. But I don't want to knock the man. Maybe he'll come on a good idea one of these days. [*Laughter*]

Assistance for Nicaragua and Panama

Q. The Nicaraguans and the Panamanians are expecting aid very soon. They are in urgent need of the aid.

The President. Exactly.

Q. And the Panamanians say that they cannot wait any longer. What can you do besides Congress? When can they expect something?

The President. I'm going to have this question replayed on Capitol Hill because you're absolutely right. There is a sense of urgency, and I would like to take the opportunity here to encourage the movement in the Congress. We've sent a proposal up on Panama; now let's get going on it. Now we're coupling it with Nicaragua; now let's [get] going on it. There's an urgency in Nicaragua, too, but Panama—very urgent. And so, we're going to keep pushing. But I think you're right on target with that hypothesis.

Economic Policy

Q. Mr. President, there was a report last week that you were so angry and upset at the Fed's failure to lower interest rates that you wouldn't reappoint Chairman Greenspan next year when his term ends. Can you comment on whether there's any thought being given yet to the question of reappointing Mr. Greenspan and the level of frustration you do feel about interest rates?

The President. No, there is no discussion of that nature at all. I'm not sure I saw the report, but I saw some speculation someplace. Maybe it was on the TV. But that's never been discussed with me. Now, if the question is, am I happy with interest rates—look, every President would like to see interest rates lower. There's no question. I don't knock the concern that some have on inflation. A President has to be concerned about inflation, too. But there's no bubbling war with Alan Greenspan, and that's what I got from the commentary I heard—that there was. But you know, going back a few years here, it's ever been thus, hasn't it? When there's some differences, it's always built into a conflict between the President and the Chairman of the Fed. And I don't want to get into that game because I don't feel that way.

Q. But is there a particular feeling at this point that the Fed is dragging its feet somewhat in getting interest rates down?

The President. I think some feel that way, and I think some probably agree with the inflationary concerns that have been expressed. But I'm not in a Fed-bashing mode. I also think it's very sensitive in terms of markets and everything else to even go as far as I have done, trying to say very little and succeeding only moderately. [*Laughter*]

President's Popularity

Q. Mr. President, you've been at near-historical public approval ratings now for well into your first term: 80 percent or more. And my question is whether you believe in spending some of this popularity on something controversial—like, say, what specifically you like about Rostenkowski's proposal—or just hoarding it. What's the goal?

The President. I don't believe it, one thing. I don't believe in polls that much.

Q. I guess the question is——

The President. Talk to Nicaragua's man; talk to Ortega's man—probably gainfully unemployed right now for missing it by a jillion points. But these things come and go, seriously. And you know where I learned it? Back in Illinois in 1980. I don't remember why, but I remember Vic Gold lecturing me on hanging your hat on polls.

That's not the way I try to call the shots on the policy. You just raised a question about China. If I had my finger in the wind, I might have done that one differently. I might have done differently about going to Cartagena if I put my finger in the wind in terms of polls, but that's not the way I run this administration. I know some think so, but that's not the point. So, I'm not going to dwell on them because tomorrow it may be very different. Then I'll have a—say, hey, wait a minute.

Q. Can I go on it for one more question? Does it become a possibility, though, that when you're at, like, 80 percent, that almost becomes an end in itself at some point? I mean it's such an extraordinary level.

The President. You mean, pull the ripcord and get out? [*Laughter*]

Q. Well, I mean——

The President. What do you mean?

Q. When you're at 80 percent, it would be tempting, I would think, just to simply protect that lead, sort of fall on the ball?

The President. No. Please believe me. That doesn't guide the decisions we take, and I've given you a couple of examples. And I'm trying to do the best I can for the country and to work with the Congress. And there's a lot of areas where I have not succeeded near as well as I would like to, but I don't live by the polls.

American Hostages in Lebanon

Q. Mr. President, last week we learned that you were so concerned about the hostages that you were willing to take a questionable call. And it might have been from the Iranian President, and then, of course, you found out it wasn't. In response, Rafsanjani made a statement saying that you had been trying to get a hold of him for a month. Did you actually then try to place a call to the real person—or could you clarify?

The President. I don't know where he got that. I saw that statement, and there was no truth in it—our trying to contact him for a month. It'd be very easy to do. I responded to an incoming call. I think the bottom line

is you have to say, would you do it again based on the information you had? And I'd say yes, I probably would. It may be difficult for somebody to get through again— [*laughter*].

But what's wrong with reaching out and touching someone—[*laughter*]—when the hostages are at stake? The hostages are at stake here, and what's wrong with trying? Look, I feel this all the time. I've talked about this—that I will go the extra mile. And when the whole story comes out on this, you all are going to be very, very fascinated with the details, very fascinated.

But I'm just telling you that it is important, it is very important to run down every avenue in terms of these hostages, and I would be remiss if I didn't. And there are things that go on, going around in back alleys and trying to find out information, and we've got to do that. I owe it to the families of those people and to those people themselves that are held hostage.

Q. Can I follow up, Mr. President?

The President. Yes.

Q. If you didn't try to reach them for a month, can you say whether you or anyone acting on your behalf did try to reach him at all?

The President. Have we been trying to reach Rafsanjani?

Q. Have you tried, yes.

The President. No, other than this one phone call that turns out to be a hoax.

Q. So, as far as you can tell, what he was saying just didn't make any sense on any level?

The President. Yes. It's very much like the rhetoric that they use from time to time. He's got some political problems at home, and we understand that. The main thing is, can we move forward and get the hostages out. And I'll repeat: Good will begets good will. And I'm satisfied that even in this instance the officials there know that nobody is trying to set them up or anything of that nature. I'm interested in saving American lives.

Soviet Reforms

Q. Mr. President, I understand that TASS [Soviet news agency] is reporting this morning that the Soviet Parliament has granted

President Gorbachev the expanded powers he wants and has been requesting. I'm interested, sir, if you side with those within the Soviet Union who fear that there are not sufficient checks and balances on this new Presidential system, that it could result in a more totalitarian Soviet Union. How do you feel this might affect your dealings with Gorbachev and whether you envision extending this fund for democracy perhaps one day to the Soviet Union itself?

The President. I answer that by saying I stay out of the internal affairs and deliberations of the Soviet Union. And they are going through a process of reform, which we support in broad terms, *perestroika.* They're going through a process of *glasnost,* which is openness, which we support. And it would be very inappropriate for the President of the United States to start passing judgment as that process of *perestroika*—democratization, if you will—moves forward.

And so, yes, the Soviets have created a new post of President, I hear, but that's their business. And we will work with, in this instance, President Gorbachev. As you know, I think we have a reasonably good relationship there, a respectful one; and I'm going to continue to work with him.

Q. Well, can you say, sir, whether you think that as you continue to work with him that will be affected in any way by these changes that have taken place, or is it going to be as it has been between you and Mr. Gorbachev? And would you see involving the Soviet Union in this fund for democracy?

The President. You mean, asking them to give money to——

Q. No, no, no. Including them, making them if not currently, as Gephardt has suggested, perhaps one day a beneficiary of this fund for democracy?

The President. I think the answer is to help in a technical way as best we can for helping the Soviets move towards market economies and free markets and those kinds of considerations. I think that's the next step we ought to take.

And there's discussion of an Eastern development bank. The question is out there whether the Soviets should be members of that bank or not. And as a matter of fact,

we have some deliberations going on as to what the U.S. position should be right now. I'm not prepared to state it, but I've been spending some time on this question. But that's an idea that was surfaced by François Mitterrand [President of France], I believe. So, there are all kinds of ways in which, down the road, we can work with the Soviet Union, but I think what they need now from us is know-how and technical knowledge, that kind of thing.

Japan-U.S. Relations

Q. Mr. President, after your meeting in Palm Springs with Prime Minister Kaifu, he took a real beating in the Japanese Diet. And I wonder if, in retrospect, were there any misunderstandings in your conversations? He was accused in Japan by his critics of having made some concessions or reached a level of detail in your discussions that some in Japan were unhappy with. Is there any clarification needed about what came out of Palm Springs?

The President. No, those reports just highlight the sensitivity of the situation in Japan. And I think that as far as I'm concerned the talks were very good. We followed up, incidentally, with close to an hour with Mr. Takeshita [former Japanese Prime Minister] yesterday and covered the same broad agenda. I didn't go into every specific, but I'm convinced that both Mr. Kaifu left Palm Springs and Takeshita will leave Washington with a far better understanding of the problems that we face. And hopefully, I have a better understanding of theirs. So, I think I'm aware of the criticism against him at home, but I think that I would just go back to the statements he made when he left Palm Springs, which I viewed as very constructive.

Q. Just one followup: You said in a speech—the day after you got back—to the Electronics Association that you had discussed telecommunications with him, and that apparently came as a surprise to some people in Japan. Was that a brief discussion, a lengthy one?

The President. A broad discussion of several categories. And I don't know in terms of the amount of time, but we left the details of all of these categories, that were so well-known as differences between the U.S. and Japan, to the experts. In fact, I think Bob Mosbacher will be going there soon, if he's not already on his way. And so, it was more broad in general, but categories mentioned.

Upcoming Meeting With Chairman Gorbachev

Q. Do you still expect the summit with Mr. Gorbachev will take place in Washington in the last 2 weeks of June?

The President. We've got to get that set soon, pin down the dates and the place. But in terms of expectation, yes.

Baseball Strike

Q. Mr. President, the announcement no one wants to hear—the delay of baseball's opening day—is imminent. Is there anything that you as the "first fan" can do— [*laughter*]—to bring the sides closer together to prevent a tragic delay of the baseball season?

The President. You know, I made a comment on that yesterday, and I misspoke because I said strike. And we got some—understandably—got some calls from some of the ballplayers saying hey, that's not technically what the situation is, please. Look, yes, I'm a ball fan, and I want to go to the opening game someplace. Last year, I went to the American League; this year I'd like to go to the National League, if possible—I don't know whether it's going to work. Maybe end up in Baltimore. But I don't want to intervene. We've already taken a battle on that up there, on another labor matter—have the Federal Government intervene. But I would simply appeal to both sides to get the matter resolved so the American people can hear that cry "Play ball!" again.

Q. I have a followup here, sir. I'm reminded by one of the senior correspondents back here that Lyndon Johnson used to lock up both sides and say, "Don't come out until you've got a settlement." Is that a prospect here?

The President. Not on this particular issue, but on some issues that could well prove to be a prospect. [*Laughter*]

President Endara of Panama

Q. Mr. President, have you been in contact with President Endara about his fast, and do you view that as a useful means of expressing the plight of the Panamanian people as they wait for U.S. aid?

The President. Well, I have not talked to him since the fast began. And I did note with interest some very supportive statements out of him after the fast began— supportive of our administration and what we're trying to do. But that's a matter for him to determine.

Assistance for Nicaragua and Panama

Q. Mr. President, in your opening statement, you appealed to Congress to pass your aid program, but you did not appeal to the American people. And one of the problems a lot of Congressmen say they're having is that foreign aid at this time is not a high priority for a lot of people. Do you think an appeal, first of all, to ordinary Americans is necessary, and what do you say to people who think that perhaps what may be seen as the first part of a peace dividend is going overseas?

The President. I think you put your finger on a good point. However, I believe that both Nicaragua and Panama have strong support from the American people. In fact, there's new information on that. But I think they raise a good point—I mean, there's a lot of domestic problems. But we're sorting this out now. And I'm convinced that when the American people understand what we're talking about, about offsetting proposals in defense, in other words not going in there and costing them more or taking it away from some other program, that it will have strong support.

But I'm not unsympathetic to that argument. But where I would differ is I think the American people would strongly support what we're saying here. They see a lot at stake for us in a totally democratic hemisphere and the success of democracy in Nicaragua.

Q. Do you feel we particularly owe it to the people of those two countries, given our military activities in both Nicaragua and Panama?

The President. Do we owe support?

Q. Do we owe money?

The President. Well, we've lifted the embargoes, and we've released the funds. So, to the degree there's anything owed, we're trying to comply with that. But what I'm proposing here is an investment in democracy. I don't think anybody would, you know, have the American people try to believe that we owe it. But it's the right thing to do, and we want to see Violeta Chamorro supported, and we want to see the Panamanian democracy succeed. So, that's the way I'd phrase it.

Q. Mr. President, let me ask you about what——

The President. I have a meeting with the Congress at 10:45, and I don't—I mean, 9:45, 9:45—sorry, accept the correction please, 9:45.

Texas Primaries

Q. It's primary day in Texas, Mr. President. Can you tell us—two questions—one——

The President. Now we're talking. [*Laughter*]

Q. ——for whom you voted in the Republican primary and, number two, do you think it should be held against a candidate if perhaps at some point in the past they used drugs, but no longer do? You've talked on that issue before. Can you go back over it for us?

The President. This is election day in Texas. I did vote in the Texas Republican primary. I will not tell you who I voted for, and I hope everybody understands. Otherwise, we'll have a quiz around here of who we voted for earlier on. It's not a proper question to reveal.

Q. But on the drugs issue, which is an issue in the primary and certainly may be in the general election, do you think it should be held against a candidate that at some point in the past they have used drugs?

The President. I think that's a matter for the voters to decide. But in my view, somebody used marijuana some time ago and is not into anything of that nature, why, no, I don't think that should be held against them.

Q. What if it were more than marijuana, sir?

The President. You're getting me involved in the Texas primary, something I don't want to do, Craig [Craig Hines, Houston Chronicle]. The polls opened down there about 2 hours ago, and I'm not about——

Q. You'll be involved in the general election, though, won't you?

The President. I'll be involved, but I'm not going to fine-tune that. I'm not going to go into that.

Soviet Compliance With Arms Reduction Agreements

Q. What about the report—the Soviet noncompliance of the INF treaty in a number of instances in East Germany? Do you think that that could throw a monkey wrench into the CFE and START talks?

The President. To the degree that there are differences on verification on INF, we've got to work those out. And we've got our experts working the problem and trying to eliminate any differences.

Q. What about the differences reported between Secretary Cheney and CIA Director Webster over the threat assessments——

The President. Just a minute.

Q. ——in the event that Gorbachev is thrown out of power?

The President. Just 1 minute on that one. As I have said before—[*laughter*]—I don't see any real disagreement here. [*Laughter*] No, I tried to answer that yesterday, and I expect I didn't lay it to rest. But I don't think anybody believes—including Cheney—that the Soviet system is going to go back to where it was in—you know, before 1980, in the middle of the eighties.

But there are differences when you go to try to predict with accuracy based on intentions. So, I've talked to them now, and I feel that they are pretty close together. And it's difficult when you have a fast-changing world, and yet you take a position like I do: We must retain a credible defense. Then you get into a big debate: Well, what is credible? And I think that's what you're seeing here.

So, I can tell you, having talked to these gentlemen, I don't think that there is this enormous defense difference between the intelligence community—and I say community—and the Secretary. I think we've come up with a prudent, well-thought-out defense plan. And there will be changes, I'm sure, after our cooperation with and consultation with Congress, but believe me, these are not diametrically different views that you're reading about.

Shall we end with this one? I really do have a 9:45.

Surplus Weapons

Q. Mr. President, here's a question that I please wish you would decide, and I think only you can. You're going to have to deal with billions and billions of surplus weapons. What are you going to do with those? There's been some indication that you've already given 1,000 tanks from Europe out of that surplus pile to Egypt. And if you keep on selling them on credit, the arms that we have, you're going to keep on creating wars in the Third World and other nations.

The President. One of the——

Q. Mr. President, would you do this at the microphone, please?

Q. Thank you.

The President. This is a departure. One of the things that is part of the negotiations on CFE is destruction of weapons—and we're talking about significant numbers. And I had a meeting yesterday with Jim Woolsey, our CFE negotiator, and he was spelling out for me just the mechanical difficulties of doing this. But nevertheless, we are determined that that will be the approach that's taken with these massive numbers of weapons. We still have security needs that we feel are enhanced by transfer of military equipment, sales of military equipment to friendly countries. So, the policy will remain as it is, but we will go forward with the destruction where that is a part of the policy.

Thank you all very much.

Note: The President's 40th news conference began at 9:18 a.m. in the Briefing Room at the White House. In his remarks, he referred to Representative Dan Rostenkowski, chairman of the House Ways and Means Committee.

Letter to Congressional Leaders Transmitting the Executive Order Terminating the National Emergency With Respect to Nicaragua
March 13, 1990

Dear Mr. Speaker: (Dear Mr. President:)

Enclosed is a copy of an Executive order that I signed today terminating the national emergency with respect to Nicaragua.

Sincerely,

GEORGE BUSH

Note: Identical letters were sent to Thomas S. Foley, Speaker of the House of Representatives, and Dan Quayle, President of the Senate. The letter referred to Executive Order No. 12707, which is listed in Appendix E at the end of this volume.

White House Fact Sheet on Economic Assistance for Nicaragua
March 13, 1990

The President has proposed the following economic assistance program for Nicaragua:

Immediate Actions

The President has determined that the

February 25, 1990, democratic election in Nicaragua has ended the unusual and extraordinary threat to the national security and foreign policy of the United States previously posed by the actions and policies of the Sandinista government. Accordingly, the President has terminated the national emergency with respect to Nicaragua and lifted all economic sanctions, including the trade embargo.

Twenty-one million dollars of existing funds will be used to provide emergency assistance, including food through PL 480, to support the democratic transition and aid in the repatriation and reintegration of the resistance and refugees.

We have begun to take steps necessary to restore Nicaragua's sugar quota and to assist the Government of Nicaragua to become eligible for preferential treatment under the Generalized System of Preferences and the Caribbean Basin Initiative, as well as the facilities offered by the Export-Import Bank and the Overseas Private Investment Corporation.

Request to Congress for FY 90

The President has requested that Congress approve a FY 90 supplemental appropriation of $300 million for economic assistance to Nicaragua. The objective of these funds are to support the Chamorro government in its efforts to democratize, demobilize, and develop, and for the private sector to restore the productive capacity of Nicaragua's economy. The funds will be used to:

- Restore productivity by providing critical agricultural supplies (seeds, fertilizer, equipment), petroleum, and health inputs (approximately $60 million);
- Fund emergency employment programs (approximately $10 million);
- Provide for the repatriation and resettlement of the resistance and refugees (approximately $45 million);
- Provide technical assistance in restructuring the economy (approximately $1 million);
- Help clear arrears of $234 million to the international financial institutions (approximately $50 million). These funds would be disbursed as part of multilateral efforts to clear the arrears and would be linked to a sound economic policy framework supported by the IMF [International Monetary Fund];
- Provide balance of payments support to restructure the economy (approximately $75 million); and
- Help fund development projects (approximately $60 million). Activities would include support for democratic institutions, repair and maintenance of basic infrastructure, education, and health.

Request to Congress for FY 91

The President intends to submit to Congress a separate request for approximately $200 million in economic assistance to Nicaragua in FY 91. Details of this assistance will be announced later.

Source of Funds

The FY 90 supplemental request to Nicaragua will be offset from the Department of Defense budget. The President is requesting Congress approve the FY 90 funds for Nicaragua, along with his January 25 request of $570 million for Panama and refugees, by April 5, 1990.

Remarks Following Discussions With President Joaquim Alberto Chissano of Mozambique
March 13, 1990

President Bush. Mr. President, it was a great pleasure to meet with you here at the White House, sir, as our very special guest. More than 2,000 years ago a prophet once said, "There are four things that can never be recaptured: the spoken word, the sped arrow, time past, and the neglected opportunity." This afternoon, President Chissano and our delegation had a very productive meeting and a very engaging working lunch. We used those opportunities to discuss important bilateral matters, including

America's strong endorsement of the Government of Mozambique's political and economic reforms. We spoke openly and frankly, and I told President Chissano that he has our strong support as he undergoes these reforms.

These reforms have enhanced the ties which link Mozambique and the United States, strengthening rights central to America: the right to vote and to own property, the right to worship as we please and to be free of violence. These reforms have buoyed the Mozambique peace process, which we amply discussed today. They have also meant more liberalization and privatization, and led Mozambique to accept the economic rehabilitation program supported by the International Monetary Fund, the IMF. For that, Mr. President, I salute you. Yet we look forward to even further reforms. So, we talked today of common concerns, like refugee issues and Mozambique's humanitarian concerns—the crisis there in humanitarian concerns, I might add.

We reviewed ongoing developments in the southern region of Africa and explored new ways to propel the trend toward political solutions and regional cooperation. In all of this, we pledge our assistance to help meet Mozambique's humanitarian and development needs, for we've seen your government take significant steps to heal divisions which threaten your nation. And we urge all parties to talk at the earliest opportunity so as to avoid further suffering.

Like many of your counterparts, President Chissano, your government has in recent years begun to open up the economy to market forces and to open up the political process, allowing a freer flow of ideas. As we've learned around the world, democracy and development are directly related; each encourages the other. So, we commend you for taking steps toward democracy parallel with those steps toward economic reform.

Mr. President, ours is the chance to act not merely for Mozambique or any single country but rather all of Africa, helping democracy enrich a continent and your continent enrich the world. Now, there's an ancient proverb which goes, "God guides whom he wills toward a straight path." The path toward progress and freedom is paved with opportunity. And today we spoke of how we can walk that path, and I must tell you, sir, I look forward to working with you toward peace and democracy in Mozambique and in the entire region. I'm so glad you came to the White House.

President Chissano. President Bush and I had an excellent meeting today. Following it, President Bush invited myself and the Mozambican delegation to join him and the American delegation for a working lunch. Mozambique and the United States relations have been moving forward and expanding ever since President Machel met here 5 years ago with President Ronald Reagan, and I believe today we have taken another giant step forward.

The Mozambique Government and the people are deeply grateful for the assistance the United States Government and the American people have been providing our people in the humanitarian emergency caused by the war and natural disasters. I also told President Bush of the gratitude of our people for United States assistance to help rebuild our railroads, restructure our economy, and develop the private sector.

I briefed President Bush about the ongoing peace process in my country. And I informed him on the decision of my government to enter into a direct dialog with RENAMO [Mozambique National Resistance] as soon as possible and about the measures already taken to bring this decision into effect.

I expressed my appreciation for the stand the United States has taken on the war in Mozambique and for the positive role it has been playing in the peace process.

My government wishes to congratulate President Bush's administration for its efforts to promote peace and democracy in southern Africa, and we make a special note of its work in Namibia and South Africa.

I have asked President Bush that the United States continue to spare no effort until peace, stability, and economic prosperity are achieved in the region of southern Africa. In recent years we have taken important initiatives towards creating the framework for further democratization and economic liberalization in Mozambique. And most recently, we put forward a draft constitution that would provide for direct election of the President and the People's Assembly based on universal suffrage, ensuring a basic set of rights for the people, and establish constitutional bases for private property.

We are a young country, only 15 years old. As we build our country and our democracy, we are grateful that we have as friends the United States of America and President George Bush.

President Bush. Thank you, sir, very much.

Note: President Bush spoke at 1:29 p.m. at the South Portico of the White House. Prior to their remarks, the two Presidents met privately in the Oval Office and with U.S. and Mozambican officials in the Cabinet Room, and then attended a luncheon in the Old Family Dining Room.

Statement by Press Secretary Fitzwater on President Bush's Meeting With President Joaquim Alberto Chissano of Mozambique
March 13, 1990

President Bush and Mozambican President Chissano met today for approximately 1½ hours, followed by a 1-hour working lunch. The primary topic of discussion was the Mozambican peace process. President Bush took particular note of President Chissano's description of the suffering caused by the war in Mozambique and strongly endorsed the decision of the Mozambican Government to begin direct discussions with RENAMO [Mozambique National Resistance] as soon as possible. President Bush also expressed his admiration for the very significant political and economic reforms underway in Mozambique. The two Presidents exchanged views on the regional situation in southern Africa, and particularly in South Africa. President Chissano expressed the gratitude of his government for assistance provided by the United States. The two leaders discussed ways in which the United States might enhance its current assistance program.

Remarks and an Exchange With Reporters at an Alternative Fuel Demonstration
March 13, 1990

The President. Obviously, the reason we're here today is to show the interest we all have—industry, the administration—in cleaner air. There's no question about that, and that's why I came over here today. This is the first commercial availability of methanol in the Washington area. I want to commend the Sun Company for taking this leadership role in helping our national efforts to reduce air pollution. And I want to thank Mr. McClements himself, the chairman, for being with us; and I would salute not only him but Ray Poling of the Ford Company, who has taken time out of his busy schedule to be with us here today, explain how all of this works in an automobile. I want to thank Chuck Imbrecht and Bob Hahn, the cochairmen of the Alternate Fuels Council, for being with us.

The clean air legislation that I proposed last year is going to go a long way toward achieving our environmental goals. And a fundamental part of this, an integral part of this program, is the clean fuels program. We're working hard—and I want to, again, thank both sides of the aisle in Congress—in a bipartisan way to enact the legislation. The Senate leadership and I, along with our top officials here—Henson Moore of the Energy Department and Jim Watkins, the Secretary; Bill Reilly of EPA; John Sununu and others—have all agreed with us on goals and on methods that will achieve our plan.

And a variety of clean fuels, no question, can help to reduce urban smog and toxic air emissions. This, in turn, is going to reduce the regulatory burden on a wide range of small businesses out there. The availability of methanol in a metropolitan area—say, like Washington—is an important step toward the widespread use of clean fuels. There are a few clean fuels in addition to methanol. Click off a couple: natural gas, propane, ethanol, reformulated gasoline, and then electricity. The flexible fuel vehicle that we see here today, one of Red's cars, a Ford Victoria, is a government fleet vehicle. By using alternative fuel vehicles, the Federal Government is trying to lead by example.

And at this time, I again want to thank both our CEO's that were here with us today. Under the direction of the Interagency Commission on Alternative Fuels—Henson Moore chairs that, the Deputy Secretary of Energy—we're moving forward to bring more alternative-fueled vehicles into our fleet. The Interagency Commission and its advisory body, the U.S. Alternative Fuels Council, have an important job in helping develop a national alternative fuels policy.

This is a part of our overall answer to those who worry about cleaning up the environment, as we do. It's a step; it's not the cure-all and the end-all. But I want to congratulate industry—in this instance, the Sun Company, Ford Motor Company—for showing fine leadership. And we will keep working with the Congress to accomplish this first major revision in the Clean Air Act since it was first written. It's sound for all of our country. And I'm delighted with the bipartisan support we've been getting. So, thank you all.

Q. Mr. President, haven't you already backed off the requirements for alternative fuel vehicles?

The President. You know, I've discovered something: Nobody ever does it exactly the way I want it done. But what we have is sound, strong, environmentally secure compromise that has the support of the best environmentalists I know of. And we're never going to placate those on the extreme side of the equation that want to do nothing or want to just shut down this country and throw every American that's got a job out of work. We've come to a good compromise, a strong compromise. And so, yes, I can fine-tune it, gripe about one phrase and one section or another, but I'm not going to do that. And I'm encouraging our Senators—both sides—to get behind this and move it out, and then prompt action in the House.

Q. But you've already thrown in the towel on a million alternative vehicles.

The President. We've thrown it in, and we're doing well, and people who take a look at it know that we've got a good, sound bill that's going to help clean up the environment—biggest breakthrough since the Clean Air Act was written. And it isn't one that's going to throw America out of work, so don't worry about that. Don't listen to the extremes on this question. Okay?

Note: The President spoke at 2:15 p.m. at a Sunoco station in Washington, DC. In his remarks, he referred to Harold A. Poling, chairman and chief executive officer of Ford Motor Co., and John H. Sununu, Chief of Staff to the President.

Letter to Congressional Leaders Transmitting the Annual Report of the United States Arms Control and Disarmament Agency
March 13, 1990

Dear Mr. Speaker: (Dear Mr. President:)

Effective and verifiable arms control treaties are important to the security of the United States and, as President Gorbachev made clear at our Malta meeting, to the Soviet Union as well. Over the past year we have undertaken new initiatives and made steady and substantial progress in our Strategic Arms Reduction Talks, Conventional Forces in Europe, Nuclear Testing, and Chemical Weapons negotiations. These steps can make a lasting contribution to a safer and more secure world for all mankind.

Because of the role of the U.S. Arms Control and Disarmament Agency (ACDA) in support of these negotiations as well as in other crucial arms control activities, I encourage all members of the Congress to read the attached 1989 annual report. The report reviews the year's arms control initiatives and negotiating efforts, as well as the activities conducted pursuant to the statutory requirements of the Arms Control and Disarmament Act, as amended.

Sincerely,

GEORGE BUSH

Note: Identical letters were sent to Thomas S. Foley, Speaker of the House of Representatives, and Dan Quayle, President of the Senate.

Message on the Observance of St. Patrick's Day, 1990
March 13, 1990

I am delighted to extend warm greetings to all those celebrating St. Patrick's Day.

As history tells us, St. Patrick led a life filled with exciting adventures and tremendous challenges. Born the son of a British city leader, he was captured by pirates as a youth and sold into slavery. After gaining his freedom, Patrick returned home, where he eventually decided to dedicate his life to God as a cleric. Soon he was to discover that God was calling him to take part in yet another extraordinary adventure—bringing the Christian faith to the people of Ireland. He spent the remaining years of his life serving God and his fellowman with tireless devotion. In so doing, he helped change forever the course of Irish history. St. Patrick's faith, courage, and compassionate spirit have lived on through the centuries, inspiring generations of men and women to follow his example of voluntary service and fervent prayer.

On St. Patrick's Day, Irish-Americans—indeed Americans of every ethnic background—happily join with the people of Ireland in celebrating the life of this remarkable man. This occasion also provides us with a wonderful opportunity to celebrate the many contributions the sons and daughters of Ireland have made to our nation. Many of those early pioneers who braved the stormy Atlantic to seek a new life in America were of Irish descent. They, like their spiritual ancestor, Patrick, helped to build a strong and proud nation through faith and hard work. On this day we also celebrate the special friendship the United States shares with Ireland—one we look forward to enriching and strengthening in the months and years to come.

Barbara joins me in sending our best wishes to all for a joyous and memorable St. Patrick's Day. May God bless you.

GEORGE BUSH

Appointment of Peter B. Teeley as United States Representative on the Executive Board of the United Nations Children's Fund
March 14, 1990

The President today announced his intention to appoint Peter B. Teeley as the Representative of the United States of America on the Executive Board of the United Nations Children's Fund. He would succeed Rita Di Martino.

Currently Mr. Teeley serves as president of Teeley and Associates, Inc., in Washington, DC. He has served as a political adviser to President George Bush for the past 9 years in several capacities, including Press Secretary to Vice President George Bush; chief spokesman, 1979–1980; and Assistant to the Vice President and Press Secretary, 1980–1985. In addition, Mr. Teeley served

as communications director on the 1988 Bush campaign; communications director and press secretary at the Republican National Committee; a Harvard fellow at the Kennedy School of Government; press secretary to the President Ford Committee; press secretary to Senator Jacob Javits, 1974–1977; and press secretary to assistant Senate minority leader Robert P. Griffin, 1970–1974.

Mr. Teeley graduated from Wayne State University (B.A., 1965). He was born January 12, 1940, in Barrow-in-Furness, England. Mr. Teeley is married, has four children, and resides in Alexandria, VA.

Remarks Following a Tour of the Potomac Electric Power Company Generating Station at Chalk Point, Maryland
March 14, 1990

The President. I want to first thank Ed Mitchell and Hula Edmonds, who have shown us around this plant—Ed being the top executive and familiar with all the economic dimension of this tremendous utility, and Hula running the plant here, described by his leader as one of the best in the business.

A few months ago, we sent to Congress—it was in July of last year—a very comprehensive Clean Air Act amendment. And these amendments had as their goal cleaning up the smog in our cities, reducing the toxic chemicals that are being emitted into our atmosphere, and halting the damage that's caused by acid rain. Now those proposals, which were the, I think, most dramatic proposed revision of the Clean Air Act in history, are subject to debate and compromise forged with the Senate leadership. And I am grateful to Democrats and Republicans alike who have come together with what we think is a very sensible approach. The Dole-Mitchell compromise substitute is now under consideration, and my

appeal again would be to urge all Members to move forward on it within the parameters hammered out in compromise by Senator Mitchell and Senator Dole.

The bill is consistent with the need to balance environmental benefits and to sustain economic growth for this country. And, Hula, I would put that in more personal terms: That means jobs for the men and women that you have under you. We cannot let this country screech to a halt, but I am determined to clean up the air. And we're going to work hard for the passage of this bill. I am confident now that it will remain intact, and I am confident that it will prevail in the Senate. And the same time, we're pursuing an equally balanced measure in the House of Representatives.

So, to get this balance, we're going to rely on market forces—incentives for technological innovation, provide the private sector with the flexibility to make emissions reductions in the most cost-effective manner possible. Ed was telling me there's megabucks involved in all of this. And we want to be as helpful as possible in making these changes as cost-effective as possible while still meeting our environmental goals.

Now, Pepco, your company, sir, like most, is committed to take these additional steps to meet these even tougher standards under the Clean Air Act, and for that we're very grateful. Under the act, we try to provide these utility companies with flexibility to meet the new and tougher standards. We give them options: burning coal with a lower sulfur content or switching to other fuels, installing new emission control technologies or utilizing some of the emerging clean-coal technologies. Providing this flexibility, we can ensure that the environmental benefits are gained at the least cost to the guy that pays the bill—the consumer. And I'm confident that a good-faith attitude toward these environmental goals prevail on the part of most of the companies, and we've seen evidence that today in projects it is going forward. We see this evidence now.

And I also must say I am very impressed with this fish culture here, because raising over a million stripers to replenish the Chesapeake Bay is a significant environmental contribution—not just for fishermen such as myself but I think it's good for the entire environmental background of the Chesapeake Bay. You've got a wildlife sanctuary here. That's good citizenship, very good citizenship. And in our new Clean Air Act, we're going to be challenging Pepco and these other great companies to do even more in terms of the environment.

So, I think we're on the road to a balanced, environmentally aggressive, economically responsible piece of legislation. And this has given me an example to get a feeling of how this energy is produced and a feeling for the kinds of people that are producing the energy, and then also to have a broad look at an environmental dimension that has not always been a part of the equation, and today it is.

And I salute you, Ed, and your associates in this company for carving out some new ground here. I hope it will serve as an example to others all across this country. So, we've had a good day here.

Q. Mr. President——

The President. Hey, listen, I had a press conference yesterday. This is a one-way street, where I do the talking and you guys——

Q. About that news conference, though, yesterday, Mr. President——

Q. Pepco says that it will cost $300 million at this plant alone—

Q. ——there are some conflicting signals coming out of there and out of Mr. Darman's briefing yesterday on taxes. Is that something that's negotiable?

The President. You've got to read all the tea leaves and listen to the nuances. I mean, it's out there, very clearly.

Q. How about the lips?

The President. Keep reading.

Q. What about the cormorants?

The President. Are you a cormorant lover?

Q. No comment.

The President. Come on, Ellen [Ellen Warren, Knight-Ridder Newspapers], you've seen those guys.

Note: The President spoke at 10:30 a.m. outside of the Pepco Aquaculture Center. In his remarks, he referred to Edward F. Mitchell, president and chief executive officer of Potomac Electric Power Co., and Hula Edmonds, general manager of the Chalk Point generating station. During his visit, the President toured the generating station, attended a briefing in the control room, and toured the aquaculture center.

Nomination of G. Philip Hughes To Be United States Ambassador to Barbados, Dominica, St. Lucia, and St. Vincent and the Grenadines
March 14, 1990

The President today announced his intention to nominate G. Philip Hughes to be Ambassador Extraordinary and Plenipotentiary of the United States of America to Barbados, and to serve concurrently and without additional compensation as Ambassador Extraordinary and Plenipotentiary of the United States of America to the Commonwealth of Dominica, to St. Lucia, and to St. Vincent and the Grenadines. He would succeed Paul Russo.

Mr. Hughes currently serves as Executive Secretary of the National Security Council, a position he held since February 1989. Prior to assuming his current duties, Mr. Hughes served as the first Assistant Secretary of Commerce for Export Enforcement, from June 1988 until February 1989. Mr. Hughes previously served as Deputy Assistant Secretary for Political-Military Affairs at the Department of State from April 1986 until June 1988. Mr. Hughes began his tenure in the Reagan administration serving as Vice President George Bush's Deputy Assistant for National Security Affairs from February 1981 to September 1985. He then joined the National Security Council staff as Director for Latin American Affairs, with responsibility for Caribbean and Mexican affairs. Mr. Hughes served previously as Assistant Director for Intelligence Policy in the Office of the Secretary of Defense from 1979 to 1981, as research fellow in defense policy studies at the Brookings Institution from 1978 to 1979, and as assistant analyst in the national security and international affairs division of the Congressional Budget Office from 1975 to 1977.

Mr. Hughes received a B.A. in political science from the University of Dayton in Ohio; an M.A. in law and diplomacy from the Fletcher School of Law and Diplomacy, Tufts University; and a master of public administration degree from the Kennedy School of Government, Harvard University. He is married to the former Victoria Knipper, and they reside in Falls Church, VA.

Appointment of Penelope Payne as Special Assistant to the President for Legislative Affairs
March 14, 1990

The President today announced the appointment of Penelope Payne as Special Assistant to the President for Legislative Affairs (Senate) at the White House.

For the past 3 years, Ms. Payne has been director of government affairs for Turner Broadcasting System, Inc., working on legislative and regulatory issues. Prior to this she served as chief counsel to the Senate Budget Committee. Ms. Payne graduated from the University of Iowa (B.A., 1978) and the George Washington University (J.D., 1982). She currently resides in the District of Columbia.

Remarks to the National Association of Manufacturers
March 15, 1990

Dan, thank you, sir. Short and sweet, right to the point. [*Laughter*] And I'm glad to be here, and I'm delighted to be back with this group. And I want to salute your president, Jerry Jasinowski.

I told Barbara that I'd be spending some time with people who have risen to the top of the financial world by controlling the disbursement of billions of dollars. She said, "You're addressing the baseball lawyers?" [*Laughter*]

But regrettably, baseball's opening day may not be on the calendar yet. But the truth is the calendar offers each of us many opening days, convenient launch points for a fresh start. Sometimes it is a new day, a new year; and now, really, it's a new decade, a decade born amid the shouts of joy and triumph, a decade full of hope, barreling with confidence towards a new century and a new era. The rollcall is exciting, exhilarating, and accelerating. We call it the Revolution of '89, but in Poland, it took about 10 years; then in Hungary, about 10 months; East Germany, 10 weeks; Czechoslovakia, 10 days; and Bulgaria and Romania right behind.

Six nations in six months—and from six different tongues we heard the same one word: freedom. The people of Central Europe believed it. They fought for it, and they deserve the credit. But take that word "freedom," pick it up out of the newsprint, turn it over, and look on the back. And more often than not, you'll find that same proud label that adorns the products you produce: "Made in America."

Eight years ago, Ronald Reagan stood before this group—your group—and issued a bold and simple challenge. He said, "America can serve as the catalyst for an era of unimagined human freedom and dignity." And the cry of that great President became the "shout heard round the world."

Back here, especially in Washington, there may be some that are still plagued by doubt. Maybe in Washington; certainly not in Warsaw. Asked if Radio Free Europe had been important to democracy in Poland,

Lech Walesa responded with a question of his own. "Would there be Earth without the Sun?" was his reply.

Maybe in Washington, but not in Wenceslaus Square. Last month Václav Havel [President of Czechoslovakia] praised our resolve, the resolve of the United States of America as "defenders of freedom," telling Congress that Czechoslovakia probably wouldn't exist today if it hadn't been for the Atlantic alliance. And just yesterday—I talked to him this morning—[West German] Chancellor Kohl told me today that just yesterday he was speaking in East Germany, and he told them that he wouldn't be there and this wouldn't be happening if it hadn't been for the United States of America. And no quotes are needed to tell you the role of American persistence and American courage in standing up for liberty in Panama and Nicaragua.

Yes, these are heady times. It's a wonderful time to be President of the United States and to be coping with this fantastic change that's taking place around the world. But the good news is it isn't only overseas because the Revolution of '89 marks the triumph not only of free ideas but also free markets. And when it comes to free markets, America continues to lead the way.

Here again, there are doubters, and I can understand that—some who worry about a slowdown. And true, our economy is not perfect. Each one of you knows that. And I don't want to paint an unrealistic picture. But look at the facts: The United States economy is the largest, strongest, most productive economy on Earth. Our standard of living is one-third higher than that of West Germany or Japan. And with less than 5 percent of the world's people, in 1988 Americans accounted for more than 25 percent of the world's production. Our GNP is more than 2½ times that of the world's number two economy, Japan. And when a small percentage of people produce a huge percentage of wealth, there's a word for it. It's called productivity, and it is spelled

"USA."

Thanks in no small part to the commitment and imagination of the people and the companies represented here in this room, last year American exports of goods and services hit an all-time high: over $600 billion. And today the United States is once again the world's number one exporter. Nineteen eighty-nine marked our seventh consecutive year of economic growth, and today we see GNP up, exports up, personal income up.

Now, some would say that every economy has its ups and downs. But take a look at what's down: The trade deficit—I'm not standing here relaxed and saying it's perfect—the trade deficit is down. The Federal deficit—still not happy with it—it's down. The prime rate—down. And last year's unemployment rate—down, the lowest since 1973.

And the good news is reaching a broad cross section of Americans. Nineteen eighty-nine unemployment rates for blacks and teenagers were the lowest since the early seventies. And for Hispanics, the 1989 rate was the lowest recorded since the Government began keeping separate data for this group back in 1980.

But we're not just talking about statistics and numbers. As Dick Darman [Director of the Office of Management and Budget] recently reminded me, "Torture numbers, and they'll confess to anything." [*Laughter*] It would take Darman to come up with that, but he did. [*Laughter*]

Well, what we're really talking about here is people—people who hold the 2½ million new jobs created just since I took office 1 year ago. For them, it means families and freedom, and it means dignity and decency because 2½ million American jobs means 2½ million American futures.

Speaking of futures, earlier I asked one CEO what he sees as the most lucrative growth industry in the 1990's. He said, "Being a lawyer connected with the Trump case." [*Laughter*]

Our people and our economy are strong, and so is our resolve. And it's going to be tested soon, as the dramatic new changes in the world produce dramatic new challenges in the world market. And so, we must prepare now to meet these challenges. And our

administration is committed to an agenda for growth. It's founded upon investing in our future, and every sound investment has its yield: America's yield is the growth dividend. The growth dividend will provide Americans with jobs and opportunity, higher living standards, and a legacy of prosperity. So, achieving solid and sustainable growth is my most fundamental domestic priority, and it's why I've proposed a strong agenda of growth initiatives.

This is a marathon. This isn't a sprint; it is a marathon. And we can't produce the products needed to capture world markets by focusing on results one quarter at a time. We need to return not only to yesterday's values but yesterday's thinking, the long-term thinking and investment-in-the-future way of doing business that produced the healthy climate that we enjoy today.

First, we need to bring more of America's investment capital back into the productive economy. And lowering the cost of capital will assure the continued investment in productive assets and human resources that are needed to keep our manufacturing sector the most competitive in the world. The bottom line: It's time for Congress to pass the capital gains tax cut. Here's what we're up against: Japan, capital gains rate, 5 percent; South Korea, 0; Taiwan, 0; West Germany, 0; Singapore, 0; Hong Kong, 0. And the list goes on. And we need your support for this critical tax cut. And America wants it done right, America wants it done responsibly, and America wants it done now. It means competitiveness, and it means jobs. And so, let them tell me that I'm favoring some tax cut for the rich; I am favoring jobs for the working man and woman in this country.

And second, we need to keep these interest rates down. And we are committed to helping that process by going to the heart of the matter. We submitted a budget that will continue to bring the Federal deficit down, and today I call on the budget committees to fulfill their legal responsibilities and come up with a budget resolution by April 1st. That is 2 weeks away. And it's time to act, the time to bring the deficit down.

And third, America needs a booster shot

of new ideas along with the infusion of new capital that our tax cut—capital gains differential—will provide: matching investment capital with intellectual capital. And so, I call on Congress to help sharpen America's competitive edge: double the budget of the National Science Foundation, bring funding for research and development to a record high, make the research and experimentation tax credit permanent, and expand the Eisenhower education grants for math and science.

And fourth, we must stand behind our work force and the quality of our products. American workers today are good workers, best in the world, but we need to keep pace. Their children are the workers of tomorrow, and we owe them a better education, with an emphasis on basic skills, the sciences, math, and engineering. And we're going to do this in partnership with the American Governors and schools, giving those in need a fair start through Project Head Start, raising our high school graduation rates to at least 90 percent. And in science and math, our goal is unambiguous: first in the world by the year 2000. You see, we've got to reestablish standards and reestablish expectations, the kind of quality control so essential to everything that America produces.

Quality is something that you—you understand it. You understand it better than most Americans. And quality in manufacturing and quality in education are intertwined. These goals are an important step towards restoring quality in education. They help focus our efforts less on input, the amount of money that goes into our schools, and more on output, the quality of the student that comes out.

The kind of basic quality control is also basic to producing quality goods. And it's being spurred on in American manufacturing by steps taken within your own ranks, steps like the prestigious, high-level competition produced by awards like those named after the late Mac Baldrige.

It's also spurred on by efforts to ensure a literate work force. We salute manufacturers' efforts like the one that Barbara, my wife, visited in Michigan recently, a model of cooperation between the Ford Motor Company and the United Auto Workers—so

many more like it that you all are involved in.

And finally, it's essential that we have a drug-free work force. One way to stop drugs at work is to make sure that it never starts—preemployment drug screening—because if you're not part of the solution, you're part of the problem.

A drug-impaired work force is one of the ways in which American competitiveness can suffer from a self-inflicted burden, but it's not the only one. So, next I call for Congress to act now to make the U.S. marketplace work better through two basic reforms: product-liability reform—to increase our competitiveness without compromising safety—and antitrust reform—to remove obstacles to joint production ventures by U.S. companies.

As I've studied the problem, and trying to work with Congress on it and working with our environmentalists and business people, I am also convinced that America's growth need not come at the expense of the environment. Our natural resources are invaluable assets, and like any other assets, they need to be maintained in order to sustain our ability to grow.

For 13 years, Congress has been unable to pass a new Clean Air Act. Two weeks ago, we reached a breakthrough, a bipartisan agreement to untangle the web of regional politics that has stopped clean air. I am very pleased to compliment the Senate leadership for their very constructive negotiations, and today I call upon the Senate to stand by the agreement and to protect our environment without saddling the bill with new subsidies and cumbersome rules.

I mentioned self-inflicted burdens, and of course not all our competitive burdens are self-inflicted. There are also foreign barriers to U.S. exports which must be addressed. And earlier this month Prime Minister Kaifu and I agreed on the need for action on what we call Structural Impediments Initiative to break down nontariff barriers to the Japanese market. And we are pressing hard to get the Japanese Government to address specific trade categories. We must move aggressively to open markets not just in Japan but around the world and expand our share of global trade. For those of you who follow the Japanese market, you'll agree with me that we need to have more openness there. I can tell you not only were the Kaifu talks good but the talks that we had with the former Prime Minister Takeshita when he was here just a handful of days ago. We have got to have them understand the seriousness of the problem we face.

I still believe that for far-reaching, fundamental reform our best hope is the proposals that we have made in the Uruguay round of the GATT negotiations. We're determined to make a level playing field. Let America compete in an arena of fair trade, and we will take on anyone, anytime, anyplace.

As in Berlin, barriers are coming down all over the world. It took years of persistence, but the ideas championed by America—freedom, democracy, competition, and investment—are flourishing because they work, because they are the best. It can be the same for American goods.

In 1986, on the eve of July 4th, a single blue laser split the darkness over New York Harbor, a manmade lightning bolt that relit the torch of a reborn Statue of Liberty. The torch has been held high ever since. And today that light continues to inspire hope from Panama to Prague, from Moscow to Managua.

Somehow, a recent bit of news seems fitting: The bald eagle, the American eagle, may soon come off the endangered species list. Ladies and gentlemen, America is back, and this time we are back to stay. And I look forward to working with this organization, your member companies, to doing what we can in government to facilitate free and fair trade to help maintain and strengthen an economy that is good for the working man and the working woman of this country.

Thank you for inviting me over. And God bless you, and God bless our great country. Thank you very much.

Note: The President spoke at 10:27 a.m. in the Grand Ballroom at the Ramada Renaissance Hotel. In his remarks, he referred to Daniel Krumm, chairman of the association.

Nomination of Robert C. Larson To Be a Member of the Oversight Board of the Resolution Trust Corporation
March 15, 1990

The President today announced his intention to nominate Robert C. Larson to be a member of the Oversight Board of the Resolution Trust Corporation for a term of 3 years. This is a new position.

Since 1974 Mr. Larson has served with the Taubman Co., Inc., in Bloomfield, MI, as chief executive officer and director, since 1988; president, since 1978; and senior vice president and director of eastern development activities, since 1974. Prior to this he was vice president of Inland Steel Development Corp. and has served in various positions in Inland subsidiaries and divisions.

Mr. Larson graduated from Carleton College (B.A., 1956). He was born June 15, 1934, in Minneapolis, MN. Mr. Larson is married, has seven children, and resides in Bloomfield Hills, MI.

Remarks and a Question-and-Answer Session at a White House Briefing for the Board of Directors of the National Newspaper Association
March 15, 1990

The President. Actually, I just came from a St. Patrick's Day lunch put on by Speaker Foley up in the Capitol. Very good hands-across-the-aisle kind of thing.

Well, welcome. We call this the White House complex. That's not the "beltway syndrome," but this is the White House complex. And you don't have to show any ID to get out of the place, so I'll put you at ease. I know it's been a pain coming in.

But I'm just delighted you all were here. I hope you've benefited from some of the briefings you've had here. And I'm delighted to see you all. We'll go to the questions, but I want to underscore some of the same points that I tried to make this morning to the National Association of Manufacturers annual Washington meeting about the economy.

The fact is that the economy remains sound and steady. The facts are these: The gross national product, up; the exports, up; personal income, up. Take a look, then, at the trade deficit; it's down. The Federal deficit—I'm not happy with it, but down. And the prime rate—far better than it was several years ago. And of course, unemployment is down. Last year's rate was the lowest in the past 16 years.

So, that is good news, but there's a great deal that we have to do to keep this expansion going. The economy at this moment isn't as robust as I'd like to see it; but we've got, basically, I think, a sound economy. Now we've got to do certain things. We've got to create incentive for investment. And I get hit in the political arena on my concept of cutting the capital gains tax, or reestablishing what we call a capital gains differential, some calling that a tax that favors the rich. I think it favors jobs. And I cited some statistics today that Japan taxes capital gains at 5 percent; Korea, Germany, Hong Kong, Taiwan tax capital gain at 0.

Now, you should be saying, "What are you doing to help us be more competitive around the world?" And the capital gains—

one of the reasons I favored it is, is I do think it will help us be much more competitive around the world. I'm also proposing to the Congress incentives to encourage research and development, so that'll keep us competitive.

Of course the most crucial investment is in the field of education. We know that we can't remain competitive or remain a world-class economy without first-class schools. So, we got together with the Governors and adopted national goals, not trying to tell the local schools what kind of curriculum to have but goals that all the Governors agreed with, and now try to go forward and try to meet those goals, such as Head Start and a literate America and then passing certain standards as the kids go from 4th-grade and 8th-grade and 12th-grade level.

And so, we've got sound goals. And if these work and if we're successful, not only in the tax end but in the education goals, then we're going to have not a "peace dividend" but a "growth dividend" and a return on our investment in expanded opportunity, more jobs, and a higher standard of living for Americans.

I made that point this morning, and I will continue to make the point that we need to do certain things to stimulate investment and savings. And that, I think, will help us become very competitive. I've had some fascinating meetings in the last couple of weeks with, first, the Japanese Prime Minister and then just a few days ago with Takeshita, former Prime Minister and very much of a power in Japan. And I did my level best to impress on these very important leaders, these friends of the United States, the need for us to have more access to their markets. So, we'll see where we end up.

But no further ado, who wants to go—yes, sir?

Soviet Political Developments

Q. I'm Jerry Moriarity [Pine-Palm Publishing], from Minnesota and Arizona. I'd like to ask you: With all the power that's gravitating into the hands of Gorbachev while the Soviet world is collapsing about him, do you see any danger of a dictatorship evolving?

The President. No, because I think there's much less danger today given what they've done in their Parliament, or in their congressional side of things. They've come out of the totalitarianism of the past. They give the new President great power, but I don't see it as a threat, and I certainly don't see it as a threat at this juncture in history.

You know, I shifted our support from going more like this: "We support reform and *perestroika*," to "We support *perestroika* and reform, and we want to see Gorbachev succeed." I am convinced that one of the reasons we've had peaceful change in Eastern Europe is because of the approach that Gorbachev himself brought to bear on the problem. And I've consulted with him, had communications from him—one, for example, on the question of Germany—and I think he's a reasonable man.

So, I'm not worried about the constitutional changes because as you look at the total picture inside the Soviet Union, you see an evolution that none of us would have believed possible 5 years ago or 3 or 2 in terms of democratic institutions. And I'm talking about the power in their Congress. They had a guy named Primakov who is the head of their Congress. And he was over here, and he came and told me—he said, "Well, I'm here to learn from the United States." And I said, "Mr. Primakov, you've come to the wrong guy in telling you what to do about the Congress. I'm not having too much luck." [*Laughter*]

But the very fact that he was here, you know, and in a spirit of very good will, getting—and I was only being semifacetious there—but it's very different, Jerry, than it used to be. It's amazingly different. I dealt with these guys back in the United Nations, and I can't tell you how different it is in terms of self-criticism on their part or debate. When you have a difference, you can do it agreeably. It doesn't have to be disagreeable like it was in the heart of the Cold War days. So, I am not overly concerned.

American Hostages in Lebanon

Q. You said in your national newscast the other day [*see news conference, March 13*] that the media and all the people there would be surprised and fascinated when the hostage situation is resolved. What did you mean by that? Can you expand on it?

The President. Well, I can't really expand, except to say I was addressing myself more to this incident of this phone call that proved to be a hoax and that I am not at liberty to discuss. In terms of the hostages, there was a wave of speculation a week or so ago that frankly confused me because we are going down every alley, we are trying every avenue to free the hostages. But there is no negotiation going on with any part of the U.S. Government or anything of that nature.

I saw the speculation, and I was wondering if it was some private initiatives on the part of lawyers or those representing the families of individuals held hostage, because I wish I could tell you that there was a serious, immediate effort that would pay off, but that isn't the case. So, when I was talking there, I was really talking about this phone call. And some of you may remember there were some cartoonists—I gave them a great deal of opportunity to have some fun at, you know, picking up the phone—"Who is this," you know, and all that. [*Laughter*]

But I would do it again because I feel—I don't know why—it weighs on me, the burden of Americans held against their will. And I don't mind taking one on the chin if I go the extra mile. I ought to do that as your President, I think. And I made the comment that the next phone call of that nature may have a little more difficulty getting through—[*laughter*]—but I'm glad we tried. So, I was talking in that context.

U.S. Economy

Q. More from the spirit of democracy, this good economy—what can be done to move some of that into the Rust Belt areas, the pockets like the Ohio Valley Rust Belt?

The President. Not sure I have a specific idea, but I'll guarantee you that if we are successful in getting the budget deficit down, then you have an economic climate in which new businesses start up. We've had a reasonable success—and I'm not crowing about it—in the creation of small businesses that are not identified with one industry. And so, I think from the Federal standpoint the best thing we can do is to see that where we do have assistance—education, and to installations going into places—that there's fairplay. But I really believe, for the Ohio Valley or wherever else it is, that just fundamentally sound fiscal policy is the answer.

I am not in favor—maybe this will be a disappointment, but I had better level with you all—in targeting funds or kind of choosing winners and losers. I don't think that is the role of the Federal Government—industrial policy in a broader sense, where you say we're going to put our efforts into one industry or another. I don't think that's the role of the Federal Government. Certainly, I don't think it's the philosophy under which I was elected.

So, there are programs. I'm strongly in favor of job retraining—Job Training Partnership Act—I think we're doing better on that. I hope our whole approach to education pays off. So, it's a general response to a very specific question.

Q. There's a growing sense of frustration across America that the standard of living in this country may be in decline. We hear the rich are getting richer, the poor are getting poorer. There are always reports that this country is no longer able to provide the standards of education, health care, housing that other nations in the industrialized world are able to give their people.

The President. We still have the highest standard of living in the world. I think if we are successful in our battle against narcotics—which is not going to be done by the Federal Government alone, but certainly I must use the bully pulpit and our National Drug Strategy I, National Strategy II to try to set a tone for the rest of the country in what can be done to fight narcotics for a successful education, antidrug fight—and then the competitiveness legislation that I've referred to—math and science education, R&D, capital gains—I believe that we will continue to have the highest living standard.

So, I am not that pessimistic, and yet I don't want to stand here with some Pollyannish attitude about the economy. There are some signs that worry me; there are some signs that make me feel that growth will continue and that the economy may be doing better now than it was a month or two ago. But I don't accept the premise that we're a second-class power or that we are in decline.

There's a marvelous book that was quoted around here about the decline of the United States. We've got some problems. But if you want to put it in a broad philosophical sense, we're winning. Our concept of freedom and democracy is winning around the world. And I sometimes wish as President that there were more funds readily available—read that less of a deficit—to help the fledgling democracies of Eastern Europe or of our own neighbors to the south, which we must never neglect.

But even then, even without the largess that we could bestow on others from budget surplus or operating in balance, we still can help countries; and we are winning in the ideological battle and the philosophical battle. And if we can make fair markets—help create market incentives and then have fair markets—I really believe we're just on the threshold of a whole age of increased living standards for the United States. But that's our goal.

American Volunteers in Nicaragua

Q. Mr. President, will you encourage the use of Peace Corps volunteers who see that aid actually gets to the poorest villagers to be a substantial part of the aid you're seeking for Nicaragua and Panama?

The President. Yes. I'm strongly in favor of the Peace Corps. I've talked to our Peace Corps Director. You know, it's not quite right there. Let me tell you something that does trouble me, though, in Nicaragua. I've answered the question because I'm a great believer in the Peace Corps. And I'll tell you, the demands for Peace Corps in some of these countries, particularly in Eastern Europe, now Poland and Czechoslovakia, is wonderful. It's a wonderful tribute to the young volunteers that go into the Peace Corps and to the concept of a great nation willing to help emerging democracies.

But I am frustrated a little bit by some of the Americans that have gone down to Nicaragua, been there for 2 years allegedly to help the people of Nicaragua. And then Nicaragua has a free and fair election, and it turns out these people were interested in helping the Sandinistas, the Sandinismos. And now they're picketing. Some of them have been—I don't know whether they're still there—in front of the U.S. Embassy because in their view the wrong people won the election. But that's not the role of the United States. If we want to help the people and there are verifiably, certifiably free elections, they ought to stay down there—if they're acting in this philanthropic way—and try to help, as the Peace Corps does in Nicaragua. Consider my spleen vented. [*Laughter*]

Federal Budget

Q. This noon you had lunch with Speaker Foley. In the spirit of St. Patrick, did you work out a deal on how to reduce defense spending?

The President. No, that has not been worked out. We've made some proposals; and he is, I think, waiting, in fairness to him, for his budget process to work. But I find him very reasonable. We differ philosophically on some of these questions. I've cited capital gains, for example. I mean, I just haven't properly sold an honorable man like Foley on what it means to create jobs, what it means to be competitive—I cited for you now the differential between what it is in Japan, what it is in Korea, and all of this—so I've got to do better in communicating with some of those people on the other side.

But on the defense, I think we must retain a reasoned defense. Colin Powell [Chairman of the Joint Chiefs of Staff] and Cheney have testified on a different kind of force. I've had strong support, vocal support, from Foley on things like our latest proposal on reducing our force levels in Europe, the proposal with Gorbachev to both reduce to 195,000 in Central Europe and then 30,000 additional troops that can be deployed under agreement with the Soviets. So, we're getting some support there, and I believe we will be able to work out an agreed defense program. I hope we will,

because I don't want to have to see defense all caught up in politics. And the rapidity of change is such that I think we are in a good position to negotiate further reductions with the Soviet Union, and that's one of the reasons I'm looking forward to the summit with Mr. Gorbachev.

Lithuania

Q. Under what circumstances would the United States begin the process and when would we begin the process of recognizing an independent Lithuania or any other Soviet republic?

The President. In the first place, we have never recognized the incorporation of the Baltic States, which you are talking about— Lithuania, Estonia, and Latvia—into the Soviet Union. It was never a question of having recognized their incorporation into the Soviet Union.

I think there are standards of control over one's country—or control over one's, in this instance, territory—that guide recognition. But I think that the best role for the United States, having encouraged self-determination, having not been willing to recognize Lithuania being incorporated into the Soviet Union, is to encourage a peaceful evolution from now on.

Lithuania, under the right of self-determination, expressed themselves. To the credit of the Soviet leaders, all the way from Ligachev [Communist Party Chairman, Agrarian Policy Commission] to Gorbachev on over, they have said: We will not use force. We're peaceful. We want to see this resolved peacefully. It is very important to the people in these Baltic States that the evolution be peaceful. And so, I am, just as in East Germany when the Berlin Wall started down—some of my political opponents were saying I was unenthusiastic about it. And I told one of our star TV commentators, well, that's the kind of person I am. I mean, some people jump with joy and do cartwheels, and I've got different genes or something. [*Laughter*]

But having said that, another political leader said, Well, you ought to go to Berlin, and the President should be seen at the wall. I had communications from the most respected leaders in East and West, several of them, saying, don't do anything silly. I mean, we're concerned now as this evolves. And sometimes caution and prudence, I think, are right. And I think in this case it proved right because that evolution has moved peacefully, and we did not provoke some kind of outbreak through exhorting there at the Berlin Wall that could have caused other countries to act differently.

I'm very pleased with the way the Lithuanian situation is developing, and we're watching it closely. We will encourage the fundamental principles of self-determination, and we will encourage the concept of peaceful change. And I hope both major parties in that discussion will continue to adhere to peaceful change.

Voice of America

Q. It seems to me that the Voice of America has been one of our best tools for exporting the ideas of democracy, and yet I understand that we want to cut their budget. Don't you think that it would be better if we just maintained the budget in order to continue to have this influence in the countries of the Eastern bloc?

The President. I'm embarrassed to say I don't have the figures, but I am not aware of any cut in the budget. Because like you, I accept your premise, your hypothesis. And you know why? Because Havel, Václav Havel, the playwright President of Czechoslovakia, expressed his not only appreciation for what the Voice of America did in keeping the hope of democracy and freedom alive but also insisted that it's essential that the Voice still go in there.

So, I don't think—can someone—we don't think that we have recommended cuts in the Voice, but maybe we could get your name. It's a good specific question. And, Barrie [Barrie Tron, Deputy Director of Media Relations], maybe you could find that, and we'll let you know the exact numbers.

But whatever the figures, believe me, there is no philosophical commitment to ratchet down or cut back on the Voice, because I agree with you that it's even more important that that message of freedom continue to be heard; and I accept the word of Havel in the process.

Now, we've got one more, and I see an urgent—I've not been very good about the left side of the room. Yes, sir?

Foreign Aid

Q. Don Mulford, Montclair Times. Does it bother you at all the proportion of the foreign aid budget going to two nations, Israel and Egypt? Irrespective of any comment on Jerusalem—*[laughter]*—is there some thought of perhaps lowering the level of the funds going there in the hope that it might promote peace—to stop funding both nations on such a large level of our resources?

The President. I would not favor that. I do favor greater flexibility for the President, which means a weakening of or an elimination of earmarking, because what's happened is a tremendous percentage, as Don points out, of our foreign aid budget is going to just a handful of countries. And you cited Israel, and I could add Egypt— well, you added Egypt—and there's Pakistan and one or two others. And by the time that money is disbursed, there is almost nothing.

And I'll give you an example. In Jamaica, I must confess that when Mr. Manley [Prime Minister] came in, based on his past record and his proximity to Cuba and his former fraternity with Mr. Castro [President of Cuba], I didn't know how it would go. Manley campaigned on a different policy this time. He said, "I'm not going to push our country into the arms of Fidel Castro." And he's been very good, and I salute him. And when I go to try to help the impoverished people of Jamaica, we have very little flexibility.

And so, I don't want to suggest cutting to good friends, but I have asked that we be accorded more flexibility, perhaps a fund that's known as a discretionary fund, for the President to be able to prioritize the interests of this country and go forward with them.

So, Bob Dole raised the question, and I saluted him for raising the question. And we will continue to work with the Congress. I think there may be some sentiment for it, but I don't think you'll see it in slashes in the budget to accomplish that end because there's some strong reasons of friendship for that and there's some powerful political forces that would argue against that.

Well, listen, thank you all very, very much. A pleasure to be with you.

Note: The President spoke at 3:34 p.m. in Room 450 of the Old Executive Office Building.

Remarks at a St. Patrick's Day Ceremony With Deputy Prime Minister Brian Lenihan of Ireland
March 16, 1990

The Deputy Prime Minister. Mr. President, it gives me great pleasure on behalf of my country, Ireland, to be present here today at the White House to present to you a bowl of shamrock from Ireland. Shamrock is the symbol of unity. St. Patrick, whose feast day we honor tomorrow, on the 17th of March, is a symbol of the values which we share with the American people. The shamrock itself, three leaves on one stem, is a symbol of unity, the essential unity between the American and the Irish peoples that has been celebrated in this manner since the time of the first President of the United States of America, George Washington.

It gives me great pleasure again to present the bowl of shamrock to President Bush.

The President. Well, *Tanaiste* [Deputy Prime Minister], we're delighted to have you here, you and Mrs. Lenihan. It's always good to see an old friend again. I will confess to something that I said in front of the Senate yesterday: Once you've had a glass of Guinness with a man in Ireland, as I have with Brian Lenihan, why, you're friends. And so, we're delighted to see you back here.

There is one thing all of us here—all Americans—are united in, and that is our desire for peace and tranquillity in Northern Ireland. We can't forget the suffering and the tragedy that plagues St. Patrick's island, and there's no place for violence in creating a new future for Northern Ireland.

Here in the United States, 43 million Americans are of Irish ancestry, and I expect many more wish that they were of Irish ancestry. And the millions of our people who share common ancestry form a bond between our nations which will never be broken. We have another bond: the beliefs and the values which hold us together as well. Ireland and America are committed to democracy, justice, and liberty.

Mention an Irish name to an American—Colleen or Bridget, Patrick or Ronald, if you will—Ronald as in Ronald Reagan—and we think of the ones we know with the sparkle in their eye, the way with a story or a song that the Irish possess like no others. Your children are making Ireland young again, creating hope and opportunity for the future, rebuilding a strong economy and a peaceful existence.

So, long live the sons and daughters of Ireland, those at home and those who live here in America. And let me close with a saying of St. Patrick's: "May the wisdom of God instruct us, may the way of God direct us, and may the shield of God defend us."

Thank you, sir. God bless Ireland, and I'm so glad you came our way.

The Deputy Prime Minister. Thank you very much.

The President. Nice to see you. Brian, glad to see you again, sir.

Note: The President spoke at 9:51 a.m. in the Rose Garden at the White House.

Nomination of Robert Marshall White To Be Under Secretary of Commerce
March 16, 1990

The President today announced his intention to nominate Robert Marshall White to be Under Secretary of Commerce for Technology. This is a new position.

Since 1986 Dr. White has served as chief technical officer and vice president for research and engineering for the Control Data Corp. in Minneapolis, MN. Prior to this, he served as vice president of research and technology for the Data Storage Products Group and Control Data Corp., 1984–1986; principal scientist for Xerox PARC, 1983–1984; manager of storage technology in the Xerox Corporate Strategy Office, 1978–1983; and manager of the solid state research area for Xerox PARC, 1971–1978. In addition, Dr. White served as NSF senior postdoctoral fellow in Cambridge, England, 1970–1971; assistant professor of physics at Stanford University, 1966–1970; NSF postdoctoral fellow at the University of California at Berkeley, 1965–1966; and visiting scientist at Osaka University in Japan, 1963.

Dr. White graduated from Massachusetts Institute of Technology (B.S., 1960) and Stanford University (Ph.D., 1964). He was born October 2, 1938, in Reading, PA. Dr. White is married, has two children, and resides in Edina, MN.

Appointment of Joseph Sewall as an Alternate Member of the Roosevelt Campobello International Park Commission
March 16, 1990

The President today announced his intention to appoint Joseph Sewall to be an alternate member on the part of the United States on the Roosevelt Campobello International Park Commission. He would succeed Lawrence Stuart.

Currently, Mr. Sewall serves as chairman and president of James Sewall and Co. in Old Town, ME. He is married, has one son, and resides in Old Town, ME.

Interview by Jim Angle of National Public Radio
March 16, 1990

American Hostages in Lebanon

Q. Why did you decide to meet with Peggy Say?

The President. Because every day I'm President, I have a heavy heart when I think of the hostages. I've met with her before, as you know. I've met with other hostage families. I think we've got to be careful that we don't send a signal to the hostage holders that make them feel there's more advantage in holding the hostages than in releasing them. So, there's a very delicate balance here.

But Peggy Say is a courageous woman. She has suffered for 5 long years. And I just got thinking that Barbara and I would like to hold her hand and say: Stay with him. You're courageous, and we respect you.

Q. How do you keep from sending the signal that you're worried hostage takers might interpret?

The President. Well, there's a delicate balance here. You don't overdo public comments. You don't have too many dramatic meetings or call public attention to this. But on the other side of the equation, if you feel something in your heart, then you try to respond with compassion and understanding. It's delicate.

Libyan Chemical Weapons Plant

Q. Mr. President, it's been 2 days now since we had the fire in Libya at the alleged chemical weapons plant in Rabta. What can you tell us? What have you learned about that fire?

The President. Very little, so far. I know that the fire is serious, and it looks like the plant is out of action. I am absolutely convinced that the plant was manufacturing bad chemicals—chemicals that would be used for killing people, chemicals to be used for chemical warfare, and therefore, I don't lament what happened. But I can't tell you I know the cause of it.

Q. Well, the White House, just before this happened, called attention to the need for vigorous action to prevent the chemical weapons plant from going any further. It looks like someone, perhaps a close ally, took you up on that.

The President. We're not sure of that. The best intelligence that I've had—and I think it's the best in the world—is uncertain as to whether this was an accident or some incident of sabotage. I have stated without fear of contradiction that the United States was not involved in any sabotage activity. But I think it would be fruitless to speculate as to whether it was an accident—there are some highly inflammable chemicals in there—or whether somebody sabotaged it. I've heard what Mr. Qadhafi has said, and he apparently is suggesting sabotage. But I don't think we know enough about it yet.

And if your question somehow relates to the predicate that we were concerned about this plant on-stream producing chemicals, you are absolutely correct. And I have made this very clear—our concern—when I met with the Italian Prime Minister. I had a talk with Mr. Chissano [President] of Mozambique on it. And I urged our diplomats to spread the word that this plant was actually not making aspirin but producing chemicals——

Q. I understand.

The President. ——for chemical weapons.

American Hostages in Lebanon

Q. Let me ask you about the hoax call in which someone pretended to be President Rafsanjani. You said that we'll all be surprised when it comes out. Can't you just tell us what it is you think we'll eventually learn?

The President. No, because there are some real sensitive matters involved. Eventually I'll be able to, but all I'll say related to that call is it was screened enough that I felt I should take the call. And I would do exactly the same thing. Maybe this is a good day to mention it because of the Terry Anderson—him being held 5 years to the day. And I will go the extra mile. It doesn't matter to me one bit if you take a few shots and people needle you because you took a phone call that was unproductive. It is my intention to continue to reach out as best I can to find any lead whatsoever that will lead to the release of these Americans and the return of Higgins' body and, hopefully, Buckley's someday.

Foreign Aid

Q. On another foreign policy issue, Mr. President, you have discouraged everyone from looking for a "peace dividend" just yet from the defense budget, but you declared one this week in order to give aid to Nicaragua and Panama. There are a lot of other countries—emerging democracies and free markets—that are lining up at the U.S. door, if you will, for aid—everyone from Czechoslovakia, Romania, possibly Lithuania someday, Mozambique, as well as Poland and Hungary. Are you going to declare a "peace dividend" for them as well, or will you find it necessary to cut other programs?

The President. I don't think I declared any "peace dividend." "Peace dividend" implies that you have earnings and you have profitability, and therefore you take the extra money and pass it out. That isn't the case here. The case is that we have two countries in Central America in which the United States has a vital stake—a vital stake in seeing that their democracies, often denied their people, now succeed.

So, this isn't the concept of a "peace dividend"; it's the concept of prioritizing the use of available funds. And I want to see the Congress move fast to pass my requests on Nicaragua. I want to see them move fast to pass my requests on Panama. And does that mean I feel happy about the levels that we can give to countries like Jamaica or other countries that are trying to help their people? No, it doesn't.

Q. Well, that's one of the problems, though. But you asked for a set amount for defense spending at one point, and you have since decided that it was safe to take some money out of that for other purposes. Isn't that a "peace dividend"?

The President. No, it's not a dividend. It's a reordering of priorities. As the world changes—and it's changing every single day—and one reassesses the threats and the risks, one can reorder priorities. And that's what I've done. Dividend—the context, the way "peace dividend" is used is, take money from defense because there's no more threat of war and spend it all on some good cause here at home. And that is a concept that I would resist only because it raises the hopes of the American people beyond fulfillment.

Financial Assistance for the Soviet Union

Q. Let me ask you about what appears to be an administration position. Do you want to prevent the Soviet Union from being able to borrow money from an Eastern European Development Bank?

The President. No, but I think they should only borrow money up to the extent of their paid-in capital. And that Eastern European Development Bank was set up—the concept being help the smaller countries in Eastern Europe who are going down democracy's road.

The Soviet Union has a long way to go before sound loans can be made there. I think they probably would admit this. And I salute Mr. Gorbachev as he is trying to reform the economy. Their first steps ought to be reform, and our first steps ought to be trying to help them with these reforms and these institutions.

Q. So you're saying he hasn't reached the threshold of change?

The President. He isn't coming in asking for large industrial loans through any bank that I know of. And this concept that we ought to go loaning money or giving money to the Soviet Union now—I don't accept that. I don't agree with that. That is not administration policy. I have a different vote from majority leader in the House on this, who proposed giving money now to the Soviet Union. And I don't think that's in America's interest, and I don't think it's needed to encourage reform and *perestroika* and *glasnost* in the Soviet Union.

Federal Budget Proposals

Q. Let me ask you about a proposal from another Member of Congress. Illinois Congressman Dan Rostenkowski raised the proposal to reduce the deficit with a combination of spending freezes, some tax increases on alcohol, tobacco, among other things. I'm a little confused about your position. For instance, Budget Director Darman now says that you won't accept any taxes that hurt economic growth. Are there taxes that don't hurt economic growth?

The President. I don't think that's what he literally said. I read that in the paper a day or so ago and then asked him what he was talking about—growth-oriented revenues increases. And that obviously leads me to my pitch to you and your listeners to enthusiastically endorse and support a capital gains tax cut because there you cut the tax and you stimulate economic activity, you create jobs, and you bring in revenue. That's what Dick intended to say. So, I'm glad to clarify it for him.

Q. So, you're saying only capital gains is the——

The President. That is what I am supporting.

Q. Mr. President, if Rostenkowski——

The President. That's the difference in the Rostenkowski plan.

Q. Right. If he's talking about a package that includes spending freezes and revenue increases of various kinds, if you're not willing to consider those things, then why even contemplate discussion on the Rostenkowski plan? It isn't just a waste of time?

The President. Look, I'm not going to sit there and say that a seasoned Member of Congress like Dan Rostenkowski, who put forward a plan, ought not do it. He did it, and it's got some very interesting concepts in there as to how he thinks the budget should be brought down. We've put our proposal on the table; now he's put a proposal on the table. Now it's the Democrat-controlled budget committees that ought to put their proposal on the table, and then we'll talk about it.

Q. Let me ask you one——

The President. That's the way it is. And so, I salute him. I have some big differences with the Rostenkowski plan, obviously. But he did it without rancor; he did it without critics trying to——

Q. I understand.

The President. ——being highly critical of the President, or something like that.

Q. Let me ask you one other point on Darman's remarks. It's been widely interpreted he's suggesting some sort of movement here. He seems to say maybe; you say absolutely no. Is this a Presidential version of a good cop-bad cop routine?

The President. I don't think so. I don't think there are any differences between me and Mr. Darman at all on it. I think there's been misinterpretation of what he said. But who knows, we're living in a changing world, and I would be remiss if I didn't talk to Dick Darman and all our people as to whether there were some fine-tuning or something we might do different in terms of our budget proposals. But we put forward a sound proposal; now let Congress say what they're for. They've all been quite critical, or a lot of them have. And now let's see what their best thinking is, and then we'll talk. I'm not saying everything has to be done exactly the way I want it done. And it won't be, so I'm glad I'm not saying that. [*Laughter*]

Administration Accomplishments and Goals

Q. Mr. President, you have ended your first year with extraordinarily high popularity ratings. Why do you think you're so popular?

The President. Jim, I hate to put anything in terms of the popularity ratings because the more I talk about that, the more chagrin I'll have to write off my face when those numbers change. But we have tried hard. I've tried to do my best. I've tried to show concern for the American people and

some of those who are less fortunate. We've tried to put forward ideas on education and antinarcotics that I think have captured the imagination and earned the support of a lot of Americans.

I think we've managed to take proper roles of leadership in the changing world. I think our policy that resulted in unprecedented free and democratic elections in Nicaragua was sensible. I feel I had strong support from the American people on what we had to do in Panama. And so, I think, to the degree there is a feeling that this administration is functioning well, it relates to those things. And there's other things as well: The economy, though soft in some areas, continues to perform.

Q. But you're looking down the road at some enormous problems, hundreds of billions of dollars worth of things that are left over from the last few years. Are you worried at all about what's going to happen to the economy if you have to spend hundreds of billions to clean up nuclear waste, to clean up the environment?

The President. I think we've got all of these things in a proper perspective, but, yes, I'm concerned about all of it. There's enormous demands from the past that are going to have to be taken care of. You put your sights on one of them. I could add cleaning up savings and loans mess. There are plenty. But fortunately, we've got an enormous gross national product, and if we manage the economy properly and lead properly on fiscal matters, that powerful engine of economic dynamism can solve a lot of the problems.

Q. Okay. I'd like to ask you more, but I think——

The President. Fifteen minutes. You don't want to bore your listeners too much, Jim. [*Laughter*]

Q. Well, I think I've got some more things that would probably keep them from getting bored.

The President. Well, thank you.

Note: The interview began at 11:14 a.m. in the Oval Office at the White House. In his remarks, the President referred to Terry Anderson, the Associated Press reporter who was kidnaped in Beirut, Lebanon, on

March 16, 1985; Peggy Say, Mr. Anderson's sister; Lt. Col. William R. Higgins, USMC, the chief of the U.N. peacekeeping force in southern Lebanon who was kidnaped near Tyre on February 17, 1988, and allegedly hanged by pro-Iranian terrorists on July 31, 1989; and William Buckley, the U.S. Em- *bassy political officer who was kidnaped in Beirut on March 16, 1984, and allegedly murdered on October 4, 1985. The interview was released by the Office of the Press Secretary on March 17. A tape was not available for verification of its content.*

Remarks and a Question-and-Answer Session With Members of the National Association of Attorneys General
March 19, 1990

The President. I did want to thank you all for coming. And Bill, I think, has had a chance to outline National Drug Strategy II. I want to thank you, Tom, for working so closely with the Federal effort, heading the attorneys general task force on all of this; and it is very, very important.

I needn't say it with him here, but I will: I am very proud of our drug czar. We don't use the name anymore with all the changes going on in the world, but—[*laughter*]—he's done a superb job. We've tried to approach it on a totally nonpartisan manner, recognizing that this problem is national and that nobody's going to make it by dealing just at the Federal level. The more I think of the solutions, the more I think the States and localities and, yes, those private Points of Light have to be involved.

And I don't know whether I should reflect Bill's optimism, but I must say I have been encouraged because as he's looked at this—he and Judge Walton and others all over this country—he senses, and I think I do, too, a certain turning around, at least in terms of public opinion, on this question. I think there was some wondering whether all of us—and this means you all—were going to stay with the antidrug fight. And when we see the numbers going down in terms of high school usage, of seniors using cocaine, it's encouraging.

And I was able to reflect, when I went to Cartagena, to the three Presidents that, yes, we recognize that our demand for these horrible narcotics was causing them enormous problems. We'd talked about it, Bill and I and others, going there—John Sununu—and we decided that right up front at that meeting we'd say, "We know we've got a demand problem." I'm surprised they thought we had to reiterate that because I've tried to make it clear to all of them that we recognize that. But there has been some feeling in South America that we didn't recognize it. And so, once we got that—say, look, there's a demand problem; here's what we're trying to do about it; now let's talk about the supply—I think we made a little headway on that.

In any event, that summit, I think, was good because we had three very strong-willed Presidents, one of whom is leading a tremendously courageous fight against the drug traffickers, come together and join us in a communique, or a statement of purpose, that I think is very helpful.

So, I would say that I'm beginning to feel a certain sense of optimism on it. We are getting marvelous support in the private sector—in the media, for example, some wonderful pro bono advertisements that—we've got a task force—have you talked about the Jim Burke effort here? Jim Burke, of Johnson and Johnson, heading a media task force [Partnership for a Drug-Free America]. The goal: $1 billion—$1 million a day for 3 years—$1 billion of pro bono advertising to fight drugs. And it's coming along.

I went out and—Bill and I—Bill, I think, set it up; and I went out and talked to the National Academy of Television Arts and a group of other leaders out there in the media. And they're taking a market—20 million kids watch cartoons every Saturday.

I don't know what that says, but nevertheless, 20 million kids watch cartoons. And they're taking all these cartoon characters, including Ninja the Turtle and Mickey Mouse and all of these, and working—not to disrupt the entertainment—but working in an antidrug message. Now, that couldn't have happened, I don't think, if it hadn't been for the focus that you all are putting on the drug problem. And it couldn't have happened, I think, without the focus that Bill Bennett and others are trying to put on it from here.

So, I stand here a little bit optimistic about how we solve it. I would say that I would like to see the Congress move forward on our crime package, and I think it's a tough one. I know there are probably disagreements in this room with certain parts of it. But I feel we've got education on the demand side of the equation, we've got interdiction, but we also have to back our law enforcement people. And you know our administration's position on things like the death penalty for drug pushers and all. And I don't want to see that reversed out in well-intentioned negotiation by certain Members of the United States Congress. So, we're going to fight for our crime package. And I think, inevitably, we're going to succeed on it. I think we will be successful, but for those who do agree with it, I'd like to ask for your help.

We've gotten some of what we've asked for: new agents, new prosecutors, new prison space. We're getting some good support already on certain parts of the package. But I must confess to a certain frustration. I really believe we have to back up our lawmen. And we're talking about an exclusionary rule that is designed to protect the truth and punish the guilty—changes there. We're talking about habeas corpus reforms to stop frivolous appeals and to allow punishment be meted out in a timely fashion. And as I say, we still favor constitutionally sound death penalty provisions. There's some battle in Congress—and maybe you've talked about this—Congress coming on to overturn retroactively certain State death penalty sentences. We're not sympathetic to that.

So, I would ask your support—this much horsepower in town—for those of you who

believe in our goals there to work with us on getting this crime package through. I understand Bill has called—[*At this point, the President sneezed.*] [*Laughter*]

Audience member. That's news.

The President. That's news. [*Laughter*] A little hay fever in the air around here. I'll tell you, I got hit with it yesterday. But they've got their job to do, and I've got mine. [*Laughter*] Sorry. Come on, you guys.

So, anyway, Bill has proposed a conference with State officials, local officials. I would urge, Tom, as many of your members that feel they can break away to participate in that, please do.

And again, thank you. I'll be glad to take a couple of questions if I haven't overstayed my welcome here. Or I'd be glad to hear from you all. I mean, this is a good chance to have at least a few shots at a two-way street and tell us what you're upset about. Don't say send money. [*Laughter*]

Tom, why don't you just come on up and tell me what's on the minds of your associates.

Mr. Miller. Thank you. Thank you for being with us, and thank you for the education in Washington—that when the President sneezes, that is news. [*Laughter*]

The President. It's not. They just like to—particularly this center row—they like to needle me a little bit. I'll get even. [*Laughter*]

Mr. Miller. Before you arrived, we had a very productive discussion with Dr. Bennett, a good give-and-take and, I think, the building blocks for some very strong cooperation between Dr. Bennett and the attorney generals. We're developing a pattern of some very close relationships with your administration in the antitrust area, the environment, in particular, and see the possibilities with Dr. Bennett. As he sat down, he suggested we get together sort of an executive group to work with him in a session in June so that—we have so much in common here. We have the bipartisanship—this is an extremely bipartisan organization. We have the drug war, and we know what that means to America and what we can accomplish. So, what we need to do is really channel the abilities, the strenghs, the resources, and the good will in this room to even greater activity. And that's what we're trying to do.

The President. Well, it is very important, and we have no complaints in terms of the cooperation at all from the State and local—the very fact that we—shift the gear from drugs a minute to education—met with the Governors and came up with six national goals. Some might not think that's enough. Some might have in mind a larger role for the Federal Government in terms of spending on education. But all of that was set aside at Virginia, at Charlottesville, Mr. Jefferson's university, to come up with some major national goals. We are not going to dictate—try to—through a lot of complicated legislation that mandates certain performance. But the thing that impressed me about the education summit was that, though there were enormous differences in political philosophy amongst the Governors and the President, we came together and set these goals. And now it's my responsibility, I'm sure, to help the Governors follow up on it.

The same thing is happening in the drug field, I think. And we've got differences—maybe you and I do, Tom—on certain facets of legislation, but I think the thing that is emerging is the need to work together to fight drugs. And you can fine-tune it in the States, and I'll tell you what I think quite directly from here.

So, I want to thank you all.

Mr. Miller. Well, we'll start from a common purpose and a lot of good will, and we get a lot done in that direction. Do you have time for a few questions?

The President. Sure. Or a few answers, I mean, if you guys got—seriously.

Mr. Miller. I think Jeff Amestoy from Vermont has a question.

Environmental Policy

Q. Mr. President, on another issue. As you know, particularly in the Northeast, the environmental matters continue to be a matter of great concern. As chair of the Attorneys General Environmental Control Committee, I want to thank you and your administration for putting the environment on the front burner and, particularly, for the relationship that the Environmental Protection Agency has redeveloped and sustained over the last 8 or 9 months with the attorneys general.

Sir, there have been conflicting reports out of Washington as to the respective roles of Administrator Reilly and Governor Sununu in terms of environmental issues, particularly in the context of the Clean Air Act. I wonder if you might address their participation in this.

The President. Well, one thing I've learned over the years, and I'm sure it's true in State governments, is everybody loves a battle—trying to figure out who's up and who's down; who's in, who's out; who's listened to, who's not. And in this case, they're both right—Sununu and Reilly. And they're working together, and they're strongly supportive of the clean air amendments. They've worked side by side in hammering out the compromises that are necessary to get legislation through.

And so, it isn't a question of one being up and the other being down, or one being in and the other being out. But I can understand the speculation on it. And where there are nuances of difference, we do it like I expect you do in the States: get everybody sitting around together and say, Now, wait a minute, here's the way it's going to be. And the President makes the decision. So, when you see that Sununu is putting words into the mouth of the President, that is the endless, inside-the-beltway speculation that a lot of people thrive on; and it happens not to be true.

And so, I think they are working very well together—and I mean it—because it is essential that they do. And Bill Reilly's got enormous credibility in the environmental community. And I think John Sununu, very respectful of where I want to see us go in terms of Federal participation in environmental matters, also knows that I am determined not to shut this country down and throw everybody out of work. And so, in this field as in others, there's compromise involved. But you get to the heart of it on the personnel side, and I would simply say, don't believe all this big feuding that's going on between EPA and the White House. And in the final analysis, I will and do take the responsibility for it.

And they're moving, Jeff; they're moving

on this clean air bill. And what I say to those that want to come at us from either the right or the left on clean air is, look, pass what we've got. George Mitchell has compromised—a very noted environmentalist, a leader in the Senate. [Senator] Bob Dole has been extraordinarily helpful in trying to reach compromise. And so, save your fire—you that want to move it one way or another—and let's pass the first major revision of the Clean Air Act since the act was written. Then we'll sort out the further amendments.

So, we've come a long way, and we still got a ways to go.

War on Drugs

Q. Mr. President, I'd like to—back on the subject of drugs—to, first of all, thank you and let you know that the Federal drug strategy is alive and well in Maine. We're working closely together with the Federal and State officials. There have been more arrests. And the teachers, including those at Kennebunk High School, are telling me that it makes a real difference and enforcement really drives the education. And I think the only comment I'd like to share with you is that I encourage you to continue to work with the private sector not just in terms of education and publicity but also to develop more meaningful employee treatment programs for their own employees as a way to help address the treatment side of this.

The President. Let me ask you while you're on your feet, if you would, because I have been concerned about the interdiction regarding the Maine coast, with that enormously complex craggy coastline. Is that still as serious a problem as it was, or do you think the interdiction efforts have resulted in less coming in?

Q. We've been successful in terms of the old marijuana shipments, which were much easier to eradicate. As the drug of choice moved towards cocaine, it's much more difficult to detect not just coastally, Mr. President, but also across the Canadian borders. But we're working very closely with the Provincial and Federal Governments in Canada and have had increasing support. It's very difficult to——

The President. It's hard to measure, too, I find, but I don't know how you all—well, thank you.

Agricultural Policy

Q. I hate to make your mind shift in so many directions, but agriculture is very important to North Dakotans, and I know the administration has not as yet submitted a new farm bill, and I just wondered what thoughts you'd have on the shape of the Federal farm legislation?

The President. Well, generally speaking, I've been pleased with the way the agricultural economy has bounded back from abysmal lows. And Clayton Yeutter is working now with the Senate and the House on a new farm bill. I am not for one of these managed-farm-economy farm bills. And we could probably discuss what that means; but I think, in broad terms, matters like the former Harkins bill, for example, will have total opposition from this administration. A farm bill that is market oriented and gives flexibility to the farmers will have the strong support of the administration.

But it is coming along, I think, in terms of negotiation. I feel a great burden to do more in the field of agricultural exports. And we've been successful in getting ag on the table for the Uruguay round, but we're still running into a tremendous resistance from some countries in terms of getting access to foreign markets. We've made some encroachments—proper encroachments—into the Japanese market, as you know. But I'm not relaxed about it; and I think you will see in whatever emerges—in the domestic side of the farm bill—it will continue to be, as was with the '85 bill, market oriented. But in terms of emphasis, we've got to expand our markets abroad, and that means we are not going to have our negotiators lighten up at all on this.

And I'm troubled about Eastern Europe—I mean, the EC Western Europe, on this because we're having difficulty getting them to understand. We've got to let them take a whole new look at their farm program. I think we'll have a more harmonious negotiation—some of it because of where this farm economy stands and some of it because I think there's general agreement on the international aspects of it.

Well, thank you all very, very much for coming by. Nice to see you.

Note: The President spoke at 10:51 a.m. in the Roosevelt Room at the White House. In his remarks, he referred to Tom Miller, at- *torney general of Iowa and president of the association; William J. Bennett and Reggie B. Walton, Director and Associate Director of National Drug Control Policy; and John H. Sununu, Chief of Staff to the President.*

Nomination of Thomas Lawrence Sansonetti To Be Solicitor of the Department of the Interior
March 19, 1990

The President today announced his intention to nominate Thomas Lawrence Sansonetti to be Solicitor of the Department of the Interior in Washington, DC. He would succeed Martin Lewis Allday.

Since 1989 Mr. Sansonetti has served as administrative assistant and legislative director for Representative Craig Thomas. Prior to this, he served as Associate Solicitor for Energy and Natural Resources in the Office of the Solicitor at the Department of the Interior in Washington, DC, 1987–1989, and founding partner of the law firm Sheehan, Stevens, and Sansonetti in Gillette, WY, 1980–1987.

Mr. Sansonetti graduated from the University of Virginia (B.A., 1971; M.B.A., 1973) and Washington and Lee University (J.D., 1976). He was born May 18, 1949, in Hinsdale, IL. Mr. Sansonetti is married and resides in Washington, DC.

Nomination of James B. Edwards To Be a Member of the Board of Directors of the Communications Satellite Corporation
March 19, 1990

The President today announced his intention to nominate James B. Edwards to be a member of the Board of Directors of the Communications Satellite Corporation until the date of the annual meeting of the Corporation in 1993. This is a reappointment.

Currently, Dr. Edwards serves as president of the Medical University of South Carolina in Charleston, SC. He is married, has two children, and resides in Mount Pleasant, SC.

Nomination of Jerry D. Jennings To Be Deputy Director of the Federal Emergency Management Agency
March 19, 1990

The President today announced his intention to nominate Jerry D. Jennings to be Deputy Director of the Federal Emergency Management Agency. He would succeed Robert H. Morris.

Since 1986 Mr. Jennings has served as Deputy Director of the Selective Service System in Washington, DC. Prior to this, he served as Executive Director of the Office of Science and Technology Policy at the

White House and Executive Director of the White House Science Council, 1982–1986, and adviser to the Assistant to the President for National Security Affairs, 1973–1982. He was a Special Agent for the Federal Bureau of Investigation in Memphis, TN, and New York City, 1968–1973, and served as special assistant to the Director of the Office of National Narcotics Intelligence, 1972–1973. In addition, Mr. Jennings was with the Central Intelligence Agency as an adviser to foreign intelligence agencies in the Far East, 1965–1968.

Mr. Jennings received his bachelor of science degree from Eastern Michigan University. He was born July 2, 1940, in Flint, MI. Mr. Jennings served in the U.S. Marine Corps. He is married, has three children, and resides in Vienna, VA.

Nomination of John K. Lauber To Be a Member of the National Transportation Safety Board
March 19, 1990

The President today announced his intention to nominate John K. Lauber to be a member of the National Transportation Safety Board for the term expiring December 31, 1994. This is a reappointment.

Dr. Lauber has served as a member of the National Transportation Safety Board since 1985. Prior to this he served as Chief of the Aeronautical Human Factors Research Office at the National Aeronautics and Space Administration's Ames Research Center at Moffett Field, CA. Dr. Lauber is married, has one child, and resides in Bethesda, MD.

Remarks on Economic Assistance for Nicaragua and Panama and an Exchange With Reporters
March 20, 1990

The President. What I wanted to say is that what I want to talk about today is Panama and Nicaragua. The changes there are dramatic in terms of democracy. Yesterday I was asked about Cuba, and of course, I'm terribly disappointed that Castro seems to be firming up his totalitarian position instead of moving towards the free and fair elections—what I think all of us here would like to see. I'd like to see him shift from that highly militarized island and let democracy have a chance.

But I think if we are helpful to Nicaragua and Panama, it will simply increase the pressure in that marvelous island of Cuba for change. And so, this is what I'd like to talk about today. And I know that the Senate and House are going to come to grips with this problem. But this is the agenda, and then anything else that's on you all's mind.

Lithuanian Independence

Q. Mr. President, are you worried that Gorbachev might make some move on Lithuania?

The President. Well, I'm glad that they're still talking peaceful change. That's essential, and they've been very good about it— the Soviets have—all through Eastern Europe. And that's what everybody wants to see, is a peaceful evolution in Lithuania. And——

Q. Then you don't think he will?

The President. ——so, that's the way it is. And I've learned not to go into a lot of hypothetical questions. I'm sure every Member here has asked questions on this subject. And we want to see democracy and freedom. We want to see self-determination. And we also want to see peaceful evolution. And that is in the interest of Eastern Europe as they begin to solidify their democracy. And so, that would be my appeal. And the second one would be please don't ask me any more hypothetical questions because I don't want to get——

Q. But it's not a hypothetical. Have you been in contact with Gorbachev on this question?

The President. Previously, yes.

Note: The President spoke at 10:05 a.m. in the Cabinet Room at the White House, prior to a meeting with congressional leaders.

Statement by Press Secretary Fitzwater on Lithuanian Independence
March 20, 1990

The Lithuanian people have freely expressed their intention to restore Lithuanian independence. The United States has consistently supported the Baltic people's right to peaceful self-determination. The United States notes that the Lithuanian Government has expressed its readiness to address all legitimate Soviet interests, including economic interests, during negotiations.

We also note repeated Soviet statements that negotiations, not force, are the proper course in this situation. We have called upon the Soviet Government to address its concerns and interests through immediate negotiations with the Government of Lithuania. We continue to urge a constructive dialog. This would be complicated by an atmosphere of intimidation and increasing tension.

In this regard, the activities and statements of the Soviet Government over the past few days are cause for concern. We are watching the situation closely.

Note: Press Secretary Fitzwater read the statement during his daily press briefing, which began at 12:08 p.m.

Statement on Transmitting the Annual National Security Strategy Report
March 20, 1990

Today I signed and forwarded to Congress the National Security Strategy Report for 1990. This report comes at a time when the international landscape is marked by change that is truly breathtaking in its character and pace. It is a time of great hope, a time when free peoples celebrate the march toward democracy that their commitment and steadfastness have helped bring about. Our national security strategy reflects these changes and joins in these hopes, but it is grounded in realism. We have arrived at a moment of historic opportunity, but continuing uncertainties and new dangers still threaten American interests and values. Today's opportunities have been created by our willingness to bear the burdens our security demands and to join in a common effort with others who share our values. Our strategy foresees many adaptations in how we go about ensuring our security, but we will not abandon the basis of our success.

This report outlines both continuities and changes in our national strategy. While addressing our strategic relationship with the Soviet Union as an inescapable priority, we will work toward a fuller integration of the Soviet Union into the broader community of nations. While contributing to the global balance in a way that only we can, we will make our military forces smaller, more agile, and better suited to likely contingencies. While keeping substantial nuclear and conventional forces in Europe as long as they are needed and wanted by our allies as part of the common defense, we will work for a new Europe, one truly whole and free. While welcoming the prospect of German unification, we join with the Government of the Federal Republic in expecting a united Germany to remain a full member of NATO, including its military structures. And while providing adequately for our defense, we will look to our economic well-being as the foundation of our long-term strength.

I look to this report to be the foundation for a productive, nonpartisan national dialog as we continue to develop and articulate a strategic approach that will take this nation and all who cherish freedom safely into the next century.

White House Fact Sheet on the National Security Strategy Report
March 20, 1990

The President today transmitted to Congress his report on the national security strategy of the United States as required by the 1986 amendment to the National Security Act. The 32-page report reflects the recent dramatic changes in the international environment and outlines U.S. policies to both shape and respond to these changes. It observes that we have reached a moment of historic opportunity, one created by the success of our postwar strategy. Highlights of the report include:

- A policy that moves beyond containment and supports the integration of the Soviet Union into the international system.
- The goal of a new Europe, whole and free, as Eastern European States rejoin the European cultural and political tradition that is their heritage.
- A commitment to a strengthened European pillar in an Atlantic alliance that remains rooted in shared values and that will continue to sustain the overall structure of stability in Europe.
- Support for German unification coming about through peaceful means, on the basis of democracy, and in the framework of Western relationships that have nurtured freedom for four decades, including full German membership in NATO.
- Continued commitment to advance the march of democracy and freedom in the Western Hemisphere.
- Recognition of the continuing importance of East Asia and the Pacific, the vital role our security ties play there, and the need to sustain a dialog with China.
- Renewed commitment to an arms control agenda broader than ever before with a goal of agreements this year in START, CFE, chemical weapons, and Open Skies.
- Recognition that our economic well-being is the foundation of America's long-term strength and that, in a new era, we must assess which risks can be ameliorated by means other than military capabilities—means like negotiations, burdensharing, economic and security assistance, economic leverage, and political leadership.
- A commitment to adapting U.S. military power to a strategy that looks beyond containment and provides us capabilities appropriate to new opportunities and challenges.
- A movement to a smaller military, one more global in its orientation, responsive to changes in warning time, and well-suited to the demands of likely contingencies. This includes improved capabilities for the unique requirements posed by potential Third World battlefields, themselves growing in complexity and lethality.

389

- Changing patterns of U.S. forward deployments as adjustments are made based on new perceptions of the threat, the improved reach of our forces, and the growing capabilities of our allies.
- Burdensharing marked by growing national specialization in defense activities. For the United States this would include nuclear and space forces, advanced technologies, strategic mobility, a worldwide presence, power projection, and a secure mobilization base.
- Identification of drug interdiction as a high-priority national security requirement.
- A restatement that deterrence of nuclear attack remains the cornerstone of U.S. strategy and meeting the requirements of strategic deterrence will remain our first priority.

The report outlines the historical roots of U.S. security strategy: our fundamental values as a people, our tradition of joining in common cause with those who share our values, our commitment to an open international economic system, and the strategic demands placed on us by geography.

The report also points out that America's basic goals are enduring:

- The survival of the United States as a free and independent nation, with its fundamental values intact and its institutions secure.
- A healthy and growing U.S. economy to ensure opportunity for individual prosperity and a resource base for national endeavors at home and abroad.
- A stable and secure world, fostering political freedom, human rights, and democratic institutions.
- Healthy, cooperative, and politically vigorous relations with allies and friendly nations.

The report explains that the fundamental challenge is to relate the means available to these enduring goals in a world marked by change that is breathtaking in its character, scope, and pace. It is clearly a time of great hope accompanied by the recognition that the future world will not automatically be a safer one for American interests or values. Elements of change that deserve special attention are:

- The democratic restructuring of Eastern Europe and the potential that exists for instability as these states enter uncharted territory.
- A shifting balance of global economic power and the danger that trade disputes could strain political and security ties.
- The proliferation of advanced weaponry, especially weapons of mass destruction and associated delivery systems, to Third World states.
- The growth of threats like illicit drug trafficking, subversion, and terrorism, which are often fed by poverty, injustice, and ethnic or religious strife.

The report also emphasizes that even with great change there will be substantial continuity. The United States will remain fully engaged in the larger world and will continue to pursue its objectives in concert with those who share its values and concerns. Our approach to security will continue to be shaped by the fact that we are a nation separated by large oceans from many of our most important friends and interests. As a global power the United States will continue to bear primary responsibility for deterring global war and will defend the interests it has in common with its allies as far forward as possible. And this will still require the presence of American forces overseas backed up by an ability to project power from the United States.

The strategy report concludes with a call for close cooperation and consultation with Congress to help construct a security structure appropriate to today's opportunities and challenges.

Remarks on Signing the Greek Independence Day Proclamation
March 20, 1990

Let me just say here—and one, apologies because we're running a couple of minutes late. But it is a great, great pleasure for me to welcome His Eminence Archbishop Iakovos, friend to everybody in this room, back to the White House, and I'm pleased to see him looking so well. Mr. Ambassador, we're just delighted to have you here, sir. It's most fitting and most appropriate. And to Secretary Derwinski and distinguished Members of Congress that are here with us today and friends of Greece, welcome.

It's my pleasure to just sign this proclamation marking the 169th anniversary of Greek independence in 1821. And I hardly need to tell this row of powerful hitters here about America's ties to Greece. You know the admiration that our Founding Fathers had for ancient Greece. The evidence is there. It's in our own Constitution, and the evidence is there in the letters our Founding Fathers exchanged with one another in charting the course for American democracy. They were all schooled in ancient Greek, and they were all schooled in Greek democracy. And you know, too, the role that so many Americans played in championing the independence of modern Greece in the last century. And this is a time for recalling the roots of our common past and a time for rejoicing in the rebirth of Greek democracy in 1974.

And it's a time, too, for noting the rich contributions so many sons and daughters of Greece—some of them in this room today—have made to the success of our own democracy. And as Greeks prepare to go to the polls on April 8th, we join with them in affirming our common devotion to liberty, to democracy, and to independence.

So, now let me sign the proclamation formally designating March 25th, 1990, as Greek Independence Day: A National Day of Celebration of Greek and American Democracy.

Note: The President spoke at 11:53 a.m. in the Roosevelt Room at the White House. The proclamation is listed in Appendix E at the end of this volume.

Message to the Senate Transmitting Amendments to the International Expositions Convention
March 20, 1990

To the Senate of the United States:

I transmit herewith amendments to the Convention of November 22, 1928, concerning International Expositions, as amended (Treaties and other International Acts Series 6548, 6549, 9948, and Treaty Doc. No. 98–1), with a view to receiving the advice and consent of the Senate to their acceptance. I also transmit, for the information of the Senate, the report of the Secretary of State on the amendments.

The main purposes of these amendments are: to halt the proliferation of world fairs by requiring 5-year intervals between such expositions, beginning in 1995; to establish a single category of "registered" international expositions (world fairs); and to create a new category of "recognized" international expositions.

I strongly support these amendments to the Convention concerning International Expositions, as amended, and recommend that the Senate give prompt consideration to the amendments and advise and consent to their acceptance.

GEORGE BUSH

The White House,
March 20, 1990.

Remarks on Signing the National Agriculture Day Proclamation
March 20, 1990

Mr. Secretary, I'm delighted to see you here. And these distinguished Members of the Congress, welcome to the White House. I'm pleased to be standing next to Clayton Yeutter, glad to see Senator Lugar, Senator Leahy, Chairman [of the House Agriculture Committee] de la Garza; and welcome. And I'm also pleased to see so many leaders of our key national agricultural organizations as I prepare officially to designate this National Agriculture Day.

And I'm grateful to the farm broadcasters for giving me this opportunity to talk directly to American farmers and ranchers, those Americans whose everyday work— work the soil—the world's most successful agricultural nation.

American agriculture is a vital resource for the world. People around the globe share in our harvests and our prayers for bountiful crops each year. And the unparalleled productivity of our farmers and ranchers makes American agriculture our greatest export earner, putting a positive balance of $17 billion into the U.S. balance of trade account last year.

Farm families embody what's good in America. They express it in the way they live and in the diligence that they apply to their craft. The spirit of rural America is found in family entrepreneurs running their own businesses; farm and ranch families willing to reach across the fence to help a neighbor; wives, husbands, children pitching in as a team to reap nature's harvest.

This administration is committed to keeping American agriculture strong. And we are committed to working with the Congress and with you, America's agricultural leaders, to provide 1990 farm legislation that gives you the management freedom and planting flexibility to run your farms at peak efficiency. Our farm bill proposal increases market orientation, improves our international competitiveness, and address-es those environmental challenges out there. Our proposal emphasizes production flexibility to allow farmers to respond more readily to market forces in making their production and marketing decisions.

We will do our part to continue aggressive agricultural research, and we will encourage new and alternative commercial uses for ag products. And I will rely heavily on the man right here, on Clayton Yeutter, to be my chief negotiator with the Congress on the farm bill. But I also would be remiss if I didn't tell you I would be relying on you and your organizations to help us pass a good, fair farm bill. Through sound fiscal policies and wise management of our resources and, God willing, good weather, rural America and American agriculture will stay strong through the nineties and beyond.

And so, now I am pleased to sign a formal proclamation designating March 20, 1990, as National Agriculture Day. And I'd like to ask the two chairmen and Dick Lugar, if you would—Senator Lugar, Senator Leahy, Congressman de la Garza—join the Secretary and me.

[*At this point, the President signed the proclamation.*]

Thank you all very much for coming. And I really mean it. We're going to need your help. And we're working with very reasonable people in the United States Congress—I know Clayton and I talked about this— we're grateful for that. But it is important that we get a good market-oriented bill. I think we can do it. And with you all's help, I'm sure we can do it.

Thank you very much.

Note: The President spoke at 3:50 p.m. in the Roosevelt Room at the White House. The proclamation is listed in Appendix E at the end of this volume.

Remarks at the Welcoming Ceremony for Prime Minister Tadeusz Mazowiecki of Poland
March 21, 1990

The President. Prime Minister Mazowiecki and all members of your distinguished delegation, and to all the many friends of Poland who have joined us here this morning, welcome to the White House. And let me first recognize three distinguished Americans, Board members of the Polish American Enterprise Fund: Chairman John Birkelund, Nicholas Rey, and Lane Kirkland.

Mr. Prime Minister, it is my great pleasure to welcome you here to Washington. Since you took office 6 months ago, we've had occasion to consult one another several times, and I've come to value your counsel, come to think of you as a friend. And today, for the first time, we meet in person, and I'm delighted to have this chance to sit down together to discuss the many changes and challenges that affect our two nations.

And of course, Barbara and I welcome this opportunity to repay in some small way the warm reception that we felt this past summer on our last visit to Poland—everywhere from the streets and squares of Warsaw to the gates of a now-historic shipyard at Gdansk. The warmth I felt in your country was a sign of the friendship between the people of our two nations, of the unbreakable bonds that link the people of Poland and the United States, not just the millions of Americans of Polish ancestry who trace their roots to the old country but all of us who share a common love of freedom.

And it's that love of freedom that lights our way today, that sparked the changes we've seen this past year—remarkable changes. On this day 1 year ago, the leaders of Solidarity and the Communist authorities were deep in the midst of those roundtable discussions. Mr. Prime Minister, you sat at the roundtable through the winter weeks of February and on into March. The fate of your nation hung in the balance. All of Poland awaited the outcome. And on April 5, 1989, Poland took its first step towards its democratic destiny. For the first time in

more than 40 years in Eastern Europe, a people's voice would speak in free elections.

Here in our country, we celebrate the Revolution of 1776; but we remember April 19, 1775, the day the Revolution began, the day the "shot heard round the world" was fired in Lexington, Massachusetts. In your country, Poles will always remember April 5th, the dawn of the Revolution of '89. The revolution that began in Poland touched off a chain reaction that changed Europe and the world. Mr. Prime Minister, those two revolutions share a common aim that unites our two nations in the cause of freedom. At Hamtramck, Michigan, nearly a year ago, I pledged America's strong support for Poland's economic reform and its democratic transition. I said then: "Liberty is an idea whose time has come in Eastern Europe." The enormous changes of this past year have indeed brought that idea, the idea of liberty, to all of Eastern Europe.

Today we welcome to the White House a great Polish patriot and patron of freedom, Tadeusz Mazowiecki, one of the founding fathers of Solidarity—a man who survived the dark days of December 1981 and the heavy hand of martial law, endured a year in prison, life in the underground, editor of the illegal newspaper of an outlawed trade union.

Mr. Prime Minister, you survived. Solidarity survived—survived and triumphed. Today you and your heroic union lead a nation—lead the Polish people from revolution to rebirth.

In the past year, Poland has taken its first steps on the path to a democratic rebirth. For the past 6 months, navigating the difficult transition to democracy has been your daily task. You've shown a great personal courage—courage in taking the necessary steps to clear away the economic wreckage of a system that produced more long lines and empty shelves than anything else. You deserve great credit for introducing a bold economic reform program which aims to build a free market economy on the ruins of central planning. All of us know this transformation, this road to reform, is not painless. The book of history teaches that the Polish people are well schooled in pain and suffering. But history also teaches a lesson about the Polish spirit: always hopeful, always strong. And today, in this time of trial, there is this difference: Poland's sacrifice is blessed by freedom—the sacrifice of a nation determined to make its destiny democracy.

Mr. Prime Minister, this is my message to the people of Poland: America wants to help Poland succeed. We want to welcome Poland as a full partner in the community of free nations. We want to see Poland prosper, see your people enjoy the fruits of free enterprise. We want to see the nation of Poland achieve its full measure of democracy and independence. In any decisions affecting the fate of Poland, Poland must have a voice.

At this time of great and turbulent change, let me assure you, sir, that the United States will remain a European power, a force for freedom, stability, and security. We see a new Europe in which the security of all European States—and their fundamental right to exist secure within their present borders—is totally assured. And in this new Europe, NATO, linking the United States to Europe in a defensive alliance of democratic states, will remain strong and united. And we want Poland and its neighbors to join with us in building a Europe whole and free.

Once again, Mr. Prime Minister, it is my privilege to welcome you to Washington and to the White House. And may God bless the people of Poland.

The Prime Minister. Mr. President, I express my deep gratitude for your invitation for me to pay this official visit to the United States. We're living in a time of great acceleration of history—acceleration which has affected my homeland, Poland, as well as Europe, and thereby, in fact, the history of the whole world. The visit which I'm now beginning is one of the visible signs of that acceleration. Our presence here today, just as that of other Eastern and Central European visitors, would not long ago have been totally inconceivable.

Yet in a special way, we have always been here. Throughout all those years, when in the name of building an ideal system we were put into enslavement, the spirit of freedom never died in our hearts. We also felt—and legitimately, I believe—that it was the same spirit which had inspired your Constitution and that the Poles persevering, working up their way to independence, was to you Americans particularly close.

Today such strivings are no longer an exclusively Polish phenomenon. The year 1989 became the year of Eastern and Central Europe, one in which that part of the world made its way toward the recovery of freedom peacefully, though not without the sacrifice of blood at the very end.

We are coming here to talk, above all, about the future—about the future of Polish-American political cooperation in the face of momentous changes in the heart of Europe, about the future of Polish-American economic cooperation, so vital in our building an economy based on free enterprise.

The United States was the first country to adopt, several years ago, the ideals of human rights as a supreme principle of its foreign policy. Poland came to be the first country in Central Europe where the ideals of human rights became the victorious program of a whole nation. It was us who sparked the process of democratic revolution across Eastern Europe. The victory of that revolution will, in a large measure, depend on our success. Therefore, we must succeed, and I do believe that we will.

The time of the present crucial acceleration of history is also one in which partnership is being put to test. Coming to you, I have no doubt that this will be genuine partnership. My conviction springs from our hitherto common experiences, particularly over the past decade when so many signs of a well-wishing attitude and affection for us were shown by the United States, both by your people and the administration. For all this, allow me today to warmly thank you, Mr. President, and the millions of Americans.

I would also like to say that your greatest contribution to the community of man is not material. In the words of your Declaration of Independence, all people are endowed by our Creator with certain inalienable rights. The ultimate inalienable right is a universal value of political freedom. That same brightly burning light of freedom has nowadays guided the peoples of Eastern and Central Europe into the splendid dawn of the 1990's. We have come here as free people. We have come from a country building a new democratic order. We have come from a country which wants to and can play a significant role in the new emerging order in Europe.

I trust that our talks will be fruitful. I trust that our meeting with America will make us stronger. This is the hope which I'm bringing with me to the White House. God bless America.

Note: The President spoke at 10:11 a.m. at the South Portico of the White House, where the Prime Minister was accorded a formal welcome with full military honors. The Prime Minister spoke in Polish, and his remarks were translated by an interpreter. Following the ceremony, the two leaders met in the Oval Office.

Remarks on Signing the Poland-United States Business and Economic Treaty
March 21, 1990

The President. Mr. Prime Minister, I'm just delighted that we've signed today this treaty concerning business and economic relations, a treaty that will greatly strengthen business and economic ties between our two countries.

I want to salute three distinguished Members of our United States Congress: Congressman Broomfield; Congressman Rostenkowski; Senator Pell, the chairman of our Foreign Relations Committee. I want to salute the newly appointed members of the Enterprise Fund Board that you just met—these distinguished Americans taking time from exceptionally busy schedules to join in as best they can to guarantee Poland's economic success. And we're looking forward to their mission and their work very much.

This treaty is very important—important not only in its content but what it says about where Poland is going. It says that Poland wants U.S. investment because this investment is good for the Polish people and vital to the growth and development of the Polish economy. In this treaty, Poland is taking a number of very substantial steps, steps that will orient the Polish economy toward the Western economic system and towards global markets. These are courageous steps, and we applaud them.

Following the steps the United States has taken to open our markets to Poland, we can now take this treaty to the U.S. business community and say, this is why you should invest in Poland. And I'm also pleased to note that this is the first economic treaty that the United States has concluded with the newly emerging democracies in Eastern Europe. And we all think that it's quite fitting that Poland is first.

This treaty is more than an investment treaty: it is a broad and comprehensive agreement that lays the basis of a new economic relationship. It's a milestone for Poland and also for the United States—a milestone on the road to a prosperous Poland and a stronger U.S.-Polish partnership.

So, once again, welcome. Would you care to say a word, sir?

The Prime Minister. Mr. President, I thank you very much for your kind words.

I also consider this treaty is very important and very significant. As I had a chance to say during our conversation before, we're tying together, linking, political change and economic change in our restructuring efforts. We believe there is a relationship between democracy and the development of an economy based on free market and free enterprise. We believe that to combine these two kinds of changes in Poland allows

395

us to make changes that reach most deep.

The treaty we have just signed is very important in this sense, because it offers a prospect for American business and for American companies to become committed and engaged in the Polish conditions and the Polish environment. The treaty offers a certain framework, and what needs to be done now is to fill it with contents. Perhaps Poland not in every respect is prepared for this kind of activity. We're having a great deal of problems. Our telephones do not work as they should, and we have many other problems. But I would like to tell you that I think people should not be discouraged by the problems which are typical of this first phase. And we will be looking forward to seeing courageous people who will be willing to come and to move through this half a year of progress.

I believe Poland is a country of big opportunity, and I believe it is a country of opportunity of opening more to the East. I think our economy could play this role, too. And I do hope that this combinative attitude to investment and business in Poland will continue to characterize our economic relationship.

Let me also join the President in expressing our thanks to the newly appointed members of the Board of the Fund that is intended to boost the development of the private sector in Poland. We want to thank them for accepting the effort of doing it. We very much count on the outcome of that Board's work and on the outcome of the Fund's activities.

Mr. President, I believe that signing this treaty is a good step, opening up our economic conduct into the future. Thank you for kindly signing this treaty personally.

Note: The President spoke at 11:45 a.m. in the Rose Garden at the White House. The Prime Minister spoke in Polish, and his remarks were translated by an interpreter.

White House Fact Sheet on the Poland-United States Business and Economic Treaty
March 21, 1990

The President and Polish Prime Minister Mazowiecki today signed a treaty concerning business and economic relations. The treaty is an important and vital step in enhancing the attractiveness of the investment and business environment in Poland.

This treaty, the first U.S. economic agreement with a newly democratic Eastern European country, is intended to encourage and facilitate U.S. investment by providing internationally recognized protections and standards. Some of the key elements of the treaty include:

- *Treatment of Investment.* U.S. investors in Poland will be treated the same as Polish nationals or investors from other countries, whichever is more favorable.
- *Expropriation.* The United States and Poland agreed to internationally recognized standards for expropriation: expropriation will be permitted only for a public purpose and must include

prompt payment at fair market value.
- *Transfer of Funds.* The Government of the Republic of Poland has agreed to permit the immediate and complete repatriation of export earnings and capital from Poland to the United States. In addition, the Poles have agreed to progressively eliminate restrictions on repatriation of U.S. investor zloty profits, with no restrictions for profits beyond 1995. Current Polish laws place a 15 percent cap on zloty profits to be repatriated.
- *Dispute Settlement.* The United States and Poland agreed to abide by internationally recognized standards for arbitration which ensure that an investor has the right to go to international arbitration after 6 months for any type of dispute.
- *Business Rights.* The treaty guarantees that U.S. firms will have the right to:

—market goods and services both at the wholesale and retail level;

—obtain access to public utilities and financial institutions;

—obtain commercial rental space and raw materials on a nondiscriminatory basis;

—conduct market studies and distribute commercial information of all kinds; and

—obtain registrations, licenses, permits, and other approvals on an expeditious basis.

• *Intellectual Property Rights.* Poland has agreed to adopt major new intellectual property standards which are among the most sophisticated in the world in areas such as:

—adherence to the Paris Act of the Berne Convention;

—copyright protection for computer software;

—product as well as process patent protection for pharmaceuticals and chemicals. The Government of the Republic of Poland will provide protection for U.S. patent holders by enacting legislation within the immediate future;

—protection for integrated circuit layout designs; and

—protection of proprietary information.

• *Ombudsman Office.* The Government of the Republic of Poland will designate a Deputy President of the Agency for Foreign Investments to serve as an ombudsman for U.S. investors. The Deputy President will serve as the government coordinator and problem-solver for U.S. investors experiencing difficulties with registration, licensing, nondiscriminatory access to utilities, and regulatory and other matters.

• *Tourism.* The United States and Poland agreed to encourage the growth of tourism and provide tourism services on a fair and equitable basis.

• *Investment Procedures.* The Government of the Republic of Poland also commits to the following procedures in applying its investment laws:

—A permit for entry of U.S. investments shall be issued automatically within 60 days, unless the U.S. investor is notified in writing of the grounds and reason for denial.

—In evaluating the impact of the proposed investment on the environment, the standards used shall be the same as those applied to domestic enterprises.

—Restrictions on the entry of U.S. investment on the grounds that it threatens Polish state economic interests shall be used only in exceptional cases and not for the purpose of limiting competition.

—In 2 years the Governments of the Republic of Poland and of the United States will review the statutory provisions on screening with a view to narrowing the scope of investments that require a formal entry permit and subsequently phasing out such permits.

Statement by Press Secretary Fitzwater on the Basel Convention on Transboundary Movement and Disposal of Hazardous Wastes
March 21, 1990

President Bush today announced that the United States will sign the Basel Convention on the Control of Transboundary Movements of Hazardous Wastes and Their Disposal. The convention prohibits exports of controlled wastes except for recycling or recovery, or except where such exports are environmentally sound and economically efficient. Safeguards required by the convention include notification to and written consent from importing countries prior to the export of controlled wastes. The convention also obligates signatories to ban the export of controlled wastes if there is reason to believe such wastes will not be managed in an environmentally sound manner in the importing country. The administration expects to implement the convention in tandem with the President's decision of March 9, 1989, to ban exports of hazardous wastes except where the United States is a party to a formal agreement with the importing country. Existing bilateral agreements with Canada and Mexico will continue to govern movements of hazardous wastes between the United States and those countries.

The United States played a leadership role in developing the convention. Forty-six countries have joined the United States in signing the convention. Following signature, the convention will be submitted to the Senate for consent to ratification. It will enter into force upon ratification by 20 governments.

Message to the Congress Transmitting the Annual Report of the National Science Foundation
March 21, 1990

To the Congress of the United States:

I am pleased to transmit the annual report of the National Science Foundation for Fiscal Year 1989. This report describes research supported by the Foundation in the mathematical, physical, biological, social, behavioral, and computer sciences; in engineering; and in science and engineering education.

Achievements such as those described here are the basis for much of our Nation's strength—its economic growth, national security, and the overall well-being of our people.

The National Science Foundation will be 40 years old in 1990. Over those years, it has played a key role in supporting this Nation's remarkable research achievements. The Foundation looks forward to the challenges and accomplishments of the new year, the new decade, and the new century.

GEORGE BUSH

The White House,
March 21, 1990.

Statement on Namibian Independence
March 21, 1990

The independence of Namibia today marks the end of colonialism in Africa and a proud beginning for the world's newest country. Americans can take pride in the role the United States played in making this transition to independence possible. Brought about in large measure by vigorous American diplomacy, the 1988 Brazzaville protocol and the New York accords cleared the way to Namibian independence and the withdrawal of all Cuban troops from Angola.

I have sent Secretary of State Baker to Windhoek as my representative at Namibia's independence ceremonies as a sign of the respect and esteem in which we hold the world's newest democracy. Secretary Baker carries the good wishes of all Americans to President Sam Nujoma and the Namibian people. We are especially gratified that Namibia's Constituent Assembly has produced a constitution that is among the most democratic in Africa and which provides an excellent basis to ensure national harmony and development.

The United States established diplomatic relations with the Republic of Namibia today, and we will take the necessary steps to exchange Ambassadors as quickly as possible. We welcome Namibia as a full trading partner and are taking steps to ensure that it is given access to the American market.

With the end of South Africa's administration, all U.S. sanctions against Namibia are being lifted.

From this promising beginning, we look forward to a warm and productive relationship with Namibia.

Toasts at the State Dinner for Prime Minister Tadeusz Mazowiecki of Poland
March 21, 1990

The President. Mr. Prime Minister and His Eminence Cardinal Szoka and distinguished guests and friends of Poland, Barbara and I are delighted to host this dinner tonight and, as I said this morning on the lawn of the White House, to return in some small measure the warm hospitality that we felt on our visits to Poland.

On our last visit this past July, that warm hospitality was coupled with a heat wave in Warsaw—ninety degrees. Would have done Washington proud last week. [*Laughter*] But everywhere we went, Barbara and I felt right at home. I don't want to inject a partisan political note into this lovely nonpartisan evening, but at one point, Barbara even saw one fellow in the square at Gdansk wearing a Bush-Quayle '88 T-shirt. [*Laughter*] I know I shouldn't have mentioned that.

But I do remember my first visit to your country, Mr. Prime Minister, in the fall of 1987. Solidarity, *Solidarność,* was outlawed, underground, but still very much alive. And I remember well meeting with members of Solidarity. And afterward, as I rode to lay a wreath at the grave of Father Popieluszko, the murdered priest, in protest the state security agents removed the Polish flag from our car. But that was in 1987.

And 2 years later I went back to Poland in the summer of 1989, and I thought back to that first visit, about that incident with that red and white Polish flag. As I was riding through Gdansk, Solidarity's birthplace, to the Monument of the Three Crosses, thousands of Poles lined the streets, in their hands thousands of American flags and, of course, the red and white of Poland, your national flag, and the banner of *Solidarność,* high above the crowd.

What a world of change in those 2 years.

On that first visit in 1987, everywhere undeniable determination, but just as undeniable, deep anxiety over the fate of Solidarity and the future of Poland. And on my return this past summer, on the eve of the Revolution of '89, everywhere we found a feeling of hope—a feeling that Poland once more held its destiny in its hand, that the time had come once more for Poland to live in freedom, for Europe to be whole and free.

Mr. Prime Minister, I assure you all Americans agree that Poland's time has come, and all our prayers are with you at this time of Poland's rebirth.

Our meetings this morning accomplished a great deal. I found a wonderful frankness. We spoke from the heart, in candor, I felt, as friends. And tonight, Mr. Prime Minister, I offer this toast to old and enduring friends, the nations of Poland and America; to the future of a free Poland. And to you, sir, Mr. Prime Minister, let me return the kind wish that your countrymen made me in the Hall of the Sejm, in the streets of Warsaw, and the square of Gdansk: *Sto lat,* may you live 100 years.

The Prime Minister. Mr. President; esteemed Mrs. Bush; your Eminence, Cardinal; ladies and gentlemen, I would also prefer to refrain from talking politics here. But I will have to speak something about politics, and please forgive me for that.

Allow me to invoke here a classical piece on modern democracy, which is at the same time a classical work on America. It is a book by Alexis de Tocqueville. De Tocqueville referred to the unstoppable march of democracy; it was 150 years ago. Nowadays, we're witnessing an enormous acceleration of that march in Nicaragua, Chile, even Mongolia, but most of all in Eastern and

Central Europe.

Democracy is a system which secures the freedom of the individual, the freedom without which no normal life is possible. Indeed, it has just been that deeply rooted need of normal life which has most strongly inspired the march observed in your country so many years ago by the famous Frenchman. It is also just to that need that, under the pressure of Eastern and Central European nations, totalitarianism is giving way—the disease of our century which had devoured tens of millions of human lives, forcing hundreds of millions of others into a dead end history for many years. We in Poland are now emerging from a long night of totalitarian oppression.

In 1939 we were ravaged by the Nazi invasion. Our people suffered more than any other on Earth. Poland lost 6 million of its citizens, half of them Polish Jews. The Third Reich was crushed, and the war ended, but to our part of Europe, peace failed to bring an order based on freedom. For the next 45 years, we were forced to live under an alien political system, a totalitarian one which was imposed on the whole Eastern and Central Europe. The Poles never accepted their fate and were the first to challenge it. They succeeded in defending peasant homesteads, churches, and their own families against the greed of the totalitarian state, even through the most difficult times. The struggle by the Polish people to preserve their dignity and franchisement played a great role in sparking the change which today has gained such momentum.

Just as we stood in the forefront of struggle, so today we wish to be in the forefront in establishing the rights and institutions of a stable, democratic order. We're making Poland a state of the rule of law, which guarantees all political freedoms to its citizens. We're building a free-market economy based on free enterprise. It is a program which calls for great sacrifices. Polish people are aware of it. We know that our economy needs to be repaired by our own effort. And so, now that this effort has been undertaken, we have the moral right to seek the support of other countries.

Today Poland enjoys such support, and I am confident that it will continue. A great share of it has come from the United States—the American Congress and personally yourself, Mr. President. Allow me to thank you for that.

Ladies and gentlemen, the changes in the Eastern and Central Europe are making the situation across the whole continent essentially different. The era of Yalta is becoming history. A need is emerging for a new structure which would operate within the parity of powers to gradually free Europe of military rivalry and bring the two separated parts closer together. Such a structure needs to be based on a solid foundation. Reconciliation between nations is possible only when they do not fear either for their present or their future. For this reason, an important component of the building must be the recognition of the Polish border along the Oder and Nysa Rivers in the form of a treaty. The direct participation in the talks about that, for Poland, was a very important matter for Poland; and it has already been guaranteed.

To create a new political facet of Europe is going to be a difficult challenge, and one calling for time and an enormous amount of work. A variety of ideas emerging, in this respect, need to become ripe, which in turn requires certain conditions. In our view, a helpful factor would be to form the Council for European Cooperation. Its job would not be to replace any of the existing organizations: it would serve as a platform whereby, within the CSC framework, work might be launched to give the ideas a concrete form. One can hardly imagine such work without a significant role on the part of the United States. After all, your country is linked to Europe by bonds of blood and by experiences of history.

Mr. President, ladies and gentlemen, after General Sikorsky visited the White House in 1943, mine is only the second-ever call by a Polish Prime Minister here. How different the circumstances and how different, I believe, the perspectives of this period in history. I would like the United States to view Poland as one of the important actors of the present-day European politics. A strong Poland engaged in building a democratic order and freed of economic difficulties will be a stable factor of the new European order, an order based on freedom, respect of human rights, and economic and political balance on the Continent. I trust that the United States, with so many of its people linked to Poland by their origin and with the affection for Poland so much alive, will see a friend in the democratic, strong, and economically sound Poland.

Permit me, ladies and gentlemen, to raise in a moment a toast to the good health and the well-being of the President of the United States.

I raise this toast also to the good health of Mrs. Barbara Bush. I wish you strength and perseverance in your difficult role here. It is well-known that the house, even if it's called White, becomes a home only upon the touch of a woman. I know how much Americans like you, and I want to tell you that so do the Poles.

I raise this toast, also, to the well-being of your great country and the millions of its citizens, as well as to our friendship, which at the Polish end has for long been extremely profound.

I raise this toast to you, Mr. President.

Note: The President spoke at 8:15 p.m. in the State Dining Room at the White House. The Prime Minister spoke in Polish, and his remarks were translated by an interpreter. The toasts were released by the Office of the Press Secretary on March 22.

Remarks at a White House Tree-Planting Ceremony
March 22, 1990

Thank you, Secretary Yeutter, Bill Reilly, and Chairman Deland, to Senators Lugar and Leahy and Congressman Kika de la Garza, the chairman also in the House Ag Committee, and distinguished Members of Congress here. I want to single out two other special friends, pioneers in this greening effort, tree planting: Trammell Crow and Margaret [Crow] from Dallas, Texas. Distinguished ladies and gentlemen—Irv, I haven't forgotten you. Irv Williams, who was introduced by Clayt, really does so much to just keep the White House grounds beautiful. And we're indebted to him every single day that we have custodianship of this lovely house. Welcome to all of you to an event which celebrates how trees can preserve and protect our great outdoors.

I want to talk just a little about the precious inheritance of trees passed from one generation to another. We see it in the great ebonies of India or the sequoias in California, the lush rainforests of South America and the evergreens of the Alps. Their very presence demands that we renew and restore the natural beauty of our land. Trees do enhance our atmosphere, providing oxygen and absorbing carbon dioxide. A tree planted today can enrich the lives of generations yet unborn.

Just think, on these grounds stands a tree planted by John Quincy Adams in 1826. Nearby is the spot where Woodrow Wilson's family so loved bay trees that they often ate lunch in a makeshift grove. And not far from here is the little-leaf linden planted in 1937 by Franklin Roosevelt for Britain's King George VI. Next to the Oval Office— there you'll find an oak tree planted by President Eisenhower. There's a swing on it. You can almost see it, over past that Suburban over there. Often our grandchild swings on it, and I expect in the future many other grandchildren of Presidents will do the same.

Trees are truly an inheritance that links generations of America. Last summer a terrible windstorm swept through Washington. I remember thinking of these trees around us and the link they provide. Truth is that Barbara and I were a little worried about them—Grover Cleveland's Japanese spiderleaf, for instance, or Herbert Hoover's oak. They're old trees, and maybe I'm beginning to feel an affinity for them with my birthday coming up, but nevertheless, they're special. For instance, the magnolia over there was planted by Andrew Jackson—the one next to the South Portico.

Thankfully, the trees here weren't damaged in that storm. Elsewhere in Washington, it was a different story: a lot of people out the next morning surveying the damage, mourning the loss of a favorite oak or an elm, regarding it with concern and affection, just as you would view a friend.

Trees can be fragile, they can be sturdy, but they are always precious. So, in the budget I submitted to Congress, I asked for $175 million to plant 1 billion trees a year. Today I'm asking Congress to approve another step to protect the environment. We call it the National Tree Trust Act of 1990. It will foster the partnership between public and private sectors to plant trees all across America.

Under our plan, we will designate a private nonprofit foundation to receive a one-time Federal grant to promote community tree planting and cultivation projects—a foundation to solicit contributions from private sources, forging cooperation between individuals, businesses, governments, and community organizations. It will sound a nationwide call for each American to become a volunteer for the environment and, most of all, plant the trees that clean our air, prevent erosion, consume carbon dioxide, and purify our water. This act can preserve the heritage of trees—their beauty that is breathtaking and their bounty that is breathgiving.

As you can imagine, the foundation's funding won't simply come out of the woodwork. In addition to the $35 million in Federal money we're proposing, the foundation will begin to raise millions of dollars more to help reforest America. The Tree Trust Act will work by using State forestry agencies and private tree-planting organizations—volunteers helping thousands of new volunteers to learn not only how and where to plant trees but how to care for them, why we need them, and how they help the environment. Our foundation will be one of a Thousand Points of Light, creating 10 billion trees of life. By planting trees in all 50 States, we'll knock Johnny Appleseed out of the Guinness Book of Records.

The National Tree Trust Act of 1990 is a key part of our national tree-planting and forest improvement initiative to be administered by the Ag Department. This two-part program involves both rural areas as well as local tree-planting programs in the cities. And it, in turn, is crucial to my America the Beautiful program, which I announced in the State of the Union.

I am proud of America the Beautiful. It will help maintain and expand our parks, wildlife refuges, forests, and public lands. I do love the outdoors, and I love exploring it with those who are the trustees of our future.

What we're doing today is planting the seeds of environmental stewardship, and that means not only planting trees but other steps just as vital—clean air, for example. Our clean air proposal promises relief from the smog, acid rain, and toxic pollution that harms trees and people. Once again, I call on the Congress to pass the bill. We're also working hard on energy efficiency and pollution prevention, clean oceans, global cooperation. Just as a tree grows, with roots and branches spreading, our efforts on all these issues will reach into the future.

Nearly a quarter of a century ago, perhaps America's greatest conservationist, Teddy Roosevelt, put it best when he called our lands and wildlife the property of unborn generations and when he said this about America's sequoias and redwoods: they "should be kept just as we keep a great and beautiful cathedral."

Today ours is the chance to keep that cathedral great and beautiful by planting not only sequoias and redwoods but poplars and maples and cypress and sassafras. And I can't think of a better time to begin than this spring, the 20th anniversary of Earth Day. Teddy Roosevelt would have loved that one.

Four weeks from now we'll celebrate it, but I thought we'd get a head start this morning. And so, I'm pleased to be able to join Barbara as she plants this eastern redbud blossoming tree in a few minutes. By comparison to other trees, it seems small today. But so, years ago, did the special tree beside me. My kids were the age of some of you when it, too, was planted by President Eisenhower. And when you're my age, Barbara's tree can be just as strong, embody just as much history, do just as much to ensure the splendor of America.

Trees are an inheritance precious to our cathedral of the outdoors. So, just look around us, and in that context, let me thank again Irv Williams—thank you, sir—and all the people of the White House grounds staff for the tender loving care they gave to our trees and flowers.

So, let us plant the trees and nurture them so that America will remain America the Beautiful for generations to come.

I am very pleased that all of you came today. And now, with no further ado, let's get on with the tree planting.

Note: The President spoke at 11 a.m. on the South Grounds of the White House. In his opening remarks, he referred to William K. Reilly, Administrator of the Environmental Protection Agency; Michael R. Deland, Chairman of the Council on Environmental Quality; and Irvin Williams, Superintendent of Grounds at the White House.

Message to the Congress Transmitting Proposed Reforestation Legislation
March 22, 1990

To the Congress of the United States:

Today I am pleased to transmit a legislative proposal entitled the "National Tree Trust Act of 1990." This proposal is a key part of my "America the Beautiful" initiative, and it would enhance the growing partnership between the public and private sectors to plant trees across America. Also transmitted is a section-by-section analysis.

President Theodore Roosevelt began this century by directing the Nation's attention to the protection of valuable public lands—America's treasure trove of parks, wildlife refuges, forests, and rangelands. As the end of the century approaches, it is appropriate that this final decade be one in which conservation, enhancement, and protection of our irreplaceable national assets rise to the forefront of national concerns. With this as our goal, my FY 1991 Budget proposes a new initiative—"America the Beautiful." Our initiative reflects my support for appropriate expansion and proper maintenance of the Nation's parks, refuges, forests, and public lands. It is also based on my determination to involve all Americans in strengthening the Nation's natural resources heritage. Finally, this initiative expresses my firm commitment to providing responsible stewardship of the country's heritage for the benefit of generations to come.

My "America the Beautiful" initiative includes three components. *First,* we propose

to expand Federal recreational land acquisition that involves activities of the Departments of the Interior and Agriculture. *Second,* the Department of the Interior is undertaking an effort—"Legacy '99"—to enhance resource protection and recreation. *Third,* we propose a national tree planting and forest improvement initiative to be administered by the Department of Agriculture. The first two components will be carried out under existing authorities. The enclosed draft legislation will permit full implementation of the third component.

Trees are one of our most valuable resources. They contribute to the environmental, economic, and social well-being of this country. They enhance biodiversity, wildlife, air and water quality, and recreational opportunities. Trees improve landscape aesthetics and property values, reduce soil erosion, and provide many valuable wood products. They also contribute to energy conservation through the shading and cooling of buildings and by serving as windbreaks.

The proposal I am transmitting to the Congress today authorizes Presidential designation of a private nonprofit Foundation to receive a one-time grant for the purpose of promoting community tree planting and cultivation projects. Second, it authorizes the Secretary of Agriculture to establish a

403

rural tree planting and forest improvement program and a community tree planting and improvement program. Third, it authorizes appropriations to the Secretary of Agriculture for a grant to permit the Foundation to begin its important work.

The Foundation will promote public awareness and a spirit of volunteerism, solicit private sector contributions, and oversee the use of these contributions to encourage tree planting and cultivation projects throughout the United States.

The Foundation will help forge cooperation among individuals, businesses, governments, and community organizations and provide financial assistance to grass-roots volunteers to plant trees. It will help draw national attention to the need for increased planting of trees in our communities where, on average, only one tree is now being planted for every four that die or are removed. It is a program that will reach every State, if not each and every community. All of our citizens will be encouraged to participate in this program.

Enactment of this proposal will permit us to harness the efforts of individuals and organizations to undertake the nationwide planting and cultivation of invaluable trees. The prompt passage of this proposal by the Congress will demonstrate our shared commitment to preserving one of our most valuable natural resources, our precious heritage of trees. Let us ensure that our descendants will be able to share our pride in referring to this land as "America the Beautiful."

GEORGE BUSH

The White House,
March 22, 1990.

The President's News Conference
March 22, 1990

The President. I don't want to have a captive audience, but there are a couple of things that I did want to say—make a statement here. I'd like to make just a few comments, after which I'll be glad to take a couple of questions.

Last week I unveiled an economic package for the new democracies of Panama and Nicaragua and urged a bipartisan effort aimed at reconstructing and developing these two countries. We have an opportunity to make this hemisphere the first to be wholly democratic; but we must act expeditiously in order to help establish firm democratic institutions, the rule of law, and human rights. And I asked the Congress last week to act quickly on the aid package, and I repeat that request today. If we are unable to resolve our differences regarding offsets, then I would be happy to have Congress authorize me to select the offsets from the defense budget in order to get economic assistance moving in the region.

We must take the lead in helping our neighbors, and we cannot look to others to make sacrifices if we ourselves cannot work in partnership in our own hemisphere. And I'd also add there are those that argue that Panama and Nicaragua are not as vital as Eastern Europe. They're wrong. This is our hemisphere. And we have a strong aid program for Eastern Europe and will continue to do so, and we can do no less for our own neighbors. The world is changing dramatically, and we must meet the challenges in every region with equal commitment and equal dedication.

In this regard today, I just concluded another meeting with the Polish Prime Minister [Tadeusz Mazowiecki] to continue the fruitful discussions that we engaged in yesterday. We discussed questions of European security, Poland's place in a new Europe. And I told the Prime Minister that we see an important role for a free, democratic, and independent Poland as a factor for stability in Europe in the future. And I reaffirmed our commitment to aiding Poland's economic recovery and its movement to democracy and our desire to stay in very close touch, consult on areas of mutual concern. We look forward to Poland joining in and building a Europe whole and free, a Europe in which the security of all states within their present borders is guaranteed, and one in which NATO will continue strong and united.

And I'd be glad to take a few questions. I'll start with Helen [Helen Thomas, United Press International].

Lithuanian Independence

Q. Mr. President, do you see a Lithuania that's whole and free in Europe? And why do you think that the Soviets are getting tough on this when they didn't move in Eastern Europe? Are they justified?

The President. Well, as you know, our position on Lithuania is, we never recognized its incorporation into the Soviet Union. I am convinced that the answer is peaceful emergence and discussion between the parties. I am pleased that Mr. Shevardnadze [Soviet Foreign Minister] reasserted his conviction that the Soviet Union would not use force. It is very important that force not be used. But I believe that they can talk and work out these problems, Helen.

Q. The Lithuanians said today they will not lay down their arms.

The President. Well, they should talk about that. I don't think either side to that difficult debate, discussion, wants to see the use of force. And so, my appeal would again be peaceful resolution through discussion of this difficult question.

Soviet Troops in Poland

Q. Mr. President, I want to ask about your meeting with the Prime Minister. Did he give you any assurances that he wants Soviet troops out of Poland? And when did he say he thought that might happen?

The President. No, he did not give assurances on that, that I recall. And I am convinced he knows that a continued presence of U.S. troops in Europe would be stabilizing and not a threat to anybody. But I don't recall his making a statement to me on that question.

Q. Well, let me ask, what's your reaction to statements by some Polish officials that there's a need for Soviet troops in Poland?

The President. Well, my reaction is: There isn't any need for Soviet troops in Eastern Europe, and the sooner they get out of there, the better. And I can understand the desire for stability and the way it's changed, but I haven't changed my position. The position of the United States is that a unified Germany should remain in NATO; the U.S. troops will be there as long as they are wanted because they are there as a stabilizing force; and that I think things would be enhanced, a peaceful evolution of all, if the Soviet troops moved out. And indeed, we're moving forward with the Soviet side on discussions of CFE. I want to have that agreement done by the time I sit down with Mr. Gorbachev.

Assistance for Nicaragua and Panama

Q. Mr. President, is it true that one of the leading Members of Congress that met with you earlier this week on Panama and Nicaragua said you simply would not be able to get the amounts of aid that you have requested? And if so, do you now feel that that aid package is in trouble?

The President. Well, one of the Members—several of them indicated to me that there might be difficulty getting what I feel is essential for Panama. But I am going to continue to reiterate the importance, not just to the United States but to the whole hemisphere, of the aid package that I have requested for both Panama and Nicaragua. But, yes, one particular Senator—I don't think I'm violating a confidence out of that meeting—indicated he thought it would be a very difficult sell. And I don't understand it, because I think the United States has a disproportionate role—others have an important role—in the evolution of democracy, making firm democracy in Nicaragua and in Panama. We've got a lot at stake in both countries. Everyone knows our security interest in Panama, particularly. But I'm equally as concerned about doing what's right by Nicaragua.

Lithuanian Independence

Q. Mr. President, your spokesman the other day cautioned the Soviet Union against using intimidation and increasing tension with Lithuania. Do you read this latest statement by President Gorbachev calling on Lithuanians to lay down their arms as intimidation?

The President. I would prefer to put emphasis on his statement that there will be no use of force. And that's where I'm going to keep the emphasis and keep reminding every party to this discussion over there: no use of force, peaceful evolution. And I think we've got to look back over our shoulders to a year ago and see how far Europe has evolved, the democracies in Europe, through peace. And there was a great deal of restraint shown by the Soviet Union in that regard. And so, I would like to say: Please continue to exercise that kind of restraint. And remember, no use of force.

Abortion

Q. Mr. President, the State of Idaho is about to enact a tough abortion law, putting severe restrictions on a woman's right to have an abortion. What do you think of that, first of all? And second of all, if the States do voice their individual positions, do you still think that a constitutional ban against abortion is necessary?

The President. I have not changed my position at all; and I think, in answer to the first part of your question, that's a matter for the State of Idaho to decide. The President of the United States has stated his position. It's my position. I feel strongly about it. And I'm not going to change it on constitutional amendment or anything else. But that matter should be debated out there, as it is being, and those people should decide that. That's what the whole Federal system is about.

Lithuanian Independence

Q. Mr. President, do you consider the Lithuanian situation an internal matter within the Soviet Union, or is there a role for outside countries, particularly the United States, to play?

The President. Role in what sense?

Q. In helping them reach whatever goal——

The President. I think the way to reach the goal is to have peaceful resolution of the problems between them that result from calm negotiation and discussion between the parties involved.

Q. But is it an internal matter within the Soviet Union?

The President. I've already told you the United States position, and that is that we do not recognize the incorporation of Lithuania into the Soviet Union. However, there are certain realities in life. The Lithuanians are well aware of them. And they should talk, as they are, with the Soviet officials about these differences.

Q. Mr. President, some of those realities include what Mr. Gorbachev has done; that is, giving the KGB more authority, restricting access to Lithuania. Is that, in fact, peaceful evolution?

The President. I wouldn't put that down as peaceful evolution; but that's a matter to be discussed between the Lithuanians themselves, having declared their independence, and the Soviet officials.

Q. But isn't that kind of a stranglehold also a form of force being used?

The President. Well, we see varying reports as to how much implementation there has been to some of these statements that come out.

Germany-Poland Border

Q. Were you able in your meeting with the Polish Prime Minister—were you able to give him any support for his request that a treaty recognizing Poland's border be initialed by both Germanys prior to the two-plus-four talks and his request that Poland have a broader role in those talks to discuss security matters besides borders?

The President. We discussed those matters. I purposely worked into my statement here the role we see for Poland in a democratic Europe—standing on its own, independent, very influential in the future. But in terms of the treaty and how the Germans enter into a treaty with the Poles—that is a matter that I haven't changed our view on it. But I think we may have a nuance of difference here. But that's a matter for the Polish Prime Minister to discuss with the leaders of Germany.

And I believe they've come a long way. They are very, very close now, far closer than I think many of us would have predicted from statements that were made a month or so ago. So, let them sort it out. It's going well. The mistrust, I think, that you sometimes read about between the parties is down. I think [West German] Chancellor Kohl has come a long way in his view. I think his leadership has been impressive and terribly important. And I would leave it there.

Q. How about two-plus-four talks, though? Do you support the broader——

The President. Two-plus-four talks? The role of the United States is, if we're talking in the two-plus-four about Poland, Poland should be there. Poland should be involved. We have a view that the two-plus-four ought to deal with certain rights and obligations that the four parties came up with right after the war. And we don't see this as the group that is going to determine the fate of all of Europe. It has a specific role to it. But if two-plus-four starts talking about Polish borders, for example, clearly, the Poles should be involved.

Lithuanian Independence

Q. Mr. President, I suppose part of the equation in Lithuania is how much maneuvering room does Gorbachev have. Does it seem to you that he has the political ability to let Lithuania go?

The President. Well, he has asserted that whatever changes take place will be peaceful. I guess I'd have to say I honestly don't know the answer to your question.

Texas Gubernatorial Election

Q. Mr. President, when your fellow Texas Republican, Mr. Williams, was in town the other day, he said that he would feel less comfortable running against a woman and that he'd have to be more cautious. Since you've been there——

The President. You're talking to an expert in the field.

Q. Well, did you give him any advice, and do you have some for him if that happens?

The President. No, I have none at all. But I know exactly what he means, and I refuse to elaborate on it for fear of complicating his life. [*Laughter*] But remember 1984. I can't forget it. And he's entitled to his opinion. Maybe he's drawing on my experience.

Soviet-U.S. Summit

Q. Mr. President, in Secretary Baker's talks with Foreign Minister Shevardnadze,

was a date set for your summit with President Gorbachev? Is that meeting likely to take place in Washington, Kennebunkport, or elsewhere?

The President. One, a date has not been set. Two, a place has not been set, but I would anticipate that the major business of the summit would be conducted in Washington, DC.

Q. When would you anticipate a date being set, sir?

The President. Soon. And the matter was raised by Jim Baker with Eduard Shevardnadze, and we should pin this down soon because you have many other meetings coming up. You have a NATO ministerial, you have the G–7 meeting [economic summit] that will be in Houston, Texas—very important meeting. We have bilaterals—I will—with President Mitterrand [of France], probably in Florida. Then we'll have one with Margaret Thatcher [Prime Minister of the United Kingdom] in Bermuda. And so, the calendar is getting full on our side, and I know it is on the Soviet side as well.

Lithuanian Independence

Q. Mr. President, you've gotten a lot of questions about Lithuania. If the Soviet Union does move with force against the Lithuanians——

The President. Too hypothetical. Stop right there. I am not going to make an answer to a hypothetical question of that nature. What possible good would come from the President of the United States, standing halfway around the world, speculating on something that he doesn't want to see happen? I mean, I could inadvertently cause something bad to happen, and I don't—I'm very sorry——

Q. Can I ask something else then, Mr. President?

The President. You can start over on a whole new question. [*Laughter*] I really don't want to go into the hypothetical.

Israeli Political Situation

Q. In another part of the world, do you think that your comments on east Jerusalem contributed to the collapse of the government there? And do you think, over the long haul, that's going to make the peace process more difficult or easier?

The President. No, I think a President, when he reiterates the standing policy of the United States Government, is doing the correct thing. I do not think it contributed to the fall of the government. These are highly complex, internal matters in the state of Israel. Who emerges, the Likud or Labor, is their problem, their right. And I will negotiate and deal openly with whoever, and talk freely and openly with whoever, emerges as the leader. But I don't believe it made a contribution, because I think if you look at the issues, both the domestic economy and the question of the peace talks, that those were the key issues in the campaign, because most people in Israel understood that I was simply reiterating a standing United States policy, one that I feel very strongly about.

African National Congress

Q. What is the status on U.S. aid for the African National Congress?

The President. I don't know how that came out. Jim Baker had some discussions about it, and I'm embarrassed to say I haven't seen the final resolution. I just don't know the answer to your question.

Q. What is your inclination?

The President. My inclination is——

Q. To be cautious.

The President. ——to be cautious. [*Laughter*]

Lithuanian Independence

Q. Mr. President, as you call for these talks between the Soviets and the Lithuanians, are you envisioning government-to-government talks?

The President. I'm envisioning—let them sort it out any way they want to. And I'm envisioning that they know how to do that, and they don't need any advice from the President of the United States on how to do that.

Q. Well, what kind of a signal does it send that we ask the Soviets to negotiate with a group that we don't recognize as a government?

The President. Look, I'm for peaceful evolution. I don't care—we're not here to sit here and say who in Lithuania ought to talk to who in Moscow. How presumptuous and arrogant that would be for any President. So, I'd say let them sort it out. They're on the right track. Lithuanians have got elected leaders, and clearly the Soviets have a strong leader. They can figure that out without fine-tuning from the United States.

Travel to Australia and New Zealand

Q. Mr. President, some Down Under questions. The Australian elections are this week. Will you take up their offer to go to Australia, and if you go, would you also follow Secretary Baker's example and meet with any New Zealand officials?

The President. Come again on the second part of it.

Q. First of all, do you plan to go to Australia at any point after the elections?

The President. Well, I have no immediate plans. But I have been invited to go to Australia, and I'm dying to go to Australia. [*Laughter*] I really would like to do it, and I think it is very important that we not neglect our friends. Bob Hawke invited me. The last thing I want to do is intervene one way or another in the Australian elections. I know the heads of both the parties there, and I don't think the U.S. ought to indicate anything of that nature. But when I say Hawke invited me—he is the Prime Minister. Barbara and I both want to go back to Australia, and I hope we'll be able to do it before the end of the year.

Q. I have a second part, sir.

The President. What was it?

Q. If you go to Australia would you also go to New Zealand, or would you follow Secretary Baker's example and meet with New Zealand officials——

The President. I'd wait and see how events were at the time. We've had some differences on—that everyone's familiar with—with New Zealand and their policy against our ships, and so I'll wait to see how that evolved. We have a strong affection for the people there. I have been to New Zealand, as you may remember. But I would take a look at where things stood at the time.

Two more and then—I'm handed—Marlin is putting the hook on me here.

Lithuanian Independence

Q. Mr. President, back to Lithuania. Were you pleased to see the Senate amendment pushed by Senator Helms on Lithuania defeated?

The President. Well, I don't feel that Senate amendment would have been helpful.

Q. Why not?

The President. For the reasons I've stated here to about 20 different questions.

Travel to Nicaragua

Q. Will you be going to Nicaragua at all for the inauguration?

The President. I will not be going to Nicaragua for the inauguration. I hope to be going to Nicaragua at some point. I, as President, don't want to neglect our own hemisphere; and so we're talking about a trip that will take us well south of the Rio Grande.

Assistance for Nicaragua

Q. A followup: If you don't get your aid in time for your deadline, what can you do to get around Congress to get aid to Nicaragua?

The President. Continue to work for it, because I believe strongly in it. And I think that it is in our interest as well as the interest of Nicaragua to support them. We see the emergence of democracy there. We saw free and fair elections, where the people said please make a dramatic change. And now we feel that we want to support those who want to move down—as the Eastern Europeans have, as other countries in our own hemisphere have—the road to democracy.

Merit Pay for Federal Workers

Q. Mr. President, have you signed off on a proposal by your Office of Personnel Management to pay workers——

The President. On broccoli? [*Laughter*]

Q. To pay government workers on a merit basis rather than on how long they serve?

The President. The concept of trying to work in merit has my strong support. I have not signed anything in the last couple of days on that. I did talk to Connie Newman, the head of OPM, the other day. We had a meeting with the heads of a lot of these agencies, and she did discuss that. But the concept of merit has my broad support, but we have to finalize the policy.

Thank you all very much.

Broccoli

Q. Mr. President, have you lost the broccoli vote?

Q. What about it, since you brought it up?

Q. Yes, can you give us a broccoli statement?

The President. Now, look, this is the last statement I'm going to have on broccoli. [*Laughter*] There are truckloads of broccoli at this very minute descending on Washington. My family is divided. [*Laughter*] I do not like broccoli. [*Laughter*] And I haven't liked it since I was a little kid, and my mother made me eat it. And I'm President of the United States, and I'm not going to eat any more broccoli. [*Laughter*]

Wait a minute. For the broccoli vote out there, Barbara loves broccoli. [*Laughter*] She's tried to make me eat it. She eats it all the time herself. So, she can go out and meet the caravan of broccoli that's coming in from Washington. [*Laughter*]

Q. Cauliflower?

Q. Lima beans?

Q. Brussels sprouts?

[*At this point, the President made a thumbs-down gesture.*]

Q. Ah-ha, thumbs down on brussels sprouts.

Note. The President's 41st news conference began at 11:15 a.m. on the South Grounds of the White House. Marlin Fitzwater was Press Secretary to the President.

Appointment of Stephen P. Farrar as Special Assistant to the President for Policy Development
March 22, 1990

The President today announced the appointment of Stephen P. Farrar as Special Assistant to the President for Policy Development.

Since March 1989 Mr. Farrar has been Associate Director for International Economic Policy, Office of Policy Development. Prior to this, he was Special Assistant to the President and Senior Director of International Economic Affairs, National Security Council. From March 1986 to September 1988, he served as Director of International Economic Affairs, National Security Council. Mr. Farrar was chief of the economic affairs branch, International Affairs Division, Office of Management and Budget, from October 1980 to March 1986. He was an international economist in the International Affairs Division, Office of Management and Budget, from November 1972 until October 1980.

Mr. Farrar received a bachelor of arts degree in 1965 from Bowdoin College and a master of science degree in foreign service in 1967 from Georgetown University. He is married to the former Kathleen D. Clark and has two children, Sheila and Scott.

Appointment of Lawrence B. Lindsey as Special Assistant to the President for Policy Development
March 22, 1990

The President today announced the appointment of Dr. Lawrence B. Lindsey of Virginia to be Special Assistant to the President for Policy Development.

Dr. Lindsey has served as Associate Director for Domestic Economic Policy, Office of Policy Development, since January 1989. In September of 1989 he was named as Executive Director of the President's Council on Competitiveness, chaired by Vice President Quayle. Prior to joining the administration, Dr. Lindsey was an associate professor of economics at Harvard University, a position from which he is now on a leave of absence. Dr. Lindsey was also a faculty research fellow at the National Bureau of Economic Research. From 1981 to 1984, he served on the staff of the Council of Economic Advisers, where he became senior staff economist for tax policy.

Dr. Lindsey received his A.B. magna cum laude from Bowdoin College in 1976, where he was elected to Phi Beta Kappa. He received his M.A. from Harvard in 1981 and his Ph.D. from Harvard in 1985 in economics. Dr. Lindsey's doctoral dissertation won the National Tax Association's Outstanding Dissertation Award in 1985. In 1988 he was the recipient of the Citicorp/Walter Wriston Award for Economic Research. He was born on July 18, 1954, in Peekskill, NY, and attended Lakeland High School. Dr. Lindsey is married to the former Susan Ann McGrath of Wakefield, RI.

Appointment of Marianne McGettigan as Special Assistant to the President for Policy Development
March 22, 1990

The President today announced the appointment of Marianne McGettigan to be Special Assistant to the President for Policy Development.

Ms. McGettigan has served as Associate Director for Legal Policy, Office of Policy Development, since July 1989. Before joining the White House, Ms. McGettigan served as counsel to Senator Warren Rudman of New Hampshire, from 1987 to 1988, and as legislative counsel to Senator Slade Gorton of Washington State, from 1981 to 1986. From 1975 to 1981, Ms. McGettigan served in the Washington State Attorney General's Office. She was president of the Washington State Governmental Lawyers' Association from 1977 to 1979.

Ms. McGettigan received her B.A. in 1972 from Clark University, Worcester, MA, and her J.D. in 1975 from Boston University. In June 1989, she was awarded an M.P.A. from Harvard University's Kennedy School of Government, where she was honored as a Lucius N. Littauer fellow.

Accordance of the Personal Rank of Ambassador to Richard J. Smith While Serving as Special Negotiator for Acid Rain Talks With Canada
March 22, 1990

The President today accorded the personal rank of Ambassador to Richard J. Smith in his capacity as Special Negotiator for Acid Rain Talks With Canada.

Mr. Smith has served as Principal Deputy Assistant Secretary for the Bureau of Oceans and International Environmental and Scientific Affairs at the Department of State in Washington, DC, 1985–1989. Prior to this, he served as Deputy Assistant Secretary for Finance and Development in the Bureau of Economic and Business Affairs, 1983–1985; deputy chief of mission at the U.S. Embassy in Ottawa, 1980–1983; country director for Canada at the Department of State, 1978–1980; member of senior seminar in national and international affairs, 1977–1978; Director of the Office of Investment Affairs, 1974–1977; and Deputy Director of the Office of International Marketing at the Department of Commerce, 1971–1973. In addition, Mr. Smith has served as a financial economist in the Office of Monetary Affairs at the Department of State, 1971; second secretary in Stockholm, Sweden, 1968–1970; assigned to the University of Michigan, 1967–1968; South Africa desk officer at the Department of Commerce, 1965–1967; vice consul in Nagoya, Japan, 1963–1965; and Foreign Service officer, 1962 to present.

Mr. Smith received a bachelor of science degree and a master of arts degree from the University of Connecticut and a master of arts degree in economics from the University of Michigan. He was born February 28, 1932, in Hartford, CT. Mr. Smith is married, has three children, and resides in McLean, VA.

Nomination of Timothy Ryan To Be Director of the Office of Thrift Supervision
March 22, 1990

The President today announced his intention to nominate Timothy Ryan to be Director of the Office of Thrift Supervision, Department of the Treasury, for a term of 5 years.

Currently Mr. Ryan serves as a partner with the law firm of Reed, Smith, Shaw and McClay, formerly Pierson, Ball and Dowd, in Washington, DC. Prior to this, he was Solicitor at the U.S. Department of Labor in Washington, DC, 1981–1983; an attorney-advisor to board member Ralph Kennedy of the National Labor Relations Board; associated with the law firm of Venable, Baetjer

and Howard in Baltimore, MD; and deputy general counsel of the President Ford Committee, 1976. In addition, Mr. Ryan served as legal counsel for the Reagan/Bush transition, 1980, and as special counsel to the George Bush for President Committee, 1988.

Mr. Ryan graduated from Villanova University (A.B., 1967) and the American University Law School (J.D., 1973). He was born June 13, 1945, in Washington, DC. Mr. Ryan served in the U.S. Army, 1962–1970. He is married, has two children, and resides in McLean, VA.

Letter to Congressional Leaders Transmitting the Annual Report on International Activities in Science and Technology
March 23, 1990

Dear Mr. Speaker: (Dear Mr. Chairman:)

In accordance with Title V of the Foreign Relations Authorization Act of Fiscal 1979, as amended (Public Law 95–426; 22 U.S.C. 2656c(b)), I am pleased to transmit the annual report on international activities in science and technology (S&T) for fiscal year 1989.

A characteristic feature of our age is the unprecedented rate of change in science and technology. In 1989, however, the rate of change in foreign affairs, particularly in Eastern Europe, has surpassed even that of science and technology. These remarkable changes in Eastern Europe have provided expanded opportunities for S&T cooperation with countries of the Eastern Bloc.

For example, on July 13, 1989, during my visit to Budapest, Hungary, I committed the United States to work with Hungary to expand bilateral research exchanges between our two peoples. Subsequent negotiations resulted in the signing of an umbrella S&T agreement less than 3 months later. In addition, because of growing concern about the environmental problems that plague

the countries of Eastern Europe, I announced the creation of a new, independent Eastern European Environment Center in Budapest, along with initiatives to improve the environmental quality of the historic city of Krakow, Poland. We will continue to look for opportunities to integrate mutually beneficial science and technology cooperation with our broad foreign policy goals that are aimed at encouraging independence, democratization, and economic growth in emerging market economies of Eastern Europe.

My desire to preserve and improve humanity's common heritage and to address issues of the environment and global change found expression in a number of other activities. During the Paris Economic Summit, I joined other heads of state in calling for decisive action to understand and protect the earth's ecological balance. The United States was instrumental in establishing the Intergovernmental Panel on Climate Change as the primary international forum on this topic. These and other efforts highlighted in this report emphasize the need for nations to work together to understand the interconnected earth system and the ways in which human activity is influencing that system.

Because science and technology are truly international activities, it is frequently the case that scientists and technologists collaborate more closely with colleagues on the other side of the globe than with those at the other end of the hall. This international dimension of science is built on the person-to-person and institution-to-institution bonds that are formed through shared education, collaboration in research and development, and communications.

We in the United States pride ourselves on open access to our educational institutions, not only for students of this country but for students around the globe. Many foreign students have been eager to take advantage of this access, because it remains a fact that the United States has the best system of graduate education anywhere in the world.

The free flow of students finds a parallel in the free flow of ideas around the world today, particularly in the area of basic scientific knowledge. Much of the international character of science derives from its universality. The United States is firmly committed to the free and open international flow of basic scientific knowledge.

This philosophy also underlies the U.S. approach to a very important subset of our scientific efforts today—namely, the megaprojects in science, such as the Superconducting Super Collider, the human genome project, and Space Station Freedom. The results of these projects are a global resource adding to the knowledge base of all countries. We are moving toward a day when the responsibility for supporting large basic science projects will be distributed around the world, reflecting the truly international character of modern scientific research and the shared financial and intellectual underpinnings of that research.

Perhaps the most important element of federally funded international cooperation in S&T is the over 600 bilateral science and technology agreements involving more than 20 U.S. agencies, 120 foreign countries, and numerous multilateral organizations. These agreements—many of which are highlighted in this report—differ from one country to another, reflecting the state of that country's development and its past relations with the scientific community in the United States. However, there are several broad principles that apply in all our international science and technology agreements: comparable access, shared responsibilities for both basic and applied research, adequate protection and fair disposition of intellectual property rights, and effective protection of sensitive knowledge.

These agreements provide exciting opportunities for cooperation between the United States and the rest of the world, but we must remain cognizant of the fact that the global marketplace is becoming increasingly competitive. The United States still has the strongest science and technology enterprise that the world has ever seen, but we no longer are in a leading position in all fields. By concentrating resources and focusing efforts, other nations have succeeded in equaling and in some cases surpassing us in specific areas of research and technology.

This is part of the orderly development of nations and is due, at least in part, to the help that we provided to other countries since the end of World War II. But the internationalization of the marketplace emphasizes that we can no longer take our leadership for granted. In an increasingly competitive world, only a continuing effort to remain at the forefront of science and technology will ensure our economic and military security.

It has become increasingly clear that science and technology, the economy, and foreign relations are inextricably intertwined. Policy decisions must be made with a clear appreciation of the scientific and technological issues surrounding those decisions. We must find more creative and effective ways to ensure that science and technology are an integral and important part of our foreign policy around the globe. We have begun that process in 1989, and I look forward to continuing that effort in 1990 and beyond.

Sincerely,

GEORGE BUSH

413

Note: Identical letters were sent to Thomas S. Foley, Speaker of the House of Representatives; Claiborne Pell, chairman of the Senate Foreign Relations Committee; and John Glenn, chairman of the Senate Governmental Affairs Committee.

Remarks on United States Economic Assistance During a Meeting With Vice President Guillermo Ford of Panama
March 23, 1990

The President. Let me just say how pleased we are to see you here. I've heard of your effective work on Capitol Hill, and it is absolutely essential that the Congress move to pass this legislation that will bring urgent, needed help to Panama. And I want to thank you for what you're doing to get that message of democracy in Panama spread across Capitol Hill, and I wish you well. I hope you'll tell your colleagues when you go back that anything we can do to help, we want to do it. But I want to assure you: The priority is passage of this legislation.

Vice President Ford. Thank you very much, Mr. President. And on behalf of the Panamanian people—this is the first time I have a chance to meet with you again after Just Cause—God bless you. We are liberated. Now we're free. And we're ready to put our act together.

It has been absolutely wonderful up on the Hill. I think all the Congressmen and the Senators have been just very understanding of our need. We have expressed the necessity of doing it as rapidly as possible. And the most important thing is that this jump start, full battery charge, will allow us to put the show on the road and not having to come back every year, knocking on doors, asking for additional help.

The infrastructure in Panama is in place, and we're ready to start working. So, I hope that Congress will really look upon it very quickly and with full support.

The President. Well, we'll keep pushing from our end. And I am encouraged. I understand you saw 102 Senators, and that's a pretty good job. [*Laughter*] Might be it just felt like that. [*Laughter*] But really, it does help, and it's good to get that message out.

Note: The President spoke at 9:30 a.m. in the Oval Office at the White House.

The President's News Conference
March 23, 1990

The President. Well, once again, let me say welcome to the White House. I'm delighted you are all here. Sometimes I'm asked about traveling, why I do it so much, and I must tell you that I really do like to travel outside of the beltway to the rest of this country. And I'm delighted that all of you have traveled here to the White House.

I'm pleased to meet with such a broad cross section of journalists. Wherever you're from, whether you came all the way in from the West Coast—and some did—or whether your organization is based right here in Washington, I'm just delighted that you're here. The organizations you represent are part of a proud journalistic tradition, serving every State, every city, community across this country. In a moment, I'll be glad to take some questions, but just a brief statement.

I'll begin with a matter critical to the future of democracy in this hemisphere. All of us have followed the unfolding of freedom in Eastern Europe, and together with Congress, we've moved to offer American assistance to support those emergency [emerging] democracies in the East. Now, that assistance is crucial; it will continue. But there's work to be done, work that I feel is every bit as important, in support of democracy right here in our own hemisphere.

Panama and Nicaragua stand at a historic moment: on the threshold of democracy. In both nations, the people have spoken in favor of freedom, but the difficult work of democracy building remains. This hemisphere, the Americas, can become the first where democracy prevails from north to south. But it cannot happen if we in the United States fail to add our strength and support to the forces of democracy.

I'm pleased you're here today because this is a matter of tremendous interest to all Americans. Whether it's out in El Paso or Paducah, Kentucky; or Rochester, New York; or Jackson Hole, Wyoming, Angus— the American people believe that what this nation stands for depends on whether we stand with people who seek freedom and democracy.

Last week, I asked the Congress to act, and act quickly, on the aid package that I've proposed to Nicaragua and Panama. I renew that call today. And let me say to Congress: If agreement cannot be reached on finding the money that is needed for this fund for democracy, I am ready to make the hard choices. With Congress' authorization—and it would require that—I am ready to select offsets from the defense budget, break the logjam, and get these much-needed resources moving into the region. With democracy at stake, we really cannot afford delay.

Let me turn now just briefly to another part of the world I know you are all interested in: Lithuania. The brave men and women of Lithuania have made known their desire to reestablish the sovereignty of the Republic of Lithuania. The United States stands with them and supports their right to self-determination. This is a complex and sensitive time when realistic, level-headed leadership is required on all sides. Lithuanian leaders have consistently demonstrated their capacity in this regard, and the United States will do nothing that will make their task more difficult.

We've repeatedly urged the Soviet Government to enter into immediate negotiations with the Lithuanian Government, which has itself called for those talks. We know that the Soviet Union has a longstanding interest in Lithuania, but those interests can only be addressed through dialog and negotiation. Any attempt to coerce or intimidate or forcibly intervene against the Lithuanian people is bound to backfire. That is inevitable.

The Soviet leadership has said again and again that it will not use force, and we welcome that. And let me repeat, we have made clear to the Soviet Union that the situation in Lithuania can only be solved peacefully.

Now I'll be glad to take some questions. Right here.

New Taxes

Q. Mr. President, we've read your lips, and we've heard your words—no new taxes. Back home in western Pennsylvania, our government leaders are saying, no new taxes that you want to be blamed for. For example, your new transportation policy would cause taxes to go up in our area, would cause transit fares to go up in our area, and our government leaders say it's a disaster. The Federal Government doesn't want to share any more credit in this, but they want the local governments to take more of a burden. And therefore, local taxes will have to raise, therefore, if you can fulfill your promise.

The President. And they feel if the Federal Government spent it all, why, then it wouldn't cost anybody at home. Is that right? They're wrong. They're just as wrong as they can be. And I was very pleased that our transportation policy was endorsed by the National Association—I believe it was—State Legislators. Wasn't it, John? So, there's a difference. I mean, I know some take the line that you asked about, but we don't feel that way at all.

We think that by removing some of the impediments to development and leaving some of the financial responsibility in the hands of the States, that's the way to go. That's the Federal system. There is a good deal of Federal money in our national transportation program.

Sanctions Against South Africa

Q. You mentioned Lithuania and Eastern Europe. I want to go back to the South African question, especially considering Secretary Baker's travels there. A lot of people now are comparing de Klerk [State President of South Africa] to Gorbachev in terms of reform, but they're still concerned about the position on sanctions. Could you address that in terms of whether——

The President. Position on what, sir?

Q. Position on sanctions.

The President. Yes.

Q. Are we going to hold the line and keep them?

The President. Well, our law requires holding the line. We've made this very clear to the South Africans. I've invited both Mr. de Klerk and Mr. Mandela to come here. We have no dates set for either one. I strongly support the Secretary of State in the dialog he has established not only with Mandela and other leaders of the ANC [African National Congress] but with Mr. de Klerk. But I don't think this is the time to change the policy on sanctions.

There's some legislation in the Congress introduced by Ron Dellums which would add to the sanction base, and I don't believe that he's going to press that legislation at all. I met with him and Bill Gray and Dean Gallo and a bipartisan delegation that was in South Africa. And they presented this to me as a unanimous view—were impressed with what they heard from Mr. de Klerk, certainly impressed with what they heard from Mr. Mandela. So, I don't think this is a time to change in either direction. But I want to see more progress.

New York Gubernatorial Election

Q. Mr. President, on the local level, in New York State [Governor] Mario Cuomo is running for election this year. The Republican Party, your party, can't even find a candidate to go up against him.

The President. This is depressing me. [*Laughter*]

Q. Is Mario Cuomo that unbeatable? Can you give your assessment of this man, and do you have any plans to help out your party in New York State?

The President. I will certainly try to help out the party in the State. I hope we can find a good, strong candidate. And, yes, the man is a formidable political opponent. There's no question about that. So, I'm not standing up here to knock Mario Cuomo.

But I'd like to have the party find a strong opponent for him and have competitive races not just in New York State but in every State. But I think you've got it sized up just about where it stands right now. I'd like to think that there would be a strong opponent for him.

Q. Would you be willing to help? Do you have any suggestions——

The President. No, I don't. I've got all the problems that I can handle right here without trying to second-guess the party in New York. But it is something that I'm interested in, of course. These gubernatorial races have a tremendous impact on my line of work—the Federal Government—because of the redistricting that will take place after the '90 elections. So, there are some key Governors' races across this country to which I will devote attention and time in the fall.

Cuba

Q. Mr. President, I'm from Miami, so my question has to do about Cuba. Tell us the policy of the United States as of now toward Cuba as the last military regime in this hemisphere and also if the United States would be willing to help the new Cuban Government after Castro is gone, like it's helping Panama and Nicaragua.

The President. Well, your question implies that Castro will be gone, but clearly the United States would rejoice in being able to help a democratically elected government in Cuba. I am convinced that the people of Cuba want the same thing that the people of Nicaragua demonstrated that they wanted, the people of Panama demonstrated that they wanted, and the rest of the countries in the hemisphere have demonstrated that they want: democracy and freedom.

And Castro has not changed. Indeed, he's swimming against the tide. And I don't believe there would be any resistance from any quarter to helping the people of Cuba once they had the right to express themselves in free and fair elections.

I don't think it will do much good, but I would encourage Castro to move toward free and fair elections. I would encourage him to lighten up on the question of human rights, where he's been unwilling to even welcome the U.N. back to take a look again. And I am not going to change the policy of the United States Government towards Mr. Castro. We're going to continue to try to bring the truth to Cuba, just as we did to Czechoslovakia and Poland and other countries.

Texas-Mexico Border Communities

Q. Your administration is opposed to a provision in the Rural Economic Development Act that would provide $30 million in loans to people living in along the Texas-Mexico border. These loans would be used to install indoor plumbing. The Texas Senate is taking up the resolution today, a plea for the administration to reconsider its opposition. These people, about 300,000, live without running water and sewage facilities—[*inaudible*]. If the administration won't make available loans, is there any other help that you might be able to offer these people?

The President. I know of the problem. I must say, with some embarrassment, I don't know of exactly where that provision stands in terms of support or not support from the administration. But it is a serious problem, and it concerns people on both sides of our border, and it's a health question. And I will try to get back to you, in El Paso, with an answer to what we might do if this provision is not supported for budgetary reasons.

Foreign Aid

Q. We asked our readers to bring their questions to you, and the question that seemed to come up most was—you referred to it today: In the face of all the problems the United States faces—homelessness, et cetera—why are we spending so much money overseas? Why don't we spend some of that money at home? Secondly, many also asked: If you want to fight the war on drugs and be the environment President and the education President, where do you plan to find the money to do that, and is it time to start reading their lips and think about raising taxes?

The President. Well, I've had very few people writing in to say please raise my taxes. But nevertheless, on why do we establish the priorities the way we do—I think it is in our own national interest to see the fledgling democracies of Eastern Europe and of this hemisphere prevail. I think, in a final analysis, it will be to our financial interest, as well, because we will help create stable democracies that will actively trade with the United States.

Secondly, I realize, having been a Member of Congress, that foreign aid is not the most popular account to vote for. I understand that. Never has been. In terms of the total percentage of the budget, it still remains a relatively small percent.

What was the other part of it?

War on Drugs

Q. The idea that you want to——

The President. Why don't we raise—yes. Well, I think——

Q. I don't think they were asking specifically for taxes, but they are questioning where you plan to get——

The President. Yes. Well, I believe that our National Strategy II—and I see Bill Bennett [Director of National Drug Control Policy] here—is receiving very strong support. We've had a tremendous increase in the amount of Federal funds that are going into the drug fight. It's close to $10 billion. What is the exact increase?

Mr. Bennett. A 70-percent increase since you took office.

The President. Since I've taken office. People don't realize this. But the exciting thing on the drug fight—I salute Bill Bennett and his efforts for what we are doing—but I honestly can say to the American people I think we are beginning to make significant progress. And I'm not simply pointing to the decline in high school senior use of cocaine—that's an important figure, down by one-third. I think there's an awareness, a national awareness now, that is going to inevitably lead to success in the war against drugs. There is certainly an international awareness that we didn't have a couple of years ago. And I was involved in it a couple of years ago—the fight.

We're getting strong cooperation from

countries around the world. We are trying to encourage the Congress to go forward with a strong law enforcement package. But I will take this opportunity to say I really do believe in my heart of hearts that we are starting to make significant progress, and we are going to keep the pressure on.

But the money that's spent by the Federal Government is a tiny percentage of the work that is being done at the State, at the local level, and also at what I think is the Points of Light level. The dynamism of individuals participating is fantastic.

Oilspills

Q. Hi, I'm from California, from Los Angeles. And tomorrow, Saturday, is the first-year anniversary of the Nation's worst oilspill, and just last month we in California averted what could have been a disaster in Huntington Beach. And experts are telling us that another one is inevitable. What is the Federal Government doing to guarantee the people of southern California that their beaches are going to be protected?

The President. I think the Federal Government, with the Coast Guard and our Department of Energy, are working very cooperatively with the environmental—and our EPA—working closely with the environmental officials in the State of California. But may I answer your question by a question? Is it proposed that we have no more tankers going into California? And if the answer to that is yes, how do you get heat, how do you get energy?

And so, what we're trying to do in this regard is to have a whole new look in the Coast Guard, Department of Transportation, EPA, looking at it as to shipping lanes to see what is the best—whether there's a way to shift the shipping lanes to avert proximity to the beaches as much as possible.

It isn't going to be possible to deny access to tankers, and we don't want that. So, what the answer is: Make it as safe as possible. But if you're saying to me, can the Federal Government guarantee that no tanker will ever again have a leak or spill oil, no, I can't do that. And I don't think any reasonable person can suggest that be done. But we can go the extra mile in terms of environmental protection—safeguarding the sea-

lanes and all of that.

Q. What about double-hulled tankers and——

The President. They're moving towards that, yes. But everything we do has a price tag, and you have to look at every suggestion—the cost benefit. Fortunately, the most recent spill, I am told, does not appear to have lasting environmental damage, and I hope that proves to be right for the people of Huntington Beach.

I'm watching very closely the situation in Alaska because I think we would all agree that the reports at this time last year were total disaster to the environment in Alaska. Now we're beginning to get a little different view of that, and I hope there's reason to be somewhat more optimistic, although that was an unacceptable incident. And that is in the courts right now, so I guess I shouldn't say too much more about it.

But we will try, because I am committed to a sensitivity in anything that has to do with the environment. But I'm not going to throw everybody in America out of work. P.S.: Please support the compromise, the clean air bill that's up before the Senate.

Senator Jesse Helms

Q. Mr. President, as you're developing your administration's responses to the emerging democracies in Eastern Europe, how much of a help or hindrance has the activities of Senator Helms been on Capitol Hill?

The President. I have great respect for Senator Helms, as you know, and I will add friendship, as well. And in terms of Eastern Europe, Jesse Helms has been out in front for a long time as a proponent of democracy in Eastern Europe. And I don't expect he's going to change his view, and I hope he doesn't.

Private Sector Education Initiatives

Q. Mr. President, I'm from Rochester, New York, and one of the issues that came up in your last visit was promotion of Kodak for its involvement in the relationship between the private sector, school boards, and the public sector. Is your administration making progress with getting enough companies directly involved in the public-private partnership, and what kind of progress have you had so far?

The President. Yes, we are, and again, it's exhortation. There is an example of what I talk about when I talk about involvement—private company being involved in helping others, or an individual being helped—those monitors or those people that Kodak lends to the school community out there, on their own, helping others. And we are seeing progress being made. Another example I could cite to you that I've seen personally is Procter and Gamble's efforts in that regard in the city of Cincinnati, and we're seeing it happen in Kansas City.

So, it's breaking out all across this country. And Kodak, to its credit, through that marvelous program of almost a magnet school concept, went into a place—what he's talking about—went into a place where the school was just—people were fleeing it, they were escaping. Not only was it they weren't performing academically but the whole environment was one of fear for the kids. And this company—along with, I might add, an enlightened school board approach—decided to do something about it. Rolled up their sleeves. They didn't come up to Washington and say please pay for it all. And it was good; it's worked just beautifully.

Yes, right here, and then I'm told we've got three or four—let's take five more. This is one. Then I'll go peacefully.

Lithuanian Independence

Q. Mr. President, I understand from your national security adviser there are rumors of a possible event tomorrow in Lithuania. Is the potential for Soviet activity in Lithuania over this weekend of particular concern right now, having seen that intelligence?

The President. I see a lot of the intelligence on this. At this moment, I can't say I'm predicting some kind of conflagration over the weekend, and I hope not. And that's why I will continue to urge, through any forum possible, a peaceful resolution to this question. I am somewhat heartened by [Soviet Foreign Minister] Shevardnadze's statement to Jim Baker just the other day in that regard. But it is a matter of considerable tension, and I hope those tensions can be released through negotiation.

District of Columbia Statehood

Q. Mr. President, you talk a lot about support for democracies around the world. There are people who think the District of Columbia ought to be one of those democracies receiving your support. There are signs that have gone up, pointing out that DC is the last colony. How far is your administration willing to go in supporting full voting representation for the Nation's Capital in Congress, or even statehood?

The President. I'm opposed to it.

Q. Even any further voting representation?

The President. Well, I'd be willing to discuss something of that nature. But I am opposed to statehood. This is a Federal city, and in my view, it should remain that. Its funds come almost exclusively from the Federal Government. And so, put me down as unsympathetic to that particular case.

National Endowment for the Arts

Q. Mr. President, there's been a lot of flak lately about the National Endowment for the Arts and its grants to numerous groups that rile some conservatives. Your administration apparently is not proposing any direct, specific standards on content for future NEA grants, and I'd like you to explain that, if possible.

The President. I will. I'd be glad to. First place, I have full confidence in John Frohnmayer, whom I've appointed—came here from Oregon to run the NEA. That's number one. Two, I am deeply offended by some of the filth that I see and to which Federal money has gone, and some of the sacrilegious, blasphemous depictions that are portrayed by some to be art. And so, I will speak strongly out opposed to that.

But I would prefer to have this matter handled by a very sensitive, knowledgeable man of the arts, John Frohnmayer, than risk censorship or getting the Federal Government into telling every artist what he or she can paint or how he or she might express themselves. So, I am against censorship, but I will try to convince those who feel differently in terms of legislation that we will do everything in our power to stop pure blasphemy. And I don't want to offend the American people by citing two horrendous examples of what I would call blasphemous material that has no business getting one cent of the taxpayers' money. Having said that, I don't know of anybody in the government or government agency that should be set up to censor what you write or what you paint or how you express yourself.

Military Base Closings

Q. This is a local issue involving a lot of jobs in Philadelphia. There's a major effort underway right now to save the Philadelphia Navy Yard, which is apparently on the Pentagon hit list of base closings. Do you get involved with those kinds of decisions? Will you?

The President. I get involved in them by recognizing that when you're trying to curtail spending and to protect the American taxpayer across this country there are going to be some tough decisions. The adage remains the same: Cut spending, but cut it in the other guy's congressional district. Be sure to cut it in somebody else's State. Don't cut it here. So, I get into it in a broad sense of saying to the Secretary of Defense: You make the tough calls. You go to the military and work with our able Chairman of the Joint Chiefs, General Powell. And you come with a list of where you can save the taxpayers money, given the changed requirements for defense around the world. You make the list, and I will support you. And I will support them, and we'll see how it works out.

Now, Congress—they have a major say in all of this. But I must say I am not sympathetic with the concept that some of our severest dove critics suddenly turn out to be tremendous hawks if you try to curtail expenditure in their own districts. And I'm not talking about the Philadelphia Navy Yard.

Academy Award Nominees

Q. Mr. President, on a quite different topic, the Oscars are this Monday, and I'm wondering if you think "Driving Miss Daisy" will win Best Picture?

The President. Now we're talking about some hard balls. I'll tell you this—and I'm going to get into trouble because—maybe I'd better not inject myself into this. But I

will just—you asked about one movie. I saw it, and I enjoyed it. But the thing that interests me—and please, Academy of Sciences or Arts, wherever you are, discount this—I have a lot of respect for Morgan Freeman, and he came here the other night, right in this room, and in a very emotional presentation, gave of his time—one of the Thousand Points of Light—to help kids in this country be inspired to learn to read. And that made a profound impression on me—that somebody with this notoriety, this fame, this acclaim as one of the great actors of our time, was willing to take his time to help some little kid somewhere out across this country.

Last one. Right here.

Coastline Cleanup

Q. Mr. President, residents of coastlands are concerned about the pollution that has washed up on their shores. Your budget cuts the reconstruction plans, and States say they can't make up the difference. What assurance can you give them that that——

The President. My answer is we're doing far better in terms of maritime pollution than I had thought we would after 1 year. And don't take my word for it; talk to the EPA Administrator, Bill Reilly. Because I read a report card—this one from environmentalists, objectively critiquing my record—and in it they were knocking, with a low mark, the progress—the marine pollution and pollution of the waters. And so, I said to Bill Reilly, "What is this? I thought we were doing better in this field." And he gave me a very stirring advocacy of the program that is doing a lot better. So, I can't address myself in terms of dollars to your question. We've got a big, fat budget, and I don't know the numbers. But I do think it's a very important area, and I think we've made dramatic progress.

And thank you all very much. I hate to cut it out here, with all these questions left, but I really do have to push on. And thank you for coming to the White House. One more—we have what is known as the shouted question as I go by. [*Laughter*]

Note: The President's 42d news conference began at 1:06 p.m. in the East Room at the

White House and was attended by regional journalists. John H. Sununu was Chief of Staff to the President. A tape was not avail- *able for verification of the content of the news conference.*

Nomination of Carl J. Kunasek To Be Commissioner on Navajo and Hopi Relocation
March 23, 1990

The President today announced his intention to nominate Carl J. Kunasek to be Commissioner on Navajo and Hopi Relocation. This is a new position.

Currently, Mr. Kunasek is a self-employed businessman in Mesa, AZ. Prior to this, he served as president of the Arizona State Senate, 1987–1989; State senator in Arizona, 1983–1989; State representative in the Arizona House of Representatives, 1973–

1983; and pharmacist and owner of three professional pharmacies in Mesa, AZ, 1961–1983.

Mr. Kunasek graduated from Creighton University (B.S., 1955). He was born May 23, 1932, in Omaha, NE. Mr. Kunasek served in the U.S. Air Force, 1955–1958. He is married, has three children, and resides in Mesa, AZ.

Statement by Press Secretary Fitzwater on the Expulsion of United States Diplomats From Lithuania
March 23, 1990

Our Embassy in Moscow today was informed that two U.S. diplomats in Vilnius were ordered to depart in 12 hours. They will comply. They will return to the U.S. consulate in Leningrad.

This action certainly adds to our concerns. It does not contribute to a lessening of tensions that would make productive dialog easier. We have protested, especially

in light of the fact that the United States has not acted in any way to exacerbate tensions.

In addition, it is unclear what specific actions have been taken against journalists. But we are opposed to any infringements on freedom of the press. The expulsion of journalists undermines the spirit of *glasnost.*

Statement on the Seventh Anniversary of the Strategic Defense Initiative
March 23, 1990

Today marks the seventh anniversary of the Strategic Defense Initiative. SDI offers an opportunity to shift deterrence to a safer and more stable basis through greater reliance on strategic defenses. Moreover, in a new international environment, as ballistic-

missile capabilities proliferate, defense against third-country threats also becomes an increasingly important benefit. Furthermore, strategic defenses can protect our security against possible violations of agreements to reduce strategic offensive weapons. In sum, in the 1990's, strategic defenses make much more sense than ever before.

Over the past 7 years, SDI has made great technological strides. In miniaturization, fast computers, powerful sensors, and dozens of other areas, SDI has pushed back the frontier of technology. In order to sustain that progress and to conduct realistic and rigorous tests of SDI concepts, we need to increase SDI's budget, even as we make real cuts in the overall defense budget. I therefore urge the Congress to support my request for SDI funding. I am committed to a robust SDI program to give us the means to defend the United States and our allies against ballistic missile attack.

Appointment of James D. Wolfensohn as a Member of the Board of Trustees of the John F. Kennedy Center for the Performing Arts
March 26, 1990

The President has announced his intention to appoint James D. Wolfensohn to be a member of the Board of Trustees of the John F. Kennedy Center for the Performing Arts, Smithsonian Institution, for the remainder of the term expiring September 1, 1996. He would succeed Joe L. Allbritton.

Currently Mr. Wolfensohn serves as president of James D. Wolf, Inc., in New York, NY. He is married, has three children, and resides in New York, NY.

Statement by Press Secretary Fitzwater on Lithuanian Independence
March 26, 1990

We have been urging a peaceful dialog to resolve this issue. The Soviets themselves have publicly and privately assured us that they have no intention of using military force to resolve the issue. We have also urged that neither side undertake any actions which could preclude the continuation of this dialog. It is incumbent that both sides maintain open communication and not take any actions that can be misinterpreted.

While I do not want to hypothesize on any eventual outcomes, it is clear that any efforts to coerce or intimidate the Lithuanian people is bound to backfire. Further actions will not lead to a lessening of the tensions, could have adverse international repercussions, and could be counterproductive for U.S.-Soviet relations.

Note: Press Secretary Fitzwater read the statement during his daily press briefing, which began at 10:02 a.m.

Nomination of Philip C. Jackson, Jr., To Be a Member of the Oversight Board of the Resolution Trust Corporation
March 26, 1990

The President today has announced his intention to nominate Philip C. Jackson, Jr., to be a member of the Oversight Board of the Resolution Trust Corporation for a term of 3 years. This is a new position.

Currently Mr. Jackson serves as an adjunct professor at Birmingham Southern College in Birmingham, AL. Prior to this he served as vice chairman of Central Bankshares of the South in Birmingham, AL. He is married, has three children, and resides in Birmingham, AL.

Accordance of the Personal Rank of Ambassador to Frederic V. Malek While Serving as Director of the 1990 Economic Summit
March 26, 1990

The President today accorded the personal rank of Ambassador to Frederic V. Malek in his capacity as director of the 1990 economic summit.

Currently Mr. Malek serves as president of Northwest Airlines in Minneapolis, MN. Mr. Malek is married, has two children, and resides in McLean, VA.

Letter to Congressional Leaders Transmitting a Report on Compliance With Arms Control Agreements
March 27, 1990

Dear Mr. Speaker: (Dear Mr. Chairman:)

Pursuant to section 52 of the Arms Control and Disarmament Act, as amended (22 U.S.C. 2592), I am pleased to transmit the enclosed report on the adherence of the United States to arms control treaty obligations and on problems related to compliance by other nations with the provisions of arms control agreements to which the United States is a party.

This report was prepared by the U.S. Arms Control and Disarmament Agency in coordination with the Departments of State, Defense, and Energy as well as the Joint Chiefs of Staff and the Director of Central Intelligence.

In previous reports to the Congress, I have made clear that the United States expects scrupulous compliance from its arms control treaty partners. For its part, the United States continues to take seriously its commitments to arms control agreements and sets rigid standards and procedures for assuring that it meets these obligations.

Sincerely,

GEORGE BUSH

Note: Identical letters were sent to Thomas S. Foley, Speaker of the House of Representatives, and Claiborne Pell, chairman of the Senate Foreign Relations Committee.

Remarks to the African Development Bank Roundtable
March 27, 1990

Being told in advance that this distinguished group was here, I just wanted to stop over and say a quick hello. I hope your meetings have been fruitful; and I hope you'll get the idea that our administration and, hopefully, Congress—over which I have no control, I might add—agrees you all are doing the Lord's work and are on the right track in terms of investment. And so, I want to come over here to welcome officially the members of the African Business Roundtable to the United States and, more particularly, to the White House.

You know, Africa—I view it as a continent with enormous potential, richly endowed with natural resources and—from my own personal experience as Ambassador to the United Nations and then as one who has traveled rather extensively in Africa—richly endowed with warm and very friendly people. And we all recognize that Africa faces tremendous challenges. I don't know how one quantifies the problems facing each continent, but I know they're tough; I know they're extraordinarily complex in Africa. Overcoming poverty—I'll never be the same as when I was in the northern part of Africa and went across the Sahel and saw some of the famine there. The disease problems—I do salute those who have worked hard in that, the United Nations and others making a significant contribution. And I hope our country has, and we will continue to try to. But I know it concerns everybody here. And then, of course, there's always unresolved, tragic and, I would say, needless armed conflicts. So, this presents a picture of not just events that adversely affect one continent—it affects a lot of them—but certainly something that I think we would all agree—these things plague Africa.

But Africa's most fundamental challenge, I think, is on the economic development side: harnessing the continent's natural and human resources side to create better and richer lives for all of the people there. Governments clearly have a role to play, and African political leaders need to create the proper economic framework for development. Donors, including the United States, have an opportunity to encourage and to support sound economic policies, moving the market forces as much as possible—private incentives, private ownership. But the key to a richer and more vibrant economy across the continent is found, I think, therefore, in the private sector, not in the hands of governments. That's why you and other African entrepreneurs represent the bright promise of Africa's economic future working, I hope, more and more with America. You're doing exactly the right thing in looking for investment opportunities at home, seeking support from private investors abroad, and working to develop mutually beneficial trade relationships.

I know that you have a busy schedule here in Washington. And I was told that you're going to see some "outside the beltway" America. We politicians always refer to Washington as "inside the beltway," meaning it's a little out of touch with the rest of the country. So, I am delighted to know that you're going to Atlanta and Dallas, in my home State of Texas—and that's where I got started in business. There's a good business ethic there, climate and feeling. I think you'll find a receptivity in that part of the world which I hope you'll see not only as hospitable but as something that's very promising economics-wise. The same thing would be true of Atlanta and throughout the rest of the country.

But I really just popped over here to wish you a very enjoyable stay. We're glad you came, and we trust that this visit will prove profitable as well as enjoyable. So, good luck in your important work. You really are on the same wavelength we are in terms of our approach to much of the evolution that's taking place in Eastern Europe and, indeed, in our own hemisphere. We think that the private sector stabilization and growth is very, very important, and I think the business groups such as this can disproportionately contribute to the well-being of the continent. So, thank you very much, and I hope we can work closely with you, President N'Diaye, and others as well, to be a catalyst for your success.

I don't know what goes next, but that's the end of my performance.

Note: The President spoke at 10 a.m. in the Indian Treaty Room at the Old Executive Office Building. Babacar N'Diaye is President of the Bank.

Remarks at a Luncheon Commemorating the Dwight D. Eisenhower Centennial
March 27, 1990

Ladies and gentlemen, welcome to the White House. Senator Dole, Speaker Foley, Commission and Foundation members, family of beloved Ike, and the distinguished foreign dignitaries that are here, Ambassadors, honored guests, I know that many of you have just come from this joint session of Congress. Let me just say welcome to the House that Ike and Mamie graced. Barbara said, You've got your nerve speaking after Walter Cronkite; Jim Robinson; Clark Clifford; Arnold Palmer; John Eisenhower, who I hear paid a magnificent tribute to his dad; and Winston Churchill—say nothing of distinguished Members of Congress. Well, somebody has to do the heavy lifting around here. [*Laughter*]

You know, every President admires other Presidents. Harry Truman was fond of Andrew Jackson. Gerald Ford studied Abraham Lincoln. And so, today I say it loudly and very proudly: I have always liked Ike. This year marks the centennial anniversary of Dwight Eisenhower's birth, a date your two groups have already done much to commemorate. And as we gather here, America still likes Ike. We like him because he was a man of character; good will was at the core. He was a healer, not a hater. And he had a deep faith in God, and he believed America to be divinely blessed.

Who will ever forget the last words he spoke on Earth: "I have always loved my wife. I have always loved my children. I have always loved my grandchildren. I have always loved my country." Second, America likes Ike because he liked us. He was one of us. We trusted him to act on behalf of us. In fact—fracturing syntax—he even spoke like us. [*Laughter*] Come to think of it, now I know why he's among my favorite Presidents. [*Laughter*]

But Ike once said, "I come from the heart of America." And so he did, enjoying what he called the great and priceless privilege of growing up in a small town. From small-town America, he learned values and ideals—what we term its culture. And he played football at the Point—followed it avidly—loved to read, loved TV westerns. Among his favorite groups was Fred Waring and the Pennsylvanians. And a few feet from here is where Ike had his famous putting green. He made golf, as I'm sure Arnold will attest to, a nationally popular sport.

And here's another reason America still likes Ike. He was intensely knowledgeable on becoming President, already a giant in foreign affairs. Of Ike it was said that he preserved civilization. Most Presidents try to save the world after they get elected. Well, he got started a little early. Few men were tested more severely. Think of it: 3 long years from the deserts of North Africa to the beaches of Normandy—3 long years, the fate of millions of brave fighting men in his hands.

And last December, off the coast of Malta, I spoke to the men of the U.S.S. *Forrestal*, where I recalled how, on D-day, Ike addressed the sailors, the soldiers, and airmen of the expeditionary force: "You are about to embark," he told them, "upon a great crusade. The eyes of the world are upon you." Ike was steadfast; he was courageous. As Supreme Commander, he met the supreme test. He helped bring peace to every corner of the world.

And finally, he was decisive, acting on

instincts that were invariably wise. You know, some critics can't figure out how Eisenhower was so successful as a President without that vision thing. Well, his vision— [*laughter*]—his vision was etched on a plaque, sitting on his desk, that many of you around here remember because you were there: "Gently in manner, strong in deed." And he used that vision not to demagog but deliver.

Listen to Ike's record of Presidential hits: 8 years of peace and prosperity, 8 years of domestic unity unparalleled in our history. He was a role model, everyone's second father. With Ike as President, father did indeed know best. And of course, he was inspired by one of the most gracious of all First Ladies, Mamie Doud Eisenhower, his wife of 52 years.

What a marvelous legacy Dwight Eisenhower left to all Americans, and how we treasure what he was and what he did. He embodied the very decade that he was President and remains the living symbol of freedom, at home and abroad. Ask anyone who shares the love of liberty: They, too,

still like Ike.

In life, he enriched us all, and now it's up to us to tell his story and so enrich our kids. And that's what your Commission and your Foundation are doing, and I thank you for it and pledge my help. And God bless this land that Ike so deeply loved.

Thank you all for coming to the White House.

Note: The President spoke at 12:37 p.m. in the State Dining Room at the White House. In his remarks, he referred to CBS News journalist Walter Cronkite; James D. Robinson III, chairman and chief executive officer of the American Express Co., Vice Chairman of the Dwight D. Eisenhower Centennial Commission, and chairman of the Eisenhower Centennial Foundation; Clark M. Clifford, who served in various capacities in the Truman, Kennedy, and Johnson administrations; golf professional Arnold Palmer; John Sheldon Doud Eisenhower, son of President Eisenhower; and British Member of Parliament Winston S. Churchill, grandson of Prime Minister Churchill.

Statement by Press Secretary Fitzwater on the Emigration of Soviet Jews
March 27, 1990

The United States has long championed the right to emigrate from the Soviet Union and has welcomed Soviet decisions enabling greater numbers of Soviet citizens to choose to leave. That many Soviet Jews are going to Israel is a historic event. The President is disappointed, therefore, at the unfortunate developments of recent days which have had the effect of severely limiting the passage out of the U.S.S.R. of large numbers of Soviet Jews heading to Israel via Hungary. Especially disturbing is the decision by the Hungarian airline Malev—citing terrorist

threats—to restrict travel opportunities for Soviet Jews.

The Polish Government has expressed its willingness to consider expanding transit for Soviet Jews through Poland. We applaud such a resolute approach and call upon other nations, particularly in Eastern Europe, to do the same. We urge Hungary's airline to reconsider its position. We also urge the Soviet Union once again to implement the agreement with Israel for direct flights.

Remarks at the Posthumous Presentation of the Congressional Gold Medal to Jesse Owens
March 28, 1990

The President. Well, this is so nice. And I was just telling Mrs. Owens I'm sorry Barbara is not here and that we view this as a very special occasion. But to Congressman Stokes and Senator Metzenbaum and then friends and teammates of the legendary Jesse Owens, welcome, all of you, to the White House.

It's my pleasure to welcome you here to the White House to honor a man who really honored his own nation—Olympic hero and an American hero every day of his life. Jesse Owens was born with the gift of burning speed, and he took that God-given talent and developed it through years of training. And he was always the fastest. One afternoon in 1935 in Ann Arbor, Michigan, he set three world records and tied a fourth—all in 45 minutes. You talk about a young guy in a hurry—well, I think maybe that was—[*laughter*]—he was the epitome of that.

As an 18-year-old in 1933, he won the city of Cleveland championship—the 100-yard dash in 9.4, tying the world record while still in high school. He burst onto the world scene in 1936, and I think every American that studies history remembers this—the 1936 Olympics, Hitler's Olympic games, the last Olympics before the outbreak of the Second World War. And the Berlin games were to be the showcase of Hitler's theories on the superiority of the master race until this 23-year-old kid named Jesse Owens dashed to victory in the 100-, the 200-, and the 400-meter relay. It was an unrivaled athletic triumph. But more than that, it really was a triumph for all humanity.

And Jesse Owens returned to this nation a hero, a household name, billed as the fastest man on Earth. But it's what he did after the spectacular performance of the Berlin games that earned him the enduring gratitude of all Americans. Jesse dedicated himself to upholding the Olympic ideal of sportsmanship and the American ideals of fairplay, hard work, and open competition.

And I know that his friend and fellow Clevelander, Harrison Dillard—now, which is Harrison? Right here, right behind you—Harrison Dillard, right here today. In 1941, at the Ohio State high school track championship, Harrison's idol, Jesse Owens—you correct me if I'm wrong, now—gave him a new pair of track shoes. And that day, Harrison Dillard won two State titles in those new shoes. And 7 years later, as we all remember, he brought home the gold medal at the 1948 Olympics in Jesse's event, that 100-meter dash, in the first games held since those Berlin games.

Jesse's example and influence extended to Olympians like Harrison Dillard and to all other athletes across the country, and he became a special ambassador for sports—a man who taught the ideals that I just mentioned were the key to success not just on the athletic field but in the game of life. And that legacy lives today through the Jesse Owens Games, a playground olympics open to kids from 8 to 15 years old all across our country; through the Jesse Owens International Trophy Award, presented each year to the best amateur athlete in America; and of course, through the Jesse Owens Foundation, which enables talented young people who can't afford college to fulfill that dream and get a degree. And I know it's a point of pride to Ruth Owens that the Jesse Owens Scholarships are awarded without regard to race, creed, or color.

And it's that legacy that we celebrate here today. And we remember Jesse Owens not only as the first athlete in Olympic history to win four gold medals. Today, 10 years since the passing of this great hero, it's my honor to add to Jesse Owens' collection a fifth gold medal—this one, as Ruth Owens said on Capitol Hill, for his humanitarian contributions in the race of life.

Mrs. Owens, it is with great pride and in honor of your late husband and his lasting achievements that I present to you this Congressional Gold Medal, the Jesse Owens

Congressional Gold Medal. And we're just delighted you came here to receive it.

Mrs. Owens. Mr. President, thank you so very much for this honor. Like your predecessors, President Ford, President Carter, who have recognized Jesse for his many contributions. Jesse achieved the unique distinction of being a legend in his own time. Despite the many honors, his greatest satisfaction came from his work with youth. Jesse's work with youth is now carried on

through, as you mentioned, the Jesse Owens Foundation, the ARCO [Atlantic Richfield Co.] Jesse Owens Games, and the International Amateur Athletic Association, spearheaded by Herb Douglas.

On behalf of the youth he still inspires, and on behalf of my family, we thank you.

Note: The President spoke at 11:50 a.m. in the Roosevelt Room at the White House.

Nomination of Michael L. Williams To Be an Assistant Secretary of Education
March 28, 1990

The President today announced his intention to nominate Michael L. Williams to be Assistant Secretary for Civil Rights at the Department of Education. He would succeed LeGree S. Daniels.

Since 1989 Mr. Williams has served as Deputy Assistant Secretary for Law Enforcement at the Department of the Treasury in Washington, DC. Prior to this, he served as Special Assistant to the Attorney General at the Department of Justice, 1989; domestic policy analyst for Bush-Quayle 1988 in Washington, DC, 1988; associate attorney with the law firm of Cotton, Bledsoe, Tighe and Dawson in Midland, TX,

1988–1989; senior trial attorney at the Department of Justice in Washington, DC, 1984–1988; and chief prosecutor and assistant district attorney in Midland, TX, 1984. In addition, he served as an attorney in private practice in Midland, TX, 1980–1984; and as an economic development planner for the Midland Chamber of Commerce, 1980–1982.

Mr. Williams graduated from the University of Southern California (B.A., 1975; M.P.A., 1979; J.D., 1979). He was born May 31, 1953, in Midland, TX. Mr. Williams is married and resides in Falls Church, VA.

Appointment of Don M. Newman as United States Representative on the Council of the International Civil Aviation Organization With the Rank of Minister
March 28, 1990

The President today announced his intention to appoint Don M. Newman to be the Representative on the Council of the International Civil Aviation Organization. The President also announced his intention to nominate Mr. Newman for the rank of Minister during his tenure of service as Representative. He would succeed Edmund Stohr.

Mr. Newman served as Acting Secretary at the Department of Health and Human Services in Washington, DC, 1989. In addition, he has served as Under Secretary at the Department of Health and Human Services, 1986–1989; Principal Deputy at the Department of Health and Human Services, 1985–1986; director of the Washington office of Indiana Governor Orr,

1980–1985; and director of the Washington office of Indiana Governor Bowen, 1973–1980. He also served as a registered pharmacist for 18 years in South Bend and Mishawaka, IN.

Mr. Newman graduated from Purdue University (B.S., 1947), Indiana University (M.S.B.A., 1972; M.B.A., 1989), and Georgetown University (J.D., 1979). He was born July 31, 1923, in Chicago, IL. Mr. Newman served in the U.S. Army Air Corps, 1943–1945. He has two children and resides in Washington, DC.

Statement on the Seizure of Nuclear Weapon Component Shipments to Iraq
March 28, 1990

The arrest of Iraqis in London raises once again the administration's deep concern about the issue of nuclear proliferation in the Middle East. Nuclear proliferation, along with the proliferation of chemical and biological weapons and intermediate range missiles, continues to pose serious threats to U.S. interests, as well as the interests of our friends in the region. These programs only serve to heighten regional tensions and exacerbate regional problems.

We again call upon nuclear suppliers to exercise special restraint in providing materials related to the development of nuclear, chemical, and biological weapons and intermediate range missiles in this volatile area. Furthermore, we urge all states in the area to adhere to the nonproliferation treaty. Iraq is a signatory of that treaty. Iraqi officials are well aware of our views on nuclear proliferation, which we have made clear on several occasions.

Remarks at the United States Olympic Committee Dinner
March 28, 1990

Senator Mitchell, thank you, George. And let me just say this: Good athletes can't run on dirty air. And George Mitchell is doing more to lead this country towards a new clean air bill than anyone else, and I am very grateful to him for his leadership there in the Senate. And thank you. I know that the minute this is over, he'll rush back up because the Senate is in session. I know he can afford to rent a tuxedo, but—[*laughter*]—he comes down, leaves, and in just a couple of minutes you turn on CNN, and there he'll be up there on the floor. So, thank you, sir, for taking time.

To you, Barney, thank you, sir, for being here and, more important even than that, for what you and your great organization are doing to support the Olympics.

To Bob Helmick and the members of the Olympic Committee, my thanks to all of you; and to Don and Vernie, for providing a little professionalism in the announcing; and to all the world-class athletes assembled here. I don't want to date—well, put it this way, I don't want to see that Bob Mathias is dated chronologically—[*laughter*]—but he and I were elected to Congress on the very same day in 1966, and I'm delighted to see my old comrade in politics here.

It's been a big day for me. I received some of the Olympic leaders in the Oval Office, and just now I've been given some wonderful Olympic sweats backstage. I'll wear them with pride and hope I don't get in trouble for impersonating an athlete. [*Laughter*]

Bar and I are leaving before dinner, and I apologize for that. We heard you were having broccoli. [*Laughter*] But we do excuse ourselves. The thing that some of you from out of town don't know, if the guy that speaks leaves before dinner, the talk is refreshingly short; and I will try to oblige you all so these guys can sit down.

But it's a special evening. And in ancient Greece—true story—competing in the games was the highest honor a citizen could receive. And back then, athletes that won didn't pay taxes for the rest of their lives. I'll get back to you on that. [*Laughter*]

Hey, listen, it's an honor to be among such talent—all of you here and many former medalists. Others are hard at work to bring home the gold in '92, '96, even '98, when, if you'll pardon the plug, we hope to see the games back in America in two of our most spectacular cities, Atlanta and Salt Lake City.

Let me put in a plug for fitness. We want to see every kid in America get and stay in shape. Arnold Schwarzenegger is doing a great job leading the President's Council on Physical Fitness, and I'd love to have each and every one of you help him in your own way. We need your support on this.

These men and women behind me represent some of America's greatest hopes and aspirations. They are portraits of pure dedication. Maybe it's their discipline that sets them apart, their natural talents, as George said, their will to win. But I think it's something more. They aspire to a kind of excellence that transcends the triumph of mind over muscle, of bodies over stopwatch, distance, high bar, hurdle. Their sense of purpose breaks through barriers of every kind. Through the hours and weeks and years of training, with every breath taken, with every heartbeat, they're moving toward a moment—and you know the oath—where they will compete "for the honor of our country and for the glory of sport." And they prove that in sport no one is advantaged. Where you come from, the color of your skin, whether you're rich, you're poor—it doesn't matter. It's just you against your opponent; it's your own limits.

Olympic athletes understand and show the world what it means simply to strive. They teach us about the triumph of the spirit, about breaking through barriers, and they speak to our highest ideals. Sometimes it's about beating odds and defying expectations. A little girl with polio from Clarks-ville, Tennessee, grew up to make the bronze medal-winning 1956 U.S. relay team. Four years later she became the first U.S. woman to win three Olympic golds. Tonight, she's fulfilling another ambition: working with the children's foundation she established. Her name: Wilma Rudolph.

During another Olympiad, an underdog discus thrower fell during practice, tore the cartilage in his ribcage. Somehow, over the next 2 days, with his torso turning shades of black, green, blue, and yellow, he made it to the finals, made one last throw, and won the gold medal. He's since become the only athlete to win gold medals in four successive Olympiads. You applauded him tonight: Al Oerter. He's with us here.

At other times, Olympians break barriers of another kind. In Berlin—we'll never forget it—in 1936, Hitler's Olympic Games were supposed to showcase his theories about the superiority of his so-called master race, until a 23-year-old black American, Jesse Owens, exploded to victories in the 100-, the 200-, and the 400-meter relay—and Hitler left the stadium. It was an athletic triumph, but more than that, it really was a victory for humanity. Ruth Owens was at the White House earlier today. She, too, I believe, is with us here tonight. She received, in her husband Jesse Owens' memory, the Congressional Gold Medal. His sprints to glory will forever be celebrated in America's heart. When Jesse Owens broke through a barrier made of man's own ignorance, the world would never be the same again.

Olympiads, like Olympians, are unique: they unite the world in purpose and principle. Something as small as a ping-pong ball brought Americans to China, paving the way for a breakthrough in relations in 1971. The world smiled then, as Zhou Enlai stood next to a 19-year-old from Santa Monica, discussing the hippie movement with him and gazing at his purple pants and his ponytail.

If Olympic competition is a drama, it's about great people and great contests, uniting mind with body, athlete with coach, player with player, toward a common purpose. Among so many of them, who could forget 1980, in a tiny town in upstate New

York, when a group of American kids—one of them here with us tonight—grabbed the American flag, took to the ice, and beat the unbeatable.

You watch an athlete in motion, and you might just see the bonds of human limits shattered in a fraction of a second, redefined forever. But the real lesson Olympic athletes teach, the hope and inspiration they offer, is that nations might aspire to the same measure of excellence in their own conduct.

If athletes have the courage to break barriers, so must nations. And if the athlete's mind and body are among the highest expressions of God's perfection, nations should aspire to the same perfection. If we could make it so—and with enough will, we can—what would we want the world to look like by the next Olympiad?

In a rebirth of the Old World, in a new Europe, we would heal the wounds of 40 years of false division on a continent made whole and free by the will of its people. In South Africa, as in every nation, we would see the abolition of racial and religious discrimination, making bigotry and bias the dusty relics of the past once and for all. In Asia and in this hemisphere, we would count the blessings of democracy, pluralism, and self-determination.

The Olympics, like democracy, are a kind of dialog, a way that nations can converse in the language of friendly competition, not deadly conflict. What nations can learn from their athletes, I believe in all my heart, can truly move the world toward greater freedom, justice, security, prosperity, and understanding.

You might say, Well, does that sound impossible? So did the 4-minute mile. So did so many barriers believed to be insurmountable, from the 29-foot long jump to the triple axel. Last year we saw a massive political barrier crumble, as young men and women joined hands atop the Berlin Wall. In 1992 we'll see skiers fly by in an icy blur of speed. We'll see sprinters explode out of the blocks so hard that the Earth may almost move. We'll see a half ton of iron hoisted skyward and a vaulting pole handled like the bow of a fine violin. We'll see tiny gymnasts defy gravity, bending the laws of physics. When the world watches those athletes, let it be reminded how much it has to learn from them. Let every nation of the world know that the only barrier remaining now is the will to make the world better.

To the once and future medalists with us tonight: You know that we admire you. You're often told that what you do brings honor to your nation. And so it does. But in these times of great change, we must do more than simply admire: we should strive to be your equals in our own pursuits. As we approach a new Olympiad, may we all remember that just as these athletes pursue a dream and serve as an inspiration for their country, America still serves as a dream and an inspiration for the entire world.

So, keep training, keep struggling, keep breaking through barriers, and the world will follow you. Thank you all. And God bless the United States of America. Thank you very, very much.

Note: The President spoke at 8 p.m. in the Regency Ballroom at the Omni Shoreham Hotel. In his remarks, he referred to Bernard Tresnowski, president of the Blue Cross and Blue Shield Association; Robert Helmick, president of the U.S. Olympic Committee; Don Criqui, of NBC Sports; and Vern Lundquist, of CBS Sports.

Remarks to the National Leadership Coalition on AIDS
March 29, 1990

The President. Well, thank you, Dr. Sullivan. And let me say at the outset of these remarks that I'm a very lucky person, and I think the country's very lucky, having Dr. Louis Sullivan as our Secretary of HHS. He's doing an outstanding job. And I want to thank Larry Williford, of Allstate; B.J. Stiles, from the coalition; and then salute Dr. June Osborn, Dr. David Rogers, and then Belinda Mason, of the AIDS Commission, with whom I just met in the Oval Office. And then, of course, my friend and the doctor to the President, who's been active in this cause for a long time, Dr. Burton Lee.

I'm delighted—and I really mean that—to be here with you today, the leaders who guide American business as it helps those suffering with HIV and AIDS. You make our hearts glad, and you make your country proud. Other generations have faced life-threatening medical crises, from polio to the plague. This virus is our challenge—not a challenge we sought; not a challenge we chose. But today our responsibility is clear: We must meet this challenge. We must beat this virus. For whether talking about a nation or an individual, character is measured not by our tragedies but by our response to those tragedies.

And for those who are living with HIV and AIDS, our response is clear: They deserve our compassion, they deserve our care, and they deserve more than a chance—they deserve a cure. America will accept nothing less. We're slashing redtape, accelerating schedules, boosting research. And somewhere out there, there is a Nobel Prize and the gratitude of planet Earth waiting for the man or woman who discovers the answer that's eluded everyone else.

We pray that that day will come soon. But until that day, until this virus can be defeated by science, there's a battle to be waged by society. Because in 1990, the most effective weapon in our arsenal against AIDS is not just medication but also education. Our goal is to turn irrational fear into rational acts.

And every American must learn what AIDS is and what AIDS is not, and they must learn now. You in this room are leaders. You already know. The HIV virus is not spread by handshakes or hugs. You can't get it from food or drink, coughing or sneezing, or by sharing bathrooms or towels or conversation. The transmission of HIV is as simple as it is deadly. In most cases, it's determined not by what you are but by what you do and by what you fail to do. Let

me state clearly: People are placed at risk not by their demographics but by their deeds, by their behavior. And so, it is our duty to make certain that every American has the essential information needed to prevent the spread of HIV and AIDS, because while the ignorant may discriminate against AIDS, AIDS won't discriminate among the ignorant.

Like many of you, Barbara and I have had friends who have died of AIDS. Our love for them when they were sick and when they died was just as great and just as intense as for anyone lost to heart disease or cancer or accidents. And probably everyone here has read the heartbreaking stories about AIDS babies and those infected by transfusions. When our own daughter was dying of leukemia, we asked the doctor the same question that every HIV family must ask: Why? Why is this happening to our beautiful little girl? And the doctor said, "You have to realize that every well person is a miracle. It takes billions of cells to make a well person, and all it takes is one cell to be bad and to destroy a whole person."

In this nation, in this decade, there is only one way to deal with an individual who is sick: with dignity, with compassion, care, and confidentiality—and without discrimination. Once disease strikes, we don't blame those who are suffering. We don't spurn the accident victim who didn't wear a seatbelt. We don't reject the cancer patient who didn't quit smoking. We try to love them and care for them and comfort them. We don't fire them; we don't evict them; we don't cancel their insurance.

Today I call on the House of Representatives to get on with the job of passing a law, as embodied in the Americans With Disabilities Act, that prohibits discrimination against those with HIV and AIDS. We're in a fight against a disease, not a fight against people. And we will not, and we must not, in America tolerate discrimination.

The disease is attacking our most precious resource, our people, especially our young; and the statistics are numbing. You know them; you heard them this morning. Just look at the quilts, the amazing quilts hanging here on the walls today. They prove that no one is a statistic. Every life has its own fabric, its own colors, its own purpose, its own soul. And like the quilts, no two are alike.

When Barbara and I left Washington for Christmas, our last stop was out there at that marvelous clinic at NIH [National Institutes of Health]. We were impressed by the determination of the people there—the doctors, researchers, nurses, health-care workers, and especially the brave people who are living with HIV. We learned a lot about caring, a lot about family, and a lot about hope. And we saw the face of humanity in the face of AIDS.

You, too, are in a powerful, unique position to influence the response to HIV and AIDS. Washing our hands of it won't help solve the problem; rolling up our sleeves will. The roster of participants at this conference is an honor roll. Allstate sponsored a landmark conference on HIV and work. Fortune magazine launched a survey on CEO's response to HIV. General Motors pledged to conduct an education program. Others are fighting the spread of HIV by fighting to keep schools and workplaces drug-free. And this is America responding to a crisis, and this is America at its best.

This epidemic is having a major impact on our health-care system. The Federal response is unprecedented. In 1982 we knew little about AIDS and spent only $8 million. But this year I have asked Congress for almost $3.5 billion to battle HIV—money for basic research, for HIV treatment and education, for protecting civil rights. From Seattle to Boston, from Dallas to Detroit, Federal grants have helped coordinate the efforts of care providers, business, and community organizations to set priorities and pool resources to meet the treatment needs of people with AIDS.

We've initiated clinical trials for promising new therapies for HIV, expanded the availability of experimental drugs, approved three new therapies that for the first time offer help to HIV-infected people before they become sick with AIDS. We've started a toll-free number where HIV patients and doctors can get state-of-the-art information on new treatments, worked with the PTA to distribute hundreds of thousands of copies of the "AIDS Prevention Guide" for use in schools and families nationwide. And

our $10 billion war on drugs is also a war on AIDS. IV drug use now accounts for some of the fastest growing infection rates, afflicting Americans that are often among those least able to get adequate medical help.

America has the most sophisticated health-care system in the world, but it is not without its problems. We face many challenges. Our system depends on private insurance and individual payments, as well as government programs. AIDS magnifies the challenges, including the challenge of expanding access, bringing costs under control, and overcoming obstacles to quality care. With these concerns in mind, I asked Dr. Louis Sullivan to lead a Cabinet-level review of health care in the 1980's. And businesses like those you represent must play a major role in helping improve our nation's health-care system.

The crisis is not over. We report tens of thousands of new cases every year. And many predict we can expect to continue to do so in this decade and even into the next century. And yet where there is life, there is hope. There are hopeful signs. To begin with, we can be encouraged by the news that current projections of the infection rate will not be as high as we thought just a year ago.

Our administration recently acted to extend AZT coverage to help HIV-infected people not yet sick with AIDS. And all 50 States now provide Medicaid coverage for AZT treatments. Thanks to these actions, more and more people will be able to live and work with HIV. Keep them in your work force, as I know many of you are already doing as leaders in this effort. They can serve many, many more productive years with no threat to you, your other workers, or your companies. It will reduce costs for everyone, and it is the right thing to do.

The pace of progress is promising. The HIV virus has been identified, isolated, and attacked with experimental treatments in a span of less than 10 years—the normal, centuries-long evolution of disease and treatment compressed into a decade. And this race against time has produced an explosion in knowledge and basic understanding about the nature of disease and immunology. Like the unexpected technological boons from *Apollo's* race to the Moon, some physicians predict the race to cure AIDS may even lead to a cure for cancer.

Dollars spent for AIDS research are dollars spent for the better health of all Americans. AIDS research strikes at the heart of many human health problems from infectious disease to aging and cancer. It includes research on a class of viruses now increasingly believed to be the cause of not only AIDS but also incurable diseases like muscular dystrophy, multiple sclerosis, and at least two of the strains of leukemia.

We're on a wartime footing at NIH and CDC, the Center for Disease Control. Tonight, like every night, the lights out there will burn late in Bethesda and Atlanta, as a group of American pioneers—selfless, dedicated workers—work to solve this problem. If they do—I should say, I'd rather put it when they do—it will be one of the greatest things our nation could do for the entire world.

We're going to continue to fight like hell, but we're also going to fight for hope. America has a unique capacity for beating the odds and astounding the world. During my own childhood, the silent, whispered terror was a mysterious killer called polio. Like HIV, the virus ignored class distinctions and geographic boundaries.

Audience member. What have you been doing for 14 months? You haven't said the "A" word yet. Say the "A" word.

The President. Let me say something about this. I can understand the concern that these people feel; and I hope, if we do nothing else by coming here, I can help them understand that not only do you care

but we care, too. And I'm going to continue to do my very, very best.

Monday would come, and kids who'd been in school on Friday were simply never seen again. Theaters were closed—you remember all that—summer camps, swimming pools.

As with AIDS, regarding polio, there was a lot of ignorance—thousands of stray cats and dogs put to death, kids sleeping with camphor inhalers, and at least one town was fumigated with DDT. And there were terrifying outbreaks in the teens, in the thirties, in the fifties. A cure was so far distant the experts refused to speculate. And then, suddenly, it was over—the dreaded iron lung, unused, cluttering hospital hallways; children again growing up in a world without fear.

Many comparisons have been made to epidemics past—cholera, smallpox, yellow fever—none of them perfect. So, let me boil down the lessons of polio to two: There was a lot of ignorance. Let's learn from that. And in the darkest of hours, hope came unexpectedly, powerfully, and with finality. Let's work hard to see that that day comes to pass.

Together, we will make a difference for those with HIV and AIDS and for all Americans. Thank you all for what you do. God bless your important work. Thank you on behalf of a grateful government.

Note: The President spoke at 11:16 a.m. in the Arlington Ballroom of the Crystal Gateway Marriott in Arlington, VA. In his remarks, he referred to Larry Williford, senior vice president of Allstate Insurance Co., and B.J. Stiles, president of the National Leadership Coalition on AIDS.

Remarks and an Exchange With Reporters Prior to a Luncheon With the Founding Directors of the Points of Light Initiative Foundation
March 30, 1990

The President. Well, today I have the pleasure of welcoming to the White House an extraordinary group of Americans. These

distinguished men and women, along with two others who couldn't be with us today, have agreed to serve as the founding directors of the Points of Light Initiative Foundation. I'm looking forward to serving as Honorary Chairman. The founding directors and I share the same vision for this foundation, and the aim of it is to make service to others central to the life and work of every individual, group, and institution in America, from our largest corporations to our smallest neighborhood associations.

Drug abuse, illiteracy, inadequate education, homelessness, hunger, environmental decay, and other critical social problems can indeed be solved. In fact, as we demonstrated Monday by naming the 100th daily Point of Light, these problems are already being solved in every corner of the Nation—men and women of all ages and organizations of every conceivable type who are tackling these problems in a direct and consequential way.

The growth and magnification of Points of Light must now become an American mission. Today we're not creating a program: we're adding a new dimension to a national movement. Block by block, neighborhood by neighborhood, life by life, we can reclaim those living in darkness. And with every American's help, we will.

Thank you, ladies and gentlemen, for being such a significant part of this major national effort. Thank you. Now we go up-stairs and have a little lunch.

Lithuanian Independence

Q. Mr. President, what did you tell Mr. Gorbachev in your message?

The President. Well, it's a confidential message, and if I told you what I told him it wouldn't be confidential. [*Laughter*]

Q. Have you heard back from him? Confidential or not?

The President. Not yet. But I believe there was some indication, in fact, that the message had been received. But as I mentioned to you all, we try to stay in close touch with world leaders, and this is just one more manifestation of that. But I want to be sure that the Soviets understand our position and understand that we're not trying to make things difficult for Lithuania or the Soviet Union or anybody else.

Q. Could you tell us what prompted you to send this message, Mr. President?

The President. Just this continual feeling of staying in touch and being sure there's no disconnect because of misinformation. Our views on the question of self-determination and all of that are well-known around the world, but I do not want to risk misunderstanding by failing to communicate. So, that's really what it's all about.

Note: The President spoke at noon in the Diplomatic Room at the White House.

Letter to Congressional Leaders Submitting a Report on Counternarcotics Intelligence Activities
March 30, 1990

Dear Mr. Chairman:

The Intelligence Authorization Act, Fiscal Year 1990 (Public Law 101–193; 103 Stat. 1711) specified that I submit a report describing how intelligence activities relating to narcotics trafficking can be integrated across the defense, law enforcement, and intelligence communities.

The Control and Coordination of Counternarcotics Intelligence Activities report prepared by the Director of Central Intelli-gence is enclosed for your information. I am pleased with the progress the Department of Defense and the intelligence community are making in the national effort to counter the flow of illegal narcotics, and I request your continued support for this program.

Sincerely,

GEORGE BUSH

Note: Identical letters were sent to David L. Boren, chairman of the Senate Select Com-

mittee on Intelligence, and Anthony C. Beilenson, chairman of the House Perma-

nent Select Committee on Intelligence.

Message to the Congress Transmitting an Amendment to the International Regulations for Preventing Collisions at Sea
March 30, 1990

To the Congress of the United States:

Consistent with the International Navigational Rules Act of 1977 (Public Law 95–75; 33 U.S.C. 1602), I transmit herewith an amendment to the International Regulations for Preventing Collisions at Sea, 1972, as amended, which was adopted at London, October 19, 1989. The Convention on the International Regulations for Preventing Collisions at Sea (72 COLREGS) was adopted at London, October 20, 1972, to replace the 1960 Collision Regulations. The 72 COLREGS entered into force July 15, 1977, and there are currently over 100 countries party to the convention. The 72 COLREGS were previously amended in November 1981 and in November 1987 to clarify technical language in the existing regulations.

This amendment modifies the language of rule 10(d) that governs the conduct of vessels in an inshore traffic zone of a traffic separation scheme adopted by the International Maritime Organization. The amendment was designed to remove the ambiguity inherent in the words "normal" and "through traffic" as used in the existing text. This ambiguity lent itself to different interpretations by coastal states anxious to limit traffic in inshore traffic zones in order to reduce the risk of pollution from collision or stranding. The new language for rule 10(d) is phrased so that the mariner should have a better understanding of his duties and obligations with regard to the use of inshore traffic zones by ships.

Consistent with section 5 of the Inland Navigational Rules Act of 1980 (section 5 of Public Law 96–591; 33 U.S.C. 2073), this proposed amendment has been considered by the Rules of the Road Advisory Council, which has given its concurrence to the amendment.

In the absence of a duly enacted law to the contrary, I will proclaim that the amendment will enter into force for the United States of America on April 19, 1991, unless by April 19, 1990, more than one-third of the Contracting Parties have notified the International Maritime Organization of their objection to the amendment.

GEORGE BUSH

The White House,
March 30, 1990.

Nomination of Rear Admiral William J. Kime To Be Commandant of the United States Coast Guard
March 30, 1990

The President today nominated Rear Adm. William J. Kime, U.S. Coast Guard, to be Commandant of the United States Coast Guard, Department of Transportation, for a term of 4 years. He would succeed Adm. Paul A. Yost, who is retiring.

Admiral Kime is commander of the 11th

Coast Guard District, headquartered in Long Beach, CA. He has served as the commander of the Central California Sector of the U.S. Maritime Defense Zone, Pacific, and as coordinator of the Pacific Region of the Office of National Drug Control Policy.

Admiral Kime graduated from Baltimore

City College in 1951, the U.S. Coast Guard Academy in 1957, and the Massachusetts Institute of Technology (M.S., 1964). He is married to the former Valerie Joan Hiddlestone.

Statement by Press Secretary Fitzwater on International Cooperation in the President's Space Exploration Initiative
March 30, 1990

The President announced today that the United States would seek an exploratory dialog with Europe, Canada, Japan, the Soviet Union, and other nations on international cooperation in the Space Exploration Initiative.

The President's announcement comes as part of a series of policy implementation decisions stemming from his address of July 20, 1989, the 20th anniversary of the *Apollo* lunar landing. On that historic occasion, the President set the future direction of the U.S. space program by proposing a long-term, continuing commitment to completing Space Station *Freedom*, returning permanently to the Moon, and sending a manned expedition to the planet Mars.

To chart this course, he asked the Vice President to lead the National Space Council in determining, among other things, the feasibility of international cooperation in this endeavor. The Council recently completed a review of potential international cooperation and concluded, in part:

• The President's Space Exploration Initiative will be of profound significance for all mankind.
• International cooperation in this endeavor is feasible and could offer significant benefits to the United States, subject to the satisfaction of national security, foreign policy, scientific, and economic interests.

Acting on the recommendations of the Vice President and the National Space Council, the President decided that:

• The United States will take a sequential and orderly approach to decisions on involving specific countries consistent with decisions made on the overall Space Exploration Initiative.
• The United States will seek an exploratory dialog with Europe, Canada, Japan, the Soviet Union, and other nations as appropriate on international cooperation on the initiative.
• The exploratory dialog will focus solely on conceptual possibilities for cooperation.
• The dialog will be based on guidelines expeditiously prepared by the National Space Council. The guidelines will be consistent with the National Space Policy, taking due account of U.S. national security, foreign policy, scientific, and economic interests.
• The National Space Council will ensure interagency coordination and review during the development of international cooperation on the initiative and provide recommendations to the President as appropriate.

These decisions by the President follow on and relate to earlier decisions on the Space Exploration Initiative announced in the White House press release of March 8, 1990.

Statement by Press Secretary Fitzwater on the Japan-United States Structural Impediments Initiative Negotiations
April 2, 1990

Prime Minister Kaifu of Japan this morning telephoned President Bush to express his interest in resolving issues related to the Structural Impediments Initiative. The Prime Minister has sent two personal emissaries to meet with the President and administration officials to emphasize the Japanese Government's commitment to progress. The two emissaries are former Ambassador to the United States Matsunaga and Deputy Foreign Minister Owada. They arrive at 10 o'clock this morning and will meet today and tomorrow with General Scowcroft and Secretary of State Baker. They will meet with President Bush on Wednesday. In addition, they will deliver a letter from Prime Minister Kaifu to President Bush concerning trade issues.

The Structural Impediments Initiative talks begin today in Washington at the State Department. The U.S. side will be headed by Richard T. McCormack, Under Secretary for Economic Affairs; Linn Williams, Deputy U.S. Trade Representative; and Charles Dallara, Assistant Secretary of the Treasury. An interim report on these meetings will be issued on April 4, with a final report produced in July.

Note: Brent Scowcroft was Assistant to the President for National Security Affairs.

Remarks at the Annual Convention of the National Association of Broadcasters in Atlanta, Georgia
April 2, 1990

Thank you for that welcome. To Messrs. Mays and Fritts, thank you both, and to all of the rest of the leaders of the NAB that are here today. And also I understand there are a lot of Members of the United States Congress here. In my line of work, you always pay your respects to the Members of Congress—[*laughter*]—in the forlorn hope that they will do it exactly my way someday. [*Laughter*] But nevertheless, I'm glad they're here.

It is my privilege this morning to be back before America's family of broadcasters, the National Association of Broadcasters. And I can't help but marvel at these huge screens as I walked in here. You know, if I were as large as my image—[*laughter*]—on these screens, imagine how easy it would be for me to get my way with the Congress. [*Laughter*] And this convention is also displayed, I'm told, on monitors throughout the arena, and from here, beamed around the world. I will try to finish each sentence without a preposition. [*Laughter*]

But there was a time when most Americans knew their Presidents distantly, from woodcut prints in the weekly newspaper. The circle of democracy in ancient Athens and Rome was even more limited, just to those within hearing range of the debates inside the Parthenon or the Forum. But today, through free over-the-air broadcasts, you have brought millions of living rooms within hearing range; you've made every home a part of the American forum. In fact, on this very day, you are providing—for the 6,000 foreign broadcasters in attendance, through your international seminars, and through USIA's WORLDNET—a seminar for the world.

Television, which began as the American forum, has become the world forum. And so, when a lone brave man stood up to a column of tanks in Tiananmen Square, the world stood with him. When the people of Prague sang the first Christmas carols in over 40 years, the world sang with them.

And when the first German took the first hammer to that wall of shame in Berlin, the world shared in an historic act of courage.

We all know that governments can censor, governments can silence, but the voice of freedom will not be stilled as long as there is an America to tell the truth. These sounds and images of the Revolution of '89 belong to the world. But it was here in America that a free people first explored how to put the airwaves into the service of democracy.

We accept regulation, but we firmly reject government programming. We reject government ownership of stations. And most of all, we reject censorship. You see, the freedom that this association enjoys—probably takes for granted—is a model for the world.

In my State of the Union Address, I spoke of the cornerstones of a free society: democracy, private investment, competitiveness, stewardship. We will see what competitiveness means just this afternoon—I'm going out to visit a General Electric plant in Cincinnati, where free workers transformed foreign investment into foreign business. Tomorrow I'm going to Indianapolis—help promote stewardship, where the city works with citizens to cultivate an urban forest. But these are not what you'd call isolated whistlestops. America's ideas are powerful, and through the power of communication, we share them with the world. After all, we live in a time when commodity prices and travel reservations and fast-breaking news flash from Hong Kong to Tokyo, Tokyo to Bonn, Bonn to Boston, all in the blink of an eye.

Roam among the hundreds of exhibits in this convention center, and you will find 22 football fields chock-full of the latest gadgets in telecommunications—personal computers and modems, fax machines, lasers, optical fibers, satellites—all strands in a growing web of world communications, a growing network linking all of us, "a global village." The information industry is not an adornment to modern life: it is the essence of who and what we are. It is truly an information age.

Last May, I discussed the future of Europe with the citizens of Mainz, a German city nestled in the green hills along the Rhine River. And it was while I was there that I appreciated anew the Biblical expression, "In the beginning was the Word." For it was in that German town that the inventor of the printing press, Johann Gutenberg, first put the scholarship of the ages into the hands of millions of knowledge-hungry readers. His one invention made possible all the pamphlets and journals of the Enlightenment and of the American Revolution, from the call to arms of Thomas Paine to the cool logic of "The Federalist Papers." You might argue that out of that one invention sprang the very idea called America.

Today, along with the word, we have the image: images projected on color television and evoked by the sounds of radio. But while Western democracy broadened as our knowledge broadened, the circle of democracy and knowledge narrowed under Communist regimes that took power on many continents. For these nations, truth was something to be twisted and stretched by the brutal hands of authority, manipulated beyond recognition. The Czech author Kundera calls this time the "kingdom of forgetting," when whole nations almost forgot their heroic histories and finest traditions. From Havana to Prague to Phnom Penh, the peoples of these lands never fully gave in to the amnesia, because even in the worst hours of repression, they could always count on a friendly voice to remind them of the truth: Radio Marti, Radio Liberty, Radio Free Europe and, God bless it, the Voice of America.

To fully appreciate what these broadcasts mean, you need only ask someone who listened to them. Sichan Siv, a young man now works on our White House staff—he's a Cambodian, an American who lived through the horrors of the killing fields. And he's told me that when the Khmer Rouge took control of a village the very first items they confiscated were the radios, for if they respected and feared anything, it was the power of free information. But even under the threat of death, men and women like Sichan Siv were so hungry for news from the outside world that they would turn on a hidden transistor radio at the lowest possible volume and then put it

439

up flush to one ear. We take free news broadcasts for granted in America, but some people risked death to hear the truth. And some people still do, and we're not going to let them down.

In the realm of ideas and ideals, there are no borders. No government should fear free speech, whether it's from entertainment programs or accurate, unbiased news about world events. And that is why Congress strongly supported TV Marti and why I strongly support TV Marti. We will scrupulously adhere to the letter of the law. But let me say again: The voice of freedom will not be stilled as long as there is an America to tell the truth.

And look, I do understand the practical concerns that some of you have about this, but I also understand that you represent the very principle TV Marti exists to serve: that free flow of ideas. Before we are business men and women, before we are doctors, lawyers, or mechanics, we are Americans. Americans have always stood for free speech, and we always will. So, I have come here to ask something of you. I ask you to stand by your traditions, the best traditions of America. I ask you, once again, to stand for TV Marti and to stand for freedom.

If we broadcast freedom, our message will be heard. After the bloodshed at Tiananmen Square and the expulsion of the VOA from China, I was heartened to see that Beijing relented a little bit and permitted a VOA correspondent to return. In the Soviet Union, publications that once vilified the Voice of America now praise it. Warm words of support even come from Izvestia. A commentator in Moscow News thanks VOA and says that it uses, and here is the quote, "our own broadening sources of information better than we do and without delay return to us what they have gathered." And now Radio Free Europe has bureaus in Warsaw, in Budapest, and VOA even has one in Moscow, an unthinkable development just a few years ago. The very fact that it is no longer considered remarkable for USIA's WORLDNET to link live programs from Washington to Kiev, or from Chicago and New York to Gdansk and Warsaw, is in itself remarkable.

How did this happen? It happened in part because of the power of truth. Czecho-slovakia's playwright-President Václav Havel paid a very personal tribute to this power in his recent visit to Washington. First he came to the White House and told me personally what this broadcasting of the truth had meant to those who were fighting for freedom. And then he visited the Voice of America and met the employees of its Czech division. It was a very poignant encounter, for though Havel didn't recognize any of them by face, he knew them all by name the instant he heard them speak.

And it's moments like that that convince me of one sure thing: I am determined that America will continue to bear witness to the truth. America must never lose its voice. Just as President Havel and others who were once under Communist domination have thanked us, I am convinced that the people of Cuba will thank us when they, too, win the liberty they yearn for.

Still, we can envision a time when the purpose of Radio Free Europe and Radio Liberty could be utterly fulfilled. But for now, these networks, along with USIA's WORLDNET and VOA, must continue in Eastern Europe until change is complete. We're still seeing the struggle for freedom, and this must continue until all that struggle is won by the forces of freedom. Free stations and newspapers are still struggling to take root. Their access to their Western colleagues is still erratic. We need to be there now more than ever before to describe and explain our own two centuries of experience in building a democracy.

We can also assist the Eastern Europeans in sharing among themselves their own experience in democracy. After all, Eastern Europeans need more than Robert's Rules of Order: they need to know how the process of reform is working with their neighbors. So, if one nation adopts a novel path to reform, pollution control, or currency law, the others need to be able to benefit from that experiment.

And we must also look ahead to the challenges of a new century. To prepare for our future role, I have directed that an interagency review be conducted of U.S. Government international broadcasting.

And of course, we will be looking for advice from many outside the Government.

After all, when it comes to setting an example of a free press, the best example must come from you. The Peace Corps is teaching English in Eastern Europe as the lingua franca of business and journalism, but it is not tasked to offer a model of journalistic excellence. Only the American press corps can pick up where the Peace Corps leaves off and provide a model of accuracy, fairness, and objectivity.

As broadcasters, you can—and you are—transferring American know-how to the East. You're working with VOA to train and orient foreign broadcasters visiting the United States. In February the director of Polish radio and television visited your headquarters, in part to seek the counsel and assistance of American broadcasters. And you've sent your representatives to meet with their counterparts inside the Soviet Union. And on top of this, you are helping Americans to invest in joint ventures to establish new radio and television networks in the East. So, most of all, I am here to recognize your energetic, international leadership. And I might make a peripheral plea: Do not neglect this hemisphere and this hemisphere's quest for democracy.

The times have changed. We need no longer act in the fine tradition of the Underground Railroad. But before the Revolution of '89, America regularly received the speeches of Lech Walesa, Václav Havel, and other brave men and women of conscience on smuggled tapes. And through the power of broadcasting, America became the courier of freedom, returning the eloquent words of these leaders back to their people, returning hope and the promise of liberty to half a dozen lands. That was our vision then; that is our vision today. And by working together, our American vision is fast becoming a reality for the world.

I can tell you many friends in this audience that there has never in my view been a more exciting or challenging time to be President of the United States. The change is mind-boggling—the changes around the world. The bid of freedom is irreversible. It's bound to happen to places denied freedom today. But the importance of your work, the importance of your commitment to open, fair journalism is unparalleled in any time in our history. So, I came here to say thank you—thank you all for what you are doing, thank you for the support you've been able to give this administration. And may God bless you. And most of all, may God bless the United States of America. Thank you all very, very much.

Note: The President spoke at 10:09 a.m. in the Thomas P. Murphy Ballroom of the Georgia World Congress Center. In his remarks, he referred to L. Lowry Mays and Eddie Fritts, joint board chairman and president of the association, respectively. Afterwards, the President examined a scale model of the proposed 1992 Olympic Village in Atlanta. In the afternoon, he traveled to Cincinnati, OH.

Remarks at a Fundraising Dinner for Gubernatorial Candidate George Voinovich in Cincinnati, Ohio
April 2, 1990

Thank you, George, very, very much. Thank you for those kind words. And be seated out there. That would mean curling up your feet. [*Laughter*] And thank you all for this very warm welcome.

I'm delighted to be here with two Members—well, three Members of Congress—but with Bill Gradison and Bob McEwen, these two distinguished Members of the Ohio congressional delegation. I'll get to this one in a minute. And let me recognize Cincinnati's next Congressman, Ken Blackwell, who's out here. Ken—right there. This is a State ticket meeting. Tomorrow Ken and I are going to figure out what I can do to assist him in that very important congressional race.

I also want to take a moment tonight to

mention a close friend of mine, a friend of so many Republicans here in this room and across the country, and I'm talking about Lee Atwater, our national chairman. During this difficult time—and he went into another hospital today in New York, I'm told—our hearts go out to him and to that wonderful family of his. And I know I speak for all when I just say we wish him our very, very best in this difficult time. And right now there's nothing more important for Lee to do than to get well, and I know that's exactly what he intends to do, given that fighting spirit. Luckily, when it comes to leadership at the RNC—and I think our very able State chairman here will attest to that—Lee is backed up by one of this party's most able politicians, a friend of mine of longstanding, Jeanie Austin, over here, who is with us tonight. And she is doing an outstanding job for the party. The Atwater-Austin ticket at our national level is hard to beat.

And that brings me then to the six members of this strong Ohio State ticket today: Jim Petro, candidate for State auditor; Senator Paul Pfeiffer, Ohio's next attorney general; your next State treasurer, Judy Brachman; and then Bob Taft, my old friend, the current Hamilton County commissioner, and Ohio's next secretary of state. I don't think he needs too much of a word around Hamilton County here.

And then, of course, the two men at the top of the ticket: Mike DeWine, one of the finest Congressmen on Capitol Hill, who's ready to come back home and be the next Lieutenant Governor of this great State. Mike, we wish you well. And of course, with you, locked in tandem, Ohio's man of the hour, the next Governor of the Buckeye State, George Voinovich. I'm here to support all of them, and you have an outstanding ticket.

Let me diverge just a minute to point out that George Voinovich says I was responsive when he was mayor of Cleveland. I don't know, I guess I want to see him elected—well, put that down as 100 percent—but I'll tell you, when you elect him the next Governor, he will be a fighter for Ohio. I can attest to it. He was mayor of Cleveland, and he was in there every single day working for the interests of Cleveland

when they interacted with the Federal Government. So, you'll have a bulldog here in Columbus, Ohio, to fight for the rights of the State, and somebody that I can work with and look forward to working with.

You know, this town—George used the baseball analogy—has seen its share of great teams, from the days of Robinson and Rose, Perez and Concepcion, Joe Morgan, Johnny Bench, right up to today's team of Davis, Larkin, and Browning. Sounds like a law firm—[*laughter*]—but this Republican lineup of Voinovich, DeWine, and Taft ranks right up there with the best of the great Reds teams ever to take the field—or, George, I noticed your plug in there for the Cleveland Indians; the same goes for them. [*Laughter*] And come "game day" this November, it's the Democrats who are going to be praying for rain. [*Laughter*]

It's always good to be back in Ohio. George says native son. I missed by a generation. It was my dad that was the native son, born in Columbus. But it's great to join you here this evening, after what George alluded to, what must be the most expensive hot dogs in the history of the State of Ohio. [*Laughter*] If marvelous Marge Schott [owner of the Cincinnati Reds baseball team] hears about this, you can bet you've seen the end of the dollar hot dog across the street at Riverfront Stadium. [*Laughter*]

You know, I know everyone here has had this day circled on the calendar for a long time. I know how the expectations build and how you feel a sense of excitement in the air. So, let me say I know how you feel right now. I was looking forward to throwing out the first pitch at the Reds' opener, but it didn't work out that way. It's all quiet across at that marvelous Riverfront Stadium. And it's not easy to tune in the Reds-Red Sox exhibition game from Plant City when you're up there on Air Force One.

But the fact is, opening day—and a new season—is just 1 week away. And in 1990—a new year and a new decade for the Republican team—it's a whole new ball game, too. It really is. The Ohio Republican Party has never had higher hopes, never had a better shot at putting this State into the Republican column and keeping it there. More and more Ohioans are looking to the

GOP to lead us into the nineties, and according to the recent polls I've seen, the GOP is now the majority party for Ohioans under the age of 25. And that bodes well not just for this next election but for this whole decade of the nineties. And every one of you here tonight is a proud member of this tough new Republican team.

This year's especially important because the impact of the 1990 elections will be felt all decade long. In the reapportionment of congressional districts that will take place after that 1990 census, Ohio, in all likelihood, stands to lose two seats. We must make sure when those districts are redrawn that the results are fair and equitable to the Republicans and, thus, to the people of Ohio. No more gerrymandering.

Right now every statewide official in Ohio is a Democrat. The election this November can guarantee three men here tonight—George Voinovich, Bob Taft, Jim Petro—a seat at the table come redistricting time. I'm telling you: This is important nationally. The GOP has made great gains in Ohio, and we don't want to see those gains erased—quite literally—by the masters of gerrymandering.

But I do believe that we have every reason to be confident. The man we're here to send to the statehouse, George Voinovich, is a triple crown winner in Ohio politics: an office holder on the city, county, and State levels—Cuyahoga County auditor and, later, county commissioner; Ohio assistant attorney general; State representative; and Lieutenant Governor. And for the past 10 years, he has been an outstanding mayor of Cleveland, a city where Democrats outnumber us—what is it—eight to one. Eight to one. The plain truth is this: You won't find anyone who knows how Ohio works better than this man, and you won't find anyone who's more ready than George Voinovich to roll up his sleeves and go to work for the entire State.

I am proud to say, George, that you and I have a lot in common: same first name—[*laughter*]—same charismatic, emotional approach to life—[*laughter*]—same approach to politics, an approach that tells us that decency and democracy are one and the same. George is a man with many qualities I admire—I might ,say I speak confidently

for the Silver Fox on this one—Barbara Bush—[*laughter*]—a man of integrity, a family man, father of three fine kids who'll be with him every step of the way in this campaign for the statehouse. One of them is here. Betsy is here someplace. Betsy, where are you? Whoops. Betsy is not here. All right, she was supposed to be. But there's always been a place for politics in the Voinovich household. George met his wife, Janet, at a political rally. And, George, I hope the hot dogs weren't as expensive as they are here. But you can count on him. You can count on this man, this experienced man, to keep his commitment to serve the public, to conduct himself and his administration with all the honor and integrity every elected official owes the people who put him in office.

But best of all, for all Ohioans, George Voinovich is a man—and I referred to this earlier—who gets things done, a proven leader in every position he's held in more than two decades in Ohio politics. And what happens here is critical for this State and for the Nation because the fact is many of the challenges we face cannot be met by Washington alone. The answers and the action will come at the State and local level. That's true whether the issue is economic growth or education or cracking down on crime and drugs. And that is the key reason that I'm looking for a partner like George Voinovich to work with here in the Ohio statehouse at Columbus.

Take the issue of crime and drugs. We're working hard—we really are—and I think we're beginning to make headway there back at the White House to implement our National Drug Strategy II and to push our tough, no-nonsense anticrime package through the Congress and into the law. We're doing all we can on the Federal level to make life tough on the criminals. We've increased funding for Federal prisons—24,000 new beds this year alone. We've called for tougher laws; stiffer penalties for crimes of violence; more Federal agents and prosecutors and judges; more certainty in sentencing; and for drug kingpins who kill the police officers, the ultimate penalty, the death penalty.

That's what we're doing in Washington.

But as a nation, we can't break the deadly grip of drugs—we can't show the criminals that prey on our citizens that we mean business—unless each and every State takes the same strong steps against crime and drugs.

It's the same when the issue is education. The President, every American family, knows how much education means for our kids and for our future. Earlier this afternoon—I wish all of you could have been with me—I toured the General Electric aircraft engines plant and saw that kind of high-tech, precision manufacturing the workers of this State and this country are capable of. Felt the pride—you could feel it as you talked to them along the line—felt the pride that they feel. That's where they build the engines, you know, for Air Force One; and it's where they're building engines in great demand in the international aircraft industry. And I can tell you, if American industry is going to keep its competitive edge in the future, American schools have got to be first-class. And education is the key.

And the States are central to real education reform. And that is the reason, as most of you know, behind last year's education summit with the Nation's Governors; and it's the guiding force behind the goals the Governors and I have agreed on, the education goals we want every student and every school to meet.

We all know those six goals: American high school students first in the world in math and science achievement by the year 2000. Raising the graduation rate to 90 percent or better. In order to make sure those diplomas mean something, we must assess our kids' progress at the crucial 4th, 8th, and then 12th grade levels. Fourth, of course, excellence in education means every American child ready to learn the day they walk into the classroom; and that's why we've stepped up funding requests for Head Start so much. Every American adult literate. Every American school drug-free.

And I know I can count on Governor Voinovich to join me in leading a crusade for excellence in our schools, to prepare every child in Ohio, every kid across this nation, to take his place in the work force of the 21st century.

Whatever the issue, whether it's keeping our streets safe, our government sound, or preparing our kids or promoting economic growth, I need friends and allies to work with me, allies like George Voinovich, Mike DeWine, Bob Taft, and the other fine members of this Ohio Republican team.

Tonight, I really came out here to ask you to go the extra mile. I thank you for your support. And I ask each and every one of you to recognize that you really are caught up in a national crusade here, because if we can win in Ohio with this clean sweep in the fall of 1990, it sets a fantastic tone for what lies ahead in the remaining 10 years of this decade. So, I'm out here to support enthusiastically and without reservation this topnotch team, to make 1990 a winning season and the 1990's a Republican decade.

Let me just say in closing, I like being President of the United States. I don't believe anybody who's had the Presidency, any of the 40 who have preceded me, could claim to have been President at a more fascinating time in terms of international affairs. And George referred to the changes that are taking place around the world, and they are fantastic. And I urge you not to just concentrate on the marvelous change in Eastern Europe, where we're trying very much to help Poland and to help Hungary and Czechoslovakia and so many other countries. But don't forget our own hemisphere. Don't forget what's happening in terms of democracy south of this border. I talked to President Aylwin of Chile and [President] Carlos Salinas of Mexico, who have enjoyed a democracy, but with whom we're working very closely. And the change in Panama and the change in Nicaragua is, to me, every bit as exciting as what's going on in Eastern Europe.

So, I am President at a fascinating time. We are Republicans at a fascinating time. And as exciting as the international environment is, I do not want to forget, and I will not, the domestic agenda. And that's what brought me here to Ohio, because I believe in this team that you see sitting here. We have the very best anywhere across the country.

Thank you very, very much for your support. And God bless you all.

Note: The President spoke at 5:50 p.m. in the Presidential Ballroom of the Westin Hotel. In his remarks, he referred to Jeanie Austin, cochairman of the Republican National Committee. Following his remarks, he attended a reception for major campaign donors. Earlier in the afternoon, the President attended a briefing and toured the facilities at the General Electric aircraft engine plant.

Statement by Press Secretary Fitzwater on Iraq's Threat To Use Chemical Weapons
April 3, 1990

We have now had the opportunity to review the text of the address given yesterday by Iraqi President Saddam Hussein. The President finds the statements about Iraq's chemical weapons capability and his threatening Israel to be particularly deplorable and irresponsible. Such statements can only exacerbate tensions and further destabilize this already volatile region. What is needed in the Middle East is not inflammatory rhetoric but concrete steps to rid the region of chemical and other unconventional weapons and to move toward peace.

Remarks at a Tree-Planting Ceremony in Indianapolis, Indiana
April 3, 1990

Well, thank you all very much. And Senator Lugar and Senator Coats; the Governor of the State, Gov. Evan Bayh; Mayor Hudnut; Director Strong; and distinguished guests and all of you ladies and gentlemen freezing out there on this spring day, I'm just delighted to be here, "back home in Indiana" again, and, as the banner says, to plant "Trees for Tomorrow" that will benefit our nation and its kids.

Not far from here is the hometown of a great former Indiana Senator who, in my view, has been an even greater Vice President—a man I trust, a Hoosier I rely on, Dan Quayle. He is serving our nation very well, thank you.

And speaking of another friend, I'm sorry Bobby Knight isn't here. It wouldn't hurt him to be around a kinder, gentler event like planting trees, but nevertheless— [*laughter*]—please give him my very best.

I'm glad to see all of you here in a city which, unlike some, can see the forest for the trees and which intends this year to plant, as your mayor just said—my old friend Bill Hudnut—30,000. Trees are in a larger sense the sanctuaries of mankind, renewing and refreshing. And many of you have grown up reading the great Hoosier poet James Whitcomb Riley, who often observed that the individual could enrich the tapestry of life. Well, so it is with trees. They renew and restore the natural magic of our world. Think of how trees enhance our atmosphere—Bill touched on it—providing oxygen and absorbing carbon dioxide, and how they enhance the environment. For their beauty is breathtaking, and their bounty, breathgiving.

Ten weeks ago I announced a new program to help preserve the wonderful legacy of our trees and, indeed, to help us conserve all natural resources. It's called America the Beautiful. It will help plant the seeds of environmental stewardship not only by planting trees but through other steps as well. America the Beautiful calls for expanded land acquisition for our national parks, wildlife refuges, forests, and public lands and funds to maintain and restore them. Our program is similar to your Clean and Green Month. It seeks clean water, clean land, clean air. In that spirit, let me note that later today the Senate will consider our clean air legislation, the first rewrite of the Clean Air Act in over a decade. I am proud of this proposal to cut smog, acid rain, and toxic pollution—to make America cleaner and safer. Tonight marks an historic vote. So, I urge the Senate to act not merely for this generation but for all generations to come.

Trees, of course, can help ensure clean air. Consider: One recent study showed that trees, much more than water, consume the carbon dioxide that is building up in our atmosphere. Research also shows that trees can lower peak energy demand in urban areas by 20 to 40 percent and that three well-placed trees around a home can reduce its air conditioning needs by 10 to 50 percent.

The record's clear: We need trees economically and environmentally. We also need them to lift our minds and our hearts. Trees are something we all can plant, for while they can be fragile or sturdy, they are always precious. And the record shows that Indianapolis is not falling down on the job of planting trees, and neither will our administration.

That's why a key part of America the Beautiful is a national tree planting and forest improvement program to be administered by our Department of the Agriculture. This program involves both rural areas as well as urban tree planting programs in great cities like Indianapolis. And to fund it I have asked Congress for $175 million for fiscal year 1991 to plant 1 billion trees a year.

Two weeks ago I also asked Congress to approve another step to protect the environment. We call it the National Tree Trust Act of 1990. It will foster the partnership between the public and private sector to plant trees all across America. Under this plan, we will designate a nonprofit foundation to receive a one-time Federal grant to promote community tree planting and cultivation projects. It will also solicit contributions from private sources; sound a nationwide call for each American to protect the environment; and most of all, plant the trees that clean our air, prevent erosion, and purify our water.

In the same spirit of our Thousand Points of Light, the National Tree Trust Act will help toward a goal of creating 10 billion trees of life, and it will complement local programs to help conservation enrich America's quality of life, programs like your Trees for Tomorrow.

Talk about cooperation, Trees for Tomorrow links individuals, private groups, and your department of parks and recreation. In April alone, 3,000 trees will be donated. This urban forestry program will help volunteers show new volunteers not only how and where to plant trees but also how to care for them, why we need them, and how they will help our precious environment.

You know, 2 weeks ago I told an audience that I'd been planting so many trees all over the country that I might have to open a branch office. [*Laughter*] I tried it once before, and it got the same groan. [*Laughter*] This one is going out of the speech from now and evermore. [*Laughter*]

I can't think of a better spot than here in Indianapolis. Just as trees grow, with roots and branches becoming stronger and deeper by the year, your effort on behalf of trees can reach far into the future.

I began by talking about two exports: Dan Quayle and basketball. Let me close by referring to an event and then a movie close to Vice President Quayle's heart.

First, the event. Three years ago, after being reelected by a landslide, he was saluted on his 40th birthday in a way each of you will appreciate. Students planted 40 trees in his honor, one at I.U. Law School, 15 at his college alma mater, 24 at his high school. Those trees reaffirm the beauty of Indiana. They embody the kindness of you, his friends.

Second, the movie. It's called "Hoosiers." You've seen it—probably memorized it. It was filmed here in three nearby towns. Yes, it's about basketball, but it also portrays, unforgettably, the beauty of Indiana. The next time you see it, look for two things: kids and trees. They're everywhere in the film, and they make the movie very special, even magical. And so it is from Evansville in the south to the Michigan State line: trees—many planted by kids—enhancing the splendor of Indiana's cathedral of the outdoors.

So, let's help these youngsters plant more trees and nurture them in this State and in all 50 States. Let's plant the Trees for Tomorrow that will bless the children of tomorrow, the generations who will inherit our Earth. Trees are an inheritance passed from one generation to another, and they symbolize the continuity of mankind.

Not far from here there's a special young man who has created a special legacy of his own, and he is in our prayers today. His name is Ryan White, and he's been fighting a courageous battle against a deadly disease and also against ignorance and fear. Ryan has helped us understand the truth about AIDS, and he's shown all of us the strength and the bravery of the human heart. So, today, as together we plant this beautiful

American elm, this symbol of new life, this first tree of your magnificent campaign, let it be Ryan's tree.

God bless that young man. God bless his family. And God bless the United States of America. Thank you all very, very much.

Note: The President spoke at 12:07 p.m. at the Trees for Tomorrow Park. In his remarks, he referred to F. Arthur Strong, director of the City of Indianapolis Department of Parks and Recreation, and Bobby Knight, Indiana University basketball coach. Earlier, prior to leaving Cincinnati, the President met with Ken Blackwell, the Republican candidate for the First Congressional District. The President also visited Derrick Turnbow, an honor student at Taft High School who was the innocent victim of a drug-related shooting.

Remarks at a Fundraising Luncheon for Senator Dan Coats in Indianapolis, Indiana
April 3, 1990

First, let me, once again, say how much I enjoyed reveling in the magic of Sandi Patti and her great music, and to see my friend Fred Travalena, again, here. Could have helped him with some of his gestures, the way it is—[*laughter*]—but he's coming along. And it's great, really, to be back in Indianapolis, with good friends like Dick Lugar and, of course, Don Cox and Margie Hill of our national committee, two great representatives there. And then, we're flying up here with our new State chairman—he's here—Keith Luce, a hard worker doing a great job to rebuild the party. And most of all, I'm pleased to be here on behalf of a man who brings your Hoosier ideas to Washington every day with great integrity and honor, and I'm talking about Dan Coats, the man of the moment. It is essential he be reelected.

I want to thank Dick Freeland and Bob Irsay and others for this tremendously successful event. I'm sorry I couldn't get over here to have lunch with you today; I wasn't allowed to. On the way over I was notified

that the Secret Service had found my food taster face down in the salad. [*Laughter*] Somebody had washed my lettuce with Perrier. [*Laughter*] It could have been worse—broccoli—could have been worse. [*Laughter*]

Throughout the eighties—the decade which saw the greatest economic expansion in U.S. peacetime history and fires of freedom begin to burn all over the world—throughout this turbulent decade, the people of Indiana had two great men representing them in the United States Senate—Dick Lugar and then, of course, Dan Quayle—a foreign policy duo that have been instrumental to the progress we've seen internationally. Dick's tenure on the Senate Foreign Relations Committee has been—I was telling this to Dick Freeland here—absolutely nothing less than superb. And I continue to depend on his wise counsel as we wrestle with a world in change.

I don't have to tell you, you know this already, how important Dan Quayle's outstanding leadership has been in crucial areas like Central and Latin America. And he's served our administration well and our nation well. So, Indiana already had a lot to be proud of in these two fine men. And now we have Dan Coats, stepping into that legacy of leadership in the United States Senate.

For the last 10 years, Dick Lugar and Dan Quayle have built this dynasty of Republican leadership in Indiana with a command of the issues that's kept America number one. In 1986 Dan Quayle was reelected by the biggest landslide of any Senate candidate in Indiana history. And yet 2 years later, Dick Lugar came along, broke the record with an even bigger winning margin. And come November my common sense tells me that the voters of Indiana will continue the tradition and give Dan Coats an even greater victory margin. It's going to happen.

So, I'm here, "back home again in Indiana," in what natives call the Crossroads of America, to talk to you today about common sense, something Hoosiers know a lot about. Indiana is the heart of the heartland, and the Hoosiers are right in the middle of an American mainstream with the kind of values that have made this nation great. And I'm talking about values like hard work and opportunity and decency and loyalty, faith and family. Everyone here believes that the family is the cornerstone of American society. Our administration has placed the family at the center of our agenda for the 1990's: to build an America where every man, woman, and child is drug-free; where schools challenge and support our kids and our teachers; and where our families can live in a clean, safe environment. Dan has been one of the biggest supporters—as Dick Lugar referred to this—Dan Coats has been one of the biggest supporters of our pro-family agenda, reaching out to families like yours with hopes and dreams for the children's futures. He is really your voice for your values.

And it's a strong voice. His work in Congress sponsoring important pro-family legislation was crucial to the progress that we've already made in strengthening the family in this country. And he's helped people in areas like education reform and family support and help for "at risk" children and families in need. In fact the Republican Party felt so strongly about his legislation that we made it a part of our national platform—mainstream values that all Americans care about. And that's why I believe we need Dan Coats in the Senate, and I know that everybody here today agrees with me on that important point.

Nothing ravages the American family more than drug abuse. Our National Drug Strategy, articulated by Bill Bennett—we call it National Drug Strategy II—which I announced last September, deals with all sides of the issue, from education and prevention to expanded treatment to stronger penalties and stepped-up enforcement. It's a tough approach, but it is a sensible approach.

No part of America is safe from the scourge of drugs. This is not simply an inner-city problem or a border problem for bureaucrats in Washington to handle. We've got to get PCP and crack off every street and out of every school in America. And it's time we got more Federal resources into the hands of those in the thick of the fight, those on the front lines. And if we are to build a better future for this country, America first must be drug-free.

As the Republican leader of the Senate subcommittee that deals with drugs, Dan knows the road ahead won't be easy, but that's another strong reason why I need him back in the Senate. I need his experience and his intelligence as we fight to take back our streets.

You know, I noticed a bunch of police officers here today and outside greeting us when we arrived at the airport, and I'd just like to say, parenthetically, we owe a great debt of gratitude to the men and women in police uniform—sheriff, whatever it is—that are protecting our kids. I think to myself—I went over the other day to the funeral home where a recognized, dedicated police officer, and this in the Maryland State Police, had been gunned down on the highway, on a major highway artery—and I thought to myself how lucky we are to have dedicated men like, in that instance, Sergeant Wolf or like some that are here today, who are dedicating themselves to protect the lives of our families and our children. It is inspirational to me.

We're talking about values, and bringing Hoosier values and Hoosier vision to Washington is important to me not just in stopping crime and drugs but also in stopping those who measure progress made solely by dollars spent. You know as I do that congressional spending is spiraling out of control—$1.2 trillion right now. And common sense tells us the American people aren't undertaxed. We need a budget process that can deal rationally with wasteful government spending. We need a line-item veto or some strong rescission legislation. And so, again I appeal to Congress: Give me what 43 Governors have—the power to cut unnecessary spending.

One of the first things that Dan Coats did when he arrived in the United States Senate was to introduce important line-item veto legislation. In fact, I haven't seen anybody move that adeptly since Chuck Person slam-dunked an opponent at Market Square Arena. Together, we're fighting to keep your taxes low and Federal spending down, and that's what I call just plain common sense.

Americans want to keep the longest peacetime expansion ever moving forward—89 months and counting. And Americans want a clean environment—we want that also. And it is my view we can do both. We can't do it if we move to the extreme. And I am not going to move to the extreme in environmental legislation, but we are going to pass and sign sound environmental legislation.

This morning, here in Indianapolis, I went over a few blocks away and planted a tree to help kick off a great community effort to protect and preserve the beauty of this wonderful city. Today, in Washington, there's also a lot at stake—Dick and Dan both know this—clean air, a safe environment, economic growth, and the jobs of thousands of Americans. The Senate today will cast—what is it, 8 p.m. tonight, I believe—an historic vote on our amendments, the first meaningful amendments to the Clean Air Act, a vote which will affect generations to come as we work to build a cleaner, safer America. It's going to take a lot of work to protect this great planet without throwing hard-working Americans out of work.

I again reject the extremists in the environmental movement who would burden our economy by mindless regulation, and I reject those who do not recognize their obligations to clean up our environment. We've got to find the middle path. Common sense tells us to find this needed balance, and we will find it.

Tonight Dan Coats will be back in the Senate to cast one of the most important votes of his life, and I know I can count on him. But I need to count on his experience, his judgment, and his concern for people not just tonight or tomorrow but in the months and the years to come. And that's why I'm counting on each and every one of you in this room to give your all for Dan Coats.

I've talked today just briefly about some of the issues that are important to me as we face the new decade. But one thing to remember: As the world changes, issues will change, but principles remain to the end. And Dan Coats is a principled man who will be a voice for your values. I know Hoosier values, and I admire them. I chose my running mate from Indiana because of them. And on November 6, when the voters of Indiana think of Dan Coats, I know they'll think of the song by another Hoosier, the great Cole Porter, called "You're the Top."

Senator Dan Coats gives voice to the values of the heartland. Nothing could be more important as we head into a new century of challenge and change. So, do what you can. Let's keep Indiana great and keep the dynasty of Republican leadership going strong. Let's continue the tradition and give this good and decent man a huge victory.

Thank you for your support. God bless the State of Indiana. God bless you all. Thank you very, very much.

Note: The President spoke at 1:11 p.m. in Hall C of the Indianapolis Convention Center. In his remarks, he referred to singer Sandi Patti; impressionist Fred Travalena; Don Cox and Margaret Hill, Indiana Republican national committeeman and committeewoman; Dick Freeland, owner of Pizza Hut of Fort Wayne, Inc.; Bob Irsay, owner of the Indianapolis Colts football team; and William J. Bennett, Director of

National Drug Control Policy.

Remarks and an Exchange With Reporters Aboard Air Force One
April 3, 1990

The President. First off, I understand that the House is voting soon on Panama and Nicaragua, and I want to thank the leadership for moving it in a timely fashion. And I hope that it will pass overwhelmingly. And then I would encourage the Senate to act immediately. It is absolutely essential that we get funding for both Nicaragua and Panama, and I will continue to keep that in my sights. It is in the best interest of the United States; it is in the best interest of democracy in our own hemisphere. And so, I would encourage the Senate to move rapidly and to vote on this matter before they consider leaving town at the end of this week. It is essential. It is priority. And I would encourage the Democrats and the Republicans in the Senate to vote promptly on this important measure to help solidify the democracies in Panama and Nicaragua.

And the second subject that concerns me is this comment out of Iraq attributed to Saddam Hussein, the President. This is no time to be talking about using chemical or biological weapons; this is no time to be escalating tensions in the Middle East. And I found those statements to be bad, and I would strongly urge Iraq to reject the use of chemical weapons. And I don't think it helps peace in the Middle East. I don't think it helps the security interests of Iraq, obviously, and it was certainly wrong. So, I would suggest that those statements be withdrawn and that—forget about talk of using chemical and biological weapons.

Assistance for Nicaragua and Panama

Q. Mr. President, Senator Mitchell says your aid package to Panama and Nicaragua have been presented as a jigsaw puzzle, and he wants to see the whole picture before he moves ahead with it.

The President. I would encourage him to move ahead promptly. There's no jigsaw puzzle when it comes to what is best for

democracy in Nicaragua and no jigsaw puzzle when it comes to what is best for Panama. One of the Panamanian leaders was up here, made a convincing case to Members of the Senate. Clearly if any leader would talk to Violeta Chamorro, they'd see the urgency of getting something done on that. I did not see Senator Mitchell's statement, but I would simply say these are laser-like requests—requests to help Nicaragua and Panama.

And in terms of our overall foreign policy, we are on the right track. And I would urge leaders to take a look at the way democracy has moved in this hemisphere, not just to these two countries but in other countries as well. So, let's keep it going, but let's give support to those who need it.

Iraqi Chemical Weapons Threat

Q. Mr. President, do we evidence that the Iraqis have new, modernized binary chemical weapons, or some new generation of chemical weapons?

The President. I've seen no evidence of that. I saw some comment about that, Norm [Norman Sandler, United Press International].

Q. They seem to refer to dual weapons——

The President. ——dual weapons, but preliminary checking—I see no evidence that that means what we think of when we talk about binary weapons.

Q. Is there any reason to feel that he was somehow provoked by threats, real or imagined, in all of this?

The President. Well, I don't know. I know what he cites, but I have no evidence that there's been any threat to his facilities inside Iran, of one kind or another.

Q. Iraq.

The President. I mean, in Iraq.

Q. But Israel could blow up their reactor several years ago.

The President. Well, maybe—you know, this is what—there's a lot speculation that he's talking about—but I've seen no evidence of this.

Q. Will you personally try to contact by Iraq, or any other channels, try to press upon him how strongly you feel at——

The President. Well, I think we've made our views to him very, very clearly through proper channels. Maybe this will help.

AIDS Patient Ryan White

Q. Are you going to try to call Ryan White's family?

The President. I don't know. It's a very delicate moment now. And I hope I made clear how strongly I feel about this young man and about his suffering. But if I thought it would help their spirits in any way, I sure would do it

Q. Any plans of visiting him?

Lithuanian Independence and the Soviet-U.S. Summit

Q. How about updates? Have you heard back from Gorbachev yet?

The President. Have I what?

Q. Have you heard back from Gorbachev? And would you expect to—from Shevardnadze?

The President. I've not had a personal reply, but that's not out of the ordinary because the Foreign Minister will be here tomorrow. I think he gets here tomorrow. And I'll be seeing him.

Q. On Friday.

The President. And that will be the chance to visit with him and see how that message went down in Moscow.

Q. Lock in the summit date?

The President. Well, I don't know that that'll be done on this visit or not. I hope

so. I'd like to get that determined. And I would repeat my desire to see this matter handled in a cool fashion, for freedom of democracy, self-determination all goes forward, but where the result is peaceful, and no use of force. So, I was a little encouraged by some comments that I read out of Lithuania yesterday, and I just would encourage the Soviets to remember the pledge to achieve a peaceful resolution to this very difficult question.

Clean Air Legislation

Q. Cut down clean air vote?

The President. Well, I hope the clean air bill goes well. I, in this instance, salute both Senator Dole and Senator Mitchell for very strong leadership. I think the White House has been very helpful in beating back unhelpful amendments. So, this is an evidence of strong bipartisan work, and it's good. I think it sets a good example. I think the country wants it. We are not going to go to either extreme: the extreme of throwing people out of work and shutting down America and stopping all economic growth, or the extreme of doing nothing about the terribly pressing environmental questions.

Mr. Fitzwater. Mr. President, we're on final approach here.

The President. Are we? How high are we, Marlin?

Mr. Fitzwater. We're at 13½ feet, sir. [*Laughter*]

The President. Thirteen and a—[*laughter*]—those people down there are ants. [*Laughter*] All right.

Note: The President spoke at 3:25 p.m., en route to Detroit, MI. Marlin Fitzwater was Press Secretary to the President. A tape was not available for verification of the content of these remarks.

Remarks at a Republican Party Fundraising Dinner in Detroit, Michigan
April 3, 1990

Thank you, ladies and gentlemen. Thank you all very, very much. Let me say that it's a great pleasure to be here. I'm glad to see Congressman Bill Shuette here. Others from the Congress were to be here, but they've got some voting going on. Especially pleased to see two great former Governors of this State: George Romney and Bill Milliken. And it's also wonderful to have our cochairman of the Republican National Committee, Jeanie Austin, here. You all know that Lee Atwater has been sick; and Jeanie, as the number two person at the Republican National Committee, is doing a superb job. I want to welcome her.

Was all this gang introduced ahead of time, I guess—down there. And of course, to salute your State party leadership: my friend Spence Abraham, the chairman; Ronna Romney and Chuck Yob, the two national committee people; and then, of course, State Senator John Engler. I'm going to say a little more about him in a little bit. And I'm glad to see Detroit City Councilman Keith Butler here tonight. And my thanks, of course, to Heinz Prechter and Randy and Mike and Paul—and I'm going to get in real trouble here—all those who did the heavy lifting on this and put together such a tremendous event. It is so well-done.

Ladies and gentlemen and honored guests, thank you for the welcome and for the privilege of being here. And it's good to be back with you all. I particularly want to pay my respects to Max Fisher and thank him, once again, for being at my side, a constant friend, loyal. And of tremendously sound advice—he gives me that all the time. It's good to be back in the State— [*laughter*]—and I need it, and I need it.

And it's good to be back in the State that produced this year's Miss USA. So, this fall we'll elect a Governor that will be Mr. GOP. [*Laughter*]

This marks my first political trip to Michigan since becoming President, although, as a baseball fan, I feel like I've been here

before. Maybe it goes back to the man I saw on television holding a sign before the recent [baseball] lockout ended. And it read, "All I ask is a chance to work." And it was great to see Sparky Anderson [manager of the Detroit Tigers baseball team] again. [*Laughter*]

Well, you've got a great State. Michigan is also basketball country. And like fans across America, I've marveled at the wizardry of your world champion Pistons, who I was honored to have in the White House last year. And actually, when I was younger, I, too, could dribble a ball with either hand, behind my back, through my legs—which got me thrown out of a lot of bowling alleys. [*Laughter*]

Sports is one reason that it's a pleasure to return to the State which was so kind to me in 1988 and helped our ticket do well. Politics is another. And let me take this chance to salute the entire Republican ticket—its candidates and especially those of you who toil so long and hard at the grassroots level.

Yet the real reason I've come to Detroit tonight goes beyond party to the very essence of this campaign. Let me put it straighter than even an Alan Trammell line drive: Your elections this November will be among the most crucial in America. This election will decide whether Michigan chooses liberal policies, which measure progress made by dollars spent and bureaucracies built, or whether it chooses Republican policies, which help people up and bureaucracies down. This election will decide whether Michigan supports a war on thugs and these drug peddlers or whether Lansing is run by those who soft-pedal the need to be really hard on crime. Finally, this election will decide whether we keep control of the State senate and gain control of the State house of representatives, and whether we have a Governor who will ensure fair reapportionment. You know, some say reapportionment has been a political gold mine for both parties, and they may be right. The Democrats walk away with the gold and we head for the hills. And it's been that way, and this election can help change that. It's that clear-cut, that important.

I know this State, I think, probably not as well as many in this room; but I feel I know this State. And I first got to know you— what Max was referring to in appropriately saluting Bill Milliken—the primary of 1980. So, tonight I make a prediction: This fall, Michigan will make the right decision by supporting Republican candidates. The right decision means a vote for Republicans at the local, county, and State level and for Michigan's next United States Senator; and most of all, it means a vote for the man who says we need new priorities, not new taxes. To repeat a slogan, "Just think what the right man can do." Your next Governor, John Engler.

Okay, so I'm slightly biased. John's a personal friend, and I wanted to come here and personally support him and the great party he represents. I know you wanted to hear a few words from a prominent national figure whose charisma can fire up a crowd and generate some excitement. [*Laughter*] Unfortunately, Bo Schembechler's [president and chief operating officer of the Detroit Tigers] still at spring training in Lakeland, so I'm here. [*Laughter*]

I will tell you, just parenthetically, we had a little receiving line inside, and many came through there and asked about Barbara's health. And let me say I'm sorry she's not here, but her health is just fine. And if this proud husband of some 46 years may be permitted, I think the Silver Fox is doing a good job for our country.

I'm delighted, just as I was a year ago, when [University of] Michigan's basketball Wolverines were welcomed to the White House. I told the national champions, "You're truly number one." Well, tonight, with apologies to you [Michigan State University] Spartan fans out there, let me say there's a song we'll be soon singing about the entire Republican ticket: "Hail to the Victors."

This year Republicans will triumph really for the best of reasons: opportunity—the opportunity that comes from fiscal sanity, less government, and freedom from crime and drugs; the opportunity which rises from increased prosperity and from the chance to think, dream, and worship as one pleases not just in Detroit and Dearborn but also Budapest and Berlin.

You know, it was 1 year ago this month that I came to Hamtramck, only 10 miles away from here, and spoke of how free speech, free elections, and the exercise of free will could change history and lives in all of Eastern Europe. Since then, of course, that's come to pass, and we've seen events even Ripley wouldn't believe. Look at Hungary: 10 days ago holding that nation's first multiparty parliamentary election since 1945. Look at Nicaragua or Czechoslovakia or, yes, that citadel of conscience, Poland— nations whose brave peoples are choosing ballots over bullets and showing how the greatest "peace dividend" is peace itself.

So far I've talked about opportunity for other nations. Republicans also can and have strengthened opportunity at home. Today thousands of Michigan men and women are in need of opportunity. Some say the way to help them is through this old adage of tax and spend. Republicans say the best way is by enacting local policies which have worked nationally. Here's America's box score: more than 20 million new jobs created since 1982, inflation at less than 5 percent, and real per capita income at record levels. Now, these statistics aren't an accident. They stem from Republican policies that work. We don't want government to spend more money; we want people to have more money to spend. So, let's elect candidates like John Engler who believe in these policies. Let's continue the longest peacetime boom in American history and bring an economic renaissance to Michigan.

You know, opportunity means different things to different people. For some, it's the chance to invest, which reminds me that it is time that Congress passed our capital gains tax cut. It is essential we get this done. For others, it's the freedom to root for the team of your choice, to vote for the candidate of your choice, or, yes, even to eat the vegetable of your choice. [*Laughter*]

There's something wrong with this country. I read a poll taken by a New England newspaper, a Boston newspaper, a national poll, that showed 79 percent of the people liked broccoli. [*Laughter*] What's wrong? Where are the 6-year-olds to stand up and join in when they've got something going for them? [*Laughter*] The other answer is they were using Ortega's pollster. [*Laughter*]

When it comes to domestic policy, opportunity really does mean many things. For instance, in child care—we're fighting that battle right now—it means the freedom to choose. So, we have proposed legislation to help low-income working Americans increase choice in child care through tax incentives, not Federal intervention. Last week the House Democratic leadership passed its child-care bill. The good news is that it's better than their previous efforts. The bad news is it costs $20 billion more than the child-care bill I sent up to Congress and that the liberal Democrats still think Big Brother knows what's best for our kids. We Republicans say parents know what's best. Keep the family strong. Do not have the Federal Government setting all the standards for child care all across this country. So, I'm going to stand up for my principles, even if I have to end up vetoing a bill labeled "child care." Child care isn't a slogan; it means the very future of our kids.

Next, there's the environment, where opportunity means an America that's clean and safe. And in that spirit, let me note that this very evening the Senate is going to vote on our clean air legislation, the first rewrite of the Clean Air Act in over a decade. In the finest tradition of American politics, this bill has bipartisan support— Senator Mitchell on the Democratic side; our very able leader, Senator Dole—working hand in hand not to win the debating points but to win cleaner air for the generation to come. I am proud of this proposal to cut smog and acid rain and toxic pollution. We've had to compromise from what I sent up originally. The Democrats have given a little bit. But it's going to work. We can and must ensure the purity of our environment. Tonight marks an historic vote, and I urge the Senate to act not merely for this generation but all the generations to come. Some think we must choose between a sound ecology and a sound economy. Republicans say we need both. America can have clean air and good jobs.

And finally, we can strengthen opportunity through two priorities where State officials, especially the Governor, play a crucial role: education, and crime and drugs.

Ten weeks ago, I announced Phase II of the 1990 National Drug Control Strategy that we unveiled last year. And we're asking Congress to spend over $10.5 billion in fiscal '91 for education, treatment, interdiction, and enforcement—about a 70-percent increase just since I took office. Now, John Engler strongly supports this program, and he'll lead the fight to toughen crime laws at the State level, just as we are trying to do at the Federal level there in Washington, DC. You in Detroit know how bad crime can be and the toll it takes on the families and on communities. And you know how some say there's always a reason for crime and drugs. Well, we say there may be a reason, but there's never an excuse. So, let's elect candidates who will help us take back the streets.

And at the same time, we must also give our kids the opportunity to learn, which is why last fall I convened really an unprecedented event: the Nation's first education summit. From that summit arose six new national educational goals that the Governors and I together announced just recently. Among them, we must see that every student starts school ready to learn—and that's one reason we stepped up a request for Head Start spending so much at the Federal level—and that each school has an environment where kids can learn. And that means making every school drug-free. And our graduation rate must be no less than 90 percent. And we want U.S. students to be first in the world in math and science by the year 2000.

We Republicans know that education is America's most enduring legacy, vital to everything we can become, and that excellence will be obtained not by spending more and more money but by demanding higher standards, greater accountability, better teachers, and greater involvement by parents and communities. And I'd add, and by giving parents more choice in where their kids go to school.

Earlier, I spoke of how liberal Democrats

measure progress made by dollars spent and bureaucracies built, and how Republicans view progress as helping people up and keeping bureaucracies down. Nothing shows the contrast more than education. Ours is the opportunity to make American education number one again, and we must seize it for ourselves and for our kids.

In closing, there's only one opportunity that I haven't mentioned: the opportunity to enjoy this marvelous meal. And ordinarily, I'd stay with you, but the Secret Service caught the cook washing my lettuce with Perrier. [*Laughter*] So, I must be going. And I do apologize for leaving. [*Laughter*] Let me leave you with the thought that opportunity can help us undertake new priorities and make those priorities come true, priorities like better schools and cleaner air, priorities like safer streets and better jobs.

Nationally, Americans have seen what Republicans can do. Now let's show them what we can do right here. Let's win the State senate, the house of representatives.

Let's elect Republican Congressmen and a United States Senator. And let's roll up our sleeves to elect John Engler Governor. We know what he will do—you know what he'll do, and I know what he'll do: He'll make the great State of Michigan even greater. I'm confident of it. I know him well. I ask you to go the extra mile and elect this outstanding man your next Governor.

Thank you all very much. Good luck on election day. And I hope I'll get invited back. And God bless the United States of America. Thank you.

Note: The President spoke at 7:08 p.m. in the Grand Ballroom at the Ritz-Carlton Hotel. In his remarks, he referred to Heinz Prechter and Randy Agley, cochairmen of the fundraising dinner; Michael Timmis, vice chairman of the Talon Corp.; Paul Borman, a Republican Party donor; and Max Fisher, honorary chairman of the fundraising dinner. Following his remarks, he returned to Washington, DC.

Remarks on Signing the Passover Message
April 4, 1990

Mr. Vice President, Mr. Secretary, and distinguished guests, welcome to the White House. Today we are marking Passover, known as the Festival of Freedom, a poignant occasion in the year that has seen freedom's lights begin to glow all over the world—in Eastern Europe, in Central and South America, in Africa, and even in the Soviet Union.

"Let my people go." Those were the words of Moses nearly 4,000 years ago, when the Israelites took the first step on the march from captivity to freedom. All Americans share in the solemn pride of millions of Jewish men, women, and children everywhere as they commemorate the Exodus. It was a journey of courage and strength toward the dream of a better tomorrow.

And today, as well, people all throughout the world have continued that epic journey, a quest for a new life of liberty and peace.

We support them in their struggle for democracy, we admire them for the strength of conviction, and we pray for their success.

This is a special time of rejoicing for the more than 15,000 Soviet Jews who have made their way to Israel this year. We are proud to have lent a helping hand, over the years, to make possible the historic emigration from the Soviet Union of those who have long sought to leave. The modern exodus is a great event for all those who delight in human freedom. The United States has worked hard to open up this lifeline, and we will continue to do everything necessary to make it possible for Soviet Jews to get to Israel, including continuing to press for direct and indirect flights. We are glad that so many will celebrate the Seder in Israel, and we're going to keep working so that many more can join them.

As we remember the Exodus, it is my deep honor to welcome Zev Raiz to the

United States after 18 years of waiting. Zev and Karmella, may you and your children enjoy many years of happiness together in your new home in Israel. For nearly two decades of darkness, you've been a brave symbol for all refuseniks. And we acknowledge and then applaud the dramatic changes that have taken place in the Soviet Union, making possible the emigration of many who have long sought to leave. But we must not—and I can assure you we will not—forget those who are left behind.

And I'd also like to welcome Natasha Stonov to the White House. I admire the courage and determination that you and Leonid, your husband, have shown through 11 long years of waiting. You have become the voice of the refusenik community, and your steadfast efforts have been invaluable to us as we strive to convince the Soviet leadership to act on its promises.

I regret that another Passover is here with Leonid still in the Soviet Union. I wish that he were here with you in America so that he, too, could experience the freedoms we enjoy. And we ask that you convey a message to Leonid and all others who still await freedom: They are not forgotten.

The Nobel laureate—a friend to so many in this room—Elie Wiesel said: "Just as despair can come to one only from other human beings, hope, too, can be given to one only by other human beings." Zev, you have given us hope. For that, we admire you. And together, we look forward to the day when no nation interferes with the faith of any of its people.

So, thank you all for being here with us on this very solemn and special occasion. And once again, I rejoice in your happiness, and we're so pleased you're here. And now I will sign this.

Note: The President spoke at 10:50 a.m. in the Roosevelt Room at the White House. The Passover message was released by the Office of the Press Secretary on April 9.

Statement by Press Secretary Fitzwater on the President's Meeting With the Special Emissaries of Prime Minister Toshiki Kaifu of Japan
April 4, 1990

President Bush met with former Ambassador to the United States Matsunaga and Deputy Foreign Minister Owada, who are Special Emissaries of Prime Minister Kaifu of Japan. The Special Emissaries delivered a letter from Prime Minister Kaifu to the President which contained details on the efforts made by the Government of Japan since the Palm Springs meeting on March 2–4. The discussion focused on the progress made in trade and economic matters.

Agreements have been concluded on supercomputers, satellites, and telecommunications; and substantial progress has been achieved in the ongoing SII process. In addition, Prime Minister Kaifu has said that he hopes an agreement will be forthcoming to resolve the forest products issue. The President was very appreciative of all of the work that has been accomplished over the last month. The President expressed his conviction that Prime Minister Kaifu deserves a very large share of the credit for settling the specific trade issues and for achieving substantial progress on SII.

The President emphasized that SII is an ongoing process and that he hopes both sides will take further steps in the final SII report in July and the resulting follow-on phase. Bringing about structural adjustments will not be easy on either side of the Pacific, but both governments are committed to achieving a positive interim SII report as well as a more comprehensive finished product in July. We have had very substantial success to date, but we must continue our efforts because neither the Japanese consumer nor the American public will be convinced until they see concrete results.

The President emphasized the vital importance of maintaining excellent relations with Japan not only in trade but with regard to security and the growing global partnership between the United States and Japan. In particular, the President complimented the Government of Japan for its

assistance efforts in Eastern Europe and in Central America. In all of these matters, the President praised the forthright and assertive leadership demonstrated by Prime Minister Kaifu and credited him with having created a new spirit of cooperation between the United States and Japan.

Remarks at the Presentation Ceremony for the National Teacher of the Year Award
April 4, 1990

Well, to the Members of the Congress and Senate that are here today, thank you all for coming, and welcome to the White House. Secretary Cavazos, Senator Pell and Representatives Lowery and Hunter, and Bill Keene and Gordon Ambach, Robert Gwinn, Norman Brown, and specially to our distinguished Teacher of the Year, Jan Gabay, Barbara and I are honored to have you all here.

The kind of people Jan represents are ambassadors to the most powerful province mankind might command, that great undiscovered realm right under your hat. For almost 40 years, the Teacher of the Year program has singled out the few, really because they represent the many. The program's goal is not to identify "the best" teacher but the best in all teachers. All teachers are different, of course, but the best have a special kind of energy that ushers ideas to minds, and ideals to souls. They unleash the imagination and turn young eyes toward brilliant constellation of human aspiration and experience.

Maybe it's the pace of history, the pulse of the natural world, or the power of reason; but whatever, America's best teachers are teaching. They all understand that learning is not a spectator sport. The value of knowledge is not in the having but in the sharing. And wisdom is not received: it is pursued.

You might have heard it said that knowledge isn't found in books. In one sense, true. There's nothing intrinsically helpful about a book—just black marks on a few

white pages. But in hands that know how to hold them, how to embrace their ideas and deliver them whole, a book can change a life forever. Those who breathe life into ancient texts have seen that power, seen those words explode in brilliance in a young mind. Through teachers and their students, the ideas of the past are sustained, and the ideas of the future are defined.

And if the life of the mind is one of both work and wonder, I'd like to introduce a man among us today who's lived that life better and longer than anyone else. He was born in 1889, the son of a former slave. He served in the First World War, became fluent in 6 languages, earned 11 degrees, and taught school until he was 81. That alone would be impressive enough. But at the age of 100, he still practices law and still attends law school seminars with the eagerness of a first-year student. Try to praise him, though, and he'll bawl you out, saying, "There's nothing extraordinary about me." And he told me that I was the second President that he's met; the first was Franklin Delano Roosevelt. [*Laughter*] But having met him, I know this is a risk to praise him, but I have to disagree with him. I hope you'll join me in commending a man who may be America's most seasoned scholar, John Morton-Finney. Would you stand up please, Mr. Morton-Finney? [*Applause*]

One lesson we might take from Mr. Morton-Finney is this: If he's still ready and willing to learn, so can we all be. And if he's always looking for new ideas and new ways of thinking, so must the entire system of American education.

A year ago this week, here in the Rose Garden, across the way, I sent legislation up to Congress to help reform and restructure America's schools. Today I want to appeal to the Members of Congress to move on those initiatives.

We've already moved in concert to bring a sense of direction to education reform. We've held the first-ever summit with the Nation's Governors, and we've set ambitious goals for our students, our schools, and ourselves—rallying points for the progress we all know is greatly needed now. But what we must remember, above all, is that education is more important than politics. And while our '91 budget request for education is the largest in American history, our progress won't be measured by bureaucracies built and dollars spent. It will be measured by results and by what our children learn and accomplish.

If we judge our students by their thinking, we must judge ourselves by our own. And there are cases of very creative thinking about education going on right now, ideas for reform that hold promise for the rest of the Nation.

In Milwaukee, Wisconsin, because of a grassroots movement made up largely of poor, inner-city parents, a new experiment in choice is applying the leverage of competition and stimulating change. Thanks to Polly Williams, once a welfare mother of four and now a State legislator, low-income parents can choose to send their kids to private nonsectarian schools, with money from the public school system's budget paying $2,500 in tuition for each student. Choice empowers people, and it puts competition to work, improving schools for every student.

In Kentucky, an entirely new philosophy of management is being put into place which is based on accountability. The school system is being decentralized, with local districts gaining control over our operations and individual schools gaining more auton-omy overall. The State is managing a new system of rewards for teachers and administrators, including biyearly awards up to $8,000 and leaving curriculum questions to the local districts.

That kind of creative thinking is government's best role in education: setting goals, providing incentives, and then demanding accountability. But as crucial as good government is, we all understand where the real action is: it's in the hands of our teachers. And that's why we're here today: to recognize a teacher who represents our best.

Her story began with a little collection of books spread out on hardpacked earth beneath a wooden stairway, where she played school with her younger sister. To Jan Gabay, those books revealed an imagined life of seekers, sages, and students—a life Jan has since chosen to make real for herself and the students she teaches. Over the past 17 years she has developed her power to motivate minds, to give kids a sense of wonder and bless them with a life of possibilities unimagined in ordinary moments.

She says her goal is to help her students find and refine the "knowledge, skill, and talent that they do not know they have." But she understands that a real education goes far beyond acquiring skills: it instills a lifelong love of learning. "Accepting simple competence," she says, "is the antithesis of what I believe education really is: an unending quest to understand the world by using one's mind and to understand the self by knowing one's heart."

Jan always tells her students that she has succeeded because of them. In that spirit, it is also true that our schools will succeed because of people like her.

So, it is an honor to have you here, Janis Gabay, and to name you the 1990 National Teacher of the Year. God bless you for all you're doing for those kids.

Note: The President spoke at 2:15 p.m. in the Roosevelt Room at the White House.

Remarks on Clean Air Legislation at a Meeting With Members of the Senate
April 4, 1990

The President. Let me just say at the outset of this meeting that I appreciate everybody's coming down. And I want to congratulate the Senate on the Clean Air Act Amendment of 1990. Senators Mitchell, Dole, Baucus, and Chafee have shown real leadership in helping us at last break the legislative logjam on clean air. And at the same time, I think everyone here would agree that a lot of work lies ahead.

Last year I submitted a bill that ensures that future generations in this country will breathe clean air; and we propose to do this through cleaner factories and power plants, cleaner cars, cleaner fuels. And we felt, and we still feel, that we can achieve our goal without major harm to the economy and without a massive job loss. And our legislation and the agreement we've worked out was very carefully balanced. The bill passed by the Senate last night reflects and is based on bipartisan consensus in support of that balanced approach: that we can have cleaner air and a growing economy which continues to produce jobs for the American people.

In that respect, there is no question that the Senate bill is a major step forward, but it is only a first step. And more progress is going to be needed if we're to achieve the balanced bill that I feel is essential. We're going to work to ensure that the bill produced by the House, and ultimately by the conference committee, does not compromise the environmental benefits or the economic balance contained in my original proposal, and certainly contained in that agreement with the Senate leadership.

So, with our friends here, I just want to thank each and every one of you who has played a constructive role in what I think is a major breakthrough, Mr. Leader. And I know Bob and I have talked about it a lot, and I think we all agree to that.

Assistance for Nicaragua and Panama

Q. Mr. President, will you ask Senator Mitchell to break the logjam on Panama and Nicaragua aid?

The President. Yes. [*Laughter*] I thought you'd never ask.

Note: The President spoke at 2:55 p.m. in the Cabinet Room at the White House.

Appointment of Wilfredo J. Gonzalez as Staff Director of the Commission on Civil Rights
April 4, 1990

The President today announced his intention to appoint Wilfredo J. Gonzalez to be Staff Director of the Commission on Civil Rights. He would succeed Joseph Al Latham, Jr.

Since 1988 Mr. Gonzalez has served as Associate Director for Equal Employment Opportunity and Civil Rights at the Department of State. Prior to this, he was Associate Administrator for Minority Small Business and Capital Ownership Development at the Small Business Administration, 1985–

1988. Mr. Gonzalez was a consultant in Washington, DC, 1985, and a White House volunteer for the Hispanic Inaugural Ball, 1984–1985. In addition, Mr. Gonzalez served in several positions at the Peace Corps, including Chief of Operations for Latin America and Deputy Director of the Peace Corps in Colombia, South America, and Director of the Peace Corps in Ghana, West Africa, 1978–1984. He served as special assistant to the Deputy Assistant Secretary at the Department of Labor, 1977–

1978; HEW fellow at the Department of Health, Education and Welfare, 1976–1977; Assistant Director for the Technical Assistant Unit for the Community Service Society Unit in New York, 1975–1976; Director of Development for ASPIRA of America in New York, 1973–1975; manpower consultant for the New York Urban Coalition, 1973; and management consultant for Costly, Miller and Sattertwaite, Inc., in Chevy Chase, MD, and New York, 1972–1973.

Mr. Gonzalez graduated from the University of Puerto Rico (B.A., 1969). He was born March 26, 1943, in San Juan, PR. Mr. Gonzalez served in the U.S. Navy, 1961–1964. He is married, has three children, and resides in Springfield, VA.

Remarks at the 20th Anniversary Dinner of the Joint Center for Political and Economic Studies
April 4, 1990

Thank you all for that warm welcome. Wendell, thank you, sir. And to Eddie Williams, my respects and thanks for having me here. And to David Kearns and Vernon Jordan, our old friend, and Jim Robinson, another, thank you all. And to Reverend Newsome, thank you, sir, for that lovely invocation. It's also good to be out on the town with our good friend Elsie Hillman, well-known to many here. And I would especially like to recognize and pay my respects to Doug Wilder, the Governor of Virginia, over here. I'm delighted.

You know, it's remarkable to think that in 1968, less than 2 years before the Joint Center was founded, there were only 200 elected black public officials in all of America. Twenty years later, there are more than 6,000—an amazing record. But what I find most heartening is the way in which black leadership in America has become an ordinary, accepted feature of our national life. This new leadership has a tremendous resource in the Joint Center for Political and Economic Studies. A philosopher once said that no problem can stand the assault of sustained thinking. If that is true, then no problem we face today is a match for the Joint Center, truly one of the leading academies of independent thought in Washington today. Eddie, we congratulate you for your steadfast leadership.

We can see for ourselves tonight that Washington is still a city that thrives on ideas. As Americans from different professions and political parties, we are together on this wonderful evening to celebrate our shared ideals. We may not agree on everything, but we agree on a few great things: liberty, equality, opportunity, and justice for all.

And not long ago, a distinguished group of 15 black publishers from across the country came for lunch at the White House; and we discussed everything from our stimulating meetings with Václav Havel, the new playwright-President of Czechoslovakia, to our struggle to battle domestically—get rid of—this nation—rid it of drugs and crime. And after lunch, we walked outside; and together we strolled out of the Oval Office, across the South Lawn and through the Diplomatic Reception Room, into the Residence and up to the Lincoln Bedroom. And it's an impressive room, with its high, imposing ceiling and its tall windows, lace curtains, and old Victorian furnishings. But you know what it is about that room that's so powerful? It's not that Lincoln slept there. In fact, he didn't. [*Laughter*] It's that he worked there and thought there and agonized there, because he made some of his greatest decisions there. It was his office and the Cabinet Room, and it was where he signed the Emancipation Proclamation.

In a display case along the wall is a copy of the Gettysburg Address, sitting on a desk in the corner, written in Lincoln's dignified hand. In fact, of the five copies he made, that he wrote out in hand, it's the only one that he actually signed. And above it is a great painting titled "Watch Meeting, Waiting for the Hour." It's a very poignant scene, depicting slaves and their friends gathered around an elderly man, a man who had never known a minute of freedom. And now that Lincoln had proclaimed January 1, 1863, as the first day of freedom, all their eyes are fixed on a watch, waiting for the stroke of midnight, waiting to be free.

It is said that Lincoln's hand shook as he dipped his quill into the ink well before he signed the Emancipation Proclamation. Perhaps he felt the weight of history. Perhaps he was weary. In any event, he waited a moment to steady his hand so that no one would think he wavered on such an important decision. Through the vision of one man, millions were freed.

Together, those of us in his room felt the greatness of the events that had taken place in there and the profound consequences of a simple stroke of the pen. In moments like these, history comes rushing back as a revelation, and that very special moment leads me to reflect on the special responsibilities of the Presidency, responsibilities that haven't changed since that midnight of freedom in 1863. Every President since has been challenged to be part of the legacy of Lincoln, the continuum of freedom.

And the day will come—and it's not far off—when the legacy of Lincoln will finally be fulfilled at 1600 Pennsylvania Avenue, when a black man or woman will sit in that Oval Office. And when that day comes, the most remarkable thing about it will be how naturally it occurs. That person will be another President, another traveler in the continuum of freedom, representing all the people of America, representing all that is best about America. You know, I meet a lot of school kids; Barbara goes to a lot of events where kids are there. And I wonder as I look at the faces of brave 10-year-olds swearing to uphold the fight against drugs: Will one of them be President? Is this the kid who will fulfill that legacy?

Now, I saw Jesse Jackson earlier, and I don't want to get anything started, so, Jesse, I'm talking about little kids. [*Laughter*] I'm not talking about some 49-year-old guy here. I like my job. [*Laughter*] Let's not rush this thing. Where did he go?

But I also know that prejudice and racial tensions still do exist in America, and that's

why I told Ben Hooks and Coretta Scott King and so many others in the civil rights movement that I would use this bully pulpit to condemn in the strongest terms racism, bigotry, and hate.

You know, black Americans have challenged me and our entire administration— my distinguished friend, Lou Sullivan, who I'm very proud of, knows this to be true— challenged us to live up to the highest ideals of the civil rights movement, and I accept that challenge. And now let me ask you to work with us to build a better America. There are new missions for the civil rights movement in the 1990's. From now on, the protection of civil rights must also mean the removal of all barriers to opportunity, for there are forms of poverty that cannot be measured or solved by dollars alone.

In fighting against poverty and for opportunity, we must draw inspiration from achievements both at home and abroad. We must draw inspiration from the civil rights and Solidarity movements and from the new hope dawning in South Africa today. For after all, the Freedom March that wound through the country roads of Selma 25 years ago leads to the cobbled streets of Warsaw and Budapest today, and now the winds of change have come to South Africa, where Nelson Mandela is a free man.

Let me just take 1 minute to discuss America's Africa policy, for change is sweeping this troubled continent. But this time, change brings opportunity. So, let us work together to help the peoples of Africa to overcome poverty, disease, starvation, and war. We're working to overcome these problems throughout Africa. And we continue to actively seek national reconciliation in Angola. And we support the efforts of President Chissano to end the fighting in Mozambique. And we are looking for ways we can help the newly independent nation of Namibia.

In Ethiopia, we stand ready to deliver tons of food to save millions facing starvation, and tragically, the war that rages there prevents our access to these people in need. And I call upon the political leaders of Ethiopia to give the highest priority to humanitarian relief by opening all available corridors for the urgent movement of food supplies, and I appeal to other members of the United Nations to use their influence to achieve this vital objective. If you ever have held in your arms, as Barbara and I did—in the Sudan it was for us—this kid that is starving—lay aside the politics. Let's get those routes open. Let's get that food to those starving people in Ethiopia.

South Africa is, of course, of special concern because we can now take hope that the age of apartheid is nearing a close. And there are new signs of flexibility and commitment both from the Government and the opponents of apartheid. President de Klerk has already taken some significant steps, lifting the ban on political parties, releasing Mandela and other political prisoners. And I salute President de Klerk for taking these steps. But even more must be done. The state of emergency must end, and political prisoners must be released. And most of all, there must be an end to the tragic cycle of violence—a task that demands great courage and resolve from all South African leaders, black and white.

The Government's attempts to enforce apartheid through force and repression have failed, and violent attacks by opponents of apartheid inside South Africa have equally failed. And most tragically, the senseless violence perpetrated by blacks against blacks has become a major impediment to rapid progress toward a negotiated settlement. All sides should follow the spirit of Martin Luther King, Jr., and renounce violence.

And such a step will nurture the climate for negotiations toward a new system based on equal rights and opportunities. It is imperative that the opposition not miss this opportunity to negotiate seriously a framework for a truly democratic South Africa, liberated from the horror of apartheid. And we are encouraged by signs that all sides share a growing commitment to the negotiating process. We stand ready to support this still-fragile process in any way we can.

Jim Baker, our Secretary of State, has just returned from South Africa, where he met with President de Klerk and the leading members of the black opposition. And he met with Nelson Mandela in Namibia. And I've also invited, as I think everybody here knows, President de Klerk and Mr. Mandela to meet with me at the White House. And I will spare no effort to bring about positive change in South Africa. But we must practice this diplomacy as a nation, and that leads me to say we must continue our programs to assist the disadvantaged majority.

American businesses that remain in South Africa must work for change. And we will make clear our strong conviction that multiparty democracy, based on a vigorous free enterprise system, represents the best model for any successful society. In short, we can all work for change. American influence is strongest when Americans speak with one voice. So, let us work together to forge a strong consensus on South Africa, one that unites all Americans of all races, of both parties in a noble cause.

In America, right here at home, we also seek the fulfillment of a noble cause: to overcome obstacles to opportunity. And in this cause let us look to the heroes of our times. Has the world known more improbable heroes than Rosa Parks and Lech Walesa? But heroes they are. Let us honor them by working together in solidarity.

But opportunity alone is not enough, for there's yet another form of poverty caused by fear. In January, in Kansas City, I saw people who had suffered from crack and crackling bursts of gunfire, not heard there since the days of the old West. And yesterday I visited a 17-year-old black high school student named Derrick Turnbow in a Cincinnati hospital. You see, Derrick was an innocent bystander who got caught in the crossfire of a shoot-out. He was shot in the head, and he's now lying there paralyzed. And the only means left to this honor student to communicate is by winking his eye. And in Alexandria, just across the Potomac, I saw another neighborhood where a crack-crazed addict had slain a policeman. And in my own old congressional district in Houston, Texas, in an area called Acres Homes, I talked with citizens who'd seen their community ravaged by pushers and decided to change all that.

Everywhere I went I found hope. I found people who have had enough of fear, had enough of crime, had enough of dope. And just as the people of East Berlin stood up for freedom, so the people of these neighborhoods are rallying together, using people power to fight for another kind of freedom: freedom from crime and drugs. Freedom from fear. We must march with them in solidarity, side by side, block by block, city by city.

And then there's yet another kind of poverty: the growing poverty of knowledge. Many young men and women in this country are simply not learning. They're not learning the basics to hold down a job or to raise a family, and that is a national disgrace. And we need to improve the quality of education for all Americans and raise our expectations for what we know our children can learn and accomplish. We must again work in solidarity to better our schools.

And that's why I'm pleased that so many of you, leaders from business—and I run a risk here, but I'd like to single out David Kearns, of Xerox—along with leaders in government, education, labor, and the media, are working together to better our schools by serving on the President's Education Policy Advisory Committee.

I've discussed just a few of the many ways in which we're trying to fight against poverty and for opportunity to build a better America, and I could go on. But my favorite story says it all. About the kid that went to church with his grandfather, and he said, "Granddad"—the preacher going on and on and on—the kid says, "What's those flags along the side of the church there?" The grandfather said, "Well, son," he said, "that's for those who died in service." And the kid said, "Oh, really? The 9 or the 11 o'clock service?" [*Laughter*]

So, I know you haven't eaten yet, and we are rudely taking off. But look, we've talked about the struggle against crime and fear, and the struggle for better education and opportunity. But the bottom line is simply this: When the morning comes, will we work together for what we have applauded tonight? I've seen your good works. I know that we will. And let us make this the time for solidarity. Martin Luther King spoke of an arc of justice, a continuum of freedom. It is our legacy, our freedom legacy, that makes the sons and daughters of this American nation like no other.

I'm just delighted to have been with you. I came over, Eddie, to say again my thanks and respects to you, sir. And to all of you, thank you, and God bless the United States of America. Thank you very, very much.

Note: The President spoke at 7:42 p.m. in the International Ballroom at the Washington Hilton Hotel. In his remarks, he referred to Wendell G. Freeland and Eddie N. Williams, chairman and president of the center, respectively; David T. Kearns, national dinner chairman and chief executive officer and chairman of the board of Xerox Corp.; James D. Robinson III, chairman, president, and chief executive officer of the American Express Co.; Elsie H. Hillman, member of the board of directors of the center; Vernon E. Jordan, Jr., master of ceremonies; Jesse Jackson, political leader and civil rights activist; Coretta Scott King, widow of Dr. Martin Luther King, Jr.; and Benjamin L. Hooks, executive director of the National Association for the Advancement of Colored People.

Excerpt From a Statement by Press Secretary Fitzwater on the Points of Light Initiative Foundation
April 5, 1990

The President was pleased to learn of the addition of George Romney as a founding director of the Points of Light Initiative Foundation. Governor Romney joins John Akers, Ray Chambers, Johnnetta Cole, Marva Collins, Michael Eisner, Roberto Goizueta, Kim Grose, James Joseph, Margaret Kuhn, Edward Malloy, Brian O'Connell, and Robert Wright as a founding director.

Note: The press release also contained biographical information on Mr. Romney.

Statement by Press Secretary Fitzwater on the Upcoming Summit With President Mikhail Gorbachev of the Soviet Union
April 5, 1990

President Bush and President Gorbachev have agreed on dates for holding their summit meeting in the United States. The summit will take place during the dates of Wednesday, May 30, and Sunday, June 3.

Remarks on the Upcoming Summit With President Mikhail Gorbachev of the Soviet Union
April 5, 1990

The President. You've got a few fans over here. This is what we call a photo opportunity. I just wanted to welcome Michael Jackson here, who has been named Artist of the Decade. And he has a tremendous following. He does good work, what we call the Points of Light concept. I just wanted to bring him out here and officially welcome him to the White House once again.

Glad you're here, sir. Very pleased you're here.

And I might say, inasmuch as I understand Marlin said that I might have a word on the summit with Mr. Gorbachev, I'm very pleased the dates have been set, and it is very important that we have these conversations. Dialog is important. And I'm looking forward to seeing Mr. Gorbachev here.

Conversations with Mr. Shevardnadze are going reasonably well, and I will receive him here in the Oval Office tomorrow. I look forward to that. This is the time for a lot of dialog and a lot of discussion, and I'm delighted that this——

Q. Where is it going to be?

Q. Why was it moved up a month, Mr. President?

The President. See what I told you was going to happen?

Note: The President spoke at 11:05 a.m. in the Rose Garden at the White House, prior to a meeting with singer Michael Jackson. In his remarks, he referred to Marlin Fitzwater, Press Secretary to the President, and Soviet Foreign Minister Eduard A. Shevardnadze.

Letter to Congressional Leaders Transmitting a Report on the Activities of the Soviet Union-United States Standing Consultative Commission
April 5, 1990

Dear Mr. Speaker: (Dear Mr. Chairman:)

In accordance with the Arms Control and Disarmament Act as amended by section 3(b) of the Arms Control and Disarmament Amendments Act of 1987 (22 U.S.C. 2578), attached is a classified report prepared by the United States Commissioner to the U.S.- U.S.S.R. Standing Consultative Commission (SCC) concerning the activities of the SCC during calendar year 1989. The report includes detailed information on all substantive issues raised by either party to the Treaty on the Limitation of Anti-Ballistic Missile Systems and the responses of the other party with regard to such issues during 1989.

Sincerely,

GEORGE BUSH

Note: Identical letters were sent to Thomas S. Foley, Speaker of the House of Representatives, and Claiborne Pell, chairman of the Senate Foreign Relations Committee.

Letter to Congressional Leaders on the Termination of the Emergency With Respect to Panama
April 5, 1990

Dear Mr. Speaker: (Dear Mr. President:)

Today I have issued an Executive order, a copy of which is attached, stating that the restoration of a democratically elected government in Panama has ended the unusual and extraordinary threat to the national security, foreign policy, and economy of the United States previously posed by the policies and actions of the Noriega regime. The order therefore terminates the Panamanian emergency declared on April 8, 1988, while preserving enforcement and blocking authorities as authorized by law.

Sincerely,

GEORGE BUSH

Note: Identical letters were sent to Thomas S. Foley, Speaker of the House of Representatives, and Dan Quayle, President of the Senate. The Executive order is listed in Appendix E at the end of this volume.

Nomination of Wendy Lee Gramm To Be a Commissioner and Chairman of the Commodity Futures Trading Commission
April 5, 1990

The President has nominated Wendy Lee Gramm to be a Commissioner of the Commodity Futures Trading Commission for the term expiring April 13, 1995, and he has also nominated her to serve as Chairman of the Commission. This is a reappointment.

Since 1988 Dr. Gramm has served as Chairman of the Commodity Futures Trading Commission. Prior to this, she served as Administrator for Information and Regulatory Affairs at the Office of Management and Budget, 1985–1988; Executive Director of the Presidential Task Force on Regulatory Relief, 1986–1988; Director of the Bureau of Economics at the Federal Trade Commission, 1983–1985; Assistant Director in the Division of Consumer Protection at the Bureau of Economics at the Federal Trade Commission, 1982–1983; and research staff member for the Institute for Defense Analyses, 1979–1982. In addition, she served in several positions at Texas A&M University, including associate professor in the department of economics, 1975–1979; director of undergraduate programs, 1974–1977; and assistant professor, 1970–1975.

Dr. Gramm graduated from Wellesley College (B.A., 1966) and Northwestern University (Ph.D., 1971). She was born January 10, 1945, in Waialua, HI. Dr. Gramm is married, has two children, and resides in Washington, DC.

Statement by Press Secretary Fitzwater on the Japan-United States Structural Impediments Initiative Negotiations
April 5, 1990

Since the March 2–4 Palm Springs meeting between President Bush and Prime Minister Kaifu, Japan and the United States have been busily engaged in strengthening the U.S.-Japan relationship by resolving ongoing trade and economic issues. An agreement has been concluded on supercomputers, and agreements in principle have been reached on satellites and telecommunications.

Today the U.S.-Japan SII working group released its interim report on the progress achieved to date. The SII talks represent an approach that may be unique in the history of bilateral trade and economic discussions. The talks were designed to identify and resolve the structural impediments that contribute to economic tensions between the two countries. Accordingly, the interim report and assessment identifies specific areas impeding the adjustment of the trade imbalance in both countries. The interim report is the first major step in a process that will include a final SII report in July as well as implementation and follow-on.

Prime Minister Kaifu and the political leadership of Japan have worked long and hard to produce the policy commitments embedded in the SII interim report. Because structural problems are deeply ingrained in both economies, complete results will not come quickly. However, the SII interim report is an important way station along the road leading to a strengthened U.S.-Japan relationship. We believe that the Prime Minister will continue to exercise his assertive leadership on these issues and that this will greatly facilitate the work on remaining economic and trade issues. Japan's inputs to the SII interim report have been very positive ones, and we look forward to further cooperation on the final report in July. For its part, the United States will continue to do its utmost to address the structural issues identified in the SII interim report as affecting the competitiveness of the U.S. economy.

As President Bush has said, the leadership of Prime Minister Kaifu has brought a new spirit of cooperation to our relationship—a positive, cooperative force which will strengthen our security relationship and enhance the U.S.-Japan global partnership while simultaneously facilitating the solution of outstanding economic differences.

Statement by Press Secretary Fitzwater on the President's Meeting With Foreign Minister Eduard Shevardnadze of the Soviet Union
April 6, 1990

The President met with Soviet Foreign Minister Shevardnadze for approximately 2 hours and 20 minutes this morning. The President's meeting follows 2 days of meeting that the Foreign Minister has held with Secretary Baker at the State Department. The 3 days of meetings encompassed the 5 baskets which have characterized our relationship over the past year: human rights, bilateral relations, regional affairs, arms control, and transnational issues.

In their discussions, the President urged continued peaceful dialog in Lithuania. The President made clear that the United States does not recognize the forcible incorporation of Lithuania into the Soviet Union. He expressed our desire for self-determination by the Lithuanian people and his concern that the Soviet Union not undertake any actions that might thwart resolution of this issue through peaceful dialog and mutual agreement.

The working group on arms control continues its work this afternoon. There are difficult technical issues yet to be resolved.

In other areas of discussion, there was a fruitful exchange of views. In particular, we pressed the Soviet Union to reconsider its position on direct flights to Israel. The United States has always supported freedom of emigration. This step by the Soviet Union would bring about the freedom of movement that we have long urged for Jewish emigrants from the Soviet Union.

In regional affairs, the two Presidents [the President and the Foreign Minister] continued the discussions on Afghanistan, Central America, Cambodia, Africa, and other regions. The President made clear once again our position on Afghanistan: that the people of Afghanistan must have the freedom of self-determination in selecting their own government.

On European affairs the issue of German unification was discussed and the United States repeated its position that a united Germany should be a full member of NATO. Both sides noted the rapid changes toward democratic and economic reform that are progressing in Eastern Europe, and both emphasized the need for these changes to continue.

Foreign Minister Shevardnadze reaffirmed President Gorbachev's commitment to *glasnost* and *perestroika*. He delivered a letter from President Gorbachev on arms control. The Foreign Minister also reiterated President Gorbachev's commitment to resolve the Lithuanian issue by open and frank dialog.

Near the end of the expanded meeting, President Bush offered his personal assessment of the U.S.-Soviet relationship. And I quote:

"Ours is a vitally important relationship. We have problems, including Lithuania. We are determined to resolve current arms control issues and move forward with the process. And finally, we acknowledge the changes in Europe and share a conviction that stability is important."

The President feels this meeting was extensive, cordial, and productive. He looks forward to the summit meeting with President Gorbachev and to this afternoon's discussions between Secretary Baker and the Foreign Minister.

Note: Press Secretary Fitzwater read the statement during his daily press briefing, which began at 1:10 p.m.

Remarks and a Question-and-Answer Session With Members of the American Society of Newspaper Editors
April 6, 1990

The President. To President Ghiglione and distinguished guests, thank you very much. It's a pleasure to be here. I see Hans-Dietrich Genscher here, the Foreign Minister of the Federal Republic of Germany, and I want to single him out and salute him and tell him how much I value the most cordial relations between the Government of the Federal Republic and the Government of the United States of America. And this man has done an awful lot to make those relations better. So, Hans-Dietrich, glad to see you here, sir.

You all understand our system, so I'm looking around to see if I see any Members of Congress to salute. [*Laughter*] But they

adjourned and have all taken off for some exotic place, I'm sure. But I am told that the Governor of the State of Michigan is here, or was to be here. But if he is, I want to pay my respects to Governor Blanchard and all the distinguished guests.

Look, my remarks will be short. After all, ours is the Information Age, so I thought I'd leave sufficient time for questions and answers. But let me just talk for a few minutes about how, as information travels from one place to another in the blink of an eye, our world has become even smaller; so that what happens in Texarkana affects Tokyo or Tbilisi. Like you, I find the Information Age fascinating. Its consequences are many, from the growing global demand for a safe and clean environment to nations uniting against the scourge of crime and drugs. The Information Age has helped liberty spread from Nicaragua to the heart of Central Europe—what I call the Revolution of '89. For as people come to know more of the free world, they demand their own world of freedom: free elections, free markets, free will unhampered by the state.

As you know, I met this morning with Foreign Minister Shevardnadze, and Lithuania was the key point of discussion. I reiterated the strong United States view that the issue must be dealt with through peaceful means. And we support the right of the Lithuanian people to self-determination. We have never recognized the forcible incorporation of the Baltic States into the Soviet Union. And I told Minister Shevardnadze that this is an issue that could adversely affect the prospects for progress in these important U.S.-Soviet relations. And I urged the Soviet Union to begin a good-faith dialog with Lithuania.

We want, and we believe the Soviets want, to make further progress in U.S.-Soviet relations. And we're working toward important agreements in the area of arms control and to make progress on human rights and the solution of these regional conflicts. I asked him to convey to President Gorbachev that I am looking forward to his visit to the United States at the end of May. This is an important time for discussion and dialog.

America's newspapers, of course, will report the news of this morning's meeting, just as they have for centuries, telling the truth, informing the public as fairly and responsibly as possible, and letting the chips fall where they may. And I know that the best example of today's Information Age will continue to be a free press.

What makes the Revolution of '89 so unprecedented is that at last an increasing number of foreign journalists are also free as well as able to write the truth without censorship or without fear—reporters, commentators, and editors abroad who have gone from instruments of the state to servants of the people.

Let me take a moment to note one journalist who is not free and who is in our thoughts. Of course, I'm talking about Terry Anderson, and we hope and pray that he will soon be free. And he, more than anyone, would be moved by the men and women who in 1989 and '90 have upheld the tradition of a courageous free press.

In Czechoslovakia, a playwright becomes President. Both his Foreign Minister and chief spokesman are former journalists persecuted by the Communist regime for years.

In Colombia, the respected editor of El Espectador is slain by assassins, but the murdered editor's brother becomes publisher and vows to fight—and does. "We cannot back down," he says. A bomb last year injured over 70 employees of that same newspaper, and most of its facilities were wiped out, totally destroyed. But the next day, an edition hits the streets, printed by a competing paper's facilities. The front-page headline says, "We Will Continue"—and they do. And let me commend those U.S. papers which bought ads in that paper to show support.

And in Nicaragua, Violeta Chamorro, former editor, wife of a murdered publisher, becomes President in certifiably free elections—President of the land that they love. Freedom of the press begets freedom of people.

This week, our talks with Japan focused on another aspect of freedom: the ability of people to trade and invest as they wish. This morning I read a quote by a Japanese businessman that demonstrated this point. He was talking about the essence of private enterprise: competition. What the Americans are saying, he said, about keeping prices low and quality high—they are talking about democracy.

Last night Japan and the United States released that interim report on our Structural Impediments Initiative designed to remove structural barriers to trade in both countries. This SII is a unique undertaking and reflects enormous amounts of hard work on each side. The Government of Japan and Prime Minister Kaifu—and I salute him—have shown true leadership. And the Prime Minister, in particular, deserves major credit. He made success on trade and economic negotiations with us his top priority, and in 1 month, we have had real success.

For the first time, Japan has committed to removing a broad array of structural barriers that constrain trade and impede imports. For its part, the United States will continue to address the structural issues identified by Japan by improving the competitiveness of our own economy—because structural problems are deeply ingrained in both economies.

Complete results will not come quickly, therefore, but they can and they must come. Neither the Japanese consumer nor the American people will be convinced that progress is at hand until they see concrete results. And this interim report shows not only substantial progress on trade issues but is an important way station leading to a strengthened U.S.-Japan relationship.

The Information Age has served as a catalyst of cooperation, a conduit of knowledge, and an advocate of freedom. As events of the past year have shown, the free press represents the very essence of that age, and you've helped write the first draft of history and breathed new life into democracy.

And for that, I thank you and congratulate you on this significant anniversary. God bless you all. Many thanks for inviting me. And now to the fun part. [*Laughter*]

Press Coverage of U.S. Troops in Combat

Mr. Ghiglione. The President has agreed to take questions. As is quite clear, members of the society only may ask questions. Please step up to one of the floor mikes, and please identify yourself by your name and your newspaper. If I may exercise the presidential prerogative, Mr. President, and ask the first question.

Given that the experience of the press pool in Panama again proved that this arrangement for covering the early stages of a military action is not working, and given that Secretary Cheney essentially told this society on Wednesday that the issue is closed, would you be willing to ask the Secretary to meet with ASNE and other press representatives to forge a plan that will work? And how soon? [*Laughter*]

The President. Sure. Knowing Dick Cheney, I expect he'd welcome such a meeting. But if there's any complications, I will encourage him to do it. And we ought to talk about a wide array of things on that press pool. I notified the Members of Congress at the time, or just before the operation began, and one of them told me that he'd already received a call from a great paper asking him about this. The person that called him had a compadre on the pool who had felt free to tell this person about it, and that person had notified a very important Member of Congress before the President could.

So, I think we should have some discussions. And I think, for those who were in the press pool and felt that they weren't given access, we certainly ought to go the extra mile to see that they get access when they get there. When you're involved in a combat situation, I don't need to tell people in this room there are constraints. But, yes, I'd welcome such a meeting, and I'd be very anxious to hear how it comes out. But I expect Dick will be glad to do it. And I want to commit my man, Marlin Fitzwater [Press Secretary to the President], to attend over there, too, because we are trying. And heaven knows, we can use some suggestions.

Middle East Peace Process

Q. Mr. President, this is a followup to a question I asked you in December here at a meeting of editors—[*laughter*]—in which your answer was that the United States definitely was not going to try to pressure Israel to negotiate with the PLO. Some people seem to see signs now that this government is pressuring Israel by trying to establish linkages between aid and the Israeli Government's performance. And also, there is speculation that President Carter's meeting the day before yesterday with Mr. Arafat [Palestine Liberation Organization leader] and Mr. Mitterand [President of France], at which Mr. Carter was given an oriental rug by Mr. Arafat, that this had the blessing of your administration. I wonder if you would care to comment on these speculations.

The President. Let me—and if I miss one, why, help me out. [*Laughter*] On President Carter, he was not acting with the blessing of, nor disapproval of, or anything else of the administration. He was acting in this meeting on his own. I knew nothing about it. And certainly the former President should be free to do his thing. That's exactly what he's doing.

In terms of pressuring Israel to meet with the PLO, that is not true, either. And there is no evidence to support the allegation that I sometimes hear that we are pressuring. What I would like Israel to do is to meet under the Baker plan and discuss peace, and I'd like to see that happen. And nobody's tied any aid into that, and for that we get some criticism. I have no intention of tying aid into it, but I will keep reiterating that, my support for the Baker plan, the Shamir plan, the Mubarak plan, all of which are really basically one and the same thing. But one of Israel's fears was that they would be compelled to talk to the PLO, and we have made very clear to them in detailed negotiations that that was not the case.

Did I leave out one part?

Q. No, that's all.

The President. Okay, sir.

Military Base Closings

Q. Rather than asking you something difficult about catching bluefish off the Maine coast, let me try to focus on something simpler, such as the downsizing of the U.S. defense economy. What responsibilities do you think the Federal Government has to places like Saco, Kittery, and Bath, Maine, for retraining and retooling as the need for guns and ships diminishes?

The President. I'm a strong believer in the Job Training Partnership Act. I think the Federal Government does have a role in retraining. I think it's been clearly set out by our very able Secretary of Labor. But I'll say this: One of the most difficult things there is—as you're trying to get control of defense costs—is to close a base, because instantly the most committed dove becomes the most flaming hawk if the base is in his or her district.

And what I'm encouraging people to do is to look at what's happened where bases and facilities have closed, and for the most part, I think you'll find that the economy compensates and takes care of people. But training should be a very important part of it. That gets me to the fundamental point that you're not going to get job opportunity

in a stagnant economy or in an economy that is in recession. So, a fundamental obligation on a President is to keep this longest peacetime expansion in history going.

But I don't worry too much about when a person is put out of work by a defense contract provided the overall economy is sound, because I think history shows the economy can absorb an awful lot of people in very different enterprises.

So, we'll keep on trying to close facilities that aren't needed, don't have priority; and it is very difficult to do that. But I know this area you're talking about. I think some areas in New England have been adversely affected, not necessarily by defense cuts. And I do think we have a role in job retraining.

Soviet-U.S. Summit

Q. Will you bring Gorbachev to Kennebunkport?

The President. I'm not sure. Well, we haven't made any determination on that. We've set the dates for this summit, and most of the summit will clearly be in Washington, DC. But beyond that the agenda, the timeframe, is open.

Lithuania and Panama

Q. After this nation has invaded a sovereign nation—Panama—aren't we being a little bit hypocritical telling the Soviet Union what to do in Lithuania?

The President. No, I don't think so, and I don't think we are telling them what to do. We're telling them what not to do. [*Laughter*] We're telling them what not to do, and that is: Don't use force. Do what you yourselves say you want to do—dialog, discuss, do not use force—because we have an awful lot at stake in the U.S.-Soviet relationship, an enormous amount at stake. It gets into arms control; it gets into human rights, the exodus of Soviet Jews; it gets into regional questions. And this is a major relationship that affects the lives of people all over the world.

I see the able Foreign Minister of the Federal Republic nodding. And I'm not going to violate a confidence, but he points out to me how important this relationship is in arms control and on the peace of an emerging democratic Europe and everything else. So, I want to keep that going. So, we're not dictating or attempting to. We couldn't do it anyway. But we are saying that we want it to be peaceful.

Of course, the Panama—I think that when you see democracy working and you see the tremendous support for what happened, you see the will of the people that was expressed in free democratic elections, and then had that will aborted by a dictator—why, I think that situation speaks for itself. My only hope is that we can move briskly forward and help that democracy, because the Congress got out of town without appropriating the funds that I wanted to see brought to bear on helping the people finalize and make more formal their democracy.

Chinese Immigration Relief

Q. Mr. President, you refer in your remarks to the Revolution of 1989, but in China there was what some people would call a counterrevolution. Do you think the Chinese students who are in this country now have a legitimate fear for their safety if they return to China? And if you do, are you willing in some more formal way to guarantee that they will have an indefinite status on their visas, perhaps in the form of the Executive order you talked about when you vetoed the congressional legislation on this subject?

The President. First, I don't know that I know the answer, but some might. And that's why I took far-reaching action that went well beyond the Pelosi bill. And I'm confident that it was the right thing to do.

You raise a technical question that is now being raised about whether I—I did say I was going to have an Executive order, and what we had was an Executive directive from the President. But I'll tell you what I am going to do. First of all, there are two provisions out there that I want to expand on. And I will have an Executive order, and it will direct the Attorney General to extend the deferral of enforced departure for Chinese nationals which is currently scheduled to expire on June 5th. This was not covered under the Pelosi bill, and it takes care of the hypothesis in your questions, because we don't want to take a chance on somebody being mistreated, brutalized if you will. And so, I think that will be helpful.

The second one is directing that steps be taken to alleviate concerns that have arisen recently about the revocation by the Chinese Government of passports belonging to Chinese nationals. This is a technical INS, Immigration Nationalization Service, question that's come up. So, these two provisions will be in the Executive order. And, then, to allay any concerns and some of these allegations against us, I will put into the Executive order all of the provisions that were in the Presidential directive that we immediately put into effect and that has been implemented by the Attorney General. And I think that will certainly convince people, those that might be skeptical, that I have every intention of keeping my word. We have kept it by this Presidential directive. But I did say Executive order, so this will formalize it in an official Executive order fashion.

Q. May I follow up briefly, sir? Would the terms of whatever this instrument is say that this is open-ended and indefinite, or will it be a postponement for a fixed period of time?

The President. Well, there are a whole bunch of provisions. This one I referred to will extend it from June 5th to 1994. I believe it's January 1st, 1994.

Federal Budget Deficit

Q. Good afternoon, Mr. President. On the outside chance that I would have an opportunity to ask a question today, I made an impromptu visit with about 30 of our readers, to ask them if they were here personally, what they might ask you. And almost invariably, they were concerned about the deficit. Why, they want to know, does it seem that everybody's talking about it, but nobody seems to be able to do anything about it?

The President. Well, we're trying to do something about it. The next move is up to the Congress. Under the law, they should have budgets by the budget committees on April 1st. Regrettably, April 1st has passed, and the Congress has not put their proposal on the table. But then, when that is done—

471

and I think the committees will be addressing themselves to that, both the budget
committee of the House, budget committee
of the Senate—when they do that, then
there will inevitably follow negotiations that
hopefully will lead to a guarantee of the
budget deficit going down.

But let me take this occasion to tell you
one of the concerns I've got. We've got a
lot of people around Washington that are
saying, hey, why don't you raise taxes? Last
week alone, we asked for a supplemental on
Nicaragua and Panama and included in
there were $2 billion of spending that we
did not request. We asked for clean air and
there were some things we had to give on
there that resulted in a great deal more
spending. And there was another—one
other provision, one other piece of legislation—I'm trying to think what it was—last
week that added—three pieces of legislation—substantially to spending.

And so, any agreement to get this budget
deficit down is going to have to have some
power in the Presidency of somewhere to
guarantee that spending will be reduced. I
use the Nicaragua-Panama as a clean shot.
We feel there was an emergency there—to
help these two democracies. We went up
there with, what I would recall, laser-like
approach, and you find that the bill is increased by about $2 billion. So, I would like
to get the deficit down. Thank God we
have a growing economy; the problem
would be a lot worse if we didn't. But that's
where it stands, and I think after I hear
from these two committees what the Congress is willing to do, why, then we can
have some serious negotiations about it.

Security Leaks

Q. Mr. President, I'd like to ask a question about leaks—not the vegetable.
[*Laughter*] Last year the Justice Department decided to take a tough stand on leaks
and to aggressively investigate them with
an eye toward prosecution. Since then
they've launched several unsuccessful leak
probes, including one much-publicized
one—cost almost a quarter of a million dollars and used 11 FBI agents for several
months, but proved inconclusive.

Isn't it time to put the taxpayers' money
to better use and lighten up on these inves-

tigations?

The President. That one has been unsuccessful. In that one, the interests of a
Member of Congress were severely damaged, I think, and he felt so. And so, a
legitimate attempt was undertaken to try to
see that there not be any breaches of this
nature. But I'll tell you this, chasing down
leaks is pretty hard to do, extraordinarily
hard to do. I don't think we've had any that
are egregious to our fundamental national
security interests. There may be some, but I
can't cite some examples for you.

So, I don't think we want to be frivolous
in this, but I believe that some things
should be protected, and sometimes they
say, well, I'm too secretive. But I don't
accept that as a serious allegation. I don't
know how to answer your question. I mean,
if there's something really bad, why, I think
we ought to find out what happened and
punish the person that does something, if
it's against the law, certainly.

But in this case, spent $250,000—you're
telling me—and didn't get anywhere, well,
I can't be defending that as particularly
prudent use of the taxpayers' money.

Q. Are you consulted before they decide
to open an investigation on a leak?

The President. I was certainly consulted
on that one and strongly supported the Attorney General of the United States.

Offshore Oil Drilling

Q. Mr. President, a lot of us in Florida are
concerned with offshore oil drilling. A lot of
us would like to see a permanent ban.
Would you discuss your position on this?

The President. My position is, there
shouldn't be a permanent ban on offshore
drilling because then I would be compelled
to ask the question: Where do we get the
energy to keep this country going and to
keep the working man and woman at work
and heat the homes? So, I don't think there
should be a ban, and I don't want to see the
United States become increasingly dependent on foreign oil. We're up close to 50
percent right now. And some remember in
this room when we had some real problems
getting oil from the Persian Gulf for one
reason or another.

Having said that, I think there will definitely be bans on certain environmentally sensitive areas. And what I don't understand is when a tanker bringing oil into California goes aground, people stop saying, hey, this proves you shouldn't have offshore drilling. I mean, do they want to ban tankers, too?

So, what we're trying to do—you're from Florida, I'll tell you—is to try to redefine sealanes so to protect the environmentally sensitive Everglades, in this case, and to not drill in areas that are highly sensitive environmentally. You're looking at a bone fisherman, one who likes to go down there and will be in a couple of weeks down at Islamorada. And I know enough about the Everglades and have been briefed enough on the environment of the Everglades to know that that ecological balance is highly sensitive. So, we will be announcing a policy that prohibits drilling in certain highly sensitive areas that will not ban—your question was broad, you didn't say just in Florida, you said offshore drilling—and we're not going to ban offshore drilling. It has been proved in my part of the country that offshore drilling can be done compatibly with sound environmental practice.

Negative Political Campaigning

Q. Mr. President, many people felt that your 1988 campaign was excessively negative. In fact, some people felt that the Willie Horton commercial was patently racist. There's a move in this country now to try to combat negative campaigning. David Broder has called it a genuine rebellion against the cheapening of our politics. And I think there are major conferences planned this year at University of Pennsylvania and Harvard.

My question is, are you aware of this movement, do you encourage it, and would you respond to it in your next campaign?

The President. I'm not aware of the conference he's talking about; I'm aware about the allegations. You repeated one. My campaign ad didn't happen to be a campaign ad by the Bush campaign that you're referring to. So, we've got to get the facts out there and deal from facts. But I'm against censorship. I think it would be extraordinarily difficult to censor. You wouldn't want it for your paper, and I don't want it for the campaign. And if there's a way to improve the quality and decency of campaigns, I'm all for it.

Q. Well, there's no suggestion of censorship here, just an appeal to more ethical campaigning.

The President. That would be fine. You might start with the Democrats in Texas. [*Laughter*] How come you didn't mention that one? I mean, I think there's a myth abroad, and people didn't want to look at the real issues. And I refuse to plead guilty to some of the charges made by, I think, rather biased sources suggesting that the campaign was something that was unique in its ugliness.

Access to Federal Information

Q. Mr. President, most of us in this room share your admiration for the benefits of a free and aggressive and an active press, and yet most of us in this room over the past few months, to name a period of time, have had great difficulty in prying information out of the Federal Government. In fact, there are many of us in this room who believe that the Federal Freedom of Information Act simply does not work.

We are faced repeatedly with delays of weeks or months or sometimes even years. We have filed countless lawsuits trying to get information about worker safety or the environment. Will you use the benefits of presence and power of your office to try to help us to report to the American people what our government is doing by improving the Federal Freedom of Information Act?

The President. I'm not sure I know enough about the mechanics of it, but yes, I would be interested if there are things we can do to streamline it and to make it more efficient because the law was passed to facilitate the distribution of information. And if that's not working, I think we should take a look at it. But I'm just not familiar with enough of the details of it to know wherein these delays take place, wherefrom these delays stem.

Q. I can almost assure you that we will be happy to provide you with those details.

The President. All right. I hope I agree with you because maybe we can get some headway, then, on this question.

Lithuanian Independence

Q. Mr. President, with the foreign press thrown out of Lithuania, the world's eyes and ears, so to speak, removed, what reasons do we and you have to believe President Gorbachev will do what he says and work to a peaceful resolution of the crisis?

The President. I'm not sure I can answer that question. But I know what I can do as President of the United States, and that is to encourage in every way possible through talks like we had today, through talks like I will be having in a couple of months with Mr. Gorbachev—encourage that kind of performance and encourage access, encourage permission to permit a free press to come there. And that's what we can do. And that's what I will do because I'm strongly in favor of fully open reporting.

I heard him ask the question. I unfortunately didn't hear the answer today; they asked him about that. But I do think that freedom of the press in these places is part of the new wave of democracy and freedom. And some formerly closed societies are going to have to adjust to it. So, I hope that I can be helpful by dealing with the top Soviet leaders and encouraging them to permit what most democracies take for granted: a free and open press. And I will try hard on that.

Cuban Detainees

Q. Mr. President, there are currently about 1,200 Cuban detainees being held in maximum security penitentiaries around the country who have not committed crimes in the United States. They are in administrative limbo. Do you plan to do anything about those situations? Some of

them have been held for as long as 8 years.

The President. I must confess I don't know about that. Detainees in what sense? Detained for what?

Q. They are under the INS being held as detainees. Their status is the same as if they were still floating around in boats off the coast.

The President. Are these people from the Mariel boat lift or something of that nature?

Q. Yes.

The President. They're in jail?

Q. They're in Federal penitentiaries held under lockdown 24 hours a day.

The President. I'm familiar with some that are held, but I must say for innocent people being held, that I'm not familiar with that. So, now I will make sure to look into that one, too. But I know that there are some in the Federal prison in Atlanta who are criminal elements who had full access to the American law, but are still there and probably will be unless the return program works. And we've tried to return to Castro—in fact, some have gone back—but I think you're talking about a broader category of presumably innocent people. I'm embarrassed to say I don't know the details of that.

Well, in any event, thank you all very much. I've enjoyed being with you.

Note: The President spoke at 2:30 p.m. in the Grand Ballroom at the J.W. Marriott Hotel. In his remarks, he referred to Terry Anderson, the Associated Press reporter who was kidnaped in Beirut, Lebanon, on March 16, 1985. Loren Ghiglione, president of the society, introduced the President and acted as moderator during the question-and-answer session.

Remarks at the 25th Anniversary Celebration of President Lyndon B. Johnson's Inauguration
April 6, 1990

Welcome. Well, what a wonderful reunion. And thanks, first, to the family, especially our esteemed friend, Lady Bird Johnson; as well as her daughters, Lynda and Luci; and the grandkids: Lynn, Nicole, Rebekah, Claudia, Catherine, and missing in action, Lucinda, who is finishing her thesis at Princeton University and, thus, cannot be with us on this special occasion—sends her mother and dad, Senator and Mrs. Robb. And, of course, our distinguished Senator, a member of the family, Chuck Robb. We're delighted he's here. [Senator] Lloyd Bentsen, I'm told, was to be here, but maybe he is not. And I don't see [Senator] Pat Moynihan, but both of them are missing in action and both wanted to be here to pay their respects.

I'm speaking for the Vice President and Mrs. Quayle and Barbara Bush when I say how very pleased we are to have all of you here. I want to single out, and I hope they're here, our fellow Texans over here: the former Speaker, Jim Wright, and Representatives Jake Pickle and Kika de la Garza, and so many other distinguished friends of President Johnson, and so many members of his Cabinet. I know I'm going in trouble with this one, because we haven't got it totally complete. But I'll just stop and say welcome to the former members of the Johnson Cabinet because there are so many. And I think it is fitting that all of you are here. I'll be in trouble if I keep singling out names. But a couple of more "thank yous" like this—keep going on this and Valenti will think he's back at the Academy Awards. [*Laughter*] And none of us can afford that.

Jack Valenti [Special Consultant to President Johnson], our dear friend—he probably described Lyndon Baines Johnson about as well as anybody ever has. Jack's book was entitled "A Very Human President," and that he surely was. "An awesome engine of a man," Jack called him, "terrorizing, tender, inexhaustibly energetic . . . loving of land, grass, and water. Engulfing, patient, impatient, caring, insightful, devoted to wife, family and friends . . . Compassionate. Courageous. And full of humor."

That about says it all, but I'll go on a little bit. LBJ's humor was matched perhaps only by his bigness of heart. At the Inaugural Ball at the Statler-Hilton, he looked at Hubert Humphrey—whose sister is with us today, I'm pleased to say—at that point, Hubert had been Vice President—there she is—had been Vice President for less than 12

hours. "There he is," LBJ exclaimed, "the greatest Vice President I've ever known." [*Laughter*]

He was a towering and passionate figure, endlessly in motion. And those in the press who think the White House is hectic today ought trade some notes with Bill Moyers. Bill was LBJ's Press Secretary for a time, and told how one day the President called him in his office and said, "Bill, I'm going to Honolulu." Bill said, "Fine, Mr. President. I'll come over and talk to you about it. Where are you?" LBJ replied, "Over Los Angeles." [*Laughter*]

Lyndon Johnson loved this country, loved her land, and loved her people. And one of my own personal heroes, Dwight Eisenhower, served as President when LBJ was majority leader in the Senate. And Ike often said that he knew that whenever the great issues of national security were concerned, Lyndon Johnson would always be a partisan of principle, not a partisan of party.

Historians will continue to argue about his legacy, as they do about the legacy of every single President. And some say the greatest thing he ever did was heal the Nation after a tragic loss. Others say it was the 1964 Civil Rights Act, or the Voting Rights Act in '65. But whatever, the greatest thing LBJ ever did—Sam Rayburn [former Speaker of the House] said there was no doubt about the best thing he ever did, and that was marrying Lady Bird Johnson.

And I think those who know Lyndon better than I would say that she was his anchor and his strength. And she never failed him. And she was always there. And as she has once again today, Lady Bird brought to the White House dignity and warmth and grace. And she was never on stage, never acting out some part, always the same genuine lady no matter what the setting. Her gift of language is a combination of both elegance and simplicity, a vivid imagery that charms our country to this very day.

Mrs. Johnson, you, too, have left this nation a very important legacy. Barbara reminds me of that every single day. And those who travel by car along the banks of the Potomac, or who walk or bicycle along its paths, are each day struck by the wonder of your gift. Friends back home tell me that the wildflowers planted along Texas highways at your direction are the prettiest ever this year. The bluebonnets and the Indian paintbrush line Interstate 10 from San Antonio to Houston. And I remember a few years back when Barbara and I were headed from Houston to College Station for a commencement up at A&M. And we skipped the chopper ride and drove so we could see your beautiful wildflowers in bloom. And today some have renewed the debate about when and where the first Earth Day was conceived, about when the environmental movement was first launched in America. But I have a feeling that it began just about the time a nation of new trees and flowers started appearing at the business end of a shovel held by Lady Bird Johnson.

The Johnsons were close to both the land and the people, and LBJ often spoke about the strength that comes from the power for good that lies out there in the fertile lands and great cities in America, about America's deep confidence in itself—its conviction that we don't have any problem that we are not big enough to solve ourselves, and always remembering that all our successes can always be improved. He tried with all his heart and to be the best President that this country ever had for the people who are pressed against the wall, whose cries are often not heard. But he heard. Lyndon Johnson heard. And he often told of spotting a tombstone he admired, somewhere out in west Texas, I believe it was. It carried just four simple words: "He done his damnedest." [*Laughter*]

Well, some say that that fabled tombstone never existed. But it does now. From the Potomac to the Pedernales, no one ever earned that epitaph more than Lyndon Baines Johnson. "He done his damnedest."

So, thank you all for coming. Thank you all for coming. And to the members of my own administration—and I think Marlin [Marlin Fitzwater, Press Secretary to the President] is here and one or two others—take heart: just 24 years from now, you too might be invited back to your own reunion. [*Laughter*] Perhaps even hosted by President Robb. [*Laughter*] President Jennifer Robb.

Note: The President spoke at 3:21 p.m. on the State Floor at the White House. In his remarks, he referred to Lynda Robb, wife of Senator Charles S. Robb and daughter of President Johnson.

Memorandum on the Delegation of Authority for Reporting on Panamanian Bank Secrecy Regimes
April 6, 1990

Memorandum for the Secretary of State

Subject: Delegation of Authority for Reporting to the Congress Pursuant to Section 104(b) of the Urgent Assistance for Democracy in Panama Act of 1990

You are hereby delegated the authority for submitting to the Congress the report on actions being taken by the Government of Panama to modify the existing bank secrecy regime required by section 104(b) of the Urgent Assistance for Democracy in Panama Act of 1990 (Public Law 101–243).

This memorandum shall be published in the *Federal Register*.

GEORGE BUSH

Statement on Chinese Immigration Relief
April 6, 1990

On November 30, 1989, I sent a directive to the Secretary of State and the Attorney General ordering that certain steps be taken to improve the immigration status of Chinese nationals in the United States. On that same day, I disapproved H.R. 2712, the Emergency Chinese Immigration Relief Act of 1989.

Since then I have recognized that there are two issues important to the Chinese nationals here that were not addressed by that bill or my November 30 directive. I have decided to issue an Executive order addressing those issues.

First, the Executive order will direct the Attorney General to extend the deferral of enforced departure for Chinese nationals, which is currently scheduled to expire on June 5 of this year, through January 1, 1994. This will provide assurance to Chinese nationals that they can remain in this country for the entire period during which the home country residence requirement for Chinese students was waived by my November 30 directive.

Second, the Executive order will direct that steps be taken to alleviate concerns that have arisen recently about revocation by the Chinese Government of passports belonging to Chinese nationals.

It has been noted that my November 30 directive was not an Executive order because it was not so entitled and was not published in the *Federal Register*. The directive, however, had precisely the same legal effect as an Executive order and extended precisely the same protections to Chinese nationals as would have been the case had it been entitled an "Executive order." Nevertheless, to allay any concerns, the new Executive order that I will issue will also reiterate the instructions to the Secretary of State and the Attorney General contained in my November 30 directive.

Note: Executive Order No. 12711 is listed in Appendix E at the end of this volume.

Statement by Press Secretary Fitzwater on the Czechoslovakia-United States Trade Agreement
April 9, 1990

On April 5, 1990, U.S. and Czechoslovak trade negotiators reached provisional agreement on the text of a trade agreement between the two countries. The President welcomes this as the first trade agreement concluded with an Eastern European country since the revolutions of 1989.

President Bush and President Václav Havel of Czechoslovakia agreed during their February 20 meeting that reestablishing a more normal trade relationship should be a top priority for both countries. The speed with which this agreement was reached is testimony to the dramatic changes occurring in Czechoslovakia's economic policies and to our shared determination to move quickly to reestablish close ties.

The agreement, along with its side letters on trade and financial matters, intellectual property, and tourism, is scheduled to be signed Thursday, April 12, by U.S. Trade Representative Carla Hills and Czechoslovak Foreign Trade Minister Andrej Barčák. Ambassador Hills and Minister Barčák will be speaking earlier in the day at a symposium on Eastern Europe sponsored by the Department of Commerce and the U.S. Chamber of Commerce.

The trade agreement, when formally approved by both sides, will provide a number of important improvements for business in each country. Most importantly, the U.S.-Czechoslovak trade relationship will be based on a most-favored-nation basis, including tariffs. This will be a significant benefit for businesses and consumers alike.

The two sides also agreed to apply the rules of the General Agreement on Tariffs and Trade (GATT) between themselves, which should put business and trade on a more certain footing. Certain explicit protections for American businesses were included, such as the right to nondiscrimination in renting office space, in paying for local goods, and in establishing bank accounts. Any hard currency earnings from trade may be repatriated immediately. In addition, the Government of Czechoslova-

kia pledged to continue its economic reform plans, including a commitment to streamline its approval procedures for foreigners and Czechoslovaks wishing to do business together. Other bilateral commitments concern intellectual property protection and tourism.

This agreement should substantially increase two-way trade between the United States and Czechoslovakia. President Bush welcomes this step as an important milestone not only in U.S.-Czechoslovak relations but also in Czechoslovakian reintegration into the global economy and the community of free nations.

Letter to Congressional Leaders Reporting on the Cyprus Conflict
April 9, 1990

Dear Mr. Speaker: (Dear Mr. Chairman:)

In accordance with 22 U.S.C. 2373(c), I am submitting to you this bimonthly report on progress toward a negotiated settlement of the Cyprus question.

This report covers the period from January 1 through early March 1990, a period marked by intensive international activity aimed at getting and keeping the intercommunal negotiating process on track. On January 18 I spoke personally with Turkish President Ozal in Washington about the desirability of having an early Cyprus negotiating session under the auspices of the United Nations Secretary General, and received President Ozal's assurances of Turkish support. The subject of Cyprus also arose briefly during the U.S. and Soviet Foreign Ministers' meeting in Moscow in early February with both Foreign Minister Shevardnadze and Secretary Baker agreeing on the need to support fully the U.N. Secretary General's "good offices" mission. State Department officials also stressed the need to support a negotiated Cyprus settlement under U.N. aegis to a group of prominent Cypriot parliamentarians who visited Washington in late January.

During this same time period, the U.N. Secretary General invited both Cypriot

President George Vassiliou and Turkish Cypriot community leader Rauf Denktash to New York. After some disagreement about dates, both leaders agreed to begin negotiations under the U.N. Secretary General's auspices in New York on February 26.

The talks opened on that date with a statement by the U.N. Secretary General and continued on Tuesday and Wednesday, February 27 and 28. A final negotiating session was held on Friday afternoon, March 2. The 4 days of talks ended without progress. At the final session on March 2, the U.N. Secretary General summed up the objective of the meetings and their results with these words:

"In line with the mandate entrusted to me by the Security Council and the 1977 and 1979 high-level agreements, the objective of the exercise of good offices is a new constitution for the state of Cyprus that will regulate the relations between the two communities in Cyprus on a federal, bicommunal and bi-zonal basis. In this effort, each community will participate on an equal footing and will also have the opportunity to express separately its consent to the arrangements reached.

"In the course of our discussion, Mr. Denktash stated that the term 'communities' be used in a manner that is synonymous with term 'peoples', each having a separate right to 'self-determination'. Mr. Denktash also proposed certain other terms for the word 'communities'. In the context of the intercommunal talks, the introduction of terminology that is different from that used by the Security Council has thus posed more than a semantic problem. Unless acceptable to both sides, any change in terminology could alter the conceptual framework to which all have thus far adhered. In the circumstances, I have come to the conclusion, regrettably, that we face an impasse of a substantive kind, which raises questions regarding the essence of the mandate of good offices given to me by the Security Council and, therefore, regarding the basis of the talks.

"In view of this, I must inform the Security Council of the situation as it exists at present and seek the Council's guidance on how to proceed."

Six days later the U.N. Secretary General sent a report to the United Nations Security Council, a copy of which is enclosed. The report reviewed what had happened and concluded with an appeal that the negotiating process not be allowed to collapse. It also noted that, despite the failure to advance the drafting of an outline of an overall agreement, "a basis for effective negotiations exists provided both leaders are prepared to take into account each other's concerns, and that both are willing to proceed within the framework of the 1977 and 1979 high-level agreements."

The U.N. Security Council considered the U.N. Secretary General's report and on Monday, March 12, unanimously adopted a new resolution, a copy of which is enclosed, which reaffirms the U.N. Secretary General's "good offices" mandate and calls upon the two parties to pursue their efforts to reach a mutually acceptable solution. Each of the two Cypriot communities has expressed its satisfaction with the Security Council resolution and has indicated a willingness to resume negotiations under U.N. auspices.

The United States, which worked to ensure a strong, effective Security Council resolution, will now work diligently in the months ahead to ensure that the intercommunal negotiations are restarted and the process of developing an agreed outline for a solution is completed. In this context we believe that each community must have the right separately to determine whether a given set of arrangements meets its essential interests. We fully support the U.N. Secretary General's mandate, which does not accept that an alternative outcome is independence for either community, partition of Cyprus, or the establishment of formal links between either community and some other state.

Achievement of a negotiated settlement to the Cyprus dispute remains a matter of priority for me and my Administration as a whole. In that connection, the White House announced on February 21, 1990, my nomination of Special Cyprus Coordinator Nelson C. Ledsky for the rank of Ambassador during his tenure in that position, subject, of course, to the advice and consent of the Senate.

Sincerely,

GEORGE BUSH

Note: Identical letters were sent to Thomas S. Foley, Speaker of the House of Representatives, and Claiborne Pell, chairman of the Senate Foreign Relations Committee.

Message on the Observance of Passover, 5750
April 9, 1990

Four thousand years ago, when Moses sounded the bold cry, "Let my people go," the Israelites began their historic journey from bondage into freedom. Today, all Americans share in the solemn pride and quiet joy of millions of Jewish men, women, and children around the world as they commemorate the Exodus.

Known as "the Festival of Freedom," Passover has a special significance this year. A great march of freedom is underway for Soviet Jewry, and this year many thousands will celebrate the Seder with their families in Israel. For these people, and for their brethren waiting to emigrate, "next year in Jerusalem" is becoming a promise fulfilled.

The call for liberty and freedom is now being heard around the world—in Eastern Europe, in Central and South America, in Africa, and even in the Soviet Union. Like the Israelites of old, determined peoples in both Hemispheres are beginning great struggles of their own, working to overcome repression and injustice and reclaiming their God-given freedom and dignity.

The call, "Let my people go," also recalls a spiritual quest, one that has been taken up by generations of men and women who have seen in the Exodus story a symbol of hope. This year, as Jews around the world gather with their loved ones to celebrate their passage to freedom, let us renew our commitment to sustaining that hopeful spirit. Let us pray that the time is approaching when, through God's providence, every human being enjoys the life and liberty He has envisioned for us.

Barbara joins me in wishing the members of the Jewish community in America and throughout the world a fulfilling Passover holiday.

GEORGE BUSH

Statement by Press Secretary Fitzwater on the Appointment of Richard L. Armitage as Special Negotiator for the Future Status of United States Access to Military Facilities in the Philippines
April 10, 1990

The President today announced the appointment of Richard L. Armitage as Special Negotiator for the future status of U.S. access to military facilities in the Philippines. Mr. Armitage most recently served as Assistant Secretary of Defense for International Security Affairs, and he has had a long career of distinguished public service. The President is pleased that he has accepted the assignment.

Discussions are expected to begin soon on the future of the U.S. military facilities, which contribute to the security of the Philippines, the United States, and the other countries of the region. We look forward to productive talks leading to the conclusion of a mutually beneficial new agreement.

Nomination of Arden L. Bement, Jr., To Be a Member of the National Science Board
April 10, 1990

The President today announced his intention to nominate Arden L. Bement, Jr., to be a member of the National Science Board, National Science Foundation, for a term expiring May 10, 1994. This is a reappointment.

Since 1980 Dr. Bement has served as vice president for technical resources for the science and technology department of TRW,

Inc., in Cleveland, OH. Prior to this, he was Deputy Under Secretary of Defense for Research and Engineering at the Department of Defense, 1979–1980, and Director of the Materials Science Office of the Defense Advanced Projects Agency at the Department of Defense, 1976–1979. He was professor of nuclear materials at the department of nuclear engineering and materials science and engineering at Massachusetts Institute of Technology, 1970–1976; manager of the fuels and materials department, 1968–1970, manager of the metallurgy research department, 1965–1968, and a senior research metallurgist for Hanford Laboratories of the General Electric Co., 1954–1965.

Dr. Bement graduated from the Colorado School of Mines (E.Met, 1954), the University of Idaho (M.S., 1959), and the University of Michigan (Ph.D., 1963). He was born May 22, 1932, in Pittsburgh, PA. He retired from U.S. Army Reserve as a lieutenant colonel. Dr. Bement is married, has eight children, and lives in Mayfield Village, OH.

Exchange With Reporters Aboard Air Force One
April 10, 1990

The President. I'll handle the diplomacy, and the commissioner will take care of the baseball. Go ahead. We've got time for one question between us.

Lithuanian Independence

Q. It sounds like the Soviets are tightening the screws on Lithuania.

The President. Well, we keep hearing that. I've made our position very clear: a peaceful resolution to this question. Because we do not recognize that the use of force would accomplish anything, other than to set back relations, and I think they know that loud and clear by now—very clear.

Soviet-U.S. Relations

Q. Any more letters exchanged between you and Gorbachev?

The President. Don't talk about internal correspondence between the heads of government. We just don't get into that, Rita [Rita Beamish, Associated Press]. I hope you understand why.

Q. How about phone calls?

The President. And phone calls. That's a correspondence. I consider phone calls and letters the same thing.

Q. You told us about the last phone call.

The President. Well, once in a while we do announce them, when we agree with the Soviets that that should be done, yes. You're right about that one, Owen [Owen Ullman, Knight-Ridder Newspapers].

Q. What did the Gorbachev response on mobile missiles do to the START talks? Is that going to complicate matters?

The President. Well, just go back and work hard. We've got a timeframe now in which there's an awful lot to be done, so I can't even predict how much will be done by the time the summit rolls around. But it's a good thing the summit date is set. It is important that we continue to talk to Mr. Gorbachev. And obviously, this will serve as a bit of a catalyst or goal for getting things done. But I don't want to overpromise and suggest that we're going to have all the details worked out by the time of the summit.

Q. Do you share the disappointment that others in the administration, Secretary Baker, and Foreign Minister Shevardnadze have expressed about the outcome of last week's discussions?

The President. No, I'm not disappointed. But, I mean, look, you deal with what's on the table; and I'm determined to see that there's no misunderstanding about the American position. And that's why I felt the visit with Shevardnadze was very good.

Anybody want to know anything about the national pastime? [*Laughter*]

Meeting With Prime Minister Mulroney of Canada

Q. What are you going to talk about?

The President. Wide array of subjects, including Europe, Central and South America, and then there are some bilateral issues. This meeting was—we talked about it for a long time, but this just seemed a wonderful way to do it. I think it's—as a baseball fan—and I think the commissioner agrees with me—this shows an interest on the part of the President, the commissioner, and the Prime Minister of Canada for baseball being

481

an international sport. And as he pointed out to me, one of the biggest drawing teams in either league is the Toronto Blue Jays, and we're going to see a beautiful baseball park as well as see a good opening game for Canada. So, I think it's good. We forget sometimes they've got two very aggressive, good ball clubs in the big leagues.

Q. Don't detract from the Rangers, right?

The President. No, we don't want to detract from them at all.

Q. ——call it the national pastime going to Canada?

The President. Well, I think we want to get them to buy into that definition. That's why we're going.

I want to get there the same time you guys do, so I want to put my seatbelt on.

Q. Are you going to throw a curve or a slider?

The President. I'm going to go with a slider this time. I've had such good luck in the last couple of years. The catcher let me down one time when he couldn't get into the dirt and grab it properly.

Q. See you later.

The President. I'll see you later.

Q. Are you working your stuff, Mr. President?

The President. No, no. Nolan will handle the fast one, and I'll go with the stuff. You know how it is, Tommie [Tom Raum, Associated Press].

We'll see you. Thanks a lot.

Note: The exchange occurred en route to Toronto, Canada, prior to the President's meeting with the Prime Minister. In his remarks, the President referred to Fay Vincent, commissioner of baseball, and Nolan Ryan, a pitcher for the Texas Rangers. A tape was not available for verification of the content of these remarks.

News Conference of the President and Prime Minister Mulroney in Toronto, Canada
April 10, 1990

The Prime Minister. I just want to tell you that the President and I have had what I consider to be an excellent meeting. We'll be meeting again over dinner before the Blue Jays inflict terrible damage upon the Rangers. [*Laughter*] But so far, our discussions have been friendly. [*Laughter*] And they've touched upon East-West relations, our trade relationships, our free trade agreement, the situation in Eastern Europe, the NATO summit, the Houston summit, the results of my recent visit to Mexico and to the Caribbean and the impacts on some American policies.

We had an excellent exchange of views. We were joined by Secretary Baker and his colleagues and Mr. Clark [Canadian Secretary of State for External Affairs] and a full Canadian delegation after, I think, the President and I had met for about an hour or so privately.

So, that, from Canada's point of view, was it. We thank you, Mr. President, for the visit of you and your colleagues. We welcome you all plus your media colleagues to Canada, and we wish you well.

The President. Well, thank you, Mr. Prime Minister. And before taking questions, let me just thank the Prime Minister and his colleagues for their hospitality. I can tell you that I find these talks extraordinarily helpful. We're in complicated international times.

And the relationship between Canada and the United States is strong. I, today, once again, found the 3 hours of talks that we had extraordinarily helpful. It is very important that Canada and the United States be on the same wavelength as much as possible.

And so, sir, I'm delighted to be here. I found that this Prime Minister tells it as it is, with no coloration; and I view that as extraordinarily helpful to the United States, the way a good friend, the head of a friendly country, should do. And he's very forceful. We have some differences; but most of the time, on these big issues that he was referring to, I think we have broad agreement with Canada. And I think, as we move into important talks—the G–7 [economic summit] meetings, our meeting that I'm planning to have with Mr. Gorbachev, and other meetings—it is very important that Canada and the U.S. are together.

So, thank you, sir. I feel it's been well-worthwhile.

Lithuanian Independence

Q. Mr. President, has the stall on arms control and Moscow's tough stand in Lithuania raised questions in your mind about Mr. Gorbachev's intentions and chances for success?

The President. No. I don't know that it's raised questions about that. I think the Secretary of State made clear to Mr. Shevardnadze [Soviet Foreign Minister]—and I believe Mr. Gorbachev knows my views—that should things deteriorate regarding peaceful solution to the question of Lithuania it would be extraordinarily difficult to move forward as rapidly as I'd like to see us move forward with them on a lot of questions. But I think on a situation that's as complicated as that one, why, you give your opinion. Our opinion is that this matter must be resolved peacefully.

We have never recognized the incorporation of Lithuania into the Soviet Union. Self-determination and freedom are hallmarks of the United States policy always. And so, be clear in talking to Mr. Gorbachev, be clear in talking to other Soviet interlocutors, and hope that they will conduct themselves in a way that can move the dramatic progress that's taken place in the last year or so even further forward.

Acid Rain

Q. Prime Minister, don't you think that you could—with the President, on the need for the U.S. and Canada—for an acid rain proposal?

The Prime Minister. The President, I think, is of the view that once the legislation passes the Congress—it's gone through the Senate, thanks to his leadership and the leadership of Senator Mitchell—when it gets through the House, perhaps this summer we can begin the process of negotiating a bilateral accord on acid rain, which I think would be a great tribute to what both of us have been seeking for both countries.

Lithuanian Independence

Q. Mr. President, on Lithuania and the Soviet Union, sir, you called the other day for what you called good-faith negotiations; and I wonder if you think it's really realistic to call for good-faith negotiations in an atmosphere where one side has tanks in the streets, has closed borders, and used troops to storm buildings?

The President. No, I think it's even more important to have good-faith negotiations when you have a situation of that nature. And I would just appeal to all sides and anyone with any influence to encourage dialog and discussion as a way to solve this very difficult and complicated problem, because the United States position is clear.

Q. If I could follow up, you spoke of the need for peaceful resolutions, but I gather the administration did not comment on the specifics—as you go along here—but does the administration care about what the details of that resolution are and whether they're in any way fair to the Lithuanian side?

The President. We care because the underpinning of our policy is self-determination, freedom, and democracy.

[*The next question was asked and answered in French, and a translation was not provided.*]

Soviet–U.S. Relations

Q. Mr. President, given the uncertainty about Soviet intentions in Lithuania, why did you agree to move up the dates of the summit? Doesn't that lock in the meeting and deny the United States the means of influencing the situation?

The President. No, it doesn't deny the United States the chance to do anything. I happen to believe when you have complications that that's a good time to talk; it's a good time to have more discussion; it's a good time to avoid difficulty, if possible, and to hammer out differences. But that wasn't why the summit meeting, as I explained to the Prime Minister earlier, was moved up. It just happened to work out that way; and they, I think, accepted a suggestion from us within 1 day that was behind the scenes. So, I want to dispel the idea that because the summit came earlier than some had expected that that had something to do with turmoil out there in anyplace around the world. But it is very important when you have difficulties brewing that you have discussion.

The Prime Minister. To complement just on that, to complement what the President has indicated, when we were in the Soviet Union, Mr. Gorbachev made it very clear that in respect to this problem that there would be—and I think I'm quoting him— "no crackdown in regard to Lithuania." And Mr. Clark, who was there, specifically sought reassurance from Mr. Shevardnadze; and he gave Mr. Clark the reassurances that he gave to Mr. Baker as well: that that was the intention of the Soviet Union, that was the policy of the Soviet Union.

They've moved along somewhat since then. But we support the approach that— both the United States and Canada have identical positions in respect of the juridical realities of Lithuania and the manner in which it was incorporated into the Soviet Union. And so, we believe that the prudence that the President has exhibited is the proper way to go.

Canada-U.S. Relations

Q. For the President. Sir, Canada's current constitutional problems involving Quebec—[inaudible]. And I was wondering if I could ask you, sir, whether you're concerned with the rather dramatic rise in independence feelings in Quebec and the future stability and unity——

The President. I think, rather clearly, that's a matter for Canada; and it's not a matter that would be helpful for me to involve myself in or the United States Government to be involved in. It's the internal affairs of Canada. We have always enjoyed superb relations with Canada, and a unified, strong Canada is a great partner—has been, and will continue to be. But I think it would be inappropriate to comment further on a matter that is not an agenda item nor one that I feel comfortable getting into.

Soviet President Gorbachev

Q. Mr. Prime Minister and then Mr. President as well, if I could get both your assessments on this. We've heard the President and his administration repeatedly say that their foreign policy is not based on the survival of one man in the Soviet Union— Mikhail Gorbachev. And yet in the current tension with Lithuania, we've seen that Mr. Gorbachev's survival is very important to you. Is that, in fact, the case? Is that a shift in policy? Should it be?

The President. Is this for me?

Q. Both of you, if you would.

The President. Well, I don't think you base the foreign policy of a country on any individual: you base it on what you think is right. In this case, Mr. Gorbachev, the President, has a record of encouraging, or certainly acquiescing in, the peaceful evolution of democratic change in Eastern Europe—so dramatic that not one single person in this room, and you can start with me and then move briskly down the aisle here, predicted it at all.

In other words, he has demonstrated that he is committed to peaceful change and the evolution of democracy—inside, as he moves forward on *perestroika*, outside, as we see a peaceful resolution to questions in Eastern Europe that, as I say, anyone would have found difficult to predict.

But again, he is a known quantity in the West. Western interlocutors like myself— and the Prime Minister can speak for himself—find a frankness there and a willingness to discuss difficult problems that has not always been the case in dealing with the Soviet Union.

But again, things happen, and I don't think that the foreign policy can be shaped on the success of any individual. I mean, I think that you have to say what's right. But this man has, I think, in terms of past Soviet leaders, demonstrated an openness and a commitment to reform and openness inside that's remarkable. So, give him credit, and deal openly. But when you have difficulties like we have today, talk frankly with him about it.

The Prime Minister. On that, I was struck by the fact that when we were in Moscow, it was just at that time that the government of Czechoslovakia—I think the day before— had been overthrown. And there were 300,000 people in Wenceslas Square listening to Mr. Dubcek. And I said to him, "Well, what do you think of this?" He said, "I think it's fine; sounds good to me." And I was struck by the fact that almost 21 years earlier his predecessor's response had been to send tanks into that same square. And so, as the President says, we're dealing with an entirely different kettle of fish; and this one is more attractive and more realistic and appears to be much more in keeping with some, if not all, of the values that we in the West defend. And there has been, with some few exceptions, a great sense of leadership and the display of reasonableness that we had not come to know in earlier Soviet leaders; and that's encouraging. It's very encouraging that the dialog with President Gorbachev be maintained.

Hostages in Lebanon

Q. ——hostages be freed in Lebanon after appeal there today by Colonel Qadhafi [leader of Libya]? The French Foreign Minister [Roland Dumas] praised high-minded—[*inaudible*]—do you believe—[*inaudible*]—marks a possible change in Libyan-U.S. relations?

The President. If, indeed, a person deserves credit for facilitating the release of people held against their will—anyone in the world—I would certainly say, fine, give the person credit. I don't know enough about the facts of this release. But a renunciation of terror by evidence that the hostages will be released and that this individual, Colonel Qadhafi, had a part in it—I would say that's very positive. But we've got some major differences with Libya that continue to exist. But look, who am I to argue on this case? If somebody can help free one hostage, any person held against his or her will, give that person credit.

Q. [*Inaudible.*]

The President. I don't know. We've talked about that a little bit today, and I don't know that it has any implications at all as it relates to the American hostages. And you know, John [John Cochran, NBC News], a few weeks ago there was a flurry of understandable excitement about the release of these people. And I had a difficulty figuring out where was all this coming from—what's driving this news flurry? And I still don't know the answer to that. But I just would repeat that good will begets good will, and a manifestation of good will would be the release of these American hostages.

NATO

Q. ——Foreign Minister Genscher [of West Germany] in Ottawa earlier suggested it was time for a redefinition of the transatlantic relationship and also a reduction in NATO. Are you and the President eye to eye on the long-term role for NATO and what comes after it?

The Prime Minister. Well, we're eye to eye on the fact that NATO and the solidarity of NATO has been responsible for preserving the peace in Europe for 50 years, and that the solidarity of NATO has been one of the key influences in bringing about the important treaties that the Soviet Union and the United States have managed to negotiate in the last 4 or 5 years, and that NATO, we believe, is an instrument for political predictability. Its existence is to the advantage both of those of us in the West and the Soviet Union. It is very important that NATO maintain its strength, but perhaps acquire a new dimension as well as the years go by.

But I don't think there's any doubt or any difference between the President and I, and we're the only two North American participants. We both have had troops in Europe since the Second World War, at great costs to both the United States and Canada. And we feel very much a part of Europe, and we want to be involved in that definition of a new architecture of Europe, as both Canada and the United States have an important role to play there. But principal, or key, to that is the solidarity of the NATO alliance.

The President. And I might add on behalf of the United States that I agree with that. And it is our responsibility to convince the Eastern Europeans, convince a unified Germany—although I hope there won't be much convincing needed—and convince the Soviet Union that the interests of stability are best served by an expanded role for NATO. Obviously, you've got different problems, different military assignments, strategy, or whatever. But here we're talking about a stable Europe, and the best answer for that is to have an expanded role for NATO. And so, I am convinced that that is the way to go, and I'm pleased that the Chancellor of Germany [Helmut Kohl of West Germany] understands that and others are beginning to understand it very, very clearly.

Q. Thank you.

North American Trade Agreement

Q. Any chance that a trilateral trade agreement with Mexico—a trilateral trade agreement for North America——

The President. Let me just say that on this one that there's no trilateral agreement being discussed. I've benefited from the debrief by Prime Minister Mulroney of a meeting that he had with President Salinas of Mexico. I will be meeting with President Salinas of Mexico. I think it is essential that Canada continue to show its extraordinary interest in matters below our border and, in this case, Mexico. And I think it is essential that the United States, interested as we are and concerned as we are about Europe, not neglect our own hemisphere. So, I learned a great deal about what I might expect when President Salinas comes to Washington by listening to Prime Minister Mulroney. But we're not talking about a trilateral agreement. We are talking about good,

sound relationships between all three of these countries.

The Prime Minister. President Salinas is struck by the leadership dimensions of the Canada-U.S. free trade agreement, and I think he sees some trading relationships to be in Mexico's direct benefit. As far as Canada's concerned, while aid to developing countries is very important, we think it's even more important that developing nations be given a chance to trade their way to greater prosperity. And a free trade agreement with some of these nations may very well be something that they're going to want to consider with the United States and other trading partners.

The President. Thank you. It's been a great pleasure.

The Prime Minister. Thank you. Wonderful pleasure.

Note: The President's 43d news conference began at 5:22 p.m. in the Founders Club Lounge at the Sky Dome, following his meetings with the Prime Minister and U.S. and Canadian officials. Following the news conference, the President was interviewed by Major League Baseball Productions and attended an informal dinner with the Prime Minister. The President and the Prime Minister then threw out the first balls of the opening game between the Toronto Blue Jays and the Texas Rangers. At the conclusion of the game, the President returned to Washington, DC.

Nomination of Dane Farnsworth Smith, Jr., To Be United States Ambassador to Guinea
April 11, 1990

The President today announced his intention to nominate Dane Farnsworth Smith, Jr., of New Mexico, a career member of the Senior Foreign Service, Class of Minister-Counselor, to be Ambassador Extraordinary and Plenipotentiary of the United States of America to the Republic of Guinea. He would succeed Samuel Eldred Lupo.

Since 1989 Dr. Smith has served as director of the economic policy staff for the Afri-

can Bureau at the Department of State. Prior to this, he served as Deputy Chief of Mission at the U.S. Embassy in Khartoum, Sudan, 1986–1989; Deputy Chief of Mission at the U.S. Embassy in Gaborone, Botswana, 1984–1986; Economic Counselor at the U.S. Embassy in Monrovia, Liberia, 1982–1984; chief of the food policy division in the Office of Food and Policy at the Economic and Business Bureau at the Department of

State, 1979–1981; international economist on the economic policy staff of the African Bureau at the Department of State, 1977–1979; senior economist in the Office of Japanese Affairs at the Department of State, 1975–1977; and an economic and commercial officer at the U.S. Embassy in Islamabad, Pakistan, 1972–1974. In addition, Dr. Smith served as consular officer at the U.S. Embassy in Dakar, Senegal, 1969–1971; international relations officer in the Office of West African Affairs at the Department of State, 1967–1969; trainer in international relations for the Peace Corps in Cambridge,

MA, 1966; Peace Corps volunteer in Asmara, Ethiopia, 1963–1965; youth assistant for the Mountainview Methodist Church in Wayne, NJ, 1962–1963; and a forest fire monitor for the Forest Service in McCall, ID.

Dr. Smith graduated from Harvard College (A.B., 1962) and the Fletcher School of Law and Diplomacy (M.A., 1966; M.A.L.D., 1972; and Ph.D., 1973). He was born December 14, 1940, in Albuquerque, NM. Dr. Smith is married, has three children, and resides in Washington, DC.

Appointment of Mrs. Potter Stewart as Alternate United States Representative on the Executive Board of the United Nations Children's Fund
April 11, 1990

The President today announced his intention to appoint Mrs. Potter Stewart to be Alternate Representative of the United States of America on the Executive Board of the United Nations Children's Fund. She would succeed Claudine B. Cox.

Since 1966 Mrs. Stewart has served as a board member and officer of the Family and Child Services in Washington, DC. Prior to this, she served as vice president and a board member of the Visiting Nurse Association of Washington, DC, 1963 to present; past president and board member of Traveler's Aid of Washington, DC, 1964 to present; member of Mainstream, Inc., 1979 to present; and a member of the advisory board of Reading is Fundamental, 1980 to present. In addition, Mrs. Stewart serves on the National Foreign Policy Association;

the Foreign Students Service Council of Washington, 1970 to present; board member of the World Affairs Council of Washington; board member of the United Way of Washington; executive committee member and vice president of the National Council on Crime and Delinquency, 1969 to present; board member and adviser for Volunteers in Probation, 1968 to present; honorary chairman and board member of the Friends of the Superior Court, 1968 to present; and a board member and adviser for the Lorton Art Program, Inc., 1978 to present.

Mrs. Stewart attended Bennington College. She was born June 3, 1919, in Grand Rapids, MI. Mrs. Stewart has three children and resides in Washington, DC.

Nomination of Patrick E. McFarland To Be Inspector General of the Office of Personnel Management
April 11, 1990

The President today announced his intention to nominate Patrick E. McFarland to be Inspector General in the Office of Personnel Management. This is a new position.

Since 1986 Mr. McFarland has served as assistant special agent in charge and as the security coordinator for the U.S. Secret Service at the White House. Prior to this, he served as assistant to the special agent in charge for the dignitary protective division, 1985–1986; assistant special agent in charge for the liaison division, 1984–1985; assistant special agent in charge for the Vice Presidential protection division, 1982–1984; special agent in the St. Louis field office, 1974–

1982; special agent for the Presidential protection division, 1969–1974; special agent for the intelligence division, 1969; and special agent in the Chicago field office, 1967–1968.

Mr. McFarland graduated from St. Louis University (B.A., 1965) and American University (M.P.A., 1986). He was born February 26, 1937, in St. Louis, MO. Mr. McFarland is married, has four children, and resides in Vienna, VA.

Statement by Press Secretary Fitzwater on the President's Physical Examination
April 12, 1990

President Bush today completed a routine physical examination at Bethesda Naval Hospital and is in excellent health. The President's examination lasted approximately 4 hours. The physical was conducted under the direction of Dr. Burton Lee, the President's personal physician.

"President Bush is in truly excellent health," Dr. Lee said. "He continues to keep extremely fit through vigorous physical activities."

An early glaucoma of his left eye was detected. Extensive visual testing revealed no loss of any aspect of his visual acuity. He will receive betagan eye drops, 1 drop every 12 hours, and will continue this medication permanently. He has had a stye in his right eye for the past week, which is almost resolved as the result of treatments

with soaks and antibiotics.

Among his test results are: chest x-ray, normal; x-rays of hips and neck, mild degenerative osteoarthritis; electrocardiogram (EKG) and stress tests, normal; urinalysis, no abnormalities; blood tests, completely normal, including cholesterol, triglycerides, and lipoprotein levels; dermatology, no significant problem or change; and his allergy problems remain minimal and unchanged.

Assisting Dr. Lee from the physician staff at Bethesda Naval Hospital were Comdr. Steven Fagan, radiologist; Comdr. Boyd Robinson, dentist; Capt. Bruce Lloyd, cardiologist; Capt. Kevin O'Connell, urologist; Capt. Ralph Sawyer, ophthalmologist; Capt. Ted Parlette, dermatologist; Comdr. Tom Jamison, rheumatologist; and Capt. William Ebbeling, allergist.

Appointment of Olin L. Wethington as Special Assistant to the President and Executive Secretary of the Economic Policy Council
April 12, 1990

The President today announced the appointment of Olin L. Wethington as Special Assistant to the President and Executive Secretary of the Economic Policy Council.

Mr. Wethington has served as a partner in the law firm of Steptoe and Johnson in

Washington, DC. Prior to this he served as Deputy Under Secretary for International Trade at the Department of Commerce, 1983–1985. During the 1988 election campaign, Mr. Wethington was an active participant in the President's international economic issues group.

Mr. Wethington graduated from the University of Pennsylvania and received his J.D. degree from Harvard Law School. He was born November 17, 1948, in Durham, NC. Mr. Wethington is married to the former Nadine Barbara Peiffer, has three children, and resides in McLean, VA.

Statements by Press Secretary Fitzwater on the President's Federal Income Tax Return
April 12, 1990

The President and Mrs. Bush's 1989 tax return shows that they have paid $101,382 in Federal income tax on an adjusted gross income of $456,780, of which $189,167 was the President's salary.

In addition, the President received $6,229 as salary while serving as Vice President during 1989. The Bushes also reported $208,274 in income from their blind trust, $804 in interest income, and $16,238 in income from other sources. A net long-term capital gain from the blind trust of $36,068 was also reported. The blind trust is managed by Bessemer Trust Co., N.A., New York City.

The President and Mrs. Bush claimed $94,702 in itemized deductions, which included $37,272 in contributions to 39 charities and $594 to charities through the blind trust. The net royalties received in 1989 of $14,282 from the President's book, "Looking Forward," were given to charitable organizations included in this list.

The President and Mrs. Bush's tax return has been reviewed by the Office of Government Ethics and will be filed in the Philadelphia regional office of the Internal Revenue Service.

Under section 212 of the U.S. Tax Code, the President is allowed to deduct the $8,000 salary as listed under the miscellaneous deductions box on statement A–1 of his 1989 tax return. This deduction has been part of the President's tax returns for the past 8 years and has been subject to annual Internal Revenue Service audits over that time.

Note: Press Secretary Fitzwater issued two separate statements during the day.

Remarks and an Exchange With Reporters at a Meeting on the Japan-United States Structural Impediments Initiative Negotiations
April 12, 1990

Q. Mr. President, how's your eye?

The President. I'll get to that in a minute. But before then, I would—the purpose of this meeting is that I want to congratulate everybody around this table, and especially Secretary Brady and Secretary Mosbacher and Ambassador Carla Hills, for the fantastic job that all of you did—working level and then Cabinet level—on this Structural Impediments Initiative team and on the other specific cases. It was well-done. I can't remember a 1-month period in our relations with Japan like the one between Palm Springs and now in the release of this interim report, and I congratulate all of you. I also want to thank and congratulate on our behalf Prime Minister Kaifu, who certainly has exemplified the best in cooperation and leadership. He's taken some very strong positions there.

Lest any of you feel like you can totally relax, there are some outstanding issues—

and I'm thinking, Carla, of the need to conclude the forest product. And so, I would just say, we've got to finish this agenda. But on satellites and supercomputers and telecommunications, I think we'd all agree, great progress has been made; and I think we ought to salute that progress. And I would say that for Prime Minister Kaifu and the other Japanese Government and party leaders—they made success on all this— trade and economic negotiations—top priority. And had they not done it, I don't believe we would have this progress.

So, my purpose here is to thank each of you, to pay my respects to the Japanese Prime Minister and thank him, but to remind them and to remind us that we're not finished yet and we want to keep on going. And I have a feeling we can get this concluded.

What's your best bet on the time, Carla, on the ongoing negotiations of forest products?

Ambassador Hills. Well, it's difficult, too, to give a specific time. We are making progress, but as you put it, Mr. President, we have more to do.

The President. What she means is everybody keep working. But thank you.

And now, to the one question—what was it?

The President's Health

Q. Your eye. They said you've got early glaucoma in your eye.

The President. I haven't felt a thing, felt it at all. I notice they said that on a report. I take a drop now, take some kind of drop— one in the morning and one at night. But the vision is very good on this. The vision thing is working well. [*Laughter*]

Is anybody interested in structural impediments or—[*laughter*]——

Q. Will your vision remain good, sir? Sometimes glaucoma is a——

The President. Yes, I think so, because they detected very little change over the last year. And literally, I don't even wear glasses for sports anymore, and I used to. So, it hasn't deteriorated that much, they told me, but there is some technical problem where I'm sticking these in there once in the morning and once in the afternoon. But the overall physical was—like everybody, you finish one and they give you a good report, you feel very, very good.

Japan-U.S. Trade

Q. Mr. President, on SII, what do you say to the people who are complaining that this won't cause any real reduction in the trade imbalance in the short term and that, over the long term, it could actually exacerbate it?

The President. Well, we have things to do on SII, and so do the Japanese. And we're addressing ourselves to the solution to fundamental problems. In our case, it's the trade deficit, and in theirs, it's some fundamental changes in their economy. So, I can't say to the American people that this is an instant short-term formula for success. It is a long-term—if we go through with all of this, as we intend and as I hope they intend and am confident they do—I think you're just paving the way for much better trade relations between the United States and Japan and other countries, as well, that trade with Japan.

So, I wouldn't put it on a short-term basis. I'd say this is part of the big picture. And along with this, we've made progress on certain categories of trade that you might say would have a shorter as well as longer term effect.

Q. Are you confident that all the promises made in these talks are going to be fulfilled?

The President. We have every intention of fulfilling everything we've agreed to, and I trust the Japanese do. And we will keep pushing for results. That's what this is all about.

East German Apology for World War II Atrocities

Q. What do you think of the East German Parliament's apology for World War II atrocities?

The President. To be very honest with you, I haven't been briefed on that and, therefore, probably shouldn't comment.

Weapon Shipments to Iraq

Q. How about the Iraqi gun?

Mr. Fitzwater. Lights. Thank you. [*Laughter*]

Q. Are you concerned about it?

The President. I've just got back from the hospital, so I've not been briefed on either of those two questions. I have expressed my concern about some of the statements emanating from Iraq. Clearly, we cooperated fully and, really, I'd say, took the lead in unearthing a plot to send material to Iraq that should not have been going there in the first place. We stopped that through the able work of our Attorney General's Department and others as well. And we've spoken out against that kind of thing. But, again, on this one, I just have not been briefed on this particular shipment.

The President's Health

Q. Mr. President, can we see the eye drops down here, sir?

The President. Which?

Q. Your eye drops, sir.

The President. Eye drops? [*Laughter*] I've got a pocketful of medicine here, but let me be sure to pull out the right one. There it is. You see, what you do is you set that to remind yourself—you all very interested in this detail? [*Laughter*]

Note: The President spoke at 3:40 p.m. in the Cabinet Room at the White House. In his opening remarks, he referred to Secretary of the Treasury Nicholas F. Brady, Secretary of Commerce Robert A. Mosbacher, and U.S. Trade Representative Carla A. Hills.

Exchange With Reporters Aboard Air Force One
April 13, 1990

Good Friday Sunrise Service

The President. ——very nice service.

Q. Were you the only person there?

The President. No. No. It was surprising. Well, there was, I'd say, about 30–40 people. Patty Presock and some came, even though they're not on the trip. But it was sweet, and it was very thoughtful of John Harper to do this—20 minutes. I'm sorry that those of you who would like to have been couldn't make it. But we just had——

Bermuda Kite-Flying Exhibition

Q. Have you ever flown a kite before?

The President. Yes. I have a large inventory of kites.

Q. You do?

The President. I'm one of the better kite flyers. And I'm often told to go fly my kite. And I have a bunch of them.

Q. What do you expect to accomplish?

Q. Mrs. Thatcher seems a little leery of the event.

The President. Of the kite-flying? It's a tradition down here.

Q. She's afraid that it might be seen as frivolous on her part.

The President. On my part?

Q. On her part.

The President. Why?

Q. It'll loosen her up a little, won't it? [*Laughter*]

The President. Helen [Helen Thomas, United Press International]! [*Laughter*]

Meeting With British Prime Minister Thatcher

Q. What do you expect to accomplish on this trip? Is it simply——

The President. A continued series of consultations. First, we had the Canadians, about 3 hours of talks. We'll probably have a little more here. Next week, François Mitterrand [President of France]. And it is extremely important that close allies stay in close touch during these times of dramatic change in Europe.

So, I would think a lot of it will be about Europe, post-German unification Europe, the present standing of relations between the Soviet Union and the United States, as well as the Soviet Union and Western Europe. So, I think that will probably dominate the conversations.

Q. Is she on the same wavelength with you on these issues in terms of——

The President. Yes. I think we're very close together on our assessment of the changes that are taking place inside the Soviet Union. But this is something I want to find out. And in this kind of a meeting, why, you can get into the nuances, and if there are differences, talk about them. And there may be some.

Q. She says she wants to persuade you that nuclear missiles should be put on German soil—modernized.

The President. We'll probably discuss that subject, and of course, our position is that this matter is really a collective decision for NATO still—and obviously with a lot of concern for how Germany will treat this. But listen, we'll talk about this and——

Q. Who seems to be the most reluctant on the pace of German unification?

The President. I don't think I can say that. I don't think I can say that, but I'll get a better feeling for that after this meeting. But we've got a special relationship with the U.K. We always have. I feel I have a very frank and open relationship with Margaret Thatcher, for whom I have tremendous respect. When I was Vice President she accorded me many courtesies, which included frank discussions at 10 Downing and over here at the Vice President's House, and then that's continued.

But if that's right, Charles [Charles Bierbauer, Cable News Network], then it's important we know that and important that I explain to her as clearly as I can U.S. policy. And then things have a way of coming together. So, I'm very——

Soviet Reforms

Q. Do you think there is a rise in Soviet military power? I mean, the hard-liners coming back in?

The President. Well, I don't know.

Q. There seems to be a lot of stories now.

The President. There's some speculation on that, but I think today is not unlike yesterday. We cannot read the tea leaves with total clarity when it comes——

Q. It's not unlike yesterday?

The President. ——to pressures inside the Kremlin. And so, we'll have to see. And I think she has some good judgment on that. Mr. Hurd is just back from—I believe he's back, her Foreign Minister—and will have talked to high Soviet leaders, has talked to them.

Q. Mr. President, are you being——

The President. And so, she'll have a good input on it. She has a very clear view of the realities of the world. That's a good subject for us to talk about.

Meeting With British Prime Minister Thatcher

Q. Sir, will you be discussing her domestic problems at all?

The President. I would be inclined to think not. I would not expect that she'd dwell on mine. [*Laughter*]

Q. What are those?

Q. What are yours?

The President. Congress. Deficits. Moving on Nicaragua-Panama. Thousands of things I want to see different.

Q. Your polls are falling. Did you know that—slightly?

The President. Well, it doesn't surprise me. As I've told you, I don't believe in them. Nor does Daniel Ortega. Get that one down. [*Laughter*] You've heard that before? Well, that's why I keep saying I don't go on these polls. I'm preparing the way when they fall further, Helen. Then I can keep saying: Don't you remember? I'm the guy who doesn't believe in these things.

Q. Is the rain going to stop you from playing golf?

The President. No. If it rains, I'm going to play. I'm going to play golf.

Q. We were afraid of that. [*Laughter*]

The President. No, but you want to—I mean, it's a Saturday morning. Why not?

Q. Well, even if it's storming? Don't you remember Malta?

The President. Yes. What else to do? What else is there to do?

Q. I hear they're bringing the *Gorky* back.

The President. The *Gorky*—[*laughter*]——

Lithuanian Independence

Q. Gorbachev says he'll get things accomplished in Lithuania without lectures. Are you lecturing him?

The President. I can understand his position, I mean, why he says that. Up until this point, he has viewed that largely, if not entirely, as an internal matter for him to work out with the Lithuanians. And because of the history, we don't view it that way. So, I can understand why he might suggest that that's in order, but I will continue to say what I think on this subject and convey my thoughts to him.

But I didn't view that as a hostile comment, but I viewed it as one of reiteration of his well-known position, just as we reiterated our well-known position when I met with those Baltic leaders the other day.

East German Apology for World War II Atrocities

Q. Mr. President, the East Germans have asked the world for forgiveness for the Holocaust. Should the world forgive them?

The President. Well, I'm one who believes in forgiveness. And for those of us who have faith, most of the teachings have ample room for forgiveness and moving on. And there's—I don't know—for our family, Easter is a very special time of year, and it's a time to take stock, and it's a time to be glad. So, I'm inclined to think we ought to forgive—not forget, necessarily, because I think you learn from history, learn what not to do wrong, how to conduct oneself.

But I'm a Christian, and I think forgiveness is something that I feel very strongly about. So, that's a personal observation. That's not a statement for our country.

Strategic Arms Reduction Talks

Q. Gorbachev—Shevardnadze [Soviet Foreign Minister] thinks that there will be a START treaty initialed—at least initialed—sort of a general agreement, framework.

The President. Well, I noticed he was quite upbeat there, and what he said about instructing his people to move forward. I viewed that as a very positive statement. And we're sending the same signals to our negotiators and policymakers, so I view that as positive.

Q. So it's possible, then, huh?

The President. Well, I don't know, Helen. I had hoped that, as you know, before. Then I think there was our feeling that things had walked back a little bit. But now that's most encouraging. I'm anxious to see [Senator] George Mitchell and get a little more detail on that.

Upcoming Summit With President Gorbachev

Q. Are you thinking of a side trip after the summit, maybe up to Maine, still?

The President. I'm not thinking anything yet on the logistics. Haven't gone beyond our last public statements on that.

Q. Do you plan to brief the NATO alliance after that summit?

The President. Personally?

Q. Yes.

The President. I don't know. There are so many visits. There's some talk about that, but then we have the G–7 meetings [economic summit] right after that. So, I don't have a plan to do it. But it is essential that they be filled in on every single detail. Maybe the Secretary of State does that.

Listen, Happy Good Friday. Nice to see you.

Note: The exchange began at approximately 7 a.m., prior to the President's departure from Andrews Air Force Base for a meeting with British Prime Minister Margaret Thatcher in Hamilton, Bermuda. Earlier in the morning, the President attended a Good Friday sunrise service at St. John's Church at Lafayette Square. Rev. John Harper was rector of the church. Patricia Presock was a Deputy Assistant to the President. During the exchange, a reporter referred to the Soviet passenger liner "Gorky," which was used as a meetingplace during the 1989 Malta summit. A tape was not available for verification of the content of the exchange.

News Conference of the President and Prime Minister Margaret Thatcher of the United Kingdom in Hamilton, Bermuda
April 13, 1990

The Prime Minister. Mr. President, ladies and gentlemen. I'm very grateful to the President for coming to Bermuda for these talks, and we've had a very full and useful discussion, lasting about 4 hours. We've discussed just about everything, and I think we agree on just about everything.

We both attach the greatest possible importance to preserving NATO as the heart of the West's defense and to keeping American forces and their nuclear weapons in Europe. We're both clear that united Germany should be part of NATO. We'll be happy to see NATO play a bigger political role within the Atlantic community. At the same time, we want to see the CSCE developed as a forum not for defense but for wider East-West political consultation and as a framework for drawing the East European countries into the mainstream of Europe. On defense, we both believe NATO will continue to need a mix of conventional and nuclear weapons, and they must be kept up to date. Whether we can make further reductions in the overall number of NATO nuclear warheads in Europe is something which will need to be considered in NATO as a whole. With so much happening, we shall need to consult particularly closely in NATO this year, and the President and I agreed to keep in very close touch on that.

We also, of course, discussed developments over Lithuania and are very much agreed that this is a problem which must be worked out by dialog and discussion. We also covered a very large number of regional issues, as well as matters such as the Uruguay round, the EBRD [European Bank for Reconstruction and Development, Eastern Europe], and relations between the European Community and the United States. We would like to see Europe and the United States together, trading and cooperating ever more closely in an Atlantic community.

So, very good talks, conducted in a very friendly atmosphere, with a very wide measure of agreement. Just as you would expect. Thank you.

The President. Thank you, Prime Minister. And first may I thank you and the Governor General [Desmond Langley] and the Premier [John W.D. Swan] of Bermuda for your wonderful hospitality. It's a pleasure to be here, not least because the Prime Minister and I have had this opportunity to sit down and consult frankly and freely and openly, at length about recent developments and what the future holds for Europe.

Naturally, we talked about the prospects of a unified Germany. We both welcome the fulfillment of the deepest aspirations of the German people to end their artificial separation. Both of our governments have supported the unification of Germany for more than 40 years, and we are glad that it is finally coming to pass in peace and in freedom.

The Prime Minister and I agree with Chancellor Kohl [Federal Republic of Germany] that Germany should remain a full member of NATO, including its military structures. And this is the view of the Federal Republic of Germany, of the entire North Atlantic alliance, and several of the countries in Eastern Europe as well. We believe that continued full German membership in NATO is in the genuine security interest of all European States. And in this context we also look forward to the continued development of the two-plus-four talks on the external aspects of the establishment of German unity. These talks will focus on bringing to an end the special Four Power rights and responsibilities for Berlin and Germany as a whole. A united Germany should have full control over all of its territory without any new discriminatory constraints on German sovereignty.

And we also had a good exchange about the situation in the Soviet Union and Lithuania. We agree that these issues must be dealt with through dialog so that the Lithuanian people's right to self-determination can be realized.

And just before coming in here, in the last few minutes, we were handed a deeply disturbing wire service report. Obviously, there's been no time to look into this matter in detail or to determine all the facts. But we have been calling on Moscow, publicly and privately, for avoiding escalatory measures in favor of dialog. And so, I'd say here: Now is no time for escalation. It's time for talk.

In talking together about the future of Europe and the Atlantic community, the Prime Minister and I discussed the opportunities which lie ahead for the North Atlantic alliance, the European Community, the Conference on Security and Cooperation in Europe—that's the CSCE—to help in building a Europe that's whole and free. The Prime Minister gave me more information about her recent proposals for the future of the CSCE, and I believe these ideas do hold a lot of promise.

These talks with Prime Minister Thatcher have been especially valuable to me. Our two countries have worked together for peace and freedom for many years now, and we've watched that cause prevail in many places and times, sometimes against great odds. The U.S.-U.K. friendship is the kind that doesn't need the words to describe it. It's a special friendship that is evident from the way we share a common vision for the future of humanity.

Thank you, Prime Minister, for a very helpful and illuminating 3 or 4 hours— whatever it's been. Thank you.

Nuclear Weapons in Europe

Q. May I ask President Bush whether you discussed the question of air-launched cruise missiles? And do you favor the basing of air-launched nuclear missiles in a united Germany?

The Prime Minister. Well, he was asking you, Mr. President. I think you'll have to get a microphone to be heard. Have we got a roving microphone? Because I'm afraid your words went into the middle distance. The question—look, while you're doing that, can we have the next question?

The President. I think he's established the ground rule that the first one goes to the Prime Minister. Were you talking to me or

her, or both?

Q. I was asking you, President Bush, because I think we know Mrs. Thatcher's answer. But I'll ask her as well. Do you think that air-launched nuclear missiles should be based in Germany, in a united Germany, as well as in Britain?

The President. I think the question of disposition of missiles is a question for the alliance. We will be having future consultations with the alliance, and I would leave it right there. Our position is that we need to do whatever it is that will fulfill America's role in helping keep the peace and in helping guarantee stability and security in Europe. So, I would leave the details of that, but I think the U.S. position is well-known. There was no change coming out of this meeting.

Lithuanian Independence

Q. I would like to ask Mrs. Thatcher: What do you think of the Gorbachev ultimatum? And also, I'd like to ask both of you, the President and Prime Minister: What can you do about it? Not only what do you think about it, but what can you do about it?

The Prime Minister. First, the President very kindly showed me the flash which he had received. And we discussed the matter, and we agreed the points which he has already made to you. The full facts are not yet known, and I would abide by the statement the President has just made.

Q. That it is deeply disturbing to you also?

The Prime Minister. I abide by the statement the President has just made. Yes, of course, we want reduction of tension so that discussion can start. And I have nothing further to add, dear.

Q. What can you do about it?

The President. Too hypothetical, Helen [Helen Thomas, United Press International]. She just said neither of us know that much about what "it" is. And I learned long ago not to go into answering a lot of hypothetical questions. But what we have done about it—and I speak for the United States—not this particular incident—but to have crystal clear, publicly and privately, to Mr. Gorbachev that coercion, escalation is not the way to go. The way to go is dialog. And I'll repeat it here. And that's what we're doing about it, right at this point, calling on them to heed these words.

Nuclear Weapons in Europe

Q. May I ask of both of you: When the Prime Minister says that all nuclear weapons need to be kept up to date, does that include all nuclear weapons, including short-range ones? And can we expect more of them to be based in the United Kingdom?

The Prime Minister. That phrase, of course, comes from the comprehensive concept which we agreed last at NATO, as you know, and the previous meeting. We agreed that all weapons, including nuclear, need to be kept up to date if they are to be effective. That does, of course, include short-range nuclear weapons as well.

Strategic Arms Reduction Talks

Q. Mr. President, earlier you said that you thought that President Gorbachev's willingness to initial a START treaty at the summit was a positive statement. What have you seen that's happened since last Friday when the negotiations were termed disappointing by both sides? Can you share with us any insight you might have on what has happened to make this encouraging?

The President. Well, only that the preliminary reports from Senator Mitchell and that delegation, I would say, was upbeat. I have not talked to them yet, though, Tom [Tom Raum, Associated Press]; and I want to do that as soon as they get back. But there was a rather thorough discussion, I'm told, and I think Gorbachev made the statement that he wanted to push his negotiators so that there would be an agreement. That's a little different slant than when Mr. Shevardnadze [Soviet Foreign Minister] left town.

Communications With President Gorbachev

Q. Is it time now to phone Mr. Gorbachev and ask him about this treaty as well as the Lithuania situation?

The President. Well, I don't know about the telephone. I use it once in a while, as you read today. And I might, and I might not. But certainly it's time to stay in close contact, and we have many ways of doing that.

South Africa

Q. Madam Prime Minister, have you and President Bush discussed at all about sanctions against the apartheid government in South Africa?

The Prime Minister. Yes, we discussed the situation in South Africa and the situation on sanctions. I described my point of view to the President, which is that, insofar as we are bound by law on sanctions—for example, through the United Nations, also orders which we have made to our Parliament in agreement with the European Community or the Commonwealth—those stand. But I took the view that as [South African] President de Klerk had, I thought, been very bold and courageous in the things that he is now doing, he should have some encouragement, and the voluntary sanctions which are not subject to orders should, therefore, be taken off. And that's why we took off the voluntary ban on investment.

Lithuanian Independence

Q. May I ask both of you if you're somewhat puzzled by this report from TASS [Soviet news agency] that Gorbachev is threatening to cut off raw materials to Lithuania? Because your Foreign Secretary, Prime Minister, Douglas Hurd, said on Wednesday that Gorbachev told him on Tuesday, I believe, that there would be no such economic blockade of Lithuania. Was that your understanding? So, are you surprised? And is the President surprised?

The President. You go ahead on Mr. Hurd. But I'll say this: Look, how can we comment on this when we've just seen about a four-line wire service report?

Q. It's a TASS report.

The President. Well, TASS report—I haven't seen the TASS report. I've told you what I've seen, and I don't think I can make conclusive judgments based on four sentences. However, I have expressed a real concern, and I do think that this is—if it proves to be accurate—is somewhat different than certainly what I would like to see coming out of there, as I've tried to make clear.

Q. Prime Minister, can you discuss what

the Foreign Secretary was told?

The Prime Minister. I understood that the undertaking given was that essential supplies would not be cut off. That, of course, is very much more limited than the expression which you gave. I haven't the precise words, but I've given you my understanding.

With regard to this particular flash, it is not precisely clear what is meant by it. And therefore, I think it inadvisable to comment further, except in the general terms; namely, that it's a reduction of tension that we now need in order to get fundamental discussions going.

Vietnamese Refugees

Q. Could I ask both of you, Mr. President and Prime Minister Thatcher, whether you had any discussion on the Vietnamese boat people, and whether the President is any closer to you, Prime Minister, on that issue?

The Prime Minister. Yes, we did discuss the Vietnamese boat people, because it's quite possible that there may be a further attempt from nonrefugee Vietnamese people to get into Hong Kong. And that will be deeply embarrassing and very, very difficult because Hong Kong is already full. But we have nothing further to report.

Arms Shipments to Iraq

Q. Mr. President, I understand that there was some discussion of what's called the gun, the Iraqi gun. Is it your sense, and I'd like to ask you both, that you need stronger controls on exports of this kind of equipment; that there needs to be something more done internationally to keep those kinds of things, whether they be guns or chemicals or what have you, out of the hands of terrorist nations?

The President. Well, anything we can do to keep guns or chemicals out of the hands of terrorist nations we should be doing. So, if this disclosure proves to be a gun and proves to be that it was being illegally shipped, I would encourage and would offer our cooperation to guarantee total banning and firming up the ban of weapons or potential weapons to countries that are illegally getting them.

But I would defer to the Prime Minister, because we were talking about this, and I

think there still is some question. But Prime Minister, am I misstating that?

The Prime Minister. Thank you. The experts are still considering and conferring as to whether it is or is not part of a gun or whether it is large steel piping. They have not yet made up their minds. If it were to prove to be part of a gun, it would require an export permit, which it has not got. And therefore, that is why it has been held up, pending consideration of precisely what it is. It is our purpose to keep such things out of the hands of the Iraqi Government.

Q. But if I could follow: This is the second incident in the last couple of weeks of weapons or parts of some sort being dealt with by the Iraqis. Is there some stronger effort needed in general to deal with the Iraqis specifically, or anyone else?

The Prime Minister. But this was a pretty strong effort. It was caught before it was loaded to see whether or not it was the kind of export that would have required an export permit, because it doesn't have one. In the meantime, they are conferring as to precisely what it is and not altogether agreeing. So, I think it's a pretty good rule: First, find the facts before you make any further comment. But the point is that, even though we don't quite know, it was apprehended and not allowed to be loaded, pending decision.

The President. And let me just add, Charles [Charles Bierbauer, Cable News Network], on your question—there has been superb cooperation between the U.K. and the United States in trying to avert such breaches in the law. And it isn't easy. And they've got laws on their books; we've got laws on our books. And if people are determined to break the law, then you have to resort to law enforcement and to intelligence to see that these bad things don't happen. And I think that great credit should be given to those in law enforcement and intelligence in the U.K. and in the United States for stopping that shipment of these alleged nuclear devices. And so, we ought to look at that half of the glass while saying if there's a way that we can tighten up export controls, certainly we ought to be doing it. And I think our people look at that all the time.

France's Role in NATO

Q. Mr. President, did you and the Prime Minister have any discussion about ways to encourage France to rejoin the military structure in NATO? And will you be raising this subject in your talks with President Mitterrand next week?

The President. No, we didn't specifically talk about that. But I will be raising with President Mitterrand the whole question of European security—question in which he is keenly interested. And one of the reasons that the Prime Minister and I have determined that we don't want to go out on a lot of new initiatives coming out of this important meeting is that we understand fully that we've got to consult with our NATO partners and our European partners. So, that subject specifically didn't come up that I recall, but I think our determination to work with France I think is well-known, but I would simply repeat it here. They are very important players in Europe, and clearly I'll be interested in discussing the broad security concerns of Europe with François Mitterrand.

Lithuanian Independence

Q. Mr. President, do you consider the latest move by the Soviets a violation of their pledge not to use force in Lithuania? And secondly, if Mr. Gorbachev carries out his threat to impose economic sanctions in 2 days if they don't rescind their call for independence, will that impact the summit?

The President. I've learned not to answer hypothetical questions, and I've told you that I can't give you more. Not that I want to avoid your question, but I simply don't know enough. I might know enough to answer a hypothetical question, but I don't think that's a prudent thing to do. And I just can't help you on that.

Europe-U.S. Relations

Q. Prime Minister, did you discuss Secretary Baker's call for a more formal treaty relationship between the U.S.A. and the European Community? And how do his ideas for a more political role for NATO fit with your ideas for the development of CSCE?

The Prime Minister. Well, we didn't discuss the first part of your question. The second, we did speak about, and I had hoped I had made it clear in my opening statement. I am very, very much in favor of increased dialog and an increased close relationship between both sides of the Atlantic community.

Therefore, giving an increased political role to NATO meets very much with my approval because I think the center of freedom and the defense of freedom is the whole Atlantic community. I have no difficulty in that. When it comes to the wider discussion, including Eastern Europe and the Soviet Union, it seems to me that the CSCE group of nations is just made for that wider political discussion. I think it's a forum in which we could draw in some of the East European nations to discussion with the United States and with the rest of Europe in a more formal and a more regular way than happens now. And I think that would be very useful for us all.

So, the one is the defense of the freedom nations having greater political contact. The other is a bridge across the divide. Both have their purpose. And they don't interfere with one another; they're complementary to one another.

The President. Might I just add that I agree wholly with what the Prime Minister has just said.

Lithuanian Independence

Q. Mr. President, this news report out of Moscow today comes a day after Senator Mitchell was reportedly told by Mr. Gorbachev that further lectures from American officials on the need for peaceful dialog were not welcome. And I wonder, sir, if you or Prime Minister Thatcher are beginning to see here the emergence of a pattern in Soviet conduct which might suggest that the policy of simply calling for restraint and not recognizing the Lithuanian Government, as it has requested, may not have been the right thing to do?

The President. No, I think we're on the right track. I, obviously, am concerned about the reports; but I did note what you reported that he said to Mitchell and that senatorial delegation. And so, I need to know a great deal more. But, look, the question is am I concerned about the report? If it proves to be accurate, the answer is yes, because it goes against the policy of dialog and a no-coercion dialog that will result in peaceful evolution of democracy and in self-determination. So, I'm concerned about the report. I'm concerned about the timing. But I just don't want to comment any further.

The Prime Minister. We're just not lecturing anyone, but we are entitled to express a view. We've frequently expressed it. This is not a problem that should be solved by force and which cannot be solved by force. It, therefore, must be solved by discussion.

We had a duty to say what we think. We still think that way, and we still think that is the only way to go. We've come a long way in relations between the Soviet Union and the free world, and we wish that improvement to continue. But it could not continue if the Soviet Union were to resolve this by force.

Soviet Political and Economic Situation

Q. Mr. President, you said that you had a full discussion on the situation in the Soviet Union. Mr. William Webster [Director of Central Intelligence] has just given a speech talking about a prolonged and deepening crisis there in the Soviet Union. Did the two of you agree in your assessments about the political situation in the Soviet Union at the moment, and would you agree with Mr. Webster's characterization of this as a crisis for Gorbachev?

The President. Lithuania being a crisis for Gorbachev?

Q. The political situation in the Soviet Union being a crisis for Gorbachev.

The President. Well, those are his words. I would say there are some very difficult problems facing him. And I would say that, in listening very carefully to the Prime Minister and then giving her my views, I think we are very close together in terms of our assessment of what the problems inside the Soviet Union right now, be they economic or as they relate to the Baltic States, other ethnic problems. The problems are enormous. And I expect both of us wish we had a little more information, because in dealing with a question of this nature, why, you never have all the facts you need.

But I feel very comfortable that I am in accord with the assessment by Prime Minis-

ter Thatcher of the situation there. And I think we have general agreement as to what the problems are, and I think we have solid agreement that we want to see a peaceful resolution to the problems as they relate to the outside world. But there are enormous problems inside the Soviet Union. And you can start and talk about the economy and the need for restructuring and reform and market incentives and a whole wide array of problems that are facing Mr. Gorbachev, and it's there that I think we need more information. Did you want to add to that?

The Prime Minister. No, nothing to add.

Lithuanian Independence

Q. Mr. President, you've been talking and calling for restraint for several weeks now, yet Mr. Gorbachev doesn't appear to be listening. In Lithuania, is there anything more you can do without sacrificing East-West relations? Is Lithuania being sacrificed to better relations or maintaining relations with the Soviets?

The President. I don't think so. I'm troubled by it, and we've made our position very clear to Mr. Gorbachev. But I know there's a great desire on the part of Americans to know what we might do, what can be done, what can the President of the United States do to force change upon somebody; and it's not that clear. If I had responses in mind, I'm not sure I'd share them with you, because I don't want to get into hypothetical situations.

As one of these reporters pointed out, it was only 24 hours ago that there was quite a different tone in report coming out of the Soviet Union. All I would keep repeating is it's highly complex, highly complicated; and the answer, in terms of smooth, ongoing relations that have no adverse effects on other things, is dialog and peaceful change.

Bombing of Pan American Flight 103

Q. I'd like to follow up. Will you in the West, both you, Mr. President, and you, Madam Prime Minister, allow an economic blockade of Lithuania?

The President. Too hypothetical. I'll let the Prime Minister speak.

May I add one word—and I wouldn't

dare to speak for the Prime Minister—but a flyer was put out relating to the victims of Pan American Flight 103. First, I want to say that the cooperation between the United Kingdom and the United States has been good in trying to track down the culprits, those that were guilty.

Secondly, we were called upon by two grieving parents, Mr. Bert Ammerman—and I don't know Dr. Swire, of Bromsgrove, England, who obviously have suffered and been hurt by the loss of loved ones. And they asked us at the conclusion of the talks to put out a joint communique condemning the terrorist attack on 103 and a renewed joint avowal to bring the perpetrators and their sponsoring nations to justice—putting terrorists on notice, et cetera. Of course, we're glad to do that. I am. I just hope that we can bring to justice those that caused this act.

Certainly, when we are asked to speak out against terrorism, I think the record of the United Kingdom and the record of the United States are very clear. But I don't think it hurts to reiterate our conviction that these dastardly terrorist acts must stop. So, we've formed a commission, and I know great inquiry has gone on in the U.K.—

Prime Minister Thatcher showing her own special brand of concern by being at the site, et cetera. And so, I would simply say to these people that appealed to us through this petition, in terms of the United States: We understand, and we do care. And we will continue to do everything we can in cooperation with the U.K. and other countries to get to the bottom of this cowardly, dastardly incident.

The Prime Minister. No one wants to solve that terrible tragedy more than we do. We have got quite a long way, but we have not yet completed the investigations. I wish we had. But we understand the feelings of all the relatives and understand why some of them are here. We, too, want it solved. We, too, wish there were far less terrorism in the world. We spend a great deal of our time and effort on trying to counter it. But we simply can't pull solutions out of the hat. It's a question of patient, continuous work on that investigation and patient, continuous determination to try to defeat terrorism.

The President. Thank you all very much.

Note: The President's 44th news conference began at 4 p.m. at Government House.

Statement by Press Secretary Fitzwater on the President's Meeting in Bermuda With Prime Minister Margaret Thatcher of the United Kingdom
April 13, 1990

The President and the Prime Minister met for 2 hours and 10 minutes and discussed a full range of international issues facing the North Atlantic alliance. Their warm and productive conversation focused on German reunification; NATO; the status of conventional forces in Europe talks; East-West relations, particularly the situation in

Lithuania; Iraq; and the status of COCOM.

President Bush and Prime Minister Thatcher have mutually supportive views on these issues. The special relationship between our two countries was evident as they considered a strong and steady Western response to the changes in Eastern Europe.

Remarks at a White House Briefing on Nicaragua
April 16, 1990

The President. Welcome to the White House. Bernie, have you been on yet?

Assistant Secretary Aronson. Yes, sir.

The President. Okay then. As you've just heard from Bernie Aronson, our chief Latin American expert, we are committed to the future of Nicaragua under democracy. And I think Fred Zeder, esteemed head of OPIC, will be briefing you in a minute; Jim Berg, of OPIC also; and Fred Schieck, of AID. And in these presentations I think that you all realize—and most of you know it already—that this is a time of tremendous change and hope and, indeed, opportunity.

Less than 2 months ago, there were a lot of pollsters looking for work after the Nicaraguan elections. But I don't think we should have been too surprised. I think the skepticism was, well, would the elections be free and fair. But given the choice, a free and fair choice between democracy and totalitarianism, people all around the world are opting for democracy. In the 7 weeks since the people have cast their ballots for peace and freedom, real progress has been made in negotiating what is really a difficult transition leading up to a peaceful transfer of power.

I've spoken several times with President-elect Violeta Chamorro since the election; and she really is, for those of you who have not met her, a woman of great moral courage, an inspiration to the people of her nation. And when she takes office in just 10 days—9 days from now, on the 25th—Nicaragua will close a painful chapter in its history and begin a new story, a new life in democracy. I have pledged to Mrs. Chamorro that the United States Government would respond in Nicaragua's hour of need.

I've called on the Congress to create what we call the Fund for Democracy, a fund to assist Nicaragua and its neighbor in Central America, Panama, as these two countries take their first critical steps on the road to democracy. I was gratified that the Congress, before adjournment, began action on our aid package, which includes $300 million for Nicaragua, but I'm disap-pointed that Congress failed to take the final steps to make the funds available before the Easter recess. That's why today I wanted to come here and to renew my plea to the United States Senate to act immediately when Congress reconvenes this week. Nicaragua and, of course, Panama, too, need these funds. With democracy at stake, there is simply no time for delay.

Government aid is crucial, but we all know that government aid alone cannot solve all the problems of Nicaragua. The business of democracy-building is a task that requires strong and steady support from the private sector, from individuals like many of you out here and those institutions that you represent.

Right now in Nicaragua I'd say the real hard work is just beginning. For the past decade, that nation has experienced terrible starvation and deprivation. And its energies were consumed, just eaten up, in that bitter civil war; its economy slowly strangled by a system of central control and mismanage-ment. Those days really have ended with the return of democracy. I'm told by Bernie and others that there's a new sense of confidence there in Nicaragua—people ready to roll up their sleeves and ready to turn things around, to build the institutions of free government and free enterprise and then create a climate for growth, to plant the seeds of peace and prosperity.

So, today I wanted to thank all of you for showing this interest, for coming here to the White House and meeting with these top members of our administration on this key question. I believe the United States of America has a great deal at stake in the success of Violeta Chamorro, but more so in democracy itself in Nicaragua.

I know that some of you are leaving tomorrow to go down there on a mission under the auspices of a private develop-ment group called Caribbean/Central American Action. And I know that OPIC is now planning a mission of its own the first week in June. I might say parenthetically that OPIC is a dynamic organization, bring-

501

ing investment and thus hope to countries all around the world now, as this new season of democracy is upon us.

I hope all of you here and all of you who take part in these special trips find it worthwhile to invest in Nicaragua. When you do, you'll be doing more than business, because I think you will really be showing the flag for, and your confidence in, democracy itself.

So, I really just want to scoot on over and wish you the very best, and please follow through. We need your commitment, and certainly Violeta Chamorro and the others that believe in democracy need your help.

Thank you all very, very much.

Note: The President spoke at 1:38 p.m. in Room 450 of the Old Executive Office Building. In his remarks, he referred to Bernard W. Aronson, Assistant Secretary of State for Inter-American Affairs; Fred M. Zeder, President and Chief Executive Officer of the Overseas Private Investment Corporation (OPIC); James D. Berg, Executive Vice President of OPIC; and Frederick W. Schieck, Acting Assistant Administrator for Latin America and the Caribbean at the Agency for International Development.

Statement by Press Secretary Fitzwater on Offsets in Military Exports
April 16, 1990

The President announced today his policy on offsets in military exports. This responds to the requirement under the FY 1989 National Defense Authorization Act, section 825, 10 U.S.C. 2505.

The President stated that the United States Government is committed to the principles of free and fair trade. Consequently, the United States Government views certain offsets for military exports as economically inefficient and market distorting.

Mindful of the need to minimize the adverse effects of offsets in military exports while ensuring that the ability of U.S. firms to compete for military export sales is not undermined, the President has established the following policy:

- No agency of the U.S. Government shall encourage, enter directly into, or commit U.S. firms to any offset arrangement in connection with the sale of defense goods or services to foreign governments.
- U.S. Government funds shall not be used to finance offsets in security assistance transactions except in accordance with currently established policies and procedures.
- Nothing in this policy shall prevent

agencies of the U.S. Government from fulfilling obligations incurred through international agreements entered into prior to the issuance of this policy.

- The decision whether to engage in offsets, and the responsibility for negotiating and implementing offset arrangements, resides with the companies involved.
- Any exception to this policy must be approved by the President through the National Security Council.

The President also noted that the time has come to consult with our friends and allies regarding the use of offsets in defense procurement. He has, therefore, directed the Secretary of Defense, in coordination with the Secretary of State, to lead an interagency team to consult with foreign nations with a view to limiting the adverse effects of offsets in defense procurement. This interagency team will report periodically on the results of these consultations and forward any recommendations to the National Security Council.

Note: The Office of the Press Secretary issued a fact sheet on the same day which provided the following additional information on offsets in military exports:

Offsets have become a common feature in the international arms trade. In the most general sense, offsets are industrial and commercial compensation practices offered or demanded in connection with the purchase of defense goods and services. While offsets also occur in civil trade and include business practices as old as barter itself, the scope and variety of offsets associated with military exports have become the focus of increasing public attention.

Some forms of offsets have become basic components of achieving defense sales and of furthering national policy goals of the U.S. and foreign governments. The objectives of a government making a foreign arms purchase often go beyond procuring arms at cost-effective prices and include considerations of the political acceptability of a foreign source; the maintenance and development of domestic defense and non-defense industries; obtaining advanced military and commercial technology; increasing employment; and other economic goals, such as conserving foreign exchange.

In this context, a U.S. seller of defense goods and services is often faced with difficult choices. The seller can elect not to offer offsets, which could result in the loss of sales because of the existence of competition willing to offer offsets. The seller can elect to offer offsets and hope to minimize their costs during implementation. The seller may face foreign government demands that obligate the seller to provide offsets as a non-negotiable condition of sales.

Because some offsets can alter the nature of defense sales transactions by including terms unrelated to price and performance of the product or service, offsets can introduce market rigidities and increased costs to the purchaser. In these circumstances, the result not only distorts trade and reduces economic efficiency but it diminishes the purchasing power of scarce defense resources.

Nomination of Charles H. Thomas To Be United States Ambassador to Hungary
April 16, 1990

The President today announced his intention to nominate Charles H. Thomas, of Maryland, a career member of the Senior Foreign Service, Class of Minister-Counselor, to be Ambassador Extraordinary and Plenipotentiary of the United States of America to the Republic of Hungary. He would succeed Robie Marcus Hooker Palmer.

Mr. Thomas served as Principal Deputy Assistant Secretary for European and Canadian Affairs at the Department of State, 1986–1989. Prior to this, he served as Deputy Assistant Secretary for European and Canadian Affairs at the Department of State, 1985–1986; Deputy Chief of Mission at the U.S. Embassy in Brussels, Belgium, 1982–1985; French language training, 1982; Director of the Office of European Security and Political Affairs, 1980–1982; Deputy Director of the Office of European Security and Political Affairs at the Department of State, 1978–1980; student at the National War College, 1977–1978; counselor for political affairs at the U.S. Embassy in Lisbon, Portugal, 1974–1977; Portuguese language training, 1974; and Executive Secretariat at the Department of State, 1973–1974. In addition, he served as Director of the Operations Center at the Department of State, 1972–1973; Deputy Director of the Operations Center, 1971–1972; director of the executive studies seminar for the Foreign Service Institute, 1969–1971; Director of the Peace Corps in Uruguay, 1967–1969; Deputy Director of the Peace Corps in Honduras, 1966–1967; desk officer for the Bureau of Inter-American Affairs for the State Department and the Agency for International Development for eastern Caribbean countries, 1964–1966; Third Secretary for the U.S. Embassy in La Paz, Bolivia, 1962–1964; vice consul for Ciudad Juarez, Mexico, 1960–1962; and Foreign Service officer for the Department of State, 1959–1960.

Mr. Thomas graduated from Harvard University (A.B., 1956). He was born June 23, 1934, in Buffalo, NY. Mr. Thomas served in the U.S. Navy, 1956–1959. He is married, has four children, and resides in Bethesda, MD.

Nomination of Alan Philip Larson To Be United States Representative to the Organization for Economic Cooperation and Development
April 16, 1990

The President today announced his intention to nominate Alan Philip Larson, of Virginia, a career member of the Senior Foreign Service, Class of Minister-Counselor, to be the Representative of the United States of America to the Organization for Economic Cooperation and Development, with the rank of Ambassador. He would succeed Denis Lamb. Currently, Dr. Larson serves as Deputy Assistant Secretary for Economic and Business Affairs at the Department of State. Dr. Larson is married, has three children, and resides in Reston, VA.

Appointment of Gerald William Ebker as a Member of the President's National Security Telecommunications Advisory Committee
April 16, 1990

The President today announced his intention to appoint Gerald William Ebker to be a member of the President's National Security Telecommunications Advisory Committee. He would succeed Vincent N. Cook. Currently, Mr. Ebker serves as vice president of IBM and president of IBM Systems Integration Division in Bethesda, MD. Mr. Ebker is married, has two children, and resides in Potomac, MD.

Appointment of Bobby Lynn Brantley as a Member of the National Commission on Agriculture and Rural Development Policy
April 16, 1990

The President today announced his intention to appoint Bobby Lynn Brantley to be a member of the National Commission on Agriculture and Rural Development Policy. He would succeed Arthur R. Brown, Jr.

Since 1986 Mr. Brantley has served as Lieutenant Governor for the State of Flori- da. Prior to this he served as an elected member of the Florida House of Representatives, 1978–1986. Lieutenant Governor Brantley was born April 6, 1948, in Atmore, AL. He served in the U.S. Marine Corps, 1968–1972. He is married, has two children, and resides in Tallahassee, FL.

Appointment of Andrew L. Lewis, Jr., as a Member of the Dwight David Eisenhower Centennial Commission
April 16, 1990

The President today announced his intention to appoint Andrew L. Lewis, Jr., to be a member of the Dwight David Eisenhower Centennial Commission. He would succeed Walter N. Thayer.

Since 1987 Mr. Lewis has served as chairman and chief executive officer of Union Pacific Corp. in Bethlehem, PA. Prior to this he was president and chief operating officer, 1986–1987. Mr. Lewis served as the Secretary of Transportation during the Reagan administration.

Mr. Lewis received a bachelor of science degree from Haverford College and a master's of business administration from Harvard Graduate School of Business. He is married, has three children, and resides in Schwenksville, PA.

Interview With Foreign Journalists
April 16, 1990

The President. This is timely in one sense because we're in the process of what appears to be organized consultations with Canada, France, and the U.K. I'm not sure that 6 months ago we envisioned this. But I am very pleased these meetings are taking place because I've tried hard as President to stay in close touch with our alliance leaders; and talks, given the rapidity of change in Eastern Europe, seemed very timely.

So, we've had two-thirds down, and one to go. And as far as the United States goes and as far as I go, I've been very pleased with the consultations—diplomacy, we'd say, frank and full. But they are very good exchanges, and I've learned from both. And I hope both [Canadian] Prime Minister Mulroney and [British] Prime Minister Thatcher have a better feel for the U.S. stance on important alliance matters.

But with no further ado, I'd be glad to take questions.

Lithuanian Independence

Q. Mr. President, one of the things that you've been talking to your coleaders about is, of course, Lithuania. Your position so far has been to suggest that the Lithuanian crisis can be resolved by dialog. I just wonder whether you think that we're approaching the moment when Western nations will have to give more direct assistance to Lithuania, particularly if there's an oil embargo.

The President. I think that's a little hypothetical, because I have been in contact with the Soviet leaders—indeed, had an opportunity to talk to Mr. Shevardnadze [Soviet Foreign Minister] right here, in that chair over there—and also have been in contact with Gorbachev. And I feel comfortable that they know the U.S. position; and I've felt that, having expressed our interest in self-determination and the peaceful evolution of all of this, that we're positioned about right. I don't think there's any question as to where I feel and, indeed, after consultation with our allies, where they feel.

But I think it's a little premature to—or perhaps a little hypothetical to suggest escalation of what we might do. I want to be sure anything we do is productive. There's been dramatic change in the world, and I don't want to inadvertently take some action that would set it back. And yet I don't want to be seen as one who is not interested in the peaceful change and in the self-determination for Lithuania.

We're in a position of never having recognized the incorporation of Lithuania, and indeed Estonia and Latvia, into the Soviet Union. So, that gives us a little bit of a standing that others might not have in terms of how we view this problem. But I just don't want to go into what we might do. I can understand the great interests in other countries and, certainly, in this country. But right now I'd like to, having expressed our concerns to the Soviets, watch the evolution here.

France's Role in NATO

Q. Mr. President, you are going to meet Mr. Mitterrand [President of France] next Thursday in Key Largo. And there has been in the French press a report about some misunderstanding in France and the U.S. about the NATO future role. Do you share any of those views, and it is true that your administration is pushing for France to get more involved in the alliance?

The President. Look, the main thing is that France and the United States be in total synchronization on alliance problems. France has a special historical position regarding the NATO alliance. But one of the reasons for having this meeting is to narrow any differences that might exist. I go down to Key Largo not feeling there are big differences with Mr. Mitterrand in this question. But I want to get his views. I want to tell him ours, and if there are differences, see if we can narrow them.

But it is my conviction that NATO will have a perhaps even more important role to play in the stability of Europe—East and West—projecting stability for East and Western Europe. And I would think that that might be shared by President Mitterrand, but I'll be talking to him about this question because there have been reports that there was a little drift and a little separation. And the best way to find that out is simply to sit and talk, as we will do there.

I can say this: that I've found my direct talks with him extraordinarily helpful in the past, and I expect this will be the same way. One of the key subjects will be security and arrangements for Europe after the unification of Germany. And that obviously will entail discussing our view for an expanded role for NATO.

His view—it doesn't exclude that but has a keen interest in a role for CSCE. And we see that. We've also talked about expanded participation in the EC, and I will try to elaborate on that with Mr. Mitterrand. So, I

know we're not egregiously apart at all. But if there are these differences, get them out on the table and talk about them.

Quebec Independence

Q. Mr. President, you say you're concerned about what might happen in Lithuania. There is also a strong independence movement in Quebec. And recently declassified State Department documents show that during the last peak of separatist sentiment in Quebec about a dozen years ago the U.S. was indeed very concerned about the prospect of a separate Quebec. Can you tell me what your concerns are about that prospect and what it could mean for U.S.-Canada relations and Quebec-U.S. relations?

The President. My experience is to stay out of a matter that's bubbling around up there in Canada right now, courageously sit on the sidelines, and say this: that we have always enjoyed the most cordial relations with a unified Canada. And that came up at a press conference we had up in Canada the other day there at the ball park. And I took the same view: that this is not a point at which the United States ought to involve itself in the internal affairs of Canada.

United Kingdom-U.S. Relations

Q. Mr. President, the British Labour Party, the opposition Labour Party, is very, very far ahead in the opinion polls in Britain at the moment. It's had an avowedly unilateralist past, and your predecessor seemed to treat it with a great deal of suspicion. I wonder if you now think that these people are people you can do business with and people you can talk to, and whether you have this sort of special relationship that you would like to have with the British Government?

The President. May I say this: that I haven't given any thought to it all because Margaret Thatcher is the head of the Government and the Prime Minister and we are in close consultation and negotiation with her.

So, I really would leave it there, because without suggesting any hostility toward opposition parties or towards—in this sense, since you asked about Labour—but I just, again, think it would be inappropriate to publicly speculate on what the U.S. might do. We do have a special relationship, and it'll continue, I'm sure. And these talks just reinforce that, these talks that I had with Prime Minister Thatcher. So, excuse me if I don't want to get into the bubbling caldron of domestic politics inside the U.K. right now.

Japan-U.S. Relations

Q. Mr. President, you seem to have had very substantial success in your relationship with Japan in the last couple of months. The SII [Structural Impediments Initiative negotiations] seems to have been moving along quite happily. I wonder whether that's a vindication of 3 years' worth of pressure from the Hill for a tough stance on trade issues.

The President. There is no question that the Hill, and indeed a lot of America, have wanted to see action taken by the Japanese. I would like to give credit to our negotiators, who are in the administrative executive branch of the Government, and also to Prime Minister Kaifu, who has taken the position that I think some of his critics here and abroad felt he wouldn't take, a position that we view quite forthcoming on SII and on specific categories of trade.

So, the jury is still out in terms of how the Hill will look at what has happened, but I've been very pleased so far that most of the leaders on Capitol Hill seem to feel that under Kaifu's leadership Japan has really moved on these important items.

But I guess the answer is, the proof of the pudding is in the eating. Also, there are certain undertakings that we make under SII. And Congress ought not to simply criticize Japan, even though I will readily concede there's been room for criticism there, and so stated. But I think we, the executive branch and the legislative branch, ought to work together now to fulfill our undertakings on investment, savings, education, budget deficits. It's a two-way street. But so far, I've been quite pleased. And—back to your question—I don't know whether it's Hill pressure, because for years Japanese leaders would come here, and hear the message from the Hill, go back; and we didn't have demonstrable progress. So, I think, in fairness, the Hill pressure has been

relatively constant.

We ought to take a look at what's different. And what's different is the way in which Prime Minister Kaifu, and indeed some of the other leaders there, have approached this problem.

NATO

Q. Mr. President, just to go back to the NATO issue, could you envision now the French being supreme commander of NATO?

The President. We're very happy with the present arrangements. You see, I think it's true in France and I know it's true in other countries: People view the U.S. presence as stabilizing, as having played a significant role in preserving a peace that, in terms of European history, is a long one. And I don't want to have this coming out in a chauvinistic sense, but I think the American people have to feel, one, the American presence is wanted. And part of the command structure, I think, contributes to the view that we have an important role to play and the Europeans want us to have an important role to play.

So, I've given no thought to any substantive changes in all of this. But if anybody has a different view, I'd be willing to hear it. But this is why I'm happy with the existing structure.

North American Trade Agreement

Q. Mr. President, your officials and Mexican officials have said they are ready to pursue, or at least consider, the idea of a free trade agreement. When you were in Toronto last week, you did say that you thought Canada should continue to show interest in trade with Mexico. Do you think it's a good idea for Canada to pursue a separate deal with Mexico; or should Canada, Mexico, and the United States sit down together and pursue a three-way deal, just as the European Community is working together?

The President. Are you talking about a free trade agreement?

Q. A free trade agreement.

The President. I think it's premature for a three-way free trade agreement. I expect Mexico feels that way; I believe that

Canada feels that way. I talked in the campaign about a North American accord and doing more together. But the sensitivities on this question in Mexico are such that we ought to let President Salinas set the pace here. And so, it is a sensitive subject there, just as some fallout from the free trade agreement with Canada and the U.S. is sensitive.

So, I think it's better to crawl before you walk, walk before you run. And the next step is to sit and talk with the President of Mexico, if this is still on his agenda, when he comes up here. And I say that because I don't want to be out saying what our meeting is going to be about. But you're right that there has been public speculation on this; indeed, different officials in our administration and Mexico have talked about it. But because of its sensitivity, I prefer to let Mexico speak for itself, and simply say I think we need to move forward in a bilateral sense, and Canada might want to move forward in a bilateral sense—that's up to them, though—before we talk about a North American accord meeting, a three-way free trade agreement.

British and French Nuclear Capabilities

Q. Mr. President, when you were in Bermuda, did you discuss with Mrs. Thatcher the status of the Trident, which as you know the Labour Party would like to include very quickly in arms control negotiations? Do you expect to discuss the French independent deterrent with Mr. Mitterrand?

The President. We touched only peripherally on that. Prime Minister Thatcher knows that she doesn't have to sell me on the French and British deterrence and the way in which they view their own nuclear capability. So, it wasn't what I would call a significant agenda item because I don't think we have any differences.

Brent [Brent Scowcroft, Assistant to the President for National Security Affairs], you were in those. Is that about the way it was? I don't think it was, unless there were some other discussions that went on not in our group.

Mr. Scowcroft. No, there wasn't an extended discussion because there aren't really any points at issue.

The President. Yes, we didn't have it as a formal agenda item.

U.S. Role in Europe

Q. Mr. President, did you like the phrase, "first among equals," as a description of your vision of America's place in the network of democratic alliances?

The President. Well, I think many of our allies look to us as the first among equals, given the blessing of the size of our gross national product and given our historic commitment to the security of others. But I don't know that—when I go sit down at a NATO meeting, I don't go there seeking a kind of recognition on that point. But I think the realities of the world are such that many look to us as essential—in this instance—the security of Europe. Certainly, we've got to be dealt with on trade matters.

And I am one who does not believe some of these elitist theories about the decline of America. I don't believe it; I don't think the American people believe it; I don't believe our allies believe it.

German Reunification

Q. Mr. President, do you think that the new Germany we've seen to come out in—one day is going to make and to cause any major problems—we being the EEC?

The President. No. Within these what?

Q. The EEC, the European Economic Community. There are some worries, you know.

The President. Yes, there are some concerns there about it, but I expect they can be sorted out. But the concept of a unified Germany does not cause me worries. I know there are perhaps nuances of difference on this one, but Germany has been a strong democracy here for a long time now—a long time. And the NATO position has been: Unification is okay. We don't worry about that at all.

But we want to stay involved as the United States. We want to be there as one who enthusiastically would deal with a unified Germany. And after this unity, there will be problems that we probably haven't even considered. But we're not opposed to it, and we don't worry about it.

Mr. Fitzwater. We're going to have to

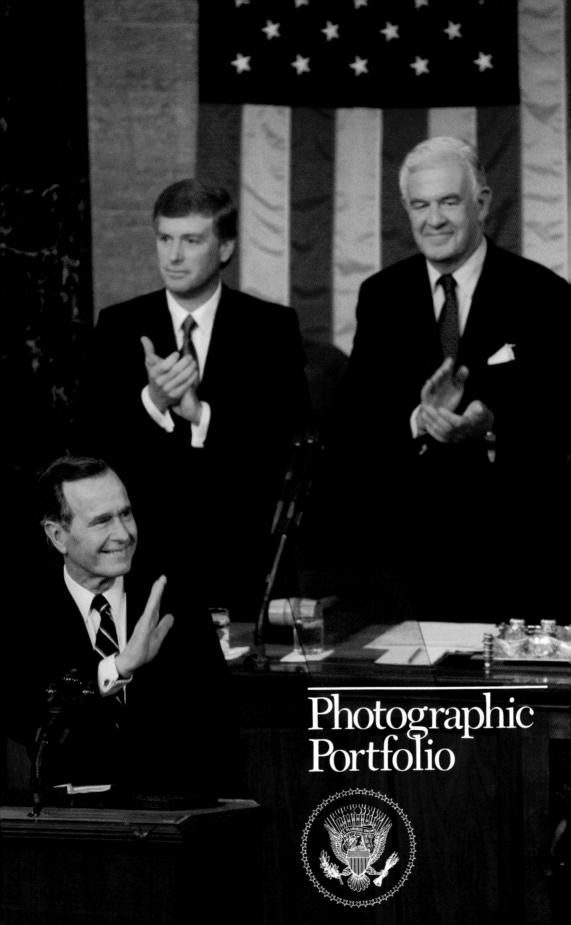

Photographic
Portfolio

erleaf: In the House Chamber
the Capitol for the State of the
ion Address to the Congress,
uary 31. *Left:* With Presidents
ne Paz Zamora of Bolivia,
gilio Barco Vargas of Colombia,
Alan Garcia Pérez of Peru at
drug summit in Cartagena,
ombia, February 15. *Below
:* Working in the Oval Office,
rch 13. *Right:* At a news
ference with Prime Minister
rgaret Thatcher of the United
gdom in Hamilton, Bermuda,
il 13. *Below:* Talking with
retary of State Baker, national
urity adviser General Scowcroft,
Press Secretary Fitzwater on
South Lawn prior to a signing
emony with Soviet President
rbachev, June 1.

Above: At the welcoming ceremony for President Mikhail Gorbachev of the Soviet Union the South Lawn, May 31. **Left:** Speaking by telephone in Islamorada, FL, to participants Earth Day events, April 22. **Above right:** Meeting with Prim Minister Toshiki Kaifu of Japan Palm Springs, CA, March 3. **Rig** Interview with magazine editors the Roosevelt Room, April 16.

Left: Meeting with Nelson Mandela in the Oval Office, June 25. **Below:** Meeting with adopted children and their paren[ts] in the East Room, January 26. **Right:** Throwing the first baseba[ll] of the season with Prime Ministe[r] Brian Mulroney of Canada at the Sky Dome in Toronto, April 10. **Overleaf:** Celebrating the 25th anniversary of Head Start in the Rose Garden, May 24.

ADOPTI♥N WORKS
FOR EVERYONE

break. If you've got a final question or two.

Q. Well, I——

The President. In the name of *egalite, fraternite.*

Q. ——stay on the sidelines just on a followup.

The President. Go ahead. Try.

Quebec Independence

Q. You have made clear your——

The President. You'll find I'm immovable——

Q. ——preference for a strong, unified Canada. Why? What difference does it make whether the United States is dealing with a separate Quebec?

The President. It makes the difference that this is the internal affair of Canada. And I learned something long ago: Do not intervene in the internal affairs of another country. That's pretty hard sometimes. In this one, it's easy.

You get another question because that was so cinchy. Go ahead.

Q. Oh, I do have another question?

The President. Yes. That's because that's just a follow-on to the other one, and it's just—look, that's a cinch, that one.

The President's Visits to Canada

Q. The question that many young Canadians sometimes ask me when I'm visiting back in Canada is: Mr. Bush has come to Ottawa—a quick trip to Ottawa, a quick trip to Vancouver, a quick trip to Toronto. He never seems to stay overnight. When he goes to Bermuda, he'll stay overnight, or he'll do this. Is there some reason that you don't like Canada, or is it too cold for you? Is there not good sporting and fishing up there? It's worth staying for?

The President. It's fantastic, but I have mean schedulers. I have invidious people there that do not let me do that which I'd like to do. And besides that, I have such a good feeling about Canada that frankly it never entered my mind if some might feel this way. But someday I will have the joy of doing that which I like best: recreating in Canada. Because I've been to Banff; I've been to the west. I know the country reasonably well. And I'd like to think that I would have a scheduler around here who would be a little more considerate and

permit me to do that.

Frankly, I think it's a good thing—the baseball recreation there—because the Blue Jays drew more, I am told, than any other team last year. They've got a fantastic stadium. And it sends a good hands-across-the-border signal. So, even though I get sheer pleasure out of going there and the little annoyance about Canada's defeat of the Texas Rangers, I think it was worthwhile for our national pastime—a game that I really enjoy.

So, I got some recreation there in that fantastic baseball stadium, but not near enough. So, if any of your readers feel there is any slight, tell them to call a man named Joe Hagin. [*Laughter*] His number is 456–1414. [*Laughter*]

British Prime Minister Thatcher

Q. Could I just ask, Mr. President, do you think that after a week in which Mrs. Thatcher was very heavily criticized and virtually written off in the American press whether her final reputation will be affected by——

The President. By what?

Q. Whether her final reputation will be affected by the pasting which she has taken in the last couple of weeks here and the differences you've had over Europe and Germany?

The President. Look, I read these polls. And I don't know what Mr. Ortega's pollster is doing now, and I don't know what the guy that said I wouldn't win because I was 17 points back in the summer of 1988 is doing now. But whether polls are right or wrong—and I don't want to denigrate all pollsters because I think there is a science there that sometimes is quite accurate. But I've just pointed out a couple of egregious errors here.

But I don't think you deal with heads of government based on whether they're up or down in the polls, or even speculate. So, I was giving you a very honest answer about the opposition. I mean, the opposition leaders would come here, we'd see them. I would think that's the way it ought to be. But I'm enough of a politician to know that people can be down one moment and then soaring like an eagle the next.

So, I missed your question just a little. What was it?

Q. I asked about her long-term reputation. Perhaps you could sum up, because whatever happens, she is coming to the end of a very long time in office. Could you say anything about what you think her long-term——

The President. No, no. That would be a matter for——

Q. ——reputation?

The President. Well, a reputation——

Q. Do you think——

The President. Oh, excuse me. I thought you meant whether she would rebound from all of this. Well, I think, at least in this country, people see her as a very courageous, principled leader who fights for her beliefs and has survived many ups and downs. So, they give her great credit. And I would be, in that vein, for courage and for—and another thing that she gets credit for here is a special feeling about the United States, a recognition that it's good for the U.K. and the U.S. to be close. I think she gets great credit from that not just in conservative circles or, say, Republican circles or IDU-affiliated circles, but across the board here in our country they see her as a tough, courageous leader who has enjoyed great success and with whom Presidents have enjoyed a very close, important relationship. It's about in there, I'd say.

Mr. Fitzwater. Thank you all very much.

Note: The interview began at 10:10 a.m. in the Oval Office at the White House. Participants included Peter Stothard, Times of London, United Kingdom; Norma Greenaway, Southam News, Canada; Michael Elliott, the Economist, United Kingdom; and Jerome Marchand, Le Point, France. Marlin Fitzwater was Press Secretary to the President. The interview was released by the Office of the Press Secretary on April 17. A tape was not available for verification of its content.

Remarks at the Opening Session of the White House Conference on Science and Economics Research Related to Global Change
April 17, 1990

Thank you very much for the welcome. I apologize for the slight delay in there. Thank you, Secretary Brady and members of the U.S. delegation; members of my Cabinet and the cochairmen of this Conference, Michael Boskin and Allan Bromley, Michael Deland. And I'm pleased to welcome this international field of distinguished high-level officials, experts all on the environment, economics, science, and energy. Welcome to the White House Conference on Global Change.

Two months ago I had the honor of addressing the Intergovernmental Panel on Climate Change. And let me recognize Bert Bolin, who is here—IPCC Chairman—here with us this morning. I see this Conference helping to accelerate the IPCC's agenda as it searches for understanding of some very critical questions, broadening the dialog by exploring the link between scientific research and economic analysis in the study of global change.

And of course, this Conference is itself another sign of the growing importance of the environment on the international agenda. Here in the United States, we've moved one step closer to a great victory for the environment, strengthening our own clean air statutes, already the world's toughest, with a comprehensive package of new clean air initiatives.

Ten months ago we renewed momentum lost in legislative stalemate for 12 years. Just this month, a clean air package cleared the United States Senate, with House action hopefully possible in May. We're moving forward on clean air legislation because it is in America's interest. But like so many of the environmental issues that concern us, we aren't the only beneficiary of a better environment.

When it comes to the environment, we are learning that local actions can have global consequences. Understanding the effects of our actions on our Earth's system is the first step to a sound environment. And the subject that led me to invite all of you here is just exactly that. I want to speak just briefly this morning so you can get on about your work. But I want to speak about what we can do over the course of the next couple of days to advance our understanding of global change. This Conference will help in three ways. First, it provides an opportunity to help sort out the science on this complex issue; to start with what we know about the Earth and this home we share, about the factors, natural as well as man-made, that cause our environment to change; and to work from what we know toward answers to the many uncertainties that abound.

Perhaps it's not surprising, when the subject is global change, that the debate often generates more heat than light. Some of you may have seen two scientists just on one of our talk shows on Sunday—respected men debating global change. One scientist argued that if we keep burning fossil fuels at today's rate, and I quote, "By the end of the next century, Earth could be nine degrees Fahrenheit warmer than today." And the other scientist saw no evidence of rapid change and warned against a drastic reordering of our economy that could cause us, in his words, "to end up the impoverished nation awaiting a warming that never comes." Two scientists, two diametrically opposed points of view—now, where does that leave us?

What we need are facts, the stuff that science is made of—a better understanding of the basic processes at work in our whole world, better Earth system models that enable us to calculate the complex interaction between man and our environment. And that's why I've asked our Congress to approve a 60-percent increase in our budget for the global change research program, an aggressive research program for which we budgeted more than $1 billion in 1991 to reduce the uncertainties surrounding global change, to advance the scientific understanding we need if we are to make decisions to maximize benefits and minimize the unintended consequences.

The second way this gathering can advance our understanding is to address the economic factor in environmental questions. We know that cleaning up our environment costs money—a lot of money—and we know it means changes in the way we work and live. Here in the United States, we're already making those changes—moving forward on clean air, planting trees through our America the Beautiful initiative, and working with other nations to find ways to halt deforestation, phasing out the use of CFC's, encouraging conservation, exploring alternative sources of fuel and energy and market-based incentives for pollution control. And yet as we move forward, all of us must make certain we preserve our environmental well-being and our economic welfare. We know that these are not separate concerns; they are two sides of the same coin. Recognizing this fact is in the interest of every nation here today. It's in the interest of the developed world and the developing world alike.

Let me focus for just a moment on the developing world. In a climate of poverty or persistent economic struggle, protecting the environment becomes a far more difficult challenge. Cold statistics don't begin to capture the harsh realities that are at stake. Development doesn't mean just another point in the gross national product, the GNP; it's measured in human lives, an end to hunger, lower infant mortality, longer life expectancy—not just quality of life but life itself.

Environmental policies that ignore the economic factor, the human factor, are destined to fail. But there's another reason to consider the economic factor when the issue is the environment. There is no better ally in service of our environment than strong economies: economies that make possible the increased efficiencies that enable us to make environmental gains, economies that generate the new technologies that help us arrest and reverse the damage that we've done to our environment. We need new economies that allow us to make vital investments in our common future.

And that brings me to the third way this

Conference contributes to a net gain in knowledge: the fact that it provides us the opportunity to form a partnership between nations and across the many disciplines represented here. Few subjects offer a greater challenge to the understanding of man than global change. And yet too often the different disciplines focusing on this question have worked in isolation, with little interchange of ideas, analysis, information. This Conference is a new departure because it brings together environmentalists and economists, experts on energy and science to search for common ground, to search the expertise each discipline can bring to this difficult and demanding concern. And this new partnership must bind nations as well. The fact of the matter is, no one nation acting alone can safeguard our Earth environment. Success requires a sense of global stewardship, an understanding that it is the Earth that endures and that all of us are no more than tenants in temporary possession of a sacred trust.

For the next 2 days, you, in essence, will be grappling with the questions, the fundamental questions, of global stewardship,

questions of global consequence. I know there's a debate raging out there, but I am confident that this approach that brings all of you experts together is the way to go.

I thank you very much for joining us here. I will be over after digesting the product of your work tomorrow to have a few more words to say. But from the bottom of my heart, I thank you for coming. There have been a lot of these environmental conferences around the world; but this one, I think, approaches the fundamentals. And we are fortunate to have here in America you experts from all around the world.

Thank you for coming. I look forward to hearing the results of your work. God bless you all. Thank you very much.

Note: The President spoke at 10:06 a.m. in the Grand Ballroom at the J.W. Marriott Hotel. In his remarks, he referred to Secretary of the Treasury Nicholas F. Brady; Michael J. Boskin, Chairman of the Council of Economic Advisers; D. Allan Bromley, Science Advisor to the President and Director of the Office of Science and Technology Policy; and Michael R. Deland, Chairman of the Council on Environmental Quality.

Remarks on the Situation in Lithuania
April 17, 1990

The President. Let me say that I understand Marlin has waived my prohibitions on saying anything at photo opportunities. But inasmuch as a lot of questions have been asked of our Press Office regarding Lithuania, I asked dispensation from our esteemed guest from Honduras, with whom I'm looking forward to visiting. And I told him if it's agreeable we would just make a brief statement about Lithuania. He acquiesced in that and was very pleasant about it.

But first, welcome, sir. We're just delighted you're here.

Let me just say on Lithuania—and this is all I'll say on it right now—obviously, we are watching the situation very, very closely. And we are waiting to see if the Soviet

announcements are implemented. Clearly, those announcements are contrary to the approach that we have urged and that others have urged upon the Soviet Union. We are considering appropriate responses if these threats are implemented.

And I'm going to leave it right there. But I would simply repeat that what we need is dialog, discussion, and a peaceful resolution of this great difficulty there.

Q. But what is your——

The President. That's all. Some missed it: I said I'd take no questions. Some missed it: I said I would take no questions.

Note: President Bush spoke at 11:13 a.m. in the Oval Office at the White House, prior to a meeting with President Rafael Callejas of Honduras. Marlin Fitzwater was Press   *Secretary to the President.*

Remarks Following Discussions With President Rafael Callejas of Honduras
April 17, 1990

President Bush. Mr. President and members of the Honduran delegation, let me again thank you for coming to the White House, all of you. We're very pleased and honored that you're here, and it's been a great and personal pleasure to meet President Callejas in his first official visit to Washington. We met before, but this was his first official visit since taking over as President.

The President is a long-time friend of the United States, dating back to his university days at Mississippi State University. And Vice President Quayle carried our warmest regards in January when he attended the President's historic inauguration, the first peaceful transfer of power to an opposition party in nearly 60 years and, indeed, an inspiring example of the democratic promise that today is spreading throughout the Americas.

I remember with great fondness the natural beauty of Honduras and the history of the Honduran people when I visited Tegucigalpa some years ago for the inauguration of your distinguished predecessor.

President Callejas and I shared very friendly and useful talks today on several subjects. We both expressed our appreciation for the stable and constructive relations shared by our two nations. The U.S. applauds Honduras' productive role in achieving a multilateral agreement on the peaceful demobilization and repatriation of the Nicaraguan resistance in conditions of safety for all concerned. We support this process and will work to ensure humanitarian assistance to those in need in both Nicaragua and Honduras as they return to their homes, their families, and their jobs, and play a vital role in helping Nicaragua establish lasting democratic institutions.

The President and I explored our mutual goals for Central America and also for our own bilateral relationship. We agreed on the importance of continuing our close cooperation in the struggle against the scourge of cocaine in our hemisphere. The U.S. remains firmly committed to helping economic development in Honduras. And we fully support President Callejas' bold economic reforms, and we are working together to help arrange new financing of Honduras' international obligations.

Mr. President, in your own Inaugural Address, you proclaimed that burning in the heart of the peoples of Central America is a flame of hope and faith in the democratic path. And, Mr. President, the people of the United States share your hope, and we share your faith. It is well-known that in Spanish the word "Honduras" means great depths. But we believe that the democratic path of which you spoke in January will lead to great heights for Honduras and for all of Central America.

Thank you for coming. We wish you Godspeed and success in your continuing talks here over the next 2 days. Thank you, sir.

President Callejas. Thank you, Mr. President. Ten years ago I came to the White House in company of a military President of Honduras. It was the beginning of a very complicated decade for Central America. Now we perceive new opportunities. We have concluded in the region, by the 25th of April, the election of democratic Presidents. And we hope that this next decade will be, in its priority, oriented to economic development and welfare.

Today, with President Bush, we have had a very cordial and fruitful meeting. We had the opportunity to discuss frankly and extensively bilateral and regional issues. I thank President Bush for the support of his administration for the efforts the Honduran people are doing in order to advance a program of economic reform. It is important that we quite well understand that there's no possibility to have democracy without economic development. And on that means the President assured us of the continued support of the United States for Honduras to recuperate its economic difficulties. I was very encouraged by the appreciation President Bush has demonstrated for the measures that we have taken.

We also discussed the regional situation. We have entered a new era in Central America. We have built upon democracy in the past decade, and now we must build an economic recovery. We have high hopes and expectations on the new prospectus of the region. With the assumption of power of Mrs. Chamorro in Nicaragua, a new page has been turned in Central America. And we all will support the efforts that the region demands and needs. This success can

only be achieved by continued support of friendly countries like the United States. And in that regard, I hope that the United States will continue to be close to the region in its new era.

I thank you, Mr. President, for your support and for your commitment to continue to give Honduras a helping hand in its effort to create a better place to live for its people. Thank you very much, Mr. President.

Note: President Bush spoke at 1:11 p.m. at the South Portico of the White House. Prior to their remarks, the two Presidents met privately in the Oval Office and with U.S. and Honduran officials in the Cabinet Room, and then attended a luncheon in the Old Family Dining Room.

Remarks on Meeting the National Collegiate Athletic Association's Men's and Women's Basketball Champions
April 17, 1990

First, let me salute our Members of Congress who are here, Senators Reid and Bryan and Representatives Bilbray and Vucanovich and Kolbe; coaches, of course, Tara VanDerveer and Jerry Tarkanian. And the athletic directors are with us, Andy Geiger, Brad Rothermel. And I also want to single out a couple from our administration, Mike Boskin and Condi Rice, of Stanford, and Sig Rogich, who was a former regent of the UNLV.

I'll try to cut this down a little, but I've got a lot to say about these guys, all of them—generic use of the term, I might add. [*Laughter*] We're here today to honor two great teams out of the West, the final two of the Final Fours, Stanford and the University of Nevada at Las Vegas, better known as the Cardinal and the Runnin' Rebels. Well, to put it simply, both teams were awesome.

The Cardinal women's basketball team won a Stanford and PAC 10 record of 32 games—in all a total of 100 individual and team records broken in this season. So, no

one was surprised when Tara VanDerveer was named the Naismith National Coach of the Year. From the very start, she installed this winning attitude so that you all began your seasons, in a sense, as champions. Coach, you've given everyone a reason to be proud down on the farm.

So has Trisha Stevens. I understand that in your career the number 35 has some significance. That's the number of points you keep reaching, game after game after game. [*Laughter*] And when you came out on the court against Auburn, you set the tone for the rest of that game. And so did Katy Steding. Three must be your magic number, considering the way you bombed the opponents with treys. Julie Zeilstra, you managed to start all 33 games this season as forward despite a problem with your Achilles heels. When the going got tough, you only got tougher.

Let me also recognize Sonja Henning. After your victory over the Lady Tigers, Stanford should light 21 candles in your honor. They say you're one-half of what is considered to be the best backcourt in women's collegiate basketball. So, let me turn, then, to your partner. You know, one of my favorite bands is the Oak Ridge Boys—[*laughter*]—so let me salute an Oak Ridge Lady, a young woman from Tennessee who went to play basketball in Palo Alto only to achieve her greatest triumph in Knoxville, 20 miles from home. It's no coincidence that Stanford senior guard Jennifer Azzi won the Margaret Wade Trophy and the James Naismith Award, the two top honors in all of women's basketball. We welcome you all; delighted you're here.

And now, we'll turn to the UNLV. Let me begin with a salute to the coach, Coach Tarkanian. I'm not saying that "Tark the Shark" has any influence on me, but the next time I'm sweating out a close vote in the Congress, don't be surprised if you see me—I'll try anything—chew on a towel. [*Laughter*]

Towel or no towel, it was the opposition that was shark-bitten. And of course, we should give the Blue Devils their due. You are, after all, the first team to trip 100 in a final.

Stacey Augmon, Stacy Cvijanovich, and David Butler, you duked it out with Duke all the way. And, David, you ought to feel at home today. Anderson Hunt, you kept the Blue Devils behind the Mason-Dixon line and made 12 of 16, to become the MVP of the Final Four. Congratulations!

And then there's Moses. You know the biblical Moses parted the waters with his staff. Moses Scurry could part the Potomac with his rebel yell. [*Laughter*] And, Larry Johnson, no wonder you're the First Team Consensus All-American. In just half an hour, you racked up 22 points, 11 rebounds, 4 steals, and 2 treys. But what impresses me the most is that while you're a probable first choice, you made it clear that you'll go for the B.A. before you go for the NBA.

And, Greg Anthony, I understand you suffered a broken jaw that had to be wired shut during the season. But you played through your pain. As vice chairman of the—this is a little political pitch here— UNLV Young Republicans—[*laughter*]—I hope you'll be coming back to Washington some day. And thank you for telling the world that your first priority is education

and that you may go on to get an M.B.A. or a law degree. That message has the right kind of impact on kids all across our great country.

And finally, let me congratulate every player in both teams—those of you on the bench as well as on the center court—and all the assistant coaches, managers, and trainers: This is your day.

In closing, let me say we're here today to celebrate another kind of championship, the kind of satisfaction that comes not from a fast break or a slam dunk but from the quiet achievement of scholarship and learning. And this is the commitment of so many, from Greg and Larry to Trisha, who aspires to be a doctor, to Chris MacMurdo, with a 3.7 average in human biology, to Stacy Parson, a social psych major who is said to be the team encyclopedia. This is the commitment of the Runnin' Rebels for teaching grade schoolers basic reading skills and geography. In fact, I understand that you'll be making at least one classroom visit here in DC, where David Butler started his schooling, at John F. Cook Elementary.

Just look at your institutions. U.S. News and World Report identified UNLV as one of the up-and-coming schools of the nineties. Little wonder—it's already one of the fastest growing universities in America. And of course, we're also familiar with the academic tradition of Stanford University. So, whether you study amid the Moorish arches of Stanford or in the modern complexes of UNLV, you're learning that when the cheering has faded and the trophy is up on the shelf you still have something to give back.

Once again, congratulations. I thank you, and God bless you all. Keep up that quest for excellence and the achievement you've all demonstrated so well. We're just delighted you all were here.

Note: The President spoke at 2:19 p.m. in the Rose Garden at the White House. In his remarks, he referred to Michael J. Boskin, Chairman of the Council of Economic Advisers; Condoleezza Rice, Director of European and Soviet Affairs for the National Security Council; and Sig Rogich, Assistant to the President for Special Activities and Initiatives.

Statement on the Death of Ralph David Abernathy
April 17, 1990

Barbara and I were deeply saddened to learn of the death of the Rev. Ralph David Abernathy. In recalling Ralph Abernathy's life, we inevitably recall the great campaigns for civil rights for black Americans in which he played such a signal part. From his father's farm in Alabama, he joined the ministry and became pastor of the First Baptist Church in Montgomery. Responding to Rosa Parks' refusal to sit in the back of a segregated bus, he and the Rev. Dr. Martin Luther King, Jr., began the Montgomery Improvement Association to ensure the success of the boycott which led in turn to the desegregation of buses in that city. Later, he and Dr. King organized the Southern Christian Leadership Conference, of which he originally served as secretary-treasurer.

Throughout, Rev. Abernathy was committed to the principle of nonviolence. As he said, "Violence is the weapon of the weak, and nonviolence is the weapon of the strong." Barbara and I join with all Americans to mourn the passing of the Rev. Ralph Abernathy, a great leader in the struggle for civil rights for all Americans and a tireless campaigner for justice.

Nomination of Anthony J. Hope To Be Chairman of the National Indian Gaming Commission
April 17, 1990

The President today announced his intention to nominate Anthony J. Hope to be Chairman of the National Indian Gaming Commission for a term of 3 years. This is a new position. Since 1987 Mr. Hope has served as senior vice president of Mutual of Omaha and United of Omaha Insurance Cos. in Washington, DC. He was born July 1, 1940, in Chicago, IL. Mr. Hope is married, has two children, and resides in Washington, DC.

Message to the Congress Reporting Budget Deferrals
April 18, 1990

To the Congress of the United States:

In accordance with the Impoundment Control Act of 1974, I herewith report three revised deferrals of budget authority now totalling $2,097,533,159.

The deferrals affect programs in Funds Appropriated to the President and the Departments of Defense and Health and Human Services. The details of the deferrals are contained in the attached report.

GEORGE BUSH

The White House,
April 18, 1990.

Note: The attachment detailing the deferrals was printed in the "Federal Register" of April 24.

Message to the Senate Transmitting the Spain-United States Convention on Taxation and Fiscal Evasion
April 18, 1990

To the Senate of the United States:

I transmit herewith for Senate advice and consent to ratification the Convention between the United States of America and the Kingdom of Spain for the Avoidance of Double Taxation and the Prevention of Fiscal Evasion with respect to Taxes on Income, together with a related Protocol, signed at Madrid on February 22, 1990. I also transmit the report of the Department of State.

The convention is the first income tax treaty to be negotiated between the United States and Spain. Based in large part on model income tax treaties developed by the Department of the Treasury and the Organization for Economic Cooperation and Development, it also reflects changes in tax law resulting from the enactment of the Tax Reform Act of 1986.

The convention provides rules governing the taxation by each State of income derived by residents of the other State. The convention also contains provisions that prevent "treaty shopping" and authorize the exchange of information and administrative cooperation between the tax authorities of the two States.

I recommend that the Senate give early and favorable consideration to the convention and protocol and give its advice and consent to ratification.

GEORGE BUSH

The White House,
April 18, 1990.

Nomination of Olin L. Greene, Jr., To Be Administrator of the United States Fire Administration
April 18, 1990

The President today announced his intention to nominate Olin L. Greene, Jr., to be Administrator of the U.S. Fire Administration, Federal Emergency Management Agency. He would succeed Clyde A. Bragdon, Jr.

Since 1982 Mr. Greene has served as State fire marshal in Salem, OR. Prior to this, he served as director of the division of State fire marshal for the State of Florida, 1973–1982; deputy State fire marshal in Miami, FL, 1969–1973; combat firefighter, fire inspector, and fire investigator for the City of Miami Fire Department, 1960–1969.

Mr. Greene attended the University of Miami and Georgia Tech. He was born January 15, 1937, in Miami, FL. Mr. Greene is married, has one child, and resides in Dallas, OR.

Remarks at the Closing Session of the White House Conference on Science and Economics Research Related to Global Change
April 18, 1990

Thank you, ladies and gentlemen. Thank you, Dr. Bromley, very much, Dr. Boskin, Mr. Deland, and Secretaries Watkins and Lujan of our Cabinet, Dr. Bolin, and distinguished delegates to this truly unprecedented conference.

After all of the hard work that's taken place here, in what I know was an atmosphere of lively debate, I would begin with thanks and a moment of perspective; for your purpose here is profoundly important to the state of nature and the fate of mankind. Your presence has offered hope for a new era of environmental cooperation around the world and the promise of a quieter, more thoughtful, more careful tenancy of nature's legacy to humanity.

You know, during these last 2 days, we've listened and learned—and I've been briefed thoroughly on some of the committee's works—learned about Brazil's new initiatives to protect the Amazon rain forest, about Nigeria's plans to remove lead from gasoline, about Mexico's promising efforts to reduce the Mexico City air pollution.

A year ago I participated in an American education summit and found the most productive sessions were those working groups. This Conference was structured with that lesson in mind. So, my thanks go to all the delegates who played such an integral role in those working groups, particularly the foreign delegates who served as cochairmen.

A growing sense of global stewardship prompted us to host this Conference. It's a sense of stewardship shared by all of you and by the nations you represent. And it arises out of a natural sense of obligation, an understanding that we owe our existence, all that we know and are, to this miraculous sphere that sustains us. Somebody told me that the evening you had over at the museum brought this into very, very clear perspective when you heard from some of the NASA people.

Such stewardship finds expression in many ways, from public demonstration to landmark legislation, but it is also rewarded in many ways, in moments unexpected and unforgettable. Nature's beauty has a special power, a resonance that at once elevates the mind's eye, and yet humbles us as well. Before nature, the works of humanity seem somehow small. We may build cathedrals, temples, mosques, monuments, and mausoleums to great men and women and high ideals, and still we know we can build no monuments to compare with nature. Our greatest creations really can't equal God's smallest.

Yet as our tools and intellect advance, we've learned of our power to alter the Earth. We understand that small actions, taken together, can have profound global consequences for the environment we share and the humanity we share it with. The importance of global stewardship can be best understood in human terms.

We also recognize that ours is an increasingly prosperous planet, with greater hopes now than ever before that more of our people in every nation may come to know an enduring peace and an unprecedented quality of life.

So, we're called upon to ensure that the Earth's integrity is preserved and that mankind's prospects for prosperity, peace and, in some regions, even survival are not put at risk by the unintended consequences of noble intentions. That's the reason we've held this conference.

The minds at work here are among the very best we have, and they are the best insurance that our actions are sound. We've gathered talent from around the world—scientists, economists, environmentalists, energy ministers, policymakers—to address the environmental and developmental future of the planet, an unprecedented cross-fertilization of disciplines and of nations. That alone, I think, is reason for hope.

But if diversity of perspective is expected, unity of purpose is crucial. In an atmosphere of uncertainty, we must foster a climate of good will and a stubborn hope that we might forge solutions without the excessive heat of politics.

Among all the challenges in our tenancy of this planet, climate change is, of course, foremost in your minds. We're leading the search for response strategies and working through the uncertainty of both the science and the economics of climate change. But there is one area where we will allow for no uncertainty, and that is our commitment to action—to sound analyses and sound policies.

To those who suggest we're only trying to balance economic growth and environmental protection, I say they miss the point. We are calling for an early new way of thinking to achieve both while compromising neither by applying the power of the marketplace in the service of the environment.

And we cannot allow a question like climate change to be characterized as a debate between economists versus environmentalists. To say that this issue has sides is about as productive as saying that the Earth is flat. It may simplify things, but it just doesn't do justice to the facts or to our future. The truth is, strong economies allow nations to fulfill the obligations of stewardship, and environmental stewardship is crucial to sustaining strong economies. If we lose sight of the forest for the trees, we risk losing both.

But above all, the climate change debate is not about research versus action, for we've never considered research a substitute for action. Over the last 2 days you've heard, formally and informally, that the United States is already taking action to stabilize and reduce emissions through our clean air legislation, our use of market-based incentives to control pollution, our search for alternative energy sources, our emphasis on energy efficiency, our reforestation initiatives, and our technical assistance programs to developing nations. These policies were developed to address a broad range of environmental concerns. In particular, our phaseout of CFC's, the impact of our Clean Air Act on emissions, our tree planting initiative, and other strategies will produce reductions in greenhouse gas emissions that will reach 15 percent in 10 years and considerably more later on.

We're also making a leading investment in climate change research—absolutely essential because it will tell us what to do next. But what bears emphasis is that we are committed to domestic and international policies that are environmentally aggressive, effective, and efficient.

And we are deeply committed to an international partnership through the IPCC [Intergovernmental Panel on Climate Change] process. We look forward to its interim assessment. And we would encourage a framework convention as a part of a comprehensive approach to address the system, sources, and sinks as a whole if a decision is made that environmental action is needed to reduce net emissions. We hope to provide a venue for the first negotiating ses-

sions here in the United States.

And finally, here in conference working groups, we've offered four new ideas: a charter for cooperation in science and economic research related to global change, possible creation of international institutes for research on the science and economics of global change, data and information transfers through a global change communications network, and a statement of principles for implementing international cooperation in scientific and economic research related to global change.

I call on you to support these suggestions. All of you here today understand climate change as one of many challenges in the call to global stewardship: ozone depletion, water supply, ocean pollution, wetlands, deforestation, biological diversity, population change, hunger, energy demand—in short, all of the interrelated issues of the global environment. Each demands our attention. Each will have great impact.

And some we can predict, and regrettably and frankly, some can't be easily anticipated. But each has a human dimension we must never forget. Understand the choices we are making; they affect us all, but in profoundly different ways. We have many paths to choose from, and some of them are fraught with risk to precious and life-giving resources; risk to geopolitical stability; and certainly, man-made limits to prosperity, most painfully reflected in the hollow eyes of hungry children and their prospects for survival.

If developed nations ignore the growth needs of developing nations, it will imperil us all. We know that even small changes in GNP growth rate often threaten adequate shelter, food, and health care for millions and millions of people. And to bear this in mind is no barrier to action. Those who have ascended the economic hill must break down the barriers to progress and assist others now making the climb. But this will only be possible if the nations of the world are linked in partnerships of every kind: scientific, economic, technical, agricultural, environmental.

Pollution is not, as we once believed, the inevitable byproduct of progress. True global stewardship will be achieved not by seeking limits to growth, which are contrary to human nature, but by achieving environmental protection through more informed, more efficient, and cleaner growth. Those who value environmental quality the most should be the most ardent supporters of strategies that tap the power of free wills and free markets, strategies that turn human nature to environmental advantage. Equally, those who value economic development most highly should be the most ardent defenders of the environment, which provides the basis for a healthy economy. Efficient strategies are the only realistic hope for developing nations to save themselves from the mistakes that developed nations have already made.

And we have made mistakes. But over the past century, we've made tremendous progress in this country, especially in the last 20 years. In the United States, automotive emission controls have brought about a new generation of cars that emit only 4 percent as much pollution as the typical 1970 model. We've cut airborne particulates by 60 percent, carbon monoxide by about 40 percent, cut sulfur emissions, and virtually eliminated lead from the air—all during a period of population growth and economic expansion. And now we want to share that knowledge—our technologies, new processes, and pollution prevention techniques—with the developing world.

Two decades ago, America, holding to its birthright of free expression, was home to a movement symbolized by Earth Day. It motivated President Nixon to sign into law a national policy to encourage productive and enjoyable harmony between man and the environment, and it set in motion a new sense of conscience that a few idealists hoped would change the world.

And it did. What began as an isolated American movement 20 years ago is now shared by over 130 countries on 7 continents. And while many thought this experiment in environmental protection would prove impossible, that you couldn't maintain both a productive economy and a healthy environment, we've learned that economic prosperity and environmental protection go hand in hand. And we've learned that worldwide, united action is essential and possible, as the Montreal protocol proved.

America and other nations must now extend an offered hand to emerging democracies in Eastern Europe and to developing societies around the world. In some, the raging fires of forests and grasslands burned for compelling but devastating economic reasons have been visible to astronauts in space. Other nations, in the struggle to support life, have been virtually stripped of the resources that sustain life.

And in Eastern Europe, whether through the tyranny of neglect or the neglect of tyrants, pollution has been unveiled as one of the Old World's cruelest dictators, an oppressor—not man but manmade. In the majestic city of Krakow that I visited a couple of years ago, monuments to great men, statues that survived countless invasions by kings and emperors, by Hitler and by Stalin, have been defaced by pollution, their medieval majesty reduced to shapeless lumps of stone.

If mankind's greatest creations cannot equal God's smallest, some may grieve that our greatest destruction is turned at times upon ourselves. Let us neither grieve nor quarrel but act on what we know can help and act in good faith. Our challenge is global stewardship: to work together to find long-term strategies that will meet the needs of the entire world and all therein.

Our convictions and my sincere belief is that environmental protection and economic growth, well-managed, complement one another and that we can serve this generation while preserving the Earth for the next and all that follow. It is an uncommon opportunity we share. And so, let us seize the moment. And together, we will succeed.

Thank you for what I believe is a significant contribution to environmental progress in the world. Thank you for coming our way. Thank you very much.

Note: The President spoke at 2:32 p.m. in the Grand Ballroom at the J.W. Marriott Hotel. In his remarks, he referred to D. Allan Bromley, Science Advisor to the President and Director of the Office of Science and Technology Policy; Michael J. Boskin, Chairman of the Council of Economic Advisers; Michael R. Deland, Chairman of the

Council on Environmental Quality; Secretary of Energy James D. Watkins; Secretary of the Interior Manuel Lujan, Jr.; and Bert

Bolin, Chairman of the Intergovernmental Panel on Climate Change.

Letter to Congressional Leaders Transmitting a Report on the United States Military Presence in East Asia
April 18, 1990

Dear Mr. Chairman: (Dear Senator:)
(Dear Congressman:)
Pursuant to section 915 of the National Defense Authorization Act for Fiscal Years 1990 and 1991 (Public Law 101–189), I am hereby transmitting classified and unclassified versions of a report on the military presence of the United States in East Asia, including the Republic of Korea. The reports include a strategic plan relating to the continued United States military presence in East Asia.
Sincerely,

GEORGE BUSH

Note: Identical letters were sent to Robert C. Byrd and Mark O. Hatfield, chairman and ranking Republican member of the Senate Committee on Appropriations; Jamie L. Whitten and Silvio O. Conte, chairman and ranking Republican member of the House Committee on Appropriations; Sam Nunn and John W. Warner, chairman and ranking Republican member of the Senate Committee on Armed Services; and Les Aspin and William L. Dickinson, chairman and ranking Republican member of the House Committee on Armed Services. The letter was released by the Office of the Press Secretary on April 19.

Nomination of James Keough Bishop To Be United States Ambassador to Somalia
April 19, 1990

The President today announced his intention to nominate James Keough Bishop to be Ambassador Extraordinary and Plenipotentiary of the United States of America to the Somali Democratic Republic. He would succeed Trusten Frank Crigler.

Since 1987 Ambassador Bishop has been Ambassador to the Republic of Liberia. Prior to this, he was Deputy Assistant Secretary for African Affairs at the Department of State, 1981–1987; Ambassador to the Republic of Niger, 1979–1981; Director of North African Affairs at the Bureau of Near Eastern and South Asian Affairs at the Department of State, 1977–1979; senior seminar student at the Foreign Service Institute in Washington, DC, 1976–1977; and Deputy Director for West Africa at the Department

of State, 1974–1976. He was a desk officer for Ghana and Togo, 1972–1974; desk officer for Chad, Gabon, Mauritius and Madagascar, 1970–1972; economic officer in Yaounde, Cameroon, 1968–1970, and Beirut, Lebanon, 1966–1968; consul in Beirut, Lebanon, 1966; vice consul in Auckland, New Zealand, 1963–1966; and a press officer at the Department of State, 1961–1963. He entered the Foreign Service in 1960.

Ambassador Bishop graduated from the College of the Holy Cross (B.S., 1960) and Johns Hopkins School of Advanced International Studies (M.I.I.P., 1981). He was born July 21, 1938, in New Rochelle, NY. He is married, has six children, and resides in Washington, DC.

Nomination of Daniel F. Evans To Be a Director of the Federal Housing Finance Board, and Designation as Chairman
April 19, 1990

The President today announced his intention to nominate Daniel F. Evans to be a Director of the Federal Housing Finance Board for a term of 7 years. Upon confirmation and appointment he will be designated Chairman. This is a new position.

Since 1985 Mr. Evans has served as a partner with the law firm of Baker and Daniels in Indianapolis, IN. Prior to this, he served as a partner with the law firm of Tabbert and Capehart, 1981–1985, and an associate and partner with the law firm of Duvall, Tabbert, Lalley and Newton, 1976–1981.

Mr. Evans graduated from Indiana University (B.A., 1971) and Indiana University Law School (J.D., 1975). He was born April 19, 1949, in Indianapolis, IN. Mr. Evans is married, has four children, and resides in Indianapolis, IN.

Nomination of Lawrence U. Costiglio To Be a Director of the Federal Housing Finance Board
April 19, 1990

The President today announced his intention to nominate Lawrence U. Costiglio to be a Director of the Federal Housing Finance Board for a term of 3 years. This is a new position.

Since 1988 Mr. Costiglio has served as a partner with the law firm of Rivkin, Radler, Dunne and Bayh in Uniondale, NY. Prior to this, he served as counsel to Certilman Haft Lebow Balin Buckley and Kremer in East Meadow, NY., 1987–1988; special counsel to the Savings Bank Association, 1984–1986; executive vice president of the Savings Bank Association of New York State, 1961–1985; attorney with the law firm of Oliver and Donnally in New York, 1959–1961, and acting deputy superintendent and counsel to the banking board, associate attorney and executive assistant to superintendent, 1957–1959. In addition, he has served as an attorney with the law firm of Finely and Lilienthal, Esqs., 1955–1957; Assistant United States Attorney for the Southern District of New York in the Criminal Division, 1951–1955; and an attorney in private law practice, 1946–1951.

Mr. Costiglio attended the College of the City of New York and graduated from Fordham University School of Law (LL.B., 1941). He was born August 8, 1916, in New York, NY. Mr. Costiglio served in the U.S. Army, 1935–1942. He is married, has four children, and resides in Woodside, NY.

Nomination of Daniel H. Carter To Be a Member of the National Commission on Libraries and Information Science
April 19, 1990

The President today announced his intention to nominate Daniel H. Carter to be a member of the National Commission on Libraries and Information Science for a term expiring July 19, 1994. This is a reappointment. Since 1986 Mr. Carter has served as president of Daniel Carter Consulting in Houston, TX. He resides in Houston, TX.

News Conference of President Bush and President François Mitterrand of France in Key Largo, Florida
April 19, 1990

President Bush. Well, it's been a great pleasure having President Mitterrand as our guest here at Key Largo, after his splendid tropical hospitality at St. Martin in December. And our meetings, starting last May at Kennebunkport, have been invaluable in ensuring close French-American cooperation during this period of historic change in Europe.

President Mitterrand and I spent most of our time today discussing the profound and encouraging transformation of Europe, and we reviewed the enormous advances towards democracy and economic reform which have occurred in Eastern Europe since we met in Paris in July.

In addition to the economic and political reforms moving forward in Eastern Europe, we discussed the welcome prospect of a unified Germany. This fulfillment of the natural aspiration of the German people is a goal which both France and the United States have supported for over two generations. President Mitterrand and I both believe that a united Germany should remain a full member of NATO, as called for by Chancellor Kohl [of the Federal Republic of Germany]. All of our allies and several Eastern European countries share this view as well.

In this context, we also look forward to the continuation of the two-plus-four talks on the external aspects of the establishment of German unity. These talks will focus on bringing to an end the special Four Power rights and responsibilities for Berlin and Germany as a whole. And we agreed that a united Germany should have full control over all of its territory, without any new discriminatory constraints on German sovereignty.

In discussing the evolution of European security, the French President and I spoke about the key role the North Atlantic alliance has played in making possible the positive changes of the past year. The alliance must remain vigorous in this critical period of transition. I told the President that the U.S. will retain militarily significant nuclear and conventional forces in Western Europe as long as our allies desire our presence as part of a common security effort, and he indicated strong French support for the continued U.S. presence.

We also discussed the progress of the European Community towards increased integration, and I repeated the unequivocal support for European unity that I'd expressed last May when we were together up there at Boston University. We agreed that as the EC evolves, closer U.S.-EC linkage and more effective channels for dialog will be required. We both believe that as the division of Europe gives way to a new era of reconciliation we must strengthen the CSCE process in ways that can enhance mutual confidence and peaceful cooperation in Europe.

We also had a thorough discussion about the situation in the Soviet Union and Lithuania. And we share a conviction that this issue must be dealt with through dialog so that the Lithuanian people's rights to self-determination can be realized. We're deeply disturbed by recent Soviet statements and activities regarding Lithuania which will clearly not improve the atmosphere, and I told President Mitterrand that the U.S. is considering appropriate measures to be taken in light of Soviet actions.

Mr. President, thank you for coming our way. I am confident that these talks have enhanced our mutual understanding. And let's hope they make a contribution to stability and peace in Europe and elsewhere.

President Mitterrand. Ladies and gentlemen, President Bush has just told you of the content of our conversations; and he, naturally, put the emphasis on the things which he considered to be the most important, which is only natural, and I will proceed likewise.

First, I'd like to say how happy I am to be meeting with the President of the United States in these circumstances, in these new circumstances. I'm extremely happy, too, to have received such warm hospitality in Key Largo. And I'd particularly like to say this to the people who have been good enough to lend us their home, to welcome us and in order that we should be able to spend some hours here, well, working admittedly, but under the extremely pleasant setting which you have in front of you. But I'd really like to express our thanks to the President of the United States, his advisers, and the people who extended their personal hospitality to us.

Well, now, to come to the substance. And I'd like to begin with three things that for France, anyway, are obvious truths. The first is that the United States and France have, in fact, always been friends and allies; and today we can say that there is nothing of importance that divides us. The second postulate is that the Atlantic alliance, in the fields defined by the treaty, provides the organic framework for the cooperation between our two countries; and this is something that should be reasserted. The third postulate is that, well, as everyone knows, or at least should know, France has a specific defense policy which she firmly intends to retain. And this is not in any way contrary to the interests of her allies, as this has been shown over the last quarter of a century.

Now, secondly, the new situation—and this is pretty obvious to everyone—a new situation is emerging in Europe. And first, Central and Eastern Europe is moving towards democracy, and these countries are also moving towards their integration— they're aspiring towards integration within the economies of the rest of the continent. Now, I feel and I have said that that part of Europe, like the other part of Europe—it would be natural for it. It is, in fact, in its calling to move towards a confederal type of structure comprising the European countries that would have a representative system of institutions.

There would be nothing against the idea, I would say—very much on the contrary— of having agreements between such a confederation and the United States of America. As to the European Community, it will, in fact, increase its movement towards integration in the field of monetary affairs, foreign policy, and security. And indeed, the most recent document in such matters is the Franco-German proposal that was published today in Paris.

Still, in the present evolution of Europe right now, we note that the talks on conventional disarmament are progressing, and this is a trend that must continue. It is true that the bringing into question of the Warsaw Pact on the part of several of its members and, secondly, the unity of Germany are things which clearly change the basic elements of the situation. I would add, also, that we hope that the talks on strategic disarmament will be brought to fruition.

In view of this situation in Europe, which is at a state of evolution, what should the alliance do? The first thing is to maintain its cohesion, and in this respect, it's necessary to reassert the need for the presence of United States forces in Europe. Secondly, support must be given to the process of unification of Germany, while at the same time taking into account the security interests of the Soviet Union, which must never be lost sight of. And of course, I'm referring to the presence within the alliance of unified Germany. Still on the question of what should the alliance do, the second answer is to make sure that one excludes from its purview no aspect of security related to the equilibrium of Europe. Thirdly, to facilitate and verify progress towards disarmament verification among allies through consultations which are always necessary. Fourthly, to seek out areas of complementarity with the other parties within which the allies find themselves together in Europe. And I would mention the CSCE and the European Economic Community. And I would add a very important additional note on this: to prepare the Europeans with the idea of playing an increased role in working for their own defense.

So, on this basis, France is prepared to participate in a common reflection on how to adapt the alliance to meet the requirements of the new times ahead. And with that in mind, I suggested to President Bush—and he agreed—that we propose to our allies to hold a summit of the alliance before the end of the year.

And lastly, a few brief remarks. Let's take the United States and the European Economic Community—we're no longer specifically within the alliance, as such yet. Now, there should be greater coordination in terms of action between the United States and the European Economic Community because economic cooperation is too piecemeal, I would say, and political cooperation is perhaps still a bit too informal. So, I think the idea should be considered of having an overall agreement on cooperation in terms of trade between the European Economic Community and the United States, just as the Community has with its main trading partners. And there could also be regular contacts in terms of political affairs at ministerial level.

Another remark on the CSCE. I have emphasized the importance of this 35-member body in the new European context. The meeting of the 35 heads of state and government in order to consider a conventional disarmament agreement reached among the 23 would make it possible to consider the future of cooperation and security in Europe. And we must always remember that the CSCE is, and has been in the past, the only place where all European countries can meet. And in this respect, the Foreign Ministers have begun working on the agenda of this future summit of the CSCE.

On Germany, I would repeat what President Bush has said: first, concerning the legitimate right—and this has been mentioned several times in France—the legitimate right for the Germans to achieve the unity of their two states. And in order to consider the consequences of this unity, the work of the four-plus-two must continue. And the problem of borders, dealt with in this framework, should be able to be solved fully and once and for all.

Now, following what President Bush has said, I would just add one thing on Lithuania. We have considered the situation as has been mentioned, and we have noted that there is a real need for opening a genuine dialog. I would add that France has never recognized the annexation of the country. But this is a phase of this stage which must be tackled in a very level-headed fashion, and in particular, it's important that the two parties should be able to talk about the specific and general aspects of the issue in a framework of overall peace. And we hope

to be able to help such a dialog.

Thank you.

American Hostages in Lebanon

Q. Mr. President, the Islamic Jihad says it's postponing the release of an American hostage in Lebanon because you refused to meet its demand to send Ambassador Kelly [Assistant Secretary of State for Near Eastern and South Asian Affairs] to Damascus. What's your reaction to that, and what's the next step?

President Bush. Well, I hadn't heard the connection with Ambassador Kelly, but I think the U.S. position is clear: We do not meet demands. Our Ambassador to Syria is back in Syria. We've been disappointed before—hopes raised only to have them dashed by excessive speculation. I would add that we are not talking to the hostage holders. I would further add we are grateful to Syria for trying to play a constructive role in what is going on. But beyond that, I can't think of anything I could say that would contribute to the release of the hostages.

Lithuanian Independence

Q. Mr. President, you said that you wanted to help the dialog between the Soviet Union and the Lithuanians. Have you in mind an initiative which France would take, you would take, or that you would take together, or that the alliance would take? How do you see the situation?

President Mitterrand. I think all initiatives should be welcomed; none should be rejected. They should all tie in with each other. France, at any rate, is prepared to act in that sense, like the United States; and France could do so on her own behalf.

Q. The Lithuanians, through Mr. Landsbergis [Lithuanian leader], have now said that the oil cutoff, in fact, has happened; so, Lithuania is facing deprivation. Apart from trying to help the dialog between Moscow and Vilnius, are you prepared to help the Lithuanian people with aid, possibly through a third agency such as the Red Cross? And this question is directed to both of you.

President Bush. I will go first, with your permission. John [John Cochran, NBC

News], we have not been able to confirm, oddly, the exact extent of any Soviet crackdown. And what is happening here today is an early stage of consultation with allies, and I think that's very important.

As you know, Secretary Baker discussed this matter with [Soviet] Foreign Minister Shevardnadze yesterday. We are in touch with the Soviets, and they know our views. And I cannot speculate beyond saying that I will discuss options with our allies as to what the United States will do in conjunction with allies or on our own. I am still hopeful that the dialog that the French President called for and that I have called for will take place.

President Mitterrand. I can but confirm what President Bush has said. Priority must be given to a dialog. Then one will have to reflect about what happens if the dialog is refused, depending on who refused the dialog. And I expressed the way I see the situation directly to the Lithuanian President in a letter that went off 48 hours ago.

Middle East Nuclear-Free Zone

Q. To the two Presidents. You have been discussing disarmament in Europe and security arrangements in the continent. Have you discussed the proposal of President Mubarak [of Egypt] for a nuclear-free zone in the Middle East, as well as all destructive arms in the area?

President Bush. That subject was not discussed between me and the President of France.

President Mitterrand. But we will have other opportunities of doing so.

Lithuanian Independence

Q. Mr. President, in your statement, you indicated that the Soviet Union had now moved beyond mere statements into action against Lithuania. In light of that, sir, since you have said repeatedly that you would defer comment on what you might do so long as it was unclear whether they were merely threats, could you tell us when you might be willing to say what you might do and whether your reluctance to say what the Soviets have done is a result of Mr. Baker's conversation with Mr. Shevardnadze?

President Bush. No, I can't tell you when the United States might do something. But my reluctance stems from trying to keep open a dialog and discussion that affects many, many countries. And I'm talking about arms control. I'm talking about solidifying the democracies in Eastern Europe. I'm talking about a lot of matters where U.S.-Soviet relations affect a lot of other countries. So, that's one question.

And I also have very much in the forefront the right of the Lithuanians to have self-determination. And what I keep coming back to and what we're trying to do through discussions like this to see if we can find a way, or discussions with the Soviet Foreign Minister, is to see if we can be helpful in getting that dialog started. But I can't help you in terms of time.

Middle East Peace Process

Q. I'm asking the two Presidents if you have some ideas of activating the deadlock peace in the Middle East and especially stopping the settlement in the Old Jerusalem. And I'm asking President Mitterrand your impressions after your meeting with President Arafat [of the Palestine Liberation Organization].

President Mitterrand. The position of France has been known for a long time. I say, alas, for a long time because events have not taken the turn that we would have hoped. Now, we on our part would have hoped for the convening of an international conference. We've also presented some observations to the Israeli leaders concerning the manner in which the election should be held.

My position is that one should reject no opportunity for moving towards peace. And I appreciate the efforts that have been made in various quarters, including by President Mubarak. Now, as to Mr. Yasser Arafat, on two occasions I've had the possibility of having talks with him in considerable depth—when he first came to visit a number of French leaders and, more briefly, during his recent visit when I received him at the same time as President Carter, where they were good enough to tell me about the results of their conversations. Since the Algiers conference, the PLO has seen with lucidity what the new perspectives are, and I think that such a move on their part should not be discouraged.

Now, as to the Israeli settlements on the West Bank, there should be no misunderstanding here. First, there can be no question of placing any restrictions, any conditions, on the fundamental right of the Jews from the Soviet Union to move about freely wherever they please. To place conditions on their destination and to ask the Soviet Union to sort people out on the basis of such criteria is something that is unacceptable, and this I have stated recently. Now, as to the settlements themselves, my reasoning is very simple: that whatever the origin of the Israelis are, whether they are from the country itself or from outside, it is not wise to multiply such settlements because they give rise to a climate of uncertainty and lack of security, which is not conducive to the general process of reconciliation.

President Bush. She asked both. Let me just say quickly, our policy has not changed. We feel the Baker plan, which originally was thought up by Mr. Shamir [Prime Minister of Israel], is the right way to go to get discussions going and to take the first major step towards peace. And we salute—I agree with my friend the President of France—of the constructive role being played by President Mubarak.

Lithuanian Independence

Q. Mr. President, you've given Mr. Gorbachev pretty generous leeway to attend to his problems at home. Is there at this point, though, a limit to your patience, to American patience, on Lithuania? Have you communicated that to him? And also isn't there a danger here that at some point he might feel a free hand to do almost anything except send in the troops to crush the independence drive?

President Bush. Yes, there are limits. And having said that, I am convinced that Mr. Gorbachev knows that there are limits in terms of this matter. And what was the second part now?

Q. Isn't there a danger here that, in view of the tolerance that you've shown, he may feel a free hand to continue moving in the direction they are now?

President Bush. I don't think there is any danger that there will be a misunderstanding on this point—none at all. We have been in touch, and I don't think there can be that big a communications gap at all.

Q. Can you cite any evidence that your restraint has led to any moderation on his part?

President Bush. Evidence in relation to the evolution of freedom in Eastern Europe? Yes. I've seen considerable constraint there. I am concerned about Lithuania. I am encouraged every time I hear them say no use of force, but I am greatly concerned by this escalation in terms of using energy to push the Lithuanians into line. But I am not concerned that there is any miscommunication or a gap of misunderstanding between the Soviets and the United States on this particular point.

European Security Arrangements

Q. President Bush, Germany and France today called for close cooperation in Europe on security matters. Do you see here any threats to the U.S. interests in Europe?

President Bush. None at all.

Q. Did you get assurances from President Mitterrand about that?

President Bush. I believe that President Mitterrand and I are very close together in our view of security arrangements for Europe, now and in the future. And I must say I felt very enlightened by the long-term view that he presented to me. So, I don't see any danger of what you asked about coming in between the United States and France, or the United States and Germany, or the United States and the rest of Europe.

Q. Mr. President, is today the first day that you learned of this confederation proposal of Mr. Kohl [Chancellor of the Federal Republic of Germany] and Mr. Mitterrand? And isn't it your view that NATO ought to play more of a role in coordinating contact between the U.S. and Europe, rather than the EC, as suggested by the other two?

President Bush. No. I think that President Mitterrand and I are very close together on the concept of NATO in the future. We're talking about the equilibrium and security of Europe, and then you include political questions that involve the equilibrium and security of Europe. So, this arrangement referred to—announcement—in my view does not adversely impact on what I've just said. The German—Helmut Kohl—you heard him stand there next to me in Camp David and reiterate his position on a unified Germany inside NATO. That, indeed, is the French position. And clearly, France has a key NATO role—slightly different in definition than other members, but clearly an ongoing commitment to exactly what the French President talked about. So, I don't see a problem here.

No, I heard about it before Mr. Mitterrand's visit.

Mr. Fitzwater. We'd like to take two final questions. Is there a French correspondent?

Hostages in Lebanon

Q. Mr. President, I'd like you to come back to Terry's [Terence Hunt, Associated Press] first question, and that is about the hostages, sir. Perhaps President Mitterrand could comment as well. The French seem to have found a formula for getting their hostages released. Did you in any way discuss that? And why, sir, is it so difficult to send Secretary Kelly to Damascus if he's there in response to the possibility of getting a hostage released and not as a negotiator?

President Bush. The answer is, we have a perfectly capable, accredited diplomat on the scene in Syria to work toward the release if it comes to that. The second answer is, the United States does not knuckle under to demands. The third answer is that, yes, I believe some of our people discussed with our French interlocutors the freeing of the French hostages, but I prefer to let President Mitterrand address himself to that. I was just delighted when they were released.

President Mitterrand. The freeing of the hostages in the earlier period, back in the beginning of 1988, took place in somewhat different circumstances than what took place last week and under different conditions compared to those prevailing for the United States hostages. Unfortunately, one has to say that each individual case of hostages is, in fact, a separate and a different case. The French government, back in 1988, the government that was in power at

that time, has always said that no special conditions had been accepted—there was no particular deal involving the release of the hostages made with the hostage-takers. And I don't think there's any reason to question that assertion.

As to the release that took place last week—there the climate was again fairly different because there is no war at present in Chad. And France is no longer in direct conflict with Libya. There was no deal involving any particular counterpart. As to the—with the hostage-takers—whose responsibilities and the connections between the responsibilities of various hostage-takers is something that's sometimes very difficult to ascertain—so, in other words, there was no—well, it was clear that the hostage-takers had no longer any particular interest in keeping these hostages. And so, what was required then was very patient diplomacy, and it really was patient because it took almost 4 years.

But France is not in any way setting herself up as a sort of model that other people should follow, because we know that the United States' problem of hostages is an extremely difficult situation, and we know that our American friends are doing all that it is their duty to do with not making any specific concessions in order to achieve the release of those hostages.

Mr. Fitzwater. Last question to the gentleman in the fourth row.

President Mitterrand. I think that we should be fair and say that we would probably not have succeeded without the contribution of Morocco, Algeria, and Egypt.

Relations With Iran and Libya

Q. This is a question to the two Presidents. Do you feel that one should be talking with countries like Iran and Libya who still do not respect our common values and who still condone terrorism?

President Mitterrand. You mentioned Iran and Libya. This could apply to others, of course. They have always said that they were not at the origin of the hostagetaking. Now, the general attitude that they have adopted on a number of issues, I think, is such that, shall we say, that one's judgment could be left open on the subject.

But we—like most countries—we have diplomatic relations with both Libya and Iran and, indeed, with many other regimes in the world that we do not like. It's always a very difficult question. At one time, we were thinking of breaking off diplomatic relations with Chile, at the time of the bloody dictatorship. But it was at the request of the democratic forces in Chile that we kept our Embassy open because it was a useful point of transit for the protection and the assistance of the people who were working in the resistance. So, it's always a very difficult question. And as far as Iran is concerned, we have diplomatic relations with Iran and Libya, and once one has such relations, like many others, I think it's probably a good idea to try to use those relations in order to try to help to get the release of the hostages.

As to the responsibility, perhaps, of those countries in the earlier taking of the hostages, there I cannot say. I would add, however, that most Western countries do business with these countries, and often on a large scale, with big companies based in the area, and in those countries. So, it's very difficult to draw the line and say this should be allowed and this should not be allowed. At any rate, what is clear is that any country that would be directly involved in hosta-getaking or that would be a clear accomplice in hostagetaking should be set outside the pale of the civilized world community.

President Bush. As you know, we have a different situation in terms of relations with Iran and Libya. So, let me just take this opportunity to repeat what I said when I first became President: Good will begets good will. And I link that to the release of American hostages. We can't have normal relations when hostages are held. And I would only add a—in our country there's this list of terrorism, and I would say a verifiable renunciation of terror is terribly important, for example, in the case of Libya, if we are to have better relations there.

Mr. Fitzwater. Thank you all very much.

Nuclear Weapons in Europe

Q. Has your administration effectively decided not to modernize the Lance missiles in Europe?

President Bush. No decision has been made on that. None.

Note: President Bush's 45th news conference began at 3:50 p.m. at the home of Carl Linder, owner of the Ocean Reef Club. Marlin Fitzwater was Press Secretary to the President. President Mitterrand spoke in French, and his remarks were translated by an interpreter.

Remarks at a Fundraising Luncheon for Senatorial Candidate Bill Cabaniss in Birmingham, Alabama
April 20, 1990

The President. Thank you for that welcome back. It is not my intention to parade naked before you. [*Laughter*] But I will say that I was delighted to be introduced here by an old friend, a guy that helped me so much to be standing here as President— Ray Scott. And I'm delighted he's with us today. And thank you for the unique introduction. And to another friend, Congressman Callahan—Sonny Callahan, from Mobile. He's running for office exactly the way one should. He has no opponent at all. [*Laughter*] And that shows you what a great job he's doing for the State of Alabama, I might say. I see we have some people from Mobile back there.

I'm glad to see our chairman, Chairman Outlaw; and our national committeewoman Jeannie Sullivan, an old-time, long-time friend and supporter. And, of course, Jerry Denton, who did a great job for this State in Washington, respected and admired as he is. Mayor Arrington, it is most gracious of you, sir, to be here to welcome me as President to your fine city. And thank you for coming. I'm delighted to see my friend Bart

Starr again—legend, of course. And Randy Owen, of Alabama—anybody that can take on a song like our National Anthem and stand up here with no note and do it that beautifully has got to be some special kind of talent. Thank you very, very much. And my special congratulations to Neil and Ann Berte and the Birmingham-Southern basketball team, which just won the NAIA [National Association for Intercollegiate Athletics] Championship. And, of course, Senator Cabaniss—and I'll get to him in a minute. And let me also mention Secretary of State Perry Hand. Joan, I called Perry from Air Force One and I expect I spoke for everyone here when I wished him a very speedy recovery and sent him our warmest best wishes. And I think Reverend Claypool put it best of all. So, we're thinking of him.

A writer once said, "Each spring in Alabama is as delicate as the wisteria in the rain and as gentle as falling in love." Well, it's great to be here in this kinder, gentler time of year—way, way away from Washington, DC. And it's also a privilege to be in Birmingham on behalf of a man who truly is a very dear friend. One of the great leaders in your State senate, soon to be a great member of the United States Senate—and I'm talking about my long-time friend, Bill Cabaniss. And I do a lot of these kinds of things, and I think it's an important responsibility of a President, but it's a delight to be back in this State to help elect a superb U.S. Senator, someone this State and my administration really need in Washington—a Senator who will make Alabama proud, a leader who will make the nation proud. And I am absolutely certain Bill Cabaniss is that man.

We go back a long way. We first met in the seventies; we've been friends for years. We're so close that not long ago Barbara and I invited ourselves, after we found that for dinner Bill and Katherine were having Ollie's pork barbecue. [*Laughter*] But you know how it goes. Twenty Secret Service men went over and swept in ahead of us. The good news is that by the time we got there they had big smiles on their faces, and the bad news is, all the barbecue was gone. [*Laughter*]

But this year, Bill Cabaniss has plenty to offer the Alabama voters: a man of charac-

ter, family man—great wife, two great kids. He values loyalty, and so do I—he worked for me back in 1980. In '88, he cast our first vote at the Republican National Convention. Like me, he's a charismatic speaker. [*Laughter*] And he also keeps things in perspective. It's like he says—he's got this degree of frankness—like he says: "It's fine that you're here, Mr. President. But if you really want to wow the crowd, bring Barbara." I will only say in that regard that the Silver Fox shares the same views that I do about the Cabaniss family, and I'm sorry she's not with us today.

Not surprisingly, these qualities that I've mentioned have endeared Bill to the voters since his election to the State legislature, just as they've impressed his peers. In 1987, Bill was named the Outstanding State Legislator by colleagues in a body then six-to-one Democratic. He's respected because he's a man of experience and judgment. He knows that only new ideas can create the new leadership needed for the decade of the 1990's. These ideas are found at every level of our Republican Party—they're the reason you don't just mean Alabama football when you refer to a Southern "Tide." Since the 1988 election, 215 former Democrat elected officials and leaders have turned Republican—179 from the South—14 from Alabama. Churchill said, "Some men change their principles for their party." These men and women changed their party for their principles. They joined us because they want to see an Alabama of growth in the nineties, an Alabama of progress, prosperity, and new ideas. The Alabama that Bill Cabaniss stands for.

One new idea is our belief that greater competitiveness and incentives mean greater growth, and one way to ensure continued growth is through a lower capital gains tax. As a businessman, Bill knows that lower taxes free more capital for investment, and that more investment means more jobs. And he knows his geography. Japan has a much lower capital gains tax, as low as 1 percent on stocks and bonds; while economies like Taiwan, Korea, Singapore, and Hong Kong don't tax capital gains at all. And these countries don't consider reducing capital gains a tax break for the rich because they think of it as an incentive to invest and create employment, create jobs—and they are absolutely right. And Bill Cabaniss supports my proposals on the capital gains tax cut. Once again, I would take this opportunity to call on the United States Congress to let the Senate and the House work their will and to pass that bill. It's time that we stop giving the edge to countries that we can match in ability and performance any day of the week.

Bill also understands that only an educated work force can be a competitive work force. Alabama needs him and I need him in that Senate to back our Educational Excellence Act of 1990. Bill and I know that there's nothing new about excellence. What is new is the idea of demanding higher standards and greater accountability, and more involvement by parents and communities to achieve it.

You know, Ray Scott says that the fish I catch aren't any bigger than his—but my stories about them are. [*Laughter*] Let me tell a story that's true. In 1961, Bill was in Airborne School in Fort Benning, Georgia. The sergeant called out, "Cah-BAN-ahs." Bill corrected him; he said, "Sir, my name is Cabaniss." Not surprisingly, at midnight he was still running laps and doing pushups. [*Laughter*] The next day, the sergeant again called, "Cah-BAN-ahs." Bill replied, "Yes, sir." The point is this—talk about a quick study. That's what we need in the Senate. We need that as this country faces enormous challenges in the decade of the nineties, like the fight against crime and drugs, our campaign for a cleaner environment. And it's the Republicans who have the new ideas to meet these challenges.

For instance, in January, we unveiled Phase II of our National Drug Control Strategy to knock out drugs and crime. We've got to toughen our laws and expand the death penalty for drug kingpins. Capitol Hill doesn't need politicians who soft-pedal the need to be hard on crime. It needs Bill Cabaniss, who believes that the penalty should be just as tough as the crime.

And when it comes to the environment, here, too, we Republicans have plenty of new ideas to make it clean and safe. After all, it was a Republican, Teddy Roosevelt, who was our first environmental President.

Teddy knew then what we know today: that we can have a sound environment and a strong economy. That means rejecting the ideas of the extremists on both sides—and we will. It means using market forces in the service of the environment—and we will. Let's keep it in mind: We don't have to throw people out of work to protect our environment.

But we must protect—and protect it we will—through new ideas, from expanding our parks to planting over a billion trees a year to banning asbestos to no net loss of wetlands. What's more, earlier this year we proposed landmark legislation, rewriting the Clean Air Act to cut smog and acid rain and toxic pollution. I'm glad to say the Senate has now passed a clean air bill—a bill that was gridlocked through the 1980's. It's been 13 years in coming. But no American should have to wait another day for cleaner air. So, I call on the House of Representatives to move promptly to produce a bill consistent with the principles that I have stated for an environmentally strong and economically sound new Clean Air Act. In that spirit, this week is the 20th anniversary of Earth Day. And I can't help thinking what a breath of fresh air Bill Cabaniss would be in Washington, DC. But we're together on this. Like me, he hopes the House will act soon and responsibly. As a staunch defender of the environment, there's one thing Bill wants to make absolutely clear—and that's Alabama.

Let me close with another issue which clearly shows the gulf between new and old ideas. I'm talking about child care. Bill's child-care position rests on that historic 'Bama trait, common sense. Like me, he supports what works. And that's why he backs our child-care program which gives parents the freedom to choose. It's a nearly $10-billion program to help low-income working Americans by increasing choice in child-care through tax incentives, not Federal intervention. You see, we want to ensure that parents, not bureaucrats, decide how to care for America's kids. And I will not see the option of religious-based child care restricted or eliminated. Bill is right when he wants to protect religious child-care centers and parents' freedom to use them.

But many liberals back the child-care legislation passed last month by the House and supported by the Democratic leadership. Let's take a look at what that bill would mean to this State and every State. The House bill would cost almost $30 billion and force many States to change their own rules. It would create a Federal committee—really, a straitjacket—to produce national child-care standards, intended to replace local standards that reflect local needs. And it would put Federal funds into more endless paperwork—creating 120 pages of new child-care law. Now, who would be hurt the most? Those who need help the most—the parents and, indeed, the kids. The truth is that we don't need this bureaucracy. It would be redundant, wasteful—and invitation for Big Brother to get involved in yet another part of our lives.

We don't want to expand the budget of the bureaucracy. We want to expand the horizons of our kids and the child-care options for the parents. So, let's reject those who measure progress simply by adding money to a proposal, who measure it by dollars spent, and instead give families the help they need to solve the child-care problem themselves. The Democratic leadership says the Federal Government knows what's best for our children. Bill Cabaniss and I say, thank you—parents do.

You can see, I hope, how much I think of Bill, how I respect him and trust him, and how much we need him in the United States Senate. To some, new ideas mean another bureaucrat to pick your pocket, but

Bill knows better, because he knows the families, the taxpayers, the working people of Alabama. His ideas will help those people and reflect the values of this State he loves so much. Bill Cabaniss unashamedly believes in patriotism, love of country, love of God. He thinks like we do. And as a U.S. Senator, he will act on your behalf. I am absolutely confident that he will stand up for a strong America, a free America, a safe America—a great America. He'll be the kind of Senator this State needs and deserves.

I came to Alabama to ask you to help this man, a public servant I admire, a wonderful friend I rely on. Help him do for America what he's already demonstrated he can do for Alabama. Thank you for this occasion. God bless the United States. And let's make Bill Cabaniss the next Senator from the great State of Alabama. Thank you all very much.

Note: The President spoke at 12:22 p.m. in the Main Exhibit Hall at the Birmingham-Jefferson Civic Center. In his opening remarks, he referred to Ray Scott, president of the Bass Anglers Society; Arthur Outlaw, chairman of the Alabama Republican Party; Senator Jeremiah Denton; Bart Starr, former professional football player; Randy Owen, musician and vocalist for the country music group Alabama; Joan Hand, wife of Alabama Secretary of State Perry Hand; Rev. John Claypool, rector of St. Luke's Episcopal Church; Katherine Cabaniss, wife of Bill Cabaniss; and Ollie McClung, restauranteur.

Remarks on Presenting a Points of Light Award to the Birmingham-Southern College Conservancy and on Signing the National Recycling Month Proclamation in Birmingham, Alabama
April 20, 1990

The President. To Will Phillips and all the others involved in this magnificent project, my thanks. I am delighted to be here with the members of the Birmingham-Southern Conservancy. Let me now salute the stu-

dents, the faculty, and staff of Birmingham-Southern who have worked together to create this important environmental initiative.

By enlisting elementary schools in neighborhood beautification efforts and working with the Cahaba River Society to involve inner-city youngsters in cleanup efforts, you are not only working to enhance our environment, you're also imparting your love for nature and concern for its well-being to the environment's future custodians, our youngest citizens. And you're helping them learn that we all have a role to play in solving some of our most pressing problems.

If we're to preserve our precious national heritage, each organization, business, individual in America must take direct and consequential action to protect our environment. So, it is my pleasure to present to you a letter designating the Birmingham-Southern Conservancy as a Point of Light.

Let me just hand this over to you, Will Phillips.

Mr. Phillips. Thank you very much.

The President. Among the many efforts this organization has undertaken, recycling is one of the finest. And I thought, therefore, it would be most fitting to have your organization and, indeed, this school be present for the signing of the proclamation designating April as National Recycling Month. And so, I'm delighted to do it. I can think of no more appropriate place to do it, inspired as I am by the work of all of you involved in this great conservation effort.

Thank you for letting me come, and now I will sign this one.

Note: The President spoke at 12:59 p.m. at the Birmingham-Southern College Recycling Center. Will Phillips was president of the conservancy. The proclamation is listed in Appendix E at the end of this volume.

Statement by Press Secretary Fitzwater on Soviet Economic Sanctions Against Lithuania
April 20, 1990

We are increasingly concerned by news reports today of an economic crackdown in Lithuania. Although our information is sketchy, we are disturbed that this signals another unfortunate step in the pressure being brought to bear on Lithuania by the Soviet Union.

The President has stepped up consultations with our allies concerning appropriate responses that the United States should take. We expect these consultations, now underway through a wide array of diplomatic channels, to be concluded early next week. At that time, President Bush will meet with congressional leaders to advise them of our consultations and to discuss possible courses of action. We continue to urge the Soviet Union to pursue a course of peaceful dialog in the hope that this matter can be resolved in a responsible manner.

Statement on the Observance of the 75th Anniversary of the Armenian Massacres
April 20, 1990

Throughout this century, the United States has had a special, enduring relationship with the Armenian people. Armenians around the world share with their friends in the United States a love of freedom, and as proud people, they have a strong commit- ment to the preservation of their heritage and culture.

Their history, though marked by a number of tragedies, nonetheless reflects their faith and the strength and resilience of their tradition. Those tragedies include the earthquake of 1988 and, most prominently, the terrible massacres suffered in 1915–1923 at the hands of the rulers of the Ottoman Empire. The United States responded to the victims of this crime against humanity by leading international diplomatic and private relief efforts.

The Armenian-American community now numbers nearly 1 million people. Those who emigrated to the United States and their descendants continue to make significant contributions to the betterment of our country in many fields of endeavor.

On this 75th anniversary of the massacres, I wish to join with Armenians and all peoples in observing April 24, 1990, as a day of remembrance for the more than a million Armenian people who were victims. I call upon all peoples to work to prevent future acts of inhumanity against mankind, and my comments of June 1988 represent the depth of my feeling for the Armenian people and the sufferings they have endured.

Remarks at a Republican Party Fundraising Dinner in Orlando, Florida
April 20, 1990

I know you're getting starved. I have to leave before the broccoli to go down to the Everglades. But I'm delighted to be here, and thank you, Governor. Let me pay my respects to Secretaries Brady, Mosbacher, Derwinski, and Skinner, four members of the President's Cabinet; and to Ambassador Fred Zeder, who's with us; and of course, the Governor that I mentioned. And it's always good to see Senator Connie Mack—doing an outstanding job in Washington for you and for us. And of course, we're privileged to have also the distinguished leader in the Senate, Senator Al Simpson from Wyoming, back here—the big, tall, skinny guy.

What a great turnout by the whole Florida delegation—the Members of Congress. They're doing an outstanding job. We could use even more. But we have a class Republican congressional delegation, and I'm proud of them every single day. And I'm delighted to salute your State chairman, Van Poole, an old friend; and, of course, pay tribute to another horseshoe-playing friend of mine, Lee Greenwood, who did us honors here in the music a minute ago; and the indefatigable Armand Hammer, properly here saluting his friend Alec; and Leo Nadeau, my tail gunner from way back when. And of course, I hope you'll understand if I salute the dinner chairman, Jeb Bush. You'll forgive a granddad one editorial comment: Didn't George P. give a good speech? It's nice to know that there's at least one charismatic silver-tongued devil in the family. [*Laughter*]

Speaking of happy events, I forgot to mention with the congressional delegation, I want to congratulate Bill Grant and his wife on the birth of their brand-new daughter, Madison. Great happiness.

And of course, my friend Alec, it's good to see you. Here's a man who breeds race horses for the same reason he works so hard for the party: only one place will do for Alec—first place.

And finally, let me just say a word—Jeanie Austin, the cochairman of our party nationally—Floridian—she's not here today. She's out with all the State chairmen—doing an outstanding job, she is, and I also might mention, along with our great Republican National Committee chairman, Lee Atwater. Lee's fighting spirit is certainly an inspiration to all of us. Everyone who knows him knows that this is one campaign he is determined to win.

Bob pointed it out, but I found it very hard to stay away from Florida. And it's not just the beaches: it's the company, the determined optimism of Florida Republicans. You certainly have every reason to be in high spirits. After all, it's here in the land of the sun and gateway to the stars that voters are rejecting the politics of the past. It's here that you are pioneering the future of

America—a Republican future.

I believe, as Bob Martinez does, as Connie Mack does, as our Congressmen do, that we can build this future, a future with a cleaner environment, great strides in education, more opportunity, and streets safe from crime. And in Florida, you need a Governor with the same vision, who will carefully balance the needs of nature and man, who will make the most of economic opportunity while protecting your special way of life. That's the kind of Governor you want, that's the kind of Governor you've got, and that's the Governor you're going to reelect this fall—Governor Bob Martinez.

It is because of Republican leadership that Florida ranks number one in the creation of new businesses and jobs, especially in high-tech manufacturing. But we call this the Sunshine State because of your quality of life. From the panhandle all the way down to the Keys, Florida is a tropical jewel glistening with rivers and marshes and freshwater swamps and beautiful beaches and mangrove forests. And I intend to work with you to help you keep it just that way.

Two weeks ago, the famous south Florida conservationist Marjory Stoneman Douglas celebrated her 100th birthday. And in her century, she's seen the vast swamp prairie of the Everglades wither to half its size. She's watched and worried as crocodiles and turtles and the Florida panther almost disappeared. She's seen rookeries of wading birds, once counted in the millions, dwindle to mere thousands. She was the first, really, to sound the alarm. She made us realize that the Everglades is the heart of Florida. We must not let it die.

Floridians want action on the Everglades, and you're getting it from Republicans because the State of Florida was willing to set aside part of the land and because of the leadership of these, your Republican congressional delegation in Washington. Because of that, I was able to sign into law a bill increasing the size of the park by more than 100,000 acres. Of course, more needs to be done, but we are determined that the Everglades will be everlasting.

To protect our natural habitats will also require local leadership. As you know, I'm honoring Americans from all walks of life who are part of that constellation of volunteers that I call a Thousand Points of Light. So, it was my pleasure this afternoon and again tonight to recognize our 122d daily Point of Light, Dr. Daniel Keith Odell, who lives right here in Orlando. You know, Dr. Odell, right here in this neighborhood, a marine biologist with Sea World, has been applying his knowledge to better the environment by learning how pollutants can harm certain marine mammals. And he's known locally for his efforts in the campaign to save the manatees. In both efforts, Dr. Odell is working to make Florida a better place to live. He is a Point of Light, like so many others here tonight.

Still, it isn't enough to preserve nature if our cities are filthy, the air we breathe foul, and our urban beaches desecrated. So, Floridians also want action on a cleaner environment, and they're getting it from Florida Republicans.

You're also getting action at the national level. In fact, as we head into Earth Day, I am pleased to announce that Tampa Bay will be included in EPA's National Estuary Program. Under this program we will bring together Federal, State, and local agencies; citizens groups; and others to develop a plan to preserve and protect the aquatic riches of Tampa Bay. Now, this program will also allow us to coordinate and focus activities of many Federal agencies and fund environmental demonstration projects in Tampa. By working together, we can preserve and protect Tampa Bay.

We will also preserve and protect other estuaries that today are also adding to the National Estuary Program: the Indian River Lagoon, also in Florida; Casco Bay, in Maine; Massachusetts Bays; the Barataria-Terrebonne Estuary Complex, in Louisiana.

At the national level, too, we've been active on clean air. And as you know, I also proposed the first major revision of the Clean Air Act since 1977, one that uses market solutions to cut acid rain and smog and other poisons in our air. And this will mean cleaner cars, cleaner fuels, cleaner factories. And if Congress passes our compromise proposal, it will mean cleaner air for America.

Floridians also want to be safe from crime, and that's another reason why they turn to Republican leadership. In Tallahassee, Republicans have toughened prison sentences and added the prison space to enforce it. And in Washington, we worked closely with your great Senator Connie Mack, your House Republican delegation to pass part of our administration's anticrime package. We share a simple philosophy: Prison sentences should be at least as tough as the criminals we convict.

Congress has provided money for new prison space and more Federal law enforcement officers, but the Democratic leadership in Congress has left too much work undone on our violent crime package. And so, I call on Congress to recognize a truth: If the kingpins who deal drugs are dealing death, then let's judge them for what they are—murderers.

And Floridians want one thing more: to give your children the education they deserve. Your business and education leaders are already working together to make Florida a world leader in math and science and computer education by 1999. What you want to do for Florida, I want to try to do for all of America. American students must be number one in math and science. Every American, every American adult, must be a literate citizen and worker. And every school in America must have a disciplined environment and, most of all, be drug-free. You see, education is critical to everything we are and can become, and that's why I've declared a new era of education reform in America, focusing not just on how much money we put into the schools but on how well educated are the kids who are coming out of the schools. Republicans focus on quality, not just on quantity. And that's why I brought all the Governors, as Bob said, together in an education summit in Charlottesville. And that's why I've promoted promising ideas like greater parental choice of schools and alternative certification of teachers.

So, when it comes to social progress, from jobs to a cleaner environment to fighting crime or educating yet another generation, the party of Lincoln is leading America while America leads the world.

Sadly, sadly, the other party has no firm principles and no new ideas to offer the world at this critical time. And that's why

Democratic voters and leaders are crossing over in record numbers. Forty-six elected Democrats in Florida alone have crossed over just since I was elected, and now I know that some political observers are busy trying to figure out the political calculus behind Bill Grant's move to our party. Well I suggest they miss the point. Bill simply shares the wisdom of Winston Churchill, who said that while some may change their principles for the sake of their party, a statesman will change parties before changing principles. And it is because of his commitment to principle that Bill Grant is a Republican leader today, and that's why he will be reelected along with these others in the fall.

Nowhere have our principles been more effective than in the international arena. Bob was talking about that. Look at the results: In the Revolution of '89 we saw freedom dawn in Eastern Europe. And now we're close—so very close—to extending the compass of freedom across the Americas. Look at the map. There was once a dictatorship, a brutal one, in Panama. But the people spoke in a democratic election, and then came Operation Just Cause, and now the people rule in Panama. And they're going to continue to rule. I might say, Connie, I wish we had more Senators like you, because we then would have passed long ago that money that we need to support the democracy in Panama and the democracy in Nicaragua. The Senate ought to move.

We all remember there was once a militant regime in Managua, but then came that election. Now the people are about to begin to rule in Nicaragua, just next week when Violeta Chamorro takes office. And of course, there is one last hardline holdout in the West—only one: Cuba. But I believe that, like its neighbors in every direction, Cuba, too, will join the ranks of free nations, making this the first totally democratic hemisphere in history. It may not happen tomorrow. It may not happen next week or next month. But it will happen. The people of Cuba will be free. I will guarantee you that.

These are historic times. These are historic achievements. And it is Republican leadership that has brought us to this moment. But to continue to work for jobs and opportunity and a better environment, a safer America and a free world, I need a Congress that will work with me, not against me. I will need partners in leadership like Bill and Ileana Ros-Lehtinen, Craig James and Andy Ireland and Cliff Stearns, just as Governor Martinez needs a Republican legislature in Tallahassee. As you know, we are just four seats away from a majority in the Florida Senate.

The political future of Florida and of all of America rests on winning these seats and reelecting Bob Martinez. The reason is simple, and it affects the voting rights of every Republican, every Independent, every Democratic voter. I am talking, of course, about the reapportionment of congressional districts after the 1990 census. We must not allow the Democrats to enact another gerrymander, a form of political manipulation that can also hurt every minority voter in Florida.

If the Democrats get their way, they'll again draw crazy, twisted lines that cut across communities, towns, and even streets without the slightest regard for the will of the people. So, remember this: In Florida, the difference between the party of big promises and the party of big achievements can be counted by four seats. We can bridge that difference. By working together, we can make sure that Florida will once again go Republican.

Thank you all for all that you have done. Thank you for all you're pledged to do—all the way down to the wire, to that victory night in November, a Republican victory. Alec, congratulations. Now, get to work Monday. Thank you all very much, and God bless you, and God bless the United States of America.

Note: The President spoke at 8:17 p.m. in the Hall E auditorium at the Orange County Convention Center. In his remarks, he referred to Secretary of the Treasury Nicholas F. Brady; Secretary of Commerce Robert A. Mosbacher; Secretary of Veterans Affairs Edward P. Derwinski; Secretary of Transportation Samuel K. Skinner; Fred M. Zeder, President of the Overseas Private Investment Corporation; Lee Greenwood, musician and lead singer of the country music group Alabama; Armand Hammer, philanthropist and businessman; Alec P. Courtelis, finance chairman of the Florida Republican Party; Leo Nadeau, crewmember in the aircraft President Bush flew in World War II; Representatives Bill Grant, Ileana Ros-Lehtinen, Craig James, Andy Ireland, and Cliff Stearns.

Remarks at the Presentation of a Point of Light Award to Reef Relief and an Exchange With Reporters in Islamorada, Florida
April 22, 1990

The President. Well, Craig and Deevon Quirolo, and guests, I'm here this morning because I want to recognize the good work, the outstanding work, of Reef Relief of Key West, Florida, as the 123d daily Point of Light.

After witnessing an alarming increase in the loss of coral reefs from anchors and excessive ocean traffic, Craig founded Reef Relief, and today Quirolo and hundreds of other individual volunteers—they volunteer their time and effort to protect these environmentally sensitive areas off the Florida Keys. These volunteers install buoys to which boats can tie up as an alternative to dropping anchor. And volunteers also participate in community education, teaching the public how to preserve and care for these precious reefs. And through a program called Marine Debris, still more volunteers participate in cleanup efforts and water quality research. I applaud them and all the volunteers associated with Reef Relief for their dedication to protecting their environment. They continue to demonstrate that individuals can and do make a difference.

And now I want to present the letter—thank you, Governor. If I could just hand that off to you, sir, with great pride in your work and say how much the whole country appreciates this effort.

Today on Earth Day and in the presence of a dedicated organization like Reef Relief, I'm also pleased to announce that I'm sending to the International Maritime Commission in London my proposal to create an Area To Be Avoided to protect the entire Florida reef track from shipping traffic. The area will extend roughly 10 miles off the Florida coast and encompass the Florida reefs which lie 5 miles off the coast. The proposal, when implemented, will instruct all vessels carrying cargoes of oil or hazardous material and all other vessels greater than 50 meters in length to avoid transiting close to the reefs.

The *Exxon Valdez* disaster has made us all painfully aware of the ecological devastation which can result from a major oil spill. The Florida coral reefs are one of the most diverse ecosystems in the world and a unique national treasure. And protecting the reefs from damage both from vessel groundings and pollution is imperative.

And I want to thank the Commandant of the Coast Guard, Admiral Paul Yost; Governor Martinez, who's worked on this; concerned Florida Congressmen such as Bill Lehman and Dante Fascell; and concerned citizens who are working together to protect this beautiful and environmentally sensitive reef area.

Thank you, sir, and well-done. The floor is yours.

Mr. Quirolo. I'd like to say on behalf of Reef Relief that we're very excited about receiving this award for this Point of Light. And we're very excited that the coral reefs of the Florida Keys have taken notice up in Washington, and we're assured that your judgment will give us future hope for the future of our living coral reefs. And I'm really excited about this because it gives us an open dialog between the actual coral reef down here in Florida and the President of the United States, and I don't think you can have a better partnership than that. And I feel assured that our future down here and the future of the reef will be in good hands.

The President. And just so his constituency will know that he faithfully fulfilled not only his conviction but what he and I both feel is an obligation for citizens to talk frankly to the President, he raised with me the very sensitive question of offshore drilling. I want to just know——

Mr. Quirolo. Good—thank you, sir. [*Laughter*]

The President. And I told him there would be an answer very, very soon. And I didn't think he'd be too disappointed.

American Hostages in Lebanon

Q. What's the word from Syria? Will a hostage be released, do you know?

The President. Look, I don't want to conduct a press conference here; but on that one, since the hopes of the American people have once again been raised, I can't tell you that I've learned anything new this morning at all. I've not talked to General Scowcroft. We'll be over there to do that right now before we go off once again to the flats out there. But I've not heard anymore about it, and so, I just don't want to be a part of raising the hopes of the families and then not have something happen. And I've said that for the last 3 months while this understandable speculation has been going on. So, I wish I could tell you, but there isn't any news that's been brought to my attention this morning. But let's hope, because this was one of the days that's been singled out where there might be some action.

Thank you all.

Q. How will you respond to that, Mr. President? You talk about good will begetting good will.

The President. Too hypothetical, Charles [Charles Bierbauer, Cable News Network]. We've got to see what happens, and I'm talking about release of all the hostages. We want every American held against his will, her will, released wherever they may be. And that's the ground rules, and that's the bottom line. And so, let's hope there's some action, but there's no point of my speculating. Put yourself in the place of these families: one day there's a picture of one of these hostages; the very next day it's another. I don't consider that a very good way to deal with the emotions and the prayers of families, frankly. So, I can't contribute any more to it.

Off we go.

Note: The President spoke at 7:05 a.m. on Cheeca Lodge Beach. Brent Scowcroft was Assistant to the President for National Security Affairs.

Remarks in a Telephone Conversation With the Earth Day 20 International Peace Climb Team
April 22, 1990

The President. Hey, Jim, can you hear me okay?

Mr. Whittaker. Hello, Mr. President, I sure can.

The President. Well, listen, I think back to our meeting in January, and here you are back at extraordinary heights. But listen, I wanted to simply send greetings on Earth Day to you and, frankly, to all the climbers with you from the United States, China, and the Soviet Union. And you know, reaching the top of Mount Everest in the name of peace and understanding reminds all of us on this special day that there is no task that's too great for the human spirit; and that means, as you reminded me when I last saw you, working together to help the environment.

So, thank you for what you're doing. I also want to congratulate your team on its very practical goal of cleaning up the debris that's been left by previous expeditions. That will set a great example for the whole world, especially from your unique vantage point there. So, we wish you well. In a sense, I wish you were here as one of the great leaders to help celebrate Earth Day. But I think what you're doing is significant and important, and I think it will send a great signal to all of us wherever we may be on the blessings of a sound environment. So, keep it up, and please give my best to everybody that's with you.

Mr. Whittaker. Well, thank you very much, Mr. President. You put it very well. We're celebrating Earth Day here on the mountain with a great cleanup effort, and especially on this Earth Day.

We've got camp 6 in. We're about ready to push to the summit. So, I figure about the first week of May we'll be standing—the climbers from each country—on the summit. And so, we'll be celebrating that event as well.

The President. Let me ask you a practical question. When I was flying airplanes a thousand years ago, they made us put an oxygen mask on at 10,000 feet. And here you are at what—right this minute—17,500? Question: How are you breathing?

Mr. Whittaker. That's correct. We're at 17,500. We've been climatized quite well to this elevation, but we've got some climbers now at the camp 6 at 27,300 feet without bottled oxygen.

The President. Oh, for heaven's sake!

Mr. Whittaker. It's amazing what the body can do.

The President. Well, it certainly is. Well, listen, keep up the great work, and thank you for taking time for this little interlude. But I hope it sends a message worldwide, not only the significance of what you're doing but of the importance of Earth Day.

Mr. Whittaker. Thank you very much, Mr. President. And thank you for being part of the team, and we'll sure tell everybody here how much you support us.

The President. Okay. And you come back to the White House and let me know how it was in reality there.

Mr. Whittaker. You bet. We'll come back and have a nice chat in the Rose Garden at a good, low elevation.

The President. Okay. Good luck. Over and out.

Mr. Whittaker. Thank you very much, Mr. President. This is base camp, Mount Everest. Over and out.

The President. Loud and clear. That's wonderful. Well done, men.

Note: The President spoke at 4:15 p.m. from Tarpon Flats in Islamorada, FL.

Remarks to Participants in the Columbia River Gorge Earth Day 20 Rally
April 22, 1990

The President. Hello, Ed. Greetings to you and, certainly, to Governor Booth Gardner. Can you hear me all right?

Listen, we just wanted to wish you well. My respects to the Governor, who was so helpful on this education conference and now taking a leadership role for the environment. And I want to welcome all. I understand you have an enormous group there assembled to celebrate Earth Day. I don't think you could have chosen a better location for this celebration. The Columbia River Gorge is so beautiful—its natural beauty—that it makes a perfect setting to celebrate your commitment to protect, preserve, and enhance our national heritage. So, to all assembled, my greetings.

The focus on Earth Day better enables all of us to build on our own successes—and there have been many—and acknowledge that so much yet remains to be done. We've got to integrate the goal of a strong economy with that of an improved environment, and we don't have to trade off a lot of jobs in order to protect and preserve. Having said that, by working together through public and private partnerships and through government at the local, State—and, yes, plenty of involvement from the Federal level—and then through individuals like you gathered in this extraordinary amphitheater, we can really make a difference.

It takes you all—dedicated individuals, committed, courageous—to make that difference. Like Frank Lockyear of Wilsonville, Oregon, who was named by us, by me as President at the White House, as the 118th Point of Light. He founded on his own, ReTree International, and his tireless work has resulted in over a million trees planted around the world. Thanks to Frank and the thousands of people like him, even more Americans will take part in building a better America. I really am confident that when we celebrate Earth Day's 30th anniversary, we will have a cleaner, a safer, and a healthier world.

It might interest you to know that just this minute I hung up from talking to Jim Whittaker 17,500 feet aboard Mount Everest, up there to send a message of environmental purity by cleaning up the debris that was left by expeditions. And now I'm talking to all of you in the beautiful gorge, and I just wish you well. Thank you for setting an example for our entire country. God bless you all.

Mr. Furia. Thank you, Mr. President. Thank you for honoring us and addressing the people gathered here at the Columbia Gorge.

The President. Is this you, Ed, or is this Booth?

Mr. Furia. No, it's me, Mr. President. We had a little technical difficulty with the microphone. I was saying that you honor all of us, not just here in the Columbia Gorge but all of us participating in Earth Days across the country, by participating with us.

The President. Well, listen, we're proud of you, and I'm proud to have weighed in here. We're going to keep up the interest from our end, and I hope that everybody there will find a way to involve himself or herself—or child—in protecting the environment and making this place just a little better for those that come on after us.

So, thanks, have a wonderful rest of the day, and thanks for taking the call. Over and out.

Mr. Furia. Over and out. Ten-four.

The President. You've got it.

Note: The President spoke at 4:21 p.m. from Tarpon Flats in Islamorada, FL, via an electronic hookup with the rally site. In his remarks he referred to Edward Furia, president of the rally, which took place at Co- *lumbia River Gorge, WA.*

Statement on the Release of Former Hostage Robert Polhill
April 22, 1990

We are pleased at the news that Robert Polhill has been freed by his captors. We are obviously happy for him, his family and friends. We also wish to thank those who had a hand in the release, particularly the Governments of Syria and Iran, whose efforts have contributed to the release of this hostage.

Our satisfaction at the release, however, is substantially tempered by the knowledge that seven other innocent Americans, as well as a number of foreign nationals, are still being cruelly held hostage in Lebanon. We cannot rest until all hostages are free. Once again, we urgently call on all parties who hold hostages or who have any influence to work to obtain the immediate and unconditional release of the remaining hostages as a humanitarian gesture.

Note: Robert Polhill, an accounting professor at Beirut University College, was kidnaped by pro-Iranian terrorists in Beirut on January 24, 1987.

Remarks on the Release of Former Hostage Robert Polhill and an Exchange With Reporters
April 22, 1990

The President. It's marvelous, this communications here. I was out there, way out on the flats, and talked to our Ambassador in Syria, prior to his going to the Foreign Ministry to greet our hostage, Mr. Polhill, and now sitting here with you all, and talking to Mount Everest and then the Columbia Gorge on the west coast. And I really think this modern-day communication is inspiring. And I want to take this opportunity to thank all at WHCA [White House Communications Agency] who do this kind of thing for the President and, indeed, for many others day in and day out. I think it's a marvelous example of their communications skills, and I'm very grateful.

Having said that, they patched me through, before this meeting here, to talk to our hostage, Mr. Polhill, to talk to his wife. And then there was a little delay because I also wanted to say hello to his mother, who is still here in the States, and I got her. And I guess what I would say is that the joy of this family knows no bounds. And I told them that Barbara and I sent our love, as I expect all Americans do. And I also told them that we were not going to forget these other hostages. I haven't. I don't intend to.

I think it's proper to thank the Syrians, who played an instrumental role in this, I understand. But this is mission uncompleted. There are other Americans held against their will. And the Polhills, all three, mentioned their concern about others. So, it's a joyous day in that sense. But I will carry the burden of the other hostages with me until every single one of them is free, and I mean it. There's not a night goes by that I don't think about it.

Q. Mr. President, what did Robert Polhill have to tell you?

The President. Well, just that he was pleased to be free. I said I could hardly hear him, and he said that his voice was a little weak. But other than that, it was just joy at being released. And everyone in our country can understand that.

541

Q. Did he have any report on the other hostages?

The President. Norm [Norman Sandler, United Press International], I really didn't ask him that, and I expect I'll get debriefed as soon as that whole process goes forward. I didn't go into any of the substance or the details of the release with him or with our Ambassador.

Q. Mr. President, you said good will begets good will. Is this the sort of gesture from Iran of good will——

The President. I'm not looking for gestures. I'm looking for the release of our hostages. And by our hostages, I mean all of them. But in terms of good will, I must say in my heart I have good will toward Syria for playing an active role in this release, yes.

Q. ——good will toward Iran. Marlin said the White House thanks both Syria and Iran. Do you have good will toward Iran?

The President. To the degree Iran's role is known in this. I can't tell you I honestly know what it is. But I'd have good will to those who facilitated the release. If that included Iran, absolutely, because I meant what I said. But I can't rejoice or say all is well until every single one of those hostages is out.

This is a cruel process. You see pictures flash, loved ones getting their hopes up, and then some hopes are dashed. And so, it's a very troubling process. I feel great joy in my heart, great happiness, but I also feel a great anxiety about those families who are separated from their loved ones still.

Q. Mr. President, is there some goodwill gesture that you can return?

The President. I'm not trying to think up any gesture. I've said right here what I think. I want all of those hostages out. We're not going to trade. I think our policy is sound. I think we have support from the hostage families. It's very important to me that we do because I want them to know exactly how much anxiety I feel about their loved ones still being held. But we're not going to change our policy. And we are going to say that we're grateful to those that facilitate the return of Mr. Polhill, but there are seven other Americans that are held against their will.

Q. Is this a test of your good will message,

Mr. President?

Q. Will you speak tomorrow with the leaders of Congress on Lithuania?

Q. Is this a test?

The President. Let me go here, and then I'll come back.

Q. Is this a test for you, Mr. President?

The President. A test of what? Every day is——

Q. Of testing your goodwill gesture?

The President. Every day is a test of my good will because I don't have forgiveness in my heart as long as one American is held against his will and as long as one family has a broken heart. And so, we're not into this mode of a test at all. It's a joyous occasion that this family is reunited, but there are seven other families that are hurting, crushed every day by the burden of this.

Soviet Economic Sanctions Against Lithuania

Q. Mr. President, do you now know what course of action you will follow in response to the Soviet tightening of the economic screws in Lithuania? And will the meeting with leaders of Congress be tomorrow?

The President. Well, I don't have any plans for a meeting tomorrow. It might be, but I don't think that's scheduled. And I can't tell you I honestly have made that determination, no.

Q. They have not already gone so far that you would act——

The President. I am not going to go into hypothetical questions. I've simply said all I want to say on that for now.

Release of Robert Polhill

Q. In thanking Iran for its apparent role in the release of Mr. Polhill, do you also hold the Iranians——

The President. Norm, I'm stopping a little short of that because I don't know what the role is.

Hostages in Lebanon

Q. ——any apparent role. Do you also hold the Iranians responsible for the other seven hostages?

The President. I don't want to assign blame, and I don't want to give credit when I don't know the facts. All I want to do is see those hostages released.

Q. Mr. President, when you say all the hostages, you say all the American hostages need to be released. What about the other Western hostages?

The President. I feel very strongly, particularly about Terry Waite [Anglican envoy], that I've met, feel that I know. But look, it's not a question of just American hostages. I think you raise a good point. It's a question of the immorality of holding hostages for whatever political end. It is an immoral practice, and it has to stop. And I'm pleased that we've seen this fascinating and wonderful development, but I can't say that the burden is lifted—not from me but from the American people and from the rest of the families and for those who share my belief that it is brutal to hold man or woman hostage against their will.

Q. Mr. President, is there any concern that without a return goodwill gesture to the hostage-takers or to Iran, for example, that this whole agonizing process just could be prolonged even further?

The President. I don't have that feeling at all. I think people that hold people hostage know the American policy. I hope there's respect for the American policy. And I am not going to change the American policy.

Q. Mr. President, why not go ahead and make the goodwill gesture if it might bring them home?

Q. Do you have any idea why they might have released Mr. Polhill today?

The President. No, I don't.

Q. Did Djerejian give you any indication that the other hostages——

Q. Why not go ahead and make the goodwill gesture if it might mean the——

The President. I'm not making gestures. I don't trade for hostages. I don't go "ante up" one step and one another. I rejoice at this release. And the American policy is sound, and it's not going to change. And I will thank those who facilitated the release, and that's exactly the way it's going to stay. And I feel the burden of these hostages— and I mean it—every single day. We say prayers about them every single night.

Note: The President spoke at 4:25 p.m. on Tarpon Flats in Islamorada, FL. Robert Polhill, an accounting professor at Beirut University College, was kidnaped by pro-Iranian terrorists in Beirut on January 24, 1987. Marlin Fitzwater was Press Secretary to the President. Edward Djerejian was U.S. Ambassador to Syria. Following his remarks, the President returned to Washington, DC.

Remarks at the Swearing-In Ceremony for Ronald W. Roskens as Administrator of the Agency for International Development
April 23, 1990

Well, welcome to this very special occasion. Vice President and Mrs. Quayle; and Secretary Baker; Ron Roskens; Ambassador Reed, who'll do the honors in a minute; Members of Congress; and distinguished guests, it's a great pleasure for me to witness the swearing-in of Ron Roskens as the Administrator of AID. Jim Baker and I are very fortunate to have such an able person head this very, very important agency.

Dr. Roskens brings proven leadership and valuable administrative experience to this job. Everybody here knows that. He was president of the University of Nebraska at Lincoln for a dozen years and before that

held an important administrative and teaching post at the University of Nebraska at Omaha and at Kent State. Being a university president these days requires substantial diplomatic skills—[*laughter*]—and I expect we'll be making good use of that talent as well.

So, Ron, you take the helm at AID at an extremely important time. Around the globe, new democracies are being born, and nations are seeking to establish free-market, democratic institutions. And your important agency will play a vital role in nurturing such transformations and in sharing our knowledge and our skills worldwide.

Today AID operates in over 70 countries, extending America's helping hand by assisting these fundamental economic reforms, improving our agricultural methods and our nutrition work, expanding access to basic education, providing humanitarian assistance, and many other tasks.

And so, in this good work, I wish you Godspeed, and I'm delighted that a man of your standing is willing to undertake this terribly important assignment.

And now we will get on with the ceremonies, Ambassador, if we could.

Note: The President spoke at 11:12 a.m. in the Roosevelt Room at the White House. In his remarks, he referred to Secretary of State James A. Baker III and Joseph V. Reed, Chief of Protocol at the Department of State.

Remarks to the National Academy of Sciences
April 23, 1990

Apologies for being late. To the distinguished members of the National Academy—all—and to Dr. Press and Dr. Ebert, Dr. Raven, Dr. Gordon, Dr. Blout—now we start on our side—Dr. Bromley—[*laughter*]—Jim Watkins, a member of our Cabinet, Admiral Truly, ladies and gentlemen, it really is an honor to be with you today.

We stand at a very interesting time. And the advice and counsel of this academy has been really crucial to American Presidents for well over a century, and I'm proud to be the latest to come over here to say thank you. We also stand at a moment of wondrous prosperity, but our wealth goes far beyond the merely material. Ours is an intellectual prosperity, unprecedented in history. For that and the health and security it affords this nation and the world, gratitude is owed to the men and women who have committed their minds and lives to science. Those devoted to such work—its patient searching, its passionate struggles—have engaged themselves in mankind's most exalted mission and the mind's manifest destiny: the search for understanding. That's what it all boils down to.

President Lincoln established this great institution in the dark hours of our nation's greatest crisis, which testifies to the enduring importance of scientific knowledge. In the years that followed, your academy has responded to urgent national needs in times of war and peace. When this magnificent building was dedicated, Calvin Coolidge predicted "a new day in scientific research. A new sun is rising," he said. He was right. The awesome scientific advances of this century, many of which you've brought about, bring us ever closer to the understanding that's required of the universe, its origins, and our own. And science has told us a stranger and more wondrous story than myth might even have written for us.

Fourscore and 10 or 20 billion years ago, the theory goes, it all began with a universe of energy and mass unimaginably hot and compressed containing everything that would become what we now see in the heavens. And then, science tells us, in one incomprehensively powerful instant, energy and matter of every kind exploded in every direction—or as a layman might explain it, somebody hit that cosmic baseball right out of the park. [*Laughter*] But while the pace of cosmic change may have begun with blinding speed and slowed down since, the pace of our scientific evolution has been rapidly accelerating, growing in intensity like a series of chain reactions in a critical mass of highly trained American gray matter, touching off scientific and technical revolutions in every direction.

Today I wanted to come over here to outline the role that this administration is playing to advance those revolutions, because as the pace of science accelerates, I believe that government must keep pace and will keep pace.

First, we've moved to better integrate science and technology into the policy process. We've created an interagency working group that will more closely link science and technology—link their considerations with the policymaking process of the Economic and Domestic Policy Councils. My assistant for science and technology, Dr. Bromley, chairs this working group and participates in those Councils, advising them on matters related to science and technology, as well as serving on the National Space Council.

And we're also committed to greater cross-fertilization with talent from the private sector on issues ranging from pure research to manufacturing performance. So, this year we created a President's Council of Advisors on Science and Technology—experts whose guidance I value and depend on. I've already had two meetings with that group myself. We'll also be looking for counsel from this academy's new manufacturing forum, just announced this month.

We want to advance America's tradition of innovation, and we intend to get the biggest bang for the Federal buck. And this administration has also taken steps to reinvigorate the Federal Coordinating Council for Science, Engineering and Technology, in order to assure that the Federal investments in R&D programs are closely integrated across these agency boundaries.

In January we sent a budget to Congress that includes a record $71 billion for research and development—an investment in a stronger economy, a more secure nation and, indeed, a brighter future. Our administration is committed to investing in the future. It's evident in the policies we're creating and the budget we're calling for, with everything from a 24-percent increase for NASA to our support of a major agricultural research initiative.

To improve the international competitiveness of American industry and our overall standard of living, we've called for a permanent extension of the research and experimentation tax credit. And we're working to lower the cost of capital and clear away regulatory burdens so that industry can make the kinds of investment that the future demands.

Along with the applied, market-driven knowledge so crucial to this country's competitive future, let me reaffirm two other priorities: first—and I'm going to keep talking about this one—math and science education. We understand that only with a new generation of scientists and engineers will your work and America's preeminence be assured. And so, we're engaged in a broad initiative of reform and restructuring in cooperation with the States. It's an effort that began with our first-ever education summit with the Nation's Governors last fall. And our goal is to make American students first in the world in science and math achievement by the end of this century and to convince more women and minorities to study science.

We're providing a number of new incentives for students, like the National Science Scholars Program that I've proposed. We're opening the doors of Federal laboratories, facilities, and agencies to students and teachers. Our budget increases funding by 26 percent to over $1 billion for science, math, and engineering education, through the Departments of Education, Energy, Interior, and others as well as the National Science Foundation and NASA.

And today I ask our industrial and business communities to create new alliances for education, mobilizing more of this nation's great technical resources for the sake of the future. We are committed to ensuring that America has the brainpower to remain at the forefront.

A second priority of this administration is basic research, the historical wellspring of this nation's well-being. Science must be able to continue seeking answers to our most fundamental questions. For such reasons, our budget calls for increasing funding for the U.S. Global Change Research Program by 57 percent to over $1 billion. And earlier this year, I reiterated my commitment to double the National Science Foundation budget by 1993. Today I want to call on Congress: Put our money where our future is. Put an increased National Science Foundation budget back on track.

Today science and technology are assuming a broader and more interrelated role in human life than ever before, and they're becoming forces for historical change. Satellites already help us study the Earth's natural systems and assess environmental threats, and the Mission to Planet Earth will further our work of global stewardship. But this past year, in the Revolution of '89, we've also seen communication satellites, along with video cameras and VCR's and fax machines, becoming a potent force for peace—both a product of science and a source of conscience—bringing the actions of nations before the eyes of the world. Pictures from Poland and South Africa, scenes on the Berlin Wall—the eye of technology has proved more powerful than chisels for breaking down barriers; etching the idea of freedom on the psyche of humanity; and setting off a wondrous, hopeful, political chain reaction worldwide.

It's no accident that many of the individuals at the center of today's worldwide political revolutions share a vision of the future based on personal freedom, openness, and freedom of inquiry. These values are shared by our political system and by science alike. Science, like any field of endeavor, relies on freedom of inquiry; and one of the hallmarks of that freedom is objectivity.

Now more than ever, on issues ranging from climate change to AIDS research to genetic engineering to food additives, government relies on the impartial perspective of science for guidance. And as the frontiers of knowledge are increasingly distant from the understanding of the many, it is ever more important that we can turn to the few for sound, straightforward advice.

The National Academy of Sciences is renowned for objectivity and immunity to partisan pressures. Your impartial guidance has been invaluable to American Presidents and to the American people for well over a century. So, I am confident that the members of this body, the most distinguished scientists in America, will continue the tradition that has been the academy's hallmark. On this I know we agree, because so many of our technical and scientific achievements have been the products of independent minds. And if the Earth-moving events of 1989 reminded us of anything at all, it's that complex bureaucracies and centralized planning don't work well in the governance of societies. We will not try to impose them on science.

Just as entrepreneurs and small businesses fuel the growth of the American economy, the backbone of American science is its brilliant array of individual investigators spread across the Nation. Among so many, think of Chester Carlson, who invented the photocopy machine in a little room over a Long Island pub, or Barbara McClintock, working alone, who made monumental discoveries in genetics nearly 50 years ago that the world began to understand only in the last decade.

Look, of course, I can't claim to comprehend how science does its work. Like many, my scientific understanding has been influenced by those Gary Larson cartoons—[*laughter*]—like the one where, after detailed calculations, Einstein discovers that time is actually money.

I'm not here as an expert but as a believer. And one of the best things government can do to support the magnificent creativity and energy of the American technical community is to locate individual scientists with talent, furnish them with adequate resources and state-of-the-art instrumentation—through agencies like our marvelous National Institutes of Health, the National Science Foundation, and then the Departments of Defense and Energy and others—to help these investigators make progress.

But there are also scientific challenges that, because of their unprecedented scope and importance, demand unusual support and international cooperation. Already, the European Space Agency, Japan, and Canada are making hardware contributions valued at more than $7 billion for Space Station *Freedom*, a key component of our Space Exploration Initiative. Combined with our total investment of about $19 billion, this will be the largest international R&D project ever undertaken.

We're exploring new ways to encourage international cooperation on the big science projects, like mapping the human genome, global change research, and the superconducting supercollider—a technological giant that will recreate the fireball of our origins and allow us to study forms of matter that haven't existed since the birth of the universe.

There's a vote coming up in Congress this week on that supercollider, so I'd like to call on the members to support that project, as well as our NASA budget. Only by doing so will we keep America on the leading edge of advancing human knowledge and pushing the limits of space exploration.

Tomorrow morning the space shuttle is scheduled to lift into the heavens the most sophisticated celestial object that mankind has ever built—the Hubble Telescope—with the power to see the ends of the universe and back to the birth of time. I understand it's half a billion times more sensitive than the human eye. You talk about the vision thing—try on the Hubble Telescope for size. [*Laughter*]

But on the southwest grounds of this great academy rests a bronze memorial to a scientist who helped define mankind's understanding of time and space, of matter and energy. Among the engravings on that memorial are words of wonder about the "joy and amazement" Einstein felt "at the beauty and grandeur of this world of which man can just form a faint notion." Your

work, the work of science, daily brings that beauty and grandeur into sharper focus.

I'm blessed to be President at this fascinating time in the history of the world, in the history of our country. And as President, I can assure you of this: My administration is committed to supporting you as you pursue the knowledge that illuminates the world, knowledge that will surely, ceaselessly continue to bring benefit to all mankind.

Thank you very much for what you do, and God bless each and every one of you. Thank you.

Note: The President spoke at 2:09 p.m. in the auditorium at the National Academy of Sciences Headquarters Building. In his opening remarks, he referred to Frank Press, James Ebert, William Gordon, and Elkan Blout, president, vice president, foreign secretary, and treasurer of the academy; and D. Allan Bromley, Science Advisor to the President and Director of the Office of Science and Technology Policy.

Remarks on Signing the Hate Crime Statistics Act
April 23, 1990

First of all, let me give a special welcome to the Members of Congress—Congress in session, taking the time to come down here—several here who were so instrumental in the passage of this bill. Senator Simon, Senator Hatch, Senator Metzenbaum, Congressman Conyers, Congressman Sangmeister, Jack Brooks—Chairman Brooks, I should say, respectfully, to a fellow Texan— [*laughter*]—and to Barbara Kennelly, and members of the civil rights community, religious leaders, and friends, welcome here. We join together to celebrate a significant step to help guarantee civil rights for every American: the passage and now the signing of the Hate Crime Statistics Act.

When I first heard that this bill had passed both Houses of Congress, I thought of a photograph in the news recently. And it's of the plaza near a Montgomery, Alabama, church where Dr. Martin Luther

King, Jr., preached during the '55 bus boycott. And in that plaza stands a new civil rights memorial inscribed with the names of 40 brave Americans who died in the civil rights struggle, each one the victim of a hate crime. On the memorial's wall, water cascades over the vow made by Dr. King on the steps of the Lincoln Memorial: "We will not be satisfied until justice rolls down like waters and righteousness, like a mighty stream."

His pledge is just as powerful today. We will not be satisfied. Justice for all has been the historic mission of the civil rights movement, and it's a mission still to be fulfilled. Bigotry and hate regrettably still exist in this country, and hate breeds violence, threatening the security of our entire society. We must rid our communities of the poison we call prejudice, bias, and discrimination. That's why I'm signing into law today a measure to require the Attorney General to collect as much information as we can on crimes motivated by religion, race, ethnicity, or sexual orientation—the Hate Crime Statistic Act.

One of the greatest obligations of this administration and of the Department of Justice is the guarantee of civil rights for all Americans. As I said in my State of the Union Address, every one of us must confront and condemn racism, anti-Semitism, bigotry, and hate not next week, not tomorrow, but right now—every single one of us. For hate crimes cannot be tolerated in a free society.

We have vigorously prosecuted Federal violations involving hate crimes. We will continue to do so. As we speak, 17 racist skinheads in Dallas are waiting to be sentenced by a Federal court for conspiring to commit hate crimes against Jewish, black, and Hispanic citizens. The mail bombings which killed a Federal judge and a NAACP lawyer are being investigated tenaciously by Federal authorities. We will not rest until the cowards who committed these senseless crimes are behind bars.

The Hate Crime Statistics Act is an important further step toward the protection of all Americans' civil rights. Our administration will work with Congress to determine whether new law enforcement measures are needed to bring hatemongers out of hiding and into the light of justice. And at the same time, by collecting and publicizing this information, we can shore up our first line of defense against the erosion of civil rights by alerting the cops on the beat.

I'm pleased to announce today that the Department of Justice has established a new toll-free phone number for reporting complaints of these hate crimes. Those incidents that can and should be prosecuted will be reported directly to the appropriate Federal, State, or local agency for action. The faster we can find out about these hideous crimes, the faster we can track down the bigots who commit them.

We must work together to build an America of opportunity, where every American is free finally from discrimination. And I will use this noble office, this bully pulpit, if you will, to speak out against hate and discrimination everywhere it exists.

Enacting this law today helps move us toward our dream: a society blind to prejudice, a society open to all. Until we reach that day when the bigotry and hate of mail bombings, and the vandalisms of the Yeshiva school and the Catholic churches we've seen recently, and so many other sad, sad incidents are no more—until that day, we must remember: For America to continue to be a good place for any of us to live, it must be a good place for all of us to live.

So, you wouldn't be here if you weren't extraordinarily interested in the work of the United States Congress. So, I want to thank each and every one of you for coming. And now I'm pleased to sign the Hate Crime Statistics Act into the law.

Note: The President spoke at 3:02 p.m. in Room 450 of the Old Executive Office Building. In his opening remarks, he referred to Representative Jack Brooks, chairman of the Judiciary Committee, and Representative Barbara B. Kennelly. H.R. 1048, approved April 23, was assigned Public Law No. 101–275.

Letter to Congressional Leaders Transmitting a Report on Compliance With the Southern Africa Tripartite Agreement
April 23, 1990

Dear Mr. Chairman:

Pursuant to the provisions of section 417(c) of the Foreign Relations Authorization Act, Fiscal Years 1990 and 1991 (Public Law 101–246; 104 Stat. 72), I am transmitting herewith a report on compliance by the governments of the People's Republic of Angola, the Republic of Cuba, and the

Republic of South Africa with the Tripartite Agreement of December 22, 1988.

Sincerely,

GEORGE BUSH

Note: Identical letters were sent to Senators Robert C. Byrd, chairman of the Appropriations Committee; David L. Boren, chairman of the Select Intelligence Committee; and Claiborne Pell, chairman of the Foreign Relations Committee; and to Representatives Anthony C. Beilenson, chairman of the Permanent Select Intelligence Committee; Dante B. Fascell, chairman of the Foreign Affairs Committee; and Jamie L. Whitten, chairman of the Appropriations Committee.*

Message to the Congress Reporting Budget Rescissions
April 23, 1990

To the Congress of the United States:

In accordance with the Impoundment Control Act of 1974, I herewith report three proposed rescissions totalling $226,883,000.

The proposed rescissions affect programs of the Departments of Agriculture and Commerce.

The details of the proposed rescissions are contained in the attached report.

GEORGE BUSH

The White House,
April 23, 1990.

Note: The attachment detailing the proposed rescissions was printed in the "Federal Register" of April 24.

Nomination of James F. Blumstein To Be Administrator of the Office of Information and Regulatory Affairs
April 23, 1990

The President today announced his intention to nominate James F. Blumstein to be Administrator of the Office of Information and Regulatory Affairs at the Office of Management and Budget. He would succeed S. Jay Plager.

Mr. Blumstein serves as a professor of law at Vanderbilt University School of Law in Nashville, TN. Prior to this, he served as the John M. Olin Visiting Professor of Law at the University of Pennsylvania Law School, 1989; senior fellow at the Vanderbilt Institute for Public Policy Studies, adjunct professor of health law at Dartmouth Medical School, and special adviser to the chancellor for academic affairs at Vanderbilt University, 1984–1985; visiting associate professor of law and policy sciences at Duke Law School and Duke Institute of Policy Sciences and Public Affairs, 1974–1975; and director of the Vanderbilt Urban and Regional Development Center, 1972–1974.

Mr. Blumstein graduated from Yale College (B.A., 1966), Yale University (M.A., 1970), and Yale Law School (LL.B., 1970). He was born April 24, 1945, in Brooklyn, NY. Mr. Blumstein is married and resides in Nashville, TN.

Message to the Congress Transmitting an Extension of the German Democratic Republic-United States Fishing Agreement
April 23, 1990

To the Congress of the United States:

In accordance with the Magnuson Fishery Conservation and Management Act of 1976 (Public Law 94–265; 16 U.S.C. 1801 *et seq.*), I transmit herewith an agreement between the United States and the German Democratic Republic extending the agreement of April 13, 1983, concerning fisheries off the coast of the United States of America, as amended. The agreement, which was effected by exchange of notes at Washington on January 16 and April 5, 1990, extends the 1983 agreement for an additional 2-year period, from July 1, 1990, to July 1, 1992.

The exchange of notes, together with the present agreement, constitute a governing international fishery agreement within the requirements of section 201(c) of the act.

U.S. fishing industry interests have urged prompt consideration of this agreement to avoid disruption of ongoing cooperative fishing ventures. I urge that the Congress give favorable consideration to the agreement at an early date.

GEORGE BUSH

The White House,
April 23, 1990.

Remarks and a Question-and-Answer Session With the National Association of Agriculture Journalists
April 24, 1990

The President. Thank you for that unique introduction—[*laughter*]—and I am—look, we're just delighted you're here—Secretary and Cooper Evans telling me that they feel it's most worthwhile. And then I was just picking the brain of my friend—brains, plural—of my friend Roger Porter; and I think he, too, has gotten something out of this. So, thank you for coming.

Unfortunately for me, this is a fairly short appearance. But I am glad that you're here—Clayton telling me this was your, what, 37th annual meeting. Your membership has covered food and ag issues that are absolutely vital. Given the press of today's world, sometimes they may not be in the headlines in the paper every day, but they're vital.

And we do understand it, and frankly I am very pleased with the team that I have in this administration—agricultural team headed by Clayton Yeutter; in the White House with Roger Porter and Cooper Evans that know this subject well; and then in our trade field, one that Clayt knows so well, and Carla Hills and her people also keenly

interested. So, I think I get good advice on it, and I think they hope I'll learn faster. But at least I feel comforted by the fact that our team is respected around the country and on Capitol Hill. So, I'll take this opportunity to thank them.

Just a quick word—Clayt said you've been very much interested in the farm bill. As you know—because I assume you've been given that green book that I have, and from that you'll see that we've forwarded some 70 recommendations to the Hill. And they are intended to fine-tune that '85 act, not dramatically change the underlying philosophy. And again, here, all of you are familiar with ag legislation. And I salute Clayton and the White House staff, too, because it isn't easy. You've got a lot of competing interests up there on Capitol Hill.

The '85 act really provided, I think, a sound underpinning for the recovery in agricultural America; and farm exports as a result, I think, have rebounded. Jotted down the figure—the low $26 billion in '86 to nearly $40 billion last year. In '89, farm income overall hit an all-time high. That is good, but we intend to build on that progress, not relax, because we known some people are still hurting.

You know, this is the Year of the Environment. We've just concluded Earth Day, and I know that there are some conflicting interests here. I happen to think agricultural America, like the rest of the country, is environmentally conscious. But I also know there are some areas where there's conflict. Clayton and Cooper were just over in the Oval Office talking to me about the wetlands question. I am committed to no loss of wetlands. I am not committed to throwing people out of work. And so, we have to balance out some of these interests. And where the regulations have gotten excessive, let us know—you can't, but your papers will, I'm sure—and we will try to see that we have a reasonable policy.

But I think we all are committed to a sound environment, and the bill proposals would help preserve this environmental interest without placing an unfair burden on the farmer. And just to put you all at ease, it isn't just agricultural America where we're trying to achieve balance: it's through the whole Ohio Valley and other places where there's a concern that we not end up with an economy in which there is no growth or where people are not able to achieve jobs. So, I guess it ends up on my desk to try to establish a proper balance, but here I'm told by your Secretary that we're getting good, strong cooperation from the farm communities on this question. So, we are proposing a stronger research program, frankly, that will help farmers and the Government make sound, and thus better, environmental decisions.

Now, I know that some have expressed an interest here on the GATT—Roger whispered to me there's some interest—and I'll be glad to take questions on Gorbachev, grain sales, and all of that. But, look, I recognize, as I think many farmers do, that agriculture is one of the most distorted sectors of trade. In the last 40 years, GATT has been successful in leveling the playing field in industrial goods by reducing these distortive trade practices while, in the same period—let's be very candid—we have not been successful, and certainly as successful

as I'd like to see us, in leveling the playing field. There's too much protection for agriculture, and it's almost doubled around the world.

And I think I'll be meeting with EC today—is it Delors?—I will be seeing him. And I will tell him what I've already said to him before as President and mentioned to him as Vice President: that we have got to make progress on the agricultural section of our negotiations in this Uruguay round. So, we are not lightening up on that. There's no tradeoff between industrial—I see Clayt nodding; he's been down that road, and he knows that's true. But if you ask me do I feel comfortable about the progress we've made, the answer is no, I want to do better. I'm trying, but I recognize I've got to do better.

So, those are some of the subjects. But let me just throw the meeting open to questions, and please, you don't have to restrict yourself to agriculture. Why don't we go one, two for openers.

Wetlands

Q. As the "environmental President," the people in Virginia, the farmers and the agricultural community in Virginia, are wondering how we can allow four agencies of the Federal Government to overrule and countermand each other in the wetlands issues—soil conservation will go onto a farm, improve the activities, even help put them in place. Years later, the EPA will come in, call them violation. The Army Corps of Engineers will come in and say, we don't see any violation. And then the Federal wildlife people will come and say, well, we'd like to have that wetland returned to a wildlife sanctuary.

Now, how—this is really——

The President. The answer to your question—and you phrased it very well, indeed, because you're talking about the complexity of the Federal Government—is to do a better job. And the concern of the farmer has been brought to our attention—do a better job in eliminating some of these overlapping jurisdictional interests.

I am committed to no net loss of wetlands. I am not committed to decisions that take productive land out of production. So,

I can only say I understand the frustration. We are trying to do a better job of getting these agencies to work together.

You've got zealots in various levels of the bureaucracy. I think we can handle it pretty well at the top. The problem is, in some areas I think the conflict that you run into is at the very local level, where one agency will come in with a mandate and another will say, Well, we've got a different one.

So, look, all I can say is, we will try very hard to get from the top on down in this instance, in this case, the clarification that is needed so we avoid this frustration to the farmer. And I'm not happy with where it stands.

Price Supports

Q. We listened to Senator Bob Kerrey this morning, who is taking the lead in the Senate on program crops, price supports. He says that the recovery, which you mention, is very fragile and that in order to continue recovery that the support system has to be based on production costs; and that could be at least $12 billion, which is considerably higher than what the administration is proposing. He says if it's not at least that much the cost in the future to make up for the problems that will be caused by not helping the farmers in production will be much greater. Can you speak to that?

The President. No, I can't. I believe in what we're trying to do. And I get criticism all day long about this economy from liberal Democrats like Bob, whom I have respect in some fields—[*laughter*]—and he's entitled to his opinion. But I place my confidence in our Agricultural Department and in what we're trying to do in the farm bill.

I'll tell you what we do have is sometimes we have just a philosophical difference of opinion. We ran into that in the campaign—this supply management approach, and I'm not sure that's what he's advocating, is not one I'm for. And I expect I'll find some advocates for the different positions sitting here, of people to whom you write. But I just have a different view than he does on this.

Secretary Yeutter. Can I just add one supplementary——

The President. Yes.

Secretary Yeutter. ——comment very quickly, because this has come up, Mr. President, before, not only with Senator Kerrey but some others, by Members of Congress determining through themselves that farm incomes are directly related only to government financial assistance.

Somehow or other, Senator Kerrey and others have forgotten that there is a market out there and that farmers get most of their income from the marketplace, and hopefully over time will get more of it from the marketplace.

All of us, including the President and myself, are concerned about the farm incomes. But that doesn't suggest that the only way to increase farm incomes is to increase Federal subsidies.

Economic Sanctions Against the Soviet Union

Q. We understand that you are considering some economic sanctions against the Soviet Union for what may or may not happen in Lithuania. I know you can't make any announcements today—couldn't give out information about it—but could you tell us whether you have ruled out——

The President. No, I can't tell you what I've ruled in and ruled out, except one area that would be very—I mention this only because we're all here today with agriculture as the matrix of this meeting. I would refer you back to statements I have made in terms of using grain as a political weapon. And I'm talking here, obviously, about the grain agreement with the Soviet Union. I am disinclined to accept any suggestions about using a grain embargo as a manifestation of our displeasure and our grief over what's happening in Lithuania. So, I won't say what I might do.

I've just concluded a very interesting meeting with the bipartisan leadership of the Congress. And I will say this: that in my view, the meeting that we have just concluded exemplifies the best in bipartisanship and the best in consultation. Out of that meeting, different Senators and different House Members will have differing views. But I can tell you, not one single person there suggested that I change my position and use the grain deal or sales of wheat to the Soviet Union as a tool to try to change the Soviets' minds on things. So, that will give you a sense of the meeting, anyway. But I have no intention of changing my mind.

What I have said on that is if we ever reached a point in our trade relations where all trade was off, then I expect the farmer would understand. But to go back to the disastrous grain embargo that hurt us with our markets and hurt our farmers worse than I think it hurt anybody else, I'm simply not going to do that.

Q. I have one of those famous two-part Washington questions for you. One, when will you share with the American people your decisions on Lithuania, since obviously the Soviet Government will know what your policy is? Do you think the American people should know it, too?

And the second part of my——

The President. Would you like me to repeat it for you right here?

Q. No, I mean on your decisions on what you're going to do and the appropriate response to Lithuania. And part number two: You've spoken to the environmental initiatives being in the farm bill. Is your administration willing to go beyond that and accept a suggestion such as a farmer should reduce use of agricultural chemicals that reduce erosion on environmentally sensitive land? Should they write 5-year programs in to reduce those certain problems? Should they keep records on pesticide use?

The President. I would refer those questions to my Secretary of Agriculture, and I will be heavily persuaded by what he tells me. On the first question, though, let me tell you that I will share with the American people my decision when I make the decision. And you know that I have not decided what will be done. And this is a highly complex situation that we're facing, and there's a lot at stake in this situation. I don't want to make—you know, remember Yogi Berra: "What happened? Why did you lose the ball game?" He said, "We made the wrong mistake." [*Laughter*] You got to think about that one. And I don't want to make the wrong mistake.

I may do something that is imprudent, but I'm encouraged by the consultation be-

cause I feel that the American people do understand my policy. And that is to handle this situation as follows: One, make very clear that the American people feel that the independence and the self-determination of Lithuania is right—a part of our very fiber, a part of our very soul—the right to self-determination. And indeed, heartened as we are by democratic change in Eastern Europe, we would like to think that the Baltic countries, whose incorporation into the Soviet Union we have never recognized, would someday enjoy that freedom. So, that's the hallmark of the policy.

Secondly, we are considering ways to encourage the Soviet Union to go forward. The whole matter could be resolved today in this matter—that if they would begin a dialog, if they would discuss peaceful change in the evolution of freedom. And I would encourage right here the Soviet Union and the Lithuanians to go forward with dialog. Right now there's a delegation from Lithuania in the Soviet Union, and let's hope they can start talking. This has a great deal of potential for the freedom that we seek for the Lithuanians, and yet have it done in a way that is not egregious to the Soviet Union. And so, therein lies the answer.

But in relation to your question—What are we going to do about it?—I will let the American people know and the Congress know when I decide to take certain action. And the decision has not been made. And once again, I'd like to say I wish you all could have been flies on the wall in the Cabinet Room, because the meeting on consultation was extraordinarily helpful. And I am very grateful—this is the first chance I've had to speak to the AP [Associated Press] or the UP [United Press International] or other reporters—very grateful for the spirit of bipartisanship, the frank discussion that took place and, indeed, the support that I felt existed around the table for the approach that I am taking.

And I think the American people are in support of that approach, and I say that with total appreciation for the strength of the feeling that Lithuanians in this country have about their own freedom. But I also am concerned about the freedom of Poland.

I'm concerned about the evolution of freedom in the other Baltic States, whose incorporation we haven't recognized. I am concerned that we not inadvertently do something that compels the Soviet Union to take action that would set back the whole case of freedom around the world.

So, it's a very complex time, and that's why I would respond to your question that I just will certainly announce it as soon as I have made any determination as to what steps should be taken. And I think you'd see that any steps we did take—if there was anything done, it would most apt to be in the economic side. But I'm not going to give up on trying to get the Soviet Union and the Lithuanians into a dialog. I think that's a constructive approach; I think that that's the approach that the American people and others around the world want. We've had extensive consultation with our allies and with friends in different parts of the world, and that approach is the approach that I think would have universal support.

Last one.

Federal Deficit Reduction

Q. Interest rates are still too high, too high—too high for industry as well as for agriculture. I think there's a general feeling out there that Congress and the White House are dealing in gimmickry to bring the deficit down. There are not serious steps of reduction even after all is said and done. Outside of capital gains, are you considering any other strategies to bring the deficit down?

The President. What's happened on that is we sent a budget proposal—some criticized it as having gimmicks. Congress, under the law, was supposed to have their budget proposals on the table by April 1st. Had a little time slippage on that. They will come forward at some point, and then we sit down and try to negotiate out the differences and move this deficit forward. But I'm glad you mentioned it, because it does affect interest rates on every quadrant, every section of our economy, and something needs to be done.

I would also say that I am still very much concerned about the spending side of the equation. And that isn't just in agriculture, it's across the whole specter. I send up a special resolution to try to send a laser-like support for Nicaragua and Panama, and the next thing you know, we've added over a billion dollars' worth of spending to that request. And next week it's something else, and yesterday it was something else.

So, I have to be the one, feeling as I do about the economy, that tries to constrain the excesses of spending. And some will say raise taxes, but what's the point of raising taxes if it just opens the floodgates to more spending. So, we're in a time period here where the Congress has the next move, and then I'm sure we'll have a negotiation that I hope will lead to real reductions in this deficit. I am somewhat encouraged by the fact that the economy continues to grow. I am very encouraged by the fact that our deficit is significantly lower percentage of our gross national product than it's been. But that is no argument to lessen our desire to get the deficit down. So, that's about where we stand.

Listen, thank you all very much for coming. Appreciate it. I appreciate your being here.

Note: The President spoke at 11:36 a.m. in the Indian Treaty Room of the Old Executive Office Building. In his opening remarks, he referred to Secretary of Agriculture Clayton K. Yeutter; Cooper Evans, Special Assistant to the President for Agricultural Trade and Food Assistance; and Roger B. Porter, Assistant to the President for Economic and Domestic Policy. Jacques Delors was President of the European Community Commission.

Remarks at a White House Briefing for the Associated General Contractors of America
April 24, 1990

This is what we call a cameo drop-by. It means you don't have to listen very long to me speaking. But as I was walking over here, my friend Sam Skinner was out there trolling around Executive Avenue in the sun on this beautiful day, and I said, come on, let's go over and say thank you to the AGC. And that's why he's here, and that's why I'm here. And I might say parenthetically that this knowledgeable Secretary of Transportation, in my view, is doing an outstanding job for our country. And I'm very, very pleased he's here with me.

I just wanted to come over really to say thank you for the support and urge your continued support on some matters that I'd like to just briefly touch on. But here's an opportunity to visit with the national, State and, I'm told, local levels of the American General Contractors.

Before I got involved in politics—and there are not many old enough to go back that far—but I, too, was in business. And I earned my livelihood with the skies as the roof—mine in the offshore drilling business. So, I have a special appreciation for the work of contractors, special appreciation for the work that you do, hard work that helps build something—build businesses and create jobs and provide opportunity and allow communities to grow and to prosper. So, this industry, the construction industry, can be proud of its most important role in the American economy.

I can't help but note a common denominator among your firms, and that is family ownership in a lot of them. The U.S. construction industry has more than 400,000 businesses ranging from really small mom-and-pop operations to substantial companies, and virtually all are family-owned. That fact helps strengthen our families, frankly, our society fabric that I must confess that I worry about, Barbara worries about. And we are committed, this administration, as Sam knows so well, to enhancing the climate so that you'll have the ability to grow and to compete.

And I will need your help and that of all Americans to weigh in on Capitol Hill. You're effective at that. I think your Senators and your Congressman, because they know that you're community oriented, listen to you. And we need your help in enacting what I think is an ambitious agenda to build a better America. And I'd be remiss, once again, if I didn't say thank you for past support, including your efforts on this capital gains tax reduction initiative, as well as your help in bolstering a choice position, a family-strengthening position, on child care.

You know, I get hit out there from Capitol Hill on a capital gains differential as being a tax cut for the wealthy. Well, if that were the case, why does Japan have a rate of about 5 percent, Korea 0, and other major countries that are coming along 0 way of taxing capital gains? And so, they can call it what they want; I'm talking about jobs for the American people; and I'm talking about the incentive, if you will, to start businesses. And I'm going to stay with this fight. But your organization, your people here in Washington, as well as many of you, have been extraordinarily, extraordinarily helpful; and I just want you to know we're going to not back off.

I know that your organization has been very interested in its zero-tolerance drug policy. You're promoting this nationwide, I'm told, through 102 chapters; and we applaud your emphasis on health and safety in the workplace. The drug fight—there's some encouraging signs. Cocaine use of high school seniors moved dramatically down in 1 year. But we've just really begun to be engaged in this battle. And I am very grateful to what I call the Points-of-Light approach, which is a volunteer approach to helping pitch in and educate the young people of this country, to change the ethic in the entertainment business on cocaine use and drug use generally, and then to be supportive of our efforts on the curtailment of crime approach—being tough on these drug dealers. And you all have been with us on most of this, and I'm very grateful to you.

Some of you might recall my memorable address that kept at least a third of you awake at your 63d annual convention in 1982—[*laughter*]—when I was Vice President. And I invoked President Johnson's memorable quote: "We can either stand with the President or paint our tails white and run with the antelopes." Well, he said it a little more graphically, but I would—[*laughter*]—you can picture it. [*Laughter*] But the tendency around here is—Sam, he's the guy who has to go up to the Hill, and our other Cabinet members. I don't have to do that so much. But there is this tendency when the going gets tough to look kind of like Custer out there. But you haven't done that, and I'm very grateful for the fact that you have stood with us on some of these tough issues.

So, now I'm here not as Vice President, with those memorable lines in mind, but as President to really again ask for that same steadfast support. I must tell you the number one objective domestically has got to be to keep this economy strong. And I am an environmentalist: I believe in leaving this Earth a little bit better than when we found it. But I'm also a believer that we've got to find a balanced approach so that we don't say to a young man or a young woman coming into the work force, sorry, we're in a no-growth mode today, and you don't have a chance for a job. And so, it's a balancing position, and I think this organization—I am told by our pros around here—understands that. So I would like to ask for your same steadfast support as we work to strengthen this economy; keep it growing; and then enact our competitiveness agenda, which will build an even better and stronger America.

And that competitiveness agenda talks about research and R&D. It talks about education. It talks about leveling the playing field internationally, of course. And I think we're making some progress there with our Japanese friends. I hope so. We'll know more very soon on that.

So, I know that our work isn't done, but I also know that I am President of the United States at perhaps the most interesting time in post-World War II history. And it is fascinating, the changes that are taking place for democracy and freedom.

And I might say to those of you who are from southern climes here, and thus maybe feel a little closer to what's happening in Central and South America, it's very encouraging what's going on there. And I would like to avail myself of your ears and attention to say I hope that the Congress will move on my request for support for Panama and Nicaragua and do it soon. I asked that they do that back in March. I asked that the legislation be finished on April 5th. And tomorrow Violeta Chamorro is being sworn in as President of Nicaragua, and we don't have that.

We have a commitment now to help those democracies, and it fits into our budget. So, if you have any spare time, please call your friendly Senator and tell him to get going and get this legislation passed, because we are a symbol up here for these countries in our own neighborhood, our own front yard, if you will. And I'd like to have that legislation intact so that our able Vice President can report that to Mrs. Chamorro when he goes down there tomorrow.

End of pitch. Thank you for your help. I hope you have a pleasant meeting in Washington, and thank you so much for all you're doing. Thank you.

Double jeopardy—you have to hear it twice. Sit down, please. [*Laughter*] I really do have to go, but he asked me just to say a word because I know Lithuania is on your minds. And we just completed a very interesting and, in my view, productive meeting with the leaders of the Senate and the House over in the Cabinet Room just before lunch.

It is an extraordinarily complicated situation. There are no easy calls. I am determined to make clear to the world that we have a stake, a fundamental stake, in self-determination for Lithuania. We have never recognized the incorporation of Lithuania into the Soviet Union. So, we have no problem that some have—the Secretary General and some countries—of considering Lithuania a part of the Soviet Union, an integral part, and thus saying any concern we express about Lithuania is mingling into the internal affairs of the Soviet Union. We don't have that dilemma because we never recognized the incorporation of Lithuania or Latvia or Estonia into the Soviet Union.

Having said that, what I'm trying to do— and I have not made a determination exactly what I will do specifically on sanction approach that many are talking about— what I am determined to do is to try to get a dialog going, or see that the Soviets and the Lithuanians get a dialog going, so they can talk about and then decide upon the peaceful evolution of democracy in keeping with our age-old principle of self-determination for people.

And I don't want to do something that would inadvertently set back the progress that has been made in Eastern Europe. And it's been dramatic progress, far faster than I think any of us here—if we went to confessional—would say we could possibly see coming up. And so, it is delicate. And you've got to look at the real options. I'm old enough to remember Hungary in 1956 and where we exhorted people to go to the barricades, and a lot of people were left out there all alone.

And so, I will continue to articulate the view that we are committed to self-determination of these Baltic countries and encourage them to indulge in a dialog, both sides, that will result in this end being achieved. Gorbachev has indicated a willingness to do this. The Lithuanians have indicated some willingness to do this. Indeed, there's a delegation in Moscow today from Vilnius. And let's hope that they can get together and start the discussion, because the progress that's been made towards democracy in Eastern Europe is mind-boggling.

We have a great stake, I think, in helping those countries in Eastern Europe. And frankly, I'd like to see the progress in the Soviet Union go forward without having some elements that are opposing Gorbachev on all of this crack down and set the clock back to a day that we all remember of a cold-war mentality and confrontation instead of negotiation in progress.

So, we're at an interesting period here, no determination having been made by your President yet as to specific action, but a determination—and I am convinced, incidentally, that the Soviet leadership knows of our adherence to this principle and to our conviction that dialog is the way to go.

So, we will see what can happen. And in the meantime, I will make clear to the Lithuanians in this country, the most patriotic, wonderful people, whose enthusiasm for independence now I can certainly understand, that we are not going to back off 1 inch from this principle of freedom and self-determination.

So, we are in an interesting period here, and I have been gratified to have the support of the American people on this one. And I'm gratified to have what appears to be good bipartisan support from the Congress at this juncture. But it's an interesting call, and we will try to handle it so progress tries to keep going instead of inadvertently setting the clock back.

I love the old expression of Yogi Berra's: You say, "What happened to the Mets, Yogi?" He said, "Well, we made the wrong mistakes." [*Laughter*] I expect in this job I'll make plenty of mistakes, but I don't want to make the wrong mistakes.

Thank you all very much.

Note: The President spoke at 1:12 p.m. in Room 450 of the Old Executive Office Building.

Statement by Press Secretary Fitzwater on President Bush's Meeting With President Jacques Delors of the European Community Commission
April 24, 1990

President Bush met today with European Community Commission President Jacques Delors to discuss the development of relations between the United States and the European Community, an important part of U.S. relations with Europe. President Delors described the Community's continuing political and economic integration and the Community's developing relations with Eastern Europe and the Soviet Union. President Bush emphasized the United States traditional and continuing support for European integration and the importance the United States attaches to the Community's role as coordinator of a broad Western effort to aid Hungary and Poland, as well as other Eastern European countries as they move toward market economies and democracy.

President Bush and President Delors discussed the roles of the United States and the European Community in a changing Europe. They both stressed the need to fur-

ther strengthen institutional links between the United States and the Community as the EC integration process progresses, and to refine procedures for continuing close political and economic consultations at all levels. President Bush said he was pleased with the progress made in this regard during the visit of Irish Prime Minister Haughey in February as President of the EC Council. The U.S.-EC Ministerial yesterday and President Bush's meeting today with President Delors should permit additional progress.

President Bush reiterated to Commission President Delors that the United States is firmly committed to improving the multilateral trading system and strengthening the GATT through agreements reached during the Uruguay round GATT negotiations scheduled to conclude in Brussels next December, and that the cooperation of the European Community is essential, particularly in the agricultural area.

Message to the Senate Transmitting a Protocol to the Canada–United States Extradition Treaty
April 24, 1990

To the Senate of the United States:

With a view to receiving the advice and consent of the Senate to ratification, I transmit herewith the Protocol signed at Ottawa on January 11, 1988, amending the Treaty on Extradition Between the United States of America and Canada, signed at Washington on December 3, 1971, as amended by an exchange of notes on June 28 and July 9, 1974. I transmit also, for the information of the Senate, the report of the Department of State with respect to the protocol.

The protocol amends the Extradition Treaty Between the United States and Canada, signed at Washington on Decem-

ber 3, 1971, as amended by an exchange of notes on June 28 and July 9, 1974. It represents an important step in improving law enforcement cooperation and combatting terrorism by excluding from the scope of the political offense exception serious offenses typically committed by terrorists; e.g., murder, manslaughter, kidnapping, use of an explosive device capable of endangering life or causing grievous bodily harm, and attempt or conspiracy to commit the foregoing offenses.

The protocol also will help to improve implementation of the current extradition treaty in several other respects. Most significant, the protocol substitutes a dual criminality clause for the current list of extraditable offenses, so that, *inter alia*, parental child abduction and certain additional narcotics offenses will be covered by the new treaty.

I recommend that the Senate give early and favorable consideration to the protocol and give its advice and consent to ratification.

GEORGE BUSH

The White House,
April 24, 1990.

Nomination of Steven E. Steiner for the Rank of Ambassador While Serving as United States Representative to the Special Verification Commission
April 24, 1990

The President today announced his intention to nominate Steven E. Steiner for the rank of Ambassador during his tenure of service as the United States Representative to the Special Verification Commission.

Since 1988 Mr. Steiner has served as the United States Representative for the Special Verification Commission. Prior to this he served as Director of Defense and Arms Control for the National Security Council at the White House, 1983–1988. Mr. Steiner graduated from Yale University (B.A., 1963) and Columbia University (M.I.A., 1966). He was born July 14, 1940, in Kittanning, PA. Mr. Steiner is married, has three children, and resides in Chevy Chase, MD.

Nomination of Ming Hsu To Be a Commissioner at the Federal Maritime Commission
April 24, 1990

The President today announced his intention to nominate Ming Hsu to be a Federal Maritime Commissioner for the remainder of the term expiring June 30, 1991. She would succeed Elaine L. Chao.

Since 1982 Mrs. Hsu has served as the Governor's special trade representative for the State of New Jersey and director of the State commerce department's division of international trade in Newark, NJ. Prior to this, she served as vice president for international trade relations for the RCA Corp. in New York, NY, and has served as director of international planning and director of marketing planning. In addition, Mrs. Hsu served as a member of the Defense Adviso-

ry Committee on Women in the Services, 1989; on the National Commission on the Observance of International Women's Year; and on the Secretary of Commerce's Advisory Committee on East-West Trade. Mrs. Hsu was awarded the Woman of the Year Award for the Asian-American Professional Women's Association, 1983.

Mrs. Hsu graduated from George Washington University School of Government Affairs (B.A., 1949), Ramapo College (LL.D., 1988), and Kean College (LL.D., 1989). She was born September 14, 1924, in Beijing, China. Mrs. Hsu is married, has one child, and resides in Westfield, NJ.

Presidential Determination No. 90–17—Memorandum on Export-Import Bank Services for Nicaragua
April 25, 1990

Memorandum for the Secretary of State

Subject: Determination Under Section 2(b)(2) of the Export-Import Bank Act of 1945, as Amended in 1986—Nicaragua

Pursuant to section 2(b)(2) of the Export-Import Bank Act of 1945, as amended in 1986, I determine that Nicaragua is no longer a "Marxist-Leninist" country; it is therefore in the national interest for the Export-Import Bank of the United States to guarantee, insure, extend credit and participate in the extension of credit in connection with the purchase or lease of any product or service by, for use in, or for sale or lease to Nicaragua.

Please transmit this determination to the Speaker of the House and to the President of the Senate.

You are authorized and directed to publish this determination in the *Federal Register.*

GEORGE BUSH

[*Filed with the Office of the Federal Register, 3:59 p.m., May 1, 1990*]

Presidential Determination No. 90–18—Memorandum on Emergency Assistance for Nicaragua
April 25, 1990

Memorandum for the Secretary of State

Subject: Determination to Authorize Assistance for Nicaragua

By virtue of the authority vested in me by section 451 of the Foreign Assistance Act of 1961, as amended, I hereby authorize the use of up to $2.5 million in funds made available under Chapter 4 of Part II of the act in fiscal year 1990 for emergency assistance to Nicaragua, notwithstanding any other provision of law.

You are requested to report this determination to the Speaker of the House of Representatives, the House Appropriations Committee, and the Senate Committees on Foreign Relations and Appropriations immediately.

You are authorized and directed to publish this determination in the *Federal Register.*

GEORGE BUSH

[*Filed with the Office of the Federal Register, 4 p.m., May 1, 1990*]

Remarks to Capital Area Community Food Bank Volunteers
April 25, 1990

Hey, listen, I'm the one that should be clapping for you all. And I want to thank Barry Scher, the chairman; and Lynn Brantley; and I guess everybody else for the tour of this Capital Area Community Food Bank. It's nice to know that all the broccoli— [*laughter*]—that my wife loves so much found a good home. And I'm told that it was well received.

It's especially fitting that I come over here today, as your President, because this is National Volunteer Week, a time to applaud those who are reaching out to those in need and to resolve to make serving others a part of America's life. I'm here to express my own thanks and the thanks of a grateful community for all that you do to address the problem of hunger in the Washington metropolitan area.

And this Capital Area Community Food Bank is a volunteer-intensive organization. In this room are some of the more than 5,500 people who volunteer to make this initiative work—distributing a minimum of 500,000 pounds of food per month. And by encouraging individuals, supermarkets, and other bulk suppliers to save their surpluses and by distributing that food to the needy in our community, those of you who are gathered here today are among those Points of Light that shine so brightly all across our country.

For the neighborhood pantries, low-income day-care centers, senior citizen lunch programs, and homeless shelters—a population served—this effort makes a difference. It makes a difference in the lives of others. And I hope that every community in the Nation will follow your lead and become, in your words, a community that cares for its own.

Thank you for demonstrating that any definition of a successful life must include serving others. You inspire me, you inspire my wife, and you inspire the country. Thank you very much.

Note: The President spoke at 10:27 a.m. at the food bank. In his opening remarks, he referred to Barry Scher and Lynn Brantley, chairman of the board and executive director of the Capital Area Community Food Bank.

Remarks Announcing Federal Budget Reform Proposals
April 25, 1990

The President. Let me welcome Senators Thurmond—I thought Pete Domenici was going to be here—certainly Dan Coats; and Tom Tauke, Lynn Martin; Representatives Craig, Penny; and of course, Secretary Brady and the Attorney General and Director Darman, General Counsel Boyden Gray.

Today I'm signing letters to send to Congress a budget reform package that would propose an amendment to the Constitution to provide a line-item veto; reiterate my previous support for the Legislative Line-Item Veto Act to enhance Presidential rescission authority; and finally, to reendorse a balanced budget amendment.

As President, I repeat the call of many of my predecessors for the line-item veto, and today I am proposing an amendment to the Constitution to accomplish this. The President needs the power to remove unnecessary expenditures that have been made a part of the appropriations bills without sacrificing entire legislative enactments. This power would give the President the same tool that 43 Governors have: the line-item

veto.

I also want to repeat my strong endorsement of August 4th of last year for the Legislative Line-Item Veto Act, which was introduced in the Senate by Senator Coats and by John McCain. I'm glad you're here, Dan; but John, I think, is in Nicaragua for the inauguration. Otherwise, he would be here as well. The House sponsors are here: Tom Tauke, Lynn Martin, Larry Craig, and Tim Penny—all out front on this issue.

The Legislative Line-Item Veto Act strengthens the rescission authority in current law. Now an appropriation can only be canceled through rescission, but Congress can reject a Presidential rescission simply by inaction. And that's precisely what's happened to the vast majority of rescission proposals since the present law went into effect in 1974. And so, I ask Congress to require an up-or-down vote on Presidential rescissions. The President needs the power to make the tough calls on spending, take the heat, and I'm perfectly prepared to do that.

The third and final element of this budget reform package is a balanced budget amendment. A balanced budget amendment, properly drafted, is both necessary and appropriate to protect the interests of a group of citizens not now able to protect themselves; and I'm talking about the citizens of future generations. Senate Joint Resolution 12, introduced by Senator Thurmond, is one such balanced budget amendment, and today I am pleased to endorse that Thurmond resolution. More than 30 State legislatures have already called for a constitutional convention for this purpose.

These three tools—a line-item veto constitutional amendment, enhanced rescission authority for the President, and a balanced budget amendment—together with political courage and discipline are vital to solving the problems of budget deficits.

So, I am prepared—I will tell all of you here—to work with Congress to enact a meaningful, credible, and effective budget reform process. Getting our fiscal house in order is crucial to our nation's long-term economic health and prosperity.

Thank you all for your leadership, and I look forward to working with you for success here.

[At this point, the President signed the letters.]

The President. So, there we are. Keep up the good work.

Lithuanian Independence

Q. Mr. President, Mr. Landsbergis [Lithuanian leader] has likened your policies to Munich. Would you care to defend yourself?

The President. I don't need any defense. The policy decisions I've taken have strong support from the American people. That's who I work for.

Note: The President spoke at 11:15 a.m. in the Roosevelt Room at the White House. In his opening remarks, he referred to Senators Pete V. Domenici and Dan Coats, and to C. Boyden Gray, Counsel to the President.

The Office of the Press Secretary issued a fact sheet on the same day which provided the following additional information on the President's budget reform proposals:

Line-item veto amendment: The amendment would give the President authority to separately approve, reduce, or disapprove any provision of a bill containing any 'item of spending authority.' 'Items of spending authority' have been broadly defined, to capture the whole range of Federal spending. They include: items of appropriation, spending authorizations, authority to borrow money on the credit of the United States or otherwise, dedications of revenues, entitlements, uses of assets, insurance, guarantees of borrowing, and any authority to incur obligations. The basic veto mechanism currently in the Constitution has been retained in the amendment. When the President exercises the item veto, he will signify in writing the portions approved or approved as reduced, which will then become law, and return disapproved portions and reductions to Congress, which will reconsider each of them just as it now does with vetoed bills.

Balanced budget amendment: The proposed amendment would require that outlays not exceed receipts, thus allowing the budget to be balanced or to run a surplus. The proposal also includes a safeguard against a resort to higher taxes as a means of complying with the constitutional mandate. The President called for a change in Senate Joint Resolution 12: that the mandate for a balanced budget be effective beginning with fiscal year 1993—the year in which the Gramm-Rudman-Hollings law requires elimination of the deficit.

Letter to Congressional Leaders on Federal Budget Reform
April 25, 1990

Dear Mr. Speaker: [*Dear Mr. President:*]

Today I am proposing to the Congress a budget reform package. In order to help restore fiscal integrity, we need a balanced budget amendment to the Constitution, a line-item veto constitutional amendment, and enhanced rescission authority for the President. These tools—together with political courage and discipline—are vital to solving the problem of budget deficits.

The most fundamental change needed in the Federal budget process is a constitutional amendment to require a balanced budget. A balanced budget amendment is both necessary and appropriate to protect the interests of a group of citizens not now able to represent themselves: the citizens of future generations. More than 30 State legislatures have already called for a constitutional convention for this purpose.

A balanced budget amendment must also include safeguards against a resort to higher taxes as a means of complying with the constitutional mandate. Senate Joint Resolution 12, a balanced budget amendment introduced by Senator Thurmond, includes such a safeguard and has my full support. There is, however, one change I would make in S.J. Res. 12: the mandate for a balanced budget should be effective beginning with fiscal year 1993. The current Gramm-Rudman-Hollings law requires elimination of the deficit by that time, and the balanced budget amendment will help ensure that the Federal budget stays in balance thereafter.

Second, as President, I repeat the call of many of my predecessors for the line-item veto. The President needs the power to remove individual and unnecessary expenditures that have been made a part of major appropriations bills without sacrificing entire legislative enactments. This power would give the President the same tool that 43 Governors have—the line-item veto.

With that power, we can put the national interest above the special interests. Therefore, I am submitting to the Congress today a proposed amendment to the Constitution granting such authority.

Finally, we need to correct the budget procedure known as rescission. Present law allows for cancellation of an appropriation only through the rescission process, in which the Congress can reject a Presidential proposal for rescission simply by inaction. That is precisely what happened to the vast majority of rescission proposals submitted by three Presidents since the present law was enacted in 1974.

Thus, I urge passage of The Legislative Line-Item Veto Act of 1989 (H.R. 3271 and H.R. 3583, companion bills to S. 1553) [(S. 1553)], which would provide enhanced rescission authority to the President. I commend, in particular, Representatives Tom Tauke, Larry Craig, Lynn Martin, and Bob McEwen for their leadership in introducing this important legislation. [I commend, in particular, Senators Dole, Domenici, Armstrong, Humphrey, McCain, and Coats for their work in drawing together this important legislation]. This legislation will provide the President with strong and effective authority to rescind appropriations that are wasteful or unnecessary.

I am prepared to work with the Congress to enact meaningful, credible, and effective budget reforms. Getting our fiscal house in order is crucial to our Nation's long-term economic health and prosperity.

Sincerely,

GEORGE BUSH

Note: Letters were sent to Thomas S. Foley, Speaker of the House of Representatives, and Dan Quayle, President of the Senate. The material appearing in brackets was contained in the letter sent to the President of the Senate.

Message to the Congress Transmitting a Joint Resolution Proposing a Line-Item Veto Constitutional Amendment
April 25, 1990

To the Congress of the United States:

I forward to you today a Joint Resolution proposing an amendment to the Constitution of the United States to authorize the President to disapprove or reduce items of spending authority and to disapprove substantive provisions contained in appropriations measures.

Amending our national charter is a profoundly serious step, and I am fully aware of the great responsibility involved in proposing such an action. My proposal, however, is supported by ample precedent. Today, the Governors of 43 of the 50 States have line-item veto authority, and for more than a century American Presidents have urged the Congress to adopt this reform at the Federal level. We have never needed it more than now. By enabling the President to open up massive omnibus spending packages and pare out wasteful and unneeded spending, this amendment would address one of the most serious and intractable issues facing the Nation today—the collapse of Federal fiscal discipline that has helped to saddle us with trillions of dollars of debt.

This amendment has been painstakingly crafted to ensure that the Congress has a chance to pass on each item lined out of a bill, using procedures essentially identical to those now in the Constitution. Its only purpose is to enable both the President and the Congress to take a closer look at the way we spend the taxpayers' money—to bring out into the sunlight the kinds of hidden, abusive spending proposals that would never make it on their own.

I look forward to working with you on this proposal, and I am confident that by enacting it we will place the Constitution and the Nation on a sounder footing than ever before.

GEORGE BUSH

The White House,
April 25, 1990.

Remarks at a White House Ceremony for the Observance of National Crime Victims' Rights Week
April 25, 1990

Welcome to the White House. And may I say I'm very pleased to see so many members of the House and the Senate here today to pay their respects to these honorees. I want to thank them for their outstanding support—Republicans, Democrats alike—on this whole concept of National Crime Victims' Week. It's always a pleasure to see our able Attorney General, who will do the honors in a minute, and in my view, he's doing an outstanding job for our country.

I'm delighted that I just signed the Presidential proclamation declaring this to be National Crime Victims' Rights Week. And I want to thank you, all of you out there who work so diligently in public service and the private sector on behalf of the victims of crime.

I'm glad to see so many of you could come—some from far away—come here to Washington. It's good to see Howard and Connie Clery again, and some of the others who have worked with the White House over the past year. Howard and Connie embody the power of voluntarism, the power of the physically challenged, and the power of a just cause—the campaign to build an America where every victim of every crime is treated with the dignity and the compassion that they deserve.

Shortly after I took office, the Attorney

General came to the Oval Office and introduced me to the seven recipients of last
year's awards. And today it's an honor for
me to stand with you again as we commemorate the great strides that we've
made toward preserving the rights of our
victimized citizens.

In the not-so-distant past, crime victims
often became the forgotten people, subjected to continued victimization by the criminal justice system. The victims' rights movement really emerged in the seventies, when
concerned Americans like one of today's
honorees, South Carolina's Dr. Dean Kilpatrick, took part in a grassroots effort to assist
victims of rape and family violence.

And the past 8 years have seen a new
emphasis placed on crime victims issues:
landmark Federal legislation, task forces led
by the President and the Attorney General,
45 States where a victims bill of rights is
now in force, and a nationwide expansion of
victim assistance and compensation programs. My administration has continued to
build on this foundation. We've backed the
Attorney General's call for full implementation of the Victim-Witness Protection Act.
We've obtained reauthorization for the
1984 Victims of Crime Act, extending the
innovative fund that turns the tables on the
bad guys by taking the criminal's money
and using it to assist and compensate the
criminal's victims. Last year, for the first
time, deposits into the fund exceeded the
legislative cap. And for 1990, $125 million
will be available for vital services to victims
of crime, $30 million over the 1989 level.
Another example of how we're protecting
victims is the fact that in securities fraud
and similar financial crimes we're regularly
seeking to recover funds to compensate the
victims of those offenses.

Through the Office for Victims of Crime,
we've also recently established new victim
assistance programs serving Native Americans in 17 States, because when violence
strikes, every American should have a place
to turn for help. Some of the best successes
have come about as a result of partnership—cooperation between Federal, State,
and local authorities; teamwork between
public and private efforts. One of today's
heroes is Mimi Olson, who has devoted 23
years to channeling victim assistance and

other services for Native American children
on the Crow Creek Sioux Reservation.

And you have Federal partners, like the
victim-witness coordinators in the U.S. Attorneys offices who not only arrange emergency services for Federal victims' assistance but also educate prosecutors about the
needs of these people—Federal victims'
needs.

And all of these efforts are important, but
we also know that the best defense is a
good offense. We're determined to stop
crime at its source, and that means tougher
laws, like the stringent drunk-driving law
Sandra Heverly helped enact in Nevada.
And it means fighting back—community pa-
trols, like the one pioneered in Boston by
Milton Cole.

Milton, in recent months, I visited your
neighborhood counterparts in Houston,
Kansas City, Santa Anna, and right across
the river over here in Virginia. And like
you, they got angry, and they got organized, and they got results.

Community results have also been magni-
fied by the power of television and the
work of yet another crime victim who refused to be further victimized: John Walsh,
of "America's Most Wanted." John says,
"Look, I was victimized once. My heart has
been broken. And I believe you take a
stand and fight back not as a vigilante but
through the system. You figure out a way to
do it with some dignity and some integrity,
and you fight back." Those are his words.
John's video version of the old post office
wanted posters have received national exposure, and the results speak for themselves: over 100 criminals nabbed in under
2 years—7 of the FBI's "10 Most Wanted."
And just this month, John's program helped
earn the conviction of a coldblooded killer
who had eluded authorities for 18 years.

The message and the popularity and effectiveness of this broadcast is simple: The
people of this country are prepared to do
whatever it takes for as long as it takes to
take back the streets, to take back what's
theirs.

And it's here where we'd like to ask your
help. I mentioned tougher laws. Congress
has approved our request for more agents,
more prosecutors, and more prisons to

catch, convict, and contain this country's most dangerous offenders. But Congress also must act on our full range of tough new anticrime proposals. Our package is in danger of being weakened in the Senate, and it's been left gathering dust in the House. And it's time to act. The American people want it done right, and they want it done responsibly, and they want it done now.

Many challenges remain. But thanks to you and your government partners, the future holds the promise for crime victims of both continued support and a continued voice.

From a community activist in Boston's public housing to one of America's most unlikely new television stars, your courageous seven personify the selfless acts of thousands of concerned Americans who strive every single day to take back the streets. And you're living proof of Father George Clemens' rallying cry in Chicago: "There are more of us than there are of them."

Congratulations, and God bless you all. Thank you.

Note: The President spoke at 11:31 a.m. in the Rose Garden at the White House. At the conclusion of his remarks, the following individuals received Department of Justice awards for outstanding public service on behalf of victims of crime: Howard and Constance Clery, Milton Cole, Sandra Heverly, Dean G. Kilpatrick, Emilia "Mimi" Olson, and John Walsh. The proclamation is listed in Appendix E at the end of this volume.

Remarks to the Bethesda-Chevy Chase Rescue Squad in Bethesda, Maryland
April 25, 1990

Thank you all very much. From George to George, thank you. [*Laughter*] President Giebel, thank you very much, and Chief Dwyer and members of this marvelous Bethesda-Chevy Chase Volunteer Rescue Squad. And of course, I want to pay my respects to our county executive, Sidney Kramer—thank him for being with us today. Congressman Curt Weldon, an old friend of mine, a current Member of the United States Congress, is the founder of the Congressional Fire Service Caucus, one of the most rapidly growing caucuses in the Congress and one that really has unanimous, across-the-aisle support. So, Curt, I'm delighted to be with you.

And of course, I don't need to say to you, her constituents, too much about my friend, your own friend, and our Representative in the United States Congress, Connie Morella. I will tell you, coming out, she wanted to be sure—you know Connie—she wanted to be sure I knew absolutely everything I needed to know; so she was telling me that it was—and she said it not in a partisan sense, but in a sense of civic commitment—that this is the heart and soul of the community. And she said that it enthusiastically let her have her announcement here, her victory celebration and, indeed, even her son's wedding reception here. [*Laughter*]

So, in addition to other good works, I salute this organization for being the heart and soul, as Connie said, of the community. This is the organization that I spoke to as a Vice Presidential nominee in 1980, and I'm certainly glad to be back.

One reason that I'm so pleased to be here is that if my speech is a disaster, relief is at hand. [*Laughter*] Then, too, there's another point that Curt and Connie and I were talking about coming out here: This week—it is National Volunteer Week, which celebrates the selfless character of the American people. National Volunteer Week salutes what I call this nation's Points of Light, this vast galaxy of individuals and businesses and schools and churches and synagogues, unions and voluntary associations working together to solve problems. This rescue squad really is a Point of Light; it is also a source of life.

Many people don't realize that fully 80 percent of America's fire protection and emergency medical service is supplied by volunteers—an amazing total, absolutely amazing. And here's the point: Volunteers who meet local emergencies—risking lives to save the lives of others, just as America's firefighters have done for more than 200 years.

You know, being here today reminds me of a story that I heard, which happened a number of years ago. It seems that 25 of Boston's top Prohibition bootleggers were rounded up in a surprise raid. And as they were being arraigned, the judge asked the usual question about occupation. The first 24 men were engaged in the same profession—each claimed to be a firefighter. Well, naturally, the judge asked the last prisoner, "And what are you?" "Your honor," he said, "I'm a bootlegger." Surprised, the judge laughed and asked, "And how's business?" He said, "Well, it would be a hell of a lot better if there weren't so many firefighters around." [*Laughter*]

Well, you get the gist. Even back in Prohibition, your numbers turned the tide. Then, as now, volunteers like you were the first responder not only to fire but also to accidents and floods and cave-ins and collapsed buildings. Then, as now, you acted as the backbone of America, showing that any definition of a successful life must include serving others.

National volunteer work—it embodies that definition, as do your 50 years of service to the Bethesda-Chevy Chase community. Talk about variety: cats rescued from treetops; children from smashed automobiles; helping victims of heart attacks; and senior citizens, alone and vulnerable, after falls within their own home. Young kids and retirees, executives and laborers—each of you, to quote the squad's original motto, has "answered the call."

Listen to an anonymous letter that appeared on your bulletin board. It talked of the comfort the B-CC Rescue Squad provides. "You can watch people's faces begin to relax just by your presence. And that gives you a special feeling." And look at the man with me here, David Dwyer, chief of the squad for the past 21 years. He's one of the heroes responsible for that feeling. And by day, he works at the NIH [National Institutes of Health]; at night, he's a volunteer— anywhere there is a need, anytime he is needed.

So, by risking your lives to save others, you are on the front lines. And those who directly take up the fight against drug abuse, illiteracy, homelessness, hunger, environmental decay, and AIDS are also on the front lines. Like you, they are finding the meaning and the adventure that all of us seek in our own lives.

We know that life itself means nothing without a cause larger than ourselves. Firefighting was such a cause when, in 1736, Ben Franklin founded one of the first volunteer companies. And so it is in 1990, with firefighters and EMS [emergency medical service] personnel today 1 million strong. I salute you, as does your community. We respect and admire you for a job well done. Today America is grateful for your special brand of skill and courage, the courage to put another's life before one's own.

Let me close with a Bible verse that defines your lives: "Greater love hath no man than this, that a man lay down his life for his friends." You and countless thousands of others like you around this great country serve strangers. You save lives, and you walk the path of engagement in the lives of those in need. And this really is the heartbeat of America and the true meaning of serving others.

Thank you for what you've done. I simply wanted to come out, down the street— through the skies, I will confess—[*laughter*]—but to say thank you from the bottom of a grateful heart. And I will try to continue to tell America how grateful we are for those who serve others. Thank you very, very much, and God bless you all.

Note: The President spoke at 2:05 p.m. outside the station house. He was introduced by George Giebel, president of the rescue squad.

Nomination of Peter Jon de Vos To Be United States Ambassador to Liberia
April 25, 1990

The President today announced his intention to nominate Peter Jon de Vos, a career member of the Senior Foreign Service, Class of Minister-Counselor, to be Ambassador Extraordinary and Plenipotentiary of the United States of America to the Republic of Liberia. He would succeed James Keough Bishop.

Since 1989 Mr. de Vos has served as Principal Deputy Assistant Secretary of State for the Bureau of Oceans and International Environmental and Scientific Affairs. Prior to this, he served as Deputy Assistant Secretary of State for Science and Technology, 1987–1989; Ambassador to the People's Republic of Mozambique, 1983–1987; Ambassador to the Republic of Guinea-Bissau and to the Republic of Cape Verde, 1980–1983; Deputy Director of Southern African Affairs

at the Department of State, 1979–1980; National War College, 1978–1979; political officer in Athens, Greece, 1975–1978; Special Assistant for the Bureau of Inter-American Affairs at the Department of State, 1973–1975; political officer in Brasilia, Brazil, 1971–1973; political officer in Sao Paulo, Brazil, 1970–1971; deputy principal officer in Luanda, Angola, 1968–1970; political officer in Naples, Italy, 1966–1968; desk officer for Brazil, 1964–1966; and a Foreign Service officer general in Recife, Brazil, 1962–1964.

Mr. de Vos graduated from Princeton University (B.A., 1960) and Johns Hopkins University (M.A., 1962). He was born December 24, 1938, in San Diego, CA. He is married and resides in Cabin John, MD.

Memorandum on Senior Executive Service Positions in the Federal Bureau of Investigation and the Drug Enforcement Administration
April 25, 1990

Memorandum for the Director of the Office of Management and Budget

Subject: Delegation of Authority to Allocate Senior Executive Service Positions to the Federal Bureau of Investigation and the Drug Enforcement Administration

By the authority vested in me as President by the Constitution and laws of the United States of America, including Section 5108 (a) of Title 5 and Section 301 of Title 3 of the United States Code, I hereby dele-

gate to the Director of the Office of Management and Budget the authority to establish and, from time to time, revise the maximum numbers of Senior Executive Service positions that may be placed in the Federal Bureau of Investigation and the Drug Enforcement Administration.

You are authorized and directed to publish this memorandum in the *Federal Register.*

GEORGE BUSH

Statement by Press Secretary Fitzwater on the President's Eye Examination
April 25, 1990

President Bush was examined today at Bethesda Naval Hospital by Dr. Harry Quigley of Johns Hopkins in Baltimore, MD, and Dr. Richard Brubaker of the Mayo Clinic in Rochester, MN, prominent experts on glaucoma.

During the President's last routine physical on April 12, an early glaucoma in his left eye was detected. Extensive visual tests at that time revealed no loss of any aspect of his visual acuity. Betagan eye drops were prescribed, 1 drop every 12 hours.

The examination today was requested by Dr. Burton Lee, the President's personal physician, to confirm the earlier diagnosis and assess the treatment strategy. "The physical findings were reviewed by the consultants and the diagnosis of exfoliation syndrome was confirmed with slightly increased intraocular pressure noted again in the left eye, one type of early glaucoma," Dr. Lee said. "Extensive testing of the eye, including detailed photographs, once again revealed no abnormalities and no visual loss. It was decided to stop the Betagan eye drops and follow him closely for now, on no treatment."

Remarks at the Welcoming Ceremony for President Carlos Andrés Pérez of Venezuela
April 26, 1990

President Bush. Welcome, all of you. It is my great honor to welcome the leader of one of South America's oldest democracies and one of Latin America's most respected statesmen, Carlos Andrés Pérez, President of Venezuela. And I am especially pleased that we welcome him today. He's just come here from Managua, just hours after attending the inauguration of Violeta Chamorro as the new President of Nicaragua—democratic Nicaragua. A great day for democracy and a great advance for the cause of freedom in our hemisphere.

President Pérez, on the morning after Nicaragua's recent elections, I remember calling you to discuss the stunning victory the Nicaraguan people had won at the ballot box. I called to confer with you because I knew how long and hard you personally had worked to bring democracy to Nicaragua. From the final days of the Somoza regime to your efforts on behalf of the Contadora group, and now to the moment of freedom's triumph, your deep personal commitment to the advance of democracy has never wavered.

Today another nation has joined freedom's ranks. For the people of all America, all the Americas, this is a time to celebrate. More than that, it's a time to dedicate ourselves to the day, perhaps not so distant, when all the people of this hemisphere live in freedom and democracy.

Mr. President, in just a few moments we'll move inside to the Oval Office and begin our consultations. But before we do, let me just say a few words about the new course your nation has chosen, about the changes your nation is making in its economic orientation, and about Venezuela's version of what I have heard described as "Perezstroika."

In the past year we've seen the thirst for freedom transform the world, and with that unquenchable desire for political freedom has come a realization that freedom is also the key to economic development. From Moscow to Managua, we've witnessed a shift from the teaching of Marx to the lessons of the free market. That shift parallels the one you've begun in Venezuela by stripping away the layers of state control that stifled development in favor of free market principles that experience proves provide fertile ground for growth.

I know this transition, with its difficult, short-term effects, has meant some pain for the people of Venezuela. But it is the kind of new beginning that will lay the foundations for future growth. It isn't an easy path, but we're convinced it is the only path to prosperity and better lives for all Venezuelans.

That's why I'm pleased to see that Venezuela and its main creditors have reached agreement under the Brady plan for dealing with debt burden, a plan that opens the way for opportunity and growth. With this agreement, Venezuela can take the next step forward toward economic vitality and growing prosperity for all its people.

That, Mr. President, is not only a testament to Venezuela energy and enterprise but, clearly, sir, to your vision and your courage. I am really looking forward to our talks. On behalf of all Americans, it is my great pleasure to meet with you here at the White House.

Once again, welcome, and may God bless the Republic of Venezuela.

President Pérez. Mr. President, Mrs. Bush, I come from a continent, Latin America, and from a nation, Venezuela, whose citizens strive to consolidate their economic and social progress and their democracy. It is to speak of these efforts that I have accepted your kind invitation, Mr. President. We will talk to each other with the same friendly sincerity that has become customary in us. I shall also meet leaders of American economic and political life, as well as outstanding representatives of your intellectual and cultural world. To all of them, we will want to express our joy at the new surge of democratization which is sweeping today's world and undoing in its wake the age of cold war and bipolarity.

We rejoice at the fact that time has come now for détente and a great joint effort aimed at facilitating economic development, social progress, equilibrium, and cooperation among nations. Latin America has much to contribute to today's world. Our continent wants to participate in shaping a world of peace—of peaceful neighborliness

and respect of human rights and the rights of the nature that is to be the heritage of our children—so as to set the foundations of a democracy and a quality of life consonant with the yearnings and possibilities of mankind.

Latin America has made progress. We have become free of dictatorships, and our democracies are being consolidated. Currently, all the countries of the region are waging their individual battles to achieve sound economies and make Latin America competitive. The Latin American continent is determined to modernize its structures, institutions, and relations, even in spite of the fact that our efforts do not always meet with proper understanding, cooperation, and encouragement.

In seeking solutions to conflicts, Latin American nations have devised their own ever more efficient mechanisms. Today Latin America is able to solve serious conflicts; and I am certain, Mr. President, that we have come to the end of all solutions that fuel the historic lack of understanding existing between our people. And in this regard, let me highlight some Latin American agreements for peace, democracy, and cooperation—such as the group of Contadora, the group of Rio, and Esquipulas II—which have set the marvelous examples of these past elections in Nicaragua.

And I come here today to Washington directly from Managua, where I attended the inauguration of a government freely elected by the people. The San José agreement is another example of the same thing. And our present economic difficulties have not prevented us from disbursing for the sake of solidarity over $3 billion as our contribution to peace and democracy. We feel full confidence in the coming new age of peace and solidarity. We trust that we will not go back to political, military, economic, and trade conditions that will place us again on an unequal footing in a world that is becoming ever more interdependent and resistant to any subservience of either the citizens of a nation to any party or sect, or some nations to others, based on their political or military might.

We want our efforts in favor of the region's peace, its democratic revival, its economic recovery, and its social harmony to be matched with support, equitable cooperation, and uniform and balanced treatment for our nations. In such a framework, we will be able to progress and contribute to the establishment of a true hemispheric community, thus bridging our traditional mutual lack of understanding, our nonencounter as I like to call it.

We must work together to solve the problems of our continent, and we will be able to do it much more successfully if we recognize the solid friendship that binds us. Between your country and mine, there is a common and complimentary interest concerning production and consumption of energy resources. We obviously need to exchange views on how to maintain an ade-

quate strategic production potential in this hemisphere. This is the hope we all have. And as your great poet Carl Sandburg said when he compared our need of cooperation to an echo that resounds further and further, we also say we have to travel further, much further, much beyond what we have achieved. And this is why I have come to meet your wonderful people and to talk to the President and other representatives of this immense, great, and admirable nation.

Note: President Bush spoke at 10:13 a.m. at the South Portico of the White House, where President Pérez was accorded a formal welcome with full military honors. President Pérez spoke in Spanish, and his remarks were translated by an interpreter.

Message to the Congress Transmitting Amendments to the China-United States Fishing Agreement
April 26, 1990

To the Congress of the United States:

In accordance with the Magnuson Fishery Conservation and Management Act of 1976 (Public Law 94–265; 16 U.S.C. 1801 *et seq.*), I transmit herewith an agreement between the Government of the United States of America and the Government of the People's Republic of China amending and extending the 1985 Agreement Concerning Fisheries off the Coasts of the United States, which was effected by exchange of notes at Washington, March 14 and 22, 1990. This agreement extends the 1985 agreement for an additional 2 years until July 1, 1992, and

amends the port access procedures contained in the 1985 agreement. The exchange of notes, together with the present agreement, constitute a governing international fishery agreement within the meaning of section 201(c) of the act.

Because of the importance of our fisheries relations with the People's Republic of China, I urge that the Congress give favorable consideration to this agreement.

GEORGE BUSH

The White House,
April 26, 1990.

Remarks at a White House Briefing for Conservative Leaders
April 26, 1990

Did I interrupt Porter? And if so—well, to Roger, my thanks if I did, and may I say hello to Doug Weed and, of course, the people that herded this outstanding group together: Jerry Falwell, Ed Prince, Mike Valerio. But in any event, I'm delighted to see

you all.

With all the traveling that I'm doing, it's a little different for me to be making an appearance so close to the White House. I was just talking to Barbara. She says, "You spend more time on the road than Charles

Kuralt." [*Laughter*]

This morning, I was talking about this, and I said, I'm looking forward this afternoon to going over and spending some time with friends, and indeed with people who were very instrumental in helping me get to be President at perhaps the most fascinating time in history, or among the most fascinating, certainly, I think, since World War II.

I'm delighted to be with a group for whom "conservatism" is not a catchword. As the past two decades show, it's a philosophy to which most Americans subscribe, and I think that's still very true across the country. Conservatives believe in Yankee ingenuity. I recall how a mother once told her son, "I have a pretty good idea that you skipped your piano lesson and played baseball." The son said he hadn't, and the mother said, "Are you sure?" And the son said, "Yes, I have a fish to prove it." [*Laughter*]

Conservatives also believe in science and technology. The more I know about the Hubble telescope, the more impressed I am. So powerful that it'll help us, I'm told, understand the black holes. What I don't understand is why anyone would want to know more about the liberal philosophy.

Conservatives share a vision. I know some reporters say I don't have a vision—sorry, I don't see it. [*Laughter*] Instead, I see a vision—I really do see a vision—as sweeping as our heritage: an America of prosperity, a world of real peace. And the question is how do we ensure that vision for our generation? As you get a little older, you think even more about the kids.

For an answer, recall how 150 years ago de Tocqueville envisioned a future that would open before us. Its possibilities were infinite, he wrote, because of America's new model, this paradigm of government. A democracy based on a free market unleashing the full energy of the human heart and mind. And that government arose from perhaps the ultimate exercise in returning power to people: the American Revolution.

Now, two centuries later, when old centralized bureaucratic systems are crumbling, the time has come for yet another paradigm; a form of government which, like the spirit of '76, gives power back to

localities and States and, most important, to the people; a model which rejects the view that progress is measured in money spent and bureaucracies built.

The first principle in our new paradigm is that as market forces grow stronger our world becomes smaller. Put another way, we must be competitive to ensure economic growth. So, I'd like to take this opportunity to urge the Congress once again—and I'm going to keep on urging this—that they pass our capital gains tax cut, spurring investment and thus creating jobs. We don't want government to spend more: we want private enterprise to thrive so that people will have more money to save, to invest, and to spend. To most Americans, I feel, that's a good idea.

As a second principle of our new paradigm—the freedom to choose. We want to reduce what government should do and increase what people can do. And so, I support a constitutional amendment, will continue to support it, restoring voluntary prayer. We need the faith of our fathers back in our schools. I haven't been President very long, but the longer I am in this job, the more strongly I feel about that.

A choice also means that parents should decide which public school is best for their kids. So, we have proposed—what many of you have been helpful to us on this—the Education Excellence Act of 1990 to provide incentives for these magnet school programs. Many States are trying out policies based on choice and finding out they work.

In this one, I want to give credit. It isn't just my party, the Republicans; it's some of the Democratic Governors are out front, way out front, on this particular theory—choice. Some only think that Big Brother can revive education, but I believe that excellence comes from higher standards, a greater accountability, and more freedom to move within a school system. And if you agree—I don't want this many influential people to go untapped or arms untwisted—if you agree with me, I would strongly solicit your help in convincing Congress that the time for this is now.

That leads me to the third principle in the new paradigm—that means the means to choose. We must empower disadvantaged Americans. So, we've unveiled a program to help the poor run or, better yet, own their public housing units. And we support a child-care tax credit for low-income working parents that enable them to care for their kids in the manner they choose. I will not see the option of religious-based child care restricted or eliminated. We're going to fight against that.

I know many liberals disagree with what I've just said and the philosophy behind it. But that's why last month the House Democratic leadership passed a bill that would cost nearly $30 billion, three times our original proposal, and force, compel, many States to change their rules. In effect, it would produce national child-care standards intended to replace local standards that meet local needs and put in place a lot more unnecessary paperwork.

Conservatives know that we don't need this bureaucracy. It would merely prove what Will Rogers once said: "Half of America does nothing but prepare propaganda for the other half to read." [*Laughter*] So, let's expand the horizons of our kids, not the budget of the bureaucracy, and through tax incentives give families the help that they need to solve their child-care problems themselves.

Next comes the fourth principle of this new paradigm: decentralization. In America, this means dispersing authority to the level closest to the source of authority—the people. Places such as Peru, for example— Hernando de Soto, the brilliant Peruvian economist, found that without any centralized bureaucratic direction the ordinary streetside entrepreneurs of Lima are producing wealth on a scale that rivals the economy officially approved by the state bureaucracy. Elsewhere in the world, decentralization has come about through nothing less than the triumph of democracy over bureaucracy.

Conservatives know that a strong defense has and will continue to help all people secure the right to think and dream and worship as they please. In Lithuania—as in Czechoslovakia and Nicaragua, Budapest, Berlin—the words of Thomas Dewey ring true: You can't beat down ideas with a club. Today freedom is on the march and will not be denied.

The fifth and final principle of the new paradigm is what I referred to earlier: We want what works. Our principles, conservative principles, were always right. And now the whole world can see that what's right is also what works. As I've said many times before, and I don't say it with arrogance, we know what works—freedom works. We are not going to let discredited ideologies block the progress of our principles. You can ask anyone in Poland or Panama: Tyranny doesn't work; freedom does.

At home, we also want what works. So, we've reached agreement with the Senate in the first rewrite of the Clean Air Act in over a decade. I call on the House to respond soon and respond responsibly. This one is difficult because I think we are all committed to leaving the Earth a little better than we found it, and yet we've got to do it in a balanced way—forward-looking, forward-leaning. But I will not accept legislation that needlessly throws a lot of Americans out of work because of lack of scientific data. I'm going to hold that line, and I would appeal for your help in urging the Congress to keep reality in mind as we go about getting ourselves out front on the cutting edge of environmental protection. I'm determined to be both a person who protects the environment and one who protects the rights of Americans to have jobs. It isn't easy, but I'm convinced that it can be done.

We've unveiled a comprehensive strategy to free America of crime and drugs. A lot of people in this room have given our planners and Roger and his able team—because of respects, you've worked very closely with Bill Bennett—to help us with this comprehensive strategy to free America of crime and drugs. We're asking Congress to expand the death penalty for drug kingpins. We need to toughen the crime laws at the State level, just as we are in Washington. My vision for the nineties is an America where punishment is at least as tough as the crime.

Just yesterday, we sent up to the Congress a three-part budget reform package that proposes an amendment to the Constitution—and I campaigned on this, so there's no surprise—to provide a line-item veto. We endorsed the Legislative Line-Item

Veto Act to strengthen the President's rescission authority and endorse a balanced budget amendment.

The time has come to enact into law these important changes. I sent up to the Congress a special piece of legislation to help Nicaragua and to help Panama. I think we have a real commitment to seeing the success of these fragile new democracies. Before it leaves the House of Representatives, billions—literally billions, plural—of spending is added to this very special legislation. I think I need the authority to make the tough decision on spending. Nobody likes to have to say no to constituents or to interests around the country, but if the Congress continues to demonstrate that they can't do it, only the President can.

So, I'd love to have your support on this package on the line-item veto, the legislative line-item veto that will strengthen the President's rescission authority; and then, of course, our commitment to this balanced budget concept. This vision, if you will, is one that I think most conservatives support. It's a vision of limited government, but unlimited opportunity—a vision to protect the family, empower the poor, and reward creativity.

I like bass fishing. There's a young bass fisherman who is a national champion, a guy named Ricky Clune. Texans will know his name. He's from Montgomery, Texas. One time I was down in Arkansas and saw him win—or, at the weigh-in—they did it— 4,000 or 5,000 people, as these bass boats were driven into the coliseum there. I couldn't believe this—4,000 or 5,000 watching people weigh fish there in the middle— but Ricky Clune, when he got up to speak, said this: "I learned to fish following my dad down the creeks in my underpants," he said, "down the creeks of Oklahoma." And then he said this: "Isn't it great to live in a country with no limits?"

I've thought about that a great deal. What we're talking about here in this con-

servative philosophy is unlimited opportunity—a vision to protect the family, empower the poor, and reward creativity. This new paradigm can fulfill it. I really would ask for your support to achieve promise, not empty promises: lifting people up, helping keep the government bureaucracies at all levels under control and, as conservatives, reject the hand of big government in favor of a Thousand Points of Light, joining hands and linking hearts.

You know, when we started talking about a Thousand Points of Light, there was a few snickers out there. I had to keep defining what I meant. But I think people understand this. I think Americans—well, since de Tocqueville took a look at America— understand it. It's real, one American wanting to help another. So, I am going to continue to say that any definition of a successful life must be the involvement in the lives of others, one American helping another. That, I think, is a fundamental part of my concept of how we can do an awful lot more to help people who are desperately in need of help in our country.

So, this is my vision—yours, I think. What a dream: to enrich America and help us to continue to lead, help us to enrich the world. I am really pleased you were here. Thanks for the privilege of addressing you. And might I say, God bless the United States of America. Thank you all very much.

Note: The President spoke at 1:35 p.m. in Room 450 of the Old Executive Office Building. In his opening remarks, he referred to Roger B. Porter, Assistant to the President for Economic and Domestic Policy; Douglas Weed, Special Assistant to the President for Public Liaison; evangelist Jerry Falwell; Edward Prince, president of Prince Corp.; and Michael Valerio, chairman of the board of Papa Tino's of America, Inc.

Nomination of General Michael J. Dugan To Be Chief of Staff of the Air Force
April 26, 1990

The President today announced his intention to nominate Gen. Michael J. Dugan, United States Air Force, to be Chief of Staff of the Air Force. He would succeed Gen. Larry D. Welch, whose term expires June 30, 1990.

General Dugan is presently serving as commander, Allied Air Forces Central Europe; commander in chief, United States Air Forces in Europe; and Air Force component commander, United States European Command. General Dugan is married and has six children. He was born February 22, 1937, in Albany, NY.

Letter to Congressional Leaders on Modifications of the Generalized System of Preferences
April 26, 1990

Dear Mr. Speaker: (Dear Mr. President:)

I am writing concerning the Generalized System of Preferences (GSP) and six current beneficiary developing countries. The GSP program is authorized by the Trade Act of 1974, as amended ("the 1974 Act").

I intend to suspend indefinitely Liberia from its status as a GSP beneficiary for failure to comply with section 502(b)(7) of the 1974 Act concerning internationally recognized worker rights. In addition, I intend to designate current beneficiaries Kiribati, Mauritania, Mozambique, Tuvalu, and Vanuatu as least-developed beneficiary developing countries, in accordance with section 504(c)(6) of the 1974 Act.

My decisions will take place at least 60 days from the date of this letter.

Sincerely,

GEORGE BUSH

Note: Identical letters were sent to Thomas S. Foley, Speaker of the House of Representatives, and Dan Quayle, President of the Senate. The letter was released by the Office of the Press Secretary on April 27.

Memorandum on Modifications of the Generalized System of Preferences
April 26, 1990

Memorandum for the United States Trade Representative

Subject: Actions Concerning the Generalized System of Preferences

Pursuant to subsections 502(b)(4) and 502(b)(7) and section 504 of the Trade Act of 1974, as amended (the 1974 Act) (19 U.S.C. 2462(b)(4), 2462(b)(7), and 2464), the President is authorized to make determinations concerning the alleged expropriation without compensation by a beneficiary developing country, to make findings concerning whether steps have been taken or are being taken by certain beneficiary developing countries to afford internationally recognized worker rights to workers in such countries, and to modify the application of duty-free treatment under the Generalized System of Preferences (GSP) currently being afforded to such beneficiary developing countries as a result of my determinations.

Specifically, after considering private sector requests for a review of the alleged violation by Costa Rica and Uruguay of the expropriation provisions of subsection 502(b)(4) of the 1974 Act, I have decided to terminate the reviews of Costa Rica and Uruguay without prejudice, noting that modification of GSP eligibility is not warranted at this time.

Second, after considering various private sector requests for a review of whether or not certain beneficiary developing countries have taken or are taking steps to afford internationally recognized worker rights (as defined in subsection 502(a)(4) of the 1974 Act) to workers in such countries, and in accordance with subsection 502(b)(7) of the 1974 Act, I have determined that Indonesia and Thailand have taken or are taking steps to afford internationally recognized worker rights, and I have determined that Liberia has not taken and is not taking steps to afford such internationally recognized rights. Therefore, I am notifying the Congress of my intention to suspend the GSP eligibility of Liberia. Finally, I have determined to continue to review the status of such worker rights in Benin, the Dominican Republic, Haiti, Nepal, and Syria.

Further, pursuant to section 504 of the 1974 Act, after considering various requests for a waiver of the application of section 504(c) of the 1974 Act (19 U.S.C. 2464(c)) with respect to certain eligible articles, I have determined to modify the application of duty-free treatment under the GSP currently being afforded to certain articles and to certain beneficiary developing countries.

Specifically, I have determined, pursuant to subsection 504(d)(1) of the 1974 Act (19 U.S.C. 2464(d)(1)), that the limitation provided for in subsection 504(c)(1)(B) of the 1974 Act should not apply with respect to certain eligible articles because no like or directly competitive article was produced in the United States on January 3, 1985. Such articles are enumerated in the list of Harmonized Tariff Schedule of the United States (HTS) subheadings in Annex A.

Pursuant to subsection 504(c)(3) of the 1974 Act, I have also determined to: 1) waive the application of section 504(c) of the 1974 Act with respect to certain eligible articles from certain beneficiary developing countries; and 2) waive the application of subsection 504(c)(2)(B) of the 1974 Act with respect to certain eligible articles from certain beneficiary developing countries. I have received the advice of the United States International Trade Commission on whether any industries in the United States are likely to be adversely affected by such waivers, and I have determined, based on that advice and on the considerations described in sections 501 and 502(c) of the 1974 Act (19 U.S.C. 2461 and 2462(c)), that such waivers are in the national economic interest of the United States. The waivers of section 504(c) of the 1974 Act apply to the eligible articles in the HTS subheadings and the beneficiary developing countries opposite such HTS subheadings enumerated in Annex B. The waivers of subsection 504(c)(2)(B) of the 1974 Act apply to the eligible articles in the HTS subheadings and the beneficiary developing countries opposite such HTS subheadings enumerated in Annex C.

These determinations shall be published in the *Federal Register*.

GEORGE BUSH

[Filed with the Office of the Federal Register, 12:19 p.m., April 30, 1990]

Note: The memorandum was released by the Office of the Press Secretary on April 27.

Statement on International Trade
April 27, 1990

After extensive discussions with Ambassador Hills, Secretary Brady, and the members of my Economic Policy Council (EPC) on the Super 301 provisions of the Omnibus Trade and Competitiveness Act of 1988, I have directed Ambassador Hills to give her highest priority to bringing the Uruguay round of multilateral trade negotiations to a timely and successful conclusion in December of this year. I believe that multilateral negotiations in GATT are the most promising route for creating new opportunities for American industry and agriculture and strengthening the global trading system.

Promoting a vibrant, open trading relationship with Japan remains a key trade priority of the administration. I have carefully reviewed with the EPC the recent progress in negotiations with Japan. Since my meeting with Prime Minister Kaifu in March, Japan has moved to address our concerns in the Structural Impediments Initiative (SII) and in bilateral negotiations involving supercomputers, satellites, and wood products. The interim SII report made a promising start toward reducing structural barriers that contribute to bilateral trade imbalances.

I am not under any illusion that the SII interim report will lead to an immediate improvement in the trade balance with Japan or an end to bilateral trade disputes. When two nations like the United States and Japan share dynamic economies, a commitment to excellence, and strong trading traditions, some commercial differences are inevitable. Nevertheless, I believe that Prime Minister Kaifu and the Japanese political leadership share my commitment to ensuring that trade strengthens rather than undermines the friendship between our nations.

Accordingly, I look forward to substantial progress with Japan in the final SII report in July and on a variety of other trade issues. I will work closely with the Congress to implement the U.S. side of the SII, particularly in the areas of savings, education, and budgetary reform.

I have directed our U.S. negotiators to seek agreement with their Japanese counterparts on a joint mechanism to monitor the implementation of SII in both nations and consider the need for further actions. This mechanism should include regular reports on actions and results.

Because last year's Super 301 investigations on India remain unresolved, I have continued the identification of India as a trade liberalization priority. I have decided not to identify any new priority countries or practices under Super 301.

Let there be no mistake. This administration is committed to free and fair trade. We want open markets and fair treatment for our products, services, investment, and ideas. We will move forward in the Uruguay round and, as appropriate, under section 301 to remove foreign barriers to American goods. I am also directing Ambassador Hills to expand her semiannual report on section 301 to review both the status of existing section 301 investigations and related initiatives in important markets such as Japan.

I have directed Ambassador Hills immediately to brief the Congress on the reasons for my decision today.

Remarks at a White House Briefing for the American Legislative Exchange Council
April 27, 1990

The President. Such enthusiasm for Sununu finishing—it's wonderful. [*Laughter*] Look, I'm just delighted to be back with this most distinguished group.

Let me say, having interrupted our Chief of Staff, how fortunate I am to have someone as Chief of Staff here in the White House who did—as Sam Rayburn often talked about—did run for sheriff. Remember what Rayburn said? He said: "Well, that guy's trouble. He never ran," he said, "never ran for sheriff." And what he really meant is didn't have a feel for the people. And John not only ran successfully for Governor of his great State but he understands and keeps reminding me of the philosophical underpinnings of our administration: decentralization and federalism, which I want to mention to you today about. And so, I am very, very pleased that he was over here, and I have great confidence in him and in Roger Porter, as well, who's up here, who handles so many of our—have you already unloaded on these guys?

Mr. Porter. No, I'm following.

The President. Following? [*Laughter*] And Roger has respect on the Hill that really is unparalleled in terms of the job that he fills and in previous administrations. And so, I'm very, very lucky.

I also have another person over here that ran for sheriff. She was the speaker—as many of you know—of her legislature. And that brings another dimension to this outreach that we're trying to do, because we learn from the input we get from people coming in here. The danger is isolation. And I know some think I'm a little frenetic in my activities, but when you get out, even if it's just driving as we did to a food bank a couple of days ago, you get a feel for what's on people's minds and what works and what we ought to try to do better. So, I'm delighted you're here in that spirit.

I want to thank Frank Messersmith, who came out and handed me a letter and told me of the support that you all are giving us, which I've already heard about, in the field of education. I want to congratulate Ellen, who's soon to become your new president—Ellen Sauerbrey. And it's also good to see Sam Brunelli, Ron Scheberle, and so many other familiar faces out there in the back benches and all across this room.

You know, before I get into the substance here, let me just talk about something that is important to America and to every State, and that is the completion of this U.S. census. Today Census Bureau workers are beginning to visit all addresses from which census forms have not been received, a mammoth undertaking. I simply want to take this opportunity to urge every American who has not returned the census form to do so, to stand up and be counted.

Now, it's great to be back among so many leaders from the States, those of you who belong to ALEC, the American Legislative Exchange Council, more than 2,300 strong. As State leaders, in alliance with leaders from the business community, you're proving every day what I mentioned at the beginning: that the government closest to the people is truly the government of the people. We've seen the wisdom of federalism vindicated over and over again.

In the sixties—just think back—the prevailing belief was that big problems required big government solutions. And of course, this country did face very real, big problems—private heartaches that, taken together, afflicted all of America. But our pockets were often deeper than our thinking.

Take the War on Poverty as a prime example. This was a unilateral war in which the Federal Government sought no allies and followed only one strategy. And we soon learned what the strategy lacked: It lacked an understanding of the problems, it lacked flexibility, and often it simply lacked programs that worked. And so, we learned a very hard lesson. And this wasn't just Democrat or Republican; it was across the aisle, across the board, across—to some degree, back then—even philosophical differences. But we learned, and good intentions can go astray. And if the Federal Government neglects State and local government, it's bound to.

So, let me say it plain and simple: I am a believer in the Jeffersonian tradition. I believe that innovation springs from these 50 laboratories of democracy. And I believe in the inherent wisdom and leadership of the States.

Federalism must be a dynamic partnership if we're to end that age-old affliction of mankind: poverty—poverty of knowledge and skills, poverty of opportunity, poverty of hope. We're going to need such a partnership if we're to meet new missions to keep expanding opportunity in this field that we were just talking about—improving education, to implement a national transportation strategy, and to fight the scourge of illegal drug use.

Our partnership must begin with an accurate account of the depth and scope of our needs that can only begin with the U.S. census, a project that needs your involvement. Again, at this moment these census workers are beginning to visit all addresses from which they haven't come back in. And we really need to get moving on this, because census data will help you make important decisions for the States. And it really fits into this theme of decentralization, part of the decentralization of government, of putting our trust where it belongs: with the people.

So, it's not enough to seek a dynamic partnership between Washington and Austin, Atlanta, and Sacramento. We must turn to our families, our schools, our small businesses; and we must often seek the achievement of public goals through private means and individual action, individual empowerment. Our partnership must include everyone if we're to fulfill our agenda—an agenda that is progrowth, profamily, and profreedom. We need this partnership to keep America growing. And that's why Congress must pass a cut in the capital gains tax this year.

For America to be competitive, we need to invest money in productive uses, generating new jobs, generating opportunities for all. We also need the partnership I referred to a second ago to keep America moving, to

implement a national transportation strategy for the 21st century. You understand that leadership must begin with those closest to our transportation problems: the States. And you understand that the States deserve a greater say in how our transportation dollars are spent. And so, I'm asking you to help others understand that our transportation strategy is, indeed, the road to the future.

And as you often stress, we also need to protect the bedrock institution of American life: the family. We are not yet certain what kind of child-care legislation this Congress will pass. But if Congress stamps out the power of the parents to choose family or church-affiliated child care, I will give that legislation a stamp of my own: I will give it the veto stamp because I am not going to accept highly centralized standards and standards that rule out participation of local churches or local family groups in solving this national problem.

We also want to bring these same principles of choice and flexibility to the way in which we educate our kids. I'll leave it to Roger Porter, who is perfectly capable—far better than I, actually—to brief you on the education goals, on our education summit, all that we can do working together. But just let me say that as I work with the Governors to bring renewed excellence to American education, I'm also looking for advice and support and, certainly, leadership. And when it comes to leadership, your federation is already supporting open enrollment plans to give parents choice in selecting their schools; alternative certification to let the talented share their knowledge; and finally, merit pay with accountability for all. So, we're not just thinking along the same lines; we're working to achieve the same goals in education.

Your federation also calls itself—and I think properly so—profreedom. What does this mean? It means working at the Federal and State levels to develop ways to liberate people from dependency on government, not bind them to it, one generation after another. And it can only mean freedom from drugs. I commend your Substance Abuse Task Force for doing an excellent job in devising a set of tough, realistic recommendations that complements and expands our National Drug Strategy, our national effort.

And finally, Americans must be free from fear. When honest working people are afraid to go to the corner grocery store or to walk home from the bus at night, then fear of crime has stolen our most precious possession—our liberty. And it is to protect this freedom and the freedom to safely walk the streets that we offered up a good crime package. I sent this crime package last year to the Hill. Congress has, to its credit, approved new prison space and more Federal law enforcement officers. But too much work remains unfinished on the rest of this crime package, the portion that concerns violent crime. And once again, I call on Congress to pass laws at least as tough as the criminals we convict.

Crime and illegal drug use, transportation, education—as we near the end of the century, these challenges that confront our nation sometimes seem bigger than our ability to solve them. And they are if we act

only as partisan Democrats or partisan Republicans, as parochial members of a region or a faction or an interest group. But by working together as Americans, I still feel that we can lick any problem, no matter how big, how complex, or how deeply rooted it may be. That's why I value our partnership, our dynamic partnership, and look forward to working with you in the years ahead.

Thank you for the tremendous support that you have given our administration, and I hope that you will continue. We are grateful to you. Thanks for coming our way, and God bless you all.

Note: The President spoke at 10:59 a.m. in Room 450 of the Old Executive Office Building. In his opening remarks, he referred to John H. Sununu, Chief of Staff to the President; Roger B. Porter, Assistant to the President for Economic and Domestic Policy; and Frank S. Messersmith, Sam Brunelli, and Ronald Scheberle, president, executive director, and chairman of the business sector of the council.

Remarks at the Presentation Ceremony for the President's Volunteer Action Awards
April 27, 1990

Welcome, everybody. Please be seated. Well, welcome all. I'm just delighted to be with you. And I was looking around because I'm told that Senator Durenberger was going to be here—I don't quite spot him. But in any event, I'm delighted that you all are here. Is Governor Kean here? There he is, way back there, and Deb—I want to say hello to the former Governor of New Jersey, who I was told was going to be here—uncharacteristically, in the back row, but nevertheless—[*laughter*]—welcome to the White House.

The famous broadcaster you all know, Paul Harvey, tells a story of a man named Vincent who lived in southern Belgium. And he was a very poor man who lived in a simple hut, dressed in an old coat, trousers made of sacking cloth. But Vincent em-

bodied the spirit of helping others. For he knew that although he had very few possessions, he still had a great gift to give. When a mining disaster struck, many villagers injured, no one fought harder to save them than Vincent did. And for days on end he cared for the injured and helped feed and clothe the needy. And years later Vincent Van Gogh, today one of the world's beloved masters, painted his famous "Starry Night." Though 100 years have passed since he put brush to canvas and created a masterpiece, the value of serving others has not changed.

I've often said that from now on any definition of a successful life must include serving others. The members of our Cabinet are taking the lead in their departments and in their trips around the country, and I'm grateful to all of them. I know that two are with us today—Secretary Lujan and Secretary Mosbacher—and if others are, I'm sorry I can't spot you right now. But we owe them a vote of gratitude for the way they're carrying this message as well.

Today it's my special honor to present the President's Volunteer Action Awards to 19 of America's Thousand Points of Light who embody that definition of success. Let me just tell you about a few of them and then we'll get on with the ceremony. There's Clarence Wilson of St. Louis, a 17-year-old high school student who watched the neighborhood where he grew up give way to crime, drug dealing, and condemned housing. And then a year ago, personal tragedy struck: a fire destroyed his home and killed his mom, his cousin, and his aunt. He decided it wasn't just a time to mourn; it was a time for action. And he began a neighborhood watch program, set up a citizens team to paint over the graffiti and encourage neighbors to cooperate with police to rid the community of drugs. Clarence, you are an outstanding example to the young people of this country. And I hope every single one of them will follow your example.

Providence House is a network of six residential facilities in New Rochelle, New York, that provide a home and a haven to women and children in crisis situations. Unfortunately, too many facilities serving women in trouble do not accept their children. Providence House is different, opening its doors to mothers and children, giving them the security they need. One of the homes in the Providence House network is creatively called My Mother's House. And it gives shelter to the children of incarcerated women, allowing them to tell their friends, truthfully, I live at My Mother's House with my mother's friends. [*Laughter*] Another one of the homes is a homeless shelter providing family and job counseling. Over 100 concerned volunteers are involved in the Providence House program. We appreciate your dedication to making a better life for these men and women.

And then there's a story—the next one. Henry Gaskins, a supervisor at the Library of Congress, who holds a doctor's degree, a doctorate in education, and his wife Mary Ann who works at NASA and also has an education degree. And they began a youth club several years ago, but soon decided that young people in the inner city needed more than just a place to go. What began as afterschool recreation soon became afterschool workshops on education and jobs, so these young people could really go places. The Gaskins began tutoring young black children for free, 6 days a week in their own home. The Freedom Youth Academy, as the kids themselves named it, soon became a reality. And now over 80 percent of the academy students, from kindergarten to 12th grade, have earned academic distinction. In fact, the high school students' SAT [Scholastic Aptitude Test] scores have improved from anywhere from 50 to 360 points, with many students going on to the Nation's very top schools. Mr. and Mrs. Gaskins, you've done so much for these young people, and we are very grateful to you.

And among the many businesses pitching in across America is the Adolf Coors Company. Nearly half the total Coors work force in the State of Colorado, about 4,000 company employees and retirees, have banded together to donate approximately 35,000 hours of service to 116 separate projects in their communities. They've participated in winter clothing drives, food drives, community health checkups, low-income housing renovations, recycling programs, special olympics. You name it, all across the board, they've done it. Must be something in the water out there, but nevertheless—[*laughter*]—it sounds grueling, 35,000 hours, but what a wonderful example. The enthusiasm that these employees have for community service really is remarkable. And every company in America should follow that lead. To all the Coors employees: Thank you for opening your hearts to your communities.

Every award recipient here today really has an amazing story. For today's winners know that only in serving others do we find the fulfillment that everyone is seeking in life. Listen to every one of the men and women here with us today, and every one will tell you that serving others enriches their own lives at least as much as it enriches the lives of those that they touch.

Each of these Americans holds the light of humanity in their hearts. And, like a candle in a steady hand, they share that light and inspire commitment in so many others. There is a bright path of goodness and love through the dark night of sadness and despair. I thank you, all of you, for what you've done. And God bless each and every one of you.

Now, Barbara and I will present the 1990 President's Volunteer Action Awards with the help of two other very special people who've devoted so much of their time and talent to helping others—Jane Kenny, the head of ACTION; and my good friend, Governor George Romney, the Chairman of VOLUNTEER: the National Center. So, could I ask you all to come forward, and we will begin.

[At this point, the awards were presented.]

The President. Well, I am also pleased to announce that Mrs. Madrid is this administration's second recipient of an award named for a great President, a good friend, the originator of the President's Volunteer Action Awards—the Ronald Reagan Award for Volunteer Excellence. This special award was created to honor the individual whose contribution to voluntarism is greatest among the winners of the President's Volunteer Action Awards. Awfully difficult choice, but, Mrs. Madrid, we'd like to present you the Ronald Reagan Award. To you, and to all of you, our warmest congratulations. And again thank you all for coming.

Note: The President spoke at 12:10 p.m. in the East Room at the White House. In his opening remarks, he referred to Debra Anderson, Deputy Assistant to the President and Director of the Office of Intergovernmental Affairs.

Designation of Edward E. Allison as Vice Chairman of the Board of Directors of the Pennsylvania Avenue Development Corporation
April 27, 1990

The President today designated Edward E. Allison as Vice Chairman of the Board of Directors of the Pennsylvania Avenue Development Corporation. He would succeed Arthur A. Fletcher.

Currently Mr. Allison serves as a partner with the law firm of McAuliffe, Kelly, Raffaelli and Siemens in Washington, DC. Prior to this, he served as an associate with Heron, Burchette, Ruckert and Rothwell in Washington, DC; senior adviser in the 1988 George Bush for President campaign; ad-

ministrative assistant to Senator and General Chairman of the Republican Party Paul Laxalt; and press secretary and administrative assistance for Senator Laxalt.

Mr. Allison received a bachelor of arts degree and a master of arts degree from the University of Nevada. He was born January 9, 1940, in Denver, CO. Mr. Allison served in the Army National Guard and the Air National Guard. He is married, has two children, and resides in Great Falls, VA.

Remarks to Participants in the Rally for Life
April 28, 1990

Well, thank you, Henry Hyde. Thank you for the introduction, and thank you, as well, for your commitment to life. Incidentally, this magnificent rally looks very, very good on television. How do I know? Because I've seen some of it.

I want to pay my respects to our able Vice President, Dan Quayle—thank him for his commitment—to other Members of Congress that are there, to Dr. Willke, to Dr. Dobson, and a special greeting to my friend—Your Eminences Cardinal O'Connor and Cardinal Hickey and others that might be in attendance.

I am very pleased to have this opportunity to express to you my deeply held views about abortion on demand. In January of this year, I addressed the March for Life on this very issue, and I said then and reaffirm now that your presence on The Mall today reminds all of us in government that Americans from all walks of life are committed to preserving the sanctity and dignity of human life. Like you, I realize that the widespread prevalence of abortion in America is a tragedy not only in terms of lives destroyed but because it so fundamentally contradicts the values that we as a nation hold dear. When I look at adopted children, I give thanks that their parents chose life.

Today, as a nation of faith and compassion, our mission must be to help more and more Americans make the right choice—the choice for life. One day your lifesaving message will have reached and influenced every American. Until then, continue to work for the day when respect for human life is sacrosanct and beyond question. I know from your devotion and selflessness that this day cannot be far away.

God bless you, and God bless life. Thank you very, very much.

Note: The President spoke at 2:20 p.m. by telephone to the rally site from the Oval Office at the White House. Participants had gathered on The Mall to affirm their commitment to outlaw abortion and their support of last year's Supreme Court decision opening the way for States to restrict abortions. In his remarks, the President referred to Representative Henry Hyde; John C. Willke, president of the National Right to Life Committee; James Dobson, president of Focus on the Family; James Cardinal Hickey, Roman Catholic Archbishop of Washington; and John Cardinal O'Connor, Roman Catholic Archbishop of New York.

Remarks at the Annual Meeting of the United States Chamber of Commerce
April 30, 1990

Thank you very, very much, John. And what do you think about that Marine Corps Band, led by Colonel Bourgeois? Aren't they first class? Thank you, ladies and gentlemen, very much. And it's always a pleasure to meet with this high-powered group. I want to pay my respects once again to Dick Lesher, the president of the chamber; to salute your outgoing chairman, John Clendenin, for the leadership that he's shown and the sacrifice that he's given over the past year; and then to salute your incoming chairman, James Baker. Not a Cabinet shakeup—[*laughter*]—I'm talking about James K. Baker, who will carry the chamber's fine tradition forward into this new decade.

And finally, let me welcome our special guests: all these Washington-area schoolchildren, right here in front. I know that you all have been looking forward to today for a long time. And after all, it's not every day that you get out of math and spelling. [*Laughter*] And I know it won't be easy to understand all the things we're talking about this morning, but there's one thing that I'm sure you can understand: You're here because you're important, because when you grow up you might just run your own business, like the people here. Or maybe you'll even run for President of the United States. It may be hard to believe, but I was once a second-grader just like you are now. [*Laughter*] So, today I want to challenge all of you to keep working hard in school. Do your very best, and don't be afraid to reach for your dreams.

And I want to challenge the Chamber of Commerce as well—that's all the rest of you who are past the second grade out there.

583

[*Laughter*] All of you know that the Governors and I have agreed on a set of national education goals, goals we must meet by the year 2000, the year these second-graders here graduate. And I'm delighted at all the Chamber of Commerce is doing to advance this great cause of excellence in education, but today I challenge you to get involved in every school and community across America. Help us make that classroom a place where miracles happen.

And before I go any further, I want to thank the chamber for its support on an issue essential to our nation's economic future. Last week I sent to the Congress a three-point plan for budget reform: one, supporting the Legislative Line-Item Veto Act; two, proposing an amendment to the Constitution to provide a Presidential line-item veto; and three, a balanced budget amendment. The chamber, together with other organizations in the Coalition for Fiscal Responsibility, has been out there on the front lines of the battle for budget reform; and I ask you now to push hard for this three-point plan. The time has come to put our fiscal house in order.

And let me say a few words about my administration's trade strategy. First, success in the Uruguay round trade talks is my top trade priority. The GATT needs strengthening. It doesn't cover services, investment, or intellectual property rights. Its rules on agricultural trade are far too weak, creating counterproductive pressures to subsidize farm exports. And we've got to strengthen GATT as a matter of principle: as a sign to the emerging democracies in Eastern Europe and in this hemisphere that free trade is the way of the future.

Second, let me just say a word about Japan. All of you know that I did not name Japan a priority country under the Super 301 provisions of the 1988 Trade Act. That does not mean that all of our problems with Japan have disappeared. We know that we could sell more American products if Japan's market were truly open. But we've been working hard on that and, I think, with impressive results. Over the past few months, we've made more progress on trade issues with Japan than at any other time I can recall. And part of the reason for this success, if you will, is that the Prime

Minister, Prime Minister Kaifu of Japan, shares our commitment to ensuring that trade strengthens rather than undermines the friendship between our nations. Now, we are going to continue to press for progress. And keep in mind, section 301 and other trade law authorities remain available to the President, and we will use all the tools at our disposal to open markets and ensure fair treatment for American products, services, American investments and ideas. I'm confident in Carla Hills, our very able and tenacious Trade Representative. I'm confident in her ability, and I'm confident we will achieve lasting results.

John Clendenin mentioned in his speech the whirlwind of the changes we've seen this past year. And last year I spoke to you on May 1, May Day, by tradition one of the great days of celebration in the Socialist world. I said then that even the Socialist world was coming to see that socialism wasn't just another economic system: it was the death of economics. And that much was clear. What none of us could have seen on the eve of May Day 1989 was how close we had come to the wholesale collapse of communism.

First in Poland, then across Eastern Europe—one nation after another broke the stranglehold of the state and embraced democracy. And here in our own hemisphere, in Panama and Nicaragua, the day of the dictator gave way to the decade of democracy. These transforming events brought freedom to tens of millions of people, and with that freedom, new challenges—digging out from under the wreckage of ruined economies, reclaiming rights and freedoms long denied. Everywhere from Prague to Panama City, the time has come to make a start in the difficult work of democracy building.

It's that challenge that I want to talk to you about today, and it's a challenge that can engage every single one of you because you and the institutions you represent are proof of the power of the private sector. Democracy prospers when it rests on the firm foundation of the free market. Think about that. What it means is that one of the chief aims of our public policy must be to involve the private sector, in all its diversity, in the business of building democracy.

That's not to say that there's no work for government to do. Government-to-government aid is essential, especially in the first days of democracy when the institutions of free government are most fragile. That's why we put together aid packages for Poland and Hungary, and that's why I continue to urge Congress to move our Nicaragua and Panama emergency aid legislation to final passage as soon as possible. It is embarrassing. Today I meet with President Endara of Panama. I've asked the Senate and the House to move on that legislation over a month ago, and they haven't done it. I call on them again today to take action in the Senate so we can help those fledgling democracies in Panama and Nicaragua.

It is frustrating to see the Congress delaying its work. Here's the facts. On this legislation, I called for aid on March 13th, to be exact, and asked that it be passed by April 5th. In the House, $800 million in domestic discretionary spending was added. The Senate added another half a billion dollars and, in committee, tacked on a contentious abortion provision. No wonder the American people get so frustrated with the way the Congress operates. Nicaragua and Panama quite simply need this aid. We've got to deliver, and we've got to show that when democracy is at stake America always extends a helping hand.

But as I've said many times, government aid alone is simply not the answer. It's more than a matter of finding enough funds: it's a matter of principle, of what we mean when we talk about building democracy. The simple truth is this: Democracy and the freedoms it enshrines can never be a gift of government.

Earlier this year, in the State of the Union, I talked about the cornerstones of free society, the building blocks of democracy, all these elements that make America what it is: competition, opportunity, stewardship, private investment. Those building blocks are what make America work. More than that, they're what makes democracy work. They're what the newly emerging democracies of this hemisphere and in Eastern Europe need to grow and prosper.

Think back to what Lech Walesa said last November when he spoke to the AFL–CIO.

Picture it—Solidarity labor leader speaking before our great AFL–CIO about the needs of the new Poland. Here is the quote: "Such is the fate of a Polish trade unionist," he said, "that he has to launch a publicity campaign for private entrepreneurship."

Lech Walesa told the Congress that he hadn't come to ask for charity—as we know that we can't create democracy by writing a check. We build democracy in other nations not by taking responsibility for their needs but by helping them take responsibility for themselves. We build democracy whenever we help individuals take their destiny into their own hands. Democracy puts the focus not on government but on the freedom of the individual, not on the state but on society, the private sector. Democracy thrives in direct proportion to the flowering of individual freedom and free enterprise.

Our administration is doing all it can to promote private sector development. The Commerce Department, under Bob Mosbacher's able leadership, has opened its Eastern Europe Business Information Center and, with the chamber, has hosted a conference on doing business in Eastern Europe. Carla Hills, our able Ambassador, and her USTR team have been negotiating with the emerging democracies to open the way for expanded trade. At Labor, we've got a great Secretary of Labor—Elizabeth Dole. She's directing programs assisting Poland on key issues such as job training and unemployment insurance. At Agriculture, most of you know Secretary Clayton Yeutter. He's doing a fine job. He's led this effort, our effort, to provide food aid and free market expertise to spearhead agricultural reform.

Today I want to turn the spotlight on one of the best-kept secrets in town—an agency called OPIC, the Overseas Private Investment Corporation. OPIC's programs have been around since the days of the Marshall plan, providing loans and risk insurance to American companies expanding into markets across the developing world. Here's a fact I know this crowd in particular will appreciate: OPIC is one government agency that actually turns a profit. Today especially, OPIC is an important tool in our overall approach to help the world's emerging democracies sustain themselves.

But we've got to be realistic. Economic growth won't come overnight. Eastern Europe sustained four decades of economic decay, and here in our own hemisphere, years of dictatorship in Nicaragua drove its economy right into the ground, destroyed the basic commercial infrastructure that makes growth possible. But with the emergence of democracy, these nations are working around the clock to jump-start their stalled economies, to make the fundamental changes needed to create a functioning free market. For democracy's sake, we've got to do all we can to help this transition take place.

Let me tell you what OPIC then is doing to strengthen the free market foundations of democracy in Panama. Just 60 days after Operation Just Cause, OPIC led an investment mission of 27 American businesspeople to meet with their counterparts in Panama. The investment agreements that came out of that 7-day mission should lead to the direct investment of more than $70 million in Panama and 400 new jobs.

Now, here's the story of one company that took part in that OPIC mission—Servrite International, a small dairy company based in New Haven, Connecticut. Servrite had plans to invest in Panama, plans that it abandoned because of the old regime. Now, with the return of democracy, Servrite is moving forward, building a modern milk processing plant in the rural province of Chiriqui. The project will create 50 new jobs and provide technical assistance to help 30 Panamanian dairy farmers get their milk to market. For Servrite, this is a good business opportunity, but for the Panamanians involved, it's more than just a paycheck: it's a chance to build a future.

We're looking then to create the same kind of opportunity for investment in Nicaragua and, of course, beyond our own hemisphere, in Eastern Europe. As we speak, OPIC's President, my good friend Fred Zeder, a successful businessman in his own right, is leading a mission to Hungary and Poland, playing matchmaker to 43 American corporations and a far larger number of Eastern Europe's aspiring entrepreneurs.

Most of you know about the $150-million deal between G.E., General Electric, and Hungary's largest electric enterprise, Tungsram. What you may not know is OPIC's leading role in making that investment possible. That's just a fraction of the interest generated so far. Already OPIC has received requests representing more than $2 billion worth of American investment in Hungary and Poland alone, for the potential for growth and the dividend for democracy are both great.

You may have heard about some of Japan's new joint ventures in Eastern Europe—Suzuki's plan to build cars in Hungary or Daihatsu's deal to do the same in Poland. There's nothing unfair about these ventures, just proof that one of our key competitors is engaged in a hardnosed hunt for good opportunities in a new market. And I've said it before, and I'll say it now: American business can outthink, outwork, outperform any nation in the world. But we can't beat the competition if we don't get in the ball game. And if American business wants to keep ahead of the competition, the time to act is now.

Government must act, too, to help energize the private sector, and today I'm announcing a new initiative under OPIC's auspices to establish an Eastern European growth fund, a magnet for the kind of investment capital that can create self-sustaining growth and responsible development. This fund will be privately managed, underwritten in part by OPIC, and backed by its political risk insurance within existing budget authorities. And when fully capitalized at $200 million, this fund will provide a significant source of new capital for promising economic ventures.

I know the chamber is already involved in expanding free market forces. I've heard about your newly created Eastern European Trade and Technical Assistance Center and about the new American Chamber of Commerce in Budapest. You are helping millions of people realize their dream of democracy.

It will be a tremendous struggle, measured not in days or months but years. But what I've seen on my visits to Poland and Hungary and what I've learned in my conversations with the new leaders of Nicaragua and Panama is that all the years of despotic rule have not crushed the human spirit. These people are determined, full of hope and dreams, and now they're free. And if our American example teaches anything, it teaches that freedom is the world's most powerful force.

It's been a great privilege to speak to all of you today. Thank you, and may God bless these little kids, and may God bless the United States of America. Thank you all very, very much.

Note: The President spoke at 10:12 a.m. at DAR Constitution Hall. He was introduced by John Clendenin, the 1989–1990 chairman of the U.S. Chamber of Commerce.

Remarks Following Discussions With President Guillermo Endara of Panama
April 30, 1990

President Bush. Mr. President—President Endara—and distinguished members of the Panamanian delegation, friends, and colleagues: It's been a pleasure and, indeed, an honor to welcome President Endara to Washington. His struggle, the struggle for prosperity and democracy in Panama, has special meaning for all Americans throughout this hemisphere. It both inspires and reminds us that the cause of freedom is as hard as it is just. And many struggle for it; some pray for it, fast for it, are beaten, shed blood for it. Guillermo Endara and his people have done all of that and more. But while the challenges they face are daunting, the people of Panama remain steadfast, for theirs is a rare privilege: to be present and serve in the rebirth of a great nation.

Two hundred and one years ago today, George Washington was sworn in on the steps of Federal Hall as the President of a newly created nation, an office he didn't seek but felt compelled to serve. He was called into the service of his country "on the eve," he said, "of an arduous struggle for its liberties." While Washington was actually aware of the responsibilities of his office and the power that attended it, he once said that "The most enviable of all titles is the character of an honest man."

President Endara, freely elected and called forth on the eve of his nation's struggle for liberty, is renowned for that character. His intelligence; his grace; his ability as a leader, as conciliator, as consensus builder have won the confidence of Panamanians and all Americans. But the struggle is not over in Panama. While democracy has been restored and the peace is now preserved, we must see that prosperity returns to the people of Panama, and that's been the principal focus of President Endara's visit and our discussions.

And now that Panama enjoys freely elected, legitimate leadership in a democracy based on equality of opportunity, the United States is working to lay a foundation for cooperative relations that will serve both nations well into the coming century. And in that light, I'd like to emphasize our commitment to the Panama Canal Treaties as a framework for the smooth and orderly transfer of canal management responsibilities to a sovereign Panama. And I'm happy to announce today the nomination of the Panamanian Administrator of the Canal: Gilberto Guardia. I want to say that both countries are eager to look beyond the 1990's to begin to consider together the future of that vitally important path between the seas, the Panama Canal.

We're committed to cooperation with Panama across the entire range of our relations—diplomatic, cultural, economic. And we're already beginning to see signs of a Panamanian renaissance, as ransacked stores are restocked and reopened, depositors and lenders are returning, and a new economic confidence is now emerging.

The four agreements that we sign here today—three on drug cooperation, the other on reentry of the Peace Corps to

Panama—are evidence of this. And still it will take time to rebuild the economy and correct the economic distortions and social dislocations of a dictatorship's corruption. Too many now find their most basic needs for food and shelter still unmet. Unemployment in Panama remains unacceptably high. And we want to help President Endara reduce it and meet the rising expectations of a liberated Panamanian people.

The liberation brought with it high expectations for a prosperous and stable future, expectations that will be fulfilled over time as democratic processes are secured and the economy revitalized. There is no risk in rising expectations when people have the means and reason to succeed. In fact, high expectations are the best motivation for economic growth and Panama's very best hope for the future.

But in the near term, we must help ensure that unfulfilled expectations do not weaken the foundations of democracy so recently restored. America is committed to Panama's future, and that's why we proposed the aid package for Panama last January. Half of that package, our trade and credit guarantees, has been approved to the great credit of the Members of Congress; but it is time to finish the job. And just as you can't cross a chasm in two small steps, the people of Panama can't hope to make the leap to liberty and prosperity with only halfhearted support from her neighbors to the north. And so, today I want to appeal to Congress. I have asked and asked again that our aid package to the newly liberated people of Panama be passed and passed swiftly. And still it waits, and with it, the future of a fledgling democracy.

Many material things may now be in short supply in Panama, but freedom is there in abundance. And with freedom, everything else follows. Panama, a nation newly reborn in liberty, can count on the support of the United States of America. We were with you in times of conflict, and we will stand with you in peace. And I'm delighted, sir, that you came to the White House.

President Endara. I have had an important meeting, a working meeting, with President Bush, during which we have ana-lyzed matters which are of interest to Panama, to the United States, and to both countries.

Democracy is on the upsurge in the world. It is being reborn in our America, and it has returned to Panama. We agree with President Bush that we must maintain it forever on the upsurge. We must nourish it always, and we must protect it day and night. It is only in freedom and as master of his own destiny that man can develop his potential in this life. The tyrannies of any kind, of any sort, must be relegated to the past. My people have suffered for 21 long years, but now it is nourishing hope and the possibility for a better future.

I have thanked President Bush on behalf of the Panamanian people for the hand of friendship which he has extended to us and the permanent consideration he has never failed to show us. On a basis of mutual respect, of serious intentions, and reciprocal trust, there are no limits at all to friendship and to understanding between the Panamanian people and the people of the United States. In this spirit, we are lighting the road to a new relationship of dignity, in equality and in freedom. And the designation of the first Panamanian Administrator of the canal is an act of justice which does honor to President Bush.

Mr. President, if you allow me, I would like to address you, my friend, President Bush. Let me, my friend, Mr. President, thank you for your kind and inspiring words. They fill our spirits with enthusiasm and optimism and gives us reason to face the future with added strength, knowing that we have such support behind our own efforts. The people of Panama will always be grateful for the support and friendship of the American people and for the sunshine of freedom we currently enjoy.

Thank you, and God bless America.

Note: President Bush spoke at 1:18 p.m. in the East Room at the White House. President Endara spoke in Spanish, and his remarks were translated by an interpreter. Prior to their remarks, the two Presidents met privately in the Oval Office and with U.S. and Panamanian officials in the Cabinet Room, and then attended a luncheon in the Old Family Dining Room.

Nomination of Gilberto Guardia Fabrega To Be Administrator of the Panama Canal Commission
April 30, 1990

The President today announced his intention to nominate Gilberto Guardia Fabrega to be Administrator of the Panama Canal Commission. He would succeed Dennis P. McAuliffe.

In 1952 Mr. Guardia founded Diaz and Guardia, an architectural and engineering company in the Republic of Panama, and currently serves as president and chairman of the board. Prior to this Mr. Guardia served as a civil engineer with the Panama Canal Co., 1951–1952. In addition, he has served on the board of directors for Fiduciary Bank of Panama and Industrial Development, S.A.; officer in the National Council of Private Enterprise, the Chamber of Commerce, Industry and Agriculture of Panama, and the Panamanian Chamber of Construction.

Mr. Guardia graduated from Santa Clara University (C.E., 1950). He was born February 13, 1930, in Panama City, Panama. Mr. Guardia is married, has three children, and resides in La Cresta, Panama.

Message to the Congress Reporting on the Transfer of Panamanian Government Assets Held By the United States
April 30, 1990

To the Congress of the United States:

1. I hereby report to the Congress on developments since the last Presidential report of October 19, 1989, concerning the national emergency with respect to Panama that was declared in Executive Order No. 12635 of April 8, 1988. This report is submitted pursuant to section 401(c) of the National Emergencies Act, 50 U.S.C. 1641(c), and section 204(c) of the International Emergency Economic Powers Act, 50 U.S.C. 1703(c).

2. On December 20, 1989, I ordered U.S. military forces to Panama to protect the lives of American citizens in Panama, to exercise the right and obligation under the Panama Canal Treaty to protect and defend the Canal, to assist the democratically elected government in Panama to return to power, and to bring General Noriega to justice in the United States. Since that date, civil order and civilian rule have been restored to Panama, and General Noriega awaits trial in the United States. On December 20, 1989, I directed the Secretary of the Treasury and the Secretary of State to lift the economic sanctions with respect to the democratically elected Government of Panama, headed by President Endara, and, in cooperation with that government, to effect an orderly unblocking of Panamanian government assets in the United States. The Panamanian Transactions Regulations, 31 C.F.R. Part 565 (the "Regulations"), administered by the Office of Foreign Assets Control ("FAC") of the Department of the Treasury, were amended accordingly to clarify that all obligations owed the Government of Panama first falling due on or after December 20, 1989, may be paid, and that property in the United States in which the Government of Panama obtains an interest on or after that date is not blocked, with the exception of payments made into certain blocked accounts for pre-December 20, 1989, obligations. The Regulations were also amended to authorize any person holding a blocked reserve account pursuant to section 565.509 ("509 Account") (1) to transfer the unadjusted gross balance of such account, with applicable interest, to the Government of Panama, or (2) to apply for a specific license to transfer an amount other than the gross balance upon concurrence of the Government of Panama.

I am enclosing a copy of the amendment to the Regulations, 55 *Fed. Reg.* 3560 (Feb. 1, 1990). This was the only amendment to the Regulations since my last report of October 19, 1989.

3. Over the past 6 months the licensing section of FAC issued fifteen (15) specific licenses authorizing U.S. companies to establish 509 accounts on their books. Since the imposition of the sanctions, a total of fifty-three (53) U.S. companies have been authorized to establish 509 accounts.

FAC is currently engaged in effecting the orderly transfer of funds to the new Government of Panama. The Panamanian Embassy and consular space in the United States have been reopened, and bank accounts have been unblocked on a case-by-case basis as requested by the new government. Upon issuance of the regulatory amendment of February 1, 1990, a mechanism was also provided to unblock amounts held in 509 accounts by general or specific license, depending on the circumstances.

Each licensed transfer of blocked funds has stringent reporting requirements, and the reports are being tracked and closely monitored. FAC has initiated a review process to examine outstanding 509 Account licenses, scrutinize open enforcement files, and identify companies that may have failed to comply with the requirements of the Regulations to either pay into Account No. 2 or establish a 509 Account.

Additional Panama compliance activities included frequent FAC staff phone contact with affected U.S. parties, numerous speeches to trade groups, such as the Council of the Americas, and publication of a Panama fact sheet entitled "What You Need to Know About U.S. Economic Sanctions."

As of March 12, 1990, FAC had released $256 million of the total $426 million blocked to the control of the Government of Panama in the manner described above. This $256 million was comprised of $82 million from escrow accounts at the Federal Reserve Bank of New York, $31 million from blocked accounts at commercial banks, and $142.8 million from 509 accounts. I am attaching a fact sheet to the end of this report outlining these transfers of blocked funds.

The $82 million released from the Federal Reserve Bank of New York consisted of the entire balance ($10.2 million) of Account No. 2, which contained payments by U.S. companies to the Government of Panama, and a portion ($72 million) of Account No. 3, which contained escrowed United States Government payments to the Government of Panama. (Account No. 1 originally contained $10.5 million of Government of Panama funds that were located in the United States prior to the sanctions. These funds were used to fund operations of the Embassy in Washington of then-President Delvalle and were completely expended before September 1, 1989.)

The $169.7 million remaining blocked consists of $122.6 million in the Federal Reserve Bank of New York that has been set aside by the Government of Panama to fund payment of Panama's arrears to international financial institutions, $1.5 million in commercial banks for which the Government of Panama has not requested unblocking, and $45.4 million in 509 accounts. The remaining 509 Account balances are subject to bilateral negotiations between the Government of Panama and U.S. firms that have both debts to and obligations owed from the Government of Panama.

4. During the most recent reporting period, FAC continued to take actions to promote compliance with the Regulations and to tighten measures to deny the illegal Noriega regime funds belonging to the Panamanian people. Despite the economic hardships sometimes involved for U.S. persons in Panama, FAC stressed the importance of complete compliance with the Regulations by all persons in the United States and all U.S. persons and their controlled Panamanian entities in Panama. Several significant enforcement actions have taken place since the last report.

In September 1989, following written notification by FAC to over 150 U.S. entities with interests in Panama and specific orders to a number of U.S. companies and their Panamanian subsidiaries to cease and desist from making indirect payments of employee income and educational taxes to the Noriega regime, all recipients of such instructions certified that they had brought themselves into full compliance with the Regulations. This initiative had the immediate effect of denying tax revenues to the Noriega regime as well as promoting full compliance with the Regulations.

As the result of this enforcement effort, several U.S. firms also presented voluntary disclosures to FAC of prior actions taken in violation of the Regulations. Other indications of willful or inadvertent noncompliance with the Regulations are being systematically investigated by FAC. The circumstances of voluntary disclosures and measures taken to ensure full compliance with the Regulations may be considered mitigating factors in seeking criminal indictments or applying FAC civil penalties under the Regulations.

In compliance with instructions from FAC, a major U.S. oil company notified the Noriega regime in late September 1989 that the Government of Panama was required to pay on a cash basis for any future fuel oil deliveries. After considerable protest, regime officials agreed to this procedure, which placed further financial pressure on the Noriega regime.

Also in September 1989, FAC initiated civil penalty actions against the Panamanian Directorate of Consular and Maritime Affairs in New York and its two principal officers, in whose bank accounts the Government of Panama had an interest. Since all Government of Panama accounts in the United States were blocked effective April 8, 1988, each unlicensed transaction involving such accounts was determined to be in violation of the Regulations.

On October 31, 1989, FAC published a notice in the *Federal Register* adding the names of Panamanian dictator General Noriega, his wife, and 32 companies to the existing list of 134 firms and individuals in Panama who act for or on behalf of Cuba. The listing of Noriega and the other entities as Specially Designated Nationals of Cuba in Panama had the effect of applying the full force of the U.S. trade and financial embargo against Cuba to Noriega and the other designated persons and firms operating in Panama. The action taken was another step to halt the channeling of funds to the illegal Noriega regime and to undermine the extensive network of commercial

and financial collusion between the Noriega and Castro regimes.

On November 27, 1989, following coordination with FAC, the U.S. Customs Service at Dallas-Fort Worth International Airport seized a helicopter part that had been imported for repair by a U.S. company. Inspection of documents revealed that the owner of the aircraft part was the Panamanian Air Force. The merchandise was seized for violation of the Regulations as an attempted unlicensed transfer of property in which the Government of Panama had an interest.

On November 30, 1989, I directed that Panamanian flag vessels not be permitted to enter U.S. ports after January 31, 1990. This measure was intended to deny the Noriega regime revenue from vessel registrations as well as illegal income in the form of bribes and kickbacks. I wanted to make it very clear that there would be no accommodation with the illegal Panamanian regime. This directive was rescinded by my directive of December 20, 1989, upon the fall of the Noriega regime, to lift the economic sanctions with respect to the new democratically elected Government of Panama and to take steps to effect an orderly unblocking of Panamanian government assets in the United States.

On January 24, 1990, FAC issued a blocking order freezing a wire transfer of $300,000 being made by a Specially Designated National of Cuba in Panama who attempting to transfer funds from its account in a London bank to a Bahamian bank, through a bank in Miami. The FAC blocking order required that the Miami bank not complete the transfer and place the $300,000 in a blocked account. This action constituted the first FAC blocking of major funds tied directly to the Noriega regime and was the first case in which an international wire transfer by a Specially Designated National of Cuba was blocked in midstream.

5. On December 20, 1989, I ordered U.S. troops into Panama to safeguard American lives, protect the integrity of the Panama Canal Treaties, assist Panama to restore democracy, and bring General Noriega to justice. I undertook this action after all peace-

ful means to resolve the crisis had been exhausted. Our action reflected the unique circumstances in Panama that evolved from our Treaty commitments and obligations and achieved all our objectives. The new government in Panama is a *de jure* government, freely elected by the Panamanian people on May 7, 1989, and certified by the Noriega-appointed Electoral Tribunal on December 27, 1989. The new government moved quickly to restore normal government functions; it has named a full Cabinet, Supreme Court, and regional and municipal authorities. The Legislative Assembly held its first session, as required by the constitution, on March 1, 1990. The Government of Panama's top priorities are economic recovery and the organizing of a civilian-controlled Public Force. Internationally, the new government has been recognized by 45 states, including Japan and major European and Latin American states. The United States is committed to assisting the democratic transition in Panama.

6. The expenses incurred by the Federal Government in the 6-month period from September 20, 1989, through March 20, 1990, which are directly attributable to the exercise of powers and authorities conferred by the declaration of the Panamanian national emergency, are estimated at $737,088, most of which represents wage and salary costs for Federal personnel. Personnel costs were largely centered in the Department of the Treasury (particularly in the Office of Foreign Assets Control, the Office of the Assistant Secretary for Enforcement, the Office of the Assistant Secretary for International Affairs, the Office of the General Counsel, and the Customs Service), the Department of State, the Federal Reserve Board, the National Security Council, and the Department of Defense.

7. On April 5, 1990, I issued Executive Order No. 12710, terminating the national emergency declared on April 8, 1988, with respect to Panama. While this order terminated the sanctions, the blocking of Panamanian government assets in the United States was continued to permit completion of the orderly unblocking and transfer of funds I directed on December 20, 1989, and to foster the resolution of claims of U.S. creditors involving Panama, pursuant to 50 U.S.C. 1706(a). The termination of the national emergency will not affect the continuation of compliance audits and enforcement actions with respect to activities taking place during the sanctions period, pursuant to 50 U.S.C. 1622(a). I will continue to report periodically to the Congress on significant developments, pursuant to 50 U.S.C. 1706(d).

GEORGE BUSH

The White House,
April 30, 1990.

Remarks and an Exchange With Reporters Prior to a Meeting With Former Hostage Robert Polhill
April 30, 1990

The President. Well, let me say that the purpose of all of this is simply to welcome Mr. and Mrs. Polhill to the White House. I just had a chance to tell him how pleased we are that he is free. And of course, this comes at a very special moment because Mr. Reed is now free, and I expect to be talking to him as soon as he finishes that initial contact and debrief over there, hopefully within the next hour or two.

But I do want to take this opportunity to thank Syria for its role in not only bringing Mr. Polhill home but its role in the Reed release; similarly, to thank Iran for its role; and simply to say that I hope this is a forerunner to the release of the other American hostages and the others from other countries held against their will. Things seem to be moving on this.

Mr. Polhill, welcome to the White House. I just can't tell you how overjoyed Barbara and I are to have both of you here.

Mr. Polhill. Thanks very much, President Bush. I feel very badly that I can't talk to you quite as well as I'd like to be able to, because there are a lot of things I want to say to the American people. But the most important thing, I think, now to say is to reinforce what President Bush has just said: that I am at this moment truly as happy for Frank and Fifi Reed as I was 8 days ago for Ferial and myself and for both families.

I sincerely hope that Frank is step two in what will be a continuing release of hostages and to bring us all back, from American hostages through all of the other countries who may be involved. The warmth and sincerity of the welcome I've received everywhere I have been, from Damascus to Wiesbaden to Washington, has been truly thrilling. Frank Reed is going to feel the way I felt because the American people are behind us and have been behind our families throughout this ordeal. And we're deeply grateful to you for that.

I'm not going to try to say very much more because I know even with the help of this device you're not going to get very much more. So, I'll just—even though I'm a bit of a ham, you see. I'd like to be able to do better, but you'll have to work with my sons, I think. Thank you so much.

Q. Mr. President, has Israel now cut a deal for the remaining Shiite prisoners?

The President. I have no knowledge of anything of that nature.

Q. Why do you think this is happening now, Mr. President? Why do you think that Iran and Syria are cooperating at this point?

The President. Well, because I hope there's a realization that holding people against their will is not the way to effect political change. I'm not suggesting in reply to your question that Syria and Iran are the ones that are holding the remaining hostages. But I can't explain the rationale, but I can express a certain gratitude that things seem to be moving. And what I feel in my heart about the return of now these two Americans is, in a sense, overwhelming. But I don't think any American can totally rejoice until the rest are free. And indeed, we can't limit our concern and our feelings to just the Americans, in my view.

So, we will just keep on track; and when, as now, there's a reason to say thank you,

certainly we'll do that. But beyond that, I just hope that the process—this is a process—I just hope it continues. I don't want to make Mr. Polhill speak again, but I feel confident I speak for him and for his wife. You heard what he said beautifully about Mr. Reed. We feel that way about all the rest of them, too.

Q. Mr. President, is there any way possible at this point to return the good will gesture?

The President. As I've said, we can't, in terms of overall relationship between countries, expect normalcy or expect vast improvement until all Americans are freed. We're not in a piecemeal basis: bidding for one human life, holding out hopes, only to have them dashed, to one American family or another. That is not the way I see, certainly, my responsibilities. But when a step is taken that goes toward that day when all hostages are released, I should say thank you. But beyond that, I can't say that I can be happy. I've tried to put myself in the place of the other families and say, hey, how about my loved one? So, this is a tough business. I just want to conduct the policy of this country in a way to facilitate the continuation of this process if, indeed, it is a process. I don't know that, and I don't expect Mr. Polhill knows it, either.

I've got time for a couple more, and I don't want to keep this tired man—make him even tireder.

Q. Mr. President, can you tell us what it is that Iran did that you're thanking them for and whether you've had any further information on whether they aided in Mr. Polhill's release?

The President. We did hear from Syria that Iran had been helpful, and it is that that I'm saying thank you for.

Q. Is it time for Israel to perhaps make a deal to release Sheik Obeid or the 400 Shiites? Or would you object if they did?

The President. I don't—certainly no objection, and that is a matter for others to determine. I've stated that holding people against their will is not a way to facilitate political change or any other kind of change. So, that's it. Last one.

Q. Sir, then are you rejecting or ruling out any type of a good will gesture towards

Iran or Syria at this time until all the Americans are released?

The President. I've said that we cannot have normalcy as long as any American is held against his will, and I think everybody understands that. But in terms of expressing appreciation to those who facilitate the release of Mr. Polhill or the release of Mr. Reed, certainly I'm prepared to do that. I've done that here today. But I can't say that that's an overwhelming expression of good will because I have on mind those other six Americans that are held.

But, look, if it's beginning to work and if, indeed, there's a process, I expect I speak for all Americans when I say I rejoice in that. But that's about where we've got to leave it, Ellen [Ellen Warren, Knight-Ridder Newspapers]. We've got to see every American returned, and that's the way it's going to be. And I'm very pleased that this Polhill release has been facilitated. And you heard him express his joy for the Reeds, and all I'd say to that is: Amen. Thank God.

Q. Sir, do we still regard Syria as a terrorism-sponsoring state?

The President. Listen, I can't take any more questions. I can't do it.

Q. A question for Mr. Polhill. A question for Mr. Polhill. Mr. Polhill, do you think there's anything that can be done to return the good will gesture at this point?

Mr. Polhill. No, I'm not conversant—you may be surprised, but I really don't know very much about what was going on around me. So, I don't think I can offer a lot of help to anyone. The only thing I can suggest is that the American people continue to show, as hostages continue to be released on a regular basis, how much we are wanted back. And I think that message might get across very clearly.

The President. That's a good point. That's a good point.

Q. Are you carrying a message to the President?

Q. Are you carrying a message from the hostage-takers?

Mr. Polhill. They said I was.

The President. Listen, I deal with these guys; you'll be out here all night. [*Laughter*]

Note: The President spoke at 5 p.m. on the South Lawn at the White House. Robert Polhill, an accounting professor at Beirut University College, was kidnaped by pro-Iranian terrorists in Beirut on January 24, 1987. In his remarks, the President referred to Frank Herbert Reed, the director of the Lebanon International School who was kidnaped by members of the Organization of the Islamic Dawn on September 9, 1986; and Sheik Abdul Karim Obeid, the senior Moslem cleric and Hizballah leader who was abducted from his home in Jibchit by Israeli forces in southern Lebanon on July 28, 1989.

Statement by Press Secretary Fitzwater on the President's Conversations With Former Hostages Frank Reed and Robert Polhill
April 30, 1990

President Bush spoke by telephone this afternoon at approximately 5:30 p.m. with Mr. Frank Reed and the American Ambassador to Syria, Mr. Edward Djerejian. The President gave Mr. Reed greetings from the American people and offered him the complete support of the United States Government as he recovers from his ordeal. The President wished Mr. Reed well and said he hoped he would soon be reunited with his wife and family.

The phone call was placed as President Bush was visiting with Mr. Robert Polhill, who was released from captivity only last week. The President put Mr. Polhill on the telephone line for a brief conversation with Mr. Reed. They exchanged warm greetings and wished each other well. The phone call lasted several minutes, and Mr. Polhill departed the White House at approximately 6:15 p.m. The President's meeting with Mr. Polhill had lasted approximately an hour.

In the meeting, Mr. Polhill said he had a private message for the President from his captors. The President received that message in private and indicated he would not discuss the message publicly. The President and Mr. Polhill had a very warm and informal meeting in which Mr. Polhill was in excellent spirits. He described his life in captivity and gave his impressions of his captors, of the confusing situation in Beirut, and of the hardship he suffered during 3½ years. He spoke of his personal ordeal of survival day by day in a hostage setting. President Bush was grateful for the conversation and told Mr. Polhill how much he admired his courage and strength during this terrible period in his life. Mrs. Bush also attended the meeting.

Note: Frank Herbert Reed, director of the Lebanon International School, was kidnaped by members of the Organization of the Islamic Dawn in Beirut on September 9, 1986. Robert Polhill, an accounting professor at Beirut University College, was kidnaped by pro-Iranian terrorists in Beirut on January 24, 1987.

Statement on the Release of Former Hostage Frank Reed
April 30, 1990

We are pleased that hostage Frank Reed has been freed by his captors. Mr. Reed had been held hostage for nearly 4 years. This is a joyous day for Mr. Reed, his family, his friends, and all Americans. With Mr. Reed's release, we have six innocent Americans that are still being held hostage in Lebanon. In addition, there are a number of foreign nationals that are being held hostage. Their predicament weighs on our mind and tempers the joy we feel today by Mr. Reed's release.

Once again, we wish to express our gratitude to all those who through their efforts helped in Mr. Reed's release. In particular, we would like to thank the Government of Syria for facilitating this release. We would also like to thank the Government of Iran for using its influence to help bring about this humanitarian step. We cannot rest, however, until all hostages are free. We urge all parties who either hold hostages or have any influence over the hostage-takers to work for the expeditious and unconditional release of the remaining hostages.

Note: Frank Herbert Reed, director of the Lebanon International School, was kidnaped by members of the Organization of the Islamic Dawn in Beirut on September 9, 1986.

Remarks on Signing the National Physical Fitness and Sports Month Proclamation
May 1, 1990

Well, welcome to the White House. I think Secretary Sullivan looks better already. [*Laughter*] And to Arnold Schwarzenegger and members of the President's Council on Physical Fitness and Sports, honored guests, ladies and gentlemen, welcome. Welcome to the White House, and a pleasure to be with all of you, especially the man who symbolizes physical fitness, Arnold Schwarzenegger.

You know, he's stronger than I thought he was. He bench-pressed the Federal budget. [*Laughter*] This weekend we had our grandson Sam LeBlond. I said, "If Arnold Schwarzenegger can do that, why can't you pick up your socks?" [*Laughter*]

But look, this morning we're here for a very special event. I want to thank all the participants. It kicks off National Physical Fitness and Sports Month. And today—I hope this doesn't get me in trouble with another vegetable—[*laughter*]—but today we're declaring war on couch potatoes. [*Laughter*] And all of us have a stake in making exercise a part of America's fitness and fitness a part of America every day. No matter what your age, sex, or physical condition, the Great American Workout can enhance the quality and longevity of each American's life.

And just look at these workout stations. Barbara and I came around and toured them all last night. In a couple of moments, we'll be visiting them again. And one involves aerobic dancing; others are for American pastimes like baseball and basketball and football and, yes, horseshoes—and a martial arts station.

And I'd like to give a special salute to the heroes here representing the Disabled and Special Olympics. Their strength and determination inspires us all.

The Great American Workout shows how fitness can reduce heart disease and stroke—lowering stress, blood pressure, cholesterol. And yet surveys show that only 40 percent of American adults exercise regularly. And among our kids fitness hasn't improved over the last decade; in fact, in some cases, it's declined. And one way to change that is by placing a new emphasis on quality physical education in our schools. Arnold briefed me on this the other day.

Only one State now requires daily physical education in its schools from kindergarten through 12th grade. So, let's encourage all 50 States.

And also, let's pledge to eat a balanced and nutritional diet, avoid excessive alcohol use and, of course, say no to drugs. And all you broccoli lovers, eat your heart out, out there. [*Laughter*] Together these steps can make America more competitive in the classroom and the factory, as well as on the playing field.

Through fitness, we can build a healthier America that's number one academically, economically, and athletically. By participating in so many sports, I'm not trying to get my picture on a Wheaties box. I love sports, as do the kids at these workout stations—kids from 6 to 65. And, yes, fitness can be an individual activity or a family affair. Either way it can help create an America that out-performs any nation in the world.

Thank you to every participant. It's my pleasure to officially proclaim National Fitness and Sports Month. And now, to quote a great golfer who often dieted but seldom exercised—Jackie Gleason—a little traveling music. Arnold, let's take a look at these workout stations. And thank you all once again.

Note: The President spoke at 7:10 a.m. on the South Grounds at the White House. In his opening remarks, he referred to Secretary of Health and Human Services Louis W. Sullivan and Arnold Schwarzenegger, Chairman of the President's Council on Physical Fitness and Sports. The proclamation is listed in Appendix E at the end of this volume.

Remarks at a White House Briefing for the Leadership of National Small Business United and the National Association of Women Business Owners
May 1, 1990

Thank you all very much. Thank you all, officials of both organizations, and welcome to Washington. Let me say I apologize; I'm afraid I might have kept you waiting for a few minutes. Let me pay my respects to the man that comes on next with all the facts, John Robson, who is a Deputy at Treasury—an enormous job. He is a successful businessman and great success in academia. Elected to come and serve his country, and he's doing a superb job. So, you're going to hear from one of our very, very best in a minute.

But as for now, a lot of dust gets kicked up around here these days. They say, if you stay too long, it's easy to forget just how well things are going in the land of the free. Last year, though, was a remarkable year for job-creating, which I think of is the matrix in this get-together here today. The entrepreneurial core of American business did well. Small businesses created over a million and a half new jobs in 1989 alone, about two-thirds of the jobs created in the entire Nation and almost equal to the entire labor force of the city of Los Angeles.

Also last year, the number of woman-owned small businesses created notably in mining, construction, and transportation increased at twice the rate of those owned by men. Nineteen eighty-nine was an important year for another reason: because it reminded us of the role that government should and shouldn't play in enterprise. It set off a collective movement toward democracy worldwide that has us all looking up from our work for a moment in wonder, bearing witness as the world confirmed the wisdom of our forefathers. They understood the importance of a limited government—those forefathers—so they fought for a social order that gave free reign to ambition and unleashed the power of individual aspiration. We rose, in fact, as a nation of upstarts who didn't know their place. This was a new idea: that government, far from fearing private initiative, should be all for it. It still seems like a new idea.

Last year, from Lima to Warsaw to Moscow to Memphis, we were reminded that the power of any economy flows not from an entrenched centralized bureaucracy elite but from the vitality of free competition, free market, and free wills. Men, women, immigrants, Americans of every kind, from every corner of this great country, are empowered by opportunities, by the degree of choice and the kind of moti-vation that only free markets can provide.

Adam Smith shocked the establishment 200 years ago with something we've realized only recently: that everyone has a natural desire and a natural right to improve their situation, to truck and barter and bargain in trade, everyone from a CEO to a kid with a pocketful of marbles. Society benefits from that creative, competitive impulse.

In this century, we defined that impulse as the American Dream. The dream has done more than endure: it is as dynamic as ever, as every one of you proves every single day. Every man and woman who builds an enterprise, from a shoeshine stand to a multinational, understands what it is I'm talking about here. It is what has made us a nation of imagination, of mavericks willing to take a gamble on the unexpected, the untried, the untested, the untraditional.

They're out there, moving in every direction and working to create new economic orders out of chaos—building empires out of garages, foreseeing needs, forming strategies, finding investors, and founding corporations of every kind. That is free enterprise. That's what we're working here to try to encourage. But it's not just free enterprise alone, free enterprise by itself: it's an entirely new way of looking at the world that no longer assumes that bureaucratic, top-down organization is the answer. Rather than stifling individual creativity and responsibility, we want to encourage initiative. This new vision of freedom and democracy is circling the globe. We want this democracy to mean opportunity for everyone.

So, we began with the lessons that our forefathers left us about limited government, which revealed an obstacle to opportunity they faced then that we face now. I'm talking, of course, about excessive taxes. Limited government must mean limited taxes. This government should not be preventing people from investing in small businesses, nor should it swallow a third of the business you've spent your life building. But that's what our taxation of capital gains does, and that's why we are working to cut the rate on long-term held assets and counting on your support.

For anyone launching a small business—whatever their age, their background, or condition—a capital gains cut makes it easier to attract start-up capital. For growing businesses, it means more investment for the long term, and for all Americans, it means opportunity and the kind of continued job creation that only new and expanding businesses bring about. So, we're fighting for this tax cut. It does, as John will tell you, raise revenue to the Treasury, creates jobs, puts us on a more equal footing with out trading partners, and underwrites American ingenuity and creativity and businesses of every kind.

We see Japan taxing capital gains at 5 percent; Korea and Taiwan, I believe, is 0. And you look around the world, and you find that those countries that are doing well in stimulating investment have much lower rates on capital gains. So, we've got to do more to fuel the kind of flexible, creative energy that drives American business. On the wide range of issues concerning business owners across this country, from deficit reduction to education to product-liability reforms—something I'm very interested in—and especially health-care cost containment, we are with you working towards solutions. And we're also encouraging the kinds of creative thinking that business will need to retain and attract talent, like flexible workplace policies, telecommuting, and choice in child care.

We greatly appreciated the well-thought-out book of policy recommendations recently produced by your two groups. We're working on a range of ideas to help business move with markets as they change, from encouraging more R&D research and experimentation to allowing joint production ventures that let American firms pool their skills, build new production facilities, and share investment risks.

But the principle that encompasses our thinking on all of these issues is something our forefathers knew and the rest of the world reminded us of last year: No state has yet managed to mandate prosperity or creativity—no state at all. And the cruelest societies are those that are static and stagnant, cultures that run counter to human nature and human aspiration. But the surest sign of a nation's kindness is the kind of social and economic mobility that it allows people. What the world learned in the Revolution of '89 is that democracy is another way of saying opportunity, that government's best role and greatest security is not in consolidating power but in empowering the individual. And the truest kindness the state can offer the people is to govern with a gentle hand.

After two centuries, we're still convinced that government should be limited. But if our experience has taught us anything, it's that the creative potential of men and women with a mission is unlimited. You are such people; you are such men and women. So, this administration salutes you and will do everything in our power to support the work you do. I've left out the major fiscal problems facing our country, but again, I'll ask John to touch on that—hammering away at keeping the deficit under control, trying to keep the lid on spending.

Let me just give you one anecdote on that. I sent legislation up in March, early March, asking the House and Senate to act on it in early April. And what it was about was helping democracy in Panama and helping democracy in Nicaragua. And there's a provision for a special supplemental in the way the Congress operates. And it was a dire emergency. And we need that, we need that money to help Violeta Chamorro [President of Nicaragua] solidify their democracy. We need it to help the people of Panama—incidentally, I had a very good visit yesterday with President Endara [of Panama]—but what happened to it? It goes up to the Congress. The House of Representatives added about $2 billion to the spending on Nicaragua and Panama. None of it related to Nicaragua. None of it related to Panama. All of it related to other priorities they had. It goes over to the Senate, and the same thing is happening. I don't know what the total is over there now, but not only did they add a lot of domestic spending but they put on contentious provisions on abortion and contentious provisions on capital punishment. No matter how one feels on these issues, that hasn't anything to do with Nicaragua; it hasn't anything to do with Panama.

I just wanted to kind of debrief here and

vent my frustration with the process, thinking that perhaps you'd understand. [*Laughter*]

But I'm not here to complain, because I feel it's a real responsibility to try to get things moving on these priorities that I think you and I share, and that is limited government, control the spending side as best you can, guard against excessive taxation, and encourage through saving and investment and as best we can to guarantee our own productivity and competitiveness into the future. I need your help, I welcome the support that you have given us, and I am very grateful you came our way. Thank you all, and God bless.

Note: The President spoke at 2:25 p.m. in Room 450 of the Old Executive Office Building.

Message to the Congress Reporting on the Economic Sanctions Against Nicaragua
May 1, 1990

To the Congress of the United States:

I hereby report to the Congress on developments since my last report of October 25, 1989, concerning the national emergency with respect to Nicaragua that was declared in Executive Order No. 12513 on May 1, 1985. This report also provides final information on total Administration expenses directly incurred in exercise of emergency authorities pursuant to that order from May 1, 1985, through my termination of the national emergency on March 13, 1990. Executive Order 12513 prohibited: (1) all imports into the United States of goods and services of Nicaraguan origin; (2) all exports from the United States of goods to or destined for Nicaragua except those destined for the organized democratic resistance; (3) Nicaraguan air carriers from engaging in air transportation to or from points in the United States; and (4) vessels of Nicaraguan registry from entering United States ports. On March 13, 1990, in Executive Order No. 12707, 55 *Fed. Reg.* 9707 (March 14, 1990), I terminated the emergency declared with respect to Nicaragua and lifted the economic sanctions imposed on that country, in response to the successful completion of a democratic presidential election in Nicaragua.

1. The declaration of emergency was made pursuant to the authority vested in the President by the Constitution and laws of the United States, including the International Emergency Economic Powers Act, 50 U.S.C. 1701 *et seq.* ("IEEPA"), the National Emergencies Act, 50 U.S.C. 1601 *et seq.* ("NEA"), chapter 12 of title 50 of the United States Code (50 U.S.C. 191 *et seq.*), and section 301 of title 3 of the United States Code. The termination of emergency and removal of sanctions were made pursuant to the authority vested in me as President by the Constitution and laws of United States, including those just noted. This report is submitted pursuant to 50 U.S.C. 1641(c) and 1703(c).

2. The Office of Foreign Assets Control ("FAC") of the Department of the Treasury issued the Nicaraguan Trade Control Regulations implementing the prohibitions in Executive Order No. 12513, effective May 7, 1985, 50 *Fed. Reg.* 19890 (May 10, 1985).

3. Since my report of October 25, 1989, fewer than 20 applications for licenses have been received by FAC with respect to Nicaragua, and the majority of these applications have been granted. Of the licenses issued in this period, some authorized exports for humanitarian purposes, covering donated articles beyond the scope of the exceptions to the export ban. Certain licenses authorized the export of equipment to *La Prensa*, the major opposition publication in Nicaragua, as well as to other opposition press groups. A license was also issued to the Free Trade Union Institute of the AFL–CIO to export equipment and supplies to the Nicaraguan Confederation of Trade Union Unity in Managua for use during the

elections that were held on February 25, 1990, in Nicaragua. Our licensing action was taken pursuant to Public Law 101–119, which was enacted by the Congress to provide assistance for free and fair elections in Nicaragua.

4. Since my last report, several cases have been referred to the FAC civil penalties division for civil penalty actions. The companies in question are based in the United States and engaged in unauthorized exports to Nicaragua from the United States. We expect at least four of these exporting companies to be assessed penalties.

In addition to cases currently under civil penalty consideration, there are approximately 34 companies under active investigation by the U.S. Customs Service. These cases involve unauthorized importation and/or exportation of goods between the United States and Nicaragua.

5. The U.S. Government expects to have greatly improved relations with Nicaragua now that the new Nicaraguan government has taken office, particularly in light of President Chamorro's commitment to democratization and to a free market economy. For these reasons, I terminated the national emergency with respect to Nicaragua on March 13, 1990.

6. The expenses incurred by the Federal Government in the period from November 1, 1989, through May 1, 1990, that are directly attributable to the exercise of powers and authorities conferred by the declaration of the national emergency with respect to Nicaragua are estimated at $119,667.48, all of which represents wage and salary costs

for Federal personnel. Personnel costs were largely centered in the Department of the Treasury (particularly in the Customs Service, as well as in FAC and the Office of the General Counsel), with expenses also incurred by the Department of State and the National Security Council.

7. For the full period of the national emergency with respect to Nicaragua (May 1, 1985, through March 13, 1990), the total expenditures of the Federal Government directly attributable to the exercise of powers and authorities conferred by the declaration of the national emergency are estimated at $1,309,783.48, all of which represents wage and salary costs for Federal personnel. Personnel costs were largely centered in the Departments of State and Treasury, and the National Security Council.

8. The February 25, 1990, democratic election in Nicaragua ended the unusual and extraordinary threat to the national security and foreign policy of the United States previously posed by the policies and actions of the Sandinista government in that country, and led to my termination of the national emergency to deal with that threat. Accordingly, this is the last periodic report that will be submitted pursuant to 50 U.S.C. 1703(c). This report also constitutes the last semiannual report and the final report on Administration expenditures required pursuant to 50 U.S.C. 1641(c).

GEORGE BUSH

The White House,
May 1, 1990.

Message to the Congress Transmitting the District of Columbia Budget and Supplemental Appropriations Request
May 1, 1990

To the Congress of the United States:

In accordance with the District of Columbia Self-Government and Governmental Reorganization Act, I am transmitting the District of Columbia Government's 1991 Budget request and 1990 Budget supplemental request.

The District's general fund 1991 operating budget request is $3,241 million. Total 1991 Federal payments anticipated in the District's budget are $540 million. The District's 1990 general fund budget supplemental request contains $111 million in cost increases and $131 million in budget authority rescissions, for a net decrease of $20 million. This transmittal does not affect the Federal budget.

There are three District budget issues to which I would direct your attention. First, I encourage you to continue the abortion funding policy that the Congress established in the District's 1989 and 1990 appropriations laws, which prohibit the use of both Federal and local funds for abortions.

Second, the 1991 Budget proposes to modify and make permanent the 1990 pilot project that requires the District of Columbia to charge Federal establishments directly for water and sewer services. Inappropriate charges and excessive usage have been eliminated through this pilot project. As a result, Federal appropriations under the

pilot program for water and sewer services for 1990 will be roughly $4 million (or about 12 percent) lower than under the old, lump-sum payment system.

Third, I ask that the Congress reinstate the President's apportionment authority over the Federal payment to the District of Columbia. Directing immediate disbursement of the Federal payment at the start of the fiscal year increases Treasury's cost of borrowing. Further, the Congress very clearly did not intend to exempt this payment from sequestration in the original Gramm-Rudman-Hollings Act as current law permits.

GEORGE BUSH

The White House,
May 1, 1990.

Statement on the Death of Henry Gregory
May 1, 1990

Barbara and I are deeply saddened by the death of Rev. Henry Gregory. As minister of the Shiloh Baptist Church of Washington, Reverend Gregory reached out to help those in need. He saw the church as a promoter of "activities that are beneficial to the interests of those without work, food, shelter, or hope," and "an advocate for people who don't have a voice." His leadership led to the construction of the church's Family Life Center, which provides both spiritual and physical help to those coping

with hardships of inner-city life. Barbara and I well remember our visits with Reverend Gregory at the Vice President's house and the White House and attending services at his church. We commend his spiritual leadership and are proud to have known him. He was an outstanding leader, and he will be missed. Our condolences go out to his wife and children, and we share the loss with his parishioners and the community he loved and served so well.

Statement by Press Secretary Fitzwater on Proposed Legislation Concerning Federal Pay Reform
May 1, 1990

Today the administration is transmitting to the Congress the Federal Pay Reform Act of 1990. This legislation would reform and modernize the pay system for the Government's white collar civilian employees. The administration's proposal will provide several interim measures to address the

most serious recruitment and retention problems and then, over the next several years, will initiate broader reforms of the pay-setting machinery. These changes will help make the system more flexible in responding to the labor market and will strengthen the ties between pay and performance.

The administration feels these changes will enable us to recruit and retain outstanding employees to continue our nation's tradition of excellence in the civil service. We urge prompt congressional enactment of this legislative proposal.

Remarks at a Fundraising Dinner for the Korean War Veterans Memorial Commission
May 1, 1990

Thank you, Ed. Thank you all. Thank you very, very much. May I thank our Secretary, Ed Derwinski, whom I knew very well when I served with him a thousand years ago in the Congress. But let me just say he's doing a superb job for the veterans of this country, and I'm very proud to have been introduced by him. I want to salute General Stilwell, an old friend, a strong friend, a man I've respected for years and with whom I worked about 15 years ago in the intelligence community, and salute all the members of the Commission, salute those honorees, those distinguished Members of Congress with us tonight, other veterans of the Korean war, other veterans. And thank all of you. And for me, it's great to be here tonight. I want to single out Chairman Lee of Samsung, whose generosity and commitment means so much to this very special evening, and thank him.

In the spring of 1951, almost 40 years ago, President Truman addressed the American people in the midst of the Korean war, saying, "In the simplest terms, what we are doing in Korea is this: We are trying to prevent a third world war." The allied men and women who fought in Korea—and who continue to guard the boundary of the Republic of Korea—fulfilled that mission and helped ensure peace in the world. Korea, the first major struggle in the nuclear age, evolved into a war of battlefield stratagem and a war of international politics; but it was a war in which we turned the tide against communism for the first time in a victory regrettably sometimes ignored by history.

And a year before President Truman spoke, tensions in the Korean Peninsula had heightened, breaking out into a bitter conflict on June 25th, 1950, when the North Koreans launched a surprise attack on the fledgling Republic in the south. And President Truman quickly made the decision to commit American troops under the leadership of General Douglas MacArthur to stop the Communist aggression. And the world watched as fighting continued throughout 1950, and then from late April through this month of May in '51, the Communists began their Spring Offensive to drive us from the peninsula. But it was our two leaders, General Jim Van Fleet, commanding the 8th Army, and General Matt Ridgway, commanding the U.N. forces, who repelled the offensive and drove Communist troops back to the north. Although they could not join us tonight, General Van Fleet and General Ridgway—ages 98 and 95, respectively—deserve our respect and our gratitude.

So, we are here tonight to remember our veterans' remote battles and their combined talents in what is often called the forgotten victory. Once this memorial, this fantastic memorial, is constructed, no American will ever forget the test of freedom our brave sons and daughters faced as they sought to stop aggression. You see, it is right that America remember that struggle in the Pusan perimeter to the landing at Inchon to the recapture and brave defense of Seoul. It is never too late for America to express her gratitude to all those who served under our flag in Korea—those who made it home and those who didn't.

Looking back at the Korean conflict, our defense of freedom laid the foundation for the march of democracy we're seeing today around the world. And that march is reflected in this memorial—in the memorial itself—with 38 soldiers from all services moving down a path toward the United States flag—the strongest symbol of freedom known throughout the world. It's those men and women honored by this memorial who joined the South Korean troops under the U.N. banner to help save a proud nation from communism, men like the Members of Congress you are saluting here tonight who served in the Armed Forces during the Korean war. Because of these brave soldiers and so many others, South Korea is now on its way to becoming one of the world's greatest economic powers with a freely elected democratic government and secure borders.

And so, to the veterans of the Korean war and to all attending, thank you for this opportunity to join you in saluting these Members of Congress, these old soldiers who have not just faded away but who have continued to serve their country in elected

office. And in closing, let me share with you a line from Tennyson, in which Ulysses looks back with his soldiers on the battles they fought as young men and tells them, "Though much has been taken, much abides."

We honor tonight the heroic hearts and strong will of our Korean war veterans, who have given so much that others might have freedom. God bless you all, and thank you for letting me come over to pay my respects to your honorees tonight. Thank you and God bless you.

Note: The President spoke at 7:45 p.m. in the Regency Gallery at the Omni Shoreham Hotel. In his opening remarks, he referred to Secretary of Veterans Affairs Edward J. Derwinski; Gen. Richard G. Stilwell, USA, Ret.; and Lee Kun Hee, chairman of the Samsung Group.

Remarks to the President's Committee on Employment of People With Disabilities
May 2, 1990

Good morning. And, Justin, thank you, my dear friend, for that most generous introduction. I'm just delighted to be with all of you. I want to say how pleased I am to see Ed Rensi and thank him for what he and his company are doing in this field of interest to all of us. I had a little opportunity just before I came in here to say hello to another person I admire very much—Patricia Neal, over here. And then I was glad to see Chris Burke again. Last time I saw him he was running wild in the White House. Not really—but he came over, and we did a little tape together. But he's doing great, and I'm so proud that he's with us here today.

I'm going to get into real trouble on all this acknowledgment; but I'm delighted, of course, to be with Justin Dart. He is truly a great humanitarian. He's one of the strongest advocates for equal rights and equal opportunity for all Americans that I've ever met, especially those with disabilities. And his hard work and perseverance through

adversity benefited all of us. And you have to forgive me for rambling on about Justin. It's just that not only is he a friend but he truly is one of the founding fathers of the Americans with Disabilities Act, one of the most important pieces of legislation to ever reach Capitol Hill.

And as I said almost 2 years ago, it is time—past time—that people with disabilities are included in the mainstream of American life. As members of a community who are actively involved in helping disabled Americans join the work force, I don't have to tell you that we face many difficulties. More than two-thirds of our fellow citizens with disabilities of working age are, indeed, unemployed; and that is intolerable. And much of that unemployment stems from lack of opportunity. And ADA, that act, will form the foundation for policies and programs that can create opportunities for Americans with disabilities to find and hold jobs and to enjoy the income and satisfaction that productive participation in society brings to us all. And no longer can we allow ignorance or prejudice to deny opportunities to millions of Americans with disabilities.

We recognize your right to equal opportunity, and we need your abilities and skills. Anybody who takes a look at the demographics in this country and looks just over the horizon into the future knows that the problem is going to be not finding jobs for people but finding people for the jobs that exist as we move towards the end of this decade. We welcome you, the disabled, into the mainstream of American life because it is your life as well as ours.

Every American should be able to join the work force to the fullest extent of their abilities. And I am hopeful that the House of Representatives will take action soon on the ADA, just as the Senate took enthusiastic action last September. I look forward to signing a bill that will address the needs of our disabled citizens. And frankly, it is my view that disabled citizens have waited long enough for equality.

Now, I was asked over here for a special purpose. And this morning I have the pleasure of sharing the stage with some truly exemplary Americans. And I wish I had time to introduce each one of them because their efforts are certainly outstanding. There is, however, one individual who de-

serves special mention. His name is David Schwartzkopf. As you saw—and I understand you've just seen this video—David has overcome some extremely tough obstacles—cerebral palsy, legal blindness, early misdiagnosis—to become a completely mainstreamed professional in a high-technology industry. Not content to merely be successful in his professional career, David is out in society doing all that he can to help other disabled Americans overcome some big hurdles. His inventions have helped visually impaired people enter the work force, his speeches have inspired management to rethink their hiring practices, and his consulting is helping to bring about equal opportunities. David gives meaning to the words dignity and independence.

And so, it is with great pleasure that I present you, David, with the President's trophy, proclaiming you the 1990 Disabled American of the Year. Congratulations for your help to so many others. Congratulations.

Note: The President spoke at 10:28 a.m. in the Ballroom at the Washington Hilton Hotel. In his remarks, he referred to Justin Dart, Chairman of the President's Committee on Employment of People With Disabilities; Edward Rensi, president and chief operating officer of McDonald's Corp.; and entertainers Patricia Neal and Chris Burke.

Remarks to the President's Youth Leadership Forum
May 2, 1990

Well, Barbara and I heard there was a good meeting going on, and we thought we'd slide over and say hello and officially welcome you to the White House. I'm delighted that my favorite Point of Light, as we call it, is with me this morning. I'm sure some of you are familiar with what we mean: Points of Light—one American helping another, group of Americans helping other Americans. And my favorite Point of Light is right here, the Silver Fox.

One of the reasons we were a little late in coming over is that we were waiting for

truly one of America's brightest stars. She's proven she's human by getting caught up in airplane delays. And of course, I'm talking about Whitney Houston, who we still hope might be along at any minute. But the airlines or somebody did not cooperate—weather or something. But in any event, she's on her way.

Look, we're here because we know that America can be really transformed by youth engaged in service. There's no problem in America that young people cannot solve or certainly help solve. This first President's

Youth Leadership Forum will demonstrate the ability of youth to identify community problems, design action plans to solve these problems, marshal community resources, and then implement those action plans.

Sometimes we adults forget the capability of young people to change the world, but you should remind all of us that youth is no barrier to great achievements. Knowing I was coming over here, I asked for some examples from history. Joan of Arc was barely 17 when she began her quest to drive the English from France. By the age of 20—I'm not recommending that you have the end results that Joan of Arc had—[*laughter*]—but I'm simply pointing this out here. By the age of 20, Mozart had composed 250 of his most beautiful pieces of music. Einstein had discovered the theory of relativity by the age of 26. And by the age of 32, Alexander the Great's empire stretched from Indiana—[*laughter*]—it included Indiana—from India to the Adriatic.

Today's young people can bring that same strength and ingenuity, courage, and sensitivity to bear on the great challenge of our day, ensuring that no American goes through life unloved, uncared for, unclaimed. Third-graders in Nebraska call elderly shut-ins each morning to offer a word of comfort and cheer. A teen in Texas has her own program providing peer-to-peer

counseling to other victims of child abuse. Countless other young people here in Washington mentor little brothers and sisters, feed the hungry, minister to the homeless, tend to the sick. Young Americans of all ages, genders, races, income levels, all backgrounds, are breaking down the invisible walls that too often separate us—standing shoulder to shoulder, each giving his or her own special gift to another and each receiving in return the fulfillment that comes only from serving others.

And if serving others can teach young people anything, it is that no matter how unfortunate your circumstances, no matter how much you need someone else, someone else needs you even more. This forum is an important event for those of you who have resolved to make service central to our daily lives, and I will be following your progress with great expectations.

And I'm just delighted to have had this opportunity to be here. I don't know what the fate is of our featured guest, but I should probably go back to work at the White House. But we did want to come over and just wish you all the best. And thank you for what you're doing, and thank you for what you're fixing to do.

Note: The President spoke at 11:33 a.m. in Room 450 of the Old Executive Office Building.

Statement by Press Secretary Fitzwater on Modifications of Export Controls for Strategic Technologies and Goods
May 2, 1990

The President is recommending to the Coordinating Committee for Multilateral Export Controls (COCOM) that significant changes be made in the list of technologies subject to export control. For over 40 years, COCOM controls have helped the allies protect our technological achievements from being exported to our adversaries. The President initiated a comprehensive study of these controls in January to reflect the changes in Eastern Europe and the Soviet Union, as well as other military priorities

that have emerged in the last year or more. The President has concluded that a complete overhaul of the control list is warranted. Therefore, the United States will recommend to COCOM the development by the end of 1990 of a new core list of goods and technologies that is far shorter and less restrictive than the present list.

The President's proposals will continue to protect our advanced technology from being exported to the Soviet Union and other adversaries. In effect, our proposals will build "higher fences around fewer goods" by focusing on those items that are the most sensitive in terms of our national security. We will be able to pinpoint a streamlined list of exports that can make a major contribution to Soviet power while changing the restrictions on items such as personal computers which are readily available throughout the world anyway.

We will propose that of the 120 categories on COCOM's industrial list 30 will be eliminated completely, and the scope of another 13 will be reduced substantially. These changes reflect specific analysis by the Department of Defense that identifies technology of crucial importance to weapons production in the Soviet Union and other countries. They have the unanimous support of all security agencies.

Careful study indicates that most of the goods and technologies that we currently control to Eastern Europe and Soviet destinations are of low strategic value and should be decontrolled. These categories include computers, telecommunications equipment, and machine tools. More specifically, these categories will include off-the-shelf personal computers and some mainframe computers for use in banking, airline reservations, etc.

We are proposing greater access for Eastern Europe to modern fiber optics equipment and some microwave telecommunications systems. Access to this technology is dependent on adoption of safeguards against diversion, such as identification of authorized uses and verification inspections.

The United States will begin consultations immediately with our allies on these changes. We think it is crucial to be able to provide maximum protection of our highly sensitive technologies while at the same time giving the Eastern Europeans access to technologies desperately needed to improve their infrastructure and modernize their industrial plants.

Note: The Office of the Press Secretary issued a fact sheet on the same day which provided the following additional information on modifications of export controls:

Core List

As a result of its evaluation, the United States recommended to its COCOM allies the development of a core list of technologies that need to be controlled to maintain the strategic technological edge that is a key component of our military strength.

The U.S. core list proposal, which is similar to a British proposal, would replace current export controls with a completely restructured list of key technologies and goods. This new list would be built from scratch. The military priorities identified by the Department of Defense's analysis would be a vital guide in identifying those technologies and goods that are militarily critical to our technological lead. The United States proposes that the new list supersede the regular COCOM lists by the end of 1990. The U.S. proposal would allow for phased or complete implementation as long as strategically critical items are fully integrated into the new list.

Decontrol in Priority Sectors

There are three priority sectors identified by COCOM for immediate or partial decontrol: computers, telecommunications equipment, and machine tools. These sectors account for a large portion of all export license applications and are key to infrastructure improvements in Eastern Europe. The United States has proposed significant decontrol in these categories as follows:

Computers. The U.S. proposal would provide for decontrol of computers to all destinations which have a Processing Data Rate (PDR) of 275 megabits per second (mps), which is half way to the China Green Line [limits of licensing to China], and favorable licensing treatment to civilian end-users all the way to the China Green Line (a PDR of 550 mps). This action would result in the decontrol of most off-the-shelf personal computers and allow access to some mainframe computers for applications in banking, airline reservations, etc.

Telecommunications Equipment. The United States proposes relaxation of controls, for example, in some cellular communications systems and some satellite ground stations, to all destinations. We are proposing for Eastern Europe greater access to modern fiber optics equipment (to a transmission level of 156 megabits) and some microwave telecommunications systems. Access to this more advanced technology is dependent on adoption of safeguards against diversion.

Machine Tools. The U.S. Government will support with a few modifications a COCOM proposal calling for significant decontrol of machine tools and their numerical controllers. This results in decontrol of many machine tools with a positioning accuracy down to the ± 2 or 3 micron level depending on the type of machine tool.

Differentiation

The United States will recommend to COCOM that more favorable licensing treatment be accorded to countries adopting COCOM-approved safeguards against diversion of controlled goods and technol-

ogies to proscribed destinations or to unauthorized end-users. Such countries would be determined to be in transition to a status of a nonproscribed destination pursuant to COCOM-agreed conditions. COCOM would be asked to develop a list of technologies and goods to which such countries would have presumed favorable treatment.

Enforcement of Export Controls

The U.S. Government continues to encourage the enforcement of the controls by its allies. It is essential to obtain the agreement of our COCOM allies to a renewed commitment to improve compliance so that the core list of identified technologies is protected. The United States will seek adherence to the previously agreed common standard levels of protection against diversion or illegal acquisition of controlled goods and technologies.

White House Statement on the Proposed Foreign Acquisition of UniSoft Group Limited
May 2, 1990

The President has decided against intervening in the possible acquisition by CMC Limited, a firm owned by the Government of India, of UniSoft Group Ltd. (UGL), a British computer software firm with a subsidiary in the United States.

The President based his decision on the results of the investigation by the Committee on Foreign Investment in the United States (CFIUS), chaired by Treasury Secretary Nicholas F. Brady. CFIUS conducted a thorough investigation of various national security issues relating to India's acquisition of UniSoft Corp., the U.S. subsidiary. UniSoft develops, markets, distributes, and customizes software operating systems.

The CMC-UniSoft investigation was conducted pursuant to section 5021 of the Omnibus Trade and Competitiveness Act of

1988. That provision, known as the Exon-Florio provision, authorizes the President to investigate and, if necessary, to suspend or prohibit a proposed foreign acquisition of a U.S. business engaged in U.S. interstate commerce. The criteria to suspend or prohibit a transaction are that the President must find:

- credible evidence to believe that the foreign investor might take actions that threaten to impair the national security;
- that existing laws, other than the International Emergency Economic Powers Act and the Exon-Florio provision itself, are inadequate and inappropriate to deal with the national security threat.

The President's News Conference
May 3, 1990

The President. Let me just open with a statement, and then be glad to take some questions.

The revolutionary changes transforming Europe are moving us from the postwar era to a new era in history beyond containment. The revolutions of 1989 that have brought democracy to Eastern Europe, the prospect of German unification, and my hope for rapid conclusion of a CFE agreement bring us close to a peaceful and more stable Europe, whole and free.

And I'll be speaking tomorrow at commencement ceremonies in Oklahoma State University about my conception of America's place in the new Europe. And I want to use this press conference today as an opportunity to highlight for you a few of the ideas I plan to discuss at greater length tomorrow.

We've arrived at this historic point by maintaining a strong partnership with our European allies. NATO will remain vital to America's place in Europe. It is a proven structure upon which to base our security and from which to promote a stable, cooperative European order.

The alliance is now ready to take on new challenges. And in order to set a new Western strategy for these times and after consulting personally with my allied colleagues, a consultation completed by Secretary Baker in Brussels today, I'm calling for a NATO summit in early summer—late June or early July, probably. The fundamental purpose of this summit should be to launch a wide-ranging NATO strategy review for the transformed Europe of the 1990's.

To provide direction for this, I suggest that this summit should address, first, the future political mission of the alliance, reaffirming its crucial role in managing and stabilizing the transformation of Europe.

Second, the alliance's conventional defenses for the future and next steps for conventional arms control. While we're still in a period of transition, as Soviet forces leave Eastern Europe and our arms control works move forward, we need to develop a new strategy for the period ahead.

And third, the role of U.S. nuclear forces in Europe. As democracy comes to Eastern Europe and Soviet troops return home, there is less need for nuclear systems of the shortest range. And in response to these new conditions, I've decided to terminate the follow-on to Lance program and cancel any further modernization of U.S. nuclear artillery shells deployed in Europe. The NATO summit should agree on broad objectives for future negotiations between the United States and the Soviet Union on the current short-range nuclear missile forces in Europe, which should begin shortly after a CFE treaty has been signed.

Fourth, the future of the Conference on Security and Cooperation in Europe, CSCE; to give it and especially its Eastern European member states a more active part in shaping Europe's future. The CSCE can help to build free societies and provide a forum for political dialog in a united Europe. My allied colleagues and I should agree to take up these ideas at the CSCE summit this fall, to be held around the signing of a CFE treaty.

The future of the United States cannot be separated from the future of Europe. And so, along with our allies, we must prepare for the magnificent opportunities that lie ahead. In these times of uncertainty and hope, NATO will continue to be vital to America's place in Europe and a bulwark of democratic values and security.

So, this is what I'll be talking about tomorrow. And it has been discussed by Jim Baker with our allies in Brussels yesterday and today.

I don't know who has the first question but—Helen [Helen Thomas, United Press International]?

U.S. Hostages in Lebanon

Q. Mr. President, you said that things were moving on the hostage front. Can I ask you what are the prospects of getting all the hostages out? They may sometimes feel like sacrificial lambs as the U.S. stands and waits. What good will gesture do you have in mind to facilitate this and expedite their release?

The President. I would have in mind any gesture that wouldn't be perceived as negotiating for the release of hostages. We have a policy; I'm going to stay with that policy.

But let me give you an example, Helen. One of the things that the Iranians are interested in is the fate of, I believe it was, four Iranians that were taken, I think, back in '82. Now, if there's some way that we can go back and get any information that would relieve the anxieties of the loved ones of those four people, we ought to do that. And it is our view—and I've said this, made this clear that it is the best information we have—that these people are not alive.

But just as we'd like a full accounting for Higgins, our heroic Marine that apparently has been killed, I can understand the Iranians wanting a full accounting, even though they know we have nothing to do with this. So, here's an area where they have said they'd like some information, and if we can get it, I think we ought to get it. And we're trying. So, if that is good will, so be it. I hope it is. That's the way I would intend it. And there may be other things we can do. But, look, I understand the anxiety of the hostage families, and I can understand the broken hearts. And that's why I'm not going to shift and act like everything is normal.

Q. Well, what are you really doing now to——

The President. I've just given you one example. And if there are others, why——

Q. And are you passing this word to Iran, and also in terms of the frozen assets and——

The President. Yes. Well, that's been going on, as you know—some discussion on frozen assets. Abe Sofaer [Legal Adviser, Department of State] has been over there, and if they view that as good will, fine. And if that can continue now in some way, fine. But that we've already discussed in open— and I'm not sure they would view that as enough, you know.

Q. Does it look brighter, though?

The President. There's a third follow-on here. I don't know, Helen, and it's an awful

good question. Look, I have tried very hard not to raise the hopes of the hostage families only to have them dashed. And there's a certain cruelty in this process when you flash a picture of a person that's held hostage and then another person appears in freedom. I welcome the release of Polhill and Reed. But I can't rejoice and say that my heart is full of great good will as long as six others are held hostage.

Yeah, Terry [Terence Hunt, Associated Press]?

Export Controls

Q. Mr. President, within the last 2 weeks, you've been considering penalties against Moscow for its treatment of Lithuania. Now, however, you're liberalizing sales of computers and other high technology to Moscow. Senator D'Amato, among others, says that now is not the time to be nice to the Soviet Union. Why have you decided on this course of reward rather than punishment?

The President. Well, I don't consider the COCOM reevaluation a policy of reward. I'll have to discuss that with Al D'Amato to see that he understands the facts, because what we're doing is putting up tighter walls around needed items that are in the national security interest. When the other items that are not on the list for pure national security now, they're going to come off. And I don't view this as giving something to the Soviets at all. So, we just have a difference of opinion with the good Senator.

Lithuanian Independence

Q. To follow up on Lithuania: Do you endorse the idea from West Germany and Britain that Lithuania suspend some of the laws pertaining to independence?

The President. I think this is a matter that Landsbergis [President of Lithuania] spoke to yesterday and indicated some flexibility there. And whatever will facilitate dialog is good. And he has seen some merit in what was suggested by Mitterrand [President of France] and Kohl [Chancellor of the Federal Republic of Germany]. And I think that is very, very positive, and let's hope it goes forward.

U.S. Hostages in Lebanon

Q. Mr. President, on hostages, didn't the ceremonious welcome that you gave Mr. Polhill here the other night and his access to you, to pass a message supposedly from his captors, send a signal to terrorists that the best way to communicate with the President of the United States is to capture an American and give him a message? And second, didn't the welcome given Polhill suggest that even citizens who disobey their government's warnings and then are captured, something their government's trying to prevent, can then be treated as heroes even by the President?

The President. Both of these considerations worry me, Brit [Brit Hume, ABC News], to be very honest with you. And I must say I enjoyed this meeting with this highly civil human being, who has a marvelous sense of humor in spite of his captivity, and I'm delighted. But what happened on that one was, we hadn't planned a great public ceremony of this nature. Timing was such that Mr. Reed came out, there was keen interest in having a response to the present, and so we accommodated this understandable interest by having a press conference. So, it wasn't timed to make a high visibility reception of Polhill.

The other thing is, he did have a message for me. And I've said I'm going to go the extra mile; I am not going to leave any stone unturned. And he brought it. He asked that it be kept confidential, and it will. And I don't think that part of it is bad.

I think that part shows that the message—I don't worry so much of the message. What I do worry about is if anybody perceives that we're putting a higher price on some human being by all of this. So, I was troubled by what you said. But I sorted it out and did my best.

Q. What about the message, sir? Can you tell us without laying it out in detail whether it taught you anything new about the situation over there?

The President. No, it did not teach me anything new about it. But it was the putting it all in one capsule that was very interesting. And I will share it discreetly with key members of our National Security Council and the intelligence community,

but I must not violate his request that the message be confidential.

Relations With Eastern-Bloc Countries

Q. Mr. President, back to Europe for a minute. Your actions speak to a policy of helping Gorbachev even though your own Defense Secretary says he's probably not going to succeed. And I think this is a question a lot of Americans would like to hear you answer: Why have you decided on Gorbachev over speaking out for American principle?

The President. I don't think I have, Lesley [Lesley Stahl, CBS News].

Q. Well, what about Lithuanian independence over Gorbachev?

The President. I don't think that's the choice. I don't think that's the choice. And let me repeat here—if anybody has any doubt about where their President stands: Of course, we favor self-determination. I don't think that's new—my saying that. And of course, we favor democracy and freedom. There's a lot at stake in all of this, and there's complications in all of this. Poland, Eastern Europe—I want those troops out, and I want to see the firming up of the democracies in Eastern Europe, and I want to see us keep this process going forward. So, our foreign policy is not based on just Mr. Gorbachev. Now, if the man has done something good and surprised everybody in this room, including me, about the acceptance of freedom and democracy in Eastern Europe—and he has—give credit for that.

But on Lithuania, there's an enormously complicated problem. And I must say I'm looking forward to visiting with the Prime Minister in a little bit—of Lithuania. But I must convince the Lithuanian-Americans that my desire for their freedom and their self-determination is just as strong as anybody else's. And I also must convince those here and around the world that we want to see the peaceful evolution that's taking place towards democracy continue. So, when Terry asked his question about dialog, that is our policy. And I'm delighted to see that Landsbergis now feels there may be some merits in this policy.

But, Lesley, we can't place this on a you-have-to-choose-between-Gorbachev-or-

Landsbergis. That's not the policy of the United States Government, nor should it be.

Soviet May Day Demonstrations

Q. Well, a followup: The May Day parade—Mr. Gorbachev was heckled. Your Defense Secretary says he doesn't think that Mr. Gorbachev can succeed with his reforms. Do you?

The President. The May Day parade? He ought to come join some of the parades I go to around here. This goes for your horse, too. I mean, you ought to see some of the expression of—[*laughter*]—look, that's the fruits of democracy. He's just learning. He's just learning. So, I wouldn't read too much into that. Yes, there's some discontent. A lot of it relates to the economy, and some of it relates, by Lithuanians inside the Soviet Union, to the handling of Lithuania.

There's a good side to all of this. I sometimes ask myself if that's true, but it is because that's the way fledgling democracies are beginning to work and that's the way our system has worked. And I don't suppose if anytime anyone points to a demonstration that gets rambunctious in the United States and points to—that means instability in the United States system; there's got to be something crazy. Because that isn't the way it works.

Federal Budget

Q. You seem to be getting serious about the budget now. You invited congressional leaders to the White House Sunday night to talk about the budget. No one in Congress believes your budget projections partly because interest rates have risen since you announced your budget. Should you revise your budget projections? And when you talk to Mitchell [Senate majority leader] and Foley [Speaker of the House of Representatives], is everything on the table? Everything negotiable, including taxes?

The President. In the first place, yes, we've been a little off on interest rates. But I will say that we've been very close to right on growth in the GNP. But I think we're required by law to come up with a new forecast later on this year.

But, look, here's what we need to do. We sent a budget up, and, okay, so nobody was too enthusiastic about it. Nobody's very en-thusiastic about the Senate budget. Nobody's very enthusiastic about the House budget, in my view—really enthusiastic.

So, what we have to do is start talking process and how we go forward. And I'm not going to sit here and do nothing. So, that process has worked. Congress was supposed to have moved by April 1st, and they didn't. Now there seems to be more action, so it seemed to me like a good time to sit down and talk process and see where we go now.

Q. You didn't say you were going to talk taxes. And beyond that——

The President. I didn't say we were going to talk any substance. This meeting that you've referred to is to sit down and meet with four leaders. Oddly, it worked out very nicely because I wanted to invite them all to come to a Presidential lecture series on Teddy Roosevelt on Sunday, and afterward we'll get together and discuss something a little more complicated.

Q. I haven't heard any "read my lips." Are taxes——

The President. No, you haven't heard it because I'm going to sit down and talk to them about what I said I was going to talk about.

Q. Can I follow on the budget?

The President. Nice try, though, John [John Cochran, NBC News]. I'm not saying—we're not into a negotiation. We're talking process. One problem about having that all out is, people are going to understandably want to know all these conditions and preconditions. But we're not there. What we are at is, we've got to move forward, and I've got to find a way to do that.

Federal Deposit Insurance Corporation Chairman Seidman

Q. Can I follow on the budget, Mr. President? It appears now the administration has acknowledged what your FDIC Chairman, Bill Seidman, had been saying all along, which is that the savings and loan bailout is going to be a lot more expensive than you initially anticipated. Why, then, are you so anxious to see him leave, and how are you going to accommodate his increased costs at a time of fiscal constraint?

The President. Hey, listen, I haven't told

you I'm anxious to see Bill Seidman leave.

Q. Aren't you saying that you wouldn't be unhappy to see him leave?

The President. Bill Seidman asked to see me a while back—came to see me. Said he was not going to fulfill the rest of his term, and we discussed that. He asked to see me to tell me that. Today he called me with the name of a successor that he enthusiastically supports. And he's done a good job. We have a significant project that he's in the middle of handling—we call it the June 30th Project—to get a lot more done with a lot of these savings and loan in a short period of time. He's agreed to enthusiastically tackle that.

And he also said, look, I understand if you might want to put your own person in there. But it's his initiative with me, and today he suggested the name of a Bill Taylor who we're very high on to take over his responsibilities. So, it's one where everyone wants to have winners and losers, and I don't think there are any. I think Seidman has conducted himself with extraordinary grace and great ability. I've known him for years, worked with him way back when.

Savings and Loan Bailout

Q. Mr. President, the costs—how to deal with the increased costs of the bailout.

The President. We've got to work with the Congress on how to deal with the cost. And right now, there's a significant review going forward to see what the costs are. The figures change all the time on you.

Defense Spending and Foreign Aid

Q. Mr. President, you talked a minute ago about fledgling democracies in Eastern Europe. Has your administration given any thought to a wholesale reevaluation of America's foreign aid requirements now that the Warsaw Pact is collapsing? And two, what's your response to those who say that we ought to take some money from the military and spend it on foreign aid for these fledgling democracies?

The President. My response to the latter part is: Everybody wants to take money from defense to do something else. And the Defense Secretary and I want to provide adequately for the defense in a changing world. And I think Dick Cheney's done a

good job up there trying to hold the line against a Congress that says, Anytime there's a need for anything, please take it out of Defense. And so, we're in a problem of my trying to hold the line, ably supported by and, in some instances, led by Dick Cheney, who's up there really fighting this battle.

What was the first part, excuse me?

Q. About a full-scale review of America's foreign aid requirements. Are you interested in doing one of those or not?

The President. Well, I'd be interested in a full-scale review. I mean, a lot of our percentage of aid goes to a handful of countries. And here we have a man coming in here today—the Prime Minister of Jamaica, Mr. Manley—who has just done a first-class job in trying to move Jamaica forward in many, many ways. And I salute him for that. But his aid was a small amount, and I believe it's been just lined out because of insufficient resources or failure to reallocate.

I've suggested that the President be given a discretionary fund out of all this foreign aid so we can accommodate a person that is trying to take his small country and firm up its democracy. So, I think a review of the nature you're talking about might be helpful, but I remember my days in Congress: Foreign aid doesn't have the constituency out there that domestic programs do.

U.S. Hostages in Lebanon

Q. Mr. President, have you done an analysis of these hostage releases, such that you conclude whether or not this is the beginning of a process that's likely to lead to all the releases? And what is the United States doing behind the scenes that might have contributed to these releases? We know you're talking to Iran through third countries, but can you give us sort of a status——

The President. I can't say that our actions facilitated the release of Reed and Polhill. I hope that the affirmation and reaffirmation of our policy might have contributed to it, but there was no behind-the-scenes negotiations that will come out that show that we pulled this off. I wish I could—I was going to say, I wish I could say that was true, but it would have to be true within these confines I've spelled out here earlier on. But we will continue to stay with the policy, trying to show good will where we can do it without violating the policy.

Q. Then have you concluded, sir, whether this is the beginning of a process of——

The President. The intelligence community's looking at that right now. The debrief of Reed and the debrief of Polhill might contribute to that. But you can rest assured that I have asked for that answer: Will this lead inevitably to the release of others? But I can't say that I've gotten any feeling that this process is destined to go forward in a short period of time. I wish it was different. I so wish it were different.

Soviet President Gorbachev

Q. Mr. President, there's a report in Europe today, citing Western intelligence sources, that on February 25th, the day of large demonstrations in Moscow, Mr. Gorbachev was perilously close to being overthrown—the Soviet Army troops were mobilized. Is it your assessment that he has come that close to facing a coup of some type within the Soviet Union?

The President. I was not advised of that by the intelligence community.

Q. Well, beyond that, sir, is there at any point, in any sense—as we've heard you say many times, you want Gorbachev and *perestroika* to survive—that you are structuring your program to assist him in any way, shape, or form? That that's why you're toeing this very difficult line between Lithuania and Moscow?

The President. I've expressed my keen interest in seeing *perestroika* succeed. Gorbachev is the architect of *perestroika*. Gorbachev conducted the affairs of the Soviet Union with great restraint as Poland and Czechoslovakia and GDR [German Democratic Republic] and other countries achieved their independence. But you can't build a foreign policy of a country on the presence of an individual. You can build it on ideas. You can build it on how do you facilitate the change toward democracy and freedom, whether it's in the countries where that's taken place or in the countries where it hasn't taken place. And so, I would

say I salute the man for what he has done. I think he's under extraordinary pressure at home, particularly on the economy; and I do, from time to time, worry about a takeover that will set back the whole process. But I have no evidence to support the incident or the timeframe that you asked about.

Q. Or any other?

The President. Or in any timeframe, yes.

China-U.S. Relations

Q. Mr. President, it's been nearly a year since the Tiananmen Square massacre. Can you point to anything in the last year in your policies that have improved the situation there after a year of trying to head off severe sanctions and keep the rhetoric down?

The President. Well, several things. I've already mentioned them, and I'd repeat— Fulbright and Peace Corps and some of these matters. But I'm disappointed. I've said that publicly before, and I am because I would like to think there would be a more vigorous response. I was pleased that they lifted martial law in Tibet the other day.

So, there are some things that are happening that are going in the right direction, but overall, I'm disappointed. And yet preserving a relationship with the People's Republic of China in the broad global context is important. So, I have no apologies. I have no feeling that I took the wrong path. I mean, we did, by Executive action, everything that the Congress would have done by legislative action—everything. And so, there wasn't any substantive difference with the Congress on this.

And so, look, I'll express a certain disappointment because I'd like to see more action, more things happen that really move the whole process forward.

Q. Do you have anything in mind other than expressing disappointment to move things along?

The President. We've got some diplomacy in mind.

Soviet Acceptance of European Realignment

Q. Do you think that your proposal of nuclear weapons in Europe will be enough for the Soviet Union to accept a reunified

Germany within NATO?

The President. Our policy on what?

Q. Your change on nuclear weapons in Europe—will that give you——

The President. You mean on the Lance follow-on?

Q. Will that be enough for the Soviet Union to accept a reunified Germany?

The President. I think they're going to accept it because that's the right thing to have happen. And I want to see that determined by the alliance and keep the solid alliance position. And I want to see the Soviets understand that it is in their interest for a U.S. presence, in their interest for an expanded NATO, in their interest in a united Germany to be inside that expanded NATO.

We got to get back to some of these backbenchers, or I'm going to catch it. You can hear the enthusiasm for that.

Arms Reduction Negotiations

Q. Mr. President, the Soviets seem to be backpedaling in both START on the cruise missiles and some of the things we think they agreed to on troop levels on CFE. Are you concerned about this? And what's your assessment now of the prospects for both a START treaty and a CFE treaty this year?

The President. We're going to have to hustle. We're going to have to hustle, and they're going to have to come forward. But I don't want to say we're not going to get a CFE agreement, and I don't want to say we're not going to get the principles of a START agreement locked in. And that's what I'd like to see happen, and the summit that's coming up serves as some incentive for that to take place.

Q. Were you concerned that they've reneged on some things the United States thought they agreed to, and does that suggest Mr. Gorbachev's not living up to his commitment to move——

The President. It suggests a lot of things. When you analyze the Soviet Union very carefully—some things that are quite disturbing if, indeed, they stay in a position where they back off. But let's hope that that can all be resolved. But if you analyze carefully that they pull back on that, then you've got to say, Why is that happening? What's the military saying who are most

affected by decisions of that nature? This is a matter of some concern.

War on Drugs

Q. Mr. President, on drugs, have you changed or are you contemplating a change in your stated administration policy which forbids active operational involvement of U.S. military forces in foreign countries?

The President. I'm not sure I understand what you're—what policy that involves active military? I want our military to be involved in interdiction. And they are involved in interdiction, and they're doing a good job in that.

Q. Will they be or have they been involved in specific operational missions, such as searching for drug cartel leaders?

The President. Inside Colombia? Be more specific, please, and I'll try to help you.

Q. Much talk about Gacha. Were they involved in the Gacha——

The President. No. U.S. troops in Colombia? No. That's the answer. Next. Do you have a followup?

Q. I have an unrelated follow.

The President. No, unrelated follow-ons are not fair.

Hostages

Q. Mr. President, on the hostages, you have frequently pressed the kidnapers to release them. You have urged Iran and Syria to do whatever they can to release them. One of the Iranians' demands—or the kidnapers' demands is the release of the 400 Shiites and Sheik Obeid that the Israelis hold. You have not pressed the Israelis to do something to facilitate a resolution of that problem. I'd like to ask you why not and why the Arab nations should not see it as a double standard?

The President. I've stated my position: that hostage-holding is unproductive towards facilitating political change. And I'll repeat it again. I want to see all hostages released. There are some, obviously, in all Muslim countries. In Israel, there's definitional problems there. But the United States is opposed to taking hostages.

Q. Why is there a definitional problem?

The President. Because some people view people that they hold as having broken their laws, and some don't. And it's not for the U.S. to make these determinations. It is for the United States to say we oppose taking of hostages and holding people against their will just to effect some kind of political change.

Arms Reduction Negotiations

Q. Mr. President, you raised the question a moment ago about what is it that the Soviet military is saying in the apparent backing off. What do you think that they are saying, and do you believe that your announcement today about missiles in Europe will change the Soviet military's attitude towards the negotiations that are currently going on?

The President. No, I'm not doing these things just to put at ease the Soviet military at all. We're doing this because we feel that it's in the alliance's interest and in the interest of world peace. But I must tell you, I sometimes do worry about the military resurgence of some kind inside the Soviet Union. Of course, I worry about that.

Baltic States Independence

Q. Mr. President, the Legislature of Latvia meets today to consider its independence. Would you advise them to be less confrontational in their approach than Lithuania was?

The President. I have no advice for them whatever. I can identify with their aspirations for freedom. I have noted that there's some nuances of difference in the way they are approaching the matter. But that is a matter for them to work out. And the answer is dialog—some would say negotiations; call it what you will—talking to each other to facilitate self-determination and independence. And that's the way they ought to do it. And I get the feeling that that's what they're about.

Q. Mr. President, with this call for dialog and with this step of meeting with the Prime Minister of Lithuania [Kazimiera Prunskiene] later today, do you see yourself assuming some sort of a mediation role between Vilnius and Moscow?

The President. If there was a role for the United States—and I've thought about that. I've talked to Brent [Brent Scowcroft, Assistant to the President for National Securi-

ty Affairs] and Secretary Baker about this. And if there was a constructive role for the United States, of course, we should fulfill that role. But there's not. And I don't see that emerging for a lot of different reasons. But if somebody said you can facilitate that through being a negotiator, which is just hard for me to conceive given the realities in the world, of course, we'd be interested in doing that. But I don't think that's a reality.

Q. A followup, sir. Do you find yourself in an unusual or odd diplomatic position in referring to this woman as the Prime Minister? Marlin Fitzwater [Press Secretary to the President] has told us that you will address her as Prime Minister, but yet you do not recognize her as the Prime Minister of an independent country.

The President. No, I don't find myself in a dilemma there.

Mrs. Bush's Commencement Address

Q. Mr. President, a small group of students at Wellesley have objected to Mrs. Bush's——

The President. Yes, Ellen [Ellen Warren, Knight-Ridder Newspapers]! [*Laughter*]

Q. Mr. President, do you believe that there is any merit to their argument that Mrs. Bush's accomplishments are largely related to her marriage to yourself? [*Laughter*] And secondly——

The President. I can't have any argument with that. [*Laughter*]

Q. Oooh.

Q. We've got a lead. [*Laughter*]

Q. ——by their hesitation to have her speak to them?

The President. Yes. And Mrs. Bush herself has put it that her ability to serve as, I think, a terribly effective Point of Light stems from the fact that she's married to the President of the United States. But I think that these young women can have a lot to learn from Barbara Bush and from her unselfishness and her advocacy of literacy and of being a good mother and a lot of other things. So, I have no objection. As Bar said yesterday, she isn't concerned that the 125 students feel this way. And I think they'll learn a lot from her. And she wants to go, and she's not concerned by it at all.

615

But she herself said, "Look, I know why I'm privileged to be able to serve in this visible fashion." She's not trying to be something she's not. The American people love her because she's something she is and stands for something.

Mexico-U.S. Relations

Q. Mr. President, do you think that the relations with Mexico have been damaged by the Machain case? And can the United States pay bounty to foreigners to abduct people in other countries?

The President. The United States has had an official system of rewards. Remember at the time of Noriega and stuff there were some rewards out. But I hope the relations haven't been damaged. The Vice President, incidentally, did a very good job in explaining the policy to President Salinas himself. Our Attorney General [Dick Thornburgh] has worked very closely with the Mexicans. We have had superb cooperation from Mexico in fighting drugs—outstanding. And so, I salute them. But, yes, there was some misunderstanding here, and I have told our key people: Eliminate the misunderstanding. We don't want misunderstanding with Mexico; we don't need it. We need continued cooperation, and we're getting continued——

Q. But in the future, are they going to continue going into Mexico—the agents of the United States?

The President. That's a matter for Mexico to decide. And if Mexico wanted to have some people work with our people here, and that could help the fight against narcotics, I would be very open to that if it fit into our fight against drugs.

I've got time for two more. One in the middle, and then, Sarah [Sarah McClendon, McClendon News], you get the last one.

Federal Deposit Insurance Corporation Chairman Seidman

Q. Mr. President, if Bill Seidman has done such an outstanding job at the FDIC in overseeing the savings and loan bailout, why didn't you prevail on him to stay on to assure continuity and an independent voice at that agency?

The President. Because I think that his decision was a personal one, and he's entitled to make it, and that's why. And I support it, and I salute him again.

Q. He didn't bring bad news about what the cost of that bailout might be, did he?

The President. Listen, if all the people who brought bad news in here were asked to do something else, it would be a little lonely. No, that's not the reason for this at all. I would ask that you talk to Bill about it.

Q. Mr. President, is this the last question?

The President. This is the last one. You've been a very good sport.

War on Drugs

Q. Sir, thank you very much. I want to know if you are going to ask permission from Congress to send U.S. troops into Peru and take $35 million of our much-needed money right now and build a military installation down there for us to train their troops to fight drug cartels?

The President. To send U.S. troops in there to do that?

Q. Are you going to ask Congress for permission to do that?

The President. I have not considered asking Congress for that. But if there's some training role that will facilitate the fight against drugs, I would be willing to consider it. But I have no intention of asking Congress at this moment for anything of that nature.

Q. Do you feel now that you have the authority to build this installation, which has been reported that you were planning to build, down there in Peru?

The President. Just a minute. I need expert advice on this. Your talking about building a facility? What facility? What facility are we talking about? We'll have to get back to you. [*Laughter*] See the kind of advice I'm getting here. [*Laughter*] No, really, I'm sorry. I just don't know about any facility. But I do know that the concept of training is a very valid concept. I don't think it requires approval from the U.S. Congress. But if the law requires me to ask, if we do something that's going to require that along the lines here, then I would ask. We're not trying to get around Congress; we work very cooperatively with them.

I have to go.

Q. One more.

The President. No, I have to—all right, one more. No, not you.

Missing Iranians

Q. Earlier you dropped a hint about the United States helping obtain the release of some Iranian hostages. Who has got them, and how can you help?

The President. These were four Iranian diplomats that were taken in Lebanon in 1982. And the Iranians don't feel that they've had a full accounting of these people. In fact, I think they still hope that those people are alive. The best information we have as an outside party to all of this is that they are not still alive.

But my point is, if Iran feels that way and the families of these four people feel that way, this is something where we should use every asset we have to disperse the lack of information, to bring them the facts if we can. See, this is something they feel strongly about. They've mentioned it to us several different times. And here's something we can do without violating our policy. It's something I'd like to do. And I think they would consider this a gesture of good will.

So, we're trying very hard. Again, I wish I felt that the answer we gave them would be different than the one—because there's a human equation here. There is some suffering here on families in Iran. So, it's——

Q. Are you doing something, though, in this specific case?

The President. What?

Q. You've spoken about the things that you could do. Are you doing something in this case?

The President. Yes, we're trying to find—it's very hard to do.

Q. How did the Iranians mention it to us? How did they mention it to us?

The President. Very carefully.

Note: The President's 46th news conference began at 10 a.m. in the Briefing Room at the White House. In his remarks, he referred to the following individuals: Lt. Col. William R. Higgins, USMC, chief of the U.N. peacekeeping force in southern Lebanon, who was kidnaped by pro-Iranian terrorists on February 17, 1988, and allegedly hanged on July 31, 1989; Robert Polhill, an accounting professor at Beirut University College who was kidnaped by pro-Iranian terrorists in Beirut on January 24, 1987; Frank Herbert Reed, the director of the Lebanon International School who was kidnaped by members of the Organization of the Islamic Dawn on September 9, 1986; and Sheik Abdul Karim Obeid, the senior Moslem cleric and Hizballah leader who was abducted from his home in Jibchit by Israeli forces in southern Lebanon on July 28, 1989.

Remarks Following Discussions With Prime Minister Michael Manley of Jamaica
May 3, 1990

The President. Mr. Prime Minister and members of the Jamaican delegation, thank you for coming to the White House. We are pleased and, indeed, honored that you are with us here today. It's been my pleasure to host Prime Minister Manley on this first official visit to Washington. Columbus may have had something going correct when he said in 1494—he called it "the fairest isle that eyes have beheld," speaking about Jamaica. And those of us who have been there, and I'm included, understand exactly what Christopher Columbus meant.

The United States and Jamaica enjoy a very close relationship, and that's because we have so many bonds of friendship and family. Some 5,000 Americans have made Jamaica their home, while 400,000 of your people have settled here in the United States, and I think that's to the enrichment of both countries. Early in this century, one Jamaican couple moved to this country. They raised a son, told him to do something with his life. Their son grew up to be the man that both Jamaicans and Americans can be very proud of, and I'm talking about our Chairman of the Joint Chiefs of Staff, General Colin Powell. I had a chance to discuss him behind his back with the Prime Minister at lunch, and he assured me that Jamaicans have that same high regard that we do for our Chairman.

In our meeting today, we not only renewed a friendship that I value, but I had a chance to express to him the total satisfaction that I feel about the cooperation between our countries. We talked about some difficult problems: the economic and financial situation. The Prime Minister, no holds barred, told me of some of the problems that he faces in terms of an external debt. That was coupled with some news he gave me about the dynamic growth in the Jamaican GNP. I commended his efforts to meet the difficult economic and developmental challenges through diversification. And then again, he's been out front on the private sector investment front, and I salute that and told him so.

The United States wants to help in these efforts, and I'm afraid I cried on his shoulder a little about some budget limitations that we face here in the United States. But we will continue to support development and growth in Jamaica. And as neighbors that share democratic traditions, we explored the historic political developments in the Caribbean and Latin America. I asked him for his views about what was happening in Central America as well as the Caribbean, and he shared them with me—a very insightful presentation.

I do appreciate his insights, and I very much appreciate the role that Jamaica plays in regional affairs. We gave particular applause to his efforts on behalf of democracy and economic reform. I think we see eye to eye on the need for that to continue. I've commissioned Secretary Brady and asked Secretary Eagleburger [Deputy Secretary of State] both to undertake some specific assignments to see how much flexibility the United States can have in helping Jamaica in the ways that would benefit their move towards more privatization, more economic growth, and more to the benefit of all Jamaican people.

So, we touched on the subject of coopera-

tion in narco-trafficking. Jamaica has been steadfast in working with us, determined to cut down this trafficking. We want to salute those individuals in Jamaica who are working in cooperation with the United States in the war on drugs. The Jamaican efforts are crucial, and we look forward to continued cooperation in this area.

So, all in all, it was just the kind of visit that I, at least, look forward to: a frank discussion between friends. We also shared with the Prime Minister our global view of our relations with the Soviet Union and our insight into developments in Eastern Europe, knowing that, though, the way we handle these matters affect countries here in the Caribbean and all around the world.

Your country's motto, sir, "Out of many, one people," and ours is "E Pluribus Unum," which is pretty much the same thing. So, we've got different people, one common aspiration, one common goal—and that's freedom. So, let's not rest until all the nations of our hemisphere enjoy the fruits of democracy and freedom. I guess what I really want to say is: Good luck, sir. I'm glad you came our way.

The Prime Minister. Mr. President and distinguished members of the administration, I'd, first of all, like to thank you very much for this invitation and for the marvelous hospitality, courtesy with which we've been received and for the very interesting discussions that this made possible.

I'd like to say to everybody that when the next winter comes, if anybody has the slightest doubt about where they should go, I refer them to the President of the United States quoting Christopher Columbus. [*Laughter*]

I might also say that I assured the President that we Jamaicans regard General Colin Powell as perhaps our most distinguished export, of whom we are very proud.

We had, as the President has said, extremely interesting discussions, and very frank. We share your delight in the increasing triumph of democracy all over the world. On the other hand, we have been concerned that some of us who have been in the trenches of democracy all along might get forgotten in the new excitement.

But I am very confident from things that we had observed in President Bush's administration and from our talks today that you do not intend to divert from our immense needs but rather to seek new ways of helping new friends—you might say, new members of the family of democracy.

I must also say that we have been very impressed with the feeling that the President has a genuine interest in this hemisphere outside of North America. We really have felt his personal interest in the Caribbean, Central America, and Latin America. And I must say, Mr. President, that even though we argue strongly not to divert resources from us but equally realize that the United States is under tremendous pressure, has tremendous problems of its responsibilities all over the world.

And I think that, to me, the most interesting and constructive single thing that came out of these talks is that we feel that when you look at debt, when you look at problems of capital formation—where do we get the capital to sustain economic development in a country like Jamaica—that

we can't so much try to find new money to throw at the problem but what we have to do is to use our ingenuity, use our sheer brains and imagination to find ways that take resources that are there and put them to work. And it has been a great source of encouragement to me, Mr. President, to feel that you and your administration are responsive to that. I think together, if we just put our imagination to work, put our brains to work, we can accomplish remarkable things.

And as I say, when next you plan to travel, Jamaica is there and within reach. Thank you very much, Mr. President. God bless you and your great country.

The President. Thank you very much. Just beautiful. Thank you, sir. That was wonderful.

Note: The President spoke at 1:18 p.m. at the South Portico of the White House. Prior to their remarks, the President and the Prime Minister met privately in the Oval Office and with U.S. and Jamaican officials in the Cabinet Room, and then attended a luncheon in the Old Family Dining Room.

Remarks at the Presentation Ceremony for the Achievement Against All Odds Awards
May 3, 1990

Thank you all. I'm surprised you're so polite. A thousand apologies for keeping you waiting. Senator Kasten and Secretary—glad to see you, Jack—and other Members of Congress and other distinguished guests, again, my official apologies. But at least you had a fair weather in which to wait in this beautiful Rose Garden; look at it that way. But to Secretary Kemp and Bob Woodson, Wayne Hedien, Members of the Congress, it's great to get outdoors again. [*Laughter*]

Perhaps you saw on the news that Millie was hanging around, just over the other side, down in the ivy down there, when something bit her on the nose. I'm not sure if it was a squirrel or a rat, but I had to investigate.

And of course, anyplace you go here—I do, as President—there's a bunch of Secret Service guys following right along. So, imagine this: the seven of us—[*laughter*]—poking around in the hedges, looking for the culprit, when, you guessed it, the sprinklers came on. [*Laughter*] So, I just want you to know there's a real life inside this magnificent complex.

But, look, we're here today because of the leadership of the Allstate Foundation and the vision of Robert Woodson and the National Center for Neighborhood Enterprise. For years, Bob has opposed the idea that big problems can only be solved by big government solutions, and he believes that no Federal program can begin to match the strength of our people and our neighborhoods. And he believes that to fight poverty, crime, and despair, we must first empower the powerless: empower Americans to help themselves; empower them to help their neighbors; empower them to become leaders, to make the coming century yet another American century.

And this is, in truth, happening, as the age of the individual dawns around the world, from Moscow to Managua. So, let's remember, in this heartland of individualism, our own American tradition of self-reliance and helping others. While government certainly has a critical role to play, we've been too willing in recent years to look first to Big Brother in Washington for the answers. And we're learning that if there is to be a better future, it must arise in the hearts of the men and women who struggle daily against poverty and ignorance and prejudice.

And so, we're here today to honor a select few—could be many of you out there—but today, we honor a select few who are creating such a future, seven people chosen to receive the first Achievement Against the Odds Award. They're not winning Oscars, they are not recipients of the Pulitzer or the Nobel, but what they have done and what they have achieved is, in truth, every bit as great and as beautiful as the work of any actor, artist, or scientist. For we have with us today seven men and women who have prevailed over handicap and heartache.

You've heard me speak of the Thousand Points of Light, my expression for that constellation of volunteers who are serving our communities, our cities, our nation, making America just a little better each day through national service. Well, some of those Points of Light, those shining stars, are with us.

Take Charles Ballard—which is Charles? Where are we? Right here—an orphan, grew up to be a teen father, chemically dependent, prison inmate. And now he's legally adopted and raised a son; earned a master's degree; founded the Teen Father Program, which helps thousands of teen fathers deal with their responsibilities.

And also Bobby Drayton. There he is— Bobby. He will tell you that he himself was twice victimized, first by epilepsy and then by an attack of self-pity. But by age 17, he had enough of feeling sorry for himself, and he decided to fight his condition through athletics, becoming one of the toughest competitors on the Howard University gymnasts team. And he also formed and headed youth programs for disadvantaged kids. Like a gymnast on the parallel bars, he balances his success—his success—with service to others.

Freddie Garcia. Freddie? Freddie Garcia grew up amid poverty, illiteracy, and too much discrimination. And in fact, some of his teachers and students actually managed to convince Freddie that he was a failure. And as so often happens, the prediction became a bit self-fulfilling, and he eventually became addicted to drugs and a criminal. But then he found his faith. He earned a degree from the Latin American Bible Institute, founded Victory Outreach of Texas, a Christian-oriented rehabilitation center which under his leadership has developed one of the most effective programs in the fight against drug addiction, alcoholism, and other life-consuming problems. A man who has come back from the precipice can best warn others of the danger of drugs, and he is such a man. And he's living proof that success is also a self-fulfilling prophecy.

Cheryl Hayes, right there—Cheryl. She's a mother who was dependent on welfare and, much worse, dependent on drugs. And now she's the head of a support group for youth with addicted family members. And she's also working hard with her family to invest 500 hours, Jack, of "sweat equity" in the home she's building with Habitat for Humanity. We congratulate you.

Or consider Kathleen Smallwood Johnson—Kathleen—whose father was murdered when she was 14 and mother was murdered when she was 16. So, at an age that for most of us is the most carefree time of our lives, she became the head of her family. And she raised her three brothers and sisters. She reentered college and graduated. She's now a successful attorney, and a mother to her late sister's three children and two children of her own, and still has time to serve others, still has time to serve her community.

Brad Linnenkamp—here we are. Brad

Linnenkamp. He calls himself physically challenged because he challenges cerebral palsy with a tenacity that most of us can only imagine. He volunteers and now works full-time as a counselor. And he has no time to worry about his own problems because he's too busy caring for others who are in a greater need than himself.

And finally, Vivienne Thompson. She's wheelchair-bound, as you can see—single parent. But Vivienne didn't let that hold her back. She often confronts the barriers—some concrete; others, sadly, of culture—that have fenced in so many disabled Americans. As an antipoverty leader in Boston, she also helped establish the first Head Start class for severely disabled, handicapped, low-income children.

Each of these seven Americans provides a definition of the word that I've learned to respect so much—learned from Jack Kemp—"empowerment." Whether they turned to a higher faith for inspiration or drew deep from strength of their souls, they represent the very best of the survival instinct in all of us and something more: a yearning to help others, to be a guiding star to someone who is lost—indeed, a Point of Light.

Zane Grey once wrote that "To bear up under loss, to smile when tears are close, to resist evil men and base instincts, to seek ever after the glory and the dream, that is what any man can do, and so be great." In this way, each of you have achieved greatness—the kind that brings out the greatness in others.

And now, Bob, let's get on with the show, to the brisk business of presenting these awards. It's all yours, sir.

Note: The President spoke at 3:31 p.m. in the Rose Garden at the White House. In his remarks, he referred to Secretary of Housing and Urban Development Jack Kemp; Robert L. Woodson, president of the National Center for Neighborhood Enterprise; and Wayne E. Hedien, chairman and chief executive officer of Allstate Insurance Co.

Statement by Press Secretary Fitzwater on the President's Meeting With Mayor Teddy Kollek of Jerusalem
May 3, 1990

The President expressed his personal admiration for Mayor Kollek. The President believes Jews and non-Jews in Jerusalem ought to act in a manner that does not threaten the city's comity or in any way prejudice prospects for the peace process. As recent events in the Christian quarter have demonstrated, the real question is not an abstract one of the rights of Jews and others but rather how these rights are implemented. The longstanding opposition of the United States to settlement activity in the territories occupied by Israel in 1967 is well known. So, too, is the position of the United States supporting a united Jerusalem whose final status is determined by negotiations.

Statement by Press Secretary Fitzwater on the President's Meeting With Prime Minister Kazimiera Prunskiene of Lithuania
May 3, 1990

The President met with Lithuanian Prime Minister Kazimiera Prunskiene for approximately 45 minutes in the Oval Office this afternoon. The President was pleased to receive a firsthand account of the current conditions from Mrs. Prunskiene, a freely elected leader of the Lithuanian people. She has provided similar information in recent days during meetings with the Prime Ministers of Norway and Sweden and the Foreign Ministers of Denmark and Canada.

The President reiterated our longstanding policy of refusing to recognize the forcible incorporation of the Baltic States into the U.S.S.R. He reaffirmed our strong support for the Lithuanian people's right to self-determination. He urged all parties to enter into a good-faith dialog. He stressed our desire to see the situation in Lithuania resolved peacefully and without intimidation. He emphasized the deep commitment of the American people to freedom and democracy around the world and the further progress of reform in the Soviet Union.

The President concluded the meeting by asking Mrs. Prunskiene to take this message back to Lithuania: "I am personally, and the United States Government is, committed to the self-determination of the people of Lithuania."

Statement by Press Secretary Fitzwater on the Establishment of a Presidential Emergency Board To Investigate Railroad Labor Disputes
May 4, 1990

The President today announced the creation, effective May 5, 1990, of a Presidential emergency board to investigate and report on the disputes between 11 railroad unions and most of the Nation's major railroads.

The creation of this Board, pursuant to section 10 of the Railway Labor Act (45 U.S.C. 160), is necessary to forestall the possibility of a crippling nationwide rail strike. The National Mediation Board has concluded that the situation is extremely critical and that it threatens substantially to interrupt interstate commerce to a degree such as to deprive various sections of the country of essential transportation service.

The Department of Transportation has advised that the railroads move over one-third of all intercity freight traffic, which involves goods valued at more than $1 billion each day. Interruption of rail service could idle nearly 200,000 railroad employees and result within 2 weeks in over 500,000 layoffs in industries served by railroads. A strike could also affect 100,000 commuters and 30,000 intercity travelers each day. The direct costs of a strike could be at least $16 million per day, and the indirect economic costs could be much higher.

In light of the immediate and devastating effects that a nationwide strike in this industry would have on the public, the President concluded that creation of a Presidential emergency board offers the best means of protecting the public interest while the parties continue their efforts to resolve their disputes.

Accordance of the Personal Rank of Ambassador to John Houston Hawes While Serving as the Open Skies Negotiator
May 4, 1990

The President has accorded the personal rank of Ambassador to John Houston Hawes, of the District of Columbia, a career member of the Senior Foreign Service, Class of Minister-Counselor, in his capacity as the Open Skies Negotiator.

Since 1989 Ambassador Hawes has served as Executive Assistant to the Under Secretary of State for Security Assistance, Science and Technology at the Department of State in Washington, DC. Prior to this, he served as Deputy Chief of Mission in Rabat, Morocco, 1987–1989; Deputy Assistant Secretary for Politico-Military Affairs, 1985–1987; Office Director for the Bureau of European and Canadian Affairs, 1982–1985; political officer in Brussels, 1980–1982; political officer in Vienna, 1978–1980; Office Director for the Bureau of Politico-Military Affairs, 1977–1978; political/military affairs officer for the Bureau of European and Canadian Affairs, 1975–1977; and Special Assistant in the Bureau of Intelligence and Research, 1974–1975. In addition, Ambassador Hawes has served in political affairs for the Bureau of Near East and South Asian Affairs at the Department of State, 1972–1974; staff assistant in New Delhi, India, 1971–1972; economic/commercial officer in Calcutta, India, 1969–1971; vice consul in Addis Ababa, Ethiopia, 1966–1968; and vice consul in Naples, Italy, 1964–1965.

Ambassador Hawes graduated from Princeton University (A.B., 1963). He was born May 23, 1941, in New York, NY. Ambassador Hawes is married, has five children, and resides in Washington, DC.

Nomination of Stephen Anthony Trodden To Be Inspector General of the Department of Veterans Affairs
May 4, 1990

The President today announced his intention to nominate Stephen Anthony Trodden to be Inspector General at the Department of Veterans Affairs. This is a new position.

Since 1986 Mr. Trodden has served as Assistant Inspector General for Auditing at the Department of Defense. Prior to this, he served as Director for Major Acquisition Programs in the Office of the Assistant Inspector General for Auditing, 1983–1986; Director for Procurement in the Office of the Assistant Secretary of Defense (Comptroller), 1981–1983; Deputy Director for Procurement in the Office of the Assistant Secretary of Defense (Comptroller), 1975–1981; Deputy Director for Research and Development in the Office of the Assistant Secretary of Defense (Comptroller), 1973–1975; technical adviser for the Directorate for Procurement in the Office of the Assistant Secretary of Defense (Comptroller), 1969–1973; project manager's staff officer for the REDEYE and SAM-D Missile Systems, 1966–1969; and industrial engineer with the United States Army Materiel Command, 1962–1966.

Mr. Trodden graduated from the University of Michigan (B.S.E., 1962) and Georgetown University Law Center (J.D., 1965). He was born December 13, 1939, in Washington, DC. Mr. Trodden is married, has two children, and resides in Arlington, VA.

Message on the Observance of Cinco de Mayo
May 4, 1990

I am pleased to send my warmest greetings to all who celebrate Cinco de Mayo.

The Mexican people prize liberty above all of life's blessings. That is why we in the United States are happy to rejoice with our southern neighbors each year on the anniversary of their great victory in the struggle for freedom and independence.

Outnumbered three to one, Mexican troops defeated invading French forces at the Battle of Puebla. We remember these brave sons of Mexico for their valor and for providing a lasting reminder that no threat or form of persecution can overcome a people's yearning for self-government. The story of this remarkable victory remains a source of hope and inspiration to freedom-loving people around the world.

In commemorating this great event in Mexican history, we also reaffirm our ties of culture and friendship with the people of Mexico and send them our good wishes. Vayan con Dios.

GEORGE BUSH

Nomination of Wallace Elmer Stickney To Be Director of the Federal Emergency Management Agency, and Appointment as a Governor of the Board of Governors of the American National Red Cross
May 4, 1990

The President today announced his intention to nominate Wallace Elmer Stickney to be Director of the Federal Emergency Management Agency. He would succeed Julius W. Becton, Jr. After confirmation, the President also announced his intention to appoint Wallace Elmer Stickney as a Governor of the Board of Governors of the American National Red Cross for a term of 3 years.

Since 1985 Mr. Stickney has served as a commissioner of the New Hampshire Department of Transportation. Prior to this, he served as special assistant for environmental affairs to Gov. John H. Sununu, 1983–1985. In addition, Mr. Stickney served as Director of the Environmental and Economic Impact Office at the Environmental Protection Agency's Region I office in Boston, MA, for more than 8 years and as Federal activities coordinator for 3 years. He served as the town engineer for the community of Salem, NH, and as an instructor at Wentworth Institute in Boston, MA. Mr. Stickney is a member of the American Society of Civil Engineers, and he served as commissioner of the Southern Rockingham Regional Planning Commission, 1975–1977.

Mr. Stickney graduated from New England College (B.S., 1959) and Harvard University (M.A., 1981). He received a master of science degree from Northeastern University. Mr. Stickney was born November 24, 1934, in Salem, NH. He is married, has four children, and resides in North Salem, NH.

Statement by Press Secretary Fitzwater on Mrs. Bush's Meeting With Former Hostage Frank Reed
May 4, 1990

Mr. Frank Reed, a recently released hostage from Lebanon, arrived at Andrews Air Force Base earlier this afternoon. At about the same time, Mrs. Bush was preparing to depart Andrews Air Force Base for a commencement address at the Southeast Community College in Cumberland, KY. Following a press conference by Mr. Reed at Andrews at about 2:45 p.m., Mr. Reed and Mrs. Bush briefly met on the tarmac near her aircraft. Mr. Reed said he was thrilled to meet Mrs. Bush and "glad to be home." Mr. Reed introduced his family to Mrs. Bush. Mrs. Bush said, "We're so glad you're home. I know the President wishes he was here to meet you."

Both parties then proceeded on to their planned destinations. Mr. Reed will undergo further medical examination at the Malcolm Grow Hospital at Andrews Air Force Base. The White House will release in Washington a photograph of this meeting as soon as possible.

Note: Frank Herbert Reed, director of the Lebanon International School, was kidnaped by members of the Organization of the Islamic Dawn in Beirut on September 9, 1986.

Remarks at the Oklahoma State University Commencement Ceremony in Stillwater
May 4, 1990

Thank you so much for that warm welcome. And thank you, Governor Bellmon, my long-time friend; President Campbell, you, sir, for your wonderful hospitality. And Senator Don Nickles, my collaborator and colleague up in Washington, DC; Congressman Wes Watkins, another graduate of this great institution—Bellmon, '42; Nickles, '71; Watkins, '60. I am delighted to be with these three distinguished public servants. I want to congratulate Chief Wilma Mankiller and Mr. Donnelly, the recipients of the coveted Bennett Awards, and say how proud I am of them. And salute the regents; the administrators; the faculty; the parents; Liz Taylor, right here; and most of all, O.S.U.'s centennial graduating class. Congratulations to each and every single one of you. I'm sorry Barbara couldn't be with me here. She did tell me to get a beer and some cheese fries over at Eskimo Joe's. Hoping at the same time they have enough T-shirts for all the grandchildren.

You know, when graduates of my vintage were sitting through ceremonies like this, right after the Second World War, we faced a world of changes, full of potential and new possibilities. Barbara and I got into a red two-door Studebaker—you still drive those, don't you, around here? [*Laughter*] But nevertheless, we drove from Connecticut down to west Texas. I've often wondered how far I'd gone if I'd made it on up to Oklahoma.

Postwar America was ready back then in 1948 for peace and prosperity. But while the free world was recovering, the nations of Eastern Europe were being "consolidated" behind an Iron Curtain. So began four decades of division in Europe—40 long

years of suspicion between two superpowers, the Soviet Union and the United States. And today you also graduate at an end of an era of conflict—but a contest of a different kind, a cold and abstract war of words and walls. Now Europe and the world have entered a new era: the Age of Freedom.

I hope you'll forgive me if I use this great forum at your great university to handle a subject of a very serious nature. It may be a little longer than you want to hear. I remember the graduation at Yale University, my school. The man giving the graduation speech got up and said, "Y is for youth." And he talked about 25 minutes. "A is for altruism." Another 32 minutes. "L is loyalty." Brushed that one off in 20 minutes. "E is for excellence." And when he finished, there was one kid out here in the audience—everyone else had fled. He looked like he was praying. And the speaker said to him, "Well, I'm glad you're saying a prayer. What are you praying for, son?" He said, "I'm praying to God and giving thanks that you didn't go to Oklahoma State University." [*Laughter*]

But I want you to bear with me because I'll be reflecting on the power and potential of democratic changes in several of these commencement addresses that I make this year. I begin today—my very first, at your great university—with a few words on the changes and America's place in the new Europe. A few of you may be wondering what a continent 4,000 miles away has to do with your class and you. Throughout our history, great upheavals in Europe have forced the American people to respond, to make deep judgments about the part we should play in European affairs. This has been true from the time of the French Revolution and the wars which followed it, to World War I and the flawed peace which ended it, on to the Second World War and the creation of the postwar order. I believe that now we are poised at another such moment—a critical time in our strategic relationship with our neighbors across the Atlantic.

Many of the graduates of America's Class of 1916 have wondered why the faraway war making headlines in their newspapers would have anything to do with them. They might have agreed with President Wilson, who that year said, "We are not interested" in the causes of the war, in "the obscure foundations from which its stupendous flood has burst forth." But a year later those classmates and their country were swept up in the torrent, carrying them to the horror of the trenches in France. Yet after the war, we again turned away from active involvement in European affairs. Instead, we sponsored a treaty to outlaw war and then, as the outlaws gained strength, the United States passed new neutrality laws. Another generation of Americans sat in the bright sun of commencement ceremonies at colleges all across our country, thinking war in Europe would somehow pass them by. But when war came, they paid an awful price, a horrible price for America's isolation. Then when the war ended, those students who—no longer questioned our role in the future of Europe. They no longer asked what Europe had to do with them because they knew the answer—everything.

About a year ago in Germany, I defined the kind of Europe our country is committed to: a peaceful, stable Europe, a Europe what I call whole and free. Today that goal is within our reach. We're entering a new Age of Freedom in a time of uncertainty, but great hope. Emerging democracies in Eastern Europe are going through social, political, and economic transformations shaking loose stagnant, centralized bureaucracies that have smothered initiative for generations. In this time of transition, moving away from the postwar era and beyond containment, we cannot know what choices the people of Eastern Europe will make for their future. The process of

change in the Soviet Union is also still unfinished. It will be crucial to see, for example, whether Moscow chooses coercion or peaceful dialog in responding to the aspirations of the Lithuanian people and nationalities within the Soviet Union. The only noble answer lies in a dialog that results in unencumbered self-determination for Lithuania.

President Gorbachev has made profound progress in his country—reforms so fundamental that the clock cannot be turned back. And yet neither can we turn the clock ahead to know for sure what kind of country the Soviet Union will be in years to come. And for the sake of the future we share with Europe, our policies and presence must be appropriate for this period of transition, with a constancy and reliability that will reassure our friends, both old and new.

My European colleagues want the United States to be a part of Europe's future. And I believe they're right. The United States should remain a European power in the broadest sense: politically, militarily, economically. And as part of our global responsibilities the foundation for America's peaceful engagement in Europe has been and will continue to be NATO. Recognizing in peace what we'd learned from war, we joined with the free nations of Europe to form an Atlantic community, an enduring political compact. Our engagement in Europe has meant that Europeans accept America as part of their continent's future, taking our interests into account across the board. Our commitment is not just in defense; it must be a well-balanced mix of involvement in all dimensions of European affairs. Because of our political commitment to peace in Europe, there hasn't been a war on the continent in 45 years. Think of your history books—not a war on the continent in 45 years. This long peace should be viewed through the long lens of history then. Europe has now experienced the longest uninterrupted period of international peace in the recorded history of that continent. The alliance is now ready to build on that historic achievement and define its objectives for the next century. So, the alliance must join together to craft a new

Western strategy for new and changing times.

Having consulted intensively with Prime Minister Thatcher recently there in Bermuda, and President Mitterrand in Key Largo in Florida, and Chancellor Helmut Kohl up in Camp David, and then by telephone or cable with NATO Secretary General Woerner and all of my other allied colleagues, I am now calling for an early summit of all NATO leaders. Margaret Thatcher, one of freedom's greatest champions of the last decade, told me that while NATO has been fantastically successful, we should be ready now to face new challenges. The time is right for the alliance to act. The fundamental purpose of this summit should be to launch a wide-ranging NATO strategy review for the transformed Europe of the 1990's. And to my NATO colleagues, I suggest that our summit direct this review by addressing four critical points: One, the political role that NATO can play in Europe. Two, the conventional forces the alliance will need in the time ahead and NATO's goal for conventional arms control. Three, the role of nuclear weapons based in Europe and Western objectives in new nuclear arms control negotiations between the United States and the Soviet Union. And four, strengthening the Conference on Security and Cooperation in Europe, CSCE, to reinforce NATO and help protect democratic values in a Europe that is whole and free.

Now, the first task the NATO summit should consider is the future political mission of the alliance. As military threats fade, the political dimension of NATO's work—always there but seldom noticed—becomes prominent. And so, at the NATO summit we should look for ways to help our German friends sustain freedom and achieve German unity, something which we and our allies have supported for over 40 years. And we should reaffirm the importance of keeping a united Germany as a full member of NATO. The alliance needs to find ways to work more closely with a vigorous European Community that is rightly asserting its own distinct views. And in Eastern Europe, governments once our adversaries are now our partners in building a new continent. And so, we must also talk

about how to encourage further peaceful democratic change in Eastern Europe and inside the Soviet Union.

But even as NATO gives more emphasis to its political mission, its guarantee of European security must remain firm. You see, our enemy today—if you think about it, what's the enemy today—our enemy today is uncertainty and instability. And so, the alliance will need to maintain a sound, collective military structure, with forces in the field backed by larger forces that can be called upon in some crisis.

And which brings me then to the second task for the NATO summit: a review of how the alliance should plan its conventional defenses. While we need to recognize that it will take some time before the Soviet military presence is gone from Eastern Europe—before those Soviet troops are taken out of Eastern Europe and before the major reductions contemplated by both sides can be implemented—we need to develop our strategy for that world now. Obviously, as I look at the equation, Soviet actions—what the Russians do—will be critical. Yet even after all the planned reductions in its forces are complete, even if our current arms control proposals are agreed and implemented, the Soviet military will still field forces dwarfing those of any other single European State—armed with thousands of nuclear weapons. Militarily significant U.S. forces must remain on the other side of the Atlantic for as long as our allies want and need them. And these forces demonstrate, as no words can, the enduring political compact that binds America's fate with Europe's democracies.

If the Soviet withdrawal continues and our arms control efforts are successful, we must plan for a different kind of military presence focused less on the danger of an immediate outbreak of war. And we must promote long-term stability and prevent crises from escalating by relying on reduced forces that show our capability and our readiness to respond to whatever may arise. The Conventional Forces in Europe Treaty which we have proposed would be the most ambitious conventional arms control agreement ever concluded. And we must finish the work on this treaty soon and plan to sign it at the CSCE summit this fall. But at the NATO summit we need to look further ahead, preparing follow-on negotiations after the conclusion of a CFE treaty. The NATO summit should develop the alliance's objectives for these talks.

Third, the NATO summit should also assess the future of U.S. nuclear forces in Europe. As democracy blooms in Eastern Europe and as Soviet troops return home and tanks are destroyed, dismantled, there is less need for nuclear systems of the shortest range. The NATO summit should accelerate ongoing work within the alliance to determine the minimum number and types of weapons that will be needed to deter war, credibly and effectively.

In light of these new political conditions, and the limited range and flexibility of these short-range nuclear missile forces based in Europe, I've reviewed our plan to produce and deploy newer, more modern, short-range nuclear missiles to replace the Lance system that's now in Europe. And we've almost finished the R&D, research and development work, for these new missiles. But I've decided, after consultation with our allies, to terminate the follow-on to Lance program. I've also decided to cancel any further modernization of U.S. nuclear artillery shells deployed in Europe. There are still short-range U.S.—and many more Soviet—nuclear missile systems deployed in Europe. And we're prepared to negotiate the reduction of these forces as well as a new set of arms control talks. And at the NATO summit, I will urge my colleagues to agree on the broad objectives for these future U.S.-Soviet negotiations and begin preparations within the alliance for these talks. I would also like to suggest that these new U.S.-Soviet arms control talks begin shortly after the CFE treaty on conventional forces has been signed.

In taking these steps, the United States is not going to allow Europe to become "safe for conventional war." There are few lessons so clear in history as this: Only the combination of conventional forces and nuclear forces have ensured this long peace in Europe. But every aspect of America's engagement in Europe—military, political, economic—must be complementary. And one place where they all come together is

in the Conference on Security and Cooperation in Europe, an organization of 35 states of Europe and North America. The CSCE is already a beacon for human rights and individual freedoms. Now, it must take on a broader role.

And so, the fourth task for this NATO summit I'm calling for is to reach common allied objectives for the future of CSCE itself. It can help the victorious forces of democracy in Eastern Europe secure their revolutions and—as they join the commonwealth of free nations—be assured a voice in a new Europe. The CSCE should offer new guidelines for building free societies—including setting standards for truly free elections, adopting measures to strengthen the rule of law, and pointing the way in the needed but painful transition from centralized, command economies to the free markets. The CSCE can also provide a forum for political dialog in a more united Europe. I agree with those who have called for regular consultations among senior representatives of the CSCE countries. We should consider whether new CSCE mechanisms can help mediate and settle disputes in Europe. I believe my allied colleagues and I should agree to take up these new ideas at a CSCE summit later this year, in conjunction with the signing of the treaty I talked to you about—that conventional force treaty, the CFE treaty.

In Eastern Europe, in this hemisphere, the triumph of democracy has cast its warm light on the face of the world like a miraculous dawn. But the outcome of this struggle for freedom is not ordained, and it's not going to be the work of miracles. All of you who graduate here today are part of a historic decision for America's engagement in the future of Europe. I am convinced that our work to protect freedom, to build free societies will safeguard our own peace and prosperity. The security of Europe and the world has become very complex in this century. But America's commitment to stability and peace is profoundly clear. Its motivation really derives from the strength of our forefathers—from the blood of those who have died for freedom and for the sake of all who live in peace. And as you leave this great university every voice, every heart's commitment to freedom is important.

There's a story about a man trying to convince his son that in the struggle for freedom every voice counts. They stood in a valley, watching the snow fall on a distant mountain. It might have been a day like today. [*Laughter*] But they stood there. "Tell me the weight of a snowflake," the man said. "Almost nothing," answered the boy. As the snow swirled around them, up on the mountain they saw an avalanche whose thunder shook the Earth. "Do you know which snowflake caused that?" the old man asked. "I don't," answered the boy. "Maybe," said the man, "like the last snowflake that moves a mountain, in the struggle for freedom a single voice makes a world of difference."

America's mission in Europe, like millions of individual decisions made for freedom, can make a voice—can make a world of difference. The cry for freedom—in Eastern Europe, in South Africa, right here in our precious hemisphere to our south—was heard around the world in the Revolution of 1989. Today, in this new Age of Freedom, add your voices to the thundering chorus.

It's a great honor for me to have been at this university. Thank you very much. God bless you. And God bless the United States of America. Thank you all. Thank you so much.

Note: The President spoke at 2:35 p.m. in Lewis Stadium at Oklahoma State University. In his opening remarks, he referred to John R. Campbell, president of the university; Wilma Mankiller, chief of the Cherokee Nation of Oklahoma; H.F. Donnelly, research associate of the OSU Center for Community Education; and Liz Taylor, the oldest living graduate of OSU. Following his remarks, the President traveled to Tulsa, where he attended a Republican fundraising reception at the Doubletree Hotel.

Remarks at the Oklahoma Foundation for Excellence Dinner in Tulsa
May 4, 1990

Thank you all very much. And thank you especially, Senator Nickles, for that warm introduction. To Governor Henry Bellmon, early supporter and friend of longstanding; Senator Boren, to whom I give enormous credit for this wonderful evening; and all the principals that led to this evening and will lead to so much more for academic excellence. And to other distinguished Members of the Congress that might be here—especially I want to pay my respects to Carl Albert [former Speaker of the House] and Mrs. Albert, who's here; and members of the foundation, honored guests, and ladies and gentlemen. I like the Sapulpa Band, too. I thought they did an outstanding job over there.

You'll be pleased, this will be a short speech. I will leave before the broccoli. [*Laughter*] Did you see the kid over there while I was speaking at Oklahoma State University holding up a sign: "George, eat your broccoli." I don't need advice from little kids about what I'm going to eat. [*Laughter*]

But earlier today I gave that speech—first, just let me say I appreciate this reception very much and am delighted to be in this State of open hearts and open skies. But let me say a word about Oklahoma State. I gave that speech over there at Oklahoma State University, and I was delighted to be there, at Stillwater. They'll never forgive me in Norman. After all, the musical "Oklahoma" says "the farmer and the cowman should be friends." It doesn't say a thing about the Sooners and Cowboys. [*Laughter*]

This evening, though, I want to talk about one thing all Americans have in common, the reason we're all here: our dedication to America's most enduring legacy. I refer, of course, to the education that is vital to everything we are and can become. It's been said there are only two bequests we can hope to give our children: one of these is roots, and the other, wings—a theme embodied, I might add, in the beautiful sculptures here. These words reaffirm that knowledge provides the foundation for every idea that takes flight in the mind of a child.

Yet today the facts are clear, and they don't make for pleasant reading. Erratic standards—Dave referred to this—an unacceptable drop-out rate, too little parental involvement, too little accountability by teachers and students, too many schools wracked by drug use, and too many kids ill-equipped to read or write. Let's be honest: Our educational system isn't making the grade.

Five years ago, a United States Senator acted to convert that grade to pass from fail—believing, like you, that if excellence breeds achievement, then excellence should be rewarded. So, David Boren set out to ensure that future generations will say of us: They taught their children well. His creation was the Oklahoma Foundation for Excellence. This foundation wisely believes that America can only be as great as her children are educated and that while the Federal Government must help, education is and should be a local and a State responsibility. Parents, teachers, local administrators—not faraway, distant bureaucrats—best understand the local needs. So, this program here affirms values as central to Oklahoma as love of freedom and of God.

First of all, the foundation reflects Oklahoma's belief in high achievement. Someone said, "Anything can have happened in Oklahoma. Practically everything has." Your work has raised private money to give $1,000 cash scholarships to the State's top 100 high school seniors. And I loved seeing those kids march across this stage just a minute ago. I salute these academic all-staters who are the true trustees of our posterity.

Next, this foundation mirrors your dedication, Oklahoma's dedication to excellence. You understand that those with the responsibility for our children's education literally hold the future in their hands. So, you're giving $5,000 each to three magnificent teachers and a superb public school administrator. I salute the recipients of the 1990

Oklahoma Medals for Excellence in Teaching and Administration. And I also want to mention that $5,000 award to the public school system that has had the most effective dropout prevention program. Keeping kids in schools is absolutely critical, and you're doing a great job.

Finally, the Foundation for Excellence reflects the belief that education can be the great uplifter and equalizer. Perhaps that great Broadway character, Oklahoma's Aunt Eller, put it best when she said, "I don't say I'm better than anybody else, but I'll be danged if I ain't just as good." Well, your idea can enrich education and help education enrich our lives.

Achievement, excellence, and equality—what a definition of Oklahoma. And I love the button that Henry Bellmon gave me here—Oklahoma, State of Excellence. What a wonderful signal that sends to everybody here and all that come here. And what a magnificent difference this movement has made in just 5 years—over $2 million raised. Today, more than 100 Oklahoma communities have local private foundations, many inspired by your lead. Think of it: Each of these foundations—I call them Points of Light—each does what the Federal Government cannot do—serve as a wonderful model for other States and localities to emulate. So, tonight I challenge every State in America to do what Oklahoma has already done: make American education a beacon of excellence. By increasing private support for public education, you've enriched academic opportunities for students all across this State. If there's any doubt, you've resolved it. When it comes to Oklahoma education, Washington doesn't know best, Oklahomans do.

The result is that today Oklahoma ranks first per capita in the number of private foundations. Yet you also know that progress made can't be measured by dollars spent alone. So, you're showing how parents, teachers, administrators, school boards can work together to help our kids—like Oklahoma's fabled pioneers—discover the unlimited frontiers of learning.

We know, of course, that it won't be easy. Let me recall how once, marking an examination written shortly before Christmas, the noted Yale scholar William Lyon Phelps came across this note: "God only knows the answer to this question. Merry Christmas." Phelps returned the paper with the annotation: "God gets an A. You get an F. Happy New Year." [*Laughter*] You remember that?

Yes, of course, education is going to meet roadblocks. But they're obstacles we can overcome. For you're not in this alone. The Federal Government does have a legitimate role. That's why a year ago we sent to the Congress our Educational Excellence Act, legislation which can help America out-think, out-work, and out-perform any nation, any day of the week.

For instance, we want to create a $500-million program by 1994 to reward schools that improve the most. And a Magnet Schools of Excellence Program—we believe parents, not Big Brother, should decide which public schools their kids attend. Our program will reward schools that cut the dropout rate; create a National Science Scholars Initiative providing incentive to excel in science, mathematics, and engineering. And recently I signed into law legislation to help schools that are hit the hardest by drug use.

Now, these steps will help our children unlock the future, give them the tools to master the new world of new technologies, and reverse the trend we saw in a recent comparison of 13-year-olds in the United States and five other countries where America placed last in mathematics and near last in science.

Most of all, our Educational Excellence Act can help make American education number one again by achieving the goals that we announced in February with Governors like Henry Bellmon. We want U.S. students to be first in math and science by the year 2000, and every American to be skilled and literate. We want every student to start school ready to learn—that means Head Start, and it means programs like it. And each school to have an environment where kids can learn—that means making every school drug-free. Finally, we want to see a graduation rate of at least 90 percent with every student competent in important subjects. Like a future graduate—Erin Amato, a third-grader from Sugarland,

Texas—who recently wrote me this letter: "Dear President Bush. I have been doing good in school I made all 'A' honor roll last 6 weeks and I hope I make it this 6 weeks also. Do you like rolls? I like rolls but I do not like broccoli." Obviously, a bright kid here. [*Laughter*] And then Erin concluded, saying, "I do like carrots. I love Texas."

Let me close with a story that I think this kid would appreciate, a story about the scholarship that, together, all of us can build. The story goes that physicist James Franck was professor at Gottingen University in Germany when Robert Oppenheimer, then only 23, was being examined for his doctorate. On emerging from the oral exam, Professor Franck said, "I got out of there just in time. He was beginning to ask me questions."

In coming years, these academic all-staters will ask many questions—questions about their faith and future, why we're here, and what we can become individually and as a nation. How can education supply some answers? The same way this administrator and these teachers have—by embodying the spirit of Oklahoma's past. Think of the heroes who settled this State. They didn't believe in government by bureaucrat. They believed in themselves. They built homes out of sod, schoolhouses from scratch. Salt Fork, Black Bear, Apache. Dirt floors, log walls. Often, supplies were limited, but there were always enough hands—pitching in, teaching classes, fighting off everything from claim-jumpers to bears.

These pioneers dreamed dreams as big as Oklahoma and made their dreams come true. Like us, they knew where the future lay: in their kids, through education. The Oklahoma Foundation for Excellence can help us achieve our dreams, so that future generations will proclaim, as the musical "Oklahoma" says, American education, "you're doing fine—OK."

Thank you for this occasion. Good luck to the Oklahoma Foundation for Excellence. And God bless each and every one of you that cares about our kids. Thank you all very, very much.

Note: The President spoke at 8:08 p.m. in

Exhibit Halls B and C of the James L. Maxwell Convention Center. Following his remarks, he traveled to Camp David, MD, for the weekend.

Remarks on Signing the Asian/Pacific American Heritage Month Proclamation
May 7, 1990

First, let me just express a warm White House welcome to Prime Minister Namaliu from Papua New Guinea. I just wanted to walk out with him, show him a little hospitality. I look forward, sir, to visiting with you this afternoon.

To Senators Inouye and Phil Gramm, welcome. To Representative Pat Saiki, my old friend, welcome back to the White House. And [Representatives] Norm Mineta; Ben Blaz; of course, Bill Broomfield; and Eni Faleomavaega—[*laughter*]—Eni, tough on your name, but I got close, didn't I? Okay. And all the Members of Congress who are with us here today, and a special welcome to Frank Horton. My heavens, Frank, because of your diligence in working with so many of your colleagues in the Congress in the support of Jeanie Jew and Ruby Moy, we established Asian/Pacific American Heritage Week.

Now, I'm proud to take one more step and proclaim this May to be the first Asian/Pacific American Heritage Month. First, let me acknowledge with respect the gentleman in the Senate who was Frank's cosponsor—someone who has left us—a great man, a great friend who wrote both haiku and lasting legislation with that same graceful fluency. And I, of course, am talking about our beloved friend, the late Senator Spark Matsunaga of Hawaii. I think this ought to be his day.

We also have with us a number of Asian and Pacific American leaders from many walks of life: Virginia Cha, I.M. Pei, Dr. Taylor Wang, Nancy Kwan, Dr. Samuel Lee, Dr. T.D. Lee. And with us, also, some distinguished Ambassadors. I also especially want to single out Governor Peter Coleman, of American Samoa, and Lieutenant Governor Benjamin Manglona, of the Northern Mariana Islands, and every member of their very distinguished delegations. Thank you all for being with us. You've come so far, and your presence is most welcome and deeply appreciated.

As I said, we're here in large measure because of the vision of Frank Horton and Spark Matsunaga. Spark's brilliant career was the culmination of a history that began 146 years ago with the arrival of Nisei, the first Japanese Americans to land on these shores. And now, people from Asia and the Pacific, from dozens of lands across a broad swath of the world that spans from the Middle East to the Philippines, have found this new homeland called America. They represent the whole range of religions—Christian, Muslim, Hindu, Buddhist. They're Arab, Iranian, Indian, Korean, Thai descent. But they will tell you that they are Americans first.

Look at the scope of America's demographic change. Cambodian, Laotian, Vietnamese neighborhoods flourish just across the Potomac River. The minaret of a mosque rises over the skyline of a Dallas suburb. The student body of a school in southern California is made up almost entirely of Hmong children. Pacific islanders have enriched the culture and heritage of Orange County. Filipinos have called America home since the first son of the Philippines arrived on these shores in 1763. All of these are subtle signs that Asian and Pacific Americans are our fastest-growing minority population. They're changing America, and they are changing America for the better.

Some Asian and Pacific Americans come from families that have lived in America for more than a century. And others have literally just arrived, by boat or jumbo jet. But all can rely on strong communities, networks of family and friends, often with the support of a church, synagogue, mosque or temple. So, whatever their background, all enjoy strong communities—a great sense of community, too. These 7 million Americans show us an example of how strong families can instill an abiding respect for the law, tenacity in the endeavor of life and work, and most of all, excellence in education.

Consider this: The last U.S. Census showed that 75 percent of Asian Americans age 25 and over had at least a high school degree—well above the national average of 66 percent. This nation is incomparably richer because of great scientists like Nobel Prize winner Dr. Yuan Lee and the late An Wang. We are richer because of the talent of Michael Chang and the courage of the late Ellison Onizuka. And we are richer because of Asian Pacific American leaders, many of them with us here today.

Count among them Elaine Chao, number two in this enormous Department of Transportation of ours; Wendy Gramm, Chairman of the Federal Commission on Commodity Future Trading; Cindy Daub, Commissioner of the Copyright Royalty Tribunal; Kyo Jhin, who will be named shortly to a senior position at the Department of Veteran Affairs; my own—I say my own—our own Sichan Siv, on the White House staff, who fled the killing fields and is now doing an outstanding job for the White House in every way; and Julia Chang Bloch, U.S. Ambassador to Nepal, our first Asian-American Ambassador.

As shown by public-spirited leaders like Spark Matsunaga and those here today, Asian Pacific Americans are beginning to excel in the field of politics, just as they have excelled in every other field. While politics is often a second-, third-, or fourth-generation profession, the time is coming when more and more Asian and Pacific Americans will seek office to lead our cities, our States, and our nation. As America looks toward the Pacific in the century ahead, we will need your insights and your leadership as never before.

You know that the future of Europe has been very much on my mind of late—I think, on the mind of all Americans. But America's destiny is also tied to the Pacific Rim. And I've lived in Asia, and I know that the fate of Asia and the Pacific is no less important to America than the future of Europe. We are encouraged by the changes in Eastern Europe and by the rise of de-

mocracy to our south right here in our own hemisphere. Make no mistake about that. But we will not neglect Asia and the Pacific. My administration is committed to promoting open trade and fighting protectionism so that the economic ties between the United States and Asia can continue to grow. Like Asian and Pacific Americans in the United States, these nations are a testament to the power of self-initiative. With time, we will create a true community of nations surrounding the Pacific Rim, bound together by commerce, a shared commitment to democracy, and an abiding friendship.

And that's why we support the emerging Asian and Pacific democracies. And that's why we advocate peaceful change, why we will remain in solidarity with the aspirations of the peoples of these many lands. And that is why America must stand for more than mere material success. America must remain the beacon of liberty, a light of hope for the troubled, the oppressed, the downtrodden. The people of this land know that it is not enough to let a man purchase what he wants. He must be allowed to say what he believes. He must be allowed to go where he wants. He must be allowed to choose his government. Economic freedom alone will not provide sufficient room for the restlessness of the human spirit.

Let us, as we celebrate the contributions of Asian Pacific Americans to our precious freedoms, remember the restless millions who remain behind. In looking for inspiration they need look no further than the success of their grandchildren, their children, their brothers, sisters, and cousins who found freedom in America. And so, it is in your honor that I sign this measure proclaiming this to be Asian/Pacific American Heritage Month.

Thank you all. May God bless you. And may God bless the United States of America.

Note: The President spoke at 11:36 a.m. in the Rose Garden at the White House. In his remarks, he referred to the following individuals: Jeanie Jew, lecturer and consultant on Asian Pacific American issues; Ruby Moy, chairperson of the Congressional

Asian/Pacific Staff Caucus; Virginia Cha, Miss Maryland 1989; I.M. Pei, architect; Taylor Wang, payload specialist for the May 1985 "Skylab I" mission; Nancy Kwan, actress; Samuel Lee, Olympic gold medalist; T.D. Lee, 1957 Nobel Prize winner for physics; Yuan T. Lee, 1986 Nobel Prize winner for chemistry; An Wang, founder of Wang Laboratories, Inc.; Michael Chang, professional tennis player; and Ellison S. Onizuka, crewmember of the space shuttle "Challenger" who was killed in the explosion of January 28, 1986. The proclamation is listed in Appendix E at the end of this volume.

Statement by Press Secretary Fitzwater Announcing Importation Restrictions on Archeological Treasures From Peru
May 7, 1990

The *Federal Register* will publish new regulations barring the importation of archeological treasures from Peru. These measures are designed to help curb looting in the Sipan region, and respond to a request for such action made to us by the Government of Peru. The discovery of important archeological sites at Sipan has unfortunately generated intense demand for these treasures in the illegal art market. The tombs of the Moche nobility, which have produced gold artifacts unlike any previously seen in the pre-Columbian cultures of Peru, have prompted looters to engage in rampant destruction of these sites in order to satisfy the illegal trade in archeological artifacts.

The United States believes that the illegal trade in cultural property does immense damage to our hemispheric cultural heritage, and is willing to cooperate with other governments of this region and elsewhere to prevent illegal trafficking in archeological treasures. This is the third such action by the United States in imposing import restrictions under the provisions of the Convention on Cultural Property Implementation Act and the 1970 UNESCO [United Nations Education, Scientific and Cultural Organization] Convention on the Means of Prohibiting and Preventing the Illicit Import, Export and Transfer of Ownership of Cultural Property. The United States imposed emergency restrictions on certain pre-Columbian artifacts from El Salvador in 1987, and on certain antique Andean textiles from Bolivia in 1989. At present, requests from the Governments of Canada and Guatemala are being considered by the Director of the U.S. Information Agency, who is advised by the President's Cultural Property Advisory Committee.

Nomination of William Bodde, Jr., To Be United States Ambassador to the Marshall Islands
May 7, 1990

The President today announced his intention to nominate William Bodde, Jr., of Maryland, a career member of the Senior Foreign Service, Class of Minister-Counselor, to be Ambassador Extraordinary and Plenipotentiary of the United States of America to the Republic of the Marshall Islands.

Since 1989 Mr. Bodde has served as the dean for senior seminar at the Foreign Service Institute at the Department of State in Washington, DC. Prior to this, he served as Deputy Assistant Secretary for European and Canadian Affairs at the Department of State, 1986–1989; consul general in Frankfurt, Germany, 1983–1986; diplomat in residence for the East-West Center in Hawaii, 1982–1983; Ambassador to Fiji, Tonga, Tuvalu, and Minister to Kiribati, 1980–1982; director of the Office of Pacific Islands Affairs at the Department of State, 1978–1980; political officer at the Department of State, 1977–1978; political officer in Bonn, Germany, 1974–1977; and political officer in Berlin, Germany, 1973–1974. In addition, Mr. Bodde has served as a political officer at the Department of State, 1970–1972; political officer in Stockholm, Sweden, 1967–1970; public information officer at the Department of State, 1965–1966; and political officer in Vienna, Austria, 1962–1965. Mr. Bodde joined the Foreign Service in 1962.

Mr. Bodde graduated from Hofstra College (B.A., 1951) and Johns Hopkins School of Advanced International Studies (M.P.P.A., 1967). He was born November 27, 1931, in Brooklyn, NY. Mr. Bodde served in the U.S. Army, 1950–1954. He is married, has three children, and resides in Maryland.

Nomination of Joseph Edward Lake To Be United States Ambassador to Mongolia
May 7, 1990

The President today announced his intention to nominate Joseph Edward Lake, of Texas, a career member of the Senior Foreign Service, Class of Counselor, to be Ambassador Extraordinary and Plenipotentiary of the United States of America to the Mongolian People's Republic. He would succeed Richard Llewellyn Williams.

Since 1987 Mr. Lake has served as director of the operations center at the Department of State in Washington, DC. Prior to this, he served as an adviser to the U.S. delegation to the 41st United Nations General Assembly, 1986; Deputy Director of the Office of Regional Affairs for the Bureau of East Asian and Pacific Affairs at the Department of State, 1985–1986; counselor and deputy chief of mission for the U.S. Embassy in Sofia, Bulgaria, 1984–1985; Chargé d'Affaires for the U.S. Embassy in Sofia, 1984; counselor and deputy chief of mission for the U.S. Embassy in Sofia, 1984; first secretary and chief of the political/economic section at the U.S. Embassy in Sofia, 1982–1984; language student in the Foreign Service Institute, 1981–1982; consul and principal officer for the U.S. consulate in Kaduna, Nigeria, 1978–1981; and second secretary and political officer for the U.S. Embassy in Lagos, Nigeria, 1977–1978. In addition, Mr. Lake has served as a political-military officer for the Office of Philippine Affairs in the Bureau of East Asian Affairs at the Department of State, 1976–1977; second secretary and political officer for the U.S. Embassy in Taipei, 1973–1976; language student for the American Embassy in China, 1971–1973; and analyst in the Office of Research for East Asia in the Bureau of Intelligence and Research at the Department of State, 1969–1971. Prior to this, Mr. Lake served in several capacities in Canada, Dahomey, and China. He joined the Foreign Service in 1962.

Mr. Lake graduated from Texas Christian University (B.A., 1962; M.A., 1967). He was born October 18, 1941, in Jacksonville, TX. Mr. Lake is married, has three children, and resides in Falls Church, VA.

Nomination of James R. Moseley To Be an Assistant Secretary of Agriculture for Natural Resources and Environment
May 7, 1990

The President today announced his intention to nominate James R. Moseley to be an Assistant Secretary of Agriculture for Natural Resources and the Environment. He would succeed George S. Dunlop.

Currently, Mr. Moseley is owner and manager of Jim Moseley Farms, Inc., in Clarks Hill, IN. Mr. Moseley received his bachelor of science degree from Purdue University in 1973. He was born June 2, 1948, in Peru, IN. Mr. Moseley is married, has six children, and resides in Peru, IN.

Remarks Following Discussions With President Jaime Paz Zamora of Bolivia
May 8, 1990

President Bush. President Paz and distinguished members of the Bolivian delegation, it really has been a great pleasure to meet with you to discuss the issues of importance to both our countries. President Paz and I first met last September at the United Nations in New York, where I was addressing the General Assembly on making the world more secure and furthering our chemical weapons agreement. Last February, we joined with our fellow Presidents from Colombia and Peru in Cartagena, where we agreed on the need to control a different type of chemical threat by securing strong international cooperation in the fight against narcotics trafficking. Today, our conversations have been wide-ranging and, from my view at least, very productive. We've discussed the deep aspirations for democracy that we share for the entire hemisphere, believing that it one day will be the first totally democratic hemisphere in the world. I am very sorry, Mr. President, that Barbara is not here. Right now, she and our son Jeb and our Chief of Staff, John Sununu, are in Central America representing the United States at the inauguration of President Calderon in Costa Rica.

But, look, the United States has been very impressed, Mr. President, by the tough economic measures that have been taken in Bolivia over the past 5 years. A strong economy is one of the building blocks of a strong democracy. So, our economic and trade discussions dealt with the improved investment climate in Bolivia and the advantages of open markets—for both the United States and Bolivia. Alternative development are two key words—alternative developments—because we share your aspiration that the people will benefit from these bold economic measures that you have taken. And so, it's in this total context that we're building a framework for the implementation of our assistance agreement with Bolivia. President Paz, both in New York and Cartagena, emphasized the importance of development assistance to his country, something that the United States has long supported. This fiscal year the U.S. will provide Bolivia with about $88 million in economic aid. And with the approval of Congress, it is my hope that our assistance next year will increase substantially.

The United States has also been impressed by what Bolivia has done during the past decade to strengthen its democratic institutions. But President Paz and I both know that the dangers facing democratic institutions—one of the dangers is this whole concept of international narcotics trafficking. And so, in Cartagena we forged an unprecedented alliance against both trafficking and use, and today we're continuing to build on our comprehensive international drug control strategy on a number of fronts.

By way of example, in the first 4 months of this year, Bolivia has eradicated more acres of illegal coca than it did all last year—just in 4 months. In fact, if the current pace of eradication is maintained, Bolivia may be able to eliminate all coca grown within its borders for illegal use. That would truly be a brave battle won in the war against drugs. And we in the United States should give total cooperation to this courageous President.

On the economic front, the United States and Bolivia will also sign an agreement creating a high-level trade and investment consultative mechanism, because we want to help Bolivia get the word out that Bolivia is a country that deserves and, indeed, needs more investment. And I told the President that I want very much to do my part—we want to do our part to help.

Bolivia is making this progress because President Paz has wisely adopted an integrated strategy of eradication, interdiction, and alternative development—I stress that again—to fight the cocaine trade. But we also realize that long-term success in the struggle depends also on the will of the people of the United States, to leave lives that are free from the temptation of drugs and to help those who are too weak to help themselves. The war against drugs is being fought in the Andes Mountains and Chaco plains of Bolivia, but it is also being fought in the schools and streets of the United States. And I am determined, Mr. President, to do my level best to reduce demand, rampant demand, in this country.

Mr. President, let me just assure you that you and your countrymen will not stand alone in the fight against cocaine, or in the drive for economic development. Because we do want what you want, and that is economic benefit for your people. So, together we're going to wage a strong fight. I look forward to continuing our relationship of cooperation and consultation. And again, it was a great pleasure welcoming you to the White House. And might I say, on a personal basis, what a pleasure it was to meet those two fine sons of yours. Welcome, sir.

President Paz. My dear friend President George Bush, and esteemed colleagues and assistants and ministers, dear friends from North America and from Bolivia. A bit before arriving here to the United States, I received a very warm letter from President Bush where he pointed out that now, more than ever, we should make our America a common home. When I read this phrase, I became very emotional, but now after having visited the President here in the White House, these feelings have become a conviction. Once again, I am convinced that you would like for us, all of us, to work jointly to make our Americas a common home. And a common home has to be taken care of. It has to be loved, it has to be nourished, and one has to help the weakest parts of the home, and among all of us, get results.

I think we are working in that spirit, Mr. President; I think we will attain it. I want you to be very certain that Bolivia, because of a sovereign decision of its people, is a full-time member working towards this common home. We are fervent allies, and we are ready to give you all of our efforts and all of our cooperation in a very clear way, in a very efficient way, to everything that would be of a common interest. And this is why I would like to thank you and express my appreciation, Mr. President, because we have found in you and your government a true understanding of what happens in our hemisphere and what happens between our relations and in Bolivia. You have understood the sacrifice that has cost our people in these economic adjustments. You have understood the hope of growth and the hope of development that the Bolivian people feel. And you have understood the effort that the Bolivians are doing to contribute to this fight against drugs. And we are aware of this common responsibility that involves Bolivia also.

You have given me the honor of citing a couple of amounts of numbers of what Bolivia has attained a few minutes ago that are completely true. And I am glad that you have understood this to make a further contribution to what we call an alternative development which will carry forward along with efficient work in interdiction and prevention.

Thank you, Mr. President, and I thank you for mentioning my children. Well, I

637

brought them to just come with me, to be with me, but also so that you could see this new youth that is growing in Bolivia. Thank you. And I know we're going to have very efficient results. And this is a new stage to our relationship.

Note: President Bush spoke at 1:36 p.m. at *the South Portico of the White House. President Paz spoke in Spanish, and his remarks were translated by an interpreter. Prior to their remarks, the two Presidents met privately in the Oval Office and with U.S. and Bolivian officials in the Cabinet Room, and then attended a luncheon in the Old Family Dining Room.*

Remarks at the Presentation Ceremony for the Small Business Person of the Year Award
May 8, 1990

Well, thank you all, and welcome to the White House. I'm sorry about the delays getting some of you all in here. But good news—you don't have to show a picture to get out of this madhouse, I've discovered. [*Laughter*]

It's good to see Secretary Mosbacher here, doing an outstanding job as our Secretary of Commerce. And I am very, very proud of him. And the same can be said for Susan Engeleiter, who is heading up the SBA and also keeping the focus where it belongs.

You know, the people that are gathered here come from 50 States and beyond, hometown heroes who are leading America into the 21st century, as the theme for this Small Business Week proclaims. And today marks a wonderful occasion not only for them but also for our nation and our future.

Small business is the backbone of the U.S. economy, creating two out of every three new jobs, employing half the private work force, accounting for 40 percent of America's total gross national product. And it's one of the reasons Americans are enjoying this longest era of peacetime growth in the history of our country. But, of course, the magic of small business is not in the power of its numbers but in the power of its dreams, of its aspirations.

And each of your businesses began as the dream of one man or one woman and soon became a dream for many others. And I look at people like Phyllis Apelbaum, one of today's finalists, whose messenger service in Chicago provides jobs for over a hundred people in transitional neighborhoods. Every job you create can mean another family with a future, another family with hope, another family with a chance for the American dream.

And as a former small business person, I know firsthand the struggles of entrepreneurs and growing businesses, the combination of adrenaline and anxiety, the adversity and the adventures that fills your days.

Iowa's Barney Roberts started his empire out of his basement. David Mathews began his ironworks on an Arkansas mountaintop without electricity or running water. Oatmeal Studios Greeting Cards were launched at a place called the Frog Hollow Craft Center. And Phyllis slept on the floor and was told no 17 times before her messenger business was licensed. By her own description, she broke the logjam when she walked into the commissioner's office—and I quote—"screamed like a fish seller on Maxwell Street." [*Laughter*] I don't know where Maxwell Street might be, but I can tell you, I can just picture it. [*Laughter*] Phyllis, don't do it here, okay? [*Laughter*]

All four are American success stories. All four know that no nation ever drowned in sweat. And all four know that good citizenship is good business, reaching out from their communities to the homeless and the Special Olympics and others.

Their rules are simple and they make sense. "People are our best assets," says Barney, "take care of them and they won't leave." And Phyllis says, "You have to love what you're doing." And David's time-proven formula for success needs just three words: "Never sacrifice quality." And Oatmeal Greeting Cards' Joe Massimino describes their brand of humor as "Not corny, not punny, not bizarre, not offensive."

I'm not the first President to recognize and appreciate the importance of smaller companies. And today is Harry Truman's birthday, and as always, he told it like it is. He said: "You don't have a prosperous country unless the little man—the farmer, the worker, the small businessman—is well-off. And when the little man prospers, big business gets along just fine."

Well, that's why one of my priorities after assuming the office was to develop Federal policies that promote and support this vital sector of our economy. We're revitalizing—thanks to Susan—the Small Business Administration. We're working to ensure the interests and concerns of small business are made part and parcel of efforts such as Federal contract procurement. And we need your support on one of this year's top legislative priorities. And of course, I'm talking on a tax cut on capital gains. Especially for small businesses and entrepreneurs, it will attract start-up capital, provide more long-term investment, create new jobs, and help level a playing field with our trading part-

ners overseas, some of whom don't tax capital gains at all.

The strength of America lies with those who are willing to take a chance in small business and build for the future. And it's here you find the determination and the ingenuity and the vision that have created the enterprises which drive our economy and enrich our lives. It is around small businesses that you find communities growing and prospering. It is here where women and minorities make their mark as business owners. It is here where you find so many of the Thousand Points of Light that are aiding those in need all across the country. We can take pride in the fact that nations around the world are using small business in the United States as a model for economic growth. So, small business is America at its best. And it's a pleasure for me to recognize those who have excelled in this vital field of endeavor.

Congratulations! Thanks, and I'm delighted you all came to the White House. And now I'll turn the podium over to Susan Engeleiter to present today's awards. Thank you all very, very much.

Note. The President spoke at 2:15 p.m. in Room 450 of the Old Executive Office Building.

Statement on the Observance of Schuman Day
May 9, 1990

On May 9, the European Community will celebrate Schuman Day. This year the occasion is particularly momentous, as it marks the 40th anniversary of the 1950 Declaration which initiated the European Coal and Steel Community and started a chain of events in European integration which has led to the strong and vibrant European Community of today. The early efforts were led by European statesmen of vision: Robert Schuman, Jean Monnet, Konrad Adenauer, Alcide de Gasperi, and Paul-Henri Spaak, among others. They foresaw clearly the need for a more integrated Europe that would reach beyond a customs

union to an entity that would integrate Europe politically and economically.

From those difficult post-war days, Americans have shared that dream and encouraged it. President Eisenhower and Secretaries Marshall and Acheson, strong supporters of European integration, foresaw that our transatlantic alliance would preserve the peace in Europe and that the example of Western economic prosperity and multiparty democracy would lead to change in the Soviet Union and Eastern Europe. The United States is proud of the role its support and presence in Europe have played in furthering European integration.

Today, we continue to support European unity. The vision of cooperation that took form 40 years ago has become a reality. It has led to a Europe that is economically strong and committed to democratic principles and an outward-looking international trading system, and we celebrate these suc-cesses with our European allies. The trans-atlantic partnership, today as in 1950, is a beacon of hope to societies in transition in Eastern and Central Europe and elsewhere.

We salute the European Community on this significant anniversary.

Statements by Press Secretary Fitzwater on the Federal Budget Negotiations
May 9, 1990

The President, the Speaker of the House [Thomas S. Foley], the Senate majority leader [George J. Mitchell], the Senate Republican leader [Robert Dole], and the House Republican leader [Robert H. Michel] have agreed to establish a special bipartisan budget negotiating group. The purpose of the special budget group is to seek bipartisan agreement on a package of measures that would have four basic objectives: First, to reduce the deficit substantially on a multiyear basis; secondly, to allow the economy to grow at a continued strong pace; third, to strengthen the budget process; and fourth, to avoid the adverse economic and programmatic effects of the stalemate that might otherwise ensue.

The President and the bipartisan congressional leadership agreed that the special budget group would function best if there were no preconditions for negotiation and if there were no negotiations through the public. The special budget group will hold its initial organizational meeting on Tuesday, May 15.

In the session this morning the leadership and the President discussed this matter for about an hour. The discussion was quite friendly, of course, and focused on procedures, on process, on participants, and on timetable. The timetable is that they would like to work as quickly as possible and complete agreement as soon as possible. There are no specific deadlines, but as I said the other day, all parties feel it's in the best interest to try to move this process forward immediately. And the first meeting on Tuesday, the 15th, will indicate a rapid pace as they proceed to deal with this issue.

———

The White House announced the members of its internal budget summit coordinating group. That group will be comprised of the President, the Chief of Staff [John H. Sununu], the Secretary of the Treasury, the Director of the Office of Management and Budget, the Secretary of Defense, the Chairman of the Council of Economic Advisers [Michael J. Boskin], the national security adviser [Brent Scowcroft, Assistant to the President for National Security Affairs], and the Assistant to the President for Economic and Domestic Policy [Roger B. Porter].

The negotiating team for the administration who will meet with the legislative bipartisan budget group will consist of the President, the Secretary of the Treasury, the Chief of Staff, and the Director of the Office of Management and Budget. This basic negotiating group will be complemented by several formal and informal subgroups. When such groups deal with tax and economic policy, the Chairman of the Council of Economic Advisers will join the negotiators; with defense policy, the Secretary of Defense and national security adviser will join; and with domestic spending programs, the Assistant to the President for Economic and Domestic Policy will join.

Note: The first statement was read by Press Secretary Fitzwater during his daily press briefing which began at 11:38 a.m.

Appointment of Raymond Philip Laverty as Deputy Administrator of the Panama Canal Commission
May 9, 1990

The President today announced his intention to appoint Raymond Philip Laverty as Deputy Administrator of the Panama Canal Commission. He would succeed Fernando Manfredo.

Currently, Mr. Laverty serves as Acting Deputy Administrator for Operations for the Panama Canal Commission in the Republic of Panama. Prior to this he served in several capacities with the Panama Canal Organization: General Manager of the Panama Canal Supply Division, Director of the Office of Executive Planning, and United States Representative to the Treaty Coordinating Committee.

Mr. Laverty graduated from the University of Notre Dame (B.A., 1954) and Boston University (M.B.A., 1958). He was born November 11, 1932, in Brockton, MA. Mr. Laverty served in the U.S. Army, 1954–1956. He is married, has three children, and resides in the Republic of Panama.

Nomination of Sylvia Alice Earle To Be Chief Scientist of the National Oceanic and Atmospheric Administration
May 10, 1990

The President today announced his intention to nominate Sylvia Alice Earle to be Chief Scientist of the National Oceanic and Atmospheric Administration, Department of Commerce. She would succeed Melvin N.A. Peterson.

Since 1981, Dr. Earle has served as founder, director, and chief executive officer of Deep Ocean Technology, Inc., in San Leandro, CA. Prior to this, she served on the board of directors for Undersea Industries, Inc., 1978–1981; and as corporate secretary-treasurer of Sea Films, Inc., and Ocean Films, Inc., of Berkeley, CA, 1976–1978. In addition, Dr. Earle has served as a part-time manager and operator of Mead Ranch in Napa, CA, 1967–1976; and co-founder and secretary-treasurer of Aquaculture International, Inc., 1967–1970. She has served as fellow, research biologist, and curator at the California Academy of Sciences since 1979; research associate at the University of California, Berkeley, from 1969 to 1981; and research fellow at the Farlow Herbarium, Harvard University, since 1967.

Dr. Earle graduated from St. Petersburg Junior College (A.A., 1953), Florida State University (B.A., 1955), and Duke University (M.A., 1956; Ph.D., 1966). She was born August 30, 1935, in Gibbstown, NJ. Dr. Earle is married, has seven children, and resides in Oakland, CA.

Remarks at the Texas A&I University Commencement Ceremony in Kingsville
May 11, 1990

Thank you, Mr. Secretary. Thank you all. What a great day! Thank you. Thank you very, very much for that welcome back, and good luck to all of you. Please be seated. What a privilege for me to be introduced by our great Secretary of Education, Lauro Cavazos. We work closely on these problems, but I guess it was a wonderfully emotional return today as we flew into this city in which he grew up—to see the excitement on his face and on his wife's face—and I felt a real part of this coming home for our great Secretary.

I want to thank your president. I can call him "the" president—President Ibañez—because Barbara and I had the chance to greet him in the White House but 6 days ago, and here he is, greeting me on his home turf. And I'm delighted, sir, to be with you.

I want to pay my respects Chancellor Adkisson, the chancellor of the whole system; of course, to our Governor, my old, close friend, Bill Clements; and to our two outstanding United States Senators, Senator Gramm and Senator Lloyd Bentsen—doing a fantastic job for our State. And of course, I'm proud to be in the home turf of Congressman Ortiz, Solomon Ortiz, who flew down with me—also your Congressman, the Congressman for many here; and another old friend of the Bush family, a distinguished chairman in the House, Kika de la Garza, Congressman from Texas and south Texas. And of course, to be introduced by another old friend—it seems like old-home week here—but Billy "Mac" McKenzie, the chairman of the whole system here. Thank you, Billy "Mac." And to Tony Armendariz, who's with me, came down—a south Texan, now a member of my team at the Federal Labor Relations Authority. He was formerly a general counsel of A&I. And then, also, another hometown boy of whom I'm very proud: David Valdez, a Kingsville favorite son. He's a photo dog, we call him. He's the head photographer at the White House. I just met with his family—that's the family that's filling up that whole bleacher over on that side there. [*Laughter*] So glad to see them.

But anyway, it's a pleasure to be back here in my home State of Texas. Congratulations also to those of you up there who paid the bills—all the families, the friends, and especially to the faculty of this great, outstanding institution. Thank you all.

And now, belatedly, I get to the main act: the Texas A&I Class of 1990. Go for it! I'm delighted to be here.

You know, when President Ibañez first contacted us about A&I's graduation, he called my son, George, Jr., up there in Dallas at the Texas Rangers Stadium; and he said that you wanted to hear a speech from a reasonably popular but aging Texan who has risen to the top of his field. And George says, "Does that mean you're inviting Nolan Ryan?" [*Laughter*]

So, I'm second choice, but I'm honored to be in the home of the legendary Javelinas, the wild hogs. And I'm deeply honored to be speaking from the hallowed space on the playing field usually reserved for "Porky." [*Laughter*] But I haven't seen the mascot today. I think he got the word that we eat pork rinds there on Air Force One. [*Laughter*]

Javelinas aren't the only wildlife native to these parts. The mesquite outside Kingsville is shot through with rattlesnake and deer, and doves rise on the warm gulf winds, soaring over the trees and the red tile roofs of Texas A&I. And south Texas is a very special place for the Bush family. I come down here nearly every December with friends, hunt just outside of Beeville—Berclair, to be exact. And let's hear it for the Berclair contingent. There's got to be at least one. [*Applause*] And as your president referred to, when I was an 18-year-old Naval Aviation cadet way back in 1943, I flew all over this country—Corpus and Cabiness and Waldron and Kingsville—and I loved every single minute of it. So, I do feel at home.

The reputation of the area is changing. When I told Barbara that I was flying down to south Texas to talk with college students and see the wildlife, she said, "Aren't you getting a bit old to be going to South Padre for spring break?" [*Laughter*]

But like springtime itself, college commencements signal a time of change. Last week at Oklahoma State University, I spoke about America's new leadership in the Atlantic alliance. Tomorrow morning up at South Carolina, we'll be talking about change among the people of Eastern Europe, people yearning to emulate not only our standard of living but also our standard of justice. But democracy isn't just the wave of the present: it's the wave of the future. And as your generation assumes a leadership role in a free world that's growing bigger all the time, others will continue to look to our shores for leadership and direction. I have proposed that one of those directions be space.

The American adventure has always had the capacity to inspire others and to astonish the world: the voyages of Columbus, the Declaration of Independence, the taming of a continent, the invention of flight. America's democracy is the world's greatest experiment in freedom and diversity, an ongoing experiment that continues to unleash the creative energy of the world's most diverse population. It's what took American pioneers to the Moon and back. It is what will take you as far as your dreams can soar.

Like Texas itself, A&I is also a place of pioneers: the first 4-year college in south Texas; a leader in bilingual education, with the first such doctoral program in the United States; home to research and innovations from natural gas engineering to snake venom to Rio Star grapefruit. And many of you are yourselves pioneers, the first in your families ever to attend college.

In America's unique democratic heritage, our pioneers commissioned themselves and took off. We are a searching people, future-oriented, impelled to push on. After graduating from my college, I took my family out West, looking for a country to test ourselves and our dreams. We found it in Texas, with enough opportunities to last many lifetimes.

Of course, Texas has always had its share of pioneers and visionaries. One was Sam Houston. Where others saw empty plains and dust, he saw farms and ranches and towns. Where others saw obstacles, he saw opportunity. But Houston could scarcely have imagined that little more than a hundred years after his death the entire planet would hold its breath as his name became the first word ever uttered on the plains and dust of another world.

It was July 20, 1969. And although *Apollo 11* had just survived one of the most harrowing landings in the history of space, the voice of Neil Armstrong was confident, strong, American. He said, "Houston: Tranquility Base here. The *Eagle* has landed." Eight words. "Houston: Tranquility Base here. The *Eagle* has landed." Eight words, and the world was changed forever.

And when America accepted the *Apollo* challenge, we rolled up our sleeves and took on a daunting and dangerous job. *Apollo 11* showed we could meet our commitments to ourselves and to the world, proof that democracy could triumph as decisively in peace as it had in war. And it lifted the spirits of a generation and raised forever the horizons of the human race. Last summer, in a speech commemorating the 20th anniversary of the *Apollo* Moon landing, I announced three major space policy objectives: First, to have space station *Freedom* up before the century is out. Second, for the new century, a permanent lunar base: "Back to the Moon, back to the future, and this time back to stay." And third, a manned expedition to Mars.

And together, these objectives form the cornerstone of my administration's far-reaching plan for investing in America's future. Our space program will, indeed, help rekindle public interest in science and mathematics, revitalize an area of our educational system that has become disturbingly weak. In fact, one of the education goals that Dr. Cavazos referred to, one that we announced in January, is to make the United States first in math and science by the year 2000. But this space program will do more. It will revolutionize everything from computers to communications, from medicine to metals, regaining and retaining America's high-tech competitive edge. It will create new technologies, new industries, and new jobs.

It's an adventure that I hope many of you will be part of. You see, it's an adventure that's already underway. The space shuttle is back and ushering in a new era of space. And it's led by a talented new generation: scientists like A&I professor John Linder, who is working here to improve shuttle communications; shuttle engineers like Ruben Zabala, A&I class of 1977; avionics experts like Primitivo Perez, the class of 1971; and new American heroes like Franklin Chang-Diaz, NASA's first Hispanic astronaut.

You are coming of age during a golden age of space, and there's no better example of this than the miracle now orbiting 380 miles above Kingsville: the Hubble Space

Telescope. It will see to the furthest reaches of the universe, to the very edges of time. It will, quite literally, even enable astronomers to see back in time, perhaps far enough back to when the Dallas Cowboys last had a winning season. [*Laughter*] You talk about history. [*Laughter*] And it's hoped that the telescope will see objects so clearly that, in theory, it could pick out the writing on a dime 100 miles away. Talk about the "vision thing."

Even while Galileo and Hubble begin looking out across space, another array of new satellites will be looking back at Earth and taking the pulse of the most important planet in the universe. You may remember of a couple years back when Time magazine named Earth "Planet of the Year." And the comedian—you remember Jay Leno, the comedian—he said: "What did you expect? All the judges came from Earth." [*Laughter*]

We call this initiative Mission to Planet Earth. It's an effort of such magnitude that it dwarfs everything in the past. A worldwide study of the complex interactions between land, sea, ice, and air, as well as between the Earth and the Sun. It's an effort of global interest in which we're inviting other nations to join. As Chairman of the National Space Council, the Vice President has just returned from Europe, where our allies expressed serious interest in both Mission to Planet Earth and in our continuing exploration of the solar system.

Initiatives like these mark a critical investment in America's future. They will help protect the environment, fuel an educational renaissance, and hone America's competitive edge. But the importance of the space program, especially the manned space program, goes deeper than that. Throughout our history, America has been a nation of discoverers. It's a part of our national character, part of our democratic heritage. In fact, Monday marks the day in 1804 when Meriwether Lewis and William Clark set out across the Mississippi to map much of what was to become the great American West. And despite Thomas Jefferson's love of machines, it's hard to imagine his sending a robot out alone to describe the wonders of the American Rockies and the Pacific coast. In the American experiment, in the experiment called democracy, there will always be a place for individual men and women with imagination and daring.

Our nation's quest for the unknown took American pioneers from the bluffs of the Mississippi to the mountains of the Moon. But today we're no longer just asking for the Moon. We've been there. We're looking further: to carry the American adventure to wherever opportunity, curiosity, and need will take us. It's time to open up the final frontier. There can be no turning back. America's space program is what civilization needs to begin this journey and to perfect the commitment to go beyond. Each time we go to the frontier and beyond, we bring back more than we hoped for. And this time we have the chance to bring back more than we can possibly imagine.

Our 1991 budget is proof positive of America's commitment to an active, exciting, and continuing presence in space—to America's leadership in space. Our proposal of $15.2 billion for NASA, an increase of 24 percent—almost $3 billion, which is the largest increase for any major agency of the government.

But leadership in space takes more than just dollars: It also takes a decision. And so, I'm announcing one today. We stand at a halfway point in our exploration of the immediate solar system: the planet Earth, its Moon, and the terrestrial neighborhood. Thirty years ago, NASA was founded, and the space race began. And 30 years from now I believe man will stand on another planet. And so, I am pleased to return to Texas today to announce a new Age of Exploration, with not only a goal but also a timetable: I believe that before *Apollo* celebrates the 50th anniversary of its landing on the Moon the American flag should be planted on Mars.

Up beneath the dome of the United States Capitol—where decisions about our space program will be made in the coming weeks—the American adventure is told in stone, a tableau of U.S. history carved around the rim of the dome itself. It begins with Columbus' arrival in the New World and ends with the first flight of the Wright brothers' plane. But you see, they got it wrong. The Wright brothers' flight doesn't mark the end of the American adventure but the beginning of a new chapter, a never-ending story, a story about a democracy where anything is possible and where no dream is too large.

We live in a century that began with great promise and hope for the idea we call democracy, then only beginning to assume an important place on the world stage. That hope has been fulfilled and surpassed beyond the wildest dreams of our Founders. And the promise of democracy is beginning to be tasted by more people in more places than ever before. It's their inspiration; and it's our strength, our heritage, and our future. And so, as this century closes, it is in America's hands to help determine the kind of people, the kind of planet, we will become in the next. We will leave the solar system and travel to the stars not only because it is democracy's dream but because it is democracy's destiny.

Around campfires, by moonlight and starlight across the ages, men and women have turned their gaze skyward and dreamed an ancient dream. And somewhere in America today, maybe right here in this stadium, there is a young man or woman who, like Neil Armstrong, will seize this dream and change the world for all time. I believe, I truly believe, that the class of '90 will leave footprints not only in the sands of our State, in the sands of Texas, but also in the sands of time and ultimately on the plains of Mars.

You who have lived this past 4 years in Kingsville know a lot about the sky. The plains of south Texas are as flat as the sea, a land without hills or impediments, a land of limitless horizons and dreams to match. It is exactly the kind of nighttime sky where the cream of America's youth—the cream of Texas A&I—can point confidently to the stars, to eternity, and to their own future, the future of this great nation, and the future of free people everywhere.

America is proud of you. We are proud of your families. And I came here to say congratulations, and thank you, and God bless the United States.

Note: The President spoke at 11:45 a.m. in Javelina Stadium on the campus of the university. In his remarks, he referred to Manuel L. Ibañez, president of the university; Perry Adkisson and William A. McKenzie, chancellor and chairman of the board of regents of the university system, respectively; and Nolan Ryan, pitcher for the Rangers baseball team. Following his remarks, the President traveled to Columbia, SC.

Nomination of Jimmy Gurule To Be an Assistant Attorney General
May 11, 1990

The President today announced his intention to nominate Jimmy Gurule to be an Assistant Attorney General for the Office of Justice Programs at the Department of Justice. He would succeed Richard Bender Abell.

Since 1989 Mr. Gurule has served as an associate professor of law at Notre Dame Law School. Prior to this, he served as an Assistant U.S. Attorney in the Criminal Division of the Office of the U.S. Attorney in Los Angeles, CA, 1985–1989; deputy county attorney in the justice division of the Salt Lake County Attorney's Office, 1982–1985; adjunct professor of law at the University of Utah College of Law, 1983–1985; and a trial attorney in the Criminal Division of the Department of Justice, 1980–1982. In addition, Mr. Gurule has served as a Special Assistant U.S. Attorney for the Southern District of Florida, 1982, and a Special Assistant U.S. Attorney for the District of Columbia, 1981.

Mr. Gurule graduated from the University of Utah (B.A., 1974; J.D., 1980). He was born June 14, 1951, in Salt Lake City, UT. Mr. Gurule is married, has three children, and resides in Granger, IN.

Nomination of J. Michael Luttig To Be an Assistant Attorney General
May 11, 1990

The President today announced his intention to nominate J. Michael Luttig to be Assistant Attorney General for the Office of Legal Counsel at the Department of Justice. He would succeed William Pelham Barr.

Since 1989 Mr. Luttig has served as Principal Deputy Assistant Attorney General in the Office of Legal Counsel at the Department of Justice. Prior to this, he served as an associate with the law firm of Davis Polk and Wardwell, 1985–1989; special assistant to the Honorable Warren E. Burger, Chief Justice of the U.S. Supreme Court, 1984– 1985; law clerk to the Honorable Warren E. Burger, 1983–1984; law clerk to the Honorable Antonin Scalia, U.S. Court of Appeals, District of Columbia Circuit, 1982–1983; and Assistant Counsel at the White House, 1981–1982.

Mr. Luttig graduated from Washington and Lee University (B.A., 1976) and the University of Virginia School of Law (J.D., 1981). He was born June 13, 1954, in Tyler, TX. Mr. Luttig is married to Elizabeth Ann Luttig, and they reside in McLean, VA.

Nomination of William Pelham Barr To Be Deputy Attorney General
May 11, 1990

The President today announced his intention to nominate William Pelham Barr to be Deputy Attorney General at the Department of Justice. He would succeed Donald Belton Ayer.

Since 1989 Mr. Barr has served as Assistant Attorney General for the Office of Legal Counsel at the Department of Justice. Prior to this, he served as a partner with the law firm of Shaw, Pittman, Potts and Trowbridge in Washington, DC, 1984–1989; a member of the domestic policy staff at the White House, 1982–1983; an associate with the law firm of Shaw, Pittman, Potts and Trowbridge, 1978–1982; and a law clerk to Judge Malcolm Wilkey of the U.S. Court of Appeals for the District of Columbia Circuit, 1977–1978. In addition, he has served with the Central Intelligence Agency, 1973–1977.

Mr. Barr graduated from Columbia University (B.A., 1971; M.A., 1973) and George Washington University (J.D., 1977). He was born May 23, 1950, in New York, NY. Mr. Barr is married, has three children, and resides in Falls Church, VA.

Nomination of Charles M. House To Be Director of the Office for Victims of Crime
May 11, 1990

The President today announced his intention to nominate Charles M. House to be Director of the Office for Victims of Crime at the Department of Justice. This is a new position.

Since 1988 Mr. House has served as operations sergeant for court services in Los Angeles, CA. Prior to this, he served in various positions for the Los Angeles County Sheriff's Department, including watch commander, 1987–1988; international liaison officer, 1980–1987; a patrol officer, 1978–1980; fraud investigator, 1977–1978; and operations planner, 1975–1977. He also served as a bailiff in the Los Angeles Superior Court System, 1966–1975.

Mr. House graduated from California State University (B.S., 1971). He was born November 17, 1935, in Austin, TX. Mr. House served in the U.S. Army, 1958–1960. He is married, has two children, and resides in Hacienda Heights, CA.

Nomination of Steven D. Dillingham To Be Director of the Bureau of Justice Statistics
May 11, 1990

The President today announced his intention to nominate Steven D. Dillingham to be Director of the Bureau of Justice Statistics at the Department of Justice. He would succeed Steven Roger Schlesinger.

Since 1988 Dr. Dillingham has served as Deputy Director for Policy and Special Programs for the Bureau of Justice Assistance at the Department of Justice. Prior to this, he served as a senior associate and project manager for Carter, Goble and Associates, Inc., 1987–1988; attorney and adviser in the Office of the General Counsel at the Department of Energy, 1986–1988; academic adviser to the law and justice task force for the American Legislative Exchange Council, 1987 to present; attorney in the Office

of General Counsel for the Office of Personnel Management, 1985–1986; special counsel on criminal law for the Senate Judiciary Committee, 1985; and assistant professor for the College of Criminal Justice at the University of South Carolina, 1981–1986. In addition, he has served in various capacities as a research analyst and a teaching associate.

Dr. Dillingham graduated from Winthrop College (B.A. 1973) and the University of South Carolina (M.P.A., 1978; J.D., 1976; and Ph.D., 1987). He was born May 12, 1952, in Orangeburg, SC. Dr. Dillingham attended the U.S. Air Force Academy, 1970–1972. He is married, has one child, and resides in Alexandria, VA.

Nomination of Robert C. Bonner To Be Administrator of the Drug Enforcement Administration
May 11, 1990

The President today announced his intention to nominate Robert C. Bonner to be Administrator of Drug Enforcement at the Department of Justice. He would succeed John C. Lawn.

Since 1989 Mr. Bonner has served as U.S. District Judge for the Central District of California in Los Angeles. Prior to this, he served as U.S. Attorney for the Central District of California, 1984–1989; in the private practice of law with the firm of Kadison, Pfaelzer, Woodard, Quinn and Rossi, 1975–

1984; Assistant U.S. Attorney for the Central District of California, 1971–1975; and a law clerk to U.S. District Judge Albert Stephens, 1966–1967.

Mr. Bonner graduated from Maryland University (B.A., 1963) and Georgetown University Law Center (J.D., 1966). He was born January 29, 1942, in Wichita, KS. Mr. Bonner served in the U.S. Naval Reserve, 1967–1971. He is married, has one child, and resides in Pasadena, CA.

Remarks at a Fundraising Reception for Governor Carroll A. Campbell, Jr., in Columbia, South Carolina
May 11, 1990

Thank you all. What a great evening here in South Carolina. Thank you very much. Thank you very much. Please be seated there. [*Laughter*] Sorry about that. It's great to be back here, back with you all. And I'm so pleased to see Congressman Floyd Spence, behind me, looking so well—doing a great job for this State up in Washington. I'm told that Congressman Ravenel was to be here from Charleston, but I don't know if he made it. But I do see the former Congressman and my friend and associate for a long time, Tommy Hartnett, over there, standing there. And of course, I want to salute the Governor and Iris and Carroll the three and Mike and Commissioner Les Tindal and Dick Greer, another longtime supporter of all the good causes in South Carolina on the political scene and certainly a friend and supporter of mine. And last, but certainly not least in this State, nor in Washington, the one and only Strom Thurmond. It's great to be with him.

It's marvelous how Carroll does it; he's always coming up with new ways to raise campaign funds. [*Laughter*] Next week he's going after that $10,000 first prize by sending his skiing tape to "America's Funniest Home Videos." [*Laughter*]

But really, it's a pleasure to be back here. And, Strom, your election is so important; and you are looking rarin' to go in the nineties, I'll tell you. [*Laughter*] And good luck, best of luck to you. I'm always tempted to ask Strom, What's your secret? But I'm afraid he'd say, Eat your vegetables. So, I'm not going to. [*Laughter*]

And let me just say how delighted I was to get that firsthand report from Lee. Barbara and I talk to him regularly, and I'm so pleased to pay his respects to this crowd of his friends. And he is staying in close touch there at the national committee, and the committee is going very well.

You know, it's a delight for Barbara and me to be back here in a State where friendships grow as easily as the yellow jasmine and back with so many South Carolina Republicans. You get the feeling things are on the move not just for the Republican Party but for the conservative cause, generally. And I am grateful for the support that I get from this Governor and this Senator and this Congressman every single day. I couldn't do without it.

When Iris—I guess I'll give her credit—and Carroll invited us to come back here, we accepted before they could change their minds because I did want to say to his friends and his supporters and then to all through the media across the State that South Carolina deserves a Governor who works hard, has demonstrated the ability to make the tough choices, who offers leadership every single day. And that is the Governor that clearly you'll reelect this coming November, and I'm talking about Carroll Campbell.

So, let me ask you to look for 1 minute at the record. South Carolina enjoys almost 200,000 more jobs today than when he took office. This is what happens when a Governor pursues policies that encourage growth, when he trusts the people to do what they do best: make a better life for South Carolina.

In fact, your Governor has done something for this State that I want to see done for America: He slashed the capital gains tax. And that meant more jobs for South Carolina. And so, I might take this opportunity to call on Congress to follow the example of this State—to open the floodgates of investment, to increase jobs and opportunity for all Americans by cutting the capital gains tax—and doing it soon. I'm going to keep on like a broken record until I get that thing done up there.

But this State is great for more than just its business climate. From the Sassafras Mountain to the home of Barbara Bush's alma mater over there, Ashley Hall, in Charleston; from the green valleys of the Piedmont—Ashley Hall has got a modest delegation back here—[*laughter*]—from the green valleys of the Piedmont to the dune-swept shoreline of Myrtle Beach, this State is special. And I know of your commitment to keep it that way. That's why Carroll has already acted against helter-skelter coastal development. He's protected the precious beaches of this State. And that's why he put together a fair, a reasonable wetlands policy, one that strives for no net loss.

On the national level, we, too, are striving for no net loss, and we seek to safeguard our beaches and redeem our wetlands. And that is going to be a crusade as long as I'm President.

As you may know, I also proposed the first major revision of the Clean Air Act since 1977, one that will sharply cut acid rain and smog and toxic pollutants. But Congress has got to respect—and thank God we have Strom there because he'll see to that—they've got to respect another kind of delicate ecology; that's the one of jobs and opportunity. So, I call on the House of Representatives not to keep America waiting for cleaner air; to pass a reasonable clean air bill in line with the compromise that we reached with the Senate leaders, not another bill that consumers and workers cannot afford.

South Carolinians also want to be safe from crime, and no one has been tougher in the war against crime and drugs than your Governor. He created this strike force that captured more than 1,800 drug offenders, confiscated literally hundreds of millions of dollars worth of drugs. But he's also reached out on the other side of the equation—with compassion, with understanding—to the most distressed neighborhoods to help them take back the streets.

While your Governor's been busy here in the State, I've been working closely with the United States Congress, with Congressmen like Floyd Spence and Arthur Ravenel and, of course, Senator Thurmond, who is the chairman of—the ranking member—he should be chairman; we lost control of the Senate, darn it all—[*laughter*]—but Senator Strom Thurmond, to provide money for new prison space, more Federal law enforcement officers. But the Democratic leadership in Congress has just left too much work undone on our violent crime package. And I call on Congress to recognize that the kingpins who are dealing

drugs and dealing death—judge them for what they are—they are murderers, and we must be tough on those people.

Finally, there's one other issue above all others, and that's the state of American education. I might say parenthetically—maybe this is wrong, but I think we all owe a vote of gratitude to Barbara for her crusading efforts in literacy and fighting to make this society more literate.

But on the government side, Carroll Campbell knows the priority for education. He's been working to make this State second to none in educational excellence. And what you are striving to do for South Carolina, I am determined to do for all of America. American students must be—we've set these national goals now—must be first in math and science. Every American adult must be a literate citizen and worker. And every school in America must have a disciplined environment and, most of all, must be drug-free. You see, education is critical to everything we are and can become. And that's why Governor Campbell was such a leader and worked so closely with me at our education summit—the first education summit with all the Governors, called there in Charlottesville, Virginia. When it comes to education, we've got to measure success not by dollars spent but by the results achieved.

In closing, let me say one thing more about Carroll and this State, something that transcends politics. South Carolina had—and he alluded to this—had a very unwelcome visitor last year, a vandal by the name of [Hurricane] Hugo. You also had a Governor, though, who moved decisively to bring people inland, to save countless lives. During those tough days, he was up to his hips in mud. Also helping with relief efforts were Members of Congress, State legislators, and mayors, and also, God bless them, the policemen and women of South Carolina, the State troopers, the Boy and Girl Scouts, whole church congregations, and too many volunteer groups to possibly name.

Everyone lost something to Hugo, and some lost everything. But no one had time—and I saw this, because Strom and I and Carroll went down there together just for a little bird's-eye view—no one had time for self-pity or worry as long as one neighbor remained stranded or needed a helping hand. In those terrible days of wind and rain, and during the long months of cleanup, that ghastly cleanup that followed, South Carolina became a point of light, giving all of America a shining example of the very best within us.

And that's the way for the greatest country on Earth; that's the American way. You know, this same spirit of openness and giving found right here in South Carolina makes America a beacon of hope for the world. Isn't it an exciting time—to see the changes for democracy and for freedom that are taking place all around the world, that have taken place just in the last 12 months. I can think of no more exciting time in history to be President of the United States than during this last year of dynamic change for democracy and freedom around the world.

I hear a lot of marvelous stories. I wish you could have seen the look on the President of Czechoslovakia's face, Vaclav Havel, the playwright. Bar and I thought it would be nice for him to see the Lincoln Bedroom in the White House, the bedroom in which Lincoln actually signed the Emancipation Proclamation. And the look on his face, as a man who was in jail and dying, or living—whatever—for freedom, stood out there, hoping against hope for freedom. It just was so moving to see this marvelous symbol of our identity there.

But I recently heard of a man living in Romania who braved arrest by possessing what the previous regime considered to be a dangerous and subversive weapon: a single American newspaper. This courageous man was so enthralled that he not only kept this paper, he read it every day

for 3 years. He memorized it, and he savored the uncensored news and the free-wheeling editorials and even the advertisements. That's how hungry the world is for the truth. That's how vital our liberty is to the oppressed. That's why America truly is a point of light for the world.

And no star in this American constellation burns brighter than the State of South Carolina. After all, historic changes are occurring around the world because of American leadership, leaders like your great Senator that stands for something, Strom Thurmond. When America needed to be protected during the Cold War years, Strom, rock-solid, standing for freedom—we'll never forget it. This country owes him a great vote of gratitude. We need his hard-won wisdom and leadership, really, as never before.

Today it's been my special honor to appear on and try to help honor someone who embodies South Carolina's determination, courage, and just plain old common sense. And of course, I'm talking again about Carroll Campbell. He's been a great Governor, and with your support, he can bring an even greater future for South Carolina.

Thank you for this magnificent turnout, this fantastic support for a great Governor. God bless the United States of America. Thank you very, very much.

Note: The President spoke at 7:12 p.m. at the Governor's Mansion. In his opening remarks, he referred to Governor Campbell's wife, Iris, and sons, Carroll and Mike; Les Tindal, South Carolina Commissioner of Agriculture; Dick Greer, chairman of the Re-Elect Governor Campbell Committee; and Lee Atwater, chairman of the Republican National Committee.

Remarks at the University of South Carolina Commencement Ceremony in Columbia
May 12, 1990

Thank you, President Holderman, distinguished officials of this wonderful university. My special respects to two great United States Senators, Senators Strom Thurmond, Fritz Hollings, over here—I'm proud to be with them today—and to Representatives Floyd Spence and Elizabeth Patterson, with us; of course, to my dear friend, your Governor, Carroll Campbell, who's a tremendous partner in our national crusade for excellence in education. I also want to say how pleased I am to be on this stage with Archbishop Iakovos, one of the great church leaders of today.

I know, looking around, that tickets were hard to come by today. It wasn't simply parking. Barbara's here. [*Laughter*] Thank goodness she's getting an honorary degree there because it was the only way I could get her a seat in this big place. [*Laughter*] But thank you for honoring her.

And she's in great company, as am I, with today's other recipients of honorary degrees. I don't know how many of you have heard me speak before, but being on stage with Andrew Lloyd Webber is about as close as I'll ever get to a dramatic presentation. [*Laughter*] Congratulations to you, sir.

And to Michael Eisner: The success that he's achieved at Disney is the envy of CEO's worldwide. His secret's simple: Just surround yourself with the best and the brightest—Dopey, Dumbo, Goofy. [*Laughter*] But what you may not know, and you should, is I salute him, too, for his commitment to this concept of Points of Light, the best impulse of America—and Michael Eisner exemplifies it—one American willing to pitch in and help another. He's a great American.

Now to you all. I've saluted—hope I have—your faculty. I should; they're outstanding—the trustees and those who govern this great institution, and to the class who I'm here to help these others honor. You've gone to school for 4 years; the last thing you want to hear is a long lecture. But I wanted to use this great university as a forum for some serious foreign policy observations. I've chosen to make each of several commencement speeches this spring a reflection on democratic change. Last week, at Oklahoma State, I focused on the new role of our Atlantic alliance. Yesterday, down in Texas, at Texas A&I, I spoke about technology and the vast frontier of space. This morning, I want to talk about a frontier of a different sort, about the new world of freedom opening up in Eastern Europe.

Now, that's pretty serious business, but I'm going to ask you to bear with me, but telling you I do remember a graduation at Yale, where the graduation speaker got up—my alma mater—Y is for youth—that took 20 minutes. A is for altruism—young people be altruistic—another 32 minutes. L for loyalty—brushed that one off in about 18 minutes. E obviously for excellence—another 32 minutes. When he left, one student left, praying. And the speaker walked down. "I see you're giving thanks to the Lord." He said, "Yes, sir, I am. I'm giving thanks that I did not go to the University of South Carolina." [*Laughter*]

So, bear with me, because we are living in exciting times. In the past year, one nation after another has pulled itself out from under communism, onto the threshold of democracy. Each has endured great suffering, tremendous economic damage. We've all seen the images of long lines and empty shelves. But what we can't see so easily, what's beneath the surface but no less real, is the moral damage, the deep scars on the spirit left by four decades of Communist rule.

Because in these regimes, the human spirit was subject to systematic assault. Religion, morality, right and wrong—any challenge to the rule of the state became the enemy of the state. Believers were persecuted, churches and cemeteries razed. Citizens were turned one against the other, enlisted into the ranks of the regime's informers. Nothing stood outside the reach of the regime, not even the past. History—well, it was rewritten to suit the needs of the present—yesterday's heroes airbrushed from the pages of history. Milan Kundera, the Czech author, called it organized forgetting.

Of course, these nations had laws. They had courts. They had constitutions. All in service to the state. They had, in name at least, rights and freedoms; in reality, the empty shell of liberty—not the rule of law but the perversion of law: rules made not to serve the will of the people but the whim of the party. That's how in Romania the law made it illegal for three or more people to have a conversation in the street. That's how in another country a man whose so-called crime was teaching others about religion was jailed for 6 months. The trumped-up charge: walking on flower beds. We will never know how many dissidents were punished as common criminals and how many millions of others were frozen by fear into silence and submission.

That's the legacy, the landscape of moral destruction. The tragic consequence of four decades of Communist rule: a breakdown of trust. From ancient times, the great minds have recognized the link between the law and trust. As Aristotle wrote: "Law is a pledge that the citizens of a state will do justice to one another"—the bond that makes the collection of individuals into a community, into a nation.

Fortunately, the moral destruction in Eastern Europe, as you all know, was not complete. Individuals somehow managed to maintain an inner strength, their moral compass; to sustain the will to break through the regime's wall of lies. They did so, as Václav Havel [President of Czechoslovakia] put it, by the simple act of "living in truth." They created "flying universities," where lecturers taught in private homes. They formed underground publishing houses and groups to monitor human rights, an authentic civil society beyond the reach of the ruling establishment. And today the builders of those civil societies no longer live underground. They are the new leaders of Eastern Europe. And they've begun to build, on the ruins of Communist rule, democratic systems based on trust.

Today I want to focus on how America can help these nations secure their freedoms, become a part of a Europe whole and free. Early this year, in the State of the Union, I talked about America's role as a shining example, about the importance of America not as a nation but as an idea alive in the minds of men and women everywhere. And that idea was, without doubt, a guiding force in the Revolution of 1989.

Let me share a story with you about a recent American visitor to Romania who asked the people she met what they needed now, what was most important to them. This simple question produced some unexpected answers. In Timisoara, one woman pulled from her purse a worn copy of TV Guide, an issue from July 1987, containing a bicentennial copy of the United States Constitution. And she held it out to the American visitor. And she said, "What we need is more of these."

And there on the streets of Timisoara—in a country where food is in short supply, where homes are without heat and streets dark at night—there a woman pins her hopes on our Constitution. What that Romanian woman wanted, what all the nations of Eastern Europe aspire to, is democratic life based on justice and the rule of law.

Poland, Czechoslovakia, and Hungary stand now, in the spring of 1990, as America stood in the summer of 1787. Who will be their Franklins, their Washingtons, their Hamiltons, their Madisons, their men and women of towering genius, the nation builders who will set in place the firm foundations of self-government? Some of them we know by name, the heroes of the Revolution of '89. But for Eastern Europe's constitution builders, the work has only now begun because the fate of freedom depends not just on the character of the people who govern but whether they themselves are governed by the rule of law.

And just as the framers of our own Constitution looked to the lessons of history, Eastern Europe's new democracies will look to their own parliamentary past, to Europe's example and, of course, to our own American Constitution. And that's why we must export our experience, our two centuries of accumulated wisdom on the workings of free government.

Already we're actively engaged with Eastern Europe and the Soviet Union with an ongoing series of exchanges bringing jurists and parliamentarians, political leaders here to the United States to meet their American counterparts. And today I'm pleased to announce four new initiatives, four steps that the United States will take to support democratic development in Eastern Europe.

First, America will continue to act to advance economic freedom. In the past year, we've committed more than $1 billion in direct economic assistance to Eastern Europe. We've extended loans and credits, opened our markets through most-favored-nation status, and promoted American investment. And today I'm pleased to announce yet another economic initiative: The Export-Import Bank will provide Poland a new line of medium-term export credits and loan guarantees for purchasing machinery, technology, and services from American suppliers.

And second, the United States will work to help ensure free and fair elections in Eastern Europe. And next week, we'll send a Presidential delegation to observe the elections in Romania and another team to next month's elections in Bulgaria.

Third, America will work to broaden the mandate of the CSCE, the Conference on Security and Cooperation in Europe. Less than a month from now, as one of the 35 nations of the CSCE, the United States will take part in a conference on human rights, including free elections, political pluralism, and the rule of law. And I've instructed Ambassador Max Kampelman, head of our delegation, to seek a new consensus on these cornerstones of freedoms, rights, and democracy. As I said last week at Oklahoma State University, we must work within the CSCE to bring Eastern Europe's new democracies into this commonwealth of free nations.

Fourth and finally, we will work to strengthen the foundations of free society in Eastern Europe. And I am pleased to announce today the creation of a Citizens Democracy Corps. Its first mission: to establish a center and a clearinghouse for American private sector assistance and volunteer activities in Eastern Europe. We know the

real strength of our democracy is its citizens, the collective strength of individual Americans. We're going to focus that energy where it can do the most good.

America has much to contribute, much it can do to help these nations move forward on the path to democracy. We can help them build political systems based on respect for individual freedoms; for the right to speak our mind, to live as we wish, and to worship as our conscience tells us we must; systems based on respect for property and the sanctity of contract; laws that are necessary not to amass fortunes, not to build towers of gold and greed, but to provide for ourselves, for our families; systems that allow free associations—trade unions, professional groups, political parties—the building blocks of a free society. We've got to help the emerging democracies build legal systems that secure the procedural rights that preserve freedom and, above all, a system that supports a strict equality of rights, one that guarantees that all men and women, whatever their race or ancestry, stand equal before the law.

In this century, we've learned a painful truth about the monumental evil that can be done in the name of humanity. We've learned how a vision of Utopia can become a hell on Earth for millions of men and women. We've learned, through hard experience, that the only alternative to tyranny of man is the rule of law. That's the essence of our vision for Europe: a Europe where not only are the dictators dethroned but where the rule of law, reflecting the will of the people, ensures the freedoms millions have fought so hard to gain.

There is still work to be done. In the Baltic States, where people struggle for the right to determine their own future, we Americans, so free to chart our own course, identify with their hopes and aspirations. For, you see, we're committed to self-determination for Lithuania and Latvia and Estonia. And ultimately, the Soviet Union itself, now committed to openness and reform, will benefit from a Europe that's whole and free. Democracy and freedom threaten absolutely no one.

We sometimes hear today that with freedom's great triumph—and, oh, what exciting times we're living in—that America's work is done. Nothing could be further from the truth. I want to close today with a story about the enduring power of the American idea and the unfinished business that awaits the generation that you proudly represent.

It's about a town called Plzen in Czechoslovakia; a town that just last week celebrated the day, 45 years ago, when it was liberated by American troops. Of course, within a few short years, Plzen's dream of freedom vanished behind the Iron Curtain, and with it, the truth about that day back in 1945. A generation grew up being taught that Plzen had been freed not by your fathers and granddads in the United States Army but by Soviet soldiers dressed in American uniforms. But the people of Plzen knew better. They never forgot. And today, finally free to speak the truth, the town invited their true liberators back. After 45 long years, those old American soldiers returned to the streets of Plzen, to the sounds of "The Star-Spangled Banner," to a hero's welcome.

Those GI's, my generation, were your age in 1945. And now it falls upon you, the graduating class of this great university, to uphold our American ideals not in times of war, thank God, but in a time of tremendous excitement, helping these nations secure the freedom that your fathers and grandfathers fought for, the freedom millions only dreamed of until today.

Once again, it's been my honor to share this special day with you, your families, and your friends. Thank you, and may God bless this great university and the class of 1990. Thank you all very, very much. Thank you.

Note: The President spoke at 11:25 a.m. at Carolina Coliseum on the campus of the university. In his remarks, he referred to James B. Holderman, president of the university; Archbishop Demetrios A. Iakovos of the Greek Orthodox Archdiocese of North and South America; composer Andrew Lloyd Webber; and Michael D. Eisner, chairman and chief executive officer of the Walt Disney Co. Following his remarks, the President traveled to Lynchburg, VA.

White House Fact Sheet on the Citizens Democracy Corps
May 12, 1990

The President announced today the creation of a Citizens Democracy Corps. The objective of this major new program is to support democratic change and market-oriented economic reform in Eastern Europe by mobilizing and coordinating American private sector initiatives.

Since the President's historic visits to Poland and Hungary and the revolutions of 1989, private Americans and voluntary organizations have stepped forward with extraordinary generosity with offers to assist the process of democratic change in Eastern Europe. To make best use of the enormous energy and creativity of the American private sector, the President supports the creation of a new center to promote these volunteer initiatives and match them with requests for assistance from Eastern Europe.

The Citizens Democracy Corps will serve as an information clearinghouse for U.S. private volunteer assistance programs for Central and Eastern Europe. It will establish an information base of technical services and equipment available from the United States on a private, volunteer basis. The Democracy Corps will also be a recipient of requests from Central and Eastern Europe for assistance in such areas as constitutional law and parliamentary procedures; English-language training; journalism, broadcasting, and publishing; public health and medical support; market economics, banking, and financial services; business law, commercial practices, and agriculture; and environmental protection.

The Citizens Democracy Corps will be the point of contact for U.S. businesses, voluntary organizations, and educational institutions that want to find out what is now being done and where further efforts are needed. The Democracy Corps could also launch new volunteer initiatives to meet the changing requirements of the region.

The President will ask prominent citizens representing a cross section of the American private sector to form a commission to direct the program and stimulate volunteer

groups. The commission and the volunteers mobilized to provide assistance will be called the Citizens Democracy Corps. While the U.S. Government will help provide initial funding, the Democracy Corps will create its own financial base so that it can become, in the full sense of the term, "citizens democracy."

Remarks at the Liberty University Commencement Ceremony in Lynchburg, Virginia
May 12, 1990

Thank you so much. And to all of you who are done medium well or medium well-done up here in the stands, I'll try not to keep you too long. [*Laughter*] But I am delighted to be here. And to Dr. and Mrs. Falwell, thank you for your hospitality. Jerry, I'm glad to have been introduced by a loyal friend. Thank you very much, sir. And to President Guillermin and my dear friend John Warner and Mayor Bryan and members of the board of trustees and the faculty, administrators, parents, and graduates, thank you for that welcome and introduction and for this most generous reception. I was privileged to address the students and faculty of this wonderful university before. And now, as then, it's good to know that if it takes divine intervention to save my remarks, help is close at hand. [*Laughter*]

I couldn't help but notice the honorees, and I would like to say that I am proud to be numbered among them—Reverend Henderson, Reverend Theis, Reverend Cox, Reverend Irvin and, of course, Mr. Williams, who's been such a benefactor to this wonderful university and to many other great causes. And let me say how it's not all just religion around here, because I recognize Eric Green over here. How many small colleges have a first-round draft choice for the National Football League? Eric, stand up there. [*Applause*] And I think we all can recognize that Eric didn't do it alone. Sam Rutigliano is a pretty good influence on these kids around here.

This afternoon, I'm honored to be back here and to join my fellow graduates. Of course, I also want you to enjoy today. Therefore, I'll renew my promise: I will be brief. After all, you've worked and studied for 4 long years, and now comes the hard part: listening to a commencement address. [*Laughter*]

Looking around campus as we flew in, I marveled at the changes since I was here last: new name, certainly a beautiful new stadium, three times as many students. And it got me to thinking how college itself has changed since my days as a undergraduate. The students are so much younger—[*laughter*]—I can't understand it—and so much smarter—that I can understand. Nowadays, with computers, bringing an apple to the teacher has a whole new meaning. [*Laughter*]

This spring, I've spoken in each of my commencement addresses about another kind of change: the democratic change that in 1989 and '90 has stirred and amazed the world. Last week, at Oklahoma State University, I discussed how this change will affect our Atlantic alliance. Yesterday in south Texas, at Texas A&I, I talked about how the American adventure in democracy inspires greater deeds here at home and around the globe. Earlier today, at the University of South Carolina, my subject was the importance of the rule of law to the emerging democracies in Eastern Europe. This afternoon, I'd like to talk about another element of democratic change, what I call individual empowerment: loving our neighbors, helping them help themselves.

True democracy, of course, has always entailed putting power in the hands of the individual. The ancient Greeks spoke of it. Millions have given their lives on behalf of it. Perhaps Woodrow Wilson said it best: "I believe in democracy because it releases the energy of every human being."

More than 200 years ago, we secured democracy through the American Revolution, ensuring rights like freedom of speech, due process under the law, and to think and dream as we choose—also, I might add, the freedom to pray as we choose, which is why I support a constitutional amendment restoring voluntary prayer. We need the faith of our fathers back in our schools. The rights of free elections, free markets, and the expression of free will form the very essence of America. And over the past year, they've become the message of America, helping liberty triumph over dictatorship in every corner of the globe.

Jerry referred to it, but look at Panama. And he referred to Romania. Look at Romania, where tyrants fell, or Hungary, holding its first multiparty parliamentary election in more than four decades. Look at Czechoslovakia, where last week U.S. soldiers returned to the small town of Plzen they freed exactly 45 years before. Finally able to celebrate, the Czechs greeted the GI's as brothers, liberators. Love united strangers. There was magic in the air.

What I call the Revolution of '89 has been a year of democratic change, and never has democratic change spawned a greater age of freedom. Nor have individuals your age had a greater chance to enrich the Earth. Yet as I said 2 weeks ago, addressing the National Prayer Breakfast, with opportunity comes responsibility. "America not only is divinely blessed, America is divinely accountable." This accountability means assuring that government does what it must and does it well, but it also means increasing what individuals can do, empowering people politically by showing them how democracy works and economically by fostering the entrepreneurship and competition and investment so crucial to private enterprise. Empowerment must also be spiritual and intellectual through the scholarship

vital to everything we are and can become. Great goals? Yes. Obtainable? You bet. By acting as what I term a Thousand Points of Light: volunteers who measure life by holding themselves accountable for the well-being of their community.

The idea of voluntarism, or community service, is rooted, first, in faith. Perhaps a little boy put it best with this simple prayer: God bless mother and daddy, my brother and sister. And, oh, God, do take care of yourself, because if anything happens to You we're all sunk. [*Laughter*] Like that boy, we believe that God requires us, as He says in Micah 6, "to act justly and to love mercy."

Community service is also grounded in our history. Think of the pioneers who tamed a wild frontier—clearing forests and building towns—or the teachers of a century ago—ill-supplied, paid less than $30 a month, often boarded in small homes with large families. They knew the future lay in children, through education. Remember Clara Barton? She, too, was a catalyst who empowered individuals. And today we have with us Art Williams, whose magnificent We Can Make a Difference program is helping to make kinder the face of the Nation and gentler the face of the world. For over 200 years, we have freely accepted, as Dwight Eisenhower said, "whatever sacrifices might be required of us." The reason: In a world with so much emphasis on imports and exports, America's major export has always been generosity.

Today, more than ever, we need to use that generosity to combat such global problems as hunger and health care, literacy and helplessness. Remember, individually, we can change a life; collectively, we can change the world. Each of you can reject membership in a "me" generation, proving that yours is the "we" generation, and in the process show how a definition of a successful life must include serving others.

Abroad, this will require real commitment—drawing inspiration from the heroes of Leipzig and the *gulags* and Tiananmen Square. In Beijing, students last year quoted Jefferson. Their image of America is not dollars but democratic ideals. We must uphold those ideals through what I call one-on-one caring. And here at Liberty, you are.

Dr. Falwell was telling me about your Kenya relief project and the annual scholarships that you offer to two students from every foreign country in the world—you talk about an academic United Nations. You've helped a children's home in Korea, a school in Costa Rica; provided medical supplies and clothing to countries in Asia and Europe. This June a student team will complete construction of a medical clinic and food distribution center in Rio de Janeiro. I salute these deeds of the heart, as you give of yourselves—missionaries in the finest sense of the word.

Yet I also challenge you to build on these deeds once you graduate. You know, there was once a mother who told her son, "I have a pretty good idea that you skipped your piano lesson and played baseball." The son said he hadn't. The mother said, "Are you sure?" The son said, "Uh-huh. And I have a fish to prove it." [*Laughter*] That's what I call American ingenuity, the kind of ingenuity that can help newly democratic countries secure the freedom and opportunity that we simply take for granted in our great country. Whether raising a family, pursuing a career, continuing your studies, or all of the above—it doesn't matter—you can help all America do as a nation what you are already doing locally.

Let me tell a story which illustrates how. It's about an American, Richard Neimeyer, who was part of an HHS initiative—paid his own way to Romania to address the needs of institutions for disabled children. A 70-year-old man greeted him in tears. "God bless you for being here," he said. "Everything about Americans is true. You are here when we need you." Finding no trained aides, no nursing schools, as many as seven babies in a crib, Dr. Neimeyer was soon to return to Romania accompanied now by nurses and doctors and therapists and hope.

This American shows how each of us can make a difference in the life of another, from Poland to Panama, not through a central bureaucratic state but, rather, individually and through the Chamber of Commerce, the Red Cross, your church, or through the Peace Corps, which is operating in Eastern Europe for the first time. In Hungary and Poland, soon to be in Czecho-slovakia, volunteers will be teaching English and providing management training. Earlier today at the University of South Carolina, I announced the creation of a Citizens Democracy Corps for Eastern Europe. It will be a clearinghouse for private voluntary organizations, assisting them and challenging their energy and initiative into programs to support Eastern Europe's transition to democracy and free market economies. Yet the need for involvement in the lives of others is not just a problem outside our borders: empowerment must be for Americans, too.

Here at Liberty, you've shown how a Thousand Points of Light can become a galaxy of people working to solve problems in their own backyard. I think of your Elim Home for Alcoholics, your Center for Urban Outreach, and the Liberty Godparent Home for Unwed Mothers. And now let America follow your lead.

Today the choices for your future are many. Make one of them, just one of them, continued commitment to community service. Be tutors at inner-city schools or candy stripers at local hospitals. Assist those without food to eat or a place to sleep or those coping with AIDS. Help not merely colleagues but strangers, stemming their desperate aloneness to make them feel needed and loved. And if you become a lawyer, ask the firm to do pro bono work. If a teacher, volunteer for counseling. Let the Office of National Service—which our administration formed last year to encourage voluntarism—let it know what you're doing. Serve at day care centers, homes for the elderly, shelters for the addicts. Join what Edmund Burke called little, but mighty, platoons. Become a light unto the world.

In this more peaceful time, when our armies can become smaller, we must mold a world where the armies of people—people helping others—can become bigger, using what has been given to us, freedom and opportunity, to give back of ourselves. Through the adventure of community service, we can unlock new frontiers of empowerment, joining hands and linking hearts to further the work of God and man.

Thank you for this special occasion. Good luck to each of you in the graduating class.

And to each of you my most heartfelt congratulations. And God bless the United States of America. Thank you very, very much.

Note: The President spoke at 4:16 p.m. in Willard May Stadium on the campus of the university. In his opening remarks, he referred to Rev. Jerry L. Falwell and A. Pierre Guillermin, chancellor and president of the university, respectively; Reverend Falwell's wife, Macel; Senator John Warner; Rev. Daniel Henderson, pastor-teacher of Los Gatos Christian Church, in Los Gatos, CA; Rev. George Theis, executive director of the Word of Life Ministry; Rev. David Cox, missionary; Rev. James Irvin, director of Pro-Missions in Memphis, TN; Arthur L. Williams, president of A.L. Williams Insurance Agency, in Atlanta, GA; Eric Green, a member of the Liberty Flames football team and first-round draft choice of the Pittsburgh Steelers; and Sam Rutigliano, coach of the Liberty Flames. Following his remarks, the President returned to Washington, DC.

Message to the Congress Reporting on the National Emergency With Respect to Iran
May 14, 1990

To the Congress of the United States:

I hereby report to the Congress on developments since the last report of November 14, 1989, concerning the national emergency with respect to Iran that was declared in Executive Order No. 12170, dated November 14, 1979, and matters relating to Executive Order No. 12613 of October 29, 1987. This report is submitted pursuant to section 204(c) of the International Emergency Economic Powers Act (50 U.S.C. 1703(c)), and section 505(c) of the International Security and Development Cooperation Act of 1985 (22 U.S.C. 2349aa–9). This report covers events through March 31, 1990, including those that occurred since the last report under Executive Order No. 12170, dated November 14, 1989. That report covered events through September 6, 1989.

1. Since the last report, there have been no amendments to the Iranian Assets Control Regulations, 31 C.F.R. Part 535 (the "IACRs"), or the Iranian Transactions Regulations, 31 C.F.R. Part 560 (the "ITRs"), administered by the Office of Foreign Assets Control ("FAC"). The major focus of licensing activity under the ITRs remains the importation of certain non-fungible Iranian-origin goods, principally carpets, which were located outside Iran before the embargo was imposed, and where no payment or benefit accrued to Iran after the effective date of the embargo. Since September 6, 1989, FAC has made 333 licensing determinations under the ITRs.

During the reporting period, the Customs Service has effected numerous seizures of Iranian-origin merchandise, primarily carpets, caviar, and pistachios, for violations of the Iranian Transactions Regulations. FAC and Customs Service investigations of these violations have resulted in forfeiture actions and imposition of civil monetary penalties amounting to $409,736. Numerous additional forfeiture and civil penalties actions are under review.

In the case of *United States* v. *Ahmad Elyasian,* the defendant was sentenced to 2 years' probation, a $3,000 fine, and the merchandise was forfeited. Criminal proceedings are pending in various jurisdictions involving several individuals and corporate entities. One arrest warrant is outstanding.

2. The Iran-United States Claims Tribunal (the "Tribunal"), established at The Hague pursuant to the Algiers Accords, continues to make progress in arbitrating the claims before it. Since the last report, the Tribunal has rendered 38 awards, for a total of 476 awards. Of that total, 341 have been awards in favor of American claimants: 210 of these were awards on agreed terms, authorizing and approving payments of settlements ne-

gotiated by the parties, and 131 were decisions adjudicated on the merits. The Tribunal has dismissed a total of 30 other claims on the merits and 65 for jurisdictional reasons. Of the 40 remaining awards, 2 were withdrawn and 38 were in favor of Iranian claimants. As of March 31, 1990, awards to successful American claimants from the Security Account held by the NV Settlement Bank stood at $1,296,219,879.08.

As of March 31, 1990, the Security Account has fallen below the required balance of $500 million 33 times. Iran has replenished the account 33 times, as required by the Algiers Accords, by transferring funds from the separate account held by the NV Settlement Bank in which interest on the Security Account is deposited. Iran has also replenished the account twice when it was not required by the Accords, for a total of 35 replenishments. This figure includes the transfer of $243 million to the Security Account on November 22, 1989, from Dollar Account No. 2 held at the Bank of England. The total amount in the Security Account as of March 31, 1990, was $643,268,583.07. The amount in the interest account as of March 31, 1990, was $118,520,896.63. The aggregate amount that has been transferred from the interest account to the Security Account is $695,648,999.39.

3. The Tribunal continues to make progress in the arbitration of claims of U.S. nationals for $250,000 or more. Over 70 percent of the nonbank claims have now been disposed of through adjudication, settlement, or voluntary withdrawal, leaving 145 such claims on the docket. The largest of the large claims, the progress of which has been slowed by their complexity, are finally being decided, sometimes with sizable damage awards to the U.S. claimant. Since the last report, eight large claims have been decided.

4. The Tribunal continues to process claims of U.S. nationals against Iran of less than $250,000 each. As of March 31, 1990, a total of 432 small claims have been resolved, 38 of them since the last report, as a result of decisions on the merits, awards on agreed terms, or Tribunal orders. Eight contested claims have been decided since the last report, raising the total number of contested claims decided to 36, 18 of which

favored the American claimant. These decisions will help in establishing guidelines for the adjudication or settlement of similar claims. To date, American claimants have also received 72 awards on agreed terms reflecting settlements of claims under $250,000. The Tribunal's current small claims docket includes approximately 200 active cases.

5. In coordination with concerned government agencies, the Department of State continues to present U.S. Government claims against Iran, as well as responses by the U.S. Government to claims brought against it by Iran. Since the last report, the Department has filed pleadings in eight government-to-government claims. The Department defended a claim concerning standby letters of credit brought by Iran against the United States in a hearing before the Tribunal. In addition, 15 claims have been settled.

6. Since the last report, nine bank syndicates have completed negotiations with Bank Markazi Jomhouri Islami Iran ("Bank Markazi," Iran's central bank) and have been paid a total of $2,403,504.53 for interest accruing for the period January 1–18, 1981 ("January Interest"). These payments were made from Dollar Account No. 1 at the Federal Reserve Bank of New York ("FRBNY"). Moreover, under the April 13, 1988, agreement between the FRBNY and Bank Markazi, the FRBNY returned $1,748,999.00 of Iranian funds to Bank Markazi. This amount includes settlement amounts for two syndicates that made no claim to the funds held on their behalf in Dollar Account No 1. All such funds were consequently returned to Bank Markazi. That transfer represents the excess of amounts reserved in Dollar Account No. 1 to pay off each bank syndicate with a claim for January Interest against Bank Markazi.

On November 3, 1989, the United States and Iran agreed to the disposition of $810 million in Dollar Account No. 2 at the Bank of England that was not needed to pay remaining claims against that account. Pursuant to that agreement, on November 22, 1989, $243 million was transferred to the Security Account and $567 million was returned to Iran. The latter payment was made in accordance with the Algiers Accords, which calls for the return of excess funds in Dollar Account No. 2 to Iran.

7. Since the last report, there have been no amendments to the Iranian Assets Control Regulations, 31 C.F.R. Part 535, administered by the Office of Foreign Assets Control. There have been no amendments to the Iranian Transactions Regulations, 31 C.F.R. Part 560, since their publication on November 17, 1988.

8. The situation reviewed above continues to implicate important diplomatic, financial, and legal interests of the United States and its nationals and presents an unusual challenge to the national security and foreign policy of the United States. The Iranian Assets Control Regulations issued pur-

suant to Executive Order No. 12170 continue to play an important role in structuring our relationship with Iran and in enabling the United States properly to implement the Algiers Accords. Similarly, the Iranian Transactions Regulations issued pursuant to Executive Order No. 12613 continue to advance important objectives in combatting international terrorism. I shall continue to exercise the powers at my disposal to deal with these problems and will continue to report periodically to the Congress on significant developments.

GEORGE BUSH

The White House,
May 14, 1990.

Nomination of Robert E. Lamb To Be United States Ambassador to Cyprus
May 14, 1990

The President today announced his intention to nominate Robert E. Lamb, of Virginia, a career member of the Senior Foreign Service, Class of Career Minister, to be Ambassador Extraordinary and Plenipotentiary of the United States of America to the Republic of Cyprus. He would succeed Bill K. Perrin.

Since 1985 Mr. Lamb has served as Assistant Secretary of State for Diplomatic Security. Prior to this, he has served in various positions at the Department of State, including Assistant Secretary for Administration, 1983–1985; Administrative Counselor in Bonn, West Germany, 1979–1983; Deputy Assistant Secretary for Passport Services, 1978–1979; Deputy Director in the Office of Passport Services, 1977–1979; Director of the Office of Personnel/Career

Management, 1976–1977; Special Assistant in the Bureau of Administration, 1974–1976; Deputy Director of the Regional Finance Center in Bangkok, Thailand, 1973–1974; and administrative officer in Kathmandu, Nepal, 1971–1973. In addition, he served as an administrative officer for the Bureau of Administration in the Office of Operations, 1969–1971; and personnel officer in career management, 1968–1969. He was assigned to the Foreign Service Institute in 1964. In 1963 Mr. Lamb entered the Foreign Service.

Mr. Lamb graduated from the University of Pennsylvania (B.A., 1962). He was born November 17, 1936, in Atlanta, GA. Mr. Lamb served in the U.S. Marine Corps, 1958–1961. He is married, has three children, and resides in Alexandria, VA.

Nomination of James Wilson Holsinger, Jr., To Be Chief Medical Director at the Department of Veterans Affairs
May 14, 1990

The President today announced his intention to nominate James Wilson Holsinger, Jr., to be Chief Medical Director at the Department of Veterans Affairs for a term of 4 years. This is a new position.

Currently, Dr. Holsinger serves as the Director of McGuire Veterans Administration Medical Center in Richmond, VA. Prior to this he served as chief of staff for the Veterans Administration Medical Center in Augusta, GA. In addition, Dr. Holsinger serves as conference lay leader for the Virginia Conference, United Methodist Church in Richmond, VA.

Dr. Holsinger graduated from Duke University (B.A., 1960; M.D., 1964; Ph.D., 1968) and the University of South Carolina (M.S., 1981). He was born May 11, 1939, in Kansas City, KS. Dr. Holsinger has served in the military since 1960 and serves as a major general in the U.S. Air Force. In this capacity, he serves as the Assistant to the Director for Logistics in the Office of the Joint Chiefs of Staff. Dr. Holsinger is married, has four children, and resides in Richmond, VA.

Remarks at the Welcoming Ceremony for President Zine El Abidine Ben Ali of Tunisia
May 15, 1990

President Bush. Mr. President, welcome back to the United States, and welcome back to the White House. I look forward to continuing the dialog that we began last November, and we are pleased to have this opportunity to welcome you to Washington for a longer visit than was possible last year.

We're especially pleased to have this opportunity to repay the fine hospitality that Tunisia showed us in 1983 and then again in 1986, when I visited as Vice President. As with those journeys, your visit continues a tradition of high-level discussions, demonstrating that our relations—dating back to 1797, and close since Tunisian independence in 1956—are still sound and growing.

True to its heritage as an ancient crossroads between Europe and Africa, Tunisia has played an effective role as intermediary between the Arab countries and the West. It's been an example of pragmatism, stability, and progress in the Middle East. And Tunisia has consistently supported a peaceful, negotiated resolution to the Middle East issues, including the Arab-Israeli conflict.

Tunisia also has an impressive record in other respects. It has the highest literacy rate in north Africa. It has always honored its debt obligations. It is persevering in the fourth year of a disciplined, market-oriented restructuring of its economy. And it's made a renewed commitment to democracy.

Your visit comes at a time of transition for north Africa. And we look forward to this opportunity to consult closely on the broad range of issues and concerns that we share. Today your friends in the Maghreb are searching for prosperity and stability. Political pluralism and market-based economies have taken root and are beginning to flourish there. Towards this, Tunisia's reforms are a potential model. We support Tunisia's commitment to democracy and a market-oriented economy, and pledge continuing assistance and cooperation in these important efforts.

It is fitting, Mr. President, that you should visit as we approach our Memorial Day services. From my visits to your homeland, I recall the moving sight of the American military cemetery in Carthage, spread out across 27 acres donated by Tunisia, a dramatic plateau between the Mediterranean and the Bay of Tunis. There in north Africa lie the graves of nearly 3,000 brave Americans who gave their lives in the allies' first major overland offensive in World War II, 3,000 Americans who will never come back home. And there in north Africa are inscribed the names of nearly 4,000 missing, 4,000 Americans whose fate will never be known.

But their sacrifice remains well-known to all. That sight reminds us that the ties between the United States and Tunisia are old and deep. And their sacrifice, like the sacrifices of freedom-loving people everywhere, reminds us of the new opportunities for both progress and peace that are today sweeping the world.

Amid this time of great change, both in the world and in the region, we look forward to our discussions with President Ben Ali, who also comes to Washington as the current President of the Arab Maghreb Union. We welcome him with a spirit of understanding and cooperation, looking forward to our conversations as allies and as friends.

Welcome back, Mr. President. God bless you and the friendship that is shared by our two nations. Thank you for coming.

President Ben Ali. In the name of God, the clement, the merciful, Mr. President, I'm conveying the warmest greetings and the most sincere expression of friendship of the Tunisian people to the American people, whom we highly regard and admire.

Indeed, we are proud of the deeply rooted friendship between our two countries, which dates as far back as 1799, when the first treaty was signed between the United States of America and Tunisia. This treaty as well as the agreement that followed do illustrate the common determination of our two countries to establish relations founded on mutual respect and close cooperation, and to undertake joint action towards upholding the noble principles in which we believe, and promoting security and peace among nations.

Mr. President, it is with great pleasure and deep gratitude that we recall the support extended by your country to Tunisia during its national struggle for freedom and independence, as well as the assistance our country has been receiving from the United States in its efforts towards achieving development and progress. Our visit comes in fulfillment of our common resolve to strengthen the bonds of friendship between our two peoples, as well as the fruitful cooperation between our countries. Indeed, Tunisia, which has entered a new era, is as firmly determined as the United States is to give these relations the attention and the support they deserve. Mr. President, we are pleased to say that we are committed as firmly as you are to the ideals of democracy, human rights, and free market economy, for such are our fundamental choices. And we are confident that you will continue supporting and strengthening these options.

We have welcomed with as much satisfaction as you have the historic changes the world is witnessing today, which mark the triumph of the noble principles in which we both believe. Indeed, such changes illustrate the determination of peoples and their legitimate aspirations to secure dignity and freedom.

Mr. President, the privileged position held by your country and the important role it plays on the international scene entails major responsibilities in the active contribution it has to make for the triumph of rightful causes: the causes of justice and freedom, as well as the support for the efforts of development and progress. All these endeavors will help establish a balance between the members of the international community in which the rights of individuals and nations are safeguarded and the security, stability, and well-being of mankind guaranteed.

Mr. President, I would like to reiterate my deep appreciation and sincere thanks for your warm welcome and kind words, and am looking forward to the valuable opportunities that my visit will provide for talks and consultation on matters of common interest in order to strengthen our bilateral relations as well as security and peace in the world. Thank you.

Note: President Bush spoke at 10:12 a.m. at the South Portico of the White House, where

President Ben Ali was accorded a formal welcome with full military honors. President Ben Ali spoke in Arabic, and his remarks were translated by an interpreter.

Statement by Press Secretary Fitzwater on the Federal Budget Negotiations
May 15, 1990

The President met for 1 hour and 40 minutes this afternoon with congressional budget negotiators to consider a Federal budget that would reduce the deficit substantially on a multiyear basis, allow the economy to continue to grow, strengthen the budget process, and avoid the adverse economic and programmatic effects of a stalemate that otherwise might ensue. The President and the negotiators agreed that it was important to reach an agreement as soon as possible. The President discussed the reasons for these summit meetings. He said there was no immediate crisis. "We are fortunate that the economy continues to grow," he said, "but it is important to act while the economy is still growing, for growth is not as strong or secure as it should be."

The President said interest rates are higher than forecast and receipts are lower. S&L related borrowing is up, so the estimated fiscal 1991 deficit is also going up.

The President concluded his opening remarks by saying, "The American people are tired of seeing the budget process seem to fail year after year. They would welcome our doing the job right and our fixing the process at the same time."

The congressional leadership gave opening remarks concerning their interest in achieving a successful agreement, and all indicated a shared responsibility by both branches of the Government to reach agreement.

Budget director Dick Darman outlined the current budget status. Several Members discussed the extent of this problem and the difficulty of the task faced by negotiators. The group concurred that they must tackle this problem in good faith and would not publicly discuss specific recommendations or proposals.

Congressman Richard Gephardt will chair the next meeting Thursday, May 17, on Capitol Hill.

Toasts at the State Dinner for President Zine El Abidine Ben Ali of Tunisia
May 15, 1990

President Bush. Mr. President and distinguished members of the Tunisian delegation, it's a great honor for Barbara and me to welcome you back to the White House— a great pleasure, a personal pleasure.

We have some things in common. Before becoming President you were an ambassador. You come from a large family, in which you take great pride. You also take pride in physical fitness, and from a youthful passion for soccer to an interest in jogging today.

And I'm told you like to keep your staffs jumping—*[laughter]*—by heading out onto the streets for surprise visits with your countrymen. You keep track of your Cabinet personally, using a home computer. Your home computer is called an Apple— *[laughter]*—mine is called John Sununu. *[Laughter]* Looking at you, I can't believe this, but I'm told that you take great pride in your role as a grandfather. You're a youthful one at that.

663

But in this country, the combination of grandchildren and computer games has produced some unexpected results. This is a true story, Mr. President. The most popular computer game in America is called Teenage Mutant Ninja Turtles. [*Laughter*] Don't worry about the translation; it doesn't make any sense in English, either. [*Laughter*]

But tonight, in a more serious vein, I want to toast a leader who, with dignity and respect, took Tunisia through a critical transition in its history. President Ben Ali's peaceful and constitutional accession to power in 1987 really marked a turning point in Tunisia's history. He boldly but wisely chose the difficult path of political and economic reform.

Tunisia's greatness as a nation goes back to the earliest foundations of Mediterranean civilization. For centuries, Carthage dominated the western Mediterranean, rivaling the splendor and the power of Rome. And Tunisia today serves as a model of pragmatic change in the Arab world—a country that looks to the future, not to the past; a country that has shunned the path of radicalism; a country that draws on the progressive tradition within its north African and Islamic heritage to address the challenges of a fast-changing world without, outside your borders. And you've already faced great challenges with the tenacious and pragmatic approach that we admire, and we will support you in your efforts.

Mr. President, in our welcoming ceremony this morning, I described the American military cemetery in Carthage, where nearly 3,000 brave Americans are buried in Tunisian soil. And let me conclude tonight with the words left on your shores by their commanding general, America's beloved President Eisenhower—Ike—when he spoke in Tunisia when he was President back in 1959.

Ike noted that he'd last visited your beautiful country exactly 16 years earlier, 1943, in the midst of a war that we thought would bring permanent peace. And he added—and this is his quote—"We have found that peace does not come just because the guns are stilled. We have to work for peace. We have to work with our hearts, with our substance, with our hands. We have to work all the time to maintain the peace and to make it more secure."

Mr. President, our talks here today reflect President Eisenhower's sentiments. They've strengthened the special friendship that is already deep and enduring; improved our understanding of each other's concerns; and laid the foundation for expanded cooperation and, yes, for expanded peace in the region and expanded peace in the world.

Earlier this morning, we enjoyed a glorious day out there on the South Lawn. And in Tunisia, it is common to compliment a visitor who brings rain. But because Washington has just weathered 2 weeks of rain, Mr. President, today we appreciate your bringing us the sunshine.

So, let me ask all of you to toast the health and success of President Ben Ali and the friendship between our two great nations. Welcome, Mr. President.

President Ben Ali. In the name of God, the clement, the merciful, Mr. President, it gives me pleasure to express to you, Mr. President, and to Mrs. Bush my thanks and gratitude for the warm welcome and kind hospitality extended to me personally and to the Tunisian delegation accompanying me. Such a warm reception sincerely reflects the mutual friendship and respect that characterize our traditional and sustained ties and represents a further step towards the consolidation of our common values of freedom, democracy, and defense of human rights.

Mr. President, ladies and gentlemen, the world is witnessing major radical changes in accordance with people's will and aspiration for freedom, democracy, and protection of dignity of individuals and of the community as a whole. Those changes reflect undoubtedly the common values that we both share. In fact, we have fully subscribed since November 7, 1987, to these very principles, as we are convinced that evolution is necessary as well as the fulfillment of the aspiration of the Tunisian people.

We have consequently reorganized the Tunisian society on a new basis to enable Tunisians to exercise their natural and legitimate rights and to live freely and democratically in a state of law and constitutional institutions. We are also committed to a policy of free market economy and open the way to private initiatives.

In view of the emergence of regional groupings and the need to find ways to deal with them, the Maghreb States have succeeded in establishing a union that I have presently the honor to chair and which is a great achievement, with a flexible and open structure which responds to the aspirations of the peoples of the region for cooperation and integrated development.

Mr. President, we have, on various occasions, called upon the international community to bring in a qualitative change in its relations, one taking into account the international détente and going beyond the international relations between advanced countries and developing ones to reach a more comprehensive concept designed for laying down a covenant for peace and progress that preserves the interests of all parties and brings about a new spirit of solidarity and justice. We believe that such an achievement is likely to provide the propitious climate which will give new impetus to the democratic process that has widely emerged on the international arena, ensure balanced development, protect our societies from the dangers of regression and extremism, and alleviate the tensions that threaten peace and security in the world.

Among the chronic factors of tensions within our region, in the Middle East and Africa, we have to mention the Palestinian-people issue and the conditions prevailing in South Africa. We believe that, owing to its weight, the position it enjoys, the influence it exerts, and its traditional and noble values, the United States can persuade Israel to respond positively to the bold initiatives taken by the Palestinian leadership and endorsed by Arab summits and to recognize the legitimate national rights of the Palestinian people. As to South Africa, while the situation is still a source of concern, despite the recent positive development, it is necessary that the international community should continue its support to leader Nelson Mandela's pledge to eradicate apartheid and build a society founded on equality and respect of democracy, standards, moral values, and international law.

Mr. President, ladies and gentlemen, my visit to your country, with which we are maintaining a traditional and deep-rooted friendship, aims at strengthening and enhancing these relations for the benefit of our two countries, as we share a commitment to freedom and democracy and work for peace, security, and stability in the world on the basis of people's right for self-determination and solidarity between nations.

Ladies and gentlemen, I invite you to stand up and join me in a toast in honor of the President of the United States and Mrs. Bush as an expression of our deepest appreciation for the feelings of friendship he expressed this morning to Tunisia—a country he visited more than once—and a tribute to the American people. Long live the Tunisian-American friendship. Thank you very much.

Note: President Bush spoke at 8:15 p.m. in the State Dining Room at the White House. In his remarks, he referred to John H. Sununu, Chief of Staff to the President. President Ben Ali spoke in Arabic, and his remarks were translated by an interpreter.

The President's News Conference
May 16, 1990

The President. Today I'm making an urgent appeal to Congress to come to the assistance of the peoples of Nicaragua and Panama. I announced my original request for $500 million in assistance to Panama on January 25th. On March 13th, I submitted my modified request for $800 million for both Nicaragua and Panama. At the time of submission, I asked the Congress for passage of the legislation by April 5th. When that date passed, I asked for passage in time for Violeta Chamorro's inauguration on April

25th. I also asked Members of Congress, in public and in private, that the bill not be loaded with extraneous items.

Members of our administration have met with the Congress to explain the content and the urgency of this request, but the Easter recess came and went with no passage. And moreover, the bill has tripled in size as extraneous items have been piled onto it. Even worse, the additional amendments include provisions that I vetoed as recently as last fall, provisions that have absolutely nothing to do with Nicaragua and Panama.

I've met repeatedly with the leadership of both Houses of the Congress to urge rapid passage. In the last several days, I've shared with them the contents of this letter that I received from President Chamorro of Nicaragua pleading for prompt passage.

The situation in Nicaragua is critical. Mrs. Chamorro's government is absolutely bankrupt, and there are strikes and demonstrations in the streets. She's asked me for an emergency bridge loan, but I can't provide that because the Nicaraguans have no assured means of repayment. And our hands are tied, and I can't provide a loan anchored on legislation which is not assured.

Panama is also in dire need of the jumpstart that our assistance will give to enable it to recover from the economic devastation of the Noriega dictatorship.

We're now facing the Memorial Day recess without the assurance that this legislation will be passed. I would like the legislation this week, certainly early next week. But I will call on the Congress to remain in session until it completes action on a bill that I can sign. We must not let this procedural gridlock in the Congress destroy the hopes for freedom in these two fledgling democracies. I feel very strongly about it, and I will again appeal to Congress to get moving on this bill.

Arms Reduction Negotiations

Q. Mr. President, officials accompanying Secretary of State Baker to Moscow say the Soviets have backtracked on earlier agreements on arms control. Does it appear unlikely that you'll have the outlines of a START treaty to sign at the summit? And how much of a setback would that be?

The President. Terry [Terence Hunt, Associated Press], I wouldn't say that it appears unlikely. I have not heard from Jim Baker since the talks have started in Moscow. I expect we'll be hearing pretty soon. But I would not predict that these matters cannot be resolved in time for the summit. But if they're not, we're going to keep on because we want a START agreement, and I'm convinced the Soviets want a START agreement.

Summit With President Gorbachev

Q. How much of a cloud has been put over the summit by the tension, the Soviet pressure on the Baltic States?

The President. I'll be able to answer that a little more after Jim comes back from Moscow, but I'd say that it has certainly put some tension on the summit. We want to see negotiations or dialog or whatever you call it—discussions between Gorbachev and the Lithuanians get going. And then I'd like to see the release of that economic pressure on Lithuania. And that would clear the air fast. But until something like that happens, there will be tension.

But we have a broad agenda of items that we must go forward on. We have negotiated with the Soviets when all of Eastern Europe was in captivity and when we had Cold War times. I'm unhappy about the state of play in the Baltics because I'd like to see them obtain their desire of freedom as soon as possible. But I feel it's important from our standpoint, the important standpoint of Eastern European countries and Western European allies and, indeed, the whole world, that we have these discussions with Mr. Gorbachev. And I look forward to them very much, and I particularly look forward to the private ones, where I can get a better feel for the problems facing him and I can tell him of our priorities in a very frank setting.

Pending Legislation

Q. Mr. President, will you sign the Panama-Nicaraguan aid bill if it contains funding for abortion? Will you sign the parental leave bill? And will you sign the civil rights act?

The President. I will not accept the Nicaragua-Panama bill with that mischievous language placed on it. It has nothing to do with Nicaragua and Panama, and it ought to be taken out. But if it comes to me that way, it'll go right back up, and we'll still urge the Congress to do what they ought to do to help these democracies.

What were the other two?

Q. The civil rights act and parental leave. You have—I mean, you removed a veto threat on civil rights, and the threat remains on parental leave.

The President. Civil rights—we're working hard to get agreement. We've had a series of meetings. I've participated in two of them. We've had three at the White House with leadership groups. Our staff is working with Congress, and I hope we can narrow the differences enough so that we can go forward together on this legislation.

And parental leave—I've got some real problems with that one, but I just have to wait until I get recommendations on it.

Federal Budget Negotiations

Q. Mr. President, the Democratic leaders who came out of yesterday's first round of the budget talks indicated that before they're going to advance any proposals at all for dealing with the problem they want to hear first the administration's discussion of how grave the problem is, and then an administration proposal or set of proposals for dealing with it. Does the administration have ready a set of budget proposals that would address the deficit fully at this time?

The President. Not fully, but Dick Darman has already begun discussions after yesterday's meeting with Congressman Gephardt. And I think that the negotiation can go forward so that both sides come to the table, say what they think, and we get an agreement. I'm confident we can get one, but this mandating who does what first—that's not going to get the job done. So, we're going to go up there—no preconditions—and have a good discussion. And I think after there's some initial posturing around we're going to make some headway. We have to make some headway.

In terms of the magnitude of the problem, I do feel that we have an obligation to be sure the Congressmen understand it. But, Brit [Brit Hume, ABC News], in this sense of going out right now to the American people, I want to go out when we have a bipartisan answer to the problem. Say, here's what the problem is, and here's what the answer. And if I go out there today, we don't have a bipartisan answer. And that's the only way this problem's going to be solved. It's not going to be done one party or another. And it is urgent enough. And when the Congress sees the data and the estimates, and then CBO [Congressional Budget Office] and OMB work with the estimates, I'm convinced that we'll have enough of a sense of urgency that we'll go forward and get a deal.

Q. Well, Mr. President, surely you must recognize that part of the reason why they're so wary is that they heard what they thought were conflicting signals from the administration, last week—you saying no preconditions; Governor Sununu [Chief of Staff to the President] suggesting something quite otherwise. First of all, what happened there? And second, what did you say to him about that?

The President. Well, I haven't said anything to him about it. But I've heard conflicting signals out of Congress from the first day I said no condition—people trying to interpret what that meant—and a wide array of blasts out of Congress, on both sides of the aisle.

But it doesn't help for me to do anything other than to cool it down and say: Look, we've got a big problem. Here's the problem, let me explain it to you all, as best OMB can. You tell us how CBO sees it. Then let's, as Lyndon [Johnson] said, reason together and try to get a deal and then make sure the American people understand how serious it is. But, Brit, I'm not going to go out there and do something that might inadvertently suggest crisis and frighten markets.

What I think we ought to do is get agreement on the size of the problem and then have a bipartisan answer. This is very sensitive stuff. Right now the markets are reasonably optimistic, and there are reasons to be optimistic about the economy. Earlier on, there were some predictions of recession, but right now it appears that most economists don't think there will be a recession. So, we're blessed by dealing with this problem at a time of some growth—not the robust growth that some of us would like to see but with some growth. And yet there are still some concerns on the part of the Fed and others on inflation, so I don't want to inadvertently send the wrong signals to the markets.

Q. Mr. President, Mr. Darman has already indicated that there is little probability of getting all the cuts that are necessary in a problem that's estimated at $100 billion. What is your predisposition towards stretching out or amending Gramm-Rudman so that you can do this at a more measured pace?

The President. Charles [Charles Bierbauer, Cable News Network], it's a very good question, very direct, and I'm not going to answer it because I am not going to go out there with a lot of suggestions to part of the problem. And I've said that. I've agreed with the Congress. I think they're not supposed to do that, either. So, we will conduct our discussions in private, and then we will have recommendations. That might be part of it, because the problem is pretty big. But I don't have a position on that because I've said there are no preconditions.

Q. Well, sir, actually your spokesman, Mr. Fitzwater, has listed some conditions. He says you wouldn't——

The President. Down with him. Down. He's—[*laughter*].

Q. You wouldn't do anything on the budget deficit, and you wouldn't advocate any solutions that would be a drag on the economy. My question to you is: Can you be persuaded that a tax exists that would not be a drag on the economy? Do you know of any such taxes?

The President. John [John Cochran, NBC News], you're trying to get me to do that which, just 1 second ago, I said I wouldn't do. And I'm trying to negotiate and to keep the negotiating process in good faith. But I just can't—if I start going into answering questions like that, no matter how much merit they have, then I start having conditions or preconditions; and I can't do that and deal in good faith with Congress.

Q. Well then, can I ask for your concept of leadership on this?

The President. Yes.

Q. You will not advocate any solutions? You will not go on prime time television to spell out the nature of the budget deficit?

The President. At the appropriate time, I will.

Q. You will? When will that be?

The President. I don't know. We got to get on with what I told you the process is. And the process is not setting preconditions, and the process is to go forward in good faith with the Congress. And I think they're dealing in good faith. I believe that the two leaders I've been dealing with want this process to go forward in this way.

Q. Is this the biggest test of your leadership on a domestic problem?

The President. I expect so.

China

Q. Mr. President, you are facing a deadline on the decision of granting most-favored-nation status to China.

The President. Yes.

Q. Can you tell us, first of all, if you've made the call? Secondly, if you haven't, what pressures do you face in terms of once again rewarding China in the absence of significant concessions or changes on their part?

The President. I have not made a decision on it. That issue is under, I would say, lively discussion. I have seen significant editorial comment that urges strongly against cutting off MFN. That comment coming from people that were quite critical of me in the way I handled the student matter. In other words, they would have preferred to see the Pelosi legislation as opposed to the executive action that I took. There's another dimension that—you ask what the thought process is here—that it relates to Hong Kong, that it is quite important in terms of trade, a significant importance. Some of the people that opposed my earlier approach are urging that MFN continue.

And so, it isn't an easy call because I don't want to send a signal that we are happy with the human rights record. I still am of the mind that having contact and working in an area where there has been progress on the economic side with China is important.

So, these are some of the ingredients we're considering right now, but it isn't that clear a call for me yet.

Q. Well, do you think that you might not grant most-favored-nation status as a way to signal them of the disappointment that you have admitted to because they haven't changed that much after Tiananmen Square?

The President. I'm not suggesting that's what I plan to do.

Family and Emergency Leave Legislation

Q. Mr. President, a lot of Republicans, especially Republican women, Congresswomen, are wondering how you could threaten to veto a bill that would guarantee job security to pregnant women and other people with family emergencies, especially since every other industrialized nation except South Africa has such a bill?

The President. I think it boils down to the concept of whether you are in favor of mandated benefits or not. And one of the complaints I get from our close proximity to the Governors and working with the Governors is, please don't mandate more benefits from the central government. So, we've had a difference. I've been quite open with my concerns about that, and yet I have great respect for the Republican women and others that you mention that differ with me on that one.

U.S. Hostages in Lebanon

Q. Mr. President, a few weeks ago when the two hostages were released, you said you hoped that it was the beginning of a process. Has anything happened since then that has encouraged you that a process is underway?

The President. No.

Q. I mean, is it that blunt? I mean——

The President. Yes. [*Laughter*]

Q. ——is it worse than that? Does it look like nothing has happened at all?

The President. I answered it as best I can. I have seen no reason to be encouraged that the process is underway. But I think I said right in this room there were certain things we could do, and we're trying to follow up—things we can do without violating some fundamental principles on negotiating or trading hostages for something.

And we're going forward there.

I remember, I mentioned trying to account for four Iranians that were taken and whom our Government feels are dead. But the Iranians are very much interested in having an accounting for that, and that is something I feel that we can move forward on. So, we're trying to get more information, although they didn't suggest, and I can confirm, that we had nothing to do with the taking of those people. But it's a matter of human concern to their families and all. So, here's an area where we might be able to facilitate matters there.

The Economy

Q. Mr. President, if you cut taxes—or if you raise taxes—I'm sorry—or if you cut spending, either way there will be a drag on the economy unless interest rates also fall. Are you operating under an assumption or some kind of guarantee from the Fed that that will happen?

The President. No, there's no such guarantee. I'd like to see interest rates falling, and I think when the fears of inflation decline one might expect interest rates to come down. But, no, I have no such guarantee.

Q. Well, are you taking, then, a gamble that even if you come up with some kind of package that it won't help the actual economic performance today?

The President. I think you raised a very good economic question, and that is: How much can be taken out of an economy, what percentage of the GNP can be taken out in terms of taxes, and not threaten the dynamism of the economy? One figure that I've heard bandied about is—I want to be careful here—but I'd say we're growing at, what, 2 percent of each—now it looks like we're growing at 2-percent growth GNP. And I'd say anything over half of that would risk doing what you say—slowing down the economy further—and that's exacerbating the problem rather than making it better.

Federal Budget Negotiations

Q. Mr. President, if I could return to the budget negotiations for a second, there's a lot of speculation—without getting into the details of the negotiations—about why you personally decided the matter was urgent enough now to resort to this process. Is it because you're afraid interest rates might stop the economic growth that you want so much? Is it because the automatic spending cuts would be too painful for the country to absorb? Or are you just frustrated that the deficit continues to restrict your ability to maneuver on a lot of issues?

The President. I want to say almost all of the above, but it's really that when you take a look at the most recent estimates—and one of the ingredients in the shortfall has been interest rates—is that the problem is of such a magnitude that we need to address it. It's more that than it is a fear of any specific categories. Just big enough that we have to do something about it, and that's why I have taken the approach I have taken.

But in here, you see, it is a place where we need to get understanding from the American people. But I want to go there saying: Look, here's the problem. Everybody's agreed on it now. We're not going to have some new organization come in and argue with the estimates, and that means getting CBO and the OMB together as much as possible. Here's a bipartisan answer—taking compromise here, give and take there—and this is what we must do as a nation on the deficit. I'm hopeful that we will be able to come forward with such an agreement that will enable me to do that.

Q. Do you have a timetable of your own?

The President. No. We talked about timetable this morning, Jerry [Gerald Seib, Wall Street Journal], but that has not been agreed with Congress. And again, I want to work with them on these answers, not do it just in——

Offshore Oil Drilling

Q. For sometime, you've hinted, Mr. President, that you would ban offshore oil drilling off the coast of Florida. Can you tell us where you are now on that decision as well as the issue in California?

The President. A while back, I said weeks and not months, and today I'll say days and not weeks because we've just concluded a meeting with those Cabinet Departments that have recommendations to make to the President. And now we've got to sort it out internally. But I can't give you an exact date, but we're getting very close to making recommendations in that regard.

Q. Can you tell me, is there a big difference in how you see the situation in Florida compared with California?

The President. I think I've already said that I'm concerned about the environmental aspects as it relates to Florida, albeit the drilling, as I was told this morning, is quite a ways offshore—the leases are. But that is a highly sophisticated and sensitive area. So, I've already said that, but I don't want to suggest that I don't feel that way about certain areas off California.

Another aspect of all this is the overall energy requirements of the country. And regrettably, I'm going to have to make a decision on this, or feel compelled to, before we have our whole energy study, which is quite important. But I have to go forward anyway without that, and it's too bad. I am increasingly concerned about our dependence on foreign oil. So, it is my responsibility, then, to balance out these needs.

Assistance for Nicaragua and Panama

Q. Mr. President, I know you're—as a former Member of the House, that you know it's not unusual for legislation to be loaded down with amendments. Have you exhausted all administrative relief for—possibility of relief for Panama and Nicaragua and contingency funds?

The President. Yes, we have. I tasked the Treasury, upon hearing from Mrs. Chamorro, to see if there is some way to arrange a bridge loan. And as I said in my statement, regrettably you can't make a bridge loan based on pending legislation; in other words, using pending legislation to bridge it, to pay it off. So, we've tried very hard on that. Indeed, I asked—through General Scowcroft [Assistant to the President for National Security Affairs]—the Secretary of the Treasury to see if we couldn't encourage private lending to help Violeta get across this difficult problem. And they run into collateral problems as well. So, it is a matter of dire urgency, and——

Q. Did you tell the Democratic leaders

that yesterday?

The President. Yes, I did.

Q. ——the budget? What did they say?

The President. They said they'd try very hard. With fairness to Speaker Foley, I talked to Congressman Jamie Whitten about it, and it is very frustrating. And I think the American people are frustrated by the inability of the Congress to do business in a prompt and orderly fashion. I believe this has the support of the American people.

Federal Budget Negotiations

Q. Mr. President, many of the participants from yesterday's budget meeting came out shaking their heads and scratching their heads in frustration at the size of the problem—as you just talked about here—magnitude of this deficit problem and the lack of trust that appeared to be in the room. In fact, one of the participants said they all turned back their papers that they had written notes on so that no one would be able to quote from them. And they all said it's going to take a lot of leadership——

The President. That was a heartening development, Jessica [Jessica Lee, USA Today].

Q. ——a lot of leadership. I'm wondering, what is it that you think you can do that can move the atmosphere forward, the atmosphere of trust, first of all, so that people will believe in the good faith that you are expressing?

The President. I think there was a meeting that involved a fair degree of trust. I don't think people think I'm trying to blindside them in the Congress. That might have been early on when I first said, Let's go, no preconditions, but I didn't get the feeling of distrust. And when people handed the papers back, it was so the process could work in an orderly fashion. And it wasn't the Republicans that suggested it, as I recall. It was a Democratic leader who said, Let's leave these and let our group that's going to meet on Thursday discuss these matters, and discuss it in as quiet a surrounding as possible, without having a big flurry out there surrounding the discussions. And so, I think I interpreted that as a determination to work together, Jessica, not the other way. I hope I'm right.

Q. But they all say that there's a stalemate about how to address the one side of the equation, the tax side of the equation, that it's going to take leadership to move things. Someone's going to have to move first now. Do you have some——

The President. That's what the process will do. No tricks.

Q. ——trick in your bag to make them forward, or are you——

The President. No tricks in the bag. But when you start a negotiation, a labor management negotiation, they get behind closed doors, and they say: Now look, here's our view. And what is yours? And reasonable people go forward and try to negotiate. So, I think the Democrats did come down—some of them—saying, Well, you should go first.

I said to them, Wait a minute, who appropriates all the money? Where's the revenue? Who's got the obligation under the Constitution to raise the revenues? So, let's not talk about who's going first. We've got a problem. We have a national problem. And I want to be a part of having the American people understand the problem, and I want to have an answer to the American people that I know can work. And it's not going to work with just Republicans or just the White House or just the Democrats.

So, I think we got over that hurdle—I hope we did—of suspicion. And I'm trying very hard here today because these are good, tough questions about procedure and substance. And I am not going to get into those. I'm going to try to keep my share of the bargain by not discussing what we might do or might not do, what my bottom line is, what my opening wedge is, because once I do that, you'll have 435 people in the House doing it and 100 in the Senate. And that isn't the way we're going to solve this national problem.

Thank you all very, very much.

U.S. Bases in the Philippines

Q. How about one on the Philippines, Mr. President?

The President. The Philippines?

Q. Yes. Do we need those bases there now as much as we did in the past?

The President. I thought our negotiator

made a very sound statement—Rich Armitage—on the Philippines, because what he pointed out is, we don't have a total blank check regarding this. And there's another point he made: And if we're not wanted there, we're not going to be there.

And so, this isn't something that is absolutely essential to the United States. They're great facilities, those two facilities, and we will negotiate in good faith. But there are certain parameters; there are certain limits to what I will do, what I will accept as President. And it's very important that we—in dealing in good faith—that the Philippine Government and its leaders know that. And that's why I strongly support—

which Rich Armitage said, or what I saw that he said on the television, which is almost that.

Q. Will we be able to protect our interests in the Pacific if we're thrown out of the Philippines?

The President. Yes, there are other ways to skin this cat. But some of them are quite expensive, and some of them are less expensive. But you can be assured I am looking at those options.

Note: The President's 47th news conference began at 12:17 p.m. in the Briefing Room at the White House.

Message to the Congress Transmitting a Report on United States Countermeasures to Political Repression in China
May 16, 1990

To the Congress of the United States:

I am transmitting herewith the report on bilateral and multilateral measures taken in response to the military crackdown in China in June 1989, pursuant to Title IX, subsection 902(c), of the Foreign Relations

Authorization Act, Fiscal Years 1990 and 1991 (P.L. 101–246).

GEORGE BUSH

The White House,
May 16, 1990.

Nomination of David Passage To Be United States Ambassador to Botswana
May 16, 1990

The President today announced his intention to nominate David Passage, of North Carolina, a career member of the Senior Foreign Service, Class of Minister-Counselor, to be Ambassador Extraordinary and Plenipotentiary of the United States of America to the Republic of Botswana. He would succeed John Florian Kordek.

Since 1989 Mr. Passage has served as Director for Africa of the National Security Council at the White House. Prior to this, he served as Director of the Office of Regional Affairs in the Bureau of African Affairs at the Department of State, 1986–1989; Deputy Chief of Mission at the U.S.

Embassy in San Salvador, El Salvador, 1984–1986; Deputy Director of the Office of Southern African Affairs at the Department of State, 1982–1984; National War College, 1981–1982; Deputy Spokesman and Director of the Office of Press Relations at the Department of State, 1979–1981; Political Counselor at the U.S. Embassy in Canberra, Australia, 1977–1979; and Special Assistant to the Secretary of State, 1975–1977. In addition, he has served in the following positions at the Department of State: as a political officer at the U.S. Embassy in Quito, Ecuador, 1974–1975; special assistant in the Bureau of Politico-

Military Affairs, 1972–1974; on the Secretariat staff, 1971–1972; in the Operations Center, 1970–1971; a pacification program analyst in Saigon, Vietnam, 1969–1970; and a political officer at the U.S. Embassy in London, England, 1966–1968. Mr. Passage

entered the Foreign Service in 1966.

Mr. Passage graduated from the University of Denver (B.A., 1964) and Georgetown University (M.S., 1966). He was born June 16, 1942, in Charlotte, NC. Mr. Passage resides in Washington, DC.

Nomination of Richard Wayne Bogosian To Be United States Ambassador to Chad
May 16, 1990

The President today announced his intention to nominate Richard Wayne Bogosian, of Maryland, a career member of the Senior Foreign Service, Class of Minister-Counselor, to be Ambassador Extraordinary and Plenipotentiary of the United States of America to the Republic of Chad. He would succeed Robert L. Pugh.

Since 1988 Mr. Bogosian has served as Director of the Office of Monetary Affairs at the Department of State. Prior to this, he served in the following positions at the Department of State: as Ambassador to Niger, 1985–1988; Director of East African Affairs, 1982–1985; chief of the aviation negotiations division, 1979–1982; Deputy Chief of Mission at the U.S. Embassy in Khartoum, Sudan, 1976–1979; and chief of the economic section at the U.S. Embassy in Kuwait, 1972–1976. In addition, he has served at the

Foreign Service Institute for Economics, 1972; in the Bureau for Intelligence and Research at the Department of State, 1969–1971; in the Bureau of Near East and South Asian Affairs at the Department of State, 1968–1969; as vice consul for the U.S. Embassy in Paris, France, 1966–1968; at the Foreign Service Institute, 1965; at the U.S. Embassy in Baghdad, Iraq, 1963–1965; in the Bureau of Near Eastern and South Asian Affairs at the Department of State, 1963; and at the Foreign Service Institute, 1962–1963. Mr. Bogosian entered the Foreign Service in 1962.

Mr. Bogosian graduated from Tufts College (A.B., 1959) and the University of Chicago (J.D., 1962). He was born July 18, 1937, in Boston, MA. Mr. Bogosian is married, has three children, and resides in Gaithersburg, MD.

Nomination of Philip S. Kaplan for the Rank of Ambassador While Serving as Deputy United States Representative to the Negotiations on Conventional Armed Forces in Europe
May 16, 1990

The President today announced his intention to nominate Philip S. Kaplan, of California, a career member of the Senior Foreign Service, Class of Minister-Counselor, for the rank of Ambassador during his tenure of service as Deputy U.S. Representative to the Negotiations on Conventional Armed Forces in Europe.

Since 1989 Mr. Kaplan has served as

Deputy U.S. Representative to the Negotiations on Conventional Armed Forces in Europe. Prior to this, he served in the following positions at the Department of State: as a senior intelligence officer, 1987–1989; Minister and Deputy Chief of Mission at the U.S. Embassy in Manila, 1985–1987; Principal Deputy Assistant Secretary of State for Policy Planning, 1981–1985; director of multilateral policy at the Bureau of International Organizations, 1979–1980; and as a member of the policy planning staff, 1975–1979. In addition, Mr. Kaplan has served on the U.S. delegation to the East-West negotiations on mutual and balanced force reductions in Vienna, Austria, 1974–1975; as political officer at the U.S. Embassy in Bonn, 1970–1974; and as an economic officer at the U.S. Mission to the European Communities in Brussels, Belgium, 1968–1970. Mr. Kaplan entered the Foreign Service in 1967.

Mr. Kaplan graduated from the University of Connecticut (B.A., 1959) and the University of California (J.D., 1962). He was born March 28, 1937, in New Britain, CT. Mr. Kaplan is married, has one child, and resides in Millbrae, CA.

Nomination of Russell Flynn Miller To Be Inspector General for the Federal Emergency Management Agency
May 16, 1990

The President today announced his intention to nominate Russell Flynn Miller to be Inspector General for the Federal Emergency Management Agency. This is a new position.

Mr. Miller currently serves as a consultant for the Central Intelligence Agency. Prior to this, he was assistant director in the office of security for the office of the President-elect, 1988–1989, and he worked for the Bush-Quayle campaign, 1988. He was a private consultant, 1986–1988. In addition, Mr. Miller worked in several capacities with the United States Synthetic Fuels Corporation, including Deputy Inspector General, 1985–1986, and Director of Investigation in the Office of the Inspector General, 1981–1985. Mr. Miller worked for the Reagan-Bush Presidential campaign, 1979–1980. Prior to that he was a career officer in the Operations Directorate at the Central Intelligence Agency.

Mr. Miller received a bachelor of arts degree from the University of Iowa and a bachelor of laws degree from Drake University College of Law. He was born October 25, 1921, in Panora, IA. Mr. Miller served in the U.S. Army, 1943–1945, and in the U.S. Army Reserve, 1946–1966. He is married, has four children, and resides in Potomac, MD.

Statement by Press Secretary Fitzwater on the Death of Sammy Davis, Jr.
May 16, 1990

The President and Mrs. Bush are deeply saddened by the death of Sammy Davis, Jr. The Bushes are longtime admirers of Mr. Davis, who has given a lifetime to bringing joy to others through his special entertainment and good will. The President and Mrs. Bush telephoned Mrs. Davis on Saturday, May 12, to extend their best wishes and prayers.

Mr. Davis has been a major figure in the entertainment world. His legacy of humor and songs, as well as charity work, will continue to be a part of future generations. The President and Mrs. Bush extend their sympathy and condolences to Mr. Davis' family and friends.

Remarks at a Meeting With the Commission on Civil Rights
May 17, 1990

Welcome to the Rose Garden and to the White House. Thank you all very much for coming. To the Attorney General and Secretary Cavazos and Secretary Sullivan, thank you for joining us; Director Newman, the same. And to Senators Dole, Hatch, and Garn, Congressman Ham Fish, thank you very much for being with us today. To Chairman Fletcher, an old friend and a man I'm very proud of, welcome, sir. To Commissioners Buckley, Ramirez, Redenbaugh, Wilfredo Gonzalez and the State Advisory Committee Chairpersons and to the distinguished leaders—I see Ben Hooks here and others of the civil rights community across this great country—it is—and I mean it—an honor to have you here today.

I think we've made it a moment that's very hopeful worldwide. In a minute from now, I'll be meeting in this marvelous Oval Office with Chancellor Kohl, talking about the dramatic changes that have taken place in the world. There is a time when the thundering cry for freedom is being heard and answered from Panama, hopefully in Johannesburg, to Warsaw. And around the world, peoples are warring against tyranny, citizens struggling against State control, economies weary of bureaucratic central planners—all are looking to America as reason for hope, the bright star by which to chart their course to freedom. And so, it's all the more crucial now that we look carefully to the kind of country we are, to the state of democracy here in the Land of Liberty. And we're called upon to ensure that this democracy means opportunity for all who call it home.

Few have worked harder to deliver the promise of democracy, to make an enduring dream a living reality, than the men and women assembled here today in this Rose Garden. And particularly, I want to give credit again to these men and women standing behind me.

From its earliest origins, the Commission on Civil Rights has been an independent, bipartisan voice for justice. And the Commissioners, the Directors, the Advisory Committees all share a cultural diversity and an intellectual and moral conviction that are truly America's best. And these men and women have earned our admiration, and today they deserve our thanks.

Joining a new Chairman—and as I said, my friend of many years, Art Fletcher—are two outstanding additions: Carl Anderson and Russell Redenbaugh. I know Bob Dole shares my admiration for Russell, a man of impressive credentials, who knows, as all Americans should know, that physical disability will not be a barrier to service in this administration. That's why I remain firmly committed to the landmark Americans for Disabilities Act to help ensure equal rights and opportunities for these Americans. And today I'd like to announce a new member of the Civil Rights Commission, Mr. Charles Pei Wang, President of the China Institute in America, an outstanding new addition.

Over the last few days, I've met to discuss pending civil rights legislation with leaders representing America's rich tapestry of cultural, religious, and ethnic diversity. And I got, as I knew I would, a lot of sound advice. Much of which I can accept. [*Laughter*] But these leaders, this Commission, the Congress, and this administration, believe me, all share a common conviction for equal opportunity. It's a responsibility that I've tried to take very seriously, especially now, when our most vital export to the world is democracy. And we must make sure that we as a nation continue to lead by example. We must see that true affirmative action is not reduced to some empty slogan and that this principle of striking down all barriers to advancement has real, living meaning to all Americans. We will leave nothing to chance and no stone unturned as we work to advance America's civil rights agenda.

This nation's progress against prejudice— from the '64 act to the Voting Rights Act to the Fair Housing and Age Discrimination in Employment Acts—it's all hinged on the principle that no one in this country should be excluded from opportunity. And so, we're committed to enacting new measures like the Hate Crimes Statistics Act, the HOPE [Homeownership and Opportunity for People Everywhere] initiative of housing, a revitalized enforcement of restrictions against employment bias. This administration seeks equal opportunity and equal protection under the law for all Americans, goals that I know are shared by Senator Kennedy and Representative Hawkins, and certainly by the four distinguished Members of Congress with us here today.

And so, we've supported efforts to ensure an individual's ability to challenge discriminatory seniority systems. We've also moved to stiffen the penalties for racial discrimination in setting or applying the terms and conditions of employment. And today, as we work to ensure that America represents democracy's highest expression, I want to begin by offering three principles that must guide any amendments to our civil rights laws. These principles are firmly rooted in the spirit of our current laws. After the extensive discussions that we've had this week, I think they're principles on which all of us, including the leadership on the Hill, can agree. And so, I will enthusiastically support legislation that meets these principles.

First, civil rights legislation must operate to obliterate consideration of factors such as race, color, religion, sex, or national origin from employment decisions. So, in essence, we seek civil rights legislation that is more effective, not less. The focus of employers in this country must be on providing equal opportunity for all workers, not on developing strategies to avoid litigation.

No one here today would want me to sign a bill whose unintended consequences are quotas because quotas are wrong and they violate the most basic principles of our civil rights tradition and the most basic principles of the promise of democracy. America's minority communities deserve more than symptomatic relief. And we want to eradicate the disease, and that will require systematic solutions, strategies that transcend statistics.

We should empower and ennoble our minority communities. We should seek systematic change that allows every American to excel. During these meetings this week, I

invited the civil rights leadership to work with me to craft a bill that moves us towards this goal. After these consultations, I am confident that this can be done. I want to sign a civil rights bill, but I will not sign a quota bill. I think we can work it out.

The second, civil rights legislation must reflect fundamental principles of fairness that apply throughout our legal system. Individuals who believe their rights have been violated are entitled to their day in court, and an accused is innocent until proved guilty. In every case involving a civil rights dispute, constitutional protections of due process must be preserved.

And third, Federal law should provide an adequate deterrent against harassment in the workplace based on race, sex, religion, or disability and should ensure a speedy end to such discriminatory practices. Our civil rights laws, however, should not be turned into some lawyer's bonanza, encouraging litigation at the expense of conciliation, mediation, or settlement.

Let me add that Congress, with respect, should live by the same requirements it prescribes for others. In '72, the Civil Rights Act of '64 was justly applied to executive agencies and State, local governments; and Congress, however, is not yet covered. This is not an assault on Congress. I'm just trying to—I've got about—[*laughter*]—but seriously, this inconsistency should be remedied to give congressional employees and applicants the full protection of the law to send a strong signal that it's both the executive branch and Congress that are in this together. And the Congress should join the executive branch in setting an example for these private employers.

Now, we seek strategies that work, putting power where it belongs: in the hands of the people. That means new ideas, like giving poor parents the power of an alternative choice in where to send the kids to school so that all can have access to the best. It means more tenant control and ownership of public housing, tax credits for child care to give parents more flexibility and choice, policies that underwrite prosperity by encouraging capital flow to businesses in poor neighborhoods. The door is open wider now than it ever has been. Together, I believe we can open it still wider.

Today an expanding economy is working in the service of civil rights. And so, let's not set the clock back. Let's look past the differences that divide us to the shared principles and the better natures that we have within us. To the civil rights leadership assembled here today—Dorothy, excuse me, I didn't see you earlier—and so many—I'm in real trouble if I single them out here. Look, I have offered you my hand and my word that together we can and will make America open and equal to all. Now, this administration is committed to action that is truly affirmative, positive action in every sense, to strike down all barriers to advancement of every kind for all people. We will tolerate no barriers, no bias, no inside tracks, no two-tiered system, and no rungless ladders. And I'm willing to take the time to make sure that this is done right, simply because it's worth doing right. Now is the time, really, to extend a hand to all that are struggling and to devote our energies to a broader agenda of empowerment, that all might join in this new age of freedom.

I am delighted that you all came here. Thank you for bringing honor to this prestigious Rose Garden and to paying tribute to our Commission here, in which I have great confidence and in which I take great pride. Thank you all very, very much.

Note: The President spoke at 10:02 a.m. in the Rose Garden at the White House. In his remarks, he referred to Constance B. Newman, Director of the Office of Personnel Management; Arthur A. Fletcher, Esther G. Buckley, Blandina C. Ramirez, Russell G. Redenbaugh, Wilfredo J. Gonzalez, and Carl A. Anderson, Chairman and Commissioners of the Commission on Civil Rights, respectively; Benjamin L. Hooks, executive director of the National Association for the Advancement of Colored People; Chancellor Helmut Kohl of the Federal Republic of Germany; and civil rights leader Dorothy Haight.

Statement by Press Secretary Fitzwater on Armenia's Expression of Appreciation to Jeb and George P. Bush for Their Earthquake Relief Efforts
May 17, 1990

On behalf of the Armenian Supreme Soviet and Council of Ministers, Soviet Ambassador Yuriy Dubinin presented medallions and certificates of appreciation to Jeb Bush and his son, George P. Bush, in gratitude for "the sincere sympathy you extended to the Armenian people during their recent misfortunes and the generous help you offered during the aftermath of the devastating earthquake that took thousands of human lives and ruined many cities and towns." The certificates note that the Armenian people "will never forget this demonstration of human charity." The presentation was made to the President by Ambassador Dubinin during a brief visit to the White House on May 14.

The earthquake struck Armenia on December 7, 1988. Jeb and his son were among the volunteers who accompanied the fourth airlift by Americares, the international medical relief agency based in Connecticut, to Armenia on December 24, 1988. The airlift carried approximately 100,000 pounds of medicines, clothing, and toys for the children of Armenia. The Bushes visited the devastated region around the Armenian capital of Yerevan and conveyed a message of sympathy from the American people to the Armenian people and especially to the children during that holiday season. The U.S. Government also provided disaster relief through the Agency for International Development's Office of U.S. Foreign Disaster Assistance.

Remarks Following Discussions With Chancellor Helmut Kohl of the Federal Republic of Germany
May 17, 1990

The President. Chancellor Kohl and I had an opportunity to follow up on our extended discussions at Camp David back in February and review the progress toward German unification and the progress in East-West relations. I'm grateful to the Chancellor, together with Minister Genscher and Minister Stoltenberg, for taking the time to come to Washington today to continue our important dialog on these historic issues before us.

What's clear from all our discussion over the past months, including our extensive talks today, is that the United States and the Federal Republic of Germany share the same approach and have the same goals regarding German unification. We both want a united Germany which enjoys full sovereignty; a united Germany which is a full member of the Western community and of the NATO alliance, including participation in its integrated military structures; a united Germany which is, as the Federal Republic has been for over 40 years, a model of freedom, tolerance, and friendly relations with its neighbors.

During our discussion today, we reviewed the talks in Bonn on May 5th among Foreign Ministers of the two German States, the United States, Great Britain, France, and the Soviet Union—those are the two-plus-four talks. Chancellor Kohl and I agreed that these talks should terminate all Four Power rights and responsibilities at the time of German unification. A united Germany should have full control over all of its territory, without any new discriminatory constraints on German sovereignty. Forty-five years after the end of the war, there is no reason that a unified democratic Germany should be in any way singled out for some special status. In keeping with the Helsinki Final Act, Germany should be fully sovereign, free to choose its own alliances and security arrangements. And we agree that U.S. military forces should remain stationed in the united Germany and elsewhere in Europe to continue to promote stability and security.

The Chancellor and I also discussed the broad issues of East-West relations. And I expressed my hope for a successful U.S.-Soviet summit at the end of this month but also reiterated my own concern, which the Chancellor shares, about the situation in Lithuania. We reaffirmed our commitment to the opening of a dialog in good faith between the Soviet leaders and Lithuanian representatives.

We also discussed the forthcoming NATO summit. It will be held in London on July 5th and July 6th. And the Chancellor and I reviewed my proposal that the summit address the political role that NATO can play in the new Europe; the conventional forces the alliance will need in the time ahead and NATO's goals for conventional arms control; the role of nuclear weapons based in Europe and Western objectives in new nuclear arms control negotiations between the United States and the Soviet Union; and the alliance's common objectives for strengthening the CSCE, Conference on Security and Cooperation in Europe.

At this time of enormous and, I would say, encouraging change in Germany and Europe as a whole, we reaffirm the continuing vital role of the North Atlantic alliance in guaranteeing stability and security. We also want that CSCE to pursue a more ambitious agenda in helping the rising democracies in Eastern Europe join the community of free nations and have a strong voice in the new Europe.

When I visited Germany last May, I spoke of the Federal Republic and the United States as partners in leadership. The remarkable changes that have occurred in this short year since then have fully confirmed that partnership, and we now look together with hope and confidence to a Germany united in peace and freedom and to a Europe whole and free.

Chancellor, thank you very much for coming, sir.

The Chancellor. Mr. President, ladies and

gentlemen, allow me to thank you, first of all, very warmly for the warm hospitality with which you have received me here today—me and the members of my delegation. We had intensive discussions in a very warm and friendly atmosphere.

Allow me to summarize my message in three points. First of all, on behalf of all Germans, I express sincere thanks to the American people, and especially to you, President Bush, for the magnificent support that you have granted from the outset and continue to grant to us Germans during this decade on our path to German unity. The Americans and Germans stood side by side at the time of the Berlin blockade and the erection of the Berlin Wall. And together we championed, not least in the difficult days of the Cold War, our vision of freedom, democracy, and human rights. Now that this vision is becoming a reality in the whole of Europe, that the Berlin Wall is being torn down and sold as souvenirs, that Germany and its former capital, Berlin, are becoming reunited, there is something that is all the more true: The friendship and partnership with the United States continue to be vital to us Germans. Naturally, this also applies to a united Germany.

A united Germany will remain a member of the North Atlantic alliance. But in view of the change occurring in Europe, in view of the triumph of human rights, democracy, pluralism, and a social market economy in the whole of Europe, the alliance must concentrate more on its traditional political role. As the threat is decreasing appreciably, the alliance must keep the initiative in the field of disarmament and arms control and review its strategy and structure accordingly.

I'm extremely grateful to you, Mr. President, for having presented important and forward-looking proposals. Together, with our allies, we shall chart the course at the NATO summit meeting in London early in July.

Mr. President, allow me to state at this opportunity here, once and again, how important it is going to be for the future of Germany and Europe that the United States take their legitimate place in Germany and in Europe as a whole.

You, Mr. President, and I agreed in our talks that in order to achieve this the three anchorages must be strengthened. That means NATO as an indispensable transatlantic security link between the European and North American democracies. Cooperation between the United States and the European Community—this is going to be of ever-growing importance in view of the completion of the internal market within the European Community by 1992 and also in view of the ever-closer political union within the European Community. What is also important is the expansion of the CSCE into a system of assured human rights, guaranteed security, and comprehensive cooperation for all 35 member countries. We continue to strive for a just and lasting peaceful order in Europe, in which the division of Europe, also as regards the date, is overcome together with the division of Germany.

Mr. President, for many of us in Germany, a dream is coming true now, is becoming reality also for me. German unity and unity of Europe are two sides of the same coin. We have a lot of reason to be grateful with regard to many who have helped us, but particularly towards our American friends. And you, Mr. President, have a very important role in all this.

Thank you very much.

Note: The President spoke at 2:08 p.m. in the Rose Garden at the White House. In his opening remarks, he referred to German Foreign Minister Hans-Dietrich Genscher and Defense Minister Gerhard Stoltenberg. The Chancellor spoke in German, and his remarks were translated by an interpreter.

Statement by Press Secretary Fitzwater on President Bush's Meeting With Acting President Arpad Göncz of Hungary
May 18, 1990

President Bush met in the Oval Office for approximately 35 minutes this morning with the Acting President of Hungary, Arpad Göncz. President Göncz is in the United States on a private visit. President Göncz was named Acting President by the new democratically elected Hungarian Parliament on May 2. Hungary will have an Acting President until new election laws are enacted this summer.

In the course of the meeting, President Bush expressed his great admiration for Hungary's progress in building democracy, and he reaffirmed the United States commitment to supporting economic growth and democracy. President Bush mentioned the Hungarian-American Enterprise Fund as a means of supporting ongoing economic

reforms and strengthening U.S. investment in Hungary. President Bush also discussed the recently announced Citizens Democracy Corps, which is designed to mobilize private voluntary assistance to Eastern Europe.

The two Presidents discussed U.S.-Soviet relations and the situation in Lithuania. They agreed on the need for opening a process of dialog between the Soviet and Lithuanian leaders as a prerequisite for creating a stable environment in which the countries of Central and Eastern Europe can consolidate their democratic reforms. President Bush also stressed the importance of maintaining a strong U.S. presence in Europe, including a military presence as a guarantee of stability. President Göncz expressed his full agreement.

Nomination of Harry W. Shlaudeman To Be United States Ambassador to Nicaragua
May 18, 1990

The President today announced his intention to nominate Harry W. Shlaudeman, of California, a career member of the Senior Foreign Service, Class of Career Minister, to be Ambassador Extraordinary and Plenipotentiary of the United States of America to the Republic of Nicaragua. He would succeed Richard Huntington Melton.

Since 1989 Mr. Shlaudeman has served as a consultant to the Department of State. Prior to this, he served as Ambassador to the Federative Republic of Brazil, 1986–1989; Ambassador at Large and the President's Special Envoy for Central America, 1984–1986; Executive Director of the National Bipartisan Commission on Central America, 1983–1984; Ambassador to Argentina, 1980–1983; Ambassador to Peru, 1977–1980; Assistant Secretary of State for Inter-American Affairs, 1976–1977; Ambassador to Venezuela, 1975–1976; Deputy Assistant

Secretary of State for Inter-American Affairs, 1973–1975; Deputy Chief of Mission in Santiago, Chile, 1969–1973; and Special Assistant to the Secretary of State, 1967–1969. In addition, Mr. Shlaudeman has served as Assistant Director for the Office of Caribbean Affairs at the Department of State and adviser to Ambassador Ellsworth Bunker, 1965–1966; Dominican Republic desk officer, 1964–1965; political officer in Santo Domingo, Dominican Republic, 1962–1964; consul in Sofia, Bulgaria, 1960–1962; political officer in Bogota, Colombia, 1956–1958; and vice consul in Barranquilla, Colombia, 1955–1956. He joined the Foreign Service in 1954.

Mr. Shlaudeman graduated from Stanford University (B.A., 1952). He was born May 17, 1926, in Los Angeles, CA. Mr. Shlaudeman is married, has three children, and resides in Washington, DC.

Nomination of Eugene L. Scassa To Be United States Ambassador to Belize
May 18, 1990

The President today announced his intention to nominate Eugene L. Scassa, of Virginia, a career member of the Senior Foreign Service, Class of Minister-Counselor, to be Ambassador Extraordinary and Plenipotentiary of the United States of America to Belize. He would succeed Robert G. Rich, Jr.

Since 1986 Mr. Scassa has served as Executive Director of the Bureau of Inter-American Affairs. Prior to this, he served as Deputy Executive Director for the Bureau of Inter-American Affairs, 1985–1986; Division Chief of the Bureau of Personnel, 1983–1985; National War College, 1982–1983; Administrative Counselor at the U.S. Embassy in Jidda, Saudi Arabia, 1980–1982; administrative and conference officer for the U.S. Mission in Geneva, 1978–1980; administrative officer for the U.S. Embassy in Reykjavik, Iceland, 1974–1977; and administrative officer for the U.S. Embassy in

Lusaka, Zambia, 1973–1974. In addition, he has served as an administrative and consular officer for the U.S. Consulate General in Monterrey, Mexico, 1971–1973; administrative officer for the U.S. Embassy in Madagascar, 1971; administrative officer and consular officer for the U.S. consulate in Mozambique, 1969–1971; Special Assistant in the Bureau of African Affairs, 1967–1969; administrative assistant for the U.S. Embassy in Libreville, Gabon, 1965–1967; communications officer for the U.S. Embassy in Quito, Ecuador, 1964–1965; and communications and records clerk for the U.S. Embassy in Panama, 1962–1964. Mr. Scassa joined the Foreign Service in 1962.

Mr. Scassa attended Geneva College, 1957–1958 and 1960–1961, and he attended Florida State University night school, 1963–1964. He was born February 6, 1939, in Monaca, PA. Mr. Scassa served in the U.S. Army, 1958–1960. He is married, has three children, and resides in Reston, VA.

Remarks at a Republican Party Fundraising Dinner in Dallas, Texas
May 18, 1990

The President. Thank you very, very much. Barbara and I are delighted to be here. And, Phil, thank you for that most generous introduction. You have the heart of old Texas in you. And for a college professor, your brevity was an appreciated departure from tradition, and your comments were far too generous. But Bar and I are just delighted to be back here.

Wasn't Yolanda Garcia marvelous, standing up here without—[*applause*]. And, Boone, this is a great party you're throwing for a great party. And so many familiar Texas faces here tonight, people that have shaped this party and served this State. First, of course, our great Governor, my friend Bill Clements. He and Rita have done an outstanding job for the State. And

to our chairman from Dallas, Fred Meyer. I'm told he did a lot of the work on this dinner—Fred. And of course, to the all-time star of Texas, Tom Landry. Where's Tom? Right there. And to Bobby Holt, the finance chairman, my pal from west Texas. And to Fort Stockton's son, Claytie Williams. I'll get to him in a bit—[*laughter*]. And to, I guess, the guy that I would always look to as my mentor in Texas politics, my dear friend John Tower, who's with us tonight. I salute him. And of course, our great statewide Republican ticket and the Victory '90 fellow over there, our son George. Glad to be with him. Go Rangers!

And again, so many wonderful friends from over so many years. Barbara and I realized on the way down here that we're talking 42 years ago next month that we moved to Texas. Of course, that was in a '47 Studebaker, and today it was in Air Force One. More leg room now. [*Laughter*] But all the same, it's just a wonderful feeling of coming home. And Texas remains larger than life in our hearts. It is a place of family and duty and loyalty and honor. But then, what more could you expect from a State whose name means "friend"?

I'd love to come back home to my friends again next October. Things have to change a little bit. I want to throw out the first ball at the opening game of the Rangers and the Astros in the World Series. We can all dream, you know. [*Laughter*] I asked George, knowing they needed a little help on the Rangers, if I could try out for the club. He said, "Don't give up your daytime job." [*Laughter*] Then he added, "Why don't you go out for the oldtimers' game?"

But also, as we flew in, there's some sadness involved in this homecoming, too, because from the plane and then from our room, Barbara and I saw some of the areas devastated by the flooding. We were astounded that we could only see the tops of some trees where the Trinity's overflowed. Two weeks ago, I signed an emergency FEMA proclamation at the request of our Governor, bringing Federal disaster aid to the beleaguered counties. And how many, Bill, now are there in the official list?

The Governor. I think it's 37.

The President. Way up there, some 37 or more counties—more counties, more counties being added.

And so, in this terrible disaster, the losses have been heavy. But the one thing that comes through to me from talking to my friends is that this State will never lose—one thing it will never lose—and that is its soul. And I heard some wonderful Texans from Liberty talking on the television today. And, yes, Texas is big, but not as big as the generous hearts and indomitable spirit of its people. So you know, when I hear the candidates of the other party, sometimes I wonder if they know the people of this State at all—know how they think, know how to listen to their voices. I realized you can explain it to them, but you can't understand it for them.

More than 40 years ago, as a salesman

peddling drilling bits out in west Texas, I crisscrossed all across west Texas in my car, from Muleshoe to Wink to Notrees, from the panhandle down, Claytie, to Fort Stockton. I learned a lot about the people then. Shared barbecues and saw their pain when they were laid off and the paychecks weren't there. Listening to the pulse of the people—that's how you hear the heartbeat of Texas, and that's how Texas gets into your blood. Sticks to you like a tumbleweed in a barbed wire fence. And you know, once it's there, it never leaves. For those of you who might be worried that I'm spending too much time in Washington or in Maine and in the Northeast in general, let me tell you that we do get homesick, and that chicken-fried lobster is no substitute for the real thing. [*Laughter*]

Coming home and seeing what the Texas GOP is doing makes me very, very proud. This is the party of inclusion. And I congratulate Claytie Williams for the kind of race he tells me he's planning to run—inclusion. And as Phil pointed out—and no one stands for this more—of idealism. No one stands for that more than Phil. And of ideas—the same. You believe that progress is not measured in money spent and bureaucracies built but in people helped. And I'm proud, very proud of this slate, this statewide slate of Republican candidates, the strongest team in the history of the State; proud that for the first time there are candidates for 15 State offices and the United States Senate.

First, of course, there's Senator Phil Gramm. Phil says he's running for reelection like he was running for sheriff in each of Texas' 254 counties. And I believe him. But when he asked to hold the budget talks there at high noon in the middle of Pennsylvania Avenue, I thought he'd gone too far. But let me say this: Thank God that this able Senator is such a key player on the high-level budget negotiations that we're undertaking in Washington now. Thank God for his common sense.

And Clayton Williams, Claytie, the next Governor of Texas—I respect what he's achieved in business, and we respect his record of success in creating jobs in his 32 years in business. We respect his commitment to fighting this insidious poison of drugs. And we respect that he has broadened the base of our party. Clayton Williams will bring his own energetic style to the Governor's office. You ought to ride in the limousine with this guy. You get ulcers just watching him jumping up and down in there. [*Laughter*] And he will stamp his brand of leadership on the Texas of the 1990's. Claytie, I am for you 100 percent. You must and you will win this race and follow Bill Clements into office. It's absolutely essential.

And the rest of this great State and local slate, men and women who make up a coalition that reflects Texas, all of Texas, as it really is and as it will be, a coalition of diverse people—Kay Bailey Hutchison; Lou Sturns; Rick Perry; Tony Garza; old friend Bob Mosbacher—Rob; Wes Gilbreath; Warren Harding; Buster Brown—you are today's Texans, with the large and generous spirit of yesterday's Texans.

You know, on Inauguration Day, I talked in the State of the Union Message about a new breeze blowing. Let me tell you, standing back here in Texas, I can feel it. It is the warm gulf breeze of a State where people are independent minded and open, as bold as its frontiers. It's the wind of a land where risktaking comes from the strength of your beliefs and where your spirit is as big as the Texas sky. Each of you in the Texas GOP has helped to open the window of the musty darkness of outdated big government. You're blowing away the stuffiness of irrelevant liberalism because your new breeze carries the new ideas Texas needs for the nineties, ideas that encourage investment in business and in the business of our children, education.

In Washington we share your belief that education is the only path to a brighter American future. It is critical to everything we are and everything we can become. And I must say, I salute Barbara Bush for her lead in trying to make this country a literate America. We've declared a new era of education reform in America. We began in September with the first education summit in American history, bringing together at Charlottesville the Nation's Governors—and I will pay tribute here—including our own Bill Clements, who took a leadership role,

brought them together to tackle this crisis.

Last winter we announced our goals— they were unanimous; they got across party lines—goals to make American education number one. Among them: American students must be the first in math and science. All children must start school ready to learn, with help from programs like Head Start. They must demonstrate competency in crucial subject areas, while we increase the percentage of graduating high school students to 90 percent. Finally, every school in America must have a disciplined environment and, most of all, be drug-free.

The curse of drugs threatens our communities, our schools, our workplaces and, most importantly—and God bless them—our children. There is no greater threat today to the health of the American family and the future of our land. The strength we bring to win the war on drugs has got to be of hurricane force. It must roar with the determination from the smallest town squares to those concrete canyons of our cities.

Our national drug control strategy is clear. The rules of the game have changed. America will no longer tolerate drug use. For too long we condoned that which we should have condemned. And those who violate the law will pay a heavy price. We will take back the streets of our country.

We must and we will stop the horror, the pollution of drugs drifting across our borders. We've designated the Houston area and the southwest border high-intensity drug trafficking areas. This means that you'll receive special Federal enforcement assistance to disrupt and dismantle drug trafficking organizations.

The additional drug legislation that our administration sent to the Hill this week contains a number of proposals that will help stop drugs and drug smugglers from breaching our borders. We've called for more border patrol agents, extending general arrest authority to them so they can enforce our drug laws as they protect our frontier. We're also proposing legislation that will permit authorities to exclude criminal aliens convicted of drug felonies.

And to win this war on drugs, we must continue the fight being waged so well by our own Governor right here in Texas, Bill

683

Clements. We need this Republican team, headed by Clayton Williams, in Austin to continue this cooperative battle. And needless to say, I need Phil Gramm in Washington, where he is a leader in the quest for drug-free communities.

But I need Phil in Washington for something else, and I alluded to it earlier: our struggle with the budget. In this last decade, not once but twice, his vision has changed the fiscal firmament of this land. On Tuesday, we convened an extraordinary, ongoing bipartisan budget summit. Phil is designated—without the ranking member on the specific committee—as a key member, one of, I think, only two in the whole process designated by the leadership. He's working closely with me at the table, providing the kind of sound fiscal advice that he's known for.

And so, education, the fight against drugs, the budget deficit—I think we're making progress, and with our Texan Republican leadership in place in Austin and Washington, we're going to make a lot more progress.

We're going to win here—you know what's at stake on redistricting across this country—we're going to win here and across the country in 1990. We have to win in 1990. If we don't, once again the opposition will gerrymander fair representation right out the window and into thin air. The Democratic leaders know that today Republicans will win in a fair fight because times are changing. Party identity, as Phil pointed out to you, is changing.

When I was running, with a spectacular lack of success, for the Senate back in 1964, my first speech was about building a two-party system in Texas. Barbara listened, and three other people listened, and that was it. [*Laughter*] And that's the gospel truth. But back then during elections, they might as well have put up a sign: Public Office Available, No Republicans Need Apply. Well, today Texas voters have put up a new sign. It tells everyone: Public Office Available,

No Outdated, Big Spending, Bureaucracy-Building, Liberal Democrats Need Apply. And that's the message.

So, the next 6 months are crucial to this State—I really feel that deep inside me—crucial to Texas and to our country itself. The future's at stake, and we've got to join together. We're going to take the Republican message to every farm and ranch, to every town and city, to every Texan willing to listen in this magnificent State of ours. And if we do, on election day the people of Texas will lift their faces and feel that Republican breeze of change, of new ideas that's sweeping our land. And then together we can face whatever challenges the future may bring because in togetherness there is strength. And in Texas togetherness is the finest kind of strength of all.

Thank you all very much for your fantastic support for our ticket. God bless the great State of Texas, and God bless America. Thank you. It's a great pleasure to be home.

Note: The President spoke at 7:41 p.m. in the Chantilly Ballroom of the Loews Anatole Hotel. In his remarks, he referred to Senator Phil Gramm, who introduced the President; T. Boone Pickens, chairman of the dinner; Rita Clements, wife of Gov. William P. Clements, Jr.; Fred Meyer, Texas Republican Party chairman; Tom Landry, former coach of the Dallas Cowboys football team; Bobby Holt, finance chairman of the dinner; former Senator John Tower; George W. Bush, general partner of the Texas Rangers baseball team; Kay Bailey Hutchison, nominee for State treasurer; Louis Sturns, nominee for Texas Court of Criminal Appeals; Rick Perry, nominee for State agriculture commissioner; Tony Garza, nominee for county judge; Rob Mosbacher, nominee for Lieutenant Governor; Wes Gilbreath, nominee for State land commissioner; Warren Harding, nominee for State comptroller; and Buster Brown, nominee for State attorney general.

Remarks at the Houston Economic Summit Headquarters and an Exchange With Reporters
May 19, 1990

The President. First, what I really wanted to do is to come by and not just see where all this is taking place but to thank all of you, the volunteers. I think the day when we got Ken and George to cochair this significant international event we were very fortunate. And I guess it goes under the heading of busy people can do the biggest and, in my sense, one of the most important jobs we've got: to be sure this runs right. Then I looked at the array of cochairmen in there, and it's impressive—the leadership of Houston, from all different parts of our great city. And Ken has told me and then George, who was up in Washington the other day and had gotten briefed on the extent of the volunteer effort here. It is unbelievable, and it is so very important.

And I might say—I don't know how many of you recognize this guy, but that's General Brent Scowcroft over here. And if we had the luxury of the time I would let him handle any of the tough questions on the— [*laughter*]—international affairs because he is, as you know, the national security adviser to the President and intimately involved in the substantive work that's going to determine whether this summit is a success or not. I am absolutely convinced from what I know already in terms of logistics and appearance and entertainment and presentation of our city to the leaders of the world and to I don't know how many thousand press will be here—but that's going to go just perfectly. And I'm very grateful to all of you. So, thank you for what you're doing.

The summit, incidentally, will be taking place at a fascinating time, as we see the evolution of democracy in Eastern Europe. We will have had the Gorbachev summit, which happens within a couple of weeks. Then just before I come down here for this—Brent and I and others, the Secretary—we will have come—in fact, I think we'll probably come directly from a NATO meeting, a meeting that we'll discuss this common subject of how will the United States stay involved in a post-German-unifi-

cation Europe. And then, of course, not only that subject will be discussed amongst our closest allies here but we'll be talking about the broad economic relations between our country. And that affects, obviously, the Government. But those discussions will have an effect on how much trade we do. Here we are in Houston with a very active port, and we're trying to guarantee the success of the Uruguay trade rounds. So, we'll have a lot at stake in terms of substance—at stake in the sense of how it affects all the business interests and people interests of the people of the United States, not just here in Houston.

So, it is an important meeting, and I am very grateful to all of you for your significant role. And one last point: I lean—I know I'm a politic—this is nonpolitical—but we depend on volunteers. And Barbara and I have both been emphasizing, and I think with some effect around the country, this concept of a Thousand Points of Light, people willing to help others. Well, in a sense, what you all are doing is that concept, because you're helping the city. When Ken told me about this concept of Houston's Clean and the committee that's all involved in this—it is a wonderfully significant event. And if it all works out the way we think it will, then we can highlight just that facet of this for the rest of our cities around the country and say, look what Houston did. Admittedly, they had a focus point, which was the summit. But other cities can do exactly the same thing. And in these times of tough financial times for some of the cities, I think we might set an example, Ken and George, for the rest of the country.

So, thank you all very, very—sorry to drop in on you—[*laughter*]—thanks a lot.

Arms Reduction Negotiations

Q. Mr. President, do you have an update from Baker?

The President. Well, Brent and I were just talking about that. And it's interesting developments, but we're not sure we know all of it yet. I think the General will be in touch and might have a little more later on. But it's—how would you describe it? Some encouraging things——

General Scowcroft. Some progress.

The President.——and some problems that still remain to be solved. So, it's a mixed review right now, but we'll keep going forward. We want the Gorbachev summit to be successful, but it's going to take some give on the Soviet side, in my view. But we're going to keep pushing.

Q. What are they not giving on, Mr. President?

The President. Well, we still have some unfulfilled arms control problems that we're all familiar with.

Note: The President spoke at approximately 9:23 a.m. in the lobby of the Kirby Mansion. In his remarks, he referred to Ken Lay and George Starke, Cochairmen of the Houston Economic Summit Committee, and Secretary of State James A. Baker III.

Remarks at the University of Texas Commencement Ceremony in Austin
May 19, 1990

Governor, thank you. Thank you very, very much. Delighted to be here. A magnificent turnout. Thank you all. Governor Clements—Bill—thank you very much for that gracious introduction. And to you and Rita, my profound thanks. I do view you as friends, and I'm very lucky for that. To Congressman Jake Pickle and Beryl, congratulations, and congratulations on the graduation of your granddaughter, Bergan Norris, out here somewhere. And to Chairman Beecherl and members of this distinguished board of regents and to Chancellor Mark and President Cunningham, distinguished platform guests, Reverend Bethune, most distinguished faculty of this great university, thank you all.

I'm pleased to be here, and there is nothing like the great outdoors. For once, it doesn't seem to matter whether you sit on the 50-yard line or not. And I understand I'm also too late for Eeyore's birthday party. But it's great to be back in Longhorn country, just the same.

I gave my first U.T. commencement address in '73, when I had just completed a tour of duty as Ambassador at the United Nations, and I am pleased to be back. And I am grateful and, indeed, honored by this honorary degree [in law]. Thank you very much for that high honor, to the regents.

So many great Americans have given this address, including a former Texas public school teacher by the name of Lyndon Johnson and, later, his wonderful wife who served this university as a regent, Lady Bird Johnson. So, I consider it the highest honor to once again address the graduates of this great institution.

The ideals of U.T. were born with Texas, when the revolutionaries of 1836 called for "a university of the first class." And Texas began dirt-poor, but Texans were rich in land and vision. And so, what began as a dream of 40 acres of pasture is now a mini-metropolis housing some of the best schools in America. Nobel and Pulitzer Prize winners rank among your faculty; National Merit scholars lead your students. So, let me say it loud and clear: The first Texans, in a sense, were wrong. This is not just a first-class university. You are graduates of a world-class university. And if I ever forget this, if I ever should forget that, our Secretary of State, Jim Baker, would remind me, and so would our own son Jeb, another proud graduate of this University of Texas.

Your splendid libraries house the manuscripts of Joyce and Hemingway and Beckett. You are justly proud of rare books and folios that resound with the rich voices of Chaucer and the Italian Renaissance, Shakespeare and Spenser. But a world-class university must have a revered tradition of its own. And so you do. It was near here that J. Frank Dobie held court with other scholars of the Southwest on the beloved Paisano Ranch, and it was here that Walter Prescott Webb scrutinized old legends and O. Henry spun new ones.

And since then, students from around the world have become a true part of the University of Texas community as U.T. has certainly become more of a part of the world. And within this wide world, you can choose to work and succeed in Paris, France, or Paris, Texas. And in short, you face the best of dilemmas, a wealth of opportunities—opportunities born of democracy.

In four commencement addresses this spring, I have examined what makes democracy such a special way of life: how democracies refuse to perish by uniting in a strong defensive alliance; how they are strengthened by the rule of law; how freedom empowers people to solve the toughest problems; and how democracy leads to progress and adventure. Tonight, in this, for me, my final commencement address of the year, I want to discuss the personal side of democracy: what it offers us and what we can make of it.

To graduate from college in America is to be as free as any man or woman can be. And now, for the first time in half a century, a new generation in Eastern Europe is reveling in freedom, throwing their caps in the air and shouting to the high heavens because finally they are free to live where they want and free to be what they want. From Austin, Texas, to Berlin to Budapest, we live during a remarkable moment in world history, an exhilarating time: the triumph of freedom.

But freedom has a constant companion: challenge. And so, I am here tonight to challenge you to make the most of our changing world, to live these remarkable times, to take risks, to do something extraordinary. This is what Jack London was getting at when he wrote: "I would rather be a superb meteor, every atom of me in magnificent glow, than a sleepy and permanent planet. The proper function of man is to live, not to exist."

And of course, you don't have to strike out for the South Seas or the wild country of Alaska like Jack London, but you can make your life an adventure. Next month will be 42 years since my own graduation. And like many of you, I, too, was presented with some choices on my graduation day: further study or maybe a law firm or a bank or the stock market, and probably for me in New York or in the East—honorable interesting professions, all. But the truly great decisions we make in life are rarely logical or practical. They spring right from the heart. And so, I packed up, Barbara and I packed, and I drove my red Studebaker from the Eastern States of our upbringing to the oil fields of west Texas. And we chose a future that would be uniquely our own. And like most Americans, we were free to live where we pleased, do what we wanted. We came of age at a time when the postwar possibilities of America seemed limitless.

But outside of America back then, the world of free choices was shrinking. Winston Churchill's prediction that an Iron Curtain would sever Europe into two hostile camps was soon fact. An Iron Curtain did cut Eastern Europe from the West and Germany from itself. And when every brick, every guard tower, and every strand of barbed wire was in place, two worlds existed: one of free people and free choice, and one of tyranny and subjugation. Eventually, millions of men and women were told what to think and study, what job to take, and where to live. Imagine, all that drive, talent, and imagination misused and wasted. Yet many still held fast to what Barbara Jordan calls conviction values. Even under the pain of death, they resisted.

This was the conviction Andrei Sakharov, who, you remember, confronted Khrushchev with the truth on above-ground nuclear testing. And that's one reason the Soviet people revere his memory today. This is the conviction of an electrician from Gdansk, who I'm proud to know, Lech Walesa, who led the Polish people to freedom. And it's the conviction of Václav Havel of Czechoslovakia, the imprisoned playwright who now leads a great nation.

Let me tell you a little incident about President Havel and a few other brave souls from the East. It was this man that I had the honor of inviting up to the White House Residence not so many days ago to see the

Lincoln Bedroom. And President Havel was in awe because he knew that this room was really President Lincoln's old office, and it was there that Lincoln worked, deliberated, agonized over a terrible war. But President Havel knew that that room is hallowed for one reason above all: It was there that President Lincoln signed the Emancipation Proclamation. It was there in that room that he freed a people, and it was there in that room that I saw President Havel moved to tears by the knowledge that freedom's bell was ringing at long last for his beloved Czechoslovakia.

What one man draws from history another finds in music. President Landsbergis of Lithuania, who adopted Beethoven's Ninth Symphony as an anthem for his people's movement, was asked why the strains of Beethoven should resound through the streets and squares of Vilnius; and he replied that it is because the Ninth is a "symphony of freedom and victory against slavery, insidiousness, and darkest hatred."

And what one finds in music another finds in words. Consider the case of a man named Cestimir Suchy, a Czech journalist who refused to describe the 1968 Soviet invasion of his country as an act of brotherly love. Mr. Suchy was fired for his honesty, but he was allowed to make a living at a new profession: washing windows. Ask him for his business card today, and it still says Suchy, Window Washer. But this is an example of the man's good humor, for now he has a job with a new title. He is the dean of journalism at Prague's Charles University. Throughout the universities of the East it is the mandarins of Marxist dogma who are now out of work.

Let me tell you one last story, that of Arpad Göncz of Hungary, who came to visit me just yesterday in the Oval Office. Like President Havel, President Göncz is also a playwright. I don't know what it is about playwrights becoming Presidents of great countries in Eastern Europe, but a former anti-Fascist fighter and newspaper editor, he was sentenced to life imprisonment during the 1956 revolution. But once released, he persevered as a dissident, and today he leads the Hungarian people as their acting President.

And so, the determination of men and women yearning to be free is simply proving tougher than the walls that surround them. Because of their courage, the free world is now more vast than anyone ever dared imagine. And this is our amazing new world of freedom. And with greater freedom comes greater opportunity—in the East and the West. Whether you will make your careers in the arts, business, law, or science, this can only be good news.

Just this morning, I toured the Houston office of what will be the site of our next economic summit with Canada, France, Great Britain, Italy, Japan, and Western Germany. When we meet, it will be more than just a comparison of balance sheets: it will be an act of fellowship between free nations. These nations stood with us through that long twilight struggle; through the painstaking building of alliances and the endless preparations for a war that must never be; through the human toil and the human toll, the sacrifice of resources that could have been used for gentler ends. And this is what the Cold War has cost Western Europe and America, but that sacrifice has been rewarded by the most precious gift of all: the dawn of new freedom and new hope for millions.

Today we see progress on many important fronts. As you know, Secretary Baker has been meeting this week with Soviet leaders to prepare for my summit conference with President Gorbachev beginning May 31. And while there is additional work to be done, I think Jim Baker's meetings represent a major step forward. This breakthrough should allow us to reach the important goal that we set in Malta: completing the major substantive elements of an historic strategic arms reduction treaty. In addition, we will be able to conclude other arms control measures with the Soviets, including an agreement on dramatic reduction in chemical weapons, as well as technical and commercial agreements. I am confident that the progress that we have made will allow this summit to be another solid step forward in the vital U.S.-Soviet relationship.

Today, as perhaps never before in history, freedom is prevailing throughout the world because freedom works. Freedom is not only right, it's practical. It's not only good, it is better. And it is because of the indomitable spirit of man that the day of the dictator is over. But there are also many extraordinary men and women to be found right here at home, like Felicitas Atabong, a student from Cameroon, who tonight will receive a degree in computer science. She just turned 19. And then there's Maggie Taylor, who graduates tonight with a bachelor of fine arts degree at the age of 70, or Irene Burnside, a nurse whose experience goes back to the Army Nurse Corps in the Pacific theater of World War II. And tonight she earns her Ph.D. in nursing with a speciality in gerontology.

But like them, you—all of you—have spent years learning, and now is the time as you leave this great university to spend your life doing. Make your Czech or Polish lessons work for the Citizens Democracy Corps. Put your Spanish in service of the Peace Corps. Or work with VISTA right here in our precious United States of America. Care for the AID babies. Love every child, in the hospital corridors of your own backyard in Austin to the beleaguered clinics of Central Africa. But whatever you do, live a life of adventure and meaning so brilliant that, like a Roman candle, it lights up the world. Dazzle us. Astonish us. Be extraordinary.

Once again, it is a delight to be back. God bless all of you graduates of this great university, and may God bless the United States of America. Hook 'em, 'Horns! Thank you very, very much. Thank you. Thank you all.

Note: The President spoke at 8:20 p.m. at the Neuhaus-Royal Athletic Complex on the campus of the university. In his remarks, he referred to Rita Clements, wife of Gov. William P. Clements, Jr.; Beryl Pickle, wife of Representative J.J. Pickle; Louis A. Beecherl, Jr., and Hans Mark, chairman of the board of regents and chancellor, respectively, of the university system; and William H. Cunningham, president of the university. The President also referred to the city's annual celebration of the birthday of Eeyore, a character from the Winnie-the-Pooh children's stories by A.A. Milne.

Remarks at the Dedication Ceremony for the Police Memorial in Portland, Oregon
May 20, 1990

Thank you, Chief Walker, and I just want to repeat what I told you: I've been looking forward very much to being here today, pay my respects to so many. And thank you for doing the introduction. Wonderfully brief—a wonderfully brief introduction. [*Laughter*]

And let me just say what a pleasure it is to have Bill Bennett with me. He is our leader in the Federal Government, all across the Federal Government, in the fight against narcotics. And in my view, he is doing not only a job of sacrifice but an outstanding job for our country, and we ought to be very, very grateful to him.

And also, one of our great Congressmen is here, Denny Smith, one of the people I count on in Washington in our efforts to fight crime, and also Secretary of State Roberts and Attorney General Frohnmayer, my great friend who is doing a fine job in this law enforcement field—has been for years—out front long before its time.

And Mayor Clark and friends, relatives, and all of us who are admirers of Portland's finest, it's a privilege to be with you and to officially dedicate a monument that embodies integrity, sacrifice and, above all, courage—just plain courage—qualities that define the essence of law enforcement officers and of the United States of America as well. In the Bible we read: "Greater love hath no man than this, that a man lay down his life for his friends." The men we salute today laid down their lives for us. We meet today to thank them on behalf of every American.

There will be 21 names on the Portland

Police Memorial, names like McCarthy, Owens, Palmer. They ranged in age from 26 to 68. Yet their story eclipses mere stone and masonry, as striking as they are. Each life was precious; each life very, very precious indeed. Each loss, searing and individual. They left behind fathers and mothers and children and wives.

The first to give his life, Thomas O'Connor, died in 1867. He was shot in a saloon, trying to break up a brawl. Like other cops of his day, his task was to civilize society. Six years ago, Stanley Pounds became Portland's last police officer killed in the line of duty. He knew, as we do, that our task must be to defend civility through America's system of law.

Achieving this will require character to rival these 21 policemen who gave of themselves and their lives, cops who knew that in a job where one sees too often man's inhumanity to man one could also prove man's fidelity to honor. They, like the disabled law enforcement officers here, are heroes of the great Pacific Northwest. We must salute them, remember them. But how?

First, in the most elemental sense, by recalling what they stood for—and against, as well. They were men of peace, fighting crime. They stood for good, against evil. They knew that black and white hats were not Hollywood fiction. They despised the cruelty of thugs who brutalize America's quiet, gentle, decent people.

Second, we can honor them by enacting laws which free our country from the fear of crime and drugs. When we ask what kind of a society the American people deserve, our answer is a nation in which law-abiding citizens are safe and feel safe. We must reject those who soft-pedal the need to be hard on crime.

One year ago this week, I stood on Capitol Hill before a group of law enforcement officials and announced my comprehensive package to combat violent crime. One year later, Congress has addressed part of the problem by providing the new Federal troops we asked for: new agents to arrest violent criminals, new prosecutors to convict them, and new prisons to hold them. But our job isn't finished; it's just begun. So, today, I call on the United States Congress to pass the major part of the Violent Crime Act, legislation that will back up our new lawmen with new laws, laws that are fair, fast, and final. Fair: an exclusionary rule designed to punish the guilty and not good cops who've acted in good faith. Fast: we need habeas corpus reforms to stop the frivolous appeals that are choking our courts. And final: fair, constitutionally sound death penalty provisions.

I hope by now the country knows my belief; I hope you know my belief: For anyone who kills a law enforcement officer, no legal penalty is too tough. And that goes for drug kingpins who threaten a Federal witness, a juror, or a judge. We want Congress to enact the steps needed to expand the death penalty not sometime, not someplace, but across our great country, America. And I mean now.

The Violent Crime Act will achieve these reforms. And yet for the past year it's gathered dust in the House, spawned weak imitations in the Senate. America deserves better, and so do the 163 police officers who died last year. And tomorrow the Senate begins debate on our crime legislation, and I call on it to honor the memory of police, both living and dead.

Now, I know some say there are reasons for crime, and I say there's never an excuse. And, yes, we support programs for rehabilitation and recovery—we should. We do. We support education, the goal of which is to keep people off drugs and away from crime. And we support counseling and other steps to prevent crime. But we cannot and we must not neglect law enforcement. When it comes to understanding, I say let's have a little more understanding and caring for the victims of crime and certainly for our law enforcement officers. And that is why our Violent Crime Act is based on three principles: Criminals must understand that if they commit crimes they will be caught; and if caught, they will be prosecuted; and if convicted, they will be punished. By taking hoods off the streets, we can, and must, take back the streets.

Already, we've acted administratively to ensure no deals when criminals use a gun. Our Violent Crime Act goes still further. Remember, it does no good to send law troops into battle wearing handcuffs. And so, I urge the Senate and, in coming weeks, the House to act quickly and build America up by opposing those who would tear America down. Together, let's pass this bill and help win our war on crime.

Yet I was talking to the attorney general coming in here. Our war on the Federal level alone isn't going to get the job done—can't be won on the Federal level alone. Here in this great State, here in Oregon, as elsewhere, you know that crime is personal; it's not remote. And so, led by Denny Smith, your outstanding Congressman, you founded Oregonians Against Crime, a citizens' crime-fighting group of 115,000 law-abiding Oregonians. We can honor the heroes of the great Pacific Northwest by doing nationally what you're doing locally.

Oregonians Against Crime successfully passed the anticrime initiative that requires repeat, violent career criminals to serve their full sentences behind bars—no parole, no temporary leave, no time off for good behavior, no weekend passes, none of this mumbo jumbo which blames the failings on the TV or on the schools or other scapegoats of society for the evil of certain individuals.

This initiative, supported by close to 1 million Oregonians, the highest vote total in this State's history, led the Oregon Legislature last year to pass a full slate of anticrime legislation, from more prison cells to tougher sentencing. You have shown the way, and every State in our country should follow. So, I call on all legislatures to boost local law enforcement through new pros-

ecutors, police, and new prisons and by toughening crime laws at the State level, including the death penalty for the killing of local enforcement officers.

This brings me then to the final way we can honor the heroes of the great Pacific Northwest. We must tell their story to generations yet unborn, like the story of two men who are with us today. One is Sergeant Earl Johnson, shot and blinded while trying to cover his fellow officers. The other, Stanley Harmon, shot by a drug addict, now a paraplegic. To you, to your colleagues: a grateful nation salutes you.

Nothing we can say here can equal the sacrifice of Americans like these. What we can do is ensure that that sacrifice was not in vain. So, let us honor the men of this memorial, acting not only through words but deeds, to ensure a future as great as America herself. This memorial will be a monument to a nation that is right-minded and resolute, a people at once unafraid and free. It's my great privilege to now open the tribute to the greatest heroes any country could have: the Portland Police Memorial.

God bless them, and God bless the United States of America. Thank you all very, very much.

Note: The President spoke at 4:35 p.m. at Memorial Coliseum. In his remarks, he referred to William J. Bennett, Director of National Drug Control Policy; Barbara Roberts, secretary of state of Oregon; and David Frohnmayer, State attorney general and Republican gubernatorial candidate.

Exchange With Reporters During a Meeting With Representative Denny Smith in Portland, Oregon
May 20, 1990

Northern Spotted Owl

Q. Hi, how are you? What are you going to do with——

The President. I'm not taking any questions here. This is what they call a photo opportunity, and I'm not taking questions,

especially on Sunday. Denny might.

Q. Denny, you're making some announcement after this, can you clue us in to what it might be?

Representative Smith. Well, it depends on how hard I'm able to twist his arm.

Q. What might it be?

Representative Smith. We've got a real big problem here with the timber supply because of the threatened and endangered species of the spotted owl, and it's important we get a fair hearing and get the opportunity to know whether we're going to have any jobs in the forest industry here.

Q. Mr. President, what's your inclination on that?

The President. My inclination is that we have a balanced policy. There's a lot of people whose livelihood is threatened out here, and I want to hear more about it from this Congressman who's been in the lead on this subject. And I've said that before, I'll say it again at the breakfast tomorrow, and I've been saying that in terms of the environment I want to be known as an environmental President, but I also want to be one who's concerned about a person's ability to hold a job and have a job. And there's a lot

at stake here on this question. One of the things I'm doing is listening very careful. I listen to the Attorney General. And Dave Frohnmayer, in whom I have great confidence, and Denny Smith—been out in front on this question a long time. So, though we had law enforcement at the last event, an area that both of them have had leadership roles in, now we've got some economic questions and some environmental questions. And so, we're listening to find out all I can about it.

Thank you, gang, for your understanding.

Note: The exchange took place at approximately 5:20 p.m. at the Portland Hilton Hotel. Denny Smith was the U.S. Representative for Oregon's Fifth District. David Frohnmayer was State attorney general and the Republican gubernatorial candidate. The northern spotted owl inhabited an area of the State that was targeted for logging.

Exchange With Reporters During a Meeting With Congressional Candidate Bob Williams in Portland, Oregon
May 20, 1990

Northern Spotted Owl

Mr. Williams. Our position is that we support strongly what you've been saying about a balanced approach——

The President. Yeah.

Mr. Williams. ——to what you have to protect the owl.

The President. Yeah, we've just simply got to find a way not to throw any of these people out of work. We have it in this question. We have it in other areas—the Clean Air Act. And I've just determined to come down on the side of the people, but——

Q. Mr. President, what about the owl?

Q. What about the owl, Mr. President?

The President. What kind of owl are you inquiring about?

Q. The owl that they say is endangered.

The President. That's the spotted one.

Q. The cute little ones.

The President. The spotted owl. I'm interested in the owl, very much so, and I'm also interested in jobs and the American family.

So, we've got a real serious problem here, but we'll find a balanced approach. That's the one you're talking about, Sandy [Sandy Gilmour, NBC News].

Q. Yes, sir, same owl.

Q. What are you going to do with President Gorbachev? Are you taking him up to Camp David?

The President. Jessica [Jessica Lee, USA Today], this is a bona fide photo opportunity, where I take questions only on the one subject that these guys want to talk about because we're not throwing this open to yet another press conference. Okay?

Q. Mr. President, are you going to change the threatened, endangered species act?

The President. Well, we're trying to find out what is the right thing to do. I'm not sure I know the answer to that yet. Except I do know the answer is we've got to be concerned about the human equation as well as the environmental equation. And I care about the working men and women of this country and what some of these changes mean to their families. So, we're trying to sort this out, and it is not easy, believe me.

Thank you all.

Note: The exchange took place at approximately 6:10 p.m. at the Portland Hilton Hotel. Mr. Williams was a candidate for the U.S. Congress in Washington State. The northern spotted owl inhabited an area of Oregon that was targeted for logging.

Remarks at a Fundraising Breakfast for Gubernatorial Candidate David Frohnmayer in Portland, Oregon
May 21, 1990

Thank you very, very much, Dave, for that wonderful introduction. It's great to be here this morning. It's good to see you, my old friend, Governor Vic Atiyeh, and of course Representative Denny Smith, one of our anticrime leaders in the United States Congress. To Lynn Frohnmayer, Dave's strong right hand, I know she's one of the mainstays of this campaign. I had my picture taken with her family. I think half the audience—this half—is all Frohnmayers. [*Laughter*] But nevertheless, that's okay. We Bushes understand that. [*Laughter*] Thank you, Lynn, for all you do in this cause.

Oregonians have a wonderful way of making you feel at home. We had a receiving line for some who have done an extraordinary amount for this successful event. I said to one most attractive young couple, I said, "Where are you all from?" He said, "Well, we're from eastern Oregon. We're in the frozen vegetable business, but we don't do broccoli." [*Laughter*] So, I was very grateful for that—[*laughter*]—sensitivity there.

I did want to single out the man who's doing so much to lead the crusade, the fight against narcotics: Bill Bennett. We had a marvelous event yesterday where we were both privileged to honor the police in Portland. Sometimes, we take for granted their service to communities like Portland—their law enforcement people. So, Bill Bennett was with me, and you should know of the confidence I have in him and the gratitude I feel for him every day for leading this all-important national fight against narcotics.

And of course, it's always a pleasure to

join your dynamic Republican leadership: My old friend Craig Berkman, the chairman; and Marylin Shannon; Don Wyant; Frohnmayer finance chairman, always dependable, Claris Poppert; Colonel Morelock. And of course, I want to congratulate and pay my respects to and once again say hello to Norma Paulus. Congratulations on your great victory. And I know Norma Paulus will be an outstanding superintendent of public instruction. When it comes to education, I believe you'll make a great team with the next Governor of Oregon, Dave Frohnmayer. I think it's going to be good for this State.

You know, Dave, as a Texan, if I was wearing that hat, I'd take it off to the Blazers. Couldn't go home to Texas if I did, but nevertheless, I want to salute them. And really, it is great to be back here in Oregon and a beautiful State. So much to do outdoors. I'd love to get in some fishing while I'm here. The way I fish, we don't have 3 weeks to spare, however. [*Laughter*] But I do remember my last trip with some wonderful adventure, going down one of your most beautiful rivers. But I'm not here today to tell fish stories. I'm here to talk for a few minutes about the future of this State, the future of our great country.

This November, there's going to be an election to decide what kind of Governor will lead Oregon into the 1990's. And I can tell you one thing: Oregon doesn't need a Governor who needs on-the-job training. Oregonians want Dave Frohnmayer, and I'm encouraged by the strong surveys and by the spirit of his campaign.

Dave's a family man. In fact, as I said, I

just met three of his five kids—Katie, Mark, and Kirsten—and believe me, I know campaigners when I see them. One of them, Kirsten, is even one step ahead of her old man—her father. [*Laughter*] She was just elected president of her high school student body. And I know how proud Dave is of her and of all of his children.

Dave is a family man and more: a native Oregonian; Rhodes Scholar; degrees from Harvard, Oxford, and Berkeley—awesome combination there; professor of law; 49 years old; 6 years in the State house of representatives; and now in his 10th year as attorney general of this State. In 1988 he was reelected with no opposition and both parties' nominations, setting the record as the largest vote-getter in Oregon State history by winning nearly a million votes. And all this before breakfast. [*Laughter*] I wish I could stick around and see what's next.

We all have an idea of what's next. After a decade as a law professor, another decade in public life, Dave has emerged as a leader in educational excellence. Now the time has come for us to support him, to help him become an education Governor. Like Dave, our administration has made excellence in education one of the top priorities. Back in September, the Nation's Governors joined me at an education summit in Charlottesville, Virginia, to set new education goals for America—not to dictate to the States, but to set educational goals for America. And in my State of the Union Address, I announced those goals: to better assess students' performance, increase our graduation rate, produce a nation of literate adults, and make our schools drug-free, assure that all children start school ready to learn through programs like Head Start, and ensure that by the year 2000 our students are first in the world in math and science achievement.

The author John Ruskin once wrote: "Education is leading human souls to what is best and making what is best out of them." By teaching our young people well, we ensure a bright future for them in commerce or public service or medicine, high-tech industries. We make the best out of America, and we build a better America. This is our legacy of freedom to future generations, and it is one that is very important

to me as President.

Part of protecting this legacy also means keeping America safe. Dave has served this State as attorney general, protecting our schools and streets from the violence of drugs and crime. During that time, he's won six out of seven cases that he's argued before the United States Supreme Court, the best record of any attorney general in the country.

Simply put, Dave Frohnmayer is the only candidate running with the experience and the determination to stand up and fight the drug dealers and violent criminals that are threatening our neighborhoods. We need Dave's take-charge attitude to take back the streets of America.

But we will also need a strategy that involves both the State and the Federal levels. So, I've asked Congress to pass tougher laws, stiffer penalties, and increase prosecutorial powers in the Violent Crime Control Act. The U.S. Senate will take up these proposals this afternoon. So, let us call on the Senate to take the next step and protect Americans with tougher laws.

Just last week my administration also sent to the Hill new proposals to stop drugs and drug smugglers from breaching our borders, to stop them cold. We've called for more border patrol agents, extending general arrest authority so they can enforce our drug laws. We're also proposing legislation that will permit Federal judges to more swiftly deport criminal aliens convicted of drug felonies. And we will also seek the power to order airborne planes suspected of drug smuggling to land. So, our message to those who traffic in human misery is clear: Keep out of America.

To those who ask if our measures are too harsh, I say that the threat to many Americans, especially those living in the inner city, is too great. Or as Benjamin Rush, a signer of the Declaration of Independence, wrote: "There are two doors to the temple of tyranny. One is government so strong that it can do whatever it pleases without regard to justice, and the other is government so weak that it cannot protect the public from the worst among themselves."

But there is another side to the drug problem, a personal side, and so, that is why

Dave seeks the same approach for Oregon that I seek for all of America: to expand the drug treatment programs. And since I took office, my administration has proposed a 68-percent increase in drug treatment funding; and now we're asking Congress, through our new legislation, to help make those dollars work better. And we want the States to develop drug treatment plans so that the right kind of treatment reaches the people who need it, especially pregnant women and drug-affected newborns.

But it's going to take a coordinated effort by our State leaders across the country to free our citizens of the revolving door approach to criminal law, a comprehensive approach to fighting drugs and crime in this State. And that's another reason why I need Dave Frohnmayer as Oregon's next Governor.

Oregonians also want a Governor who understands this beautiful State. From the Snake River to the Pacific coast, Dave knows and loves Oregon, knows and loves its precious environment. As an outdoorsman, he's deeply concerned, as I am, about preserving and protecting our environment. It's going to take a lot of work to protect this great planet and its wildlife without throwing hard-working citizens out of a job. I reject those who would totally ignore the economic consequences on the spotted owl decision. The jobs of many thousands of people—it's a human equation—the jobs of many thousands of Oregonians and whole communities are at stake. But I also think that we ought to reject those who don't recognize their obligation to protect our delicate ecosystem. Common sense tells us to find a needed balance. And together, I am convinced that we can work to find that balance.

We also need to find a balance when it comes to clean air. I am committed to a cleaner environment, and that's why I've proposed the first major revisions in the Clean Air Act in more than a decade. I want Congress to pass a bill that will sharply cut acid rain, smog, toxic pollutants, but Congress has got to respect another kind of delicate ecology: that of jobs and opportunity. So, I call on the House not to keep America waiting for cleaner air, to pass a reasonable clean air bill in line with the

compromise that we hammered out with those Senate leaders—both sides of the aisle—not another bill that consumers and workers cannot afford.

Here in Oregon, you have a strong Republican team that we need to send back to the United States Capitol. I just can't tell you how much I enjoy working with your friend and mine, Senator Mark Hatfield— very important that he be reelected—and the Smith duo, Bob and Denny. Denny, who is with us here this morning, is a key member of our administration's efforts on Capitol Hill. All of these leaders, along with our own Bob Packwood, are tackling the problems of crime and drugs, the environment, and education. But this great team really needs a Governor back home to get the job done right.

You know, at my invitation, Dave came to the White House last fall to talk about these issues and other issues. Maybe he popped in to see his brother—and I might say, I am very proud of John Frohnmayer and what he's trying to do for this country.

But anyway, Dave's a forceful and passionate spokesman for the people of this great State. He's a fighter. He believes in the people of Oregon. He believes in the principles this State has stood for since Thomas Jefferson sent Meriwether Lewis and William Clark on their noble expedition across the unknown wilderness. They spent the winter of 1805 near the mouth of the great Columbia River, where a memorial still stands in their honor. And it was 87 years ago today that another great leader and outdoorsman, President Theodore Roosevelt, laid the cornerstone of that memorial and spoke to the people of Oregon: "Let us carry on the task that our forefathers have entrusted to our hands, and let us resolve that we shall leave to our children and our children's children an even mightier heritage than we received in our turn." Those are the words of one of the great conservation Presidents.

Well, Dave Frohnmayer is a man of integrity, achievement, and honor; a man who will leave Oregon an even mightier heritage than the one left to him. I'm proud to say that he's got a good friend in Washington pulling for him on election night. So, let's keep Oregon great; let's keep it Republican; and this November, let's make Dave Frohnmayer the next Governor of this great State.

Thank you all, and God bless you. And now you can have your breakfast. Thank you very much.

Note: The President spoke at 8 p.m. in the Grand Ballroom of the Portland Hilton Hotel. In his remarks, he referred to David Frohnmayer's wife, Lynn; William J. Bennett, Director of National Drug Control Policy; Craig Berkman, Oregon Republican Party chairman; Marylin Shannon and Don Wyant, Oregon's Republican national committeewoman and committeeman; Lt. Col. Mervin L. Morelock, divisional commander of the Salvation Army; and John Frohnmayer, Chairman of the National Endowment for the Arts. The President also referred to the Portland Trail Blazers basketball team, who had recently eliminated the San Antonio Spurs from the National Basketball Association playoffs, and the northern spotted owl, which inhabited an area of Oregon that was targeted for logging.

Remarks to Members of Self Enhancement, Incorporated, in Portland, Oregon
May 21, 1990

Well, good morning everybody. Thank you for coming out. I'm just delighted to be here to salute Self Enhancement, Inc. You've got the sign right there. And I love that motto, "Life has options." This worthwhile organization was selected as our 69th daily Point of Light, setting an example for the entire country.

Back in 1981—some of you guys were just real little ones then, some might not have even been there—Self Enhancement began as a summer camp for student athletes, and today it's a full-service program dedicated to the total development of disadvantaged young people. Some 700 young people are provided with a positive alternative to drugs and crime and their activities during school hours and after school to improve study skills; expand knowledge; and learn personal responsibility, communication, employment tips. Youngsters whose future was once bleak, can, thanks to Self Enhancement, look forward to futures bright with promise, limited only by their dreams.

And Self Enhancement is providing what these young people need most: not money or a job but something worth so much more, a sense of dignity and self-worth. This group teaches them to believe in themselves and to care about themselves. Once these youngsters find the greatness within them, there can be absolutely no stopping them.

So, keep up the great work. To all of you adults connected with this program, you have my profound thanks and the gratitude of our country, and to all you kids involved, stay in there and get the job done. You've got great and exciting lives ahead of you.

Thanks for coming out to say hello. Thank you all very much.

Note: The President spoke at 8:53 a.m. at Portland International Airport prior to his departure for Los Angeles, CA.

Remarks to Oakwood Community Members in Los Angeles, California
May 21, 1990

Well, it's a beautiful day, and I'm delighted to be here. Thank you, Foster Webster, for inviting me into your home today. I'm pleased to have with me today Director Bill Bennett, who's doing such an outstanding job leading our country's fight against drugs. And of course, another leader in that fight, your own great United States Senator, Pete Wilson. But here in Los Angeles you also have a talented and dedicated chief of police, a man I respect greatly, Daryl Gates, with us here today—doing a great job and doing it right.

I also want to mention Jim Hahn with us, your city attorney, and your city councilperson Ruth Galenter, here today. Thank you to the community of Oakwood for this welcome and for the extraordinary example of neighborhood unity and dedication which you set for us all. You're truly a Point of Light. Daryl Gates says that's no point of light: this is a beacon of light for the entire country, leading others out of the darkness.

The world which we see now from Mr. Webster's front yard is a good one. Carved on the face of this community is a message of family and future. We see a neighborhood united no longer out of fear but out of strength. This world is one of hope, but the world of this community's memory is not. This vivid world which still haunts many here was a cruel one, one whose inhumanity and hopelessness dominated their lives, where drugs and crime made them prisoners of fear.

And it's from this shattered world that the members of the Oakwood neighborhood crafted a new dream. They wanted to be free in their own homes. So, working with the police, they decided to reclaim their streets, to reclaim their children, to reclaim their future. And they are succeeding.

The first time some neighbors met with the police to discuss what they could do, two police cars were parked outside a resident's home while the officers talked with the people inside. But on the corner across the street, in defiant mockery of the police, drug dealers continued to sell their poison. It was a world of drive-by shootings; of frustrated anger that exploded in gang graffiti, vandalism, armed robberies and, above all, the obsessed tragedy of drug abuse. It was a world held captive to crime; a world without center, without safety, without sense.

But since the community undertook its quest to clean up their streets, police estimate that drug- and gang-related crimes in Oakwood have declined 44 percent. The darkness of drugs, crime, and fear is being banished; and in its place shines the light of honor, respect, and family pride. When the legendary bird called the phoenix was destroyed by fire, it rose again from its own ashes, reborn stronger than ever. Oakwood is a phoenix. It's a magnificent reminder of the power of the human heart.

I want to tell you the story of two boys who grew up here right in these neighborhoods. It's not his name, but let's call the first one Michael. A few years ago, a picture of Michael might have shown him playing baseball down the block—loving the game, loving the moment. But later would come other pictures—one of him around the corner from the baseball diamond he loved, selling drugs in its shadow; another of him in gang colors, his gun blazing into the night. Today we see a final picture: His heart hollow, his eyes empty, he drags himself bitterly through the prison he now calls home. He is lost to us now. His life was as brief as the frozen image in that first photograph of innocent youth, when his eyes were looking brightly toward a future he will never see.

Yet in Oakwood, the memory of the emptiness of his lost life will last forever; so will the emptiness left by the devastation of his own neighborhood, shattered by his street-side dealing, rampages of violence, his shootings. For he was Oakwood. His life was the route to take a few years ago when you grew up here with nothing but drugs and crime and hate as your models.

But finally there came a moment when the people of this community could no longer bear what they lived with every day: the wasted lives of those who terrorize and who are terrorized. Michael may never have a second chance, but the Oakwood residents became determined that the rest of their community would have a second chance, a chance to face the sun together.

Let's call the next boy Paul. Last month, when neighbors were holding their candlelight vigil for a drug-free community, a woman noticed a little kid, a little 6-year-old boy at the side, just watching on curiously. "What's going on?" he asked. She explained that the vigil celebrated his neighborhood's rebirth. Then she asked him where his parents were. "I don't have any," he answered. It turned out he lived with his grandmother and his uncle, a drug dealer. The boy walked away. The woman thought, Well, that's the sad end of another sad story. But a little while later, as the vigil continued, she saw him again, shyly joining the others. Dressed in his best clothes, he stood in the soft light of a hundred candles, with a candle of his own in one hand, his grandmother's hand in the other.

If Oakwood had continued the way it was going, Paul, too, might have been lost to us, in the tragedy of death or the blank-eyed hopelessness of prison. Instead, he can now grow up playing on a community baseball team coached by the policemen Michael and his gang had spent their young lives taunting. He will help his neighbors paint over the violent graffiti with which Michael's gang had scarred the face of the neighborhood. He will grow up knowing that there is an alternative to drugs and crime, and its name is hope.

That's what we celebrate today. More than this community's freedom from the oppression of crime and despair, we celebrate their hope, their determination, their spirit. In a special way, when the first people decided to take back their community, they lit the first candle of hope. When more and more of their neighbors joined them, their unified spirit shone with a light that banished the darkness of despair.

Thanks to the vision, courage, and wisdom of the residents of Oakwood, we are today witnessing the wonder of a rebirth. It's more than a rebirth of community: it's a rebirth of hope, of life, and of the future. And so, today I am proud to name the Oakwood community the 148th national Point of Light for the inspiration and the example that you are setting for our entire country. Oakwood proves that no community has to accept things as they are. Americans don't have to live in fear. Crime, drugs, hunger, homelessness, and so many other social problems can be driven from every community if every community cares enough to light the candle of hope.

God bless each and every one of you for what you're doing, setting an outstanding example for our great country. And God bless the United States of America. Thank you all.

Note: The President spoke at 12:07 p.m. outside the home of Foster Webster, chairman of the Oakwood Beautification Committee. In his remarks, the President referred to William J. Bennett, Director of National Drug Control Policy.

Remarks to the Council of the Americas
May 22, 1990

Thank you for that welcome, and thank you, Secretary Baker. Jim Baker's just back from a very interesting and highly significant trip to the Soviet Union, which I'm sure you've all read about. From my standpoint, it went very well indeed. I think he's done a lot of clearing the way for what I hope will be a highly successful meeting with Mr. Gorbachev not so many days away from now. I want to thank him. Normally, he's not awake this close to his jet lag recovery—it takes him a little longer—but he was looking forward to being here. But he had a tough and grueling trip, and it's still, I'm sure, on him. But I thank you very much for being here today.

To David Rockefeller, my friend and the chairman of the Council of the Americas, I want to thank you. David came to see me a while back and told me of the emphasis that he felt should properly be placed on Central America, South America—the Americas—something he's stood for for a long time. But I will address myself to some of those concerns in a minute. But I want to thank him. I want to thank Ambassador Landau and Kim Flower; and, of course, pay my respects to my trusted right arm in the White House in foreign affairs, General Brent Scowcroft, who is head of the National Security Council; to Bernie Aronson, for whom I have great respect and with whom I personally work very closely on a lot of these matters—he, Jim and I and Brent—matters affecting our common interests here today.

I am pleased once again to speak to this most influential group, pioneers, if you will, in the private-sector effort to expand trade investment between the United States and Latin America. I'm delighted to address this gathering after what has been a remarkable year of change.

I told a group out in Oregon yesterday, I can't think of a more fascinating time in the recent history of our country, certainly in the Nuclear Age, to be President of the United States. Over the past 12 months, it sometimes seemed that the eyes of the world rest solely on Eastern Europe, on the miraculous transformation that's taken place there. Our friends in Latin America have watched these historic events unfold with inspiration, certainly with awe, but also, I know, with an unmistakable sense of anxiety—and it was this that David was talking to me about—concern that our active involvement in Europe will mean a decline in the United States interest in Latin America.

I'm here today to assure you, just as I've assured the many Latin American leaders with whom I've met, that the events of the past year have increased our interests in this region, strengthened our desire to forge a new partnership with the growing forces of freedom in Latin America, because the fact is, the great drama of democracy is unfolding right here in our own hemisphere. Think about the tremendous gains made for freedom just this past year. When I spoke here last May, the people of Panama were preparing to go to the polls, even as the dictator of Panama was preparing to steal the election. And in Nicaragua, civil war raged, the Sandinistas ruled, and the brave men and women of the Nicaraguan opposition were just beginning the long campaign that led to this year's great victory for democracy.

In Central America—Nicaragua and Panama; in South America—Paraguay and Chile. All across the Americas, today more people live under freely elected governments than ever before; and we are closer than ever before to the day when all the people of the Americas, North and South, will live in freedom. Even in Haiti, the scene of so much human suffering and anguish and turmoil, the provisional government has now announced its intention to hold free elections. This Thursday, I will be meeting with the new leader of Haiti, where we're sure to discuss ways that we can support democracy in Haiti.

In all of Latin America, only Cuba remains—Castro's island—isolated, totally out of step with the democratic tide. But today we're celebrating the anniversary of Cuban independence. And let me say with certainty that even in Cuba the dream of democracy can only be pushed back a little, only deferred; it will never be destroyed.

As we in the United States welcome our Central and South American neighbors into the ranks of democracy, we must offer them our help and something more: we must offer them our respect, the respect due one free nation from another, and the outstretched hand of partnership.

I've been working with Jim and Brent and others to strengthen our ties. Just this year alone, I've met with Presidents Barco [Colombia], Paz [Bolivia], and Garcia [Peru], at the Andean drug summit in Cartagena. It was a good meeting, incidentally. Here in Washington, I've hosted Presidents Carlos Andrés Pérez [Venezuela], Paz Zamora, Cristiani [El Salvador], and Endara

[Panama], Collor de Mello [Brazil], Calderon [Costa Rica], and Callejas [Honduras], and Prime Minister Manley [Jamaica] as well. And in each case, I've come away from our talks with a strong sense of optimism, and I believe every one of those leaders left the White House knowing that the U.S. is engaged as never before in the future of this hemisphere.

While from country to country conditions differ, we know now that our challenge is to consolidate democracy and accelerate development. That means advancing the intellectual revolution now sweeping Latin America, a movement away from stale statist doctrines; away from dictatorships of the right and the left; toward democracy, free government, free enterprise; toward the true political and economic empowerment of the people themselves.

That means encouraging, for the first time in many cases, genuine free market reform. Even in the countries that claim no kinship with communism, true free enterprise did not exist. In practice, economies were often organized to ensure the prosperity of the people in power, not to open an avenue toward upward mobility for anyone ready and willing to work.

Peruvian economist Hernando de Soto describes the maze of bureaucratic barriers that stood in the way of the entrepreneur and stifled economic growth in his country. De Soto also shows how much Lima, Peru's capital, owed its economic vitality to what he calls the informal sector, the thousands of individual and enterprising individuals doing business without the consent of the state. De Soto's prescription, and mine—is to free this economic force, unleash the million sparks of energy and enterprise, let the incentive of reward inspire men and women to work to better themselves and their families.

Already, Latin America is discovering this path. In Brazil and Bolivia, in Argentina, Venezuela, Mexico, Costa Rica, and Jamaica, free market reforms are going forward, creating space for private initiative to take hold and flourish. And as they succeed and as they reap the rewards that will follow this—I would say what will certainly be a painful transition—these nations will bring others along in their wake.

We in the United States must do all we can to ensure the future of free markets in the Americas because our nation has a stake in the economic health of this hemisphere. We know that since the late seventies Latin America's share of all U.S. trade dropped from 10 percent of all U.S. exports down to 7 percent. And yet last year, for the first time ever, two-way trade between the United States and Latin America topped $100 billion. As that trade continues to grow, so will the link between our prosperity and the prosperity of our Latin American partners.

Let me provide just a few statistics to drive home this point. Last year the Colombian economy grew 3 percent; U.S. exports to Colombia rose 9 percent. Mexico's economy grew 3 percent, and U.S. exports to that country climbed 21 percent. In Chile, with an overall growth rate of 10 percent, U.S. exports increased by triple that rate—more than 30 percentage points.

The most effective way to ensure expansion of trade between the United States and Latin America is for all countries of the hemisphere to support a successful Uruguay round. The ambitious agenda in the Uruguay round, including proposals for significant multilateral tariff reductions, will benefit our Latin American trading partners. We are committed to the expansion of trade and investment liberalization, and we seek Latin American support for these very important objectives. In addition, the strengthened debt strategy launched last spring has reinvigorated market-oriented economies and reinvigorated the reforms in Latin America. These economies help provide the needed foundation for democracy itself.

That's why I'm so pleased to report on the progress we've made this past year under the Brady plan. Mexico, Venezuela, Costa Rica have all reached agreements with their creditors on ways to reduce their debt, ways to complement their efforts to restructure their economies along free-market lines, because in the long term, the free market remains the only path to sustained growth.

We all know the private sector plays a crucial role. Taking advantage of new investment opportunities is good for business; but at this critical moment, there's something beyond the bottom line, something that can't be measured simply in terms of GNP. The role the Council of the Americas can play—expanding trade and strengthening the private sector—that role contributes not just to economic growth but to the growth of democracy itself.

Now, there is, of course, an important role for government to play as well, especially during the difficult days of transition from dictatorship to democracy. That's why, frankly, I've called on Congress to provide $800 million in emergency economic aid to Panama and Nicaragua. We have a big stake in this. This aid is critical.

A little over a week ago, I received a letter from President Chamorro, Violeta Chamorro, just 3 weeks into her term in office, telling me that Nicaragua was bankrupt. And yet, for more than 2 months now, this emergency aid has been bogged down on Capitol Hill. To give you an idea of the magnitude of this problem, in March I requested $800 million for Panama and Nicaragua, asking that this bill be finished on April 5th—April 5th. It's now May 22d, and the funds for Panama and Nicaragua have been reduced by $80 million, even though $1.4 billion in extra spending has been added to this legislation. Finally, it appears the Congress may act this week on this vital measure. For the people of Nicaragua and Panama, meanwhile, democracy hangs in the balance.

So, let me again say to the Congress: The fate of freedom rests in your hands. Do the work of democracy and pass this emergency aid package now.

Today I began by speaking about the changes that have riveted world attention on Europe. Part of the power of the story is that it can be told in intensely personal terms, as the story of the dissident playwright who is now President or of the electrician who came to symbolize his people's hopes for freedom. Democracy's advance in Latin America has produced its share of heroes, and today I'll close with three from one country alone, Latin America's newest democracy, Nicaragua.

For 4 years, beginning in 1979, the year the Sandinistas took power, Enrique Dreyfus was head of Nicaragua's Supreme Council of Private Enterprise, a private-sector group in many ways similar to this one. His criticism of Sandinista rule put him on the Sandinista black list and landed him in prison. Today, with the Sandinistas swept from power, Enrique Dreyfus is not just free from persecution, he is Nicaragua's new Foreign Minister.

In 1985 members of the Sandinista internal security force beat Sofonias Cisneros for criticizing the way the Sandinistas had politicized the schools. Today Mr. Cisneros is Minister of Education.

And on July 10th, 1988, opposition leader Myriam Arguello was beaten, taken from her home in the middle of the night by Sandinista police, tried, and sentenced to 6 months in prison. Today Myriam is President of Nicaragua's freely elected National Assembly.

These three stories underscore in personal terms the truly revolutionary political change that's taken place not just in Nicaragua but across the Americas, change that proves beyond doubt that the day of the dictator is over and democracy's day has come.

For our part, we in the United States must do all we can to help secure for all the Americas the freedom, the peace, and the prosperity we enjoy. Please, keep up, more now than ever, your important work in guaranteeing that democracy succeeds in this precious hemisphere of ours. Thank you for what you're doing, and God bless the United States of America. Thank you all very much.

Note: The President spoke at 11:30 a.m. in the Loy Henderson Conference Room at the Department of State. In his remarks, he referred to Secretary of State James A. Baker III; George Landau, president of the council; Ludlow Flower III, managing director of the council and vice president of the Americas Society; Brent Scowcroft, Assistant to the President for National Security Affairs; and Bernard W. Aronson, Assistant Secretary of State for Inter-American Affairs.

Statement by Press Secretary Fitzwater on the Killing of Palestinian Laborers in the Israeli-Occupied Gaza Strip
May 22, 1990

The President wishes to extend his sympathies to the families of the Palestinian workers who lost their lives in the tragic killings in Israel on Sunday, May 20. The President is also deeply troubled by the violent aftermath to these deaths. Besides expressing condolences to the families of all those who have lost their lives amidst the subsequent violence, the President calls upon the Israeli security forces, as well as others, to act with maximum restraint. Additional bloodshed and loss of life will only compound the tragedy.

It is not enough, however, to deplore what has happened and to call for restraint. It is essential to address the political issues that lie at the core of the region's strife. Based on experience, we believe that violence in the Middle East will continue and

possibly grow so long as there is an absence of a promising peace process that nourishes hope among Israelis and Palestinians alike.

The United States remains committed to promoting such a political process. We believe that the initiative of the Government of Israel, which the United States has been trying to implement, offers the best path to a negotiating process that would protect Israel's security, further the legitimate political rights of Palestinians, and bring about a broader reconciliation between the State of Israel and its Arab neighbors. We look forward to the quick emergence of an Israeli government that is capable of making decisions on issues of peace and is committed, just as we are, to moving ahead on the peace process.

Statement on Signing the Biological Weapons Anti-Terrorism Act of 1989
May 22, 1990

I am pleased today to sign S. 993, the "Biological Weapons Anti-Terrorism Act of 1989." This Act will impose new criminal penalties against those who would employ or contribute to the dangerous proliferation of biological weapons, and it will add teeth to our efforts to eradicate such horrible weapons. I salute the bipartisan consensus in the Congress that has demonstrated its support for this humanitarian objective and the leadership's commitment to our shared goal of destroying forever the evil shadow these weapons have cast around the world.

The United States has renounced these weapons, as have all civilized countries, by joining the Biological Weapons Convention of 1972. Scrupulous compliance with the obligations of that Convention and similar prohibitions against the use of chemical

weapons are essential to the security of all mankind. I call upon the leaders of all nations to join us in our drive to rid the world of biological and chemical weapons and to do everything in their power to stop the proliferation of these weapons of mass destruction. We must halt and reverse the threat that comes from such weapons and their proliferation. This Act that I sign today is a measured but important step in that direction.

GEORGE BUSH

The White House,
May 22, 1990.

Note: S. 993, approved May 22, was assigned Public Law No. 101–298.

Remarks at the Presentation Ceremony for the "E" Star Awards
May 23, 1990

To distinguished Members of Congress and other guests, welcome to the White House. It's a pleasure to have two of our administration's top trade team people here today: Secretary Bob Mosbacher and Ambassador Carla Hills. These two are working every single day, day and night, to open markets for American goods and services. And in my view, they're successful, and I am grateful to both of them. And I also want to single out Susan Engeleiter, head of the SBA here; and all Members of the Congress, once again, welcome.

For American business, confronting protectionist barriers is like having a door shut rudely in your face. And more and more, American business is looking to Carla to open the door and Bob to help them through it. But in the end, it is up to American business to step beyond the open door to enter foreign markets, and that's why I'm here today to present the "E" Awards, honoring American firms that have been such outstanding competitors abroad. Later on I'll let you know what the "E" stands for, but first—it does not stand for Elvis, I was asked to point out. [*Laughter*]

Before I get to the awards, let me talk trade. I believe the protectionist path leads to closed markets, lower living standards, unemployment in our country; and so, our direction is to open markets, expanding trade, and negotiating a set of clear and enforceable rules to govern world trade. And this is the path to prosperity and growth and high employment, and that's why my top trade priority for this year is an ambitious multilateral agreement. We must conclude that Uruguay round of global trade talks by December. And unfortunately, world trade has outgrown the rules of the GATT, of the General Agreement on Tariffs and Trade, that served us so well for four decades.

The United States and almost a hundred other nations, representing more than 85 percent of the world's trade, are working with us to revise and improve GATT's rules. And this is what we're striving to achieve:

First, we seek to reform agricultural trade, a market inadequately covered by GATT rules and badly distorted by subsidies and trade barriers that cost farmers and consumers alike hundreds of billions of dollars. There simply cannot be a successful conclusion to the Uruguay round without fundamental agricultural reform. Second, we want to expand market access. We challenge our trading partners to join us in creating a world of sharply reduced tariffs. Thirdly, the United States wants to curb hundreds of billions of dollars of trade-distorting subsidies. And we believe that entrepreneurs should compete on the basis of price and quality, not on the basis of government's deep pockets. Fourth, we want to ensure that the rules we have and those that we are negotiating apply to developing countries so these countries are no longer at the margin of the trading system. Fifth, we want to develop fair rules for new areas— services, investment, intellectual property— not covered under current GATT rules. Sixth and finally, we want to create swift and effective means to resolve trade disputes.

All told, we're striving to incorporate roughly $1 trillion worth of goods and services, a third of the world's trade, that is not sufficiently covered by rules of fair play. In our efforts, we will, of course, work closely with our friends in the Congress and the business community as well, especially the private sector advisers, many who are here today. But time is short; our task is great. I call on our trading partners to move these negotiations forward at the Organization for Economic Cooperation and Development meeting this month and at our Houston economic summit in early July.

This round of GATT is an ambitious undertaking, the last, best chance for the world to enter the next century with free and fair trade for all. So, let me be blunt: To the United States, no agreement is better than a bad agreement.

Even as we're driving at full speed to complete the round, the United States is also making progress in market-opening negotiations with Japan, in keeping the flow of goods and services open with Canada and Mexico, by intensifying our dialog with the dynamic states of the Pacific rim, and by ensuring that America will have access to Europe after creation of this historic single market in 1992.

We're also negotiating trade and investment agreements with the democratic governments of Eastern Europe and engaging in market-opening initiatives with Latin America. They stand to reap enormous gains from the Uruguay round and other steps to integrate their economies into this big global trading system; but the United States will also gain from their new found freedom to invent, to invest, and to imagine. Our objective is to anchor these countries in the ideal of freedom—economic as well as political freedom. And so, we're striving for free trade not just because it is good for America but because it is good for all mankind.

As the winds of freedom blow down old barriers and liberalize markets from Managua to Warsaw, we must be prepared to take advantage of this historic opportunity to compete and to win. And that's why today I directed the Economic Policy Council to undertake a Commercial Opportunities Initiative to encourage American business to move competitively into foreign markets. The EPC will implement this initiative through a working group called the Trade Promotion Coordinating Committee, TPCC, to be chaired by Bob Mosbacher, our Secretary of Commerce. This Committee will for the first time harness all the resources of the Federal Government to serve American exporting businesses. It will provide a focal point for business and industry in the markets of the world's emerging democracies. And I'm also directing the Committee to promote U.S. businesses in new or neglected markets through official Presidential trade missions, missions to be headed by the Secretary of Commerce.

And so, that is an overview of our trade picture. And now for the "E" Awards, a word. At the height of the Second World War, "E" Awards were presented to those war plants in recognition of excellence in production. In a time of peace, we used the

"E" symbol to celebrate excellence in American exports. And as it turns out, this is a very appropriate time to confer these awards.

You see this week, the Commerce Department is joining with State and local governments, international trade groups, and universities throughout the Nation to celebrate World Trade Week. And this week, I think we really have something to celebrate: last Thursday's announcement that U.S. exports in March hit $33.3 billion—a record high.

And this is yet another sign that America remains a superpower in world trade. But America's exporting strength is no accident, as all of you here today know. It's the result of the hard work of leaders like our Secretary of Commerce and our dynamic Trade Representative, Carla Hills, here with us here today, but first and foremost, it's because of the leadership of the American worker, the American farmer, the American entrepreneur.

You and all the other "E" and "E" Star Award winners that we honor today started the decade off in a winning spirit. And you've done something more than just represent your firms: you've represented American drive and creativity to the world. And for that, you have our gratitude and my congratulations and my thanks.

And so, it's a pleasure now to join Bob and Carla in presenting this prestigious award for exporting excellence to 11 outstanding companies that have earned the highest level "E" Award, the "E" Star. And now, Bob, if you will take over from here.

[At this point, the awards were presented.]

Thank you all very much. Thank you for coming, and congratulations to all these winners. Now everybody else go out there and work harder. Thanks a lot.

Note: The President spoke at 2:04 p.m. in the Rose Garden at the White House. In his remarks, he referred to Susan S. Engeleiter, Administrator of the Small Business Administration. The "E" Star Award was presented to the following individuals: Jan R. Endresen, president of Aerotech World Trade Corp.; Harvey L. Herer, president of the American Bureau of Collections; William P. Farrell, president of the American Hardware Manufacturers Association; William E. Fisher, chief operating officer of Applied Communications, Inc.; J.S. Brown III, president of Bruce Foods Corp.; Jonathan M. Kemper, president of Commerce Bank of Kansas City; Robert W. Reid, Jr., president of the Jacobsen Division of Textron, Inc.; Bill Aossey, Jr., president of Midamar Corp.; Dan Williams, president of the Mid-South Exporters' Roundtable; Herman Proler, chairman of the board of Proler International Corp.; and William F. Welsh II, president of Valmont Industries.

The Office of the Press Secretary issued a fact sheet on the same day which contained the following additional information on the Trade Promotion Coordinating Committee (TPCC):

The TPCC will for the first time unify and streamline Federal trade promotion activities, including: collection and analysis of market information; trade events, including trade missions, and identification of agents and distributors; dissemination of information on export financing; representation of U.S. business interests with officials of foreign governments and international organizations; assistance in identifying joint venture partners and foreign research and development projects; and counseling on foreign standards, testing, and certification requirements.

TPCC members include the Departments of Commerce, State, Treasury, Agriculture, Defense, Energy, and Transportation; the Office of Management and Budget; the Office of the U.S. Trade Representative; the Council of Economic Advisers; the Export-Import Bank; the Overseas Private Investment Corporation; the U.S. Information Agency; the Agency for International Development; the Trade and Development Program; and the Small Business Administration.

Nomination of William B. Milam To Be United States Ambassador to Bangladesh
May 23, 1990

The President today announced his intention to nominate William B. Milam, of California, a career member of the Senior Foreign Service, Class of Minister-Counselor, to be Ambassador Extraordinary and Plenipotentiary to the People's Republic of Bangladesh. He would succeed Willard Ames De Pree.

Since 1985 Mr. Milam has served as Deputy Assistant Secretary of State for International Finance and Development. Prior to this, he served as Deputy Chief of Mission for the U.S. Embassy in Yaounde, Cameroon, 1983–1985; Director of the Office of Monetary Affairs, 1980–1983; Deputy Director of the Office of Monetary Affairs, 1977–1980; international economist in the Office of Fuels and Energy, 1975–1977; financial economist for the U.S. Embassy in London, United Kingdom, 1973–1975; and financial economist in the Office of Monetary Affairs, 1970–1973. In addition, Mr. Milam was in training at the University of Michigan, 1969–1970; an economic officer and Mali desk officer for the Bureau of African Affairs, 1967–1969; in economic training for the Foreign Service Institute, 1967; an assistant economic officer in Monrovia, Liberia, 1965–1967; and vice consul in Martinique, French West Indies, 1962–1964. He entered the Foreign Service in 1962.

Mr. Milam graduated from Sacramento City College (A.A., 1957), Stanford University (A.B., 1959), and the University of Michigan (M.A., 1970). He was born July 24, 1936, in Bisbee, AZ. He is married and resides in Washington, DC.

Nomination of James Daniel Phillips To Be United States Ambassador to the Congo
May 23, 1990

The President today announced his intention to nominate James Daniel Phillips, of Kansas, a career member of the Senior Foreign Service, Class of Minister-Counselor, to be Ambassador Extraordinary and Plenipotentiary of the United States of America to the People's Republic of the Congo. He would succeed Leonard Grant Shurtleff.

Since 1986 Ambassador Phillips has served as the Ambassador to the Republic of Burundi. Prior to this, he served as consul general for the U.S. consulate general in Casablanca, Morocco, 1984–1986; Office Director for the Bureau of International Organizations, 1981–1984; student at the National War College, 1980–1981; Permanent Chargé d'Affaires for the U.S. Embassy in Banjul, Gambia, 1978–1980; Deputy Chief of Mission for the U.S. Embassy in Luxembourg, 1975–1978; first sec-retary at the U.S. Embassy in Paris, France, 1971–1975; economic officer in the Office of European Community Affairs, 1968–1971; and second secretary at the U.S. Embassy in Kinshasa, Zaire, 1967–1968. In addition, Mr. Phillips served as vice consul and consul for the U.S. consulate in Lubumbashi, Zaire, 1965–1967; third secretary for the U.S. Embassy in Paris, 1963–1965; and a foreign service generalist, 1961–1963. Mr. Phillips entered the Foreign Service in 1961.

Mr. Phillips graduated from Wichita State University (B.A., 1952; M.A., 1958). He attended the University of Vienna, 1956–1957, and Cornell University, 1958–1961. He was born February 23, 1933, in Peoria, IL. Mr. Phillips is married, has five children, and resides in Washington, DC.

Nomination of Thomas W. Simons, Jr., To Be United States Ambassador to Poland
May 23, 1990

The President today announced his intention to nominate Thomas W. Simons, Jr., of the District of Columbia, a career member of the Senior Foreign Service, Class of Minister-Counselor, to be Ambassador Extraordinary and Plenipotentiary of the United States of America to the Republic of Poland. He would succeed John R. Davis, Jr.

Currently Dr. Simons is diplomat-in-residence, visiting scholar, and adjunct professor of history at Brown University in Providence, RI. Prior to this, he served as Deputy Assistant Secretary of State for European and Canadian Affairs; member of senior seminar in foreign policy, 1985–1986; Director for Soviet Union Affairs at the Department of State, 1981–1985; Counselor for Political Affairs at the U.S. Embassy in London, United Kingdom, 1979–1981; Deputy Chief of Mission at the U.S. Embas-sy in Bucharest, Romania, 1977–1979; and chief of the external reporting unit in the political section of the U.S. Embassy in Moscow, 1975–1977. In addition, Dr. Simons served as a member of the policy planning staff, 1974–1975; international relations officer (MBFR and CSCE) in the Bureau of Politico-Military Affairs at the Department of State, 1972–1974; council on foreign relations international fellow at the Hoover Institution in Stanford, CA, 1971–1972; political officer at the U.S. Embassy in Warsaw, Poland, 1969–1971; consular officer at the U.S. Embassy in Warsaw, 1968–1969; Polish language training, 1967–1968; and secretary of delegation and technical secretary for the U.S. delegation to the 6th round of trade negotiations in the GATT, 1964–1967.

Dr. Simons graduated from Yale University (B.A., 1958) and Harvard University (M.A., 1959; Ph.D., 1963). He was born September 4, 1938, in Crosby, MN. Dr. Simons is married, has two children, and resides in Washington, DC.

The President's News Conference
May 24, 1990

The President. Today, after long and thorough deliberation, I have determined that MFN [most-favored-nation] trade status for China should be extended for a year. MFN is not a special favor; it is not a concession; it's the basis of everyday trade. And taking MFN away is one thing I said I would not do; that is, in doing that, take steps that would hurt the Chinese people themselves. I do not want to do that.

To express America's outrage at the tragedy of Tiananmen, the Congress and my administration promptly enacted sanctions against China. These sanctions remain basically unchanged today. And while implementing those sanctions, I have repeatedly made clear that I did not want to hurt the Chinese people. And this was a difficult decision, weighing our impulse to lash out in outrage that we all feel—weighing that against a sober assessment of our nation's long-term interests.

I concluded that it is in our best interest and the interest of the Chinese people to continue China's trade status. Not to do so would hurt the United States. Trade would drop dramatically, hurting exporters, consumers, and investors. China buys about $6 billion a year of American aircraft and wheat and chemicals, lumber and other products. Lose this market, and we lose American jobs: aircraft workers in the West, farmers in the Great Plains, high-tech employees in the Northeast.

Our economic competition will not join us in denying MFN. Without MFN, an average of 40 percent higher costs for Chinese imports will turn into higher prices for American consumers. Hong Kong weighed on my mind. Hong Kong would be an innocent victim of our dispute with Beijing. Twenty thousand jobs and $10 billion could be lost in a colony that is a model of free enterprise spirit. The United Kingdom and China's neighbors have urged me to continue MFN. Korea, Japan, Thailand, Singapore, even Taiwan made clear that MFN should be retained.

In recent weeks, China has taken modest steps that appear intended to show responsiveness to our concerns. Beijing lifted martial law in Tibet, restored consular access there, giving us a chance to judge the situation for ourselves. Two hundred eleven detainees were recently released and then their names provided for the first time. While we welcome these and earlier steps, they are, let's face it, far from adequate. And I am not basing my decision on the steps that the Chinese have taken so far.

Most important of all, as we mark the anniversary of Tiananmen, we must realize that by maintaining our involvement with China we will continue to promote the reforms for which the victims of Tiananmen gave their lives. The people in China who trade with us are the engine of reform, an opening to the outside world. During the past 10 years, we've seen our engagement in China contribute to the forces for justice and reason that were peacefully protested in Beijing. And our responsibility to them is best met not by isolating those forces from contact with us or by strengthening the hand of reaction but by keeping open the channels of commerce and communication.

Our Ambassador [James R. Lilley] came to see me here in the Oval Office the other day and told me that not only the people that he's in contact with but the students there, the intellectuals there, all favor—there in China—favor the continuation of MFN. So, this is why I've made the decision I have made.

And I will be glad to respond to questions. I understand, Helen [Helen Thomas,

United Press International], you are first.

Savings and Loan Crisis

Q. Mr. President, every day the American people read a different figure on the savings and loan debacle. What is the true figure? What does it all mean? What are you going to do about it? And what is the impact on the average taxpayer? Do you know the true figure?

The President. We don't know the impact on the taxpayer yet. We do know that we are going to protect the depositors, and that's what this is all about. It isn't protecting any savings and loan people; it is protecting the depositors. Nick Brady testified on an array of figures because we don't know a specific figure. But he gave some broad parameters yesterday that are on the record.

And what we're going to do about it is have negotiations with the Congress, and out of this I'm sure we will have an answer Congress agrees with. And incidentally, I'm pleased with the way those talks are going—that we'll figure out what to do. We can't brush this problem under the rug. It's been building for 20 years, and it is something that causes me great concern.

Q. Well, is it going to go as high as $300 billion, $500 billion? Do you have any ballpark?

The President. We don't think so. And I would simply refer you to the Secretary of the Treasury's testimony.

Trade With China

Q. Mr. President, it's been a year now since the world has watched China mow its own people down in Tiananmen Square. How can we expect the prodemocracy movement fighters around the world to have faith in the United States when they see a reward to Beijing such as the MFN?

The President. I made clear, Tom [Thomas Raum, Associated Press], I don't think this is a reward to Beijing. I think it is very important we keep these commercial contacts. I think it is in the interest of the United States that we keep these contacts. MFN is based on emigration, and emigration has continued from China at respectable levels. And so, that is why I'm making this decision.

And what irks me is when some of the people up on the Hill accuse me of being less interested than they are in human rights. I think we're on the right track here. I've cited the number of countries that agree with us. I've cited the fact that the students and the intellectuals in China itself agree with what I've just done. And so, it is not a favor we're doing. I have cited the need to balance out the interest of others, including Hong Kong, which is under enormous pressure from the refugee situation there. And so, this decision is the proper decision. And it has nothing to do with saying we're condoning human rights excesses. I took the lead a year ago at the G–7 [economic summit of industrialized nations] meeting in Paris and got our allies to join in sanctions that still exist. So, I'm glad you asked it because then I vented a spleen here.

Q. But, sir, if it's not a favor, how do you square this with our policy on denying the same status to the Soviet Union, based on the fact that they haven't codified their emigration policy?

The President. Because the MFN is related to emigration. And the Soviets have not passed the necessary emigration legislation.

Q. Mr. President, is it time now for——

The President. And China does have the proper policy.

Cambodia–U.S. Relations

Q. Is it time now, sir, for a review of our policy toward Cambodia, in light of the expressed willingness of the government there to permit international supervised elections and in light of the fact that our policy has thrown widespread condemnation for helping, directly or indirectly, the Khmer Rouge?

The President. We've seen some inaccurate reporting on whether we were sending arms in there, and we are not. And we are reviewing our Cambodian policy. It's very complicated. And, listen, anytime we can get free and certifiably fair elections, we should be encouraged by that. I'm troubled by it because it isn't clear in Cambodia at all.

Q. Were you made particularly uncomfortable, sir, by the fact that our support for the non-Communist resistance has the effect at least, since they are fighting alongside the Khmer Rouge of helping the notorious Khmer Rouge?

The President. To the degree it has any effect to help them, yes, I am uncomfortable about. But when we have this kind of compromise that has been worked out, at this juncture, I think we're on the right track. But there's a discomfort level, Brit [Brit Hume, ABC News], because of the brutality of the Khmer Rouge. And if anybody even perceives that we're trying to help those people, why, then it does cause discomfort. But I think we're on the right track. We are reviewing the whole policy now.

Lithuanian Independence

Q. Mr. President, this morning the Soviet Government, specifically the Prime Minister [Nikolai Ryzhkov], rejected Lithuania's latest compromise offer to get talks going. Are you disappointed that Moscow seems to be persisting in this hard line? And what do you plan to tell President Gorbachev about Lithuania when you see him?

The President. Michael [Michael Gelb, Reuters], I was encouraged when the Prime Minister [of Lithuania, Kazimiera Prunskiene]—having made her swing of the United States and other countries—Prunskiene went to Moscow. I was encouraged when she was received by Mr. Gorbachev. I can't tell you I'm encouraged about where it stands right now. I have told you, told the American people, that this Lithuanian situation and, indeed, the situation regarding the Baltics, whose incorporation into the Soviet Union we have never recognized, does cause certain tensions. And Jim Baker had a very frank discussion with President Gorbachev about that. He understands from Jim Baker and, frankly, from me directly how we feel about this.

So, I wish I could give you a more optimistic assessment, but the only answer to this question lies in dialog between the affected parties. And I was encouraged when Prunskiene met with Mr. Gorbachev, but I have no reason now to report to the American people further encouragement.

Q. If I could follow up: About a month or so ago, you said that you thought Mr. Gor-

bachev was showing willingness to compromise and the Lithuanians only showing some willingness to compromise. Is that still your assessment, or have you viewed a balance on that?

The President. Well, you're presenting me with some semantic difference that I did not intend to make. But I'm not here to assess blame; what I am here to do is to try to encourage dialog on this important question. It is extraordinarily difficult for both sides. And I think President Gorbachev is concerned not just about the Baltics but about other Republics. And I think the Lithuanians, understandably, are concerned about their freedom and their right to self-determination, although the Soviet Union still says self-determination is proper. They've got a difference on referendum; they have other differences.

Trade With China

Q. Mr. President, critics of this decision on China believe it is based too heavily on a blind faith that you have of those leaders based on your experience as envoy over there. What message does this send to the younger generation of Chinese leaders who are going to come along and replace those in power now?

The President. It says that economic contacts are the best way to keep the economic reforms going forward. It says that the more economic contacts we have with China, the more they're going to see the fruits of free-market economies. I've told you that the students in China, according to our Ambassador, want to see this MFN continue. And so, it should send no message other than that isolation is bad and economic involvement is good.

And the whole fact that we've had economic involvement, I think, has moved China more towards reform than if we hadn't had it. And so, I want to see it continue. And that is the message to the people because it has—some will interpret the way you've said, and I will say it has nothing to do with that. It has nothing to do with that at all. We have certain sanctions in place; they remain in place. China has got an emigration policy going that qualifies, and you have the interests of—Taiwan says keep it going, Hong Kong says keep it going. Three editorials in this country—well, maybe many, many more, I think—who were upset with the fact that I opted for executive action instead of legislation all support continuation of MFN. And those people who were on my case, if you will, about the decision I took, which I still think was the correct decision, are now saying continue MFN.

Q. You're satisfied that these students, who now say that they favor the policy, aren't doing that under some duress since the crackdown by the regime in Beijing?

The President. No, because I think you wouldn't see all these other interests out there if it was simply that. Maybe there's some pressure on them; I don't know. But that's not what our Ambassador is telling me.

Federal Budget Negotiations

Q. Your favorite subject, taxes. Some of the polls are——

The President. Texas?

Q. Taxes. [*Laughter*] Several polls, including one broadcast last night, are showing that most Americans think that there will be taxes and, in fact, they think you'll go along with taxes. And about half say they're willing to go along with taxes themselves if the case can be proven that taxes are needed. Does this give you more leeway as you make your decisions?

The President. Look, I have stated right here at this podium that I'm not going to go into the details of what might be discussed up there. I've said that there's no preconditions. I'm satisfied with the way the process is going. Indeed, I should give credit to [Representative] Mr. Gephardt for the conduct of these initial meetings. Our people— Dick Darman, Nick Brady, John Sununu [Chief of Staff to the President]—up there, all working in good faith.

And I've seen those surveys, but it is way too early to start talking about remedies here. I want to let that process go forward; and then when I get agreement, I will go out and say to the American people, Here's what we recommend. And I'm not going to prejudge it.

Q. Can I just follow that up on the timeframe?

The President. Yes.

Q. You're going to host the economic summit in Texas in early July. By that time, do you think you must have gone to the American people to suggest remedies? Do you not want to go into the economic summit and say to your fellow world leaders, Well, we really haven't resolved this, and I don't have anything to tell you fellows?

The President. I think the G–7 leaders know of my determination to do something about the budget deficit. So, I don't have the timeframe linked into progress or lack of progress by the time the summit meets in Houston.

Q. Some of the Democrats up on the Hill——

The President. Yes, Lesley [Lesley Stahl, CBS News]?

Q. ——Mr. President, say that you're ducking the tough issue by saying what you just said: that you're not going to tell the American people what's at stake.

The President. Yes, I've heard that criticism.

Q. They want you to outline the problem and explain to the American people that it's going to take sacrifice. Are you ready to do at least that?

The President. I'm going to outline the problem when we get agreement so we can go forward with the solution. If I outlined the problem now, I'd rely on some of the fact that the Congress appropriates all the money and raises all the revenues. That's their obligation. And I'm not one to dwell on surveys recently, but I will point out that people understand that the Congress bears a greater responsibility for this. But I'm not trying to assign blame. That's why I'm not doing it right now. [*Laughter*] That's why I'm not doing it. That's why I'm saying we're going to sit and talk. Because if I go out now and say what I think without keeping in mind the need to get some progress, I might say something like I just said, and I don't want to do that. [*Laughter*]

Q. They're going to come back at you today up on the Hill, and they're going to say, See, he's not showing leadership. What's your answer to that?

The President. My answer is, I am. We've

gotten these people together. I've said there's no preconditions; let's talk. And I think it's making progress. You're going to always have some people on the fringes sniping at you. That goes with this territory. But I think we're on the right track, and we'll try to do our best to get a deal.

Trade With the Soviet Union

Q. Mr. President, come back to the earlier questions about MFN for the Soviet Union. While you point out that there's no emigration law there as yet, the Soviets are moving towards that. Is there any additional—and some people would suggest Lithuania is an additional condition—under which you do not want to extend MFN at this point to the Soviet Union?

The President. Well, I think there's a political climate in this country that would make it extraordinarily difficult to grant it. But that is not a bridge we're having to cross at this juncture because the legislation is not in place in the Soviet Union.

Q. It is a bridge that you're going to have to cross when that legislation is in place, and it seems to be when rather than——

The President. Well, but let's hope there's some progress on the Lithuanian question, because I think many feel there's a direct linkage there. And I must say it concerns me.

Q. In what way, sir?

The President. Because I want to see these negotiations start, and I want to see this emigration law pass. And there's a lot of things going on that are going to affect the whole climate of the economic aspects of this summit.

Upcoming Summit With President Gorbachev

Q. I'd like to ask you about the climate of the summit. The Soviets have slowed down the negotiations on conventional arms control. You're not going to be signing a START treaty, which we've been led to believe was going to be the centerpiece of this summit. It looks like there won't be any kind of trade treaty signed. Has the summit changed from one of consolidating gains and moving ahead to just trying to get the relationship back on track?

The President. I wouldn't phrase it exactly that way. You may recall that I mentioned in here—in answer to the question, "Who's the enemy?"—instability, unpredictability; and it would seem to me that I would repeat that. And I don't want to have two ships pass in the night—Soviet Union and the United States. And we've got a lot to talk about.

I don't want to, by answering the question this way, indicate I don't think there will be significant progress on START. I hope we can move things forward on CFE. Indeed, I was heartened by what Shevardnadze [Soviet Foreign Minister] and Genscher [West German Foreign Minister] talked about yesterday. That was somewhat encouraging. Chemical weapons—I hope I've expressed with great enthusiasm and passion my desire to do something about chemical weapons, and it looks to me like we're very, very close there.

So, we've got a lot of things that I think will be seen properly as progress, but there's enormous problems that just need to be talked about where I can't say there will be an answer. And I would refer you to the highly complex question of German unification: where forces will be deployed, and whose forces will be deployed after German unification. We've got questions on borders. We've got a lot of things to discuss that might not result in a signed agreement.

Q. Considering all those things, especially the Lithuanian situation, has your personal relationship with Mr. Gorbachev changed coming into this summit?

The President. Well, I have to wait and see what he says when he gets here. But I feel that the man has got some enormous problems. He's made some enormous progress. I think he knows, from talking to Jim Baker after he got back, that we're not trying to undermine him or make life complicated for him. But we have certain differences with the Soviet Union, which I'll be perfectly prepared to talk about.

So, you know, it's a good question, and we were talking about it before coming in here. Because I don't want to overpromise, but I don't want to act like I think it's just some kind of a dance out there on this meeting because what we're going to talk about is really substantive. And I think the part where we can sit and talk at Camp David there—I'm glad the Soviets have agreed to that because I think it's in that kind of a session after which I would probably be better able to answer the question you asked about the relationship itself.

Violence in the Israeli-Occupied Territories and the Middle East Peace Process

Q. Mr. President, the conflict in Israel between the Israelis and the Palestinians seems to become increasingly violent. Do you think the Israelis at this point are acting appropriately and responsibly?

The President. I've called on both sides for restraint. I've called on the Israeli forces to show constraint. I'm worried about it. I'm troubled about the loss of human life in this area. I'm deeply troubled about—well, totally human life, but I think particularly of children in this kind of situation. The answer is to get these talks going. I will do everything I can to get the talks for peace going. And so, we're talking. I was on the phone yesterday, I think it was, with Mubarak [President of Egypt]. And we had very good talks—pre-Baghdad summit—with Ben Ali [President of Tunisia] here, who represents a friendly country. We're talking to a lot of people about how that can go. But, yes, I am very troubled by this.

Q. But, Mr. President, is there anything the United States can do with its enormous clout with Israel to push the Israelis to be more open to these peace talks?

The President. The problem we face right now is this—almost an interregnum—there's no firm decisionmaking government in place. So, we're in a bit of hiatus because of that.

Mexico-U.S. Relations

Q. Do you think that the relations with Mexico are going to be damaged now that Mexico is asking for the extradition or the return of Dr. Alvarez Machain?

The President. No.

Q. And I'd like to follow up.

The President. The answer is no. Go ahead and follow up.

Q. Yes. What can be done in that case? Are you going to return him?

The President. I'm not going to get into that because we have some matters in the

court on that question. But the reason I answer—and I wasn't being flip about it—that relationship is too important that no incident is going to disrupt it. The respect I feel for President Salinas is shared by the American people. The determination to keep this relationship that has already moved forward continuing to move forward is shared by the American people.

Today I'll be meeting with some parliamentarians, a group, incidentally, that I've belonged to 20—let's see how many—20-some years ago. And I'm sure some of these questions will come up. But I'm not going to go into anything that might conflict with the legal problem. But I did be sure that the President of Mexico knows that we did not grab that doctor and—Americans did not do that. I think that has helped somewhat.

Gun Control

Q. Mr. President, your administration has raised the likelihood of a veto of Senate legislation that bans several types of semiautomatic weapons. And we see that you're supporting Republican legislation that doesn't even include your own proposal which would have restricted the ammunition capacity of these weapons. Why is it that you insist on having a different standard for these domestically produced weapons than you do for imports?

The President. Look, Rita [Rita Beamish, Associated Press], I have not changed my position on ammunition clips. I read in the paper somewhere that we had changed it, backed off of that position. That isn't true. I sent a crime bill, however, to the Congress, and I'd like to see it enacted—a law enforcement bill. Congress knows of the difficulties. You saw it passed yesterday by one vote—this ban. I am not supporting that.

And I wish the Congress wouldn't keep adding matters of this nature. Let's get a good strong anticrime bill, and then we can have an open debate again on whatever they want to talk about. But all I can do is perfect legislation by saying, Here's what I can accept, and here's what I can't. And if they want to add something on these clips, that's fine; it would have my strong support. The automatic weapon part does not have my strong support.

Q. Mr. President, are we going to see then your administration and your people on the Hill pushing to get that provision back in a law?

The President. Consider this a strong pitch for it right now.

Federal Budget Negotiations

Q. Mr. President, what happened to your promise to balance the budget without raising taxes? Are we going to make it?

The President. Are we going to make the promise? Things are complicated out there on this subject. We're trying very hard to get a budget agreement, and that's the way it is, and we'll see how we go. And I reported I think that we've started off now, in a bipartisan nature, doing a good job. I wish we could control the spending side better. I refer you once again—I don't want to ruin the last minute getting Nicaragua-Panama passed, but I sent it up there at $800 million, and it's now $2-plus billion. But we'll keep plugging away, and I'd like to do it exactly the way I propose. I'm now enough of a realist to realize that it might not be done exactly that way.

Now, here's my problem. I have a 10 a.m. meeting with the leader of Haiti [President Ertha Trouillot], and we've got some problems there that we're trying to help to resolve. So, I can take two more. One. Two.

Arms Reduction Negotiations

Q. Mr. President, I'd like to ask about the news reports coming out, in the aftermath of the Moscow meetings with Secretary Baker, that you were not as pleased with the outcome of those talks, especially pertaining to START, as Secretary Baker was.

The President. There is no light between us on that at all. The administration has a unified position. It is a sound position. There's no point just before you sit down to say, They caved; they gave more than we did. But I am very satisfied with where we stand. All I want to do is be sure we can move forward and get these deals finalized, and we may not be able to do that. But it doesn't help for me to go out and say who gave the most, who knuckled under, who took the most heat—too much pressure. I support what Jim Baker reported to me was where we stand at this juncture in negotiations.

I'll tell you what troubles me is that we're not—somebody asked the question here— not further along on conventional forces. But the strategic arms talks are going very well. We still haven't got a firm deal, as you know.

But to get back to your question, there isn't any daylight between the White House and the State Department or the arms control community or Defense. The proposals that Jim Baker is talking about has the strong support of the Joint Chiefs and of the Secretary of Defense. So, this is very encouraging that the administration is united. Now, we're going to have some criticism. Many times you make a deal, you have editorials out there telling you exactly how it should be done. But I am confident that we're on the right track.

Follow up, and then we go over for one more to Frank [Frank Murray, Washington Times].

Q. You mentioned your concern about the stall in the conventional force talks, and some people are saying that conventional forces is now the real litmus test for Soviet intentions, given the developments in Eastern Europe. If they don't pull those troops back out of Eastern Europe, then that tells you something about their ultimate intentions.

The President. Well, I think that that's a good point and one that I expect the Soviets would want to dispel through action, because I don't get the feeling that they are opposed to CFE agreements. I do think, for complicated reasons involving Eastern Europe, that the talks haven't gone as far or as fast as I would like to see them.

But read carefully what Shevardnadze and Genscher allegedly talked about yesterday, and Genscher will be here talking about that. And maybe we can find some way at the summit or before the summit to move CFE forward. It's important, and I think it does send a bad signal if the Soviets look like they are refusing to go forward and don't want to, say, pull forces out of countries in accordance with previous deals.

Statehood for the District of Columbia

Q. Mr. President, a few weeks ago, in answer to a question about statehood for DC, you suggested that voting representation might be a better alternative and you would consider it. What consideration have you given, and what——

The President. None so far, and I am opposed to statehood for the District.

Q. Could you please explore the representation question? What did you have in mind when you talked about that?

The President. About what?

Q. About voting representation rather than——

The President. Haven't really got it in mind; interested in talking about it. Have done nothing about it at all except to continually restate my opposition—because this is a Federal city—to statehood for the District.

Q. So, the statehood bill now pending would be vetoed?

The President. Well, I haven't even seen the legislation. I don't know whether the Senate and the House have agreed on a bill. But I think my position is very clear, and I'm not going to sign a statehood bill. And so, I don't want to be under any false colors on this. I've said that over the years, and I have not changed my position.

Thank you.

Q. Sir, just to follow up on that——

The President. That's a followup on a followup. I've got to go see the President of Haiti.

Q. Yes, sir. You premised your opposition to statehood the last time on the inordinate share of Federal funds that went into the local budget. And I think it has been clarified to some extent. Could you just tell us why you're opposed to it?

The President. Marlin [Marlin Fitzwater, Press Secretary to the President] had to clean up what I said. [*Laughter*]

Q. Right. Could you tell us why you're opposed to statehood, since that is not a factor?

The President. Because it's a Federal city. That's it.

Thank you very much.

Note: The President's 48th news conference began at 9:33 a.m. in the Briefing Room at the White House.

Presidential Determination No. 90–21—Memorandum on the Renewal of Most-Favored-Nation Trade Status for China
May 24, 1990

Memorandum for the Secretary of State

Subject: Determination Under Subsection 402(d)(5) of the Trade Act of 1974— Continuation of Waiver Authority

Pursuant to the authority vested in me under the Trade Act of 1974 (Public Law 93–618), January 3, 1975 (88 Stat. 1978) (hereinafter "the Act"), I determine, pursuant to subsection 402(d)(5) of the Act, 19 U.S.C. 2432(d)(5), that the further extension of the waiver authority granted by subsec-

tion 402(c) of the Act will substantially promote the objectives of section 402 of the Act. I further determine that the continuation of the waiver applicable to the People's Republic of China will substantially promote the objectives of section 402 of the Act.

You are authorized and directed to publish this determination in the *Federal Register.*

GEORGE BUSH

Message to the Congress on the Renewal of Most-Favored-Nation Trade Status for China
May 24, 1990

To the Congress of the United States:

I hereby transmit documentation referred to in subsection 402(d)(5) of the Trade Act of 1974 with respect to a further 12-month extension of the authority to waive subsections (a) and (b) of section 402 of the act. These documents constitute my decision to continue in effect this waiver authority for a further 12-month period.

I include as part of these documents my determination that further extension of the waiver authority will substantially promote the objectives of section 402. I also include my determination that continuation of the waiver applicable to the People's Republic of China will substantially promote the objectives of section 402. The attached documents also include my reasons for extension of the waiver authority and for my determination that continuation of the waiver currently in effect for the People's Republic of China will substantially promote the objectives of section 402.

An additional document and determination with respect to Czechoslovakia will be forwarded under separate cover.

GEORGE BUSH

The White House,
May 24, 1990.

Statement by Press Secretary Fitzwater on the Renewal of Most-Favored-Nation Trade Status for China
May 24, 1990

The President informed the Congress today that he will extend China's most-favored-nation (MFN) status for another year. In notifying Congress of his decision, the President emphasized that he remains deeply concerned about human rights violations in China.

The President found the MFN decision to be an extremely difficult one. He is personally disappointed that the Chinese Government has not taken more decisive steps to demonstrate a commitment to internationally accepted human rights. While there have been modest gestures, such as lifting of martial law and renewing our consular access in Tibet and the release of 211 more detainees, these are clearly inadequate. The United States and many other Western countries and the President himself have repeatedly called upon China to initiate a process leading to real improvements in human rights. The President nonetheless concluded that not to renew MFN would harm rather than help U.S. interests and concerns. He also is determined to help and not harm the people of China, who aspire for a better and more open life.

Extending MFN will substantially promote freedom of emigration, the objective of section 402 of the 1974 Trade Act and an explicit requirement for China's continuing eligibility for most-favored-nation status. China has continued to permit emigration to the United States without interruption over the past 12 months. Approximately 17,000 Chinese nationals received U.S. visas to emigrate from the mainland in 1989, most for the purpose of family reunification.

The commercial opportunities created by MFN trade status give millions of Chinese workers and thousands of enterprises a stake in China's market-oriented reforms and opening to the West. They also make possible a wide range of contacts with Americans and American institutions that expose Chinese students, workers, teachers, and officials to our free enterprise system and political values. MFN status is essential for maintaining our commercial relationship with China and to avoid a costly trade war that will hurt business interests and consumers in both countries. In 1989 U.S.-China trade amounted to $18 billion, and China was our 10th largest trading partner worldwide.

MFN also bolsters confidence in Hong Kong's free enterprise economy, which is heavily dependent on U.S.-China trade and the health of industries in southern China. Not to continue MFN for China would deliver a terrible blow to Hong Kong, costing as many as 20,000 jobs and reducing the colony's GNP by as much as 2.5 percent. Hong Kong should not be the innocent victim of our disappointment with the Chinese administration.

We have also heard support expressed for continuation of China's MFN status from Taiwan, the United Kingdom, the Republic of Korea, Japan, and others in the Asian-Pacific region.

As we approach the anniversary of the tragedy in Beijing, we pay tribute to its victims by continuing to sustain as high a level of people-to-people contact and commerce as we can. The U.S. Government intends to press vigorously during the coming year for significant improvement in China's human rights practices. We want to see China's people enjoy the full scope of human rights to which people all over the world are entitled.

In the notification to Congress, the President reaffirmed that the sanctions against China he authorized in June 1989 remain in force. They include suspension of arms exports, the suspension of high-level government exchanges, and opposition to all multilateral development bank loans to China except those aimed at addressing basic human needs. U.S. policy remains that normal relations with China are not possible until China takes further major steps to respect human rights and returns to the path of reform.

Statement by Press Secretary Fitzwater on President Bush's Meeting With Provisional President Ertha Pascal Trouillot of Haiti
May 24, 1990

President Bush met at 10 a.m. in the Oval Office with Ertha Pascal Trouillot, Provisional President of Haiti. President Bush expressed admiration and respect for President Trouillot and welcomed her commitment, and that of the Haitian people, to hold a free and fair election. In this regard, President Bush took note of the invitation by the Haitian Government to the U.N. and OAS to provide technical assistance and election observers. President Bush expressed hope that an election date be set soon and that the Haitian Government and Armed Forces take all necessary steps to enhance respect for human rights and ensure a secure environment for the election campaign and the balloting. President Bush said the United States will support Haiti's transition to democracy with election aid.

The two Presidents also discussed Haiti's economic situation and U.S. assistance. We have announced $18 million in PL–480 food assistance to Haiti ($6 million now and $12 million in the first quarter of fiscal year 1991) and are examining other ways to assist Haiti's development.

Remarks at a White House Ceremony Celebrating the 25th Anniversary of Head Start
May 24, 1990

Well, good morning, and welcome to this beautiful morning in the Rose Garden. And Representative Kildee's here. I appreciate your coming, sir. And to others, welcome. It's a great pleasure to have you here. Connie Horner, Mary Gall, great to see both of you. Let me congratulate you, Connie, as number two in this enormous HHS for what she's doing, and, Mary, to your continued commitment to our young.

First of all, happy 25th birthday to Head Start. Like all birthday parties, today we celebrate both where we've been and where we will be tomorrow.

In May 1965, on a beautiful spring day right here in the Rose Garden, a great idea came into being. President Lyndon Johnson first spoke of a new initiative that he would soon propose: Head Start. And he said then that the program would—here were his words—"rescue these children from the poverty which otherwise could pursue them all their lives. The project," he went on, "is designed to put them on an even footing with their classmates as they enter school."

Since that day, Head Start has reached over 11 million children, providing comprehensive development services to nearly half a million low-income children every year. Head Start provides these children not only with preschool education and social skills but with health and nutrition services as well. Virtually all of the children enrolled in Head Start get the medical attention they need, and for many children, Head Start gives them their best meal of the day.

Everyone agrees Head Start is a program that works for children by enhancing their educational performance and really fostering success in life. Head Start also works for families by offering child care and child development programs for parents, which builds self-confidence, and by encouraging a commitment to improve their lives and the lives of the children. And it works for the thousands of communities nationwide where Head Start graduates give so much right back to society by helping to build strong families and strong neighborhoods.

Today almost a third of the 80,000 Head Start staff members across America are current or former Head Start parents themselves—80,000—parents like Eugenia Boggus, here with us today, who is now president of the National Head Start Association. Where is she? You stand up. Thank you.

Or Claude Endfield of White River, Arizona. When she enrolled her child in a White Mountain Apache Indian Head Start program in 1973, she was unemployed. She became a volunteer at the Head Start center, then a Head Start teacher, and today is program chairman of the early child development department at Northland Pioneer College in Arizona. Head Start, you see, gave her the skills and confidence she needed to turn her whole life around.

But as vital as the parents and the staff are to the success of Head Start, we must especially congratulate the kids. Many—some of you kids here are grown up now—but they are grown up now, and because they were given an equal chance at the starting block, they crossed the finish line on their own and most of them winners.

Seba Johnson, for example, attended Head Start as a child in the Virgin Islands and, at the age of 14, became the first black woman skier to participate in the winter Olympics, representing the Virgin Islands. Today she lives in Nevada, where she is training for the next winter Olympics, and is volunteering her time to help celebrate Head Start's 25th anniversary.

Carlos Jimenez of Meadville, Pennsylvania, who was a Head Start student back in 1977. This year Carlos is graduating from high school, third in his class of 320. A National Honor Society member, Carlos will attend college in California this fall.

Or another example, Carl Brenner, who is with us today. Carl? Where's Carl? Right here. Oh, here's our man, right here. He's now going to be performing. Also a Head

Start alumnus. Graduated first in his high school class. Now a senior cadet out at the U.S. Air Force Academy in Colorado.

These kids earned a lot of attention with their brilliant success stories, but there are also quiet ones, special children that otherwise might get overlooked. Take the example of Timothy Combs from Buffalo, West Virginia, a child born with Down's syndrome who wasn't yet talking when he enrolled in Head Start at the age of 3. Head Start provided Timothy with speech therapy, help for his hearing problem. And 2 years later, Timothy was able to enroll in public school, where he continues to get the special attention that began in Head Start.

There are so many stories to tell and so many Americans to thank in Head Start centers all around the country. In fact, over 600,000 committed volunteers, each one a Point of Light, are giving their all to make Head Start a national treasure. The kids we have with us today are from Head Start programs throughout the Washington area. And by getting them ready to learn today, we ensure that they too will have success stories to share tomorrow.

It's because of children like these, and parents and staff like many of you here,

that at the historic education summit last September in Charlottesville I asked every Governor in the Nation to join in our commitment to quality programs like Head Start and give every poor child a chance to start school ready to learn. We proposed— our administration—the largest one-time funding increase in the history of Head Start, a half a billion dollars. And I know that the Congress will join me in giving Head Start the best 25th birthday present possible, enough—and I salute Representative Kildee in this regard—enough money to enroll as many as 180,000 more children in this successful program.

As they say, that's a gift that keeps on giving by enriching the lives of the kids, strengthening our families, and building our communities. To everyone who has supported Head Start for so many years, thank you, and God bless each and every one of you. Thank you very, very much.

Note: The President spoke at 11:04 a.m. in the Rose Garden at the White House. In his remarks, he referred to Constance Horner and Mary S. Gall, Under Secretary and Assistant Secretary for Human Development Services at the Department of Health and Human Services.

Message to the House of Representatives Returning Without Approval the Amtrak Reauthorization and Improvement Act of 1990
May 24, 1990

To the House of Representatives:

I am returning herewith without my approval H.R. 2364, the "Amtrak Reauthorization and Improvement Act of 1990."

H.R. 2364 contains an unprecedented new regulatory review requirement and represents a step backward for the entire rail industry.

This new regulatory burden would interfere with the ability of the Nation's largest freight railroads to obtain needed capital or to change existing capital structure. The provision would institute for the first time, and for the railroad industry alone, Govern-

ment review and approval of acquisitions by entities that are not actual or potential competitors, including a carrier's own management or employees. This requirement is an unwarranted regulatory roadblock to financial restructuring of the railroad industry.

There is already adequate authority to protect the public interest in acquisition situations. Acquisitions of railroads by other railroads are now closely scrutinized under existing law to prevent reductions in competition. Dispositions of rail line segments are also subject to scrutiny when appropriate. Any financing of an acquisition, whether or not by another carrier, that involves the issuance of securities or new obligations by the target carrier is subject to review as well. This review focuses on the acquisition's effect on the public interest and on the carrier's ability to provide service. Current law is therefore more than sufficient to protect shippers and the general public.

The rejuvenation of the rail industry since 1980 is due in large part to the Congress's decision to lift outdated and counterproductive Government oversight from the railroads. The result was the creation of a favorable environment for capital investment for the first time in decades. The new regulatory hurdle in H.R. 2364 would counter this progress by adding uncertainty to refinancing and by delaying the infusion of cash when it may be most needed. Further, this delay and uncertainty would likely drive up the railroad industry's cost of capital, which could ultimately jeopardize the industry's financial stability and endanger needed rail service. For no justifiable reason, the bill could inhibit the future flexibility of Class I freight railroads to use capital restructuring to adapt to ever-changing markets and economic circumstances.

Existing law is adequate to ensure protection of the public interest when railroad acquisitions are being proposed. Because H.R. 2364 would impose a new, unprecedented, and unjustified regulatory review requirement for railroad acquisitions, I am compelled to veto the bill.

GEORGE BUSH

The White House,
May 24, 1990.

Nomination of Roger Gran Harrison To Be United States Ambassador to Jordan
May 24, 1990

The President today announced his intention to nominate Roger Gran Harrison, of Colorado, a career member of the Senior Foreign Service, Class of Minister-Counselor, to be Ambassador Extraordinary and Plenipotentiary of the United States of America to the Hashemite Kingdom of Jordan. He would succeed Roscoe Seldon Suddarth.

Since 1989 Dr. Harrison has served as a diplomat-in-residence at Colorado College. Prior to this, he served as Deputy Assistant Secretary of State for Defense and Arms Control for the Bureau of Politico-Military Affairs, 1987–1989; Political Counselor at the U.S. Embassy in Tel Aviv, Israel, 1985–1987; first secretary for the U.S. Embassy in London, United Kingdom, 1981–1985; officer in charge for NATO political affairs, 1979–1981; an associate professor at the Air Force Academy, 1977–1979; and a member of the national security staff, 1975–1977. In addition, Dr. Harrison has served as a Special Assistant at the Politico-Military Bureau, 1973–1975; second secretary in Warsaw, Poland, 1970–1973; and vice consul in Manila, Philippines, 1967–1969. Dr. Harrison entered the Foreign Service in 1967.

Dr. Harrison graduated from San Jose State College (B.A., 1965) and Claremont Graduate School (Ph.D., 1979). He was born May 25, 1943, in San Jose, CA. Dr. Harrison is married, has two children, and resides in Arlington, VA.

Statement on the House of Representatives Action on Clean Air Legislation
May 24, 1990

I congratulate the House of Representatives on passage of the Clean Air Amendments of 1990 last night. The overwhelming backing it received shows that the American people strongly support steps to reduce acid rain, smog, and air toxics emissions. I am particularly pleased that the legislation is similar in approach, structure, and content to the bill the administration submitted last summer.

The bill includes an acid rain program that will permanently reduce sulfur dioxide emissions by 10 million tons while employing an innovative emissions trading system; a new program to promote clean alternative fuels in cars, trucks, and buses; and a new standard to use the best technology to cut air toxics emissions. Such provisions represent major steps forward in breaking the logjam which has existed for too long on the subject of clean air.

I especially want to congratulate Chairman Dingell, Congressman Lent, and Congressman Waxman, and the administration team of Governor Sununu, Administrator Reilly, and Roger Porter for helping to steer the legislation through the House.

While the administration remains opposed to certain provisions, such as the Wise amendment, we are confident that these can and will be addressed in conference. We look forward to working with conferees from the House and the Senate to produce quickly a final package that will help bring cleaner air to all Americans.

Interview With Martyn Lewis of BBC–1, British Television
May 24, 1990

Upcoming Summit With President Gorbachev

Q. Mr. President, your Secretary of State talked yesterday of hard choices to be made on both sides. What are the main difficulties facing you and President Gorbachev as you sit down at the table next week at the summit?

The President. Well, of course, there's a cloud of tension because of the Baltic States. I determined long ago that it was important that this summit meeting go forward and be successful, and yet I would be misleading you if I didn't say that the inability to get dialog going there between the Lithuanians and the Soviets does cause a lot of concern to a lot of us here in the United States.

Secondly, I'd like to think we can move the conventional force talks further along than they are now. I think in START [strategic arms reduction talks] we're in reasonable shape, although it won't be ready for a treaty signing. On the chemical weapons side, I think there could well be good news for the free world and everybody in the world if they share my concern about reduction and eventual elimination of chemical weapons.

The European questions are not solved by a long shot. How, for example, does post-German unification Europe look? Who will be calling the shots? What's the role for the United States in terms of stability?

So, all of these questions will be on the table, and I look forward to a very frank and full discussion. One thing I've found is Mr. Gorbachev will lay it on the table, and I think I owe it to him to let him know how we in the alliance feel and how we in the United States feel on our bilateral.

Lithuanian Independence

Q. Mr. President, taking those one at a time, Lithuania and the other Baltic States are struggling for the kind of freedom and independence that is right at the heart of the American ideal. Are you in any sense embarrassed that your pursuit of arms control success is in fact preventing you from saying what you would like to say about Lithuania?

The President. I don't think it is preventing me, because what I say about Lithuania is, Lithuania is entitled to self-determination, to determine their own future. You see, our country has never recognized the incorporation of Lithuania into the Soviet Union. But where it could be a problem is some say because we feel that way—and we do passionately—and because talks are not going forward between the Lithuanians and the Soviets, therefore you ought to not have this meeting or set this summit meeting back. I don't feel that way. But I don't think it diminishes my personal commitment to freedom and democracy because we talk with the Soviets.

I would give you an example. We talked to the Soviets when Czechoslovakia wasn't free and Hungary wasn't free and Poland wasn't free. And so, we have a broad agenda there. And I'd like to feel that Mr. Gorbachev wants to go forward with what he says he's for, that is, eventual self-determination. But I don't feel a conflict there.

Q. But if Mr. Gorbachev continues to deny the Lithuanians and the other Baltic States self-determination, the right to go independent, will you not be forced to sacrifice the arms control treaty at some stage?

The President. You know something, I've learned long ago not to answer questions quite that hypothetical, with respect, because we can conjure up a lot of scenarios, good and bad, and answer; but that I don't think is helpful on the eve of his visit here. But believe me, I will have an opportunity, as our Secretary of State did just within the last week, to reaffirm the United States commitment to freedom and to self-determination.

Q. You don't feel that you are sacrificing Lithuania on the order of arms control expediency?

The President. I don't think so. And our agenda with the Soviet Union has far more to do with a lot of other subjects, too, than just arms control. But may I answer your question with a rhetorical question? When we talked to the Soviet Union when Czechoslovakia was what we call captive nation—Hungary was and Poland was— were we sacrificing their freedom in discussing arms control with the Soviet Union? Now, the world would clearly say of course you weren't, as long as we adhere to our principle of self-determination and freedom. So, that's the way I'd respond to my critics.

Soviet-U.S. Relations

Q. And you're saying that arms control is the most important thing on your agenda, and you will go for that come what may?

The President. No, I'm not saying that's the most important. That's what you're saying or suggesting or asking me if I'm saying. We have a lot of regional problems that we discuss with the Soviet Union. We have the whole question of post-German unification Europe that is very, very important to the people in the U.K. and France and other NATO countries. We have the questions of German participation in NATO—a vital question.

So, I'm not trying to set out for you priorities. Do I think arms control is important? Yes. Are we working with diligence to try to have a good arms control agenda? Absolutely. But I can't tell you that's the only thing that drives the meetings between me and Mr. Gorbachev. I want to talk to him frankly about things in Europe and in this hemisphere, and I don't want these two gigantic ships to pass in the night because of misunderstanding.

President Gorbachev

Q. Finally, Mr. President, do you think that Mr. Gorbachev is going to survive, that he's going to be the person you'll be negotiating with in a year's time, given the pressures that he has from the democrats and the radicals on one hand and from the military on the other?

The President. I'm inclined to think the answer to your question is yes, but it is not my role as President of the United States to try to sort out who should lead the Soviet Union. In Mr. Gorbachev I see a man who has presided over dramatic changes in Eastern Europe that benefit freedom and benefit mankind, if you will, and so I give him credit for that.

I see somebody who's talking about *perestroika* and reform inside—and openness, *glasnost*—inside the Soviet Union, and I give credit for that.

But Soviet leadership is up to the Soviet people. And I don't think one's foreign policy can be determined or be predicated on one person—can't be. But I think most Western leaders feel that in Mr. Gorbachev we have a man with whom we can talk frankly, with whom we agree on many principles; a man who has many problems, internal problems, facing him—I'm talking about predominately economic problems—a man who has tried to work with us constructively on many fields. So, that's why we're going to approach this summit with

great openness, and yet there are outside events—and you mentioned Lithuania—outside concerns that put a little bit of a tension on this meeting.

But in terms of my sitting down, up at Camp David, and talking frankly with Mr. Gorbachev, he's the kind of person you can do that with. And I believe that that's useful to every country—that the United States deal in this manner with Mr. Gorbachev. But that is not to say we have no problems.

Q. Mr. President, thank you very much for talking to the audience.

The President. Thank you for coming all this way. Thank you sir.

Note: The interview began at 2:39 p.m. in the Family Dining Room at the White House.

Interview With Gerd Helbig of ZDF, German Television
May 24, 1990

German Reunification

Q. Mr. President, after Secretary [of State] Baker's visit in Moscow, it seems as if we and you can't have both at the same time speedy unification of Germany and full membership in NATO and full sovereignty. What can be done at the summit to make it more acceptable to Mr. Gorbachev?

The President. A full discussion of the unification question and then postunification Europe. And that would include Germany in NATO. I feel incumbent on me to try to convince Mr. Gorbachev that there is no threat to the Soviet Union with a unified Germany and with a U.S. presence and with Germany as a full member of NATO. Now, the Soviets don't agree with what I've just said. But here's one of the good things about this kind of a summit: We'll sit down, he'll tell me his views, and I will tell him that he has absolutely nothing to fear from that formulation.

Conventional Force Reductions in Europe

Q. The crucial point for Europe and the world powers are the reduction talks on

troops in Vienna, and they seem to be stalled. Now, what are you willing to do to get them going again and have a treaty at the end of your meetings?

The President. I was very much interested in the fact that [West German] Foreign Minister Genscher and [Soviet] Foreign Minister Shevardnadze had talks that appeared to offer some optimism on the conventional force formulation. So, Genscher will meet with our Secretary of State, and then the Secretary and General Scowcroft [Assistant to the President for National Security Affairs] and I and others who are responsible for U.S. policy will be seeing if, out of those talks, we have some hints as to what we can do on our side to move the process forward.

Very candidly, I am a little disappointed in conventional force. I thought we would have the agreement further along. It is in the interests of everyone in the free world and, I think, the Soviets to move faster on conventional force agreement. So, I'm hoping that the optimism that I detected out of the Shevardnadze-Genscher talk will give us some leads as to what we can do to encourage the Soviets to come along a little more there.

NATO

Q. You proposed this summit of NATO leaders in London in July.

The President. Yes.

Q. And major shift and change in the alliance strategy is on the agenda. Can it be far-reaching enough to be acceptable to Mr. Gorbachev?

The President. I don't know. And it's a very good question. But historically, they've seen NATO as an enemy. And we've seen the Soviets as an enemy. Today the enemy, in my view, is instability, unpredictability, not sure—lack of confidence in each other. So, if we have a NATO that has a broader mission, I believe we can convince the Soviets that that is in their interest. We've not sought territory from any country over the years. And I think they don't need to have inordinate fears of a unified Germany. So, we've got to talk all this out with Mr. Gorbachev.

German Reunification

Q. Do you think that the monetary and economic and military offers and concessions of Germany towards the Soviet Union are too generous or even dangerous?

The President. Well, I think that's a matter for Germany and the Soviet Union to work out. But I see nothing that contradicts the United States interests in anything that they have decided or might decide in that regard. We have supported German unification. We've been out front in the United States.

And you know, what's touching to me is the emotion with which many Germans have told me that their—well, I don't want it to come out wrong, but their thanks to the United States for this position. But it's the right position, and I hope the people of Germany understand that we have confidence in a unified Germany. We have confidence in the contribution that the Federal Republic has made for 50 years to democracy and to freedom. And so, when I stand up for these principles of a unified Germany, I

do it from the heart, because I believe this.

Upcoming Meeting With President Gorbachev

Q. When you last met with Mr. Gorbachev in Malta, it was anticipated that this meeting in Washington would be a big success. If not, would you consider it a major setback?

The President. No, I would not, because we're living in fascinating but rapidly changing times, and when we were talking in Malta not so many months ago, the question of the Baltic States and the Republics was not right in the middle of that TV screen. And that happened. On the other hand, the rapidity of German unification wasn't on the table then. And that happened. Some good things happen; some things that are less good happen; and some that concern us greatly, like the freedom of the people of Lithuania—that's in a difficult phase right now.

So, I approach this meeting: Here's the hand we're dealt, here's what's on the table today. Now how do we, as mature people who want peace, and we, the United States, committed to democracy—ours and others—how do we conduct ourselves in dealing with the Soviet power and with Mr. Gorbachev, who has dramatically changed things in the world and changed things inside the Soviet Union?

So, we've got some big problems here, but we also have a lot of common ground, more common ground than anyone would have dared predict even 2 years ago or 1 year ago or even when we met in Malta. So, it's a mixed bag, and I'm going to do my best to keep things moving forward on arms control, the reduction of regional tensions, seeking agreement with the Soviet Union on unification of Germany, and post-German unification Europe. There's a lot of things to discuss.

Q. Mr. President, thank you very much for your time.

The President. Thank you, sir, very much.

Note: The interview began at 2:50 p.m. in the Family Dining Room at the White House.

Interview With Christian Malar of Channel 5, French Television
May 24, 1990

Soviet Relations With the West

Q. Mr. President, thank you very much for welcoming us here in the White House first. My first question would be: Gorbachev is reluctant to take drastic decisions concerning disarmament, especially concerning the integration of the new Germany to NATO. Do you still maintain that you have to help him if he doesn't make any effort, I should say, in your direction?

The President. No, I don't think we have to help him. I think we ought to do what's, in my case, the interests of the United States, and clearly in the interests of the alliance. But Gorbachev has handled up until now change in Eastern Europe with great ability. And so, I will approach him and make my case for a Germany in NATO. But I have to sell him on the fact that this presents no threat to the Soviet Union. It doesn't present a threat; indeed, a NATO with a broader mandate, I think, helps provide for stability in Europe.

Q. But, Mr. President, do you think that Gorbachev is blocked in a certain way by, I would say, his military high-ranking chief?

The President. I don't think we know that, but that's certainly a concern. But I gather he's in pretty strong control now, but facing enormous problems. But it's not my role to figure out whether Gorbachev is having a problem with his right or his left; it's mine to deal with what's on the table. And what's on the table is a strong Soviet leader, clearly in charge, with whom we have a lot of business items.

And they range from contentious ones, like the Lithuania problem, to more reconcilable problems, like arms control, and to some other difficult ones, like a post-German unification Europe.

NATO

Q. Mr. President, you are thinking of a new structure of NATO—military NATO structure. Would you include France in it?

The President. Listen, the more France wants to be involved in that, the better it is. Now, I'm well aware of the historical problems, but, yes, I think—and I talked to President Mitterrand, for whom, incidentally, I have not only respect but affection. And so, I can talk rather frankly with him. And I talked to him about a broader role for NATO, and I had the feeling that on some of the things I was talking about he understood. I don't want to put words in his mouth, but we have the kind of relationship where I can tell him why I think an expanded role for NATO will be the best way, certainly, for the shorter run for the U.S. to make a role of contributing to stability in Europe.

Middle East Peace Process

Q. The situation is deteriorating in the Middle East. What can you and Gorbachev do to bring back peace in the area?

The President. I'm not sure that Bush and Gorbachev, working as a team, can do anything about it. I am sure that what has to happen is these talks have to get going. And our Secretary of State, supported by this President, has been doing our level best—working with Mubarak [President of Egypt], working originally with Shamir's [Prime Minister of Israel] own plan to try to get talks going. But I am very concerned about it. And I think of the needless loss of life and those—as I told a press conference today, maybe what moves me the most is the children. And you know, you see these little kids hurt, and we have to do better. But I don't think it's a U.S.-Soviet role that's going to solve this problem.

Communism and Muslim Fundamentalism

Q. What would you fear most today, Mr. President, communism or the growing of Muslim fundamentalism?

The President. Well, I haven't thought about that in terms of priorities. Communism is on the wane; it's on the way out. In our hemisphere, there's only one left, and that's Castro. And I don't know what he believes, but he darn sure can't be excited about the way things are going for good, old Communists—going down the drain. And I think when you see people have a free choice, nobody's speaking up: Hey, I want to have a Communist government. It just isn't happening. And so, I don't fear communism at all. I don't like that ideology, and so, I worry about that.

But in terms of Muslim fundamentalism, the real extremes there, I am concerned about that. We lived through a terrible time in Iran. We still have difficulties there. But I'm hopeful some day we can have better relations because I think Mr. Rafsanjani is showing a sense of reasonableness in some areas that perhaps his predecessor didn't feel he could show or didn't feel like showing. So, I worry about this problem.

Q. Mr. President, I know that you can express yourself in French. I remember in the past when I saw you for the first time.

The President. Mais non. [*Laughter*] *Je parle seulement un peu. J'ai besoin de pratiquer.* [I speak only a little. I need to practice.]

Q. Oui. But could you, before the summit, deliver a little message, short message I can understand—[*laughter*]—to the French people before the summit. What would you like to say to them?

The President. I'm afraid it would be embarrassing—[*laughter*]—and they might

think I was putting—I love the French language. *J'étudiais pendant onze ans à l'école et l'université. Mais j'ai besoin de pratiquer.* [I studied for 11 years in school and in college. But I need to practice.] But I don't want to insult the French people by making them think I speak French.

Q. The French don't speak much English. The French—[*laughter*]

The President. No, I will try. I will try—*J'essayerai faire*—to bring about—*la paix*—the peace. And to work for peace. And whether it's English or French, I have a strong feeling with Mr. Mitterrand [President of France] and others in France that we have an obligation, the French have an obligation, to work so that our grandchildren will live in peace. And I wish I could say it in French because it's a beautiful language.

Q. I want to thank you very much, Mr. President. I hope to see you again, and I wish you all the best for the future.

The President. Well, thank you for coming all the way on the Concorde. Thank you. *Grand plaisir. Merci.* [A great pleasure. Thank you.]

Note: The interview began at 2:59 p.m. in the Family Dining Room at the White House.

Statement on Signing a Bill Amending Indian Laws
May 24, 1990

Today I am signing S. 1846, a bill "To make miscellaneous amendments to Indian laws, and for other purposes." Our Constitution contemplates a special relationship between the Federal Government and Indian tribes, and I applaud the Congress for acting once again to fulfill our obligation to the tribes. S. 1846 contains many provisions that will permit Federal agencies to administer more effectively laws affecting Indians. S. 1846 also contains, however, a provision that raises a serious concern.

The Supreme Court has made clear that the Congress and the executive branch may

act to benefit members of Indian tribes, as opposed to Indians defined as a racial category, and I fully support efforts to provide such assistance. I am very concerned, however, that section 2(a)(6) of the bill authorizes racial preferences, divorced from any requirement of tribal membership, that will not meet judicial scrutiny under the Constitution. Accordingly, I am hereby directing interested Cabinet Secretaries to consult with the Attorney General to clarify and resolve this issue.

Notwithstanding this concern, I am approving S. 1846 because it does contain beneficial provisions.

GEORGE BUSH

The White House,
May 24, 1990.

Note: S. 1846, approved May 24, was assigned Public Law No. 101–301. The statement was released by the Office of the Press Secretary on May 25.

Nomination of Paul L. Ziemer To Be an Assistant Secretary of Energy
May 25, 1990

The President today announced his intention to nominate Paul L. Ziemer to be an Assistant Secretary of Energy for Environment, Safety and Health. He would succeed Ernest C. Baynard III.

Since 1983 Dr. Ziemer has served as head of the School of Health Sciences at Purdue University. Prior to this, he served in various positions at Purdue University, including acting head for the School of Health Sciences, 1982–1983; acting head for the bionucleonics department, 1982; associate head of the School of Health Sciences, 1979–1981; associate head for the bionucleonics department, 1971–1981; professor of health physics, 1969; associate professor of health physics, 1966–1969; assistant professor of health physics, 1962–1966; and a radiological control officer, 1959–1982. In addition, Dr. Ziemer has served as health physicist for the Oak Ridge National Laboratory, 1959; radiological physics fellow at Vanderbilt University and Oak Ridge National Laboratory, 1957–1958; physicist for the U.S. Naval Research Laboratory in Washington, DC, 1957; and a mathematics trainee for the U.S. Naval Research Laboratory, 1956.

Dr. Ziemer graduated from Wheaton College (B.S., 1957), Vanderbilt University (M.S., 1959), and Purdue University (Ph.D., 1962). He was born June 28, 1935, in Toledo, OH. Dr. Ziemer is married, has four children, and resides in West Lafayette, IN.

Nomination of Calvin A. Kent To Be Administrator of the Energy Information Administration
May 25, 1990

The President today announced his intention to nominate Calvin A. Kent to be Administrator of the Energy Information Administration at the Department of Energy. He would succeed Helmut A. Merklein.

Currently Dr. Kent serves as the Herman W. Lay Professor of Private Enterprise at Baylor University in Waco, TX, and director of the Center for Private Enterprise, and as an adjunct professor of law at the Baylor Law School. Prior to this, he served as a professor of economics at the University of South Dakota and chief economist for the South Dakota Legislature. In addition Dr. Kent served as vice chairman of the South Dakota Municipal Power Association.

Dr. Kent graduated from Baylor University (B.A., 1963) and the University of Missouri (M.A., 1965; Ph.D., 1967). He was born September 8, 1941, in Kansas City, KS. Dr. Kent is married, has two children, and resides in Waco, TX.

Statement by Deputy Press Secretary Hart on President Bush's Telephone Conversations With Presidents Violeta Chamorro of Nicaragua and Guillermo Endara of Panama
May 25, 1990

President Bush this morning called President Chamorro of Nicaragua and President Endara of Panama to inform them of the congressional passage of the Panama-Nicaragua aid bill.

President Chamorro and President Endara expressed their gratitude for the congressional action and thanked President Bush for his efforts on behalf of their countries. They stated that this is a major step forward in solidifying and supporting the growth of democracy in Panama and Nicaragua. President Bush expressed his support of their efforts and stated the continued U.S. desire for close relations and for the continued partnership with Panama and Nicaragua and the rest of Latin America.

President Bush will sign the aid bill as soon as he receives it. It is expected the bill may arrive as early as today or tomorrow.

Statement on Signing the Dire Emergency Supplemental Appropriations Bill
May 25, 1990

Today I have signed into law H.R. 4404, the Dire Emergency Supplemental Appropriations Act of 1990.

The Act provides $720 million in emergency funding to assist Panama and Nicaragua. I am pleased that this Act supports our efforts to restore peace and to support the emerging democracies in Panama and Nicaragua. The funds will help the citizens of these nations to rebuild their economies after years of economic mismanagement and privation. As further economic progress is made in Panama and Nicaragua, their democracies will grow stronger and add to the stability of Central America.

The Act provides additional funds for several mandatory programs, including $1.2 billion for Food Stamps and $0.4 billion for veterans' programs. The Act also funds immediate needs for several discretionary programs, including the 1990 Census, disaster relief following recent floods, Veterans Medical Care, and NASA.

I regret that the Congress has used this important legislation to enact many special interest provisions that are not in response to dire emergencies, and that Defense programs rather than domestic discretionary appropriations were used as offsets. I note that section 205 of the Act would infringe upon my constitutional authority over the conduct of diplomacy by requiring the inclusion of a particular provision in certain international agreements, and by imposing preconditions on my ability to enter into those agreements. I shall construe section 205 consistently with the Constitution and therefore shall regard it as advisory. Notwithstanding these concerns, the need to provide immediately for the legitimate emergency needs of Panama and Nicaragua is sufficient to counterbalance the Act's objectionable characteristics.

GEORGE BUSH

The White House,
May 25, 1990.

Note: H.R. 4404, the Dire Emergency Supplemental Appropriations for Disaster Assistance, Food Stamps, Unemployment Compensation Administration, and Other Urgent Needs, and Transfers, and Reducing Funds Budgeted for Military Spending Act of 1990, approved May 25, was assigned Public Law No. 101–302.

Exchange With Reporters in Kennebunkport, Maine
May 28, 1990

U.S.S. "Iowa" Explosion

Q. Mr. President, can I ask you a quick Memorial Day question?

The President. Yes.

Q. Do you believe Clayton Hartwig——

The President. Who?

Q. Do you believe Clayton Hartwig——

The President. I have no opinion on that.

Q. ——is owed an apology by the Navy?

The President. I have no opinion on it. I think they're looking into it, and I really have no judgment. But if the man is proved innocent of these allegations, clearly there should be a statement to that effect. But I can't judge it from what—I haven't read the report, and just all I've seen is the headlines on it.

Q. Do you think it's a testament of how the Navy conducted its investigation, sir?

The President. Can't assess it until I get all the facts.

Q. Have you requested one—requested a report from——

The President. They'll get that to me within about—well, I don't know how long, but clearly, I'm interested in it. I haven't requested it, but it will come to me, I'm sure.

Upcoming Summit With President Gorbachev

Q. Are you ready for Thursday?

The President. Thursday? Yes. I've got some more work to do, but I've been reading my briefing books. We have two big ones here. I've got about—almost through the first one, and I'll get the second one done tonight. And then we'll have 2 days of intensive consultations to bring us up to date on where we go. But I think I know the issues, and I'm sure that all our people do. There's nothing that's changed in the last few days.

So, German unification, Germany's role in NATO, arms control, START, conventional forces, chemical weapons, nuclear treaties. We've got some commercial agreements. We've got a discussion of their political problems and ours. And we've got a big agenda, and I'm looking forward to the meeting.

Soviet Political Stability

Q. ——for Gorbachev. Every day a new headline, things are getting worse——

The President. Well, because he has enormous problems. But it's not our business as the United States to sort out the other person's economic problems. We've got some of our own. But it is our business to understand them, to make clear to him what we can do and those things we can't do, and so, I'm taking a lot of time to try to assess the economic situation there. We had some very good briefings on that the other day by some outside experts—Steve Cohen and others.

Q. Do you agree with Secretary Baker that he's in more danger of being overthrown from below than——

The President. I don't think that's my business to sort that out. I deal with the Soviet leader that's there in place, coming to the United States to discuss these matters. And I think we spend too much time trying to figure out how long a leader in any country will be there. I mean, this man has survived. I've given him, I think, appropriate credit for the dramatic changes in Eastern Europe, conducting himself in a manner that none of us would have predicted possible 2 years ago. And so, I'll deal with him. And my own personal opinion is that he's pretty darn strong there, and I say that after talking to an awful lot of Soviet experts.

Q. Is most-favored-nation status become even more critical now, considering the economic straits——

The President. Well, it's not on the table because, as you know, there's an emigration law that's required; and there's no evidence that such a law is going to be on the agenda at this time. We thought it was, but it doesn't look like it. So, I don't think that issue will be an action item. I expect it will be talked about because as they move towards a free-market economy, trade with the West is vitally important to them. And I'd say that certain items are very important to us as well, and I've told you that the Baltic States is one situation that concerns me enormously.

We'd better get going.

Q. Do you expect any "Gorby" surprises?

The President. I don't think so. I don't know. You always hear about that. I don't think so.

You guys got the honor.

Q. Do you have any surprises for him?

The President. No. [*Laughter*]

Q. You can tell us. [*Laughter*]

The President. I hope golf doesn't come to the Soviet Union. If he has to put up with what I put up with, why, it might shatter him. These guys! [*Laughter*]

Note: The exchange began at 7:20 a.m. on Cape Arundel Golf Course. Gunner's Mate Clayton M. Hartwig, USN, was accused by the Navy of setting off an explosion aboard the U.S.S. "Iowa." Experts outside the Navy suggested that the cause of the explosion was accidental. Stephen F. Cohen was director of the Russian studies program at Princeton University.

Remarks at a Memorial Day Ceremony in Kennebunkport, Maine
May 28, 1990

Thank you, Stedman. Our thanks to our able State representative, Stedman Seavey. I see his family is here. And my thanks to those from Kennebunk High School, Kennebunk Junior High School, the elementary, and also the recording band back there. Thank you for this. And let me just tell you that Barbara Bush is looking forward to speaking at the Kennebunk graduation not so many days from now. I salute Wally Reid, who puts on this little piece of Americana every year, this marvelous parade that symbolizes not just for the people in Maine but for the people across the country what Memorial Day is all about. I salute the color guard; and I would like to draw the attention of those who maybe didn't notice it to the POW-MIA flag back here, this black flag with white symbols, because we must never forget those who are unaccounted for wherever they may be. And I also want to thank Reverend Pat Adams, my pastor, for her remarks.

Let me just say that on this very special Memorial Day, in a world literally crying out for peace, we have a lot to be thankful for. We should never forget the veterans, those who served their country well, particularly those who gave their lives. I can assert to you, as the Commander in Chief of the United States Armed Forces, that we have never had a better fighting force than

we have today; and we should be grateful to every man and woman that wears the uniform of the United States of America.

I have a special guest with me here today who is the Secretary of Transportation; and in that role, he is, as you know, the top official for the United States Coast Guard—Secretary Sam Skinner. I'd like him to just say hello here. And I guess everybody in Maine, certainly along the coast, is grateful to that fantastic service, the U.S. Coast Guard. And I might say that I know what a fantastic job they are doing in trying to save our country through interdiction from the threat of narcotics.

We thank God on this Memorial Day for all who served. I can assert to you that the day of the dictator is over. The day of the dictator is over, and democracy and freedom are winning all around the world. On this Memorial Day, I'm especially grateful to the young men who gave their lives in Panama. Panama—now joining the free countries, the countries who practice democracy right here in our own hemisphere. And I'm grateful to every one of those fine kids, those who gave their lives and those who fought with such courage.

On this special day, we think of those people who are not free, and we hope that they will have the blessings that I'm afraid too often we take for granted in this country. Stedman says, and I go—I leave here this afternoon, do a little more preparation, and then on Thursday we meet at the summit—I meet with President Gorbachev of the Soviet Union. And things have changed dramatically. There's no question that we have a better chance now for a lasting world peace, but there are still some enormous problems out there. And this country must remain strong. We must remain committed to the values that have made us great over the last 200-plus years. So, I go to the summit with open arms to welcome the President of the Soviet Union. But we must stand on our principles when we discuss world peace. We must stand on our principles when we discuss the stability in Europe or the fate of the countries around the world that yet are not free. And that's exactly what I plan to do—refurbished, I might add, by these beautiful 4 days right here in our beloved Kennebunk-port.

So, I really just came here as Commander in Chief of the Armed Forces of this country to thank God for those who serve with such distinction and such patriotism, and then, as one who served many years ago in World War II, to thank heavens for the veterans, those who sacrificed their lives and those who serve with such distinction and are with us here today and other such ceremonies all across the country. It is great to be an American. God bless the United States of America. Thank you all very, very much.

Note: The President spoke at 10:45 a.m. at Dock Square. In his remarks, he referred to Wally Reid, retired businessman and former owner of the Green Heron Inn; and Patricia Adams, United Church of Christ minister for the First Congregational Church of Kennebunkport.

Remarks at the Welcoming Ceremony for President Mikhail Gorbachev of the Soviet Union
May 31, 1990

President Bush. Friends and distinguished guests, welcome to all of you, especially our guests from the Soviet Union. It is my great honor to welcome to the White House the President of the Soviet Union, Mikhail Gorbachev.

Mr. President, just over a year ago I said that the United States wanted to move beyond containment in its relations with the Soviet Union toward a new era, an era of enduring cooperation. When we last met in Malta, we agreed to accelerate our efforts on a full range of issues. Today differences remain, of course, but in the short 6 months since the Malta summit, we've made encouraging progress. I want this summit to take us farther still, and I know that that is your view as well, Mr. President.

We've seen a world of change this past year. Now, on the horizon, we see what, just 1 short year ago, seemed a distant dream: a continent cruelly divided, East from West, has begun to heal with the

dawn of self-determination and democracy. In Germany, where the Wall once stood, a nation moves toward unity, in peace and freedom. And in the other nations of the most heavily militarized continent on Earth, at last we see the long era of confrontation giving way to the prospect of enduring cooperation in a Europe whole and free. Mr. President, you deserve great credit for your part in these transforming events. I salute you, as well, for the process of change you've brought to your own country.

As we begin this summit, let me stress that I believe we can work together at this historic moment to further the process of building a new Europe, one in which every nation's security is strengthened and no nation is threatened. Around the world, we need to strengthen our cooperation in solving regional conflicts and building peace and stability. In Nicaragua, for example, we've shown that we can work together to promote peaceful change. In Angola, our support for an early resolution of that country's tragic conflict—is a resolution acceptable to the Angolan people—is now paying off. So, let us expand this new spirit of cooperation not merely to resolve disputes between us but to build a solid foundation for peace, prosperity, and stability around the world.

In that same spirit, Mr. President, let me quote the words of one of your nation's great minds, one of the world's great men in this or any age, Andrei Sakharov. Fourteen years ago, he wrote: "I am convinced that guaranteed political and civil rights for people the world over are also guarantees of international security, economic and social progress." Sakharov knew that lasting peace and progress are inseparable from freedom, that nations will only be fully safe when all people are fully free.

We in the U.S. applaud the new course the Soviet Union has chosen. We see the spirited debate in the Congress of People's Deputies, in the Soviet press, among the Soviet people. We know about the difficult economic reforms that are necessary to breathe new vigor into the Soviet economy. And as I've said many times before, we want to see *perestroika* succeed. Mr. President, I firmly believe, as you have said, that there is no turning back from the path you have chosen.

Since our meeting in Malta, we've reached agreements in important areas, each one proof that when mutual respect prevails progress is possible. But the agreements we've reached cannot cause us to lose sight of some of the differences that remain. Lithuania is one such issue. We believe that good faith dialog between the Soviet leaders and representatives of the Baltic peoples is the proper approach, and we hope to see that process go forward.

Over the next 4 days, we're not going to solve all of the world's problems. We won't resolve all of the outstanding issues that divide us. But we can and will take significant steps toward a new relationship.

This summit will be a working summit in the strictest sense of the term, one where we mark the real progress we've made by signing new agreements and where we address the differences that divide us in a spirit of candor, in an open and honest search for common ground. In a larger sense, though, that the success of this summit depends not on the agreements we will sign but on our efforts to lay the groundwork for overcoming decades of division and discord, to build a world of peace in freedom.

Mr. President, together, your great country and ours bear an enormous and unique responsibility for world peace and regional stability. We must work together to reduce tensions, to make the world a little better for our children and grandchildren. And to this end, I pledge you my all-out effort.

Mr. President, you've brought us a beautiful day, and you've brought back Mrs. Gorbachev—that brings joy to all of our hearts. A hearty welcome to her as well. So, it is my privilege to welcome you to the White House. And may God bless our peoples in their efforts for a better world. Welcome, sir.

President Gorbachev. Mr. President, Mrs. Bush, ladies and gentlemen, comrades, thank you for this welcome. May I also greet all Americans on behalf of the peoples of the Soviet Union.

My present visit to the United States is a confirmation that Soviet-U.S. relations are acquiring greater stability, clarity, and predictability. I am convinced that both the Soviet people and the Americans approve such changes. I think that they are also properly appreciated throughout the world. Therefore, it is the great responsibility of the President and myself to make sure that the capital of trust and cooperation accumulated in recent years is protected and constantly increased.

I remember well my first visit to the United States, and not only because I saw America for the first time then. During those days in December 1987, President Reagan and I signed the treaty on the elimination of INF [intermediate-range nuclear force] missiles. That was truly a watershed not only in our relations but in the history of modern times. It was the first step taken together by two powerful countries on the road leading to a safe and sensible world.

Since then, our two great nations have

traveled a long way toward each other. Thousands of American and Soviet citizens; dozens of agencies, private companies, and public organizations are involved in political and business contacts, humanitarian exchanges, scientific and technological cooperation.

In the same years, the world around us has also changed beyond recognition. Mr. President, this generation of people on Earth may witness the advent of an irreversible period of peace in the history of civilization. The walls which for years separated the peoples are collapsing. The trenches of the cold war are disappearing. The fog of prejudice, mistrust, and animosity is vanishing.

I have come to the United States with the impressions still fresh in my mind of how our people celebrated the 45th anniversary of the victory over nazism and of my meetings with war veterans. I recently had many meetings with my countrymen. They all understand the importance of Soviet-U.S. relations. They look upon their improvement with the hope that the tragedies of the 20th century—those horrible wars—will forever remain a thing of the past. I think that this is what the Americans want, too.

Mr. President, living up to these hopes of our two nations is your mission and mine. This meeting is part of it. My colleagues and I have come to do serious work in order to make a decisive step toward an agreement reducing the most dangerous arms, which are increasingly losing their political significance, and to provide further impetus to interaction between our two countries—interaction and, of course, cooperation in solving international problems in trade, scientific, technological, and humanitarian fields; in cultural exchanges; in expanding information about each other; and in people-to-people contacts.

We want progress in relations between the Soviet Union and the United States of America. I am looking forward to meetings with the Americans and, to the extent possible, getting to know better your unique and great country.

On behalf of Mrs. Gorbachev and myself and of all those who have come with me to your Nation's Capital, I thank once again President George Bush and Mrs. Bush and all those present here for this warm welcome.

Note: President Bush spoke at 10:14 a.m. on the South Lawn of the White House, where President Gorbachev was accorded a formal welcome with full military honors. President Gorbachev spoke in Russian, and his remarks were translated by an interpreter.

Remarks and an Exchange With Reporters on the Soviet-United States Summit
May 31, 1990

The President. Well, I'll just say, at the end of a very interesting day, that the talks have gone reasonably well. The mood is very positive in the sense that I had a very good, and I mean genuinely—not in a diplomatic sense—very good, exchange for a couple hours this morning with President Gorbachev. I'm very well pleased with the ground we've covered. This afternoon's meeting—the tone was positive. Differences remain.

We talked about the German question there. I believe President Gorbachev indicated after the meeting that he didn't think the whole question of Germany would be resolved. Certainly, we're not in any position to resolve that entire question, but when he said that the differences had been narrowed somewhat—I'm taking some heart from that. And we'll continue these discussions tomorrow.

But I think, given the difficulties of some of the problems we face, the talks have gone, certainly, as well as I could have expected up to now. We still have a lot of discussion. We've touched on almost every contentious issue, as well as spelling out the areas of which we have common interest, where things are going very well between us.

So, that's the report for tonight; and tomorrow, why, we'll be able to say a little bit more. But I won't go into details because we've agreed we're going to talk about them.

Trade Agreement

Q. None of us understand why you can't sign a trade agreement if it's all wrapped up.

The President. We haven't said whether we can sign a trade agreement or not yet.

Q. Why?

The President. We haven't discussed that yet.

German Reunification

Q. Mr. Gorbachev said you've instructed the Foreign Ministers to discuss something that emerged today about Germany, sir. Could you tell us about that?

The President. No, because we agreed we wouldn't. We agreed we'd let them discuss it. I think when I heard what President Gorbachev said—that's exactly what we had agreed he would talk about. So, we're just going to stay with that guidance.

Q. When will they meet again?

The President. I don't know. Probably tomorrow.

Q. Was there some narrowing of differences that made you decide the Foreign Ministers should get together or some specific details you have them working on?

The President. That was a proposal that President Gorbachev made, and I think the Foreign Ministers need to discuss in great detail the subjects we discussed to see. But I must say, Michael [Michael Gelb, Reuters], I took some heart from that. I was encouraged by that. Our position has been stated and restated, and we'll see where we go. But I think the important point is, we've talked very frankly—no rancor there. And let's hope some of the differences have been narrowed. But when he says this whole German question will not be solved in a meeting of this nature, I would agree with that. We consult our allies, and he knows that. He knows we have a lot of

consultation. But basically, my position is the same as it was when I went into the meetings, but I'm listening very carefully—listening to their views and trying to understand their position.

Q. Did he offer something specific for the Foreign Ministers to discuss on Germany?

The President. I think they do have some specifics to discuss, but that can be discussed after they get through talking——

Q. Mr. President, did you offer any concessions? Did you give him anything in return?

The President. No. I want to stay with the guidance that we agreed on. But our position is well-known, and——

Q. You gave nothing?

The President. ——the fundamentals have not changed.

Q. You gave nothing at all?

The President. The fundamentals have not changed.

Soviet-U.S. Differences

Q. Has he taken offense to your stand on Lithuania or your remarks today in the arrival ceremony?

The President. He didn't seem to take offense to anything. He knows that we have differences. I've been very up front with him, and he's been very, very direct and up front with me. So, that's one of the good things about the meeting. Great powers have differences. Sometimes they haven't been able to talk about them in a civil way. We are talking about them in a very civil way. I commend him for that approach. It's one I like, it's one I understand, and it's one I think benefits not just the United States and the Soviet Union but a lot of other countries as well.

Trade Agreement

Q. Would a trade bill be contingent on what you hear on Lithuania?

The President. We're going to discuss the details of that—probably get into some of that tomorrow.

German Reunification

Q. Does he feel that he has a proposal to talk about on Germany—means that he is more ready to come your way than you are to his, sir?

The President. We're not dealing on that. Look, we agreed to some guidance, he and I, and I'm going to stick with it. And he did, and I think that's a good sign. We're in the middle of some discussions about where it stands.

Summit Tone

Q. Why do you think it is going so well? Both of you have talked about a really good relationship that—the two of you have talked about the hours he's spent here. Why do you think this time there has been such—is it a good chemistry?

The President. Well, I don't know. That's a good question. I feel very comfortable with him. I feel very free to bring up positions that I know he doesn't agree with. And as I've said, that hasn't always been the case. There have been times when people banged their shoes when they didn't agree. That's not the mood or the tone of this meeting. And we both realize we're engaged in very, very historic and important work here. I think when these meetings are over people in this country are going to be pleased with some of the positions he takes concerning U.S. interests. And hopefully, I can be reassuring to people in the Soviet Union about the kind of relationship we want. But the tone of it is important so that we can try to "narrow differences."

Lithuanian Independence

Q. Mr. President, does either side have a better understanding of the other's position on Lithuania now? Have you narrowed any differences?

The President. That subject has been discussed, but not in the plenary meetings and not in great detail yet. It will certainly be discussed in more detail.

Q. You said you were heartened by the discussion on Germany. Was there any reason for similar encouragement on Lithuania?

The President. As I say, that matter has not been discussed. And I can't quantify for you my hopes on each important question, and that is an important question.

German Membership in NATO

Q. Mr. President, has he backed off anything since his comment yesterday about

dictating to the Soviets?

The President. I don't recall. You mean, something he said in Canada?

Q. Yes, sir.

The President. I think when I said out there that we're dealing from positions of unique responsibility, I think he understood that I have certain respect for the standing of the Soviet Union and I'm not attempting to dictate. But I clearly am entitled to and will put forward the views of the American side as forcefully as I can. But you don't get any progress if you give the impression that you're in a situation of dictation. The age of the dictator is over. Remember my speech a while back?

Q. Mulroney [Prime Minister of Canada] seems to think that most of the West is insensitive to what the Soviets suffered in World War II.

The President. I think Mulroney, with whom I've talked twice in the last 2 days, knows very well the United States is not insensitive to the fact that the Soviets lost 27 million lives in the war. And I know Mr. Gorbachev understands that I'm quite sensitive to that. I think he's also sensitive to the fact that a lot of American kids lost their lives. It might have been that I was only one of the two of us who was old enough to remember from being there.

Q. That's why he doesn't want Germany in NATO as a military——

The President. You're putting words into his mouth.

Q. Mr. President, is there any change in his ability to negotiate——

Length of the Summit

Q. Will you have enough time in 3 days, or is that too short a period of time?

The President. Well, I don't know. I think the Camp David meeting, where we have a lot of one-on-one time, is going to be fruitful. I think we've got to do better on— simultaneous, as opposed to consecutive, translation speeds things up. And today in the Oval Office we had the longer version, so I'd like to move that up a little bit. But I guess there's never enough time when you're dealing with an agenda that is this important. We've got regional questions that we haven't touched on yet. We have more refinement on—each side to refine its views on the European questions. We have arms control that's still being talked about behind the scenes, but that he and I have not gone into. So, we've got a big agenda. Whether we'll have enough time to do everything that he wants and that I want, I don't know.

I am convinced that, out of this meeting, we will narrow differences and the two ships are less apt to pass in the night based on simple misunderstanding. And I'm convinced of that because I can talk very frankly with him. And when he talks, I listen, and when I talk, he listens. We're not shouting at each other. There's not a rancor in there. And once in a while, both of us, if we feel strongly about something, we might get a little more passionate than the rest of the time in presenting our views. But I'm very pleased with that mood of his wanting to understand the United States position, my having the opportunity to express it. And I hope he understands the receptivity on my part.

German Reunification

Q. Mr. President, may I try once more on the question of Germany, sir?

The President. You can try, but I'm not going to give you any more because we agreed with the President of the Soviet Union on the guidance—if you want me to read it to you again, I'll get my notes. I can't help you on it. Nice try. Another question, though, maybe.

President Gorbachev and Soviet Domestic Problems

Q. Mr. President, have you noticed a change in the Soviet President since Malta? Have his domestic problems constrained him at all in your talks?

The President. He's 6 months older. No, I don't really—I don't——

Q. Has he brought up his own domestic problems and offered that as a stumbling block in these solutions?

The President. No. He's not done that. He's not trying to hide anything, nor is he wringing his hands. To me, there is a certain—I don't know whether Brent [Brent Scowcroft, Assistant to the President for National Security Affairs] felt this way—but a

certain strength and confidence that was there in Malta and certainly is still there now. And you can feel that. I mean, this wasn't just a casual observation. I felt strongly about that. So, I don't feel a weakened presence or anything of that nature. I feel a man determined to do his job.

Q. Do you think there is anything you can or should do to help him in the short term?

The President. I'm going to do what's in the national interest of the United States—our security interests, our global interests. And working closely with the Soviet Union—a lot of questions—is in our interest. So, with that approach in mind, I think maybe he can go away feeling that he's got people here that are not just dealing with some innate animosity towards the Soviet Union. We're in a fantastic era of change. We focus on the problems at meetings like this; but we ought not to neglect the fact that we're sitting here, talking to the head of the Soviet Union at a time when Eastern Europe, for the most part, enjoys the democratic process and enjoys a freedom that none of us would have predicted possible. A lot of that is because of the way in which Mr. Gorbachev has conducted himself.

So, there's some problems out there. But we ought not to overlook the fact that we've come a long, long way, and there is less tension in terms of world catastrophe. But there are still some big problems. So, it's that kind of an approach that I'm bringing to these meetings.

Arms Reduction Negotiations

Q. Sir, was there any progress today on START or CFE?

Q. Conventional weapons? What about conventional? You haven't talked about that. Any problems on——

The President. That's going on, but didn't come up—the arms control agenda was not discussed today.

Q. Do you think he'll invite you to Moscow?

President Gorbachev's Meeting With American People

Q. Did you watch him when he got out of the car down there at 15th Street?

The President. No, I didn't see that.

Q. A big crowd.

The President. Was it?

Q. A big crowd. Yes. I hear he's taken your advice about parades.

The President. How was it received?

Summit Discussions

Q. When did he last indicate that he was hoping there would be more in-depth discussions? Weren't there in-depth discussions today?

The President. I thought they were in depth.

Q. He didn't seem to feel that way.

The President. I think he thinks they were in depth.

President Gorbachev's Meeting With American People

Q. Did you talk with him about the hand-shaking out on the street, pressing the flesh, working——

The President. No, we didn't discuss that.

Q. You didn't really settle anything today, did you?

President Bush's Exchange With Reporters

Q. Did you come out here because you felt you weren't in the game, and he was getting all the publicity by talking to us?

The President. Michael, I knew you'd want a debriefing. You know how I'm jealous about air time. [*Laughter*] It's one of my driving factors is to be sure you're on for 30 seconds. You know how I am. [*Laughter*]

Good seeing you guys. You've got to stop laughing. [*Laughter*]

Note: The exchange began at 6:26 p.m. in the Rose Garden at the White House.

Excerpts of White House Fact Sheets on Soviet-United States Scientific and Commercial Agreements
May 31, 1990

OCEAN STUDIES AGREEMENT

- Provides for a broad range of oceanographic research cooperation, use of port facilities in each other's countries, and far-reaching scientific exchanges.
- Intellectual property rights (IPR) provisions are included.
- Results of joint studies will be published openly.
- Shared use of research vessels will result in substantial savings for both sides.

EXPANDED CIVIL AVIATION AGREEMENT

- Total passenger and cargo flights per side would increase from 7.6 Boeing-727 equivalents/week to 15.1 immediately; to 42 on April 1, 1991; to 58 on April 1, 1992.
- U.S. airlines could increase services to Moscow and Leningrad. They would gain new rights over the North Atlantic to four additional cities and over the Pacific to two additional cities.

- Soviet airlines could increase services to New York and Washington. They would gain new rights over the Atlantic to two additional cities (with onward service to South America) and over the Pacific to two additional cities.
- Each side could designate up to seven airlines to serve the other, with no more than two passenger airlines per side serving a city pair.
- A charter article would be added guaranteeing each side annual approval of 100 charter flights over the Atlantic, within certain national constraints, and positive consideration of charter flight requests over the Pacific.
- Soviet airlines would retain unrestricted rights to sell tickets in the United States. Until Soviet currency becomes convertible for purchase of air transportation, U.S. airlines could only sell tickets in the U.S.S.R. for hard currency. To ensure U.S. sales access to Soviet

citizens in absence of ruble convertibility, Soviet airlines would sell ruble tickets on U.S. airlines equal to 8.75 percent of our airlines' round-trip capacity, and remit the profits to U.S. airlines in hard currency.

MARITIME TRANSPORTATION AGREEMENT

• The agreement commits both parties to eliminate discriminatory treatment, although it permits Soviet shippers to pay Soviet carriers in rubles as an interim measure.
• The agreement contains no provisions for cargo-sharing, but does require Soviets to charter U.S.-flag carriers for Soviet Government controlled bulk cargoes whenever U.S. carriers are available on terms and conditions equal to or better than those offered by non-U.S. carriers. U.S. carriers wish-

ing to participate in bilateral bulk trade are encouraged to inform Soviets of their interest, time availability, and price.
• The agreement establishes a forecast mechanism to trigger consultations on U.S. liner trade. The agreement goes into effect following the conclusion of first joint forecast, expected to take place within a few months of signature.
• It grants 2-day reciprocal notification access to 42 U.S. and 42 Soviet ports.
• Soviet-flag vessels are permitted to re-enter U.S. cross-trades, subject to Soviet assurances with regard to past Soviet predatory rate practices.

Note: This item contains information excerpted from three fact sheets released by the Office of the Press Secretary.

Toasts at the State Dinner for President Mikhail Gorbachev of the Soviet Union
May 31, 1990

President Bush. Friends and distinguished guests, and especially President and Mrs. Gorbachev, Barbara and I are delighted to welcome you to the White House to share bread and salt with us on this special evening.

We're now nearing the end of a momentous day, the first of 4 in this Washington summit. And tomorrow, Mr. President, comes the moment that so many have been waiting for, a day when expectations will be at a fever pitch. That's right, tomorrow Barbara and Raisa go to Wellesley College. [*Laughter*]

And back here at the White House, sir, we will meet again, this time to sign our names to a series of agreements that signify the progress that our two nations have made in forging a new relationship, agreements on everything from nuclear testing and chemical weapons to expanded contacts between the people of America and the people of the Soviet Union. These agreements are a continuation of all that began

in Malta just 6 months ago, a foundation we can build on, proof that differences can be resolved even while others remain. And let me assure President Gorbachev: Whatever deep differences divided us in the past, the United States and the American people approach every issue with a sincere belief that our two nations can find common ground. Indeed, because of our unique positions in the world, we must find common ground.

We meet at a time of great and historic change in the Soviet Union, in Europe, and around the world. Such profound change is unsettling, but also exhilarating. And we don't shrink from the challenges before us, but we welcome them, determined to build the foundations of enduring peace and security.

Mr. President, you deserve great credit for the course that you have chosen, for the political and economic reforms that you have introduced, and for creating within the Soviet Union this commitment to change. As I said this morning when I welcomed you to the White House, we want to see *perestroika* succeed. We want to see this transition now underway in the Soviet Union maintain its momentum.

Mr. President, it's said that your country is the land of possibilities. You have demonstrated the truth of that statement. And we've seen this past year that ours is a world of possibilities, that our time is a time of historic change, a time when men and nations can transform history, can turn possibility into progress, into peace. So, let us raise our glasses to our guests, President and Mrs. Gorbachev, to the growing friendship between American and Soviet people and to the possibilities now open to us, to the prospect of progress and lasting peace.

President Gorbachev. Mr. President, Mrs. Bush, ladies and gentlemen, allow me on behalf of Mrs. Gorbachev and myself and all the members of our delegation to thank you for your warmth and for the kind words of President Bush.

We share the assessment of President Bush that we have done fruitful work today, and I'm sure that as a result of this meeting our countries will go to a new level of cooperation. Even now our relations, to which history assigned such an important role in the events and lessons of the 20th century, differ dramatically from what they were before the 1985 Geneva summit. To achieve this, we have worked together.

The enemy image is becoming a thing of the past. Ideological stereotypes are fading away. We have begun to understand each other's motives. As we are changing and becoming closer to each other, we have not ceased to be different. But it turns out that that is not so bad. Quite the opposite: it is useful, for diversity is a vital force of development.

The world, too, has changed beyond recognition. It has made significant progress toward a new period of genuine peace in its long history. I think we can say with confidence that the most important and decisive step in this direction was made by our countries. Our two countries had the will, common sense, and understanding of the situation and of the imperatives of the future to embark on a long and difficult road which led from Geneva via Reykjavik, Washington, Moscow, and New York to

Malta, and now once again to Washington.

Today I would like to repeat here what I said to the President 6 months ago at Malta. The Soviet Union does not regard the United States as its enemy. We have firmly adopted the policy of moving from mutual understanding through cooperation to joint action. Today, when I was meeting some American intellectuals at the Soviet Embassy, I said to them this: "Yes, indeed, we used to be enemies, or almost enemies. Now we are, maybe, rivals, at least to some extent. And we want to become partners. We want to go all the way to become friends."

Improved Soviet-American relations have reduced the threat of war. This is the main achievement of these years. We have concluded close to 20 bilateral agreements in various fields. There has been an unprecedented expansion of exchanges among our people—and that is especially valuable—from schoolchildren to prominent personalities in the fields of science and the economy. I think that the work we have been doing together with President Bush during these days can be considered as another step toward a more humane and just world.

I cannot say yet how we are going to conclude this meeting, what the results would be. That would be premature. But I think that my talk today with the President and also the meeting of the delegations makes it possible to expect major results from this meeting, and maybe even major results, the biggest results, compared to all the other meetings in previous Soviet-American summits. Maybe I'm too optimistic, but let's wait and see. We have 2 days. I believe that maybe we will have those major results.

I feel that we're now witnessing the emergence of a general idea which is conquering people's minds on the eve of the 21st century: it is the idea of unity. To make this idea a reality is a truly monumental challenge. The world's diversity and its complex problems are such that we can only do it by synthesizing, or at least interlinking, the aspirations, values, achievements, and hopes of different nations.

In the world confronted with the nuclear, environmental, and other threats, global unity means a chance for the survival of our civilization. But mankind cannot be merely a community of survival. It should be a community of progress, progress for all, the East, the West, the North, the South, the highly developed, and the less fortunate. But today we have to rethink the whole idea of progress. Mankind's ascent toward the realization of the idea of its history should not result in irreparable damage to the environment, in the exploitation of man or entire nations, or in irreversible moral and ethical losses.

It is a difficult and novel task to build a new civilization. Coming from a country in which more than 100 nationalities live together, we know that, perhaps better than anyone else, our own house is in need of an overhaul and a fundamental restructuring along the lines of reason and justice. We are aware of the magnitude of this undertaking, unprecedented in the history of mankind.

Judging by the response of the rest of the world to our *perestroika*, we can conclude that it is a necessary and desirable element of mankind's political and philosophical potential. That is why, while rethinking that potential and restructuring ourselves, we believe that we are making a contribution to the cause of universal development and universal unity.

We have not yet completed the task of creating a durable democratic system in our country, but I am convinced that the re-

serves of our society's energy already committed to this great undertaking are enough to bring it to its completion. I can say this firmly: We shall act on the basis of our values; we shall move resolutely but prudently.

The goal of our policy is to bring our society to a qualitatively new level. This will enable us to be predictable participants in the international process, partners to all who want a secure, just, and free world. In building this world, we count on long-term cooperation of the United States of America.

The most important developments in relations between our two countries and in world politics are probably yet to come. It is important not to lose sight of our goal, to resist the temptation of trying to secure unilateral advantages. Let us move ahead while overcoming both current and future problems and roadblocks. Let us cooperate and work together.

To the health of Mrs. Barbara Bush and to your health, Mr. President, to the success and well-being of all those present here, to a life worthy of today, and to our common and better future. Thank you.

Note: The President spoke at 8:20 p.m. in the State Dining Room at the White House. President Gorbachev spoke in Russian, and his remarks were translated by an interpreter.

Exchange With Reporters Following a Meeting With President Mikhail Gorbachev of the Soviet Union
June 1, 1990

President Bush. We had a very good talk this morning, very good talk.

President Gorbachev. Yes, it was a good talk. The important thing is that we get results. And I think that we will get results, specific results.

Q. ——press out here, Soviet press. [*Laughter*]

President Gorbachev. I hope so.

President Bush. Certainly, there will be on some things. You can put that in the

bank.

Q. There are problems; there are complications?

President Bush. We always have complications, but we measure it not by whether the glass is half empty or the glass is half full.

President Gorbachev. I will say this: We have gone two-thirds of the road in our talks. We have had mostly one-on-one discussions with the President. Right now we were discussing the central question of the 50-percent START reductions, and in this the main—the forces of our delegations participated, and we made a lot of progress. We have also tomorrow. I think we'll negotiate in a good setting. There's a lot of fresh air there, and I think we'll work and think more expansively, and I think that we'll complete our discussions successfully.

I think we can already say that this meeting is going to be an important one. And it can become even more productive and more important. Whether it is just important or very important, that will be decided tomorrow.

Q. [Inaudible]

President Bush. ——significant accomplishment if it all works out. It will be viewed by the American people anyway as enormously important. So, I felt positive about that one.

Thank you all.

Q. Thank you. We very much appreciate it.

President Bush. Not at all. See you later.

Note: The exchange began shortly after 1 p.m. in the Rose Garden at the White House. President Gorbachev spoke in Russian, and his remarks were translated by an interpreter. A tape was not available for verification of the content of the exchange.

Remarks on Signing Soviet-United States Bilateral Agreements
June 1, 1990

President Bush. President Gorbachev, again, welcome to the White House. Mr. President, you and I set a course 6 months ago off the island nation of Malta. And at that time we agreed on an agenda, much of which was completed for this week's summit. Of course, our Malta agenda remains unfinished, but we've made great progress in the last 6 months and in the last 2 days.

We're about to sign agreements concerning many areas of vital interest to our countries and to the world, and to record specific understandings in joint statements that are being published today.

First, we'll sign a bilateral agreement that will, for the first time, eliminate the great majority of the chemical weapons that our countries have stockpiled over the years. And let this landmark agreement quickly lead to a global ban on chemical weapons.

Secondly, we will be signing protocols on limiting nuclear testing. After long, sometimes arduous negotiations, we both agreed on unprecedented improvements for on-site verification of the Threshold Test Ban Treaty and the Peaceful Nuclear Explosions Treaty.

Third, we will sign a major new agreement that updates and expands our 1973 agreement on the peaceful uses of atomic energy. This new agreement provides for substantial U.S.-Soviet cooperation in atomic energy research and civilian nuclear safety.

In addition, President Gorbachev and I are issuing a joint statement recording major agreed provisions of a strategic arms reduction treaty as well as a joint statement in which we agree to future negotiations on nuclear and space arms designed to enhance stability and reduce the risk of war. We're also issuing a statement on the conventional armed forces in Europe, committing us to intensify the pace of the Vienna negotiations and to reach rapid agreement on all outstanding issues. You see, we agree that a CFE treaty is an indispensable foundation for the future of European security.

There are many other agreements the United States and the Soviet Union are signing or announcing during this summit, agreements that represent hard work and a lasting achievement not just by our governments but also for the peoples. For example, an agreement to establish a U.S.-Soviet park across the Bering Strait. This park will preserve the unique natural, environmental, and cultural heritage of the Bering Sea region of Alaska and Siberia. Just as a bridge of land once joined our two continents, so let a bridge of hope now reach across the water to join our two peoples in this spirit of peaceful cooperation.

In this same spirit, President Gorbachev and I will sign an agreement that realizes our Malta objective of expanding undergraduate exchanges by 1,000 students on both sides, allowing more of our young people to experience firsthand each other's culture and politics, to live as friends. And out of simple acts of friendship, a profound revelation eventually arises: the people of the world have more in common than they have in conflict.

In just a few moments, Secretary of State Baker and Foreign Minister Shevardnadze will also sign four important new agreements concerning maritime boundaries, ocean studies, civil aviation, and a long-term grains agreement. Minister Shevardnadze and Transportation Secretary Skinner will sign a fifth agreement on maritime transportation. President Gorbachev and I are also signing a commercial agreement and are looking forward to the passage of a Soviet emigration law.

President Gorbachev, I am very gratified by what we've accomplished over the last few days and determined to build on this solid foundation. The agreements we record today and those yet to come will advance the cause of peace—agreements in the best interests of both our nations and all nations.

Not long ago, some believed that the weight of history condemned our two great countries, our two great peoples to permanent confrontation. Well, you and I must challenge history, make new strides, build a relationship of enduring cooperation. We may not agree on everything, and indeed we don't agree on everything, but we believe in one great truth: the world has waited long enough; the cold war must end. And so, today with gratitude in my heart for all those on the Soviet side and the United States side that worked so hard at all levels to bring these agreements to fruition, I say let's renew our pledge and build a more peaceful world.

President Gorbachev. Mr. President, ladies and gentlemen, comrades, first of all, I would like to thank President George Bush for presenting so well the results of our work that we've been doing over these days in Washington. So, I have a problem: What shall I talk about? [*Laughter*] So, I think that I will do some thinking aloud in this context.

I would say that maybe this room has seen many important events and many agreements signed, but I think that what is happening now and what you have listed as the results of our work together represents an event of momentous importance not only for our two countries but for the world.

President Franklin D. Roosevelt half a century ago spoke of a world in which four essential freedoms will triumph: freedom of speech, freedom of worship, freedom from want, and freedom from fear. And this ideal has not yet been attained in the world, and it could not be attained in the world of animosity and confrontation. And therefore, while liberating the world from fear, we are making steps towards a new world; and this is the important work of our two nations, of our two peoples.

What is very important, I think, is that we do not just declare our commitment to moving toward a healthier international environment, toward better international relations, toward a nonviolent world; we are taking practical steps in that direction. And what you have just listed and what we'll be signing during this visit, I think, is a confirmation that both our declarations are right in that they seek to justify the hopes of our peoples and that we're also taking those practical steps. The important steps that we are taking today illustrate the degree of agreement between our two countries, despite the fact that—and here I quite agree with you—that there are things on which we disagree and there are differing views that we have on certain questions. But that area of disagreement is being narrowed in the course of our work together. What we will be signing, I think, is the best demonstration that we are ready to participate at the level of our responsibility in building a new civilization.

There are still many difficult challenges awaiting us. It is evident that to dismantle that monumental artifact of the cold war, the accumulated arsenals of mutual destruction, is not at all a simple or even an entirely safe thing to do. The slightest imbalance and due haste or lack of equilibrium in this process may dangerously destabilize the overall international situation. But I'm sure that if we take a balanced and responsible approach, if we take into account the concerns and positions of each other even when we disagree, if we do all that, I'm sure that we will be able to move ahead more resolutely and more vigorously.

Mr. President, you have just mentioned Malta. Mr. President, I'm pleased to note that the turbulent developments of recent months after Malta have not led us astray from the goal we set together. So, I believe that we have passed the first test.

Mr. President, let me reaffirm here something that I've been saying to you during our one-on-one talks. We have had many such talks during this summit, and I welcome this style of negotiating. But let me reaffirm to both of our peoples that the Soviet Union is committed to the objective set at Malta: completing before the end of this year the preparation of the START treaty. I believe that this goal is attainable even though it is difficult.

I also can confirm what you have said:

that we have agreed during our talks that this year we will seek to sign a treaty at the Vienna talks. And of course, we believe that in that case that will be the CSCE European security summit meeting. I think we already have good results and a good potential to work.

I believe that this is all possible as a result of the efforts of both sides over the past few years, including the efforts in which you, sir, have participated vigorously and actively and with great foresight in order to expand our relationship and to build on the capital of trust in our relations.

It would seem that I've said even more than I intended to say. I think it means that I'm human in the sense that I'm emotional. I would like to say that we've done a great deal in order to assure the success, and I would like to congratulate our two nations. And I would like also to shake your hand, Mr. President, so that we congratulate each other.

Note: The President spoke at 6:13 p.m. in the East Room at the White House. President Gorbachev spoke in Russian, and his remarks were translated by an interpreter.

Soviet-United States Joint Statement on the Treaty on Strategic Offensive Arms
June 1, 1990

The President of the United States George Bush and the President of the Union of Soviet Socialist Republics Mikhail S. Gorbachev discussed the status of the Treaty on the Reduction and Limitation of Strategic Offensive Arms. The two Presidents expressed their satisfaction with the great progress which has been made in the negotiations on this Treaty. In particular, they welcomed the mutually acceptable solutions which have been found in major issues in the talks and reaffirmed their determination to have the Treaty completed and ready for signature by the end of this year. They instructed their negotiating teams in Geneva to accelerate their work to complete the Joint Draft Text recording the

details of these solutions in order to fulfill this goal.

The START Treaty will be a major landmark in both arms control and in the relationship between the United States of America and the Union of Soviet Socialist Republics. It results from the recognition by both sides of the special obligation they bear to reduce the risk of outbreak of nuclear war, enhance strategic stability, and strengthen peace and international security. As such, the START Treaty will signal a turning point in U.S.-Soviet arms control efforts toward a more rational, open, cooperative, predictable and stable relationship. The Treaty will complement to a remarkable degree the important political changes which have recently begun to remove the hostility and suspicion and will facilitate the reduction of the sizeable stockpiles of strategic offensive arms which now exist.

The benefits of this Treaty are many. For the first time ever, both sides will carry out significant reductions in strategic offensive arms—up to 50 percent in certain categories. More importantly, these reductions will be designed to make a first strike less plausible. The result will be greater stability and a lower risk of war.

Major agreed provisions of the Treaty are as follows:

The total number of deployed ICBMs and their associated launchers, deployed SLBMs and their associated launchers and heavy bombers will be reduced to no more than 1600; within this total deployed heavy ICBMs and their associated launchers will be reduced to no more than 154;

The total number of warheads attributed to deployed ICBMs, deployed SLBMs and heavy bombers will be reduced to no more than 6000. Of these, no more than 4900 will be warheads on deployed ICBMs and deployed SLBMs, no more than 1540 will be warheads on heavy ICBMs, and no more than 1100 will be warheads on mobile ICBMs;

The aggregate throw-weight of the deployed ICBMs and SLBMs of each side will be limited to an agreed level which will be approximately 50 percent below the existing level of the aggregate throw-weight of deployed ICBMs and SLBMs of the Union of Soviet Socialist Republics as of a date to be determined. This limit will not be exceeded for the duration of the Treaty;

Heavy bombers equipped for long-range nuclear air-launched cruise missiles (ALCMs) will be distinguishable from other heavy bombers. Heavy bombers equipped for nuclear armaments other than long-range nuclear ALCMs will be counted as one delivery vehicle against the 1600 limit and will be attributed with one warhead against the 6000 limit;

Heavy bombers equipped for long-range nuclear ALCMs will be counted as one delivery vehicle against the 1600 limit and shall be attributed with an agreed number of warheads against the 6000 limit. Existing and future U.S. heavy bombers equipped

for long-range nuclear ALCMs will be attributed with 10 warheads each. Existing and future Soviet heavy bombers equipped for long-range nuclear ALCMs will be attributed with 8 warheads each;

Within the 1600 limit on delivery vehicles the United States of America may have no more than 150 heavy bombers equipped for long-range nuclear ALCMs that are attributed with 10 warheads each. The Union of Soviet Socialist Republics may exceed that number of heavy bombers by 40 percent. If the United States of America exceeds the 150 number, each additional heavy bomber equipped for long-range nuclear ALCMs will be attributed with the number of long-range nuclear ALCMs for which it is actually equipped. If the Union of Soviet Socialist Republics exceeds 210 heavy bombers equipped for long-range nuclear ALCMs, each such heavy bomber will be attributed with the number of long-range nuclear ALCMs for which it is actually equipped;

Existing and future U.S. heavy bombers may be equipped for no more than 20 long-range nuclear ALCMs; existing and future Soviet heavy bombers may be equipped for no more than 12 long-range nuclear ALCMs;

Long-range ALCMs will be considered those with a range in excess of 600 kilometers. Future long-range non-nuclear ALCMs will not be considered nuclear if they are distinguishable from long-range nuclear ALCMs. There will be no restrictions on deploying such ALCMs on aircraft not limited by the Treaty.

Reductions will be carried out in three phases over a period of seven years. Specific, equal interim levels for agreed categories of strategic offensive arms will be achieved by the end of each phase of reductions;

The numerical limitations provided for by the Treaty will be achieved and complied with through conversion or elimination in accordance with agreed procedures.

Sea-launched cruise missiles (SLCMs) will not be constrained in the START Treaty. Each side will provide the other with a unilateral declaration of its policy concerning nuclear SLCMs and, annually for the duration of the Treaty, with unilateral declarations regarding its planned deployments of nuclear long-range SLCMs, i.e., those with a range in excess of 600 kilometers. Those declarations will be politically binding. In the annual declarations the maximum number of deployed nuclear SLCMs for each of the following five Treaty years will be specified, provided that the number declared will not exceed 880. In the declarations of policy it will be specified that the United States of America and the Union of Soviet Socialist Republics will not produce or deploy nuclear sea-launched cruise missiles with multiple independently targetable warheads. The sides reaffirmed their 1987 Washington Summit Joint Statement to continue to seek "mutually acceptable and effective methods of verification".

Except as specifically prohibited, modernization and replacement of strategic offensive arms may be carried out.

The START Treaty will include specific prohibitions on certain categories of strategic offensive arms, basing modes and activities. The following are among the bans under the START Treaty:

—new types of heavy ICBMs;
—heavy SLBMs and launchers of heavy SLBMs;
—mobile launchers of heavy ICBMs;
—new types of ICBMs and SLBMs with more than 10 reentry vehicles;
—flight testing and deployment of existing types of ICBMs or SLBMs with a number of reentry vehicles greater than the number specified in the Washington Summit Joint Statement of December 1987;
—rapid reload of ICBM launchers;
—long-range nuclear ALCMs equipped with multiple independently targetable warheads.

The far-reaching reductions and other constraints contained in the Treaty will be accompanied by the most thorough and innovative verification provisions ever negotiated.

Taken together, the START Treaty's comprehensive verification regime will create a degree of transparency in the military sphere which would have been unthinkable only a short time ago. It will not only provide for effective verification of the obliga-

tions of the Treaty, but will also greatly increase the mutual confidence which is essential for a sound strategic relationship. In addition, this verification system can provide a model which may be incorporated into future agreements. The verification regime under development includes:

- On-site inspections: For the purpose of ensuring verification of compliance with the Treaty, each side will, on the basis of reciprocity, conduct twelve kinds of on-site inspections, as well as continuous monitoring of mobile ICBM production facilities, in accordance with agreed procedures. *Inter alia,* each side will conduct short-notice inspections at facilities related to strategic offensive arms, including inspections to verify the numbers of reentry vehicles on deployed ballistic missiles, inspections to verify elimination of strategic offensive arms and facilities related to them, suspect site inspections, and various exhibitions.
- National technical means of verification: For the purpose of ensuring verification, each side will use national technical means of verification at its disposal in a manner consistent with generally recognized principles of international law. The Treaty will include a series of cooperative measures to enhance the effectiveness of national technical means of verification. There will be a ban on interference with such means;
- Ban on denial of telemetric information: The sides agreed to make on-board technical measurements on ICBMs and SLBMs and to broadcast all telemetric information obtained from such measurements. Except for strictly limited exceptions, there will be a ban on any practice, including the use of encryption, encapsulation or jamming, that denies full access to telemetric information;
- Information exchange: Before signature of the Treaty the sides will exchange data on the numbers, locations and technical characteristics of their strategic offensive arms. These data will be updated on a regular basis

throughout the lifetime of the Treaty;
* A comprehensive agreement on the manner of deployment of mobile ICBM launchers and their associated missiles and appropriate limitations on their movements so as to ensure effective verification of adherence to the numerical limitations provided for in the Treaty. In addition, the number of non-deployed ICBMs for mobile launchers will be limited and mobile ICBMs will be subject to identification through the application of unique identifiers, or tags.

To promote the objectives of the Treaty, the sides will establish the Joint Compliance and Inspection Commission.

The sides have agreed that the Treaty will have a duration of 15 years, unless superseded earlier by a subsequent agreement. If the sides so agree, the Treaty can be extended for successive five year periods, unless superseded.

The progress outlined above fulfills the aim, set forth by the Presidents of the United States of America and the Union of Soviet Socialist Republics during their Malta meeting, of agreeing upon the basic provisions of the strategic offensive arms Treaty by the time of their Washington meeting. The two Presidents express confidence that the Foreign Ministers and the delegations of the two countries at the Geneva talks will be able to reach agreement in the remaining months on the outstanding issues that are still being negotiated.

Note: The joint statement was made available by the Office of the Press Secretary but was not issued as a White House press release.

Soviet-United States Joint Statement on Future Negotiations on Nuclear and Space Arms and Further Enhancing Strategic Stability
June 1, 1990

The United States of America and the Union of Soviet Socialist Republics, building on the results of the current negotiations, agree to pursue new talks on strategic offensive arms, and on the relationship between strategic offensive and defensive arms. The objectives of these negotiations will be to reduce further the risk of outbreak of war, particularly nuclear war, and to ensure strategic stability, transparency and predictability through further stabilizing reductions in the strategic arsenals of both countries. This will be achieved by seeking agreements that improve survivability, remove incentives for a nuclear first strike and implement an appropriate relationship between strategic offenses and defenses.

In order to attain these objectives, the sides have agreed as follows:

First. This year the sides will complete work on the Treaty Between the United States of America and the Union of Soviet Socialist Republics on the Reduction and Limitation of Strategic Offensive Arms. Following the signing of the Treaty, the sides will hold consultations without delay regarding future talks and these important talks will begin at the earliest practical date. Both sides in these future talks will be free to raise any issues related to any strategic offensive arms.

Within the existing negotiating framework on Nuclear and Space Arms in Geneva, the two sides will continue negotiations on ABM and space without delay. Thus, in the future talks the two sides will discuss strategic stability issues of interest to them, including the relationship between strategic offensive and defensive arms, taking into account stabilizing reductions in strategic offensive arms and development of new technologies. The sides will work toward the important goal of reaching an early outcome in these negotiations.

Second. The United States of America and the Union of Soviet Socialist Republics, as is the case in the emerging START

Treaty, will, in the new negotiations, seek to reduce their strategic offensive arms in a way consistent with enhancing strategic stability. In the new negotiations, the two sides agree to place emphasis on removing incentives for a nuclear first strike, on reducing the concentration of warheads on strategic delivery vehicles, and on giving priority to highly survivable systems.

In particular, the two sides will seek measures that reduce the concentration of warheads on strategic delivery vehicles as a whole, including measures related to the question of heavy missiles and MIRVed ICBMs. Effective verification will be provided by national technical means, cooperative measures, and on-site inspection.

Third. Having agreed on the need to ensure a predictable strategic relationship between the United States of America and the Union of Soviet Socialist Republics, the sides will, for the entire duration of the START Treaty, exchange, at the beginning of each calendar year, information on planned changes in the numbers of strategic offensive arms as of the end of the current year.

Fourth. The sides will pursue additional measures to build confidence and ensure predictability of the military activities of the United States of America and the Union of Soviet Socialist Republics that would reduce the possibility of an outbreak of nuclear war as a result of accident, miscalculation, terrorism, or unexpected technological breakthrough, and would prevent possible incidents between them.

Fifth. The sides believe that reducing the risk of outbreak of nuclear war is the responsibility not only of the United States of America and the Union of Soviet Socialist Republics, and that other States should also make their contribution toward the attainment of this objective, in particular in the field of nonproliferation of nuclear weapons. They call upon all States to consider the new opportunities for engagement in mankind's common effort to remove the risk of outbreak of nuclear war worldwide.

Accordingly, the United States of America and the Union of Soviet Socialist Republics will give these future negotiations the highest priority so that the benefits of strengthened stability can be realized as soon as possible.

Note: The joint statement was made available by the Office of the Press Secretary but was not issued as a White House press release.

Soviet-United States Joint Statement on Conventional Armed Forces in Europe
June 1, 1990

President Bush and President Gorbachev agreed that early conclusion of an agreement on conventional armed forces in Europe (CFE) is essential to the future stability and security of the continent. A CFE agreement will constitute the indispensable foundation for new European relationships and for a future security architecture in Europe. The Presidents reaffirmed the commitment they made at their meeting in Malta in December 1989 to conclude a CFE agreement by the end of 1990. They agreed further that the forthcoming summit of the CSCE nations should be held after the CFE agreement is ready for signature.

In the course of their talks, the Presidents committed themselves to intensifying the pace of the negotiation in Vienna and to reaching rapid agreement on all outstanding issues.

Note: The joint statement was made available by the Office of the Press Secretary but was not issued as a White House press release.

Soviet-United States Joint Statement on the Establishment of a Soviet-United States International Park in the Region of the Bering Strait
June 1, 1990

The Presidents of the United States of America and of the Union of Soviet Socialist Republics, expressing support for the expansion of bilateral cooperation in the field of environmental protection and in the preservation of cultural heritage, endorse the intention of the two countries to create, in the region of the Bering Strait, a U.S.-Soviet International Park embracing protected terrestrial and aquatic areas.

Both leaders recognize that elements of natural and cultural heritage of the Bering region represent a common heritage of the American and Soviet peoples. Thousands of years ago, across a land bridge uniting the Asian and American continents, the first arrivals came to North America. Later, the sea divided the continents but failed to destroy the ecological, cultural and spiritual community of the inhabitants of Beringia. This community has remained essentially undisturbed by the influences of historical change.

Both leaders recognize that the creation of an international park would facilitate permanent recognition of the unity of this heritage and secure a framework for joint efforts in its preservation.

During 1990–1991, both countries will undertake the following practical steps:

—preparation and signature of a protocol on the creation of a complex of specially designated protected terrestrial and aquatic areas; and

—determine all organizational details connected with the functioning of the park.

Continuing close cooperation regarding the international park, between the representatives of both countries, may take the form of regular meetings of senior park management officials, the exchange of park personnel for professional training and orientation, joint research and consultations on planning and exchange visits to both sides of the park for touristic and cultural purposes, in particular by native populations.

The two sides express their confidence that establishment of the international park will serve the development of U.S.-Soviet cooperation in the protection of nature, and the activities of local populations in preserving the unique natural and cultural heritage of the Bering region.

Note: The joint statement was made available by the Office of the Press Secretary but was not issued as a White House press release.

The Office of the Press Secretary issued a fact sheet on the same day which provided the following additional information on the establishment of the Soviet-U.S. international park:

The U.S.-U.S.S.R. joint report "International Park Program, Beringian Heritage Cooperation" was endorsed as the framework for establishing an international park by the end of 1991.

The Bering Land Bridge National Reserve will be the initial companion site to be linked with a Soviet protected area on the Chukotskiy Peninsula.

Excerpts of White House Fact Sheets on Soviet-United States Bilateral Agreements
June 1, 1990

TRADE AGREEMENT

At Malta, President Bush proposed targeting the June summit for completion of a MFN (most-favored-nation trade status)

commercial agreement, provided that the Soviets approve and implement new emigration legislation. New emigration legislation passed the first reading in the Supreme Soviet in November. The Second Supreme Soviet reading, which would codify the law, was set for May 31. No serious opposition has appeared, but the press of other business could delay final passage. We have emphasized to the Soviets at all levels the importance of expeditious passage.

This agreement breaks much new ground in commercial agreements with the Soviets. Specifically, it:

- provides improved market access, for example, by prohibiting adoption of standards which are discriminatory or designed to protect domestic production;

- facilitates business by establishing expedited accreditation procedure for commercial offices, allowing offices to hire directly local and third-country employees on mutually agreed terms, permitting access to all advertising media, and allowing companies to engage and serve as agents and to conduct market studies; and

- offers strong intellectual property rights protections by reaffirming commitments to the Paris Convention and the Universal Copyright Convention, obligating adherence to the Bern Convention for the Protection of Literary and Artistic Works, providing copyright protection for computer programs and data bases and protection for sound recordings; providing product and process patent protection for virtually all areas of technology; and providing comprehensive coverage of trade secrets.

The Soviets have reaffirmed their commitment, once they receive MFN and USG lending restrictions (Stevenson and Byrd amendments) are lifted, to resume lend-lease repayments.

LONG-TERM GRAINS AGREEMENT

- The new agreement is to take effect January 1, 1991.

- The Soviets are required to buy a minimum of 10 million metric tons of grain from the United States annually (up from 9 million metric tons), including at least 4 million metric tons of wheat; 4 million metric tons of feed grains (corn, barley, or sorghum); and 2 million additional metric tons of either wheat, feed grains, or soybeans/soymeal, with soy measures counted double for purposes of quantity.

- The Soviets may buy up to 14 million metric tons annually (up from 12 million metric tons) without prior consultation with the Department of Agriculture.

U.S.-U.S.S.R. CHEMICAL WEAPONS DESTRUCTION AGREEMENT

The U.S.-U.S.S.R. Bilateral Agreement

The key provisions of the destruction agreement are:

- Destruction of the vast bulk of declared stocks to begin by the end of 1992.

- Destruction of at least 50 percent of declared stocks by the end of 1999.

- Declared stocks are to be reduced to 5,000 agent tons by 2002.

- Both countries will stop producing chemical weapons upon entry into force of this agreement, without waiting for the global chemical weapons ban.

- On-site inspections during and after the destruction process to confirm that destruction has taken place.

- Annual exchanges of data on the stockpile levels to facilitate monitoring of the declared stockpiles.

- Details of the inspection procedures will be worked out by December 31, 1990.

- Both countries will cooperate in developing and using safe and environmentally sound methods of destruction.

- The United States and U.S.S.R. will take steps to encourage all chemical weapons-capable states to become parties to the multilateral convention.

Both countries took an initial step in this direction by exchanging data on declared chemical weapons stockpiles in December

1989 and by initiating verification experiments to build confidence and gain experience for a chemical weapons ban treaty.

This agreement will be submitted to Congress for its review and approval.

A Global Chemical Weapons Ban

The bilateral U.S.-Soviet agreement was designed to provide new impetus to the conclusion of a comprehensive, verifiable global chemical weapons ban at the earliest possible date. Toward that end:

- Both countries have agreed to accelerate their destruction of chemical weapons under a global chemical weapons convention so that by the eighth year after it enters into force, the United States and U.S.S.R. will have reduced their declared stocks to no more than 500 agent tons.
- The United States and U.S.S.R. will propose that a special conference be convened at the end of the eighth year of a multilateral convention to determine whether participation in the convention is sufficient to complete the elimination of chemical weapons stocks over the following 2 years.

THE NUCLEAR TESTING PROTOCOLS

Verification Methods

- Two verification protocols being signed at the Washington summit will provide for effective verification of compliance with the treaties.
- Verification methods for Threshold Test Ban Treaty (TTBT) and Peaceful Nuclear Explosions Treaty (PNET) include hydrodynamic yield measurement, on-site inspection, and some seismic monitoring on the territory of the testing party. The U.S. hydrodynamic method is CORRTEX [Continuous Reflectrometry for Radius versus Time Experiments] is the most accurate nonintrusive technique the United States has found. CORRTEX determines the yield by measuring, at the detonating site, the rate at which the supersonic shock wave in the ground crushes coaxial cable buried near the explosive device. On-site inspections permit each side to take core samples and rock

fragments from the area of the explosion to confirm geological/geophysical data near the explosion. Seismic monitors measure distant shock waves produced by the explosion (as in measuring earthquakes) in order to arrive at an estimate of the explosive yield.

- National technical means also will be used to monitor all explosions.

How the Protocols Work

- PNET verification: Both sides have the right to hydrodynamic measurement (CORRTEX for the United States) for explosions with planned yields above 50 kilotons; the right to on-site inspections for explosions with planned yields above 35 kilotons; the right to a local seismic network for a group explosion above 150 kilotons.
- TTBT verification: the right to hydrodynamic measurements of nuclear weapons tests with planned yields above 50 kilotons; on-site inspection for tests with planned yields above 35 kilotons; in-country seismic monitoring for tests with planned yields above 50 kilotons, using three designated seismic stations off the test site but within the testing party's territory; special provisions for monitoring unusual cases: tests with nonstandard geometries, tests with multiple nuclear explosions; in each of the first 5 years of the treaty, if a side does not have at least 2 tests with planned yields above 50 kilotons, the other side may use hydrodynamic measurement that year on up to 2 tests with planned yields below 50 kilotons.
- Required notifications under TTBT (PNET notifications are similar): Each June, the parties will inform each other of the number of explosions with planned yields above 35 kilotons and 50 kilotons for the following calendar year. No later than 200 days prior to the planned date of any explosion, the other side would have the right, under protocol provisions, to monitor; the testing party must provide notification of the planned date, location, and whether the planned yield exceeds 35

or 50 kilotons. Within 20 days of receipt of such notification, the verifying party must inform the testing party whether it plans to carry out verification activities, and, if so, which type.

- Under both treaties, joint commissions will be used to discuss implementation and verification issues.
- Once the protocols are signed, the administration will seek Senate advice and consent as to ratification of the TTBT and the PNET and their protocols.

CUSTOMS COOPERATION AGREEMENT

- The agreement provides for mutual assistance between the customs services of the United States and the U.S.S.R.
- The agreement provides the basis for cooperative activity in deterring and detecting narcotic trafficking.
- The agreement is designed to strengthen cooperative measures which the two services typically undertake.
- The agreement provides a formal basis for cooperation in areas of customs law enforcement assistance, export control, and commercial fraud.

U.S.-U.S.S.R. MARITIME BOUNDARY AGREEMENT

- The parties agree that the line described as the "western limit" in the 1867 U.S.-Russia convention ceding Alaska is the maritime boundary along its entire length.
- Further, the agreement contains innovative provisions to ensure that all areas within 200 miles of either coast fall under the resource jurisdiction of one or the other party. The U.S.S.R. transfers to the United States jurisdiction in three "special areas" within 200 miles of the Soviet coast, beyond 200 miles of the U.S. coast, and on the U.S. side of the maritime boundary. The United States transfers to U.S.S.R. jurisdiction in one "special area" within 200 miles of the U.S. coast, beyond 200 miles of the Soviet coast, and on the Soviet side of the maritime boundary.

CULTURAL CENTERS AGREEMENT
- The Centers—constituted as non-diplo-

matic, nonprofit institutions—will be opened in Washington and Moscow.
- The Center Directors and one Deputy Director for each side are to have diplomatic titles and be accredited by their governments to their respective Embassies, with this exception: Center personnel, properties, and papers will not have diplomatic status.
- The Centers will carry out a variety of functions, e.g. operating libraries; sponsoring seminars, films, and performances; and providing student counseling and language instruction.
- The public is guaranteed free, unrestricted access to the Centers.
- The U.S. Center in Moscow has the right to use rubles to cover domestic operating expenses.
- Occupancy and opening dates will be determined by mutual agreement on basis of reciprocity.
- The agreement is to take effect after an exchange of notes confirming each side has completed the domestic measures required for implementation.

AGREEMENT ON EXPANSION OF UNDERGRADUATE UNIVERSITY EXCHANGES

- Increase existing exchanges (750 U.S. and 250 Soviet) by 250 students both ways in academic year 1991–1992.
- Increase targeted numbers to 1,500 each way by 1995–1996, subject to availability of funds.
- Mix of private and U.S. Government funding (arrangements to be determined) to cover the costs of the Soviet participants in the United States; the U.S.S.R. is to cover all in-country costs for Americans.
- Participants on both sides are to be chosen on basis of academic excellence and language proficiency.
- Participants would pursue full-time academic work in a variety of disciplines, including agriculture. The preferred length of the students' participation would be 1 year, though shorter periods would be considered.

MEMORANDUM OF UNDERSTANDING TO INCREASE CIRCULATION OF AMERICA AND

SOVIET LIFE MAGAZINES

- The memorandum of understanding (MOU) amends the 1989–1991 Program of Cooperation under General Exchanges Agreement.
- The MOU provides for increased circulation of America and Soviet Life magazines up to 250,000 copies in 1991.
- The distribution of both magazines after 1991 is to be governed solely by demand.
- Each side may print commercial advertising and distribute unsold copies of its magazine at official premises, cultural centers, and exhibitions under its sponsorship.

Note: This item contains information excerpted from eight fact sheets released by the Office of the Press Secretary.

Toasts at a Dinner Hosted by President Mikhail Gorbachev of the Soviet Union
June 1, 1990

President Gorbachev. Mr. President, Mrs. Bush, ladies and gentlemen, comrades, we have completed the second full day of talks, but I would like to sum things up. This meeting is only a stage, though a major one, in the gigantic and forward-looking project of *perestroika* and Soviet-American relations.

We are going to have at least two more meetings with President Bush this year alone: one at the Conference on Security on Cooperation in Europe, where I hope a treaty reducing conventional arms in Europe will be signed, and the other to sign a treaty reducing strategic offensive arms.

I believe that the agenda for 1990 that we approved at Malta can be implemented. We may reach greater heights in building a new Soviet-American relationship only by setting our sights higher and higher while abandoning all that was nurtured by the ideology and geopolitics of the cold war.

In assessing the outcome of our talks, I believe I can say that they have demonstrated a growing mutual understanding between the U.S.S.R. and the United States, which means progress in sustaining the profound and positive changes underway in the world. In this regard, our in-depth discussion of the problems and prospects of the European process was no doubt a useful one. It has served to clarify views and positions, and brought in new arguments for consideration and exploration of acceptable solutions.

It is quite natural that we focused on the external aspects of German unification. As we see it, two processes should be completed: that of the final postwar settlement, and that related to the internal issues of interforming the two parts of Germany into a single state. We believe that those two processes form the substance of the period of transition which when completed will result in the cancellation of the rights of the four victorious powers; the rights which, incidentally, stem from the outcome of the war and not from the division of Germany. The transition will end in the emergence of a new sovereign state.

At the same time we believe that the discussion is not over, that it continues. And there may be more than one approach. We have to consider all of them together, including also our allies. What is acceptable in the final analysis is only a jointly developed approach which would not prejudice anybody's interest or erode the overall process of positive changes in Europe and in the world. Those changes are the principle achievement of recent years and the main product of growing trust between us and of the growing awareness that our civilization is one.

A very important result of this summit is the agreements we have signed today and the official statements we have made. They demonstrate that our joint policy of moving from constructive understanding to constructive interaction is bearing fruit. There is no doubt that this has been made possible—and I would say that what happened today is a confirmation of what I'm going to say—this has been made possible only in the environment produced by our meeting with President George Bush at Malta.

The Soviet Union and the United States had to conduct a major and, I would say, courageous reassessment of how they viewed each other and the world. They had to realize that our mutual isolation was an anomaly and that human civilization is indivisible. Therefore, it is quite logical that the agreements we have signed reflect our common readiness to obtain greater interdependence from people-to-people communication and cooperation in vitally important areas and through reinforcing the legal framework of Soviet-American relations. The package of our new agreements also reflects the special role the Soviet Union and the United States play in building bridges of understanding and trust between the East and the West.

In particular, I would like to call your attention to the agreement on trade. This agreement takes on special relevance since it has been concluded at a time of a dramatic change of direction in the Soviet economy which is crucial for the future of *perestroika*. I am convinced that the Soviet people will appreciate the fact that the United States, the President of the United States, is signing this agreement to normalize Soviet-American commercial relations at this moment of special importance for our country.

Now that we have recorded the progress we have made and laid down guidelines for the future, I would like to express the hope that the ship of Soviet-American relations will continue to sail on this course. It is clear that there are still some disagreements between us as to the optimal structure of our relationship. But this area of disagreement is being narrowed while the area of trust, agreement, and cooperation is expanding. An indication of the sincerity and seriousness of our countries' intentions is that we have started a difficult process of revising what appeared to be eternal concepts of the role of military power in safeguarding national security. In taking a radically different approach to security, we should not forget people who were ahead of their time. Andrei Sakharov is one of them.

One of the fathers of nuclear super weapons, Sakharov had the courage of his convictions to uphold to the end that force could no longer play a role in relations among states. Sakharov taught us another lesson, too: One should not fear dogma, nor be afraid of appearing naive. Political decisions that truly meet peoples' best interests should be based on the realities of life, not on contrived schemes.

Today our society is going through a complex, and sometimes dramatic, but promising process of *perestroika* on a democratic and humane basis with full respect for human rights and freedoms. *Perestroika* is also a contribution to building a new world, for we are searching for answers to the questions that confront in one way or another with greater or lesser intensity all nations and, indeed, all mankind.

We believe that once we are clear of the thorns on this path we have chosen, we shall not only reach new frontiers in our country's history but also help to build a new civilization of peace. We are ready to do that, together with the United States of America.

I would like to propose a toast to a future of peace for the Soviet and the American people, and for all nations on Earth. To idealism and the idealists. To the health of the President of the United States of America, Mr. George Bush, and Barbara Bush. To the health and well-being of all present here. To the happiness of our children and grandchildren.

President Bush. Mr. President and Mrs. Gorbachev, Barbara and I would like to thank you for this splendid dinner and for your wonderful hospitality and for your most interesting and gracious remarks. Yesterday we welcomed the Gorbachevs back to Washington still filled with memories of the things we shared in Malta: friendship, cooperation, seasick pills. [*Laughter*]

For us here in this country, Mr. President, this week began with our observance of our Memorial Day, a day for not only remembrance of those who gave their last full measure of devotion but also for recommitment to the ideal that they shall not have died in vain.

And the week has now ended with a new memorial, a living memorial marked by historic agreements on both nuclear and chemical arms. And they've been shaped by a remembrance of shared interests and a recommitment to forging a just and lasting peace. And they stand as a memorial not to the past but to the future, a memorial to wars that need never be fought, to the hardship and suffering that need never be endured.

This afternoon we signed a landmark agreement to destroy the great majority of our chemical weapons. And we issued a joint statement recording major agreed provisions of a strategic arms reduction treaty. And the President and I also signed a commercial agreement, and we're looking forward to the passage of a Soviet emigration law. And we also agreed on this long-term grain agreement.

But true peace takes more than just laying down of arms. It also requires the reaching out of hands. And you know, Americans and Soviets have often tended to think of our two countries as being on opposite sides of almost everything, including the opposite sides of the world. But we share an important northern border, and we are, in fact, next door neighbors across the Bering Sea.

Today, we've also signed an agreement fixing our maritime boundary in the Bering Sea area and announced our agreement to establish a U.S.-Soviet park across the Bering Strait, a new gateway to the Arctic and a new gateway to the future.

Mr. President, I learned that the name of your home town out in the northern Caucasus, Privolnoye, can mean spacious or free.

President Gorbachev. Thank you for mentioning it.

President Bush. I know my pronunciation was bad, but I'm sure I'm right when I say it means spacious or free. [*Laughter*]

President Gorbachev. Great pronunciation—can mean both.

President Bush. Well, anyway, it reminded me of the new breeze, the new spirit of freedom that we've seen sweep across Europe and around the globe. I sensed it last summer, speaking in front of the shipyard gates to the people of Gdansk. And I told them because Americans are so free to dream, we feel a special kinship with those who dream of being free. Today that kinship is quickly becoming a shared spirit, a spirit that inspires millions here in our nation, in your own, and around the world.

So, ladies and gentlemen, I invite all of you to join me in a toast to our gracious hosts, the President and Mrs. Gorbachev. To lasting peace, and to this wonderful spirit of freedom.

Note: President Gorbachev spoke at 7:55 p.m. in the Golden Dining Room at the Soviet Embassy. He spoke in Russian, and his remarks were translated by an interpreter.

Exchange With Reporters Following Meetings at Camp David, Maryland, With President Mikhail Gorbachev of the Soviet Union
June 2, 1990

Meetings With President Gorbachev

Q. President Bush, how was the meeting?

President Bush. Just a minute, wait until I get out of this thing. [*Laughter*]

President Gorbachev. In today's discussions with the President I rate them no less than the conversations we had yesterday and the day before yesterday, over the past 2 days. We worked very constructively and fruitfully, and I think that had we not had this day like today my visit would have been different. But the discussions we have had today make it possible for me to state with full responsibility and in a balanced manner the full and two things: there is really ample opportunity for our cooperation, even though there are some real problems to which neither the President nor myself turn a blind eye to. And I set high store by the personal relationship that the President and myself have established, the personal rapport between us.

We showed a great responsibility, both to our people as well as to the peoples of other nations. But this kind of personal rapport that we have established enables us to approach all problems in a better way by presenting argumentation and reaching a certain balance.

Q. But will you reassess your position on Germany as a result of these informal talks?

President Gorbachev. We discussed that, and the President and myself are going to mention the subject tomorrow. We exchanged views on this question, too. But there's one point that has to be borne in mind: for all the importance of our positions and responsibilities, we must remember that we are all part of this process. There is also the six—the two-plus-four formula. There are also interests of other European nations involved. And I think the President and myself took that into account. It's been a big day, indeed.

Q. On what issues did you make progress today?

President Bush. I would simply say that my assessment of the meetings and President Gorbachev's are in close parallel. He pointed out there's some differences, and I'll point out there's some differences. But as I said yesterday, I see this glass not half empty but half full, and more. And I think the point is, we've been able to discuss these differences and the common ground in a very civil way. I will repeat what I have said before: that President Gorbachev has presided over and, indeed, led in ways that have brought about significant change. That change benefits mankind and it benefits U.S.-Soviet relations.

So, some will argue that we haven't solved all the problems. To me, that's not the point. The point is, we have an awful lot of common ground. We sat there today and talked about regional problems, not in the sense of dividing up the world—maybe that would have happened years ago—but in terms of ironing out problems, achieving common ground as we looked at a lot of regional problems. We did the same thing yesterday and the day before on bilateral problems.

So, at the end of the day here in Camp David, no neckties, very relaxed. The only thing that went wrong is, I pride myself as a horseshoe player, and President Gorbachev picked up a horseshoe, never having played the game to my knowledge, and literally, literally—all you horseshoe players out there—threw a ringer the first time. [*Laughter*] Really. And I like to think—there's not much more to say.

President Gorbachev. Well, I couldn't give in, after all. [*Laughter*]

President Bush. But there's a more significant point. And that is that he pointed out in a very warm and friendly atmosphere at dinner that a horseshoe in the Soviet Union, when posted in one's house, symbolizes warmth and friendship. That made an impression on me.

Bilateral Agreements

Q. Mr. President, "close enough" is only good enough usually in horseshoes.

President Bush. Yes.

Q. But you went ahead and signed the trade agreement despite the differences on Lithuania.

President Bush. Exactly. And the maritime agreement and the grain agreement and a lot of other agreements, including arms control agreements.

Q. Despite the difference on Lithuania.

President Bush. And this, in my view, is the interest of the United States. The agreement we signed on arms, the agreement we signed on trade, maritime, Bering Straits. Why do you single out one agreement? I look at the overall relationship. If somebody wants to argue with me, fine, we'll take him on. I'm doing what I think is in the best interest of the United States of America.

President Gorbachev. Goodbye.

President Bush. You got it. Thank you all.

President Gorbachev. Thank you.

President Bush. We'll see you guys.

Note: The exchange began at 8:15 p.m. on the grounds of Camp David. In his opening remarks, President Bush referred to the golf

cart that he was riding in. President Gorba- *were translated by an interpreter.*
chev spoke in Russian, and his remarks

Soviet-United States Joint Statement on Ethiopia
June 2, 1990

The U.S. and USSR discussed relief requirements and the prospects for a political solution to Ethiopia's internal conflict. They welcome the Ethiopian government's agreement to permit relief food to enter northern Ethiopia through the Port of Massawa under a UN sponsored relief effort, and they believe that such operations would not compromise the unity and territorial integrity of Ethiopia. They also welcomed the agreement expressed by the Ethiopian government to have UN representatives present in the course of the negotiations between the Ethiopian government and the Eritreans.

In addition, to deal with the growing problems of starvation, the U.S. and the USSR are prepared to work together and combine their assets. U.S. food will be transported on Soviet aircraft to demonstrate our joint commitment to responding to this tragic humanitarian problem.

Recognizing the continuing political and military conflicts that exacerbate the problems of starvation and recognizing also the lack of momentum on peace talks, the U.S. and USSR will support an international conference of governments under the auspices of the UN on settlement of conflict situations in the Horn of Africa.

Note: The joint statement was made available by the Office of the Press Secretary but was not issued as a White House press release.

Soviet-United States Joint Statement on the Environment
June 2, 1990

During the state visit of Mikhail S. Gorbachev, President of the USSR, at the invitation of George Bush, President of the United States, the two sides affirmed their serious concern about the health of the global environment, and their commitment to expand U.S.-Soviet cooperation in the field of environmental protection and the study of global change. Mindful of their obligations under international environmental conventions, and committed to continued international discussion aimed at other understandings on matters of common concern, the sides emphasized the need for practical and effective joint measures on environmental protection.

The United States and the USSR attached great importance to full and open exchange of environmental data, and to careful coordination of existing global atmospheric, terrestrial and ocean monitoring systems. Accordingly, they endorsed intensified bilateral cooperation in areas of environmental, ecological and pollution monitoring, and in related research.

The United States and the Soviet Union noted with satisfaction their agreement to establish, by the end of 1991, a Beringian International Park in the region of the Bering Strait. On other bilateral matters, they also pledged to facilitate contacts and cooperation between their respective nongovernmental environmental organizations.

Note: The joint statement was made available by the Office of the Press Secretary but was not issued as a White House press release.

News Conference of President Bush and President Mikhail Gorbachev of the Soviet Union
June 3, 1990

President Bush. Good morning, everybody. Please be seated. Well, when President Gorbachev and I were at Malta, we agreed that we would try to build a fundamentally different U.S.-Soviet relationship, one that would move beyond containment to an era of enduring cooperation. At the time, no one knew the momentous events that would unfold around the world. And our task is, if anything, more urgent, and the case for a new U.S.-Soviet relationship more compelling, because the opportunities before us are so great.

We've not shied away from discussing issues about which we disagree. There were some tough ones before us, particularly the aspiration of the Baltic peoples, a cause which the United States fully supports. I think it's a mark of how far the U.S.-Soviet relationship has come that in all our exchanges, whether about issues on which we agreed or disagreed, the spirit of candor and openness, a desire not just to understand but to build bridges, shone through.

President Gorbachev and I had intensive discussions on the transforming events in Europe, events that have put before us our best chance in four decades to see Europe whole and free. I stressed that the long-held aspirations of the German people should be met without delay. On the matter of Germany's external alliances, I believe, as do Chancellor Kohl and members of the alliance, that the united Germany should be a full member of NATO. President Gorbachev, frankly, does not hold that view. But we are in full agreement that the matter of alliance membership is, in accordance with the Helsinki Final Act, a matter for the Germans to decide.

Over the last 6 months and in Washington this week, we made great progress in our mutual effort toward building a more peaceful and stable world. We signed a very important chemical weapons accord, nuclear testing protocols and gave a political push to others, including negotiations to reduce U.S.-Soviet strategic nuclear forces

and conventional military forces in Europe. I'm also hopeful that the good discussion between President Gorbachev and—the one we had about the importance of "open skies"—we'll revive those negotiations. We discussed regional issues and human rights in considerable detail, made progress in the economic sphere, concluding a commercial agreement, a long-term grains agreement.

In closing, let me say how productive I really feel the last few days have been. President Gorbachev and I have agreed to meet on a regular basis, perhaps annually. Both of us would like to think that we can get together more often with less formality because, you see, we're now at a stage in the U.S.-Soviet relationship, and indeed in world history, where we should miss no opportunity to complete the extraordinary tasks before us.

Mr. President, it's been a pleasure having you here, sir.

President Gorbachev. Ladies and gentlemen, comrades, what has happened over these days enables me to characterize this summit meeting as an event of enormous importance, both for our bilateral relations and in the context of world politics. President Bush has listed the results of the work that we have done together here, which enables you to see the scope, the scale, of this work and, I think, confirms the conclusion that I have drawn.

I agree with President Bush fully, who many times emphasized that we took Malta as a point of departure. And it is Malta that added momentum to the process which, of course, given all the difficulties and disagreements which we have and which we do not deny, still leads us to a qualitatively new relationship with the U.S.S.R. and the U.S.A. The atmosphere and the results of this meeting make it possible for us to speak, really, of a new phase of cooperation, which the President has just mentioned.

I believe that this transition is both the result and a factor for further changes that affect all countries. The constructive spirit of these days, the spirit of responsibility in which we discussed all questions, have made our success possible; and that's very important because that has a stabilizing effect on the entire international situation at a time when we are addressing fundamental issues of civilization.

I would not want to now give a listing of all that we discussed, to mention all the agreements, all the important questions and statements that we have made and that have a lot of potential for the future. But let me still mention what is most important: We signed the main provision for a treaty on the reduction of strategic arms. And I would like to emphasize that this is the first time that we're not just limiting but we will be reducing the most devastating means of warfare. And I hope that we will sign the treaty itself this year. We also signed a statement about the future treaty negotiations on nuclear and space arms. We have agreed to make sure that we will complete the Vienna talks this year and sign an agreement on conventional arms at a European summit by the end of this year. Not everything depends on us, but this is our position; we want to achieve that.

We also discussed problems relating to the European process; specifically, external aspects of German unification. I cannot say that we have reached agreement, but that does not mean that our efforts were futile. Many new arguments emerged as a result of these discussions, and new, possible perspectives. We have clarified our positions, and it is our position that we will continue discussion in order to find a mutually acceptable solution. We could not resolve this issue in Washington with the two of us. There is also the two-plus-four formula and other European countries which are concerned and which want to see a mutually acceptable solution, a solution acceptable to all of us. The position of the Soviet Union is that we have to find solutions that would fit into the overall positive trend of changes in Europe and in the world that would strengthen and not erode security.

I would like, in particular, to emphasize the importance of our dialog at Camp David, where we talked during the day yesterday; and this is a new phase in strengthening mutual understanding and trust be-

tween us. We really discussed all world problems. We compared our political perspectives, and we did that in an atmosphere of frankness, a constructive atmosphere, an atmosphere of growing trust. We discussed, specifically, such urgent international issues as the situation in the Middle East, Afghanistan, southern Africa, Cambodia, Central America. That is just some of what we have discussed. I would not want to go into detail right now. I think that you will probably seek to get clarification on this. But anyway, I think that the Camp David dialog was very important.

We have agreed to make a special statement on Ethiopia, to support efforts to reestablish peace there and also, with the help of the United Nations, to give humanitarian relief to the Ethiopian people.

Speaking of bilateral relations, we have some important political achievements here. Specifically, there is movement on such important areas as trade agreement, grain trade, agreement on civil aviation cooperation, maritime agreement, peaceful uses of the atomic energy science and technology, and education.

While we and the President were working—and our Ministers were also discussing things—there were important contacts and discussions with the various American companies. And some important decisions were made, such as Chevron, that will be participating in the exploration of the Tengiz oil fields. That will mean an investment of about 10 billion rubles. A group of our academicians were here with me, and they had a good discussion which resulted in the signing of a memorandum of intent with IBM, which will participate in the program of using computers for education in the Soviet Union. I think that this economic area and other areas create a good foundation for our political dialog and creates a kind of solid pillar of support for our cooperation.

I would like to express my profound gratification at this work that we have done together with President George Bush. I appreciate very much him as a political leader who is able, in a very human way and in a politically responsible way, to engage in dialog and cooperation. We spent many hours together and were able to come to know each other very well. I don't know whether anyone will be ever able to say that we know each other totally well or completely. I think that would take many, many years. But now we have a good human relationship and, I think, a good human atmosphere between us.

The President has said, and I would like to confirm this, that we have decided to have regular meetings on a working basis in a businesslike manner, and this is really what is necessary. I would like to tell you that I've invited President George Bush, the President of the United States, to visit the Soviet Union, to come for a state visit to our country, in concluding—and that is something that is not within the framework of the official negotiations but was part of our visit.

I would like to say both to the Americans and to the Soviet people that here we—the Soviet delegation—we have felt very good feelings of the American people, feelings of solidarity, and a lot of interest from the Americans toward what we are doing in the Soviet Union for *perestroika*. I have felt that on many occasions in my short exchanges with the Americans and also in various talks. I would like to thank all Americans for that, and they certainly can expect reciprocity from the Soviet Union for that.

And finally, we, the two of us, were discussing things of concern to us, various regions, various problems affecting the lives of other countries; but that does not mean that we were trying to decide anything for others anyway. We remembered always that what we were doing must be useful not only for our countries but for the world—and of course, specifically, for the Third World.

And let me, at this, wrap up my initial remarks at this press conference.

German Reunification and Membership in NATO

Q. I'd like to ask both Presidents about Germany. President Bush, you've mentioned that you still have a disagreement about a united Germany being in NATO. In any concrete sense, did you narrow your differences on this subject, and are any al-ternatives being seriously considered?

President Bush. I'm not sure we narrowed them. I feel I understand President Gorbachev's position. But I know this for fact certain: I had every opportunity to explain in considerable detail why I felt a united Germany in NATO would be stabilizing, would be important for the stability of a post-German unification Europe.

So, I can't say whether we narrowed them; but the benefit of a meeting like this is, once again, you can talk in great frankness about it. I have no suspicion about his position, and I hope he has no suspicion about mine. And we've got collective decisions to take with NATO allies on matters of this nature, but in the final analysis, it's the question for Germany to decide that. And maybe we're closer on that, but I would defer to President Gorbachev.

President Gorbachev. Since I have already made quite a few remarks on many occasions during these days on this subject, I will confine myself to comments which I think important in order to emphasize the thinking on this score and in order for us to understand better what we are after. We're not insisting that it should be an option of the Soviet Union. We are not saying that this should be a version by the United States of America or anybody else's option.

What we are talking about is an option—or a solution of external problems related to Germany unification which would organically incorporate the European process and improvement of international politics as a whole—so that a solution of these issues would help enrich this process and make it more stable and reliable. We're opposed to any options whatever it may come from. We ourselves are not going to offer one that would weaken these processes or create difficulties for the unfolding processes in the European continent. We've not going to put spokes in the wheels, as it were. So, I believe the fact that the President, myself, and our colleagues have devoted a great deal of time to this issue—we have thrashed out this idea very, very thoroughly—I think has been very helpful and beneficial because we will continue our debates on this.

Rapport Between Presidents Bush and Gorbachev

Q. I have this question to address to you. You have just mentioned President Bush as having qualities of a statesman. Could you tell us what role they played in helping you make so many accomplishments at this summit meeting and advance in the solution of many problems that seem to be intractable?

President Gorbachev. I can reiterate what I have said, and I can add the following: Mr. Bush and I met each other a bit earlier before finding ourselves in this position together. And during my contacts with him, I felt—and it was during my first visit here in 1987—that this is the kind of person to do business with, to build our relations with. Then we had contacts at Governors Island, which persuaded me even more of that.

We have maintained correspondence between us, and perhaps Malta was exactly the point where President Bush and I could get to know each other even better and to engage in some thinking on one-on-one meetings. I must say that everything began with discovering the fact that President Bush and myself have a desire to do business informally, which is very, very important. If we added to this the fact that each of us, while being himself and while representing their own people, should react in a responsible fashion to everything and in context of the real role played by the Soviet Union and the United States of America, we could very well imagine the human compatibility which exist between people and which enables them to create a kind of atmosphere that makes it possible to clarify the root causes of some particular processes.

I can say that this dialog is well underway. And as to yesterday's meetings at Camp David, they were a great accomplishment in and by themselves. This is my assessment, and I think the fact that we have established a rapport will be very important.

Israeli-Occupied Territories and the Middle East Peace Process

Q. This is a two-pronged question for both Presidents. Beyond words, what guarantees can you give the Palestinians that the decisions you made on emigration will not result in the further usurpation of their lands? And why is it that President Gorbachev has shown so much human sympathy for the Palestinians, while the U.S. vetoes even a U.N. look at their plight under military siege?

President Bush. Did you have a particular order you wanted us to answer that question in? [*Laughter*]

Q. If you can.

President Bush. The United States policy on settlement in the occupied territories is unchanged and is clear. And that is: We oppose new settlements in territories beyond the 1967 lines—the stated, reaffirmed policy over and over again. Now, we do not oppose the Secretary-General sending an emissary to the Middle East to look at this important question. The question is compounded, however, when you see, on the eve of the discussion of that, an outrageous guerrilla attack on Israel launched from another country. That is unacceptable to the United States. Having said that, the position of our country is we do not think that it needs U.N. troops or U.N. Security Council missions, but we do favor Mr. Goulding, a representative of the Secretary-General, going there.

So, when the question came—and we differed with the Soviet Union; indeed, we differed with many of our other allies on this question—it is our view that the most productive way to handle that question was to have an emissary from the Secretary-General, not, as the other countries in the Security Council favored, a Security Council delegation go there.

Q. But, Mr. President, you agree that there have been settlements, even though this has been our policy for many years?

President Bush. Yes, I agree there are settlements that go contrary to the United States policy; and I will continue to represent the policy, reiterate the policy, and try to persuade the Government of Israel that it is counterproductive to go forward with additional settlements in these territories. Our objective is to get the parties to the peace table. And our Secretary of State has worked diligently with the Israelis, and I've tried to do my best to get them talking.

And that's what we think is the most immediate step that is needed. And I will continue to reiterate American policy and continue to push for peace talks.

President Gorbachev. Just a moment. I'd like to respond, too. You formulated your question in precise terms, namely: What kind of guarantees can we issue so that those who want to leave—those who have chosen Israel as their place of residence—those who leave from the Soviet Union should not be resettled on occupied territories?

This is not a simple question, and this is what I have to say in this connection. The Soviet Union is now being bombarded by a lot of criticism from Arab countries lately. I have had meetings with President Assad of Syria and President Mubarak of Egypt. Those were very important talks with them. Nevertheless, this was the question that was also raised by them in acute terms—the question of guarantees now. We are facing the following situation.

Either, after these meetings and exchanges with the President of the United States of America on this particular issue, our concern would be heeded in Israel and they will make certain conclusions or else we must give further thought to it in terms of what we can do with issuing permits for exit. And some people are raising the matter in these terms in the Soviet Union, namely: As long as there are no assurances from the Israelis that this is not going to be done by them for the—to postpone issuing permits for exit, to put it off. But I hope they will heed what the two Presidents strongly advise them, that they should act in a wise fashion. Perhaps this is what I would like to express by way of reacting.

President Boris N. Yeltsin of the Russian Republic

Q. My question is addressed to Comrade Gorbachev. Your relationship with President Bush, *perestroika* activities well-assured inside, but there is a cooling of interest. Everybody's concerned with internal matters at home. Taking advantage of this opportunity, I'd like to ask you what do you think of your relationship with Yeltsin? Are you going to offer an olive branch of peace to each other?

President Gorbachev. I don't think you have chosen the best place for clarifying our internal problems. [*Laughter*] But *c'est la vie,* as they say—[*laughter*]—there is real life. There are certain processes underway back home. And I thought I tried to respond to this question when I was in Canada. As soon as I stepped out of the plane, they asked me this particular question. And I said that what I was worrying about most was a kind of an impasse which emerged at the Congress itself, because there is no strong preponderance. It took really three rounds for Comrade Yeltsin to gain a majority of votes, by just a few votes, to be elected. So, the situation remains.

And I said that in recent days something has happened which calls for thinking on our part. Comrade Yeltsin, with respect to some very serious, important, political, fundamental issues, has changed his position. At least he has introduced clarity. And I said if this is not a political gain for him to hold high office it is one thing. A certain approach can be adopted on the basis of that, and we could certainly forecast a certain kind of developments in the Supreme Soviet and in Russia.

But if this is nothing but a maneuver and he will return to what he has been doing in recent years—not only critical terms if Americans believe this is to be constructive but also in destructive activities, destructive efforts. He went as far as to fertilize in the framework of *perestroika* our efforts with ideas regarding forms of life where we are making a turnaround in all spheres. So, if he is going to come back to this, then, of course, his chairmanship will certainly complicate these processes. I should say that, after that he gave an interview and people began to see that he is changing again, the very next day he was interrogated at a session. He tried to explain his position.

In short, I always say life will place everything in proper perspective. Now that we have reached a phase of radical, fundamental change where everybody is supposed to show great responsibility for their country, where we're changing everything, now that we're about to make a radical change in our economy, it is all very serious. Everything will become clear pretty soon what Comrade Yeltsin is after.

Soviet-U.S. Trade

Q. Mr. President, President Bush, I'd like to ask you about the trade agreement that you signed yesterday, already a matter of some political controversy and criticism in this country. Secretary Baker has indicated it will not go to Congress for its action until the Soviet codification of its new emigration policies. Does that mean, sir, that when that law is passed in the Soviet Union that you are prepared to go ahead as well with most-favored-nation trading status for the Soviet Union, or will that further step require some action, some loosening, some shift on the Baltics?

President Bush. We had a chance to discuss the Baltics, and I made clear that the Baltics—I think I said it at a U.S. press conference several weeks ago—caused some tensions. But the linkage is between the trade agreement and the emigration legislation. I'm not going to send that legislation up—and I've tried to be very frank—until the Soviet Union has completed action on the legislation guaranteeing the right of emigration.

Q. Well, what about, sir, the further step of actually granting most-favored-nation status?

President Bush. I've given our position in the linkages between the emigration, and that's it.

Q. May we take it, then, sir, that most-favored-nation status would then be forthcoming if this emigration law is codified?

President Bush. We'll cross that bridge when we get to it. But the trade agreement linkage is between the—MFN is hooked into the emigration law being passed. That's it.

We have other agreements—the grain agreement, and we have a maritime agreement. And the difference of position we have on the Baltics, you might say, is one of the thorns in the side of an overall relationship. We've always had a difference on this. We have not recognized the incorporation of the Baltic States into the Soviet Union; that's been the historic position of the United States. But that concern, you might say, affects a wide array of issues that we have with the Soviet Union.

Frankly, I've been very pleased. First place, I've tried to be very frank with President Gorbachev not just here but before he came here, saying the difficulties that I face. And Jim Baker was very frank with [Soviet Foreign Minister] Eduard Shevardnadze, saying the problems we face. I think it is important in this emerging relationship that we share as directly as we can with the Soviet side the political problems we face. We've got a Congress that has its rights. They have every right to look at what I've signed and every obligation to do that and make their judgment as to whether it's in the best interests.

I signed the trade agreement because I am convinced that it is in the best interests of the United States. I believe the same thing about the grain agreement. I believe the same thing about the maritime agreement. But I don't want to mislead the American people and say that I have lessened my concern over the Baltic States. I've tried to be frank with the Soviet side on this. But the linkage—back to your question—the linkage with trade is on MFN—emigration law being passed. And then we go forward.

Negotiating Strengths and Weaknesses

Q. In connection with this meeting, there was a lot of speculation about weak and strong points—somebody speaks from a position of strength, someone from a position of weakness. How would you define what a strong position is, a position of strength? What is the place where a factor of force or strength holds? What are the components of force? What makes politics strong? This is a question that is addressed to both Presidents.

President Gorbachev. Let me begin first in order to let President Bush have a little rest. [*Laughter*] I think this is a certain speculation on this score. Both during the preceding period and in the course of our talks, we have been representing our peoples and countries, well aware of what the dialog is all about. And I think to assume that someone—myself or President Bush—can dictate to each other or to the Soviet Union is absurd. This would be the greatest misconception, on the basis of which no progress could ever be made.

I think that this idea is suggested because at this point in time the Soviet Union is deep into profound change. And since fundamental change is involved, we are walking away from one particular way of life toward different forms of life: we're changing our political system; we're introducing a new model in economy. All these are fundamental things, indeed. Debates are underway. Doubts are being expressed. Views are being compared. And this is very important because what is at stake is our destiny.

Of course, when you look from outside—well, we ourselves can feel the strain of our society; it is very much politicized. But a look from outside, without knowing all the subtleties, without knowing all the depth of sentiments—one could certainly arrive at some erroneous conclusions. Hence, the question of how long will Gorbachev stay in his office and how this whole *perestroika* will end and so on and so forth.

Even this, I think, fits into this process of profound change, and perhaps this is something we cannot do without. But the most important thing is that everything that is happening confirms not only the fact that we're cleaning up our courtyard, we are really revamping our entire society. We are trying to adapt it to human needs on the basis of freedom and democracy. We want to make it more open toward the outside world. That is the essence, and therein, Soviet people do not differ. And I hope there are no differences on that among the journalistic corps.

Perhaps some part of society thinks otherwise, but the question is how to do all this to avoid losing everything that we should keep and jettison everything that we don't need, that stands in the way. I don't think we have ever tackled tasks like this in the history of our country. I don't know whether anybody else has been able to resolve so many tasks within such a short period of time. So, it is for this particular reason that we appreciate so highly the fact that the whole world understands this correctly.

So, from this particular perspective, I wish to state—and this goes to show the farsightedness of President Bush and his colleagues, to say nothing of the American public, which overall understands what is happening in the Soviet Union today, understands that this is something that we need. Above all, of course, it's up to us to solve all of these problems; but of course, everybody understands full well that this is something that the whole world, all the nations, need. For without such changes, without a stronger, balanced, harmonized world, we will not accomplish our objectives.

So, today the pivotal point of world politics is *perestroika* in the Soviet Union, not because we are there but because this is an objective reality.

President Bush. May I simply add that the United States is not trying to deal from strength or weakness. I tried to say this at the welcoming ceremony for President Gorbachev. We have a unique responsibility to deal with world peace. No other countries have the same degree of responsibility that the Soviet Union and the United States have. So, we're not looking for winners or losers. We salute reforms that make our systems more compatible on the economic side, on the human rights side, the openness side. But we're not looking for trying to achieve advantage. We sat down here, one-on-one, and tried to hammer out agreements and get closer together on vital matters affecting other countries.

And it is because of the standing of the Soviet Union and the standing of the United States in the world that we have responsibilities. So, I can tell you—all the journalists from the Soviet side, the European journalists—the United States is dealing with mutual respect here. We salute the changes, of course. But we have a unique responsibility in the world. And I plan to—one of the things I'm pleased about in our agreement is that we will be meeting more often now, and we can't miss an opportunity to enhance stability and peace in the world. So, that's where I'm coming from on your question.

Mr. Fitzwater. Let's turn to the international press.

Soviet-U.S. Relations

Q. Following on President Bush's comment, on a scale that had adversaries at one end and allies at the other, would you now say that each other's country was more of an ally than an adversary?

President Bush. I don't want to get into semantics. "Alliances" have a connotation to some that they might not have for another. "Adversaries" sometimes convey the concept of hostility or enmity. In my view, we've moved a long, long way from the depths of the cold war. We've moved towards a—I don't quite know how to quantify it for you, but we could never have had the discussions at Camp David yesterday or as we sat in the Oval Office a couple of days before with President Gorbachev 20 years ago. We all know that. So, there's been dramatic move. And the more this reform and openness takes place, the more compatible the relationship becomes. Neither of us tried to cover over the differences.

So, I know that's too general for you, but that's where I'd leave it.

NATO's Future and German Reunification

Q. Question to President Bush, if I may, to follow up my colleague's one. Are there circumstances under which you would be prepared to recommend the total dissolution of NATO? What's the threat that still keeps it in business?

And a question to President Gorbachev, too. How long do you think the transition period should last before the responsibilities of the Four Powers run out—the four victorious powers in World War II?

President Bush. You want me to start with that one?

As I look at the world, the threat is unpredictability and stability—or instability is the threat. We feel that a continued U.S. presence in Europe should not be seen as hostile to the Soviet interests, but indeed, we hope a continued U.S. presence there will be seen as something that's stabilizing. And NATO is the existing machinery that we feel, with an expanded mission, can best provide that stability. And herein, we have a difference with the Soviet Union.

But it is that, rather than some kind of cold war mentality, that drives our decision to, one, remain in Europe and two, to try to have a broader role for NATO. Under article II of the NATO treaty, there is language put in there, I'm told, by Lester Pearson years ago that provides a broader than just

military assignment for NATO. So, we see this as not exclusive to an expanded role for CSCE, not contradictory to the aspirations of many Europeans for an expanded EC, but as a way in which we can continue without hostility to anyone to provide a stabilizing presence.

President Gorbachev. I'd like to respond to this extremely important question if I may.

First, as an overall statement of the fact, it seems to me that if some kind of option is suggested, one that would replace or would be accompanied by replacing an isolation on the European continent, either of the United States of America or of the Soviet Union, then I would say in no uncertain terms—and I could even make a forecast—that that particular option would be doomed. It would be doomed in the sense that it would be difficult to put into effect, but what matters most, it would lead to exacerbation rather than improvement in the situation. For that reason, we believe that we will not be able to make any further progress in restructuring international relations, including in the main European area, without an active participation of the United States of America and the Soviet Union. These are realities, and there's also a great sense of responsibility behind those realities. This is the first point.

The second point now. Yes, indeed, we believe that the option which we think will be found eventually and which will provide powerful momentum and which would contribute to the strengthening of the European process must necessarily include some kind of a transition period during which we could join our efforts to conclude a final document, exhausting thereby the rights we are endowed with as the victorious Four Powers under the results of the Second World War. These are the issues that were raised by history itself; and so, therefore, in the framework of international law it must be brought to conclusion.

A concurrent unification of Germany and its presence would mean the coincidence of these two events. This would mean that this would be an independent and sovereign state. I really don't know, and I wouldn't like to engage in speculation about the timeliness. But I think that we must be very, very active now so as to ensure some kind of synchronization between the internal processes which lead to the unification of Germany and the settlement of external aspects so that they would be combined.

I can see, and I offered, many options in our position. Those options are there, and it seems to me there are some points the American side has noticed. I am expressing my supposition. I am not saying that I heard this from the President. But I think they have something to think about, and I think we will give serious thinking to the U.S. position, too.

Q. President Gorbachev, on the subject of NATO membership for a united Germany, you have complained in the past about Western sensitivity to your security concerns. Some of your aides say privately that a united Germany could belong to NATO and your security concerns could be satisfied by both a limited American presence in Germany and, primarily, by strict limits on German troops and armaments. The real problem, they say, is psychological: a matter of national pride. They say that if you accept Germany in NATO it will be a humiliating admission to the Soviet people that you've lost the cold war.

In your talks with President Bush, were you frank about this? Is this a problem for you? And, President Bush, have you considered this problem yourself in your own thoughts?

President Gorbachev. First, I do not think that whatever I am saying on this extremely important question of world politics appears to be a complaint from me or from the Soviet Union—"this would be humiliating for the Soviet Union" to pass, you said, around—to come here to Washington or to Bonn or elsewhere—this is out of the question. And please bear that in mind. This is the first point.

The second point is: You know there is a process underway, a beneficial process, and look how far we have progressed in this process. We're entitled to raise the question in these terms. Each subsequent step must strengthen it rather than weaken it. We have a right to that. Take, for example, our negotiations on 50-percent reductions in strategic offensive arms. If this whole nego-

tiating process were to be depicted to you in its entirety, you would certainly see the kind of battles we are having on each and every point. Why? Because nobody really wants his security to be diminished.

Incidentally, our own position is that we find it unacceptable that we should have greater security than the United States of America. In a situation like this, we won't be able to move forward. I would recommend to all our partners to give some thought to this position. If decisions are made of the kind that will cause concern to the Soviet Union, this would not be beneficial to the Soviet Union; this would not be beneficial to others as well.

So, the question arises: a united Germany, its advent on the horizon—all this is very important and serious. While applauding the Germans' desire to be united, we must at the same time think about ways of preserving the balance that has been emerging and taking shape for decades.

Here is the central point. If we were to adopt only one point of view, then I would think that it would not be complete, for it gives rise to concerns. And if that is the case, then if there were no other way out— but I believe that such a way out will be found to mutual satisfaction—but if this were to be the only option and some would like to impose it on us and say that we reject this, then we should go back and see where we are. What's happening to our security? What should we be doing with our Armed Forces, which we are both reforming and reducing? What should we do about Vienna? How should we behave there? All these are matters of strategic importance for everything happening in Europe; it is really the highest level of strategy.

This is one way, one pathway, which gives rise to some doubts or suspicions, one that can certainly slow down things. But there is another pathway that we are offering—let it be American or German or British. We are not claiming to have it as our own. We are claiming one thing only: We want to see an option that would strengthen everything in Europe rather than weaken things.

As to the second part: It's a question of pride? Well, I'd say that the problem is not pride, really, if today I have to remind you once again that we lost 27 million people in the fronts, in partisan detachments—27 million people during World War II. And 18 million people were wounded and maimed. Then I think it's not a matter of pride, but of justice—supreme justice. For these sacrifices of our people enable us to raise these matters with all nations, and we have a moral right to do so, so that everything that was obtained at such tremendous costs—that so many sacrifices would not spell new perils. So, this is what I wanted to say, and I think that this is what should be said.

President Bush. Mr. President, may I simply add, in answer to your question, the answer is no because our policy is not predicated on pride or on humiliation or on arrogance. It is predicated on what do we see, from the U.S. standpoint, is the best for the future, best for stability and peace in Europe and elsewhere. So, the considerations that you asked about have nothing to do with the formulation of U.S. policy on these important questions. I'm just going to do what I think is best for the United States and the rest of the free world and the Soviets. So, we're not dwelling on what you asked about.

Soviet Relations With Pacific Nations

Q. Mr. Gorbachev, you say that you have established new relations with the United States. Could you tell us how you are going to develop the process in the area of the Pacific Ocean and whether you're going to convene some kind of representative conference or meeting to discuss those matters with representatives of different zones?

President Gorbachev. It seems to me that I have already expressed myself in rather a great detail on this score. And it also seems to me that what I said back in Vladivostok, in Krasnoyarsk, remains today. And I reiterate that approach. And it seems to me that this is not a thing of the past, for the processes are beginning to develop in that region, too, which is inhabited by billions of people. One way or another things will be more complex with due regard for the real specifics over there. We must act with due regard for those specifics without copying blindly the European process, but borrowing something from it.

At this time, I can say that what happened with armaments, with INF [intermediate-range nuclear force] missiles along the border with China, and the kind of dialog which is underway now between countries and, finally, the fact that we have traveled a certain distance toward a settlement of the situation of Afghanistan—all these are signs showing that there is a positive process emerging over there.

Of course, I think this road will be longer and more thorny. But still, it is especially necessary over there because those peoples need an opportunity to reallocate their resources to overcome a lot of social problems that have been accumulated. This is number one.

And number two, I'd like to say that, following the intensive contacts we have had and the dialog that we are developing with India and now with China and other countries, such as Indonesia, I am planning to go on a visit to Japan so as to open that area for discussions. So, we're going to intensify our efforts in that direction.

I wish to say right away that here, too, we must cooperate with the United States of America. I said this before in my statements; and now, too, I wish to reiterate it once again in the presence of the President of the United States of America.

Lithuanian Independence

Q. This question is directed to President Bush, but, President Gorbachev, feel free to join in, of course. Mr. President, about 6 weeks ago you suggested your patience was nearing an end in regards to the Lithuanian situation. I was wondering if that's still the case. If not, what has changed? And specifically, have you received any assurances that the embargo will be lifted?

President Bush. No, there have been no such assurances. I'm not sure anything has changed. I don't recall placing it that my patience is nearing an end. I've tried to make clear to everybody that we have not recognized the incorporation of these Baltic States into the Soviet Union and, therefore, we have a difference with the Soviet Union. They consider this an internal matter; and we say that, having not recognized the inclusion, why, we have a different problem.

But we had some good discussions of this. I've been encouraged to see discussions going on over there between various leaders. And let's hope the matter can be resolved, because I haven't lessened my view as to people's aspirations for self-determination, and I feel strongly about that. That's a hallmark of American belief and policy, and I haven't changed one bit on that. But I would turn it over to President Gorbachev, who has a different view on it.

President Gorbachev. I really don't even know what I can tell you now, because 2 days ago, in a meeting with representatives of the congressional leadership, I explained our position in great detail. It seems to me that our position is constructive and convincing.

Our Constitution has recorded the right for each people to make a choice for self-determination up to and including secession. We did not have a mechanism that would regulate the implementation of that right. Now we have it recorded in the law. So, we are reforming our federations. We are expanding the Republics' sovereign rights. And we hope that a full federation is something that we are in vital need of to resolve all the problems that have been accumulated. This is our conviction; this is the way we're acting. And shortly, in the next few days, there is to be a Federation Council meeting convened to consider specific steps, dates, and ways of resolving this particular problem in specific, concrete terms.

Perhaps this particular process will develop in a way that would imply the presence of different levels of federative ties, just like various ties or links between the Republics. This will be a new process, new forms of links of the kind that would be in consonant with the purposes of our *perestroika*, with the goals of reforming our federation. This is one direction.

If, nevertheless, in the framework of this process, some Republic or other is going to raise this question—and I'm sure they will—they must be addressed and dealt with in the framework of the constitutional process. We want to see this happen precisely on the basis of the Constitution. Any other different approach leads only to an impasse. And the experience that we have by now not only with respect to Lithuania but also

with respect to other Republics in terms of dealing with ethnic problems, where some people are trying to resolve the problem by different methods, without due regard for the Constitution, leads to exacerbation, aggravation, and confrontation. And this is not beneficial either for people, for their families, or for the economy, or for the overall atmosphere in our country.

The President of the Soviet Union, just like the President of the United States of America—and I happen to know the American Constitution—have as one of their main responsibilities to defend and protect the constitutional system. I swore an oath of allegiance to the Constitution; and for that reason, we are prepared and willing to address any issue, including those that have been raised by the Supreme Soviet of the Lithuanian SSR, in the framework of the constitutional process. This implies a referendum, incidentally. As to the referendum, those who have engineered this kind of solution, if I may say so, regarding the statehood of Lithuania, will also address our own option and let the people decide.

After they make a choice, I'm sure no fewer than 5 or 7 years would be required for us to sort things out. There will be this divorce proceeding underway, for there are 800,000 non-Lithuanians who live there. Defense, missiles, navy—they're all there. Today Lithuania's territory includes five areas that used to belong to Byelorussia. Stalin ceded Klaipeda, which the Soviet Union, as the basis of the results of World War II, received just as it did Kaliningrad in Eastern Prussia. It received Lithuanian territories. So, they raise this question: to return to Russia these lands.

Recently, I held a press conference with President Mitterrand of France, just as I am doing now with President Bush here. And I said: Listen, in order to make a decision how to act with respect to overseas territories such as Caledonia, France has projected a period of 10 years. How is it possible for us to resolve issues such as this overnight, when people met pending the opening of the Third Congress of People's Deputies and put the question to the vote? Is that a responsible policy really, I ask myself. I really think that we are acting in accordance with the mandate from the Third Congress of People's Deputies. And we have a vast reserve of good will and constructive spirit; and we do our best in order to resolve, on the basis of constitutional approaches, this particular issue. But any other way would be unacceptable.

I keep referring to—well, I'm not asking the President to come over to us and bring order to our house. But I keep saying that President Bush would have resolved an issue like this within 24 hours, and he would have restored the validity of his Constitution within 24 hours in any State. [*Laughter*]

But we are going to resolve it. We are going to do it ourselves. With full responsibility, I wish to declare here now for all of you to know that we are anxious to see this issue resolved in such a way as everybody's interest would be taken into account and within the Constitution's framework.

Note: President Bush's 49th news conference began at 10 a.m. in the East Room at the White House. President Gorbachev spoke in Russian, and his remarks were translated by an interpreter. Marlin Fitzwater was Press Secretary to President Bush.

Presidential Determination No. 90–22—Memorandum on the Waiver of Requirements for Most-Favored-Nation Trade Status for Czechoslovakia
June 3, 1990

Memorandum for the Secretary of State

Subject: Determination Under Subsection 402(d)(5) of the Trade Act of 1974— Continuation of the Waiver Applicable to the Czech and Slovak Federal Republic

Pursuant to the authority vested in me under the Trade Act of 1974 (Public Law 93–618) ("the Act"), I determine that the continuation of the waiver applicable to the Czech and Slovak Federal Republic will

substantially promote the objectives of Section 402 of the Act, 19 U.S.C. 2432.

You are authorized and directed to publish this determination in the *Federal Register.*

GEORGE BUSH

Note: The memorandum was released by the Office of the Press Secretary on June 4.

Letter to Congressional Leaders on the Waiver of Requirements for Most-Favored-Nation Trade Status for Czechoslovakia
June 3, 1990

Dear Mr. Speaker: (Dear Mr. President:)

I hereby transmit my determination that continuation of the waiver applicable to the Czech and Slovak Federal Republic will substantially promote the objectives of Section 402 of the Trade Act of 1974. The attached documents, referred to in Section 402(d)(5) of the Trade Act of 1974, include my reasons for my determination that continuation of the waiver in effect for the

Czech and Slovak Federal Republic will substantially promote the objectives of Section 402.

Sincerely,

GEORGE BUSH

Pursuant to section 402 of the Trade Act of 1974, I have today determined that continuation of the waiver currently applicable to the Czech and Slovak Federal Republic will substantially promote the objectives of section 402 of the Act. My determination is attached and incorporated herein.

The Czechoslovak Government has already instituted reforms ensuring freedom of emigration for all of its citizens. The reform government of Vaclav Havel has implemented sweeping liberal emigration policies, eliminating virtually all the emigration restrictions of the previous communist regime. Under the new travel regulations issued by the Government of the Czech and Slovak Federal Republic on January 1, 1990, potential emigrants need only a valid passport and a foreign immigrant visa. Passports are now issued routinely and are valid for travel to all countries. Citizens no longer need exit visas to travel. All pending bilateral family reunification cases have been resolved.

Further, since I waived application of the Jackson-Vanik amendment on February 20, 1990, new laws have been passed guaranteeing freedom of religion, freedom of speech, freedom of association, and freedom of the press. Czechoslovakia's ethnic groups have agreed that interethnic disputes should be resolved by constitutional means.

Note: Identical letters were sent to Thomas S. Foley, Speaker of the House of Representatives, and Dan Quayle, President of the Senate. The letter and attachment were released by the Office of the Press Secretary on June 4.

Soviet-United States Joint Statement on Nonproliferation
June 4, 1990

The United States of America and the Union of Soviet Socialist Republics oppose the proliferation of nuclear weapons, chemical weapons, missiles capable of carrying such weapons, and certain other missiles and missile technologies. The more nations that possess such weapons, the more difficult it will be to realize the desire of people everywhere to achieve effective arms control and disarmament measures and to reduce the threat of war. Weapons proliferation can provoke or intensify insecurity and hostility among nations, and threatens mankind with warfare of unprecedented destructiveness.

Our discussions over the past months point the way to a new era in relations between our two countries. We have taken major steps toward concluding agreements to reduce our own strategic nuclear arsenals, to bring limits on nuclear testing into force, and to reach a global ban on chemical weapons. Together with the nations of Europe, we are taking unprecedented steps to reduce existing conventional weaponry as part of a process of building a lasting structure of European security. The progress we are making and the commitments we have made in these bilateral and multilateral arms control efforts clearly demonstrate that arms reductions can contribute to increased security, even when there have been long-standing and deep-seated differences between countries.

The historic steps we have taken to improve U.S.-Soviet relations and to cooperate in the interests of international stability create the possibility of even closer and more concrete cooperation in the areas of nuclear, chemical, and missile non-proliferation.

With these considerations in mind, The United States and the Soviet Union:

- Declare their commitment to preventing the proliferation of nuclear weapons, chemical weapons, and missiles capable of carrying such weapons and certain other missiles and missile technologies, in particular those subject to the provisions of the Missile Technology Control Regime (MTCR);
- Agree to work closely together and with other members of the international community to develop and to put

into action concrete measures against the proliferation of these types of weapons; and

- Call on other nations to join in a renewed commitment to effective non-proliferation measures as a means of securing international peace and stability and as a step toward the effective limitation worldwide of nuclear weapons, chemical weapons, missiles, and missile technology.

The two sides have taken specific actions to advance these commitments.

Nuclear Weapons Non-Proliferation

In order to prevent the proliferation of nuclear weapons, the United States and the Soviet Union:

- Reaffirm their steadfast and long-lasting commitment to prevent the proliferation of nuclear weapons and to strengthen the international nuclear weapons non-proliferation regime;
- Reaffirm their strong support for the Treaty on the Non-Proliferation of Nuclear Weapons (NPT) and agree that it continues to make an invaluable contribution to global and regional security and stability;
- Urge all countries which have not yet done so to adhere to the NPT;
- Urge all NPT parties to implement scrupulously their International Atomic Energy Agency (IAEA) safeguards obligations under the Treaty;
- Affirm their intention to cooperate together and with other Treaty parties to ensure a successful 1990 Review Conference on the Treaty on the Non-Proliferation of Nuclear Weapons which would reaffirm support for the objectives of the Treaty and its importance to international security and stability;
- Support the Treaty for the Prohibition of Nuclear Weapons in Latin America (the Treaty of Tlatelolco) and urge all countries in the region to bring it into force at an early date;
- Reiterate their continuing commitment to strengthening the IAEA, whose unique system of safeguards has contributed to the widespread peaceful use of nuclear energy for social and economic development;
- Support increased international cooperation in the peaceful uses of nuclear energy under IAEA safeguards;
- Call on all non-nuclear-weapons states with unsafeguarded nuclear activities to place these activities under international safeguards;
- Agree on the need for stringent controls over exports of nuclear-related material, equipment and technology, to ensure that they will not be misused for nuclear explosive purposes, and urge all other nations capable of exporting nuclear-related technology to apply similarly strict controls;
- Continue to support efforts to improve and strengthen the international nuclear export control regime;
- Support discussions among states in regions of nuclear proliferation concern for the purpose of achieving concrete steps to reduce the risk of nuclear proliferation, and, in particular, join in calling on the nations of the Middle East, Southern Africa, and South Asia to engage in and pursue such discussions;
- Agree to continue their regular, constructive bilateral consultations on nuclear weapons non-proliferation.

Missile and Missile Technology Non-Proliferation

In order to stem the proliferation of missiles and missile technology, the United States and the Soviet Union:

- Have signed the Treaty between the United States of America and the Union of Soviet Socialist Republics on the Elimination of Their Intermediate-Range and Shorter-Range Missiles, demonstrating that controls on—indeed the elimination of—such missiles can enhance national security;
- Reaffirm their intention that the START Treaty be signed by the end of the year;
- Affirm their support for the objectives of the Missile Technology Control Regime, covering missiles, and certain equipment and technology relating to missiles capable of delivering at least

500 kilograms of payload to a range of at least 300 kilometers and they call on all nations that have not done so to observe the spirit and the guidelines of this regime;

- Are taking measures to restrict missile proliferation on a worldwide basis, including export controls and other internal procedures;
- Have instituted bilateral consultations to exchange information concerning such controls and procedures and identify specific measures to prevent missile proliferation;
- Agree to work to stop missile proliferation, particularly in regions of tension, such as the Middle East;
- To this end, affirm their intent to explore regional initiatives to reduce the threat of missile proliferation, including the possibility of offering their good offices to promote such initiatives;
- Recall that they favor international economic cooperation including cooperation aimed at peaceful space exploration, as long as such cooperation could not contribute to missile proliferation;
- Appeal to all countries—to exporters of missiles and missile technology as well as purchasers—to exercise restraint, and express their willingness to continue their respective dialogues with other countries on the non-proliferation of missiles and missile technology.
- Are resolved, on their part, to continue to work to strengthen such international restraint with respect to missile and missile technology proliferation.

Chemical Weapons Non-proliferation

In order to stem the use and proliferation of chemical weapons, the United States and the Soviet Union:

- Declare that a multilateral, effectively verifiable chemical weapons convention banning the development, production and use of chemical weapons and eliminating all stocks on a global basis is the best long-term solution to the threat to international security posed by the use and spread of chemical

weapons, and that non-proliferation measures are considered a step toward achieving such a convention;
- Will intensify their cooperation to expedite the negotiations in Geneva with the view to resolving outstanding issues as soon as possible and to finalizing the draft convention at the earliest date;
- Have instituted bilateral confidence building measures, including chemical weapons data exchange and reciprocal site visits;
- Have just signed a trailblazing agreement on destruction and non-production of chemical weapons and on measures to facilitate the multilateral convention on chemical weapons;
- Commit themselves, in that agreement to take practical measures to encourage all chemical weapons-capable states to become parties to the multilateral convention;
- Having declared their possession of chemical weapons, urge other states possessing chemical weapons to declare their possession, to commit to their destruction, and to begin immediately to address, through research and cooperation, the need for chemical weapons destruction capability;
- State that they themselves will not proliferate chemical weapons;
- Have instituted export controls to stem the proliferation of chemical weapons. These measures are not intended to hinder or discriminate against legitimate peaceful chemical activities;
- Have agreed to conduct bilateral discussions to improve the effectiveness of their respective export controls to stem the proliferation of chemical weapons;
- Conduct regular bilateral consultations to broaden bilateral cooperation, including the reciprocal exchange of information on the problems of chemical weapons proliferation;
- Confirm their intent to pursue political and diplomatic actions, where specific cases give rise to concerns about the production, use or spread of chemical weapons;
- Join with other nations in multilateral efforts to coordinate export controls,

exchange information, and broaden international cooperation to stem the proliferation of chemical weapons;

• Reaffirm their support for the 1925 Geneva Protocol banning the use of chemical weapons in violation of international law;

• Are taking steps to strengthen the 1925 Geneva Protocol by:

—Encouraging states that are not parties to accede;

—Confirming their intention to provide active support to the United Nations Secretary General in conducting investigations of reported violations of the Protocol;

—Affirming their intention to consider the imposition of sanctions against violators of the Protocol, including those under Chapter VII of the United Nations Charter;

—Agreeing to consult promptly in the event of a violation of the Protocol to discuss possible bilateral and multilateral actions against the offender, as well as appropriate assistance to the victims of such violation;

• Agree that the presence and further proliferation of chemical weapons in areas of tension, such as the Middle East, is particularly dangerous. The two countries therefore affirm their intent to explore regional initiatives in the Middle East and other areas, including the possibility of offering their good offices to promote such initiatives as:

—Efforts to broaden awareness of the dangers of chemical weapons proliferation and its negative impact on implementation of the multilateral convention on chemical weapons;

—Bilateral or multilateral efforts to stem chemical weapons proliferation, including the renunciation of the production of chemical weapons;

—Efforts to destroy chemical weapons in advance of the multilateral convention on chemical weapons, as the United States and the Soviet Union are doing.

The United States and the Soviet Union call on all nations of the world that have not already done so to join them in taking comparable, effective measures to stem chemical weapons proliferation.

Note: The joint statement was made available by the Office of the Press Secretary but was not issued as a White House press release.

Soviet-United States Joint Statement on Bering Sea Fisheries Conservation
June 4, 1990

In the course of the state visit by the President of the Union of Soviet Socialist Republics to the United States of America, the sides reviewed problems posed by the development of an unregulated multi-national fishery for pollock in the central Bering Sea. In light of the magnitude of that fishery, which accounts for more than one-third of the total annual catch of pollock in the Bering Sea, the situation is of serious environmental concern. In particular, there is a danger to the stocks from overfishing. This may result in significant harm to the ecological balance in the Bering Sea and to those U.S. and USSR coastal communities whose livelihoods depend on the living marine resources of the Bering Sea.

The sides agreed that urgent conservation measures should be taken with regard to this unregulated fishery. The sides noted that, in accordance with international law as reflected in the relevant provisions of the 1982 United Nations Convention on the Law of the Sea, all concerned states, including coastal states and fishing states, should cooperate to ensure the conservation of these living resources. To this end, both sides noted that they would welcome cooperative efforts towards the development of an international regime for the conservation and management of the living marine resources in the central Bering Sea.

Note: The joint statement was made available by the Office of the Press Secretary but was not issued as a White House press release.

Soviet-United States Joint Statement on Cooperation in Peaceful Uses of Atomic Energy
June 4, 1990

During the state visit of Mikhail S. Gorbachev, President of the USSR, at the invitation of George Bush, President of the United States, the sides concluded a new U.S.-USSR Agreement on Scientific and Technical Cooperation in the Field of Peaceful Uses of Atomic Energy. This Agreement strengthens the longstanding framework for important research in a number of fields of mutual interest, including controlled thermonuclear fusion, fundamental properties of matter, and civilian nuclear reactor safety.

Recognizing the need to manage responsibly the development and utilization of nuclear power, the two sides have agreed on cooperation in the study of the health and environmental effects of past, present and future nuclear power generation, and in strengthening operational safety practices in civilian nuclear reactors. The sides intend to develop and implement promptly a mutually beneficial joint program of work in these fields under this Agreement. They also agreed to explore the possibilities for cooperation in the management of hazardous and radioactive waste.

Note: The joint statement was made available by the Office of the Press Secretary but was not issued as a White House press release.

Soviet-United States Joint Statement on the International Thermonuclear Experimental Reactor
June 4, 1990

At their meeting in Geneva in 1985, the leaders of the United States and the Soviet Union emphasized the importance of the work aimed at utilizing controlled thermonuclear fusion for peaceful purposes, and advocated the widest practical development of international cooperation in obtaining this essentially inexhaustible source of energy for the benefit of all mankind.

The International Thermonuclear Experimental Reactor (ITER) project, involving joint efforts by the USSR, the United States, Japan and the European Community, under the aegis of the International Atomic Energy Agency, is making significant progress towards this end. A conceptual design will soon be completed.

Noting with satisfaction the results being attained under this project, the United States and the Soviet Union look forward to continued international efforts aimed at promoting further progress in developing controlled thermonuclear fusion for peaceful purposes.

Note: The joint statement was made available by the Office of the Press Secretary but was not issued as a White House press release.

Soviet-United States Joint Statement on Technical Economic Cooperation
June 4, 1990

The two sides reiterated their commitment to the program of technical economic cooperation outlined by Presidents Bush and Gorbachev at Malta in December and expressed a desire to expand the scope and number of joint projects. This program is a concrete expression of U.S. and Soviet commitment to work together in support of economic perestroyka. Its goal is to advance the process of market-oriented economic reform by sharing experience and expertise regarding the problems and opportunities involved in building market structures and institutions.

Projects and contacts currently underway at the expert level include statistical cooperation, development of small businesses, establishment of financial markets, banking reform, and tax administration. The two sides also had useful discussions on economic policy issues during visits by the Soviet Minister of Finance and State Bank Chairman to Washington, and the Chairman of the President's Council of Economic Advisors and the Chairman of the Federal Reserve Board to Moscow.

The two sides will work to expand the scope of current cooperation projects and in particular to develop new projects in areas of special interest, including anti-trust issues, enterprise management, and economic education. The two sides also noted that private exchanges and projects can be consistent with and complement technical cooperation. Both sides believe that technical economic cooperation is in their mutual benefit in promoting the successful development of market-oriented reforms.

Note: The joint statement was made available by the Office of the Press Secretary but was not issued as a White House press release.

Exchange With Reporters at a Briefing for Cabinet Members on the Soviet-United States Summit
June 4, 1990

Q. What was the applause all about, Mr. President?

The President. Scintillating personality, I guess? [*Laughter*]

Q. Something we don't know about happen at the summit?

Q. Scintillating results?

The President. I'm very pleased with the results of the summit. And I think the American people are. I think maybe that was manifested by the welcome I was given here.

Maybe it is a good time to thank everybody around this table and the White House staff and staffs in the various Departments because often—Jules knows this for the work he's done here and abroad—we don't really adequately get to thank the people in the Government, career people or appointed people, who flesh out the agreements and work up the agenda and deal behind the scenes with no credit, no sitting at the head table. And this meeting, with a broad array of issues, convinces me that I am very fortunate to have this Cabinet team and to have the White House staff, as energetic as it is, and General Scowcroft and his people—doing a superb job on preparation—and then the Departments themselves that work for everybody around this table. And I know Jim Baker would second the motion.

So, I am pleased with the results. And I think the reception from the American people was rather clear. There are some problems. We never said there wouldn't be. We had a chance to describe the problems.

And that's it, because this is what they call a modified photo opportunity. [*Laughter*]

Q. How many allies did you call?

The President. I'm not going to take any questions; I took them all yesterday. And Marlin will give you that; but the mood from the allies so far, the ones I've talked to, have been very, very positive. And that is important when you're dealing with issues of this nature. Let me elaborate, Helen [Helen Thomas, United Press International]—I will now modify the modification.

I did talk with Helmut Kohl yesterday, and I talked to Margaret Thatcher yesterday. And I'm not going to put words in their mouth, but I was very pleased with their response. And then I talked to President Reagan, to give him a briefing as to what he might anticipate at his breakfast. So, I did that after the meeting. But we'll have to wait and see what the response is from around the world, but so far our experts have been very pleased.

Note: The exchange began at 10:08 a.m. in the Cabinet Room at the White House. In his remarks, he referred to Julius L. Katz, Deputy U.S. Trade Representative; Brent Scowcroft, Assistant to the President for National Security Affairs; Marlin Fitzwater, Press Secretary to the President; Helmut Kohl, Chancellor of the Federal Republic of Germany; and Margaret Thatcher, Prime Minister of the United Kingdom.

Statement by Press Secretary Fitzwater on the President's Meeting With Secretary-General Javier Perez de Cuellar de la Guerra of the United Nations
June 4, 1990

The President met today with United Nations Secretary-General Javier Perez de Cuellar. Following a meeting, the President hosted a working luncheon in honor of the Secretary-General. They discussed United Nations activities and matters of mutual interest, and they noted the increased role the U.N. has been playing in the changing world.

The President explained that the United States will soon release an additional $62.5 million to the United Nations to pay current dues. The President reaffirmed to the Secretary-General his view that the United States should meet its financial obligations to the United Nations, which are solemn international obligations made by the United States after full consultation with Congress. He expressed his hope that Congress will provide the necessary funds, including payment of arrears.

Appointment of Edith E. Holiday as Assistant to the President and Secretary to the Cabinet
June 4, 1990

The President has appointed Edith E. Holiday to be Assistant to the President and Secretary of the Cabinet. She would succeed David Bates.

For the past 21 months Ms. Holiday has served in the Treasury Department, most recently as General Counsel, 1989–1990. Prior to this, she served as Assistant Secretary of the Treasury for Public Affairs and Public Liaison and Counselor to the Secretary, 1988–1989; chief counsel and national financial and operations director for the Bush-Quayle 1988 Presidential campaign; director of operations for George Bush for President, 1987–1988; and special counsel for the Fund for America's Future, 1985–1987. In addition, Ms. Holiday has served as Executive Director for the President's Commission on Executive, Legislative, and Judicial Salaries, 1984–1985; an attorney with the law firm of Dow Lohnes and Albertson, 1983–1984; an attorney with the law firm of Reed Smith and McClay, 1977–1983; and legislative director for United States Senator Nicholas F. Brady, 1982.

Ms. Holiday graduated from the University of Florida (B.S., 1974; J.D., 1977). She was born in Middletown, OH. Ms. Holiday is married to Terrence B. Adamson; has one child, Kathlyn, and one stepson, Terrence Morgan Adamson; and resides in Atlanta, GA, and Washington, DC.

Statement by Press Secretary Fitzwater on the Appointment of William Frederick Sittmann as Executive Secretary of the National Security Council
June 4, 1990

The President today announced the appointment of William Frederick Sittmann as Executive Secretary of the National Security Council.

Mr. Sittmann is a native of Decatur, IN. He attended the University of Richmond in Richmond, VA, and received a B.A. degree in political science and history. Following his graduation, he served in the Foreign Service with the State Department from 1974 to 1982. From 1982 through 1985, Mr. Sittmann served in the White House as a Special Assistant to President Reagan. He then joined the Washington, DC, firm of Michael K. Deaver and Associates before assuming the position of vice president of Kissinger Associates, Inc., a New York consulting firm. Mr. Sittmann has served since June 1989, as the Deputy Executive Secretary of the National Security Council.

Mr. Sittmann is married to the former Anne Marie Schlichter. They have one daughter, Meredith, and reside in Alexandria, VA.

Nomination of David H. Leroy To Be Nuclear Waste Negotiator
June 4, 1990

The President today announced his intention to nominate David H. Leroy to be Nuclear Waste Negotiator. This is a new position.

Currently, Mr. Leroy serves as an attorney with Leroy Law Offices in Boise, ID. Prior to this, he served as Lieutenant Governor of Idaho, 1983–1987; Idaho attorney general, 1979–1983; Ada County prosecuting attorney, 1974–1978; deputy prosecuting attorney for Ada County, 1973–1974; and an associate attorney with the law firm of Rothblatt, Rothblatt, Seijas and Peskin in New York, NY, 1971–1972.

Mr. Leroy graduated from the University of Idaho (B.S., 1969; J.D., 1971) and New York University School of Law (M.L., 1972). He was born August 16, 1947, in Seattle, WA. Mr. Leroy is married, has two children, and resides in Boise, ID.

Statement on the Anniversary of the Suppression of the Demonstrations at Tiananmen Square
June 4, 1990

One year ago, as China commenced the brutal suppression of peaceful demonstrators around Tiananmen Square, I deeply deplored the decision to use force. Two days later, on June 5, I again deplored the violence, emphasizing that the demonstrators in Tiananmen Square were advocating basic human rights, including freedom of expression, freedom of the press, and freedom of association. These are freedoms that are enshrined in both the U.S. Constitution and the Chinese Constitution, and are goals we support around the world. America will always stand with those who seek greater freedom and democracy—this is the strongly felt view of my administration, of our Congress, and most important, of the American people.

China's citizens, through massive demonstrations in scores of cities, were expressing the same yearnings and aspirations we have seen in so many places in the world during the last several years. The peoples of the Philippines, the Republic of Korea, Taiwan, Mongolia, Panama, Nicaragua, Czechoslovakia, East Germany, Bulgaria, Poland, Hungary, Romania, the Soviet Union, South Africa, and Burma have expressed those desires with their lives, their voices, and their votes. The institutions that each chooses to adopt will vary, but the values of democracy and freedom underlie the movements in all of them.

Transforming China—with its 4,000 year-old civilization, its own distinct and extraordinary traditions, an undeveloped economy, and an historically authoritarian political system—is a monumental task. China made great strides from 1978 to 1988 in the face of difficulties, and the dramatic growth in U.S.-China relations during those 10 years was testimony to that progress. I remain deeply concerned by the lack of respect for internationally recognized human rights in China today, and urge a rapid return to the most positive course set before Tiananmen occurred.

As China's people and leaders seek to recover from the wounds of Tiananmen, they should find inspiration in the modern, universal urge for freedom and democracy. At the same time, they will find guidance in those benevolent traditions of China which emphasize righteousness and justice.

The world watched with awe the restraint of the peaceful demonstrators in Tiananmen, the people of a great nation seeking freedom and economic modernization. The world will continue to watch in the years ahead with the hope that China will turn decisively away from repression and toward the path of reform. The American people and government—who value good relations with the Chinese people and government—stand ready to develop this relationship as China resumes that path.

Remarks at a Ceremony Honoring the GI Bill
June 5, 1990

Thank you all. And I'm delighted to be here with two members of my Cabinet: Dick Cheney, who's doing an outstanding job leading America's defense forces, and of course, Sam Skinner, our very able Secretary of Transportation. Chairman of our Joint Chiefs is here, General Colin Powell, Secretary Stone, Secretary Rice. General

Gray was to be here, and there he is. And I'm going to omit somebody, so I'll stop right there. But just welcome all of you.

And I also want to recognize, single out, so many Members of the United States Congress that are here today. I'm delighted that you are. And, of course, the representatives of the Armed Forces. Most of all, I guess we got to pay tribute to the distinguished Representative from the State of Mississippi, the Chairman of the House Veterans Affairs Committee, and the Army veteran for whom this historic bill was named, our old friend, my old friend, Sonny Montgomery.

Sonny—I got to hand it to Sonny. He and I were elected to Congress on exactly the same day many years ago. And he's the one who's got his name on both a major, significant piece of legislation and a gigantic building—Air National Guard complex down in Mississippi.

But today, I'm very pleased and honored to welcome you to the Rose Garden and to have this opportunity to tell you personally just how important I believe this program is. From the time it was first launched in 1944, the original GI bill was a huge, bold, and successful experiment, an ongoing experiment in which young men and women from all walks of life are given not only a choice but also a chance: a chance for a higher education and their own piece of the American dream.

In 1945, October, Barbara and I joined the ranks of more than 40,000 couples who headed to college that year on the original GI bill. America's schools were soon swamped with prefab housing and trailers. And by 1946 and 1947, the flood tide had crested, and more than 2½ million veterans had embarked on getting their education.

The GI bill has special importance to me, and special importance to the peace and prosperity that America has enjoyed during the 46 years since it first began. The GI bill changed the lives of millions by replacing old roadblocks with paths of opportunity. And, in so doing, it boosted America's work force, it boosted America's economy, and really, it changed the life of our nation.

And thanks to people like Congressman Montgomery and other leaders here from both the Senate and the House today, the GI bill has continued to successfully improve and evolve. And I remember some of the tough battles that were fought to get the new bill through Congress. Sonny interrupted one marathon conference session with a rather unique reminder of the needs of the military and of his own commitment to stick it out. He brought in C-rations. Well, I've tried C-rations, and eating them

on the Hill is my definition of serious commitment.

The success of Sonny's effort is evidence in the young American heroes we salute today, the men and women here representing America's armed services and symbolizing the one millionth participant in the Montgomery GI bill. Airmen like Alabama's Jeramie Brown, who leaves for Munich tomorrow to help tell the story of America through the Armed Forces Network. The Coast Guard's Keith Pyle, who was part of the honor guard last month at the wreath-laying ceremony at the Tomb of the Unknown Soldier. Medical specialists like the Army's Linda Meidling, who's been on the dean's list at Stockton State College since 1987. And reservists like Chicago's Teryl Speights, who puts in time with two jobs: reading x-rays at the West Side V.A. Hospital and reading radar screens at Glenview Naval Air Base. Those are definitely two jobs, Teryl, that you don't want to get mixed up. [*Laughter*]

But for America, as for these individuals, the payback has been terrific. Today, the Montgomery GI bill ranks among the most practical and cost-efficient programs ever devised and represents one of the best Federal investments since Betsy Ross bought needle and thread.

To begin with, right now the program is more than paying for itself, and even as payouts increase, four decades of experience have taught us that the increased earnings of these educated GI's also mean increased tax revenues for America. And the additional education its participants receive continues to produce a technological gain for our country.

Even more important are the improvements in our Armed Forces. The Montgomery GI bill has been an important component in the success of America's all-volunteer forces. And let me just repeat here what Colin Powell and the other Chiefs have told me over and over again: we have never had better men and women in the Armed Forces than we have today. This program contributes to savings because better educated recruits mean training costs and attrition have gone down, while productivity and morale have gone up.

This bill is playing an important role in promoting excellence in our Armed Forces. And it's also playing an important role in promoting excellence in education. Several of its components—choice, flexibility, competitiveness—parallel some of the most important components of the Educational Excellence Act that we sent to the Congress last April, a critical first step in our efforts to revitalize quality in America's schools. It was passed by the Senate in February. And I believe it's time for the House to act now. So, let's make this year of change, a year of progress in education. Let's strike a blow for excellence, and let's get that legislation passed.

Education is our most enduring legacy, vital to everything we are and can become. And the Montgomery GI bill is a powerful example of what is right about education in America. Our Armed Forces and our system of higher education are today the envy of the world. And so, I'm here to thank you for your important work, the work you do in defending our nation's freedom; in educating our nation's youth; and in ensuring that, whether in military might or educational excellence, the United States of America stands second to none.

Thank you for coming to the White House today. And God bless you in your efforts. And God bless the United States of America. Thank you all very, very much.

Note: The President spoke at 11:27 a.m. in the Rose Garden at the White House. In his remarks, the President referred to Secretary of the Army Michael P.W. Stone, Secretary of the Air Force Donald B. Rice, and Commandant of the Marine Corps Gen. A.M. Gray, Jr.

Appointment of the 1990–91 White House Fellows
June 6, 1990

The President today announced the appointments of the 1990–91 White House fellows. This is the 26th class of fellows since the program was established in 1964. Twelve fellows were chosen from nearly 1,000 applicants who were screened by 11 regional panels. The President's Commission on White House Fellowships, chaired by Ronna Romney, interviewed the 33 national finalists prior to recommending the 12 persons to the President. Their year of government service will begin September 1, 1990.

Fellows serve for 1 year as special assistants to the President's principal staff, the Vice President, and members of the Cabinet. In addition to the work assignments, the fellowship includes an education program that parallels and broadens the unique experience of working at the highest levels of the Federal Government. The program is open to U.S. citizens in the early stages of their careers and from all occupations and professions. Federal Government employees are not eligible, with the exception of career Armed Forces personnel. Leadership, character, intellectual and professional ability, and commitment to community and national service are the principal criteria employed in the selection of fellows.

Applications for the 1991–92 program are available from the President's Commission on White House Fellowships, 712 Jackson Place, NW, Washington, DC 20503.

The 1990–91 White House fellows are:

Andrew I. Batavia, of Washington, DC. Mr. Batavia is the Director of the Health Services Research Program at the National Rehabilitation Hospital Research Center in Washington, DC. He is also a faculty member of the department of community and family medicine of the Georgetown School of Medicine in Washington and has authored over 20 publications on issues of health care and disability policy. Mr. Batavia graduated from the University of California at Riverside (B.A., 1980). He received an M.S. degree in health services research from Stanford Medical School in 1983 and graduated from Harvard Law School (J.D., 1984). Mr. Batavia was born June 15, 1957, in Brooklyn, NY.

Samuel Dale Brownback, of Topeka, KS. Mr. Brownback serves as the secretary of agriculture in the State of Kansas. A specialist in agricultural law, he has taught at Kansas State University and has written numerous articles and two books on the subject. Mr. Brownback graduated from Kansas State University (B.S., 1979) and from the University of Kansas (J.D., 1982). Mr. Brownback was born September 12, 1956, in Garnett, KS.

Robert Bruce Chess, of Palo Alto, CA. Mr. Chess is the president of Penederm, a biotechnology company he cofounded in 1986. A successful entrepreneur with both a technology and business background, he has started two companies and helped in the establishment of three others during the past 6 years. Mr. Chess graduated from California Institute of Technology (B.S., 1978) and from Harvard Graduate School of Business (M.B.A., 1980). He was born January 31, 1957, in Inglewood, CA.

Jody Ann Greenstone, of Greenville, SC. Ms. Greenstone is a vice president in public finance with the Robinson-Humphrey Co., Inc., a subsidiary of Shearson Lehman Hutton. Her interest in the improvement of housing in South Carolina has afforded her the opportunity to serve as a member of the board of the South Carolina Low Income Housing Coalition and as an appointee to the South Carolina Affordable Housing Council. Ms. Greenstone graduated from the University of Michigan (B.A., 1979) and from the University of Virginia School of Law (J.D., 1982). She was born March 18, 1958, in Philadelphia, PA.

Robert R. Grusky, of Croton-on-Hudson, NY. Mr. Grusky is a vice president in the investment banking division of Goldman, Sachs & Co. He actively supports the Hackley School in Tarrytown, NY, where he serves as a member of the alumni board of directors and as an adviser to the investment committee of their board of trustees. Mr. Grusky graduated from Union College (B.A., 1979) and from the Harvard Business School (M.B.A., 1985). He was born August 19, 1957, in New York City.

Willie Arthur Gunn, of Fort Lauderdale, FL. Captain Gunn serves in the U.S. Air Force as a circuit defense counsel for a five-State region in the western United States, defending service members in complex criminal cases. He also serves as vice chairperson of the National Bar Association's military law section. Captain Gunn graduated from the U.S. Air Force Academy (B.S., 1980) and from Harvard Law School (J.D., 1986). He was born December 14, 1958, in Birmingham, AL.

Randall Herman Kehl, of Albuquerque, NM. Major Kehl serves in the U.S. Air Force as an attorney in the office of the Judge Advocate General, Washington, DC. He has been a member of the adjunct law faculty at the University of Alaska, and in 1989 the American Bar Association honored him as the Outstanding Young Military Service Lawyer of the Year. Major Kehl graduated from the U.S. Air Force Academy (B.S., 1976) and from the Graduate School of Business Administration, University of North Dakota (M.B.A., 1980). He graduated from the School of Law, Pepperdine University (J.D., 1983). Major Kehl was born May 18, 1954, in Furstenfeldbruck, Germany.

John William Miller, of Annapolis, MD. Lieutenant Commander Miller is a flight officer in the U.S. Navy. He is presently assigned as a leadership section head in the department of leadership and law at the U.S. Naval Academy, Annapolis, MD. In 1984 he was selected as the Fighter Wing One Radar Intercept Officer of the Year and the Atlantic Fleet Naval Flight Officer of the Year. He graduated from the U.S. Naval Academy in 1979 and is a recent graduate of the Naval War College. Lieutenant Commander Miller was born October 2, 1957, in Chicago, IL.

Eric McLaren Phillips, of Maplewood, NJ. Mr. Phillips is currently a district manager within AT&T International Communications Services, Basking Ridge, NJ. In 1989, he received an Outstanding Service Award from AT&T Bell Laboratories for his exceptional contribution in his field of electrical engineering and computer science. Mr. Phillips graduated from McMaster in Canada (B.S., 1976) and from New York University (M.B.A., 1983). He was born October 19, 1952, in Dundee, Mahaicony, Guyana.

Edward Augustus Rice, Jr., of Yellow Springs, OH. Major Rice is currently assigned as a rated force manager in the directorate of plans and operations, U.S. Air Force, Washington, DC. He is a distinguished Air Force pilot and graduated with highest distinction from the College of Naval Command and Staff at the Naval War College in Newport, RI. Major Rice graduated from the U.S. Air Force Academy (B.S., 1978) and from Embry Riddle Aeronautical University (M.S., 1987). He was born March 31, 1956, in Albuquerque, NM.

Joseph E. Samora, Jr., of Albuquerque, NM. Mr. Samora is chairman of the New Mexico Public Service Commission. In 1988, he was selected by the American Bar Association's young lawyers division's Barrister magazine as one of "20 Young Lawyers in the United States Who Make a Difference." He graduated from the University of New Mexico (B.A., 1978) and from the University of New Mexico School of Law (J.D.,

779

1982). Mr. Samora was born September 6, 1955, in Albuquerque, NM.

Kimberly Till, of Prattville, AL. Ms. Till is an international management consultant with Bain & Co. in London, England. In 1980–81, she was selected as a Henry Luce scholar and spent a year working in Japan on trade and investment projects. She graduated from the University of Alabama (B.A., 1977), from Duke University School of Law (J.D., 1980), and from the Harvard Graduate School of Business Administration (M.B.A., 1983). Ms. Till was born September 22, 1955, in Bainbridge, MD.

Message to the Congress Transmitting the Annual Report on Environmental Quality
June 6, 1990

To the Congress of the United States:

The people of this country share a deeply rooted love and concern for the environment. We have been blessed with a wealth of natural resources that enrich our physical and spiritual lives, and throughout our history we have recognized our responsibility to protect those resources for the generations to come.

Even as the pioneers traveled west to civilize a wild and seemingly endless frontier, there were Americans who understood that the Nation's natural resources had to be conserved for the future. In 1871, long before all of the continental states were incorporated into the Union, two million acres were set aside to create Yellowstone, our first national park.

The consequences of thoughtless exploitation of our natural resources began to be noticed more than a century ago. In 1908, President Theodore Roosevelt convened at the White House a national conference on conservation, where he said: "The wise use of all our natural resources, which are our national resources as well, is the great material question of today." That conference was a historical landmark in the development of public policy to protect and manage this country's natural resources.

Our national environmental ethic was expressed with particular clarity and conviction in 1970. On the first day of that year, President Nixon signed the National Environmental Policy Act, which created the Council on Environmental Quality and incorporated environmental awareness into the planning processes of the Federal Government. On the last day of 1970, the President signed the Clean Air Act, the Nation's first comprehensive environmental protection law. During that year, the Environmental Protection Agency and the National Oceanographic and Atmospheric Administration were established. And on April 22, 1970, millions of Americans voiced their environmental hopes and concerns on Earth Day.

This long national tradition of natural resource stewardship and environmental protection continues today, and in many ways it is stronger than ever. During the last 20 years we have built on the work begun in 1970, and the results have been remarkable. Possible effects on the environment are now weighed carefully whenever Federal agencies plan major actions. Our scientists have developed pollutant detection and control technologies that are far more effective than anything available in 1970. Environmental laws are now enforced, and environmental crimes punished, at every level of government, and enforcement officials have more legal and technical tools at their disposal than ever before. Besides spending billions of dollars a year to capture pollutants before they enter the air or water, American companies are beginning to invest in production materials and processes that generate much less pollution. And governments around the world are working together in unprecedented ways to solve pollution problems that affect the global quality of life.

We can be proud of our environmental track record. In many ways we have set an example for the rest of the world, and other nations continue to look to the United States for environmental leadership. Over the past year, as the countries of Eastern Europe shook off their chains and took charge of their own political and economic lives, they turned to us for help in reversing decades of environmental neglect.

This 1989 Report to the Congress on Environmental Quality is a retrospective—a look back at the ways our national environmental ethic has evolved over the past 20 years. And in looking back, the report also suggests a fair measure of hope for the future.

We have not solved all our environmental problems. Some we have only begun to understand. But over the past 2 decades we have proven to ourselves, and to the rest of the world, that we are willing to act on our beliefs. If the best prophet of the future is the past, as Lord Byron once wrote, then our children and grandchildren can look forward to the same good health, clean environment, and abundant natural resources that so many Americans have been so fortunate to share.

GEORGE BUSH

The White House,
June 6, 1990.

Nomination of Roy M. Huffington To Be United States Ambassador to Austria
June 6, 1990

The President today announced his intention to nominate Roy M. Huffington, of Texas, to be Ambassador Extraordinary and Plenipotentiary of the United States of America to the Republic of Austria. He would succeed Henry Anatole Grunwald.

Dr. Huffington has served as owner of Roy M. Huffington, Inc., 1956 to present, and as president, chairman of the board, and director and treasurer since 1958. Prior to this, he served as a field geologist, senior geologist, and division exploration geologist with the Humble Oil and Refining Co., 1946–1956; instructor in geology at Harvard University, 1942; and as a teaching fellow at Harvard University, 1939–1942.

Dr. Huffington graduated from Southern Methodist University (B.S., 1938) and Harvard University (M.A., 1941; Ph.D., 1942). He was born October 4, 1917, in Tomball, TX. Dr. Huffington served in the U.S. Navy, 1942–1945. He is married, has two children, and resides in Houston, TX.

Nomination of Hugh Kenneth Hill To Be United States Ambassador to Bulgaria
June 6, 1990

The President today announced his intention to nominate Hugh Kenneth Hill, of California, a career member of the Senior Foreign Service, Class of Minister-Counselor, to be Ambassador Extraordinary and Plenipotentiary of the United States of America to the People's Republic of Bulgaria. He would succeed Sol Polansky.

Since 1988 Mr. Hill has served as counselor and then chief of the Senior Officer Division at the Department of State. Prior to this, he served as Deputy Chief of Mission for the U.S. Embassy in Lusaka, Zambia, 1984–1988; Deputy Chief of Mission for the U.S. Embassy in Sofia, Bulgaria, 1982–1984; Deputy Director of the Office of Security Assistance and Foreign Military Sales in the Bureau of Political-Military Affairs, 1980–1982; management analyst in the Bureau of Management Operations, 1978–1980;

781

human rights officer in the Bureau of Human Rights at the Department of State, 1976–1978; and political officer for the U.S. Embassy in Belgrade, Yugoslavia, 1973–1976. In addition, Mr. Hill has served as a desk officer for the Federal Republic of Germany in the Office of German Affairs at the Department of State, 1970–1972; vice consul/consul for the U.S. mission in West Berlin, 1968–1970; vice consul for the U.S. consulate general in Frankfurt am Main,

West Germany, 1966–1968; and vice consul for the U.S. consulate general in Jerusalem, 1965–1966. He entered the Foreign Service in 1964.

Mr. Hill graduated from the University of California (B.A., 1959; M.A., 1964). He was born June 14, 1937, in Cushing, TX. Mr. Hill served in the U.S. Army, 1961–1963. Mr. Hill is married, has three children, and resides in Bethesda, MD.

Nomination of Frederick Vreeland To Be United States Ambassador to Burma (Myanmar)
June 6, 1990

The President today announced his intention to nominate Frederick Vreeland, of New York, to be Ambassador Extraordinary and Plenipotentiary of the United States of America to the Union of Burma (Myanmar). He would succeed Burton Levin.

Since 1989 Mr. Vreeland has served as vice president of John Cabot International College in Rome, Italy. Prior to this, he served as contributing editor of Conde Nast Traveler in New York, 1988; director of Aspen Institute in Rome, Italy, 1985–1987; counselor and political officer for the U.S. Embassy in Rome, 1978–1985; political officer for the U.S. Embassy in Paris, 1971–1978; political and security officer for the U.S. mission to the United Nations in New York, 1967–1971; deputy chief of the eco-

nomic section for the U.S. Embassy in Rabat, Morocco, 1963–1967; temporary aide to the National Security Council at the White House, 1963; and political officer for the U.S. Embassy in Bonn, Germany, 1959–1963. In addition, he has served as an economic officer for the U.S. mission in Berlin, Germany, 1957–1959; and economic officer for the U.S. mission in Geneva, Switzerland, 1952–1957. Mr. Vreeland entered the Foreign Service in 1952.

Mr. Vreeland graduated from Yale University (B.A., 1951). He was born June 24, 1927, in Danbury, CT. Mr. Vreeland served in the U.S. Naval Reserve, 1945–1947. He is married, has two children, and resides in Rome, Italy.

Nomination of Aurelia Erskine Brazeal To Be United States Ambassador to Micronesia
June 6, 1990

The President today announced his intention to nominate Aurelia Erskine Brazeal, of Georgia, a career member of the Senior Foreign Service, Class of Minister-Counselor, to be Ambassador Extraordinary and Plenipotentiary of the United States of America to the Federated States of Micronesia.

Since 1987 Ms. Brazeal has served as Minister-Counselor for Economic Affairs for the U.S. Embassy in Tokyo. Prior to this, she served as a member of the Senior Seminar, 1986–1987; Deputy Director for Economics at the Department of State, 1984–1986; in the Economic Bureau of the Office of Development Finance at the Department of

State, 1982–1984; economic officer in Tokyo, 1979–1982; review officer for the Treasury Department Secretariat, 1977–1979; Uruguay/Paraguay desk officer, 1974–1977; and watch officer and line officer for the Secretariat staff at the Department of State, 1973–1974. In addition, she has served as an economic reports officer in the Economic Bureau at the Department of

State, 1971–1972; and a consular and economic officer for the U.S. Embassy in Buenos Aires, 1969–1971. Ms. Brazeal entered the Foreign Service in 1968.

Ms. Brazeal graduated from Spelman College (B.A., 1965) and Columbia University (M.I.A., 1967). She was born November 24, 1943, in Chicago, IL.

Accordance of the Personal Rank of Ambassador to John F. Maisto While Representing the United States at the Organization of American States
June 6, 1990

The President today accorded the personal rank of Ambassador to John F. Maisto, of Virginia, a career member of the Senior Foreign Service, Class of Minister-Counselor, in his capacity as Vice Chairman of the U.S. delegation to the OAS General Assembly, and as Head of the U.S. delegation to the Inter-American Council for Education, Science, and Culture (CIECC) and the Inter-American Economic and Social Council (CIES).

Since 1989 Mr. Maisto has served as Deputy U.S. Representative to the Organization of American States. Prior to this, he served as Deputy Chief of Mission for the U.S. Embassy in Panama, 1986–1989; in political affairs for the Bureau of East Asian and Pacific Affairs, Department of State, 1984–1986; deputy office director for the Philippines in the Bureau of East Asian and Pacific Affairs, 1982–1984; political officer at the U.S. Embassy in Manila, Philippines, 1978–1982; political officer at the U.S. Em-

bassy in San José, Costa Rica, 1975–1978; international relations officer for the Bureau of Inter-American Affairs in the Office of Andean Affairs, 1973–1975; and an international relations officer for the Operations Center and Special Assistant in the Office of the Counselor of the Department, 1972. In addition, Mr. Maisto has served as an economic and commercial officer at the U.S. Embassy in La Paz, Bolivia, 1969–1972, and administrative assistant for the Foreign Service Institute at the Department of State, 1968–1969. Mr. Maisto entered the Foreign Service in 1968. He served in the U.S. Information Agency, 1963–1968. Mr. Maisto was assistant cultural affairs officer, 1966–1968, and he served at the BiNational Center in Cochabamba, Bolivia, 1963–1966.

Mr. Maisto graduated from Georgetown University (B.S.F., 1961) and San Carlos College (M.A., 1962). He was born August 28, 1938, in Braddock, PA. Mr. Maisto is married, has one child, and resides in Washington, DC.

Nomination of William Eric Andersen To Be Administrator of the Wage and Hour Division at the Department of Labor
June 6, 1990

The President today announced his intention to nominate William Eric Andersen to

be Administrator of the Wage and Hour Division at the Department of Labor. He would succeed Paula V. Smith.

Currently Mr. Andersen serves as Deputy Assistant Secretary for the Employment Standards Administration at the Department of Labor in Washington, DC. Prior to this he served as an attorney with the law firm of Baker, Worthington, Crossley, Stransberry and Woolf in Johnson City, TN.

Mr. Andersen graduated from the U.S. Military Academy (B.S., 1976) and Vanderbilt Law School (J.D., 1984). He was born September 28, 1954, in Bristol, TN. Mr. Andersen served in the U.S. Army, 1976–1981. He is married, has one child, and resides in Washington, DC.

Letter to Congressional Leaders Transmitting National Forest and Rangeland Management Proposals
June 7, 1990

Dear Mr. Speaker: *(Dear Mr. President:)*

I am pleased to transmit my Statement of Policy for the Recommended 1990 RPA Program regarding Federal management and use of our Nation's natural resources pursuant to the Forest and Rangeland Renewable Resources Planning Act (RPA) of 1974 (16 U.S.C. 1606). Accompanying the Statement of Policy is the *RPA Assessment of the Forest and Rangeland Situation in the United States, 1989,* and the Secretary of Agriculture's recommended program entitled *The Forest Service Program for Forest and Rangeland Resources: A Long-term Strategic Plan.*

The Secretary of Agriculture's proposed program provides important guidance for the conservation and wise use of the Nation's natural resources. The proposal recommits the Forest Service to multiple-use principles, while emphasizing the importance of seeking a proper balance among resources and the commitment to a healthy environment. It is a strategy that will help to ensure a proud legacy of diverse forests and rangelands for future generations of Americans.

Sincerely,

GEORGE BUSH

Note: Identical letters were sent to Thomas S. Foley, Speaker of the House of Representatives, and Dan Quayle, President of the Senate.

Statement by Deputy Press Secretary Glen on the Termination of the State of Emergency in South Africa
June 7, 1990

We welcome the announcement of the ending of the state of emergency in South Africa, except in Natal. This is another significant step toward creating a climate conducive to negotiations that will lead to a democratic, nonracial South Africa. This announcement builds on earlier decisions by President de Klerk to release Nelson Mandela and certain other political prisoners, to unban the ANC [African National Congress] and other organizations, and to permit free political debate to take place in South Africa.

Much work remains to be done by all sides. The issue of the remaining political prisoners needs to be resolved. The continuing climate of violence and intimidation must be transformed. The senseless killings in Natal Province must end.

However, we are encouraged by the remarkable progress that has been made in recent months. With this latest move, the

Government has moved to meet almost all of the opposition's requirements to enter into negotiations. We look forward to the early beginning of a negotiating process.

Remarks at a Fundraising Luncheon for Governor Tommy Thompson in Milwaukee, Wisconsin
June 7, 1990

Thank you all very much. Thank you, Tommy, very, very much—and all of you—for that warm welcome. I'm pleased to be joined today by several illustrious people—one, my very able chief of the Small Business Administration, Wisconsin's own Susan Engeleiter, who is with me here today. And also, one of our most able and effective Cabinet Secretaries, Sam Skinner, the Secretary of Transportation, is here. I want to recognize some of Wisconsin's own. Here today is the man who led the Bucks for so many years, the fellow with that soft-shooting touch and the size 19 shoes, Bob Lanier somewhere out there. [*Laughter*] And Pat Richter, who recently brought the national champs to the White House—he's here with us today, and John McLaughlin and Pete Vukovich and so many others—so many of Wisconsin Republicans' leading lights. I would be remiss—I won't single out any of them, except for my friend John MacIver, my patron in the world of Wisconsin politics. And of course, I want to salute our ticket with a special welcome to your next secretary of state, Bob Thompson, who made the switch to the GOP just last week, and we are going to support him 100 percent.

I'm proud, of course, to show my support for the hardest working man in Wisconsin, Governor Tommy Thompson—hardest working and, if my polling data is right, best known, because I understand there's a poll out that shows that Tommy's better known than anyone in the State, even the American League MVP on the Brewers, Robin Yount. I guess that puts him all in a league by himself.

We've seen a world of change this past year, and Tommy alluded to it—unforgettable images of what I call the Revolution of '89. And now, in 1990, we've entered a new period of democracy-building, a renaissance, if you will—a renaissance of freedom. Let me share a story with you—and there are so many emotional stories coming out of Eastern Europe—but a story about an American visitor on a recent trip to Romania who asked the people she met what they needed most. Listen to a surprising answer: In a country where food is in short supply, where the streets are dark at night and the homes lack heat, one Romanian woman pulled from her purse a worn copy of an American magazine, a 3-year-old issue, with a special bicentennial copy of the U.S. Constitution. And she told the American, "What we need now is more of these." You've got to think about that answer and what it means for America, for the moral example we owe the world, for the material help we must provide—not just American aid but expertise—to people the world over who seek only to have for themselves and their families the freedoms that we enjoy and sometimes take for granted.

And we're entering a new era—Tommy alluded to it here—in U.S.-Soviet relations as well. Just this past Sunday, President Gorbachev paid a visit to your neighbors in Minnesota. I'm pleased to be here today in the great State of Wisconsin, pleased to share with you my thoughts on what I believe was a very productive Washington summit.

We signed a number of agreements: deep reductions in our chemical weapons arsenals; agreement on reaching rapid closure on major outstanding issues governing a strategic arms treaty, a START treaty; protocols on nuclear testing; agreements on trade and grain sales. But perhaps even more important than the agreements we signed is the progress we made in understanding the great political challenges that we face. A united Germany in NATO, the future of the Baltics, regional problems— these aren't questions that can be solved simply or in one single summit meeting. But we make progress on these difficult issues whenever we speak with candor, without animosity, about our aims and interests. I am grateful to Mr. Gorbachev for the forthright spirit in which he addressed every issue on the table, and I take it as proof that we have indeed entered a new era in our relations with the Soviet Union.

Of course, we have differences. You're reading now, post-summit, a lot of analysis of what I might have done different or what they should have done. Of course, we have differences. I want to see Lithuania have its freedom. We are committed to self-determination for the Baltic States. And although I take great pleasure and joy and am pleased that the emigration of Soviet Jews is at an all-time high, I want to see unfettered emigration. We differ on Cuba and, for now, on a united Germany in NATO and on many other issues as well. But as I chatted informally with President Gorbachev up there at Camp David, I kept thinking that this new Soviet leader, committed to reform and openness, is indeed a remarkable man. It was a good summit.

Today I want to focus on the new era that we're entering here at home, on the challenges that will command our attention in the decade ahead. You all know the three R's. Well, today I want to talk about the three E's: the economy, education, and the environment—three areas that Governor Thompson and I agree are crucial to the citizens of this State and every State.

Let me start with the economy, America's great engine of progress. And let's start right here in Wisconsin. Think about the turnaround since Tommy Thompson's been in office. You heard some of the statistics: unemployment down, income up—rising faster than the national average. Two hundred thousand new jobs in the first Thompson term—and he's pledged to 200,000 more the second time around.

We're working to do the same nationally: to maintain a business climate conducive to growth, one that opens the door to entrepreneurs, the small business men and women who are America's great jobs machine. And I am committed to taking decisive action against the Federal budget deficit, to keep our record 91-month economic recovery going strong.

We're also working to strengthen America's competitive edge abroad. My administration's top trade priority is to lower barriers to free and fair trade the world over, to bring the Uruguay round trade talks to a successful completion by the end of this year. And let me tell you, any trade agreement we sign will be an agreement that is good for the American farmer, for American agriculture. It has to be that way.

Every State and city and town in America is going to feel the impact of the global market. Governor Thompson knows this; he knows it well. And that's why he's worked to open Wisconsin industry to the world, to expand business-to-business contacts with Japan and South Korea and establish export markets. This guy doesn't miss an opportunity for the farmers of this State, either. He was the only Governor at last week's state dinner at the White House for President Gorbachev. He tried out his Russian—I think he was saying, "Eat more cheese." [*Laughter*] No, actually, the star of this one is Sue Ann. She sat right there next to President Gorbachev, and we Bushes took great pride in that. He was looking at one of our very best first ladies, I'll tell you. Tommy had to settle for a seat next to Secretary of State Baker. [*Laughter*] So, I guess if the Soviets start importing Wisconsin cheddar you have a right to thank—maybe Tommy—probably Sue Ann. [*Laughter*]

But when it comes to long-term economic opportunity, education is the key. Among the agreements that we signed at the summit was one expanding U.S.-Soviet education exchanges, exchanges that will allow that American and Soviet students to live and learn in one another's lands so that the foreign becomes familiar.

Those education exchanges are in keeping with the crusade for excellence in education now gaining momentum across this country. It's no surprise to me that Wisconsin is the scene of one of the most interesting experiments in education reform or that Tommy Thompson's the catalyst for change.

Tommy's told me about the Milwaukee Choice Program. Starting next school year, nearly 1,000 underprivileged kids from Milwaukee's inner-city schools are going to have a chance to attend the private, nonsectarian school of their choice, with the State supplying their share of tax dollars for tuition. And I think we all see that when schools compete to attract students that can't help but raise the overall level of education.

Tommy found an ally in his fight for Milwaukee Choice in a former welfare mother and Democrat named Polly Williams, a woman who had heard a lifetime's worth of wornout excuses on what's wrong with our schools. And now some might say that's an unlikely alliance. Not if they know Tommy Thompson. What matters to him is what works—forging consensus with people who share his burning desire to get the job done. In education reform, that means parents, parents who are tired of waiting for the system to work for them, parents who are ready to reform the system, ready to make it work.

I'm counting on my friend Tommy to spread the word that the Federal Government will also do its part to help make our schools better. Over a year ago, I sent Congress an education bill, a seven-point plan for school reform, built on the bedrock concepts of parental choice, flexibility, innovation—initiatives aimed in encouraging excellence by rewarding our teachers, our students, our schools for what works. It's been over a year, and I am still waiting for a bill to sign into law. So, where is the Congress when our schools need help? It's time to get serious about our schools and take some commonsense steps to make them better. I want your support for that Education Excellence Act.

Well, we mentioned the economy and education, and now there's a third E, the environment—and here again, an issue with what I would call international dimensions. Last week at the summit, we established a U.S.-Soviet Bering Sea Park to preserve the unique natural environment in that string of islands that mark the border between our two nations.

Right here in Wisconsin, I know the environmental ethic is strong. And Tommy's pledge to plant 110 million trees by the year 2000—that fits right into our America the Beautiful Initiative: to plant a billion trees a year for the next 10 years. And I support all that Wisconsin is doing to preserve our precious natural heritage, and I ask your help: Work with me to keep the pressure on in Washington. Send Congress a signal to pass a sound and sensible clean air package—and pass it soon. It's been 13 long years since we last strengthened the Clean Air Act, and let's make 1990 the year that we take action on the environment.

And let me say I believe we can have a sound national environmental policy without throwing a lot of working men and women out of work. I'm convinced that we can find a proper balance on these important questions.

It's been my pleasure to come out here today to this beautiful State on a typical Wisconsin day. [*Laughter*] I remember the last time I was here. It didn't seem quite like this somehow. But I'll take his word for it if this is the way it is all the time. But nevertheless, it's been a pleasure to come here and speak with all of you.

You know, right here in the auditorium, almost 80 years ago, Teddy Roosevelt came to meet with the citizens of Milwaukee. His speech that day saved his life—literally. He was shot by a deranged assassin while on his way here. And TR had his draft speech folded up in his jacket pocket, where it helped blunt the bullet. Tough guy. He delivered the speech anyway. But the moral is: It's not whether a speech is long or short; what matters most is how thick it is. [*Laughter*]

So, let me thank all of you for this warm welcome back to your wonderful State of Wisconsin and commend you on all that Wisconsin has to be proud of. As other States search for solutions to today's challenges, you can say: Take a look at what works. Take a look at Wisconsin.

And to the citizens of this great State, who will go to the polls in November to choose a Governor, I say: Take a look at Tommy Thompson, at all he's done to turn this State around and all he'll do the next 4 years working hard for Wisconsin. I am proud that he is my friend, and I am proud

787

to enthusiastically endorse him for another term as Governor of the State of Wisconsin.

God bless you, and God bless the United States of America. Thank you very much.

Note: The President spoke at 12:30 p.m. at Mecca Auditorium. In his remarks, he referred to Bob Lanier and John McLaughlin, former members of the Milwaukee Bucks basketball team; Pat Richter, athletic director at the University of Wisconsin; Pete Vukovich and Robin Yount, former member and current member of the Milwaukee Brewers baseball team; John MacIver, chairman of the Wisconsin Bush/Quayle 1988 campaign committee and the Committee to Reelect Governor Thompson; and Sue Ann Thompson, wife of the Governor.

Remarks at a Fundraising Dinner for Gubernatorial Candidate Jim Edgar in Chicago, Illinois
June 7, 1990

Thank you, Jim Edgar, for that very generous introduction. Please, you all be seated, will you? [*Laughter*] I like this kind of event, though. No broccoli, no head table. It's wonderful. [*Laughter*] Please don't send it in. [*Laughter*] First, let me just be a little emotional as I pay my respects to Governor Jim Thompson and Jayne, who are with us tonight. What a magnificent service this man has rendered this State over all these years. A good friend, and a great—really, in the best sense, public servant. I also want to say a word—this is Jim Edgar's evening, and I'll tell you what I think about him in a minute. But I have a friend in Washington who I want to see stay there. And I'm talking about Lynn Martin—Barbara's and my great friend who is running for the U.S. Senate over here. Really, as I look at the problems in my trying to fulfill the agenda upon which I was elected, it really is significant and important that Illinois have a Republican in that seat and have a capable one like Lynn Martin. So, please, do your best.

I want to pay my respect to other Republicans here tonight—George Ryan, an old friend; Pate Philip, the same; Lee Daniels, Jim Ryan, Greg Baise, Susan Suter, Bob Kustra. And of course, we have two congressional candidates. Maybe more, but I saw these guys out at the helicopter—Manny Hoffman and Wally Dudycz. We need your support for them as well. A plug for a local Illinois boy that's making good in Washington—Sam Skinner, our able Secretary of Transportation—flew out here with me. And what a job he's doing for his country.

I'm glad to be back here. Last time I was here, people started—there was a handful of people in the front, started yelling to me about Nicaragua. And I said, Nicaragua will someday be democratic. Two months later, it was. So I hope we have a few—they were protesting something or other. But it made me feel at home.

Let me just say a word about those—[*Laughter*]—let me say a word in great seriousness about the people outside. These are decent, honorable people who feel strongly about the freedom of Lithuania. And I feel strongly about the self-determination and the freedom of Lithuania. So, there's no difference between us at all on that. And if our policy is successful, let's hope that they will have the same self-determination and freedom that Poland and Hungary and Czechoslovakia and other countries now enjoy, thanks to the changes in the Soviet Union and thanks to the foreign policy of the United States of America over the years. Let me say about—I love Illinois. It's lively. It's wonderful and it's lively.

Audience member. What about AIDS?

The President. Hey, listen—not only are we—let me just address myself to that subject. Last time it was Nicaragua; this time it's AIDS. The Federal Government is doing far more in terms of research on AIDS to help this horrible national crisis than it's ever done in the past. And it will continue to. And with compassion and caring, that problem, too, someday must be solved.

Now, back to where we were—[*laughter*]—the man of the hour, Jim Edgar. Let me say this—he takes every aspect of his job seriously. He takes an activist approach, one that makes government work for the people of Illinois, work for the good of this State.

So, I want to talk this evening a little bit about what he's done, all he can do. But let me just share with you a couple of more developments in the world, if I might—to say a few comments about the recently completed summit with President Gorbachev, because it does affect not only the lives of the Lithuanians and other Baltic States but so much else in terms of the United States itself and our European allies. Every superpower summit is shaped by history. I believe that last week's summit can alter history. Our many hours of talk led to, frankly, much better understanding. I've dealt with the Soviets since I was Ambassador to the United Nations in 1971. And others here have—in business and perhaps in government as well. But there's all the difference in the world today in terms of candor and frankness. No longer the hostility and the outrage and the banging of the shoe, but reason. When you have differences, at least you can get them out on the table. And I think that is a good thing—a good reason for itself to have a meeting with President Gorbachev.

We had a breakthrough agreement on chemical weapons. I don't know why, but Barbara and I talk about these issues when we go home. And one that's always concerned me is the goal of trying to eliminate chemical weapons—to ban them from the face of the Earth. We signed a good agreement with the Soviet Union. They're meeting our proposal that I made at the United Nations just last fall. We agreed on a joint statement on strategic arms limitation—these, the most destabilizing of weapons, cutting those SS–18's in half; and that's good. We agreed to go forward and pursue negotiations on nuclear and space arms. We signed protocols allowing unprecedented improvements for on-site verification in limiting nuclear testing. Who would have thought years ago with that closed society

that we would now have an agreement on on-site verification to be sure both sides keep their words. That is progress in this relationship. We agreed to increase our cooperation in atomic energy testing and civilian nuclear safety.

But most important to Illinois, I think, we signed a long-term grain agreement, one that will bring grain to Soviet consumers and business to the farmers of Illinois. And I am not going to let food be used as a political weapon. I remember the failed Carter embargo, and we're not going to have that kind of foreign policy anymore. We negotiated a trade deal with the Soviets, an agreement that depends on the passage of key emigration laws within the Soviet Union. Certainly, I believe that's in the best interest of the United States, and it will mean an improved trade relationship between our two countries, expanded markets for American goods and services, expanded markets for Illinois workers and farmers. And it will mean, through economic interaction, a continuation of this *perestroika*, this reform and openness inside the Soviet Union itself.

So, I'm delighted that we did it. There is a danger—Mike Ditka might want to trade a couple of Bears for Soviet weightlifters, but we'll see how all that works out.

No, but I am very pleased with this. I realize we've got a long way to go, but we've made progress. With a safer world come other challenges—many of them right here at home. Challenges like a better environment, better schools, safer streets. You need someone now to continue in Jim Thompson's footsteps. Someone who will continue to move this state on those key issues in the right direction. That's why I am convinced Jim Edgar will be your Governor. I like this sign. I like this sign that—and a philosophy that is summed up by this sign—let the future begin. And he has been a dynamic Secretary of State, creatively using his position to begin that future today.

For example, he's been a leader in the fight against drunk driving, initiating tough new laws and heightening public awareness. His persistence has paid off. Traffic deaths in Illinois have been reduced by one-fifth. Jim Edgar and I can also work together to make a better future for America. For example, we can work together to preserve wetlands, to clean up toxic wastes. And just as he will work for a cleaner Illinois, I will continue to work with Congress in Washington to bring about a cleaner environment for all Americans. That is why I have proposed the first major revisions in the Clean Air Act in more than a decade. I want Congress to pass a bill that will sharply cut acid rain, smog, toxic pollutants. But Congress has to respect another kind of delicate ecology—that of jobs and opportunity. We can do both: have a cleaner environment and still keep this state and other states growing.

So, I really would like to take this opportunity with this many present to call on the United States Congress not to keep America waiting any longer for clean air. We've made a compromise. It's a good one. It is a sound one. And now, the Congress ought to act so I can put my John Hancock on a good clean air bill. I get so frustrated at times.

And Jim and I talk about these other issues. And I believe the future should begin with safer streets, an America free of crime. Look, as Secretary, he has shut down sixty auto theft operations and illegal security operations that prey on the unsuspecting. And as Governor, he will work in Springfield for tougher laws against those who sell the drugs and those who commit violent crimes. So, you see, we share a simple philosophy. If dealing drugs is dealing death, then let's get those big dealers to have what they deserve, and I mean the ultimate penalty. We cannot condone and coddle these drug criminals.

We need the tougher laws and the stiffer penalties and more prosecutorial powers proposed in our Violent Crime Control Act. And again, I call on the United States Congress to pass the major parts of our Violent Crime Act, new laws that are fair, fast and final. Fair: an exclusionary rule designed to punish the guilty and not to punish good cops who have acted in good faith. We owe a lot to the men on the street, men in blue, and women as well. And fast: We need reforms to stop the often repetitive appeals that are choking our courts. And final: fair, constitutionally sound provisions for the death penalty, for the ultimate penalty. And

we want Congress to enact the steps needed to expand the death penalty—not sometime, not some other place, but now. And the U.S. Senate fortunately has begun debate on these measures. But now is the time for them to take the next step and protect Americans. And we can protect Americans by passing laws that are at least as tough as the criminals we convict.

A cleaner environment, a crackdown on crime—they're important issues. But Jim and I also believe—and we had a marvelous experience today at one of your wonderful schools—also believe that education really is the paramount issue; for the state, the classroom today is the state of the union tomorrow. And so, as chief executives, we will also work to make American education second to none.

We visited this school, this Farnsworth Elementary today. And I met some of the top principals—the school principals in the entire area here—listened to their concerns and ideas about quality education. An impressive group of people saving the lives and helping our kids every single day. And then, just a little later, I sat down—did Barbara's bit—I sat down with the first, second, and third graders. And you know, when their principal told them that the most important man in the world was coming to their class, one little boy looked around and said: "Oh yeah? So where's Michael Jordan?" Well, I finally got around to telling them about my responsibilities, and what I'm doing now that Congress is on recess. You should have seen their eyes light up at the word "recess". But, nevertheless, some things never change. [*Laughter*] And then I read them a story—a story about reading, actually. And I saw the bright faces, and I heard the laughter, and I answered the question of curious third-grade minds. And one thought stays with me from that experience: these kids really do deserve the best education that America can offer. And we must not let these children down.

That's why last September—and I want to again thank Jim Thompson for his key role in this—we asked the Nation's Governors to join us at an education summit, the first ever held with Governors of any kind of a summit, at Charlottesville in Virginia. And it was there that we agreed to set national education goals for our students, our teachers and ourselves. And in my State of the Union address, I announced these goals: To improve students' academic performance, increase our graduation rate, produce a nation of literate adults, and make our schools drug-free, ensure that all children start school ready to learn—and that means more vigorous Head Start, more fully-funded Head Start programs, too—and ensure that by the year 2000 our students are first in the world in math and science achievement.

And you know what? Just after that speech, that State of the Union, I received a telegram from our candidate, your friend and mine, Jim Edgar. And he was first to make a commitment, pledging to lead Illinois into a new era on education—at the foremost of moving the nation to reach these education goals. He committed himself and now he's ready to move into that Governor's office and follow up on what Jim has done. And he's leading another effort that is related—one which is very close to my heart, and one in which Barbara Bush has been such an outstanding leader—and I'm talking about our national campaign against illiteracy.

And so what Jim is doing is living up to the highest ideals, the Republican ideals of Abraham Lincoln and Teddy Roosevelt—to imaginatively use the limited resources of government to share opportunity, to bring enlightenment. And when a leader truly cares, and gives a darn, and truly wants to make a difference, people can tell that. American people aren't dumb. They can sense it immediately if somebody cares. And that's why Jim does so well downstate. And that's why he is the one Republican who does so very well right here in Chicago.

And so I've come here today not just to thank you for your support for Jim Edgar—I've come here to say something to Chicago as well. For too long, too many have felt as if they live outside of the American political process. For too long, they have believed elections are irrelevant to their own futures,

their very lives. And I'm here today to throw open the doors of the two-party system. I am asking this city to take a good hard look at the Republican Party and all of its candidates. And I'm inviting Chicago to return to the party of Lincoln where it belongs.

I was a minute late coming down because I was on the phone to tomorrow's birthday girl, the one who did so well at Wellesley, if I might take some pride in Barbara Bush. And she asked me—you know, you can put the hook on me, but let me just make one comment about that. I was calling some of the world leaders after the Gorbachev summit. And I talked to the Prime Minister of Japan and Germany's Chancellor, you know, and the President of Brazil and others. And I called Margaret Thatcher, and she didn't want to talk about the Gorbachev summit; she wanted to talk, because she had seen live on television over there—she'd seen Barbara Bush speaking at Wellesley. So, I was very proud of her assessment of what went on.

When I was on the phone to Bar a few minutes ago, she asked me to give Brenda a hug. That was easy—I did that upstairs—and to wish the Edgars the very, very best. Because you see, she, like me, considers them close friends. And we know a great opportunity for a great State when we see one. Thank you for your support. Now, go out and work hard for Jim Edgar. Thank you very, very much. Thank you. Good to see you.

Note: The President spoke at 6:39 p.m. in the Ballroom at the Hyatt Regency Hotel. In his remarks, he referred to Lieutenant Governor George Ryan; Pate Philip and Lee Daniels, Illinois Senate and House minority leaders; Jim Ryan, State's attorney for DuPage County; Greg Baise and Susan Suter, candidates for treasurer and State comptroller; Robert Kustra and Wally Dudycz, Illinois State senators; State representative Manny Hoffman; Mike Ditka, coach of the Chicago Bears; and Michael Jordan, a member of the Chicago Bulls basketball team.

Remarks at a Fundraising Breakfast for Governor Terry Branstad in Des Moines, Iowa
June 8, 1990

Thank you all very much. Thank you, Terry. Thank you, Governor Branstad. I'm just delighted to be back with so many friends. I was looking around for Chuck Grassley, who is doing an outstanding job in the Senate. I assume he's back there, but I want to just put in a plug for our Senator.

But I see one who I want very much to be in the Senate, and I'm talking about my old friend Tom Tauke. We've got to elect him. And, Tom, keep up the great work. And of course, perhaps my oldest Iowa friend and a guy that's helped me today a lot as President—helped me in the past very much, indeed—and I'm talking about Jim Leach over here, a Member of Congress in the eastern part of the State.

I'm going to get in trouble, but I also want to single out Jim Lightfoot and Fred Grandy. But I think both of them are in Washington, working. And I might add that now we have this important second district coming up, and I'm for Jim Nussle. He came out to the airport last night, and I want to see him win this race. We do not want to lose seats in the United States Congress. And the strength's not just with Governor Branstad at the top of this ticket, and Tom Tauke and others, when you have candidates like Burt Day and Varel Bailey over here, whom I've known forever—I don't want to date him—[*laughter*]—I mean, put him outdated, put it that way—[*laughter*]—Beverly Anderson and Edward Kelly. And then, another old friend that—I guess he's a household word by now. He's just being sworn-in as the national president of the State Auditors. And I'm talking, of course, about Dick Johnson. I wish he were here, but I wish him well, too.

I don't want to forget the party organization, because when we move into an election year, the party organization means something. It's terribly important, as so many of you out here know, that the candidates are backed with a strong party structure, led by Rich Schwarm over here, our chairman; Gwen Boeke, our national committeewoman; and Marvin Pomerantz, who—gosh, everybody knows him. Ask somebody to get some money raised—get Marv to head it up, I'll tell you. And it's not simply that; it's his judgment and his experience and the respect level that he brings to anything he's interested in.

Of course, I'm going to get in trouble as I look around this room—but Charlotte Mohr and my old friend George Wittgraf. I don't think she's here, but I do want to pay an emotional tribute to Mary Louise Smith, who followed me as national chairman when I left being chairman of the Republican Party. And we've remained good, close friends. I'm told that she's in Washington today.

The last time I was at this particular hotel was the night before the Iowa caucuses—[*laughter*]—and today I've come back to this great State to let Terry in on my secret formula for political success. [*Laughter*] But I'm confident he'll win Iowa anyway.

Now let me put a little different spin on this. I'll tell you something I know very well—and I mean it, and the Silver Fox knows this, too—that's Barbara—[*laughter*]—that I would not be President of the United States if it hadn't been for Iowa, albeit in 1980. It was very important. And I look around this room, and I see so many people into whose homes I and Barbara and our kids have intruded. And I remain very grateful because I know just exactly how I got here—having an opportunity to serve as President in this most fascinating of times. So, I came to say thank you as well as support for our great Governor, Terry Branstad.

So, for me, it is great to be back in the Hawkeye State. Whenever I'm here, I take the advice of a great Iowan, the "Duke," John Wayne, who once said, "Talk low, talk slow, and don't say too much." [*Laughter*] So, as I look at all these pages, I may be—[*laughter*]. But you can't say enough about what another great Iowan—and I mean that—this Governor, Terry Branstad, has done for this State. You look at his background: a family man, attorney, farmer—served three times in the Iowa House of Representatives and then a term as Lieutenant Governor before being elected Iowa's youngest Governor ever.

Look at his record: he's running for his third consecutive term as Governor. Over the past 7 years, Terry has turned the State economy around through sensible fiscal policies and by staying with the controlling of spending. He put education at the top of his agenda, ensuring world-class status for Iowa's school system. He's one of America's leading Governors, elected by his peers as chairman of the National Governors' Association. Iowa needs this kind of experience and leadership; and frankly, if you believe as I do that a lot of the best answers are found in the States and at the local level, so does America need Terry Branstad to continue as Governor of this State.

Terry touched on the Governors' summit that we had at Charlottesville. He and I worked closely together at that summit in Virginia last September, where he played a key role—and I mean this—a key role in his position as head of the Governors. You know, exactly 26 years ago today, former President Eisenhower addressed that same group, saying, "Our best protection against bigger government in Washington is better government in the States." Well, that's still true today, and Terry Branstad proves that every single day.

My last visit to this great State was just a few days after the Malta summit, at an appearance on behalf of the next Senator over here, my friend Tom Tauke. We laid a solid foundation for progress at Malta, and I shared many things with President Gorbachev: dialogs, cooperation, and Dramamine. [*Laughter*]

I told Iowans that night that President Gorbachev and I had just agreed to new initiatives nurturing Europe's tide toward democracy, accelerating arms control, and expanding trade. I'd like to talk to you this morning about some of the progress we've made at the Washington summit and what it means for Iowans and, indeed, for all Americans.

This historic summit has furthered the process of peace by working toward a safer world and a stable, new Europe, one in which every nation's security is strengthened and no nation is threatened. In a spirit of cooperation and hope, President Gorbachev and I reached a number of new agreements that will affect the lives of all Americans. Among them is a bilateral agreement, between the Soviet Union and us, to eliminate, for the first time, the great majority of these ghastly chemical weapons that our countries have stockpiled over the years. That is progress. At long last, we have also signed new protocols that will allow 15-year-old nuclear testing treaties to be ratified as well as a major new agreement that updates and expands our 1973 agreement on peaceful uses of atomic energy. And we made substantial progress on our negotiations governing reductions in both these strategic arms, these deadly, destabilizing weapons—these SS-18's and others. And also in conventional forces, I think we did make progress, though we haven't signed a CFE treaty. And we issued joint statements in both these areas.

These agreements, we hope, represent the beginning of the end of the Cold War. And I think I represent all Americans when I hope that we are having now a new relationship of enduring cooperation between the Soviet and American peoples, cooperation further strengthened with new agreements on trade and grain sales.

And while our trade deal with the Soviets, properly, in my view, depends on the passage of key emigration laws within the Soviet Union, the trade agreement we negotiated is, in my view, in the best interest of the United States because an improved trade relationship between our two countries means expanded markets for American goods and services and expanded markets for, in your case, Iowa corn and soybeans. And, in fact, the new U.S.-Soviet grain agreement signed at the summit calls for at least 40 million metric tons of grain to be purchased by the Soviets over the next 5 years. And that's nothing but good news for agricultural America. Our task is to keep moving forward and to keep Iowa productive and to keep America strong.

But despite all our progress, let's be candid, we cannot lose sight of the significant differences that remain between our two countries. Lithuania is one difference. And I urged the Soviet President to establish a good-faith dialog between the Soviet leaders and the Baltic peoples. And the United States will continue to speak out on behalf of peoples rightfully yearning for freedom and self-determination. We must never retreat from our commitment for democracy and freedom.

The question of a unified Germany is not one that will be solved by the United States alone. When I leave here, I stop off in Nebraska and then fly home to have yet another meeting with the Federal [Republic of Germany] Chancellor—with Chancellor Helmut Kohl—to talk about this very important question, that affects not only the stability of Europe but greatly affects the interests of the United States. But it's not going to be solved by the U.S. alone, nor is it one that will be solved quickly or easily. In the final analysis, I think we would agree that it's a question for the people of Germany to decide. But the United States remains committed to German membership in NATO as a part of a stable Europe, whole and free.

As one who has strongly supported the exodus of Soviet Jews, and it is a question of fundamental rights and fundamental integrity of a country, I am pleased to see that after last year's record-setting total emigration of 72,000 Soviet Jews, this year's emigration rate may become the highest ever. And we must keep the door to freedom open for these Soviet Jews.

And I've said often that we want *perestroika* to succeed, and we do. As a world leader in agriculture, farm technology, and education, you, Iowa, can play a significant role in making that happen. In fact, you already are helping *perestroika* succeed. Many people here may remember the first American-Soviet summit in the United States, back in 1959. After his meetings with President Eisenhower, Chairman Khrushchev toured Des Moines. And he was obsessed with the vision of productivity that he had seen on American farms and with the idea of growing corn. And yet because the Soviet system was not a free enterprise system, one with open markets and good distribution and production incentives

or any of the economic freedoms we enjoy, its experiment in collective farming was a dismal failure.

As a young man, Mikhail Gorbachev witnessed the struggle of the Russian farmers. He went on to become the Party Secretary of Agriculture, some may have forgotten that. And by the time President Gorbachev and I sat down at the table last week, a delegation of collective farmers had already journeyed 5,000 miles to the fields of Iowa to learn from our system, the most efficient and bountiful in the entire world. And how amazed—how amazed Chairman Khrushchev would have been at the interaction between the American farmers and the Soviet farmers.

Under the leadership of Governor Branstad, Iowa is forging a new sense of cooperation between its citizens and the Soviet people. In fact, 2 years ago, Terry signed an agreement making Iowa a sister State with President Gorbachev's native region, the Stavropol district.

But another way to help *perestroika* succeed is through education, learning about each other's countries and peoples. In Washington last week we agreed to increase undergraduate exchanges by 1,000 students, college students, on both the American and Soviet sides. This agreement will allow more of our young people to learn firsthand about each other's culture and politics. Here in Iowa, learning and education have always been a priority. Your internationally renowned writers workshop at the University of Iowa is living proof of that, and with a Soviet writer currently in the international writing program.

You've got a Governor who puts education at the top of his list. At the education summit with the Nation's Governors last September, Terry really made a difference—it wasn't just the cameo appearance of the chairman—he made a difference. And he's made a difference right here in this State, ensuring that your State's education system is one of the best in the entire country, with Iowa students ranked first in ACT scores in America. And Iowans can brag—they've got the fifth highest percentage [rate] of high school graduates in the entire country. And like Terry, we've made education one of our top priorities at the national level. And so, we can do nationally, we must do nationally, what you've done locally.

Under Terry's leadership—and after he personally journeyed to the Soviet Union twice for the negotiations—Iowa State University became the first institution in the United States to forge a relationship with a Soviet academic institution, the Agricultural Academy of Science. So far, Iowa has received five Soviet official delegations to discuss trade and education ties. In fact, a Soviet trade representative will be coming into the State in just a few days.

I came to you today to talk about Terry Branstad and our work together for a better America and a better world. His dedication to this State and nation is what drew Terry Branstad into public service, and it's what keeps him working so hard for the future of this State and for America's future as well. You see, we need him to remain in the Governor's chair. We need his experience, his energy, and then this proven ability.

This decade is fast becoming known, for quite obvious reasons, as the decade of democracy, the decade of opportunity. But to make those goals a reality, we will need leadership. Terry Branstad has been providing that leadership to his State and nation for nearly 20 years. And they say, "The

Time is Right" for Iowa. Well, "The Time is Right" for Terry Branstad to continue to lead Iowa forward into the new decade of democracy and opportunity.

Let me say once again, and I did talk to Barbara this morning, she seemed unexcited about her 65th birthday, but nevertheless, I—[*laughter*]—just a couple of observations since some in the receiving—she's doing just great. And I thought she was superb up there at Wellesley University, representing the values of this—[*applause*]. And so she joins me in saying to our friends in Iowa, thank you. Thank you for your support for this outstanding Governor.

And thank you for giving Barbara and me the opportunity to serve the greatest country on the face of the Earth. God bless you all. And God bless America.

Note: The President spoke at 8:11 a.m. in the Iowa Ballroom of the Des Moines Marriott. In his remarks, he referred to Representatives Jim Lightfoot and Fred Grandy; Burtwin Day, candidate for State treasurer; Varel Bailey, candidate for State secretary of agriculture; Beverly Anderson, candidate for State secretary of state; Edward Kelly, candidate for State attorney general; Charlotte Mohr, cochairperson of Governor Branstad's reelection committee; and George Wittgraf, a former member of the Bush for President Committee.

Exchange With Reporters Aboard Air Force One
June 8, 1990

Middle East

Q. Are you going to make a decision on the PLO, or have you made one?

The President. Well, we're discussing all of that. No decision has been made.

Q. Do you want to override the veto?

The President. Incidentally, I had a very interesting phone call from [Egyptian] President Mubarak just a few minutes ago. We discussed a wide array of subjects of interest to the Middle East, and both of us still committed to getting these peace talks going forward. And it's been complicated,

as you know. But we're going to keep on trying. So, there's no answer to your question right now.

Q. Have you ascertained the responsibility for that attack?

The President. Well, I just said, I don't really want to say anything more about it now. I've expressed my outrage about the attack. And indeed, I'd like to—maybe I could take this opportunity to express my outrage about all violence in the Middle East and in this troubled area of the world. But this one was horrendous. There was no rationale for it, other than, in my view, terror, and that is clearly something that is unacceptable to us. So, we're trying to figure out a little more about this and see where we go. But I'm not prepared to make an announcement of policy at this point.

Q. When you say the Middle East is more difficult——

The President. Well, everything there. Every time you get something started, why, there seems to be some outbreak. I'm still outraged by the holding of American hostages, and I understand that—what is it—Sutherland's——

Q. Five years.

The President. Five years as of tomorrow, or today.

Q. Terry Anderson.

The President. Well, Anderson—no, but the other——

Q. Seven.

The President. Yes. And so, I have this on my mind all the time. All of these things have a way of coming together, but on this one, why, we just haven't made a final decision.

Q. How do you approach [Israeli Prime Minister] Shamir forming a right wing government?

The President. Well, that's an internal matter for Israel. But they know the policy of the United States. The policy of the United States is firm: that we want the peace talks to begin, to get going. After all, Shamir, to his credit, was one of the originators of this; Mubarak with his points helping, Jim Baker actively involved with both sides on this. So, it has to go forward, and that is the answer. And I'm not going to—I mean, Israel can do what it wants in its government, and I'll work with whoever the country puts forth as the government. But they know the policy of the United States in terms of peace talks. So, we're going to stay——

Q. Is the peace process harder because of this, sir?

The President. Well, I'm not going to say that. Let's see. Maybe it will go forward, but I've read speculation on that. But I think it's not really officially done yet, either. So, we've got a little time there to see what happens. But the world is crying

out for negotiations on this question. It's happening in many other places around the world, and it's essential that it go forward. So, we'll see what happens. We'll keep going on it.

But anyway, I hope you've enjoyed this swing through the Midwest. It's good to get out of Washington, DC.

Veto of Amtrak Bill

Q. How about the veto on the Amtrak? Do you think you can——

The President. I don't know. I think it's going to be very close in the Senate, and we'll see what happens.

Condoleezza Rice

Q. Have you gotten a report on the Condi Rice incident yet?

The President. Not yet, except I have great regret about it any time a staffer is handled in that nature. But I'm satisfied from what I do know about it that it was a big, big mistake. And nothing egregious—or singling her out—of any kind. But it's not good—I mean, to treat staff people—and I have great respect for the Secret Service and the way they do their job. But there was an excess here, and she understands it, and she understands how upset I've been with it. But we'll get to the bottom of it, and just make every effort to see there's no recurrence.

Cold War

Q. Gorbachev says the Cold War is over, sir. You just say it's the beginning of the end. Do you have a difference of opinion with him on that?

The President. I don't know. We've got a difference of semantics, don't we?

Q. Is the Cold War over?

The President. As I say, I don't know. We've got to wait and see how we resolve all these problems out here. There's plenty of them around. I felt that the summit moved in the right direction regarding that question.

Soviet-U.S. Relations

Q. Did Baker report any progress in the [Soviet Foreign Minister] Shevardnadze meeting?

The President. Yes, he did, as a matter of

fact. I talked to him a couple of days ago, Lori [Lori Santos, United Press International]. I didn't talk to him yesterday. He'll be back tonight. I'm having this dinner for [West German Chancellor] Helmut Kohl, which will be interesting in the wake of the Baker trip. I think Jim will be—if he can keep his eyes open, he'll be there.

Q. What kind of progress?

The President. Well, we'll wait and see. But I think he felt a certain degree of optimism. I'll tell you one thing, that all these leaders that I talked to around the world were very encouraged with what they thought happened at the summit and the tone of it. I just talked a few minutes ago with Michael Manley, Prime Minister of Jamaica.

Michael Manley

Q. How is he feeling?

The President. Well, I don't know. He sounded pretty good, but I think he's been quite sick because they told me he was not routinely taking phone calls. But I was impressed with his spirit, certainly been impressed with what he's trying to do for his country. But my point is, he was very generous in his assessment of the summit from their standpoint, a small country in the Caribbean. But I'm afraid he's had some health difficulties, and he's—mainly pulmonary at this point.

Soviet Union

Q. Gorbachev faces much more ethnic turmoil back there. Did he get into that with you?

The President. Yes, we talked about it. We talked about that, we talked about the federation—the republic's problems, but he was determined to go back and lead. And I think there will be a meeting coming up soon of the republics, and that will be very interesting and hopefully productive. We want to see this evolution of democracy and freedom and openness inside the Soviet Union as well continue. And that's what's at stake here.

Q. Sir, could you foresee a solution where there would be a Soviet military enclave in Lithuania?

The President. I don't go to any hypothesis on something of that nature. Let's just hope the process continues, so that self-determination is fulfilled. That's our aspirations. Really is—comes back to freedom. Freedom. Choice. But we can't fine-tune all the individual decisions that they might work out—with agreements they might work out with each other. It's not our role.

Terrorist Raid in Israel

Q. Sir, are you disappointed that the PLO has not spoken out following that attack?

The President. I would like to see Mr. Arafat [Yasser Arafat, chairman of the Palestine Liberation Organization] speak out. One of the members of the PLO council spoke out very strongly against it. But I'd certainly like to see Arafat speak out and denounce it because part of our discussions and dialog was predicated on the renunciation of terror. In my view, this is sheer terror. So, I'd like to see that happen.

Q. But you're not ready to assign responsibility?

The President. I'd like to see that happen.

Note: The exchange took place shortly after 10:40 a.m. en route to Omaha, NE. An early question referred to a terrorist raid on an Israeli beach on May 30, and a later question referred to an incident in which a Secret Service agent reportedly shoved Condoleezza Rice, a Director of European and Soviet Affairs for the National Security Council, while she was attending the departure ceremony for President Mikhail Gorbachev of the Soviet Union. A tape was not available for verification of the content of this exchange.

Remarks at a Fundraising Luncheon for Senatorial Candidate Hal Daub in Omaha, Nebraska
June 8, 1990

Thank you all. Hal, thank you so very much for that warm and most generous welcome, and to all of you for that warm welcome back to Nebraska. To Governor Orr, let me say how important I think your reelection is. You've done a good job, and I want to see you back for another term here. I'm sorry that Virginia's not here, but I see Congressman Bereuter. We've got a good delegation, a strong Nebraska delegation in Washington. We need more. And so, when I salute Doug Bereuter, I wouldn't speak for him, but I know that he would welcome more Republican support in the House. And thus, I want to single out Ally Milder, who's running as a candidate in the Second District and urge strong support for her. We got a good candidate.

I'm delighted I heard P.J. Morgan's remarks out there and his enthusiastic support for Hal. And I might say one of the things I take pride in is just before his election, he found time to come back to the Oval Office so we could publicly give the abrazo, and I was right. He's doing a superb job, I'll tell you, for this city. And the voters were certainly right on that one.

And I want to salute our chairman, Chairman Riffel. I want to say how pleased I am to see Bob Kasten, an outstanding Senator from Wisconsin, who was one of the leaders in the Senate. And he's out here to join me in showing our unified and strong support for our candidate here. To Father Val Peter, who's so well-known, so well respected by both Barbara and me and so many around the country. My greetings to you, sir. And to Rabbi Nadoff, as I understand the situation here, he's one of the great leaders of the Jewish community all across this State.

And I'll just mention, sir, in a minute, how pleased I was at the recent summit to have a very frank discussion with President Gorbachev about the need to keep this high level of Soviet Jews emigrating from the Soviet Union going forward. I am convinced we're on the right track. And we're going to not let up until we get even more of those people able to go home and able to join their families.

And I want to salute Cindy Daub, a member of my team in a sense and long-time friend. If Hal has about half as much energy as Cindy, I expect he's got it made already. [*Laughter*] But, anyway, ladies and gentlemen and friends, it's a pleasure to be back in one of America's greatest and most Republican States—two things that go together as naturally as the Cornhuskers and winning football.

And today, I am here to support a candidate who, like those Cornhuskers, has made a difference in Nebraska. And he's one of you. And he's never failed to speak for you. My friend, your next United States Senator, Hal Daub. He has my enthusiastic endorsement.

We've known each other since the early seventies. And I wanted to come here and personally endorse him. And one reason is his great family. Another, we heard some of it today, his Main Street values and his career of dedication. And Hal isn't going to get to the Senate on PAC money, incidentally. He'll get there on shoe leather and hard work. And then, there's the reason you may not know. As a kid, Hal wanted to be a musical conductor.

Peony Park, of course, is where Lawrence Welk made his debut. And Cindy tells me that Hal still wakes up chanting, "A one and a two," and you know how it is out there. [*Laughter*] But Lawrence Welk, he played champagne music. And this November, Republicans will be playing a victory march because the people of Nebraska know Hal Daub has made a difference—as a lawyer, businessman, four-term Congressman. And starting in January, he'll mean even more to a State whose compass, as one writer said, is the Sun, the distant hilltops, and its own resolution.

Now people say it doesn't matter anymore. There is a frustration, I'm afraid. Some say it doesn't matter who's elected to the Senate or which party controls it. And that's like saying it doesn't matter if Nebraska beats OU [Oklahoma University]. [*Laughter*] But, so in a moment, I'd like to talk about the Hal Daub difference and how it can benefit Nebraskans from the bluffs of the Missouri to the Wyoming line. And first, though, Hal referred to it—let me just speak about the summit that President Gorbachev and I held last week in Washington which can make a difference by benefiting Nebraska and the world.

Every summit between America and the Soviet Union is shaped by history. And I believe that last week's summit will alter history. In 4 days of talks, we discussed the power of freedom to dismantle walls between nations. And because the greatest peace dividend is a safer, more democratic world, we signed agreements concerning areas of interest to both our countries and recorded bilateral understandings in several joint statements.

First, we signed a bilateral agreement that will, for the first time, eliminate the great majority of chemical weapons that have been stockpiled over the years. And our common goal is nothing less than a global ban on these devastating chemical weapons. And second, I joined President Gorbachev in signing protocols on limiting nuclear testing. And they will create unprecedented improvements for on-site verification on the Threshold Test Ban Treaty and PNET, the Peaceful Nuclear Explosions Treaty. And the third agreement updates and expands our 1973 pact on the peaceful uses of atomic energy, increasing our cooperation in atomic energy research and civilian nuclear safety. You know, that tragic Chernobyl accident shows that the fate of our planet eclipses ideology and nation. And the agreements we signed can help create a better future for the community of nations.

You know, there is an old Russian story that reflects the spirit of last week's summit—a spirit of friendship growing as knowledge grows. It concerns a traveler walking to another village. And who, coming upon a woodsman, asked how much further he had to go. The woodsman said he didn't know. Whereupon the traveler, angered, continued down the road. And at that point the woodsman called out to him, "Stop. It will take you 15 minutes." And the traveler then asked why he didn't tell him that in the first place. "Because," the woodsman said, "I didn't know your stride."

Last week President Gorbachev and I learned more about each other's stride. And so, in addition to our agreements, we also signed understandings. We released a joint statement on strategic arms limitations, recording our agreement on major outstanding issues governing a START treaty. We pledged to continue future negotiations on nuclear and space arms. And we also issued a statement on conventional armed forces in Europe, the CFE area. A CFE agreement is crucial to a Europe that is whole and free.

In particular, let me talk about the trade agreement that Hal referred to, and an agreement that we negotiated that will relax barriers between East and West, creating new markets for American products and, in the process, new jobs for American workers. As he reminded me, President Gorbachev used to be the Party Secretary for Agriculture. And he knows that an improved trade relationship between our two countries means a greater demand for American goods and services.

In our talks, we also agreed that selling our grain to the Soviet Union will benefit both our nations. So, the new U.S.-Soviet grain agreement we signed at the summit calls for at least 40 million metric tons of grain to be purchased by the Soviets over the next 5 years. Incidentally, I have not changed my views on using food as a political weapon. I still remember that disastrous grain embargo put into effect by President Carter. And to that I say: Never again! We are not going to use food for that purpose.

Now, look, let me be candid. Serious differences still remain. Of course they still remain between us and the Soviets. We must heed the desire of self-determination in the Baltic republics and elsewhere while protecting the rights of minority populations. I can identify with those Lithuanian-Americans outside this building, proudly holding that flag. And I want to see that they have the self-determination that other nations are achieving all across this world.

We must see that German reunification adheres to the wishes of the German people while respecting the views of other nations. And when I leave here, I'm heading back to Washington to have yet another meeting with [West German] Chancellor Kohl at the White House to discuss post-unification Europe and what it means after Germany is unified. And moreover, while I am pleased that the emigration of Soviet Jews is at an all-time high, I want to see unfettered emigration. And I believe Gorbachev is a leader willing, as Lincoln said, "to think anew." And I believe that because look at the changes that have taken place in Eastern Europe with his encouragement as well as his acquiescence. And he is committed inside to reform, and he faces these enormous economic problems. And as I told him, though, I will not send our new agreement on trade to Congress until the Soviet Legislature passes key emigration laws.

I've often said we want *perestroika* to succeed. And I believe that. I believe it's in the interest of the United States that those internal reforms keep going forward, as they move towards economic reform and more human rights. And I believe that the steps I've outlined can help it triumph. But America can't do it alone, and we need the support of our allies. And our administration needs the support of Senators who will actively support these historic new directions in foreign policy.

At the summit we talked of many issues that will confront your great State, the State of Nebraska, and, indeed, America. But this country also faces a lot of important domestic challenges. So, let me shift now because we need the support of Senators who can make a difference for America at home as well as abroad.

And one of those challenges, of course, is agriculture. As you know, in the late eighties, farm income hit near-record levels. Our job is to make good news even better. Our grain agreement will help, and so will passing our administration's capital gains tax cut proposal. I wish that Senate would get on and do something about it.

What's more, we need a new farm bill that emphasizes market-oriented farm policies, giving producers more flexibility to decide what crops to grow. And our new farm bill—of course, it's got to be even-handed and level-headed, leading, in turn, to a lower Federal deficit, lower interest rates, and increased choice for farmers and consumers. And so, I need Hal Daub to make these objectives a reality. We agree on this philosophy. And I want to see him in the United States Senate.

Another issue that's absolutely critical to the America of the nineties is education. And last week President Gorbachev and I signed an agreement to expand undergraduate exchanges by 1,000 students on both sides. You see, I believe that as these students interact—those Soviet students here—that that further enhances the changes that are taking place. And I think when our students go there, the people in Russia can learn a great deal about the American ethic, the American commitment to family and freedom and democracy, just from the interchange with the students.

On the domestic front, I wish Hal Daub were in the Senate now to help our kids by urging his colleagues, as Bob Kasten is doing, to pass our Educational Excellence Act of 1989 because this legislation would promote excellence and choice and flexibility in our education system. For 1 year, some Members of Congress have stalled for a whole year, stalled on this bill. And again, it is time for action now. In addition, Hal supports something that happened this past Monday that I feel strongly about, the Supreme Court ruling that affirms student religious groups' equal access to public high schools. I'm pleased by this ruling. To Omaha's own Bridget Mayhew, my congratulations—in the forefront of all of this.

And finally, we must act on another issue that we discussed at the summit, and that Hal alluded to here, and that I've talked to your Governor about many times. And I'm talking about the environment, cleaning up our air. We need to keep America what a child once called, "the nearest thing to Heaven. And lots of sunshine, places to swim, and peanut butter sandwiches." [*Laughter*] So, I call on the House-Senate conference committee, which will begin work soon, to send me clean air legislation that I can sign.

Issues like world peace, agriculture, the

environment, and education are not merely American questions. They affect every part of the world from the Midwest to the Ukraine. And we must do our part, and we will. To questions that confront America, Hal Daub really will help provide answers, answers that make a difference, and mirror what an author said of Nebraska's plains: "Men began to dream." Today, like the pioneers before them, Nebraskans still dream impossible dreams and make them a reality, relying on Nebraska values to build the Main Street of America, an American example to the world.

Hal Daub understands those values. He'll support those values in the United States Senate. I'm delighted to have been here. I wish that Barbara were here on her big birthday, the hero of Wellesley. I'm very, very proud of her. And she asked me to tell you that she, too, supports the Daubs, all out, in this important race. So, let's all go out and help Hal make a difference for Nebraska and the Nation.

Thank you for this wonderful occasion. It's a great pleasure to be back in the State of Nebraska. Thank you all, and God bless you.

Note: The President spoke at 12:57 p.m. in the ballroom of Peony Park. In his remarks, he referred to Representative Virginia Smith; P.J. Morgan, mayor of Omaha; Norman Riffel, State Republican Party chairman; Val Peter, executive director of Boys Town; and Isaac Nadoff, Rabbi Emeritus of Beth Israel Synagogue.

Remarks to Members and Supporters of MAD DADS in Omaha, Nebraska
June 8, 1990

First, thank all of you for that warm welcome, and thank you, John Foster. And to the Governor of this State, Governor Orr; and to the mayor of this great city, P.J. Morgan; and of course to Eddie Staton and Robert Tyler, George Garrison, Lafayette Nelson, and all of you wonderful, inspiring MAD DADS, MAD MOMS, MAD KIDS— MAD everything—I'm glad to be here with you today to meet you. And we've just had a wonderful visit with these men, these MAD DADS that I've just clicked off their names, right next door here, briefing me on how this organization is coming together and what it's doing to help the kids of Omaha, not just this neighborhood but, through its example, the kids of America— all the kids across this country.

And so, I will carry back with me to Washington the story of this extraordinary war for decency waged in a parking lot and on this street and across the streets of this community. And you are truly what I call a Point of Light, a beacon for others to turn to in the grim and lonely darkness of their despair. And we are grateful to each and every one of you that are involved in this program.

Your Reverend Tyler put it this way about drugs and gangs and emptiness: "Used to be," here's what he'd call it, "a cancer festering in the heart of north Omaha." Well, you've done some radical surgery, my friends, on that cancer. And you've ripped it out, and you've replaced it with the healing balm of love—caring about the other guy.

And of course, I'll take back with me to Washington, in a few minutes, the lesson of how this revolution began, how you transformed tragedy into hope. And I'll tell others of last May, when Sean Foster, a college student with no ties to gangs or drugs, was beaten viciously by the member of a gang; and of how his father, John, took one look at his bloodied son and something inside him exploded. He took to the streets to find his son's attackers. He never did, but what he did find serves his community, and all of us, much better.

He found that the streets belonged not to the families but to the gangs, not to hope but to the drug dealers, not to a bright future but to a brutal cycle of violence and crime. And John Foster found that voice within him to shout: "This madness must stop."

So, this angry father and his friends formed MAD DADS. In the last year, along with more than 550 others who have joined them, they have become the dominant presence on their previously devastated streets. And they're father figures who take a hard line against the drugs and the gangs which are the predators, but speak softly, put their arm around and hug the kids who are the victims.

Your MAD DADS logo behind me tells the story: the outstretched, caring hand of the loving father who embraces positive change, and the fist of determination of the strong father who resolves to be the force behind that change.

And these good, strong men who talk with pain in their hearts about pain on the streets take action. They paint over gang graffiti to proclaim that they're reclaiming the city. Nightly, they patrol the killing grounds of their streets, going out, as one said, with nothing but "a radio, a conversation, and a prayer." They speak to schools, they provide protection from gang threats, they sponsor events, counsel, and I guess most of all, they care. They are fathers to a neighborhood desperately in need of family. In the shifting shadows of midnight street-corners, they reach out to the lost sons of other men. But most importantly, they're there. They are simply there. And they care. And they are voices crying in the dark: "See us and fear; see us and believe; see us and hope."

The handful of determined neighbors who formed MAD DADS were those voices. They shouted out against this meaningless violence that they saw leading today's young men and women into self-destruc-

tion, and one by one, others joined them in their cry of protest. And now their world is filled with a lion's roar, supremely strong, fiercely proud, challenging, and redeeming.

And so, we are today witnessing the wonder of a rebirth. It's more than a rebirth of community: it is a rebirth of hope, of respect for life, and of the future. And so, MAD DADS, for the inspiration and the example you set, I am proud to have honored you as our nation's 126th daily Point of Light.

If every community could band together as you have, we could see the MAD DADS' spirit of caring spread, street by street, neighborhood by neighborhood, city by city. Crime, drugs, and hopelessness can be and will be banished from the shadows of our great land when each individual cares enough to add his or her voice to the growing chorus of outrage.

The government wants to help: the Federal Government, the State government, the city government. But far more important—and we will do our level best—but far more important is that spirit exemplified by the men that we honor here today.

Thank you for all that you do in the name of love. God bless you, and God bless these wonderful children. Thanks for giving them a chance, and God bless the future of the United States of America. Thank you all very, very much. Thank you. Good luck to you, kids. Thank you all.

Note: The President spoke at 2:16 p.m. in a lot at 30th and Spencer Streets. In his opening remarks, he referred to John Foster, Eddie Staton, Robert Tyler, George Garrison, and Lafayette Nelson, chairman of the board, president, secretary treasurer, vice president, and director of field security of MAD DADS, respectively. Following his remarks, the President returned to Washington, DC.

Remarks and an Exchange With Reporters Following Discussions With Chancellor Helmut Kohl of the Federal Republic of Germany
June 8, 1990

The President. Well, let me just say in the beginning here that we were delighted to have Chancellor Kohl back at the White House for a small dinner—one more step in the very close consultations that the United States has with the Federal Republic. We are in general and, I'd say, firm agreement on how we both look at Europe now. And once again, Chancellor Kohl, it was a pleasure having you here, sir. And thank you very much for your courtesy in coming to us this soon again. I'm very grateful to you.

The Chancellor. Mr. President, thank you very much for these warm words of welcome. This was a very good opportunity to meet with you only a few days after your meetings with President Gorbachev, on the occasion of my short visit to New York and to Boston—the University of Harvard. And I should like to make use of this opportunity to thank you, Mr. President, for the friendly and very effective support which you have shown to us once again—to us Germans—during this visit. After all, we're seeing an historic hour here in world politics, in European politics, in the whole process of German politics, and it is of particular importance at this particular point in time that the relationship between the United States and the Europeans, also between the Germans and the United States, and particularly between the two of us personally, should be so excellent at this very point in time.

And let me say how pleased I am that, again today, we were able to work together, to work also in the whole field of preparation for the NATO summit meeting, to prepare also for our meeting during the world economic summit meeting in Houston, Texas.

I think we can now expect you to ask questions. I should like to ask you for your understanding; I have only limited time because I fly back to Germany. And you know what a pleasant experience it is to fly by night.

German Membership in NATO

Q. Mr. President, during your talks, were you able to come up with any options between the two of you that would allow Germany to remain in NATO, as you've insisted, and, at the same time, some kind of options that would calm the Soviets' worries, give them assurances about the things they're concerned about?

The President. Well, I think Chancellor Kohl and I agree—clearly we agree on Germany, a united Germany, remaining as a full participating partner in NATO. There's no difference of even nuance between the Federal Republic and the United States on that point. We also agree that the Soviets have understandable interest in all of this.

But we did not try to fashion, Rita [Rita Beamish, Associated Press], some compromise at this juncture; but we will be talking about an expanded role for NATO. I will be consulting with Chancellor Kohl before the NATO meeting, and then at the NATO meeting, we will be talking to the other leaders in NATO about how we lay to rest any concerns that the Soviets might have by having an expanded role that certainly will be seen to be as unthreatening to the Soviet Union. But we had no formula that we agreed on. Now, maybe the Chancellor would like to add to that.

The Chancellor. First of all, I should like to underline that our position, the position of the President and my own position, are completely identical as regards the question of membership in NATO for a united Germany. To me it is totally clear that membership in NATO for a united Germany is of existential importance. Any singling out, any neutralization, always means isolation. And out of the isolation of Germany, which happened during the twenties, a lot of bad things came about. We want that the unified Germany is part of NATO, part of the community of free nations, and part of the European Community so that in both cases we are bound in and that we are under no circumstances in any way isolated.

Secondly, I actually think that we're on a good way now, in spite of all the discussions. I've never expected that this important question could be solved overnight. I have always said the internal aspects, the intra-German aspects, must be settled until unification and the external aspects. That, after all, is the purpose behind the two-plus-four negotiations—the negotiations, the talks, which united the two German States, the United States of America, the United Kingdom, France, and the Soviet Union. And we have always said we will need two to three rounds of talks. And we have just now completed the first round. But our objective will remain, and we stand a good chance that this will be possible to complete this by fall.

And of course, we as Germans, as a matter of course, are in this whole process also going to bear in mind the Soviet security. And it's going to be important that NATO and the Warsaw Pact meet in a good atmosphere. The President has already made proposals, and we're going to talk about this. I'm optimistic that a good message is going to come out also in this sense from the London NATO summit meeting.

The President. Is there a question from the German press?

Visit of Prime Minister Lothar de Maizière of the Democratic Republic of Germany

Q. Chancellor Kohl, did you talk about the first coming visit of the East German head of government, de Maizière? Did the President ask you about your opinion? You do know de Maizière quite well.

The Chancellor. Yes, of course, we did talk about this—a matter of course.

The President. Let me simply add that he will be cordially received here in the White House. We're looking forward to that visit, and I think it's just one more step that demonstrates the magnificent changes that have taken place over the past year and a half. So, he will be well-received here in the White House—he and those with him.

German Membership in NATO

Q. Mr. President, in the wake of the Baker-Shevardnadze talks recently this week, and as the Secretary has just re-turned, do you hear anything new from the Soviets in terms of their willingness to swallow Germany's staying in NATO?

The President. I don't think anything to report on that. But I think as these talks go forward—the talks we had with Mr. Gorbachev here, the talks that Jim Baker had with [Soviet Foreign Minister] Shevardnadze over there—I'd like to think we can be very helpful in narrowing the differences that we all know exist. I felt, without being able to document it, that we narrowed the differences at Camp David.

But it is my intention to continue to try to convince Mr. Gorbachev that there is no threat, indeed, to the Soviet Union from a united Germany in NATO and, indeed, in a NATO that has an expanded political role. And I think Jim would like to feel—I don't want to put words in his mouth—that perhaps he made some progress in this regard. But for the U.S. side, we're going to just keep on pushing to that end because it is the right answer and it is not threatening to the Soviet Union.

NATO's Purpose and Strategies

Q. Mr. President, Chancellor Kohl—to both of you—you both have made reference to the upcoming NATO summit meeting in July. Do you anticipate that out of that summit meeting there will be a clear statement of new purpose for NATO, perhaps fundamental changes in the alliance's military strategy, on the subjects of no first use, forward deployment, that sort of thing?

The Chancellor. We're working on that. And of course, this summit meeting is being met with great expectations; and we're trying to fulfill them because the world, after all, has changed very much, if you think of the fact that we saw the Warsaw Pact summit meeting just recently happening and that within the normal rotation procedure which is applicable there Lothar de Maizière was in the chair of that meeting.

The President. To that I would simply add we are determined to more clearly define what we're talking about. I wouldn't look for the final and only answer to come out of that summit meeting. We've got a lot of consultation between now and then. But I think what we'll see emerging after the

NATO summit is a common direction for this expanded concept. But I don't think, Frank [Frank Sesno, Cable News Network], that it's going to be every "t" crossed and every "i" dotted.

Upcoming German Elections

Q. Can I ask the Chancellor if he has reached an agreement with the East German Prime Minister about the date of the election for January, as has been reported?

The Chancellor. There is no agreement to this effect at the moment because we are in the habit of doing our work stage by stage, taking it as it comes. And our most important job of the next 2 weeks is going to be to see in the People's Chamber in the GDR the state treaty ratified and to see to it that it is also ratified in the German Bundestag and the Bundesrat. And I'm convinced that both Parliaments are going to ratify that treaty. And then, as of the 1st of July, we're going to see the deutsche mark introduced in the German Democratic Republic and also a market economy. And that, of course, obviously, is going to have enormous consequences. And very soon, out of that, discussion is going to evolve. And I'm waiting for that one, and I'm very calm about it. And it's only fair and reasonable that here the German Democratic Republic should have the first say. But the election is going to be soon. That's what I think.

German Troop Levels

Q. Chancellor Kohl, would you be willing, as a way out of the impasse over the size of the German army, to offer voluntarily some limits, some ceiling on the size of the German army, to the Soviets as an assurance?

The Chancellor. The strength of the future German army is not a private matter to be decided only by Germans; it's a question which is of enormous importance for the overall security configuration of Europe. And I'm strictly against any going it alone by the Germans—assuming a single or separate course. What we need now is more and more confidence and trust, and trust and confidence can only grow out of friendly consultations.

And of course, hidden behind your question is also a question directed against the Warsaw Pact and NATO. And that is to say it is a question which is connected with the Vienna negotiations. And we, the Germans, are ready to participate in a reasonable solution for the future.

German Membership in NATO

Q. Mr. President, you and Secretary Baker and Chancellor Kohl have all expressed some optimism that you could somehow reduce the Soviets' fears of a unified Germany. Can you be specific, sir, on why you have reason to be optimistic that your differences are narrowing?

The President. Because the facts are on our side. I mean, I don't think anyone inside the Soviet Union would fear—with the changes going on in the Soviet Union, I think it's much more likely we can find common ground. Secondly, I think that Mr. Gorbachev himself accepts the concept that U.S. forces in Europe are stabilizing and not threatening. So, you have these two points to build on.

And I can't be too specific on it, Ellen [Ellen Warren, Knight-Ridder], but I just have the feeling from some of the things that were said not just at Camp David but in that Cabinet Room over there—that they understand that. They also paid some lip service, gave some credibility to the idea that a country could decide what alliance it wanted to be in. So, these points make me feel that we can, indeed, make progress and convince Mr. Gorbachev and his associates that the solution that we strongly favor is not threatening to them, indeed, will be the most compelling in terms of adding to the stability of Europe.

And you're seeing other countries in Eastern Europe begin to accept that concept— some enthusiastically. So, I think we're making progress, but I can't make a prediction as to how totally successful we're going to be. But we're going to keep on trying because the facts are on our side: A united Germany in NATO will not be threatening to the Soviet Union. A U.S. presence will not be threatening to the Soviet Union. So, we've just got to keep on making our case. Do you want to add to that, Helmut?

The Chancellor. No.

The President. Well, thank you all very much. The Chancellor must fly on to Germany, and I must fly on elsewhere. [*Laughter*]

Note: The President spoke at 9:05 p.m. in the Rose Garden at the White House. The Chancellor spoke in German, and his remarks were translated by an interpreter.

Statement by Press Secretary Fitzwater on President Bush's Dinner With President Carlos Salinas de Gortari of Mexico
June 10, 1990

President Bush hosted a private dinner in the White House this evening for President Carlos Salinas de Gortari of Mexico. President Salinas is in the United States on a private visit to address the Business Roundtable. He will meet with Secretary Baker on Monday, June 11, and with Vice President Quayle on Tuesday, June 12.

At dinner, the two leaders discussed a wide range of bilateral and international affairs. President Bush discussed his recent meeting with President Gorbachev and his consultations with European leaders. The Presidents discussed the status of our mutual efforts to fight the spread of narcotics. President Bush reiterated our desire to continue close cooperation with Mexican authorities.

The Presidents focused considerable discussion on economic issues. In 1989 trade between the two countries totaled $52 billion. U.S. exports to Mexico were $25 billion. The United States has $5.5 billion in direct foreign investment in Mexico.

Both leaders believe that the United States and Mexico would each derive substantial and long-term benefits from a comprehensive bilateral trade agreement. They agreed that bilateral efforts to maximize trade and investment opportunities can and should complement the trade liberalization achieved in the Uruguay round of the GATT.

Consultations on the free trade issue will continue tomorrow with Members of Congress and in President Salinas' meeting with Secretary Baker. Both leaders agreed on a future course of increased economic and political cooperation between the two countries.

A reception before dinner was attended by the Vice President; Secretary of the Treasury Brady; Secretary of Commerce Mosbacher; U.S. Trade Representative Carla Hills; the President's national security adviser, General Scowcroft; Ambassador Negroponte [U.S. Ambassador to Mexico]; and William Pryce, of the National Security Council.

Mexico-United States Joint Statement on Negotiation of a Free Trade Agreement
June 11, 1990

During their June 10 meeting in Washington, the Presidents of Mexico and the United States held discussions on bilateral relations, with the particular purpose of broadening and strengthening economic relations between the two countries. Both Presidents agreed that their two countries

must look to the future and devise ways to meet the challenges of the 1990s and the next century, establishing a climate of greater stability and confidence for trade and investment.

The Presidents share a commitment to forge a vigorous partnership for sustained economic growth and opportunity—one which will open markets, so that trade and investment can expand further.

The two Presidents have determined that a comprehensive Free Trade Agreement is the best vehicle to achieve these ambitious objectives and, therefore, agree to move in a timely manner toward that end. They are convinced that free trade between Mexico and the United States can be a powerful engine for economic development, creating new jobs and opening new markets.

Accordingly, they have directed Ambassador Carla A. Hills, the United States Trade Representative, and Dr. Jaime Serra Puche, the Minister of Commerce and Industrial Development of Mexico, to undertake the consultations and preparatory work needed to initiate such negotiations, in accordance with each country's internal procedures, and to report back to the two Presidents as soon as practicable, but in any event before their next meeting in December.

The Presidents agreed that the greatest possible mutual benefit would derive from an agreement that entails the gradual and comprehensive elimination of trade barriers between the two countries, including: the full, phased elimination of import tariffs; the elimination or fullest possible reduction of non-tariff trade barriers, such as import quotas, licenses and technical barriers to trade; the establishment of clear, binding protection for intellectual property rights; fair and expeditious dispute settlement procedures; and means to improve and expand the flow of goods, services, and investment between the United States and Mexico.

The Presidents reaffirmed their commitment to the multilateral trading system and the General Agreement on Tariffs and Trade. They agreed that a successful conclusion of the Uruguay Round of multilateral trade negotiations by December is their highest priority, since this would yield the greatest benefit to both countries. They pledged to work toward that end. They also concluded that bilateral efforts to expand trade and investment opportunities can and should complement the trade liberalization achieved in the Uruguay Round.

The Presidents agreed that they would stay in close personal touch on this issue and review progress during President Bush's visit to Mexico in December 1990.

Remarks at the Presentation Ceremony for the Drug-Free School Recognition Program Awards
June 11, 1990

Thank you all very much. Welcome, Secretary Cavazos and all of you, the principals, the students, parents, teachers, and friends. I'm delighted to have you here in the Rose Garden today. We're here to celebrate a cause that's near and dear to your hearts and mine: the battle to free our schools and our children from the poisonous plague of drugs. We're so proud to honor the 51 schools named as winners in our 1989 to '90 Drug-Free School Recognition Program.

You've distinguished yourselves and your country by substantially reducing alcohol, tobacco, and other drug use among your students. And each school represented here today has been selected because they have a clear no-drug-use policy, established enforcement procedures, and an ongoing plan to remain or become totally drug-free. You're each stars on your own, and together you form a constellation of hope, illuminating the blackness of the night's sky.

We've established these awards because nothing should be more important to us than the young people of America. And because they are our future, they trust us to leave our land healthy and at peace and our values strong and true so that the world they inherit will be a good one. And they trust us to prepare them to take advantage of the opportunity that the world has to offer.

You know, education means more than

807

just teaching our children the skills that are needed to hold a job; it's also about passing on to each new generation the values that serve as the foundation and cornerstone of our free society: loyalty, compassion, courage, and the ability to make the crucial distinctions between the right and wrong. But to get the finest education in our schools, we must get the drugs out.

As President, I have seen much and heard even more, but as a parent, few stories have wrenched me as hard as those about schoolchildren trapped in this evil nightmare of drugs. We've seen the tragic devastation that drugs cause, seen how they're draining the lifeblood of our best and greatest hope. We've heard the stories, have thought about the young lives being wasted. And finally, as a nation, we declared: This is war, and let the victory begin with each one of us.

We must win our war on drugs by persuading our young people that drugs are not "cool," that drugs will chew them up and spit them out, and that they must see that the choice of drugs over self-reliance is the choice of death over life. But you know, ultimately the most important weapons in the war on drugs are the least tangible ones: self-discipline, courage, support from family, and faith in one's self. The answer is traditional values. And if we want to stop our kids from putting drugs in their bodies, we must first ensure that they have good ideas in their heads and moral character in their hearts.

And that's exactly what the 51 schools that we honor here are doing. But actions not words, speak most vividly, most poignantly. Listen to the extraordinary stories of some of the schools represented here today.

Almost half a century ago, a scene from a movie captured the hearts of Americans: An older boy, troubled but now reformed, carries a younger boy. And when a priest offers to relieve him of his burden, the boy quietly but firmly refuses. "He ain't heavy," he says, "he's my brother." The movie was "Boys Town."

In 1990 the extraordinary mission of this community continues, inspiring its students to take responsibility for their lives and the lives of those around them. A model town for "at risk" teens, it teaches right from wrong in a loving environment that stresses self-respect and moral values. It's a healing balm that restores lost youngsters physically, mentally, and spiritually.

A visitor to Boys Town High School once said: "Here, they make the kids want to resist drugs by showing them that they're people who deserve respect—from themselves as well as from others. I've never seen kids so in touch with themselves."

And, for the real truth of this place, here's what one Boys Town High student said: "There are lots of holes in my life that were filled with pain. And now I'm going to fill them with joy."

Another place where kids are finding joy is the Mollie Ray Elementary School in Orlando, Florida. Principal Paul Van Mitchell is a hero with faith in commonsense values which have never failed us when we've had the courage to live up to them.

The school is in what's been called an ugly environment with pretty kids. Paul and his staff are warriors defending what's beautiful by destroying what's evil. They provide special after-school drug prevention programs for the most "at-risk" students and have an open-door mentor program. And Paul has also inspired a community-wide drug program and is part of a task force to combat drugs.

And another principal-hero, Robert McCarley, of Crockett Junior High School in Odessa, Texas, is also the backbone of that school's drug-free program. He set up a hotline where kids can call and report drug use. Robert has transformed the school from one run by three gangs to one with a proud and successful no-use policy.

But it is Robert's own example that shines as a proud beacon, a North Star for all to follow. For years, he and his wife have taken problem kids into their home. And then came Ginger, an abused child from a family filled with drugs. She was malnourished, depressed, and failing school. And after a year with them, she is now healthy, well-adjusted, making A's and B's. And this is the most wonderful news of all: The McCarleys are adopting Ginger.

I've told you three stories today, but behind each school here are similar tales of joy and success, tales that show people are working together toward our national education goals. The Governors of the U.S. and I agree: By the year 2000, every school in America will be free of drugs and violence. I know that with people like you to inspire them, others will follow until every school in America is safe. And with people like you, America's future will be bright beyond our dreams.

Today we honor these 51 schools from across our country, selected from hundreds—literally hundreds—nominated by public and private education's groups. You're from 25 States and include 42 public

and 9 private schools, from elementary to high schools. You're being saluted today as the finest in the Nation, and you should be very proud of your achievements and your legacy. And I am proud of you.

Congratulations, and God bless you for your unselfish example. Thank you for what you're doing; keep up the great work. Thank you all very much. Now, Dr. Cavazos will pass out the awards.

Note: The President spoke at 11:08 a.m. in the Rose Garden at the White House.

Exchange With Reporters on the Supreme Court Decision Overturning a Federal Flag Desecration Statute
June 11, 1990

Q. Mr. President, are you going to renew your flag amendment now?

The President. Absolutely.

Q. What's your next step?

The President. I don't know. We just heard the decision. But I'm not in any way pulled back from my conviction that that's what we need. And I think some of us said ahead of time that this legislative approach would not be upheld, and apparently the Court has decided that. So, I will continue to press for what I strongly believe is in the best interest of this country.

Q. Do you believe that's the public appetite for an amendment?

The President. I hope so.

Note: The exchange took place at 11:23 a.m. in the Rose Garden at the White House. On June 11, the Supreme Court of the United States ruled that a law making it a crime to burn or deface the American flag violated the free-speech guarantee of the first amendment. A tape was not available for verification of the content of this exchange.

Statement by Press Secretary Fitzwater on the President's Meeting With Prime Minister Lothar de Maizière of the German Democratic Republic
June 11, 1990

The President met for approximately 2 hours today with Prime Minister Lothar de Maizière of the German Democratic Republic, first in the Cabinet Room and then at a working lunch in the Residence. It was the first meeting ever held between an American President and an East German Prime Minister.

The President expressed his admiration for Prime Minister de Maizière's role in the GDR's democratic transformation and reiterated the goal the United States has long shared with the German people: German unity in peace and freedom.

The bulk of their discussion was on German unification. The President and

Prime Minister de Maizière agreed that a united Germany should enjoy full sovereignty from the time of unification, with no discriminatory constraints on its sovereignty, and that Germany should be free to choose its own alliance arrangements as stipulated in the Helsinki Final Act. They also discussed the future of Germany in NATO and agreed on the continuing vital role of the alliance and of U.S. forces stationed in Europe as guarantors of stability and security.

The President reviewed the results of the U.S.-Soviet summit and discussed Prime Minister de Maizière's recent meetings with President Gorbachev at the Warsaw Pact meeting in Moscow. The President outlined his proposals for a transformed Atlantic alliance, further negotiations on conventional and nuclear forces, and a stronger role for the CSCE process. He and Prime Minister de Maizière agreed that these steps were important to demonstrate to the Soviet Union that a united Germany in NATO is no threat to Soviet security.

Exchange With Reporters
June 12, 1990

The President's Birthday

The President. It's a vast improvement. [*Laughter*] Helen [Helen Thomas, United Press International], where's yours?

Q. I don't know what they're running for. [*Laughter*]

The President. No answers—only those wearing hats get their question answered. [*Laughter*]

Q. Touché.

The President. One birthday question.

Q. Have you gotten a birthday card from the President of the Soviet Union?

The President. No, I have not—that I'm aware of. But I've got to be careful; he may well have sent something.

German Membership in NATO

Q. Mr. President, have you seen his latest remarks where he's proposed associate membership for Germany in NATO and the Warsaw Pact?

The President. That matter was discussed here. So, I haven't seen any recent remarks, except I saw a proposal of some consideration, and of course, that has been discussed with the leaders in Eastern Europe. It's been discussed here, and our position is well-known to him, which is that a unified Germany should be in NATO with no conditions. But the more talking we do, the more convinced I am that they will see that what we're proposing is most stabilizing and is best for the Soviet Union as well as Western Europe and Eastern Europe. So, we'll keep on trying. But these ideas—let them float them out there. And we'll listen, and we'll discuss them without rancor.

Thank you all very much.

Note: The exchange began at 10:05 a.m. in the Cabinet Room at the White House, prior to a meeting with Republican congressional leaders. The reporters entered the room wearing birthday hats.

Letter to Congressional Leaders on the Canada-United States Free Trade Agreement
June 12, 1990

Dear Mr. Chairman:

Pursuant to section 103 of the United States-Canada Free-Trade Agreement Implementation Act of 1988 (Public Law 100–

449), I am pleased to submit the attached report and related documents pertaining to a proposed action to accelerate elimination of duties on designated products under the United States-Canada Free-Trade Agreement.

Sincerely,

GEORGE BUSH

Note: Identical letters were sent to Lloyd

Bentsen, chairman of the Senate Finance Committee, and Dan Rostenkowski, chairman of the House Ways and Means Committee. Proclamation 6142, which implemented the accelerated schedule of duty elimination under the agreement, was printed in the "Federal Register" of May 30 and is listed in Appendix E at the end of this volume.

Remarks Upon Receiving a Replica of the Iwo Jima Memorial and an Exchange With Reporters
June 12, 1990

The President. Well, first, my profound thanks to Mr. Felix de Weldon. A great pleasure, sir, having you here in the Rose Garden, and of course my old friend Senator Mark Hatfield. Mr. de Weldon has just presented me with this beautiful replica of the memorial, which he designed. It's of a battle in which Senator Hatfield served, the battle of Iwo Jima.

You all know the story: Early in 1945, 8 square miles of black sand and volcanic rubble, and gallant marines fought hand to hand, yard by yard; and finally, Mount Suribachi. And when the marines reached the top, six men raised a piece of pipe upright, and from one end floated a flag. And in the most famous image of World War II, a photograph was taken; and from it came, ultimately, the Iwo Jima Memorial. This memorial embodies self-expression and opportunity and democracy for all.

And, well, so does another symbol that I'd like to talk about here today: concern for the American flag and what it represents. That concern is not new. For instance, 75 years ago, President Woodrow Wilson said: "A patriotic American is never so proud of his flag as when it comes to mean to others, as to himself, a symbol of liberty." He knew that the flag was more than mere fabric; rather, a mosaic of values and of liberty.

What that flag encapsules is too sacred to be abused. You all know yesterday's Supreme Court decision. It wasn't surprising. One year ago this month, many of us

deeply concerned about protecting the American flag from willful desecration predicted that any congressional legislation would be declared unconstitutional. I take no joy that this prediction has been upheld.

Accordingly, I want to take the chance today to renew my commitment to the surest, safest way to guarantee that, while speech remains free, flag desecration is unacceptable and must carry a price, and, yes, a constitutional amendment to protect the truly unique symbol of all that we are and that we believe. Our constitutional amendment will preserve the widest conceivable range of options for free expression. It applies only to the flag. Its language is simple but eloquent: The Congress and the States shall have power to prohibit the physical desecration of the flag of the United States.

Our forefathers, with remarkable foresight, provided a mechanism for amending the Constitution. And they wished it to be used sparingly and wisely, and it has been, and it must today. Just as the Constitution is a unique symbol of America, so is our flag.

And as Justice Stevens said so eloquently last year when he spoke of the ideas of liberty: "If those ideas are worth fighting for, and our history demonstrates that they are, it cannot be true that the flag that uniquely symbolizes their power is not itself worthy of protection from unnecessary desecration." Amending the Constitution to protect the flag is not a matter of partisan politics. It's not a Democrat nor a Republican issue. I don't see it as either liberal or conservative. It's an American issue. And so, I call on the Congress to act by July 4th, this nation's birthday. I know that honest and patriotic Americans may differ on this question, but I am absolutely convinced that this is the proper course for our country. I feel it deep in my heart because the flag and what it means is carried in the hearts of all Americans.

Henry Ward Beecher once said: "A thoughtful mind, when it sees a nation's flag, sees not the flag, not the flag only, but the nation itself." Through a constitutional amendment, let us honor the greatest symbol of this great country.

And now, Mr. de Weldon and Senator, thank you very much for coming to the Rose Garden, and thank you for this magnificent presentation. It is most appropriate, and I'm proud to have it at my side as I express my heartfelt support for this important constitutional step. Thank you very much, sir. Thank you.

Flag Desecration

Q. Senator Hatfield, are you in favor of this amendment?

Q. Mr. President, what do you say to those who say every country has a flag, but only we have the Bill of Rights. It's never been amended; why should we amend it today?

The President. I say that the forefathers provided for amendment of the Constitution, including the Bill of Rights, and that the flag is a unique symbol. I can't speak for the other countries, but I can speak for how strongly I feel about this being the unique symbol of the United States. And it should be protected. The Congress tried to protect it by legislation; that legislation did not stand up. And it wasn't Republicans alone or Democrats alone; it was Republicans and Democrats that voted for that legislation. When it was knocked down by the Court, I feel there's no other way to go but this constitutional amendment, which was provided for. So, that's what I say. I keep emphasizing the word "unique" symbol of the United States of America.

Q. But isn't burning it free speech, sir?

Q. Mr. President, if it's not a partisan matter——

The President. No, there's some—let me get this question right here—because the Court has determined that there are excesses to free speech. And I would like to see one of these excesses be the burning of the American flag. So, yes, I am all for free speech, but I am for protecting the flag against desecration. The law books are full of restrictions on free speech, and we ought to have this be one of them. Shouting "fire" in a crowded theater is a good one for you.

Q. Mr. President, but that endangers people. Does burning the flag endanger people?

The President. Yes. It endangers the fabric of our country, and I think it ought to be outlawed.

Q. If it's not a matter of partisan politics, Mr. President, why are members of your party already gearing up to put together 30-second campaign commercials dealing with their opponents' votes?

The President. I know nothing about those campaign commercials, and I expect both sides will be talking about their position on this issue. I disagree with what I heard the chairman of the Democratic Party [Ronald H. Brown] say when he made a political comment about this. And I'm putting it in what I think is best for the United States. I feel strongly about it. That's my answer.

Any others? Yes, Brit [Brit Hume, ABC News]? I get credit for a press conference now. I've been asked more than three questions. So, I want to put this down as number 56.

Q. Senator Hatfield, could we hear your position on this issue, sir?

Senator Hatfield. It's the President's press conference, not mine.

Q. Will you be commenting on this during the election?

The President. You're darn right. I want this done now. I hope it will be out of the way by the time of the election.

Q. Will you talk about individual Member's of Congress position on this?

The President. I will talk about the fact that I think the flag should be protected by a constitutional amendment.

Palestine Liberation Organization

Q. Can I ask a question on another topic? Have you made up your mind on continuing or not continuing the PLO dialog?

The President. No, no decision on that yet.

Q. How close are you?

The President. John [John Cochran, NBC News], I can't help you on how close. There's quite a bit going on behind the scenes, but I just can't tell you. Incidentally, I had a talk with President Mubarak [of Egypt], and that subject came up today. But I'm not prepared to make my decision known on that yet.

Q. Are you giving Arafat [Yasser Arafat, chairman of the PLO] some more time?

The President. I want to see that terroristic act condemned and those who did it condemned.

Nelson Mandela

Q. We've heard reports, Mr. President, that the CIA was involved in Nelson Mandela's arrest in 1962. Would you offer him an apology when he arrives here?

The President. I don't know what I'll do about that. But I'm very pleased that he's coming here; I'm very pleased that he is free. I saw a story about that, but I cannot attest to it. I haven't looked into it yet.

Q. Was that an appropriate role for the CIA then or now?

The President. What role?

Q. To be involved in the—essentially turning over someone——

The President. I can't comment on that matter.

Any other questions?

The President's Birthday

Q. How does it feel to be 66?

The President. Slightly worse than being 65, but not bad, not bad. In fact, this has been a happy birthday. I started off kind of regretting it, but along comes Mr. de Weldon. I'm not saying he says this is a birthday present, because this has been in the mill, but it's been a very good one. I feel like a spring colt. I'm ready to take two more questions, and that's it. It's been a good birthday. I hadn't thought so, but good cake, good cards, and not bad.

Offshore Oil Drilling

Q. ——decision on offshore oil drilling?

The President. Very soon now.

Baltic States

Q. Have you heard from Gorbachev——

Q. We've been hearing that a lot.

Q. ——on Germany?

The President. About the German question?

Q. The German question and also the fact that Gorbachev is meeting with the Baltic States representatives.

The President. I think that's a heartening development. I hope that out of that comes a further step towards self-determination for the Baltics. And I view dialog, John, as something that's very important. I've said all along that we want dialog to go forward because he knows that I have a difference with him on the status of Lithuania—the United States never having recognized its incorporation into the Soviet Union.

Last one. Who's got it?

Nolan Ryan

Q. Nolan Ryan?

The President. Nolan Ryan. [*Laughter*] Well, I just hung up talking to Nolan about 1:30. I said, "Where are you?" And he said, "Well, I'm out at the ballpark." And I think it was a magnificent performance. I loved what he said—and it's typical of Nolan, because I've known him for a long time—giving credits to his teammates. He told me that his wife and his son had gotten there 5 minutes before the game started. I said, "Well, had you told them you were going to pitch a no-hitter?" He hadn't gone quite that far. But, look, here's this guy—what's Nolan—43, and just the tops, a top human being and a top performer. And it's a great symbol for the kids around this country that love baseball as much as I do. It was a wonderful moment, I'll tell you. I wish I'd been there.

Thank you all very much.

Q. Is that why you feel better about 66?

The President. Yes, that's one of the reasons.

Note: The President spoke at 4:08 p.m. in the Rose Garden at the White House. On

June 11, Nolan Ryan, a pitcher for the *hitter against the Oakland Athletics.*
Texas Rangers baseball team, pitched a no-

Nomination of Kenneth Noel Peltier To Be United States Ambassador to Comoros
June 12, 1990

The President today announced his intention to nominate Kenneth Noel Peltier, of Texas, a career member of the Senior Foreign Service, Class of Minister-Counselor, to be Ambassador Extraordinary and Plenipotentiary of the United States of America to the Federal and Islamic Republic of Comoros.

Mr. Peltier served as Executive Director for the Bureau of European and Canadian Affairs from 1985 to 1988. Prior to this, he served as Counselor for Administrative Affairs at the U.S. Embassy in Kinshasa, Zaire, 1983–1985; administrative officer for the U.S. Embassy in Ouagadougou, Burkina Faso, 1982–1983; administrative officer for USOECD [U.S. Organization for Economic Cooperation and Development], Paris, France, 1979–1982; and on a training assignment at the École Nationale d'Administration in Paris, France, 1978–1979. In addition, Mr. Peltier has served as an assignments officer in Africa for the Bureau of Personnel for the Department of State, 1976–1978; administrative officer for the U.S. Embassy in Antananarivo, Madagascar, 1974–1976; general services officer for U.S. Embassy in Fort Lamy, Chad, 1972–1974; and foreign service officer for the Foreign Service Institute, 1971–1972. He joined the Foreign Service in 1971.

Mr. Peltier graduated from the University of Missouri (B.A., 1967) and the University of Texas (M.B.A., 1971). He was born June 9, 1944, in Boston, MA. Mr. Peltier is married, has three children, and resides in Arlington, VA.

Nomination of George Fleming Jones To Be United States Ambassador to Guyana
June 12, 1990

The President today announced his intention to nominate George Fleming Jones, of Texas, a career member of the Senior Foreign Service, Class of Minister-Counselor, to be Ambassador Extraordinary and Plenipotentiary of the United States of America to the Co-operative Republic of Guyana. He would succeed Theresa Anne Tull.

Since 1989 Mr. Jones has served as vice president for State Department affairs for the American Foreign Service Association in Washington, DC. Prior to this, he served as Deputy Chief of Mission for the U.S. Embassy in Santiago, Chile, 1985–1989; Deputy Chief of Mission for the U.S. Embassy in San José, Costa Rica, 1982–1985; Director of the Office of Regional Political Programs, 1980–1982; Deputy Director of the Office of Regional Political Programs in the Bureau of Inter-American Affairs at the Department of State, 1978–1980; National War College, 1977–1978; Political Counselor at the U.S. Embassy in Guatemala, Guatemala, 1974–1977; and political adviser at the U.S. Mission to the International Atomic Energy Agency in Vienna, Austria, 1971–1974. In addition, he was assigned to the Department of State, 1967–1971, and served in the U.S. Embassy in Caracas, Venezuela, 1963–1966; the U.S. Embassy in Accra, Ghana, 1961–1963; and the U.S. Embassy in Quito, Ecuador, 1958–1960. Mr. Jones joined the

Foreign Service in 1956.

Mr. Jones graduated from Wabash College (A.B., 1955), the Fletcher School of Law and Diplomacy (A.M., 1956), and Stanford University (M.A., 1967). He was born June 27, 1935, in San Angelo, TX. Mr. Jones is married and resides in Fairfax, VA.

Nomination of Richard V. Bertain To Be an Associate Director of ACTION
June 12, 1990

The President today announced his intention to nominate Richard V. Bertain to be Associate Director for the ACTION Agency for the Office of Domestic and Anti-Poverty Operations.

Since 1978 Dr. Bertain has served as superintendent and assistant superintendent for business services for the El Segundo Unified School District in California. Prior to this, he served as assistant superintendent for business services for the Palm Springs Unified School District in California, 1978; management consultant and president of the American Educational Services in Los Angeles, CA, 1971–1978; deputy superintendent of schools, acting planning director, and special consultant to the superintendent for the Glendale Unified School District in California, 1969–

1971; deputy of secondary schools and high school principal for the Culver City Unified School District in California, 1967–1969; and assistant to the superintendent of the Beverly Hills Unified School District in California, 1963–1967. In addition, he has served on the advisory council of the Boy Scouts of America and is a sustaining member of Young Men's Christian Association.

Dr. Bertain graduated from St. Mary's College (A.B., 1951), California State University (M.A., 1960), and Harvard University Graduate School of Education (Ed.D., 1964). He was born July 4, 1930, in Scotia, CA. Dr. Bertain served in the U.S. Navy, 1955–1957. He is married, has six children, and resides in West Hills, CA.

Remarks at a Reception for Supporters of the Annual Republican Congressional Fundraising Dinner
June 12, 1990

Welcome, everybody, for many a return engagement. And Barbara and I are delighted to have you here. Once again, we're in your debt. First, let me single out our chairman of tonight's dinner, under the theory that you get a busy person to get in and get the job done. The committee, the blind committee—because nobody wanted to take the blame nor the credit—said, "We'll go get Howard Baker; we'll try." And sure enough he accepted, and sure enough I think tonight we have the most successful dinner ever.

And just to guarantee that—as I walked up here, I'm sure you wondered what the deep, dark secret was that Howard told me—that thanks to the generosity of Armand Hammer, to the tune of $500,000, that we're now over the top and going strong. So, Armand, my great vote of thanks to you.

And that is a very nice supplement to what so many others have done, either through wearing out the telephone—guys like Jack McDonald, my old colleague in the House, who I understand is modestly standing back here but should be hanging from the rafters because of his performance, probably the leading ticket seller or participant in that manner, according to Howard. And then, of course, Carl Lindner and Dwayne Andreas—just stars in this, and I am very grateful to them. But in the same vein, I'm grateful to every single person here, you who did the heavy lifting out there and most of the work. So, thank you all very much because this comes at an important time in what we feel could be an historic year.

The dinner I hope will be fun if we can see each other across a rather intimate ballroom over there—[*laughter*]. But nevertheless, it's marvelous. Let me just say a word about it, and I really should defer to Don Nickles, who's our superb chairman on the Senate side, and Guy, on the House side, and, of course, the National Committee weighing in in a great way on all this, too. And I want to thank them. But they are better to comment on the day-to-day political activity.

But you know the litany: The party in power loses seats in an off year, historically. Well, we want to change that. And I had a report from both Senator Nickles and Congressman [Guy] Vander Jagt when I met in the Cabinet Room with the leadership of the party this morning on the Hill—our Hill leadership—Dole, Michel, et cetera. Without kind of putting too optimistic a spin on it, the Senate report was very strong, and the House report—where everyone knows we have a great difficulty because of the locking in of incumbency—even there, Guy was able to give us a pretty upbeat report.

And I can tell you I'm going to try to do my share. The Vice President has been magnificent—Dan Quayle—in what he's been able to do in helping candidates raise money. The recruitment, I think I can say without putting words in the mouths of these two, has gone well. The party under Lee Atwater and Mary Matalin is pitching in. Jeanie Austin doing a good job on that as well. So, the team is together, and the importance of the year is enormous.

I don't want to overlook the Governors' races because they are key when you look at this concept of redistricting that we're going to have to grope with in the years ahead. And we have some very key Governors' races out there. And the Republican Governors Association has been active and strong in doing their part.

So, we're getting the assistance, and we're getting the financial support, thanks to the approach that many of you have taken to this. But again, the election is important. I know Howard Baker is probably better able to speak to this than anybody else here. But the difference between controlling one body in the Congress and not is night and day in terms of how a President can operate. And Howard saw it when he so effectively led the Senate majority when he was Senate leader. And you could move the agenda. The President would campaign on certain things, and then he'd be able to at least be sure they were considered.

The way it is now in the Senate, as Don knows, we're playing—our leader is doing a superb job. Bob Dole is just outstanding, and he and I are working very closely together for the same objectives. But the problem is, with the numbers the way they are, it is very difficult to get our agenda placed ahead of their agenda. And the result is we're often playing defense and trying to amend a proposal that's far different philosophically than what we would have proposed in the first place.

So, we're keeping working on it, and I'm very pleased that we've been able to get some things done. Sometimes you measure progress by keeping bad things from happening. And I don't know what's going to happen at 6:15 p.m. on our veto override. We've got a technical bill up there that has a technicality that even some of our own Republicans are having difficulty with. But we've been very lucky that the vetoes have been sustained and not overridden. We may take one on the chin here today or in the next few days on another issue.

But generally, the Republican side has stayed together enough to be able to negate very unhappy legislation. Now I'd like to take that a step forward this fall and make it a more optimistic process, where we can take the offense and get done the things that join us all together as Republicans, and those who come from a more conservative side of the ledger when it comes to the free economy, free market, and all of those kinds of points.

I might—just looking around the room, I know of the interest of so many here in the international aspects. I just would say a word on the summit meeting that we had with Gorbachev. I was very pleased with it—not that we solved all the problems, the tough problems of the Baltic States. We're different. I told him very candidly and very frankly and, indeed, at an open press conference, sitting side to side. We could talk about our differences without rancor and without people getting all upset with each other the way it used to be.

We've got differences on the Baltic States, and I'm very pleased that now he's back there talking to the three leaders of the three Baltic States. And I'm hopeful that that can be resolved so we can get a dialog going and get the economic blockade lifted and then move forward in these areas that are very important not just to Gorbachev and the Soviet Union but in my view to the United States. And I'm talking about a freer, more open trading system where we can interact with each other more on the economic side, because I firmly believe that is in the interest of our country. And I know it is in the interest of markets and of an economy that has got to change and will change. But the more we interact with them, in my view, the more dramatic the change and the sooner the change can come.

And so, the meeting with Gorbachev was a good one. We made some progress on a lot of subjects. One near and dear to my heart—they accepted our proposals that lead to a ban on chemical weapons, which I think is a very civilized thing to be talking about in the year 1990. And I just wanted you to know that the tone of these meetings were quite different than anything that has transpired before, although the last Reagan-Gorbachev summit did have a very good climate, too.

The man is facing enormous problems at home. It is my view that we need to keep our eyes open, that we need to keep our country strong, that we don't want to be naive in the treatment with any country. But I just thought that you ought to know that the mood of it was good, and I think it will lead to an understanding on questions such as the Baltic States or a unified Germany being a full, participating member in NATO or whatever the question was. It's a wonderful challenge that so many of you—that all of you, really—have given me and, I would say, to the star of Wellesley, too, to represent this country at this very special time in our history. We like—I won't speak too confidently for Barbara—but we like every single minute of it. [*Laughter*]

It's a challenge, it's a great challenge, and I will never forget how we got here. And we got here just exactly through the generosity and commitment of people in this room, just as other future Senators are going to get to the Senate as a result of that same generosity, just as a wide new group of new courageous young Congressmen are going to get to the Congress for the same very reason.

So, once again, our heartfelt thanks to you for what you're doing. Thank you. And I look forward to seeing you all, I think, at a large dinner later on. Thank you for making it such a success.

Note: The President spoke at 4:37 p.m. in the East Room at the White House. In his remarks, he referred to Jack McDonald, Carl Lindner, and Dwayne Andreas, members of the President's Dinner leadership committee; and Lee Atwater, Mary Matalin, and Jeanie Austin, chairman, chief of staff, and cochairman of the Republican National Committee. Mrs. Bush spoke at the Wellesley College commencement ceremony. A tape was not available for verification of the content of these remarks.

Remarks at the Annual Republican Congressional Fundraising Dinner
June 12, 1990

Thank you very, very much. Thank you all. What a wonderful evening. Please be seated, and Guy, thank you for that wonderful introduction and also for the great job you are doing as chairman of the House campaign committee. We are very, very grateful to you.

I think that's Dan Quayle way down there. But let me point out what an outstanding job Dan is doing for our country and for our party. He's carried this message of opportunity practically a quarter of a million miles around the world. And we are very grateful to him, and I am very lucky that he is my Vice President, your Vice President.

I also want to single out and salute our two great leaders with whom I work so closely every day and to whom I'm very grateful. To Bob Dole, our outstanding leader in the United States Senate, my thanks. Today was just another bit of his handiwork, coming against the odds to carry that veto vote up there, and I'm grateful to him and to his colleagues. And of course, to Bob Michel, our indefatigable leader in the House—my sincere thanks to you, Bob, for working so closely with our administration. I want to thank Don Nickles and simply suggest that he keeps up the great work that he's doing for the Senate campaign committee. We've got a lot riding this fall, and Don is doing a great job.

Also, thanks to our wonderful host tonight, the man who is our outstanding dinner chairman, and I'm talking about Senator Howard Baker, who really has thrown himself into the breach and produced these magnificent results. Howard, thanks so much.

I want to thank all of our dinner leadership: Dwayne Andreas and Carl Lindner, especially, and Armand Hammer and my dear friend and former colleague—the one that, I'm told, on an individual basis, made the most calls or got the most done working for Howard Baker—and I'm talking to my former colleague Jack McDonald, who did

an outstanding job on these ticket sales. It's a pleasure to see all of you, and I thank you for your hard work and dedication.

I want to acknowledge the outstanding men and women of my Cabinet, and I count my blessings every single day for the kind of administration we have. We can fight like cats and dogs in that Cabinet Room, and then we go out and stay close together, working for a common cause, a common objective. I'm very fortunate, and I know it. And I count my blessings for the Cabinet and for our Chief of Staff and for those others in the executive branch who are with us here tonight.

Let me mention a man who is not with us tonight, a good friend and one of the most dynamic chairmen this party has ever seen. I, too, am talking about Lee Atwater. You know, he is a real pro, a real professional. And I just can't wait till he's back full-time in that saddle again, leading the party to more victories in the future.

I think all of us, especially those of us who are 66, remember a few losses over the years, too. I remember when I was running, with this spectacular lack of success, for the Senate back in 1964. My first speech was about building a two-party system in Texas. Barbara listened. Literally, three other people listened, and that was it. That was the whole thing. I'm pleased to see now a few more people here tonight.

But I understand some of you circulated a petition complaining that the only reason I was invited to speak tonight was because I'm Barbara Bush's husband. Guy put it very well, and perhaps generously. But I thought Barbara did a wonderful job at Wellesley, and I was very, very proud of her.

I'll tell you a story that's the gospel truth. I called Margaret Thatcher [Prime Minister of the United Kingdom] up to debrief her on the Gorbachev summit, as I did with Kohl [Helmut Kohl, Chancellor of the Federal Republic of Germany] and Mitterrand [François Mitterrand, President of France] and the other leaders of Western Europe. And Margaret, before I could get a word in—some of you know her, and she makes her point of view early—but she said, "Please, I watched Barbara's speech, and please tell her I thought it was magnificent." Here she was all the way across the Atlantic. She didn't want to talk about the Gorbachev summit; she wanted to talk about what Bar said up at Wellesley.

But a little-known secret is, Barbara did try to get me to go, too. She told me that I might as well face up to the fact that she was invited only because of the popularity and prominence of, as she put it, "the sweet soul who shares my bedroom at the White House." [*Laughter*] I said, "They invited you to Wellesley because of Millie?" [*Laughter*]

But you know, I just returned from the Midwest on a trip for some great Republican candidates, where I talked about this meeting that I felt was a very successful summit—the one we held with President Gorbachev.

And over the past year—remarkable change—we have seen literally, as Howard alluded to, millions of people freed from the bonds of tyranny; and we felt this new breeze of freedom sweep away decades of oppression. And it was the Republican policy of peace through strength coupled with our unyielding commitment to freedom and democracy that helped breathe life into the Revolution of '89 and provided us the opportunity to make so much progress at the Washington summit 2 weeks ago, a policy so successful in the 1980's because of the vision and the leadership of many people, but none more than my predecessor, President Ronald Reagan. I remember some cynics saying—when he stood in Berlin and said, "Mr. Gorbachev, take down this Wall"—I remember some critics coming at him from the left. The Wall is down, and I think some of that is due to the steadfast conviction of the last President of the United States.

You know, President Gorbachev and I worked together during these 4 days to further the process of peace by working toward a safer world, a stable new Europe, one in which every nation's security is strengthened and no nation is threatened.

And important differences? Of course they still remain: self-determination for Lithuania, to which we are committed, and the question of a unified Germany in NATO, which will contribute to the stability of a post-German unification Europe. But the summit was a success, and real progress was made.

I've also come here tonight to set a few things straight. Apparently there are some people whose sense of priorities is out of whack. And I'm talking about the people who believe that there is no difference between the Republican and the Democratic Parties. But there's a big difference. On our side, the Republican side, lies opportunity, empowerment, free market solutions to critical problems. Republican wants power in the hands of people, not in the hands of big government.

And what's scaring the heck out of our opponents is the simple fact that this fall they're up against the Republican record: the longest peacetime economic expansion in the history of the United States, the lowest unemployment rate in 16 years, and almost 22 million jobs created. And Republicans are the ones who want to keep this economy strong, and we fought every step of the way against those who want to bring America to a grinding halt. And we're fighting against mandated benefits that would burden every small business in America. We're fighting against mindless redtape, more tax-and-spend programs. And we are the ones who support a balanced budget amendment and, certainly, the line-item veto because with a more sane budget process, we know that we can build a better America.

Republicans are the ones who sent the Violent Crime Control Act to the Congress last year, with tougher penalties and enforcement measures. This administration is leading the charge to take back the streets, and we will win that battle. We are the party that brought you the Education Excellence Act and the education summit—for the first time developing national goals for our schools, for the first time in American history, so that American students can be the best in the entire world.

And we care about the environment.

Take a look at the record. We sent to the Congress the first major overhaul of the Clean Air Act in over a decade because we must protect our planet for our children and their children. But this administration also believes in market-oriented policies, policies that protect our planet and keep hard-working Americans on the job.

These are just a few of the greatest hits from the Republican record. But as everyone here knows, achieving more depends on winning more elections for Congress. We can beat our Democratic opponents on the issues when the fight's a fair one; but we lose, and the American people lose, when the fight's rigged because of Democratic gerrymandering. This year's election also presents an opportunity for us to regain a majority in the United States Senate. I feel it in my bones. We can get the majority in the Senate, and we can end the Democratic stranglehold on the U.S. Congress.

Our goal is to build a better America for our children and for those who will come after them in the next century. Our goals are ambitious, but we have the best candidates and the best supporters in the entire country to get us there. And many of them are you. Many of them are right here in this room.

Republicans all across America are making a difference in our party, in our country, and in the lives of others: people like David Kirschner of Hanna-Barbera, who joined with other industry leaders to use the unique power of television cartoons to teach children at an early age to avoid the temptation of drugs, or Lod Cook over here, who's led Atlantic Richfield to become one of the most aggressive companies, mobilizing its work force to engage in what I call a Thousand Points of Light—to engage in community service, helping the other guy. And there are so many others like them here tonight who make up this Grand Old Party. We do call them Points of Light. We can and will continue to make a difference for those who are hurting, those who are in need. And that's what building a better America is all about.

Thank you all for this glorious evening. Thank each and every one of you for caring, for your commitment. God bless you all. And aren't we lucky to live in the United States of America at this fascinating time of change in the world. Thank you very, very much.

Note: The President spoke at 9:48 p.m. in Hall A at the Washington Convention Center. In his opening remarks, he referred to Representative Guy Vander Jagt and John H. Sununu, Chief of Staff to the President.

The President's News Conference With the Regional Reporters Association
June 13, 1990

Baltic States

The President. Sorry for keeping you. Thank you very much. I'm very glad to meet with you all today—leaders of the RRA—for the newspapers and media represented in this room provide a daily, some times hourly, forum for the American people. From the large dailies in New York and Denver and Houston to the Watertown Daily Times, and from the cable networks to the radio affiliates, you cover regions as well as the Nation, and you provide this vital bridge from Washington to your own hometowns.

You also provide a bridge to the world, and I would like to start today's conference by just a very brief comment on the significant change that's occurred in the Soviet Union. You see, we applaud President Gorbachev's meeting with the Baltic Presidents. For some time, we've urged a peaceful resolution of this confrontation, one that will result in dialog—negotiation, if you will—in lifting of this economic blockade against Lithuania.

So, I hope that what we saw yesterday is

a first step in a dialog that will lead to the self-determination that we strongly support. In any event, I think it was good news. I don't want to overstate it, but I was very, very pleased to see this occur in the wake of what I think was a successful summit meeting.

Now I'll be glad to respond to questions. I don't know how we're going to do this. We need a moderator.

High School Dropout Rate

Q. Mr. President, the Tennessee General Assembly passed a law this year in which they will take away the driver's licenses of any high school students who drop out until they're 18 years old. And I wondered if that's the kind—would be a good national policy to keep more students in school.

The President. I'd be interested to know how it works. One of the great things about our educational system is its diversity. I'd be very interested to see if that works because I have been very much concerned about the dropout rate. I've been concerned not just as it affects everybody but there are certain groups that are most adversely affected where the numbers are very high on dropout. So, without going any further, I'd simply like to know how it works, and perhaps in our whole educational approach, we could use that as an example of something that will help correct the abysmal dropout rate that we have in this country.

Niobrara River Scenic River Designation

Q. The House is voting this week on a scenic river bill for the Niobrara River in Nebraska. Why is your administration opposed to this bill, and will you veto it?

The President. That has not come to me yet, and I cannot comment on it in detail at all. I'm very sorry I can't help you on it.

Offshore Oil Drilling

Q. Mr. President, you said a few weeks ago that your decision on offshore drilling was a few days away. It's been more than a few days.

The President. How much is a few days? You said a few weeks ago. Let's not get into semantics.

Q. About 2 weeks ago. When are you

going to announce a decision?

The President. Okay, that's only 14. I don't know. I really don't. But it's a matter of——

Q. What's the delay?

Mr. President. Just wanting to be sure that I have all the information I need. We're still getting opinions. It's a very hot item as you know, but we'll have a decision, as I said, within days.

Mexico-U.S. Free Trade Agreement

Q. Mr. President, some Northeastern border States are worried this week about the future of their economic relationship with the north. You agreed or promised this week to lay the groundwork this year for a free trade agreement with Mexico very similar to the deal struck 18 months ago with Canada. The feeling in some Northern States seems to be that an abundance of cheap Mexican labor might undermine business links with Canada. My question to you is: How would you protect the Canadian free trade agreement from that cheap Mexican labor in the event of a deal?

The President. We're a long way from an agreement with Mexico. But in principle, I am strongly in favor of a free trade agreement with Mexico. We had a very good discussion—I did Sunday night—with President Salinas [of Mexico] at our house. You know, every time you try to work out a free trade agreement—and this was true of the Canadian one—you hear a lot of horror stories. But I think the pluses so far outweigh the negatives that it's worth pursuing. I haven't even really gotten into thinking about what an adverse effect on Canada of a free trade agreement with Mexico, if that was your question, or of border States.

I do know that I live in a border State, in Texas. And I've talked to several of the leaders who come from Texas in the Congress—and they are very important ones, people that have some say on this—and they're all very enthusiastic in principle. I expect there will be some organized labor opposition to some aspects of it, but we really haven't gotten that far. I would simply respond to the concerns that you ask about by saying the benefits will far outweigh any negative aspects, in my view.

Maine Gubernatorial Race

Q. Mr. President, you also live in another border State sometimes.

The President. Probably more than the other one right now. [*Laughter*]

Q. Some Maine Democrats are sort of viewing the Maine gubernatorial race as a political test of strength between yourself and Senate Majority Leader George Mitchell. Governor McKernan, the Republican, was one of your earliest supporters. Former Governor Brennan, who is running as a Democrat, appointed Mitchell to the Senate. You're a part-time resident of the State of Maine, so I assume you have some interest in the race. Is this a test of strength between yourself and Mitchell, and if it is, who is going to win?

The President. No. I don't think it's a test of strength between any other outside observers. But what I do think is that it's very important that Jock McKernan be reelected Governor of Maine. And I am strongly for him, and I hope that I can help him. And I think I know something about that State because I have a great affinity for it and connection with it, as you point out. So, I would simply say I want to do everything I can to help Jock McKernan. He's an outstanding Governor, and I think he is locked in a tough battle there with Joe Brennan.

Neil Bush

Q. Mr. President, your son Neil's lending practices while a boardmember of Silverado Savings and Loan will cost taxpayers $106 million. How should Neil make restitution, and are you not providing the FBI the enforcement tools it requested because Neil might get caught in the web?

The President. I don't accept your premise at all, and I don't think the Congress does, either.

Environmental Policy and Employment

Q. As you know, your administration opposes the provision in the Clean Air Act that the House passed to compensate workers displaced from the Clean Air Act. Would you apply that same sort of logic to the Pacific Northwest—in that workers could be displaced by the listing of the spotted owl—would you want to help those workers out in some form of compensation?

The President. I want to help them out in the decision. I do not support—I think what you're referring to was the Byrd amendment that was debated. And I oppose that, and I would oppose a similar amendment, but I am very much concerned about the potential loss of jobs as a result of this spotted owl problem. I want those 30,000 families to understand that we care very much about that. But I cannot say that I would support the very kind of amendment that I opposed. But I hope that we can have a resolution of this problem that will not result in throwing 30,000 families out of work.

Terrorism and Iran

Q. Mr. President, more than 30 Syracuse University students were killed in the bombing of Flight 103, and it's been about a month since the Commission on Aviation Terrorism released its report. I'm wondering what you plan to do to implement the recommendations in the report. I'm wondering also, since aviation experts and terrorism experts have said that Iran paid for the bomb in the flight, why you have unfrozen Iranian assets and reached out to Iran?

The President. We aren't sure where the guilt lies on that. I wish I could say to the suffering members of the families who were here in this room not so many weeks ago that we knew definitively. We do have a mechanism set to follow up on Ann McLaughlin's report. The NSC [National Security Council] will coordinate that for me.

Some of the recommendations can be implemented really quickly, some will require some time, and I'm not sure I will accept them all. We've just gotten that report a couple of weeks ago. But it was very good work. And the thing I liked about the meeting with the families—at least I had an opportunity to dispel some concerns I think that they felt: that there was a lack of caring here about this.

On Iran, there has been very limited progress; and there will not be a normalization of relations with Iran, I'm afraid, until all of our hostages are out. They asked me, you know, at the time of the release of two, what good will I could exhibit, saying good will begets good will.

Incidentally, the minor adjustments in the—what do you call it, on the Iran sanctions, Iran money that was held up, and our money that was held up—came out very far in favor of United States interest. But it was a small amount of the overall problem that was discussed. But we cannot have normalized relations until we make more progress on getting the hostages out. It's like saying, Okay, two are out, but four are still kidnaped. So, for each one, you make some deal. I'm not going to do that.

Clean Air Legislation

Q. Mr. President, Mr. Porter, your domestic aide, said you would actually veto the Clean Air Act if the conference committee puts in the House amendment which does provide special unemployment and retraining aid for those who are made jobless by the Clean Air Act. Is that so?

The President. I'm not sure I can address it in that much detail. I tried to answer the question over here, and I just have to stay with that until I—I've learned something in this job: You don't make decisions until you have all the facts. And I don't have all of them here, and I don't want to go into a hypothetical example like that.

Once in awhile, we do that. Once in awhile we say, If this isn't changed, we'll put down a veto on it. And I think I try to do that so as to shape the legislation early on. On this one, I'd need to know more before I'd take that position.

Federal Assistance for Depressed State Economies

Q. Mr. President, the economies in the Northeast right now are going through some really tough times. Could you comment, please, about what the role of the Federal Government should be to help these States out?

The President. The role should be the same as it was when Texas and the Southwest were going through some very difficult times 2 years ago. And indeed, some areas of that State and others are still going through it. And that is to provide an economic climate in which there is job opportunity. I don't believe that the Federal Government has a kind of what I would call an industrial policy role in alleviating a prob-

lem that's on a certain city or a certain State. The Federal Government has the obligation to try to provide an economic climate in which prosperity can prevail and thus lift up the lives of all Americans. And then we have some specific other roles. But if you're talking about impacted aid, I don't believe that's the proper response.

Way in the back, only because we haven't been back there. These two. One, and then——

Cuba-U.S. Relations

Q. Mr. President, as you know, the people are quite interested and concerned about our relations with Cuba. I'm interested in knowing what you think of the Soviet proposal that the United States loosen its economic embargo of Cuba as a step toward the Soviet Union reducing its subsidies for Cuba.

The President. I've got a better idea: The Soviets ought to stop spending $5 billion a year in Cuba. I think that would be enormously helpful to get for the Cuban people what most every other country in this hemisphere has and clearly what many in Eastern Europe are enjoying—democracy and freedom.

So, my suggestion would be: If that totalitarian and brutal society were not propped up by an enormous subsidy from the Soviet Union, I have every reason to believe that Cuban people would have a right to achieve the freedom that other countries have achieved. So, that's where I'd start on that question, and I would not accept the idea that this is a time to change our policy toward Fidel Castro [President of Cuba].

Larry McAfee

Q. Mr. President, I understand your domestic policy staff has been working on the case of Larry McAfee, the fellow with the respirator in Alabama. I'd like to know what steps they've taken and how soon someone might be able to give him an answer about whether he'll be able to live in his own house and help support himself.

The President. I'm embarrassed to say that one has not come to me. But we should get an answer, David [David F. Demarest, Jr., Assistant to the President for Communications], to that before you leave here. I mean, I want you to have it. It's not come to me yet.

Taxes

Q. Governors, including Governor Bill Clinton of Arkansas, have complained repeatedly in the past that your no-new-taxes pledge that you made at the Republican Convention in 1988 has dramatically limited the ability to raise needed tax revenues at the State and local level. Did you intend for "Read my lips!" to apply to the local level?

The President. No, it's a good question, and I think I've spoken out on that. I know I have before, because certain States have found that they have had to raise revenues. And I am not about to criticize, and have not criticized, Governors, Democrat or Republican, who have gone that route, or ballot proposals that take an opposite view from that. What I'm talking about is the Federal role. And so, I'm glad to have a chance to clear it up, and it's a very good question.

We'll take two more on the aisle here.

Environmental Policy and Employment

Q. A followup to the earlier question on the spotted owl. Were you saying that you are trying to influence Mr. Turner's [John F. Turner, Director of the U.S. Fish and Wildlife Service] decision on whether the owl should be listed?

The President. No. We have very limited control over that. I'm saying I care very much about environmental concerns, and I care very much about family concerns. It's tough when a person is thrown out of work in this country, and we've got to keep in mind family concerns as well as environmental concerns. But I'm glad you raised it because, really, the act provides a certain mechanism for addressing problems of this nature. And the administration has very little way to get involved in that.

Space Exploration

Q. You've spoken optimistically about the need for a space station—it's going to cost about $35 billion, four times its original estimate—a Moon-Mars mission, which could cost as much as $500 billion over the next

30 years. How do you get Congress, at a time when NASA is notorious for cost overruns and when they've got to tighten the budgets everywhere, to go along with your vision for space, or in the alternative, how do you convince the American public that this is not just a grandiose, feel-good plan from the White House?

The President. Well, of course, some of the proposals we're talking about are stretched out over many years. But you know, I've been very pleased that Congress has been willing, in difficult fiscal times, to support a meaningful space program. I think it is important not only to be out front in terms of scientific achievement but also to recognize that what Sally Ride [shuttle astronaut] called a visit to planet Earth, I believe, is important. In other words, there's benefits that come to medical science and to environment and to everything else from having a very active space program.

And you put it well because there's a tremendous demand for dollars in a budget, especially when you have an enormous deficit to face, like we're doing. And so, I've been pleased that our proposals have had broad supports, crossing party lines, Democrat and Republican, in the sense of support for the objectives in space that I've spelled out. And I hope that support remains because I think there is benefit to the United States and I think it's always been our heritage, our pride, to reach out and be on the cutting edge of science. And so, I think the American people will continue to support that. You ask how the people—I don't believe Congress would be supporting it if the American people looked at it quite differently.

I really do have to go, and thank you all very much.

Q. Mr. President, will you do this again?

The President. Now, wait a minute, you're changing this again. You already asked two questions. Get out of here. [*Laughter*] Thank you all very much. You have a question—aw, aw, no two questions. [*Laughter*]

Q. Will you do this again? Will you do this again?

The President. This is a walking exit. This is a walking exit. I may not answer it if it's not the kind in general.

Transportation Policy

Q. With airline deregulation and Greyhound bankruptcy, many cities have lost their airline and inner city bus services. Does the Federal Government have a responsibility to preserve transportation options for rural America?

The President. I think the Federal Government would like to see options preserved, and they'll like to see it done by supply and demand. I would like to see it done not by the Federal Government coming in and saying you've got to have this carrier here and that mode of transportation there but by having the market provide the transportation that is often essential, and that's the way of it. But I am concerned when you have a major carrier like Greyhound having the fiscal problems they do because it could be enormous interstate inconvenience. So, we're taking a look at that one right now.

Thank you all very much.

Note: The President's 50th news conference began at 11:14 a.m. in Room 450 of the Old Executive Office Building.

Nomination of Townsend B. Friedman, Jr., To Be United States Ambassador to Mozambique
June 13, 1990

The President today announced his intention to nominate Townsend B. Friedman, Jr., of Illinois, a career member of the Senior Foreign Service, Class of Counselor, to be Ambassador Extraordinary and Plenipotentiary of the United States of America to the People's Republic of Mozambique. He would succeed Melissa Foelsch Wells.

Since 1987 Mr. Friedman has served as Director of the Office of Southern European Affairs at the Department of State. Prior to this, he served as Deputy Director of the Office of Southern European Affairs, 1986–1987; Political Counselor at the U.S. Embassy in Athens, Greece, 1983–1986; student at the National War College, 1982–1983; political officer at the U.S. Embassy in Buenos Aires, Argentina, 1979–1982; labor-political officer at the U.S. Embassy in Buenos Aires, Argentina, 1978–1979; and political officer at the U.S. Embassy in Athens, Greece, 1975–1978. In addition, he has served as a Special Assistant for Policy Planning, 1973–1974; Special Assistant to the Counselor, 1973; information officer at the Department of State, 1972; political officer at the U.S. Embassy in Santiago, Chile, 1968–1972; staff aide at the U.S. Embassy in Santiago, Chile, 1967–1968; analyst for the Bureau of Intelligence and Research at the Department of State, 1965–1967; vice consul in Porto Alegre, Brazil, 1964–1965; and a junior officer at the U.S. Embassy in Rio de Janeiro, Brazil, 1962–1964. Mr. Friedman joined the Foreign Service in 1962.

Mr. Friedman graduated from Cornell University (B.A., 1962). He was born January 4, 1940, in Chicago, IL. Mr. Friedman is married, has two children, and resides in Potomac, MD.

Nomination of Richard C. Brown To Be United States Ambassador to Uruguay
June 13, 1990

The President today announced his intention to nominate Richard C. Brown, of Maryland, a career member of the Senior Foreign Service, Class of Minister-Counselor, to be Ambassador Extraordinary and Plenipotentiary of the United States of America to the Oriental Republic of Uruguay. He would succeed Malcolm Richard Wilkey.

Since 1990 Mr. Brown has served as special adviser for International Security Affairs at the Department of Defense. Prior to this, he served as Deputy Assistant Secretary of Defense for Inter-American Affairs, 1988–1990; Deputy Chief of Mission at the U.S. Embassy in Montevideo, Uruguay, 1985; Director of the Office of Caribbean Affairs, 1984–1985; Director of the Grenada Task Force, 1983–1984; Deputy Director of Caribbean Affairs at the Department of State, 1982–1983; student at the National War College, 1981–1982; staff member for Latin American Affairs on the National Security Council, 1978–1981; Deputy Chief of Mission at the U.S. Embassy in Port Louis,

Mauritius, 1976–1978; principal officer for the U.S. consulate in Recife, Brazil, 1974–1976; and political officer for the U.S. consulate general in Rio de Janeiro, Brazil, 1972–1974. In addition, he has served as Special Assistant to the Assistant Secretary of State for Inter-American Affairs, 1969–1972; political officer for the U.S. consulate general in Barcelona, Spain, 1967–1969; provincial officer in Vietnam for the Agency for International Development, 1965–1966; in Vietnamese language training for a Foreign Service Institute, 1964–1965; and projects officer for Special Information Project on Cuba, 1963–1964. Mr. Brown joined the Foreign Service in 1963.

Mr. Brown graduated from George Washington University (B.S., 1960; M.S., 1961). He was born November 1, 1939, in Tulsa, OK. Mr. Brown is married, has two children, and resides in Chevy Chase, MD.

Statement by Press Secretary Fitzwater on the Violence in Romania
June 14, 1990

The United States condemns in the strongest possible terms the rioting of the past 2 days and the government-inspired vigilante violence that departs from the commonly accepted norms of democracy and the rule of law. We are concerned that the deplorable events of the past 2 days are being used to justify the suppression of legitimate dissent in Romania. This under-

scores the urgent need for Romania's newly elected leaders rapidly to establish the rule of law and to demonstrate in action their expressed commitment to genuine democratization.

Note: Press Secretary Fitzwater read the statement during his daily press briefing, which began at 10:03 a.m.

Remarks Following Discussions With Prime Minister Chatchai Chunhawan of Thailand
June 14, 1990

The President. To our visitors, Prime Minister Chatchai, Minister Sitthi—Foreign Minister—and all the honorable members of the delegation: It has been a pleasure to host this delegation from Thailand, one of America's oldest friends and closest allies.

Prime Minister Chatchai is a distinguished emissary from a noble land. From

the temples and palaces of Bangkok to the teak forests and fertile rice paddies of the provinces, the Kingdom of Thailand is a land proud in its independent history, rich in its resources, and steadfast in its culture and faith. But in this era of breathtaking change, in Asia and around the world, what is most remarkable about Thailand is that it has combined a double-digit economic growth with the emergence of parliamentary democracy.

As His Royal Majesty King Bhumibol reminded a joint session of Congress 30 years ago this month, the word "Thai" actually means "free." Thailand is the only country in Southeast Asia that maintained its independence throughout the colonial era. So, even though our peoples live on opposite sides of the globe, our countries are joined by a common vision. And we have made freedom our common cause. And in freedom, our nations have found an abiding friendship.

In our discussions, the Prime Minister and I agreed on the importance of maintaining a U.S.-Thai security relationship. I told him that while regional circumstances and world conditions have changed, America's commitment under the Manila Pact to Thailand's security and integrity remain firm.

America is proud of her role in the Pacific—a commitment that has fostered peace and freedom and economic development among democratic friends like Thailand. But the Prime Minister and I agreed that much work remains, and I expressed our profound appreciation for Thailand's long cooperation in providing asylum to Indochinese refugees and assured him that we will continue to welcome to America our share of Vietnamese refugees presently residing in Thailand.

And we also talked about resolving the tragic conflict in Cambodia. And we agreed that both our countries should continue our diplomatic efforts to end the violence, to achieve a comprehensive solution that meets the aspirations of the Cambodian people by assuring genuine self-determination through free and fair elections under U.N. auspices and in the presence of an international peacekeeping force.

The Prime Minister's visit comes shortly before a meeting in Singapore on greater economic cooperation among the Pacific Basin countries. And Thailand and the five other ASEAN nations are key to the success of this promising initiative.

I assured the Prime Minister of America's commitment to closer cooperation, to a successful conclusion to the Uruguay round of trade negotiations this year, and to mutually beneficial economic growth.

In the spirit of collective effort that extends back to our first economic treaty back in 1833, the Prime Minister and I agreed to establish a joint U.S.-Thai Committee for Commercial Cooperation, chaired by the Secretary of Commerce for the United States and by Thailand's Minister of Commerce. This committee will develop opportunities for bilateral cooperation in trade and investment while promoting greater commercial activity between the United States and Thailand.

Thailand is now enjoying a diversified and rapidly expanding economy, a stable government, and a business community attractive to foreign investors. We are working closely with the Thai people to assure that the mutual benefits of economic growth as well as environmental protection in joint science and technology efforts.

But there's one kind of business we agree we will not tolerate, and that is narcotics. It's a challenge of global proportions, and we look forward to expanding cooperation with Thailand in suppressing the production and trafficking of these poisons. And I assured the Prime Minister we were going to continue our battle on the demand side of the narcotics equation.

Mr. Prime Minister, relations between our countries now span some 150 years, and we share many goals in common. But what unites us is our commitment to peace, prosperity, and to the freedom that makes peace and prosperity possible. So, as you and your delegation depart after what we feel were very productive meetings and cordial discussions, we wish you the very best. Good luck and Godspeed, sir.

The Prime Minister. Mr. President, it is a great honor for me to be here at the White House on this auspicious day when the Americans throughout the United States are celebrating Flag Day, a day of great pride for all Americans. It is also with a sense of pride that we Thai look upon our relationship with this great nation. I have expressed to President Bush my hope that we would be able to build upon our 157 years of friendship and cooperation and together forge a closer and active partnership into the future.

With the more favorable trends of international relations, our two countries are committed more than ever to work together in bringing peace to Cambodia and to end the suffering of the Cambodian people. We will do all we can to accelerate the ongoing peace process. In this regard, we are prepared to work with the United States and the other permanent members of the United Nations Security Council to obtain our common objective of comprehensive peace in Cambodia through a free and fair election. We look upon the United States active participation in the Cambodian peace process and a United States presence as a stabilizing role in the region as being vital to peace and stability of Southeast Asia.

In our economic relations, we have agreed to set up consultative mechanism on all aspects of our economic relation, which I hope could lead to a new framework for economic cooperation and partnership between our two countries. Such a mechanism would allow us to regularly discuss any potential trade issues before they become trade disputes. It would also serve as a vehicle to promote the constructive areas of economic cooperation, especially in Thai investment, which is bound to assume greater significance in our economic relation in the future. United States technology is second to none, and so United States investment should be second to none.

Mr. President, I share with you your concern on the need to rid our societies of the menace of drugs. It is tearing apart the very fabrics of our societies. Our efforts must be directed at both the supply and demand side of this problem. On our part, His Majesty the King is particularly concerned about the problem and has urged the Government to take serious steps to tackle it. I pledge to you the full support of the Thai Government in the war against drug trafficking.

These are the important issues which President Bush and I discussed. These are the issues that our two governments will be working on in the days and months ahead. Lastly, I would like to thank President Bush and the United States Government for the warm and cordial reception accorded to us.

Thank you, sir. Mr. President, thank you.

The President. Mr. Prime Minister, thank you. Glad you were here.

Note: The President spoke at 1:23 p.m. at the South Portico of the White House. Prior to their remarks, the two leaders met privately in the Oval Office and with U.S. and Thai officials in the Cabinet Room, and then attended a luncheon in the Old Family Dining Room.

Statement by Press Secretary Fitzwater on President Bush's Meeting With President Andrés Rodriguez Pedotti of Paraguay
June 15, 1990

President Bush met with Paraguayan President Andrés Rodriguez this morning. President Rodriguez is here on a private visit en route to the Far East.

President Bush expressed his support for the democratization process underway in Paraguay. The country held its first truly open and free election last year. Press freedom has been established. And the opposition is free to speak out and organize.

The two Presidents also discussed the question of drugs. President Bush told President Rodriguez that we would like to cooperate more intensively with Paraguay to prevent drug traffickers from establishing a foothold in that country.

President Rodriguez expressed the hope that GSP benefits for Paraguay would be restored as a result of the hearings now scheduled to begin on June 27.

Remarks at a White House Ceremony Marking the Entry of the Peace Corps into Central Europe
June 15, 1990

Thank you all very much, and welcome to the drizzly Rose Garden. [*Laughter*] But we're very pleased you're here on this special day. And I want to thank Paul Coverdell for his leadership during this exciting period, this new period in the history of the Peace Corps. I'm delighted that Secretary Mosbacher is here, and Secretary Eagleburger and Robson and, of course, Chief Justice Burger. It's a pleasure to welcome you back to the White House. And we're honored to have the representatives of the Hungarian and Polish Governments here as well, Ron Roskens, the head of AID, and so many former Peace Corps veterans, Members of Congress here today. I'll be careful; I'm sure I'll omit some. But I see Silvio and Jim Leach, Tom Petri, and Chris Shays and others. Jerry Lewis was supposed to be here—and Silvio Conte I mentioned—for this historic sendoff rally. Most of all, we're honored to have this opportunity to salute a dedicated, committed group of talented Americans who were here to take leave of these shores and become the first Peace Corps volunteers to serve in Eastern Europe. And today we're very pleased to welcome all of you, to tell you just how exciting and important we believe that this new mission will be.

From the time it was first launched in 1961, the Peace Corps has been a thrilling and an ambitious undertaking—lofty in principle and yet, in its day-to-day struggle with challenging circumstances around the world, as practical and down-to-earth as government ever gets. The United States Peace Corps built its reputation the old-fashioned way—step by step, village by village, family by family—bringing the world a bit closer, one friendship at a time. For nearly 30 years it has drawn 120,000 idealistic Americans from all walks of life and sent them to the far corners of the Earth. And for nearly 30 years, the men and women of America's Peace Corps have built bridges of understanding and good will between the peoples of the United States and the peoples of scores of other nations. And today we launch a new people-to-people effort through which the citizens of America, Poland, and Hungary can work together in the exhilarating process of building new democratic societies.

Paul says that in many ways it is as if the Peace Corps had been in training for this historical moment. It shows that our mission, our desire for peace, knows no political or geographic boundaries. I agree with what he has said. Barbara and I have traveled all over the world, and the experience has taught us one important lesson: History is made not simply by nations but by their people. And that's why your efforts are so very, very important.

With your arrival in Poland and Hungary, the Peace Corps will serve in 70 nations, including half of all the developing nations. And our volunteers do battle against the age-old enemies of humankind—famine, illiteracy, poverty, and disease.

I think back to 1985, when we visited the famine-stricken regions of Africa and saw firsthand the heartbreaking conditions of those lands. And I remember visiting our Peace Corps project and witnessing the quiet heroism of young Americans whose efforts were providing relief and whose lives were truly making a difference. Tomorrow you will set sail for a different region, and you'll encounter a different kind of hunger, a different kind of craving from that which Bar and I saw in Africa.

But the hunger is powerful, and the need is real for the nourishment of free ideas and the sustenance of free enterprise. Václav Havel, Czechoslovakia's beloved playwright-turned-President, spoke of this need when he addressed that magnificent joint session of Congress just last spring. And he said, "We must all learn many things from you, from how to educate our offspring, how to elect our representatives, all the way to how to organize our economic life so that it will lead to prosperity and not to poverty."

The key you carry with you will be the English language—what Paul calls the language of commerce and understanding. And just as national literacy has long been the key to power, so today English literacy has become the key to progress. Like your liberty, your language came to you as a birthright and a credit to the dreams and sacrifices of those who came before. And today you're investing that birthright in the ancient dreams and the new ideas of far-away peoples and their own nations reborn. Your investment is America's investment in the consolidation of democracy and independence in Central and Eastern Europe. Peace Corps programs in Poland and Hungary, and then soon in Czechoslovakia, are another tangible element of America's sustained commitment to Central and Eastern Europe's democratic transformation toward a Europe whole and free.

The 121 Points of Light gathered today—make that 122—[*laughter*]—gathered today in the Rose Garden represent 121 reasons why this new Peace Corps initiative is bound to succeed: pioneers like Margaret Mary McGill, an Adrian Dominican Sister who has also pioneered the use of bilingual classrooms; recent graduates like Katherine Uderstadt, who taught math and reading to second graders in Massachusetts public housing; lifelong public servants like Wash-ington's own Felix Lapinski, a veteran educator who has tutored in English across three continents; and volunteers like Belle Rothberg, who has taught English to Spanish-speaking working people. Born to Polish immigrants before the Great War, teaching has kept Belle as young as her ideas. She recently even taught a course on the American Dream. And Belle says—the quote here—"I remember my mother's yearning for the Vistula, and I have longed to walk in her footsteps. I love to teach, and I want to teach, continue to teach as long as I can."

Now, that's one great ambition, and that pretty much says it all—speaks well of a great nation. To Belle and to all of you, we wish you Godspeed in this very important journey and wisdom and strength in the challenges ahead. Congratulations. Thank you for what you're doing for this country. Thank you for what you're doing for the people of the world. And God bless you all. Thank you very much for coming.

Note: The President spoke at 9:30 a.m. in the Rose Garden at the White House. In his opening remarks, he referred to Paul D. Coverdell, Director of the Peace Corps; Deputy Secretary of State Lawrence S. Eagleburger; Deputy Secretary of the Treasury John E. Robson; and Representatives Silvio O. Conte, Jim Leach, Thomas E. Petri, Christopher Shays, and Jerry Lewis.

Message to the House of Representatives Returning Without Approval the Hatch Act Reform Amendments of 1990
June 15, 1990

To the House of Representatives:

I am returning herewith without my approval H.R. 20, the "Hatch Act Reform Amendments of 1990." This bill would alter unacceptably the provisions of Federal law, commonly known as the Hatch Act, that bars Federal employees from active participation in partisan politics.

As one who has devoted much of his life to public service, I take great pride in the integrity of our Federal work force. Thus, to protect Federal employees from political pressure and preserve the impartial, even-handed conduct of Government business, I am obligated to disapprove H.R. 20.

Originally enacted in 1939 as a bulwark against political coercion, the Hatch Act has successfully insulated the Federal service from the undue political influence that would destroy its essential political neutrality. It has been manifestly successful over the years in shielding civil servants, and the programs they administer, from political exploitation and abuse. The Hatch Act has upheld the integrity of the civil service by assuring that Federal employees are hired and promoted based upon their qualifications and not their political loyalties. It also has assured that Federal programs are administered in a nonpartisan manner, which is critical to maintaining the public's confidence and trust in the operations of Government.

H.R. 20 would effectively repeal the Hatch Act's essential prohibitions on partisan political activity by Federal civil servants. It also would convert the present rule that partisan politicking by Federal civil servants is prohibited, into a presumption that such partisan campaigning should be encouraged.

Under this legislation, Federal employees would be able to participate actively in partisan political campaigns and hold official positions in political parties; actively endorse partisan political candidates in the public media; and solicit political contributions in most situations from other employees who are members of the same "employee labor organization" for that organization's political action committee. The obvious result of the enactment of H.R. 20 would be unstated but enormous pressure to participate in partisan political activity.

History shows that such a reversal in the role of partisan politics in the ethic of public service would inevitably lead to repoliticizing the Federal work force. The sanctions provided in the bill would add little if anything to the effectiveness of existing criminal prohibitions. Moreover, experience with enforcement of criminal antipatronage laws shows that the Federal criminal justice process is ill-suited to the task of protecting Federal employees from subtle political coercion. Public servants who are subjected to direct or indirect partisan political pressures understandably would often be reluctant to file criminal complaints against their superiors or peers, possibly putting their livelihoods in jeopardy. They deserve better protection than that.

Overt coercion is difficult enough by itself to guard against and detect. The more subtle forms of coercion are almost impossible to regulate, especially when they arise in a climate in which the unspoken assumption is that political conformity is the route to achievement and security. Such a climate leads inexorably to subtle, self-imposed pressures on employees to conform, or appear to conform, to whatever political tendency will assure greater job security.

After all the debate, no real need to repeal the existing Hatch Act has been demonstrated. Under present law, the Hatch Act allows Federal employees to engage in a variety of forms of political expression. Only forms of active participation on behalf of partisan political causes and candidates are barred. The Supreme Court has twice determined that these limits on active partisan political activity are constitutional. These rules provide reasonable balance between participation in the political process by Federal civil servants and the need to protect them from harassment and coercion that would jeopardize the fair and impartial operation of the Government. H.R. 20 poses a grave threat to that delicate balance.

Indeed, the lack of any grass-roots clamor for repeal of the Hatch Act either now, or at any time during its 50-year existence, testifies to the support this statute has received within the ranks of the Federal civil service and among the general public.

I am firmly convinced that any appreciable lessening of the current protections afforded to Federal civil servants by the Hatch Act will lead to the repoliticization of the civil service and of the programs it administers. We cannot afford, in the final decade of this century, to embark on a retreat into the very worst aspects of public administration from the last century.

GEORGE BUSH

The White House,
June 15, 1990.

Nomination of Timothy J. McBride To Be an Assistant Secretary of Commerce
June 15, 1990

The President today announced his intention to nominate Timothy J. McBride to be an Assistant Secretary of Commerce for Trade Development. He would succeed Michael Philip Skarzynski.

Since 1989 Mr. McBride has served as a Special Assistant to the President of the United States. Prior to this, he served as Personal Aide to the Vice President of the United States, 1985–1989; Deputy Director of the Vice Presidential Advance Office, 1985; consultant to the Republican National Convention Arrangements Committee in Dallas, TX, 1984; and a small business management consultant in Coral Springs, FL, 1982–1984.

Mr. McBride graduated from Eastern Michigan University (B.B.A., 1982). He was born October 10, 1958, in Orange, CA. Mr. McBride resides in Alexandria, VA.

Nomination of W. Lee Rawls To Be an Assistant Attorney General
June 15, 1990

The President today announced his intention to nominate W. Lee Rawls to be an Assistant Attorney General for the Office of Legislative Affairs. He would succeed Carol T. Crawford.

Since 1988 Mr. Rawls has served as a managing partner with the law firm of Baker, Worthington, Crossley, Stansberry and Woolf in Washington, DC. Prior to this, he served as a partner with the law firm of Vinson and Elkins, 1986–1988; resident director of Keleher and McLeod, P.A., 1985–1986; administrative assistant for Senator Pete V. Domenici, 1982–1985; manager of Federal Government relations for the Penzoil Co., 1980–1982; and administrative assistant and legislative director for Senator Pete V. Domenici, 1977–1980. In addition, Mr. Rawls served as a professional staff member for the Senate Committee on Environment and Public Works, 1975–1977; manager of government affairs for the Water Pollution Control Federation, 1974–1975; and legislative specialist in the Office of Legislation and Subcommittee Director for Senator Howard H. Baker for the Environmental Protection Agency, 1971–1974.

Mr. Rawls graduated from Princeton University (B.A., 1966) and George Washington University (J.D., 1977). He was born November 20, 1944, in Newport, RI. Mr. Rawls served in the U.S. Navy, 1967–1970. He is married, has three children, and resides in Kensington, MD.

Designation of Anne E. Brunsdale as Vice Chairman of the United States International Trade Commission
June 15, 1990

The President today announced his intention to designate Anne E. Brunsdale as Vice Chairman of the United States International Trade Commission for the term expiring June 16, 1992. This designation will be effective June 16, 1990. She would succeed Ronald Cass.

Since 1989 Ms. Brunsdale has served as Chairman of the United States International Trade Commission in Washington, DC. Ms.

Brunsdale graduated from the University of Minnesota (B.A., 1945; M.A., 1946) and Yale University (M.A., 1949). She was born October 1, 1923, in Minneapolis, MN. Ms. Brunsdale resides in Washington, DC.

Statement by Press Secretary Fitzwater on the Soviet-United States Short-Range Nuclear Forces Negotiations
June 15, 1990

On June 8, the Soviets proposed that short-range nuclear forces (SNF) negotiations in Europe begin before a conventional forces in Europe (CFE) agreement is reached. The President has stated that SNF negotiations should begin after the conclusion of a CFE agreement. In addition, NATO strategy is based on maintaining an adequate mix of nuclear and conventional weapons. NATO will be discussing its approach to SNF negotiations over the next few months, most notably at the upcoming summit in London.

NATO has significantly and unilaterally reduced its nuclear forces over the past decade. In addition, the United States is canceling the follow-on to the Lance and will not be progressing with the modernization of nuclear artillery in Europe. The Soviet offer of unilateral cuts, therefore, would be welcome since it would parallel NATO's actions. The Soviets have a preponderance of forces in this category in Europe, and any unilateral reduction can help enhance predictability and stability.

The position of NATO, as articulated in the Turnberry North Atlantic Council Communique of June 9, is that negotiations on U.S. and Soviet SNF systems in Europe should begin shortly after a CFE agreement is concluded.

Statement by Press Secretary Fitzwater on the Review of Regulatory Issues by the Council on Competitiveness
June 15, 1990

The President today designated the Council on Competitiveness, chaired by Vice President Quayle, as the appropriate council to review issues raised in conjunction with the regulatory program under Executive Order 12498. The President has also directed the Council on Competitiveness to exercise the same authority over regulatory issues as did the Presidential Task Force on Regulatory Relief under Executive Order 12291, which established the administration's regulatory review process.

In taking these actions, the President reaffirmed his commitment to regulatory relief and the use of cost-benefit principles to remove unnecessary regulatory burdens from American businesses, workers, and consumers.

Statement by Chief of Staff Sununu on the Establishment of an International Fund for the Termination of Chlorofluorocarbon Production
June 15, 1990

The administration will propose a fund, operated and administered by the World Bank, to assist less developed countries (LDC's) in phasing out the production of CFC's by the year 2000. The President's proposal is intended to allow the parties to the Montreal protocol to conclude an acceptable agreement on a package of amendments. The proposal includes specific requirements addressing the uses of the fund, the precedential nature of the fund, the administration of the fund, assessments, control of the fund, and voting rights within the fund.

The President's proposal is structured to reflect the unique circumstances that create the need for a fund specifically designed to assist LDC's in phasing out CFC's in a nonprecedential framework. This approach meets the President's essential criteria for any such funding mechanism:

—First, there is adequate scientific evidence of the causes and effects—in this case, of ozone depletion.
—Second, there is strong evidence that the steps to be taken, under the amended protocol, will successfully address the problem.
—Third, the resources needed to address the problem are reasonable and predictable.

The President expects the parties to the Montreal protocol to successfully conclude negotiations on a package of amendments to the protocol next week in London. The administration's proposal will be offered at that time. The President's proposal is designed to meet the financial needs of LDC's as they transition from the production of ozone-depleting substances to environmentally safe alternatives. At the same time, it addresses previously stated, significant U.S. concerns about the use and management of the fund and the concern that there be no precedent-setting nature to such aid.

The United States has been a world leader in efforts to control emissions that adversely affect the ozone layer: The United States outlawed the use of CFC aerosol propellants in 1978, strongly supported the initial negotiations that led to the Vienna Convention for the Protection of the Ozone Layer in 1985, and was among the first to sign the Montreal protocol in 1987.

Nomination of Stephen D. Potts To Be Director of the Office of Government Ethics
June 18, 1990

The President today announced his intention to nominate Stephen D. Potts to be Director of the Office of Government Ethics, Office of Personnel Management, for a term of 5 years. He would succeed Frank Q. Nebeker.

Since 1961 Mr. Potts has served as a partner with the law firm of Shaw, Pittman, Potts and Trowbridge in Washington, DC. Prior to this, he served as vice president of Cherokee Life Insurance in Nashville, TN, 1959–1961, and as an associate attorney with the law firm of Farris, Evans and Evans in Knoxville, TN, 1957–1959. He has served in the U.S. Army Judge Advocate General's Corps in the Defense Appellate Division at the Department of Defense in Washington, DC, 1955–1957.

Mr. Potts graduated from Vanderbilt University (A.B., 1952; LL.B., 1954). He was born November 20, 1930, in Memphis, TN. Mr. Potts served in the U.S. Army, 1954–1957. He is married, has three children, and resides in Bethesda, MD. Mr. Potts has won five national father-son tennis championships.

Message to the Congress Transmitting the Annual Report on Radiation Control for Health and Safety
June 19, 1990

To the Congress of the United States:

In accordance with section 360D of the Public Health Service Act (42 U.S.C. 2631), I am submitting the report of the Department of Health and Human Services regarding the administration of the Radiation Control for Health and Safety Act during calendar year 1989.

The report recommends that section 360D of the Public Health Service Act that requires the completion of this annual report be repealed. All the information found in this report is available to the Congress on a more immediate basis through the Center for Devices and Radiological Health Center technical reports, the Radiological Health Bulletin, and other publicly available sources. This annual report serves little useful purpose and diverts agency resources from more productive activities.

GEORGE BUSH

The White House,
June 19, 1990.

Nomination of Edward William Gnehm, Jr., To Be United States Ambassador to Kuwait
June 19, 1990

The President today announced his intention to nominate Edward William Gnehm, Jr., of Georgia, to be Ambassador Extraordinary and Plenipotentiary of the United States of America to the State of Kuwait. He would succeed W. Nathaniel Howell.

Currently Mr. Gnehm serves as Deputy Assistant Secretary of State for Near East and Southeast Asian Affairs. Prior to this he served as Deputy Assistant Secretary of Defense for Near Eastern and Southeast Asian Affairs. In addition, Mr. Gnehm served as Deputy Chief of Mission at the U.S. Embassy in Amman, Jordan. He has served as a career Foreign Service officer in Sanaa, Yemen Arab Republic; Riyadh, Saudi Arabia; Damascus, Syria; Lebanon; Tunisia; Vietnam; and Nepal.

Mr. Gnehm graduated from George Washington University (B.A., 1966; M.A., 1968). He was born November 10, 1944, in Carrollton, GA. Mr. Gnehm is married, has two children, and currently resides in Potomac, MD.

Nomination of Genta Hawkins Holmes To Be United States Ambassador to Namibia
June 19, 1990

The President today announced his intention to nominate Genta Hawkins Holmes to be Ambassador Extraordinary and Plenipotentiary of the United States of America to the Republic of Namibia. This is a new position.

Since 1988 Mrs. Holmes has served as Deputy Chief of Mission for the U.S. Embassy in Pretoria, South Africa. Prior to this, she served as Deputy Chief of Mission for the U.S. Embassy in Port-au-Prince, Haiti, 1986–1988; Deputy Chief of Mission for the U.S. Embassy in Lilongwe, Malawi, 1984–1986; member of the Board of Examiners, 1983–1984; member of the 25th Executive Seminar in National and International Affairs, 1982–1983; and Assistant Administrator for Legislative Affairs at the Agency for International Development, 1979–1982. In addition, Mrs. Holmes has served in the Bureau of Congressional Relations at the Department of State, 1978–1979; in the congressional fellowship at the American Political Science Association, 1977–1978; as chief of the economic and commercial section for the U.S. Embassy in Nassau, Bahamas, 1974–1977; in the Office of Development Finance for the Economic Bureau at the Department of State, 1973–1974; in the Office of Economic Opportunity at the New York Regional Office, 1972–1973; as special assistant to the Ambassador and youth officer at the U.S. Embassy in Paris, France, 1968–1971; and in the Office of Special Assistant to the Secretary of State for Refugee Affairs, 1966–1968.

Mrs. Holmes graduated from the University of Southern California (B.A., 1962). She was born September 3, 1940, in Anadarko, OK. Mrs. Holmes is married and resides in Washington, DC.

Message to the Senate Transmitting the Poland-United States Business and Economic Relations Treaty
June 19, 1990

To the Senate of the United States:

With a view to receiving the advice and consent of the Senate to ratification, I transmit herewith the Treaty between the United States of America and the Republic of Poland Concerning Business and Economic Relations, with Protocol and four related exchanges of letters, signed March 21, 1990, at Washington. I transmit also, for the information of the Senate, the report of the Department of State with respect to this treaty.

This treaty is the first to be transmitted to the Senate under my initiative to strengthen economic relations with East European countries, in support of the political and economic reforms taking place there. It will encourage, facilitate, and protect U.S. investment and business activity in Poland. The treaty also will serve to stimulate the growth of the private sector and of market institutions in that country. The treaty is fully consistent with U.S. policy toward international investment. A tenet of this policy, reflected in this treaty, is that U.S. direct investment abroad and foreign investment in the United States should receive fair, equitable, and nondiscriminatory treatment. Under this treaty, the parties also agree to international law standards for expropriation and compensation; free financial transfers; and procedures, including international arbitration, for the settlement of disputes.

I recommend that the Senate consider this treaty as soon as possible and give its advice and consent to ratification of the treaty, with protocol and related exchanges of letters, at an early date.

GEORGE BUSH

The White House,
June 19, 1990.

Remarks at the Great Outdoors Award Dinner
June 19, 1990

Thank you all very much for that warm introduction and that special honor. And thanks—I think it's the Marines I see down there in the glow. [*Laughter*] I thank them especially for providing the music tonight, and David Humphreys and Galey Coleman here and Sheldon. I understand we have some distinguished Senators or Congressmen. Every time you announce them, somebody says, "Oh, they're not here. They're off voting someplace." [*Laughter*] But Senators Burns and Roth, Ron Marlenee, Congressman Hiler and, of course, my friend Derrick Crandall and Stu Northrop and Dick Nunis over here and Jeff Napier.

Look, it's a great pleasure for me to be with you tonight, and I will be relatively brief, speaking before the broccoli. I've got to get out of here and get back home. [*Laughter*] But really, what an honor to accept this Sheldon Coleman Great Outdoors Award. He was a great friend, I bet, to everybody in this room and to many others across the country—a great friend of nature, and his influence is still with us today in so many ways: in partnerships for the outdoors that he encouraged throughout his entire life. And like the lanterns that bear his name, glowing beside the tents and RV's across this country, those partnerships do shine bright with promise for the environment—the precious environment we share.

I am deeply honored that you consider me worthy of this award, and I imagine there was some controversy. [*Laughter*] Some might say that the award should have gone to a more accomplished outdoorsperson. It probably should have gone to the only person I know who can fish and read at the same time: Barbara Bush [*Laughter*]

Look, there's some fishermen out here. Please understand my frustration. [*Laughter*] We're looking for these damn bluefish, and—[*laughter*]—Barbara's reading away, studying, reading—"Oh, I've got a fish." And I'm out there working and studying and changing bait, and nothing happens. [*Laughter*] But I don't worry when somebody reaches into the tackle box and pulls out a lure like a Mepps Spinner or a Johnson Silver Spoon, because I've got the Silver Fox. [*Laughter*]

And like every pursuit in the great outdoors, fishing is a great equalizer, whether you're out there with a friend or a head of state or one of the grandkids. You get out there; and you just simply love it, just like the other 60 million American men, women, and children who fish from boats and beaches and bridges and riverbanks all across this great country.

I remember, fishing off the Saco River in Maine, there was a guy with a belly that made one of these sumo wrestlers, or whatever they are, look skinny, you know. [*Laughter*] And he's standing out there, fishing with his grandson; and I come by in our cigarette [boat] with our couple, trolling, I admit, nice and slow. And the guy yells out, "Only in America." [*Laughter*] And you know, he was absolutely right. [*Laughter*] Here we were. It was just very special, and all of us have our own tales to tell. [*Laughter*]

But all of you understand how time spent in nature, in camping or hiking or fishing, frees up the mind, restores the soul, and makes memories—tranquil, peaceful, wonderful memories that stay with you the rest of your life. Among the greatest joys that Barbara and I have ever known have been exploring the outdoors with our kids and our grandkids. You saw George P. here with us. Look at the majesty, then, of the Grand Tetons through the eyes of a 13-year-old grandson, teach a grandkid a few mysteries of the ocean, and you're powerfully reminded that our kids will truly inherit the Earth.

You don't even have to leave home. Every summer on vacation, up at our house there at Kennebunkport, we put up a tent—I don't want to prejudice any other vendors here or manufacturers. [*Laughter*] But I call Sheldon Coleman and say, "Hey listen, I need a tent." This was several years ago. And I get a tremendous kick out of— that same tent goes up every year—and I get a tremendous kick—you don't have to leave home—hearing the nighttime giggles of the grandchildren out there. It's wonderful. You see them reading by a lantern and telling stories, hear them whispering to each other before they drop off to sleep with the sea pounding away in the background.

These are special moments, moments in the outdoors, and they are all very, very special. So, preserving nature for future generations demands special effort. And I've been very happy to support the public-private partnerships like this Wallop-Breaux—was Dingell-Johnson—but the Wallop-Breaux Trust Fund to protect our wetlands and preserve and enhance the boating and fishing, and by encouraging private partnerships like Ducks Unlimited and groups like the American Recreation Coalition and the Recreation Roundtable to engage this nation in a new spirit of renewal. I want to try my very hardest to do my part to help build that spirit.

In this year's budget, we included funds to help save the Everglades and to implement the historic North American Waterfowl Management Plan, to stop the tragedy of thousands of birds dying at the Stillwater Wildlife Refuge. But the cornerstone of our program was something called America the Beautiful, to expand our parks, our forests, and wildlife refuges; to promote recreation; and, yes—one of the ones that I'm most interested in—to plant a billion trees a year in America.

Tonight I want to ask for your help. I've seen too many budgets frittered away on other priorities. We all agree that trees are good for our water and good for air, good for our communities. So, take this message with you, please, to the legislative branch: Don't leave our tree planting initiative out on a limb.

Groups like this one are helping us build a new ethic of stewardship in America. And you know, I do believe that we have reason to be hopeful. This year, in a tradition that dates back to President Taft, I was presented with the first salmon caught in the 1990 season in the Penobscot River in Maine. It was a tradition that died back in the 1950's because the river had deteriorated so much. But this year, a State fisheries spokesman said they had the biggest opening day that he could recall. Right here in Washington, DC, the once-polluted Potomac River is now a site for first-class bass fishing tournaments.

I was fishing in Pintlala, Alabama, with Ricky Clune, a kid from Montgomery, Texas, one of the great bass fishermen in this country. And Rick—I'll never forget his winning a bass tournament. If you haven't been to one of these weigh-ins, you ought to go. Four or five thousand people in a stadium when these guys come trailering their fishing boats in and bringing out the bass. And I'll never forget Rick Clune, when he won Bass Masters Championship, saying that he learned to fish when he was in his underwear following his dad in the creeks of Oklahoma. And he said, "Isn't it great to live in a country with no limits." And I like that, and I think he's right.

He was telling me in Pintlala this winter, he said, "You don't have to come all the way down here to Alabama to fish." He said, "The Potomac River is back. You can go right across from the Pentagon and get good 5-, 6-, 7-pound bass out there." And he was right. I think it's an exciting thing that you all are doing for this country, helping us bring back these fantastic resources that regrettably we took for granted maybe 10 or 20 years ago.

So, I'm honored that you'd grant me the Great Outdoors Award, in the memory of Sheldon Coleman. He was a great inspiration to me. I knew him personally. I loved that remarkable spirit that you all remember, and I salute his memory. I'm also here to tip my hat to all of the individuals in America, like yourselves, who are raising awareness, raising money, and sometimes raising hell to preserve—[*laughter*]—our natural heritage for future generations. Sometimes that does mean conflicts, but I believe that the efforts we put into finding constructive partnerships will take us much farther than debate and contention. We need to spend less time arguing and more time working on solutions.

All of you here tonight have the creativity, the will, and the love of the outdoors to create new private partnerships to protect this nation's natural beauty. So, let me encourage each of you: Help us build momentum for a new spirit of American stewardship. As your President, I will not ever miss any opportunity at all to go fishing, to go hiking, to go camping—[*laughter*]—to go out in my boat. I want to do my part. And

so, I'll go to work early in the morning and sometimes go home late at night, but I'll be damned if I'm going to let anybody keep me from the great outdoors.

Thank you all very, very much. I'm honored to be with you. Thank you so much.

Note: The President spoke at 8:23 p.m. in the ballroom at the Vista International Hotel. In his remarks, he referred to David Humphreys, chairman of the board of the American Recreation Coalition; Galey Coleman, the widow of Sheldon Coleman, Sr.; Sheldon C. Coleman, Jr., chairman of Sheldon Coleman Enterprises; Representative Ron Marlenee; Derrick Crandall, president of the American Recreation Association; Stuart Northrop, chairman of the executive committee of Huffy Corp.; Richard Nunis, president of Walt Disney Attractions; and Jeff Napier, president of the National Marine Manufacturers Association.

Remarks at a Fundraising Luncheon for Governor Guy Hunt in Huntsville, Alabama
June 20, 1990

Thank you, ladies and gentlemen. Thank you for that warm welcome back to Huntsville. Thank you very much, all of you. These guys that did that extra applauding over here, you young guys, you can have my broccoli when they serve the lunch. [*Laughter*]

I want to thank Governor Hunt and his family, who I had a chance to meet with earlier, especially Helen. I'm glad to see her looking so fit, working so hard on the campaign trail. I want to pay my respects to Mayor Folmar and Anita, other friends of longstanding—he of Montgomery fame. And it's great to see so many others. John Grenier was there to greet me when I got off the plane, and we go back a long, long time. And of course, another old, close, personal friend that Barbara asked me to convey her love to, and I'm talking about Bill Cabaniss, who's running such a great race for the United States Senate. We've got to have him elected.

And I'm pleased to see our chairman, Arthur Outlaw. And I'm told Jean Sullivan is here, though I didn't see her. And there is someone here today, in addition, that I really need in Washington, DC—someone who can help the fight to win the battle against drugs, someone that is committed to expanding and protecting our space program, and someone who stands for a strong national defense. And I'm talking about your next Congressman from this district, Albert McDonald. We've got to see him elected. We need that Fifth District seat.

It's great to be back, back in what the song calls sweet home Alabama. In fact, I've recently been down this way—several months now—first, recently to Birmingham and, prior to that, doing a little bass fishing in Pintlala. Considering my record as a fisherman, the bass have nothing to worry about, nothing at all. [*Laughter*] But I loved every minute of it, and I want to be invited back. And we had a reception over here—

and I will spare her the embarrassment—but a beautiful Alabamian said to me—how she got this past the Secret Service, I don't know—what she meant was: You're a lousy fisherman, and I think I can help. And she reached into her pocket and pulled out a rubber, kind of a pink-looking frog, or something of that nature—a worm, exactly. And I thanked her very, very much, because when we get out of Washington, we talk about the things that really matter. [*Laughter*]

This time I've come to Alabama, though, with a more serious purpose in mind. This State is so special and so unique, so who can say what best captures the spirit of Alabama? Is it the voices of the choir in Montgomery's Dexter Baptist Church or the ornate balconies and French windows of Mobile? Or is it the hustle of that dynamic Birmingham business or the quiet intensity of this fantastic space center? This much we can say: Alabama is diverse, and Alabama needs a Governor who understands what it means to serve all of the people. And that's exactly the kind of Governor you've got. And come November, that's the man that Alabama must and will reelect. And of course, I'm talking to Guy Hunt, your friend and mine.

I'm told that a New York Daily News reporter was recently touring the State with Guy, and he literally was astonished by what he saw. The reporter spoke with admiration of how your Governor strives to bring in new businesses and tourists and how he inspires this whole State to come together, to pull together. This New Yorker saw for himself what Alabamians have seen for almost 4 years now: Leadership works.

And Guy Hunt is a leader who switches from one area of expertise to another with all the grace of Bo Jackson out there going from baseball to football. Look at how he helped create the most new jobs in Alabama history. Just look at the way in which he established a first-of-its-kind program to transfer NASA technology to apparel manufacturers, small businesses, and universities all across this State.

But Guy believes, and I believe, that government has certain serious obligations. One, of course, is our national security. But there's another one, and I'm talking about the protection of the people. And so, when it comes to this fight against crime, the country preacher from Holly Pond in Cullman County is as tough as Elliot Ness. And I think the people in Alabama understand that, and we certainly understand it and appreciate it in Washington. You see, we share a simple philosophy: We will not condone or coddle the drug criminals. And he agrees with me that if dealing drugs is dealing death, then let's give those major narcotics dealers what they deserve: the ultimate penalty.

America needs the tougher laws, stiffer penalties, and criminal justice system—the reforms proposed in our Violent Crime Control Act. And that's why I am hopeful that the Senate leaders will work with me to pass the major parts of our Violent Crime Act, new laws that are fair but also fast and final. Fair: assure that those who are guilty are held accountable for their actions. Fast: we need reforms to stop the repetitive appeals that are choking our courts. And finally: constitutionally sound provisions for the death penalty, particularly for those who are major dealers in narcotics or those who take the lives of a police officer.

And let me just say a quick word on another constitutional issue. And it's a debate going on right now; and I'm trying to do it in a nonpartisan way because this issue, in my view, should be above partisanship. But I do believe that our flag is a unique symbol. And until the recent Supreme Court decision, I'm told that 48 States had spoken, 48 States had laws protecting the flag against desecration. And that meant that the people of the States were speaking. And I strongly believe we should use the amendatory procedures wisely provided by the framers to pass a carefully drawn, narrow amendment to make the burning of the American flag a crime. And I'm going to fight for it with everything I have.

Another area of concern that I share with the Governor is the fate of our environment. He and Bill Cabaniss and I were talking about the natural wonders of this State on the way down here—the fate of our environment. From the estuaries of Mobile Bay to the lakes and misty mountains of the north, Alabama truly is beautiful, and it's beautiful in part because this Governor is working to preserve your very special quality of life. We're also working in Washington with the Congress to bring about a cleaner environment for all America. In fact, that is why I have proposed the first major revisions in the Clean Air Act in more than a decade. We can have clean air and clean water while respecting another kind of delicate ecology: that of jobs and opportunity.

A cleaner environment, safer streets, more jobs—all these are absolutely critical to our future. But if there is a paramount issue—and we have to click them all off there and try to—if we had to put them in a list, you can't overlook education because the state of the classroom today really is the state of our Union tomorrow.

We believe in asking more of our teachers, our children, and ourselves. And that's why I was very grateful to have Governor Hunt at my side at the recent education summit in Charlottesville, Virginia—the first time such a summit had ever been convened. And at the summit, we agreed to develop America's first national education goals, not to inflict our views onto the State education system but to set broad national goals. And we agreed to ensure our kids—that they master important subject areas, math and science being part of it; to boost graduation rates; to make this nation a nation of literate adults; to kick drugs out of our schools; and to see that all children start school ready to learn through vigorous programs like Head Start. And then we agreed to one thing more: to ensure that our students by the year 2000 are first in math and science achievement. America should not accept second place to any nation when it comes to education and the quality of the education for our kids.

When it comes to making a difference in the world, America has always been first. And we've already seen the difference America is helping to make in what I call this magnificent Revolution of 1989, a struggle of the democracy-building that continues to this day.

Let me share a story about an American visitor on a recent trip to Romania—a troubled land that it is—who asked the people she met what was most important now, what they needed most. And listen to one surprising answer: In a country where the streets are dark at night and the homes lack heat, one Romanian woman pulled from her purse a worn copy of an American magazine—a 3-year-old issue, with a special bicentennial copy of the United States Constitution. And she said, "What we need now is more of these."

And this is the moral example that our great country owes the world. Some may say the goals we set for ourselves and the example we offer the world are too ambitious. And I say only great ambitions can galvanize a nation; only great examples can change the world. When the first rockets lifted off the pad at Cape Canaveral—rockets built at Redstone—the eyes of America were already on the Moon. We need once again to work together as a people so that our future will be as bright as that Redstone rocket. And with the leadership of Guy Hunt, I know that your possibilities will be as limitless as the stars over Alabama.

Guy Hunt is the right Governor to lead Alabama in the nineties. I believe he would agree with me that this is a fascinating time to be Governor of your great, progressive, forward-moving State. And I might say parenthetically, as I look back over my shoulder at the recent history of this country, I can't think of a more fascinating time to be President of the United States of America than today.

I am very grateful for the support that you're showing for Guy Hunt. I'm very grateful for the fact that many people in this room made it possible for me—and, I might say, for the Silver Fox, Barbara, to be at my side as we undertake the duties of the Presidency.

Thank you for your support in the past, and now—not that you haven't paid for this hamburger—but go out and work extra hard for Guy Hunt. Alabama needs him, and I need him. Thank you all. And God bless you, and God bless our wonderful country.

Note: The President spoke at 12:22 p.m. in the North Hall of the Von Braun Civic Center. In his remarks, he referred to Helen Hunt, wife of the Governor; Emory M.

Folmar, mayor of Montgomery, and his wife, Anita; John Grenier, chairman of Friends for Guy Hunt; Arthur Outlaw, chairman of the Alabama Republican Party; and Jean Sullivan, Republican national committeewoman.

The President's News Conference in Huntsville, Alabama
June 20, 1990

The President. Well, first, I want to thank our hosts here at the Center and thank Admiral Truly, who is doing an outstanding job at NASA, for coming down here and thank Mr. Lee and all the others. It's inspiring to be here, and it just reinforces my conviction that we must have a vigorous, forward-looking space program. And I'm convinced we will. But I think anybody who sees the dedication of the workers here and then hears what the possibilities are will be supportive. But I salute the workers here in Huntsville and across our whole space agency.

But today I have an announcement I'd like to make, and then I'll be glad to take a few questions here.

Well, based on the recommendation of the Secretary of State, I have decided to suspend the dialog between the United States and the PLO, pending a satisfactory response from the PLO of steps it is taking to resolve problems associated with the recent acts of terrorism, in particular, that May 30th terrorist attack on Israel by the Palestinian Liberation Front, a constituent group of the PLO.

By way of background, on December 14, 1988, Yasser Arafat, speaking on behalf of the PLO Executive Committee, recognized Israel's right to exist. He accepted the United Nations Security Council Resolutions 242 and 338, and he renounced terrorism. Now, subsequently, the United States announced that because the PLO had met our longstanding conditions for dialog we would begin a substantive dialog with the PLO. And at the time, we applauded Chairman Arafat for taking these essential steps. And we have conducted such a dialog with the PLO through our Embassy in Tunis.

Over the past 18 months, representatives of the United States and the PLO regularly exchanged views about the political and security situation in the region. On balance, we believe that these exchanges contributed to progress in the peace process.

On May 30th, 1990, the Palestinian Liberation Front attempted a seaborne terrorist infiltration into Israel. Palestinian Liberation Front Leader Abu Abbas represents the PLO on the Executive Committee of the PLO. The size of the force and the geographical target area strongly indicate that civilians would have been the target.

That day we issued a statement deploring this attempted terrorist attack. On May 31st, we raised this incident with the PLO in Tunis. We told them that it could not avoid responsibility for an attempted terrorist action by one of its constituent groups and needed to take steps to deal with the matter by condemning the operation, disassociating itself from it, and by also beginning to take steps to discipline Abu Abbas, the perpetrator.

We've given the PLO ample time to deal with this issue. To date, the PLO has not provided a credible accounting of this instance or undertaken the actions outlined above. The U.S. does take note of the fact that the PLO has disassociated itself from this attack and issued a statement condemning attacks against civilians in principle, but as we previously indicated this is not sufficient—this alone is not sufficient.

The U.S.-PLO dialog has demonstrated that it can advance the Arab-Israeli peace process. And at the same time, the dialog is based on the assumption that the PLO is willing to abide by the conditions it accepted in December, 1988, including renunciation of terror.

At anytime that the PLO is prepared to take the necessary steps, we are prepared to promptly resume the dialog. In the meantime, we would hope and expect that the peace process would proceed as intended and without delay. We remain committed to the pursuit of a comprehensive settlement of the Arab-Israeli conflict and to a just and lasting peace. And as is often stated, it is our view that such a peace must be based on those two resolutions, U.N. Resolution 242 and 338, and the principle implicit therein of territory for peace, and provide for Israel's security and Palestinian political rights.

We believe that Palestinian participation is vital to any successful process and that there are real opportunities for Palestinians in this process. We strongly hope that Israelis, Palestinians, and the Arab States will recognize these opportunities and take the necessary steps to create an environment in which a viable peace process can thrive.

We denounce violence in the area and call upon all parties to eschew violence and terror and opt instead for dialog and negotiation. We're prepared to continue working with the parties toward this end.

I'll be glad to take a few questions.

Middle East Peace Process

Q. Mr. President, doesn't your announcement of today, coupled with Secretary Baker's words that the Israelis should call the White House when they're serious, mean that the U.S. position in the peace process, though, in the Middle East is dormant right now?

The President. John [John Mashek, Boston Globe], it's not moving forward right now. And the offer still stands. I have sent a letter to Prime Minister Shamir [of Israel]. I have very specifically asked questions that relate to seriousness about the peace process. But I would like to see the peace process move forward. Nothing herein should indicate anything different. Because here we are simply taking a narrow shot at terrorism.

Norm [Norman Sandler, United Press International]—excuse me, I forgot my protocol.

Savings and Loan Crisis

Q. Mr. President, yesterday, Marlin [Marlin Fitzwater, Press Secretary to the President] seemed to have lit a fairly short

political fuse with his comments on the S&L bailout in accusing the Democrats of having a big part in that mess. Are you ready to play that game this election year and blame the Democrats for a problem that others have laid on years of kind of permissive regulation by the Reagan administration?

The President. Norm, you're almost getting me into the fight by the way you ask the question, but I know I'm not going to. No, I want to get the savings and loan problem solved. And Marlin, properly, seeing a couple of shots across my bow from certain distinguished Members of the United States Senate, decided not to acquiesce in those attacks without some response. What he did was appropriate.

But what I'm trying to do is not respond to individuals and to simply keep moving forward on this process and not try to be out there saying here's who's to blame and here's who's not to blame. But it was interesting because I think you're right, a spark seemed to be ignited there. And I think more important than continuing to pour fuel on that spark is to work cooperatively with Congress in trying to get this mess solved. And of course, that is a part of what will be discussed in the budget process.

I would say to the American people on this one: The obligation is to protect the depositor. That's what our obligation is. And another obligation is to prosecute those who have broken the law, and there has been an active prosecution underway. I talked with Dick Thornburgh at lunch yesterday. I got some impressive numbers—of the numbers of cases that are being followed up on now—and I expect we'll see plenty more. So, protect the depositor; put those that are guilty into the dock, where they belong; and see that they are brought to responsibility for what they've done.

Q. Do you, in retrospect, though, agree with the argument that deregulation or unregulation of the savings and loans, the financial industry, occurred too quickly, went too far in the eighties?

The President. Well, I think—in looking back—I think some of the excesses of the loan policies are rather obvious. Basically, we made some proposals, I think, in that task force that I headed that might have corrected some of the abuse. But I don't want to argue in favor of reregulation of industries. But I will say that I think some of the loan policies instituted after the changes were made were foolish and were certainly ill-advised. And the result is a pounding for the original purpose of the S&L's, which was primarily financing housing in this country.

Palestine Liberation Organization

Q. Is it true that none of our allies, with the exception, of course, of the Israelis, wanted you to suspend these talks with the PLO? And you said you have given the PLO enough time. I mean, why now? Is there some reason it's happening today?

The President. No, I don't think of any reason today, and I didn't set in my mind *x* numbers of days. But, John [John Cochran, NBC News], I think there will be a lack of agreement with what I've done here on the part of some of our strongest allies. And I know this is true on the part of some of the most reasonable and moderate Arab States. But I would simply remind them of the conditions upon which the dialogs started in the first place, and I would also remind them that if they look at this statement and remedial action is taken the dialog from the U.S. side can promptly be restored.

Israeli-Occupied Territories

Q. Mr. President, at the same time you're having this trouble with the PLO, you've also got a new Israeli government that has an avowed policy of settling in the West Bank more rapidly than it's been settled in the past. How are you going to deal with that government? What's your policy going to be on aid toward that government, specifically on housing guarantees for Soviet emigrants?

The President. Jerry [Gerald Seib, Wall Street Journal], my position on settlement in the territories is probably as well-known as anything. And our policy is not to have new settlements, and our policy is certainly not to finance new settlements. Is that responsive, or is there another part to your question?

Q. This is a specific question now, though, of whether we'll provide housing guaran-

tees for Soviet emigrants—$400 million.

The President. But not to settle in the post-'67 territory—in the territories beyond the '67 lines.

Q. Are you going to seek specific new guarantees from this new government that that won't happen with that money?

The President. Well, I will, and I hope I'm successful. But I think there is no question that the Shamir government knows my position on this, knows the standing position of the United States.

Economic Sanctions Against South Africa

Q. Mr. President, as you know, Nelson Mandela [South African antiapartheid leader] arrived in the United States today, and you're going to meet with him next week. What are you going to tell him on the sanctions question? And the second part: There have been reports some weeks ago that the United States Central Intelligence Agency was involved in the process that led to his arrest many years ago, and there have been suggestions that you should apologize on behalf of the United States Government and the American people. Will you do that?

The President. No, I will take my leadership on that question from Mr. Mandela, who put it very well when he said let bygones be bygones. And that is not to agree with or disagree with the charge.

On the second point—your first, my second: The sanctions under the law cannot be lifted until certain additional steps are taken by South Africa. Let me be very clear. I salute Mr. de Klerk [President of South Africa] for what he's done. He's come a long, long way. And I salute Mr. Mandela for his approach to De Klerk. I think that demonstrates a willingness to talk that few of us might have predicted a couple years ago.

But there still are things that have to be done under our law in order to lift the sanctions, and I've listed them here. But anyway, you don't want to go into the details on it—but if you do I'll be glad to click them off for you. But in any event, there has to be progress. And I'd like to find a way to show Mr. de Klerk that we, the United States, are grateful for this new approach that is having South Africa evolve to a much more open society and, hopefully one day, to one which is colorblind in terms of participation in the political process. But I can't lift the sanctions under existing U.S. law.

But I'm looking forward to talking to Mr. Mandela about this. There are black leaders in South Africa that disagree with him on this question of sanctions. Foremost of those that come to mind is Mr. Buthelezi, with whom I have talked about this question. And I historically have not felt that, certainly, adding to the sanction base would help at all. And I had some original reservations about sanction approach, but I will say that it seems to—if you can credit sanctions with the evolution towards democracy in South Africa, I'd have to say, well, it seems there are some good things to it.

But it's delicate because I want to find a way to show our appreciation to De Klerk, and yet I don't want to pull the rug out from under Mr. Mandela.

Economic Assistance for the Soviet Union

Q. Mr. President, are you planning to support a G–7 initiative to offer economic aid to the Soviet Union at next month's economic summit? And if so, what has caused you to change your mind about the wisdom of such a program?

The President. No, I'm not planning to do that. And I expect, though, that matter may be discussed. I've tried to be very up-front with Mr. Gorbachev, when he was here, about difficulties in terms of financial support. I talked to him in Malta about that. Indeed, we presented him with a list of things that might be done to improve our ability to work in full cooperation with him on that. But I don't plan a new initiative.

And yet I want to see *perestroika* continue. I haven't changed my view that economic reform is important, and I recognize that support from the West can well help the economy. But there's an awful lot of reform that has to take place in the market, in the distribution systems. There are some political problems that we have that I've discussed very frankly with Mr. Gorbachev, not the least of them $5 billion a year going down to Cuba. So, we've still got some problems there. But discount the fact that

we are planning some bold new initiative. On the other hand, I'm perfectly prepared to talk to our allies on any subject, and I think that will probably be one of them.

Q. There are reports that President Mitterrand [of France] will propose such a plan. Do you expect that?

The President. Well, the Germans are interested, too. I'm not saying we're not interested but I'm saying there are some formidable obstacles.

Palestine Liberation Organization

Q. Back on the PLO. One of the theories passed around in your own administration was that the intent of this terrorist attack was to derail the peace process. Are you at all concerned that by suspending the dialog you're playing into the hands of the hardliners like Abu Abbas? And is there also a danger——

The President. Yes. Let me stop you there just to respond so I don't forget the question. Yes, I am concerned about that. Go ahead. [*Laughter*]

Q. Well, if you're so concerned about it then why did you take the stand?

The President. Well, because we had to weigh the whole question; and the question was complicated by the fact that there were three specific undertakings, one of which, a very important one in my view, has clearly been violated. It's not an easy call because I know some feel that the PLO dialog is totally unproductive, and as I indicated in this statement, I don't. The question up here was: Well, do our allies—will they agree with the steps that I've taken here in Huntsville today? And the answer is no; some of them will not agree because they do feel that the dialog has kind of helped calm things in some parts of the Middle East.

So, what the answer to it is, is for the PLO to take the action that I've called for and to satisfy us that those who were responsible will be disciplined and condemn this specific act. It's not enough to simply reiterate one's concern on terror.

Q. If I may follow up?

The President. Please.

Q. Is there a danger, too, that those Palestinians who had put some hope in the

845

dialog between the PLO and the U.S. might now throw up their hands in desperation and resort to violence?

The President. Well, I hope that's not the case, and yet I would refer you to my last paragraph or two of the statements when I did call for no violence. And I think it's fair to say that anytime you're dealing with something as complicated as the Middle East you worry about that. But I hope that's not the case. And I hope they'll see in my statement a rather temperate view here: that we're specific in calling for the condemnation of this particular terrorist act; that once that is done, in keeping with Arafat's undertaking, that we can resume talks.

There has been a frustration, Jim [Jim Miklaszewski, NBC News], in the Arab world that this dialog has not resulted in more progress. And I understand the frustration. I don't happen to agree with it. I think things are better because we've had the dialog. But Israel has strongly objected to it; and some Palestinians have been, as we can clearly see, concerned about it. But I believe we ought to try to find a way to get it back at some point.

Q. But the flip side of that coin, if I might: As you grappled with this, did you worry, and are you worried now, that Israel will just take this and say, See, we've been right about the PLO all along, and we won't talk to them?

The President. I'm not so troubled on that because I think they will see here that I am not accepting the premise that there is no good to come from talking to the PLO. So, I don't worry too much about that point.

Middle East Peace Process

Q. Do you see Mr. Shamir as too hardline, as the kind of leader who is going to say, Well, we were right, and therefore, we'll stay away from the table even longer?

The President. Well, I'm hoping that's not the case. And one of the reasons I sent him this long and lengthy letter was to make clear to him that it is our view the peace process ought to go forward. And it's going to be difficult for him, but it must go forward. And it must go forward along the lines of what originally was the Shamir plan, and then it became—Mubarak [President Hosni Mubarak of Egypt] got interested and

he played a useful role in it. Then Jim Baker got involved and done a heroic job in trying to get the talks going.

So, I hope that the U.S. will have a useful role to play, regardless of the step I've taken here in the PLO, because as we all know, we were not proposing that the PLO be at the table. This was a charge made against us by some in Israel, and that doesn't happen to be the case. And I think the government knows that.

Family and Medical Leave Legislation

Q. Mr. President, during the campaign you said often that we've got to find a way that people who have children won't be threatened with the loss of their jobs, and now you're saying that that has to be a voluntary position on the part of employers to give parental leave. How does that fulfill your campaign promise for people who work for employers who won't give voluntary leave, and what do you have to say to those people?

The President. You've got to keep working for them until they do because my campaign promise did not go to what they call mandated benefits. Just to be sure I was right we looked it up again yesterday. But my position has not changed, and I see that I must convince some Republicans as well as many Democrats that it hasn't changed.

Q. Do you have any point of view on how you're going to convince these employers? Many of them say if it's not a mandatory requirement, why should they do it?

The President. Well, I have a great faith that collective bargaining and market forces move towards progress. And we've seen it in the private sector, and I want to see it faster and quicker in the private sector without burdening every business by the same formula of mandated benefits.

Palestine Liberation Organization

Q. Mr. President, you specified that the PLO dialog has been positive and productive, but you haven't really told us in what way. Could you be a little more specific about that? What productivity do you see in it?

The President. I think the very fact we are talking can—and that's one of the reasons I would hope that it can be restored—can eliminate differences. And I would like to feel that the PLO, because of our dialog, doesn't see us as quite the hostile country that once they did. There's all kinds of small points that are taken up by our Ambassador Pelletreau in Tunis that I think have reduced the levels of misunderstanding.

I don't want to leave you the wrong impression: that I think the dialog has resulted in a more dynamic peace process. But I do think that it's good, and I think that it encourages moderation within the PLO ranks. I think we lose sight of the fact that Arafat did something that was predicted no Palestinian leader could do when he recognized Israel's right to exist as a state. And some might say, Well, it's about time. And I'm one of them. But that was quite a step forward. It was quite a step forward when he recognized Resolution 242, and I think that was positive. And then I think we've had a chance to solidify those gains, modest though they might have been, through dialog. But I can't point to the fact that that has really solved the question of Middle East peace. I just feel that talking offers more potential than stiff-arming each other. And yet we can't digest it as long as this terroristic act is sticking in our throat. And properly so, as a country that decries international terrorism.

Space Program Funding

Q. A question about space. How serious are you about this lunar base and Mars mission proposal? Would you go so far as to veto the bill that contains NASA appropriations if Congress decides to delete all the money?

The President. I haven't even contemplated any veto strategy. I'd like to get what I want. I think it's in the national interest. I think that the United States must remain way out front on science and technology; and this broad program that I've outlined, seed money that I've asked for, should be supported. But I think it's way too early to discuss veto strategy. We took one on the chops in a House committee the other day, and I've got to turn around now and fight for what I believe.

Q. Mr. President, how far will you go to

protect the NASA budget in the future? Can you remove it from HUD and give it some security?

The President. It's pretty hard, given the way Congress functions, and that is a function of the Congress, not of the executive branch—to decide under what committees these budgets are worked. But I think it is fair to say that I will fight for a fully funded space program. We've put forward what I think is a bold one. I've taken some shots—saying, Hey, how can you propose something this big when we have such a large deficit? And I understand the question. But we're talking about stretched-out financing, and we're talking about, hopefully, a continued dynamic economy. And between the two, we can accommodate this goal if we all get with it.

Palestine Liberation Organization

Q. Was there not a need here, sir, to not appear to be indulging to the PLO at a time when the administration has been tougher than perhaps any recent administration has been with Israel?

The President. That's not what made my decision. And I don't know that we've been tougher. I'm the President of the United States. The United States has a policy. And I'm supposed to, I think, go forward with our policy. And one of the big problems we've had is the question—between ourselves and the Israeli Government—is this question of settlements. But I wouldn't read my decision here to go as follows: He made this decision because he's concerned about a complicated relationship with Israel at this point. That's not why I made the decision, but some may read it as that. But we're staying with our concept on the peace process, and we are staying with our policy on settlements. And this action that I've taken today is consistent with our policy on antiterror.

Violence and Terrorism in the Middle East

Q. Mr. President, do you feel that Israel has committed acts of terrorism when it bombs Palestinians?

The President. We spoke out on the recent violence in the Gaza. And please note my last comment calling for peaceful

847

resolution to these questions as opposed to violence and international terror. And that's the way I would respond on that.

Governor Guy Hunt of Alabama

Q. Mr. President, sir, can we go back to why you're here in Huntsville, sir? If you are here to help raise money for Governor Guy Hunt's gubernatorial campaign——

The President. I'm not standing right here to do that, but I was downtown doing exactly that. And I hope we were successful because I am totally committed to his reelection. I have respected the progress the State of Alabama has made under his leadership. And as I look at the way my philosophy of government works, the Governors are very, very important on all this. I cite not just the education summit, in which I worked closely with Guy, but this whole concept that the States and localities have a significant role to play not just in the money end of it but in the whole setting of objectives and goals. So, I'm glad you raised it; and, yes, that part of the trip was strongly to support him, to support other political leaders, too.

Q. You have goals for your space initiative. Do you believe Governor Hunt can help you reach some of those by being so strong in the Tennessee Valley?

The President. I think he's a proponent of the space program that I've set forth. I think he's got great credibility with other Governors. If I'm not mistaken, I think he's hosting the national Governors down here, and that will give him to have an opportunity to make the case for space or any other initiatives for. But he is seen by other Governors to know what he's talking about in this area and clearly to be a strong proponent. So, I guess the bottom line is, yes, I think Governor Hunt here can be helpful to

our objectives in terms of a vibrant space program.

Tennessee Valley Authority Appointment

Q. Mr. President, are you going to nominate or appoint Governor Hunt's nominee to the TVA board?

The President. I don't know that I'm going to carry my enthusiasm that far. [*Laughter*] But he's made a strong case for a person that he believes in, and he did it in his typical way, typical of Guy Hunt: right, direct. He told me exactly why he favored a certain nominee and then seemed to be saying, look, I recognize that you have a lot of factors to weigh in this decision. But I leave here understanding exactly why he has taken the position he has, and the position has respect. And I'm not prepared to discuss further what I might or might not do in this TVA—you're talking about the TVA appointment.

Q. Did you say how long you would take to make an appointment?

The President. Matter of days. [*Laughter*]

Offshore Oil Drilling

Q. What about OCS [outer continental shelf]?

The President. A few days, a few days. Not for him, for this.

Thank you all very much.

Note: The President's 51st news conference began at 1:40 p.m. in the Space Exploration Initiative Exhibition Room at the George C. Marshall Space Flight Center. In his opening remarks, he referred to Richard H. Truly, Administrator of the National Aeronautics and Space Administration, and T.J. Lee, Director of the Center. Prior to the news conference, the President toured the facilities and was briefed by the Center's staff.

Remarks to Employees of the George C. Marshall Space Flight Center in Huntsville, Alabama
June 20, 1990

Dick, Admiral Truly, I'm very glad to be here. Let me just say something very personal: I can't tell you how fortunate the country is to have Admiral Truly lead

NASA through these very exciting times. I salute him, and I'm very grateful to him. And I'm pleased to be here with the Governor of this State, a man whose unwavering support for the space program is so well-known. I want to thank Jack Lee, the director of this center and my tour guide today. I'm grateful to him. There is no quiz. If there was I would probably fail, because I am mightily impressed with the dedicated NASA workers, men and women, young and old, who are doing such a superb job on the cutting edge of science.

I was sorry we were a little late getting started. These arrangements affect everything. Even I couldn't find a parking place. [*Laughter*] Reminds me of my days in college. Everybody would gather around to get cooled off watching me strike out.

But nevertheless, I really am pleased to be back in Alabama, back in Huntsville. And I'm very proud of this State, proud of this special facility. The Marshall Space Flight Center is the birthplace of America's first satellite, America's first space station, and the world's first Moon rocket; and it was here with Saturn 5 that humankind began its historic journey to the stars.

Because of these traditions, Huntsville has a special importance to America and, indeed, to the entire world. And it has a special importance to me, as well. It was to Huntsville that I journeyed in the fall of 1987 to give a campaign—for me, at least, a first major address on space. And on that October day 2½ years ago, I promised to create a National Space Council, chaired by the Vice President. I pledged to underwrite Mission to Planet Earth, to boost space science, and to launch a dynamic new program of both manned and unmanned exploration of the solar system.

And today I'm pleased to return to Marshall to report that we have made good on these promises. And we've done it the old-fashioned way, done it the American way—step by step, program by program, all adding up to the most ambitious and far-reaching effort since Marshall and *Apollo* took America to the Moon.

The Space Council I proposed is not only up and running but under the dynamic leadership of our Vice President. It's lead-ing the way into the 21st century. Mission to Planet Earth, a bold and unprecedented initiative to preserve our precious environmental heritage, has been plucked off the drawing board and placed in the hands of the scientists who will make it happen. And now that the shuttle program has put America back in space, we stand at the dawn of a new era in space science, with wonders like that magnificent Hubble Space Telescope and the fantastic voyage of *Galileo* to Jupiter.

Exactly 11 months ago, I was at the Air and Space Museum in Washington to commemorate a special anniversary for you who work at the Marshall Space Flight Center: the 20th anniversary of *Apollo 11*'s thunderous journey to the Moon. And standing with Neil Armstrong and dozens of other astronauts, I announced three major space policy objectives: first, to have space station *Freedom* up before the century is out, and second, for the new century, a permanent lunar base. And we're going back to the Moon, back to the future, and this time back to stay. And the third objective was refined last month in Texas, where I went to announce a new age of exploration with not only a goal but a 30-year timetable. I declared—permit me to read it again—before *Apollo* celebrates the 50th anniversary of its landing on the Moon, the American flag should be planted on Mars.

Being first in space is not just America's dream: it is indeed our destiny. And to see this happen, we're matching rhetoric with resources. Our budget proposes $15.2 billion for NASA, an increase of nearly 25 percent and the largest increase for any major agency of the United States Government.

Now for the bad news. Unfortunately, not everyone on Capitol Hill shares this commitment to investing in America's future. And last week, the House Appropriations Subcommittee for Space voted to pull the plug on this historic undertaking, completely gutting the seed money we proposed for the Moon-Mars mission.

But you know, space used to be a bipartisan effort, just a plain American effort. And the last time a President visited Marshall, John F. Kennedy compared those who were uncertain about America's leadership in space to those in Queen Isabella's court who counseled, in effect, "Turn back. Leave the riches and rewards for other nations and braver hearts."

Some say the space program ought to wait, that we should only go forward once the social problems today are completely solved. But history proves that that attitude is self-defeating. Had Columbus waited until all the problems of his time were solved, the timbers of the *Santa Maria* would be rotting on the Spanish coast to this very day. And instead, he went forward, he ventured forth, and his travels brought Spain to the zenith of her stature as a nation.

Many an American schoolkid has read the story of Columbus' doubters and shook their heads in disbelief that these naysayers could have been so shortsighted. We must not let the children of the future shake their heads at our behavior. And right now, in the funding wars on Congress, we face a central question—the question of whether America will continue to be a pioneering nation.

And when John F. Kennedy stood before the Congress in 1961 and spoke about the Moon, he spoke to a nation of pioneers. Now some in Congress appear ready to give up on that pioneering spirit, to turn their sights inward, to concede that America's days as a leader in space have passed. Well I, for one, am not ready to give up. America has always been and will always be a nation of pioneers. I may not be around in the year 2019, but all of you guys will, and a lot of people out here in this marvelous, young, vigorous work force will. And on that special day 30 years from now, I want you to think back to the commitment that we made here today as you look at the TV monitors, maybe right here at Marshall, and

watch the first American plant his feet on Mars. It's going to happen. With your work and our support it is going to happen.

During the *Apollo* era, America's space efforts grew at unprecedented rates. The Government hired the biggest and the best scientific force in history, and colleges and universities swelled with applicants and graduates in science and engineering. And it produced a golden age of American technology and advancement, an age that, today, we can recapture and begin anew.

Wernher von Braun was the giant who, in a sense, put Huntsville on the map. And when someone asked him what it would take to build a rocket to reach the Moon, Von Braun replied simply, "The will to do it." And so, I'm here today at this monument to daring, this monument to imagination that Von Braun built, and call on the American Congress to step forth with the will that the moment requires. Don't postpone greatness. History tells us what happens to nations that forget how to dream. The American people want us in space. So, let us continue the dream for our students, for ourselves, and for all humankind.

Thank you for your dedicated work to this great country of ours. God bless the United States of America. Thank you for this warm, warm welcome. Thank you very much. Thank you.

Note: The President spoke at 2:26 p.m. on the grounds of the Center. In his remarks, he referred to Richard H. Truly, Administrator of the National Aeronautics and Space Administration, and Gov. Guy Hunt of Alabama. Following his remarks, the President traveled to Charlotte, NC, where he participated in a Point of Light recognition ceremony at Charlotte/Douglas International Airport for the Duke Power Co.

Nomination of Edwin D. Williamson To Be Legal Adviser of the Department of State
June 20, 1990

The President today announced his intention to nominate Edwin D. Williamson to be Legal Adviser of the Department of State. He would succeed Abraham D.

Sofaer.

Since 1964 Mr. Williamson has been with the law firm of Sullivan and Cromwell, serving as a partner in Washington, DC, since 1988; partner in New York, NY, 1979–1988 and 1971–1976; resident partner in London, England, 1976–1979; and an associate, 1964–1970.

Mr. Williamson graduated from the University of the South (B.A., 1961) and New York University School of Law (J.D., 1964). He was born September 23, 1939, in Florence, SC. Mr. Williamson served in the U.S. Marine Corps Reserve, 1958–1960. He is married, has three children, and resides in Washington, DC.

Nomination of C.M. Schauerte To Be Federal Insurance Administrator of the Federal Emergency Management Agency
June 20, 1990

The President today announced his intention to nominate C.M. Schauerte, of Texas, to be Federal Insurance Administrator of the Federal Emergency Management Agency. He would succeed Harold T. Duryee.

Since 1972 Mr. Schauerte has served as vice president of government affairs for the American General Corp. in Houston, TX. Mr. Schauerte received a bachelor of arts degree, bachelor of journalism degree, and a master of arts degree from the University of Missouri. Mr. Schauerte served in the U.S. Air Force, 1949–1951. He is married, has four children, and resides in Houston, TX.

Nomination of James M. Stephens To Be a Member of the National Labor Relations Board, and Designation as Chairman
June 20, 1990

The President today announced his intention to nominate James M. Stephens to be a member of the National Labor Relations Board for the term of 5 years expiring August 27, 1995. This is a reappointment. Upon confirmation, he is to be designated Chairman.

Since January 1988 Mr. Stephens has been Chairman of the National Labor Relations Board in Washington, DC, and served as a member, 1985–1988. Prior to this he was labor counsel of the Senate Committee

on Labor and Human Resources, 1981–1985. Mr. Stephens was assistant counsel, 1977–1978, and then associate counsel, 1978–1981, for the associate minority labor counsel of the House Committee on Education and Labor.

Mr. Stephens graduated from Wittenberg University (B.A., 1968) and Case Western Reserve University (J.D., 1971). He was born September 16, 1946, in Rochester, NY. He is married, has two children, and resides in Vienna, VA.

Nomination of John N. Raudabaugh To Be a Member of the National Labor Relations Board
June 20, 1990

The President today announced his intention to nominate John N. Raudabaugh to be a member of the National Labor Relations Board for the remainder of the term expiring December 16, 1992. He would succeed John E. Higgins, Jr.

Presently Mr. Raudabaugh serves as a partner with the law firm of Constangy, Brooks and Smith in Atlanta, GA. Prior to this he was a partner with Powell, Goldstein, Frazer and Murphy in Atlanta, GA.

Mr. Raudabaugh graduated from the Wharton School of Finance and Commerce, University of Pennsylvania (B.S., 1968); Cornell University School of Industrial and Labor Relations (M.S., 1974); and the University of Virginia Law School (J.D., 1977). He served in the U.S. Navy, 1968–1972. He was born July 12, 1946, in Sioux City, IA. Mr. Raudabaugh is married and resides in Atlanta, GA.

Appointment of Norman Sisisky as a Member of the Board of Trustees of the James Madison Memorial Fellowship Foundation
June 20, 1990

The President today announced his intention to appoint Norman Sisisky to serve in an advisory capacity as a member of the Board of Trustees of the James Madison Memorial Fellowship Foundation for the remainder of the term expiring October 3, 1990. He would succeed James R. Olin. He will also be appointed for a term expiring October 3, 1996.

Mr. Sisisky is presently serving his fourth term as a United States Representative for the Fourth District of Virginia. Prior to this he was a Virginia State legislator. Representative Sisisky graduated from Virginia Commonwealth University (B.S., 1949). He was born June 9, 1927, in Baltimore, MD. In addition, he served in the U.S. Navy. He is married, has four children, and resides in Petersburg, VA.

Nomination of Earl Roger Mandle To Be a Member of the National Council on the Arts
June 20, 1990

The President today announced his intention to nominate Earl Roger Mandle to be a member of the National Council on the Arts, National Foundation on the Arts and the Humanities, for a term expiring September 3, 1994. He would succeed Raymond J. Learsy.

Since 1988 Mr. Mandle has served as the Deputy Director of the National Gallery of Art. Prior to this, he was director of the Toledo Museum of Art, 1977–1988, and associate director, 1974–1976. He was associate director of the Minneapolis Institute of Arts, 1967–1974.

Mr. Mandle graduated from Williams College in 1963 and New York University (M.A., 1967). He was born May 13, 1941, in Hackensack, NJ. He is married, has two children, and currently resides in Washington, DC.

Nomination of Bert W. Corneby To Be Superintendent of the United States Mint at West Point
June 20, 1990

The President today announced his intention to nominate Bert W. Corneby, of New York, to be Superintendent of the Mint of the United States at West Point, NY, Department of the Treasury. He would succeed Clifford M. Barber.

Since 1985 Mr. Corneby has served as deputy commissioner of finance for the County of Orange in Goshen, NY. Prior to this, he served as partner/manager for ALFA Market in Central Valley, NY, 1982–1985; general manager for Vornado, Inc., Sutton Place Catalog Showrooms in Rahway, NJ, 1981–1982. Mr. Corneby

served in several capacities at the Grand Union Co. Grand Catalog Showrooms in Ridgewood, NJ, including vice president/division general manager, 1978–1981; operations vice president, 1975–1978; administrative vice president, 1973–1975; director of personnel, 1972–1973; and in the supermarket division, 1959–1972.

Mr. Corneby graduated from West Virginia Wesleyan College (B.S., 1959). He was born December 15, 1937, in Scranton, PA. Mr. Corneby is married, has three children, and resides in Monroe, NY.

Remarks at a Fundraising Dinner for Senator Jesse Helms in Charlotte, North Carolina
June 20, 1990

Thank you, Senator. Thank you all very, very much. Thank you, Jesse. Thank you very, very much, Jesse, for that very warm introduction. And I am so pleased to be here. And to Dot Helms, my respects. Barbara sends her love. To our outstanding Governor, Jim Martin, a friend of longstanding, my respects, and to his cohort from across the way, Carroll Campbell, another close friend. The Carolinians are lucky—they've got it made with these two Governors. I want to salute another friend, the Congressman from this district who's making such a superb record for himself and for North Carolina values in the United States Congress, Alex McMillan, going strong. And I'm very proud of him. Another old friend—I don't want to date Jim Gardner in a sense, but he and I were elected to the Congress on exactly the same day several years ago. And I am proud of him as he serves this State as Lieutenant Governor.

I want to salute the Mayor, Sue Myrick; our chairman, Jack Hawk; old friends of mine, Jack and Helen Laughery, who do so much for the cause and with whom I spent

a nervous primary night in this State 2 years ago. Roger Milliken, from Spartanburg down here, right across the way; strong supporter of the Republican Party and the conservative cause. And, of course, the real star of tonight's show—a truly great North Carolinian with an unparalleled record of success, loved by his fans, feared by his opponents. You all know him—professional wrestler Ric "Nature Boy" Flair, down here. Ric, I was thinking you ought to team up with my friend, the Chairman of the national Fitness Council, Arnold Schwarzenegger. You know, Conan the Republican. [*Laughter*] And maybe the two of you could bench-press the Federal budget. I'm glad you're here.

And I don't have what they call in baseball "rabbit ears"—you know, the guy that always hears the heckling from the sidelines—but I did notice some protest going on outside as we were coming in tonight. And they're upset because they think that the only reason I was invited to speak this evening is because I'm Barbara Bush's husband. [*Laughter*] I thought it came out pretty well—Bar Bush, seven; Wellesley, you know what. [*Laughter*]

Anyway, it's a pleasure to be with you in the birthplace of one of America's greatest religious leaders, too, a friend of all of ours, the Reverend Billy Graham. And what's more, I am privileged this evening to salute one of America's most dynamic political leaders, a steadfast champion of what he believes—what he believes. And, of course, I'm talking about Senator Jesse Helms, my friend.

You know, it's been said that Jesse Helms is a political partisan. He still maintains that "One Flew Over the Cuckoo's Nest" was really the title of a film on the 1972 Democratic Convention. [*Laughter*] Yet partisanship really is only a small part of the Jesse Helms story. The son of a police chief, Jesse worked his way through school. Later, telling the plain truth as a columnist and commentator. And as a Senator with seniority and prestige, he's been a clear, strong voice for North Carolina, reflecting this State's motto: To be rather than to seem.

The theme of this campaign is "you know where Jesse stands." Yet I'd like to talk about the Jesse Helms you may not know about. Not just professionally—I'm talking personally. And why his reelection isn't a partisan crusade but a national necessity. The Jesse Helms that I know and that all of us that orbit around that Senate from time to time know is a man of courtesy, unfailing courtesy, and conviction. He isn't a trendy follower who flows with the current. He's a visionary who alters the tide. Sam Ervin put it best: "Jesse is one of the few men with the courage to stand up for what he believes." And the Jesse Helms I know also embodies the values of North Carolina's good, quiet, and decent people—people who pay their taxes and believe in hard work and have a love of country and of God. And like them, Jesse's a man of integrity, a great family man—lovely wife, Dot, and three great kids, six grandchildren. And a man of kindness and humanity.

Let me tell you a revealing story. Barbara and I have two adopted grandchildren, the younger christened in the Rose Garden 2 weeks ago. And they are a constant source of happiness in our lives. Well, 28 years ago,

at Christmas, Jesse and Dot were reading a story about a boy with cerebral palsy living in a Greensboro orphanage. And asked what he would most like from Santa Claus, the boy had said, a mother and a father. And soon after, Jesse and Dot visited that boy and they adopted him—became his mother and father. Brought him through several operations. And today, he's a successful businessman with a family of his own. Like Barbara and I, Dot and Jesse know the joy of adoption. And I know we all salute them for bringing the caring light of love to another.

And that is the Jesse Helms I know—a parable of character. The character which led Jesse to go out and buy glasses for the son of a woman in Johnson County whom he heard couldn't see the blackboard, or caused him to help Durham's Thuy Doan. Having escaped from Vietnam, she tried for 7 years to get her mother out. And Jesse reunited her family.

Let's face it: people don't always agree with him, but they always respect him. And where does Jesse stand? You know where. He places principle and people above partisan politics—strengthening the United States of America. By way of example, look first at foreign policy, where naturally, the liberal Democrats want us to make reckless defense cuts. And as long as I'm President, there's as much chance of that happening as there is of Mike Krzyzewski going to the Boston Celtics. It isn't going to happen.

And the truth is, a strong national defense has and is helping to build a more democratic world. Consider: Earlier this month, President Gorbachev and I held our Washington summit, and we signed an agreement to update and expand our 1973 pact on the peaceful uses of atomic energy. Another agreement on nuclear testing will create unprecedented improvements for on-site verification—a course that Jesse has urged since the 1970's. And President Gorbachev and I also issued a joint statement on conventional armed forces in Europe in which both sides committed themselves to intensify the pace of the negotiations in Vienna and agreed that such a treaty is essential to the future security of Europe. And furthermore, we also agreed to hold future negotiations on nuclear and space arms once the START treaty is concluded.

The great humorist Will Rogers once said, "A man in the country does his own thinking—but you get him into town and he soon will be thinking second-handed." In North Carolina, even city folks are commonsense country thinkers. And you understand that giving peace a chance does not mean taking a chance on peace. As we build upon our new relationship with the Soviet Union— and I'm going to keep on trying there— America must heed the desire for self-determination for the Baltic Republics. And we will. And I was pleased to see last week's meeting between President Gorbachev and the Presidents of these three Republics. And those talks began a dialog that we hope can lead to a peaceful resolution of this situation, an end to the Soviet economic blockade of Lithuania, and freedom for millions more.

And as we work to consolidate the positive change of the past year, we must also maintain the policies and institutions that made that change possible: a strong NATO, with Germany remaining a full member, and a strong American military presence in Europe as guarantors of stability, security, and freedom. Carolinians know these challenges can only be met through an America unafraid to adjust but committed to remain strong. You see, weakness will not preserve the peace that our national defense policies have helped us win. And I need Senators who will help our defense maintain that peace.

And where does Jesse stand? You know where Jesse stands: for a safer, more secure, and stable world. And turning to America, a lot of challenges also remain. And so, quoting Asheville's own Thomas Wolfe, let's "look homeward." And here, too, I need Jesse Helms to keep standing up for what's right.

A noted preacher once said, "A thoughtful mind, when it sees a nation's flag, sees not the flag only but the nation itself." And yet, what would we say to the brave men and women who fought and died for the Stars and Stripes if they were alive today? Forty-eight States had laws protecting the flag against desecration. Forty-eight States. And those laws were effectively struck down when the Supreme Court ruled that flag-burning is protected by the Constitution. Now, I know this is an emotional issue on which Americans of good faith can and do disagree. As I look at it, it's not a Republican issue or Democrat, or even a liberal or conservative issue. To me, it is an American issue.

And our forefathers, with remarkable insight, knew that the Constitution must evolve in order to be contemporary. And so, they provided a mechanism for amending this sacred and marvelous document. And like us, they knew that the flag is the unique symbol of America. And I emphasize that word "unique." I honestly can't believe that they would condone burning it under the cover of free speech. The constitutional amendment we have proposed is carefully drawn. And here's what it says: "The Congress and the States shall have power to prohibit the physical desecration of the flag of the United States." I will fight for that amendment, and I am proud to have Jesse Helms at my side.

And Jesse and I, of course, agree on many other issues—things that I think we all agree could be called value issues. An example: Jesse believed that kids should have the right to have voluntary prayer in the classroom—and so do I. As an old-fashioned guy, he believes in fiscal sanity. And when it comes to solving problems, liberals measure progress made by dollars spent. And Jesse and I, on the other hand, want to clean up the deficit through proposals requiring a balanced budget and a line-item veto. If the Congress can't make these cuts, give the President what 43 Governors have, and let him have a shot at it.

And finally, there's the issue of fighting crime. And last May I outlined our Violent Crime Act. And at its heart is the belief that for anyone killing a law enforcement officer, no legal penalty is too tough. Liberals oppose the death penalty. And where does Jesse stand? Where I do: We want to eliminate loopholes that allow these, the worst criminals, to escape just punishment. And what's more, we want to expand its coverage to include major drug traffickers. Not sometime, not someplace but right now all across America.

I'm told that Jesse's favorite movie is "Patton." And in closing, let me recite the words of Patton telling his troops that in coming months they would often wonder whether they'd retreat under fire. "Don't worry about it," he advised them. "I can assure you, you will all do your duty." For 18 years Jesse Helms has done his duty, acting as a United States Senator to protect what Mayberry's own Aunt Bee, of the beloved "Andy Griffith Show," called "home and people's feelings, and how they grew up." He continues to lead with the civility and conscience that is a metaphor for North Carolina and with a spirit that would make even General Patton proud.

Two years ago, after an operation, Jesse—typical of him—disobeyed the doctor's order by leaving his sickbed early to hit the campaign trail for me and Dan Quayle. And I'll never forget how he literally stood up to support me. And tonight, I came down here to pledge him my support. You know where Jesse stands: for a safe, strong, and moral America. And I need him in the United States Senate, so let's keep him there—for your sake, for North Carolina's sake, and for America's sake.

And thank you for this occasion. And let's reelect Jesse Helms. And God bless the United States of America. Thank you.

Note: The President spoke at 7:25 p.m. in Liberty Hall at the Merchandise Mart. In his remarks, he referred to Jack Hawk, chairman of the State Republican Party; Jack Laughery, president of Hardees; Roger Milliken, president of Milliken Industries; Mike Krzyzewski, coach of the Duke University basketball team; and author Thomas Wolfe. Mrs. Bush spoke at the Wellesley College commencement ceremony. Following his remarks, the President returned to Washington, DC.

Remarks at the Ribbon-Cutting Ceremony for the Children's Inn at the National Institutes of Health in Bethesda, Maryland
June 21, 1990

What a beautiful day! Thank you, Dr. Sullivan. And I love the music, too. I love to sing. We heard you when we were just getting ready to come out here. Thank you very much. I guess I needn't tell this group, infiltrated by so many doctors and friends from NIH, of my high regard for our Secretary of HHS, Dr. Sullivan. I'm just delighted he's with me and very proud to be introduced by him. I really want to single out those who have worked so hard, recognizing that I might, by omission, risk offending. But Bar and I've had this warm welcome here, and then we've been reading up on the hard work that's gone into it. Certainly, I want to single out Debbie Dingell for her commitment, Dr. Pizzo, Dr. Raub, Dr. Vagelos, Alan Kay, Carmala Walgren, Chris Downey, Kathy Russell, and—again, excuse me, I'll stop there—but everybody else as well.

It's good to see so many friends and believers from the Hill over here—from Capitol Hill, those who are giving this project a lot of heartfelt support—Congressmen Dingell and Downey and Walgren and Morella and Lowery. Welcome to all. And a special greeting to the kids, the parents, and the friends who have come down from NIH this morning.

I have been so impressed by what I've learned about the unique concept of Children's Inn. Barbara and I have talked about it, and she's told me of this wonderful concept. It's an extraordinarily sensitive idea to provide this place of refuge and renewal so that sick children and their families can live together during treatment. I am very moved to be here today to see how joyously your vision of caring has been realized. This is a story of how dreams come true, and if you believe with all your heart and work with all your might, dreams do come true.

Yours is also an inspiring message of bravery, sacrifice, and hope that can bring together individuals, political parties, professionals, volunteers, private businesses, and then the Government itself. The Children's Inn, this extraordinary home for those who need it most, is a remarkable lesson in unity of purpose and caring. As brilliant Points of Light in the hard, dark world of battling illness, you've given this rare and loving gift, and you've shown your belief in the shining role which family support plays in the treatment of a sick child.

Carmala and Debbie and Chris and all of the congressional spouses, your vision and compassion and caring touch us all very deeply. Dr. Pizzo, your professional commitment to this dream has lasted a decade; the remarkable legacy that you've helped to create will last for generations. And, Dr. Vagelos, you and Merck & Co. have embodied in a most exemplary way the ideal of corporate responsibility, utilizing the unique talents and gifts that your company has to give. And then to NIH: Your generous gift of land and medical expertise has and will change the lives of many of the children and so many, many others. Your leadership and gifts, both spiritual and physical, have made this dream an astonishing reality.

The lesson of the Inn will show us all that the most important part of life is a very simple one: taking time to hold a hand, share a laugh, wipe away a tear. Many people will be doing exactly that to comfort the 36 families who will live at this Inn: people like resident manager Kate Higgins and her staff; people like the volunteer fundraisers and more than 4,000 donors who have raised over $7 million for construction and who will continue to raise $500,000 a year for operating expenses; people like those at the Clinical Center and the entire campus of NIH, who have been involved in caring for decades, in planning for years, and in construction since last August. I think it's wonderful that over 3,000 of you came to tour this place earlier this week. And Debbie said that—knowing her, I'm sure there were a few arms twisted—but nevertheless, she said that most of you have volunteered to help, and I would encourage the others to listen to her message.

We can't forget those who simply care, like the eighth graders at Baker Intermedi-

ate School in Damascus, Maryland, who made a squadron of 35 toy airplanes for the Inn.

But above all, it will be the families themselves who will be providing the love. As your Children's Inn slogan says: "There is a closeness that can only come from the family."

Let me give you an example of the importance of the family bond in bringing new hope to a sick child. Today 10-year-old Breanne Schwantes can swim up to 54 laps a day, plays hard with her sisters and cousins, and is so concerned about the penguins in Antarctica that she even wrote a letter to me about them. But she could have spent these last 10 years in a world bounded by her hospital room walls, like others with her illness, for Breanne has osteogenesis imperfecta, brittle bone disease. But what is more important is that she also has her loving parents, Terry and Theresa, and sister, Elizabeth.

When Breanne's condition was diagnosed, Theresa gave up her Ph.D. work, saying nothing else mattered except devoting herself to the health of her daughter and the health of her family. And she says: "We decided that our gift to Breanne would be that she have a life that was full and joyous and that all of our lives would be truly lived." And now, whether at home in Wisconsin or in the Schwantes' second home here at NIH, those who know Breanne say it is her family's depth of support that has given this child her life.

There is nothing that hurts more than a child afraid of the darkness whose cries go unheard, a lonely child whose tiny spirit is wrapped up in a brave fight too big for its years. And that is what this splendid cause, your splendid cause, so eloquently recognizes.

As I thought about why I was so deeply touched by the sensitivity of your concept, I remembered Barbara's words a couple of weeks ago at Wellesley. To me they sum up the spirit of this place: that the family is the key to everything. She told the graduates there, you may remember, "You will never regret not having passed one more test, not winning one more verdict, or not closing one more deal. You will regret, however, time not spent with a husband, a friend, a child, or a parent."

We share the belief that the family is the bright center of love and life itself. Quite simply: Family comes first.

Those of you who are parents of these special, gravely ill children share something. You learn to carve out your daily lives with the tools of courage, faith, and love.

Dr. Vagelos and Dr. Pizzo and the Friends of the Children's Inn are people of exceptional goodness, and we are very, very grateful to them. And I also want to thank the nurses, the nurses who hold these kids in their arms and take care of them, and all the other fine people here at NIH who help and care. And to the families of these kids— you live with a special grace. You who spend precious time with these kids, these intensely ill children, have learned the true meaning of the prayer of St. Francis:

"Where there is despair, let me sow

hope; where there is darkness, light; and where there is sadness, joy."

You've had the extraordinary opportunity to bring joy and strength to each other, and that is the greatest strength of all.

Thank you, and God bless this wonderful work right here at this very special Inn. And now off to cut the ribbon.

Note: The President spoke at 10:14 a.m. outside the Children's Inn. In his remarks, he referred to Secretary of Health and Human Services Louis W. Sullivan; Philip Pizzo, Chief of Pediatrics at the National Cancer Institute; William F. Raub, Deputy Director of the National Institutes of Health; P. Roy Vagelos, chairman and chief executive officer of Merck & Co., Inc.; Carmala Walgren, Debbie Dingell, Chris Downey, Alan Kay, Kathy Russell, and Katie Lowery, president, vice president, secretary, and members of the board of directors of Friends of the Children's Inn, respectively.

Remarks Congratulating the Detroit Pistons on Winning the National Basketball Association Championship
June 21, 1990

The President. Well, thank you all very much. Deja vu all over again, as Yogi Berra would say. [*Laughter*] To the Members of the Senate—both Senators—and several Members of the House delegation from Michigan, welcome to the steamy Rose Garden. There hasn't been so much excitement around here since Michael Jackson swung out through that door a while back. But I want to welcome you all back and to say to the deputy commissioner here, Russ Granik, and all distinguished guests, welcome to the White House. Bill Davidson and General Manager McCloskey and, of course, Coach Daly and all the proud members of the Pistons, we're very proud of you. I'm delighted to welcome all of you here to the Rose Garden to join in honoring the world champion Detroit Pistons on this repeat performance.

I know that—one serious note—that it is a bitter-sweet victory for one member of the

Pistons team—I should say the Pistons family. And I'm talking about Joe Dumars. And our hearts go out to you and to your family on your loss. And all of us admire the strength and the dignity that you displayed these last very difficult weeks.

You know, today is a proud day for the Pistons; it's one for the record books. You've become only the third team in pro basketball history to win the NBA championship back to back. First the Celtics, then the Lakers, and now the Detroit Pistons. And each great team has a trademark style, the Pistons being no exception. The style starts with Chuck Daly, voted Coach of the Year by Gentlemen's Quarterly—[*laughter*]— who knows it's not just how you play, it's how you look. How he made it some of us don't know. But anyway—[*laughter*]——

In Detroit, it's defense, the take-no-prisoners, wall-to-wall pressure that held Pistons' opponents under 100 points for 44 times this season and 13 of the 20 games in the playoffs. And the key is to keep that focus, play with the same intensity for the full 48 minutes. And that's the Pistons' brand of basketball that has captivated the hearts of this country. Take the fifth and final game. The Trailblazers had a tough team. They played the Pistons dead-even all game long—47 minutes, 59.3 seconds to be exact. Good, but not good enough. And in the last, seven-tenths of a second, Vinnie Johnson nailed a jumper, and the Pistons nailed another championship banner to the rafters in the Palace.

And on a team with this tremendous talent, it's no surprise to find some of pro basketball's very best. I should start, I guess, with everybody's MVP, Isiah Thomas, the kind of guy who gets lost in a crowd until you toss in a basketball out there. And his game goes into overdrive in the playoffs. Listen to these stats: In the last 7 minutes of game 1, Isiah scored 16 points. Or game 4—30 points in the second half. And of course, the final, last Thursday night, Isiah led the way with a team-high 29 points. That concludes today's reading from Isiah. [*Laughter*]

Detroit got championship-level play all series long, all season long, from every member of the team. Instant offense from Mark Aguirre, Joe Dumars. Aggressive—I see their families are here. [*Laughter*] Aggressive defense from John Sally and the NBA's number one defensive player, Dennis Rodman. And there's the front court—James Edwards and, of course, my old friend, Mr. Congeniality over here, Bill Laimbeer. [*Laughter*] James' nickname may be Buddha, but I know no one is ever going to call Bill Laimbeer Gandhi. [*Laughter*] Kinder and gentler maybe, but not peaceful.

In any event, key contributions along the way from Jerome Henderson and Scott Hastings, David Greenwood, William Bed-ford, all under the guidance of the great coach, Coach Daly, and his topnotch staff. There may be 5 men out there on the court, but no one knows better than this proud Piston team that it takes a 12-man effort and more to bring home the title 2 years in a row.

So, I want to welcome you here today, welcome you back, true champions that you are. Once again, my sincere congratulations to you, to the city of Detroit, the home of the world champion Pistons. Maybe I'll see you next year, too.

Thank you all very much.

Isiah Thomas. As they said in "Poltergeist," "We're back!" [*Laughter*]

On behalf of the Detroit Pistons—well, let me say one other thing. Vice President Quayle, sir, you've come to see us play twice. [*Laughter*] The first time was in Indiana, and I think we ended up losing by about, what was it, 30 that night? It was the worst game we played all season. So, we're happy and everything that he's going to come and watch us play again in Detroit. So, he comes to the final game, and that's the only game we lose in the finals. [*Laughter*] We lose it in overtime. Thanks for all your support. [*Laughter*]

Now, on behalf of the Detroit Pistons, my teammates, the whole organization, we again would like to present President Bush with a Piston jersey. And even though we may be number one, he's also number one. Thank you.

The President. Thank you very much. Thank all of you guys.

Note: The President spoke at 2:17 p.m. in the Rose Garden at the White House. In his remarks, he referred to Russ Granik, executive vice president of the National Basketball Association, and William Davidson and Jack McCloskey, managing partner and general manager of the Detroit Pistons, respectively.

Designation of Susan M. Coughlin as Vice Chairman of the National Transportation Safety Board
June 21, 1990

The President today designated Susan M. Coughlin to be Vice Chairman of the National Transportation Safety Board for a term of 2 years. She would succeed James L. Kolstad.

Since 1989 Mrs. Coughlin has served as a member of the National Transportation Safety Board. Prior to this she served as Deputy Administrator of the Federal Railroad Administration at the Department of Transportation in Washington, DC, 1987–1989. Mrs. Coughlin has served in various capacities for the Export-Import Bank of the United States in the Office of Public Affairs and Publications, Washington, DC, including Acting Vice President, 1986–1987, and as Deputy Vice President, 1983–1986. In addition, she has served as an officer in intergovernmental relations in the Office of the Secretary at the Department of Transportation, 1981–1983.

Mrs. Coughlin graduated from Moravian College (B.A., 1972). She was born March 17, 1946, in Naval Station, MD. Mrs. Coughlin is married, has four children, and resides in Washington, DC.

Letter to Congressional Leaders Reporting on the Cyprus Conflict
June 22, 1990

Dear Mr. Speaker: (Dear Mr. Chairman:)

In accordance with Public Law 95–384 (92 Stat. 739; 22 U.S.C. 2373(c)), I am submitting to you this bimonthly report on progress toward a negotiated settlement of the Cyprus question.

This report covers the period from mid-March through mid-May 1990, a time marked by intense activity in both Cypriot communities, as well as international efforts at resuming direct intercommunal negotiations.

In northern Cyprus elections were held on April 22 and May 6, 1990, which reconfirmed the positions of leadership and authority long held by Mr. Rauf Denktash and the Turkish Cypriot National Unity Party, respectively. Observers have since interpreted these electoral successes as endorsements by the Turkish Cypriot community of existing Turkish Cypriot policies and intercommunal negotiating positions.

In the south, the arrest of a Greek Cypriot youth who crossed into northern Nicosia, defaced a public building, and was arrested and jailed by the Turkish Cypriot police led to a series of demonstrations by Greek Cypriot students along the U.N.-controlled buffer zone. These demonstrations and protests intensified as the intercommunal negotiations in New York ended in early March without a positive result. For some days the checkpoint near the Ledra Palace was closed, thus effectively blocking travel between the two communities on Cyprus. In addition, a handful of young Greek Cypriots managed to dart through the lines and commit small acts of vandalism, which led to further arrests and jailings by Turkish Cypriot authorities. Several of these Greek Cypriots remain in northern Cyprus jails.

While elections and heightened tensions were the order of the day in Cyprus, strong efforts continued by the United Nations Secretary General, supported by the United States and others, to find a way to restart direct intercommunal negotiations aimed at completing an outline for a Cyprus settlement. Toward this end, I discussed the Cyprus situation personally with Prime Minister Thatcher during our meeting in Bermuda in early April, and my Cyprus Coordinator, Ambassador Nelson Ledsky, held 4 hours of talks with President Vassiliou in New York in late April.

During this same time period the United

Nations Secretary General met separately with the Turkish Foreign Minister and President Vassiliou of Cyprus. There were also extensive conversations about Cyprus during President Vassiliou's official visit to Canada on April 30–May 1.

Finally, on May 15, I nominated to the Senate Robert E. Lamb, a distinguished career Foreign Service Officer, as Ambassa-dor to Cyprus.

Sincerely,

GEORGE BUSH

Note: Identical letters were sent to Thomas S. Foley, Speaker of the House of Representatives, and Claiborne Pell, chairman of the Senate Foreign Relations Committee.

Remarks to United States Attorneys
June 22, 1990

Thank you all, and welcome back to Washington, many of you. For those here, my thanks to you as well for the job you're doing. I want to thank Secretary Brady for being with us, Nick, and of course my valued counselor and friend, the Attorney General, Dick Thornburgh, who is doing an outstanding job for our country. And I'm grateful to him every single day that I'm President.

To the prosecutors and crimefighters, you know what—when I told the grandchild that's with me there in the White House now that I'd be spending some time with some of America's finest crimefighters, Noelle asked me if I'd be sure to bring back an autograph from Dick Tracy. [*Laughter*] We just saw that show in the White House.

But nevertheless, true villains are drawn from life, not from primary colors; and where financial fraud is concerned, it takes a discerning mind and a determined spirit to distinguish the incompetent from the fraudulent, the unlucky from the unlawful. And this nation is very fortunate to be able to look to you, the United States attorneys of America, to make these tough calls. And we depend on you as you work with the FBI and other investigative and regulatory agencies to sift through piles upon piles of documents and understand that in the cold numbers of a ledger can be found the tragedy of an embezzled pension, the heartache of stolen savings.

White-collar crime is not as dramatic as violent crime, but white-collar crime still ruins lives, and it murders the fondest dreams of whole families. And it takes a snake, a coldblooded snake, to betray the trust and innocence of hard-working people. And so, if we have to look under rocks to find these white-collar criminals, then we will leave no stone unturned.

This administration, from our first days in office, has worked with Congress to crack down on white-collar criminals—to crack down on fat-cat financiers who launder the smell of blood out of drug money and white-collar crooks who cheat the elderly out of their life's hard work, and to bring to justice government contractors who steal by the numbers. You already know of the 37 convictions from the Ill Wind probe of Federal defense contractors, and you already know of the 127 people rounded up in Operation Polar Caps crackdown on drug financiers.

And let me say I wanted you here today to also thank you because there are signs that we are starting at long last to make credible progress in the war on drugs. Dick and Nick Brady and I have just come from a meeting with Bill Bennett [Director of National Drug Control Policy]—a report on where we stand; and we're beginning to get the sense—and I think the country is beginning to get the sense—that we will, indeed, win this war on drugs.

You already know that among cases involving abuse of HUD contracts, the Department of Justice has already obtained 65 convictions this fiscal year, including 21 convictions in Oklahoma alone, while courts have ordered almost $2½ million in restitution in that State, more than half of which will come from an executive who has a 5-year reservation in prison. And in all, the Government has won 10,000 financial fraud convictions since 1985. And just last year alone, the Department of Justice aggressively won almost 800 convictions in major financial institution fraud cases—cases involving more than $100,000 each.

But the most critical financial fraud problem we've faced is the—Dick referred to it—the savings and loan crisis. Working closely with Congress, we succeeded in obtaining many critical regulatory reforms, but a great deal of wrongdoing had already taken place, had already occurred. And so, in the third week of my administration, I directed the Attorney General to give cases of S&L fraud the highest priority; and he did just exactly that. And when it comes to civil action, we have sought restitution to protect taxpayers through tens of thousands of civil suits leveled against S&L executives, owners, and borrowers. And when it comes to criminal action, we aim for a simple, uncompromising position: Throw the crooks in jail.

And this aggressive attitude is paying off, and in 3 years, we've won more than 150 S&L convictions: $100 million ordered in restitution—$100 million; more than 400 years in prison terms meted out. And I know that because of you and your firm support there will be much, much more. I am grateful to each and every one of you that is fighting hard to bring these people to justice.

Consider all that is happening. An S&L chairman gets 30 years in the celebrated case in Dallas, Texas. An S&L CEO in Santa Rosa is sentenced to prison, and the courts ordered almost $7 million in fines and restitution. In Illinois, top officers of an S&L go to prison and are ordered to pay $17 million. Now, these cheats have cost us billions, and they will pay us back with their dollars, and they'll pay us back with years of their lives.

These prosecutions are the result of a determined effort, an effort which we are boosting with 202 FBI agents, 100 more FBI accounting technicians, and 118 more United States attorneys. The Dallas Task Force has been particularly successful, obtaining 52 convictions. So successful, in fact, that Attorney General Thornburgh is expanding the task force concept to 27 cities.

Now, we could have been moving even faster, but very candidly, Congress did not act on my request for $36.8 million in additional investigatorial and prosecutorial resources for 1989. And further, approval of my request that Dick talked about for $50 million for the current fiscal year was delayed.

Under Secretary Brady's leadership, the IRS is aggressively pursuing individuals suspected of tax fraud in connection with failed savings and loan institutions, while the Resolution Trust Corporation is adding about 300 members to its investigative staff this year to become part of a new national investigative network. The FDIC is pursuing more than 1,200 cases of fraud and negligence against thrift officials—attorneys, accountants—and has collected more than $120 million in damages this year. Treasury's Office of Thrift Supervision, the OTS, has also required 664 institutions to agree to terminate unsafe and unsound practices, remove more than 150 senior thrift officers and directors, and issued 111 cease and desist orders to stop unsafe and unsound practices.

Throughout it all, our men and women in the Federal agencies are doing a great job, from the halls of Justice and Treasury to the passport clerk who recovered $3 million in cash, jewelry, and gold by keeping a former savings and loan owner from skipping the country.

We're learning a lot from our successes, and so, I'm here today to back new legislative and administrative action. In further ways, we can crack down on white-collar crime. First, let me declare my support for a proposed amendment to the Omnibus Crime bill to enhance and enforce the civil and criminal penalties for fraud against financial institutions. This legislation, sponsored by leaders—Bob Dole, Republican leader, and Bob Michel, by Senators Heinz and Garn, as well as Congressmen Hiler and Wylie—will strengthen our investigative and prosecutorial tools in the service of justice, and it will provide added protection to the victims of crime.

We want to allow the use of court-approved wiretaps in investigating bank fraud. And we also want Congress to authorize Federal regulatory agencies to ask the courts to freeze the corporate and personal assets of defendants in civil cases involving financial institution fraud so that they will not leave the taxpayers high and dry. And we want to prevent rip-off artists from using bankruptcy as a strategy to avoid paying damages.

Now, these are some of the legislative steps that we can and must take, but we must also build on our recent successes by taking further administrative action. The Attorney General will establish within this great department, the Department of Justice, a new unit to direct and sharpen the Department's actions even further while helping to coordinate actions with other Agencies.

Where new problems emerge in S&Ls we'll need to get involved fast, and that's why Attorney General Thornburgh and Secretary Brady have created a new approach: rapid response teams against fraud—teams of razor-sharp prosecutors and auditors recruited from their Departments and other Agencies striking city by city, teams that will jump right into the paper chase, teams that will hit the trail while that trail is still hot. These teams will be deployed to help you. You're on the cutting edge, you U.S. attorneys. And I am confident that they will work well with you.

I have already seen the men and women of these two Departments working together, sharing a tenacious spirit born of a thirst for justice. Of course, we will always quantify the importance of our work together in terms of billions of dollars lost, but perhaps it is more appropriate to remember why this mission is so important to so many people—a thought that will sustain you in the months to come as you sip that cold coffee long after everyone else has gone home. You'll be working late because you will not let those people be forgotten: savers whose hard work and honest trust must and will be protected, elderly people whose faith in the future must be preserved. It's your duty—I would say it is your sacred duty—to right these wrongs, to stand up for the vulnerable against the unscrupulous, the guileless against the conniving.

We will not rest until the cheats and the chiselers and the charlatans spend a large chunk of their lives behind the bars of a Federal prison. You do a difficult job in a spirit of professionalism. Sometimes you come under fire—partisan political fire. And I will do my level best to see that the facts are out there so that the American people can understand and appreciate, as I do, the job that you all are doing. I can thank you, only thank you, on behalf of all Americans for this dedication, this dedication that you bring to the people's work.

I want to thank all of you for coming here to Washington, and may God bless each and every one of you. Thank you for what you're doing. We want to support you 100 percent. Many, many thanks.

Note: The President spoke at 11:12 a.m. in the Great Hall at the Department of Justice.

Statement by Press Secretary Fitzwater on the Renewal of the Hungary-United States Trade Agreement
June 22, 1990

The President has renewed the bilateral trade agreement between the United States and the Republic of Hungary. Under the agreement, which went into effect in 1978, the United States and the Republic of Hungary grant each other most-favored-nation tariff treatment. The President based his decision on, among other criteria, a satisfactory balance of concessions in trade and services between the two countries during the life of the agreement.

The administration will seek further negotiations in the near future with the newly elected Hungarian government on investment matters, intellectual property protections, and other measures aimed at increasing trade and business contacts between the two countries.

In renewing the bilateral trade agreement with Hungary, the President reaffirmed support for the Republic of Hungary's commitment to market mechanisms and the country's continued movement toward trade liberalization and nondiscriminatory practices with her trading partners.

Japan-United States Joint Statement on the 30th Anniversary of the Entry into Force of the United States-Japan Treaty of Mutual Cooperation and Security
June 22, 1990

On this historic day 30 years ago, representatives of the United States and Japan exchanged instruments of ratification and put into effect the U.S.-Japan Treaty of Mutual Cooperation and Security, an agreement which is the very foundation of the overall relationship between our two countries and provides the framework for peace and stability in Asia.

The past three decades have witnessed remarkable progress and prosperity among the free nations of the Pacific region. Such progress would not have been possible but for the framework for peace and stability that the Treaty has provided. As we consider the important role that the Treaty has played over these years, our respect deepens for the wise judgment made by our predecessors.

With our combined economic strength, our steadfast security relationship, and our common adherence to political and economic freedom, the United States and Japan, working together, constitute a force for positive change in the world.

We are partners for peace, and the foundation of our partnership is the Treaty of Mutual Cooperation and Security. In the coming decades, as we pursue our global partnership, the Treaty will remain a vital instrument for ensuring the freedom and security of our two nations and promoting peace and prosperity throughout the world. On this occasion, therefore, we hereby renew our commitment and efforts steadfastly to maintain and effectively implement the U.S.-Japan Treaty of Mutual Cooperation and Security.

Remarks Prior to Discussions With Nelson Mandela
June 25, 1990

The President. Welcome to all of you. It is a great pleasure, a sincere pleasure, for Barbara and me to welcome to the White House Mr. and Mrs. Mandela—Mr. Mandela, a man who embodies the hopes of millions. In our meetings this morning, he and I will talk about the future of South Africa, and it is my sincere hope that these talks will be productive discussions that will contribute to positive change toward true democracy and the dismantling once and for all of apartheid.

We meet at a time of transition for South Africa. We applaud the recent steps President de Klerk and the Government of South Africa have taken to expand the rights and freedoms of all South Africans. These are positive developments, steps toward a fully free and democratic future that we all wish to see for all of the people of South Africa. In order for progress to continue, we must see on all sides a clear commitment to change.

864

All parties must seize the opportunity to move ahead in a spirit of compromise and tolerance, flexibility and patience. And from all parties, we look for a clear and unequivocal commitment to negotiations leading to peaceful change. I call on all elements in South African society to renounce the use of violence in armed struggle, break free from the cycle of repression and violent reaction that breeds nothing but more fear and suffering. In the words of the great Martin Luther King, Jr., "Let us not seek to satisfy our thirst for freedom by drinking from the cup of bitterness and hatred."

Mr. Mandela, in the eyes of millions around the world, you stand against apartheid, against a system that bases the rights and freedoms of citizenship on the color of one's skin. That system is repugnant to the conscience of men and women everywhere, repugnant to the ideals that we in America hold so dear. No system that denies the rights that belong to each and every individual can endure forever. Apartheid must end.

The United States, committed to the concept of free market and a productive private sector, is ready to do its part to encourage rapid and peaceful change toward political and economic freedom. We will continue to urge American firms that are still doing business in South Africa to play a progressive role in training and empowering blacks and building a foundation for future prosperity.

But while the reform process has moved forward—and it has—apartheid remains a reality, and genuine democracy a dream. Our sanctions have been designed to support change. And when the conditions laid down in our law have been met, then, and only then, will we consider, in consultation with the Congress, whether a change in course will promote further progress through peaceful negotiations.

Mr. Mandela, we in this country support the struggle against apartheid. For two centuries, we had our own battles. America fought its own battles to promote the standard of equal rights. It was here at the White House—in a room now obscured by these coverings because we're repainting the White House—but it's right there, in the midst of the Civil War, that Abraham Lin-

coln signed the Emancipation Proclamation, that great beacon of light and hope. In the room where this historic document was signed, even now we feel the power of the undeniable truth that guided Lincoln's hand: that all men must be free.

In this past year, freedom has made great gains. A terrible chapter of oppression has ended for millions of men and women in Eastern Europe, in Asia, and in this hemisphere. People have defeated, through peaceful means, dictatorships that promised freedom and progress but delivered only poverty and repression. The triumph is far from universal. There are still those who rule through force and terror. But the events of this past year have been clear: The future belongs not to the dwindling ranks of the world's dictators but to democracy, the millions of friends of freedom the world over.

Mr. Mandela, you said many years ago, before the first of your 10,000 days in prison, that there is no easy walk to freedom. Your years of suffering, your nation's suffering—they've borne that out. But just as, this past year, so many millions of people in Eastern Europe and elsewhere tasted freedom, so, too, South Africa's time will come.

As Martin Luther King said on the steps of the Lincoln Memorial, we cannot walk alone. Sir, we here in America walk in solidarity with all the South Africans who seek through nonviolent means democracy, human rights, and freedom.

Once again, it is a sincere privilege to welcome you to the White House, and may God bless you and all the people of South Africa. Welcome, sir.

Mr. Mandela. Mr. President, it is an honor and a pleasure for my wife, my delegation, and I to be welcomed by you. This is a continuation of the rousing welcome which we have received from the people of New York and Boston, of black and white. That welcome has far exceeded our wildest expectations. We look forward to visiting Atlanta and other cities because we are confident that the warm welcome we have received is not confined to New York, Boston, and Washington. That mood expresses the commitment of all the people of the United

States of America to the struggle for the removal of apartheid.

One thing that is very clear, and it has been made even more clear in the remarks by the President, is that on the question of the removal of apartheid and the introduction of a nonracial democracy in our country we are absolutely unanimous. That is something that we have always known because the people of America and the President, in particular, have spoken in this regard in very clear and firm terms. And this has been a source of great encouragement to our people. To receive the support of any government is, in our situation, something of enormous importance; but to receive the support of the Government of the United States of America, the leader of the West, is something beyond words. If today we are confident that the dreams which have inspired us all these years is about to be realized, it is, in very large measure, because of the support we have got from the masses of the people of the United States of America and, in particular, from the Government and from the President.

There are very important political developments that have taken place in our country today, and it is my intention to brief the President as fully as possible on these developments. We are doing so because it is necessary for him to understand not only in broad outline what is happening in our country, he must be furnished with the details which may not be so available to the public so that the enormous assistance that he has given us should be related to the actual developments in the country.

I will also ask the President to maintain sanctions because it is because of sanctions that such enormous progress has been made in the attempt to address the problems of our country.

I will also inform him about developments as far as the arms struggle is concerned. The remarks that he has made here are due to the fact that he has not as yet got a proper briefing from us. I might just state in passing that the methods of political action which are used by the black people of South Africa were determined by the South African Government. As long as a government is prepared to talk, to maintain channels of communication between itself and the governed, there can be no question of violence whatsoever. But when a government decides to ban political organizations of the oppressed, intensifies oppression, and does not allow any free political activity, no matter how peaceful and nonviolent, then the people have no alternative but to resort to violence.

There is not a single political organization in our country, inside and outside Parliament, which can ever compare with the African National Congress in its total commitment to peace. If we are forced to resort to violence, it is because we had no other alternative whatsoever. But even in this regard, there have been significant developments which I hope to brief the President on. I am also going to brief the President on the key role which the ANC now occupies in the country as a result of his efforts to mobilize the entire country around the question of peace.

We have and are addressing the question of black unity. We are also addressing ourselves to means and methods of helping Mr. de Klerk to maintain his position with confidence and to go on with the negotiations without looking over his shadow. We have already started important initiatives in trying to mobilize the white community, not only those who support him but even the right wing, because we are the only organization in the world that can help Mr. de Klerk to maintain his position.

And I am going to urge on the President not to do anything without a full consultation with the ANC in regard to any initiative which he might propose to take in order to help the peace process in the country. As people who are operating inside, and as the architects of the peace process, it is absolutely necessary for everybody who wants to be of assistance in the struggle of the black people inside the country and who want to help promote the peace process to have a full consultation with the ANC before any step is taken.

Finally, Mr. President, I would like to congratulate you and President Gorbachev for the magnificent efforts that you are making in order to reduce international tensions and to promote peace. It is my hope that governments throughout the world will follow your example and attempt to settle problems between governments, and between governments and dissidents inside its country, by peaceful methods. You and comrade Gorbachev have opened a chapter in world history which might well be regarded as the turning point in many respects. And here we congratulate you and

wish you every success.

Note: The President spoke at 10:42 a.m. at the South Portico of the White House. Following their remarks, the President and Mr. Mandela met in the Oval Office and then attended a luncheon in the Old Family Dining Room.

Statement by Press Secretary Fitzwater on Fang Lizhi's Departure From China
June 25, 1990

Dr. Fang Lizhi and his wife, Li Shuxian, have left the U.S. Embassy in Beijing to proceed to the United Kingdom. The United States Government welcomes the PRC Government's decision to facilitate the departure of Dr. Fang and his wife for rea-

sons of Dr. Fang's health and well-being and to permit Dr. Fang to pursue his important research in astrophysics. This humanitarian action is a farsighted, significant step that will improve the atmosphere for progress in our bilateral relations.

Statement by Press Secretary Fitzwater on the Acquisition of Norton Company by BTR of the United Kingdom
June 25, 1990

The President has decided against intervening in the possible acquisition of Norton Co. by BTR plc of the United Kingdom. Norton Co. manufactures abrasive products and engineering materials, including advanced ceramics. In addition, Norton has engaged in extensive research and development of advanced ceramics and diamond films.

The President based his decision on the results of the investigation by the Committee on Foreign Investment in the United States (CFIUS), chaired by Treasury Secretary Nicholas F. Brady. CFIUS conducted a thorough investigation of various national security issues relating to this possible acquisition.

The BTR-Norton investigation was con-

ducted pursuant to section 5021 of the Omnibus Trade and Competitiveness Act of 1988. That provision, known as the Exon-Florio provision, authorizes the President to investigate and, if necessary, to suspend or prohibit a proposed foreign acquisition of a U.S. business engaged in interstate commerce. The criteria to suspend or prohibit a transaction are that the President must find: credible evidence that leads him to believe that the foreign investor might take action that threatens to impair the national security; that existing laws, other than the International Emergency Economic Powers Act and the Exon-Florio provision itself, do not provide adequate and appropriate authority to protect the national security.

Statement on the Federal Budget Negotiations
June 26, 1990

I met this morning with the bipartisan leadership—the Speaker, the Senate majority leader, the Senate Republican leader, the House majority leader, and the House Republican leader—to review the status of the deficit reduction negotiations.

It is clear to me that both the size of the deficit problem and the need for a package that can be enacted require all of the following: entitlement and mandatory program reform, tax revenue increases, growth incentives, discretionary spending reductions, orderly reductions in defense expenditures, and budget process reform to assure that any bipartisan agreement is enforceable and that the deficit problem is brought under responsible control. The bipartisan leadership agree with me on these points.

The budget negotiations will resume promptly with a view toward reaching substantive agreement as quickly as possible.

Note: The statement referred to Thomas S. Foley, Speaker of the House of Representatives; George J. Mitchell, Senate majority leader; Robert Dole, Senate Republican leader; Richard A. Gephardt, House majority leader; and Robert H. Michel, House Republican leader.

Message on the Observance of Independence Day
June 26, 1990

Each July 4th, people across the United States pause to celebrate the continued success of our Nation's great experiment in self-government. It is a day marked by joyous gatherings with family and friends, by colorful parades and brilliant displays of fireworks—all the fanfare and festivities that befit a celebration of our freedom.

On this Independence Day, we have added cause for rejoicing: during the past year, in nations that once bore the heavy yoke of totalitarianism, freedom-loving men and women have triumphed over regimes maintained by intimidation and force. The seeds of democratic thought planted on these shores 214 years ago have also taken root around the world.

I am convinced that the people of the United States have inspired many of these changes—by word, deed, and example—particularly during the past 45 years. Recognizing the cause of freedom as universal, we have steadfastly defended human rights around the world, holding true to the belief "that all men are Created equal, that they are endowed by their Creator with certain unalienable rights, that among these are Life, Liberty, and the Pursuit of Happiness."

Indeed, it is our devotion to these timeless ideals that has made the United States a model of freedom and a source of hope to so many. Today, as we raise the flag in celebration, we can take great pride in all that it represents. For millions of people around the globe, Old Glory has bid a warm welcome, marking a place of refuge from tyranny and persecution. For millions of others, it has represented the liberty to which all men are heirs. To us, may it always be the cherished symbol of freedom's first home and most steadfast ally on earth.

All Americans have my best wishes for a safe and happy Independence Day. I offer special greetings and a heartfelt salute to those who will be observing the Fourth in Veterans Hospitals and at military installations far from home. The freedom and peace we enjoy would not be possible without your courage and sacrifice. May God bless you.

GEORGE BUSH

Nomination of Michael Martin Skol To Be United States Ambassador to Venezuela
June 26, 1990

The President today announced his intention to nominate Michael Martin Skol, of Illinois, to be Ambassador Extraordinary and Plenipotentiary of the United States of America to the Republic of Venezuela. He would succeed Otto J. Reich.

Since 1988 Mr. Skol has served as Deputy Assistant Secretary of State for the Bureau of Inter-American Affairs. Prior to this, he served as Director of the Office of Andean Affairs, 1987–1988; Minister-Counselor for the U.S. Embassy in Bogota, Colombia, 1985–1987; Deputy Director of the Bureau of Inter-American Affairs in the Office of Policy Planning and Coordination at the State Department, 1982–1985. In addition, Mr. Skol has served as Political Counselor in San José, Costa Rica, 1978–1982; commer-cial attaché in Rome, 1976–1978; economic/commercial officer in Naples, 1975–1976; and commercial attaché in Santo Domingo, Dominican Republic, 1972–1975. He also served as a desk officer at the State Department Bureau of Inter-American Affairs for Paraguay and Uruguay, 1971–1972, and Costa Rica, 1970–1971; a political officer in Saigon, Vietnam, 1967–1968; and a political officer in Buenos Aires, Argentina, 1966–1967. Mr. Skol entered the Foreign Service in 1965 and became a member of the Senior Foreign Service in 1984.

Mr. Skol graduated from Yale University (B.A., 1964). He was born October 15, 1942, in Chicago, IL. Mr. Skol is married and resides in Washington, DC.

Statement on Outer Continental Shelf Oil and Gas Development
June 26, 1990

I have often stated my belief that development of oil and gas on the outer continental shelf (OCS) should occur in an environmentally sound manner.

I have received the report of the interagency OCS Task Force on Leasing and Development off the coasts of Florida and California and have accepted its recommendation that further steps to protect the environment are needed.

Today I am announcing my support for a moratorium on oil and gas leasing and development in Sale Area 116, Part II, off the coast of Florida; Sale Area 91, off the coast of northern California; Sale Area 119, off the coast of central California; and the vast majority of Sale Area 95, off the coast of southern California, until after the year 2000. The combined effect of these decisions is that the coast of southwest Florida and more than 99 percent of the California coast will be off limits to oil and gas leasing and development until after the year 2000.

Only those areas which are in close proximity to existing oil and gas development in Federal and State waters, comprising less than 1 percent of the tracts off the California coast, *may* be available before then. These areas, concentrated in the Santa Maria Basin and the Santa Barbara Channel, will not be available for leasing in any event until 1996, and then only if the further studies for which I am calling in response to the report of the National Academy of Sciences satisfactorily address concerns related to these tracts.

I am also approving a proposal that would establish a National Marine Sanctuary in California's Monterey Bay and provide for a *permanent* ban on oil and gas development in the sanctuary, and I am asking the Secretary of the Interior to begin a process that may lead to the buyback and cancellation of *existing* leases in Sale Area 116, Part II, off southwest Florida.

In addition, I am directing the Secretary

of the Interior to delay leasing and development in several other areas where questions have been raised about the resource potential and the environmental implications of development. For Sale Area 132, off the coasts of Washington and Oregon, I am accepting the recommendation of the Secretary that further leasing and development activity be deferred until a series of environmental studies are completed, and directing that no such activity take place until after the year 2000. I am also canceling Lease Sale 96, in the Georges Bank area of the North Atlantic, and directing that no leasing and development activity take place in this area until after the year 2000. This will allow time for additional studies to determine the resource potential of the area and address the environmental and scientific concerns which have been raised.

Finally, I am today directing the Secretary to take several steps to improve the OCS program and respond to several of the concerns expressed by the task force. My goal is to create a much more carefully targeted OCS program, one that is responsive to local concerns, to environmental concerns, *and* to the need to develop prudently our nation's domestic energy resources. Although I have today taken these strong steps to protect our environment, I continue to believe that there are significant offshore areas where we can and must go forward with resource development.

While I believe that a leaner OCS program will ultimately be more effective, Americans must recognize that the OCS program is a vital source of fuel for our growing economy. My desire is to achieve a *balance* between the need to provide energy for the American people and the need to protect unique and sensitive coastal and marine environments.

Note: The Office of the Press Secretary issued a fact sheet on the same day which provided the following additional information on outer continental shelf development:

Guiding Principles

The President's decisions were based on the following principles:

(1) *Adequate Information and Analysis.* Adequate scientific and technical information regarding the resource potential of each area considered for leasing and the environmental, social, and economic effects of oil and gas activity must be available and subjected to rigorous scrutiny before decisions are made. No new leasing should take place without such information and analysis.

(2) *Environmental Sensitivity.* Certain areas off our coasts represent unique natural resources. In those areas, even the small risks posed by oil and gas development may be too great. In other areas, where science and experience and new recovery technologies show development may be safe, development will be considered.

(3) *Resource Potential.* Priority for development should be given to those areas with the greatest resource potential. Given the inexact nature of resource estimation, particularly offshore, priority should be given to those areas where earlier development has proven the existence of economically recoverable reserves.

(4) *Energy Requirements.* The requirements of our nation's economy for energy and the overall costs and benefits of various sources of energy must be considered in deciding whether to develop oil and gas offshore. The level of petroleum imports, which has been steadily increasing, is a critical factor in this assessment.

(5) *National Security Requirements.* External events, such as supply disruptions, might require a reevaluation of the OCS program. All decisions regarding OCS development are subject to a national security exemption. If the President determines that national security requires development in the areas of these three lease sales or in other areas, he has the ability to direct the Interior Department to open the areas for development.

General OCS Decisions

The President also decided that:

(1) Air quality controls for oil and gas development offshore California should be substantially the same as those applied onshore.

(2) Immediate steps should be taken to improve the ability of industry and the Fed-

eral Government to respond to oilspills off-shore, regardless of their source.

(3) Federal agencies should develop a plan to reduce the possibility of oilspills off-shore from whatever source, including and especially from tanker traffic. This plan should include moving tanker routes fur-ther away from sensitive areas near the Florida Keys and the Everglades.

Restructuring the OCS Program

The President directed Interior Secretary Lujan to take three actions to improve the overall OCS program:

(1) Improve the information needed to make decisions on OCS development by conducting the studies identified by the Na-tional Academy of Sciences and studies to explore new technologies for alleviating the risks of oilspills from OCS platforms and new oil and gas drilling technologies, such as subsea completion technology.

(2) Target proposed sale areas in future OCS 5-year plans to give highest priority to areas with high resource potential and low environmental risk. This will result in offer-ing much smaller and more carefully select-ed blocks of tracts.

(3) Prepare a legislative initiative that will provide coastal communities directly affect-ed by OCS development with a greater share of the financial benefits of new devel-opment and with a larger voice in decision-making.

Lease Sale 96 in the North Atlantic

The President also directed Interior Sec-retary Lujan to consult with the Governors of the States whose residents would be af-fected by future development of oil and gas in the North Atlantic.

Message to the Congress Reporting Budget Deferrals
June 26, 1990

To the Congress of the United States:

In accordance with the Impoundment Control Act of 1974, I herewith report two revised deferrals of budget authority now totalling $2,547,688,227.

The deferrals affect programs in Interna-tional Security Assistance and the Depart-ment of State. The details of the deferrals are contained in the attached report.

GEORGE BUSH

The White House,
June 26, 1990.

Note: The attachment detailing the pro-posed deferrals was printed in the "Federal Register" of July 11.

Statement by Press Secretary Fitzwater on the President's Meeting With Thorvald Stoltenberg, United Nations High Commissioner for Refugees
June 26, 1990

President Bush met June 26 at the White House with the United Nations High Com-missioner for Refugees, Thorvald Stolten-berg. The President expressed his apprecia-tion and U.S. support for the important worldwide humanitarian work of UNHCR.

President Bush and High Commissioner Stoltenberg discussed the issue of Vietnam-ese boat people and the overall issue of po-tential population movements in the coming years. The President restated the U.S. position in support of first asylum in Southeast Asia and against involuntary repatriation to Vietnam under current conditions there. It was agreed that the United States would continue to be in touch with the High Commissioner on the issue of preserving first asylum in Southeast Asia.

Remarks at a White House Barbecue for Members of Congress
June 26, 1990

The President. Glen, thank you. Thank you all very much. You really turned it on tonight.

Let me just say to everybody how pleased—I think I speak for all of you—we are to have Glen here—40 albums, 4 gold singles, and 4 special awards, one of the great musical talents in our country and a friend to everybody out here. And we are very, very pleased, Glen. Thank you for that marvelous, lively performance.

Mr. Campbell. You are quite welcome, sir. Thank you, everybody.

The President. And all this wonderful band of yours. We're delighted to have you all here. And let me say to the Members of the Congress that Barbara and I are delighted that you came down here—a good, relaxed evening and a beautiful night at the White House. We've got a lot of work ahead, but I think at least as far as we're concerned from this end of Pennsylvania Avenue it's been a joy. We're delighted you were here. Now, make yourselves at home, and thank you once again, Glen Campbell. Thank you so much.

Mr. Campbell. Thank you, Mr. President. Thank you a lot.

Note: The President spoke at 8 p.m. on the South Lawn at the White House.

Nomination of George F. Murphy, Jr., To Be Inspector General of the United States Information Agency
June 27, 1990

The President today announced his intention to nominate George F. Murphy, Jr., to be Inspector General of the U.S. Information Agency. He would succeed Anthony J. Gabriel.

Since 1988 Mr. Murphy has served as Deputy Director for the U.S. Arms Control and Disarmament Agency in Washington, DC. Prior to this, he served as a consultant to the nuclear industry, 1986–1987; director of the Senate National Security Office, 1977–1986; executive director of the Joint Committee on Atomic Energy, 1975–1977; deputy director of the Joint Committee on Atomic Energy, 1968–1975; and a professional staff member on the Joint Committee on Atomic Energy, 1958–1968. In addition, Mr. Murphy worked for the Central Intelligence Agency, 1950–1958.

Mr. Murphy graduated from Harvard College (A.B., 1949). He was born May 1, 1924, in Boston, MA. Mr. Murphy served in the U.S. Army Air Corps, 1942–1946. He is married, has two children, and resides in Bethesda, MD.

Statement on Signing a Bill Protecting Natural and Cultural Resources in New Mexico
June 27, 1990

I take great pleasure in signing into law S. 286, an Act to establish the Petroglyph National Monument and the Pecos National Historical Park in New Mexico, and to resolve various New Mexico land issues.

West of Albuquerque, New Mexico, the major landscape feature is the West Mesa, marked by a 17-mile long basalt escarpment and five volcanic cones. Within the area are an estimated 15,000 to 17,000 petroglyphs, which are designs carved or pecked into the rock. Establishment of the Petroglyph National Monument will provide an excellent opportunity to form a strong partnership among the Federal Government, the State of New Mexico, and the City of Albuquerque to ensure the protection of seriously threatened ancient Pueblo Indian and Spanish rock art. Cost sharing will be an important component of the success of this joint effort, and I look forward to a successful partnership.

S. 286 also will expand the existing 365-acre Pecos National Monument into the 5,865-acre Pecos National Historical Park. This will allow for expanded protection and recreation programs in an area rich in cultural resources.

I wholeheartedly support the measures contained in S. 286 because they will ensure the protection of rich natural and cultural resources within the State of New Mexico that are now seriously threatened.

GEORGE BUSH

The White House,
June 27, 1990.

Note: S. 286, approved June 27, was assigned Public Law No. 101–313.

Remarks Announcing the Enterprise for the Americas Initiative
June 27, 1990

Thank you all very much for coming to the White House, and it is my pleasure to welcome so many distinguished guests with such strong interests in the vital Latin American and Caribbean region. Let me recognize the many members of the diplomatic corps that are here and extend to you a warm welcome—from Latin America, particularly, and the Caribbean, Europe, Japan. Members of our Cabinet—Nick Brady and Secretary Baker, Carla Hills, Secretary Mosbacher—delighted you're here. Chairman of the Council of Economic Advisers, Mike Boskin, is here. Bill Webster, welcome. And of course, we're delighted to see Alan Greenspan, Chairman of the Federal Reserve Board, here and then an old friend, Barber Conable, of the World Bank, and Richard Erb, from the IMF. And Ricky Iglesias, an old friend of the Bushes, and we welcome him, of the IDB, and so many leading lights in the business and financial communities. To all of you, then, a welcome.

In the past 12 months, every one of us, from the man in the White House to the man on the street, has been fascinated by the tremendous changes, the positive changes, taking place around the world. Freedom has made great gains not just in Eastern Europe but right here in the Americas; and we've seen a resurgence of democratic rule, a rising tide of democracy, never before witnessed in the history of this beloved hemisphere. And with one exception, Cuba, the transition to democracy is moving towards completion, and we can all sense the excitement that the day is not far off when Cuba joins the ranks of world democracies and makes the Americas fully free.

With one exception, that's the case. But

873

the political transformation sweeping the rest of Latin America and the Caribbean has its parallel in the economic sphere. Throughout the region, nations are turning away from the statist economic policies that stifle growth and are now looking to the power of the free market to help this hemisphere realize its untapped potential for progress. A new leadership has emerged, backed by the strength of the people's mandate, leadership that understands that the future of Latin America lies with free government and free markets. In the words of Colombia's courageous leader, Virgilio Barco—President Barco: "The long-running match between Karl Marx and Adam Smith is finally coming to an end" with the "recognition that open economies with access to markets can lead to social progress."

For the United States, these are welcome developments, developments that we're eager to support. But we recognize that each nation in the region must make its own choices. There is no blueprint, no one-size-fits-all approach, to reform. The primary responsibility for achieving economic growth lies with each individual country. Our challenge in this country is to respond in ways that support the positive changes now taking place in the hemisphere. We must forge a genuine partnership for free-market reform.

Back in February, I met in Cartagena [Colombia] with heads of the three Andean nations, and I came away from that meeting convinced that the U.S. must review its approach not only to that region but to Latin America and the Caribbean as a whole. And I asked Treasury Secretary Brady to lead a review of U.S. economic policy towards this vital region, to make a fresh assessment, if you will, of the problems and opportunities we'll encounter in the decade ahead. And that review is now complete, and the results are in, and the need for new economic initiatives is clear and compelling.

All signs point to the fact that we must shift the focus of our economic interaction towards a new economic partnership because prosperity in our hemisphere depends on trade, not aid. And I've asked you here today to share with you some of the ideas, some of the ways we can build a broad-based partnership for the nineties—to announce the new Enterprise for the Americas Initiative that creates incentives to reinforce Latin America's growing recognition that free-market reform is the key to sustained growth and political stability.

The three pillars of our new initiative are trade, investment, and debt. To expand trade, I propose that we begin the process of creating a hemispherewide free trade zone; to increase investment, that we adopt measures to create a new flow of capital into the region; and to further ease the burden of debt, a new approach to debt in the region with important benefits for our environment.

Let's begin with trade. In the 1980's, trade within our hemisphere trailed the overall pace of growth in world trade. One principal reason for that: overrestrictive trade barriers that wall off the economies of our region from each other and from the United States at great cost to us all. These barriers are the legacy of the misguided notion that a nation's economy needs protection in order to thrive. The great economic lesson of this century is that protectionism still stifles progress and free markets breed prosperity. To this end, we've formulated a three-point trade plan to encourage the emerging trend toward free-market reform that are now gathering forces in the Americas.

First, as we enter the final months of the current Uruguay round of the world trade talks, I pledge close cooperation with the nations of this hemisphere. The successful completion of the Uruguay round remains the most effective way of promoting long-term trade growth in Latin America and the increased integration of Latin nations into the overall global trading system. Our aim in the Uruguay round is free and fair trade, and through these talks we are seeking to strengthen existing trade rules and to expand them to areas that do not now have agreed rules of fairplay. And to show our commitment to our neighbors in Latin America and the Caribbean, we will seek deeper tariff reductions in this round on products of special interest to them.

Second, we must build on the trend we see toward free markets and make our ultimate aim a free trade system that links all of the Americas: North, Central, and South. And we look forward to the day when not only are the Americas the first fully free, democratic hemisphere but when all are equal partners in a free trade zone stretching from the port of Anchorage to the Tierra del Fuego.

I'm announcing today that the U.S. stands ready to enter into free trade agreements with other markets in Latin America and the Caribbean, particularly with groups of countries that have associated for purposes of trade liberalization. And the first step in this process is the now-announced free trade agreement with Mexico. We must all recognize that we won't bring down barriers to free trade overnight; changes so far-reaching may take years of preparation and tough negotiations. But the payoff in terms of prosperity is worth every effort, and now is the time to make a comprehensive free trade zone for the Americas our long-term goal.

And third, I understand that some countries aren't yet ready to take that dramatic step to a full free trade agreement. And that's why we're prepared to negotiate with any interested nation in the region bilateral framework agreements to open markets and develop closer trade ties. Such agreements already exist with Mexico and Bolivia. Framework agreements will enable us to move forward on a step-by-step basis to eliminate counterproductive barriers to trade and towards our ultimate goal of free trade. And that's a prescription for greater growth and a higher standard of living in Latin America and, right here at home, new markets for American products and more jobs for American workers.

Promoting free trade is just one of three key elements in our new Enterprise for the Americas Initiative. And our second pillar is increased investment.

The competition for capital today is fierce, and the key to increased investment is to be competitive, to turn around the conditions that have discouraged both foreign and domestic investment—reduce the regulatory burden, clear away the thicket of bureaucratic barriers that choke off Latin America's aspiring entrepreneurs.

In one large Latin city, for instance, it takes almost 300 days to cut through the redtape to open a small garment shop. In another country, the average overseas caller has to make five phone calls to get through, and the wait for a new telephone line can be as long as 5 years. And that's got to change.

Investment reform is essential to make it easier to start new business ventures and make it possible for international investors to participate and profit in Latin American markets. In order to create incentives for investment reform, the United States is prepared to take the following steps:

First, the United States will work with the Inter-American Development Bank to create a new lending program for nations that take significant steps to remove impediments to international investment. The World Bank could also contribute to this effort.

And second, we propose the creation of a new investment fund for the Americas. This fund, administered by the IDB, could provide up to $300 million a year in grants in response to market-oriented investment reforms in progress in privatization. The U.S. intends to contribute $100 million to the fund, and we will seek matching contributions from Europe and Japan.

But in order to create an attractive climate for new investment, we must build on our successful efforts to ease the debt burden. That's the third pillar of this new Enterprise for the Americas Initiative.

Many nations have already undertaken painful economic reforms for the sake of future growth, but the investment climate remains clouded, weighted down by the heavy debt burden. Under the Brady plan, we are making significant progress. The agreements reached with Mexico and Costa Rica and Venezuela are already having a positive impact on investment in those countries. Mexico, to take just one example, has already seen a reversal of the destructive capital flight that drained so many Latin American nations of precious investment resources. That's critical. If we restore confidence, capital will follow.

As one means of expanding our debt strategy, we propose that the IDB add its efforts and resources to those of the International Monetary Fund and the World Bank to support commercial bank debt reduction in Latin America and the Caribbean, and as in the case of World Bank and IMF, IDB funds should be directly linked to economic reform.

While the Brady plan has helped nations reduce commercial bank debt, for nations with high levels of official debt—debt owed to governments rather than private financial institutions—the burden remains heavy. And today, across Latin America, official debt owed to the U.S. Government amounts to nearly $12 billion, with $7 billion of that amount in concessional loans. And in many cases, the heaviest official debt burdens fall on some of the region's smallest nations, countries like Honduras and El Salvador and Jamaica.

That's a problem we must address today. As the key component in addressing the region's debt problem, I am proposing a major new initiative to reduce Latin America and the Caribbean's official debt to the United States for countries that adopt strong economic and investment reform programs with the support of international institutions.

Our debt reduction program will deal separately with concessional and commercial types of loans. On the concessional debt, loans made from AID or Food for Peace accounts, we will propose substantial debt reductions for the most heavily burdened countries. And we will also sell a portion of outstanding commercial loans to facilitate these debt-for-equity and debt-for-nature swaps in countries that have set up such programs. These actions will be taken on a case-by-case basis.

One measure of prosperity and the most important long-term investment any nation can make is environmental well-being. As part of our Enterprise for the Americas Initiative, we will take action to strengthen environmental policies in this hemisphere. Debt-for-nature swaps are one example, patterned after the innovative agreements reached by some Latin American nations and their commercial creditors. We will also call for the creation of environmental trusts, where interest payments owed on restructured U.S. debt will be paid in local currency and set aside to fund environmental projects in the debtor countries.

These innovative agreements offer a powerful new tool for preserving the natural wonders of this hemisphere that we share. From the vistas of the unspoiled Arctic to the beauties of the barrier reef off Belize to the rich rain forests of the Amazon, we must protect this living legacy that we hold in trust. For an increasing number of our neighbors, the need for free-market reform is clear. These nations need economic breathing room to enact bold reforms, and this official debt initiative is one answer, a way out from under the crushing burden of debt that slows the process of reform.

I know there is some concern that the revolutionary changes we've witnessed this past year in Eastern Europe will shift our attention away from Latin America; but I want to assure all of you here today, as I've assured many democratic leaders in Central and South America and the Caribbean and Mexico, the United States will not lose sight of the tremendous challenges and opportunities right here in our own hemisphere. And indeed, as we talk with the leaders of the G-24 about the emerging democracies in Europe—I've been talking to them also about their supporting democracy and economic freedom in Central America. Our aim is a closer partnership between the Americas and our friends in Europe and in Asia.

Two years from now, our hemisphere will celebrate the 500th anniversary of an epic event: Columbus' discovery of America, our New World. And we trace our origins, our shared history, to the time of Columbus' voyage and the courageous quest for the advancement of man. Today the bonds of our common heritage are strengthened by the love of freedom and a common commitment to democracy. Our challenge, the challenge in this new era of the Americas, is to secure this shared dream and all its fruits for all the people of the Americas—North, Central, and South.

The comprehensive plan that I've just outlined is proof positive the United States is serious about forging a new partnership with our Latin American and Caribbean neighbors. We're ready to play a constructive role at this critical time to make ours the first fully free hemisphere in all of history. Thank you all for coming, and God bless the peoples of the Americas. Thank you very, very much, indeed.

Note: The President spoke at 2:48 p.m. in the East Room at the White House. In his opening remarks, he referred to William H. Webster, Director of Central Intelligence; *Barber B. Conable, Jr., President of the International Bank for Reconstruction and Development, also known as the World Bank; and Richard D. Erb, Deputy Managing Director of the International Monetary Fund. The President also referred to the Group of 24, the industrialized democracies that pledged support for economic and political reform in Poland and Hungary.*

Message to the Congress Reporting Budget Rescissions
June 28, 1990

To the Congress of the United States:

In accordance with the Impoundment Control Act of 1974, I herewith report eight proposed rescissions totalling $327,375,000.

The proposed rescissions affect programs of the Department of Defense. The details of the proposed rescissions are contained in the attached report.

GEORGE BUSH

The White House,
June 28, 1990.

Note: The attachment detailing the proposed rescissions was printed in the "Federal Register" of July 6.

Statement on the Japan-United States Trade Negotiations
June 28, 1990

Last year the United States and Japan launched a new cooperative endeavor in economic policy called the Structural Impediments Initiative. This initiative is designed to address underlying structural problems in both of our economies with the goal of contributing to more open and competitive markets and to the reduction of payments imbalances. A joint working group was formed to identify and solve these problems. Over the past year, these discussions have demonstrated the constructive and cooperative spirit which characterizes the relationship between our two countries.

The joint report of the SII working group has just been issued in Tokyo, following up an interim report issued in April. I welcome and endorse this joint report. Both countries have identified structural impedi-

ments, taken initial corrective actions, and made commitments to take further steps to resolve a wide range of structural problems. We expect that the structural policy actions to be taken will have a positive effect on our economies, encouraging open and competitive markets, promoting sustained world economic growth, contributing to a reduction in global payments imbalances, and enhancing the quality of life in both Japan and the United States. Although our efforts on SII are bilateral, the effects will be beneficial for the entire world.

I particularly welcome the clear commitment by Japan to reduce further its current account surplus and view the SII process as an important framework in which the underlying causes of trade imbalances can be removed.

Removing structural impediments is a

two-way street. As Japan tackles its structural problems, so must the United States. In particular, I look forward to working closely with the Congress on efforts to strengthen both public and private saving and to reduce our budget deficit through the negotiations now underway.

Both our governments recognize that further effort will be necessary in order to address fully these structural problems and to maintain the momentum of our adjustment efforts. I am pleased that an effective follow-on mechanism has been established. Continuing success on SII can help us move away from trade disputes, thus allowing us to focus our efforts on more positive activities as we continue to develop a global partnership between our two countries.

The personal efforts of Prime Minister Kaifu were responsible in large measure for the substantial progress on our joint effort to address these structural problems. I commend Prime Minister Kaifu for his strong and courageous political leadership. I look forward to a full range of discussions with Prime Minister Kaifu when we meet July 7 in Houston.

Message to the Congress Transmitting the Annual Report of the Federal Council on the Aging
June 28, 1990

To the Congress of the United States:

In accordance with section 204(f) of the Older Americans Act of 1965, as amended (42 U.S.C. 3015(f)), I hereby transmit the Annual Report for 1989 of the Federal Council on the Aging. The report reflects the Council's views in its role of examining programs serving older Americans.

GEORGE BUSH

The White House,
June 28, 1990.

Message to the Senate Transmitting Protocols to Soviet-United States Treaties on Underground Nuclear Testing
June 28, 1990

To the Senate of the United States:

I transmit herewith, for the advice and consent of the Senate to ratification, the Protocol to the Treaty Between the United States of America and the Union of Soviet Socialist Republics on the Limitation of Underground Nuclear Weapon Tests, and the Protocol to the Treaty Between the United States of America and the Union of Soviet Socialist Republics on Underground Nuclear Explosions for Peaceful Purposes (the Protocols). The Protocols were signed at Washington on June 1, 1990. I transmit also, for the information of the Senate, the Report of the Department of State on the Protocols, including section-by-section analyses of the Protocols and letters exchanged by the Heads of Delegation to the Nuclear Testing Talks, which will implement certain aspects of the Protocol to the Treaty on the Limitation of Underground Nuclear Weapon Tests.

The Protocols provide for effective verification of compliance with the Treaty on the Limitation of Underground Nuclear Weapon Tests, signed on July 3, 1974, and the Treaty on Underground Nuclear Explosions for Peaceful Purposes, signed on May 28, 1976 (the Treaties). These Treaties, which limit the yield of nuclear weapon tests and individual nuclear explosions for peaceful purposes to no more than 150 kilotons, were transmitted to the Senate for its advice and consent to ratification on July

29, 1976. The Protocols replace, and should be substituted for, the protocols that were submitted with the Treaties at that time. In addition, the Administration remains committed to the nuclear testing treaty safeguards that were submitted to the Senate in 1987, which are essential to the national security and to the maintenance of a credible nuclear deterrent.

The Protocols represent the successful culmination of several years of effort to provide for effective verification of compliance with the Treaties. Negotiations to develop new Protocols to verify compliance with limits established by the Treaties began in November 1987 and continued until May 1990, when the Protocols were completed. The Protocols provide for a variety of activities related to verification, including the

use of the hydrodynamic yield measurement method. Operational changes in the U.S. nuclear test program, including changes at the Nevada Test Site, which implementation of the verification measures will entail were considered carefully and have been judged manageable and therefore acceptable in the interests of effective verification.

I believe these Treaties are in the national interest. Therefore, I urge the Senate to give early and favorable consideration to the Treaties including their Protocols and to give its advice and consent to their ratification.

GEORGE BUSH

The White House,
June 28, 1990.

Nomination of Robert S. Mueller III To Be an Assistant Attorney General
June 28, 1990

The President today announced his intention to nominate Robert S. Mueller III to be an Assistant Attorney General for the Criminal Division at the Department of Justice. He would succeed Edward S.G. Dennis, Jr.

Since 1988 Mr. Mueller has served as a partner with the law firm of Hill and Barlow in Boston, MA. Prior to this, he served in the Office of the U.S. Attorney, District of Massachusetts, in several capacities: Deputy U.S. Attorney, 1987–1988; U.S. Attorney, 1986–1987; First Assistant U.S. Attorney, 1985–1986; and Chief of the Criminal Division, 1982–1985. In addition, Mr. Mueller served in the Office of the United

States Attorney, Northern District of California, in several capacities: Interim Chief of the Criminal Division, 1981–1982; Chief of Special Prosecutions Unit, 1980–1981; Assistant U.S. Attorney in the Criminal Division, 1978–1980; and Assistant U.S. Attorney in the Civil Division, 1976–1977.

Mr. Mueller graduated from Princeton University (B.A., 1966) and the University of Virginia (J.D., 1973). He served in the U.S. Marine Corps, 1967–1970, and was awarded the Bronze Star, two Navy Commendation Medals, and the Purple Heart. He was born August 7, 1944, in New York, NY. Mr. Mueller is married, has two children, and currently resides in Weston, MA.

The President's News Conference
June 29, 1990

The President. Good morning, everybody. I'm leaving in a few hours and will be gone from Washington for several days. Congress is about to close up shop for the Fourth of July holidays. And so, I thought it would be a good idea to bring you up to date on a wide array of current topics and respond to your questions.

During the next 2 weeks, the U.S. will join its allies in considering a number of crucial political, security, and international economic issues. And seldom in the last 40 years have such questions had such direct impact on the lives of all Americans. Today in the U.S., we are carefully examining the historic changes in Eastern Europe, size of our military forces, our ability to compete in world markets, the assistance that we provide to help emerging democracies, and the size and priorities of our own budget, and how to continue the 90 months of economic expansion that we've enjoyed. These issues are not abstract. Every American has a stake in how we as a nation address these very complex questions. On July 5th and 6th in London, the NATO alliance will gather to forge a new direction for the future. And at the Houston economic summit, we will press for progress in the Uruguay round of trade negotiations, discuss economic support for various countries, and review progress on the environment.

These international concerns are reflected in many of the decisions I made just this week. First, we're doing what is necessary to assure continuation of the economic expansion, now in its 90th month, and we want to keep it going.

We now estimate a deficit of over $150 billion in fiscal 1991, not counting the costs of the savings and loan cleanup. And this means that unless Congress acts there will be a cutoff in October of nearly $100 billion in government services under the sequester provisions of the Gramm-Rudman-Hollings. The potential results: draconian cuts in defense, student grants, and a wide array of other necessary domestic services.

To avoid this, tough decisions must be made. Leadership is needed, and that is exactly what administration officials are seeking to provide and, indeed, in these talks, I believe, are providing. The budget negotiations now underway are a make-or-break effort at responsible government. The congressional budgeting process must succeed. The negotiators are facing tough questions about where to make cuts and where to raise the revenues.

These are not decisions that anyone relishes. They are decisions that Democrats and Republicans alike have got to face with candor and courage. Frankly, I believe that ultimately good politics is rooted in good government. I'm optimistic that we can get a budget agreement legislated which not only tells the world that America puts its fiscal house in order but also will garner the full support of the American people.

Secondly, this week we reached an agreement with the Japanese on a structural impediments initiative that's going to help to open markets and create new opportunities for business and commerce.

Next, we took an important step toward increasing jobs, opportunity, and economic prosperity throughout our own hemisphere—Enterprise for the Americas—an innovative and, I think, visionary plan for increased trade and investment with Latin America and the Caribbean. The response from south of our border has been overwhelmingly positive. This included a new proposal on official debt in the hemisphere which will help our neighbors in Latin America and the Caribbean resume the process of growth.

We developed a plan for protecting our coastal resources, this OCS [outer continental shelf oil and gas development] decision, while also endeavoring to protect energy independence.

As I leave for the Fourth of July holiday and then from there to the NATO summit, and then to the Houston economic summit, I just wanted to assure you that America will squarely face the challenges of leadership that are before us, both domestically and in terms of international affairs.

Tax Revenue Increases

Q. Mr. President, I'd like to ask you about your reversal on no new taxes. Do you consider that a betrayal of your promise? And what do you say to Republicans who complain that you've robbed them of the same campaign issue that helped get you elected?

The President. I think—what I consider it is a necessary step to get stalled budget negotiations moving. I am very encouraged with the approach taken now by Republicans and Democrats in these important discussions that are going on. I'm not going to discuss details—what I'll accept and what I won't accept—but things are moving, and I think that much more important today is getting this deficit down, continuing economic expansion, and employment in this country. So, that's the way I'd respond to it.

Q. Can people trust politicians if they make statements and are willing to break them?

The President. You know, I recall a previous flurry when I was Vice President, and there was some economic plans proposed back in '82 that caused a furor—something like we're hearing now. And the President, in my view, did what was right. And so, I think that we're on the right track. I think that the arrows have been flying—front, back, sideways—but that's what I get paid for. I think we're on the right track now. I think we'll have strong support from both sides of the aisle.

Q. Mr. President, but do you believe it will hurt your credibility?

The President. No, not in the long run.

Q. Why not? People are already questioning——

The President. Because what people are interested in are jobs, economic growth. People know this deficit is bad. People know that we're going to have to take some action. And that's why I think not.

Q. What will you say to American people who said you made a promise, no new taxes, now you've——

The President. I'd say I take a look at a new situation. I see an enormous deficit. I see a savings and loan problem out there that has to be resolved. And like Abraham Lincoln said, I'll think anew. I'm not violat-

ing or getting away from my fundamental conviction on taxes, anything of that nature, not in the least. But what I've said is on the table, and let's see where we go. But we've got a very important national problem, and I think the President owes the people his judgment at the moment he has to address that problem. And that's exactly what I'm trying to do.

Look, I knew I'd catch some flak on this decision—just those two words—but I've got to do what I think is right, and then I'll ask the people for support. But more important than posturing now or even negotiating is the result. Do we continue to provide jobs for the American people, and do we continue to provide economic growth, and do we try to stop saddling the generations on the way up, the young people, with absolutely unacceptable deficits?

Savings and Loan Crisis

Q. What will you do with the savings and loan situation? Is there any way to do a budget with that still coming out of general revenue, or do you have to push the whole issue off to the side?

The President. We can't push it off to the side: We've got to solve the problem. My interest on that one, incidentally, is to protect the depositor, put the people that broke the law in jail. And that is exactly what the policy that we proposed did. We came in here and 18 days after taking office initiated a very important savings and loan policy. And the size of the savings and loan problem is terrible. And we're trying very hard to go after the criminals and to have in place rules and regulations so that this will never happen again and to protect the depositors. Those are the three key elements of what I'm trying to do.

Q. But where do you pay for it? Is it out of the taxes the Government takes in every year from the American taxpayer?

The President. Well, we have to. People are going to have to pay for it. And it goes as a part of all our expenditures I'm talking about. There has got to be a remedy.

Middle East Peace Process

Q. Mr. President, on another subject. Prime Minister Shamir [of Israel] has sent you——

The President. Good, Michael [Michael Gelb, Reuters]. I was hoping we'd get to another one. [*Laughter*]

Q. We can go back and do taxes later. Prime Minister Shamir has sent you what appears to be a pretty tough letter ruling out flatly talks with any Palestinians with any sort of authority. Do you feel the peace process is deadlocked, and are you concerned that the hardliners, the voices of extremism, now have the upper hand throughout the region?

The President. I'm concerned about a deadlock in the peace process. We have received the Shamir letter; came over to me late last night. The analysis process between NSC [National Security Council] and State has just started, so I can't give you or provide the American people with a response to that letter. But, yes, I am very concerned about a high centering of the peace process.

And we've had a plan, and it is a sound plan, and I want to see it go forward. So, we will be analyzing the Shamir response very, very carefully and, hopefully, then go back and say: Find some way; find some material in the response that permit us to get these talks going again. It is essential. The status quo is unacceptable to everybody. But I can't give you right now whether I think the letter is negative or positive or something of that nature.

Q. Well, can you see any way to get this peace process going unless the Israelis show some willingness to talk to Palestinians with some authority?

The President. I think there has got to be discussion with Palestinians, and that has to happen. And we will push and find ways to make it happen if we can. We're halfway across the world, but we are not going to give up on that kind of solution to this problem. We have to do that. But if we get totally stiff-armed on the [Secretary of State] Baker approach, or what was the Shamir plan, Mubarak's [President of Egypt] help on it—he could have his name on it—then we go back to the drawing board because we're not going to sit here and do nothing.

Federal Budget Negotiations

Q. Mr. President, I'm sorry, but I'd like to go back to taxes.

The President. Lesley [Lesley Stahl, CBS News], I thought you'd want to get back to that.

Q. I'm sorry. I know it's hard for you. I can tell it is, and it's difficult.

The President. It's not hard.

Q. Okay, if it's not hard, could you clarify what seems to be a fuzzing up of the issues by some Republicans who are trying to say that your new statement isn't new? Are you telling the American people that this budget outcome is going to be higher taxes?

The President. I'm telling the people that there are negotiations going on right now. There are no preconditions, and everything is on the table. We will see where we come out. And when we get an agreement that is supported by Democrats and Republicans alike—and if I think it's a good agreement—I will then tell the American people clearly why they need to support it—what's at stake for them in terms of jobs, continued growth in this economy.

Q. You're not saying it. You're not saying we have to raise taxes. Why aren't you saying those words?

The President. I'll tell you—sorry I missed your point. We've agreed with the Democratic leaders that we would not discuss the details of what's going on in these discussions, and we're not going to do that. If and when we come up with a program that raises revenues—and our original budget talked about that—and if there are taxes in it, why, then I will go out there and advocate strong bipartisan support for this. But if I get into going into each kind of tax that's discussed or each kind of budget reform or each kind of spending cut, I will be doing something that I have asked our negotiators and the Congress not to do.

Q. Yes, but when you say in your statement tax revenues are required, is that the same as taxes?

The President. And I say budget reforms are required, and I say spending cuts are required. So, let's see where we come out on that.

Q. Is it taxes?

The President. Is what taxes?

Q. What you're saying. Are you saying higher taxes are required?

The President. Lesley, I've told you what I've said, and I can't help you anymore. Nice try.

Q. You said we needed candor.

The President. You've got it. You've got it. You've seen the arrows coming my way, and that's fine. But let people interpret it anyway——

Q. A lot of people——

The President. Well, I want to leave it the way I said I would so the negotiators are free to discuss a wide array of options, including tax increases. Does that help?

Q. No. [*Laughter*]

Tax Revenue Increases

Q. Mr. President, you mentioned a couple of times that you're getting arrows from all directions. One newspaper headline that declared "Read My Lips: I Lied." Is this kind of criticism justified? Is it fair? Do you deserve it?

The President. Well, I expected it, but I think the deserving of it—the proof of the pudding is going to be in the eating and how it comes out. Because I think the American people recognize that the budget is greater than we had predicted and the Democrats had predicted. The economy has been slower. And so, we'll just wait and see how we come out. But, no, I can't say I didn't expect to hear some campaign words played back to me, and it's been fairly intense.

But I'll tell you, I've been more relaxed about it than I thought it would be. I went back into history and took a look at what others have had to go through in this job. So, it hasn't been as tense. You know, we had some congressional candidates over there yesterday—people running. And they don't want to see tax increases. Some of them—I could see them: How are we going to handle this? We don't want to be rude to the President, but we feel strongly. So, one or two of them, a couple of them, spoke up. And I could totally empathize with what they were going through. We didn't have time because it was about a 45-second handshake. But if we had, I'd have said: Now, look, you've got to look at the big picture here. Stay with your position. Advocate what you believe and what you tell your constituents what you'll try to do.

Then just stay a little bit openminded so when we get an agreement—and I hope we will—that is good for the country that you can say, Well, we can accept this. Because we're going to need support from Republicans and Democrats alike, to say nothing of the American people. But I think the people will support it. I think they want to see jobs and economic growth, and that is what is at stake here.

Federal Budget Negotiations

Q. But within hours after you released the statement, some of your staff members—Chief of Staff John Sununu, for one—was up on the Hill trying to assure conservative Republicans that nothing's changed. At this point, whose lips should the American people believe?

The President. I think what he was talking about is that everything is on the table. Nothing's changed. I saw a lot of interpretations of what he said, but I've not seen a statement or anything of that nature. You've got various interpretations from various political factions. You've seen the Democratic study group has put out a mandate of what has to happen to have it just exactly their way. We have people that feel very strongly on our side. And so, this we expected. We expected Members of Congress who have strong convictions on how to approach this problem to weigh in. We expected editorial comment. We expected, as I say, some of the slings and the arrows.

But I just have a comforting feeling after 2 or 3 days now that if I do my job right—and that is to help facilitate the negotiations—and then we can get a bipartisan agreement. And then I can go to the American people and say: Look, we've all had to give or take a little on this. But this agreement is going to be good for future generations. It's going to be good for the economy. It's going to be good for jobs. Then people will say: Look, we support the President.

Tax Revenue Increases

Q. Mr. President, can you walk us through your thinking just a little bit? Was there one particular moment when you realized you were going to have these campaign promises played back at you all day?

The President. The minute I decided that we would go forward on a joint statement, which I felt was necessary to get the budget process moving. But I'd had a preview of coming attractions because when we said no preconditions—maybe that wasn't the exact word—but no preconditions, arrows started flying. And I understand this. I've been in the political wars. But I am also President, and I've got to try now to look at the big picture and the welfare of this country and put it ahead of my own strongly held preferences and everything else. And that's exactly what's happening. The process has started to move forward as a result of that statement with a seriousness that I applaud.

Q. Could you talk a little bit about what led you to feel that you needed to——

The President. Is this a third followup? That's unfair.

Q. No, a second. Second for me.

Q. Lesley got eight followups.

Q. But could you talk more about what led you to believe that that statement was necessary? Was there some moment of epiphany? Was there any particular bit of data that—[*laughter*]——

The President. You mean, did I suddenly get hit with the lightning? No, I suddenly was presented with the fact from Democrats and Republicans and our three able negotiators, in whom I have tremendous confidence, we've got to do something to get the process going for it. But I don't recall any—because I'm not changing my view on taxes. I'm just saying everything's on the table. We may have to do something here. But if I were going to go back and, say, do it my way, we'd figure out a way that would be somewhat less controversial than this approach has been.

Q. Mr. President, if it were so comforting and good for the country, why didn't you do it a year ago?

The President. Because we've got a problem, that of far greater magnitude today, because we've had a much slower economy than anybody predicted. And that has meant revenue shortfalls, and that means bigger budget deficits, and that means more burden for future generations of Americans and unacceptably high interest rates. And so that is why I——

Q. Are you saying the economy is in some kind of trouble now that these problems——

The President. I'm saying the economy is sluggish. And I think a deficit package that is seen to be a real one will have an ameliorating effect on that and, hopefully, will result in lower interest rates and thus have a more vibrant, a more robust economy.

NATO Summit

Q. You talked about the next NATO summit as a milestone. Next Friday, what are we going to see? Are we going to see a totally different NATO? How different will it be?

The President. No, but we're going to see a NATO that makes very clear to the world, one, that it's purely defensive and, two, it has a broadened agenda beside just military—building on article II of the NATO document, the founding document. That's what you'll see. I can't help you with the details because we obviously haven't even met yet.

Q. Will there be any American proposals there at NATO—something entirely new?

The President. I was asked the other day at a meeting with some foreign journalists whether there would be—I don't know that they used the word "bombshells," but big surprises. I don't anticipate that, but let's wait and see what happens when we get there. The NATO goal at this juncture should be to convince President Gorbachev that a reconstituted NATO with Germany as a full member is not a threat to the Soviet Union, but rather provides stability for Europe and thus will guarantee the continuance of the longest peace that Europe has had in its history.

Tax Revenue Increases

Q. Mr. President, you're a great student of the American electorate. Have you concluded that the American public is more willing to consider and accept new taxes to deal with the deficit?

The President. Not particularly. If you say to a guy, do you want to pay more taxes—I haven't found anybody that would say that. But I think if we do our job properly and they understand the magnitude of the problem at hand in terms of this deficit and then we make a proposal that is fair on the revenue side, on the spending side, and then on the reform side so that we don't get in this mess again—and I'm going to restrain myself from putting the blame on Congress—[*laughter*]—because it's hard to constrain spending, so we need some reforms—then I think if they see all three of these things and they see it's fair that people will support this.

Q. Would you, under any circumstances, consider increasing income tax rates?

The President. I've said and told the leaders that I'm not going to go into the details. They are not going into the details of what they will or won't accept. And the only way to accomplish a negotiation is to keep faith with that approach. And they are doing that, Republicans as well as Democrats, so I'm not going to go into the details.

Q. Income taxes are on the table, too?

The President. I'm not saying what's on or off. I've made my statements on that, and I'm just going to go forward. I've got preferences, strongly held preferences that people are familiar with, but I'm not going to reiterate them because more important than my posturing or protecting from arrows coming from one direction is getting a deal that's fair and good for the American people.

Yes, Maureen [Maureen Dowd, New York Times]. Then we'll go to the back. The middle—sorry.

Q. Mr. President, I wonder if you can try to explain today why you made the no-new-taxes promise in the first place? At the time, the deficit was absolutely horrendous, the savings and loan situation was absolutely horrendous, and most people greeted your promise with a fair amount of cynicism, saying taxes were eventually going to be needed to bring down the deficit. Can you sort of blame people for now looking back——

The President. No, I don't want to blame anybody.

Q. No, I'm just saying can you blame people for looking back and saying, Well, maybe he didn't really mean it the whole time?

The President. I can understand people saying that. I think it's wrong, but I can understand it. I'm presented with new facts. I'm doing like Lincoln did: think anew. And I'm thinking anew. I've still got the principles that underline my political philosophy. It hasn't changed my view about whether—you know, taxes. But we've got a major problem facing this country. I have the responsibility, leading the executive branch, to get things moving, to get a solution.

The budget deficit is bigger, far bigger. I had thought I could do a better job on getting spending down and perhaps getting the reforms of the budget process that I also talked about. So, we're not talking about just in the campaign talking about one aspect. I was talking about reform, I was talking about spending constraints and not having everything go exactly my way. Now we've got to address ourselves to a worse problem, Maureen, than any of us visualized back then.

Federal Budget Negotiations

Q. Mr. President, throughout the '88 campaign, you kept saying—and this was a quote—"The surest way to kill economic growth in this country is to raise taxes." Now you're telling us that the reason you're thinking anew about raising taxes is to make sure that you sustain economic growth. And yet you also told us that you're not changing your views about taxes. Exactly what are your views about taxes?

The President. Wait until you see the agreement that comes out. That will be my view as what has to happen, hopefully, within a month of 1990. That will be my views, faced with a problem very different than the problem facing the Presidency in the end of 1988.

Taxes and Economic Growth

Q. Well, can you just say—do you believe that taxes kill economic growth, or do you believe that higher taxes——

The President. I think taxes wrongly applied can kill economic growth. And, yes, I do think that. So, I think we've got to be very careful as to how we get this formula to see that we don't kill off economic growth. You've got to look at the overall gross national product when you talk about that, too.

Q. Why didn't you say that during the campaign, Mr. President?

The President. Well, I don't think anybody did such a good, penetrating job of questioning, and because the problem is different. The problem is quite different, Owen [Owen Ullmann, Knight-Ridder Newspapers], today than it was then.

Tom [Tom DeFrank, Newsweek] and John [John Mashek, Boston Globe]. Patience is what it is.

Federal Budget Negotiations

Q. Some Members of Congress and some members of your own staff are saying that your three able negotiators, as you just described them, have signaled one important possible deal. And that is, if the Democrats will give you your capital gains tax cut, you're prepared to go along with eliminating the bubble on the high end of the tax rates scale.

The President. We're going to leave all——

Q. Is that a fair——

The President. No, it's not a fair—I'm not sure your dope is correct, either. But I just don't want to violate this concept of confidentiality while we're in the negotiating stage, and so I can't respond to it. But I wouldn't put too much trust in that one.

Tax Revenue Increases

Q. Mr. President, if your statement here this morning represents your latest thinking, why is it that a whole flock of conservative Republicans have already disavowed your position, considering it a tacit request that taxes will be increased?

The President. For the same reason that that same response occurred in 1982, John. We have people who feel very strongly on this question, and I'm one of them. But I've got to make the case for the broader addressing, ourselves, of this problem here. But I can understand that.

Q. It doesn't give you any pause that this fall you're going to be out campaigning for Republican candidates who disagree with you on taxes——

The President. No.

Q. ——as well as abortion and perhaps other issues?

The President. No. We've always had differences with me on all those issues, one way or another, one side or another. But we also have a matrix of a party that is opposed to tax and spend, who wants to constrain spending and who wants reform. I still feel a fundamental part of that, even though we're talking now about an agreement that will hopefully cover all three aspects of that. If it doesn't, there won't be an agreement, I guess.

Q. Mr. Secretary—[laughter]—Mr. President.

The President. Do you have a message for me? [Laughter] This is going to work out. This is going to work out, don't worry about it. [Laughter]

Economic Assistance for the Soviet Union

Q. Yesterday, the Secretary of State, Mr. Baker, seemed to duck a question that encompassed two of your dilemmas. One is the specter of taxes, but the other is the pressure from the allies, which you'll see in NATO and then again at Houston, to help the Soviet Union, to give them actually more than technical aid. Have you changed your thinking? Are you moving toward some sort of agreement with the allies?

The President. We have some differences in the alliance on this question. Are you talking about just strictly the aid to the Soviet Union? I've tried to be very frank and up-front not only with the allies but with the Soviets on the difficulties we have at this juncture, because there has got to be economic reform there, market reform, and all kinds of changes that I believe Gorbachev wants to see take place. But they have to be in place for the United States to go forward. Then we have a political agenda that we've tried to be very frank about. Secretary Baker has presented it in considerable detail to Mr. Shevardnadze [Soviet Foreign Minister], and I had a chance to touch on it with President Gorbachev.

You see, it is hard for the American people to say: Why put x billions of dollars of money into the Soviet economy when it's not reformed, when they're spending 18 percent of their gross national product on military, and when they're spending an estimated $5 billion in Cuba? Some of our allies might not be as concerned about that last point as we are. I'm very concerned about it.

So, we want to try to be of assistance in reform. We can do a lot in terms of helping institutionally. The EBRD [European Bank for Reconstruction and Development], in which we are a participant, now has in place some facility for future lending. But I don't want to misrepresent this to our allies nor to the Soviets. And that's why I say we've got difficulties with this that perhaps transcend the difficulties that others have.

Q. And you will not oppose the allies giving direct aid, though?

The President. I want to talk to them about it, but I don't think we should tell Mr. Kohl [Chancellor of the Federal Republic of Germany] what his lending policy or finance policy should be. It's understandable. He's a neighbor. They've got quite different problems with the Soviet Union than we do. But normally, it's best to have the alliance act in concert. And I expect we'll be talking about this not only at Houston but perhaps at the summit at NATO.

Q. Mr. President, do you believe that we reporters are being somewhat naive when we suggest in our stories that——

The President. Yes, because I didn't recognize you. I recognized him. [*Laughter*] I'll come back to it, Frank [Frank Murray, Washington Times].

Tax Revenue Increases

Q. A senior economic adviser in the last administration was fond of telling us that economic expansions don't die, bad policies kill them. Now that you're admitting that the economy is growing sluggish enough that tax revenue increases are needed, what policies went wrong? Why do we need this budget agreement so badly now?

The President. In theory I'm not sure I disagree with that. In practice, provided everything is kept in proper perspective in terms of the total GNP, revenue increase would not kill off economic growth. You've got to see what the size of it is, what form it takes, whether it's accompanied by incentives for growth—something I'm very much interested in. So, you can't look at one piece of the package at this point, as we're talking about solving a major deficit prob-

lem. And you also have to consider the total size of the deficit as it relate to our economy.

Q. Well, sir, what I was asking is what went wrong? Why is it necessary now? Is this——

The President. Yes. I think we got slower economic growth than had been anticipated and, thus, fewer revenues, thus, a bigger deficit. We have a law requiring us to get the deficit down to certain levels, and so you've got a combination: the discipline that the Gramm-Rudman-Hollings causes and economic growth not being as robust as we predicted. And that is why we've got to do something right now.

Frank, yes.

Q. Mr. President, in your research of what's happened to others, have you concluded that we're naive to suggest that the public takes campaign promises seriously?

The President. No. I think people are smarter than a lot of us think they are, including me, and I think they're fair. And I go back to the experiences of previous people that have been in this office who say one thing in a campaign; come in and keep that pledge, if you're talking about taxes, for quite a while; and then see that there's an enormous problem facing the Nation that requires a bipartisan answer. And if I had control of this Congress, both Houses, we might not even be talking about this today. But there's a different feeling here, and I've got to see the country go forward. And I've got to take the heat that comes from certain quarters, political and other, and I'm prepared to do that because I think I'm on the right track and I think in the final analysis the American people will understand that.

Q. And you think the public understands this and takes this into account when they hear campaign pledges?

The President. Well, I've seen polling figures that indicate that. But I don't want to suggest that all politicians are cynical. Certainly when I was making comments of that nature, I was convinced that I could stay the course, and we did for a long time, and we may now, but let's see where we go on this negotiation. Because more important than how people look at what I've said is

887

what happens to the economy, what happens to jobs, what happens to economic growth.

So, when you make a change that people see as a dramatic shift, you've got to batten down the hatches and take the heat. But I really am not trying to misrepresent my position. I feel comfortable about that because I've gone back and done a little research and seen these firestorms come and go—people who feel just as strongly on one side or another of an issue as I do and haven't gotten their way exactly. That's the American system, and I've got to work with it. Congress can—they can go out, everybody up there can go out and take a position, but it's only the President that has the responsibility for the whole executive branch approach to it.

Couple more and then I'm going.

Q. Mr. President, how do you explain to the country why you're treating this as essentially a Washington insider's game right now? Why not explain to the public what your list of priorities are within the spending and tax issues? Are there no longer any lines to be drawn in the sand based on your convictions on these areas?

The President. Yes, and they will be drawn in the negotiations. And then I'm going to do exactly what you're talking about. I'm going to tell the American people why this bipartisan agreement, which I'm still hopeful we'll get, is essential to the national interest.

Q. The Republicans have gotten a lot of mileage in the last several elections out of what the Democrats think has been shameless demagoguery on the tax issue. By assuming that you get this bipartisan agreement, haven't you basically undercut that argument for your party? Hasn't your party now lost that issue?

The President. Some will say so, but not if I go out and do my part and if I remind them of history. Take a look at the reaction in 1982, and it didn't have that kind of an adverse effect.

Sarah [Sarah McClendon, McClendon News Service]? Sarah, you thought I'd never——

U.S. Support of NATO Allies

Q. Here's a way, sir, I think you can solve your problems. [*Laughter*] You're going to NATO, and you're going to try to reform it. Research shows that you could save a $150 billion to $160 billion by cutting out the support that we give to other foreign countries by paying for their defense of Europe. Now, why, in the name of God, don't you cut down the spending that you're putting on NATO when we're really paying this for other countries that are going to the summit with you?

The President. Because I believe that a strong NATO is in the national security interest of the United States. I think it is in our interest that Europe has kept the peace for 40-some years, that it is going more and more the democratic route. And we have a stake in it. Every taxpayer in the United States has a stake in world peace. And that's why I feel as I do about it.

Last one.

Neil Bush

Q. Mr. President, going back to the S&L scandal, your son Neil has been involved in one of those failed S&L's in Colorado. And I'm wondering if you've discussed this issue with him. Are you convinced that he is not guilty of any wrongdoing? And are you convinced, also, that a government that you head will be able to fairly investigate his role?

The President. Yes, to your last question. And I have—what dad wouldn't—full confidence in the integrity and honor of my son. And I will stay out of anything to do with the investigation, but this is a fine young man. Everyone that knows him and saw him testify feels he's a fine young man. But yet the system's got to go forward, and I'm convinced that if he has done something wrong the system will so state. And if he hasn't, I hope it's fair enough to say: Hey, the boy did nothing wrong.

Q. Have you discussed this issue with him?

The President. Only in that broad parental way. But making clear—and he would be the last to ask me, in any way, to get involved in any side or the other. I do think that those that allege misconduct ought to speak up and say what it is. But it's not been easy for him. He's probably the most sensitive of our four boys, maybe second most sensitive—I can't quantify this for you with all four of them—but he's a good kid. And it's not easy. He's held his head up. He, too, has taken a few shots on this. But he's had some good defenders from both sides of the aisle. And the system is going to work, whether it's the President's son or somebody else. And to suggest that it doesn't undermines the basic integrity of the American process, the American system. But it's not easy for him, but he'll do okay.

Mayor Marion Barry of the District of Columbia

Q. Mr. President, have you seen the Marion Barry tape, and what's your reaction?

The President. I thought I'd get asked that, and I am simply not going to get into that matter. It is not appropriate. It's a matter for in the courts. Please forgive me for not commenting on that one.

Thank you all very much.

Note: The President's 52d news conference began at 9:32 a.m. in the Briefing Room at the White House.

Letter to Congressional Leaders on the Designation of Bahrain as a Beneficiary Developing Country
June 29, 1990

Dear Mr. Speaker: (Dear Mr. President:)

I am writing to inform you of my intent to add Bahrain to the list of beneficiary developing countries under the Generalized System of Preferences (GSP). The GSP program is authorized by the Trade Act of 1974, as amended ("the 1974 Act").

Bahrain was a GSP beneficiary from the inception of the program in 1976 to July 1, 1988. Proclamation No. 5805 of April 29, 1988, terminated Bahrain as a designated beneficiary developing country under the GSP pursuant to section 504(f) of the 1974 Act. Section 504(f) provides that if the President determines that the per capita gross national product (calculated on the basis of the best available information, including that of the World Bank) for any beneficiary country for a calendar year subsequent to 1984 exceeds the applicable limit for the determination year in question, such country shall not be treated as a beneficiary developing country under this Act after the close of a 2-year period. Based on the best available information, it was determined that Bahrain's per capita gross national product for the calendar year 1985 had exceeded the applicable limit provided in section 504(f).

The World Bank has now revised its per capita GNP statistics for Bahrain, indicating that Bahrain did not exceed the GSP statutory limit for 1985 or succeeding years. On the basis of these revised statistics, I have determined that the previous determination in Proclamation No. 5805 that the per capita gross national product of Bahrain for calendar year 1985 exceeded the applicable limit under section 504(f) of the 1974 Act was erroneous, and the restrictions of section 504(f)(1) of the 1974 Act are therefore inapplicable to Bahrain. I have further determined, pursuant to sections 502(a) and (c) of the 1974 Act and having due regard for the eligibility criteria set forth therein, that it is appropriate to designate Bahrain as a beneficiary developing country for purposes of the GSP.

This notice is submitted in accordance with section 502(a)(1) of the Trade Act of 1974, as amended.

Sincerely,

GEORGE BUSH

Note: Identical letters were sent to Thomas S. Foley, Speaker of the House of Representatives, and Dan Quayle, President of the Senate.

Statement on the Copenhagen Declaration of the Conference on Security and Cooperation in Europe
June 29, 1990

Last May, in a commencement address at the University of South Carolina, I identified free elections, political pluralism, and the rule of law as the cornerstones of freedom and urged that they be enshrined among the principles of the 35-nation Conference on Security and Cooperation in Europe (CSCE). I am pleased to report that this morning, the 35 nations of the CSCE Conference in Copenhagen adopted a document laying precisely that foundation for freedom. I commend the U.S. delegation, under the direction of Ambassador Max M. Kampelman, for its major role in that historic achievement.

With the Copenhagen Declaration, the CSCE has sought and reached an historic new consensus. The nations of Europe—along with the United States, Canada, and the Soviet Union—have now committed themselves to the path of democracy based on justice, peace, security, and cooperation. The promise of the 1975 Helsinki accords now has become a program of democratic action. This is the most significant step forward that the CSCE has taken since the inception of the Helsinki process.

This program of action has been shaped and embraced by our NATO allies, the neutral and nonaligned European States, the Soviet Union, and the emerging democracies of Central and Eastern Europe. It brings together nations, large and small, and opens the house of democracy—the commonwealth of free nations I have spoken about—to all of Europe's peoples. Together, the CSCE signatory nations now stand before their own peoples and before the world community on the solid ground of shared democratic values. Together, we now must put our program of democratic action to work fulfilling the promise of a Europe whole and free.

Message to the House of Representatives Returning Without Approval the Family and Medical Leave Act of 1990
June 29, 1990

To the House of Representatives:

I am returning herewith without my approval H.R. 770, the "Family and Medical Leave Act of 1990." This bill would mandate that public and private employers with 50 or more employees, and the Federal Government, provide their employees with leave under specified circumstances.

In vetoing this legislation with its rigid, federally imposed requirements, I want to emphasize my belief that time off for a child's birth or adoption or for family illness is an important benefit for employers to offer employees. I strongly object, however, to the Federal Government mandating leave policies for America's employers and work force. H.R. 770 would do just that.

America faces its stiffest economic competition in history. If our Nation's employers are to succeed in an increasingly complex and competitive global marketplace, they must have the flexibility to meet both this challenge and the needs of their employees. We must ensure that Federal policies do not stifle the creation of new jobs, nor result in the elimination of existing jobs. The Administration is committed to policies that create jobs throughout the economy—serving the most fundamental need of working families.

The strong American labor market of the past decade is a sign of how effectively our current labor policies work. Between 1980 and 1989, the United States created more than 18 million new jobs. In contrast, within European countries, where mandated benefits are more extensive and labor markets less flexible, job growth has been weak. Between 1980 and 1989, all of Europe generated only 5 million new jobs. As a Nation, we must continue the policies that have been so effective in fostering the creation of jobs throughout our economy. H.R. 770 is fundamentally at odds with this crucial objective.

H.R. 770 ignores the realities of today's work place and the diverse needs of workers. Some employees may believe that shorter paid leave is more important than the lengthy, unpaid leave mandated by this legislation. Caring for a sick friend, aunt, or brother might be just as critical to one employee as caring for a child is to another. In other cases, some employees may prefer increased health insurance or pension coverage rather than unpaid family and medical leave.

Choosing among these options traditionally has been within the purview of employer-employee negotiation or the collective bargaining process. By substituting a "one size fits all" Government mandate for innovative individual agreements, this bill ignores the differing family needs and prefer-

ences of employees and unduly limits the role of labor-management negotiations.

We must also recognize that mandated benefits may limit the ability of some employers to provide other benefits of importance to their employees. Over the past few years, we have seen a dramatic increase in the number of employers who are offering child care assistance, pregnancy leave, parental leave, flexible scheduling, and cafeteria benefits. The number of innovative benefit plans will continue to grow as employers endeavor to attract and keep skilled workers. Mandated benefits raise the risk of stifling the development of such innovative benefit plans.

My Administration is strongly committed to policies that recognize that the relationship between work and family must be complementary, and not one that involves conflict. If these policies are to meet the diverse needs of our Nation, they must be carefully, flexibly, and sensitively crafted at the work place by employers and employees, and not through Government mandates imposed by legislation such as H.R. 770.

GEORGE BUSH

The White House,
June 29, 1990.

Statement on Signing a Bill Calling Upon the United Nations to Repeal General Assembly Resolution 3379
June 29, 1990

I have today signed S.J. Res. 246, a joint resolution of Congress "calling upon the United Nations to repeal General Assembly Resolution 3379," which declared Zionism to be "a form of racism and racial discrimination." S.J. Res. 246 requests the President to report periodically to the Congress on progress made to repeal the resolution.

The United States vigorously opposed the 1975 adoption of the pernicious proposition, in United Nations General Assembly (UNGA) Resolution 3379, that Zionism is a form of racism. We continue to work actively for its renunciation. It is long overdue that all of the member states of the United

Nations join us in renouncing UNGA Resolution 3379.

For these reasons, I wholly agree with the sentiments underlying this congressional repudiation of a totally counterproductive UNGA resolution. By signing S.J. Res. 246, I add my full endorsement as President of the United States, and the person charged by the Constitution with maintaining the foreign relations of this Nation, to this otherwise nonbinding expression of congressional sentiment.

At this time, I also want to reaffirm U.S. determination to pursue efforts toward a comprehensive, just, and lasting Middle

East peace. In our view, this peace must be achieved on the basis of United Nations Security Council Resolutions 242 and 338 and the principle of territory for peace. It must provide for Israel's security and recognition and for Palestinian political rights. We strongly hope that Israelis, Palestinians, and the Arab states will take the necessary steps to create an environment in which a viable peace process can thrive.

GEORGE BUSH

The White House,
June 29, 1990.

Note: S.J. Res. 246, approved June 29, was assigned Public Law No. 101–317.

Appendix A—Digest of Other White House Announcements

The following list includes the President's public schedule and other items of general interest announced by the Office of the Press Secretary and not included elsewhere in this book.

January 1

In the morning, the President and Mrs. Bush left Houston, TX, and traveled to Montgomery, AL, where they visited the home of Ray and Susan Scott. In the evening, they returned to Washington, DC.

January 2

The President met at the White House with:
—the Vice President; John H. Sununu, Chief of Staff to the President; Brent Scowcroft, Assistant to the President for National Security Affairs; and members of the CIA briefing staff;
—John H. Sununu, Chief of Staff to the President.

In the morning, the President and Mrs. Bush traveled to Lincoln, MA, to attend funeral services for Alexander Ellis II, the President's brother-in-law. In the afternoon, the President and Mrs. Bush returned to Washington, DC.

January 3

The President met at the White House with:
—the Vice President; John H. Sununu, Chief of Staff to the President; Brent Scowcroft, Assistant to the President for National Security Affairs; and members of the CIA briefing staff;
—Secretary of State James A. Baker III;
—John H. Sununu, Chief of Staff to the President.

In the evening, the President telephoned Gen. Maxwell Thurman, commander of SOUTHCOM, to discuss the situation in Panama.

January 4

The President met at the White House with:
—the Vice President; John H. Sununu, Chief of Staff to the President; Brent Scowcroft, Assistant to the President for National Security Affairs; and members of the CIA briefing staff;
—the Vice President, for lunch;
—Secretary of Defense Richard B. Cheney;
—John H. Sununu, Chief of Staff to the President.

In the morning, the President spoke by telephone with Pope John Paul II about the situation in Panama.

January 5

The President met at the White House with:
—the Vice President; John H. Sununu, Chief of Staff to the President; Brent Scowcroft, Assistant to the President for National Security Affairs; and members of the CIA briefing staff;
—Attorney General Richard L. Thornburgh;
—Secretary of State James A. Baker III;
—John H. Sununu, Chief of Staff to the President.

January 6

In the evening, the President and Mrs. Bush attended a performance of "A Tuna Christmas" at the John F. Kennedy Center for the Performing Arts.

January 8

The President met at the White House with:
—the Vice President; John H. Sununu, Chief of Staff to the President; Brent Scowcroft, Assistant to the President for National Security Affairs; and members of the CIA briefing staff;
—John H. Sununu, Chief of Staff to the President.

In the morning, the President met with Katherine Donihi in Orlando, FL, to thank her for her volunteer activities.

January 9

The President met at the White House with:
—the Vice President; John H. Sununu, Chief of Staff to the President; Brent Scowcroft, Assistant to the President for National Security Affairs; and members of the CIA briefing staff;
—the Vice President, for lunch;
—Secretary of the Treasury Nicholas F. Brady;
—Ilona Hardy, head of the Hungarian Stock Exchange;
—John H. Sununu, Chief of Staff to the President.

January 10

The President met at the White House with:

—the Vice President; John H. Sununu, Chief of Staff to the President; Brent Scowcroft, Assistant to the President for National Security Affairs; and members of the CIA briefing staff;

—editors of Business Week magazine, for an interview;

—Secretary of State James A. Baker III;

—John H. Sununu, Chief of Staff to the President.

In the morning, the President telephoned Violeta Chamorro, Nicaraguan Presidential candidate and editor of La Prensa, who was undergoing medical treatment in Houston, TX.

The President declared that a major disaster existed in farming communities of the Rio Grande Valley in Texas as a result of the severe winter freeze that began on December 21. He directed the Federal Emergency Management Agency to provide assistance to supplement State and local recovery efforts.

January 11

The President met at the White House with:

—the Vice President; John H. Sununu, Chief of Staff to the President; Brent Scowcroft, Assistant to the President for National Security Affairs; and members of the CIA briefing staff;

—Secretary of Education Lauro F. Cavazos;

—the Education Policy Advisory Committee;

—John H. Sununu, Chief of Staff to the President.

January 12

The President met at the White House with:

—the Vice President; John H. Sununu, Chief of Staff to the President; Brent Scowcroft, Assistant to the President for National Security Affairs; and members of the CIA briefing staff;

—Foreign Minister Gerard Collins of Ireland;

—Asian-American Republicans.

In the morning, the President traveled to Cincinnati, OH.

January 15

In the afternoon, the President returned to the White House from a weekend stay at Camp David, MD.

The President declared that a major disaster existed in farming communities in Florida as a result of the severe winter freeze that began on December 23. He directed the Federal Emergency Management Agency to provide assistance to supplement State and local recovery efforts.

January 16

The President met at the White House with:

—the Vice President; John H. Sununu, Chief of Staff to the President; Brent Scowcroft, Assistant to the President for National Security Affairs; and members of the CIA briefing staff;

—the Vice President, for lunch;

—John H. Sununu, Chief of Staff to the President.

In the afternoon, the President visited the home of Thomas and Corena Jones, public housing tenants in Alexandria, VA, to discuss antidrug efforts in the neighborhood. The President was accompanied by Secretary of Housing and Urban Development Jack Kemp; William Cleveland, Alexandria city councilman; and Ramona Younger, leader of the Alexandria Public Housing Residents Council. He then went to the Charles Houston Community Center, where he met with Alexandria residents and activists involved in antidrug and tenant ownership efforts. Following the meeting, he returned to the White House.

January 17

The President met at the White House with:

—the Vice President; John H. Sununu, Chief of Staff to the President; Brent Scowcroft, Assistant to the President for National Security Affairs; and members of the CIA briefing staff;

—Secretary of State James A. Baker III;

—John H. Sununu, Chief of Staff to the President.

The White House announced that Robert M. Gates, Assistant to the President and Deputy for National Security Affairs, will meet with President Corazon C. Aquino and Secretary of National Defense Fidel Ramos in Manila to convey President Bush's continuing strong commitment to democracy in the Philippines and to discuss the security situation and the Government's economic and military programs.

January 18

The President met at the White House with:

—the Vice President; John H. Sununu, Chief of Staff to the President; Brent Scowcroft, Assistant to the President for National Security Affairs; and members of the CIA briefing staff;

—Glenn "Bo" Schembechler, coach of the University of Michigan football team.

The President declared that a major disaster existed in Lewis County, WA, as a result of severe storms and flooding that began on January 6. He directed the Federal Emergency Management Agency to provide assistance to supplement State and local recovery efforts.

January 19
The President met at the White House with the Vice President; John H. Sununu, Chief of Staff to the President; Brent Scowcroft, Assistant to the President for National Security Affairs; and members of the CIA briefing staff.

In the morning, the President traveled to Atlanta, GA, where he addressed the National Association of Home Builders. In the afternoon, he traveled to Florida, where he toured Everglades National Park.

January 21
In the afternoon, the President returned to the White House from a weekend stay at Camp David, MD.

January 22
The President met at the White House with:
—the Vice President; John H. Sununu, Chief of Staff to the President; Brent Scowcroft, Assistant to the President for National Security Affairs; and members of the CIA briefing staff;
—Benjamin Hooks, executive director of the National Association for the Advancement of Colored People;
—Secretary of Defense Richard B. Cheney;
—John H. Sununu, Chief of Staff to the President.

The White House announced that the President recess-appointed the following individuals to be members of the Board of Directors of the Legal Services Corporation:

For a term expiring July 13, 1990:

Howard H. Dana, Jr., of Maine. He would succeed Thomas F. Smegal, Jr. Currently Mr. Dana serves as a partner with the law firm of Verrill and Dana in Portland, ME.

Luis Guinot, Jr., of Puerto Rico. He would succeed Michael B. Wallace. Currently Mr. Guinot serves as an attorney with the law firm of Kelley, Drye and Warren in Washington, DC.

Penny L. Pullen, of Illinois. She would succeed William Clark Durant. Currently Ms. Pullen serves as State representative and house minority leader for the 55th district in Illinois.

Xavier L. Suarez, of Florida. He would succeed Basile Joseph Uddo. Currently Mr. Suarez serves as the mayor of Miami and as a partner with the law firm of Tew, Jordan and Schulte in Miami.

George W. Wittgraf, of Iowa. He would succeed Paul B. Eaglin. Currently Mr. Wittgraf serves as a partner with the law firm of Sayre and Wittgraf in Cherokee, IA.

For a term expiring July 13, 1992:

John F. Collins, of Massachusetts. He would succeed Robert A. Valois. Currently Mr. Collins is self-employed.

Jo Betts Love, of Mississippi. Ms. Love would succeed Lorain Miller.

Guy Vincent Molinari, of New York. He would succeed Claude Galbreath Swafford. Currently former Congressman Molinari serves as borough president of Staten Island.

Jeanine E. Wolbeck, of Minnesota. She would succeed Hortencia Benavidez.

January 23
The President met at the White House with the Vice President; John H. Sununu, Chief of Staff to the President; Brent Scowcroft, Assistant to the President for National Security Affairs; and members of the CIA briefing staff.

January 24
The President met at the White House with:
—John H. Sununu, Chief of Staff to the President; Brent Scowcroft, Assistant to the President for National Security Affairs; and members of the CIA briefing staff;
—the Vice President and Senate Republican leaders, for breakfast;
—Secretary of State James A. Baker III;
—John H. Sununu, Chief of Staff to the President.

The President announced his intention to nominate the following individuals to be members of the National Commission on Libraries and Information Science. These are reappointments.

For a term expiring July 19, 1994:

Daniel W. Casey, of New York. Mr. Casey served a 5-year term on the National Commission on Libraries and Information Science.

Elinor H. Swaim, of North Carolina. For 4 years, Ms. Swaim has served as chairman of the North Carolina Library Commission.

For the remainder of the term expiring July 19, 1993:

Wanda L. Forbes, of South Carolina. Since 1984 Ms. Forbes has served as a member of the National Commission on Libraries and Information Science.

Charles E. Reid, of New Jersey. Mr. Reid currently serves as senior vice president of the Weingarten Group in Iselin, NJ.

The President declared that a major disaster existed in the western coastal area of Oregon as a result of severe storms and flooding that began on January 6. He directed the Federal Emergency Management Agency to provide assistance to supplement State and local recovery efforts.

January 25
The President met at the White House with:
—the Vice President; John H. Sununu, Chief of Staff to the President; Brent Scowcroft, Assistant to the President for National Security Affairs; and members of the CIA briefing staff;
—Secretary of the Treasury Nicholas F. Brady;

—John H. Sununu, Chief of Staff to the President.

In the afternoon, the President presented the Presidential Commendation to the National Football League Charities and former commissioner of the National Football League Pete Rozelle in the Diplomatic Reception Room.

The President announced his intention to appoint the following individuals to be members of the Committee for the Preservation of the White House:

Wendy A. Cooper, of Maryland. She would succeed Mrs. John F. Kennedy. Currently she serves as curator of decorative arts for the Baltimore Museum of Art in Baltimore, MD.

Mrs. Dorothy M. Craig, of Texas. She would succeed Mrs. Hugo Neuhaus, Jr.

Mrs. Charles W. Engelhard, of New Jersey. This is a reappointment.

Jonathan Leo Fairbanks, of Massachusetts. He would succeed Mrs. Ogden Phipps. Currently Mr. Fairbanks serves as the Katharine Lane Weems curator of American decorative arts and sculptor at the Museum of Fine Arts in Boston, MA.

Mark Hampton, of New York. He would succeed Mrs. Clare Boothe Luce. Currently Mr. Hampton is an interior designer for Mark Hampton, Inc., in New York, NY.

William Kloss, of the District of Columbia. He would succeed Wiley T. Buchanan, Jr. Currently Mr. Kloss is a self-employed art historian, writer, curator, lecturer, and consultant.

Richard C. Nylander, of New Hampshire. He would succeed Gertrude Adams Mellon. Currently Mr. Nylander serves as curator of collections at the Society for the Preservation of New England Antiquities in Boston, MA.

John Wilmerding, of New Jersey. He would succeed Mrs. Lucille Gannon Murchison. Currently Mr. Wilmerding is the Christopher Binyon Sarofim professor in American art at the department of art and archeology at Princeton University and visiting curator at the Henry R. Luce Center for the Study of American Art at the Metropolitan Museum of Art.

The President announced his intention to nominate Ronald William Roskens, Administrator-designate of the Agency for International Development at the U.S. International Development Cooperation Agency, to be a member of the Board of Directors of the Inter-American Foundation for the remainder of the term expiring September 20, 1992, and announced his intention to appoint him as Special Coordinator for International Disaster Assistance.

January 26
The President met at the White House with:
—Republican mayors;
—the Vice President; John H. Sununu, Chief of Staff to the President; Brent Scowcroft, Assistant to the President for National Security

Affairs; and members of the CIA briefing staff;
—Natan Shcharanskiy;
—Secretary of State James A. Baker III;
—John H. Sununu, Chief of Staff to the President.

The President announced his intention to designate Charles E. Reid, of New Jersey, as Chairman of the National Commission on Libraries and Information Science upon confirmation by the Senate.

January 27
In the afternoon, the President attended the Alibi Club luncheon, and in the evening, he attended the Alfalfa Club dinner.

January 28
In the morning, the President and Mrs. Bush attended services at the John Wesley Zion Church, where the President addressed the congregation.

January 29
The President met at the White House with:
—the Vice President; John H. Sununu, Chief of Staff to the President; Brent Scowcroft, Assistant to the President for National Security Affairs; and members of the CIA briefing staff;
—the congressional leadership;
—British Foreign Secretary Douglas Hurd;
—Secretary of the Treasury Nicholas F. Brady.

In the afternoon, the President and Mrs. Bush hosted a reception on the State Floor for the Republican Eagles, a group of major donors to the party.

In the evening, the President and Mrs. Bush attended the Republican Eagles inaugural gala at the John F. Kennedy Center for the Performing Arts.

January 30
The President met at the White House with:
—the Vice President; John H. Sununu, Chief of Staff to the President; Brent Scowcroft, Assistant to the President for National Security Affairs; and members of the CIA briefing staff;
—Dewey Stokes, chairman of the National Fraternal Order of Police, and members of the National Fraternal Order of Police Board;
—John H. Sununu, Chief of Staff to the President.

January 31
The President met at the White House with:
—the Vice President; John H. Sununu, Chief of Staff to the President; Brent Scowcroft, As-

sistant to the President for National Security Affairs; and members of the CIA briefing staff;
—the congressional leadership;
—Secretary of State James A. Baker III;
—the Cabinet;
—John H. Sununu, Chief of Staff to the President.

The President telephoned Chairman Mikhail Gorbachev of the Soviet Union to discuss the U.S. proposal to reduce conventional forces in Central and Eastern Europe to 195,000 on each side.

The White House announced that President Bush has invited President Václav Havel of Czechoslovakia to make a working visit to the United States. President Havel has accepted the invitation and will meet with President Bush at the White House on February 20.

The White House also announced that the President has invited Prime Minister Tadeusz Mazowiecki of Poland to make an official visit to the United States. The Prime Minister has accepted the invitation and will meet with the President at the White House in March.

The following individuals will comprise the Presidential delegation to attend the 25th anniversary celebration of The Gambia's independence on February 18:

Delegation Chairman:

George W. Bush, managing general partner, Texas Rangers, and Laura Bush.

Delegates:

Elsie Hillman, Republican National Committeewoman from Pennsylvania.
Capt. John Young, NASA astronaut.
Stan Scott, president, Crescent Distributing Co.
Warren Iliff, director, Dallas Zoo.

February 1
The President met at the White House with:
—John H. Sununu, Chief of Staff to the President; Brent Scowcroft, Assistant to the President for National Security Affairs; and members of the CIA briefing staff;
—conservative Christian leaders;
—the Vice President, for lunch;
—John H. Sununu, Chief of Staff to the President.

The President transmitted to the Congress the third biennial report of the Interagency Arctic Research Policy Committee (February 1, 1988, to January 31, 1990) and the report on the operation of the Generalized System of Preferences (GSP) program.

February 2
The President met at the White House with John H. Sununu, Chief of Staff to the President; Brent Scowcroft, Assistant to the President for

National Security Affairs; and members of the CIA briefing staff.

In the morning, the President traveled to Knoxville, TN.

February 3
In the morning, the President met with his science advisers.

February 4
In the afternoon, the President returned to the White House from a weekend stay at Camp David, MD. Later, the President and Mrs. Bush hosted an "In Performance at the White House" concert.

February 5
The President met at the White House with:
—the Vice President; John H. Sununu, Chief of Staff to the President; Brent Scowcroft, Assistant to the President for National Security Affairs; and the CIA briefing staff;
—Jewish community leaders;
—Secretary of Defense Richard B. Cheney.

In the morning, the President telephoned Prime Minister Yitzhak Shamir of Israel to offer his condolences over the terrorist killings of Israeli academics on February 4.

At noon, the President had lunch with Representatives G.V. (Sonny) Montgomery and John Paul Hammerschmidt in the House Members Dining Room at the Capitol.

The President transmitted to the Congress the following:
—the 10th annual report of the Federal Labor Relations Authority, covering fiscal year 1988;
—the annual report on hazardous materials transportation, covering calendar year 1988; and
—the Saint Lawrence Seaway Development Corporation annual report, covering calendar year 1988.

February 6
The President declared that a major disaster existed in the Commonwealth of the Northern Mariana Islands as a result of Typhoon Koryn, which struck the area on January 15 and 16. He directed the Federal Emergency Management Agency to provide assistance to supplement State and local recovery efforts.

The President transmitted to the Congress a $570 million package of fiscal year 1990 supplementals that included the following:
—$500 million for increased aid to Panama, as announced by the President on January 19th;
—$70 million for increased refugee assistance;

—appropriations language that would allow the U.S. Governor of the International Bank for Reconstruction and Development to purchase shares in a general capital increase of the Bank.

The budget authority and outlays for these requests would be fully offset by transfers and deferrals from the Department of Defense.

The President transmitted to the Congress the following:

—the annual report of the Commodity Credit Corporation for fiscal year 1988;
—the 1989 annual report on Alaska's mineral resources; and
—the 18th annual report on Federal advisory committees for fiscal year 1989.

February 7

The White House announced that the President has invited Chancellor Helmut Kohl of the Federal Republic of Germany to make a working visit to the United States. Chancellor Kohl has accepted the invitation and will meet with the President at Camp David on February 24 and 25.

The White House announced that the President has invited Prime Minister Charles J. Haughey of Ireland to make a working visit to the United States. Prime Minister Haughey has accepted the invitation and will meet with the President at the White House on February 27.

February 8

The White House announced that the President has invited Secretary General Manfred Woerner of the North Atlantic Treaty Organization to make a working visit to the United States. Secretary General Woerner has accepted the invitation and will meet with the President at Camp David on February 10 and 11.

February 9

The President met at the White House with:
—the Vice President; John H. Sununu, Chief of Staff to the President; Brent Scowcroft, Assistant to the President for National Security Affairs; and the CIA briefing staff;
—the Vice President, for lunch;
—crewmembers of the space shuttle *Discovery.*

The White House announced that President Bush has invited President Alberto Chissano of Mozambique to make a working visit to the United States. President Chissano has accepted the invitation and will meet with President Bush on March 13.

The President declared that a major disaster existed in the Territory of American Samoa as a result of Hurricane Ofa, which struck the area on February 2. He directed the Federal Emergency Management Agency to provide assistance to supplement State and local recovery efforts.

In the afternoon, the President went to Camp David, MD, for the weekend.

February 11

In the afternoon, the President and Mrs. Bush returned to the White House from a weekend stay at Camp David, MD. They taped a television program to be aired by the American Broadcasting Company honoring literacy workers and volunteers.

February 12

The President met at the White House with:
—the Vice President; John H. Sununu, Chief of Staff to the President; Brent Scowcroft, Assistant to the President for National Security Affairs; and members of the CIA briefing staff;
—Secretary of the Treasury Nicholas F. Brady;
—John H. Sununu, Chief of Staff to the President.

In the evening, the President hosted a state dinner for President Denis Sassou-Nguesso of the Congo in the State Dining Room.

February 13

The President met at the White House with:
—the Vice President; John H. Sununu, Chief of Staff to the President; Brent Scowcroft, Assistant to the President for National Security Affairs; and members of the CIA briefing staff;
—the Cabinet and advisers, to discuss issues related to the upcoming drug summit in Cartagena, Colombia;
—John H. Sununu, Chief of Staff to the President.

The President announced his intention to nominate the following individuals to be members of the Board of Directors of the Inter-American Foundation for a term of 6 years:

Frank D. Yturria, of Texas. This is a new position. Upon confirmation he will be designated Chairman. Currently Mr. Yturria serves as a rancher and banker in Brownsville, TX.

Norton Stevens, of New York. This is a new position. Currently Mr. Stevens serves as an associate with Donaldson Enterprises in New York, NY.

The President announced his intention to nominate the following individuals to be members of the Board of Directors of the State Justice Institute:

For a term expiring September 17, 1991:

Terrence B. Adamson, of Georgia. He would succeed Lawrence H. Cooke. Currently Mr. Adamson serves as a partner with the law firm of Dow, Lohnes and Albertson in Atlanta, GA.

Vivi L. Dilweg, of Wisconsin. She would succeed Rodney A. Peeples. Currently Mrs. Dilweg serves as the

Brown County Circuit Judge, Branch II, for general jurisdiction in Green Bay, WI.

For a term expiring September 17, 1992:

Carl F. Bianchi, of Idaho. He would succeed Larry P. Polansky. Currently Mr. Bianchi serves as the administrative director of the courts for the State of Idaho.

James Duke Cameron, of Arizona. This is a reappointment. Currently Mr. Cameron serves as justice for the supreme court in the State of Arizona.

Janice L. Gradwohl, of Nebraska. This is a reappointment. Currently Mrs. Gradwohl serves as judge for the county court for the third judicial district in Lancaster County, NE.

Malcolm M. Lucas, of California. He would succeed Ralph J. Erickstad. Currently Mr. Lucas serves as the chief justice of California and chairman of the Judicial Council of California in San Francisco, CA.

The President announced his intention to appoint the following individuals to be members of the U.S. Holocaust Memorial Council:

For a term expiring January 15, 1995:

Charles S. Ackerman, of Georgia. He would succeed Eli Zborowski. Currently Mr. Ackerman serves as president and chief executive officer of Ackerman and Co. in Atlanta, GA.

Catherine Zachs Gildenhorn, of Maryland. She would succeed Sigmund Strochlitz. Currently Mrs. Gildenhorn serves as a consultant in Chevy Chase, MD.

William J. Lowenberg, of California. This is a reappointment, and he will be reappointed as vice chairperson. Currently Mr. Lowenberg serves as vice chairperson of the U.S. Holocaust Memorial Council in San Francisco, CA.

Julius Schatz, of New York. This is a reappointment. Currently Mr. Schatz serves as a consultant on federations and Jewish elder seminars for the American Jewish Conference in New York, NY.

For a term expiring January 15, 1994:

John T. Pawlikowski, of Illinois. This is a reappointment. Currently Mr. Pawlikowski serves as a Servite priest and professor of social ethics at Catholic Theological Union in Chicago, IL.

The President designated the following individuals:

Edward E. Hood, Jr., of Connecticut, to be Chairman of the President's National Security Telecommunications Advisory Committee. He would succeed Paul H. Henson. Currently Mr. Hood serves as vice chairman and executive officer of the General Electric Co. in Fairfield, CT.

Robert E. Allen, of New Jersey, to be Vice Chairman of the President's National Security Telecommunications Advisory Committee. He would succeed Edward E. Hood. Currently Mr. Allen serves as chairman and chief executive officer of AT&T in New York, NY.

February 14

The President met at the White House with:
—the Vice President; John H. Sununu, Chief of Staff to the President; Brent Scowcroft, Assistant to the President for National Security

Affairs; and members of the CIA briefing staff;
—Beverly Chapman, Disabled American of the Year;
—Vanessa Vance, Easter Seal poster child;
—representatives of the Non-Commissioned Officers Association;
—Secretary of State James A. Baker III;
—John H. Sununu, Chief of Staff to the President.

The White House announced that the President has invited Prime Minister Giulio Andreotti of Italy to visit Washington. The Prime Minister has accepted the invitation and will meet with the President at the White House on March 6.

February 16

The President met at the White House with:
—the Vice President; John H. Sununu, Chief of Staff to the President; Brent Scowcroft, Assistant to the President for National Security Affairs; and members of the CIA briefing staff;
—the Cabinet;
—the Vice President, for lunch;
—Secretary of State James A. Baker III.

The President announced his intention to appoint the following individuals to be members of the Advisory Committee for Trade Policy and Negotiations for terms of 2 years:

W.L. Lyons Brown, Jr., of Kentucky. This is a reappointment. Currently Mr. Brown serves as chairman and chief executive officer of the Brown Forman Corp. in Louisville, KY.

A.W. Clausen, of California. He would succeed Mark Sheperd, Jr. Currently Mr. Clausen serves as chairman and chief executive officer of the Bank America Corp. in San Francisco, CA.

Robert W. Galvin, of Illinois. He would succeed Robert H. Beeby. Currently Mr. Galvin serves as chairman of the board of Motorola, Inc., in Schaumburg, IL.

Stanley C. Gault, of Ohio. This is a reappointment. Currently Mr. Gault serves as chairman and chief executive officer of Rubbermaid, Inc., in Wooster, OH.

Maurice R. Greenberg, of New York. This is a reappointment. Currently Mr. Greenberg serves as president and chief executive officer of the American International Group, Inc., in New York, NY.

Philip E. Lippincott, of New Jersey. This is a reappointment. Currently Mr. Lippincott serves as chairman of the board, president, and chief executive officer of Scott Paper Co. in Philadelphia, PA.

Richard M. Morrow, of Illinois. He would succeed Peter J. Wallison. Currently he serves as chairman and chief executive officer of the AMOCO Corp. in Chicago, IL.

Edmund T. Pratt, Jr., of New York. This is a reappointment. Currently he serves as chairman of the board and chief executive officer of Pfizer, Inc., in New York, NY.

George H. Weyerhaeuser, of Washington. He would succeed Mike Curb. Currently Mr. Weyerhaeuser serves as chairman and chief executive officer of the Weyerhaeuser Co. in Tacoma, WA.

John A. Young, of California. He would succeed Edson W. Spencer. Currently Mr. Young serves as president and chief executive officer of Hewlett-Packard in Palo Alto, CA.

In the afternoon, the President went to his home in Kennebunkport, ME, for the holiday weekend.

February 19

In the afternoon, the President returned to the White House from a weekend stay at his home in Kennebunkport, ME.

The President declared that a major disaster existed in the central part of Alabama as a result of severe storms, tornadoes, and flooding that began on February 3. He directed the Federal Emergency Management Agency to provide assistance to supplement State and local efforts.

February 20

The President met at the White House with:
—the Vice President; John H. Sununu, Chief of Staff to the President; Brent Scowcroft, Assistant to the President for National Security Affairs; and members of the CIA briefing staff;
—Chancellor Franz Vranitzky of Austria;
—Members of Congress and their constituents.

The President announced his intention to appoint Nina J. Stewart, of Maryland, to be Executive Director of the President's Foreign Intelligence Advisory Board. She would succeed Fred Ralph Demech, Jr. Currently Mrs. Stewart serves as Acting Executive Director of the President's Foreign Intelligence Advisory Board in Washington, DC.

The President announced his intention to appoint the following individuals to be members of the Board of Directors of the Pennsylvania Avenue Development Corporation for a term of 6 years expiring October 26, 1994:

Walter John Ganzi, Jr., of the District of Columbia. He would succeed Arthur A. Fletcher. Currently Mr. Ganzi serves as president and chairman of the board of the Palm Management Corp. in Washington, DC.

Jayne Brumley Ikard, of the District of Columbia. She would succeed Henry A. Berliner, Jr. Currently Mrs. Ikard serves as a public affairs consultant at the Joint Center for Political Studies in Washington, DC.

The President announced his intention to appoint the following individuals to be members of the National Critical Materials Council:

D. Allan Bromley, Director of the Office of Science and Technology Policy. He would succeed Donald P. Hodel. Upon appointment, he will be designated Chairman.

T.S. Ary, Director of the Bureau of Mines. He would succeed Thomas Gale Moore.

W. Henson Moore, Deputy Secretary of Energy. He would succeed William F. Martin.

February 21

The President met at the White House with:
—the Vice President; John H. Sununu, Chief of Staff to the President; Brent Scowcroft, Assistant to the President for National Security Affairs; and members of the CIA briefing staff;
—congressional leaders;
—national board members of Mothers Against Drunk Driving;
—publishers of African-American publications;
—Secretary of State James A. Baker III;
—John H. Sununu, Chief of Staff to the President.

In the late afternoon, the President and Mrs. Bush hosted a reception and concert in the East Room for National Symphony Orchestra artistic director Mstislav Rostropovich.

The President announced his intention to appoint the following individuals to be members of the President's Council on Physical Fitness and Sports:

Suzanne P. Timken, of Ohio. She would succeed Mark Saginor. Upon appointment she will be designated Vice Chairman. Currently Ms. Timken serves as a lecturer and public speaker in Canton, OH.

Barbara Jane Blalock, of New Hampshire. She would succeed Bernard Cahill. Currently Ms. Blalock serves as vice president of sales for Pandick New England in Boston, MA.

Myrna L. Partrich, of Michigan. She would succeed Robert Levy. Currently Mrs. Partrich serves as coowner of the Work Out Co. Exercise Studio in Birmingham, MI.

Cory SerVaas, of Indiana. She would succeed Donn Moomaw. Currently Dr. SerVaas serves as editor and publisher of the Saturday Evening Post and president and medical research director of the Benjamin Franklin Literacy and Medical Society in Indianapolis, IN.

Christine I. Silkwood, of Texas. She would succeed Wayne Newton. Currently Ms. Silkwood serves as president of Silkwood Enterprises in Houston, TX.

Peter G. Vidmar, of California. He would succeed Jere Thompson. Peter Vidmar was the premier male gymnast for the United States in the 1984 Olympics and currently serves as owner of Vidmar and Co. in Irvine, CA.

Gary C. Visconti, of California. He would succeed David A. Werblin. Currently Mr. Visconti serves as president of the Southern California Olympians and president of Pro Skates, Inc., in Culver City, CA.

February 22

The President met at the White House with:
—the Vice President; John H. Sununu, Chief of Staff to the President; Brent Scowcroft, As-

sistant to the President for National Security Affairs; and members of the CIA briefing staff;

—His Royal Highness, Prince Bandar bin Sultan bin 'Abd al-'Aziz, the Ambassador from Saudi Arabia;

—His Royal Highness, Charles, the Prince of Wales, for lunch.

The President announced that the following individuals will comprise the U.S. delegation to the inauguration of President Luis Alberto Lacalle of Uruguay, March 1.

Delegation Chairman:

Dick Thornburgh, United States Attorney General, and Ginny Thornburgh.

Delegates:

Wales H. Madden, Jr., attorney and businessman, Amarillo, TX.

Thomas W. Moseley, former executive, GATX Corp., Gates Mills, OH.

Remedios Diaz-Oliver, chief operating officer and executive vice president, American International Container, Inc., Miami, FL.

Gaddi H. Vasquez, county supervisor, Orange County, CA.

Malcolm R. Wilkey, U.S. Ambassador to Uruguay.

The President announced that the following individuals will comprise the U.S. delegation to the United Nations Commission on the Status of Women, which will convene in Vienna, Austria, from February 26–March 9:

Head of Delegation:

Juliette Clagett McLennan, Representative of the United States to the United Nations Commission on the Status of Women.

Alternates:

Theresa Elmore Behrendt, fundraising consultant, Bush/Quayle '88.

Jennifer Dunn, chairman, Washington State Republican Committee.

Bonnie Guiton, special adviser to the President for consumer affairs.

Elsie Vartanian, assistant majority leader, New Hampshire House of Representatives; president of the national Republican Legislators Association; New Hampshire Republican national committeewoman and northeastern vice chairman.

Adis Maria Vila, Assistant Secretary of Agriculture for Administration.

The President announced his intention to appoint the following individuals to be members of the Commission of Fine Arts for a term of 4 years:

Joan Abrahamson, of California. She would succeed Diane Wolf. Currently Dr. Abrahamson serves as president of the Jefferson Institute in Beverly Hills, CA.

J. Carter Brown, of the District of Columbia. This is a reappointment. Currently Mr. Brown serves as director of the National Gallery of Art in Washington, DC.

Robert A. Peck, of the District of Columbia. He would succeed Carolyn Deaver. Currently Mr. Peck serves as an associate with the law firm of Jones, Day, Reavis and Pogue in Washington, DC.

February 23

The President met at the White House with:

—the Vice President; John H. Sununu, Chief of Staff to the President; Brent Scowcroft, Assistant to the President for National Security Affairs; and members of the CIA briefing staff;

—Prime Minister Jan P. Syse of Norway;

—Arthur A. Fletcher, newly appointed Chairman of the Commission on Civil Rights;

—the Vice President, for lunch;

—members of the Overseas Private Investment Corporation-sponsored investment mission to Panama;

—Secretary of State James A. Baker III;

—John H. Sununu, Chief of Staff to the President.

The President declared that a major disaster existed in the northwestern part of Georgia as a result of severe storms and tornadoes that began on February 10. He directed the Federal Emergency Management Agency to provide assistance to supplement State and local efforts.

In the afternoon, the President and Mrs. Bush went to Camp David, MD, for the weekend.

February 26

The President met at the White House with:

—the Vice President; John H. Sununu, Chief of Staff to the President; Brent Scowcroft, Assistant to the President for National Security Affairs; and members of the CIA briefing staff;

—Michael J. Boskin, Chairman of the Council of Economic Advisers;

—Secretary of Defense Richard B. Cheney;

—John H. Sununu, Chief of Staff to the President.

The President transmitted the 1988 annual report on the administration of the Federal Railroad Safety Act of 1970.

The President announced his intention to appoint the following individuals to be members of the President's Intelligence Oversight Board:

James R. Thompson, Jr., of Illinois. He would succeed W. Glenn Campbell. Upon his appointment he will be designated Chairman. Currently James R. Thompson serves as the Governor of Illinois.

Amos A. Jordan, Jr., of Virginia. He would succeed Charles Tyroler II. Currently Dr. Jordan serves as vice chairman of the board of trustees and as the Henry Kissinger chair in national security policy at the

Center for Strategic and International Studies in Washington, DC.

The White House announced that the following individuals will comprise the Presidential delegation to Moroccan Throne Day, March 3:

Delegation Chairman:

Caspar W. Weinberger, former Secretary of Defense, and Jane Weinberger

Delegates:

Dorothy Bush LeBlond, of Maine

Betsy H. Heminway, Connecticut State cochairman, Bush/Quayle '88

Jack C. Jansing, chairman of the board, Independent Election Corp. of America

Shelley Bush Jansing, of New York

February 27

The President met at the White House with:
—the Vice President; John H. Sununu, Chief of Staff to the President; Brent Scowcroft, Assistant to the President for National Security Affairs; and members of the CIA briefing staff;
—congressional leaders;
—Jennifer Carol Price, national poster child for asthma and allergy;
—child-care constituency groups;
—Walter Momper, governing mayor of Berlin;
—Secretary of Agriculture Clayton K. Yeutter;
—John H. Sununu, Chief of Staff to the President.

The President transmitted to the Congress the annual report on mine safety and health activities for fiscal year 1988.

The President announced his intention to nominate the following individuals to be members of the Board of Directors of the Overseas Private Investment Corporation for a term expiring December 17, 1992:

J. Carter Beese, Jr., of Maryland. He would succeed Donley L. Brady. Currently Mr. Beese serves as a partner with Alex Brown and Sons in Baltimore, MD.

Donald Burnham Ensenat, of Louisiana. He would succeed Mitchell E. Daniels, Jr. Currently Mr. Ensenat serves as managing director of Hoffman, Sutterfield, Ensenat and Bankston in New Orleans, LA.

The President transmitted to the Congress the 1990 trade policy agenda and 1989 annual report on the Trade Agreements Program.

February 28

The President met at the White House with:
—the Vice President; John H. Sununu, Chief of Staff to the President; Brent Scowcroft, Assistant to the President for National Security Affairs; and members of the CIA briefing staff;

—Chief Mangosuthu Gatsha Buthelezi of South Africa.

The White House announced that the President telephoned Chairman Mikhail Gorbachev of the Soviet Union to discuss developments in Nicaragua and Eastern Europe.

The President announced his intention to appoint the following individuals to be members of the Board of Directors of the Student Loan Marketing Association:

Harry R. King, of Kentucky. He would succeed Edward A. McCabe. Upon appointment he will be designated Chairman. Currently Mr. King serves as principal of the Cypress Creek Co. in Louisville, KY.

Stan Huckaby, of Tennessee. He would succeed Earl S. Smittcamp. Currently Mr. Huckaby serves as owner and founder of Huckaby and Associates in Alexandria, VA.

The President announced his intention to nominate the following individuals to be members of the Board of Regents of the Uniformed Services University of the Health Sciences:

Clarence S. Avery, of California, for a term expiring June 20, 1995. He would succeed Ann S. Peterson. Currently Dr. Avery serves as a staff surgeon at Nathaniel C. Holderman Hospital in Yountville, CA.

George Tryon Harding IV, of Ohio, for a term expiring May 1, 1995. This is a reappointment. Currently Dr. Harding serves as a clinical professor of psychiatry at Ohio State University, College of Medicine, in Worthington, OH.

The President declared that a major disaster existed in Hamilton and Polk Counties in Tennessee as a result of severe storms and flooding that began on February 15. He directed the Federal Emergency Management Agency to provide assistance to supplement State and local recovery efforts.

March 1

The President announced his intention to nominate the following individuals to be members of the National Science Board, National Science Foundation:

Peter H. Raven, of Missouri, for a term expiring May 10, 1994. He would succeed William A. Nierenberg. Currently Dr. Raven serves as the director of the Missouri Botanical Garden and Engelmann professor of botany at Washington University in St. Louis, MO.

Benjamin S. Shen, of Pennsylvania, for a term expiring May 10, 1994. He would succeed Norman C. Rasmussen. Currently Dr. Shen serves as the Reese W. Flower professor of astronomy and astrophysics at University of Pennsylvania.

The President announced his intention to appoint Wade F. Horn to be a member of the National Commission on Children for a term expiring March 31, 1991. He would succeed Dodie Truman Borup. Currently Dr. Horn serves as

Commissioner and Chief of the Children's Bureau at the Department of Health and Human Services in Washington, DC.

The President announced his intention to appoint Mark Victor Rosenker to be a member of the American Battle Monuments Commission. He would succeed Freda J. Poundstone. Currently Mr. Rosenker serves as vice president of the Electronic Industry Association in Washington, DC.

The President announced his intention to appoint Francis B. Schulte to be a member of the President's Education Policy Advisory Committee. This is a new position. Currently Most Reverend Schulte is the Archbishop of New Orleans in New Orleans, LA.

The President announced his intention to appoint the following individuals to be members of the Advisory Council on Historic Preservation:

William J. Althaus, mayor of York, PA, for a term of 4 years expiring June 10, 1993. This is a reappointment.

Gov. Michael Newbold Castle, of Delaware, for a term of 4 years expiring June 10, 1993. This is a reappointment.

March 2

In the afternoon, the President traveled to Palm Springs, CA, where he participated in a welcoming ceremony for Prime Minister Toshiki Kaifu of Japan. In the evening, the President and Mrs. Bush hosted a dinner for the Prime Minister at the Annenberg residence in Palm Springs.

The President selected the following individuals as members of the U.S. delegation to the World Conference on Education for All, which will meet in Thailand, March 5–9:

Delegation Chairman:

Thomas H. Kean, president, Drew University, and former Governor of New Jersey

Delegates:

John R. Bolton, Assistant Secretary of State for International Organization Affairs

Julie Cooke, Director of Projects for Mrs. Bush

James E. Duffy, national spokesman, Project Literacy, and former president of the American Broadcasting Corp.

Observers:

Christopher T. Cross, Assistant Secretary of Education for Educational Research and Improvement

Bradley Langmaid, Acting Assistant Administrator for Science and Technology, Agency for International Development

The President announced his intention to appoint the following individuals to be members of the American Battle Monuments Commission:

William Campbell, of California. He would succeed Preston H. Long. Mr. Campbell is a retired State senator in California and currently serves as the president of the California Manufacturing Association.

Ronald D. Ray, of Kentucky. He would succeed Armistead Jones Maupin. Currently Mr. Ray serves as an attorney with the law firm of Ray and Morris in Louisville, KY.

March 4

In the evening, the President returned to the White House from Palm Springs, CA.

March 5

The President met at the White House with:

—the Vice President; John H. Sununu, Chief of Staff to the President; Brent Scowcroft, Assistant to the President for National Security Affairs; and members of the CIA briefing staff;

—the Cabinet;

—Secretary of the Treasury Nicholas F. Brady;

—John H. Sununu, Chief of Staff to the President.

March 6

The President met at the White House with:

—the Vice President; John H. Sununu, Chief of Staff to the President; Brent Scowcroft, Assistant to the President for National Security Affairs; and members of the CIA briefing staff;

—John H. Sununu, Chief of Staff to the President.

The President declared that a major disaster existed in the central part of Illinois as a result of a severe ice storm that began on February 14. He directed the Federal Emergency Management Agency to provide assistance to supplement State and local recovery efforts.

The President announced his intention to nominate the following individuals to be members of the Board of Directors of the Corporation for Public Broadcasting:

Henry J. Cauthen, of South Carolina, for a term expiring March 1, 1994. He would succeed Howard D. Gutin. Currently Mr. Cauthen serves as president of the South Carolina Educational Television Network in Columbia, SC.

Lloyd Kaiser, of Pennsylvania, for a term expiring March 1, 1994. This is a reappointment. Currently Mr. Kaiser serves as president of QED Communications in Pittsburgh, PA.

The President has directed Salvatore R. Martoche, Assistant Secretary of the Treasury for Enforcement, to act as Director of the Office of Thrift Supervision. It is expected that Mr. Martoche will serve until a new Director is in place.

March 7

The President met at the White House with:

—the Vice President; John H. Sununu, Chief of Staff to the President; Brent Scowcroft, Assistant to the President for National Security

Affairs; and members of the CIA briefing staff;
—Secretary of Commerce Robert A. Mosbacher, for lunch;
—Secretary of State James A. Baker III;
—John H. Sununu, Chief of Staff to the President.

The President transmitted to the Congress a report on the results of investigations to determine the effect of imports on the national security during fiscal year 1989.

March 8
The President met at the White House with:
—the Vice President; John H. Sununu, Chief of Staff to the President; Brent Scowcroft, Assistant to the President for National Security Affairs; and members of the CIA briefing staff;
—the Vice President, for lunch;
—John H. Sununu, Chief of Staff to the President.

In the afternoon, the President recorded two public service announcements at McDonough Memorial Gymnasium at Georgetown University.
The President announced the U.S. delegation to the inaugural ceremonies of the President-elect of the Republic of Chile, His Excellency Patricio Aylwin Azocar, to be held in Santiago, Chile, on March 11:

Personal Representative of the President to Head the Delegation:
Dan Quayle, Vice President of the United States of America

Representatives of the President, With the Rank of Special Ambassador:
Edward M. Kennedy, United States Senator from the State of Massachusetts
Bernard Aronson, Assistant Secretary of State for Inter-American Affairs
Charles A. Gillespie, Jr., U.S. Ambassador to the Republic of Chile

The President announced the U.S. delegation to the inaugural ceremonies of the President-elect of the Federative Republic of Brazil, His Excellency Fernando Collor de Mello, to be held in Brasilia, Brazil, on March 15:

Personal Representative of the President to Head the Delegation:
Dan Quayle, Vice President of the United States of America

Representatives of the President, With the Rank of Special Ambassador:
Marilyn Quayle, wife of the Vice President of the United States of America
Richard Huntington Melton, U.S. Ambassador to the Federative Republic of Brazil

March 9
The President met at the White House with:
—the Vice President; John H. Sununu, Chief of Staff to the President; Brent Scowcroft, Assistant to the President for National Security Affairs; and members of the CIA briefing staff;
—Secretary of State James A. Baker III;
—John H. Sununu, Chief of Staff to the President.

In the afternoon, the President and Mrs. Bush went to Camp David, MD, for the weekend.

March 11
In the afternoon, the President returned to the White House from a weekend stay at Camp David, MD.

March 12
The President met at the White House with:
—the Vice President; John H. Sununu, Chief of Staff to the President; Brent Scowcroft, Assistant to the President for National Security Affairs; and members of the CIA briefing staff;
—Secretary of Defense Richard B. Cheney;
—John H. Sununu, Chief of Staff to the President.

March 13
The President met at the White House with:
—the Vice President; John H. Sununu, Chief of Staff to the President; Brent Scowcroft, Assistant to the President for National Security Affairs; and members of the CIA briefing staff;
—Republican congressional leaders;
—John H. Sununu, Chief of Staff to the President.

The President sent to the Congress a proposed fiscal year 1990 supplemental request for $300 million for aid to Nicaragua.

March 14
The President met at the White House with:
—the Vice President; John H. Sununu, Chief of Staff to the President; Brent Scowcroft, Assistant to the President for National Security Affairs; and members of the CIA briefing staff;
—Federal agency chiefs, for lunch;
—Secretary of State James A. Baker III;
—Edward J. Moskal, president of the Polish American Congress;
—Baptist editors and community leaders;
—John H. Sununu, Chief of Staff to the President.

The White House announced that the President and Prime Minister Margaret Thatcher of the United Kingdom have agreed to an informal meeting in Bermuda on April 13. The President will return to Washington, DC, on April 14.

The President announced his intention to appoint the following individuals to be members of the Federal Service Impasses Panel for terms expiring January 10, 1995:

Edwin D. Brubeck, of Indiana. He would succeed Thomas A. Farr. Currently Mr. Brubeck serves as a business representative for the Indiana State Building Trades Council in Indianapolis, IN.

Charles A. Kothe, of Oklahoma. He would succeed Jean T. McKelvey. Currently Mr. Kothe serves as special consultant to the Chairman of the Equal Employment Opportunity Commission; consultant to the University of Tulsa, College of Business Administration; and an attorney with the law firm of Pray, Walker, Jackman, Williamson, Marler in Oklahoma.

The White House announced that President Bush and President François Mitterrand of France have agreed to meet in Florida on April 19.

In the afternoon, President Bush spoke by telephone with President Guillermo Endara of Panama. The two Presidents discussed U.S. assistance for Panama and the war on drugs.

In the evening, the President and Mrs. Bush attended a performance of "Stardust" at the John F. Kennedy Center for the Performing Arts.

March 15

The President met at the White House with:
—the Vice President; John H. Sununu, Chief of Staff to the President; Brent Scowcroft, Assistant to the President for National Security Affairs; and members of the CIA briefing staff;
—Members of Congress;
—Rev. Lazslo Tokes, hero of the Romanian revolution;
—John H. Sununu, Chief of Staff to the President.

In the morning, the President spoke by telephone with Chancellor Helmut Kohl of the Federal Republic of Germany. The President and the Chancellor discussed the manner in which German-Polish border questions would be addressed.

In the evening, the President spoke by telephone with President-elect Violeta Chamorro of Nicaragua. They discussed U.S. assistance for Nicaragua and the Central American peace process.

March 16

The President met at the White House with:
—the Vice President; John H. Sununu, Chief of Staff to the President; Brent Scowcroft, Assistant to the President for National Security

Affairs; and members of the CIA briefing staff;
—Secretary of State James A. Baker III;
—John H. Sununu, Chief of Staff to the President;
—the Vice President, for lunch.

The President announced the designation of the following U.S. Directors for the Polish-American Enterprise Fund and for the Hungarian-American Enterprise Fund:

Polish-American Enterprise Fund:

John P. Birkelund, chief executive officer, Dillon, Read & Co. (chairman)

Lane Kirkland, president, AFL–CIO

Zbigniew Brzezinski, Center for Strategic and International Studies

Charles Harper, chairman and chief executive officer, CONAGRA

Nicholas Rey, managing director, Bear, Stearns and Co.

Hungarian-American Enterprise Fund:

John Whitehead (chairman)

Daniel Burke, chief executive officer, Capital Cities/ABC

George Gould, vice chairman, Klingenstein Fields & Co.

Robert Hormats, vice chairman, Goldman Sachs International

Paul Marer, Indiana University

The President transmitted a classified report on foreign intelligence activities within the United States to the Committee on Foreign Relations and the Select Committee on Intelligence of the Senate and to the Committee on Foreign Affairs and the Permanent Select Committee on Intelligence of the House of Representatives.

In the afternoon, the President and Mrs. Bush went to Camp David, MD, for the weekend.

March 18

In the afternoon, the President and Mrs. Bush returned to the White House from a weekend stay at Camp David, MD.

March 19

The President met at the White House with:
—the Vice President; John H. Sununu, Chief of Staff to the President; Brent Scowcroft, Assistant to the President for National Security Affairs; and members of the CIA briefing staff;
—Emilio and Gloria Estefan, members of the Miami Sound Machine, a popular music group;
—the Vice President, for lunch;
—the executive committee of the National Conference of Republican County Officials;
—Secretary of the Treasury Nicholas F. Brady;
—John H. Sununu, Chief of Staff to the President.

905

In the morning, the President attended the swearing-in ceremony in the Old Executive Office Building for Gov. James R. Thompson as Chairman of the Intelligence Oversight Board.

March 20
The President met at the White House with:
—the Vice President; John H. Sununu, Chief of Staff to the President; Brent Scowcroft, Assistant to the President for National Security Affairs; and members of the CIA briefing staff;
—the congressional leadership, to discuss legislation providing assistance for Nicaragua and Panama;
—President-elect Rafael Angel Calderon of Costa Rica;
—John H. Sununu, Chief of Staff to the President.

In the morning, the President spoke by telephone with Chancellor Helmut Kohl of the Federal Republic of Germany. They discussed the national parliamentary elections in the German Democratic Republic and German reunification.

The President announced his intention to nominate James Henry Michel to be a member of the Board of Directors of the Inter-American Foundation for the remainder of the term expiring September 20, 1992.

The President transmitted to the Congress the annual report of ACTION for fiscal year 1988.

March 21
The President met at the White House with:
—the Vice President; John H. Sununu, Chief of Staff to the President; Brent Scowcroft, Assistant to the President for National Security Affairs; and members of the CIA briefing staff;
—William H. Webster, Director of Central Intelligence;
—Secretary of Defense Richard B. Cheney;
—John H. Sununu, Chief of Staff to the President.

The President transmitted to the Congress the 23d annual report of the United States-Japan Cooperative Medical Science Program for the period of July 1988 to July 1989.

March 22
The President met at the White House with:
—the Vice President; John H. Sununu, Chief of Staff to the President; Brent Scowcroft, Assistant to the President for National Security Affairs; and members of the CIA briefing staff;
—Prime Minister Tadeusz Mazowiecki of Poland;
—leaders of the National Conference of Catholic Bishops;

—members of the Commission on Minority Business Development;
—the Episcopal Council for Advice, for lunch;
—John H. Sununu, Chief of Staff to the President.

In an Oval Office ceremony in the morning, the President presented the Cancer Courage Award to Dave Dravecky of the San Francisco Giants.

The President declared that a major disaster existed in Alabama as a result of severe storms and flooding that began on March 15. He directed the Federal Emergency Management Agency to provide assistance to supplement State and local recovery efforts.

The President appointed the following individuals to be members of the Commission on Minority Business Development:

Hernando G. Caampued, of California. Currently Mr. Caampued serves as principal and founder of H.G. Caampued and Associates in Milpitas, CA.

Fern R. Espino, of Michigan. Currently Dr. Espino serves as dean of student development for GMI Engineering and Management Institute in Flint, MI.

David K. Lam, of California. Currently Dr. Lam serves as president and chief executive officer of the Expert Edge Corp. in Palo Alto, CA.

Wright Lowenstein Lassiter, Jr., of Texas. Currently Dr. Lassiter serves as president of El Centro College in Dallas, TX.

Sybil Collins Mobley, of Florida. Currently Dr. Mobley serves as dean of the School of Business and Industry at Florida Agricultural and Mechanical University.

William Hodges Mobley, of Texas. Currently Dr. Mobley serves as president of Texas A&M University in College Station, TX.

Maria Elena Torano Pantin, of Florida. Currently Mrs. Pantin serves as president and owner of Maria Elena Torano Associates, Inc., in Miami, FL.

Abel R. Quintela, of Texas. Currently Mr. Quintela serves as president of ACO Machine and Tool, Inc., in Odessa, TX, and as vice president of Alpha Sales and Rental Co. in Odessa, TX.

March 23
The President met at the White House with:
—the Vice President; John H. Sununu, Chief of Staff to the President; Brent Scowcroft, Assistant to the President for National Security Affairs; and members of the CIA briefing staff;
—members of the President's Council of Advisors on Science and Technology;
—John H. Sununu, Chief of Staff to the President.

In the afternoon, the President and Mrs. Bush went to Camp David, MD, for the weekend.

March 25

In the afternoon, the President and Mrs. Bush returned to the White House from Camp David, MD.

In the evening, the President and Mrs. Bush attended the Ford's Theatre gala.

March 26

The President met at the White House with:
—the Vice President; John H. Sununu, Chief of Staff to the President; Brent Scowcroft, Assistant to the President for National Security Affairs; and members of the CIA briefing staff;
—members of McDonald's Capital Classic all-star high school basketball teams;
—John H. Sununu, Chief of Staff to the President;
—Secretary of Defense Richard B. Cheney.

In the morning, the President telephoned Barbara Tomblinson, who was named as the 100th daily Point of Light.

March 27

The President met at the White House with:
—the Vice President; John H. Sununu, Chief of Staff to the President; Brent Scowcroft, Assistant to the President for National Security Affairs; and members of the CIA briefing staff;
—the international trans-Antarctica expedition;
—former President Jimmy Carter, to discuss the Middle East peace process;
—John H. Sununu, Chief of Staff to the President.

In the afternoon, the President hosted a reception on the State Floor for members of the National Republican Senatorial Committee Senatorial Trust.

In the evening, the President attended the National Republican Senatorial Committee Chairman's Club dinner in the Indian Treaty Room of the Old Executive Office Building.

The President announced his intention to appoint the following individuals to be members of the Independent Commission to Review National Endowment for the Arts Grant Making Procedures. These are new positions.

John Thomas Agresto, of New Mexico. Currently Dr. Agresto serves as president of St. John's College in Santa Fe, NM. He has served as president of the Madison Center, 1989, and Deputy Chairman of the National Endowment for the Humanities in Washington, DC, 1985–1989.

Theresa Elmore Behrendt, of New York. Mrs. Behrendt served as the White House Liaison to the Arts and Humanities from 1982 to 1984.

Leonard Garment, of the District of Columbia. Currently Mr. Garment serves as senior partner with the law firm of Dickstein, Shapiro and Morin in Washington, DC.

Charles Kinsley McWhorter, of New York. Currently Mr. McWhorter serves as a consultant in the public affairs department of the AT&T Co. in New York, NY. Mr. McWhorter served as a member of the National Council on the Arts, 1970–1976.

March 28

The President met at the White House with:
—the Vice President; John H. Sununu, Chief of Staff to the President; Brent Scowcroft, Assistant to the President for National Security Affairs; and members of the CIA briefing staff;
—congressional leaders;
—Secretary of State James A. Baker III;
—Representatives C. Christopher Cox, Richard J. Durbin, John Miller, and Bill Sarpalius, to discuss U.S. policy on Lithuanian independence;
—John H. Sununu, Chief of Staff to the President;
—Robert H. Helmick, president of the U.S. Olympic Committee.

In the evening, the President telephoned Prime Minister Margaret Thatcher of the United Kingdom to discuss the situation in Lithuania.

March 29

The President met at the White House with:
—the Vice President; John H. Sununu, Chief of Staff to the President; Brent Scowcroft, Assistant to the President for National Security Affairs; and members of the CIA briefing staff;
—Secretary of Education Lauro F. Cavazos, to discuss the Secretary's recent trip to Mexico;
—the leadership of the National Commission on AIDS;
—John H. Sununu, Chief of Staff to the President;
—Senator Edward Kennedy, to discuss the Senator's recent trip to the Soviet Union.

In the afternoon, the President attended the White House Communications Agency service awards ceremony at Bolling Air Force Base, VA.

In the evening, the President telephoned Prime Minister Robert Hawke of Australia to congratulate him on his reelection.

The President sent a written message to Chairman Mikhail Gorbachev of the Soviet Union concerning the situation in Lithuania.

March 30

The President met at the White House with:
—the Vice President; John H. Sununu, Chief of Staff to the President; Brent Scowcroft, Assistant to the President for National Security

Affairs; and members of the CIA briefing staff;

—members of the boards of directors of the Polish and Hungarian Enterprise Funds;

—representatives of the Catholic Golden Age and the Catholic Daughters of the Americas;

—John H. Sununu, Chief of Staff to the President.

In the morning, the President received his District of Columbia, Maryland, and Virginia fishing licenses.

The President announced his intention to designate the following individuals to be members of the Board of Visitors to the U.S. Naval Academy for the terms expiring December 30, 1992:

FitzGerald Bemiss, of Virginia. He would succeed C. Fred Chambers. Mr. Bemiss is currently a consultant in Richmond, VA, and has served as president of Fitz-Gerald and Co. in Richmond, VA.

John C. Fitch, of Texas. He would succeed Lynn S. Wyatt. Mr. Fitch has served as executive vice president of the construction division for SEDCO, Inc., in Houston, TX.

March 31

In the morning, the President received his daily intelligence briefing.

In the evening, the President and Mrs. Bush attended the Gridiron Dinner at the Capital Hilton Hotel.

April 1

The President and Mrs. Bush met in Glen Burnie, MD, with the family of Maryland State Police Cpl. Theodore D. Wolf, who was slain March 29 after he stopped a car on Interstate 95.

April 2

In the morning, Prime Minister Toshiki Kaifu of Japan telephoned the President to discuss the ongoing trade negotiations between the two countries.

The President announced that the following individuals comprise the U.S. delegation to the inauguration of President Rafael Angel Calderon of Costa Rica, May 8:

Delegation Chairman:

Barbara Bush, the First Lady of the United States.

Delegates:

Roger Ailes, president, Ailes Communications, New York, NY

Jeb Bush, chairman, Bush Klein Realty, Inc., Miami, FL

Don Luis Ferre, former Governor of Puerto Rico, Guaynabo, PR

John Sununu, Chief of Staff to the President, and Nancy Sununu

The President announced that the following individuals comprise the U.S. delegation to the

celebration of Australian-American Friendship Week, May 4–10, in Canberra, Australia:

Delegation Chairman:

Adm. James D. Watkins, USN, Ret., Secretary of Energy, and Sheila Watkins

Delegates:

Jerry Weintraub, chairman and chief executive officer, Weintraub Entertainment Group, Inc., Los Angeles, CA, and Jane Weintraub

Melvin F. Sembler, Ambassador of the United States to Australia

April 3

The President declared that a major disaster existed in the western part of Florida as a result of heavy rains and flooding that began March 15. He directed the Federal Emergency Management Agency to provide assistance to supplement State and local recovery efforts.

The President announced his intention to appoint Kent M. Black to be a member of the President's National Security Telecommunications Advisory Committee. He would succeed Donald J. Yockey. Currently Mr. Black serves as president of electronics operations at the Rockwell International Corp. in Texas.

The President announced his intention to appoint Glenn E. Watts to be a member of the U.S. Holocaust Memorial Council for a term expiring January 15, 1995. This is a reappointment. Currently Mr. Watts serves as president emeritus of the Communications Workers of America of the AFL–CIO, in Washington, DC.

April 4

The President met at the White House with:

—the Vice President; John H. Sununu, Chief of Staff to the President; Brent Scowcroft, Assistant to the President for National Security Affairs; and members of the CIA briefing staff;

—Foreign Minister Hans-Dietrich Genscher of West Germany, to discuss the Conference on Security and Cooperation in Europe and the situation in Lithuania;

—Secretary of State James A. Baker III;

—black Republican elected officials.

April 5

The President met at the White House with:

—the Vice President; John H. Sununu, Chief of Staff to the President; Brent Scowcroft, Assistant to the President for National Security Affairs; and members of the CIA briefing staff;

—congressional leaders;

—singer Michael Jackson;

—the Vice President, for lunch;

—Democratic congressional leaders;

—John H. Sununu, Chief of Staff to the President.

In an Oval Office ceremony, the President signed the National Safe Boating Week proclamation.

April 6
The President met at the White House with:
—the Vice President; John H. Sununu, Chief of Staff to the President; Brent Scowcroft, Assistant to the President for National Security Affairs; and members of the CIA briefing staff;
—Secretary of State James A. Baker III;
—Susan Butcher, winner of the 1,158-mile Anchorage-to-Nome dogsled marathon;
—John H. Sununu, Chief of Staff to the President.

In the morning, Prime Minister Toshiki Kaifu of Japan telephoned the President to discuss the ongoing trade negotiations between the two countries.
In the afternoon, the President and Mrs. Bush went to Camp David, MD, for the weekend.

April 8
In the afternoon, the President and Mrs. Bush returned to the White House from a weekend stay at Camp David, MD.

April 9
The President met at the White House with:
—the Vice President; John H. Sununu, Chief of Staff to the President; Brent Scowcroft, Assistant to the President for National Security Affairs; and members of the CIA briefing staff;
—members of the Cabinet;
—John H. Sununu, Chief of Staff to the President.

In an Oval Office ceremony, the President received diplomatic credentials from Ambassadors John Schwank Duran of Guatemala, Virgil Constantinescu of Romania, Rita Klimova of Czechoslovakia, Nassib Lahoud of Lebanon, Eduardo Vallarino of Panama, and Moussa Sangare of Guinea.
In another Oval Office ceremony, the President presented the President's Award for Distinguished Federal Civilian Service to Laurence Legere, former defense adviser to the U.S. Ambassador to NATO and senior civilian representative of the Secretary of Defense in Europe.

April 10
The President met at the White House with:
—the Vice President; John H. Sununu, Chief of Staff to the President; Brent Scowcroft, Assistant to the President for National Security

Affairs; and members of the CIA briefing staff;
—Secretary of the Treasury Nicholas F. Brady;
—Richard Burt, former U.S. Ambassador to the Federal Republic of Germany and United States Negotiator for Strategic Nuclear Arms.

The White House announced that the President and Mrs. Bush recorded an antisubstance abuse message for the "Cartoon All-Stars to the Rescue" television program, which is part of CBS's Stop the Madness antidrug campaign. The show will be televised on April 21.

April 11
The President met at the White House with:
—the Vice President; John H. Sununu, Chief of Staff to the President; Brent Scowcroft, Assistant to the President for National Security Affairs; and members of the CIA briefing staff;
—Baltic-American community leaders, to discuss the independence of Latvia, Estonia, and Lithuania;
—Secretary of State James A. Baker III;
—John H. Sununu, Chief of Staff to the President.

In the evening, the President attended a fundraising reception for Senator Strom Thurmond of South Carolina at the National Press Club.

April 12
The President met at the White House with:
—the Vice President, for lunch;
—members of the White House Conference on Science and Economics Research Related to Global Change;
—John H. Sununu, Chief of Staff to the President.

April 13
In the morning, the President traveled to Hamilton, Bermuda, where he met with Prime Minister Margaret Thatcher of the United Kingdom and U.S. and British officials at Government House.
In the afternoon, the President and the Prime Minister attended a working luncheon at Government House and participated in a Good Friday kite-flying exhibition with local schoolchildren. The President then met again with the Prime Minister and U.S. and British officials. After their meeting, the President and the Prime Minister participated in a tree planting ceremony.
In the evening, the President attended a reception aboard the H.M.S. *Arrow* and a dinner hosted by the Prime Minister at Government House. Following the dinner, the President went to the consulate general's residence in Chelston, where he stayed overnight.

April 14

In the afternoon, the President left Bermuda and traveled to Camp David, MD, for the weekend.

April 15

In the afternoon, the President returned to the White House from a weekend stay at Camp David.

April 16

The President met at the White House with:
—the Vice President; John H. Sununu, Chief of Staff to the President; Brent Scowcroft, Assistant to the President for National Security Affairs; and members of the CIA briefing staff;
—First Deputy Prime Minister Goh Chok Tong of Singapore;
—Secretary of Defense Richard B. Cheney;
—John H. Sununu, Chief of Staff to the President.

In the morning, the President and Mrs. Bush participated in the annual White House Easter Egg Roll.

April 17

The President met at the White House with:
—the Vice President; John H. Sununu, Chief of Staff to the President; Brent Scowcroft, Assistant to the President for National Security Affairs; and members of the CIA briefing staff;
—Prime Minister Geoffrey Henry of the Cook Islands;
—Senator George J. Mitchell and a Democratic congressional delegation;
—Senator Robert Dole and a Republican congressional delegation;
—John H. Sununu, Chief of Staff to the President.

April 18

The President met at the White House with:
—the Vice President; John H. Sununu, Chief of Staff to the President; Brent Scowcroft, Assistant to the President for National Security Affairs; and members of the CIA briefing staff;
—the Vice President, for lunch;
—Secretary of State James A. Baker III;
—John H. Sununu, Chief of Staff to the President.

In the afternoon, the President hosted an Earth Day reception in the Rose Garden at the White House.

The President transmitted to the Congress the annual report of the National Endowment for the Humanities for fiscal year 1989.

April 19

President Bush met with President François Mitterrand of France at the Farmer residence in Key Largo, FL, and participated in a working luncheon.

Later, the two Presidents attended a reception and dinner at the home of Carl Linder, owner of the Ocean Reef Club, where President Bush stayed overnight.

April 20

The President announced that the Vice President will head a Presidential delegation to the inauguration of Nicaraguan President Violeta Chamorro on April 25. The following Members of Congress and distinguished citizens have been named to the delegation:

Mrs. Quayle
Senator Richard Lugar (R–IN)
Senator Chris Dodd (D–CT)
Senator David Durenberger (R–MN)
Senator Patrick Leahy (D–VT)
Senator Connie Mack (R–FL)
Senator John McCain (R–AZ)
Senator Claiborne Pell (D–RI)
Senator Harry Reid (D–NV)
Senator Terry Sanford (D–NC)
Gov. Bob Martinez of Florida
Representative Rod Chandler (R–WA)
Representative Mickey Edwards (R–OK)
Representative Jim Slattery (D–KS)
Representative Tom Tauke (R–IA)
Representative Anthony Beilenson (D–CA)
Representative Henry Hyde (R–IL)
Representative Ileana Ros-Lehtinen (R–FL)
Representative Cass Ballenger (R–NC)
Representative Barbara Vucanovich (R–NV)
Representative Bob Dornan (R–CA)
Representative Steve Solarz (D–NY)
Paul Coverdell, Director of the Peace Corps
Ambassador Joseph Reed, Chief of Protocol
Bernard W. Aronson, Assistant Secretary of State for Inter-American Affairs
Ambassador Jeane Kirkpatrick
Carol Hallett, Commissioner of Customs
Jeb Bush, chairman, Bush Klein Realty, Inc., Miami, FL
Allen Weinstein, Center for Democracy

Following the inauguration, the Vice President will travel to Mexico to meet with President Carlos Salinas de Gortari.

The President announced that five sites have been added to the Environmental Protection Agency's National Estuary Program. The five new areas are: Barataria-Terrebonne Estuarine Complex, LA; Casco Bay, ME; Indian River Lagoon, FL; Massachusetts Bays, MA; and Tampa Bay, FL.

In the evening, the President traveled to Orlando, FL, where he took a walking tour of Sea

World and presented a Point of Light Award to Daniel K. Odell, a research biologist at the Stranded Animal Research Area. Later, the President attended a fundraising dinner for the Florida Republican Party at the Orange County Convention Center. Following the dinner, he traveled to Islamorada, FL, where he stayed overnight.

April 22
The President returned to the White House after a 3-day trip to Alabama and Florida.

April 23
The President met at the White House with:
—the Vice President; John H. Sununu, Chief of Staff to the President; Brent Scowcroft, Assistant to the President for National Security Affairs; and members of the CIA briefing staff;
—Deputy Secretaries from each Cabinet agency, for lunch;
—Secretary of the Treasury Nicholas F. Brady;
—John H. Sununu, Chief of Staff to the President.

In the morning, the President participated in a proclamation signing ceremony in the Rose Garden for National Volunteer Week and in a tribute to daily Points of Light and government employees in community service.

In the afternoon, President Bush telephoned King Hussein I of Jordan to discuss Middle East issues. He also telephoned President Hafiz al-Assad of Syria to discuss the hostage situation in the Middle East and to thank Syria for its role in the release of Robert Polhill.

The White House announced that the President asked the Congress to consider several amendments to the fiscal year 1991 request for appropriations. In addition, he asked the Congress to consider several fiscal year 1990 supplemental requests. He concurrently sent the Congress a special message proposing rescissions that would offset the increased fiscal year 1990 costs that result from the supplemental requests. As required by law, he submitted two requests for fiscal year 1990 supplemental appropriations for the legislative branch and two fiscal year 1991 budget amendments for the judiciary.

April 24
The President met at the White House with:
—the Vice President; John H. Sununu, Chief of Staff to the President; Brent Scowcroft, Assistant to the President for National Security Affairs; and members of the CIA briefing staff;
—congressional leaders, to discuss the U.S. response to Soviet economic sanctions against Lithuania;

—the Vice President, for lunch;
—the University of Wisconsin Badgers, the National Collegiate Athletic Association hockey champions;
—Secretary of State James A. Baker III;
—John H. Sununu, Chief of Staff to the President.

The President announced his intention to nominate Andrew Camp Barrett to be a member of the Federal Communications Commission for a term of 5 years from July 1, 1990. This is a reappointment.

April 25
The President met at the White House with:
—the Vice President; John H. Sununu, Chief of Staff to the President; Brent Scowcroft, Assistant to the President for National Security Affairs; and members of the CIA briefing staff;
—John H. Sununu, Chief of Staff to the President.

In the afternoon, the President attended a reception for the Connecticut Republican Party in the Indian Treaty Room of the Old Executive Office Building.

The President transmitted to the Congress the annual report of the National Endowment for Democracy for fiscal year 1989.

The President appointed Gen. Colin L. Powell, Chairman of the Joint Chiefs of Staff, to be a Governor of the Board of Governors of the American National Red Cross for a term of 3 years. He would succeed William J. Crowe, Jr.

The President appointed Jan B. Vlcek, of Maryland, to be the Federal Representative of the United States to the Western Interstate Nuclear Board. He would succeed Lawrence F. O'Donnell. Currently Mr. Vlcek serves as a partner with the law firm of Sutherland, Asbill and Brennan in Washington, DC.

The President announced his intention to designate the following individuals to be members of the Board of Directors of the Rural Telephone Bank:

Charles H. Bronson, Jr., of Florida. Mr. Bronson would succeed William F. Stake. Currently he is a self-employed rancher in Satellite Beach, FL.

Bruce L. Gardner, of Maryland. Mr. Gardner would succeed John William Bode. Currently he serves as Assistant Secretary for Economics at the Department of Agriculture in Washington, DC.

Roland R. Vautour, of Vermont. This is a reappointment. Mr. Vautour serves as Under Secretary for Small Community and Rural Development at the Department of Agriculture in Washington, DC.

Adis Maria Vila, of Florida. Ms. Vila would succeed John J. Franke, Jr. Currently she serves as Assistant Secretary for Administration at the Department of Agriculture in Washington, DC.

April 26

The President met at the White House with:
—the Vice President; John H. Sununu, Chief of Staff to the President; Brent Scowcroft, Assistant to the President for National Security Affairs; and members of the CIA briefing staff;
—the National Cattlemen's Association leadership;
—winners of the JFK Representative Volunteer of the Year Award;
—John H. Sununu, Chief of Staff to the President.

In the afternoon, the President and Mrs. Bush attended a reception for the Republican Congressional Leadership Council at the National Museum of Women in the Arts.

In the evening, President Bush hosted a state dinner for President Carlos Andrés Pérez of Venezuela on the State Floor.

April 27

The President met at the White House with:
—the Vice President; John H. Sununu, Chief of Staff to the President; Brent Scowcroft, Assistant to the President for National Security Affairs; and members of the CIA briefing staff;
—John H. Sununu, Chief of Staff to the President.

The President announced his intention to designate the following individuals to be members of the Board of Visitors to the United States Military Academy, for terms expiring December 30, 1992:

John H. Lindsey, of Texas. He would succeed William D. Mounger. Currently Mr. Lindsey serves as owner of the Lindsey Insurance Agency in Houston, TX.

Sally Freeman McKenzie, of Texas. She would succeed George B. Price. Currently Mrs. McKenzie serves on the board of directors for Pier One Imports in Dallas, TX.

April 28

In the evening, the President attended the annual White House Correspondents Association dinner.

April 30

The President met at the White House with:
—the Vice President; John H. Sununu, Chief of Staff to the President; Brent Scowcroft, Assistant to the President for National Security Affairs; and members of the CIA briefing staff;
—Secretary of Defense Richard B. Cheney;
—John H. Sununu, Chief of Staff to the President.

May 1

The President met at the White House with:
—the Vice President; John H. Sununu, Chief of Staff to the President; Brent Scowcroft, Assistant to the President for National Security Affairs; and members of the CIA briefing staff;
—congressional leaders, to discuss funding for the space program;
—Secretary of State James A. Baker III;
—John H. Sununu, Chief of Staff to the President.

The President announced his intention to appoint the following citizens of the Republic of Panama to be members of the Board of the Panama Canal Commission:

Luis A. Anderson. This is a reappointment. Currently Mr. Anderson serves as general secretary of the Inter-American Regional Labor Organization of Workers in Mexico.

Cecilia E. Alegre. She would succeed Oyden Ortega Duran. Currently Dr. Alegre serves as a tenured professor in the department of humanities at the Universaida de Panama and as a director of the Panamanian Commission for Human Rights.

Alfredo N. Ramirez. He would succeed Carlos Valarde Ponce. Currently Mr. Ramirez serves as a senior partner with the law firm of Alfaro, Ferrer, Ramirez and Aleman in the Republic of Panama.

Joaquin J. Vallarino, Jr. He would succeed Carlos Ozores Typaldos. Currently Mr. Vallarino serves as chairman of the board and chief executive officer of the Panama Coca Cola Bottling Co. in the Republic of Panama.

May 2

The President met at the White House with:
—the Vice President; John H. Sununu, Chief of Staff to the President; Brent Scowcroft, Assistant to the President for National Security Affairs; and members of the CIA briefing staff;
—the Vice President, for lunch;
—John H. Sununu, Chief of Staff to the President.

May 3

The President met at the White House with:
—the Vice President; John H. Sununu, Chief of Staff to the President; Brent Scowcroft, Assistant to the President for National Security Affairs; and members of the CIA briefing staff;
—John H. Sununu, Chief of Staff to the President.

In the morning, the President hosted a breakfast in the State Dining Room to commemorate the National Day of Prayer.

The President declared that a major disaster existed in the eastern part of Texas as a result of severe storms, flooding, and tornadoes. He directed the Federal Emergency Management Agency to provide assistance to supplement State and local recovery efforts.

In the afternoon, the President hosted a reception for the Episcopal Church Foundation board of directors in the Residence.

In the evening, the President attended the National Republican Senatorial Committee Inner Circle gala at the Sheraton Washington Hotel.

May 4

The President met at the White House with the Vice President; John H. Sununu, Chief of Staff to the President; Brent Scowcroft, Assistant to the President for National Security Affairs; and members of the CIA briefing staff.

In the morning, the President traveled to Stillwater, OK.

May 6

In the afternoon, the President hosted a lecture on Theodore Roosevelt by Prof. David McCullough of Harvard University, the second in the Presidential Lecture Series.

In the evening, the President met at the White House with Representatives Thomas S. Foley and Robert H. Michel and Senators George J. Mitchell and Robert Dole to discuss the budget. John H. Sununu, Chief of Staff to the President; Richard G. Darman, Director of the Office of Management and Budget; and Secretary of the Treasury Nicholas F. Brady also attended the meeting.

May 7

The President met at the White House with:
—the Vice President; John H. Sununu, Chief of Staff to the President; Brent Scowcroft, Assistant to the President for National Security Affairs; and members of the CIA briefing staff;
—Manfred Woerner, Secretary General of the North Atlantic Treaty Organization;
—Prime Minister Rabbie Namaliu of Papua New Guinea;
—Commissioners from each of the independent Federal regulatory agencies.

In the evening, the President hosted a reception for the Advertising Council on the State Floor.

May 8

The President met at the White House with:
—the Vice President; John H. Sununu, Chief of Staff to the President; Brent Scowcroft, Assistant to the President for National Security Affairs; and members of the CIA briefing staff;
—Republican congressional leaders;
—Secretary of the Treasury Nicholas F. Brady.

May 9

The President met at the White House with:
—the Vice President; John H. Sununu, Chief of Staff to the President; Brent Scowcroft, Assistant to the President for National Security Affairs; and members of the CIA briefing staff;
—congressional leaders;
—crewmembers of the space shuttle *Atlantis*;
—Secretary of State James A. Baker III;
—John H. Sununu, Chief of Staff to the President;
—Secretary of the Treasury Nicholas F. Brady.

In the morning, in an Oval Office ceremony, the President signed the Wildfire Disaster Recovery Act of 1989.

In the afternoon, the President hosted a reception on the State Floor for the Republican Eagles, a group of major donors to the party.

The President transmitted to the Congress the 1988 annual reports of the Departments of Labor and Health and Human Services and the Occupational Safety and Health Review Commission.

The President announced his intention to nominate the following individuals to be members of the National Council on the Humanities:

For a term expiring January 26, 1996:

Bruce D. Benson, of Colorado. Mr. Benson would succeed Kathleen S. Kilpatrick. Currently he serves as owner and president of Benson Mineral Group, Inc., in Golden, CO.

For a term expiring January 26, 1994:

Billie Davis Gaines, of Georgia. Dr. Gaines would succeed Jeffrey Hart. Currently she serves as president of Horizon Productions in Atlanta, GA.

Gary L. McDowell, of the District of Columbia. Dr. McDowell would succeed Rita Ricardo-Campbell. Currently he serves as vice president for legal and public affairs at the National Legal Center for the Public Interest in Washington, DC.

Jeanne J. Smoot, of North Carolina. Dr. Smoot would succeed Ellis Sandoz. Currently she serves as a tenured full professor at North Carolina State University in the English department.

May 10

The President met at the White House with:
—the Vice President; John H. Sununu, Chief of Staff to the President; Brent Scowcroft, Assistant to the President for National Security Affairs; and members of the CIA briefing staff;
—Donald Draayer, superintendent of Minnetonka public schools in Excelsior, MN, and School Superintendent of the Year;
—the Vice President, for lunch;
—John H. Sununu, Chief of Staff to the President.

In the afternoon, in an Oval Office ceremony, the President signed the resolution designating Infant Mortality Awareness Day. Later, he hosted a reception on the State Floor for the Republican Eagles, a group of major donors to the party.

The President announced his intention to nominate the following individuals:

Michael S. Gelacak, of Virginia, to be a member of the U.S. Sentencing Commission for the remainder of the term expiring October 31, 1991. He would succeed Michael K. Block. Currently Mr. Gelacak serves as an attorney with the McNair law firm, P.A., in Washington, DC.

A. David Mazzone, of Massachusetts, to be a member of the U.S. Sentencing Commission for a term expiring October 31, 1995. Mr. Mazzone would succeed Stephen G. Breyer. Currently he serves as U.S. district judge in Boston, MA.

May 11
In the morning, the President traveled to Kingsville, TX.

May 14
The President met at the White House with:
—the Vice President; John H. Sununu, Chief of Staff to the President; Brent Scowcroft, Assistant to the President for National Security Affairs; and members of the CIA briefing staff;
—Ronald F. Lehman II, Director of the U.S. Arms Control and Disarmament Agency, to discuss the status of arms reduction agreements;
—President Abdou Diouf of Senegal;
—members of the National Troopers Coalition;
—civil rights leaders, to discuss civil rights legislation;
—Secretary of Defense Richard B. Cheney;
—John H. Sununu, Chief of Staff to the President.

May 15
The President met at the White House with:
—the Vice President; John H. Sununu, Chief of Staff to the President; Brent Scowcroft, Assistant to the President for National Security Affairs; and members of the CIA briefing staff;
—members of the President's Commission on Aviation Security and Terrorism, to receive the Commission's report on its investigation of the December 21, 1988, terrorist bombing of Pan American Flight 103 which crashed in Lockerbie, Scotland, and its appraisal of U.S. airline security systems and counterterrorism measures;
—family members of the victims of Pan American Flight 103, to discuss aviation security;
—congressional leaders, for the first session of the budget negotiations;

—John H. Sununu, Chief of Staff to the President.

The President declared that a major disaster existed in Arkansas as a result of severe storms and flooding that began on May 1. He directed the Federal Emergency Management Agency to provide assistance to supplement State and local recovery efforts.

May 16
The President met at the White House with:
—the Vice President; John H. Sununu, Chief of Staff to the President; Brent Scowcroft, Assistant to the President for National Security Affairs; and members of the CIA briefing staff;
—members of the Cabinet, to discuss administration policy on offshore oil drilling in Florida and California;
—Hispanic-American leaders, to discuss civil rights legislation;
—community leaders, to discuss civil rights legislation;
—Recording for the Blind Award winners;
—Members of Congress, to discuss administration policy on offshore oil drilling in Florida and California;
—John H. Sununu, Chief of Staff to the President.

The President transmitted to the Congress the annual report of the Department of Transportation for fiscal year 1988.

The President announced his intention to appoint the following individuals to be members of the Independent Commission to Review National Endowment for the Arts Grant Making Procedures. These are new positions:

John Brademas, of New York. Currently Dr. Brademas is the president of New York University in New York, NY.

David E. Connor, of Illinois. Currently Mr. Connor is president of David E. Connor and Associates in Peoria, IL.

Marcia Laing Golden, of Kansas. Currently Mrs. Golden serves on the executive board of the Association of Community Arts Agencies of Kansas and has served as immediate past president.

Kay Huffman Goodwin, of West Virginia. Currently Mrs. Goodwin is a member of the National Endowment for the Arts National Advisory Council on the Arts and Education.

Joan W. Harris, of Illinois. Currently Mrs. Harris is a trustee of the Harris Foundation and commissioner of the department of cultural affairs in Chicago, IL.

Kitty Carlisle Hart, of New York. Currently Mrs. Hart is the chairman of the New York State Council on the Arts in New York, NY, and is an actress and singer.

Peter N. Kyros, Jr., of California. Currently Mr. Kyros is a general partner for the western division of the Potomac Investment Associates in Westlake Village, CA.

Rosalind W. Wyman, of California. Currently Mrs. Wyman is owner and president of Rosalind Wyman Consultants, Inc., in Los Angeles, CA.

The President announced his intention to appoint the following individuals to be members of the Board of Directors of the Federal National Mortgage Association for terms ending on the date of the annual meeting of the stockholders in 1991. These are reappointments:

Al Cardenas, of Florida. He will be the mortgage industry representative. Currently Mr. Cardenas serves as director of Greenberg, Traurig, Hoffman, Lipoff, Rosen and Quentel, P.A., in Miami, FL.
Henry C. Cashen II, of the District of Columbia. He will serve as a public member. Currently Mr. Cashen serves as an attorney with the law firm of Dickstein, Shapiro and Morin in Washington, DC.
George L. Clark, Jr., of New York. He will be the real estate representative. Currently Mr. Clark serves as president of George L. Clark, Inc., in Brooklyn, NY.
J. Brian Gaffney, of Connecticut. He will serve as a public member. Currently Mr. Gaffney serves as a partner with the law firm of Gaffney, Pease and DiFabio in New Britain, CT.
Christine D. Reed, of California. She will be the homebuilding representative. Currently Mrs. Reed serves as executive director of the Building Industry Association of Southern California for the Orange County Region in Santa Ana, CA.

The President announced that the following individuals will comprise the Presidential delegation to observe the elections in Romania, May 17–23:

Delegation Chairman:

Gov. Garrey Carruthers of New Mexico and Katherine Carruthers

Delegates:

Mary Jo Arndt, Republican national committeewoman, Illinois
Ellen R. Conant, chairman, St. Louis County Council, Missouri
Victor Gold, national correspondent, Washingtonian magazine, Virginia
Alan Green, Jr., U.S. Ambassador to Romania
Howard Lamb, State senator, Nebraska

May 17

The President met at the White House with:
—the Vice President; John H. Sununu, Chief of Staff to the President; Brent Scowcroft, Assistant to the President for National Security Affairs; and members of the CIA briefing staff;
—Members of Congress, to discuss administration policy on offshore oil drilling in Florida and California;
—John H. Sununu, Chief of Staff to the President.

The White House announced that President Bush will meet with President Ertha Pascal Trouillot of Haiti on May 24 and President Virgilio Barco Vargas of Colombia on June 5, to continue a series of high-level meetings with Latin American and Caribbean leaders.

The White House also announced that the President will meet with Prime Minister Constantine Mitsotakis of Greece on June 6.

The President announced his intention to appoint Charles Pei Wang to be a member of the Commission on Civil Rights for a term expiring December 5, 1995. He would succeed Murray Friedman. Currently Mr. Wang is president of the China Institute in America in New York, NY.

May 18

The President met at the White House with:
—the Vice President; John H. Sununu, Chief of Staff to the President; Brent Scowcroft, Assistant to the President for National Security Affairs; and members of the CIA briefing staff;
—Prince Philip, Duke of Edinburgh;
—the Vice President, for lunch.

The President announced that Armando Valladares will continue to serve as the U.S. Representative on the Human Rights Commission of the Economic and Social Council of the United Nations.

In the afternoon, the President and Mrs. Bush traveled to Dallas, TX.

In the evening, following a State Republican Party fundraising dinner, the President and Mrs. Bush traveled to Houston, TX, where they spent the night.

The President declared that a major disaster existed in Hawaii as a result of lava flows from the Kilauea Volcano. He directed the Federal Emergency Management Agency to provide assistance to supplement State and local recovery efforts.

The President also declared that a major disaster existed in Oklahoma as a result of heavy rains, tornadoes, and flooding that began on April 14. He directed the Federal Emergency Management Agency to provide assistance to supplement State and local recovery efforts.

May 19

In the morning, the President toured areas along the Trinity River flooded by recent severe storms.

Later that morning, the President participated in the Doug Sanders Kingwood Celebrity Classic Golf Tournament at the Deerwood Country Club.

May 20

In the afternoon, the President traveled from Houston, TX, to Portland, OR, where he met with State legislative candidates.

May 21

In the early afternoon, the President attended a State Republican Party fundraising luncheon. Following the luncheon, the President returned to Washington, DC.

May 22

The President met at the White House with:

—the Vice President; John H. Sununu, Chief of Staff to the President; Brent Scowcroft, Assistant to the President for National Security Affairs; and members of the CIA briefing staff;

—Republican congressional leaders, to discuss their legislative agenda;

—the Vice President, for lunch;

—Secretary of State James A. Baker III;

—Cuban-Americans, on the 88th anniversary of Cuba's independence from Spain;

—John H. Sununu, Chief of Staff to the President.

The President announced his intention to appoint the following individuals to be members of the Advisory Commission on Intergovernmental Relations for terms of 2 years:

Victor H. Ashe, of Tennessee. He would succeed William E. Hudnut III. Currently Mr. Ashe serves as the mayor of Knoxville, TN.

Robert Michael Isaac, of Colorado. This is a reappointment. Currently Mr. Isaac serves as the mayor of Colorado Springs, CO.

Joseph A. Leafe, of Virginia. He would succeed Arthur J. Holland. Currently Mr. Leafe serves as the mayor of Norfolk, VA.

The President announced his intention to nominate Michael T. Bass to be a member of the National Council on the Humanities, National Foundation on the Arts and the Humanities, for a term expiring January 26, 1994. He would succeed James Clayburn La Force, Jr. Currently Mr. Bass is the president of the Bass Group in Pensacola, FL.

The President announced his intention to appoint Patrick A. Domenico to be a member of the Nuclear Waste Technical Review Board for a term expiring April 19, 1994. This is a new position. Currently Dr. Domenico is the David B. Harris professor of geology at Texas A&M University in College Station, TX.

The President announced his intention to designate Johnny Yune to be a member of the Board of Governors of the United Service Organizations, Incorporated, for a term of 3 years. He would succeed Gordon D. Walker. Currently Mr.

Yune serves as an entertainer for KOJAP & Co. in Beverly Hills, CA.

May 23

The President met at the White House with:

—the Vice President; John H. Sununu, Chief of Staff to the President; Brent Scowcroft, Assistant to the President for National Security Affairs; and members of the CIA briefing staff;

—Secretary of State James A. Baker III;

—John H. Sununu, Chief of Staff to the President.

The President announced his intention to appoint the following individuals to be members of the Board of Directors of the Federal Home Loan Mortgage Corporation for a term ending on the date of the next annual meeting of the voting common stockholders in 1991. These are new positions:

George L. Argyros, of California. Currently Mr. Argyros serves as chief executive officer and president of Arnel Development Co. in Costa Mesa, CA.

Thomas Ludlow Ashley, of the District of Columbia. Currently Mr. Ashley serves as president of the Association of Bank Holding Companies in Washington, DC.

Woodward Kingman, of the District of Columbia. Currently Mr. Kingman serves as an investment management consultant, and he is a former President of the Government National Mortgage Association.

In the evening, the President hosted a barbecue for the White House press photographers. Later, he attended the Patrick Henry Foundation dinner.

May 24

The President met at the White House with:

—the Vice President; John H. Sununu, Chief of Staff to the President; Brent Scowcroft, Assistant to the President for National Security Affairs; and members of the CIA briefing staff;

—delegates to the Mexico/United States Interparliamentary Conference;

—John H. Sununu, Chief of Staff to the President.

In an Oval Office ceremony, the President presented the Blind and Handicapped Workers of the Year Awards.

In the evening, the President attended a fundraising reception for Senator Larry Pressler.

The President declared that a major disaster existed in Missouri as a result of severe storms and flooding that began on May 15. He directed the Federal Emergency Management Agency to provide assistance to supplement State and local recovery efforts.

May 25

The President met at the White House with the Vice President; John H. Sununu, Chief of Staff to the President; Brent Scowcroft, Assistant to the President for National Security Affairs; and members of the CIA briefing staff.

The President participated in an Oval Office ceremony in observance of National Missing Children's Day.

In the morning, the President traveled to Kennebunkport, ME, for the weekend.

The President announced his intention to nominate Rosalie Gaull Silberman to be a member of the Equal Employment Opportunity Commission for a term expiring July 1, 1995. Upon confirmation she will be designated Vice Chairman. This is a reappointment. Currently Mrs. Silberman serves as Vice Chairman of the Equal Employment Opportunity Commission in Washington, DC.

The President announced his intention to designate the following individuals to be members of the Board of Visitors of the United States Air Force Academy:

Phyllis Levitt Kaminsky, of Pennsylvania, for a term expiring December 30, 1992. She would succeed Charles B. Wilkinson. Currently Mrs. Kaminsky serves as senior international adviser for Ruder Finn, Inc., a public relations and communications firm.

Harry Jonathan Pearce, of Michigan, for a term expiring December 30, 1992. He would succeed Holly Coors. Currently Mr. Pearce serves as vice president and general counsel of General Motors Corp. in Detroit, MI.

May 26

The President declared that a major disaster existed in western Iowa as a result of severe storms and flooding that began on May 18. He directed the Federal Emergency Management Agency to provide assistance to supplement State and local recovery efforts.

May 28

In the afternoon, the President and Mrs. Bush returned to the White House from a weekend stay at their home in Kennebunkport, ME.

May 29

The President met at the White House with:
—the Vice President; John H. Sununu, Chief of Staff to the President; Brent Scowcroft, Assistant to the President for National Security Affairs; and members of the CIA briefing staff;
—the Vice President, for lunch;
—John H. Sununu, Chief of Staff to the President.

Throughout the day, the President attended meetings at the White House in preparation for

the upcoming summit with President Mikhail Gorbachev of the Soviet Union.

In a ceremony in the Residence, the President received diplomatic credentials from Ambassadors Jaime de Ojeda y Eiseley (Spain), Patricio Silva Echenique (Chile), Abid Hussain (India), Charles M. Nyirabu (Tanzania), Roger Issombo (Congo), and Alexander A. Bessmertnykh (Soviet Union).

In the evening, President Bush had a telephone conversation with Prime Minister Brian Mulroney of Canada to discuss the Prime Minister's meetings with President Gorbachev in Ottawa on May 29.

May 30

The President met at the White House with:
—the Vice President; John H. Sununu, Chief of Staff to the President; Brent Scowcroft, Assistant to the President for National Security Affairs; and members of the CIA briefing staff;
—John H. Sununu, Chief of Staff to the President.

In the morning, the President had a telephone conversation with Chancellor Helmut Kohl of the Federal Republic of Germany to discuss the upcoming summit with President Mikhail Gorbachev of the Soviet Union.

Throughout the day, the President attended meetings at the White House in preparation for the upcoming summit.

The President announced his intention to appoint the following individuals to be members of the Cultural Property Advisory Committee for terms expiring April 25, 1992:

Jack A. Josephson, of New York. He would succeed John J. Slocum. Currently Mr. Josephson serves as president of Sellers and Josephson, Inc., in Norwood, NJ.

Harold Mark Keshishian, of the District of Columbia. He would succeed James G. Crowley III. Currently Mr. Keshishian serves as president of Mark Keshishian and Sons, Inc., in Chevy Chase, MD.

Frederick William Lange, of Colorado. He would succeed Denver Fred Wendorf, Jr. Currently Dr. Lange serves as an adjunct associate professor of anthropology at the University of Colorado and as curator of anthropology at the University of Colorado Museum in Boulder, CO.

The President announced his intention to appoint the following individuals to be members of the Intergovernmental Advisory Council on Education for the terms indicated:

John K. Andrews, Jr., of Colorado, for a term expiring July 27, 1994. This is a reappointment. Upon appointment he will be designated Chairman. Currently Mr. Andrews serves as president of the Independence Institute in Golden, CO.

917

Hugh D. Shine, of Texas, for a term expiring July 27, 1993. This is a reappointment. Currently Mr. Shine serves as an investment consultant for Dean Witter Reynolds, Inc., and as a State representative for District 53 in Temple, TX.

Josephine J. Wang, of Maryland, for a term expiring on July 27, 1993. She would succeed Paul M. Jenkins. Currently Mrs. Wang serves as an elementary school teacher in Rockville, MD.

Addison Graves Wilson, of South Carolina, for a term expiring on July 27, 1993. He would succeed John M. Engler. Currently Mr. Wilson is a partner with the law firm of Kirkland, Taylor, Wilson, Moore, Allen and Deneen, P.A., in Columbia, SC.

The President announced his intention to appoint the following individuals to be members of the Korean War Veterans Memorial Advisory Board:

John Patrick Comer, of Massachusetts. He would succeed Conrad Hausman. Currently Mr. Comer serves as the national commander of the American Legion and executive director of Quincy Housing Authority in Quincy, MA.

John S. Staum, of Minnesota. He would succeed John B. Curcio. Currently Mr. Staum serves as the national commander-in-chief of Veterans of Foreign Wars and with Sales Club Supplies in Minneapolis, MN.

The President announced his intention to nominate Christopher A. Hart to be a member of the National Transportation Safety Board for the remainder of the term expiring December 31, 1992. He would succeed Joseph Trippe Nall. Currently Mr. Hart serves as managing partner with the law firm of Hart and Chavers in Washington, DC.

The President announced his intention to nominate Gopal Sivaraj Pal to be a member of the Board of Regents of the Uniformed Services University of the Health Sciences for a term expiring June 20, 1995. He would succeed M. Robert Hill, Jr. Currently Dr. Pal serves as a dentist in general practice in Washington, DC.

May 31

The President met at the White House with:

—the Vice President; John H. Sununu, Chief of Staff to the President; Brent Scowcroft, Assistant to the President for National Security Affairs; and members of the CIA briefing staff;

—John H. Sununu, Chief of Staff to the President.

In the morning, President Bush met privately in the Oval Office at the White House with President Mikhail Gorbachev of the Soviet Union.

In the late afternoon, President Gorbachev returned to the White House, and the two Presidents met in the Cabinet Room with U.S. and Soviet officials.

June 1

The President met at the White House with the Vice President; John H. Sununu, Chief of Staff to the President; Brent Scowcroft, Assistant to the President for National Security Affairs; and members of the CIA briefing staff.

In the morning, President Bush met in the Oval Office at the White House with President Mikhail Gorbachev of the Soviet Union.

In the afternoon, President Gorbachev returned to the White House, and the two Presidents met in the Oval Office, following the signing of bilateral agreements in the East Room.

June 2

In the morning, President and Mrs. Bush and President and Mrs. Gorbachev left the White House for Camp David, MD, where the two Presidents continued their discussions.

In the evening, President and Mrs. Bush hosted an informal dinner for President and Mrs. Gorbachev at Camp David. Following the dinner, President and Mrs. Gorbachev returned to the Soviet Embassy in Washington, DC, while President and Mrs. Bush returned to the White House.

June 3

In the morning, President and Mrs. Bush met privately with President and Mrs. Gorbachev at the White House.

Following the joint news conference in the East Room of the White House, President and Mrs. Gorbachev traveled to Minneapolis, MN.

In the afternoon, President Bush telephoned Prime Minister Margaret Thatcher of the United Kingdom and Chancellor Helmut Kohl of the Federal Republic of Germany to discuss the recently concluded summit with President Mikhail Gorbachev of the Soviet Union.

In the evening, President Bush telephoned former President Reagan to discuss President Gorbachev's upcoming meeting with President Reagan.

June 4

The President met at the White House with:

—the Vice President; John H. Sununu, Chief of Staff to the President; Brent Scowcroft, Assistant to the President for National Security Affairs; and members of the CIA briefing staff;

—Secretary of Defense Richard B. Cheney;

—John H. Sununu, Chief of Staff to the President.

The President announced his intention to nominate Andrew C. Hove to be a member of the Board of Directors of the Federal Deposit Insurance Corporation for a term expiring February 28, 1993. Upon confirmation he will be designated Vice Chairman. This is a new position. Currently Mr. Hove serves as chairman of the board and chief executive officer of Minden Exchange Bank and Trust Co. in Minden, NE.

The President announced his intention to appoint S. Thomas Gagliano to be a member of the Commission on Railroad Retirement Reform. He would succeed Gregory W. Baise. Currently Mr. Gagliano serves as executive director of the New Jersey Transit Corp. in Newark, NJ.

The President announced his intention to nominate the following individuals to be members of the Board of Directors of the Commodity Credit Corporation:

Catherine Ann Bertini, of Illinois. She would succeed John William Bode. Currently Mrs. Bertini serves as Assistant Secretary of Agriculture for Food and Consumer Services.

Keith D. Bjerke, of North Dakota. He would succeed Milton J. Hertz. Currently Mr. Bjerke serves as Administrator for the Agricultural Stabilization and Conservation Service at the Department of Agriculture.

Bruce L. Gardner, of Maryland. He would succeed Ewen M. Wilson. Currently Dr. Gardner serves as Assistant Secretary of Agriculture for Economics.

Jo Ann Doke Smith, of Florida. She would succeed Kenneth A. Gillis. Currently Mrs. Smith serves as Assistant Secretary of Agriculture for Marketing and Inspection.

In the evening, the President telephoned Prime Minister Toshiki Kaifu of Japan to discuss the recently concluded summit with President Mikhail Gorbachev of the Soviet Union.

June 5

The President met at the White House with:
—the Vice President; John H. Sununu, Chief of Staff to the President; Brent Scowcroft, Assistant to the President for National Security Affairs; and members of the CIA briefing staff;
—congressional leaders, to discuss the recently concluded summit with President Mikhail Gorbachev of the Soviet Union;
—President Virgilio Barco Vargas of Colombia;
—John H. Sununu, Chief of Staff to the President.

In the morning, President Bush telephoned President François Mitterrand of France to discuss the recently concluded summit with President Mikhail Gorbachev of the Soviet Union.

The President declared that a major disaster existed in Indiana as a result of severe storms, flooding, and tornadoes that began on May 15. He directed the Federal Emergency Management Agency to provide assistance to supplement State and local recovery efforts.

The President transmitted to the Congress the annual report of the Corporation for Public Broadcasting for fiscal year 1989 and the inventory of Federal funds distributed to the public telecommunications entities by Federal Departments and Agencies for fiscal year 1989.

June 6

The President met at the White House with:
—the Vice President; John H. Sununu, Chief of Staff to the President; Brent Scowcroft, Assistant to the President for National Security Affairs; and members of the CIA briefing staff;
—Secretary of Defense Richard B. Cheney;
—President Roh Tae Woo of the Republic of Korea;
—Prime Minister Constantine Mitsotakis of Greece;
—Lane Kirkland, president of the American Federation of Labor and Congress of Industrial Organizations, and senior trade union leaders from the seven industrialized nations participating in the upcoming economic summit;
—John H. Sununu, Chief of Staff to the President.

The White House announced that the following individuals will comprise the Presidential delegation to observe the elections in Bulgaria, June 7–12:

Chairman:

Gov. Henry Bellmon of Oklahoma and Shirley Bellmon

Delegates:

Richard D. McLellan, attorney with Dykema, Gossett in Michigan

Marshall L. Miller, attorney with Bishop, Cook, Purcell and Reynolds in the District of Columbia

Jack Perry, former U.S. Ambassador to Bulgaria, director of the Dean Rusk program in international studies and professor of political science at Davidson College in North Carolina

Sol Polansky, U.S. Ambassador to Bulgaria

Eunice B. Whittlesey, Republican national committeewoman from New York

The White House announced that the following individuals will comprise the Presidential delegation to Madagascar in celebration of its 30th anniversary of independence on June 26:

Chairman:

Col. Frederick D. Gregory, USAF, NASA astronaut, and Barbara Gregory, of Texas

Delegate:

Howard Walker, U.S. Ambassador to Madagascar

The President announced his intention to nominate the following individuals to be members of the National Council on Disability:

Larry Brown, Jr., of Maryland, for a term expiring September 17, 1992. He would succeed Theresa Lennon Gardner. Currently Mr. Brown serves as business and community relations manager for the integrated systems operations of the Xerox Corp. in McLean, VA.

Michael B. Unhjem, of North Dakota, for the remainder of the term expiring September 17, 1990. He would succeed Justin Dart. He will be nominated for an additional term expiring September 17, 1993. Currently Mr. Unhjem serves as vice president for corporate affairs and legal counsel for Blue Cross, Blue Shield of North Dakota in Fargo, ND.

Helen Wilshire Walsh, of Connecticut, for a term expiring September 17, 1990. She would succeed Nanette MacDougall. She will also be nominated for an additional term expiring September 17, 1993. Currently Ms. Walsh serves on the board of trustees of Nathaniel Witherell and on the board of directors of the Rehabilitation Institute of Chicago.

June 7

The President met at the White House with the Vice President; John H. Sununu, Chief of Staff to the President; Brent Scowcroft, Assistant to the President for National Security Affairs; and members of the CIA briefing staff.

In the morning, the President traveled to Milwaukee, WI.

June 8

The White House announced that the President approved a request by Robert O. Harris, Chairman of Emergency Board No. 219, created by Executive Order No. 12714, to extend the reporting deadline of the Board. The Board will now be required to report to the President not later than September 15, 1990. The Board is investigating a dispute between railroads represented by the National Carriers' Conference Committee of the National Railway Labor Conference and their employees.

In the evening, the President returned to Washington, DC, where he hosted a dinner in the Residence for Chancellor Helmut Kohl of the Federal Republic of Germany. Following the dinner, the President went to Camp David, MD, for the weekend.

June 10

In the afternoon, the President returned to the White House from a weekend stay at Camp David, MD, and attended the christening of his grandson Charles Walker Bush in the Rose Garden.

June 11

The President met at the White House with:
—the Vice President; John H. Sununu, Chief of Staff to the President; Brent Scowcroft, Assistant to the President for National Security Affairs; and members of the CIA briefing staff;
—administration officials, to discuss the budget;
—the National Collegiate Athletic Association women's championship lacrosse teams from

Harvard University and Ursinus College and the men's championship lacrosse teams from Syracuse University and Hobart College;
—John H. Sununu, Chief of Staff to the President.

The President announced his intention to nominate the following individuals to be members of the Boards of Trustees of the Federal Old-Age and Survivors and the Federal Disability Insurance Trust Fund, the Federal Hospital Insurance Trust Fund, and the Federal Supplementary Medical Insurance Trust Fund for terms of 4 years:

Stanford G. Ross, of the District of Columbia. He would succeed Suzanne Jaffe. Currently Mr. Ross serves as a senior partner with the law firm of Arnold and Porter in Washington, DC.

David M. Walker, of Virginia. He would succeed Mary Falvey Fuller. Currently Mr. Walker serves as partner and national director of compensation and benefits practice for Arthur Andersen and Co. in Washington, DC.

The President announced his intention to appoint the following individuals to be members of the Advisory Commission on Intergovernmental Relations for terms of 2 years:

Gov. John Ashcroft, of Missouri. This is a reappointment.

Gov. Booth Gardner, of Washington. He would succeed Theodore Schwinden.

State Senator David Nething, of North Dakota. This is a reappointment.

Gov. Stan Stephens, of Montana. He would succeed John Henry Sununu.

The President announced his intention to nominate Benjamin F. Marsh to be a member of the Foreign Claims Settlement Commission of the United States for the term expiring September 30, 1992. He would succeed Robert J. Kabel. Currently Mr. Marsh serves as a partner with the law firm of Marsh and McAdams in Maumee, OH.

The President approved and sent to the Congress the following fiscal year 1991 budget amendments:
—two requests totaling $300 million for the President's initiative to provide special assistance for Eastern Europe. These amendments would make $230 million available for bilateral assistance and $70 million available for the U.S. subscription to paid-in capital for the European Bank for Reconstruction and Development;
—technical appropriations language to provide a program limitation for the Inter-American Development Bank;
—an appropriations language amendment that would enable the Department of Defense to pay National Guard and Reserve military

personnel for support activities performed for law enforcement agencies involved in antinarcotics work.

June 12

The President met at the White House with:
—the Vice President; John H. Sununu, Chief of Staff to the President; Brent Scowcroft, Assistant to the President for National Security Affairs; and members of the CIA briefing staff;
—Republican congressional leaders;
—President Amata Kabua of the Marshall Islands;
—John H. Sununu, Chief of Staff to the President.

The President announced his intention to nominate the following individuals to be members of the Board of Trustees of the Harry S. Truman Scholarship Foundation for the terms indicated:

John Ashcroft, of Missouri, for a term expiring December 10, 1993. He would succeed Terry Edward Branstad. Currently John Ashcroft serves as Governor of Missouri.

Richard C. Hackett, of Tennessee, for a term expiring December 10, 1993. He would succeed Robert Michael Isaac. Currently Richard Hackett serves as mayor of Memphis.

The President announced his intention to appoint the following individuals to be members of the Committee for Purchase from the Blind and Other Severely Handicapped:

Nell Carney, of Virginia. She would succeed Susan S. Suter. Currently Ms. Carney serves as Commissioner of the Rehabilitation Services Administration at the Department of Education in Washington, DC.

Mervin J. Flander, of Nevada, for a term expiring December 21, 1994. Currently Mr. Flander serves as chief of the bureau of services to the blind in the rehabilitation division of the department of human resources for the State of Nevada in Carson City, NV.

Richard P. Seiter, of the District of Columbia. He would succeed Gerald M. Farkas. Currently Dr. Seiter serves as Assistant Director of Federal Prison Industries for the Federal Prison System at the Department of Justice in Washington, DC.

June 13

The President met at the White House with:
—the Vice President; John H. Sununu, Chief of Staff to the President; Brent Scowcroft, Assistant to the President for National Security Affairs; and members of the CIA briefing staff;
—Secretary of State James A. Baker III;
—former French President Valéry Giscard D'Estaing;
—John H. Sununu, Chief of Staff to the President.

The White House announced that the President will travel to Yorba Linda, CA, to attend the dedication and formal opening of the Richard Nixon Presidential Library and Birthplace on July 19.

June 14

The President met at the White House with the Vice President; John H. Sununu, Chief of Staff to the President; Brent Scowcroft, Assistant to the President for National Security Affairs; and members of the CIA briefing staff.

June 15

The President met at the White House with the Vice President; John H. Sununu, Chief of Staff to the President; Brent Scowcroft, Assistant to the President for National Security Affairs; and members of the CIA briefing staff.

In the morning, the President went to Camp David, MD, where he hosted a picnic for Cabinet senior staff.

June 17

In the afternoon, the President returned to the White House from a weekend stay at Camp David, MD.

June 18

The President met at the White House with:
—the Vice President; John H. Sununu, Chief of Staff to the President; Brent Scowcroft, Assistant to the President for National Security Affairs; and members of the CIA briefing staff;
—Secretary of Defense Richard B. Cheney;
—John H. Sununu, Chief of Staff to the President.

The President transmitted to the Congress a report on the feasibility of establishing a National Drug Operations Center for the integration, coordination, and control of all drug interdictions.

The President announced his intention to appoint Damon J. Keith to be a member of the Commission on the Bicentennial of the United States Constitution. He would succeed William Lucas. Currently Mr. Keith serves as a judge for the U.S. Court of Appeals for the Sixth Circuit in Detroit, MI.

June 19

The President met at the White House with:
—the Vice President; John H. Sununu, Chief of Staff to the President; Brent Scowcroft, Assistant to the President for National Security Affairs; and members of the CIA briefing staff;
—congressional leaders;
—Attorney General Dick Thornburgh, for lunch;

—President Sam Nujoma of Namibia;
—the Recreation Roundtable.

The President transmitted to the Congress the annual report of the Department of Housing and Urban Development, which covered calendar year 1988.

June 20
The President met at the White House with the Vice President; John H. Sununu, Chief of Staff to the President; Brent Scowcroft, Assistant to the President for National Security Affairs; and members of the CIA briefing staff.

In the morning, the President traveled to Huntsville, AL.

June 21
The President met at the White House with:
—the Vice President; John H. Sununu, Chief of Staff to the President; Brent Scowcroft, Assistant to the President for National Security Affairs; and members of the CIA briefing staff;
—Ken Lay and George Strake, Cochairmen of the Houston Economic Summit Committee;
—the Vice President, for lunch;
—members of the International Chamber of Commerce, to discuss the upcoming Houston economic summit;
—former Japanese Foreign Minister Shintaro Abe.

In the evening, the President hosted a reception in the Residence for the retirement of Adm. Paul A. Yost, Jr., Commandant of the U.S. Coast Guard.

June 22
The President met at the White House with the Vice President; John H. Sununu, Chief of Staff to the President; Brent Scowcroft, Assistant to the President for National Security Affairs; and members of the CIA briefing staff.

The President declared that a major disaster existed in Illinois as a result of severe storms, tornadoes, and floods that began on May 15. He directed the Federal Emergency Management Agency to provide assistance to supplement State and local recovery efforts.

In the afternoon, the President traveled to Camp David, MD, for the weekend.

June 24
In the afternoon, the President returned from a weekend stay at Camp David, MD.

June 25
The President met at the White House with:
—John H. Sununu, Chief of Staff to the President; Brent Scowcroft, Assistant to the Presi-

dent for National Security Affairs; and members of the CIA briefing staff;
—Republican congressional Federal budget negotiators;
—Secretary of the Treasury Nicholas F. Brady;
—John H. Sununu, Chief of Staff to the President.

In the evening, the President and Mrs. Bush hosted a barbecue for members of the diplomatic community on the South Lawn.

June 26
The President met at the White House with:
—John H. Sununu, Chief of Staff to the President; Brent Scowcroft, Assistant to the President for National Security Affairs; and members of the CIA briefing staff;
—Foreign Minister Ahmed Esmat Abdel Meguid of Egypt, to discuss the Middle East peace process and the suspension of U.S. talks with the Palestine Liberation Organization;
—police officers from Milton, MA;
—the National Collegiate Athletic Association women's championship softball team from the University of California at Los Angeles and the men's championship baseball team from the University of Georgia;
—Secretary of Defense Richard B. Cheney;
—John H. Sununu, Chief of Staff to the President.

The President announced his intention to appoint John F.W. Rogers to be Chairman of the Advisory Council on Historic Preservation for a term of 4 years expiring June 10, 1993. This is a reappointment. Currently Mr. Rogers serves as executive vice president of the Oliver Carr Co. in Washington, DC.

The President announced his intention to nominate Elmer B. Staats to be a member of the Board of Trustees of the Harry S. Truman Scholarship Foundation for a term expiring December 10, 1995. This is a reappointment. From 1966 to 1981, Dr. Staats served as Comptroller General of the General Accounting Office in Washington, DC.

The President announced his intention to appoint John Charles Gartland to be a member of the National Council on Vocational Education for a term expiring January 17, 1991. He would succeed Gertrude McDonald. Currently Mr. Gartland serves as director of Washington affairs for the Amway Corp. in Washington, DC.

June 27
The President met at the White House with:
—John H. Sununu, Chief of Staff to the President; Brent Scowcroft, Assistant to the Presi-

dent for National Security Affairs; and members of the CIA briefing staff;
—Secretary of State James A. Baker III;
—John H. Sununu, Chief of Staff to the President.

June 28

The President met at the White House with:
—the Vice President; John H. Sununu, Chief of Staff to the President; Brent Scowcroft, Assistant to the President for National Security Affairs; and members of the CIA briefing staff;
—the Vice President, for lunch;
—John H. Sununu, Chief of Staff to the President.

The President announced his intention to reappoint the following individuals to be members of the Advisory Committee for Trade Policy and Negotiations for terms of 2 years:

Allen F. Jacobson, of Minnesota. Mr. Jacobson currently serves as the chairman and chief executive officer of the 3M Co. in St. Paul, MN.

John A. Rollwagen, of Minnesota. Mr. Rollwagen currently serves as the chairman and chief executive officer of Cray Research, Inc., in Minneapolis, MN.

Jack Sheinkman, of New York. Mr. Sheinkman currently serves as president of the Amalgamated Clothing and Textile Workers Union, AFL–CIO, CLC, in New York, NY.

Gordon B. Zacks, of Ohio. Mr. Zacks currently serves chairman of the board and chief executive officer of the R.G. Barry Corp. in Columbus, OH.

June 29

The President met at the White House with:
—the Vice President; John H. Sununu, Chief of Staff to the President; Brent Scowcroft, Assistant to the President for National Security Affairs; and members of the CIA briefing staff;
—Peter Ueberroth, former commissioner of baseball, and Trammell Crow, major donor to the Republican Party;
—Secretary of State James A. Baker III.

The President announced his intention to nominate Joyce Elaine Tucker to be a member of the Equal Employment Opportunity Commission for the remainder of the term expiring July 1, 1991. She would succeed Clarence Thomas. Cur-

rently Mrs. Tucker serves as director of the Illinois Department of Human Rights in Chicago.

The President approved and sent to the Congress the following fiscal year 1991 budget amendments:

—Budget amendments for the Department of Energy (DOE) would provide an increase of $20.1 million for various energy supply, research, and development programs, and an increase of $27 million for environmental restoration and waste management activities. These increases would be fully offset by a $47.1 million decrease in atomic energy defense activities, reflecting reduced requirements for naval fuel. Another DOE amendment reduces the estimate of uranium supply and enrichment revenues and reduce total program needs based on lower power costs.
—An increase of $575 thousand for the Office of Personnel Management would expand the operation of the Federal Quality Institute.
—An amendment would provide the National Archives and Records Administration with $879 thousand to cover 50 percent of the proposed January 1991 3.5 percent Federal pay raise.
—An increase of $225 thousand for the Office of Government Ethics would cover the increased workload resulting from the Government Ethics Act of 1989.
—An additional $12 million for the legislative branch would be used to reconstruct the Senate Subway Transportation System, and additional appropriations language for the judiciary would enable an adjustment in the salaries of Justices and judges.

In the afternoon, the President and Mrs. Bush traveled to their home in Kennebunkport, ME.

June 30

The President declared that a major disaster existed in California as a result of wildland fires that began on June 26. He directed the Federal Emergency Management Agency to provide assistance to supplement State and local recovery efforts.

In the evening, the President had a telephone conversation with African National Congress leader Nelson Mandela. Mr. Mandela thanked the President for their recent meeting.

Appendix B—Nominations Submitted to the Senate

The following list does not include promotions of members of the Uniformed Services, nominations to the Service Academies, or nominations of Foreign Service officers.

Submitted January 23

Everett Ellis Briggs,
of New Hampshire, a career member of the Senior Foreign Service, Class of Career Minister, to be Ambassador Extraordinary and Plenipotentiary of the United States of America to the Republic of Portugal.

Paul C. Lambert,
of New York, to be Ambassador Extraordinary and Plenipotentiary of the United States of America to the Republic of Ecuador.

Edward Morgan Rowell,
of California, a career member of the Senior Foreign Service, Class of Minister-Counselor, to be Ambassador Extraordinary and Plenipotentiary of the United States of America to Luxembourg.

Susan Jane Koch,
of the District of Columbia, to be an Assistant Director of the United States Arms Control and Disarmament Agency, vice William H. Fite, resigned.

Douglas Alan Brook,
of Virginia, to be an Assistant Secretary of the Army, vice Ken Kramer, resigned.

Colin Riley McMillan,
of New Mexico, to be an Assistant Secretary of Defense, vice Jack Katzen, resigned.

Enrique Mendez, Jr.,
of Puerto Rico, to be an Assistant Secretary of Defense, vice William E. Mayer, resigned.

Thomas W. Corbett, Jr.,
of Pennsylvania, to be United States Attorney for the Western District of Pennsylvania for the term of 4 years, vice J. Alan Johnson, resigned.

Julie E. Carnes,
of Georgia, to be a member of the United States Sentencing Commission for a term expiring October 31, 1995, vice Paul H. Robinson, resigned.

Gary C. Byrne,
of California, to be Administrator of the Rural Electrification Administration for a term of 10 years, vice Harold V. Hunter, resigned.

L. Joyce Hampers,
of Massachusetts, to be an Assistant Secretary of Commerce, vice Orson G. Swindle III, resigned.

Barbara Everitt Bryant,
of Michigan, to be Director of the Census, vice John G. Keane, resigned, to which position she was appointed during the last recess of the Senate.

Antonia Coello Novello,
of the District of Columbia, to be Surgeon General of the Public Health Service for a term of 4 years, vice C. Everett Koop, resigned.

D'Wayne Gray,
of Virginia, to be Chief Benefits Director, Department of Veterans Affairs (new position).

Malcolm S. Forbes, Jr.,
of New Jersey, to be a member of the Board for International Broadcasting for a term expiring April 28, 1992 (reappointment).

Annice M. Wagner,
of the District of Columbia, to be an Associate Judge of the District of Columbia Court of Appeals for the term of 15 years, vice Julia P. Cooper Mack, resigned.

The following-named persons to be Associate Directors of the Office of Science and Technology Policy (new positions):

William D. Phillips, of Missouri.
Eugene Wong, of California.

Ervin S. Duggan,
of South Carolina, to be a member of the Federal Communications Commission for a term of 5 years from July 1, 1989, vice Patricia Diaz Dennis, resigned.

Donald Robert Quartel, Jr.,
of Florida, to be a Federal Maritime Commissioner for the term expiring June 30, 1994, vice Edward J. Philbin, term expired.

David W. Mullins, Jr.,
of Arkansas, to be a member of the Board of
Governors of the Federal Reserve System for the
unexpired term of 14 years from February 1,
1982, vice H. Robert Heller, resigned.

Edward W. Kelley, Jr.,
of Texas, to be a member of the Board of Governors of the Federal Reserve System for a term of
14 years from February 1, 1990 (reappointment).

Jessica L. Parks,
of Georgia, to be a member of the Merit Systems
Protection Board for the remainder of the term
expiring March 1, 1995, vice Samuel W. Bogley.

The following-named persons to be Members of
the National Council on Disability for the terms
indicated:

*For the remainder of the term expiring Septem-
ber 17, 1991:*

Mary Matthews Raether, of Virginia, vice Phyllis D. Zlotnick, term expired.

For a term expiring September 17, 1992:

Sandra Swift Parrino, of New York (reappointment).
Alvis Kent Waldrep, Jr., of Texas (reappointment).

Anthony Hurlbutt Flack,
of Connecticut, to be a member of the National
Council on Disability for a term expiring September 17, 1991, vice John F. Mills.

Dennis M. Devaney,
of Maryland, to be a member of the National
Labor Relations Board for the term of 5 years
expiring December 16, 1994 (reappointment), to
which position he was appointed during the last
recess of the Senate.

Clifford R. Oviatt, Jr.,
of Virginia, to be a member of the National
Labor Relations Board for the remainder of the
term expiring August 27, 1993, vice Wilford W.
Johansen, resigned, to which position he was appointed during the last recess of the Senate.

Tommy G. Thompson,
of Wisconsin, to be a member of the Board of
Directors of the National Railroad Passenger Corporation for a term of 4 years, vice Robert D.
Orr, resigned.

James L. Kolstad,
of Colorado, to be Chairman of the National
Transportation Safety Board for a term of 2
years, vice James Eugene Burnett, Jr., term expired.

Velma Montoya,
of California, to be a member of the Occupational Safety and Health Review Commission for the
remainder of the term expiring April 27, 1991,
vice Robert E. Rader, Jr., resigned.

Ronald M. Holdaway,
of Wyoming, to be an Associate Judge of the
United States Court of Veterans Appeals for the
term of 15 years (new position).

Withdrawn January 23

Samuel W. Bogley,
of Maryland, to be a member of the Merit Systems Protection Board for the term of 7 years
expiring March 1, 1995, vice Dennis M. Devaney,
resigned, which was sent to the Senate on January 3, 1989.

Submitted January 24

Raymond C. Clevenger III,
of the District of Columbia, to be United States
Circuit Judge for the Federal Circuit, vice Oscar
H. Davis, deceased.

Alan D. Lourie,
of Pennsylvania, to be United States Circuit
Judge for the Federal Circuit, vice Daniel M.
Friedman, retired.

David H. Souter,
of New Hampshire, to be United States Circuit
Judge for the First Circuit, vice Hugh H. Bownes,
retired.

Robert H. Hodges, Jr.,
of South Carolina, to be a Judge of the United
States Claims Court for a term of 15 years, vice
John L. Napier, resigned.

Joseph M. Hood,
of Kentucky, to be United States District Judge
for the Eastern District of Kentucky, vice Scott
Reed, retired.

James F. McClure, Jr.,
of Pennsylvania, to be United States District
Judge for the Middle District of Pennsylvania,
vice William J. Nealon, retired.

Lawrence M. McKenna,
of New York, to be United States District Judge
for the Southern District of New York, vice William C. Conner, retired.

John S. Martin, Jr.,
of New York, to be United States District Judge
for the Southern District of New York, vice
Edward Weinfeld, deceased.

John D. Rainey,
of Texas, to be United States District Judge for the Southern District of Texas, vice Gabrielle K. McDonald, resigned.

James K. Singleton, Jr.,
of Alaska, to be United States District Judge for the District of Alaska, vice James M. Fitzgerald, retired.

William M. Nickerson,
of Maryland, to be United States District Judge for the District of Maryland, vice Herbert F. Murray, retired.

Daniel B. Sparr,
of Colorado, to be United States District Judge for the District of Colorado, vice John P. Moore, elevated.

Norman H. Stahl,
of New Hampshire, to be United States District Judge for the District of New Hampshire, vice Martin F. Loughlin, retired.

Jack N. Engor,
of Colorado, to be United States Marshal for the District of Colorado for the term of 4 years, vice Charles L. Dunahue.

Donald W. Tucker,
of Arizona, to be United States Marshal for the District of Arizona for the term of 4 years, vice John W. Roberts.

John Wesley Bartlett,
of Massachusetts, to be Director of the Office of Civilian Radioactive Waste Management, vice Ben C. Rusche, resigned.

Bradley Gordon,
of Virginia, to be an Assistant Director of the United States Arms Control and Disarmament Agency, vice Kathleen C. Bailey, resigned.

Submitted January 25

Charles M. Herzfeld,
of New Jersey, to be Director of Defense Research and Engineering, vice Robert Clifton Duncan, resigned.

Donald Jay Yockey,
of California, to be Deputy Under Secretary of Defense for Acquisition, vice Milton L. Lohr, resigned.

Robert H. Gentile,
of Ohio, to be an Assistant Secretary of Energy (Fossil Energy), vice James Allan Wampler, resigned.

D'Wayne Gray,
of Virginia, to be Chief Benefits Director, Department of Veterans Affairs, for a term of 4 years (new position).

Ronald William Roskens,
of Nebraska, to be Administrator of the Agency for International Development, vice M. Alan Woods, deceased.

Ronald William Roskens,
of Nebraska, to be a member of the Board of Directors of the Inter-American Foundation for the remainder of the term expiring September 20, 1992, vice M. Alan Woods, deceased.

C. Anson Franklin,
of Virginia, to be an Assistant Administrator of the Agency for International Development, vice Thomas R. Blank, resigned.

The following-named persons to be members of the National Commission on Libraries and Information Science for the terms indicated:

For a term expiring July 19, 1993:

   Wanda L. Forbes, of South Carolina (reappointment).
   Charles E. Reid, of New Jersey (reappointment).

For a term expiring July 19, 1994:

   Daniel W. Casey, of New York (reappointment).
   Elinor H. Swaim, of North Carolina (reappointment).

John R. Dunne,
of New York, to be an Assistant Attorney General, vice William Bradford Reynolds, resigned.

Withdrawn January 25

William Lucas,
of Michigan, to be an Assistant Attorney General, vice William Bradford Reynolds, resigned, which was sent to the Senate on May 1, 1989.

D'Wayne Gray,
of Virginia, to be Chief Benefits Director, Department of Veterans Affairs, (new position), which was sent to the Senate on January 23.

Submitted January 29

Richard J. Hankinson,
of Virginia, to be Inspector General, Department of Justice (new position—P.L. 100–504).

Submitted January 30

Gerald A. Cann,
of Maryland, to be an Assistant Secretary of the Navy, vice Thomas F. Faught, Jr., resigned.

Jacqueline E. Schafer,
of Virginia, to be an Assistant Secretary of the Navy, vice Everett Pyatt, resigned.

Joyce T. Berry,
of the District of Columbia, to be Commissioner on Aging, vice Carol Fraser Fisk, resigned.

Frederick M. Bernthal,
of Tennessee, to be Deputy Director of the National Science Foundation, vice John H. Moore, resigned.

Philip R. Lochner, Jr.,
of Connecticut, to be a member of the Securities and Exchange Commission for the remainder of the term expiring June 5, 1991, vice David S. Ruder, resigned.

Submitted January 31

Michael Lorne Moodie,
of Maryland, to be an Assistant Director of the U.S. Arms Control and Disarmament Agency, vice Lynn Marvin Hansen, resigned.

Donald L. Ivers,
of New Mexico, to be an Associate Judge of the United States Court of Veterans Appeals for the term of 15 years (new position).

Submitted February 5

Erich W. Bretthauer,
of Nevada, to be an Assistant Administrator of the Environmental Protection Agency, vice Vaun A. Newill, resigned.

Charles J. Chamberlain,
of Illinois, to be a member of the Railroad Retirement Board for the term of 5 years from August 29, 1989 (reappointment).

Glen L. Bower,
of Illinois, to be a member of the Railroad Retirement Board for the remainder of the term expiring August 28, 1992, vice Thomas J. Simon.

Submitted February 6

Richard E. Bissell,
of Virginia, to be an Assistant Administrator of the Agency for International Development, vice Nyle C. Brady, resigned.

Tommy G. Thompson,
of Wisconsin, to be a member of the Board of Directors of the National Railroad Passenger Corporation for the remainder of the term expiring April 27, 1990, vice Robert D. Orr.

Submitted February 20

Deane Roesch Hinton,
of Illinois, a career member of the Senior Foreign Service, with the personal rank of Career Ambassador, to be Ambassador Extraordinary and Plenipotentiary of the United States of America to the Republic of Panama, to which position he was appointed during the recess of the Senate from November 22, 1989, to January 23, 1990.

Jonathan Moore,
of Massachusetts, to be the Representative of the United States of America on the Economic and Social Council of the United Nations, with the rank of Ambassador.

Shirin Raziuddin Tahir-Kheli,
of Pennsylvania, to be the Alternate Representative of the United States of America for Special Political Affairs in the United Nations, with the rank of Ambassador.

Samuel A. Alito, Jr.,
of New Jersey, to be United States Circuit Judge for the Third Circuit, vice John J. Gibbons, retired.

Stephen M. McNamee,
of Arizona, to be United States District Judge for the District of Arizona, vice Charles L. Hardy, retired.

Robert H. Cleland,
of Michigan, to be United States District Judge for the Eastern District of Michigan, vice James P. Churchill, retired.

Graham C. Mullen,
of North Carolina, to be United States District Judge for the Western District of North Carolina, vice James B. McMillan, retired.

Robert E. Jones,
of Oregon, to be United States District Judge for the District of Oregon, vice James M. Burns, retired.

John J. Adair,
of Virginia, to be Inspector General, Resolution Trust Corporation (new position).

Brig. Gen. Arthur E. Williams, USA,
to be a member and President of the Mississippi River Commission.

The following-named persons to be members of the Board of Directors of the State Justice Institute for the terms indicated:

For a term expiring September 17, 1991:

Terrence B. Adamson, of Georgia, vice Lawrence H. Cook, resigned.

Vivi L. Dilweg, of Wisconsin, vice Rodney A. Peeples, term expired.

For a term expiring September 17, 1992:

Carl F. Bianchi, of Idaho, vice Larry P. Polansky, term expired.

James Duke Cameron, of Arizona (reappointment).

Janice L. Gradwohl, of Nebraska (reappointment).

Malcolm M. Lucas, of California, vice Ralph J. Erickstad, term expired.

Robert H. Swan,
of Utah, to be a member of the National Credit Union Administration Board for the term of 6 years expiring August 2, 1995, vice David L. Chatfield, resigned.

Herman Jay Cohen,
an Assistant Secretary of State, to be a member of the Board of Directors of the African Development Foundation for the remainder of the term expiring September 22, 1991, vice Chester A. Crocker.

The following-named persons to be members of the Board of Directors of the Inter-American Foundation for terms of 6 years:

Norton Stevens, of New York (new position).
Frank D. Yturria, of Texas (new position).

Submitted February 21

E.U. Curtis Bohlen,
of Maine, to be Assistant Secretary of State for Oceans and International Environmental and Scientific Affairs, vice Frederick M. Bernthal, resigned.

Nelson C. Ledsky,
of Maryland, a career member of the Senior Foreign Service, Class of Minister-Counselor, for the rank of Ambassador during his tenure of service as Special Cyprus Coordinator.

William Hughes Graves III,
of Mississippi, to be Director of the National Institute on Disability and Rehabilitation Research, vice David B. Gray, resigned.

LeGree Sylvia Daniels,
of Pennsylvania, to be a Governor of the United States Postal Service for the term expiring December 8, 1998, vice John Lathrop Ryan, term expired.

Submitted February 23

James Henry Michel,
of Virginia, to be an Assistant Administrator of the Agency for International Development, vice Dwight A. Ink, resigned.

Jack D. Shanstrom,
of Montana, to be United States District Judge for the District of Montana, vice James F. Battin, retired.

Submitted March 5

John C. Foltz,
of Ohio, to be Administrator of the Federal Grain Inspection Service, vice W. Kirk Miller, resigned.

The following-named individuals to be members of the National Science Board, National Science Foundation, for terms expiring May 10, 1994:

Peter H. Raven, of Missouri, vice William A. Nierenberg, term expired.

Benjamin S. Shen, of Pennsylvania, vice Norman C. Rasmussen, term expired.

Submitted March 6

Samuel Grayson Wilson,
of Virginia, to be United States District Judge for the Western District of Virginia, vice Glen M. Williams, retired.

D. Brock Hornby,
of Maine, to be United States District Judge for the District of Maine, vice Conrad K. Cyr, elevated.

Lynne Vincent Cheney,
of Wyoming, to be Chairperson of the National Endowment for the Humanities for a term of 4 years (reappointment).

Submitted March 7

Jo Anne B. Barnhart,
of Delaware, to be Assistant Secretary for Family Support, Department of Health and Human Services (new position).

The following-named persons to be members of the Board of Directors of the Corporation for Public Broadcasting for terms expiring March 1, 1994:

Henry J. Cauthen, of South Carolina, vice Howard D. Gutin.

Lloyd Kaiser, of Pennsylvania (reappointment).

Submitted March 8

Adriane J. Dudley,
of the Virgin Islands, to be a Judge of the District Court of the Virgin Islands for a term of 10 years, vice Almeric L. Christian, retired.

Arthur F. Van Court,
of California, to be United States Marshal for the Eastern District of California for the term of 4 years (reappointment).

Submitted March 19

Morris Lee Thompson,
of Kansas, to be United States Attorney for the District of Kansas for the term of 4 years, vice Benjamin L. Burgess, Jr., resigned.

Submitted March 20

Stephen D. Easton,
of North Dakota, to be United States Attorney for the District of North Dakota for the term of 4 years, vice Rodney S. Webb, resigned.

Thomas Lawrence Sansonetti,
of Wyoming, to be Solicitor of the Department of the Interior, vice Martin Lewis Allday.

Robert Marshall White,
of Minnesota, to be Under Secretary of Commerce for Technology (new position).

Julian W. De La Rosa,
of Texas, to be Inspector General, Department of Labor, vice James Brian Hyland, resigned.

Karen L. Gillmor,
of Ohio, to be Director of the Women's Bureau, Department of Labor, vice Jill Houghton Emery, resigned.

James B. Edwards,
of South Carolina, to be a member of the Board of Directors of the Communications Satellite Corporation until the date of the annual meeting of the Corporation in 1993 (reappointment).

Jerry D. Jennings,
of Michigan, to be Deputy Director of the Federal Emergency Management Agency, vice Robert H. Morris, resigned.

John K. Lauber,
of Maryland, to be a member of the National Transportation Safety Board for the term expiring December 31, 1994 (reappointment).

Robert C. Larson,
of Michigan, to be a member of the Oversight Board of the Resolution Trust Corporation for a term of 3 years (new position).

Keith McNamara,
of Ohio, to be a member of the Board of Directors of the State Justice Institute for a term expiring September 17, 1992, vice Joseph Wentling Brown, term expired.

Submitted March 21

James Henry Michel,
of Virginia, to be a member of the Board of Directors of the Inter-American Foundation for the remainder of the term expiring September 20, 1992, vice M. Alan Woods, deceased.

Withdrawn March 21

Ronald William Roskens,
of Nebraska, to be a member of the Board of Directors of the Inter-American Foundation for the remainder of the term expiring September 20, 1992, vice M. Alan Woods, deceased, which was sent to the Senate on January 25, 1990.

Submitted March 29

Don Melvin Newman,
of Indiana, for the rank of Minister during his tenure of service as the Representative of the United States of America on the Council of the International Civil Aviation Organization.

Michael L. Williams,
of Texas, to be Assistant Secretary for Civil Rights, Department of Education, vice LeGree S. Daniels, resigned.

Submitted March 30

Richard W. Vollmer, Jr.,
of Alabama, to be United States District Judge for the Southern District of Alabama, vice William Brevard Hand, retired.

Submitted April 4

Wendy Lee Gramm,
of Texas, to be a Commissioner of the Commodity Futures Trading Commission for the term expiring April 13, 1995 (reappointment).

Wendy Lee Gramm,
of Texas, to be Chairman of the Commodity Futures Trading Commission (reappointment).

Submitted April 18

Dane Farnsworth Smith, Jr.,
of New Mexico, a career member of the Senior Foreign Service, Class of Minister-Counselor, to be Ambassador Extraordinary and Plenipotentiary of the United States of America to the Republic of Guinea.

Charles H. Thomas,
of Maryland, a career member of the Senior Foreign Service, Class of Minister-Counselor, to be Ambassador Extraordinary and Plenipotentiary of the United States of America to the Republic of Hungary.

Alan Philip Larson,
of Virginia, a career member of the Senior Foreign Service, Class of Minister-Counselor, to be the Representative of the United States of America to the Organization for Economic Cooperation and Development, with the rank of Ambassador.

Richard F. Suhrheinrich,
of Michigan, to be United States Circuit Judge for the Sixth Circuit, vice Albert J. Engel, retired.

David C. Norton,
of South Carolina, to be United States District Judge for the District of South Carolina, vice Solomon Blatt, Jr., retired.

The following-named persons to be Associate Judges of the Superior Court of the District of Columbia for the term of 15 years (new position):

Mary Ellen Abrecht, of the District of Columbia.
Kaye K. Christian, of the District of Columbia.
Frederick D. Dorsey, of the District of Columbia.
Ellen Segal Huvelle, of the District of Columbia.
Jose M. Lopez, of the District of Columbia.
Joan Z. McAvoy, of the District of Columbia.
Gregory E. Mize, of the District of Columbia.
Patricia A. Wynn, of the District of Columbia.

Patrick E. McFarland,
of Virginia, to be Inspector General, Office of Personnel Management (new position).

Arden L. Bement, Jr.,
of Ohio to be a member of the National Science Board, National Science Foundation, for a term expiring May 10, 1994 (reappointment).

Submitted April 19

Joseph G. Schiff,
of Kentucky, to be an Assistant Secretary of Housing and Urban Development, vice J. Michael Dorsey.

Anthony J. Hope,
of California, to be Chairman of the National Indian Gaming Commission for a term of 3 years (new position).

Olin L. Greene, Jr.,
of Oregon, to be Administrator of the United States Fire Administration, vice Clyde A. Bragdon, Jr., resigned.

Submitted April 20

James Keough Bishop,
of New York, a career member of the Senior Foreign Service, Class of Minister-Counselor, to be Ambassador Extraordinary and Plenipotentiary of the United States of America to the Somali Democratic Republic.

Daniel H. Carter,
of Texas, to be a member of the National Commission on Libraries and Information Science for a term expiring July 19, 1994 (reappointment).

The following-named persons to be Directors of the Federal Housing Finance Board for the terms indicated:

For a term of 3 years:

Lawrence U. Costiglio, of New York (new position).

For a term of 7 years:

Daniel F. Evans, Jr., of Indiana (new position).

Submitted April 24

Steven E. Steiner,
of Maryland, a career member of the Senior Foreign Service, Class of Minister-Counselor, for the rank of Ambassador during his tenure of service as United States Representative to the Special Verification Commission.

Jimmy C. Carter,
of Georgia, to be United States Marshal for the Southern District of Georgia for the term of 4 years, vice Larry James Stubbs, term expired.

James F. Blumstein,
of Tennessee, to be Administrator of the Office of Information and Regulatory Affairs, vice S. Jay Plager, resigned.

Andrew Camp Barrett,
of Illinois, to be a member of the Federal Communications Commission for a term of 5 years from July 1, 1990 (reappointment).

Ming Hsu,
of New Jersey, to be a Federal Maritime Commissioner for the remainder of the term expiring June 30, 1991, vice Elaine L. Chao, resigned.

James S. Halpern,
of the District of Columbia, to be a Judge of the United States Tax Court for a term expiring 15

years after he takes office, vice Meade Whitaker, retired.

Withdrawn April 24

Victor Stello, Jr.,
of Maryland, to be an Assistant Secretary of Energy (Defense Programs), vice Sylvester R. Foley, Jr., resigned, which was sent to the Senate on July 24, 1989.

Submitted April 25

Peter Jon de Vos,
of Florida, a career member of the Senior Foreign Service, Class of Minister-Counselor, to be Ambassador Extraordinary and Plenipotentiary of the United States of America to the Republic of Liberia.

James J. West,
of Pennsylvania, to be United States Attorney for the Middle District of Pennsylvania for the term of 4 years, vice David Dart Queen, resigned.

Submitted April 26

Kenneth L. Ryskamp,
of Florida, to be United States Circuit Judge for the Eleventh Circuit, vice Paul H. Roney, retired.

Submitted April 30

James L. Webb,
of Oklahoma, to be United States Marshal for the Eastern District of Oklahoma for the term of 4 years, vice Laurence C. Beard, retired.

Pamela Talkin,
of New York, to be a member of the Federal Labor Relations Authority for a term of 5 years expiring July 1, 1995 (reappointment).

Submitted May 7

William Bodde, Jr.,
of Maryland, a career member of the Senior Foreign Service, Class of Minister-Counselor, to be Ambassador Extraordinary and Plenipotentiary of the United States of America to the Republic of the Marshall Islands.

Joseph Edward Lake,
of Texas, a career member of the Senior Foreign Service, Class of Counselor, to be Ambassador Extraordinary and Plenipotentiary of the United States of America to the Mongolian People's Republic.

Gary E. Shovlin,
of Texas, to be United States Marshal for the Middle District of Pennsylvania for the term of 4 years, vice Matthew Chabel, Jr.

Stephen Anthony Trodden,
of Virginia, to be Inspector General, Department of Veterans Affairs (new position).

Wallace Elmer Stickney,
of New Hampshire, to be Director of the Federal Emergency Management Agency, vice Julius W. Becton, Jr., resigned.

Submitted May 8

Karen LeCraft Henderson,
of South Carolina, to be United States Circuit Judge for the District of Columbia Circuit, vice Kenneth W. Starr, resigned.

A. Raymond Randolph,
of Maryland, to be United States Circuit Judge for the District of Columbia Circuit, vice Spottswood W. Robinson III, retired.

James R. Moseley,
of Indiana, to be an Assistant Secretary of Agriculture, vice George S. Dunlop, resigned.

Submitted May 10

Gilberto Guardia Fabrega,
a citizen of the Republic of Panama, to be Administrator of the Panama Canal Commission, vice Dennis P. McAuliffe.

Sylvia Alice Earle,
of California, to be Chief Scientist of the National Oceanic and Atmospheric Administration, vice Melvin N.A. Peterson, resigned.

The following-named persons to be members of the United States Sentencing Commission for the terms indicated:

For the remainder of the term expiring October 31, 1991:

Michael S. Gelacak, of Virginia, vice Michael K. Block, resigned.

For a term expiring October 31, 1995:

A. David Mazzone, of Massachusetts, vice Stephen G. Breyer, term expired.

The following-named persons to be members of the National Council on the Humanities for the terms indicated:

For a term expiring January 26, 1994:

Billie Davis Gaines, of Georgia, vice Jeffrey Hart, term expired.
Gary L. McDowell, of the District of Columbia, vice Rita Ricardo-Campbell, term expired.
Jeanne J. Smoot, of North Carolina, vice Ellis Sandoz, term expired.

For a term expiring January 26, 1996:

Bruce D. Benson, of Colorado, vice Kathleen S. Kilpatrick, resigned.

Submitted May 11

Paul V. Niemeyer,
of Maryland, to be United States Circuit Judge for the Fourth Circuit, vice Harrison Winter, retired.

John H. McBryde,
of Texas, to be United States District Judge for the Northern District of Texas, vice Eldon B. Mahon, retired.

Charles W. Pickering, Sr.,
of Mississippi, to be United States District Judge for the Southern District of Mississippi, vice Walter L. Nixon, Jr.

Frederick P. Stamp, Jr.,
of West Virginia, to be United States District Judge for the Northern District of West Virginia, vice William M. Kidd, retired.

Submitted May 14

Steven D. Dillingham,
of South Carolina, to be Director of the Bureau of Justice Statistics, vice Steven Roger Schlesinger, resigned.

Jimmy Gurule,
of Utah, to be an Assistant Attorney General, vice Richard Bender Abell, resigned.

Charles M. House,
of California, to be Director of the Office for Victims of Crime (new position).

Lourdes G. Baird,
of California, to be United States Attorney for the Central District of California for the term of 4 years, vice Robert C. Bonner, resigned.

Submitted May 15

Robert E. Lamb,
of Georgia, a career member of the Senior Foreign Service, Class of Career Minister, to be Ambassador Extraordinary and Plenipotentiary of the United States of America to the Republic of Cyprus.

James Wilson Holsinger, Jr.,
of Virginia, to be Chief Medical Director, Department of Veterans Affairs, for a term of 4 years (new position).

Jonathan R. Steinberg,
of Maryland, to be an Associate Judge of the United States Court of Veterans Appeals for the term of 15 years (new position).

Submitted May 16

G. Philip Hughes,
of Virginia, to be Ambassador Extraordinary and Plenipotentiary of the United States of America to Barbados, and to serve concurrently and without additional compensation as Ambassador Extraordinary and Plenipotentiary of the United States of America to the Commonwealth of Dominica, Ambassador Extraordinary and Plenipotentiary of the United States of America to Saint Lucia, and Ambassador Extraordinary and Plenipotentiary of the United States of America to Saint Vincent and the Grenadines.

David Passage,
of North Carolina, a career member of the Senior Foreign Service, Class of Minister-Counselor, to be Ambassador Extraordinary and Plenipotentiary of the United States of America to the Republic of Botswana.

Richard Wayne Bogosian,
of Maryland, a career member of the Senior Foreign Service, Class of Minister-Counselor, to be Ambassador Extraordinary and Plenipotentiary of the United States of America to the Republic of Chad.

Philip S. Kaplan,
of California, a career member of the Senior Foreign Service, Class of Minister-Counselor, for the rank of Ambassador during his tenure of service as Deputy United States Representative to the Negotiations on Conventional Armed Forces in Europe.

Russell Flynn Miller,
of Maryland, to be Inspector General, Federal Emergency Management Agency (new position).

Submitted May 18

Michael Boudin,
of the District of Columbia, to be United States District Judge for the District of Columbia, vice John H. Pratt, retired.

Harry W. Shlaudeman,
of California, a career member of the Senior Foreign Service, Class of Career Minister, to be Ambassador Extraordinary and Plenipotentiary of the United States of America to the Republic of Nicaragua.

Eugene L. Scassa,
of Virginia, a career member of the Senior Foreign Service, Class of Minister-Counselor, to be Ambassador Extraordinary and Plenipotentiary of the United States of America to Belize.

Carol Bagley Amon,
of New York, to be United States District Judge for the Eastern District of New York, vice Mark A. Costantino, retired.

Submitted May 23

William B. Milam,
of California, a career member of the Senior Foreign Service, Class of Minister-Counselor, to be Ambassador Extraordinary and Plenipotentiary of the United States of America to the People's Republic of Bangladesh.

James Daniel Phillips,
of Kansas, a career member of the Senior Foreign Service, Class of Minister-Counselor, to be Ambassador Extraordinary and Plenipotentiary of the United States of America to the People's Republic of the Congo.

Thomas W. Simons, Jr.,
of the District of Columbia, a career member of the Senior Foreign Service, Class of Minister-Counselor, to be Ambassador Extraordinary and Plenipotentiary of the United States of America to the Republic of Poland.

Michael T. Bass,
of Florida, to be a member of the National Council on the Humanities for a term expiring January 26, 1994, vice James Clayburn La Force, Jr., term expired.

Submitted May 24

Roger Gran Harrison,
of Colorado, a career member of the Senior Foreign Service, Class of Minister-Counselor, to be Ambassador Extraordinary and Plenipotentiary of the United States of America to the Hashemite Kingdom of Jordan.

Submitted June 5

Federico A. Moreno,
of Florida, to be United States District Judge for the Southern District of Florida, vice Alcee L. Hastings.

Michael L. Johnson,
of Idaho, to be United States Marshal for the District of Idaho for the term of 4 years, vice Blaine Skinner.

Albert Z. Moore,
of Ohio, to be United States Marshal for the Northern District of Ohio for the term of 4 years, vice Earl L. Rife, resigned.

Paul L. Ziemer,
of Indiana, to be an Assistant Secretary of Energy (Environment, Safety and Health), vice Ernest C. Baynard III, resigned.

Calvin A. Kent,
of Texas, to be Administrator of the Energy Information Administration, vice Helmut A. Merklein, resigned.

Rosalie Gaull Silberman,
of the District of Columbia, to be a member of the Equal Employment Opportunity Commission for a term expiring July 1, 1995 (reappointment).

Andrew C. Hove,
of Nebraska, to be a member of the Board of Directors of the Federal Deposit Insurance Corporation for a term expiring February 28, 1993 (new position).

Christopher A. Hart,
of the District of Columbia, to be a member of the National Transportation Safety Board for the remainder of the term expiring December 31, 1992, vice Joseph Trippe Nall, deceased.

David H. Leroy,
of Idaho, to be Nuclear Waste Negotiator (new position).

Gopal Sivaraj Pal,
of Virginia, to be a member of the Board of Regents of the Uniformed Services University of the Health Sciences for a term expiring June 20, 1995, vice M. Robert Hill, Jr., term expired.

The following-named persons to be members of the Board of Directors of the Commodity Credit Corporation:

Catherine Ann Bertini, of Illinois, vice John William Bode, resigned.
Keith D. Bjerke, of North Dakota, vice Milton J. Hertz, resigned.
Bruce L. Gardner, of Maryland, vice Ewen M. Wilson, resigned.
Jo Ann Doke Smith, of Florida, vice Kenneth A. Gillis, resigned.

Submitted June 6

Hugh Kenneth Hill,
of California, a career member of the Senior Foreign Service, Class of Minister-Counselor, to be Ambassador Extraordinary and Plenipotentiary of

the United States of America to the People's Republic of Bulgaria.

John W. Raley, Jr.,
of Oklahoma, to be United States Attorney for the Eastern District of Oklahoma for the term of 4 years, vice Roger Hilfiger, resigned.

Submitted June 7

Aurelia Erskine Brazeal,
of Georgia, a career member of the Senior Foreign Service, Class of Minister-Counselor, to be Ambassador Extraordinary and Plenipotentiary of the United States of America to the Federated States of Micronesia.

Roy M. Huffington,
of Texas, to be Ambassador Extraordinary and Plenipotentiary of the United States of America to the Republic of Austria.

Frederick Vreeland,
of New York, to be Ambassador Extraordinary and Plenipotentiary of the United States of America to the Union of Burma (Myanmar).

Joel F. Dubina,
of Alabama, to be United States Circuit Judge for the Eleventh Circuit, vice Robert S. Vance, deceased.

William Eric Andersen,
of Tennessee, to be Administrator of the Wage and Hour Division, Department of Labor, vice Paula V. Smith, resigned.

The following-named persons to be members of the National Council on Disability for the terms indicated:

> Larry Brown, Jr., of Maryland, for a term expiring September 17, 1992, vice Theresa Lennon Gardner, resigned.
> Michael B. Unhjem, of North Dakota, for the remainder of the term expiring September 17, 1990, vice Justin Dart, resigned.
> Michael B. Unhjem, of North Dakota, for a term expiring September 17, 1993 (reappointment).
> Helen Wilshire Walsh, of Connecticut, for a term expiring September 17, 1990, vice Nanette Fabray MacDougall, term expired.
> Helen Wilshire Walsh, of Connecticut, for a term expiring September 17, 1993 (reappointment).

Withdrawn June 7

Debra Russell Bowland,
of Louisiana, to be Administrator of the Wage and Hour Division, Department of Labor, vice

Paula V. Smith, resigned, which was sent to the Senate on June 8, 1989.

Submitted June 8

Andrew C. Hove,
of Nebraska, to be Vice Chairperson of the Board of Directors of the Federal Deposit Insurance Corporation (new position—P.L. 101–73).

Constance Horner,
Under Secretary of Health and Human Services, to be a member of the Board of Directors of the National Consumer Cooperative Bank for a term of 3 years, vice Ewen M. Wilson.

Withdrawn June 8

Ewen M. Wilson,
an Assistant Secretary of Agriculture, to be a member of the Board of Directors of the National Consumer Cooperative Bank for a term of 3 years, which was sent to the Senate on January 3, 1989.

Submitted June 11

Robert C. Bonner,
of California, to be Administrator of Drug Enforcement, vice John C. Lawn, resigned.

Randall R. Rader,
of Virginia, to be United States Circuit Judge for the Federal Circuit, vice Jean Galloway Bissell, deceased.

William M. Skretny,
of New York, to be United States District Judge for the Western District of New York, vice John T. Curtin, retired.

Fred L. Foreman,
of Illinois, to be United States Attorney for the Northern District of Illinois for the term of 4 years, vice Anton R. Valukas, resigned.

The following-named persons to be members of the Boards of Trustees of the Federal Hospital Insurance Trust Fund, the Federal Old-Age and Survivors Insurance Trust Fund and the Federal Disability Insurance Trust Fund, and the Federal Supplementary Medical Insurance Trust Fund:

For terms of 4 years:

> Stanford G. Ross, of the District of Columbia, vice Suzanne Denbo Jaffe.
> David M. Walker, of Virginia, vice Mary Falvey Fuller.

Benjamin F. Marsh,
of Ohio, to be a member of the Foreign Claims Settlement Commission of the United States for

935

the term expiring September 30, 1992, vice Robert J. Kabel, term expired.

Withdrawn June 11

The following-named persons to be members of the Boards of Trustees of the Federal Hospital Insurance Trust Fund, the Federal Old-Age and Survivors Insurance Trust Fund and the Federal Disability Insurance Trust Fund, and the Federal Supplementary Medical Insurance Trust Fund for terms of 4 years, which were sent to the Senate on January 3, 1989:

Mary Falvey Fuller, of California.
Suzanne Denbo Jaffe, of New York.

Submitted June 12

The following-named persons to be Associate Judges of the Superior Court of the District of Columbia:

For terms of 15 years:

John Henry Bayly, Jr., of the District of Columbia, vice Iraline Green Barnes, retired.
Linda Turner Hamilton, of the District of Columbia, vice Carlisle Edward Pratt.

Submitted June 13

Kenneth Noel Peltier,
of Texas, a career member of the Senior Foreign Service, Class of Minister-Counselor, to be Ambassador Extraordinary and Plenipotentiary of the United States of America to the Federal and Islamic Republic of the Comoros.

George Fleming Jones,
of Texas, a career member of the Senior Foreign Service, Class of Minister-Counselor, to be Ambassador Extraordinary and Plenipotentiary of the United States of America to the Co-operative Republic of Guyana.

The following-named persons to be members of the Board of Trustees of the Harry S. Truman Scholarship Foundation:

For terms expiring December 10, 1993:

John Ashcroft, of Missouri, vice Terry Edward Branstad, term expired.
Richard C. Hackett, of Tennessee, vice Robert Michael Isaac, term expired.

Submitted June 14

Richard C. Brown,
of Maryland, a career member of the Senior Foreign Service, Class of Minister-Counselor, to be Ambassador Extraordinary and Plenipotentiary of the United States of America to the Oriental Republic of Uruguay.

Townsend B. Friedman, Jr.,
of Illinois, a career member of the Senior Foreign Service, Class of Counselor, to be Ambassador Extraordinary and Plenipotentiary of the United States of America to the People's Republic of Mozambique.

Richard V. Bertain,
of California, to be Associate Director of ACTION, vice Daniel F. Bonner, resigned.

Submitted June 18

Timothy John McBride,
of Michigan, to be an Assistant Secretary of Commerce, vice Michael Philip Skarzynski.

Stephen D. Potts,
of Maryland, to be Director of the Office of Government Ethics for a term of 5 years, vice Frank Q. Nebeker, resigned.

Submitted June 19

Edward William Gnehm, Jr.,
of Georgia, a career member of the Senior Foreign Service, Class of Minister-Counselor, to be Ambassador Extraordinary and Plenipotentiary of the United States of America to the State of Kuwait.

Genta Hawkins Holmes,
of California, a career member of the Senior Foreign Service, Class of Minister-Counselor, to be Ambassador Extraordinary and Plenipotentiary of the United States of America to the Republic of Namibia.

Submitted June 22

W. Lee Rawls,
of Maryland, to be an Assistant Attorney General, vice Carol T. Crawford, resigned.

Stanley A. Twardy, Jr.,
of Connecticut, to be United States Attorney for the District of Connecticut for the term of 4 years (reappointment).

Submitted June 26

Michael Martin Skol,
of Illinois, a career member of the Senior Foreign Service, Class of Minister-Counselor, to be Ambassador Extraordinary and Plenipotentiary of the United States of America to the Republic of Venezuela.

Elmer B. Staats,
of the District of Columbia, to be a member of the Board of Trustees of the Harry S. Truman

Scholarship Foundation for a term expiring December 10, 1995 (reappointment).

Withdrawn June 26

Eric M. Javits,
of New York, to be Ambassador Extraordinary and Plenipotentiary of the United States of America to the Republic of Venezuela, which was sent to the Senate on July 11, 1989.

Submitted June 27

George F. Murphy, Jr.,
of Maryland, to be Inspector General, United States Information Agency, vice Anthony J. Gabriel, resigned.

937

Appendix C—Checklist of White House Press Releases

The following list contains releases of the Office of the Press Secretary which are not included in this book.

Released January 8

Advance text:
Remarks to the American Farm Bureau Federation in Orlando, FL

Fact sheet:
American farming and rural America

Released January 11

Transcript:
Press briefing on the President's meeting with Prime Minister Anibal Cavaco Silva of Portugal—by Raymond G.H. Seitz, Assistant Secretary of State for European and Canadian Affairs

Released January 12

Advance text:
Remarks at Robert A. Taft High School in Cincinnati, OH

Advance text:
Remarks to the Chamber of Commerce in Cincinnati, OH

Released January 19

Advance text:
Remarks at the annual convention of the National Association of Home Builders in Atlanta, GA

Advance text:
Remarks at a fundraising dinner for Gov. Bob Martinez in Miami, FL

Released January 22

Announcement:
Redecoration of the Oval Office with private funds

Advance text:
Remarks at the American Spectator annual dinner

Released January 23

Advance text:
Remarks to the law enforcement community in Kansas City, MO

Released January 24

Announcement:
Nomination of Raymond C. Clevenger III to be United States Circuit Judge for the Federal Circuit

Announcement:
Nomination of David H. Souter to be United States Circuit Judge for the First Circuit of New Hampshire

Announcement:
Nomination of William M. Nickerson to be United States District Judge for the District of Maryland

Announcement:
Nomination of Jack N. Engor to be United States Marshal for the District of Colorado

Announcement:
Nomination of Robert H. Hodges to be a United States Claims Court Judge

Announcement:
Nomination of Joseph M. Hood to be a United States District Judge for the Eastern District of Kentucky

Announcement:
Nomination of Alan D. Lourie to be a United States Circuit Judge for the Federal Circuit

Announcement:
Nomination of John S. Martin, Jr., to be United States District Judge for the Southern District of New York

Announcement:
Nomination of James F. McClure, Jr., to be United States District Judge for the Middle District of Pennsylvania

Announcement:
Nomination of Lawrence M. McKenna to be United States District Judge for the Southern District of New York

Announcement:
Nomination of John D. Rainey to be United States District Judge for the Southern District of Texas

Announcement:
Nomination of James K. Singleton to be United States District Judge for the District of Alaska

Announcement:
Nomination of Daniel B. Sparr to be United States District Judge for the District of Colorado

Announcement:
Nomination of Norman H. Stahl to be United States District Judge for the District of New Hampshire

Announcement:
Nomination of Donald W. Tucker to be United States Marshal for the District of Arizona

Released January 25

Advance text:
Remarks at a luncheon for newspaper publishers

Transcript:
Press briefing on the administration's budget outlays for the war on drugs in fiscal year 1991—by William J. Bennett, Director of National Drug Control Policy

Transcript:
Press briefing on U.S. aid to Panama—by Deputy Secretary of the Treasury John Robson and Deputy Secretary of State Lawrence Eagleburger

Released January 26

Fact sheet:
President's Head Start Initiative

Transcript:
Press briefing on the gross national product for the fourth quarter of 1989—by Michael J. Boskin, Chairman of the Council of Economic Advisers

Released January 29

Transcript:
Press briefing on the President's fiscal year 1991 budget—by Secretary of the Treasury Nicholas F. Brady; Richard G. Darman, Director of the Office of Management and Budget; and Michael J. Boskin, Chairman of the Council of Economic Advisers

Fact sheet:
The President's fiscal year 1991 budget

Advance text:
Remarks at the annual convention of the National Religious Broadcasters

Released January 30

Transcript:
Press briefing on the proposed Savings and Economic Growth Act of 1990, the President's fiscal year 1991 budget, and the State of the Union Address—by Secretary of the Treasury Nicholas F. Brady

Announcement:
Nomination of Donald L. Ivers to be an Associate Judge of the United States Court of Veterans Appeals

Released January 31

Advance text:
Address before a joint session of the Congress on the state of the Union

Fact sheet:
Address before a joint session of the Congress on the state of the Union

Fact sheet:
National education goals

Released February 1

Transcript:
Press briefing on the President's education goals, budget, and achievements—by Secretary of Education Lauro F. Cavazos

Transcript:
Press briefing on the President's agenda, fiscal year 1991 budget, and State of the Union Message—by John H. Sununu, Chief of Staff to the President

Released February 2

Fact sheet:
Science and technology accomplishments and initiatives of the Bush administration

Fact sheet:
CATIC/MAMCO divestment

Advance text:
Remarks to students and faculty of the University of Tennessee at Knoxville

Released February 6

Fact sheet:
1990 Economic Report of the President

Advance text:
Remarks to U.S. troops at the National Training Center at Fort Irwin in Barstow, CA

Advance text:
Remarks at a fundraising breakfast for Gov. Kay Orr in Omaha, NE

Released February 8

Advance text:
Remarks at a fundraising dinner for the Ohio Republican Party in Columbus

Released February 9

Announcement:
Nomination of Stephen M. McNamee to be United States District Judge for the District of Arizona

Announcement:
Nomination of Graham C. Mullen to be United States District Judge for the Western District of North Carolina

Announcement:
Nomination of Robert H. Cleland to be United States District Judge for the Eastern District of Michigan

Announcement:
Nomination of Samuel A. Alito to be United States Circuit Judge for the Third Circuit

Released February 12

Announcement:
Nomination of Robert E. Jones to be United States District Judge for the District of Oregon

Released February 13

Transcript:
Press briefing on the drug summit in Cartagena, Colombia—by Brent Scowcroft, Assistant to the President for National Security Affairs

Transcript:
Press briefing on the results of the annual survey of drug use among high school seniors and young adults—by Secretary of Health and Human Services Louis W. Sullivan; Under Secretary of Education Ted Sanders; and William J. Bennett, Director of National Drug Control Policy

Fact sheet:
U.N. Convention Against Illegal Traffic in Narcotic Drugs and Psychotropic Substances

Released February 15

Fact sheet:
Drug summit in Cartagena, Colombia—bilateral agreements

Fact sheet:
Drug summit in Cartagena, Colombia—Declaration of Cartagena

Released February 20

Transcript:
Press briefing on President Bush's meeting with President Václav Havel of Czechoslovakia—by Raymond G.H. Seitz, Assistant Secretary of State for European and Canadian Affairs

Released February 22

Advance text:
Remarks at the centennial celebration of the Johns Hopkins University Medical Institutions in Baltimore, MD

Released February 23

Announcement:
Nomination of Jack D. Shanstrom to be United States District Court Judge for the District of Montana

Released February 26

Fact sheet:
National goals for education

Released February 28

Statement:
The President's telephone conversation with Chairman Mikhail Gorbachev of the Soviet Union—by Marlin Fitzwater, Press Secretary to the President

Advance text:
Remarks at a fundraising luncheon for congressional candidate Susan Molinari in Staten Island, NY

Announcement:
Nomination of Leo A. Giacometto to be United States Marshal for the District of Montana

Announcement:
Nomination of Dexter W. Lehtinen to be United States Attorney for the Southern District of Florida

Advance text:
Remarks at a fundraising dinner for gubernatorial candidate Pete Wilson in San Francisco, CA

Released March 1

Advance text:
Remarks at the California Chamber of Commerce Centennial Dinner in Los Angeles, CA

Released March 5

Advance text:
Remarks to members of the National PTA Legislative Conference

Released March 6

Announcement:
Nomination of Samuel G. Wilson to be United States District Judge for the Western District of Virginia

Announcement:
Nomination of D. Brock Hornby to be United States District Judge for the District of Maine

Transcript:
Press briefing on the President's meeting with Prime Minister Andreotti of Italy—by Raymond G.H. Seitz, Assistant Secretary of State for European and Canadian Affairs

Advance text:
Remarks to the American Society of Association Executives

Released March 7

Advance text:
Remarks at the American Electronics Association luncheon

Released March 8

Transcript:
Press briefing on national transportation policy—by Secretary of Transportation Samuel K. Skinner

Announcement:
Nomination of Adriane J. Dudley to be a Judge of the District Court of the Virgin Islands

Announcement:
Nomination of Arthur F. Van Court to be United States Marshal for the Eastern District of California

Released March 13

Fact sheet:
The President's clean fuels program

Released March 14

Fact sheet:
Potomac Electric Power Company's Chalk Point Generating Station

Released March 15

Advance text:
Remarks to members of the National Association of Manufacturers

Released March 16

Excerpt:
Interview by Jim Angle of National Public Radio

Released March 19

Announcement:
Nomination of Stephen D. Easton to be United States Attorney for the District of North Dakota

Announcement:
Nomination of Morris Lee Thompson to be United States Attorney for the District of Kansas

Released March 21

Transcript:
Press briefing on the President's meeting with Prime Minister Tadeusz Mazowiecki of Poland—by Raymond G.H. Seitz, Assistant Secretary of State for European and Canadian Affairs

Fact sheet:
Basel Convention on the Control of Transboundary Movements of Hazardous Wastes and Their Disposal

Released March 22

Fact sheet:
Tree-planting ceremony

Fact sheet:
National Tree Trust Act of 1990

Announcement:
Nomination of Stanley F. Birch, Jr., to be United States Circuit Judge for the Eleventh Circuit

Released March 27

Announcement:
Nomination of Daniel J. Horgan to be United States Marshal for the Southern District of Florida

Released March 28

Advance text:
Remarks at the U.S. Olympic Committee dinner

Released March 29

Advance text:
Remarks to the National Leadership Coalition on AIDS

Released March 30

Announcement:
Nomination of Richard W. Vollmer, Jr., to be United States District Judge for the Southern District of Alabama

Fact sheet:
Founding directors of the Points of Light Initiative Foundation; luncheon with the President

Released April 2

Advance text:
Remarks at the annual convention of the National Association of Broadcasters in Atlanta, GA

Advance text:
Remarks at a fundraising dinner for gubernatorial candidate George Voinovich in Cincinnati, OH

Released April 3

Advance text:
Remarks at a tree-planting ceremony in Indianapolis, IN

Advance text:
Remarks at a fundraising luncheon for Senator Dan Coats in Indianapolis, IN

Advance text:
Remarks at a Republican Party fundraising dinner in Detroit, MI

Released April 4

Advance text:
Remarks at the 20th anniversary dinner of the Joint Center for Political and Economic Studies

Released April 5

Announcement:
Nomination of Richard F. Suhrheinrich to be United States Circuit Judge for the Sixth Circuit

Released April 9

Fact sheet:
Czechoslovakia-U.S. trade agreement

Released April 10

Advance text:
The President and Mrs. Bush's antisubstance abuse message for the "Cartoon All-Stars to the Rescue" program, which will be televised April 21

Announcement:
Nomination of David C. Norton to be United States District Judge for the District of South Carolina

Announcement:
Nomination of Mary Ellen Abrecht, Kaye K. Christian, Frederick D. Dorsey, Ellen Segal Huvelle, Jose M. Lopez, Joan Z. McAvoy, Gregory E. Mize, and Patricia A. Wynn to be Associate Judges of the Superior Court of the District of Columbia

Released April 12

Transcript:
Press briefing on the White House Conference on Science and Economic Research Related to Global Change—by William K. Reilly, Administrator of the Environmental Protection Agency; D. Allan Bromley, Science Advisor to the President and Director of the Office of Science and Technology Policy; Michael J. Boskin, Chairman of the Council of Economic Advisers; Michael R. Deland, Chairman of the Council on Environmental Quality; and W. Henson Moore, Under Secretary of Energy

Released April 17

Transcript:
Press briefing on President Bush's meeting with President Rafael Callejas of Honduras—by Bernard W. Aronson, Assistant Secretary of State for Inter-American Affairs

Released April 18

Advance text:
Remarks at the closing session of the White House Conference on Science and Economics Research Related to Global Change

Fact sheet:
U.S. initiatives affecting global climate change

Released April 20

Advance text:
Remarks at a fundraising luncheon for Senatorial candidate Bill Cabaniss in Birmingham, AL

Transcript:
Statement by Press Secretary Fitzwater on the Presidential delegation to the inauguration of President Violeta Chamorro of Nicaragua

Advance text:
Remarks at a fundraising dinner for the Florida Republican Party in Orlando, FL

Fact sheet:
National Estuary Program

Released April 23

Announcement:
Nomination of Jimmy C. Carter to be United States Marshal for the Southern District of Georgia

Released April 24

Announcement:
Nomination of James S. Halpern to be a Judge of the United States Tax Court

Released April 25

Announcement:
Nomination of Kenneth L. Ryskamp to be United States Circuit Judge for the Eleventh Circuit

Announcement:
Nomination of James J. West to be United States Attorney for the Middle District of Pennsylvania

Fact sheet:
Budget reform proposals

Released April 26

Transcript:
Press briefing on President Bush's meeting with Carlos Andrés Pérez of Venezuela—by Bernard W. Aronson, Assistant Secretary of State for Inter-American Affairs

Released April 30

Announcement:
Nomination of James L. Webb to be a United States Marshal for the Eastern District of Oklahoma

Transcript:
Press briefing on President Bush's meeting with President Guillermo Endara of Panama—by Bernard W. Aronson, Assistant Secretary of State for Inter-American Affairs

Released May 1

Advance text:
Remarks at a fundraising dinner for the Korean War Veterans Memorial Commission

Released May 2

Fact sheet:
Comprehensive U.S. proposal for modernizing the Coordinating Committee for Multilateral Export Controls (COCOM)

Released May 4

Announcement:
Nomination of Gary E. Shovlin to be a United States Marshal for the Middle District of Pennsylvania

Advance text:
Remarks at the Oklahoma Foundation for Excellence dinner in Tulsa

Released May 8

Transcript:
Press briefing on President Bush's meeting with President Jaime Paz Zamora of Bolivia—by Bernard W. Aronson, Assistant Secretary of State for Inter-American Affairs

Announcement:
Nomination of Karen L. Henderson to be United States Circuit Judge for the District of Columbia Circuit

Announcement:
Nomination of A. Raymond Randolph to be United States Circuit Judge for the District of Columbia Circuit

Released May 10

Announcement:
Nomination of Paul V. Niemeyer to be United States Circuit Judge for the Fourth Circuit

Announcement:
Nomination of John H. McBryde to be United States District Judge for the Northern District of Texas

Announcement:
Nomination of Frederick P. Stamp, Jr., to be United States District Judge for the Northern District of West Virginia

Announcement:
Nomination of Charles W. Pickering to be United States District Judge for the Southern District of Mississippi

Released May 11

Advance text:
Remarks at the Texas A&I University commencement ceremony in Kingsville

Advance text:
Remarks at a fundraising reception for Gov. Carroll A. Campbell, Jr., in Columbia, SC

Released May 12

Advance text:
Remarks at the Liberty University commencement ceremony in Lynchburg, VA

Released May 14

Announcement:
Nomination of Jonathan R. Steinberg to be an Associate Judge of the U.S. Court of Veterans Appeals

Announcement:
Nomination of Lourdes G. Baird to be U.S. Attorney for the Central District of California

Released May 15

Transcript:
Press briefing on President Bush's meeting with President Zine El Abidine Ben Ali of Tunisia—by John H. Kelly, Assistant Secretary of State for Near Eastern and South Asian Affairs

Released May 17

Announcement:
Nomination of Michael Boudin to be U.S. District Judge for the District of Columbia

Statement:
The President's upcoming meetings with foreign leaders—by Marlin Fitzwater, Press Secretary to the President

Released May 18

Announcement:
Nomination of Carol Bagley Amon to be U.S. District Judge for the Eastern District of New York

Advance text:
Remarks at a Republican Party fundraising dinner in Dallas, TX

Released May 19

Transcript:
Press briefing on the visit of Secretary of State James A. Baker III to the Soviet Union—by Brent Scowcroft, Assistant to the President for National Security Affairs

Advance text:
Remarks at the University of Texas commencement ceremony in Austin

Excerpt:
Remarks at the University of Texas commencement ceremony in Austin

Released May 21

Advance text:
Remarks at a fundraising breakfast for gubernatorial candidate David Frohnmayer in Portland, OR

Advance text:
Remarks to Oakwood community members in Los Angeles, CA

Released May 23

Transcript:
Press briefing on the upcoming summit with Soviet President Mikhail Gorbachev—by Secretary of State James A. Baker III

Fact sheet:
The administration's trade strategy

Released May 25

Announcement:
Nomination of Michael L. Johnson to be U.S. Marshal for the District of Idaho

Released May 29

Announcement:
Nomination of Federico A. Moreno to be U.S. District Judge for the Southern District of Florida

Released May 31

Transcript:
President Mikhail Gorbachev's exchange with reporters upon arriving at the White House

Transcript:
President Mikhail Gorbachev's exchange with reporters following a meeting with President Bush

Announcement:
Gifts exchanged between President and Mrs. Bush and President and Mrs. Gorbachev at the state dinner

Announcement:
Menu and description of the state dinner for President Mikhail Gorbachev of the Soviet Union

Announcement:
Guest list for the state dinner for President Mikhail Gorbachev of the Soviet Union

Fact sheet:
Ocean studies agreement

Fact sheet:
Expanded civil aviation agreement

Fact sheet:
Maritime transportation agreement

Advance text:
Toasts at the state dinner for President Mikhail Gorbachev of the Soviet Union

June 1

Fact sheet:
Beringian Heritage International Park

Fact sheet:
Conventional armed forces in Europe treaty

Fact sheet:
Peaceful uses of atomic energy agreement

Transcript:
Press briefing on the Soviet-U.S. summit in Washington—by Secretary of State James A. Baker III

Fact sheet:
Commercial agreement

Fact sheet:
Long-term grains agreement

Fact sheet:
U.S.-U.S.S.R. chemical weapons destruction agreement

Fact sheet:
Nuclear testing protocols

Fact sheet:
Customs cooperation agreement

Fact sheet:
U.S.-U.S.S.R. maritime boundary agreement

Fact sheet:
Cultural centers agreement

Fact sheet:
Agreement on expansion of undergraduate university exchanges

Fact sheet:
Memorandum of understanding to increase circulation of America and Soviet Life magazines

June 2

Announcement:
Guest list and menu for dinner honoring President and Mrs. Gorbachev at Camp David, MD

June 4

Fact sheet:
Arms nonproliferation

Released June 5

Announcement:
Nomination of Albert Z. Moore to be U.S. Marshal for the Northern District of Ohio

Released June 6

Announcement:
Nomination of Joel F. Dubina to be U.S. Circuit Judge for the Eleventh District

Announcement:
Nomination of John W. Raley, Jr., to be U.S. Attorney for the Eastern District of Oklahoma

Released June 7

Advance text:
Remarks at a fundraising reception for gubernatorial candidate Jim Edgar in Chicago, IL

Released June 8

Advance text:
Remarks at a fundraising breakfast for Gov. Terry Branstad in Des Moines, IA

Advance text:
Remarks at a fundraising luncheon for senatorial candidate Hal Daub in Omaha, NE

Advance text:
Remarks to members and supporters of MAD DADS in Omaha, NE

Released June 11

Announcement:
Nomination of Randall R. Rader to be U.S. Circuit Judge for the Federal Circuit

Announcement:
Nomination of William M. Skretny to be U.S. District Judge for the Western District of New York

Announcement:
Nomination of Fred L. Foreman to be U.S. Attorney for the Northern District of Illinois

Released June 12

Announcement:
Nomination of John Henry Bayly, Jr., to be an Associate Judge of the Superior Court of the District of Columbia

Announcement:
Nomination of Linda Turner Hamilton to be an Associate Judge of the Superior Court of the District of Columbia

Advance text:
Remarks at the annual Republican congressional fundraising dinner

Released June 14

Transcript:
Press briefing on the President's meeting with Prime Minister Chatchai Chunhawan of Thailand—by Richard H. Solomon, Assistant Secretary of State for East Asian and Pacific Affairs

Released June 15

Statement:
The Consumer Price Index in May and the merchandise trade deficit in April—by Marlin Fitzwater, Press Secretary to the President

Released June 19

Advance text:
Remarks at the Great Outdoors Award dinner

Released June 20

Advance text:
Remarks at a fundraising luncheon for Gov. Guy Hunt in Huntsville, AL

Advance text:
Remarks to employees of the George C. Marshall Space Flight Center in Huntsville, AL

Fact sheet:
Chronology of the President's space exploration program

Released June 21

Announcement:
Nomination of Fred I. Parker to be U.S. District Judge for the District of Vermont

Announcement:
Nomination of Stanley A. Twardy, Jr., to be U.S. Attorney for the District of Connecticut

Released June 22

Transcript:
Press briefing on the President's meeting with Nelson Mandela—by Herman Cohen, Assistant Secretary of State for African Affairs

Released June 25

Transcript:
Remarks by Nelson Mandela after meeting with the President

Transcript:
Press briefing on the President's meeting with Nelson Mandela—by Herman J. Cohen, Assistant Secretary of State for African Affairs

Released June 26

Fact sheet:
Presidential decisions concerning oil and gas development on the outer continental shelf

Released June 27

Statement:
Address on U.S. economic policies toward Latin America and the Caribbean—by Marlin Fitzwater, Press Secretary to the President

Advance text:
Remarks announcing the Enterprise for the Americas Initiative

Transcript:
Press briefing on the Enterprise for the Americas Initiative—by Secretary of the Treasury Nicholas F. Brady

Fact sheet:
Enterprise for the Americas Initiative

Released June 28

Transcript:
Press briefing on the upcoming NATO summit in London—by Secretary of State James A. Baker III

Released June 29

Announcement:
Nomination of Anthony L. Bennett to be U.S. Marshal for the District of Minnesota

Announcement:
Nomination of Joe D. Whitley to be U.S. Attorney for the Northern District of Georgia

Announcement:
Nomination of Joseph M. McLaughlin to be U.S. Circuit Judge for the Second Circuit

Appendix D—Acts Approved by the President

S.J. Res. 229 / Public Law 101–261
To designate April 1990 as "National Prevent-A-Litter Month"

Approved March 31

S. 2231 / Public Law 101–262
Energy Policy and Conservation Act Extension Amendment of 1990

Approved April 4

S. 1521 / Public Law 101–263
To provide for an increase in the maximum rates of basic pay for the police force of the National Zoological Park

S.J. Res. 250 / Public Law 101–264
Designating April 1990 as "National Recycling Month"

S.J. Res. 266 / Public Law 101–265
Designating March 1990, as "United States Naval Reserve Month"

Approved April 5

S.J. Res. 190 / Public Law 101–266
Designating April 9, 1990, as "National Former Prisoners of War Recognition Day"

Approved April 6

H.J. Res. 500 / Public Law 101–267
To designate April 6, 1990, as "Education Day, U.S.A."

Approved April 9

H.R. 2692 / Public Law 101–268
To amend the Woodrow Wilson Memorial Act of 1968 to provide that the Secretary of Education and two additional individuals from private life shall be members of the Board of Trustees of the Woodrow Wilson International Center for Scholars

S. 2151 / Public Law 101–269
To permit the transfer of the obsolete submarine U.S.S. Requin to the Carnegie Institute in Pittsburgh, Pennsylvania, before the expiration of the 60-day waiting period that would otherwise be applicable to the transfer

Approved April 10

H.R. 4099 / Public Law 101–270
To suspend section 332 of the Agricultural Adjustment Act of 1938 for the 1991 crop of wheat

Approved April 11

S. 388 / Public Law 101–271
Federal Energy Regulatory Commission Member Term Act of 1990

Approved April 18

S. 1813 / Public Law 101–272
To ensure that funds provided under section 4213 of the Indian Alcohol and Substance Abuse Prevention and Treatment Act of 1986 may be used to acquire land for emergency shelters

S. 1949 / Public Law 101–273
To amend the Labor Management Relations Act of 1947 to permit parties engaged in collective bargaining to bargain over the establishment and administration of trust funds to provide financial assistance for employee housing

Approved April 23

H.R. 3968 / Public Law 101–274
To further delay the applicability of certain amendments to the Public Health Service Act that relate to organ procurement organizations

H.R. 1048 / Public Law 101–275
Hate Crime Statistics Act

Approved April 25

S.J. Res. 242 / Public Law 101–276
Designating the week of April 22 through April 28, 1990, as "National Crime Victims' Rights Week"

Approved April 30

S. 1096 / Public Law 101–277
To provide for the use and distribution of funds awarded the Seminole Indians in dockets 73, 151, and 73–A of the Indian Claims Commission

Approved May 1

H.R. 2334 / Public Law 101–278
To redesignate the Post Office located at 300 East Ninth Street in Austin, Texas, as the "Homer Thornberry Judicial Building"

S.J. Res. 258 / Public Law 101–279
To authorize the President to proclaim the last Friday of April 1990 as "National Arbor Day"

Approved May 4

H.J. Res. 553 / Public Law 101–280
To make technical changes in the Ethics Reform Act of 1989

S. 2533 / Public Law 101–281
To amend the Federal Aviation Act of 1958 to extend the civil penalty assessment demonstration program, and for other purposes

Approved May 8

S.J. Res. 236 / Public Law 101–282
Designating May 6 through May 12, 1990, as "Be Kind to Animals and National Pet Week"

Approved May 9

H.R. 3802 / Public Law 101–283
To designate May 1990 as "Asian/Pacific American Heritage Month"

S.J. Res. 153 / Public Law 101–284
Designating the third week in May 1990 as "National Tourism Week"

S.J. Res. 230 / Public Law 101–285
To designate the period commencing on May 6, 1990, and ending on May 12, 1990, as "National Drinking Water Week"

H.R. 1011 / Public Law 101–286
Wildfire Disaster Recovery Act of 1989

Approved May 10

H.J. Res. 546 / Public Law 101–287
Designating May 13, 1990, as "Infant Mortality Awareness Day"

S. 1485 / Public Law 101–288
To grant the consent of Congress to the Quad Cities Interstate Metropolitan Authority Compact entered into between the States of Illinois and Iowa

S.J. Res. 224 / Public Law 101–289
To designate the month of May 1990, as "National Trauma Awareness Month"

S.J. Res. 241 / Public Law 101–290
To designate the week of May 6, 1990 through May 13, 1990, as "Jewish Heritage Week"

H.R. 756 / Private Law 101–3
For the relief of Shelton Anthony Smith

Approved May 17

H.R. 922 / Public Law 101–291
To designate the building located at 1515 Sam Houston Street in Liberty, Texas, as the "M.P. Daniel and Thomas F. Calhoon, Senior, Post Office Building"

H.R. 1472 / Public Law 101–292
To establish the Grand Island National Recreation Area in the State of Michigan, and for other purposes

H.R. 4637 / Public Law 101–293
To amend Public Law 101–86 to eliminate the 6-month limitation on the period for which civilian and military retirees may serve as temporary employees, in connection with the 1990 decennial census of population, without being subject to certain offsets from pay or other benefits

H.J. Res. 453 / Public Law 101–294
Designating May 1990 as "National Digestive Disease Awareness Month"

H.J. Res. 490 / Public Law 101–295
Commemorating May 18, 1990, as the 25th anniversary of Head Start

S. 1853 / Public Law 101–296
To award a congressional gold medal to Laurance Spelman Rockefeller

Approved May 22

H.R. 2890 / Public Law 101–297
To designate the Federal Building and United States Courthouse located at 750 Missouri Avenue in East St. Louis, Illinois, as the "Melvin Price Federal Building and United States Courthouse"

S. 993 / Public Law 101–298
Biological Weapons Anti-Terrorism Act of 1989

Approved May 23

S.J. Res. 275 / Public Law 101–299
Designating May 13, 1990, as the "National Day in Support of Freedom and Human Rights in China and Tibet"

Approved May 24

S. 2300 / Public Law 101–300
To provide financial assistance to the Simon Wiesenthal Center in Los Angeles, California, for the education programs of the Museum of Tolerance

S. 1846 / Public Law 101–301
To make miscellaneous amendments to Indian laws, and for other purposes

Approved May 25

H.R. 4404 / Public Law 101–302
Dire Emergency Supplemental Appropriations for Disaster Assistance, Food Stamps, Unemployment Compensation Administration, and Other Urgent Needs, and Transfers, and Reducing

Funds Budgeted for Military Spending Act of 1990

Approved May 29

H.R. 1805 / Public Law 101–303
To amend title 5, United States Code, to allow Federal annuitants to make contributions for health benefits through direct payments rather than through annuity withholdings if the annuity is insufficient to cover the required withholdings, and for other purposes

H.R. 3961 / Public Law 101–304
To redesignate the Federal building at 1800 5th Avenue, North in Birmingham, Alabama, as the "Robert S. Vance Federal Building and United States Courthouse"

Approved May 30

H.R. 3910 / Public Law 101–305
1992 National Assessment of Chapter 1 Act

Approved June 6

H.R. 644 / Public Law 101–306
East Fork of the Jemez River and the Pecos River Wild and Scenic Rivers Addition Act of 1989

S.J. Res. 231 / Public Law 101–307
To designate the week of June 10, 1990 through June 16, 1990, as "State-Supported Homes for Veterans Week"

S.J. Res. 267 / Public Law 101–308
To authorize and request the President to designate May 1990 as "National Physical Fitness and Sports Month"

Approved June 18

S.J. Res. 251 / Public Law 101–309
Designating "Baltic Freedom Day"

H.J. Res. 516 / Public Law 101–310
To designate the week beginning June 10, 1990, as "National Scleroderma Awareness Week"

Approved June 25

H.R. 4612 / Public Law 101–311
To amend title 11 of the United States Code regarding swap agreements and forward contracts

S. 2700 / Public Law 101–312
To authorize the Secretary of Veterans Affairs to proceed with a proposed administrative reorganization of the regional field offices of the Veterans Health Services and Research Administration of the Department of Veterans Affairs, notwithstanding the notice-and-wait provisions in section 210(b) of title 38, United States Code

Approved June 27

S. 286 / Public Law 101–313
To establish Petroglyph National Monument and Pecos National Historical Park in the State of New Mexico, and for other purposes

Approved June 28

S.J. Res. 245 / Public Law 101–314
Designating July 3, 1990, as "Idaho Centennial Day"

H.J. Res. 575 / Public Law 101–315
To designate June 25, 1990, as "Korean War Remembrance Day"

S.J. Res. 264 / Public Law 101–316
To commemorate the 50th anniversary of the National Sheriffs' Association

Approved June 29

S.J. Res. 246 / Public Law 101–317
Calling upon the United Nations to repeal General Assembly Resolution 3379

The texts of the proclamations and Executive orders are printed in the Federal Register (F.R.) at the citations listed below. The documents are also printed in title 3 of the Code of Federal Regulations and in the Weekly Compilation of Presidential Documents.

PROCLAMATIONS

EXECUTIVE ORDERS

Appendix F—Points of Light Recognition Program

The President named the following individuals and institutions as exemplars of his commitment to making community service central to the life and work of every American. The daily recognition program, which began on November 22, 1989, was a national tribute to voluntarism. The recipients for the period covered by this volume are listed in chronological order.

Senior Health and Peer Counseling Center, of Santa Monica, CA

Sophia Jeffery, of Springfield, MA

Senior Center Foster Grandparents Program, of Charlottesville, VA

MOVE (Mobilization of Volunteer Efforts), of Winooski, VT

Jefferson County Community Center, of Lakewood, CO

Katherine Donihi, of Altamonte Springs, FL

Little Vikings Program, of Arlington, TX

Neil J. Houston House, of Roxbury, MA

Higher Achievement Program, of Washington, DC

Cincinnati Youth Collaborative, of Cincinnati, OH

Herbert Chamberlain, of Rochester, NY

St. Vincent de Paul-Joan Kroc Center, of San Diego, CA

Marsha G. Johnson, of Cleveland, OH

Marilyn M. Murphy, of Stamford, CT

Kelley R. Edwards, of Lilburn, GA

Mary's House, of Rockville, MD

Sheila Fitzpatrick, of Harrisburg, PA

Diane Wurst, of Polk, NE

Get Involved Before Your Kids Do, of Appleton, WI

Beth, Kerry, and Megan Kerby, of Troy, MI

Principle of the Alphabet Literacy System (PALS), of New Orleans, LA

Gallia Academy High School Key Club, of Gallipolis, OH

Residents of Yoncalla, OR

Dan Conrad, of Minnetonka, MN

Michael Carlton Noyes, of Levant, ME

Youth Aware, of San Francisco, CA

Daniel James Greene, of David, KY

Phyllis Lydia Green, of Long Grove, IA

Rev. Michael Lewis, of Tampa, FL

Salvation Army Hope Center, of St. Louis, MO

"Friends," of Fargo, ND

Holy Rosary Family Center, of Columbus, OH

Alan Waters, of Daleville, AL

Pamela Calhoun, of Sparks, NV

Project Good Turn, of Missoula, MT

Men on the Move and ESTEEM (Early Start Toward Educational Excellence and Maturity), of Cordele, GA

South San Jose Neighborhood Association, of Albuquerque, NM

Seniors Serving Schools Program, of Shawnee Mission, KS

Self Enhancement, Inc., of Portland, OR

Lou and Lola Stouffer, of Terra Alta, WV

ActionAIDS, of Philadelphia, PA

Stacy Lynn Priest, of Little Rock, AR

Project Aware, of Jackson, MS

Daisy Patricia Hitchcock, of Louisville, KY

George Simmons, of Provo, UT

Save the Bay, of Providence, RI

Orangeburg School District Five, of Orangeburg, SC

The Shoulder, of Houston, TX

Joseph A.A. Fournier, of Augusta, GA

Black Hills Regional Ski for Light, of Rapid City, SD

Stop the Violence Movement, of Milwaukee, WI

Edith Lewis, of Garland, TX

Cheyenne Botanic Gardens, of Cheyenne, WY

Zenobia White, of Des Moines, IA

Page Attacks Trash, of Page, AZ

Project Chesed, of Miami Beach, FL

Dr. Jonathan Soderstrom, of Oak Ridge, TN

Robert and Jacquelyn Corrigan, of Gorham, NH

Julia Goldstein, of University City, MO

Robert Low, of Waianae, HI

Joseph Ziskovsky, of Shoreview, MI

Building and Construction Trades Council of Alameda County, of Oakland, CA

Toni Allee, of Norfolk, VA

Jesse Sanchez Berain, of Boise, ID

Pauline Hord, of Memphis, TN

William Warner Johnson, of Washington, DC

Glaxo, Inc., of Research Triangle Park, NC

Joan Stairs and Juanita Suggs, of New Castle, IN

VYTAL (Volunteer Youth Training and Leadership), of Pittsburgh, PA

Barbara Tomblinson, of Kansas City, MO

Michael Garber, of Waterbury, CT

Madison House, of Charlottesville, VA

Rod Gorham, of Scarborough, ME

Good Shepherd Center for Homeless Women, of Los Angeles, CA

BABES (Beginning Alcohol and Addiction Basic Education Studies), of Cleveland, OH

Jean Mary Barton, of Wappingers Falls, NY

Ravendale Area Revitalization Project (R.A.R.E.), of Detroit, MI

Our Town Family Center, of Tucson, AZ

Martin and Ida Alexander, of Nashville, TN

Nickolas Monreal, Jr., of San Antonio, TX

Ai Yokota, of Sacramento, CA

Dayton Power and Light Co., of Kettering, OH

Listening Ear, of East Lansing, MI

Dr. Gayle Arnold, of Richmond, VA

Hands, Feet, and Mouth, of Smyrna, GA

United Technologies Community Teams, of United Technologies Corp.

Action Elementary School Volunteer Program, of East Lebanon, ME

Frank H. Lockyear, of Wilsonville, OR

Residents of Stowe, VT

William and Suzanne Sterling, of Sequim, WA

Birmingham-Southern College Conservancy, of Birmingham, AL

Daniel Keith Odell, of Orlando, FL

Reef Relief, of Key West, FL

Midnight Basketball League, Inc., of Hyattsville, MD

Donald Edwin Horton, of Minneapolis, MN

MAD DADS, of Omaha, NE

Lawndale Community Church Ministry, of Chicago, IL

Shelley Joyce Spell, of Houston, TX

Giraffe Project, of Langley, WA

Futures for Children, of Albuquerque, NM

Intergenerational Project, of Santa Clara, CA

Norman Asselstine, of Flint, MI

Skating Association for the Blind and Handicapped, of Amherst, NY

Hispanic Employees Association of Pacific Gas and Electric Co., of Fresno, CA

Phillip A. Wiley, of Broken Arrow, OK

Volunteers for Medical Engineering, Inc., of Baltimore, MD

Jan Zwetsch, of Spokane, WA

The Seeing Eye, Inc., of Morristown, NJ

Youth Service Charleston, of Charleston, SC

David Scott Lessen, of Woodmere, NY

Venture House, of Wichita, KS

Vietnam Veterans Workshop, Inc., of Boston, MA

Anne Ross Fairbanks, of Troy, NY

Mack Stolarski, of Williamsburg, VA

Eva D. Filice, of Salinas, CA

Student Programs for Urban Development, of Worcester, MA

Ann S. Dryburg, of Brownsville, PA

Residents of Oakwood, a subdivision of Venice, CA

Project Child, of Boca Raton, FL

Interfraternity Association Town Watch, of Philadelphia, PA

Meals on Wheels, of Greenville, SC

Joan Mary DeMarsh, of Palmetto, FL

Retired Senior Volunteer Program (RSVP) Sewing Circle, of Salina, KS

Dr. Ray Simmons, of Brownsville, TX

Anna Senior Nelson, of Kingston, PA

Bridgerland Literacy Program, of Logan, UT

National Association for the Southern Poor, of Durham, NC

El Paso Boys' Club Association, of El Paso, TX

Geraldine Ellen Engle, of Taft, CA

Yellowstone Recovery Corps, of Yellowstone National Park, WY

Central Alabama Laubach Literacy (CALL) Council, of Montgomery, AL

Special Needs Projects, Inc., of Idyllwild, CA

Kum Ba Yah Association, of Lynchburg, VA

Sandra Lee Eadie, of Las Vegas, NV

Barbara De Ridder Cotrell, of Little Silver, NJ

Ruth Brinker, of San Francisco, CA

Project NorthStar, of Washington, DC

Austin Adopt-A-School, of Austin, TX

Street Smart Program, of Denver, CO

Sarah Howell East Nutt, of Staunton, VA

Saturday Work-Day, of Panama City, FL

Athens Tutorial Program, of Athens, GA

Hospice of San Joaquin, of Stockton, CA

Kansas 4-H CARES (Chemical Abuse Resistance Education Series), of Manhattan, KS

Barbara Jill Clark, of Sioux Falls, SD

Needle's Eye, of Youngstown, OH

First African Methodist Episcopal Church, of Los Angeles, CA

Capt. Al Lewis, of Philadelphia, PA

Interfaith Ministries, Inc., of Wichita Falls, TX

Alice Oakley, of Kennewick, WA

Let's Help, of Topeka, KS

Dean Cornett, of Paint Lick, KY

Pearl Kling, of Cheboygan, MI

Subject Index

ABC Television—898
AFL–CIO. *See* Labor & Congress of Industrial Organizations, American Federation of
AID. *See* Development Cooperation Agency, U.S. International
AIDS
  See also Health and medical care
  National Leadership Coalition on—431
  National Commission on—907
ASEAN. *See* South East Asian Nations, Association of
Abortion—67, 83, 123, 406, 583, 601, 666
Achievement Against All Odds Awards—619
Acres Homes War on Drugs—115
ACTION—128, 815, 906
Action Elementary School Volunteer Program, East Lebanon, ME—958
ActionAIDS, Philadelphia, PA—957
Ad Hoc Group Against Crime, Kansas City, MO—73, 74
Adoption—66, 67, 118, 123
Advancement of Colored People, National Association for the—3, 27, 28, 111, 895
Advertising Council—12, 913
Advisory committees and commissions, Federal—23, 241, 898
Aeronautics and Space Administration, National—140, 152, 158, 334, 518, 545, 547, 644, 848
Afghanistan, administration policies—467
Africa
  See also specific country
  Economic growth—424
  President's views—205, 424
Africa Tripartite Agreement, Report on Compliance With the Southern—548
African Americans. *See specific subject;* Civil rights
African Development Bank—424
African Development Foundation—217
African National Congress. *See* South Africa, reforms, political and economic
Afro-American (Black) History Month, National—127
Agency. *See other part of subject*
Aging, Administration on. *See* Health and Human Services, Department of
Aging, Federal Council on the—878
Agricultural Trade Policy Advisory Committee—23
Agriculture
  Administration policies—22–24, 186, 385, 392, 550–552, 786, 800
  Free market policies—23, 385
  General Agreement on Tariffs and Trade (GATT). *See* Commerce, international

Agriculture—Continued
  Grain embargoes—552, 799
  President's views—22, 392
  Rural development—68
  Soviet-U.S. trade agreement—748, 793, 799
  Water quality, role—23
Agriculture, Department of
  Assistant Secretary—636
  Budget—21
  Commodity Credit Corporation—898, 919
  Conservation, role—446
  Forest and rangeland resources planning, report—784
  Forest Service, U.S.—784
  Grain Inspection Service, Federal—307
  Rural Telephone Bank—911
  Secretary—22, 23, 68, 186, 385, 392, 403, 404, 550–553, 585, 784, 902
Agriculture Day, National—392
Agriculture Journalists, National Association of—550
Agriculture and Rural Development Policy, National Commission on—504
Air Force, Department of the
  Air Force Academy, U.S.—917
  Chief of Staff—575
  Strategic Air Command—187
Alabama
  Birmingham-Southern College Conservancy—532
  Flooding—900, 906
  Governor—839, 848
  President's visits—529, 532, 839, 842, 848
  Republican Party events—529, 839
Alaska
  Dogsled marathon—909
  Mineral resources, 1989 report—898
Alfalfa Club—896
Algeria, consular convention with U.S.—279
Alibi Club—896
Allstate Insurance Companies—433, 619
Alternative Fuels, Interagency Commission on—363
Ambassadors. *See specific country*
American. *See other part of subject*
Americare—87
Americas, Council of the—809
Amtrak Reauthorization and Improvement Act of 1990—718
Angola
  Conflict resolution—32, 204, 461
  Tripartite agreement, report on compliance—548

A–1

Name Index

Williams, Irvin—401, 403
Williams, Michael L.—428, 930
Williams, S. Linn—438
Williamson, Edwin D.—850
Wilmerding, John—896
Wilson, Addison G.—918
Wilson, Clarence—581
Wilson, Ewen M.—935
Wilson, Pete—170, 288
Wilson, Samuel G.—929
Wittgraf, George W.—895
Woerner, Manfred—204, 219, 272, 627, 898, 913
Wolbeck, Jeanine E.—895
Wolf, Theodore D.—448, 908
Wolfensohn, James D.—422
Wong, Eugene—62, 925
Woodson, Robert L.—619
Woolsey, R. James—359
Wright, Robert C.—463

Wurst, Dian—957
Wyman, Rosalind W.—915
Wynn, Patricia A.—931

Yeutter, Clayton K.—22, 23, 68, 186, 385, 392, 550–553, 585, 784, 902
Yockey, Donald J.—92, 927
Yokota, Ai—491
Yost, Paul A., Jr.—538, 922
Young, John A.—900
Young, John W.—897
Younger, Ramona—894
Yturria, Frank D.—898, 929
Yune, Johnny—916

Zacks, Gordon B.—923
Zaydan, Muhammad. *See* Abu Abbas
Zeder, Fred M.—69, 501, 586
Ziemer, Paul L.—726, 934
Ziskovsky, Joseph—957
Zwetsch, Jan—958

Document Categories List